T0359328

# OXFORD
## UNIVERSITY PRESS

Oxford University Press is a department of the University of Oxford.
It furthers the University's objective of excellence in research, scholarship,
and education by publishing worldwide. Oxford is a registered trademark
of Oxford University Press in the UK and in certain other countries.

Published in Australia by
Oxford University Press
Level 8, 737 Bourke Street, Docklands, Victoria 3008, Australia.

© Oxford University Press 2019

The moral rights of the author have been asserted.

First published 1986
Second edition 1998
Third edition 2005
Fourth edition 2010
Fifth edition 2019

Reprinted 2020, 2022 (twice), 2023

Published by arrangement with Oxford University Press, Oxford.
Based on *The Little Oxford Dictionary*, Seventh edition
© Oxford University Press 1969, 1980, 1986, 1994

The *Oxford Little Dictionary of Current English*, Seventh edition was originally published in English in
1994 by Oxford University Press, Great Clarendon Street, Oxford, OX2 6DP, United Kingdom. This
adaptation is published by arrangement. Oxford University Press Australia is solely responsible for
this adaptation from the original work.

A catalogue record for this
book is available from the
National Library of Australia

ISBN 9780190319335

**Reproduction and communication for educational purposes**
The Australian *Copyright Act 1968* (the Act) allows educational institutions that are covered by
remuneration arrangements with Copyright Agency to reproduce and communicate certain
material for educational purposes. For more information, see copyright.com.au.

Botanical cover illustrations by Ink and Spindle
Typeset by Newgen KnowledgeWorks Pvt. Ltd., Chennai, India
Printed in Hong Kong by Sheck Wah Tong Printing Press Ltd.

Oxford University Press Australia & New Zealand is committed to
sourcing paper responsibly.

**Disclaimer**
Links to third party websites are provided by Oxford in good faith and for information only. Oxford
disclaims any responsibility for the materials contained in any third party website referenced in this work.

**Acknowledgement of Country**
Oxford University Press acknowledges the Traditional Owners of the many lands on which we
create and share our learning resources. We acknowledge the Traditional Owners as the original
storytellers, teachers and students of this land we call Australia. We pay our respects to Elders,
past and present, for the ways in which they have enabled the teachings of their rich cultures
and knowledge systems to be shared for millennia.

**Warning to First Nations Australians**
Aboriginal and Torres Strait Islander peoples are advised that this publication may include
images or names of people now deceased.

FIFTH
EDITION

Australian Mini

# Oxford
## Dictionary

Australia's bestselling dictionaries

Edited by Mark Gwynn and Amanda Laugesen

OXFORD
UNIVERSITY PRESS

# Preface

The *Australian Mini Oxford Dictionary* is the smallest member of the Oxford family of Australian dictionaries, and is written for those who need a compact guide to the spelling and meaning of words in the English language today.

This new edition has been thoroughly updated to reflect the ongoing work of the Australian National Dictionary Centre and Oxford Dictionaries. Many new words, phrases, and compounds have been added, while the existing entries have been extensively modified to reflect changes in both International and Australian English.

The dictionary provides many alternative spellings and includes helpful advice where there might be doubt about the formation or spelling of inflected forms; difficult plural forms of nouns and those inflections of verbs and comparative adjectives that are not wholly straightforward are spelt out in full. Assistance is given for those usages that may be disputed or controversial, and special usage notes are provided in cases that require more information or explanation.

This edition of the *Australian Mini Oxford Dictionary* has been supported by the resources of the Australian National Dictionary Centre. We thank the team at Oxford University Press Australia (especially Joanna Lake and Anne McKenna) for their ongoing support and publishing expertise.

Mark Gwynn
Amanda Laugesen

# Abbreviations

Abbreviations in general use (such as *etc.*, *i.e.*) are explained in the dictionary itself.

| | | | |
|---|---|---|---|
| abbr. | abbreviation | n. | noun |
| adj. | adjective | Naut. | Nautical |
| adv. | adverb | neg. | negative |
| arch. | archaic | N.Engl. | Northern English |
| Aust. | Australian | n.pl. | noun plural |
| aux. | auxiliary | NZ | New Zealand |
| Brit. | British | offens. | offensive |
| colloq. | colloquial(ly) | orig. | originally |
| comb. | combination; combining | Parl. | Parliament(ary) |
| conj. | conjunction | Philos. | Philosophy |
| contr. | contraction | phr. | phrase |
| | | pl. | plural |
| derog. | derogatory | poet. | poetical |
| dial. | dialect | Polit. | Politics |
| | | prep. | preposition |
| Econ. | Economics | pron. | pronoun |
| Electr. | Electricity | propr. | proprietary term |
| ellipt. | elliptical(ly) | RC Ch. | Roman Catholic Church |
| emphat. | emphatic | | |
| esp. | especially | ref. | reference |
| euphem. | euphemism | rel. | relative |
| Gk | Greek | S.Afr. | South African |
| Gram. | Grammar | Scot. | Scottish |
| hist. | with historical reference | sing. | singular |
| | | superl. | superlative |
| | | symb. | symbol |
| imper. | imperative | Theatr. | Theatre |
| int. | interjection | US | American; in American use |
| iron. | ironical | | |
| joc. | jocular | usu. | usually |
| Math. | Mathematics | v. | verb |
| Med. | Medicine | v.aux | auxiliary verb |
| Mus. | Music | v.refl. | reflexive verb |

# Proprietary terms

This dictionary includes terms that are, or are asserted to be, proprietary terms or trademarks. Their inclusion does not mean that they have acquired for legal purposes a non-proprietary or general significance, nor is any other judgement implied concerning their legal status. In cases where the editors have some evidence that a word is used as a proprietary name or trademark, this is indicated by *propr.*, but no judgement concerning the legal status of such words is made or implied thereby.

**Do you have a query about words, their origin, meaning, use, spelling, pronunciation, or any other aspect of Australian or international English?**

Then write to the Australian National Dictionary Centre, Canberra ACT 0200 (email andc@anu.edu.au). All queries will be answered using the full resources of the *Australian National Dictionary* and the *Oxford English Dictionary*.

# Aa

**A** *abbr.* ampere(s). □ **A1, A2, A3, A4** standard paper sizes, each half the previous one, e.g. A4 = 297 × 210 mm.

**a** *adj.* **1** one, some, any. **2** in, to, or for each; per.

**aardvark** *n.* African mammal with tubular snout and long tongue.

**aback** *adv.* □ **taken aback** disconcerted.

**abacus** *n.* frame with wires along which beads are slid for calculating.

**abalone** *n.* mollusc with edible flesh, having shallow shell lined with mother-of-pearl.

**abandon** ● *v.* desert; give up (hope etc.) ● *n.* freedom from inhibitions. □□ **abandonment** *n.*

**abandoned** *adj.* deserted; uninhibited, unrestrained.

**abase** *v.* humiliate; degrade. □□ **abasement** *n.*

**abashed** *adj.* embarrassed, disconcerted.

**abate** *v.* make or become less strong etc. □□ **abatement** *n.*

**abattoir** *n.* place where animals are slaughtered for food.

**abbess** *n.* female head of abbey of nuns.

**abbey** *n.* (building occupied by) community of monks or nuns.

**abbot** *n.* male head of abbey of monks.

**abbreviate** *v.* shorten. □□ **abbreviation** *n.*

**ABC** *abbr.* Australian Broadcasting Corporation.

**abdicate** *v.* give up or renounce or resign from (throne etc.) □□ **abdication** *n.*

**abdomen** *n.* part of body containing stomach, bowels, reproductive organs, etc. □□ **abdominal** *adj.*

**abduct** *v.* carry off illegally, kidnap. □□ **abduction** *n.* **abductor** *n.*

**aberrant** *adj.* showing aberration. □□ **aberrance** *n.*

**aberration** *n.* deviation from normal type or accepted standard; distortion.

**abet** *v.* (abetted) encourage or assist in wrongdoing. □□ **abetter** *n. Law* **abettor**.

**abeyance** *n.* temporary disuse; suspension.

**abhor** *v.* (abhorred) detest; regard with disgust. □□ **abhorrence** *n.*

**abhorrent** *adj.* detestable.

**abide** *v.* bear, tolerate. □ **abide by** keep (a promise etc.); accept (consequences) etc.

**abiding** *adj.* enduring, permanent.

**ability** *n.* **1** capacity, power. **2** cleverness, talent.

**ab initio** *adv.* from beginning.

**abject** *adj.* wretched; lacking all pride. □□ **abjection** *n.* **abjectly** *adv.* **abjectness** *n.*

**abjure** *v.* renounce; repudiate. □□ **abjuration** *n.*

**ablaze** *adj. & adv.* on fire; glittering; excited.

**able** *adj.* having power or ability. □□ **ably** *adv.*

**ablutions** *n.pl. formal* process of washing oneself.

**abnegate** *v.* give up, renounce.

**abnormal** *adj.* not normal; unusual. □□ **abnormality** *n.* **abnormally** *adv.*

**aboard** *adj. & prep.* on or into (a ship, aircraft, etc.)

**abode** *n.* dwelling place.

**abolish** *v.* put end to existence or practice of. □□ **abolition** *n.*

**abominable** *adj.* very bad or unpleasant. □□ **abominably** *adv.*

**abominate** v. detest, loathe.
□□ **abomination** n.

**aboriginal** ● adj. indigenous, inhabiting land from the earliest times; (usu. **Aboriginal**) of Australian Aboriginal people. ● n. **1** aboriginal inhabitant; (usu. **Aboriginal**) aboriginal Australian. **2** colloq. Aboriginal language.

**aborigine** n. aboriginal inhabitant; (usu. **Aborigine**) aboriginal Australian.

> **Usage** Both *Aborigine(s)* and *Aboriginal(s)* are used to refer to the indigenous people of Australia. In many contexts, however, it is preferable to use the terms *Aboriginal person* and *Aboriginal people*.

**abort** v. (cause to) expel a foetus prematurely; end prematurely and unsuccessfully.

**abortion** n. premature expulsion of foetus from uterus; operation to cause this. □□ **abortionist** n.

**abortive** adj. fruitless, unsuccessful.

**abound** v. be plentiful.

**about** adv. & prep. **1** near; here and there; in circulation. **2** approximately. **3** in connection with. **4** so as to face in opposite direction. □ **about-face** (also **about-turn**) change of opinion or policy. **be about to** be on the point of (doing).

**above** adv. & prep. at or to a higher point (than); beyond the level or understanding of. □ **above board** without deception.

**abracadabra** int. magic word.

**abrasion** n. rubbing or scraping away; resulting damaged area.

**abrasive** ● adj. causing abrasion; harsh. ● n. substance used for grinding or polishing.

**abreast** adv. **1** side by side and facing same way. **2** up to date with; well-informed (about).

**abridge** v. shorten by using fewer words. □□ **abridgement** n.

**abroad** adv. **1** in or to foreign country. **2** in circulation.

**abrogate** v. repeal, abolish (law etc.). □□ **abrogation** n.

**abrupt** adj. sudden, hasty; curt; steep. □□ **abruptly** adv. **abruptness** n.

**ABS** abbr. anti-lock braking system.

**abscess** n. swelling containing pus.

**abscond** v. go away secretly or illegally. □□ **absconder** n.

**abseil** v. descend (a cliff face etc.) by using a rope fixed at a higher point.

**absence** n. **1** being away. **2** lack of.

**absent** adj. **1** not present or existing. **2** lacking. □ **absent oneself** go or stay away. **absent-minded** with one's mind on other things; forgetful. □□ **absently** adv.

**absentee** n. person not present. □ **absentee vote** *Aust.* formal vote cast on election day in electorate other than that in which elector resides. □□ **absenteeism** n.

**absinthe** n. wormwood-based aniseed-flavoured liqueur.

**absolute** adj. complete, unrestricted. □ **absolute majority** majority over all others combined; more than half. **absolute monarchy** government in which absolute power is invested in the monarch; state governed in this way. □□ **absolutely** adv.

**absolution** n. formal forgiveness of sins.

**absolutism** n. principle of government with unrestricted power. □□ **absolutist** n.

**absolve** v. free from blame or guilt.

**absorb** v. incorporate; assimilate; take in (heat, etc.); deal with easily, reduce intensity of; engross attention of. □□ **absorption** n.

**absorbent** adj. able to absorb moisture.□□ **absorbency** n.

**absorbing** adj. engrossing; intensely interesting.

**abstain** v. 1 refrain (from indulging in). 2 decline to vote.□□ **abstainer** n. **abstention** n.

**abstemious** adj. moderate or ascetic, esp. in eating and drinking. □□ **abstemiousness** n. **abstemiously** adv.

**abstinence** n. act of abstaining, esp. from food or alcohol.

**abstract** ● adj. 1 of or existing in theory rather than practice; not concrete. 2 (of art etc.) not representational. ● v. 1 remove. 2 summarise. ● n. 1 summary. 2 abstract idea, work of art, etc. □□ **abstraction** n.

**abstracted** adj. inattentive. □□ **abstractedly** adv.

**abstruse** adj. hard to understand, obscure.

**absurd** adj. wildly inappropriate; ridiculous, illogical.□□ **absurdity** n. **absurdly** adv.

**abundance** n. plenty; more than enough; wealth.□□ **abundant** adj.

**abuse** ● v. use improperly; misuse; insult verbally; maltreat. ● n. misuse; insulting language; corrupt practice; maltreatment. □□ **abusive** adj.

**abut** v. (abutted) border (upon); touch or lean (on).

**abysmal** adj. extremely bad; dire. □□ **abysmally** adv.

**abyss** n. deep chasm.

**AC** abbr. 1 alternating current. 2 Companion of the Order of Australia.

**a/c** abbr. account.

**acacia** n. flowering tree or shrub; wattle.

**academia** n. world of scholars.

**academic** ● adj. 1 scholarly; of learning. 2 of no practical relevance. ● n. teacher or scholar in university etc.□□ **academically** adv.

**academician** n. member of Academy.

**academy** n. place of specialised training; (Academy) society of distinguished scholars, artists, scientists, etc.

**acanthus** n. herbaceous plant with spiny leaves.

**a cappella** adj. & adv. (of choral music) unaccompanied.

**accede** v. formal agree to.

**accelerate** v. increase speed (of); (cause to) happen earlier. □□ **acceleration** n. **accelerator** n.

**accent** ● n. 1 style of pronunciation of region or social group. 2 emphasis. 3 prominence given to syllable by stress or pitch. 4 mark on letter indicating pronunciation. ● v. 1 emphasise. 2 write or print accents on.

**accentuate** v. emphasise, make prominent.□□ **accentuation** n.

**accept** v. 1 willingly receive. 2 answer (invitation etc.) affirmatively. 3 regard favourably. 4 receive as valid or suitable.□□ **acceptance** n.

**acceptable** adj. worth accepting; tolerable.□□ **acceptability** n. **acceptably** adv.

**access** ● n. way of approach or entry; right or opportunity to reach, use, or visit. ● v. gain access to.

**accessible** adj. reachable or obtainable; easy to understand. □□ **accessibility** n.

**accession** ● n. 1 taking office, esp. as monarch. 2 thing added. ● v. record addition of (new item) to library etc.

**accessory** n. 1 additional or extra thing. 2 person who abets or is privy to illegal act.

**accident** n. 1 unintentional and unfortunate esp. harmful event. 2 event without apparent cause. 3 unexpected event.

**accidental** *adj.* happening or done by chance or accident.
□□ **accidentally** *adv.*

**acclaim** ● *v.* welcome or applaud enthusiastically. ● *n.* public praise, applause. □□ **acclamation** *n.*

**acclimatise** *v.* (also **-ize**) adapt to new climate or conditions.
□□ **acclimatisation** *n.*

**accolade** *n.* praise given.

**accommodate** *v.* **1** provide lodging or room for. **2** adapt, harmonise, reconcile. **3** do a favour for.
□□ **accommodation** *n.*

**accommodating** *adj.* obliging.

**accompaniment** *n.* **1** instrumental or orchestral support for solo instrument, voice, or group.
**2** accompanying thing.

**accompany** *v.* **1** go with; escort. **2** *Mus.* play accompaniment for.
□□ **accompanist** *n. Mus.*

**accomplice** *n.* partner in crime.

**accomplish** *v.* succeed in doing; achieve, complete.
□□ **accomplishment** *n.*

**accomplished** *adj.* clever, skilled.

**accord** ● *v.* be consistent or in harmony. ● *n.* agreement; consent.
□ **of one's own accord** without being asked.

**according** *adv.* □ **according to** as stated by; in proportion to.

**accordingly** *adv.* **1** as circumstances suggest or require. **2** consequently; therefore.

**accordion** *n.* musical reed instrument with concertina-like bellows, keys, and buttons.

**accost** *v.* approach and speak boldly to.

**account** ● *n.* **1** narration, description. **2** arrangement at bank etc. for depositing and withdrawing money etc.; statement of financial transactions with balance.
● *v.* consider as. □ **account for** give a reckoning of; explain; kill; overcome.

**accountable** *adj.* responsible; required to account for one's conduct.

**accountant** *n.* professional keeper or verifier of accounts.
□□ **accountancy** *n.*

**accoutrements** *n.pl.* equipment, trappings.

**accredited** *adj.* officially recognised; generally accepted.

**accretion** *n.* growth by accumulation or organic enlargement; an addition.

**accrue** *v.* come as natural increase or advantage, esp. financial.
□□ **accrual** *n.*

**accumulate** *v.* acquire increasing number or quantity of; amass, collect; grow numerous. □□ **accumulation** *n.* **accumulative** *adj.* **accumulator** *n.*

**accurate** *adj.* precise; conforming exactly with truth etc. □□ **accuracy** *n.* **accurately** *adv.*

**accursed** *adj.* **1** under a curse. **2** *colloq.* detestable, annoying.

**accusative** *n.* grammatical case expressing the direct object.

**accuse** *v.* charge with fault or crime; blame. □□ **accusation** *n.* **accusatory** *adj.*

**accustom** *v.* make used (to).

**ace** ● *n.* **1** playing card with single spot. **2** expert. **3** unreturnable serve in tennis. ● *adj. colloq.* excellent.

**ACE inhibitor** *n.* class of drugs used for the treatment of high blood pressure.

**acerbic** *adj.* harsh and sharp.
□□ **acerbity** *n.*

**acetate** *n.* compound of acetic acid, esp. the cellulose ester; fabric made from this.

**acetic** *adj.* of or like vinegar.

**acetone** *n.* colourless volatile solvent of organic compounds.

**acetylene** *n.* flammable hydrocarbon gas, used esp. in welding.

**ache** ● *n.* continuous dull pain. ● *v.* suffer from or be the source of ache.

**achieve** v. reach or attain by effort; accomplish (task etc.); be successful. □□ **achievement** n.

**Achilles heel** n. person's vulnerable point.

**Achilles tendon** n. tendon attaching calf muscles to heel.

**achromatic** adj. free from colour. □□ **achromatically** adv.

**acid** ● n. **1** Chem. any of a class of substances that contain hydrogen and neutralise alkalis. **2** colloq. LSD.
● adj. sour. □ **acid rain** rain made acid by pollution. □□ **acidic** adj. **acidity** n.

**acknowledge** v. **1** recognise, accept the truth of. **2** confirm receipt of (letter etc.); show that one has noticed; express gratitude for. □ **acknowledgement of country** Aust. formal acknowledgement of traditional Aboriginal custodians of a particular area by a speaker who is not a member of the local Aboriginal community. □□ **acknowledgement** n. (also **acknowledgment**)

**acme** n. highest point.

**acne** n. skin condition with red pimples.

**acolyte** n. assistant, esp. of priest.

**acorn** n. fruit of oak.

**acoustic** ● adj. **1** of sound or sense of hearing. **2** Mus. without electrical amplification. ● n.pl. (**acoustics**) qualities of a room that affect the way sound carries in it. □□ **acoustically** adv.

**acquaint** v. make aware of or familiar with.

**acquaintance** n. being acquainted; person one knows slightly. □□ **acquaintanceship** n.

**acquiesce** v. agree, esp. tacitly; raise no objection. □□ **acquiescence** n. **acquiescent** adj.

**acquire** v. gain possession of. □ **acquired immune deficiency syndrome** see AIDS.

**acquisition** n. (esp. useful) thing acquired; acquiring, being acquired.

**acquisitive** adj. keen to acquire things.

**acquit** v. (**acquitted**) declare to be not guilty. □ **acquit oneself** conduct oneself, perform. □□ **acquittal** n.

**acre** n. in imperial system, measure of land, 4840 sq. yds, 0.405 ha.

**acreage** n. number of acres.

**acrid** adj. bitterly pungent.

**acrimonious** adj. bitter in manner or temper. □□ **acrimony** n.

**acrobat** n. performer of acrobatics.

**acrobatic** ● adj. involving spectacular gymnastic feats.
● n.pl. (**acrobatics**) acrobatic gymnastic feats.

**acronym** n. word formed from initial letters of other words.

**acrophobia** n. abnormal dread of heights.

**across** prep. & adv. **1** to or on other side (of). **2** from one side to another side (of).

**acrostic** n. poem etc. in which first (or first and last) letters of lines form word(s).

**acrylic** n. synthetic fibre made from organic substance.

**ACT** abbr. Australian Capital Territory.

**act** ● n. **1** thing done; deed; process of doing. **2** item of entertainment. **3** pretence. **4** main division of play. **5** decree of legislative body.
● v. **1** behave. **2** perform actions or functions. **3** have effect. **4** perform in play etc.; pretend; play part of.

**acting** adj. serving temporarily as.

**actinium** n. radioactive element (symbol Ac).

**action** n. **1** process of doing or acting. **2** battle. **3** lawsuit.

**actionable** adj. providing grounds for legal action.

**activate** v. make active; bring into action. □□ **activation** n.

**active** *adj.* **1** working, operating. **2** energetic. □□ **actively** *adv.*

**activism** *n.* policy of vigorous action, esp. for political cause. □□ **activist** *n.*

**activity** *n.* an action; particular pursuit.

**actor** *n.* **1** person who acts in play, film, etc.; person who behaves in way that is not genuine. **2** participant in an action or process.

**actress** *n.* female actor.

**ACTU** *abbr.* Australian Council of Trade Unions.

**actual** *adj.* **1** existing, real. **2** current. □□ **actuality** *n.*

**actually** *adv.* in fact, really.

**actuary** *n.* statistician, esp. one calculating insurance risks and premiums. □□ **actuarial** *adj.*

**actuate** *v.* cause to move, function, act.

**acuity** *n.* sharpness, acuteness.

**acumen** *n.* keen insight or discernment.

**acupressure** *n.* = SHIATSU.

**acupuncture** *n.* medical treatment using needles in parts of body to stimulate nerve impulses. □□ **acupuncturist** *n.*

**acute** *adj.* **1** keen, penetrating; shrewd. **2** (of disease) coming quickly to crisis. □ **acute accent** the accent ´. **acute angle** angle of less than 90°. □□ **acutely** *adv.*

**AD** *abbr.* (in dates) after supposed date of Christ's birth. (from Latin *Anno Domini* = in the year of the Lord)

**adage** *n.* maxim, proverb.

**adagio** *adv. Mus.* in slow time.

**adamant** *adj.* stubbornly resolute. □□ **adamantly** *adv.*

**Adam's apple** *n.* cartilaginous projection at front of neck.

**adapt** *v.* make or become suitable for new use or conditions. □□ **adaptable** *adj.*

**adaptation** *n.* **1** adapting; being adapted; thing that has been adapted. **2** process by which organism etc. becomes suited to its environment.

**adaptor** *n.* device for making equipment compatible; device for connecting several electrical plugs to one socket.

**ADD** *abbr.* attention deficit disorder; condition with symptoms such as hyperactivity and poor concentration.

**add** *v.* **1** join as increase or supplement. **2** unite (numbers) to get their total. **3** say further.

**addendum** *n.* (*pl.* **addenda**) thing to be added; material added at end of book.

**adder** *n.* small venomous snake.

**addict** *n.* person addicted, esp. to drug; *colloq.* devotee. □□ **addiction** *n.*

**addicted** *adj.* dependent on a drug as habit; devoted to an interest.

**addition** *n.* adding; person or thing added. □□ **additional** *adj.*

**additive** *n.* substance added, esp. to colour, flavour, or preserve.

**addle** *v.* **1** muddle, confuse. **2** make (an egg) rotten.

**address** ● *n.* **1** place where person lives or organisation is situated. **2** *Computing* location of item of stored information; location on World Wide Web. **3** speech delivered to audience. ● *v.* **1** write postal directions on. **2** speak or write to. **3** direct one's attention to.

**addressee** *n.* person to whom letter etc. is addressed.

**adduce** *v.* cite as proof or instance.

**adenoids** *n.pl.* enlarged lymphatic tissue between nose and throat, often hindering breathing. □□ **adenoidal** *adj.*

**adept** *adj.* skilful.

**adequate** *adj.* sufficient, satisfactory. □□ **adequacy** *n.* **adequately** *adv.*

**adhere** v. 1 stick fast. 2 behave according to (rule etc.); give allegiance.□□ **adherence** n. **adherent** adj.

**adhesion** n. 1 adhering. 2 unnatural union of body tissues due to inflammation.

**adhesive** ● adj. sticky, causing adhesion. ● n. adhesive substance.

**ad hoc** adv. & adj. for one particular occasion or use; impromptu.

**adieu** int. goodbye.

**ad infinitum** adv. without limit; for ever.

**adipose** adj. of fat; fatty.

**adjacent** adj. 1 lying near; adjoining. 2 (of pair of angles) formed on the same side of a straight line when intersected by another line. □□ **adjacency** n.

**adjective** n. word modifying or ascribing characteristics to noun or pronoun.□□ **adjectival** adj.

**adjoin** v. be next to and joined with.

**adjourn** v. postpone; break off; transfer to another place. □□ **adjournment** n.

**adjudge** v. pronounce judgement on; pronounce or award judicially.

**adjudicate** v. act as judge etc.; adjudge.□□ **adjudicator** n.

**adjunct** n. subordinate or incidental thing.

**adjure** v. charge or request solemnly or earnestly.□□ **adjuration** n.

**adjust** v. alter slightly; become familiar with, adapt to.□□ **adjustable** adj. **adjustment** n.

**adjutant** n. army officer assisting superior in administrative duties.

**ad lib** ● v. (ad libbed) improvise. ● adj. improvised. ● adv. to any desired extent.

**administer** v. 1 manage (business affairs). 2 give or hand out.

**administrate** v. act as manager (of). □□ **administrator** n.

**administration** n. 1 administering; management of public or business affairs.□□ **administrative** adj.

**admirable** adj. 1 deserving admiration. 2 excellent. □□ **admirably** adv.

**admiral** n. naval officer of highest rank.

**admire** v. regard with approval, respect, or satisfaction. □□ **admiration** n. **admirer** n. **admiring** adj. **admiringly** adv.

**admissible** adj. 1 worth accepting or considering. 2 allowable.

**admission** n. 1 acknowledgement (of error etc.) 2 (right of) entering. 3 entrance charge. 4 person admitted to hospital.

**admit** v. (admitted) 1 acknowledge. 2 recognise as true. 3 confess to. 4 let in. 5 take (patient) into hospital. 6 allow as possible.

**admittance** n. 1 admitting. 2 being admitted, usu. to a place.

**admittedly** adv. as must be admitted.

**admixture** n. thing added.

**admonish** v. 1 reprove. 2 warn. □□ **admonishment** n. **admonition** n. **admonitory** adj.

**ad nauseam** adv. to a sickening extent.

**ado** n. 1 fuss. 2 trouble.

**adobe** n. sun-dried brick.

**adolescent** ● adj. between childhood and adulthood. ● n. adolescent person.□□ **adolescence** n.

**adopt** v. 1 take (child) as one's own. 2 accept responsibility for. 3 formally approve (report etc.) □□ **adoption** n.

**adoptee** n. adopted person.

**adoptive** adj. because of adoption.

**adorable** adj. 1 deserving adoration. 2 delightful, charming.

**adore** v. 1 love intensely. 2 worship. 3 like very much.□□ **adoration** n. **adorer** n.

**adorn** v. 1 add beauty to. 2 decorate. □□ **adornment** n.

**adrenal** adj. close to kidneys.

**adrenalin** n. stimulative hormone secreted by adrenal glands.

**adrift** adv. & adj. drifting; powerless; out of order.

**adroit** adj. dexterous, skilful.

**ADSL** abbr. asymmetric digital subscriber line, technology for transmitting digital information over standard telephone lines.

**adsorb** v. attract and hold thin layer of (gas or liquid) on its surface. □□ **adsorbent** adj. & n. **adsorption** n.

**adulation** n. great praise; excessive flattery.

**adult** ● adj. 1 mature, grown-up. 2 euphem. sexually explicit. ● n. adult person. □□ **adulthood** n.

**adulterate** v. debase by adding other substances. □□ **adulteration** n.

**adultery** n. sexual infidelity to one's partner. □□ **adulterer** n. **adulterous** adj.

**advance** ● v. 1 move or put forward. 2 lend (money). ● n. 1 a forward movement; progress. 2 a loan; a rise in price. 3 (**advances**) attempts to establish friendly relationship. ● adj. done etc. beforehand. □□ **advancement** n.

**advantage** ● n. 1 beneficial feature; benefit, profit; superiority. 2 Tennis next point after deuce. ● v. benefit, favour. □ **take advantage of** make use of; exploit. □□ **advantageous** adj.

**advent** n. 1 arrival. 2 (**Advent**) season before Christmas.

**adventure** n. unusual and exciting experience; enterprise. □□ **adventurer** n.

**adventurous** adj. venturesome, enterprising.

**adverb** n. word indicating manner, degree, circumstance, etc. used to modify adjective, verb, or other adverb.

**adverbial** ● n. word or phrase that functions as an adverb. ● adj. functioning as an adverb or adverbial.

**adversary** n. enemy, opponent. □□ **adversarial** adj.

**adverse** adj. unfavourable; harmful; opposing; contrary. □□ **adversely** adv.

**adversity** n. misfortune.

**advertise** v. promote publicly to increase sales; make generally known.

**advertisement** n. public notice advertising something.

**advertorial** n. advertisement written in form of news item, editorial, etc.

**advice** n. recommendation on how to act; information.

**advisable** adj. to be recommended. □□ **advisability** n.

**advise** v. give advice to; recommend; inform.

**advisedly** adv. deliberately.

**adviser** n. (also **advisor**) person who gives advice in a particular field.

**advisory** adj. giving advice.

**advocacy** n. support or argument for cause etc.

**advocate** ● n. 1 person who speaks in favour. 2 person who pleads for another. ● v. recommend by argument.

**adze** n. axe with blade at right angles.

**aegis** n. protection; support.

**aeolian** adj. wind-borne.

**aeon** n. (also **eon**) long or indefinite period.

**aerate** v. expose to air; charge with carbon dioxide. □□ **aeration** n.

**aerial** ● n. device for transmitting or receiving radio signals. ● adj. from the air; existing in the air; like air; involving aircraft.

**aerobatics** n.pl. feats of spectacular flying of aircraft.

**aerobics** n.pl. vigorous exercises designed to increase oxygen intake. □□ **aerobic** adj.

**aerobridge** n. (also **air bridge**) portable bridge used at airports to connect passenger terminal and aircraft.

**aerodynamics** *n.pl.* study of interaction between air and solid bodies moving through it. □□ **aerodynamic** *adj.*

**aerofoil** *n.* structure with curved surfaces (e.g. aircraft wing) designed to give lift in flight.

**aeronautics** *n.pl.* science or practice of motion in the air. □□ **aeronautical** *adj.*

**aeroplane** *n.* powered flying vehicle with fixed wings.

**aerosol** *n.* pressurised container releasing substance as fine spray.

**aerospace** *n.* earth's atmosphere and outer space; technology of aviation in this region.

**aesthete** *n.* person who appreciates beauty.

**aesthetic** ● *adj.* of or sensitive to beauty; artistic, tasteful. ● *n.* set of principles underlying the work of a particular artist etc. □□ **aesthetically** *adv.* **aestheticism** *n.*

**aesthetics** *n.* study of beauty, esp. in art.

**aetiology** *n.* (also **etiology**) study of causation or of causes of disease. □□ **aetiological** *adj.*

**afar** *adv.* at or to a distance.

**affable** *adj.* friendly; courteous. □□ **affability** *n.* **affably** *adv.*

**affair** *n.* 1 thing to be done; business. 2 temporary sexual relationship.

**affect** *v.* 1 produce effect on. 2 pretend. □□ **affecting** *adj.* **affectingly** *adv.*

> **Usage** Do not confuse *affect* with *effect*, 'bring about'.

**affectation** *n.* assumed or contrived manner; pretentious display.

**affected** *adj.* pretended; full of affectation.

**affection** *n.* 1 fond feeling, goodwill. 2 mental state, emotion. □□ **affectionate** *adj.* **affectionately** *adv.*

**affidavit** *n.* written statement on oath.

**affiliate** ● *v.* attach to, adopt, or connect to as member or branch. ● *n.* affiliated person etc. □□ **affiliation** *n.*

**affinity** *n.* attraction for; close resemblance.

**affirm** *v.* 1 state emphatically or publicly. 2 declare one's support for. 3 offer emotional support or encouragement; give (life) a heightened sense of value. □□ **affirmation** *n.*

**affirmative** ● *adj.* affirming, saying yes. ● *n.* affirmative statement. ● *int.* yes. □ **affirmative action** recruitment or promotion etc. policies favouring those who are disadvantaged.

**affix** ● *v.* attach; add signature etc. ● *n.* addition; prefix, suffix.

**afflict** *v.* distress physically or mentally. □□ **affliction** *n.*

**affluent** *adj.* rich. □□ **affluence** *n.*

**afford** *v.* 1 have enough money, time, etc. for. 2 be able to spare. 3 be in a position. 4 provide.

**afforest** *v.* convert into forest; plant with trees. □□ **afforestation** *n.*

**affray** *n.* breach of peace by fighting or rioting in public.

**affront** ● *n.* open insult. ● *v.* 1 insult openly. 2 embarrass.

**afield** *adv.* to or at distance.

**AFL** *abbr.* Australian Football League.

**aflame** *adv. & adj.* 1 in flames. 2 very excited.

**afloat** *adv. & adj.* 1 floating; at sea; on board ship. 2 out of debt.

**afoot** *adv. & adj.* happening, going on.

**afore-** *comb. form* before, previously.

**aforethought** *adj.* (after noun) premeditated.

**afraid** adj. **1** alarmed, frightened. **2** (I'm afraid) used to express polite or formal apology or regret.

**afresh** adv. anew; with fresh start.

**African** ● adj. of or relating to Africa or its people, customs, or languages. ● n. native of Africa; person of African descent.

**aft** adv. at or towards stern or tail.

**after** ● prep. **1** following in time. **2** in view of. **3** despite. **4** behind. **5** in pursuit or quest of. **6** about, concerning. **7** in allusion to or imitation of. ● conj. later than. ● adv. **1** later. **2** behind. ● adj. later. □ after-effect an effect persisting after its cause has gone.

**afterbirth** n. placenta discharged from uterus after childbirth.

**aftermath** n. consequences.

**afternoon** n. time between midday and evening.

**aftershave** n. lotion used after shaving.

**afterthought** n. something thought of or added later.

**afterwards** adv. later, subsequently.

**again** adv. **1** another time. **2** as previously. **3** in addition.

**against** prep. **1** in opposition or contrast to. **2** into collision or contact with. **3** to the disadvantage of. **4** in anticipation of. **5** as compensating factor to. **6** in return for.

**agar** n. gelatinous substance obtained from seaweed, used in food etc.

**agate** n. stone streaked with bands of colour.

**age** ● n. **1** length of past life or existence. **2** (ages) colloq. long time. **3** historical period. ● v. (aged, ageing) (cause to) show signs of age; grow old; mature.

**aged** adj. of the age of; old.

**ageism** n. prejudice or discrimination on grounds of age. □□ ageist adj.

**ageless** adj. never growing or appearing old.

**agency** n. **1** business or premises of agent. **2** intervention.

**agenda** n. **1** list of items to be considered at a meeting; things to be done. **2** underlying intentions of a particular person or group.

**agent** n. **1** person acting for another in business etc. **2** spy. **3** person or thing producing effect.

**agent provocateur** n. person employed to detect suspected offenders by tempting them to do something illegal.

**agglomerate** ● v. collect into mass. ● n. mass, esp. of fused volcanic fragments. ● adj. collected into mass. □□ agglomeration n.

**agglutinate** v. stick as with glue. □□ agglutination n. agglutinative adj.

**aggrandise** v. (also -ize) increase power, rank, or wealth of; make seem greater. □□ aggrandisement n.

**aggravate** v. **1** make worse or more serious. **2** colloq. annoy. □□ aggravation n.

**aggregate** ● n. **1** sum total. **2** crushed stone. ● adj. collective, total. ● v. collect together, unite. □□ aggregation n.

**aggression** n. hostile behaviour or feelings. □□ aggressive adj. aggressor n.

**aggrieved** adj. having a grievance.

**aghast** adj. amazed and horrified.

**agile** adj. **1** quick-moving, nimble. **2** of a method of project management characterised by division of tasks into short phases of work and frequent reassessment and adaptation of plans. □□ agility n.

**agist** v. take in and feed (livestock) for payment. □□ agistment n.

**agitate** v. **1** disturb, excite; campaign, esp. politically. **2** shake briskly. □□ agitation n. agitator n.

**AGM** abbr. annual general meeting.

**agnostic** ● n. **1** person who believes that existence of God is not provable.

**2** person who is non-committal about a certain thing. ● *adj.* of agnosticism; claiming lack of knowledge of and hence commitment to.
□□ **agnosticism** *n.*

**ago** *adv.* in the past.

**agog** ● *adj.* eager, expectant. ● *adv.* eagerly, expectantly.

**agonise** *v.* (also **-ize**) undergo mental anguish; (cause) to suffer agony.

**agony** *n.* extreme mental or physical suffering. □ **agony aunt** person who gives advice to correspondents in a newspaper, magazine, etc.

**agoraphobia** *n.* abnormal fear of open spaces. □□ **agoraphobic** *adj.* & *n.*

**agrarian** *adj.* of land or its cultivation.

**agree** *v.* **1** hold or reach a similar opinion. **2** consent. □□ **agree with 1** suit health or digestion of. **2** approve of.

**agreeable** *adj.* **1** pleasing. **2** willing to agree. □□ **agreeably** *adv.*

**agreement** *n.* act or state of agreeing; arrangement, contract.

**agriculture** *n.* cultivation of soil and rearing of animals. □□ **agricultural** *adj.*

**agronomy** *n.* science of soil management and crop production.
□□ **agronomist** *n.*

**aground** *adj.* & *adv.* on (to) the bottom of shallow water.

**ague** *n.* **1** shivering fit. **2** (*arch.*) malarial fever.

**ahead** *adv.* in advance; in front; in the lead.

**AI** *abbr.* **1** artificial intelligence. **2** artificial insemination.

**aid** *v.* & *n.* help.

**aide-de-camp** *n.* (*pl.* **aides-de-camp**) officer assisting senior officer.

**AIDS** *n.* (also **Aids**) acquired immune deficiency syndrome, disease in which there is severe loss of the body's cellular immunity, greatly lowering resistance to infection and malignancy.

**aikido** *n.* Japanese form of self-defence.

**ail** *v.* be ill or in poor condition.

**aileron** *n.* hinged flap on aeroplane wing.

**ailment** *n.* minor illness or disorder.

**aim** ● *v.* intend, try; direct or point. ● *n.* purpose or object; directing of weapon etc. at object.

**aimless** *adj.* purposeless.
□□ **aimlessly** *adv.*

**ain't** *colloq.* am not, is not, are not, has not, have not.

> **Usage** The use of *ain't* is not considered correct in standard English.

**air** ● *n.* **1** mixture chiefly of oxygen and nitrogen surrounding the earth; atmosphere overhead. **2** impression given. **3** a tune. ● *v.* **1** expose (clothes, room, etc.) to air, ventilate. **2** express and discuss publicly. □ **air bag** car safety device that inflates in a collision to protect driver or passengers. **air conditioning** system controlling humidity and temperature of air in building or vehicle. **air force** branch of armed forces using aircraft.

**airborne** *adj.* carried by air or aircraft; (of aircraft) in flight.

**aircraft** *n.* (*pl.* **aircraft**) machine capable of flight. □ **aircraft carrier** ship carrying and acting as base for aircraft.

**airgun** *n.* gun with missile propelled by compressed air.

**airing** *n.* **1** exposure to air for drying etc. **2** public expression of an opinion in this way.

**airlift** ● *n.* the large scale transport of supplies by aircraft. ● *v.* transport in this way.

**airline** *n.* a company providing an air transport service.

**airlock** n. **1** stoppage of the flow in a pipe, caused by air bubble. **2** device allowing gas to escape from airtight fermentation vessel etc.; airtight compartment giving access to a pressurised chamber.

**airmail** n. mail carried by aircraft.

**airman** n. (pl. **airmen**) member of air force, esp. below rank of officer.

**airplay** n. playing of a recording on radio.

**airport** n. airfield with facilities for passengers and goods.

**airspace** n. air and skies above a country and subject to its control.

**airstrip** n. strip of ground suitable for take-off and landing of aircraft.

**airtight** adj. **1** impermeable to air. **2** colloq. without flaws.

**airwaves** n.pl. radio waves used in broadcasting.

**airway** n. **1** regular route of aircraft. **2** ventilating passage; passage for air into lungs.

**airwoman** n. (pl. **airwomen**) female member of air force, esp. below rank of officer.

**airworthy** adj. (of aircraft) fit to fly. □□ **airworthiness** n.

**airy** adj. (**airier**) **1** well-ventilated. **2** flippant. □□ **airily** adv.

**aisle** n. **1** passage between rows of seats. **2** side part of church.

**ajar** adv. & adj. (of door) slightly open.

**aka** abbr. (also **a.k.a.**) also known as.

**akimbo** adv. (of arms) with hands on hips and elbows out.

**akin** adj. **1** related. **2** similar.

**Akubra** n. Aust. propr. shallow-crowned wide-brimmed hat, esp. one of felted rabbit fur.

**à la** prep. colloq. in the style of.

**alabaster** ● n. translucent usu. white form of gypsum. ● adj. **1** of alabaster. **2** white, smooth.

**à la carte** adv. & adj. with individually priced dishes.

**alacrity** n. **1** briskness. **2** readiness.

**alarm** ● n. **1** warning of danger etc. **2** warning sound or device. **3** alarm clock. **4** frightened expectation. ● v. **1** frighten, disturb. **2** warn. □□ **alarming** adj.

**alarmist** n. person spreading needless alarm.

**alas** int. expressing grief or regret.

**albatross** n. **1** long-winged stout-bodied seabird. **2** Golf score of three strokes under par for hole.

**albeit** conj. although.

**albino** n. (pl. **albinos**) person or animal lacking pigment in skin, hair, and eyes. □□ **albinism** n.

**album** n. **1** book for displaying photographs, stamps, etc. **2** collection of recordings issued as single item on CD, record, or another medium.

**albumen** n. egg white.

**albumin** n. water-soluble protein found in egg white, milk, blood, etc.

**alchemy** n. medieval chemistry, esp. seeking to turn base metals into gold. □□ **alchemist** n.

**Alcheringa** n. (also **Alchuringa**) Aust. = DREAMTIME.

**alcohol** n. colourless volatile liquid, esp. as intoxicant present in wine, beer, spirits, etc., and as solvent, fuel, etc.; liquor containing this; other compound of this type.

**alcoholic** ● adj. of, like, containing, or caused by alcohol. ● n. person addicted to drinking alcohol. □□ **alcoholism** n.

**alcopop** n. ready-mixed soft drink containing alcohol.

**alcove** n. recess in wall of room, garden, etc.

**al dente** adj. (of pasta, vegetables, etc.) cooked so as to be still firm when bitten.

**alderman** n. elected local government councillor.

**ale** n. beer.

**alert** ● adj. **1** watchful. **2** ready to take action. ● n. **1** alarm. **2** state or period of special vigilance. **3** signal on device that prompts the user to do something or attracts their attention. ● *v.* warn.

**alfalfa** *n.* lucerne; sprouted seeds of this used as salad vegetable.

**alfredo** *n.* cream-based pasta sauce with garlic and parmesan cheese.

**alfresco** *adv. & adj.* in the open air.

**algae** *n.pl.* water plants with no true stems or leaves. □□ **algal** *adj.*

**algebra** *n.* branch of mathematics using letters to represent numbers. □□ **algebraic** *adj.*

**algorithm** *n.* process or rules for (esp. computer) calculation etc.

**alias** ● *adv.* also known as. ● *n.* assumed name.

**alibi** *n.* proof that one was elsewhere, esp. when a crime was committed; *colloq.* an excuse.

**alien** ● *adj.* **1** unfamiliar. **2** repugnant. **3** foreign. **4** of beings from another world. ● *n.* **1** foreign-born resident who is not naturalised. **2** a being from another world.

**alienate** *v.* **1** estrange. **2** transfer ownership of. □□ **alienation** *n.*

**alight** ● *adj.* on fire; lit up. ● *v.* get down or off; come to earth, settle.

**align** *v.* **1** place in or bring into line. **2** ally (oneself etc.) □□ **alignment** *n.*

**alike** ● *adj.* similar, like. ● *adv.* in similar way.

**alimentary** *adj.* of or providing food or nourishment.

**alimony** *n.* money payable to divorced or separated spouse.

**alive** *adj.* living; alert; lively.

**alkali** *n.* substance that neutralises acids, turns litmus blue, and forms caustic solutions in water. □□ **alkaline** *adj.* **alkalinity** *n.*

**alkaloid** *n.* plant-based nitrogenous compound often used as drug, e.g. morphine, quinine.

**all** ● *adj.* the whole amount, number, or extent of. ● *n.* **1** all people or

things concerned. **2** the whole of. □ **all but** almost. **all-clear** signal that danger is over. **all in** exhausted. **all out** using maximum effort. **all right** satisfactory, satisfactorily; in good condition.

**allay** *v.* **1** diminish. **2** alleviate.

**allege** *v.* declare without proof. □□ **allegation** *n.* **allegedly** *adv.*

**allegiance** *n.* loyalty; duty of subject or citizen.

**allegory** *n.* story etc. with meaning or message represented symbolically. □□ **allegorical** *adj.*

**allegro** *Mus.* ● *adv. & adj.* in lively tempo. ● *n.* allegro passage or movement.

**alleluia** *int. & n.* (also **hallelujah**) praise to God.

**allergen** *n.* substance causing allergic reaction. □□ **allergenic** *adj.*

**allergy** *n.* adverse reaction to certain substances. □□ **allergic** *adj.*

**alleviate** *v.* make (pain etc.) less severe. □□ **alleviation** *n.*

**alley** *n.* (*pl.* **alleys**) narrow street or passage; enclosure for skittles, bowling, etc.

**alliance** *n.* formal union or association; relationship resulting from shared interests.

**allied** *adj.* **1** connected or related. **2** associated in an alliance.

**alligator** *n.* large reptile of the crocodile family.

**alliteration** *n.* rhyming of consonant sounds. □□ **alliterative** *adj.*

**allocate** *v.* assign. □□ **allocation** *n.*

**allopathy** *n.* treatment of disease by conventional means. □□ **allopathic** *adj.*

**allot** *v.* (**allotted**) apportion or distribute to (person).

**allotment** *n.* small piece of land; share; allotting.

**allotrope** *n.* one of different physical forms of element.

**allow** *v.* **1** permit. **2** assign fixed sum to. **3** provide or set aside for purpose.

4 admit, concede. □□ **allowable** *adj.*
**allowably** *adv.*

**allowance** *n.* 1 amount or sum allowed, esp. regularly. 2 deduction, discount.

**alloy** ● *n.* mixture of metals. ● *v.* 1 mix (metals). 2 debase by admixture.

**allspice** *n.* spice obtained from berry of pimento plant; this berry.

**allude** *v.* make allusion (to).

**allure** ● *v.* attract, charm, or entice. ● *n.* attractiveness, charm. □□ **allurement** *n.*

**allusion** *n.* passing or indirect reference. □□ **allusive** *adj.*

**alluvium** *n.* deposit left by flood, esp. in river valley. □□ **alluvial** *adj.*

**ally** ● *n.* nation or person formally cooperating or united with another, esp. in war. ● *v.* combine in alliance (with). □□ **allied** *adj.*

**alma mater** *n.* one's university, school, or college.

**almanac** *n.* (also **almanack**) 1 annual calendar, usu. including important dates, astronomical data, etc. 2 annual directory or handbook.

**almighty** *adj.* 1 infinitely powerful. 2 *colloq.* very great.

**almond** *n.* kernel of fruit related to peach; tree bearing this.

**almost** *adv.* all but, very nearly.

**alms** *n.pl. hist.* money given to the poor.

**aloe** *n.* plant with bitter juice.

**aloft** *adj. & adv.* high up, overhead.

**alone** ● *adj.* without company or help; lonely. ● *adv.* only, exclusively.

**along** ● *prep.* beside or through (part of) the length of. ● *adv.* 1 onward, into more advanced state. 2 with oneself or others. 3 beside or through (part of) thing's length.

**alongside** *adv.* close to side of ship, wharf, etc.

**aloof** ● *adj.* distant, unsympathetic. ● *adv.* away, apart.

**alopecia** *n.* loss of hair; baldness.

**aloud** *adv.* audibly.

**ALP** *abbr.* Australian Labor Party.

**alp** *n.* high mountain. (**the Alps**) those in south-eastern Australia, those in Switzerland and adjacent countries.

**alpaca** *n.* shaggy S. American llama-like animal; its long wool; fabric made from this.

**alpha** *n.* 1 first letter of the Greek alphabet (A, α). 2 first of a series of items, categories, forms, etc. 3 dominant animal or human in particular group. □ **alpha and omega** beginning and end.

**alphabet** *n.* set of letters or signs used in a language. □□ **alphabetical** *adj.*

**alphabetise** *v.* (also **-ize**) put into alphabetical order.

**alphanumeric** *adj.* containing both letters and numbers.

**alpine** ● *adj.* of high mountains. ● *n.* plant growing on mountains or in rock gardens.

**already** *adv.* before the time in question; as early as this.

**alright** *adv.* all right.

> **Usage** Although *alright* is widely used, it is considered incorrect by many people.

**Alsatian** *n.* = German shepherd.

**also** *adv.* in addition, besides.

**alt-** *comb. form* alternative.

**altar** *n.* table for religious service; table for offerings to deity.

**altarpiece** *n.* painting behind altar.

**alter** *v.* change. □□ **alteration** *n.*

**altercation** *n.* dispute, wrangle.

**alterity** *n. formal* state of being other or different.

**alternate** ● *adj.* 1 every other. 2 (of things of two kinds) alternating. ● *v.* 1 arrange or occur by turns. 2 go repeatedly from one to another. □□ **alternately** *adv.* **alternation** *n.*

**alternative** ● *adj.* available as another choice; offering a different approach from the conventional one. ● *n.* any of two or more possibilities; choice. □□ **alternatively** *adv.*

> **Usage** The adjective *alternative* is often confused with *alternate*, which is used correctly in 'there will be a dance on alternate Saturdays'.

**alternator** *n.* dynamo generating alternating current.

**although** *conj.* despite the fact that.

**altimeter** *n.* instrument measuring altitude.

**altitude** *n.* height, esp. of object above sea level or horizon.

**alto** *n.* (*pl.* **altos**) 1 highest adult male voice; musical instrument with second or third highest pitch in its group. 2 = CONTRALTO.

**altogether** *adv.* 1 totally. 2 on the whole. 3 in total.

> **Usage** Note that *altogether* means 'in total', as in *six rooms altogether*, whereas *all together* means 'all at once' or 'all in one place' as in *six rooms all together*.

**altruism** *n.* unselfishness as principle of action. □□ **altruist** *n.* **altruistic** *adj.*

**alum** *n.* colourless compound used in medicine and dyeing.

**alumina** *n.* 1 aluminium oxide. 2 emery.

**aluminium** *n.* silvery light and malleable metallic element resistant to tarnishing bt (symbol Al).

**alumna** *n.* (*pl.* **alumnae**) female former pupil or student.

**alumnus** *n.* (*pl.* **alumni**) former pupil or student.

**alveolus** *n.* (*pl.* **alveoli**) 1 any of many tiny air sacs of lungs allowing rapid gaseous exchange. 2 bony socket for root of tooth. □□ **alveolar** *adj.* **alveolate** *adj.*

**always** *adv.* at all times; whatever the circumstances.

**Alzheimer's** *n.* progressive mental deterioration due to generalised degeneration of the brain.

**AM** *abbr.* 1 amplitude modulation. 2 Member of the Order of Australia.

**a.m.** *abbr.* before noon (*ante meridiem*).

**amalgam** *n.* 1 mixture, blend. 2 alloy of mercury used in dentistry.

**amalgamate** *v.* mix, unite. □□ **amalgamation** *n.*

**amass** *v.* heap together; accumulate.

**amateur** *n.* 1 person who engages in pursuit as pastime not profession. 2 person with limited skill. □□ **amateurish** *adj.* **amateurism** *n.*

**amaze** *v.* fill with surprise or wonder. □□ **amazement** *n.* **amazing** *adj.*

**Amazon** *n.* one of a mythical race of female warriors; (**amazon**) strong or athletic woman.

**ambassador** *n.* 1 diplomat living abroad as representative of his or her country. 2 promoter. □□ **ambassadorial** *adj.*

**amber** *n.* 1 yellow translucent fossil resin; colour of this. 2 yellow traffic light meaning caution. □ **amber fluid** *Aust. colloq.* beer.

**ambergris** *n.* waxlike substance from sperm whale used in perfumes.

**ambidextrous** *adj.* able to use either hand equally well.

**ambience** *n.* surroundings, atmosphere. □□ **ambient** *adj.*

**ambiguous** *adj.* 1 open to more than one interpretation; not having one obvious meaning. 2 not clear or decided. □□ **ambiguity** *n.*

**ambit** *n.* scope, bounds.

**ambition** *n.* determination to succeed; object of this. □□ **ambitious** *adj.*

**ambivalent** n. having mixed feelings towards person or thing.
□□ **ambivalence** n.

**amble** ● v. walk at leisurely pace, stroll. ● n. leisurely pace.

**ambo** n. Aust. ambulance officer.

**ambrosia** n. something delicious.

**ambulance** n. vehicle for taking patients to hospital.

**ambulatory** adj. of or for walking.

**ambush** ● n. surprise attack by people hiding; hiding place for this. ● v. attack from ambush; waylay.

**ameliorate** v. make or become better.□□ **amelioration** n.

**amen** int. (in prayers) so be it.

**amenable** adj. 1 responsive. 2 capable of being won over. 3 answerable (to law etc.).

**amend** v. make minor alterations in; correct error in.□□ **amendment** n.

> **Usage** Amend is sometimes confused with emend, 'remove errors from'.

**amenity** n. pleasant or useful feature of place; public toilet.

**amenorrhoea** n. Med. absence of menstruation.

**American** ● adj. of America; of the US. ● n. American person.
□ **American football** form of football played on field marked as gridiron.

**americium** n. artificially made radioactive element (symbol **Am**).

**amethyst** n. violet or purple semiprecious stone.

**amiable** adj. friendly and pleasant, likeable.□□ **amiability** n. **amiably** adv.

**amicable** adj. friendly.□□ **amicably** adv.

**amid** prep. (also **amidst**) in the middle of; during.

**amino acid** n. organic acid found in proteins.

**amiss** ● adj. wrong; faulty. ● adv. wrongly; badly.

**amity** n. friendship.

**ammeter** n. instrument for measuring electric current.

**ammonia** n. pungent strongly alkaline gas; solution of this in water.

**ammonite** n. mollusc with spiral shell found as fossil.

**ammunition** n. 1 bullets, shells, grenades, etc. 2 information usable in argument.

**amnesia** n. loss of memory.
□□ **amnesiac** adj. & n.

**amnesty** n. general pardon.

**amniocentesis** n. (pl. **amniocenteses**) sampling of amniotic fluid to detect foetal abnormality.

**amnion** n. (pl. **amnia**) innermost membrane that encloses embryo.

**amniotic** adj. of the amnion.
□ **amniotic fluid** fluid surrounding foetus in uterus. **amniotic sac** fluid-filled sac that contains and protects foetus in uterus.

**amoeba** n. (pl. **amoebae** or **amoebas**) single-celled organism capable of changing shape.□□ **amoebic** adj.

**amok** adv. □ **run amok** be out of control.

**among** prep. (also **amongst**) 1 surrounded by. 2 included in or in the category of. 3 from the joint resources of. 4 between.

**amoral** adj. beyond morality; without moral principles.

**amorous** adj. showing or feeling sexual desire.

**amorphous** adj. shapeless, vague.

**amortise** v. (also -**ize**) gradually extinguish (debt) by regular instalments.

**amount** ● n. total of anything; quantity. ● v. (**amount to**) 1 add up to; be the equivalent of. 2 develop into; become.

**amp** n. 1 ampere. 2 amplifier.

**ampere** n. SI unit of electric current.

**ampersand** n. the sign '&' (= and).

**amphetamine** n. synthetic stimulant drug.

**amphibian** n. amphibious animal or vehicle.

**amphibious** adj. living or operating on land and in water.

**amphitheatre** n. round open building with tiers of seats surrounding central space.

**ample** adj. plentiful, extensive; more than enough. □□ **amply** adv.

**amplify** v. 1 increase strength of (sound, electrical signals). 2 add detail to (story etc.) □□ **amplification** n. **amplifier** n.

**amplitude** n. 1 spaciousness. 2 maximum departure from average of oscillation, alternating current, etc.

**ampoule** n. small sealed capsule holding solution for injection.

**amputate** v. cut off surgically (limb etc.) □□ **amputation** n. **amputee** n.

**amulet** n. charm worn against evil.

**amuse** v. 1 cause to laugh or smile. 2 interest, occupy. □□ **amusing** adj.

**amusement** n. being amused; thing that amuses, esp. mechanical device for entertainment at fairground etc.

**amygdaloid** adj. almond-shaped.

**an** adj. the form of 'a' used before vowel sounds.

**anabolic steroid** n. synthetic steroid hormone used to build up bone and muscle.

**anabranch** n. Aust. arm of river that separates from, and later rejoins, the main stream.

**anachronism** n. attribution of custom, event, etc. to wrong period; thing thus attributed; out-of-date person or thing. □□ **anachronistic** adj.

**anaconda** n. large snake of S. America that kills prey by constriction.

**anaemia** n. (also **anemia**) deficiency of red blood cells or their haemoglobin, causing pallor and lack of vitality. □□ **anaemic** adj.

**anaesthesia** n. (also **anes-**) artificially induced insensibility to pain.

**anaesthetic** (also **anes-**) ● n. substance producing anaesthesia.
● adj. producing anaesthesia.

**anaesthetist** n. (also **anes-**) person who administers anaesthetics. □□ **anaesthetise** v.

**anagram** n. word or phrase formed by rearranging letters of another.

**anal** adj. 1 of the anus. 2 (in full **anal retentive**) excessively orderly and fussy. □□ **anally** adv.

**analgesic** n. & adj. (a drug) relieving pain. □□ **analgesia** n.

**analogous** adj. comparable.

**analogue** (also **analog**) ● n. analogous or parallel thing.
● adj. (usu. **analog**) (of clock etc.) using continuous rather than discrete variables to represent change.

**analogy** n. comparison between one thing and another; correspondence or partial similarity.

**analyse** v. perform analysis on. □□ **analyst** n.

**analysis** n. (pl. **analyses**) detailed examination or study; statement of result of this.

**analyte** n. substance whose chemical constituents are being identified and measured.

**analytic** adj. 1 (also **analytical**) of or using analysis. 2 (**analytics**) systematic computational analysis of data or statistics.

**anaphylaxis** n. (pl. **anaphylaxes**) acute allergic reaction to an antigen (e.g. bee sting) to which the body has become hypersensitive. □□ **anaphylactic** adj.

**anarchism** n. belief that government and law should be abolished. □□ **anarchist** n. **anarchistic** adj.

**anarchy** n. total disorder, esp. political. □□ **anarchic** adj.

**anathema** *n.* detested thing.

**anatomy** *n.* (science of) animal or plant structure.□□ **anatomical** *adj.*

**ancestor** *n.* person, animal, or plant from which another has descended or evolved; prototype.

**ancestry** *n.* lineage; ancestors collectively.□□ **ancestral** *adj.*

**anchor** ● *n.* **1** metal device used to moor ship to sea bottom; stabilising thing. **2** anchorman or anchorwoman. ● *v.* **1** secure with anchor; fix firmly. **2** act as anchorman or anchorwoman. □□ **anchorage** *n.*

**anchorman** *n.* someone who plays crucial part; coordinator, esp. compère of radio or TV program.

**anchorwoman** *n.* female anchorman.

**anchovy** *n.* small strong-flavoured fish of herring family.

**ancient** *adj.* of times long past; very old.

**ancillary** ● *adj.* providing essential support; subsidiary, auxiliary. ● *n.* ancillary worker; auxiliary.

**and** *conj.* **1** together with, added to. **2** next, then.

**andante** *Mus.* ● *adv. & adj.* in moderately slow time. ● *n.* andante passage or movement.

**androgynous** *adj.* hermaphrodite; sexually ambiguous.

**android** *n.* **1** robot with human appearance. **2** *propr.* (Android) open-source operating system used for smartphones and tablet computers.

**andrology** *n.* branch of medicine concerned with diseases etc. specific to men.

**anecdote** *n.* short amusing or interesting story about a real incident or person; account regarded as unreliable or hearsay. □□ **anecdotal** *adj.*

**anemometer** *n.* instrument for measuring wind force.

**anemone** *n.* plant with white, red, or purple flowers.

**aneroid barometer** *n.* barometer measuring air pressure by action of air on a box containing a vacuum.

**aneurism** *n.* (also **aneurysm**) excessive enlargement of an artery.

**anew** *adv.* **1** again. **2** in different way.

**angel** *n.* **1** attendant or messenger of God, usu. represented as human with wings. **2** virtuous or obliging person. □□ **angelic** *adj.* **angelically** *adv.*

**angelica** *n.* aromatic plant; its candied stalks.

**anger** ● *n.* extreme displeasure. ● *v.* make angry.

**angina** *n.* (in full **angina pectoris**) chest pain brought on by exertion, owing to poor blood supply to heart.

**angiogram** *n.* photograph taken by radiography of blood vessels after radio-opaque dyes have been injected.

**angle**[1] ● *n.* **1** space between two meeting lines or surfaces, esp. as measured in degrees. **2** corner. **3** point of view. ● *v.* **1** move or place obliquely. **2** present (information) in biased way.

**angle**[2] *v.* fish with hook and line; seek objective indirectly.□□ **angler** *n.*

**Anglican** ● *adj.* of Church of England or church in communion with it, as Anglican Church of Australia. ● *n.* member of Anglican Church.

**Anglo-** *comb. form* English or British.

**angora** *n.* fabric made from hair of angora goat or rabbit.

**angry** *adj.* (**angrier**) **1** feeling or showing anger. **2** (of wound etc.) inflamed, painful.□□ **angrily** *adv.*

**angst** *n.* anxiety; neurotic fear; guilt.

**angstrom** *n.* unit of wavelength measurement.

**anguish** *n.* severe mental or physical pain.□□ **anguished** *adj.*

**angular** *adj.* **1** having sharp corners or (of person) features; lean and bony. **2** (of angle) measured by angle. □□ **angularity** *n.*

**anigozanthos** *n.* Aust. plant commonly known as kangaroo paw.

**aniline** *n.* colourless oily liquid used in dyes, drugs, and plastics.

**animal** ● *n.* **1** living organism with sense organs and nervous system; any such being other than human. **2** brutish person. ● *adj.* **1** of or like animal. **2** carnal.

**animate** ● *adj.* having life; lively. ● *v.* enliven; give life to.

**animated** *adj.* **1** lively, living. **2** (of film etc.) using animation. □□ **animator** *n.*

**animation** ● *n.* **1** liveliness; being alive. **2** technique of film-making by photographing sequence of drawings etc. to create illusion of movement; manipulation of electronic images using computer to create moving images.

**anime** *n.* Japanese animation, often intended for mature audience.

**animism** *n.* belief that inanimate objects and natural phenomena have souls. □□ **animist** *n.* **animistic** *adj.*

**animosity** *n.* hostility.

**animus** *n.* hostility, ill feeling.

**anion** *n.* ion with negative charge.

**anise** *n.* plant with aromatic seeds.

**aniseed** *n.* seed of anise.

**ankle** *n.* joint connecting foot with leg.

**anklet** *n.* ornament worn around ankle.

**ankylosis** *n.* stiffening of joint by fusion of bones.

**annals** *n.pl.* narrative of events year by year.

**annatto** *n.* (also **anatto**) orange-red dye from a tropical fruit, used as food colouring.

**anneal** *v.* heat (metal, glass) and cool slowly, esp. to toughen.

**annelid** *n.* segmented worm, e.g. earthworm.

**annex** *v.* **1** add as subordinate part. **2** take possession of. □□ **annexation** *n.*

**annexe** *n.* (also **annex**) supplementary building; addition to document.

**annihilate** *v.* destroy utterly. □□ **annihilation** *n.*

**anniversary** *n.* yearly return of date of event; celebration of this.

**Anno Domini** see AD.

**annotate** *v.* add explanatory notes to. □□ **annotation** *n.*

**announce** *v.* make publicly known. □□ **announcement** *n.* **announcer** *n.*

**annoy** *v.* anger or distress slightly; be troublesome to. □□ **annoyance** *n.*

**annual** ● *adj.* reckoned by the year; recurring yearly. ● *n.* book etc. published yearly; plant living only one year. □□ **annually** *adv.*

**annuity** *n.* **1** yearly grant or allowance. **2** investment yielding fixed annual sum for stated period.

**annul** *v.* (**annulled**) declare invalid; cancel, abolish. □□ **annulment** *n.*

**annular** *adj.* ring-shaped.

**anode** *n.* positive electrode.

**anodise** *v.* (also **-ize**) coat (metal) with protective layer by electrolysis.

**anodyne** ● *adj.* pain-relieving; soothing. ● *n.* anodyne drug etc.

**anoint** *v.* apply oil or ointment to, esp. ritually.

**anomaly** *n.* irregular or abnormal thing. □□ **anomalous** *adj.*

**anon** *adv. arch.* soon.

**anon.** *abbr.* anonymous.

**anonymous** *adj.* **1** of unknown name or authorship. **2** featureless. □□ **anonymity** *n.*

**anorak** *n.* waterproof usu. hooded jacket.

**anorexia** *n.* **1** lack of appetite. **2** (in full **anorexia nervosa**) obsessive desire to lose weight by refusing to eat. □□ **anorexic** *adj. & n.*

**another** ● adj. additional or different. ● pron. additional or different person or thing.

**answer** ● n. **1** something said or done in reaction to a question, statement, or circumstance. **2** solution to problem. ● v. **1** make answer or response (to). **2** suit. **3** be responsible. **4** correspond to (esp. description).

**answerable** adj. **1** responsible. **2** that can be answered.

**ant** n. small insect living in complex social group.

**antacid** ● adj. preventing or correcting acidity. ● n. antacid agent.

**antagonise** v. (also -ize) provoke.

**antagonism** n. active hostility. □□ **antagonist** n.

**Antarctic** ● adj. of the south polar region. ● n. this region.

**ante-** prefix before.

**anteater** n. mammal that eats ants.

**antecedent** ● n. preceding thing or circumstance. ● adj. previous.

**antechinus** n. small marsupial mouse.

**antedate** v. **1** precede in time. **2** give earlier than true date to.

**antediluvian** adj. of time before Noah's flood; antiquated.

**antelope** n. animal resembling deer.

**antenatal** adj. before birth; of pregnancy.

**antenna** n. **1** (pl. antennae) insect's or crustacean's feeler. **2** (pl. antennas) aerial.

**anterior** adj. **1** nearer the front. **2** prior.

**ante-room** n. small room leading to main one.

**anthem** n. **1** song adopted by country or by group as expression of identity. **2** piece of music to be sung in religious service.

**anther** n. part of flower's stamen containing pollen.

**anthology** n. collection of poems, essays, stories, etc.

**anthracite** n. hard kind of coal burning with little flame or smoke.

**anthrax** n. disease of sheep and cattle transmissible to humans, usu. affecting skin and lungs.

**anthropocentric** adj. regarding humankind as centre of existence.

**anthropoid** ● adj. human in form. ● n. anthropoid ape.

**anthropology** n. study of humankind, esp. societies and customs. □□ **anthropological** adj. **anthropologist** n.

**anthropomorphism** n. attributing of human characteristics to god, animal, or thing. □□ **anthropomorphic** adj.

**anti-** prefix opposed to; preventing; opposite of; unconventional.

**antibiotic** ● n. substance that can inhibit or destroy bacteria etc. ● adj. functioning as antibiotic.

**antibody** n. protein formed in blood in reaction to substance that it then destroys.

**anticipate** v. **1** expect, look forward to. **2** forestall (action, person, or thing). □□ **anticipation** n. **anticipatory** adj.

**anticlimax** n. disappointing conclusion to something significant.

**anticlockwise** ● adv. in direction opposite to clockwise. ● adj. moving anticlockwise.

**antics** n.pl. foolish behaviour.

**anticyclone** n. system of winds rotating outwards from area of high pressure, producing fine weather.

**antidepressant** ● n. drug etc. alleviating depression. ● adj. alleviating depression.

**antidote** n. medicine etc. used to counteract poison.

**antifreeze** n. substance added to water (esp. in vehicle's radiator) to lower its freezing point.

**antigen** n. foreign substance causing body to produce antibodies.

**anti-hero** n. (pl. **anti-heroes**) central character lacking conventional heroic qualities.

**antihistamine** n. drug that counteracts effect of histamine, used esp. to treat allergies.

**anti-lock** adj. (of brakes) not locking when applied suddenly.

**antimony** n. brittle silvery metallic element (symbol Sb).

**antinomy** n. contradiction between two reasonable beliefs or conclusions; conflict between two laws or authorities.

**antipasto** n. (pl. **antipasti**) Italian appetiser.

**antipathy** n. strong aversion or dislike.□□ **antipathetic** adj.

**antipodes** n.pl. places diametrically opposite each other on the earth, esp. (also **Antipodes**) Australasia in relation to Europe.□□ **antipodean** n. & adj.

**antipyretic ●** adj. preventing or reducing fever. **●** n. antipyretic drug.

**antiquarian ●** adj. of or dealing in antiques or rare books. **●** n. person who studies or deals in antiques.

**antiquated** adj. old-fashioned.

**antique ●** n. old valuable object, esp. piece of furniture. **●** adj. **1** of or existing since old times. **2** old-fashioned.

**antiquity** n. ancient times; relic from ancient times.

**anti-Semitic** adj. hostile to or prejudiced against Jewish people. □□ **anti-Semite** n. **anti-Semitism** n.

**antiseptic ●** adj. counteracting sepsis by destroying germs. **●** n. antiseptic substance.

**antiserum** n. serum containing antibodies against specific antigens.

**antisocial** adj. opposed or harmful to society; not sociable.

**antithesis** n. (pl. **antitheses**) direct opposite; contrast.□□ **antithetic** adj. (also **antithetical**).

**antitoxin** n. antibody counteracting toxin.□□ **antitoxic** adj.

**antivenene** n. (also **antivenom**) antiserum effective against specific poisons in venom of snakes and spiders etc.

**antiviral ●** adj. **1** (of drug etc.) effective against viruses. **2** (also **antivirus**) (of software) designed to detect, remove, or offer protection against computer viruses. **●** n. antiviral drug etc.

**antler** n. branched horn of deer.

**antonym** n. word opposite in meaning to another, e.g. *bad* is an antonym of *good*.

**antrum** n. natural cavity in body, esp. in bone.

**anus** n. excretory opening at end of alimentary canal.

**anvil** n. iron block on which metals are worked.

**anxiety** n. troubled state of mind; worry.

**anxious** adj. troubled, uneasy in the mind. □□ **anxiously** adv.

**any** adj. one or some from a quantity; every.

**anybody** adj. any person.

**anyhow** adv. **1** anyway. **2** not in orderly manner.

**anyone** pron. anybody.

**anything** n. any item.

**anyway** adv. in any case.

**anywhere** adv. & pron. (in or to) any place.

**Anzac** n. soldier in Australian and New Zealand Army Corps serving in Gallipoli campaign during First World War; member from the armed services of Australia and New Zealand.□ **Anzac biscuit** Aust. biscuit made with rolled oats, golden syrup, etc. **Anzac Day** Aust. 25 April.

**AO** abbr. Officer of the Order of Australia.

**aorta** *n.* main artery, carrying oxygenated blood from heart. □□ **aortic** *adj.*

**apart** *adv.* separately; into pieces; to or at a distance.

**apartheid** *n.* racial segregation.

**apartment** *n.* single room; a flat.

**apathy** *n.* 1 lack of interest. 2 indifference. □□ **apathetic** *adj.*

**ape** ● *n.* 1 tailless monkey-like primate. 2 imitator. ● *v.* imitate. □□ **apelike** *adj.*

**aperient** ● *adj.* laxative. ● *n.* laxative medicine.

**aperitif** *n.* alcoholic drink before meal.

**aperture** *n.* opening or gap, esp. variable one letting light in camera.

**apex** *n.* highest point or level.

**aphasia** *n.* loss of verbal understanding or expression, resulting from brain damage.

**aphid** *n.* sucking insect that infests plants.

**aphorism** *n.* short wise saying. □□ **aphoristic** *adj.*

**aphrodisiac** ● *adj.* arousing sexual desire. ● *n.* aphrodisiac substance.

**apiary** *n.* place where bees are kept. □□ **apiarist** *n.*

**apiculture** *n.* bee-keeping.

**apiece** *adv.* for each one.

**aplomb** *n.* self-assurance.

**apocalypse** *n.* 1 destructive event. 2 revelation, esp. about end of the world. □□ **apocalyptic** *adj.*

**Apocrypha** *n.pl.* biblical writings not forming part of accepted canon.

**apocryphal** *adj.* of doubtful authenticity; invented.

**apogee** *n.* 1 highest point; climax. 2 point furthest from earth in orbit of moon.

**apolitical** *adj.* not interested in or involved in politics.

**apologetic** *adj.* expressing regret. □□ **apologetically** *adv.*

**apologise** *v.* (also **-ize**) make apology.

**apologist** *n.* person who defends by argument.

**apology** *n.* regretful acknowledgement of offence or failure; explanation.

**apoplexy** *n. dated* 1 a stroke. 2 *colloq.* extreme anger. □□ **apoplectic** *adj.*

**apostasy** *n.* abandonment of belief, faith, etc.

**apostate** *n.* person who renounces belief. □□ **apostatise** *v.* (also **-ize**)

**a posteriori** *adj. & adv.* from effects to causes.

**apostle** *n.* 1 leader of reform. 2 (**Apostle**) any of twelve men sent by Christ to preach the gospel. □□ **apostolic** *adj.*

**apostrophe** *n.* punctuation mark (') indicating possession or marking omission of letter(s) or number(s).

**apothecary** *n. arch.* pharmaceutical chemist.

**apotheosis** *n.* (*pl.* **apotheoses**) 1 deification. 2 glorification or sublime example of thing.

**app** *n.* computer application; application (form).

**appal** *v.* (**appalled**) dismay, horrify.

**apparatus** *n.* equipment for scientific or other work.

**apparel** *n. formal* clothing. □□ **apparelled** *adj.*

**apparent** *adj.* 1 obvious. 2 seeming. □□ **apparently** *adv.*

**apparition** *n.* 1 thing that appears, esp. of startling kind. 2 ghost.

**appeal** ● *v.* 1 request earnestly or formally. 2 be attractive. 3 resort to for support. 4 apply to higher court for revision of judicial decision. 5 *Cricket* ask umpire to declare batter out. ● *n.* 1 appealing. 2 request for aid. 3 referral of case to higher court. 4 attractiveness.

**appear** v. **1** become or be visible. **2** seem. □□ **appearance** n.

**appease** v. **1** make calm or quiet, esp. conciliate (aggressor) with concessions. **2** satisfy (appetite etc.) □□ **appeasement** n.

**appellant** n. person who appeals to higher court.

**appellation** n. formal name, title.

**append** v. attach, affix, add. □□ **appendage** n.

**appendectomy** n. (also **appendicectomy**) surgical removal of appendix.

**appendicitis** n. inflammation of appendix.

**appendix** n. (pl. **appendices** or **appendixes**) **1** tubular sac attached to large intestine. **2** subsidiary matter at the end of a book etc.

**appertain** v. be relevant; relate (to).

**appetiser** n. thing eaten or drunk to stimulate appetite.

**appetising** adj. (esp. of food) stimulating the appetite.

**appetite** n. natural craving, esp. for food etc.; inclination, desire.

**applaud** v. express approval (of). □□ **applause** n.

**apple** n. roundish firm fruit; tree bearing this.

**appliance** n. device etc. for specific task.

**applicable** adj. appropriate, relevant. □□ **applicability** n.

**applicant** n. person who applies for job etc.

**application** n. **1** formal request. **2** applying; substance applied. **3** relevance; use. **4** diligence. **5** computer program designed to fulfil a particular purpose.

**applicator** n. device for applying ointment etc.

**appliqué** n. piece of fabric attached ornamentally.

**apply** v. **1** formally request. **2** be relevant. **3** make use of. **4** put or

spread (on). □ **apply oneself** give one's attention and energy.

**appoint** v. **1** assign job or office to. **2** fix (time etc.)

**appointee** n. person appointed.

**appointment** n. **1** arrangement to meet or visit at specified time. **2** job.

**apportion** v. share out. □□ **apportionment** n.

**apposite** adj. appropriate; well expressed.

**apposition** n. placing side by side.

**appraise** v. estimate value or quality of. □□ **appraisal** n.

**appreciable** adj. significant, considerable.

**appreciate** v. **1** (highly) value. **2** be grateful for. **3** understand, recognise. **4** rise in value. □□ **appreciative** adj.

**appreciation** n. **1** appreciating; being appreciated. **2** full understanding of a situation. **3** increase in monetary value.

**apprehend** v. **1** arrest. **2** understand. □□ **apprehension** n.

**apprehensive** adj. uneasy, fearful. □□ **apprehensively** adv.

**apprentice** ● n. person learning trade by working for agreed period. ● v. engage as apprentice. □□ **apprenticeship** n.

**apprise** v. inform.

**approach** ● v. **1** come nearer (to) in space or time. **2** be similar or approximate to. **3** set about. **4** make tentative proposal to. ● n. **1** act or means of approaching. **2** approximation. **3** technique. **4** Golf stroke from fairway to green. **5** part of aircraft flight before landing.

**approachable** adj. friendly, easy to talk to.

**approbation** n. approval, consent.

**appropriate** ● adj. suitable, proper. ● v. **1** take possession of. **2** devote (money etc.) to special purposes. □□ **appropriately** adv.

**appropriation** n. **1** appropriating; being appropriated. **2** assignment of something to a special purpose; thing so assigned, esp. sum of money.

**approval** *n.* approving; consent.

**approve** *v.* sanction; regard with favour.

**approx.** *abbr.* approximately.

**approximate** ● *adj.* fairly correct or accurate; near to actual. ● *v.* be very similar. □□ **approximately** *adv.* approximation *n.*

**appurtenances** *n.pl.* belongings; accessories.

**Apr.** *abbr.* April.

**apricot** ● *n.* small orange-yellow peachlike fruit; its colour. ● *adj.* orange-yellow.

**April** *n.* fourth month.

**a priori** ● *adj.* 1 from cause to effect. 2 not derived from experience. 3 assumed without investigation. ● *adv.* 1 deductively. 2 as far as one knows.

**apron** *n.* 1 garment protecting front of clothes. 2 part of stage in front of curtain. 3 area on airfield for manoeuvring or loading.

**apropos** ● *adj.* 1 appropriate. 2 *colloq.* in respect of. ● *adv.* 1 appropriately. 2 incidentally. 3 concerning.

**apse** *n.* arched or domed recess, esp. at end of church.

**apt** *adj.* 1 appropriate, suitable. 2 having a tendency. 3 quick to learn.

**aptitude** *n.* talent; ability, esp. specified.

**aqua** *n. & adj.* aquamarine.

**aqualung** *n.* = SCUBA.

**aquamarine** ● *n.* bluish-green beryl; its colour. ● *adj.* bluish-green.

**aquaplane** ● *n.* board for riding on water, pulled by speedboat. ● *v.* (of vehicle) glide uncontrollably on wet surface.

**aquarium** *n.* (*pl.* **aquariums** or **aquaria**) tank for keeping fish etc.; building containing a number of these.

**Aquarius** *n.* eleventh sign of zodiac, the Water-carrier. □□ **Aquarian** *adj. & n.*

**aquarobics** *n.pl.* aerobic exercises performed in water.

**aquatic** *adj.* growing or living in water; in or on water.

**aqueduct** *n.* structure carrying waterway over valley.

**aqueous** *adj.* of or like water.

**aquifer** *n.* layer of water-bearing rock or soil.

**aquiline** *adj.* 1 of or like an eagle. 2 (of nose) curved.

**Arab** *n. & adj.* (member) of Semitic people of Middle East.

**arabesque** *n.* 1 *Ballet* posture with one leg extended horizontally backwards. 2 decoration with intertwined leaves, scroll work, etc.

**Arabic numerals** *n.pl.* symbols 1, 2, 3, etc.

**arable** *adj.* (of land) suitable for crop production.

**arachnid** *n.* creature of class comprising spiders, scorpions, etc.

**arbiter** *n.* 1 arbitrator. 2 person influential in specific field.

**arbitrage** *n.* buying and selling of stocks etc. to take advantage of varying prices in different markets. □□ **arbitrageur** *n.*

**arbitrary** *adj.* 1 random. 2 capricious, despotic. □□ **arbitrarily** *adv.*

**arbitrate** *v.* settle disputes between others. □□ **arbitrator** *n.*

**arbitration** *n.* settlement of disputes by arbitrator; *Aust.* compulsory settlement of industrial dispute by arbitrator appointed by industrial court.

**arboreal** *adj.* of or living in trees.

**arboriculture** *n.* cultivation of trees and shrubs.

**arbour** *n.* (also **arbor**) shady garden alcove enclosed by trees etc.

**arc** ● *n.* 1 part of circumference of circle or other curve. 2 luminous

discharge between two electrodes.
**3** (in a novel etc.) development or resolution of the narrative or principal theme. ● *v.* **1** form electric arc. **2** move in a curve.

**arcade** *n.* **1** covered walk, esp. lined with shops. **2** series of arches supporting or along wall. **3** enclosed place containing games machines etc.

**Arcadian** *adj.* ideally rustic.

**arcane** *adj.* mysterious, secret.

**arch**[1] ● *n.* curved structure supporting bridge, floor, etc. as opening or ornament. ● *v.* form into arch.

**arch**[2] *adj.* self-consciously or affectedly playful.

**archaeology** *n.* (also **archeology**) study of ancient cultures, esp. by excavation and interpretation of material remains. □□ **archaeological** *adj.* **archaeologist** *n.*

**archaic** *adj.* belonging to former or ancient times; (of word) no longer in ordinary use.

**archaism** *n.* archaic word or phrase.

**archangel** *n.* angel of highest rank.

**archbishop** *n.* bishop of highest rank.

**archdeacon** *n.* Anglican cleric next below bishop. □□ **archdeaconry** *n.*

**archdiocese** *n.* archbishop's diocese. □□ **archdiocesan** *adj.*

**arch-enemy** *n.* chief enemy.

**archery** *n.* shooting with bow and arrows. □□ **archer** *n.*

**archetype** *n.* original model; typical example. □□ **archetypal** *adj.*

**archipelago** *n.* (*pl.* **archipelagos**) group of islands; sea around this.

**architect** *n.* **1** designer of buildings etc. **2** person who brings about specified thing.

**architecture** *n.* **1** design and construction of buildings; style of building. **2** *Computing* conceptual structure of computer. □□ **architectural** *adj.*

**architrave** *n.* **1** moulded frame around doorway or window. **2** main beam laid across tops of classical columns.

**archive** ● *n.* collection of documents or records; place where these are kept. ● *v.* **1** place in archive. **2** *Computing* transfer (data) to less frequently used file. □□ **archivist** *n.*

**archway** *n.* arched entrance or passage.

**Arctic** ● *adj.* **1** of the north polar regions. **2** (**arctic**) *colloq.* very cold. ● *n.* Arctic region.

**ardent** *adj.* eager, fervent, passionate. □□ **ardently** *adv.*

**ardour** *n.* (also **ardor**) zeal, enthusiasm.

**arduous** *adj.* hard to accomplish; strenuous.

**area** *n.* **1** extent or measure of surface. **2** region. **3** space for specific purpose. **4** scope, range.

**arena** *n.* **1** centre of amphitheatre. **2** scene of conflict. **3** sphere of action.

**areola** *n.* (*pl.* **areolae**) circular pigmented area, esp. around nipple. □□ **areolar** *adj.*

**arête** *n.* sharp mountain ridge.

**argon** *n.* inert gaseous element (symbol Ar).

**argot** *n.* jargon or slang of a group or class.

**argue** *v.* **1** exchange views, esp. heatedly. **2** give reasons for opinion. □□ **arguable** *adj.* **arguably** *adv.*

**argument** *n.* **1** (esp. heated) exchange of views. **2** reasoning. **3** summary of book etc. □□ **argumentation** *n.*

**argumentative** *adj.* fond of arguing.

**argy-bargy** *n. joc.* dispute, wrangle.

**aria** *n.* song for one voice in opera, oratorio, etc.

**arid** *adj.* dry, parched. □□ **aridity** *n.*

**Aries** *n.* first sign of zodiac, the Ram. □□ **Arian** *adj. & n.*

**arise** v. (arose, arisen, arising)
**1** originate. **2** result. **3** emerge. **4** rise.

**aristocracy** n. ruling class; nobility.

**aristocrat** n. member of aristocracy.
□□ **aristocratic** adj.

**arithmetic** ● n. science of numbers;
use of numbers, computation. ● adj.
(also **arithmetical**) of arithmetic.

**ark** n. (in Bible) ship in which Noah
escaped the Flood.

**arm** ● n. **1** upper limb of the human
body; raised side part of chair etc.
**2** (**arms**) weapons. **3** division of a
company or organisation. ● v. equip
with arms; make (bomb) ready to
explode. □□ **armful** n.

**armada** n. fleet of warships.

**armadillo** n. (pl. **armadillos**)
S. American mammal with plated
body.

**Armageddon** n. final disastrous
conflict; in the Bible, the last battle
between good and evil before the
Day of Judgement.

**armament** n. military weapon etc.

**armature** n. **1** rotating coil or coils of
dynamo or electric motor. **2** iron bar
placed across poles of magnet.
**3** framework on which sculpture is
moulded.

**armchair** n. chair with raised sides.

**armistice** n. truce.

**armorial** adj. of heraldic arms.

**armour** n. protective covering worn
in fighting; metal plates etc.
protecting ship, car, tank, etc.;
armoured vehicles. □□ **armoured** adj.

**armpit** n. hollow under arm at the
shoulder.

**army** n. **1** organised force armed for
fighting on land. **2** very large number.
**3** organised body.

**aroma** n. **1** smell, esp. a pleasant
one. **2** subtle quality. □□ **aromatic** adj.

**aromatherapy** n. inhalation,
massage, etc. using essential oils and
plant extracts to promote health and
well-being. □□ **aromatherapist** n.

**around** adv. & prep. **1** in a circle or
curve; so as to surround someone or
something; so as to cover a whole
area or group. **2** so as to face in a
different direction; facing in a
particular way. **3** to a place by a
particular route; colloq. to someone's
home. **4** so as to surround or enclose.
**5** going past (an obstacle) and curving
to go back along the other side.
**6** visiting in a series; seeing the whole
of. **7** approximately.

**arouse** v. **1** induce (esp. emotion).
**2** awake from sleep. **3** stir into activity.
**4** stimulate sexually. □□ **arousal** n.

**arpeggio** n. (pl. **arpeggios**) notes of
musical chord played in succession.

**arrack** n. alcoholic spirit made esp.
from rice.

**arraign** v. indict, accuse; find fault
with. □□ **arraignment** n.

**arrange** v. **1** put in order. **2** plan or
provide for. **3** take measures. **4** come
to agreement. **5** Mus. adapt
(composition). □□ **arrangement** n.

**arrant** adj. downright, utter.

**array** ● n. **1** imposing or
well-ordered series or display.
**2** ordered arrangement. **3** literary
outfit or dress. ● v. **1** deck, adorn.
**2** set in order. **3** marshal (forces).

**arrears** n.pl. **1** outstanding debt.
**2** what remains to be done.

**arrest** v. **1** lawfully seize. **2** stop.
**3** catch attention of. ● n. **1** arresting,
being arrested. **2** stoppage.

**arrive** v. reach destination; reach
(conclusion); colloq. become
successful; be born. □□ **arrival** n.

**arrogant** adj. proud and overbearing.
□□ **arrogance** n. **arrogantly** adv.

**arrogate** v. claim without right.
□□ **arrogation** n.

**arrow** n. pointed missile shot from
bow.

**arrowroot** n. nutritious starch.

**arse** n. (US **ass**) colloq. buttocks or
anus.

**arsenal** *n.* place where weapons and ammunition are made or stored.

**arsenic** *n.* **1** semi-metallic element (symbol As). **2** strongly poisonous compound of this.

**arson** *n.* act of maliciously setting fire to building, forest, etc. □□ **arsonist** *n.*

**art** *n.* **1** production of something beautiful; paintings and sculptures. **2** (arts) subjects other than sciences; creative activities, e.g. painting, music, writing. □ **art house** cinema that specialises in showing films that are experimental or artistic.

**artefact** *n.* (also **artifact**) **1** object made by a human being. **2** something observed in a scientific experiment etc. that is not naturally present but occurs as a result of the preparative or investigative procedure.

**arteriosclerosis** *n.* hardening and thickening of artery walls.

**artery** *n.* **1** blood vessel carrying blood from heart. **2** main road or railway line. □□ **arterial** *adj.*

**artesian bore** *n.* (also **artesian well**) *Aust.* well in which water rises by natural pressure through a vertically drilled hole.

**artful** *adj.* crafty, sly. □□ **artfully** *adv.*

**arthritis** *n.* condition in which there is pain and stiffness in the joints. □□ **arthritic** *adj.* & *n.*

**arthro-** *comb. form* of a joint.

**arthropod** *n.* animal with segmented body and jointed limbs, e.g. insect, spider, crustacean.

**artichoke** *n.* **1** (in full **globe artichoke**) plant with flowers of leaflike scales used as vegetable. **2** (in full **Jerusalem artichoke**) type of sunflower with root eaten as vegetable.

**article** ● *n.* **1** item or thing. **2** short piece of non-fiction in newspaper etc. **3** clause of agreement etc.

● *v.* employ under contract as trainee. □ **definite article** the word 'the'. **indefinite article** the word 'a' or 'an'.

**articulate** ● *adj.* **1** fluent and clear in speech. **2** having joints.

● *v.* **1** pronounce distinctly; express clearly. **2** connect with joints. □□ **articulately** *adv.* **articulation** *n.*

**articulated** *adj.* **1** (of insects, crustaceans, etc.) having the body and limbs composed of segments joined together; (of bus, semitrailer, etc.) with sections connected by flexible joint.

**artifice** *n.* trick; cunning; skill, ingenuity.

**artificer** *n.* inventor; craftsperson.

**artificial** *adj.* not originating naturally; man-made. □ **artificial intelligence** development of computers to do things normally requiring human intelligence. □□ **artificiality** *n.* **artificially** *adv.*

**artillery** *n.* heavy guns used in land warfare; branch of army using these. □□ **artilleryman** *n.*

**artisan** ● *n.* skilled worker or craftsperson. ● *adj.* (of food or drink) made in a traditional or non-mechanised way using high-quality ingredients.

**artist** *n.* **1** person who practises any art, esp. painting. **2** artiste. **3** person skilled at a particular task. □□ **artistic** *adj.* **artistically** *adv.* **artistry** *n.*

**artiste** *n.* professional entertainer.

**artless** *adj.* **1** guileless, ingenuous. **2** natural. **3** clumsy. □□ **artlessly** *adv.*

**arty** *adj.* (**artier**) pretentiously or affectedly artistic.

**as** ● *adv.* to the same extent. ● *conj.* **1** in the same way that. **2** while, when. **3** since, seeing that. **4** although. ● *prep.* in the capacity or form of.

**asafoedita** *n.* strong-smelling spice.

**asap** *abbr.* (also **a.s.a.p.**) as soon as possible.

**asbestos** *n.* fibrous silicate mineral; heat-resistant or insulating substance made from this.

**asbestosis** *n.* lung disease resulting from inhalation of asbestos fibres.

**ascend** *v.* 1 rise. 2 climb, go or come up.

**ascendant** *adj.* rising.

**ascension** *n.* ascent, esp. (**Ascension**) of Christ into heaven.

**ascent** *n.* 1 ascending, rising. 2 upward slope or path etc.

**ascertain** *v.* find out for certain.

**ascetic** ● *adj.* severely abstinent; self-denying. ● *n.* ascetic person. □□ **asceticism** *n.*

**ascorbic acid** *n.* vitamin C.

**ascribe** *v.* attribute. □□ **ascription** *n.*

**ASEAN** *abbr.* Association of South East Asian Nations.

**asepsis** *n.* absence of sepsis or harmful bacteria; aseptic method in surgery. □□ **aseptic** *adj.*

**asexual** ● *adj.* 1 without sexual feelings or associations. 2 (of reproduction) not involving fusion of gametes; without sex or sexual organs. ● *n.* asexual person. □□ **asexually** *adv.*

**ash** *n.* 1 N. hemisphere tree with silver-grey bark; any similar Australian tree. 2 powdery residue left after burning. 3 (**the Ashes**) trophy in cricket between Australia and England.

**ashamed** *adj.* embarrassed by shame; reluctant owing to shame.

**ashen** *adj.* grey, pale.

**ashore** *adv.* to or on shore.

**Asian** ● *adj.* of or relating to Asia or its people, customs, or languages. ● *n.* native of Asia; person of Asian descent.

**aside** ● *adv.* 1 to or on one side. 2 out of consideration. ● *n.* words spoken aside, esp. by actor to audience.

**asinine** *adj.* 1 asslike. 2 stupid.

**ASIO** *abbr.* Australian Security Intelligence Organisation.

**ask** ● *v.* 1 call for answer to or about. 2 seek to obtain from another person. 3 invite. ● *n. colloq.* task; request.

**askance** *adv.* sideways. ● **look askance** at look with distrust or disapproval.

**askew** ● *adv.* crookedly. ● *adj.* oblique; awry.

**aslant** ● *adv.* at a slant. ● *prep.* obliquely across.

**asleep** *adj. & adv.* in or into state of sleep.

**asparagus** *n.* plant of lily family; its edible shoots.

**aspect** *n.* 1 viewpoint, feature, etc. to be considered. 2 appearance, look. 3 side facing specified direction.

**asperity** *n.* harshness or sharpness of temper.

**aspersion** *n.* derogatory remark.

**asphyxia** *n.* suffocation.

**asphyxiate** *v.* suffocate. □□ **asphyxiation** *n.*

**aspic** *n.* clear savoury jelly.

**aspidistra** *n.* house plant.

**aspirant** ● *adj.* aspiring. ● *n.* person who aims to achieve something.

**aspirate** ● *n.* sound of 'h'. ● *v.* 1 pronounce with 'h'. 2 draw (fluid) by suction from cavity etc.

**aspiration** *n.* 1 desire, ambition. 2 aspirating.

**aspirator** *n.* apparatus for aspirating fluid.

**aspire** *v.* have ambition or strong desire.

**aspirin** *n.* drug that relieves pain and reduces fever; tablet of this.

**ass** *n.* 1 donkey. 2 *colloq.* stupid person. 3 *US* = ARSE.

**assail** *v.* attack physically or verbally. □□ **assailant** *n.*

**assassinate** *v.* kill for political or religious motives. □□ **assassin** *n.* **assassination** *n.*

**assault** ● *n.* violent physical or verbal attack; *Law* threat or display

of violence against person.
● v. make assault on.

**assay** ● n. test of metal or ore for ingredients and quality. ● v. make assay of.

**assemble** v. put together parts of; bring or come together.

**assembly** n. assembling; assembled group, esp. as legislative body etc.

**assent** v. agree; consent.
● n. consent, approval.□□ assenter n.

**assert** v. declare; enforce claim to.
□□ assertion n.

**assertive** adj. tending to assert oneself; forthright, positive.
□□ assertively adv. assertiveness n.

**assess** v. 1 estimate size or quality of; estimate value of (property etc.) for taxation. 2 fix amount of (tax, fine, etc.) □□ assessable adj. assessment n. assessor n.

**asset** n. 1 property with money value. 2 useful quality; person or thing having this.

**assiduous** adj. persevering, hard-working.□□ assiduity n. assiduously adv.

**assign** v. 1 allot, appoint; fix (time, place, etc.) 2 designate or set (something) aside for specific purpose.□□ assignable adj. assigner n. assignor n. Law

**assignation** n. 1 arrangement to meet. 2 assigning, being assigned.

**assignee** n. Law person to whom right or property is assigned.

**assignment** n. 1 task or mission. 2 written work required from student. 3 assigning, being assigned.

**assimilate** v. absorb or be absorbed into system; make like.
□□ assimilable adj. assimilation n. assimilative adj.

**assist** v. help.□□ assistance n.

**assistant** n. helper; subordinate worker.

**associate** ● v. 1 connect mentally; join, combine. 2 have frequent

dealings. ● n. partner, colleague; friend, companion. ● adj. 1 joined, allied. 2 of lower status.

**association** n. group organised for joint purpose; associating, being associated; connection of ideas.

**assonance** n. rhyming of vowel sounds.

**assorted** adj. of various sorts, mixed.

**assortment** n. diverse group or mixture.

**assuage** v. soothe; appease.

**assume** v. 1 take to be true. 2 simulate. 3 undertake. 4 take on (aspect, attribute, etc.)
□□ assumption n.

**assurance** n. 1 declaration. 2 insurance, esp. of life. 3 certainty; self-confidence.

**assure** v. tell (person) confidently; promise.

**assured** adj. 1 sure, confident. 2 insured.

**assuredly** adv. certainly.

**astatine** n. radioactive element (symbol At).

**aster** n. plant with bright daisy-like flowers.

**asterisk** n. symbol (*) used to indicate omission etc.

**astern** adv. 1 in or to rear of ship or aircraft. 2 backwards.

**asteroid** n. one of many small rocky bodies revolving around sun between Mars and Jupiter.

**asthma** n. condition marked by difficulty in breathing.□□ asthmatic adj.

**astigmatism** n. eye or lens defect resulting in distorted images.
□□ astigmatic adj.

**astonish** v. surprise, amaze.
□□ astonishment n.

**astound** v. astonish greatly.

**astral** adj. of or from the stars.

**astray** adv. & adj. away from proper path.

**astride** ● *adv.* with one leg on each side. ● *prep.* astride of.

**astringent** ● *adj.* 1 causing contraction of body tissue. 2 severe, austere. ● *n.* astringent substance. □□ astringency *n.*

**astrology** *n.* study of influence of planets, stars, etc., on human affairs. □□ astrologer *n.*

**astronaut** *n.* person trained to travel in spacecraft.

**astronautics** *n.pl.* science of space travel and its technology. □□ astronautical *adj.*

**astronomical** *adj.* (also **astronomic**) 1 of astronomy. 2 vast, gigantic. □□ astronomically *adv.*

**astronomy** *n.* science of celestial bodies. □□ astronomer *n.*

**astrophysics** *n.pl.* study of physics and chemistry of celestial bodies. □□ astrophysical *adj.* astrophysicist *n.*

**astroturf** *n. propr.* artificial grass surface, esp. for sports fields.

**astute** *adj.* shrewd. □□ astutely *adv.* astuteness *n.*

**asunder** *adv. literary* apart.

**asylee** *n.* person who has left their native country to seek political asylum in another.

**asylum** *n.* 1 sanctuary. 2 political asylum. 3 *hist.* mental institution.

**asymmetry** *n.* lack of symmetry. □□ asymmetric(al) *adj.*

**at** *prep.* expressing position, point in time or space, engagement in activity, value or rate, or motion or aim towards.

**atavism** *n.* 1 reappearance of remote ancestors. 2 reversion to earlier type. □□ atavistic *adj.*

**ataxia** *n. Med.* imperfect control of bodily movements. □□ ataxic *adj.*

**ate** see EAT.

**atheism** *n.* belief that no God exists. □□ atheist *n.* atheistic *adj.*

**atherosclerosis** *n.* formation of fatty deposits in arteries.

**athlete** *n.* person who engages in athletics, exercises, etc. □ athlete's foot infectious fungal condition of foot.

**athletic** ● *adj.* 1 of athletes or athletics. 2 physically strong or agile. ● *n.* (**athletics**) track and field events, e.g. running, jumping, and throwing. □□ athletically *adv.* athleticism *n.*

**atlas** *n.* book of maps.

**atmosphere** *n.* 1 gases enveloping earth, other planet, etc. 2 tone, mood, etc. of place, book, etc. 3 unit of pressure. □□ atmospheric *adj.*

**atoll** *n.* ring-shaped coral reef enclosing lagoon.

**atom** *n.* smallest particle of chemical element that can take part in chemical reaction; this as source of nuclear energy; minute portion of thing.

**atomic** *adj.* concerning atoms or atomic energy. □ atomic bomb bomb deriving its power from atomic energy. atomic energy energy obtained from nuclear fission.

**atomise** *v.* (also -**ize**) reduce to atoms or fine spray. □□ atomiser *n.*

**atonal** *adj. Mus.* not written in any key. □□ atonality *n.*

**atone** *v.* make amends.

**atonement** *n.* atoning; (in religious contexts) reparation or expiation for sin.

**atrium** *n.* (*pl.* **atriums** or **atria**) 1 either of upper cavities of heart. 2 (usu. skylit) central court, esp. rising through building of several storeys.

**atrocious** *adj.* very bad; wicked. □□ atrociously *adv.*

**atrocity** *n.* wicked or cruel act.

**atrophy** ● *n.* wasting away, esp. through disuse. ● *v.* suffer atrophy; cause atrophy in.

**attach** *v.* fix to something else; join; attribute or be attributable (to). □□ attachment *n.*

**attaché** *n.* specialist member of ambassador's staff. □ attaché case small case for carrying documents.

**attack** ● v. **1** try to hurt or defeat using force. **2** criticise adversely. **3** act harmfully on. **4** vigorously apply oneself to. **5** *Sport* try to score against. ● n. **1** act of attacking. **2** sudden onset of illness. □□ **attacker** n.

**attain** v. reach; gain, accomplish; arrive at (goal etc.) □□ **attainable** adj. **attainment** n.

**attar** n. perfume made from rose petals.

**attempt** ● v. try to accomplish or master. ● n. attempting; endeavour.

**attend** v. **1** be present at; go regularly to. **2** give attention to; deal with. **3** escort, accompany. □□ **attendance** n.

**attendant** ● n. person attending, esp. to provide service. ● adj. **1** accompanying. **2** waiting.

**attention** n. **1** act or faculty of applying one's mind; consideration; care. **2** *Mil.* erect attitude of readiness.

**attentive** adj. paying attention. □□ **attentively** adv.

**attenuate** v. make thin or weaker. □□ **attenuation** n.

**attest** v. certify validity of; bear witness to. □□ **attestation** n.

**attic** n. space or room immediately under roof of house.

**attire** ● n. clothes, esp. formal. ● v. clothe.

**attitude** n. **1** opinion, way of thinking; behaviour reflecting this. **2** bodily posture; pose. **3** *colloq.* individuality, self-confidence. □□ **attitudinal** adj.

**attorney** n. (pl. **attorneys**) person, esp. lawyer, appointed to act for another in business or legal matters.

**attorney-general** n. (pl. **attorneys-general** or **attorney-generals**) (chief) law minister in an Australian government and in some other countries.

**attract** v. (of magnet etc.) draw to itself or oneself; arouse interest or admiration in.

**attraction** n. attracting, being attracted; person or thing that attracts; attractive quality.

**attractive** adj. attracting, esp. interest or admiration; pleasing. □□ **attractively** adv.

**attribute** ● v. regard as belonging to or as written, said, or caused by, etc. ● n. **1** quality ascribed to person or thing; characteristic quality. **2** *Computing* piece of information that determines properties of a field or tag in a database or string of characters in a display. □□ **attributable** adj. **attribution** n.

**attributive** adj. *Gram.* (of a word) placed before word it describes.

**attrition** n. gradual wearing down.

**attune** v. **1** adjust. **2** *Mus.* tune.

**atypical** adj. not typical. □□ **atypically** adv.

**aubergine** n. = EGGPLANT.

**auburn** adj. (usu. of hair) reddish-brown.

**auction** ● n. sale in which each article is sold to highest bidder. ● v. sell by auction.

**auctioneer** n. person who conducts auctions.

**audacious** adj. daring, bold; impudent. □□ **audacity** n.

**audible** adj. that can be heard. □□ **audibility** n. **audibly** adv.

**audience** n. **1** group of listeners or spectators; people giving attention to something. **2** formal interview.

**audio** n. sound or reproduction of sound. □ **audio-visual** using both sight and sound.

**audit** ● n. official scrutiny of accounts. ● v. (**audited**) conduct audit of. □□ **auditor** n.

**audition** ● n. test of performer's ability. ● v. assess or be assessed at audition.

**auditorium** n. (pl. **auditoriums** or **auditoria**) part of theatre etc. for audience.

**auditory** adj. of hearing.

**au fait** adj. conversant.

**Aug.** abbr. August.

**auger** n. tool with screw point for boring holes.

**augment** v. make greater; increase. □ **augmented reality** technology that superimposes a computer-generated image on a user's view of the real world.□□ **augmentation** n.

**au gratin** adj. cooked with crust of breadcrumbs or melted cheese.

**augur** v. portend, serve as an omen.

**August** n. eighth month.

**august** adj. venerable, imposing.

**au naturel** adj. & adv. uncooked; (cooked) in simplest or most natural way.

**aunt** n. (also **auntie, aunty**) **1** sister or sister-in-law of one's father or mother. **2** unrelated woman friend of parent(s).

**aura** n. distinctive atmosphere; subtle emanation.

**aural** adj. of ear or hearing. □□ **aurally** adv.

**aureole** n. (also **aureola**) halo.

**au revoir** int. & n. goodbye (until we meet again).

**auricle** n. **1** atrium of heart. **2** external ear of animals.□□ **auricular** adj.

**auriferous** adj. yielding gold.

**auscultation** n. listening to sound of heart etc. to help diagnosis.

**auspice** n.□ **under the auspices of** with the patronage of.

**auspicious** adj. promising; favourable.

**Aussie** colloq. ● n. **1** Australian. **2** Australia. ● adj. Australian.

**austere** adj. severely simple; morally strict; stern.□□ **austerity** n.

**austral** adj. **1** southern. **2** (**Austral**) of Australia or Australasia.

**Australasian** adj. of Australia and SW Pacific islands.

**Australia** n. **1** continent in Southern hemisphere bounded by Indian, Southern, and Pacific Oceans. **2** federated States and Territories making up the Commonwealth of Australia.□ **Australia Day** 26 Jan., anniversary of British settlement at Sydney Cove in 1788.

**Australian** ● adj. of or relating to Australia or its people etc. ● n. native of Australia; person of Australian descent.□ **Australian Rules** form of football played by teams of eighteen on oval field.

**Australiana** n. books, documents, artefacts, etc., relating to or characteristic of Australia and its history.

**Australite** n. small piece of dark meteoric glass.

**autarchy** n. absolute rule.

**autarky** n. self-sufficiency.

**authentic** adj. of undisputed origin; genuine; trustworthy. □□ **authentically** adv. **authenticity** n.

**authenticate** v. establish as true, genuine, or valid.□□ **authentication** n.

**author** n. ● **1** writer of book etc. **2** originator. ● v. be author or originator of.□□ **authorship** n.

**authorise** v. (also -**ize**) **1** give authority to (person). **2** sanction officially.□□ **authorisation** n. **authorised** adj.

**authoritarian** ● adj. favouring or enforcing strict obedience to authority. ● n. authoritarian person.

**authoritative** adj. reliable, esp. having authority.

**authority** n. **1** power or right to enforce obedience; person with this. **2** person with specialised knowledge.

**autism** n. developmental disorder characterised by difficulty in social interaction and communication and by restricted or repetitive patterns of thought and behaviour.□□ **autistic** *adj.*

**auto-** *comb. form* self; own.

**autobiography** *n.* story of one's own life.□□ **autobiographer** *n.* **autobiographical** *adj.*

**autocracy** *n.* absolute rule by one person.□□ **autocrat** *n.*

**autocross** *n.* motor racing across country or on dirt tracks.

**autocue** *n. propr.* screen etc. from which speaker reads television script.

**autograph** ● *n.* signature, esp. of celebrity. ● *v.* sign or write on in one's own handwriting.

**autoimmune** *adj.* (of diseases) caused by anti-bodies produced against substances naturally present in the body.

**automate** *v.* control by automation.

**automatic** ● *adj.* mechanical, self-regulating; done without thinking. ● *n.* automatic machine, car, or firearm.

**automation** *n.* use of automatic equipment in place of manual labour.

**automobile** *n.* motor car.

**automotive** *adj.* of motor vehicles.

**autonomous** *adj.* self-governing; free to act independently. □□ **autonomy** *n.*

**autopilot** *n.* device for keeping aircraft or ship on set course automatically.

**autopsy** *n.* post-mortem.

**autumn** *n.* season between summer and winter.□□ **autumnal** *adj.*

**auxiliary** ● *adj.* giving help or support. ● *n.* a helper.□ **auxiliary verb** *Gram.* verb used in forming tenses of other verbs.

**avail** ● *v.* be of use or help. ● *n.* effectiveness, advantage.□ **avail oneself** use, profit by.

**available** *adj.* ready to be used; obtainable.□□ **availability** *n.*

**avalanche** *n.* **1** mass of snow and ice rapidly sliding down mountain. **2** sudden abundance.

**avant-garde** ● *n.* innovators, esp. in the arts. ● *adj.* new; pioneering.

**avarice** *n.* greed for wealth. □□ **avaricious** *adj.*

**avatar** *n.* **1** (in Hinduism) descent of a deity etc. to earth in bodily form. **2** *Computing* movable icon representing person in cyberspace etc.

**Ave.** *abbr.* avenue.

**avenge** *v.* inflict retribution on behalf of; exact retribution for.

**avenue** *n.* road or street.

**aver** *v.* (averred) *formal* assert, affirm.

**average** ● *n.* something midway between two extremes; mean, median, mode; a standard regarded as usual. ● *adj.* **1** usual, ordinary; *colloq.* mediocre. **2** found by making an average. ● *v.* amount on average to; do on average; estimate average of.

**averse** *adj.* opposed, disinclined.

**aversion** *n.* strong dislike.

**avert** *v.* **1** turn away. **2** ward off.

**aviary** *n.* large cage or building for keeping birds.

**aviation** *n.* flying of aircraft. □□ **aviator** *n.*

**avid** *adj.* eager, greedy.□□ **avidity** *n.* **avidly** *adv.*

**avocado** *n.* (*pl.* avocados) dark green pear-shaped fruit with creamy flesh.

**avoid** *v.* keep away or refrain from; escape; evade.□□ **avoidable** *adj.* **avoidance** *n.*

**avoirdupois** *n.* system of weights based on pound of 16 ounces.

**avow** *v.* declare.□□ **avowal** *n.*

**avuncular** *adj.* like or of an uncle.

**AWACS** *abbr.* airborne warning and control system.

**await** *v.* wait for.

**awake** ● v. (awoke, awoken, awaking) wake. ● adj. not asleep; alert.

**award** ● v. give or order to be given as payment, penalty, or prize. ● n. 1 thing awarded. 2 Aust. determination of industrial court, commission, or tribunal.

**aware** adj. having knowledge or realisation.□□ **awareness** n.

**awash** adj. covered with water; awash with full of.

**away** ● adv. 1 to or at a distance; into non-existence. 2 constantly, persistently. ● adj. (of match etc.) played on opponent's ground.

**awe** ● n. reverential fear or wonder. ● v. inspire with awe.

**aweigh** adj. (of anchor) raised clear of sea bed.

**awesome** adj. 1 inspiring awe. 2 colloq. excellent.

**awful** adj. 1 extremely bad or unpleasant. 2 (used as intensifier) excessive, large.□□ **awfully** adv.

**awhile** adv. for a short time.

**awkward** adj. 1 difficult to use or handle. 2 clumsy, having little skill. 3 embarrassed. 4 inconvenient.

**awl** n. small tool for piercing holes, esp. in leather.

**awning** n. fabric roof, shelter.

**AWOL** abbr. absent without leave.

**awry** ● adv. 1 crookedly. 2 amiss. ● adj. 1 crooked. 2 unsound.

**axe** ● n. 1 chopping tool with heavy blade. 2 (the axe) dismissal (of employee). 3 abandonment of project etc. ● v. (axed, axing) remove by abolishing or dismissing.

**axiom** n. 1 established principle. 2 self-evident truth.□□ **axiomatic** adj.

**axis** n. (pl. axes) line through centre of object, around which it rotates if spinning.□□ **axial** adj.

**axle** n. rod on which wheel is fixed or turns.

**ayatollah** n. religious leader in Iran.

**aye** ● (also ay) adv. arch. & dial. yes. ● v. (in voting) I assent.

**azalea** n. kind of rhododendron.

**azan** n. Muslim call to ritual prayer.

**azimuth** n. angular distance between point below star etc. and north or south.□□ **azimuthal** adj.

**Aztec** n. & adj. (member) of indigenous people dominant in Mexico before Spanish conquest of 16th century.

**azure** adj. & n. (of) deep sky-blue colour.

**B** n. (B, 2B, 3B, etc.) (of a pencil lead) soft; softer than H and HB.

**b.** abbr. born.

**B&S** n. (also **B&S ball**) Aust. formal dance for unattached young people.

**BA** abbr. Bachelor of Arts.

**babble** ● v. chatter indistinctly or foolishly; (of a stream) murmur.
● n. babbling talk or sound.

**babe** n. 1 baby. 2 colloq. attractive person.

**babel** n. confused noise.

**baboon** n. large monkey.

**baby** n. very young child or animal.
□□ **babyish** adj.

**babysit** v. (babysat, babysitting) look after child while its parents are out.
□□ **babysitter** n.

**baccarat** n. gambling card game.

**bachelor** n. 1 unmarried man.
2 person with university first degree.

**bacillus** n. (pl. **bacilli**) rod-shaped bacterium.□□ **bacillary** adj.

**back** ● n. 1 surface or part that is furthest from front; rear part of human body from shoulders to hips; corresponding part of animal's body.
2 (in Australia) part of the interior that is remote from settlements or from water. 3 defensive player in hockey, football etc. ● adv. 1 at or towards the rear; in or into a previous time, position, or state. 2 in return. ● v. 1 go backwards. 2 help, support. 3 lay a bet on. 4 Mus. accompany. 5 Aust. (of sheepdog) run across backs of yarded sheep. ● adj. 1 situated behind.
2 Aust. remote. 3 past, not current.
□ **back down** give up claim; withdraw argument. **back out** withdraw from agreement. **back-pedal** reverse one's previous decision or commitment.

**back seat** inferior position or status.

**back up** 1 support. 2 Computing make copy of (data).

**backache** n. pain in one's back.

**backbencher** n. ordinary MP not holding senior office.

**backbiting** n. spiteful talk.

**backbone** n. column of small bones down centre of back.

**backchat** n. colloq. answering back rudely.

**backdate** v. declare to be valid from earlier date.

**backfire** v. 1 make explosion in exhaust pipe. 2 produce undesired effect.

**backgammon** n. game played on board with draughts and dice.

**background** n. 1 back part of scene etc. 2 inconspicuous position.
3 person's education, social circumstances, etc. 4 explanatory information etc.

**backhanded** adj. 1 performed with back of hand turned forwards. 2 said with underlying sarcasm.

**backhander** n. 1 backhanded stroke. 2 colloq. a bribe, a reward for services.

**backlash** n. violent hostile reaction.

**backlist** n. publisher's list of books available.

**backlog** n. arrears of work.

**backpack** n. rucksack.
□□ **backpacker** n.

**backside** n. colloq. buttocks.

**backslide** v. slip back from good behaviour into bad.

**backspace** v. move computer cursor one space back.

**backspin** n. backward spinning movement of ball.

**backstop** n. 1 thing placed at the rear of something as a barrier or support; emergency precaution or last resort. 2 Aust. a help; a support.

**backstrap** n. boneless cut of lamb from near ribs.

**backstreet** ● n. side street. ● adj. secret and illegal.

**backstroke** n. swimming stroke performed on back.

**backtrack** v. retrace one's route; reverse one's opinion.

**backup** n. 1 a support, a reserve. 2 Computing copy of data made in case of loss or damage.

**backward** adj. 1 directed backwards. 2 slow in learning. 3 shy.

**backwards** adv. 1 away from one's front. 2 back foremost, in reverse of usual way. 3 into worse state. 4 into past. 5 back towards starting point.

**backwash** n. 1 backward flow of water. 2 after-effects of action or event.

**backwater** n. 1 stretch of stagnant water in river not reached by the current. 2 place unaffected by progress or new ideas.

**backyard** n. yard at back of house.

**bacon** n. cured meat from back and sides of pig.

**bacteriology** n. study of bacteria.

**bacterium** n. (pl. bacteria) microscopic organism. □□ **bacterial** adj.

**bad** adj. (worse, worst) 1 inadequate, defective; unpleasant; harmful. 2 decayed; ill, injured. 3 serious, severe. 4 wicked; naughty. 5 incorrect; not valid.

**bade** see BID.

**badge** n. small flat emblem worn as sign of office, membership, etc. or bearing slogan etc.

**badger** ● n. nocturnal burrowing mammal of Europe etc. with black and white striped head. ● v. pester.

**badly** adv. (worse, worst) 1 in bad manner. 2 very much; severely.

**badminton** n. game played with racquets and shuttlecock.

**baffle** ● v. perplex; frustrate. ● n. device that hinders flow of fluid or sound. □□ **bafflement** n.

**bag** ● n. 1 soft open-topped receptacle; piece of luggage, handbag. 2 colloq. large amount. 3 amount of game shot by one person, number of wickets taken by bowler. ● v. (bagged) 1 secure, take possession of; put in bag. 2 hang loosely, bulge. 3 colloq. criticise.

**bagatelle** n. 1 game in which small balls are struck into holes on inclined board. 2 a mere trifle.

**bagel** n. ring-shaped bread roll.

**baggage** n. luggage.

**baggy** adj. (baggier) hanging loosely.

**bagpipes** n. pl. musical instrument with windbag for pumping air through reeded pipes.

**baguette** n. long thin French loaf.

**Bahasa Indonesia** n. official language of Indonesia.

**bail** ● n. 1 security given for released prisoner's return for trial. 2 either of two crosspieces resting on stumps in cricket. ● v. 1 give bail for and secure release of (prisoner). 2 (also bale) scoop water out of. □ **bail out** rescue.

**bail up** Aust. (of bushranger) make (person) hold up arms to be robbed; accost.

**bailiff** n. sheriff's officer who executes writs, carries out distraints, etc.

**bailiwick** n. area of authority or interest.

**bait** ● n. food to entice prey; allurement. ● v. 1 harass (person); torment (chained animal). 2 put bait on (hook, trap, etc.); add poison to food.

**baize** n. usu. green felted woollen material, used for coverings etc.

**bake** v. cook or become cooked by dry heat, esp. in oven; harden by heat. □ **baking powder** raising agent for cakes etc. □□ **baker** n.

**bakery** n. place where bread and cakes are made or sold.

**baklava** n. rich sweetmeat of pastry, honey, and nuts.

**balaclava** n. (in full **balaclava helmet**) usu. woollen covering for head and neck.

**balalaika** n. Russian triangular-bodied guitar-like musical instrument.

**balance** ● n. 1 even distribution of weight or amount. 2 weighing apparatus. 3 regulating apparatus of clock etc. 4 difference between credits and debits; remainder. ● v. 1 bring or come into or keep in equilibrium. 2 compare by comparing.

**balcony** n. outside balustraded or railed platform with access from upper floor; upper tier of seats in theatre etc.

**bald** adj. 1 lacking some or all hair on scalp; without fur, feathers, etc.; with surface worn away. 2 direct. □□ **baldly** adv. **baldness** n.

**balderdash** n. nonsense.

**bale** ● n. bundle of merchandise or hay. ● v. make up into bales.

**baleful** adj. menacing; malignant, destructive.

**balk** = BAULK.

**ball** n. 1 spherical object or mass; usu. spherical object used in game; rounded part or mass; delivery or pass of ball in game. 2 formal social gathering for dancing; colloq. enjoyable time. 3 (balls) colloq. testicles. 4 (balls) colloq. strength; courage. □ **ball bearing** ring of small steel balls reducing friction between moving parts of machine; one of these balls. **balls-up** colloq. mess; confused or bungled situation. **ball-up**

*AFL* bouncing of ball by umpire to start or restart play. **have someone by the balls** colloq. have someone in one's power. **on the ball** colloq. alert.

**ballad** n. 1 poem or song narrating popular story. 2 slow sentimental song.

**ballast** ● n. heavy material stabilising ship, controlling height of balloon, etc.; coarse stone etc. as bed of railway or road. ● v. provide with ballast.

**ballcock** n. device with floating ball, controlling water level in cistern.

**ballerina** n. female ballet dancer.

**ballet** n. dramatic or representational style of dancing to music. □□ **balletic** adj.

**ballistic** adj. of projectiles.

**ballistics** n.pl. science of projectiles and firearms.

**balloon** ● n. small inflatable rubber toy or decoration; large inflatable flying bag, esp. one with basket below for passengers. ● v. (cause to) swell out like balloon; travel by balloon. □□ **balloonist** n.

**ballot** ● n. vote recorded on slip of paper; voting by this. ● v. (**balloted**) (cause to) vote by ballot.

**ballpark** ● n. 1 baseball ground. 2 colloq. area of activity or responsibility. ● adj. colloq. approximate.

**ballpoint** n. pen with ball as its writing point.

**ballroom** n. large room where dances are held.

**ballyhoo** n. loud noise, fuss; noisy publicity.

**balm** n. 1 aromatic ointment; thing that heals or soothes. 2 aromatic herb.

**balmy** adj. (**balmier**) mild, fragrant, soothing.

**baloney** n. (also **boloney**) colloq. nonsense.

**balsa** n. lightweight tropical American wood used for making models etc.

**balsam** n. **1** ointment. **2** tree yielding balsam. **3** any of several flowering plants. □□ **balsamic** adj.

**baluster** n. short supporting rail.

**balustrade** n. railing supported by balusters, esp. on balcony.

**bamboo** n. tropical giant woody grass; its hollow stem.

**bamboozle** v. **1** colloq. cheat. **2** mystify.

**ban** ● v. (banned) prohibit officially. ● n. formal prohibition.

**banal** adj. trite, commonplace. □□ **banality** n.

**banana** n. long curved yellow tropical fruit; treelike plant bearing it.

**band** ● n. **1** flat strip or loop of thin material. **2** stripe. **3** group of musicians. **4** organised group of criminals etc. **5** range of values, esp. frequencies or wavelengths. ● v. **1** unite. **2** put band on. **3** mark with stripes.

**bandage** ● n. strip of material for binding wound etc. ● v. bind with bandage.

**bandanna** n. large patterned square of cloth for wearing around head.

**bandicoot** n. marsupial of Australia and New Guinea with long pointed head.

**bandit** n. robber, esp. of travellers. □□ **banditry** n.

**bandolier** n. (also **bandoleer**) shoulder belt with loops or pockets for cartridges.

**bandwagon** n. □ **climb on the bandwagon** join group likely to succeed.

**bandwidth** n. **1** range of frequencies within a given band; transmission capacity of a computer network etc. **2** energy or mental capacity required to deal with a situation.

**bandy** ● v. pass to and fro; exchange words. ● adj. (bandier) (of legs) curved wide apart at knees.

**bane** n. cause of ruin or trouble.

**bang** ● n. **1** loud short sound. **2** sharp blow. ● v. **1** strike or shut noisily. **2** (cause to) make bang. ● adv. **1** with a bang. **2** colloq. exactly.

**banger** n. **1** colloq. sausage. **2** loud firework.

**bangle** n. rigid bracelet or anklet.

**banish** v. **1** condemn to exile. **2** dismiss from one's mind. □□ **banishment** n.

**banisters** n.pl. (also **bannisters**) uprights and handrail of staircase.

**banjo** n. (pl. **banjos**) round-bodied guitar-like musical instrument. □□ **banjoist** n.

**bank** n. **1** a slope, esp. at side of river; raised mass of earth etc. **2** row of lights, switches, etc. **3** establishment for safe keeping of money; place storing reserve supply. ● v. **1** build up into mound or bank; tilt sideways in rounding a curve. **2** place money in bank. **3** base one's hopes.

**banknote** n. printed strip of paper, plastic, etc., issued as currency.

**bankrupt** ● adj. unable to pay one's debts. ● n. a bankrupt person. ● v. make bankrupt. □□ **bankruptcy** n.

**banksia** n. Australian tree or shrub, having usu. leathery leaves and dense flower spikes.

**banner** n. **1** large portable cloth sign bearing slogan or design; flag. **2** advertisement on website in form of box etc.

**banns** n.pl. announcement of intended marriage read in church.

**banquet** ● n. sumptuous esp. formal dinner. ● v. (banqueted) attend banquet; give banquet for.

**bantam** n. kind of small domestic fowl.

**bantamweight | barney**

**bantamweight** *n.* weight between featherweight and flyweight (esp. in boxing).

**banter** ● *n.* good-humoured teasing. ● *v.* tease; exchange banter.

**banyan** *n.* (also **banian**) type of fig tree.

**bap** *n.* soft bread roll.

**baptise** *v.* (also **-ize**) administer baptism to; give name to.

**baptism** *n.* admission to Christian church with ceremonial use of water and usu. with name-giving. □□ **baptismal** *adj.*

**Baptist** *n.* member of church practising adult baptism by immersion.

**bar** ● *n.* **1** long piece of rigid material, a strip; a barrier. **2** counter or room for serving alcoholic drinks etc. **3** prisoner's enclosure in lawcourt. **4** section of music between vertical lines. **5** barristers, their profession. **6** unit of atmospheric pressure. ● *v.* fasten or keep in or out with bar; obstruct, prohibit; exclude. ● *prep.* except.

**barb** ● *n.* **1** backward-facing point on arrow, fish hook, etc. **2** hurtful remark. **3** beardlike filament at mouth of some fish. ● *v.* fit with barb.

**barbarian** ● *n.* uncultured or brutish person. ● *adj.* uncultured; uncivilised.

**barbaric** *adj.* **1** brutal, cruel. **2** rough and uncultured.

**barbarity** *n.* **1** savage cruelty. **2** barbaric act.

**barbarous** *adj.* uncultured, cruel.

**barbecue** (also **barbeque**) ● *n.* meal cooked over charcoal etc. out of doors; party for this; grill etc. used for this. ● *v.* cook on barbecue. □ **barbecue stopper** *Aust.* important topic of public discussion.

**barbell** *n.* iron bar with removable weights, used for weightlifting.

**barber** *n.* person who cuts men's hair.

**barbican** *n.* outer defence, esp. double tower over gate or drawbridge.

**barbiturate** *n.* sedative derived from barbituric acid, an organic acid.

**barcode** *n.* machine-readable code in the form of a pattern of stripes printed on commodity.

**bard** *n.* poet. □□ **bardic** *adj.*

**bardi** *n.* *Aust.* edible larva or pupa of beetle or moth.

**bare** ● *adj.* not clothed or covered; not adorned; scanty. ● *v.* uncover, reveal.

**bareback** *adv.* on horseback without a saddle.

**barefaced** *adj.* shameless, undisguised.

**barely** *adv.* only just, hardly.

**bargain** ● *n.* **1** agreement on terms of sale etc. **2** cheap thing. ● *v.* discuss terms of sale etc.

**barge** ● *n.* long flat-bottomed cargo boat on canals or rivers. ● *v.* move clumsily. □ **barge in** intrude.

**baritone** *n.* adult male singing voice, between tenor and bass; singer with this voice.

**barium** *n.* white metallic element (symbol Ba).

**bark** ● *n.* **1** sharp explosive cry of dog. **2** tough outer layer of tree. ● *v.* **1** make sharp harsh sound of dog; utter in sharp commanding voice. **2** scrape skin off accidentally.

**barley** *n.* cereal used as food and in spirits; (also **barleycorn**) its grain. □ **barley sugar** sweet made of boiled sugar.

**bar mitzvah** *n.* religious initiation of Jewish boy at 13.

**barmy** *adj.* (**barmier**) *colloq.* crazy.

**barn** *n.* building for storing grain etc.

**barnacle** *n.* small shellfish clinging to rocks, ships' bottoms, etc.

**barney** *colloq.* ● *n.* noisy quarrel. ● *v.* argue.

**baro-** *comb. form* of pressure or weight.

**barometer** *n.* instrument measuring atmospheric pressure. □□ **barometric** *adj.*

**baron** *n.* **1** member of lowest rank of the nobility. **2** powerful businessman etc. □□ **baronial** *adj.*

**baroness** *n.* woman holding rank of baron; baron's wife or widow.

**baronet** *n.* holder of hereditary title below baron but above knight. □□ **baronetcy** *n.*

**baroque** ● *adj.* (esp. of 17th- & 18th-c.) European architecture and music) ornate and extravagant in style; complicated, elaborate. ● *n.* baroque style.

**barque** *n.* kind of sailing ship.

**barrack** *v.* shout or jeer (at); (**barrack for**) *Aust.* support, encourage (team etc.) □□ **barracker** *n.*

**barracks** *n.pl.* buildings for soldiers to live in.

**barracouta** *n.* long slender fish of southern oceans.

**barracuda** *n.* large tropical marine fish.

**barrage** *n.* **1** concentrated artillery bombardment. **2** rapid succession of questions or criticisms.

**barramundi** *n.* *Aust.* freshwater fish valued as food.

**barrel** *n.* **1** large round container with flat ends. **2** tubelike part, esp. of gun.

**barren** *adj.* **1** unable to bear young. **2** unable to produce fruit or vegetation. **3** unprofitable, dull. □□ **barrenness** *n.*

**barricade** ● *n.* barrier, esp. improvised. ● *v.* block or defend with this.

**barrier** *n.* **1** fence etc. barring advance or access. **2** obstacle to communication etc.

**barring** *prep.* except.

**barrister** *n.* person entitled to practise as advocate in any court.

**barrow** *n.* **1** wheelbarrow; cart pulled or pushed by hand. **2** ancient grave mound.

**barter** ● *v.* exchange goods etc. without using money. ● *n.* trade by bartering.

**basal** *adj.* of, at, or forming base.

**basalt** *n.* dark volcanic rock. □□ **basaltic** *adj.*

**base** ● *n.* **1** lowest part; part on which thing rests or is supported; basis; headquarters. **2** substance capable of combining with an acid to form a salt. **3** each of four stations to be reached by batter in baseball. **4** number on which system of counting is based. ● *v.* use as base or foundation or evidence for forecast. ● *adj.* dishonourable; of inferior value.

**baseball** *n.* team game in which runs are scored by hitting ball and running around a series of four bases.

**baseless** *adj.* unfounded, groundless.

**basement** *n.* floor below ground level.

**bash** ● *v.* **1** strike bluntly or heavily. **2** *colloq.* attack violently. ● *n.* **1** heavy blow. **2** *colloq.* attempt. **3** party. □□ **basher** *n.* **bashing** *n.*

**bashful** *adj.* shy, diffident.

**basic** ● *adj.* forming a basis; fundamental. ● *n.* (usu. **basics**) fundamental facts or principles. □□ **basically** *adv.*

**basil** *n.* aromatic herb.

**basilica** *n.* ancient Roman hall with apse and colonnades; similar church.

**basilisk** *n.* mythical reptile with lethal breath and look.

**basin** *n.* **1** round vessel for liquids or preparing food in; washbasin. **2** hollow depression; round valley; area drained by river; sheltered mooring area.

**basis** *n.* (*pl.* **bases**) foundation; main principle or ingredient; starting point for discussion etc.

**bask** v. relax in warmth and light; revel (in).

**basket** n. **1** container made of woven canes, wire, etc.; amount held by this. **2** the goal in basketball; goal scored.

**basketball** n. team game in which the aim is to throw ball through high hooped net.

**bas-relief** n. sculpture or carving projecting slightly from background.

**bass**¹ ● n. **1** lowest adult male voice; singer with this. **2** colloq. bass guitar, double bass. **3** low-frequency sound of radio, stereo, etc. ● adj. lowest in pitch; deep-sounding. □□ **bassist** n.

**bass**² n. (pl. **bass**) N. hemisphere fish of the perch family; similar Australian fish.

**bassinet** n. child's cradle or carrying basket.

**bassoon** n. bass instrument of oboe family. □□ **bassoonist** n.

**bastard** n. **1** dated illegitimate child. **2** colloq. difficult or awkward or unpleasant person or thing. □□ **bastardy** n.

**bastardry** n. cruel or malicious behaviour.

**baste** v. **1** moisten (roasting meat) with fat etc. **2** sew with long loose stitches; tack.

**bastion** n. projecting part of fortification; thing regarded as protection.

**bat** ● n. **1** implement with handle for hitting ball in games; player batting in game. **2** mouselike nocturnal flying mammal. ● v. (**batted**) perform or strike with bat in a game. □□ **batter** n.

**batch** n. set of people or things dealt with as group.

**bated** adj. □ with bated breath very anxiously.

**bath** ● n. container for sitting in and washing body; its contents; act of washing in it; vessel of liquid for immersing something. ● v. wash in bath.

**bathe** v. immerse oneself in water, esp. to swim or wash; immerse in or treat with liquid; (of sunlight etc.) envelop.

**bathos** n. lapse from sublime to trivial; anticlimax. □□ **bathetic** adj.

**batik** n. method of dyeing textiles by waxing parts to be left uncoloured; fabric printed in this way.

**batman** n. army officer's servant.

**bat mitzvah** n. religious initiation of Jewish girl at 12 years and one day old.

**baton** n. thin stick for conducting orchestra etc.; short stick carried in relay race; stick carried by drum major; staff of office; police officer's truncheon.

**batrachian** ● n. amphibian that discards gills and tail, esp. frog or toad. ● adj. of batrachians.

**batsman** n. (pl. **-men**) player batting in cricket etc.

**batt** n. rectangular block of insulation material for installation in ceiling etc.

**battalion** n. large army unit.

**batten** ● n. long narrow piece of squared timber or metal, esp. used to hold something in place. ● v. strengthen or fasten with battens.

**batter** ● v. strike hard and repeatedly. ● n. **1** mixture of flour and eggs beaten up with liquid for cooking. **2** player batting in baseball, cricket, etc.

**battery** n. **1** portable container of cell or cells for supplying electricity. **2** series of cages for intensive breeding and rearing of poultry. **3** set of connected or similar instruments etc. **4** emplacement for heavy guns. **5** Law physical violence inflicted on person.

**battle** ● *n.* prolonged fight, esp. between armed forces; contest.
● *v.* struggle.

**battleaxe** *n.* medieval weapon.

**battlefield** *n.* place of battle.

**battler** *n. Aust.* person who strives doggedly against the odds.

**batty** *adj.* (**battier**) *colloq.* crazy.

**bauble** *n.* showy trinket.

**baulk** (also **balk**) ● *v.* be reluctant; hinder. ● *n.* **1** a hindrance. **2** starting area on billiard table.

**bauxite** *n.* claylike mineral, chief source of aluminium.

**bawdy** *adj.* (**bawdier**) humorously indecent.□□ **bawdiness** *n.*

**bawl** *v.* shout or weep noisily.

**bay** ● *n.* **1** part of the sea within wide curve of shore. **2** a recess. **3** laurel, esp. type used as herb. **4** deep cry of large dog or of hounds in pursuit.
● *v.* make deep cry of dog.
● *adj.* (of horse) reddish-brown.
□ **bay window** window projecting from outside wall of house.

**bayonet** *n.* stabbing blade attachable to rifle.

**bazaar** *n.* **1** oriental market. **2** sale of goods, esp. for charity.

**bazooka** *n.* anti-tank rocket-launcher.

**BC** *abbr.* (of a date) before Christ.

**bcc** ● *abbr.* blind carbon copy (used as an indication that a duplicate should be or should be sent to another person without the knowledge of the main recipient). ● *v.* send such a copy.

**be** ● *v.* **1** exist, occur. **2** have certain position, quality, or condition. ● *v.aux.* (used to form tenses of other verbs).

**beach** ● *n.* sandy or pebbly shore of sea, lake, etc. ● *v.* run or haul (boat etc.) on to shore.

**beacon** *n.* signal fire on hill or pole; visible warning or guiding device;

radio signal helping fix position of ship or aircraft.

**bead** ● *n.* small ball of hard material pierced for threading with others on string; drop of liquid. ● *v.* adorn with bead(s) or beading.

**beading** *n.* moulding like series of beads.

**beady** *adj.* (**beadier**) (of eyes) small and bright.

**beagle** *n.* small hound.

**beak** *n.* bird's horny projecting jaws; any similar projection.

**beaker** *n.* lipped glass vessel for scientific experiments.

**beam** ● *n.* **1** long piece of squared timber or metal used in house-building etc. **2** ray of light or other radiation. **3** bright smile.
● *v.* **1** send out (light etc.); shine.
**2** smile radiantly.

**bean** *n.* plant with edible seeds in long pods; seed or pod of this or of coffee etc.

**beanie** *n.* close-fitting knitted cap.

**bear** ● *n.* heavy thick-furred mammal; toy like this. ● *v.* (**bore**, **borne**) **1** carry, support; have in one's heart or mind. **2** endure. **3** be fit for. **4** produce; give birth to. **5** take (a specified direction). **6** exert pressure.

**beard** ● *n.* facial hair on chin etc.; part on animal (esp. goat) or on wheat etc. resembling beard.
● *v.* oppose, defy.□□ **bearded** *adj.*

**bearing** *n.* **1** outward behaviour, posture. **2** relevance. **3** device reducing friction where a part turns. **4** compass direction.

**beast** *n.* **1** animal, esp. wild mammal. **2** brutal person. **3** *colloq.* disliked person or thing.□□ **beastly** *adv.*

**beat** ● *v.* (**beat, beaten, beating**) **1** strike repeatedly or persistently; inflict blows on. **2** overcome, surpass. **3** exhaust, perplex. **4** whisk (eggs etc.) vigorously. **5** shape (metal etc.) by blows. **6** pulsate. **7** mark (time of music) with baton, foot, etc. **8** move or cause (wings) to move up and down. **9** make (path etc.) (as if by) trampling. ● *n.* **1** main accent in music or verse. **2** strongly marked rhythm of popular music etc. **3** stroke on drum. **4** throbbing. **5** police officer's route or area; one's habitual round. ● *adj. colloq.* exhausted, tired out. □ **beat-up** *Aust.* exaggerated or fake news report etc.

**beatific** *adj.* **1** making blessed. **2** *colloq.* blissful.

**beatify** *v.* **1** *RC Ch.* declare to be blessed, as first step to canonisation. **2** make happy. □□ **beatification** *n.*

**beatitude** *n.* blessedness.

**Beaufort scale** *n.* scale of wind speeds.

**beautician** *n.* specialist in beauty treatment.

**beautiful** *adj.* **1** having beauty. **2** excellent. □□ **beautifully** *adv.*

**beautify** *v.* make beautiful. □□ **beautification** *n.*

**beauty** *n.* combination of qualities that pleases the sight or other senses or the mind; person or thing having this.

**beaver** ● *n.* large amphibious broad-tailed rodent that builds dams. ● *v.* work hard.

**becalm** *v.* deprive (ship) of wind.

**because** *conj.* for the reason that.

**beck** *n.* □ **at someone's beck and call** always ready to obey a person's orders.

**beckon** *v.* summon by gesture; entice.

**become** *v.* (**became, become, becoming**) **1** turn into; begin to be. **2** look well on, suit.

**becquerel** *n.* SI unit of radioactivity.

**bed** *n.* **1** place to sleep or rest, esp. piece of furniture for sleeping on. **2** garden plot. **3** bottom of sea or river; flat base on which thing rests.

**bedaub** *v.* smear with paint etc.

**bedclothes** *n.pl.* sheets, blankets, etc.

**bedding** *n.* **1** mattress and bedclothes. **2** litter for animals.

**bedeck** *v.* adorn.

**bedevil** *v.* (**bedevilled**) trouble, confuse; torment. □□ **bedevilment** *n.*

**bedlam** *n.* uproar and confusion.

**bedraggled** *adj.* dishevelled, untidy.

**bedridden** *adj.* confined to bed through illness.

**bedrock** *n.* **1** solid rock beneath loose soil. **2** basic facts or principles.

**bedroom** *n.* room for sleeping in.

**bedsitter** *n.* (also **bedsit, bedsitting room**) one-roomed unit of accommodation used for both living and sleeping in.

**bedspread** *n.* covering for bed.

**bee** *n.* four-winged stinging insect, collecting nectar and pollen and producing wax and honey.

**beech** *n.* smooth-barked glossy-leaved European etc. tree; any similar Australian tree.

**beef** ● *n.* **1** meat from an ox, bull, or cow. **2** muscular strength. **3** *colloq.* a complaint. ● *v. colloq.* complain.

**beefy** *adj.* (**beefier**) having solid muscular body.

**beehive** *n.* **1** artificial shelter for bees. **2** busy place.

**beeline** *n.* □ **make a beeline for** go straight or rapidly towards.

**beep** ● *n.* short high-pitched sound. ● *v.* emit beep.

**beer** *n.* alcoholic drink made from fermented malt etc., flavoured esp. with hops. □□ **beery** *adj.*

**beet** *n.* plant with fleshy root used as vegetable (beetroot) or for making sugar (sugar beet).

**beetle** ● *n.* **1** insect with hard protective outer wings. **2** tool for ramming or crushing things. ● *v.* **1** *colloq.* hurry, scurry. **2** overhang, project.

**beetroot** n. beet with dark red root, used as vegetable.

**befall** v. (**befell, befallen, befalling**) *poet.* happen; happen to.

**befit** v. (**befitted**) be appropriate for.

**before** adv. & prep. & conj. at earlier time (than); ahead, in front of; in preference to.

**beforehand** adv. in advance.

**befriend** v. act as friend to; help.

**befuddle** v. 1 make drunk. 2 confuse.

**beg** v. (**begged**) 1 ask for as gift or charity; request earnestly or humbly. 2 (of dog) sit up expectantly with forepaws off ground. □ **beg the question** invite an obvious question; assume the truth of a thing to be proved.

**beget** v. (**begot, begotten, begetting**) *literary* be father of; give rise to.

**beggar** ● n. 1 person who lives by begging. 2 colloq. person. ● v. 1 reduce to poverty. 2 be too extraordinary for (belief, description, etc.)

**beggarly** adj. 1 mean. 2 poor, needy.

**begin** v. (**began, begun, beginning**) perform first or earliest part of (activity); be first to do thing; come into being.

**beginner** n. learner.

**beginning** n. time at which thing begins; source, origin; first part.

**begonia** n. plant with ornamental foliage and bright flowers.

**begrudge** v. grudge; feel or show resentment at or envy of; be dissatisfied at. □□ **begrudgingly** adv.

**beguile** v. 1 charm. 2 divert; delude; cheat. □□ **beguilement** n.

**begum** n. (in India, Pakistan, and Bangladesh) Muslim woman of high rank; (**Begum**) title of married Muslim woman.

**behalf** n. □ **on behalf of** in aid of; as representative of; in the interests of.

**behave** v. 1 act or react in specified way. 2 conduct oneself properly; work well (or in specified manner).

**behaviour** n. (also **behavior**) way of behaving. □□ **behavioural** adj.

**behead** v. cut head from (person); execute thus.

**behest** n. *literary* command; request.

**behind** ● prep. 1 in or to rear of. 2 hidden by, on farther side of. 3 in past in relation to. 4 inferior to. 5 in support of. ● adv. 1 in or to rear. 2 on far side. 3 remaining after others' departure. 4 in arrears. ● n. 1 colloq. buttocks. 2 AFL scoring kick earning one point.

**behold** v. (**beheld, beholding**) take notice, observe.

**beholden** adj. under obligation.

**behove** v. 1 *formal* be incumbent on. 2 befit.

**beige** ● n. pale sandy fawn colour. ● adj. of this colour.

**being** n. existence; nature; existing person etc.

**belabour** v. (also **belabor**) attack physically or verbally.

**belated** adj. coming (too) late. □□ **belatedly** adv.

**belay** ● v. secure (rope) by winding it around peg, rock, etc. ● n. belaying.

**bel canto** n. singing marked by full rich tone.

**belch** ● v. emit wind from stomach through mouth; (of volcano, gun, etc.) emit (fire, smoke, etc.) ● n. act of belching.

**beleaguer** v. vex; harass.

**belfry** n. bell tower; space for bells in church tower.

**belie** v. (**belying**) give false impression of; fail to confirm, fulfil, or justify.

**belief** n. act of believing; what one believes; trust, confidence; acceptance as true.

**believe** v. accept as true; think; have faith or confidence in; trust word of. □□ **believable** adj. **believer** n.

**belittle** v. disparage.
□□ **belittlement** n.

**bell** n. hollow esp. cup-shaped usu.
metal object emitting musical sound
when struck; sound of bell;
bell-shaped thing.

**belladonna** n. deadly nightshade;
drug obtained from this.

**belle** n. beautiful or most beautiful
woman.

**belles-lettres** n.pl. writings or
studies of purely literary kind.

**bellicose** adj. eager to fight.

**belligerent** ● adj. engaged in war
or conflict; given to constant fighting;
pugnacious. ● n. belligerent nation
or person. □□ **belligerence** n.

**bellow** ● v. emit deep loud
roar. ● n. loud roar.

**bellows** n.pl. device for driving air
into fire, organ, etc.

**belly** n. cavity of body containing
stomach, bowels, etc.; front of
body from waist to groin;
underside of animal; cavity or bulging
part of anything.

**bellyful** n. 1 enough to eat. 2 colloq.
more than one can tolerate.

**belong** v. 1 be property of, assigned
to, or member of. 2 fit socially; be
correctly placed or classified.

**belongings** n.pl. possessions,
luggage.

**beloved** ● adj. much loved.
● n. much loved person.

**below** ● prep. 1 under; lower than;
less than. 2 unworthy of. ● adv. at or
to lower point or level.

**belt** ● n. 1 strip of leather etc.
worn around waist. 2 continuous
band in machinery. 3 distinct strip of
colour etc. 4 seatbelt. 5 region,
district. 6 colloq. heavy blow.
● v. 1 put belt around. 2 colloq.
thrash. 3 colloq. move rapidly.
□ below the belt unfair.

**beltway** n. US 1 highway encircling
an urban area. 2 Washington DC, esp.

as representing the perceived
insularity of the US government.

**bemoan** v. lament; complain about.

**bemuse** v. puzzle, bewilder.

**bench** n. 1 long seat, usu. without
arms; strong work table. 2 office of
judge or magistrate; lawcourt. 3 Sport
area at side of playing field, for coach
and reserve players.

**benchmark** n. 1 surveyor's mark.
2 a standard or point of reference.

**bend** ● v. (bent, bending) 1 force
into curve or angle, be altered this
way. 2 incline from vertical. 3 bow,
stoop. 4 interpret or modify (rule) to
suit oneself. 5 (force to) submit.
● n. 1 bending, curve. 2 bent part of
thing. 3 (the bends) colloq.
decompression sickness.
□□ **bendable** adj. **bendy** adj.

**bender** n. colloq. wild drinking spree.

**beneath** ● prep. 1 below, under.
2 unworthy of. ● adv. below,
underneath.

**benediction** n. utterance of blessing.
□□ **benedictory** adj.

**benefaction** n. 1 charitable gift.
2 doing good.

**benefactor** n. person who has given
financial or other help.

**beneficent** adj. doing good; actively
kind. □□ **beneficence** n.

**beneficial** adj. advantageous.
□□ **beneficially** adv.

**beneficiary** n. receiver of benefits.

**benefit** ● n. 1 advantage, profit.
2 insurance or social security
payment. 3 performance or game of
which proceeds go to charity.
● v. (benefited) 1 do good to.
2 receive advantage or gain.

**benevolent** adj. wishing to do good;
kind and helpful; charitable.
□□ **benevolence** n.

**benighted** adj. intellectually or
morally ignorant.

**benign** adj. 1 kindly, gentle;
favourable; salutary. 2 Med. mild, not

malignant. □□ **benignity** n. **benignly** adv.

**bent** see BEND. ● adj. **1** curved or having angle. **2** colloq. dishonest, illicit. **3** set on doing or having. ● n. a natural skill or liking. □ **bent on** seeking or determined to do.

**benumb** v. make numb; deaden; paralyse.

**benzene** n. chemical obtained from petroleum and coal tar, used as solvent, fuel, etc.

**benzine** n. liquid mixture of hydrocarbons used as solvent in dry-cleaning.

**benzol** n. unrefined benzene.

**bequeath** v. leave by will; transmit to posterity.

**bequest** n. bequeathing; thing bequeathed.

**berate** v. scold.

**bereave** v. deprive of a relative, friend, etc., esp. by death. □□ **bereavement** n.

**bereft** adj. deprived.

**beret** n. round flat brimless cap.

**beriberi** n. nervous disease caused by deficiency of vitamin $B_1$.

**berk** n. fool; stupid person.

**berkelium** n. artificial radioactive metallic element (symbol Bk).

**berley** Aust. ● v. (also **berley-up**) scatter ground bait on water to attract fish. ● n. ground bait.

**berry** n. any small round juicy stoneless fruit.

**berserk** adj. □ **go berserk** go into an uncontrollable destructive rage.

**berth** ● n. **1** sleeping place. **2** ship's place at wharf; adequate room for ship. **3** position in an organisation or event. ● v. **1** moor (ship) in berth. **2** provide sleeping place for.

**beryl** n. transparent (esp. green) precious stone; mineral species including this and emerald.

**beryllium** n. white metallic element (symbol Be).

**beseech** v. (besought, beseeching) entreat; ask earnestly for.

**beset** v. (beset, besetting) attack or harass persistently.

**beside** prep. **1** at the side of; near. **2** compared with. □ **beside oneself** frantic with worry. **beside the point** irrelevant.

**besides** ● prep. **1** in addition to. **2** apart from. ● adv. also; as well.

**besiege** v. **1** lay siege to. **2** crowd around eagerly. **3** assail with requests.

**besmirch** v. soil, dishonour.

**besotted** adj. infatuated.

**besought** see BESEECH.

**bespeak** v. (bespoke, bespoken, bespeaking) **1** engage beforehand. **2** be evidence of.

**bespoke** adj. made for a particular customer or user.

**best** ● adj. most excellent or desirable; most beneficial. ● adv. better than any others; to highest degree. ● v. get the better of. ● n. highest standard that one can reach; that which is best. □ **best man** bridegroom's chief attendant at wedding. **best part of** most of.

**bestial** adj. **1** cruel. **2** of or like beasts. □□ **bestiality** n.

**bestiary** n. medieval treatise on beasts.

**bestir** v. (bestirred) □ **bestir oneself** exert or rouse oneself.

**bestow** v. confer as gift. □□ **bestowal** n.

**bestride** v. (bestrode, bestridden, bestriding) stand astride over.

**bet** ● v. (bet or betted, betting) **1** risk sum of money etc. on basis of outcome of unpredictable event. **2** colloq. feel certain. ● n. act of betting; amount staked.

**beta** n. second letter of Greek alphabet (B, β). □ **beta blocker** drug used to prevent increased cardiac activity. **beta version** piece of software that is made available for testing before its general release.

**betake** v. (**betook**, **betaken**, **betaking**) □ **betake oneself** go.

**betatron** n. apparatus for accelerating electrons.

**bête noire** n. (pl. **bêtes noires**) particularly disliked person or thing.

**betide** v. happen to.

**betoken** v. be sign of.

**betray** v. **1** be disloyal to (a friend, one's country, etc.); give up or reveal treacherously. **2** reveal involuntarily. **3** be evidence of. □□ **betrayal** n.

**betroth** v. cause to be engaged to marry. □□ **betrothal** n.

**better** ● adj. **1** of a more excellent kind. **2** partly or fully recovered from illness. ● adv. **1** in better manner. **2** to greater degree. ● n. **1** better thing or person. **2** person who bets. ● v. improve (upon); surpass.

**betterment** n. improvement.

**bettong** n. Aust. rat-kangaroo.

**between** ● prep. **1** in or into space or interval. **2** separating. **3** shared by. **4** to and from. **5** taking one or other of. ● adv. between points or limits.

**bevan** n. Aust. colloq. uncultured or unsophisticated person.

**bevel** ● n. **1** slope from horizontal or vertical in carpentry etc.; sloping surface or edge. **2** tool for marking angles. ● v. (**bevelled**) impart a bevel to.

**beverage** n. drink.

**bevy** n. company, flock.

**bewail** v. mourn for; wail over.

**beware** v. be on one's guard.

**bewilder** v. perplex, confuse. □□ **bewilderment** n.

**bewitch** v. enchant; cast spell on.

**beyond** ● prep. at or to further side of; outside range or understanding of; more than. ● adv. at or to further side; further on.

**bezel** n. **1** sloped edge of chisel. **2** oblique face of cut gem. **3** groove holding watch glass or gem.

**bi** colloq. n. & adj. bisexual.

**bi-** comb. form two; twice.

**biannual** adj. occurring etc. twice a year.

**bias** ● n. **1** predisposition, prejudice. **2** distortion of statistical results. **3** edge cut obliquely across weave of fabric. **4** Sport bowl's curved course due to its lopsided shape. ● v. (**biased** or **biassed**) give a bias to, influence.

**biathlon** n. athletic contest in skiing and shooting or cycling and running.

**bib** n. **1** cloth put under child's chin while eating. **2** top part of an apron etc.

**Bible** n. **1** Christian or Jewish scriptures. **2** (**bible**) colloq. authoritative book. □□ **biblical** adj.

**bibliography** n. list of books of any author, subject, etc. □□ **bibliographer** n. **bibliographical** adj.

**bibliophile** n. lover or collector of books.

**bicameral** adj. having two legislative chambers.

**bicarbonate** n. **1** any acid salt of carbonic acid. **2** (in full **bicarbonate of soda**) compound used in cooking and as antacid.

**bicentenary** n. 200th anniversary.

**bicentennial** ● n. bicentenary. ● adj. recurring every 200 years.

**biceps** n. muscle with double head or attachment, esp. that at front of upper arm.

**bicker** v. argue pettily.

**bicuspid** ● adj. having two cusps. ● n. bicuspid premolar tooth.

**bicycle** ● n. pedal-driven two-wheeled vehicle. ● v. ride bicycle.

**bid¹** ● n. 1 offer of a price, esp. at auction. 2 statement of number of tricks player proposes to win in card game. 3 an attempt. ● n. (bid, bidding) make a bid (of); offer. □□ bidder n.

**bid²** v. (bid or bade, bidden, bidding) command; say as greeting.

**biddable** adj. obedient.

**bidding** n. command, invitation.

**bidet** n. low wash basin that one can sit astride to wash genital and anal regions.

**biennale** n. art etc. exhibition held every two years.

**biennial** ● adj. lasting 2 years; recurring every 2 years. ● n. plant that flowers, fruits, and dies in second year.

**bier** n. movable frame on which coffin or corpse rests.

**biff** colloq. ● n. sharp blow.
● v. strike.

**biffo** n. Aust. colloq. fight.

**bifid** adj. divided by cleft into two parts.

**bifocals** n.pl. spectacles with lenses that have two segments, assisting both distant and close focusing.

**bifurcate** v. divide into two branches; fork. □□ bifurcation n.

**big** adj. (bigger) large in size, amount, or intensity. □□ biggish adj.

**bigamy** n. crime of making second marriage while first is still valid.
□□ bigamist n. bigamous adj.

**bight** n. 1 bay, recess of coast. 2 loop of rope.

**bigot** n. obstinate and intolerant adherent of creed or view.
□□ bigoted adj. bigotry n.

**bike** ● colloq. n. bicycle, motorcycle. ● v. ride bike.
□□ biker n.

**bikie** n. colloq. member of motorcycle gang.

**bikini** n. woman's two-piece swimsuit.

**bilateral** adj. 1 of, on, or with two sides. 2 between two parties.
□□ bilaterally adv.

**bilby** n. Aust. small burrowing marsupial bandicoot.

**bile** n. 1 bitter fluid secreted by liver to aid digestion. 2 bad temper; peevishness. □□ biliary adj.

**bilge** n. 1 nearly flat part of ship's bottom; (in full bilge water) foul water that collects there. 2 colloq. nonsense.

**bilingual** adj. of, in, or speaking two languages. □□ bilingualism n.

**bilious** adj. 1 affected by disorder of the bile. 2 bad-tempered.

**bilk** v. 1 colloq. cheat. 2 avoid payment of.

**bill¹** ● n. 1 statement of charges for goods, work done, etc. 2 draft of proposed law. 3 poster. 4 program of entertainment. 5 banknote.
● v. 1 send statement of charges to. 2 announce; advertise as.

**bill²** n. 1 bird's beak. 2 muzzle of platypus.

**billabong** n. Aust. arm of river, made by water flowing from mainstream into backwater, anabranch, or lagoon; dry bed of such formation.

**billboard** n. large outdoor board for advertisements.

**billet** n. 1 lodging for troops. 2 temporary lodging in household for member of sporting team etc.; person so billeted. ● v. place in a billet.

**billiards** n. game played with cues and three balls on cloth-covered table.

**billion** n. 1 thousand million; (now rarely) million million. 2 (billions) colloq. very large number.
□□ billionth adj. & n.

**billow** ● n. great wave; any large mass. ● v. rise or move in billows.
□□ billowy adj.

**billy** n. **1** Aust. (in full **billycan**) tin or enamel outdoor cooking pot. **2** colloq. **bong**.

**billy goat** n. male goat.

**bimbo** n. (pl. **bimbos**) attractive but unintelligent young woman.

**bin** ● n. **1** large rigid receptacle or container. **2** each of a series of ranges of numerical value into which data are sorted in statistical analysis. ● v. discard or reject.

**binary** adj. **1** of two parts, dual. **2** of system using digits 0 and 1 to code information.

**bind** ● v. (**bound, binding**) **1** tie or fasten tightly; restrain; (cause to) cohere; compel; impose duty on. **2** edge with braid etc. **3** fasten (pages of book) into cover. ● n. colloq. nuisance. □□ **binder** n.

**bindi-eye** n. (also **bindy-eye**) Australian plant bearing barbed fruits; its fruit.

**binding** ● n. **1** a book cover. **2** a braid etc. for edging. ● adj. obligatory.

**binge** colloq. ● n. bout of excessive eating, drinking, etc.; spree. ● v. indulge in a binge.

**bingle** n. **1** colloq. collision. **2** fight, skirmish.

**bingo** n. gambling game in which each player marks off numbers on card as they are called.

**binocular** adj. for both eyes.

**binoculars** n.pl. instrument with lens for each eye, for viewing distant objects.

**binomial** ● n. algebraic expression of sum or difference of two terms. ● adj. consisting of two terms.

**bio-** comb. form **1** biological. **2** life.

**biochemistry** n. chemistry of living organisms. □□ **biochemical** adj. **biochemist** n.

**biodegradable** adj. able to be decomposed by bacteria or other living organisms.

**biodiversity** n. diversity of plant and animal life.

**bioengineering** n. **1** application of engineering techniques to biological processes. **2** use of artificial tissues or organs to replace parts of body.

**biofuel** n. fuel derived from living matter.

**biogas** n. gaseous fuel, esp. methane.

**biography** n. written account of person's life. □□ **biographer** n. **biographical** adj.

**biological** adj. of biology or living organisms. □□ **biologically** adv.

**biology** n. study of living organisms. □□ **biologist** n.

**biome** n. large naturally occurring community of fauna and flora adapted to particular conditions in which they occur.

**bionic** adj. having electronically operated body parts.

**biopsy** n. examination of tissue removed from living body for diagnosis.

**biorhythm** n. biological cycle thought to affect person's physical or emotional state.

**biosecurity** n. measures taken to protect population against harmful biological or biochemical substances.

**biosphere** n. earth's crust and atmosphere containing life.

**biotechnology** n. branch of technology exploiting biological processes, esp. using microorganisms, in industry, medicine, etc.

**biotope** n. area with particular habitat that supports a particular community of flora and fauna.

**bipartisan** adj. of or involving two (esp. political) parties.

**bipartite** adj. of two parts; involving two parties.

**biped** ● n. two-footed animal. ● adj. two-footed.

**biplane** n. aeroplane with two sets of wings, one above the other.

**bipolar** *adj.* **1** having two poles or extremities. **2** suffering from bipolar disorder. □ **bipolar disorder** mental illness characterised by alternating periods of elation and depression.

**birch** *n.* tree with thin peeling bark.

**bird** *n.* feathered egg-laying animal, usu. able to fly.

**birdie** *n. Golf* hole played in one under par.

**biretta** *n.* square cap of RC priest.

**biro** *n. propr.* (*pl.* **biros**) ballpoint pen.

**birth** *n.* emergence of young from mother's body; origin, beginning; ancestry, inherited position. □ **birth control** contraception.

**birthday** *n.* anniversary of day of one's birth.

**birthmark** *n.* unusual coloured mark on skin at birth.

**biscuit** *n.* **1** flat thin unleavened cake, usu. crisp and sweet. **2** fired unglazed pottery. **3** light brown colour.

**bisect** *v.* divide into two (usu. equal) parts. □□ **bisection** *n.* **bisector** *n.*

**bisexual** ● *adj.* feeling sexual attraction to people of both sexes. ● *n.* bisexual person. □□ **bisexuality** *n.*

**bishop** *n.* **1** senior Christian clergyman, usu. in charge of diocese. **2** mitre-shaped chess piece.

**bishopric** *n.* office or diocese of bishop.

**bismuth** *n.* **1** reddish-white metallic element (symbol Bi). **2** compound of it used medicinally.

**bison** *n.* wild ox of Europe or N. America.

**bisque** *n.* rich soup.

**bistro** *n.* (*pl.* **bistros**) small informal restaurant.

**bit** ● *v. see* **bite**. ● *n.* **1** small piece or amount; short time or distance. **2** mouthpiece of bridle. **3** cutting part of tool. **4** *Computing* binary digit.

**bitch** ● *n.* **1** female dog, fox, or wolf. **2** *offens.* spiteful woman. **3** *colloq.*

unpleasant or difficult situation or thing. **4** *colloq.* complaint, whinge. ● *v.* **1** speak spitefully. **2** *colloq.* complain, whinge.

**bitcoin** *n.* type of cryptocurrency.

**bite** ● *v.* (**bit**, **bitten**, **biting**) **1** nip or cut into or off with teeth. **2** sting. **3** penetrate, grip. **4** accept a bait. **5** *Aust. colloq.* borrow money from. ● *n.* **1** act of biting; a wound made by this. **2** small amount to eat.

**bitter** ● *adj.* **1** having sharp pungent taste, not sweet. **2** showing or feeling resentment. **3** harsh, virulent; piercingly cold. ● *n.* **1** bitter beer. **2** (**bitters**) liquor with a bitter flavour. □□ **bitterly** *adv.* **bitterness** *n.*

**bittern** *n.* wading bird of heron family.

**bitty** *adj.* (**bittier**) made up of bits.

**bitumen** *n.* tarlike mixture of hydrocarbons derived from petroleum; tarred road. □□ **bituminous** *adj.*

**bivalve** ● *n.* aquatic mollusc with hinged double shell. ● *adj.* with such a shell.

**bivouac** ● *n.* temporary encampment without tents. ● *v.* (**bivouacked**, **bivouacking**) make, or camp in, a bivouac.

**bizarre** *adj.* strange; eccentric; grotesque.

**blab** *v.* (**blabbed**) talk or tell foolishly or indiscreetly.

**black** ● *adj.* **1** of very darkest colour; like coal; having dark skin. **2** dismal, gloomy; hostile; evil. ● *n.* **1** black colour or thing. **2** (usu. **Black**) member of human group having dark-coloured skin. □ **black armband** black band worn around arm to indicate mourning. **black box** flight recorder. **black belt** (holder of) highest grade of proficiency in judo, karate, etc. **black dog** depression or melancholy. **black hole** region in outer space from which matter and radiation cannot escape. **black market** illicit traffic in prohibited commodities. **black sheep** member of family etc. regarded as a disgrace. **black spot** place of danger or difficulty. **black tie** man's formal evening dress. **in the black** with credit balance, not in debt.

**blackberry** n. dark edible fruit of bramble.

**blackbird** n. European songbird.

**blackbirding** n. *Aust. hist.* kidnapping of Pacific Islanders as slave labour for Queensland sugar etc. plantations.

**blackboard** n. board for writing on with chalk.

**blackbutt** n. Australian eucalypt with fire-charred fibrous bark on lower trunk.

**blackcurrant** n. small black fruit; shrub on which it grows.

**blacken** v. 1 make or become black. 2 slander.

**blackguard** n. villain, scoundrel. □□ **blackguardly** adj.

**blackhead** n. black-topped pimple.

**blacklist** n. list of people etc. in disfavour. ● v. put on blacklist.

**blackmail** n. extortion of payment in return for silence; use of threats or pressure. ● v. extort money etc. from thus. □□ **blackmailer** n.

**blackout** n. 1 temporary loss of consciousness or memory. 2 loss of power, radio reception, etc.

**blacksmith** n. smith who works in iron.

**bladder** n. 1 sac in humans and other animals, esp. that holding urine. 2 inflated sac in seaweed etc. 3 inflatable inner lining of football.

**blade** n. 1 cutting part of knife etc.; razor blade. 2 flat part of oar, spade, propeller, etc.; flat narrow leaf of grass etc.; flat bone in shoulder.

**blame** ● v. assign fault or responsibility to; assign responsibility for (error etc.) to. ● n. responsibility for bad result; blaming, attributing of responsibility. □□ **blameless** adj.

**blanch** v. 1 make or grow pale. 2 peel (almonds etc.) by scalding. 3 immerse (vegetables etc.) briefly in boiling water. 4 whiten (plant) by depriving it of light.

**blancmange** n. sweet opaque jelly of flavoured cornflour and milk.

**bland** adj. mild; tasteless; insipid; gentle, suave. □□ **blandly** adv.

**blandishments** n.pl. flattering or coaxing words.

**blank** ● adj. 1 not written or printed on. 2 without interest, result, or expression. ● n. 1 blank space. 2 cartridge containing no bullet. □ **blank cheque 1** cheque with amount left blank for payee to fill in. 2 *colloq.* unlimited freedom of action. **blank verse** verse without rhyme. □□ **blankly** adv.

**blanket** ● n. large esp. woollen sheet as bed covering etc.; thick covering layer. ● adj. general, covering all cases or classes. ● v. cover.

**blare** ● v. sound or utter loudly; make sound of trumpet. ● n. blaring sound.

**blarney** n. cajoling talk; flattery.

**blasé** adj. bored or indifferent, esp. through familiarity.

**blaspheme** v. treat religious name or subject irreverently; talk irreverently about.

**blasphemy** n. (instance of) blaspheming. □□ **blasphemous** adj.

**blast** ● n. 1 strong gust. 2 explosion; destructive wave of air from this. 3 loud note from wind instrument, car horn, whistle, etc. 4 *colloq.* severe reprimand. ● v. 1 blow up with explosive. 2 (cause to) make explosive sound. 3 blight.

**blatant** adj. flagrant, unashamed. □□ **blatantly** adv.

**blather** (also **blether**) ● *n.* foolish talk. ● *v.* talk foolishly.

**blaze** ● *n.* **1** bright flame or fire; brilliant light or display. **2** white mark on animal's face; mark cut in bark of tree to mark a route.
● *v.* burn or shine brightly or fiercely.
□ **blaze a trail** mark out a route; pioneer.

**blazer** *n.* jacket without matching trousers, esp. part of uniform.

**blazon** *v.* **1** proclaim. **2** describe or paint (coat of arms).□□ **blazonment** *n.* **blazonry** *n.*

**bleach** ● *v.* whiten in sunlight or by chemical process. ● *n.* bleaching substance or process.

**bleak** *adj.* exposed, windswept; dreary, grim.

**bleary** *adj.* (**blearier**) dim-sighted, blurred.

**bleat** ● *v.* **1** utter cry of sheep, goat, etc. **2** speak plaintively.
● *n.* bleating cry.

**bleed** ● *v.* (**bled**, **bleeding**) **1** emit blood; draw blood from. **2** *colloq.* extort money from. **3** (of plant) emit sap. **4** (of dye) come out in water. ● *n.* a haemorrhage.

**bleep** ● *n.* intermittent high-pitched sound. ● *v.* make bleep; summon by bleep.□□ **bleeper** *n.*

**blemish** ● *n.* flaw, defect, stain.
● *v.* spoil, mark, stain.

**blench** *v.* flinch, quail.

**blend** ● *v.* mix smoothly; mingle; purée in electric blender.
● *n.* a mixture.

**bless** *v.* **1** ask God to look favourably on. **2** consecrate. **3** glorify (God). **4** thank. **5** make happy.

**blessed** *adj.* **1** holy. **2** *euphem.* damned, cursed. **3** *RC Ch.* beatified.

**blessing** *n.* **1** act of declaring, seeking, or bestowing (esp. divine) favour; person's sanction or support; grace said at meals. **2** benefit, advantage.
□ **blessing in disguise** apparent

misfortune that eventually has good results.

**blight** ● *n.* **1** plant disease caused esp. by insects; such insect. **2** harmful or destructive force. ● *v.* **1** affect with blight. **2** destroy; spoil.

**blimp** *n.* small non-rigid airship.

**blind** ● *adj.* **1** without sight; without foresight, understanding, or adequate information.
**2** (in cookery) without a filling.
**3** closed at one end. ● *v.* make blind; rob of judgement.
● *n.* **1** a screen, esp. on a roller, for a window. **2** a pretext.□□ **blindly** *adv.* **blindness** *n.*

**blindfold** ● *v.* cover eyes of (person) with tied cloth etc.
● *n.* cloth etc. so used. ● *adj. & adv.* **1** with eyes covered. **2** without due care.

**blink** ● *v.* **1** shut and open eyes quickly. **2** shine unsteadily, flicker. ● *n.* **1** act of blinking. **2** momentary gleam.□ **on the blink** (of a machine) not working properly; out of order.

**blinker** ● *n.* **1** leather piece fixed to bridle preventing horse from seeing sideways. **2** flashing light on car etc. indicating direction of turn.
● *v.* obstruct sight or understanding of.

**blip** *n.* **1** minor deviation or error; temporary problem. **2** quick popping sound. **3** small image on radar screen.

**bliss** *n.* perfect joy.□□ **blissful** *adj.* **blissfully** *adv.*

**blister** ● *n.* small bubble on skin filled with watery fluid; any swelling resembling this. ● *v.* become covered in blisters; raise blister on.

**blistering** *adj.* sharp; intense; severely critical.

**blithe** *adj.* cheerful, happy; carefree, casual.□□ **blithely** *adv.* **blitheness** *n.* **blithesome** *adj.*

**blitz** *colloq.* ● *n.* intensive (esp. aerial) attack. ● *v.* 1 inflict blitz on. 2 defeat convincingly.

**blizzard** *n.* severe snowstorm.

**bloat** ● *v.* inflate, swell. ● *n.* (also **bloating**) disease of livestock characterised by accumulation of gases in stomach.

**blob** *n.* small drop or spot.

**bloc** *n.* group of governments etc. sharing common purpose.

**block** ● *n.* 1 solid piece of hard material; compact mass of buildings; large building divided into flats or offices; large quantity treated as unit. 2 *Aust.* building allotment; tract of rural land. 3 pad of paper for drawing or writing on. 4 obstruction. 5 pulley mounted in a case. ● *v.* obstruct; prevent the movement or use of.

**blockade** ● *n.* surrounding or blocking of place by enemy. ● *v.* subject to blockade.

**blockage** *n.* obstruction.

**blockbuster** *n.* something very successful.

**blockchain** *n.* system in which records are maintained across several computers that are linked in a peer-to-peer network.

**blog** ● *n.* regularly updated website or webpage that is written in an informal or conversational style. ● *v.* add material to or regularly update blog. □□ **blogger** *n.*

**blogosphere** *n.* personal websites and weblogs collectively.

**bloke** *n. colloq.* man, fellow.

**blond** (of woman usu. **blonde**) ● *adj.* light-coloured, fair-haired. ● *n.* blond person.

**blood** ● *n.* 1 usu. red fluid circulating in arteries and veins of animals. 2 killing, bloodshed. 3 passion, temperament. 4 race, descent. 5 relationship. ● *v.* initiate (person). □ **blood bin** (in sports) any place off field to which player who is bleeding

is sent. **blood sports** sports involving killing. **blood vessel** tubular structure conveying blood within body.

**blooded** *adj.* initiated.

**bloodshot** *adj.* (of eyes) red from dilated veins.

**bloodstained** *adj.* stained with blood.

**bloodstream** *n.* blood circulating in body.

**bloodsucker** *n.* creature that sucks blood; person who extorts money.

**bloodthirsty** *adj.* eager to kill or wound.

**bloody** ● *adj.* (**bloodier**) 1 stained with blood. 2 involving bloodshed, cruel. 3 *colloq.* cursed. ● *adv. colloq.* extremely. ● *v.* stain with blood. □ **bloody-minded** *colloq.* deliberately uncooperative.

**bloom** ● *n.* 1 flower; flowering state. 2 prime, freshness. 3 fine powder on fruit etc. ● *v.* 1 bear flowers; be in flower. 2 flourish. □□ **blooming** *adj.*

**blossom** ● *n.* flower; mass of flowers on tree. ● *v.* 1 open into flower. 2 thrive.

**blot** ● *n.* 1 spot of ink etc. 2 disgraceful act; blemish. ● *v.* (**blotted**) 1 make blot on; stain. 2 dry with blotting paper.

**blotch** *n.* 1 inflamed patch on skin. 2 irregular patch of colour. □□ **blotchy** *adj.*

**blotto** *adj. colloq.* very drunk.

**blouse** ● *n.* 1 woman's shirtlike garment. 2 type of military jacket. ● *v.* make (bodice etc.) full like blouse.

**blow** ● *v.* (**blew, blown, blowing**) 1 send out current of air or breath; move or flow as current of air does; move, sound, or shape by this; puff and pant. 2 (of fuse) melt. 3 *colloq.* depart suddenly (from). 4 break with explosion. 5 *colloq.* squander. ● *n.* 1 act of blowing. 2 hard stroke with hand, tool, or weapon; stroke in

shearing. **3** disaster, shock.
□ **blow-out 1** burst tyre. **2** increase in budget deficit etc. **blow over** fade away. **blow up** explode, shatter by explosion; inflate; exaggerate; enlarge (photograph); lose one's temper.

**blowfly** n. fly that lays its eggs on meat.

**blowie** n. Aust. colloq. blowfly.

**blowy** adj. windy.

**blubber** ● n. whale fat. ● v. sob noisily.

**bludge** Aust. colloq. ● v. **1** evade responsibility or work. **2** impose on others; cadge, scrounge. ● n. act of bludging; undemanding job. □□ **bludging** adj. & n.

**bludgeon** ● n. heavy club. ● v. **1** beat with bludgeon. **2** coerce.

**bludger** n. Aust. colloq. idler, person who makes little effort; person who appears to live off the efforts of others; sponger.

**blue** ● adj. **1** coloured like a clear sky. **2** sad, depressed. **3** colloq. indecent. ● n. **1** blue colour or thing. **2** Aust. colloq. argument; mistake or blunder. □ **blue-blooded** of aristocratic descent. **blue metal** broken blue stone used in road-making. **blue-screen** special-effects technique used in films in which scenes shot against a blue background are superimposed on other scenes. **blue-sky** creative or visionary and unconstrained by practicalities.

**blueberry** n. edible blue-black berry; shrub bearing this.

**bluebottle** n. jellyfish with crest, and tentacles that have poisonous sting.

**blueprint** n. blue photographic print of building plans; detailed scheme.

**blues** n.pl. **1** bout of depression. **2** melancholic music of African-American origin.

**Bluetooth** n. propr. wireless technology for interconnecting mobile phones, computers, etc.

**bluey** n. **1** Aust. swag, luggage. **2** heavy woollen outer garment.

**bluff** ● v. pretend to have strength, knowledge, etc. ● n. **1** bluffing. **2** broad steep cliff or headland. ● adj. **1** blunt, frank, hearty. **2** with steep broad front.

**blunder** ● n. serious or foolish mistake. ● v. make blunder; move clumsily.

**blunnies** n.pl. Aust. stout leather boots.

**blunt** ● adj. **1** without sharp edge or point. **2** direct, outspoken. ● v. make blunt. □□ **bluntly** adv. **bluntness** n.

**blur** ● v. (**blurred**) make or become less distinct; smear. ● n. a smear; indistinct appearance.

**Blu-ray** n. propr. very high-definition optical disk for video, storage of data, etc.

**blurb** n. promotional description, esp. of book.

**blurt** v. utter abruptly or tactlessly.

**blush** ● v. become red-faced with embarrassment or shame. ● n. blushing; pink tinge.

**bluster** ● v. **1** behave pompously. **2** storm boisterously. ● n. noisy pompous talk; empty threats. □□ **blustery** adj.

**BMX** n. bicycle racing on dirt tracks; bike for this.

**BO** abbr. colloq. body odour.

**boa** n. **1** large snake that kills its prey by crushing it. **2** long stole of feathers or fur.

**boar** n. uncastrated male pig; wild pig.

**board** ● n. **1** thin piece of sawn timber; flat piece of wood or stiff material; surfboard. **2** daily meals supplied in return for payment or services. **3** committee; directors of a company. **4** Aust. part of shearing shed floor upon which sheep are shorn. ● v. **1** cover or block with boards. **2** enter (ship, aircraft, or vehicle). **3** receive, or provide with, meals and accommodation for payment. □ **on board** on or in ship, aircraft, or vehicle.

**boarder** n. person who boards with someone; resident pupil.

**boardies** n.pl. Aust. colloq. boardshorts.

**boardroom** n. room in which board of directors etc. meets.

**boardshorts** n.pl. long shorts, orig. as used by surfboard riders.

**boast** ● v. **1** declare one's achievements etc. with excessive pride. **2** have (desirable thing).
● n. **1** boasting. **2** thing one is proud of.□□ **boastful** adj.

**boat** ● n. **1** small vessel propelled by engine, oars, or sails; ship. **2** long low jug for gravy etc. ● v. go in boat, esp. for pleasure.□ **boat people** refugees travelling by sea.

**boater** n. flat straw hat with straight brim.

**boatswain** n. (also **bosun**) ship's officer in charge of equipment and crew.

**bob** ● v. (**bobbed**) **1** move quickly up and down. **2** cut (hair) in bob. **3** curtsy. ● n. **1** bobbing movement. **2** hairstyle with hair hanging evenly above shoulders.

**bobbin** n. spool or reel for thread etc.

**bobble** n. small woolly ball on hat etc.

**bobcat** n. propr. small earth-moving machine.

**bobsleigh** n. (also **bobsled**) racing sledge steered and braked mechanically.

**bocconcini** n.pl. small balls of mozzarella.

**bode** v. be sign of, portend.

**bodgie** Aust. colloq. ● n. something flawed or worthless. ● adj. **1** worthless, flawed. **2** false; (of name) assumed. ● v. put (something)

together in a dishonest or incompetent way.

**bodice** n. part of woman's dress above waist.

**bodily** ● adj. of the body. ● adv. **1** as a whole (body). **2** in person.

**bodkin** n. blunt thick needle for drawing tape etc. through hem.

**body** n. **1** physical structure of person or animal; person's or animal's trunk. **2** corpse. **3** main part. **4** group of people regarded as unit. **5** quantity, mass, piece of matter. **6** colloq. person. **7** full or substantial quality of flavour, tone, etc.

**bodyguard** n. escort or personal guard.

**boffin** n. colloq. expert.

**bog** n. **1** (area of) wet spongy ground. **2** colloq. toilet.□□ **boggy** adj.

**bogan** n. Aust. colloq. usu. derog. person who is regarded as being uncultured or unsophisticated.

**bogey** n. (pl. **bogeys**) **1** Golf score of one more than par for hole. **2** (also **bogy**) something causing fear.

**boggle** v. be surprised or baffled.

**bogong** n. (in full **bogong moth**) large brown moth of southern Australia.

**bogus** adj. sham, spurious.

**bohemian** ● n. socially unconventional person, esp. artist or writer. ● adj. socially unconventional.□□ **bohemianism** n.

**bohrium** n. chemical element (symbol Bh).

**boil** ● v. bubble up with heat, reach temperature at which liquid turns to vapour; bring to boiling point.
● n. inflamed swelling producing pus.

**boiler** n. tank etc. for heating water or turning it to steam.

**boisterous** adj. **1** noisily cheerful. **2** violent, rough.

**bolar** n. Aust. cut of beef adjacent to the blade.

**bold** *adj.* **1** confident, adventurous, brave. **2** impudent. **3** distinct, vivid. **4** (in full **boldface** or **-faced**) printed in thick black typeface.□□ **boldly** *adv.* **boldness** *n.*

**bole** *n.* trunk of tree.

**bolero** *n.* **1** Spanish dance. **2** woman's short open jacket.

**boll** *n.* round seed vessel of cotton, flax, etc.

**bollard** *n.* short thick post in street etc.; post on quay or ship for securing rope.

**bollocks** *n.pl. colloq.* **1** testicles. **2** nonsense, rubbish.

**bolshie** *adj. colloq.* rebellious, uncooperative.

**bolster** ● *n.* long cylindrical pillow. ● *v.* encourage, support, prop up.

**bolt** ● *n.* **1** door fastening of metal bar and socket; large metal pin with thread, secured with rivet or nut. **2** discharge of lightning. **3** bolting. **4** roll of fabric. ● *v.* **1** fasten with bolt; keep in or out by bolting door. **2** dart off, run away; (of horse) escape from control. **3** gulp down unchewed. **4** run to seed.

**bomb** ● *n.* **1** container filled with explosive, incendiary material, etc., designed to explode and cause damage. **2** (**the bomb**) atomic bomb. **3** *colloq.* old or unreliable motor vehicle. ● *v.* **1** attack with bombs; drop bombs on. **2** *colloq.* fail badly.

**bombard** *v.* **1** attack with heavy guns etc. **2** question or abuse persistently. **3** *Physics* direct stream of high-speed particles at.□□ **bombardment** *n.*

**bombardier** *n.* artillery NCO below sergeant.

**bombast** *n.* pompous language; hyperbole.□□ **bombastic** *adj.*

**bomber** *n.* aircraft equipped for bombing; person using bombs.

**bomblet** *n.* small bomb.

**bombora** *n.* (also **bommie**) *Aust.* dangerous stretch of broken water over submerged reef or rock; the reef or rock itself.

**bona fide** *adj. & adv.* genuine.

**bonanza** *n.* source of wealth, prosperity, good luck, etc.

**bonbon** *n.* **1** = CRACKER (sense 1). **2** lolly, sweet.

**bond** ● *n.* **1** something that unites or restrains; binding agreement; emotional link. **2** certificate issued by government or company acknowledging that money has been lent to it and will be repaid with interest. **3** term(s) under which offender is released by court of law. **4** (also **bond money**) amount payable at beginning of tenancy against property damage by tenant or non-payment of rent. ● *v.* unite with a bond. □ **in bond** stored in customs warehouse until duties are paid.

**bondage** *n.* slavery; subjection to constraint.

**bone** ● *n.* **1** any of separate parts of vertebrate skeleton. **2** (in Aboriginal ritual practice) bone pointed at someone to bring bad luck or death. ● *v.* **1** remove bones from. **2** (also **point the bone**) (in Aboriginal ritual practice) influence (person at whom bone is pointed) with intention of causing bad luck or death.

**bonfire** *n.* open-air fire.

**bong** *n.* water pipe for smoking marijuana etc.

**bongo** *n.* (pl. **bongos** or **bongoes**) either of pair of small drums played with fingers.

**bonhomie** *n.* geniality.

**bonk** ● *v.* **1** hit, bump. **2** *colloq.* have sexual intercourse (with). ● *n.* **1** abrupt sound of heavy impact. **2** *colloq.* sexual intercourse.

**bonnet** *n.* **1** woman's or child's hat tied under chin. **2** hinged cover over vehicle's engine.

**bonny** *adj.* (**bonnier**) *Scot.* healthy looking, attractive.

**onsai** n. (pl. **bonsai**) dwarfed tree or shrub; art of growing these.

**onus** n. extra benefit or payment.

**on voyage** int. have good trip.

**ony** adj. (**bonier**) thin with prominent bones; of or like bone.

**onzer** Aust. colloq. ● n. person or thing exciting admiration. ● adj. excellent, first-rate.

**oo** int. **1** expression of disapproval or contempt. **2** sound intended to surprise.

**oob** n. colloq. **1** a mistake. **2** woman's breast.

**oobook** n. Aust. owl with characteristic two-note call.

**ooby** n. silly or awkward person. □ **booby prize** one given to competitor with lowest score. **booby trap** hidden trap as practical joke; hidden bomb.

**oodie** n. Aust. burrowing rat-kangaroo.

**oofhead** n. Aust. colloq. fool, simpleton.

**oofy** adj. Aust. colloq. foolish; big and stupid; blokey.

**ook** ● n. **1** sheets of paper bound in a cover; literary work filling this; main division of literary work. **2** record of bets made. **3** (**books**) set of records or accounts. ● v. **1** reserve or buy in advance; engage (entertainer etc.). **2** take personal details of (offender).

**ookcase** n. piece of furniture with shelves for books.

**ookie** n. colloq. bookmaker.

**ookkeeping** n. the systematic recording of business transactions.

**ookmaker** n. person whose business is taking of bets.

**ookmark** ● n. **1** strip of paper etc. to mark place in book. **2** record of address of website etc. made to enable quick access. ● v. make bookmark of (address etc.).

**ookworm** n. **1** person fond of reading. **2** grub that eats holes in books.

**boom** ● v. **1** make deep resonant sound. **2** have period of prosperity. ● n. **1** booming sound. **2** prosperity. **3** long pole; floating barrier. □ **boom gate** movable barrier that controls traffic access to certain places.

**boomer** n. Aust. large adult male kangaroo.

**boomerang** ● n. **1** curved flat hardwood missile used orig. by Aboriginal people for hunting etc., and often of kind returning to thrower. **2** plan etc. that recoils on originator. **3** thing lent which lender insists must be returned. ● v. **1** act as boomerang. **2** (of plan etc.) backfire.

**boon** n. a benefit. □ **boon companion** a favourite.

**boor** n. ill-mannered person. □□ **boorish** adj.

**boost** ● v. **1** promote, encourage; increase, assist. **2** push from below. ● n. boosting.

**booster** n. **1** device for increasing power or voltage. **2** auxiliary engine or rocket for initial speed. **3** dose renewing effect of earlier one.

**boot** ● n. **1** outer foot-covering reaching above ankle. **2** luggage compartment of car. **3** colloq. firm kick, dismissal. ● v. **1** kick. **2** eject forcefully. **3** make (computer) ready. □ **boot camp** US military training camp for new recruits.

**booth** n. **1** temporary structure used esp. as market stall. **2** enclosure for telephoning, voting, etc.

**bootleg** adj. smuggled, illicit. □□ **bootlegger** n.

**bootscooting** n. line dancing.

**booty** n. **1** loot, spoil. **2** colloq. prize.

**booze** ● colloq. n. alcoholic drink. ● v. drink alcohol, esp. excessively. □□ **boozer** n. **boozy** adj.

**boracic** adj. of borax.

**borax** n. salt of boric acid used as antiseptic.

**border** ● *n.* edge or boundary; flower bed around part of a garden. ● *v.* put or be border to; adjoin.

**bore** ● *v.* 1 see BEAR. 2 weary by dullness. 3 make (a hole) with a revolving tool. ● *n.* 1 boring person or thing. 2 a hollow inside a cylinder; its diameter. 3 tidal wave in an estuary. 4 *Aust.* artesian bore.□□ **boredom** *n.*

**bored** *adj.* feeling weary and impatient because one is unoccupied or lacks interest in one's current activity.

**boric acid** *n.* acid used as antiseptic.

**born** *adj.* 1 existing as a result of birth. 2 of natural ability or quality; destined.□ **born-again** newly converted and enthusiastic about religion etc.

**borne** see BEAR.

**boron** *n.* chemical element very resistant to high temperatures (symbol B).

**boronia** *n.* small Australian shrub with usu. aromatic foliage and highly-perfumed flowers.

**borough** *n.* urban local government area.

**borrow** *v.* get temporary use of (something to be returned); use another's (idea, invention, etc.). □□ **borrower** *n.*

**bosom** ● *n.* 1 person's breasts. 2 *colloq.* each of woman's breasts. 3 enclosure formed by breast and arms. 4 emotional centre. ● *adj.* intimate.

**boss** ● *n.* 1 employer, manager, or supervisor. 2 round knob or stud. ● *v.* give orders to.

**bossy** *adj.* (**bossier**) *colloq.* domineering.□□ **bossiness** *n.*

**bosun** (also **bo'sun**) = BOATSWAIN.

**bot** *n. Aust. colloq.* cadge.

**botany** *n.* study of plants. □□ **botanic(al)** *adj.* **botanist** *n.*

**botch** (also **bodge**) ● *v.* bungle; repair clumsily. ● *n.* bungled or spoilt work.

**both** ● *adj. & pron.* the two (not only one). ● *adv.* with equal truth in two cases.

**bother** ● *v.* 1 cause trouble, worry, or annoyance to; pester. 2 take trouble. ● *n.* 1 person or thing that bothers. 2 nuisance; trouble, worry. □□ **bothersome** *adj.*

**Botox** *n. propr.* drug used to treat muscular conditions and for cosmetic surgery.

**bottle** ● *n.* narrow-necked container for storing liquid etc. ● *v.* 1 put into bottles; preserve (fruit etc.) in jars. 2 restrain (feelings etc.).

**bottlebrush** *n.* 1 Australian shrub with flower spikes shaped like cylindrical brush. 2 cylindrical brush for cleaning inside bottles.

**bottleneck** *n.* point at which flow of traffic, production, etc., is constricted.

**bottom** ● *n.* 1 lowest point or part. 2 buttocks. 3 less important end of table, class, etc. 4 ground under water. 5 basis, origin. ● *adj.* lowest; last. ● *v.* reach its lowest level; touch bottom (of).□□ **bottomless** *adj.*

**botulism** *n.* poisoning caused by bacillus in badly preserved food.

**boudoir** *n.* woman's private room.

**bougainvillaea** *n.* tropical plant with large coloured bracts.

**bough** *n.* branch of tree.

**bought** see BUY.

**bouillon** *n.* clear broth.

**boulder** *n.* large rounded rock.

**boulevard** *n.* broad tree-lined avenue.

**bounce** ● *v.* 1 (cause to) rebound. 2 *colloq.* (of a cheque) be returned by bank when there are no funds to meet it. 3 rush boisterously. 4 *AFL* bounce the ball, esp. at start of game. ● *n.* 1 a rebound. 2 *colloq.*

swagger, self-confidence. **3** *AFL* ball-up. □□ **bouncy** *adj.*

**bouncer** *n.* **1** person employed by a nightclub etc. to prevent unwanted people entering or to eject them from the premises. **2** *Cricket* ball bowled fast and short so as to rise high after pitching.

**bouncing** *adj.* big and healthy.

**bound** • *v.* **1** see BIND. **2** run with a jumping movement. **3** limit, be a boundary of. • *n.* **1** bounding movement. **2** (usu. **bounds**) the limit of something. • *adj.* going in a specified direction. □ **out of bounds** beyond the permitted area.

**boundary** *n.* **1** line marking limits. **2** *Cricket* a hit crossing limit of field; runs scored for this. □ **boundary rider** *Aust.* person employed to ride round the fences etc. of a cattle or sheep station and keep them in good order.

**bounteous** *adj. poet.* bountiful.

**bountiful** *adj.* generous; ample.

**bounty** *n.* **1** generosity. **2** official reward. **3** gift.

**bouquet** *n.* **1** bunch of flowers. **2** scent of wine. **3** compliment. □ **bouquet garnis** (*pl.* **bouquets garnis**) bunch of herbs for flavouring stews etc.

**bourbon** *n.* whisky from maize and rye.

**bourgeois** *adj.* conventionally middle-class.

**bourgeoisie** *n.* bourgeois class.

**bout** *n.* **1** period of exercise, work, or illness. **2** wrestling or boxing match.

**boutique** *n.* **1** small shop selling fashionable clothes etc. **2** (business) producing individual or high-class products.

**bouzouki** *n.* Greek form of mandolin.

**bovine** *adj.* **1** of cattle. **2** stupid, dull.

**bow**¹ *n.* **1** weapon for shooting arrows. **2** rod with horsehair stretched along

its length, for playing violin etc. **3** a knot with loops in a ribbon or a string.

**bow²** • *n.* bending of head or body in greeting, respect, etc. • *v.* bend in this way; bend downwards under weight; submit.

**bow³** *n.* front end of boat or ship.

**bowdlerise** *v.* (also **-ize**) expurgate. □□ **bowdlerisation** *n.*

**bowel** *n.* **1** intestine; (**bowels**) innermost parts.

**bower** *n.* arbour; secluded place, esp. in garden.

**bowl**¹ • *n.* **1** round, deep dish for food etc.; contents of this; hollow rounded part of spoon etc. **2** heavy ball weighted to run in curve; (**bowls**) game played with these. • *v.* **1** send rolling along ground; go fast and smoothly. **2** *Cricket* send ball to batter; dismiss by knocking bails off with ball. □ **bowl over** knock down; overwhelm with surprise or emotion.

**bowler** *n.* **1** person who bowls in cricket; player of bowls. **2** (in full **bowler hat**) hard felt hat with rounded top.

**bowser** *n.* **1** *Aust.* petrol pump. **2** tanker for fuelling aircraft etc.

**bowyang** *n.* *Aust. dated* either of pair of straps worn around trouser legs below knee.

**box**¹ • *n.* **1** container, usu. flat-sided and firm; amount contained in box. **2** compartment in theatre, lawcourt, etc. **3** = *post-office box*. **4** (**the box**) *colloq.* television. **5** enclosed area or space. **6** shield for genitals in sports. • *v.* put in or provide with box. □ **box office** ticket office at theatre etc. **box seat** best or most favoured position.

**box²** • *v.* **1** fight with fists as sport. **2** slap (person's ears). • *n.* slap on ear.

**box³** *n.* Australian tree with close-grained timber and fibrous bark; evergreen European shrub with small dark green leaves; its wood.

**boxer** n. person who boxes. □ **boxer shorts** men's loose underpants like shorts.

**boxing** n. fighting with fists, esp. as sport.

**Boxing Day** n. day after Christmas.

**boy** n. male child. □□ **boyhood** n. **boyish** adj.

**boycott** ● v. refuse social or commercial relations with; refuse to handle or buy (goods). ● n. such refusal.

**boyfriend** n. regular male companion or lover.

**bra** n. woman's undergarment supporting breasts.

**brace** ● n. 1 device that holds things together or in position; (**braces**) straps supporting trousers from shoulders; wire device for straightening teeth. 2 a pair.
● v. give support or firmness to.

**bracelet** n. ornamental band or chain worn on wrist or arm.

**brachiosaurus** n. long-necked plant-eating dinosaur.

**bracken** n. 1 large coarse fern. 2 mass of these.

**bracket** ● n. 1 support projecting from vertical surface; shelf fixed to wall with this. 2 each of a pair of marks — ( ), [ ], < >, or { } — used to enclose words or figures. 3 group classified as similar or falling between limits. ● v. 1 enclose in brackets. 2 group in same category.

**brackish** adj. (of water) slightly salty.

**bract** n. leaflike part of plant growing before flower.

**brag** ● v. (**bragged**) talk boastfully. ● n. boastful statement or talk.

**braggart** n. boastful person.

**Brahman** n. (also **Brahmin**)
1 member of Hindu priestly caste.
2 Indian breed of cattle.

**braid** ● n. 1 woven band as edging or trimming. 2 plait of hair.
● v. 1 plait. 2 trim with braid.

**braille** n. system of writing and printing for the blind, with patterns of raised dots.

**brain** ● n. 1 organ of soft nervous tissue in skull of vertebrates. 2 (also **brains**) intelligence. 3 colloq. intelligent person. ● v. 1 dash out brains of. 2 colloq. strike hard on head.

**brainchild** n. person's invention or plan.

**brainstorm** n. violent mental disturbance; sudden mental lapse; spontaneous discussion in search of new ideas.

**brainwash** v. force (person) to change views by exerting great mental pressure.

**brainwave** n. a bright idea.

**brainy** adj. (**brainier**) intellectually clever.

**braise** v. stew slowly in closed container.

**brake** ● n. device for stopping or slowing wheel or vehicle; thing that impedes. ● v. apply brake; slow or stop with brake.

**bramble** n. wild thorny shrub, esp. blackberry. □□ **brambly** adj.

**bran** n. husks separated from flour.

**branch** ● n. 1 limb or bough of tree. 2 lateral extension or subdivision of river, railway, family, etc. 3 local office of business etc. ● v. diverge, divide.

**brand** ● n. 1 particular make of goods. 2 identifying mark made with hot metal. ● v. mark with brand.
□ **brand new** completely or obviously new.

**brandish** v. wave or flourish.

**brandy** n. strong spirit distilled from wine or fermented fruit juice.

**brash** adj. vulgarly self-assertive; impudent. □□ **brashly** adv. **brashness** n.

**brass | breakneck**

**brass** ● n. **1** yellow alloy of copper and zinc; brass objects; brass wind instruments; *colloq.* money; brass memorial tablet. **2** *colloq.* effrontery. ● adj. made of brass.

**brasserie** n. restaurant, orig. one serving beer with food.

**brassica** n. plant of cabbage family.

**brassière** n. = BRA.

**brassy** adj. (**brassier**) **1** of or like brass. **2** bold and vulgar.

**brat** n. *derog.* ill-behaved child.

**bravado** n. show of boldness.

**brave** ● adj. able to face and endure danger or pain. **2** splendid, spectacular. ● v. face bravely or defiantly.□□ **bravely** adv. **bravery** n.

**bravura** n. brilliance of execution; music requiring brilliant technique.

**brawl** ● n. noisy quarrel or fight. ● v. **1** engage in brawl. **2** (of stream) run noisily.

**brawn** n. **1** muscular strength. **2** pressed meat from pig's or calf's head.

**brawny** adj. muscular.

**bray** ● n. cry of donkey; harsh sound. ● v. make a bray; utter harshly.

**braze** v. solder with alloy of brass.

**brazen** adj. **1** shameless. **2** of or like brass. □ **brazen it out** face or undergo defiantly.□□ **brazenly** adv.

**brazier** n. pan or stand holding burning coals.

**brazil nut** n. large three-sided S. American nut.

**breach** ● n. **1** breaking or neglect of rule, duty, promise, etc. **2** breaking of relations; quarrel. **3** gap. ● v. **1** break through; make gap in. **2** break (law etc.).

**bread** n. **1** baked dough of flour, usu. leavened with yeast. **2** *colloq.* money.

**breadfruit** n. fruit resembling new bread when roasted; tropical tree bearing it.

**breadline** n. □ **on the breadline** living in extreme poverty.

**breadth** n. **1** broadness; distance from side to side. **2** freedom from mental limitations or prejudices.

**breadwinner** n. member of family who earns money to support the others.

**break** ● v. (**broke**, **broken**, **breaking**) **1** divide or separate other than by cutting; fall into pieces. **2** damage; become unusable. **3** fail to observe or keep (a promise or law). **4** make or become discontinuous. **5** make a way suddenly or violently; appear suddenly. **6** reveal (news). **7** surpass (record). **8** (of ball) change direction after touching the ground. **9** (of waves) curl over and foam. **10** (of voice) change in quality at puberty or with emotion. **11** (of stock) stampede; (of athlete) get off mark prematurely. ● n. **1** breaking. **2** gap; interval. **3** sudden dash. **4** *Cricket* deflection of ball on bouncing. **5** points scored in one sequence at billiards etc. **6** point at which the swell of a wave 'breaks'. □ **break a leg** *Theatr.* do well, good luck. **break down** fail; collapse; give way to emotion; analyse. **break even** make gains and losses that balance exactly. **break in** intrude forcibly, esp. as thief. **2** interrupt. **3** accustom to habit.

**breakable** adj. easily broken.

**breakage** n. broken thing, breaking.

**breakbeat** n. (in dance music etc.) sample of syncopated drum beat forming rhythm.

**breakdancing** n. acrobatic style of street dancing.□□ **breakdance** n. & v. **breakdancer** n.

**breaker** n. heavy breaking wave.

**breakfast** ● n. first meal of day. ● v. have breakfast.

**breakneck** adj. dangerously fast.

**breakthrough** *n.* breaking through; major advance in knowledge or negotiation.

**breakwater** *n.* wall built out into sea to break force of waves.

**bream** *n.* 1 marine fish valued as food. 2 freshwater perch.

**breast** *n.* 1 either of two milk-secreting organs on woman's chest; chest; part of garment covering this; joint of meat from upper front part of body. 2 seat of emotions.
● *v.* 1 contend with. 2 reach top of (hill).

**breastbone** *n.* bone connecting ribs in front.

**breaststroke** *n.* swimming stroke performed face downwards with circular arm and leg movements.

**breath** *n.* air drawn into or expelled from lungs; slight movement of air.

**breathalyser** *n.* instrument for measuring alcohol in breath.
□□ **breathalyse** *v.*

**breathe** *v.* 1 take air into lungs and send it out again. 2 live. 3 utter or sound, esp. quietly. 4 pause. 5 send out or take in (as) with breath.

**breather** *n. colloq.* short period of rest.

**bred** see BREED.

**breech** *n.* back part of rifle or gun barrel.

**breeches** *n.pl.* short trousers fastened below knee.

**breed** ● *v.* (**bred, breeding**) produce offspring; propagate; raise (animals); yield, result in; arise, spread; bring up, train. ● *n.* stock of animals within species; race; lineage; sort, kind.
□□ **breeder** *n.*

**breeding** *n.* good manners resulting from training or background.

**breeze** ● *n.* 1 gentle wind. 2 *colloq.* easy task. ● *v. colloq.* saunter casually.

**brethren** *n.pl. arch.* brothers.

**breve** *n.* 1 *Mus.* note equal to two semibreves. 2 mark ( ˘ ) indicating short or unstressed vowel.

**brevity** *n.* conciseness; shortness.

**brew** ● *v.* 1 make (beer etc.) by infusion, boiling, and fermenting. 2 make (tea etc.) by infusion. 3 begin to develop. ● *n.* amount brewed; liquor brewed. □□ **brewer** *n.*

**brewery** *n.* factory for brewing beer etc.

**briar** *n.* thorny bush, wild rose.

**bribe** ● *n.* something offered to influence person to act in favour of giver. ● *v.* persuade by this.
□□ **bribery** *n.*

**bric-a-brac** *n.* cheap ornaments, trinkets.

**brick** ● *n.* block of baked clay used in building; rectangular block.
● *v.* close or block with brickwork.
□ **brick veneer** covering of brick applied to timber frame; house built with this.

**bride** *n.* woman on her wedding day or shortly before or after it. □□ **bridal** *adj.*

**bridegroom** *n.* man on his wedding day or shortly before or after it.

**bridesmaid** *n.* unmarried woman or girl attending bride at wedding.

**bridge** ● *n.* 1 structure providing way across river, railway, etc.; connection between two points or groups. 2 captain's raised platform on ship. 3 upper bony part of nose. 4 card game derived from whist. ● *v.* be or make bridge over; span as if with a bridge.

**bridgework** *n.* dental structure covering gap.

**bridle** ● *n.* headgear for controlling horse etc.; restraining thing.
● *v.* 1 put bridle on, control, curb. 2 express resentment, esp. by throwing up head and drawing in chin.

**brief** ● *adj.* of short duration; concise; scanty. ● *n.* set of information and instructions, esp. to barrister about a case. ● *v.* employ (barrister); inform or instruct in advance. □□ **briefly** *adv.*

**briefcase** *n.* case for carrying documents etc.

**briefs** *n.pl.* short pants or knickers.

**brig** *n.* two-masted square-rigged ship.

**brigade** *n.* military unit forming part of division; organised group of workers etc.

**brigadier** *n.* army officer commanding brigade or of similar status.

**brigalow** *n. Aust.* wattle with dark furrowed bark and silver foliage; (the brigalow) area of country dominated by brigalow.

**brigand** *n.* member of robber gang.

**bright** *adj.* 1 emitting or reflecting much light; shining; vivid. 2 clever. 3 cheerful; hopeful, encouraging. □□ **brighten** *v.* **brightly** *adv.* **brightness** *n.*

**brilliant** ● *adj.* 1 bright; sparkling. 2 highly talented. 3 *colloq.* excellent. ● *n.* diamond of finest quality. □□ **brilliance** *n.* **brilliantly** *adv.*

**brim** ● *n.* edge of vessel; projecting edge of hat. ● *v.* (**brimmed**) fill or be full to brim.

**brimstone** *n. arch.* sulphur.

**brindled** *adj.* brown with streaks of other colour.

**brine** *n.* saltwater; sea water.

**bring** *v.* (**brought, bringing**) convey; cause to come. □ **bring about** cause to happen. **bring out** show clearly. **bring up** look after and train (growing children).

**brink** *n.* edge of precipice etc.; furthest point before danger, discovery, etc.

**brinkmanship** *n.* act of pursuing dangerous course to brink of disaster.

**briny** *adj.* of brine or sea; salty.

**briquette** *n.* block of compressed coal dust as fuel.

**brisk** *adj.* quick, lively; active. □□ **briskly** *adv.*

**brisket** *n.* animal's breast, esp. as joint of meat.

**bristle** ● *n.* short stiff hair, esp. one used in brushes etc. ● *v.* 1 (of hair) stand upright. 2 cause to bristle. 3 show irritation. 4 be covered (with) or abundant (in). □□ **bristly** *adj.*

**British** *adj.* of Britain or its people.

**brittle** *adj.* fragile, apt to break.

**bro** *n. colloq.* brother; male friend.

**broach** *v.* 1 raise for discussion. 2 pierce (cask) to draw liquor.

**broad** ● *adj.* 1 large across, extensive. 2 full, clear. 3 explicit. 4 general. 5 tolerant. 6 coarse. 7 (of accent) markedly strong. ● *n.* broad part. □ **broad-minded** having tolerant views. □□ **broaden** *v.* **broadly** *adv.*

**broadband** *n.* high-speed network for transmission of a range of frequencies including video and audio.

**broadcast** ● *v.* 1 transmit by radio, television, etc.; take part in such transmission. 2 scatter (seed etc.); disseminate widely. ● *n.* radio, television, etc. program or transmission. □□ **broadcaster** *n.* **broadcasting** *n.*

**broadsheet** *n.* large-sized newspaper.

**broadside** *n.* 1 vigorous verbal attack. 2 firing of all guns on one side of ship.

**brocade** *n.* fabric woven with raised pattern.

**broccoli** *n.* vegetable with greenish flower heads.

**brochure** *n.* pamphlet, booklet, esp. containing descriptive information.

**brogue** *n.* 1 strong shoe with ornamental perforations; rough shoe of untanned leather. 2 marked accent, esp. Irish.

**broil** v. grill.

**broke** ● v. see BREAK. ● adj. colloq. having no money.

**broken** ● v. see BREAK. ● adj. 1 (of person) reduced to despair. 2 (of language) spoken imperfectly. 3 interrupted.□ **broken-hearted** overwhelmed with grief. **broken-in** comfortable through habitual use or familiarity. **broken record** used to refer to a person's constant and annoying repetition of a particular statement or opinion.

**broker** ● n. person who buys and sells goods or assets for others. ● v. arrange or negotiate (an agreement).□□ **broking** n.

**brokerage** n. broker's fee or commission.

**brolga** n. large Australian crane with grey plumage and red skin on its head.

**brolly** n. colloq. umbrella.

**bromance** n. colloq. intimate non-sexual relationship between two men.

**bromide** n. binary compound of bromine, esp. one used as sedative.

**bromine** n. poisonous liquid non-metallic element with choking smell (symbol Br).

**bronchial** adj. of two main divisions of windpipe or smaller tubes into which they divide.

**bronchitis** n. inflammation of bronchial mucous membrane.

**bronco** n. (pl. **broncos**) wild or half-tamed horse of the western US.

**brontosaurus** n. large plant-eating dinosaur.

**bronze** ● n. brown alloy of copper and tin; something made of this. ● adj. make or become suntanned.

**brooch** n. ornamental hinged pin.

**brood** ● n. 1 bird's young produced at one hatch. 2 (female animal) kept for breeding. ● v. 1 worry or ponder, esp. resentfully. 2 (of hen) sit on eggs.

**broody** adj. 1 (of hen) wanting to brood. 2 sullenly thoughtful. 3 colloq. CLUCKY.

**brook** ● n. small stream. ● v. tolerate; allow.

**broom** n. 1 long-handled sweeping brush. 2 any of various shrubs with esp. yellow flowers.

**Bros** abbr. brothers.

**broth** n. thin meat or fish stock.

**brothel** n. 1 premises for prostitution. 2 Aust. colloq. very untidy room etc.

**brother** n. 1 man or boy in relation to his siblings. 2 close male friend. 3 member of male religious order. 4 fellow human being.□ **brother-in-law** wife's or husband's brother; sister's husband.□□ **brotherly** adj.

**brotherhood** n. 1 relationship (as) between brothers. 2 (members of) association for mutual help etc.

**brought** see BRING.

**brow** n. 1 forehead; eyebrow. 2 projecting or overhanging part.

**browbeat** v. (**browbeat**, **browbeaten**, **brow beating**) intimidate, bully.

**brown** ● adj. 1 colour as of dark wood or rich soil. 2 dark-skinned, suntanned. ● n. brown colour, paint, or clothes etc. ● v. make or become brown.□ **browned off** colloq. fed up. □□ **brownish** adj.

**brownie** n. 1 benevolent elf. 2 small square of chocolate cake with nuts. 3 (**Brownie**) junior Guide.

**browse** ● v. 1 look around casually; read or scan superficially. 2 feed on leaves, twigs, etc. ● n. browsing.

**browser** n. 1 person or animal that browses. 2 Computing program used to search for and access documents on World Wide Web.

**brucellosis** n. bacterial disease, esp. causing abortion in cattle.

**bruise** ● n. discoloration of skin caused by blow or pressure; similar damage on fruit etc. ● v. inflict bruise on; be susceptible to bruises.

**bruiser** n. colloq. tough brutal person.

**bruit** v. spread (report or rumour).

**brumby** n. Aust. wild horse.

**brunch** n. combined breakfast and lunch.

**brunette** n. woman with dark brown hair.

**brunt** n. chief impact of attack etc.

**brush** ● n. 1 cleaning or hairdressing or painting implement of bristles. 2 fox's tail. 3 skirmish. 4 brushing. 5 undergrowth.
● v. 1 use brush on. 2 touch lightly, graze in passing. □ **brush off** reject curtly; snub. **brush up** smarten; study and revive one's knowledge of.

**brushtail** n. Aust. any of several native animals with a bushy tail.

**brushwood** n. undergrowth; cut or broken twigs.

**brusque** adj. abrupt, offhand. □□ **brusquely** adv. **brusqueness** n.

**brussels sprout** n. vegetable with small cabbage-like buds on stem.

**brutal** adj. savagely cruel; merciless. □□ **brutalise** v. **brutality** n. **brutally** adv.

**brute** ● n. 1 cruel person; colloq. unpleasant person. 2 animal other than human. ● adj. 1 unthinking; cruel, stupid. 2 animal-like. □□ **brutish** adj.

**BSc** abbr. Bachelor of Science.

**bubba** n. (also **bub**, **bubby**) Aust. colloq. young child.

**bubble** ● n. 1 thin sphere of liquid enclosing air or gas; air-filled cavity in glass etc. 2 transparent domed canopy. ● v. 1 rise or send up bubbles. 2 make sound of boiling. 3 show great liveliness.

**bubbler** n. drinking fountain.

**bubbly** ● adj. 1 full of bubbles. 2 exuberant. ● n. colloq. champagne.

**bubonic** n. (of plague) marked by swellings, esp. in groin and armpits.

**buccaneer** n. pirate; adventurer. □□ **buccaneering** n. & adj.

**buck** ● n. 1 male deer, hare, or rabbit. 2 article placed before dealer in game of poker. 3 colloq. dollar. ● v. 1 (of horse) jump vertically with back arched. □ **bucks' party** (also **bucks' night**) Aust. all-male celebration, esp. in honour of man about to marry. **buck up** colloq. hurry up; cheer up. **pass the buck** shift responsibility (and possible blame).

**bucket** ● n. 1 round open container with handle, for carrying or drawing water etc.; amount contained in this. 2 colloq. large quantity. 3 compartment or scoop in waterwheel, dredger, or grain elevator. ● v. colloq. 1 (esp. of rain) pour heavily. 2 denigrate (person). □ **bucket list** colloq. number of experiences etc. that a person hopes to have before they die.

**buckjump** Aust. ● v. (of horse) leap with head down, legs drawn together, and back arched. ● n. buckjumping; buckjumping event. □□ **buckjumper** n.

**buckjumping** n. Aust. 1 action of horse leaping with head down, legs drawn together, and back arched. 2 equestrian event in which each competitor attempts to remain on an unbroken horse as long as possible.

**buckle** ● n. clasp with hinged pin for securing belt or strap etc. ● v. 1 fasten with buckle. 2 (cause to) crumple under pressure. 3 fasten seatbelt.

**Buckley's** n. (in full **Buckley's chance**) Aust. colloq. little or no chance.

**buckram** n. coarse linen etc. stiffened with paste etc.

**buckwheat** n. seed of plant related to rhubarb.

**bucolic** adj. of shepherds; rustic, pastoral.

**bud** ● n. 1 projection from which branch, leaf, or flower develops. 2 flower or leaf not fully open.

- *v.* (**budded**) form buds; begin to grow or develop; graft bud of (plant) on another plant.

**Buddhism** *n.* Asian religion based on the teachings of Buddha.
□□ **Buddhist** *n.* & *adj.*

**buddy** *n. colloq.* friend, mate.

**budge** *v.* move slightly.

**budgerigar** *n.* small Australian parrot that is popular as pet.

**budget** ● *n.* plan of income and expenditure; amount allowed. ● *v.* allow or arrange for in budget. □□ **budgetary** *adj.*

**budgie** *n. colloq.* budgerigar.
□ **budgie smugglers** *Aust.* close-fitting male swimming briefs made of stretch fabric.

**budo** *n.* martial arts, and the code on which they are based.

**buff** ● *adj.* 1 of yellowish beige colour. 2 *colloq.* in good physical shape; muscular. ● *n.* 1 buff colour. 2 *colloq.* enthusiast. 3 velvety dull yellow leather. ● *v.* 1 polish. 2 make (leather) velvety.

**buffalo** *n.* (*pl.* **buffalo** or **buffaloes**) any of various kinds of ox; bison.

**buffer** *n.* 1 something that reduces effect of impact. 2 *Computing* temporary memory area or queue for data. ● *v.* act as a buffer to.

**buffet**[1] *n.* 1 room or counter where refreshments are sold; self-service meal of several dishes set out at once. 2 sideboard.

**buffet**[2] ● *v.* (**buffeted**) strike repeatedly. ● *n.* a blow, esp. with hand.

**buffoon** *n.* clown; jester; silly person.
□□ **buffoonery** *n.*

**bug** ● *n.* 1 small insect. 2 *colloq.* virus, infection. 3 concealed microphone. 4 *colloq.* error in computer program etc. 5 *colloq.* obsession, enthusiasm, etc.
● *v.* (**bugged**) 1 conceal microphone in. 2 *colloq.* annoy.

**bugbear** *n.* 1 cause of annoyance. 2 object of baseless fear.

**bugger** *coarse colloq.* ● *n.* 1 unpleasant or awkward person or thing, person of specified kind. 2 person who performs buggery. ● *int.* damn.

**buggerise** *v. coarse colloq.* mess about; fool aimlessly (with).

**buggery** *n.* anal intercourse.

**buggy** *n.* 1 small sturdy motor vehicle. 2 light horse-drawn vehicle for one or two people.

**bugle** ● *n.* brass instrument like small trumpet. ● *v.* sound bugle.
□□ **bugler** *n.*

**build** ● *v.* (**built**, **building**) construct by putting parts or material together. ● *n.* bodily shape. □ **build up** publicity; increase. **built-in** forming part of structure. **built-up** covered with buildings. □□ **builder** *n.*

**building** *n.* 1 house or other structure with roof and walls. 2 action or trade of constructing something; development of something over period of time.

**bulb** *n.* 1 rounded base of stem of some plants. 2 bulb-shaped thing or part; light bulb.

**bulbous** *adj.* bulb-shaped; bulging.

**bulbul** *n.* songbird of Africa and Asia, usu. with distinctive crest.

**bulge** ● *n.* irregular swelling; *colloq.* temporary increase. ● *v.* swell outwards. □□ **bulgy** *adj.*

**bulimia** *n.* (in full **bulimia nervosa**) disorder in which overeating alternates with self-induced vomiting, fasting, etc. □□ **bulimic** *adj.* & *n.*

**bulk** ● *n.* size; magnitude, esp. when great; the majority; large quantity. ● *v.* seem in size or importance. ● *adj.* 1 *colloq.* many. 2 a lot of. □ **bulk bill** *Aust.* (of doctor etc.) choose reduced fees paid by the government, rather than bill patients fully.

**bulky** *adj.* (**bulkier**) large, unwieldy.

**bull** *n.* **1** male of ox, whale, elephant, etc. **2** bullseye of target. **3** papal edict. **4** *colloq.* nonsense. □□ **bullish** *adj.*

**bulldog** *n.* strong dog with large head.

**bulldozer** *n.* powerful tractor with a device for clearing ground.

**bullet** *n.* **1** small pointed missile fired from rifle, revolver, etc. **2** small solid circle printed before each item in list etc.

**bulletin** *n.* short official statement; short broadcast news report.

**bullion** *n.* gold or silver in lump, or valued by weight.

**bullock** ● *n.* castrated bull. ● *v.* work tirelessly. □□ **bullocking** *n.*

**bullocky** *Aust.* ● *n.* driver of team of bullocks. ● *adj.* of bullock driving or rural life generally.

**bullroarer** *n. Aust.* sacred object used in Aboriginal ceremony, consisting of piece of wood attached to cord and swung around to make sound.

**bullseye** *n.* centre of a target.

**bully** ● *n.* person who harms and intimidates others. ● *v.* seek to harm, intimidate, or coerce someone. □ **bully off** put ball into play in hockey by two opponents striking sticks together.

**bulrush** *n.* tall rush; papyrus.

**bulwark** *n.* **1** defensive wall, esp. of earth; protecting person or principle. **2** ship's side above deck.

**bum** *n.* **1** buttocks. **2** *colloq.* loafer; dissolute person.

**bumble** *v.* **1** speak in rambling way. **2** be inept; blunder.

**bumblebee** *n.* large bee with loud hum.

**bump** ● *n.* **1** dull-sounding blow or collision; swelling caused by it. **2** uneven patch or raised area on road etc. ● *v.* **1** come or strike against with bump; hurt thus. **2** move along with

jolts. □ **bump into** *colloq.* meet by chance. **bump off** *colloq.* murder. □□ **bumpy** *adj.*

**bumper** ● *n.* **1** horizontal bar on motor vehicle to reduce damage in collision. **2** *Cricket* ball rising high after pitching. ● *adj.* unusually large or abundant.

**bumpkin** *n.* rustic or awkward person.

**bumptious** *adj.* self-assertive, conceited.

**bun** *n.* **1** small sweet bread roll or cake often with dried fruit. **2** hair coiled and pinned to the head.

**bunch** ● *n.* cluster of things growing or fastened together; lot; *colloq.* group, gang. ● *v.* **1** arrange in bunch(es); gather in close folds; form into group or crowd.

**bundle** ● *n.* collection of things tied or fastened together; set of nerve fibres etc.; *colloq.* large amount of money. ● *v.* **1** tie into bundle. **2** throw or move carelessly. **3** send away hurriedly. □ **drop one's bundle** *Aust. colloq.* go to pieces; panic.

**bung**[1] ● *n.* stopper, esp. for cask. ● *v.* **1** stop with bung. **2** *colloq.* throw.

**bung**[2] *adj. Aust.* broken down; useless.

**bungalow** *n.* cottage; shack; sleepout.

**bungee jumping** *n.* sport of jumping from a height attached to a **bungee**, an elasticated cord or rope.

**bunger** *n.* loud firework.

**bungle** ● *v.* mismanage, fail to accomplish; work clumsily. ● *n.* bungled attempt or work.

**bunion** *n.* swelling on foot, esp. on side of big toe.

**bunk** *n.* shelflike bed. □ **do a bunk** *colloq.* run away.

**bunker** *n.* **1** container for fuel. **2** reinforced underground shelter. **3** sandy hollow in golf course.

**bunkum** n. nonsense, humbug.

**bunny** n. 1 child's name for rabbit. 2 victim, dupe. 3 scapegoat.

**Bunsen burner** n. small gas burner used in scientific work.

**bunting** n. flags and other decorations; loosely-woven fabric for these.

**bunyip** n. Aust. 1 monster inhabiting swamps and lagoons. 2 imposter.

**buoy** ● n. anchored float as navigational mark etc.; lifebuoy.
● v. 1 keep afloat. 2 encourage.

**buoyant** adj. 1 apt to float. 2 resilient. 3 exuberant. □□ **buoyancy** n.

**burble** v. 1 talk ramblingly. 2 make bubbling sound.

**burden** ● n. 1 thing carried; load; oppressive duty, expense, emotion, etc. 2 refrain of song, theme.
● v. load, encumber; oppress.
□□ **burdensome** adj.

**bureau** n. (pl. **bureaux** or **bureaus**) 1 writing desk with drawers. 2 office or department for specific business; government department.

**bureaucracy** n. government by central administration; government officials, esp. regarded as oppressive and inflexible; conduct typical of these. □□ **bureaucrat** n.

**burgeon** v. grow rapidly; flourish.

**burger** n. colloq. hamburger.

**burgher** n. citizen, esp. of town in continental Europe.

**burglary** n. illegal entry into building with intent to commit theft or other crime.

**burgle** v. commit burglary (on). □□ **burglar** n.

**burgundy** n. red wine orig. from Burgundy in France; purplish red colour.

**burial** n. burying, esp. of corpse; funeral.

**burin** n. tool for engraving copper or wood.

**burlesque** n. 1 mocking imitation, parody. 2 variety show, often including striptease.

**burly** adj. large and sturdy.

**burn** ● v. (**burned** or **burnt, burning**) 1 (cause to) be consumed by fire; blaze or glow with fire; (cause to) be injured or damaged by fire, sun, or great heat; use or be used as fuel; produce (hole etc.) by fire or heat; brand; give or feel sensation or pain (as) of heat. 2 record data on CD or DVD. ● n. 1 mark or injury made by burning. 2 (also **burn-off**) Aust. clearing of vegetation by burning; area so cleared. □□ **burner** n.

**burnish** v. polish by rubbing.

**burnout** n. 1 reduction of substance to nothing through use or combustion. 2 failure of electrical component through overheating. 3 physical or mental collapse caused by overwork or stress. □□ **burnt-out** adj.

**burnt** see BURN.

**burp** v. colloq. belch; make (baby) belch.

**burr** n. 1 whirring sound; rough sounding of r. 2 rough edge on metal etc.; surgeon's or dentist's small drill. 3 clinging seed vessel or flower head.

**burrow** ● n. hole dug by animal as dwelling. ● v. 1 make burrow; make by digging. 2 investigate or search.

**bursar** n. 1 treasurer, esp. of college. 2 holder of bursary.

**bursary** n. grant, esp. scholarship.

**burst** ● v. (**burst, bursting**) 1 fly violently apart or give way suddenly, explode. 2 rush, move, speak, be spoken, etc. suddenly or violently. ● n. bursting, explosion, outbreak, spurt.

**bury** v. 1 place (dead body) in earth or tomb; put or hide underground; cover up. 2 involve (oneself) deeply.

**bus** ● n. 1 (**buses**) large public vehicle, usu. travelling fixed route.

2 *Computing* signal route allowing for direct communication between components of computer.
● *v.* (**buses, bussed, bussing**) 1 go by bus. 2 transport by bus.

**bush**[1] ● *n.* 1 shrub, clump of shrubs. 2 *Aust.* natural vegetation; tract of land covered in this; uncultivated land. 3 *Aust.* rural as opposed to urban life; the country as opposed to town or city. ● *adj.* 1 *Aust.* of (land covered in) natural vegetation. 2 (of artefacts) made with branches, saplings, etc. 3 (of Aboriginal people) living outside white society. 4 (of fauna and flora) indigenous to Australia. 5 (of domestic animals) having become wild. 6 (of rural, as opposed to urban, life. 7 amateur, untrained. 8 (in Aboriginal English) traditional or Aboriginal as opposed to European.

**bush**[2] *n.* 1 metal lining of axle hole etc. 2 sleeve giving electrical insulation.

**bushed** *adj. colloq.* 1 lost. 2 exhausted. 3 bewildered.

**bushel** *n.* imperial measure of capacity for corn, fruit, etc. (8 gallons or 36.4 litres).

**bushfire** *n.* fire burning (often extensive) areas of natural vegetation.□ **bushfire brigade** *Aust.* volunteer fire-fighting organisation.

**bushie** *n.* (also **bushy**) *Aust. colloq.* person who lives in the country.

**bushman** *n. Aust.* person skilled in travelling and surviving in bush; person who lives in the bush; unskilled country labourer.

**bushranger** *n. Aust. hist.* person engaging in armed robbery, esp. living in bush as outlaw.□□ **bushrange** *n.*

**bushwalk** *n. Aust.* hike in the bush.

**bushwhack** *v.* 1 clear ground in bush country; live or travel in bush country. 2 (as **bushwhacked** *adj.*) *Aust.* utterly exhausted.□□ **bushwhacker** *n.*

**bushy** *adj.* (**bushier**) covered with bush; growing thickly.

**business** *n.* 1 one's occupation or profession; one's own concern; task, duty; serious work. 2 (in Aboriginal English) traditional lore and ritual. 3 (difficult or unpleasant) matter or affair. 4 thing(s) needing attention or discussion. 5 buying and selling, trade; commercial firm.□□ **businessman** *n.* **businesswoman** *n.*

**businesslike** *adj.* efficient, systematic, practical.

**busk** *v.* perform esp. music in street etc. for tips.□□ **busker** *n.*

**bust**[1] ● *n.* sculptured head, shoulders, and chest; the bosom. ● *v.* (**busted** or **bust, busting**) *colloq.* burst; break.□ **go bust** *colloq.* become bankrupt.

**bustard** *n.* large swift-running bird.

**buster** *n.* strong squally wind, esp. from south.

**bustier** *n.* strapless close-fitting bodice.

**bustle** ● *v.* move busily and energetically. ● *n.* 1 excited activity. 2 *hist.* padding worn under skirt to puff it out behind.

**busy** *adj.* (**busier**) occupied or engaged in work etc.; full of activity; (of telephone line) engaged.□□ **busily** *adv.*

**busybody** *n.* meddlesome person.

**but** ● *conj.* however, on the other hand; otherwise than. ● *prep.* except; apart from. ● *adv.* only.

**butane** *n.* hydrocarbon used in liquefied form as fuel.

**butch** *adj. colloq.* masculine; tough-looking.

**butcher** ● *n.* 1 person who sells meat, person who slaughters animals for food. 2 brutal murderer. ● *v.* 1 slaughter or cut up (animal). 2 kill wantonly or cruelly. 3 *colloq.* ruin through incompetence.□□ **butchery** *n.*

**butler** *n.* chief male servant of household.

**butt** ● *n.* 1 large cask or barrel. 2 thicker end, esp. of tool or weapon. 3 stub of cigarette, cheque, etc. 4 mound behind target. 5 (**butts**) shooting range. 6 object of ridicule etc. 7 *colloq.* buttocks. ● *v.* 1 push with head. 2 meet or place edge to edge.

**butter** ● *n.* yellow fatty substance made from cream, used as spread and in cooking; substance of similar texture. ● *v.* spread, cook, or serve with butter.

**butterfly** *n.* 1 insect with four large often brightly coloured wings. 2 swimming stroke with both arms lifted at same time.

**buttermilk** *n.* liquid left after butter has been churned from cream.

**butterscotch** *n.* hard toffee made from butter, brown sugar, etc.

**buttock** *n.* either protuberance on lower rear part of human trunk; corresponding part of animal.

**button** ● *n.* 1 disc or knob sewn to garment as fastener or for ornament; small round object resembling a button. 2 small device on a piece of electronic equipment that is pressed to operate it. ● *v.* fasten (as) with buttons.

**buttonhole** ● *n.* 1 slit in cloth for button. 2 flower(s) worn in lapel buttonhole. ● *v. colloq.* accost and detain (reluctant listener).

**buttress** ● *n.* support against wall. ● *v.* support or strengthen.

**buxom** *adj.* plump and rosy; large and shapely.

**buy** ● *v.* (**bought**, **buying**) 1 obtain in exchange for money etc.; procure by bribery, bribe; get by sacrifice etc. 2 *colloq.* accept, believe. ● *n. colloq.* purchase. □□ **buyer** *n.*

**buyout** *n.* purchase of controlling share in a company; buying of company by people who work for it.

**buzz** ● *n.* 1 hum of bee etc. 2 sound of buzzer. 3 low murmur. 4 hurried activity. 5 *colloq.* telephone call. 6 *colloq.* thrill. ● *v.* 1 hum. 2 summon with buzzer. 3 move busily; be filled with activity or excitement. 4 *colloq.* fly (aircraft) fast and very close to.

**buzzard** *n.* large bird of hawk family.

**buzzer** *n.* electrical buzzing device as signal.

**buzzword** *n.* fashionable technical word; slogan.

**by** ● *prep.* 1 near, beside, along. 2 through action, agency, or means of. 3 not later than. 4 past. 5 via. 6 during. 7 to extent of. 8 according to. ● *adv.* 1 near. 2 aside. 3 in reserve. 4 past.

**bye** *n.* 1 *Cricket* run scored from ball that passes batter without being hit. 2 *Sport* status of competitor etc. not having a match in a particular round.

**by-election** *n.* election of MP to replace one who has died or resigned.

**bygone** *adj.* past, departed.

**by-law** *n.* regulation made by local government authority etc.

**byline** *n.* line naming writer of newspaper article.

**BYO** *abbr.* bring-your-own, esp. alcoholic drinks.

**bypass** ● *n.* main road around town or its centre; alternative passage provided by surgery for circulating blood through heart. ● *v.* avoid, go around (town, difficulty, etc.)

**by-product** *n.* substance produced during the making of something else; secondary result.

**bystander** *n.* person present but not taking part.

**byte** *n. Computing* group of eight binary digits, often representing one character.

**byword** *n.* notable example; familiar saying.

# Cc

**C** ● *abbr.* Celsius; centigrade.
● *n.* (as Roman numeral) 100.

**c.** *abbr.* **1** century. **2** cent(s). **3** (also **ca**) circa, about.

**cab** *n.* **1** taxi. **2** driver's compartment in truck, train, crane, etc.

**cabal** *n.* **1** secret intrigue. **2** political clique.

**cabana** *n.* **1** hut or shelter at beach or swimming pool. **2** spicy sausage, eaten cold.

**cabanossi** *n.* spicy sausage, eaten cold.

**cabaret** *n.* entertainment in restaurant etc.

**cabbage** *n.* **1** vegetable with green or purple leaves forming round head. **2** *colloq.* dull or inactive person.

**cabernet sauvignon** *n.* variety of black grape; wine made from this.

**cabin** *n.* **1** small shelter or house, esp. of wood; room or compartment in aircraft, ship, etc.

**cabinet** *n.* **1** cupboard or case for storing or displaying things. **2** (**Cabinet**) committee of senior ministers in government.

**cabinetmaker** *n.* skilled furniture maker.

**cable** ● *n.* encased group of insulated wires for transmitting electricity etc.; thick rope of wire or hemp. ● *v.* send (message) or inform (person) by cable. □ **cable car** small cabin pulled by a moving cable for carrying passengers up and down mountains etc.

**caboose** *n.* kitchen on ship's deck.

**cacao** *n.* bean from which cocoa and chocolate are made; tree bearing it.

**cache** ● *n.* **1** hiding place for treasure, supplies, etc.; things so hidden. **2** (in full **cache memory**) high-speed computer memory used to enhance performance. ● *v.* put in cache.

**cachet** *n.* prestige; distinguishing mark or seal.

**cack-handed** *adj. colloq.* **1** clumsy. **2** left-handed.

**cackle** ● *n.* **1** clucking of hen etc. **2** raucous laugh; noisy chatter.
● *v.* emit cackle; chatter noisily.

**cacophony** *n.* harsh discordant sound. □□ **cacophonous** *adj.*

**cactus** *n.* (*pl.* **cacti** or **cactuses**) plant with thick fleshy stem and usu. spines but no leaves.

**cad** *n. dated* man who behaves dishonourably. □□ **caddish** *adj.*

**cadaver** *n.* corpse. □□ **cadaverous** *adj.*

**caddie** (also **caddy**) ● *n.* golfer's attendant carrying clubs etc. ● *v.* act as caddie.

**caddy** *n.* small container for tea.

**cadence** *n.* **1** rhythm. **2** fall in pitch of voice. **3** tonal inflection. **4** close of musical phrase.

**cadenza** *n. Mus.* virtuoso passage for soloist during concerto.

**cadet** *n.* **1** young trainee for armed services, police force, journalism, etc. **2** member of military training corps in secondary school. □□ **cadetship** *n.*

**cadge** *v. colloq.* get or seek by begging.

**cadmium** *n.* soft bluish-white metallic element (symbol **Cd**).

**cadre** *n.* basic unit, esp. of servicemen; group of activists etc.

**caecum** *n.* pouch between small and large intestines.

**Caesarean** ● *adj.* (of birth) effected by Caesarean section. ● *n.* (in full **Caesarean section**) delivery of child by cutting into mother's abdomen.

**caesium** n. (also **cesium**) soft silver-white element (symbol **Cs**).

**caesura** n. pause in line of verse.

**cafe** n. (also **café**) small coffee house or restaurant.

**cafeteria** n. self-service restaurant.

**cafetière** n. coffee pot with plunger for pressing animals; similar.

**caffeine** n. alkaloid stimulant in tea leaves and coffee beans.

**caffe latte** n. (also **cafe latte**) coffee with milk.

**caftan** n. = KAFTAN.

**cage** • n. structure of bars or wires, esp. for confining animals; similar open framework; esp. lift in mine etc. • v. confine in cage.

**cagey** adj. colloq. cautious and non-committal. □□ **cagily** adv.

**cahoots** n.pl. colloq. □ **in cahoots** (with) in collusion.

**cairn** n. mound of stones.

**caisson** n. watertight chamber for underwater construction work.

**cajole** v. persuade by flattery, deceit, etc. □□ **cajolery** n.

**Cajun** adj. in style of French Louisiana.

**cake** • n. **1** mixture of flour, butter, eggs, sugar, etc. baked in oven. **2** flattish compact mass. • v. **1** form into compact mass. **2** cover (with sticky mass).

**calabash** n. gourd-bearing tropical American tree; bowl or pipe made from gourd.

**caladenia** n. Aust. terrestrial orchid with showy flowers.

**calamari** n. squid etc. used as food.

**calamine** n. powdered zinc carbonate and ferric oxide, used as skin lotion.

**calamity** n. disaster. □□ **calamitous** adj.

**calcareous** adj. of or containing calcium carbonate.

**calciferol** n. vitamin ($D_2$) promoting calcium deposition in bones.

**calciferous** adj. yielding calcium salts, esp. calcium carbonate.

**calcify** v. harden by depositing of calcium salts. □□ **calcification** n.

**calcine** v. decompose or be decomposed by strong heat. □□ **calcination** n.

**calcium** n. soft grey metallic element (symbol **Ca**).

**calculate** v. ascertain or forecast by exact reckoning; plan deliberately. □□ **calculable** adj. **calculation** n.

**calculated** adj. done with awareness of likely consequences; designed.

**calculating** adj. scheming, mercenary.

**calculator** n. device (esp. small electronic one) for making mathematical calculations.

**calculus** n. (pl. **calculuses** or **calculi**) **1** branch of mathematics dealing with rates of variation. **2** stone formed in body.

**calendar** n. system fixing year's beginning, length, and subdivision; chart etc. showing such subdivisions; list of special dates or events.

**calender** • n. machine in which cloth, paper, etc. is rolled to glaze or smooth it. • v. press in calender.

**calf** n. (pl. **calves**) **1** fleshy hind part of human leg below knee. **2** young cow, bull, elephant, whale, etc.

**calibrate** v. **1** mark (gauge) with scale of readings. **2** correlate readings of (instrument) with standard. **3** find calibre of (gun). □□ **calibration** n.

**calibre** n. **1** internal diameter of gun or tube; diameter of bullet or shell. **2** strength or quality of character; ability, importance.

**calico** n. cotton cloth.

**californium** n. radioactive metallic element (symbol **Cf**).

**caliph** n. hist. Muslim ruler.

**call** • v. **1** shout to attract attention; utter characteristic cry; summon;

command, invite; rouse from sleep.
**2** communicate (with) by telephone
or radio. **3** make brief visit. **4** name;
describe or address as. **5** *Aust.*
broadcast description of a race in
progress. ● *n.* **1** a shout; bird's cry.
**2** invitation, demand; need;
vocation. **3** telephone
communication. **4** short visit. **5** *Aust.*
broadcast description of a race in
progress. □ **call off** cancel. **call option**
right to buy stock at fixed price on
fixed date. □□ **caller** *n.*

**calligraphy** *n.* beautiful handwriting;
art of this. □□ **calligrapher** *n.*
**calligraphic** *adj.*

**calling** *n.* profession, occupation;
vocation.

**calliper** *n.* (also **caliper**) **1** (**callipers**)
compasses for measuring diameters
etc. **2** metal support for weak leg.

**callistemon** *n.* = BOTTLEBRUSH.

**callisthenics** *n.pl.* (also **calisthenics**)
exercises for fitness and grace.
□□ **callisthenic** *adj.*

**callosity** *n.* callus.

**callous** *adj.* **1** unfeeling, insensitive.
**2** (also **calloused**) (of skin) hardened.
□□ **callously** *adv.* **callousness** *n.*

**callow** *adj.* inexperienced, immature.

**callus** *n.* (*pl.* **calluses**) area of hard
thick skin.

**calm** ● *adj.* **1** tranquil, windless. **2** not
agitated. ● *n.* calm condition or
period. ● *v.* make or become calm.
□□ **calmly** *adv.* **calmness** *n.*

**calorie** *n.* unit of heat, amount
needed to raise temperature of one
gram (**small calorie**) or one kilogram
(**large calorie**) of water by 1°C.

**calorific** *adj.* producing heat.

**calumny** *n.* slander; malicious
representation. □□ **calumnious** *adj.*

**calve** *v.* give birth to (calf).

**Calvinism** *n.* branch of Protestantism
following teachings of John Calvin.
□□ **Calvinist** *n.* & *adj.*

**calx** *n.* (*pl.* **calces**) powdery residue
left after heating of ore or mineral.

**calypso** *n.* W. Indian song with
improvised usu. topical words.

**calyx** *n.* (*pl.* **calyces** or **calyxes**) leaves
forming protective case of flower in
bud.

**cam** *n.* projection on wheel etc.,
shaped to convert circular into
reciprocal or variable motion.

**camaraderie** *n.* friendly
comradeship.

**camber** ● *n.* convex surface of road,
deck, etc. ● *v.* build with camber.

**cambric** *n.* fine linen or cotton fabric.

**came** SEE COME.

**camel** *n.* **1** long-legged ruminant with
one hump (*Arabian camel*) or two
humps (*Bactrian camel*). **2** fawn
colour.

**camellia** *n.* evergreen flowering
shrub.

**camembert** *n.* kind of soft creamy
cheese.

**cameo** *n.* **1** small piece of hard stone
carved in relief. **2** short literary sketch
or acted scene. **3** small part in play or
film.

**camera** *n.* **1** apparatus for taking
photographs or for making motion
film or television pictures.
**2** equipment for converting images
into electrical signals.

**camisole** *n.* woman's lightweight
vest.

**camomile** *n.* (also **chamomile**)
aromatic herb.

**camouflage** ● *n.* disguising of
soldiers, tanks, etc. so that they blend
into background; such disguise;
animal's natural blending
colouring. ● *v.* hide by camouflage.

**camp** *n.* **1** place with temporary
accommodation in tents; place where
troops are lodged or trained. **2** *Aust.*
Aboriginal living place. **3** group of
people with the same ideals.

**4** affected or exaggerated behaviour. ● **v.** **1** sleep in tent; live in camp. **2** *Aust.* (of sheep or cattle) flock together. ● **adj.** **1** affected, exaggerated. **2** *colloq.* homosexual.

**campaign** *n.* **1** organised course of action, esp. to gain publicity. **2** series of military operations.
● **v.** take part in campaign.
□□ **campaigner** *n.*

**campanology** *n.* study of bells; bell-ringing. □□ **campanologist** *n.*

**campdraft** *n.* *Aust.* equestrian event in which a steer is driven round a set course.

**camper** *n.* **1** person who camps. **2** (also **campervan**) motor vehicle with beds.

**camphor** *n.* pungent white crystalline substance used in medicine and mothballs.

**campus** *n.* grounds of university or college.

**camshaft** *n.* shaft carrying cam(s).

**can¹** *v.aux.* (**can, could**) be able or allowed to.

**can²** ● *n.* **1** sealed container for preservation of food or drink. **2** (**the can**) *colloq.* prison.
● **v.** (**canned**) **1** put or preserve in can. **2** *colloq.* disparage; criticise. **3** *colloq.* cancel.

**canal** *n.* artificial inland waterway; tubular duct in plant or animal.

**canapé** *n.* small piece of bread or pastry with savoury topping.

**canard** *n.* unfounded rumour.

**canary** *n.* **1** small songbird with yellow feathers. **2** *Aust. hist.* convict in Australia.

**canasta** *n.* card game resembling rummy.

**cancan** *n.* high-kicking dance.

**cancel** *v.* (**cancelled**) **1** revoke, discontinue (arrangement). **2** delete. **3** mark (ticket, stamp, etc.) to invalidate it. **4** annul. **5** neutralise, counterbalance. □□ **cancellation** *n.*

**Cancer** *n.* fourth sign of zodiac, the Crab. □□ **Cancerian** *adj.* & *n.*

**cancer** *n.* malignant tumour; disease in which this form. □□ **cancerous** *adj.*

**candela** *n.* SI unit of luminous intensity.

**candelabrum** *n.* (*pl.* **candelabra**) large branched candlestick or lamp holder.

**candescent** *adj.* glowing (as) with white heat. □□ **candescence** *n.*

**candid** *adj.* **1** frank. **2** (of photograph) taken informally, usu. without subject's knowledge. □□ **candidly** *adv.*

**candidate** *n.* person nominated for, seeking, or likely to gain office, position, award, etc.; person entered for exam. □□ **candidacy** *n.* **candidature** *n.*

**candied** *adj.* encrusted or preserved in sugar.

**candle** *n.* cylinder or block of wax or tallow enclosing wick that gives light when burning.

**candour** *n.* (also **candor**) frankness.

**candy** *n.* (in full **sugar candy**) sugar crystallised by repeated boiling and slow evaporation.

**cane** *n.* hollow jointed stem of giant reeds or grasses or solid stem of slender palm, used for wickerwork or as walking stick, instrument of punishment, etc.; sugar cane.
● **v.** beat with cane; weave cane into (chair etc.)

**canine** ● *adj.* of a dog or dogs.
● *n.* **1** dog. **2** (in full **canine tooth**) tooth between incisors and molars.

**canister** *n.* small container for tea etc.; cylinder of shot, tear gas, etc.

**canker** *n.* **1** disease of trees and plants; open wound in stem of tree or plant. **2** ulcerous ear disease of animals. **3** corrupting influence.
● *v.* infect with canker; corrupt.
□□ **cankerous** *adj.*

**cannabis** n. hemp plant; parts of it used as narcotic; marijuana.

**canned** adj. 1 pre-recorded. 2 sold in can. 3 *colloq.* drunk. 4 *colloq.* cancelled.

**cannelloni** n.pl. tubes of pasta stuffed with savoury mixture.

**cannibal** n. person or animal that eats its own species. □□ **cannibalism** n. **cannibalistic** adj.

**cannon** ● n. 1 (pl. **cannon**) large gun. 2 hitting of two balls in one shot in billiards. 3 (in full **cannon bit**) smooth round bit for horse.
● v. collide.

**cannot** v.aux. can not.

**canny** adj. shrewd, thrifty.

**canoe** ● n. light narrow boat, usu. paddled. ● v. travel in canoe. □□ **canoeist** n.

**canon** n. 1 general law, rule, principle, or criterion. 2 member of certain RC religious orders; member of cathedral chapter. 3 set of writings accepted as genuine; literary works etc. regarded as significant. □□ **canonical** adj.

**canonise** v. (also **-ize**) declare officially to be the saint. □□ **canonisation** n.

**canopy** n. 1 covering suspended over throne, bed, etc. 2 sky. 3 overhanging shelter. 4 rooflike projection. 5 uppermost layers of foliage etc. in forest. ● v. supply or be canopy to.

**cant**[1] ● n. 1 insincere pious or moral talk. 2 language peculiar to class, profession, etc. 3 jargon. ● v. use cant.

**cant**[2] ● n. 1 slanting surface, bevel. 2 oblique push or jerk. 3 tilted position. ● v. push or pitch out of level.

**can't** cannot.

**cantabile** *Mus.* ● adv. & adj. in smooth flowing style. ● n. cantabile passage or movement.

**cantaloupe** n. (also **cantaloup**) rockmelon.

**cantankerous** adj. bad-tempered, quarrelsome. □□ **cantankerously** adv. **cantankerousness** n.

**cantata** n. *Mus.* composition for vocal soloists and usu. chorus and orchestra.

**canteen** n. 1 restaurant for employees in office, factory, etc. 2 shop for provisions in barracks or camp; school shop selling lunches etc. 3 case of cutlery. 4 soldier's or camper's water flask.

**canter** ● n. horse's pace between trot and gallop. ● v. (cause to) go at canter.

**cantilever** n. bracket or beam etc. projecting from wall to support balcony etc.; beam or girder fixed at one end only. □□ **cantilevered** adj.

**canto** n. division of long poem.

**canton** n. subdivision of country, esp. Switzerland.

**canvas** n. 1 strong coarse cloth used for sails and tents etc. and for oil painting; a painting on canvas. 2 strong open-weave fabric used for tapestry etc. 3 racing boat's covered end.

**canvass** v. 1 solicit votes (from). 2 ascertain opinions of. 3 seek custom from. 4 propose (idea etc.) □□ **canvasser** n.

**canyon** n. deep gorge.

**cap** ● n. 1 soft brimless hat, often with peak; head covering worn as part of uniform; cover or top. 2 explosive device for toy pistol. 3 contraceptive diaphragm.
● v. (**capped**) 1 put a cap on; form the top of. 2 set an upper limit. 3 provide fitting climax or conclusion to.

**capable** adj. competent, able; having ability, fitness, etc. for. □□ **capability** n. **capably** adv.

**capacious** adj. roomy. □□ **capaciousness** n.

**capacitor** n. device for storing electric charge.

**capacity** ● n. 1 power to contain, receive, experience, or produce. 2 maximum amount that can be contained etc. 3 mental power. 4 position or function. ● adj. fully occupying available space etc.

**cape** n. 1 short cloak. 2 headland, promontory.

**capeesh** int. colloq. do you understand?

**caper** ● v. jump playfully. ● n. 1 playful leap. 2 prank. 3 colloq. activity or occupation. 4 bramble-like shrub; one of its pickled buds, for use in sauce etc.

**capillarity** n. rise or depression of liquid in narrow tube.

**capillary** ● adj. 1 of hair. 2 of narrow diameter. ● n. capillary tube; one of delicate blood vessels intervening between arteries and veins.

**capital** ● n. 1 chief town or city of country or region. 2 money etc. with which company starts in business; accumulated wealth. 3 (of letter of alphabet) of kind used to begin name or sentence. 4 head of column or pillar. ● adj. 1 involving punishment by death. 2 most important. 3 dated colloq. excellent.

**capitalise** v. (also -ize) 1 convert into or provide with capital. 2 write (letter of alphabet) as capital; begin (word) with capital letter. □□ capitalisation n.

**capitalism** n. economic and political system dependent on private capital and profit-making.

**capitalist** ● n. person using or possessing capital; advocate of capitalism. ● adj. of or favouring capitalism. □□ capitalistic adj.

**capitulate** v. surrender. □□ capitulation n.

**capon** n. castrated rooster.

**cappuccino** n. frothy milky coffee.

**caprice** n. 1 whim. 2 lively or fanciful work of music etc.

**capricious** adj. subject to whims; unpredictable. □□ capriciously adv. capriciousness n.

**Capricorn** n. tenth sign of zodiac, the Goat. □□ Capricornian adj. & n.

**capsicum** n. plant with edible fruits; sweet pepper; red, green, or yellow fruit of this. □□ capsicum spray oil extracted from cayenne pepper, used esp. by police to ward off attackers etc.

**capsize** v. (of boat) be overturned; overturn (boat).

**capstan** n. thick revolving cylinder for winding cable etc.

**capsule** n. 1 small soluble case enclosing medicine. 2 detachable compartment of spacecraft or nose of rocket. 3 enclosing membrane. 4 dry fruit releasing seeds when ripe. □□ capsular adj.

**captain** ● n. 1 chief, leader. 2 commander of ship. 3 pilot of civil aircraft. 4 military officer. ● v. be captain of. □□ captaincy n.

**caption** ● n. wording appended to illustration or cartoon; wording on cinema or television screen; heading of chapter, article, etc. ● v. provide with caption.

**captious** adj. fault-finding.

**captivate** v. fascinate; charm. □□ captivation n.

**captive** ● n. confined or imprisoned person or animal. ● adj. taken prisoner; confined; unable to escape. □□ captivity n.

**captor** n. person who captures (person, place, etc.)

**capture** ● v. 1 take prisoner; seize. 2 record accurately in words or pictures. 3 cause (data) to be stored in a computer. ● n. 1 act of capturing; thing or person captured.

**car** n. 1 motor vehicle for driver and small number of passengers. 2 railway carriage of specified type. **3** passenger compartment of lift, balloon, etc.

**carabiner** *n.* (also **karabiner**) coupling link with a safety closure, used by rock climbers.

**carafe** *n.* glass container for water or wine.

**caramel** *n.* sugar or syrup heated until it turns brown; kind of soft toffee.☐☐ **caramelise** *v.* (also **-ize**)

**carapace** *n.* upper shell of tortoise or crustacean.

**carat** *n.* unit of weight for precious stones (200 mg); measure of purity of gold (pure gold = 24 carats).

**caravan** *n.* **1** vehicle equipped for living in and usu. towed by car. **2** people travelling together. ☐☐ **caravanner** *n.*

**caraway** *n.* plant with small aromatic fruit (**caraway seed**) used in cakes etc.

**carbide** *n.* binary compound of carbon.

**carbine** *n.* kind of short rifle.

**carbohydrate** *n.* energy-producing organic compound of carbon, hydrogen, and oxygen; food containing a lot of carbohydrates.

**carbolic** *n.* (in full **carbolic acid**) kind of disinfectant and antiseptic.

**carbon** *n.* **1** chemical element (symbol C). **2** occurring as diamond, graphite, and charcoal, and in all organic compounds. ☐ **carbon copy** exact copy. **carbon dating** method of determining age of something by measuring decay of radiocarbon within it. **carbon footprint** amount of carbon dioxide produced by particular person, group, etc. **carbon sink** forest, ocean, etc., viewed in terms of its ability to absorb carbon from the atmosphere.

**carbonate** ● *n.* salt of carbonic acid. ● *v.* **1** impregnate (e.g. soft drink) with carbon dioxide. **2** aerate. **carboniferous** *adj.* producing coal.

**carbonise** *v.* (also **-ize**) reduce to charcoal or coke; convert to carbon; coat with carbon. ☐☐ **carbonisation** *n.*

**carborundum** *n.* compound of carbon and silicon used esp. as an abrasive.

**carbs** *n.pl. colloq.* dietary carbohydrates.

**carbuncle** *n.* **1** severe skin abscess. **2** bright red jewel.

**carburettor** *n.* apparatus mixing air with petrol vapour in internal combustion engine.

**carcass** *n.* (also **carcase**) **1** dead body of animal. **2** framework. **3** worthless remains.

**carcinogen** *n.* substance producing cancer. ☐☐ **carcinogenic** *adj.*

**carcinoma** *n.* (*pl.* **carcinomas** or **carcinomata**) cancerous tumour.

**card** ● *n.* **1** thick stiff paper or thin pasteboard etc.; piece of this for writing or printing on, esp. to send greetings, to identify person, or to record information; credit card; playing card. **2** program of events. ● *v.* clean or comb (wool etc.) with wire brush or toothed instrument.

**cardamom** *n.* seeds of SE Asian aromatic plant, used as spice.

**cardboard** ● *n.* pasteboard or stiff paper. ● *adj.* flimsy, insubstantial.

**cardiac** *adj.* of the heart.

**cardigan** *n.* knitted jacket.

**cardinal** ● *adj.* **1** chief, fundamental. **2** deep scarlet. ● *n.* one of RC dignitaries who elect Pope.☐ **cardinal number** number denoting quantity rather than order, e.g. 1, 2, 3, etc. (compare ORDINAL).

**cardio-** *comb. form* of the heart.

**cardiogram** *n.* record of heart movements.

**cardiograph** *n.* instrument recording heart movements.☐☐ **cardiographer** *n.* **cardiography** *n.*

**cardiology** *n.* branch of medicine concerned with heart. □□ **cardiologist** *n.*

**cardiopulmonary** *adj.* of heart and lungs.

**cardiothoracic** *adj.* of heart and organs of chest.

**cardiovascular** *adj.* of heart and blood vessels.

**care ●** *n.* **1** protection and provision of necessities; supervision. **2** serious attention and thought; caution to avoid damage and loss. **●** *v.* feel concern or interest. □ **care for** look after; feel affection for; like, enjoy.

**careen** *v.* turn (ship) on side for repair; move or swerve wildly.

**career ●** *n.* way of making one's living; profession; course through life. **●** *v.* move swiftly or wildly.

**carefree** *adj.* light-hearted; joyous.

**careful** *adj.* painstaking; cautious; taking care; not neglecting. □□ **carefully** *adv.* **carefulness** *n.*

**careless** *adj.* lacking care or attention; unthinking, insensitive; light-hearted. □□ **carelessly** *adv.* **carelessness** *n.*

**carer** *n.* person who cares for sick or elderly person, esp. at home.

**caress ●** *v.* touch lovingly. **●** *n.* loving touch.

**caret** *n.* mark indicating insertion in text.

**caretaker ●** *n.* person in charge of maintenance of building. **●** *adj.* taking temporary control.

**careworn** *adj.* showing effects of prolonged worry.

**cargo** *n.* (*pl.* **cargoes** or **cargos**) goods carried on ship or aircraft. □ **cargo pants** loose-fitting trousers with large patch pockets down each leg.

**Caribbean** *adj.* of the West Indies.

**caribou** *n.* N. American reindeer.

**caricature ●** *n.* grotesque usu. comically exaggerated representation. **●** *v.* make or give caricature of. □□ **caricaturist** *n.*

**caries** *n.* decay of tooth or bone.

**carillon** *n.* set of bells sounded from keyboard or mechanically; tune played on this.

**caritas** *n.* spiritual love of humankind; charity.

**carjacking** *n.* hijacking of car.

**cark** *v.* **1** (of cow) caw. **2** (of person) speak raucously. **3** *Aust.* die; break down completely.

**carminative ●** *adj.* relieving flatulence. **●** *n.* carminative drug.

**carmine** *adj.* & *n.* vivid crimson.

**carnage** *n.* great slaughter.

**carnal** *adj.* worldly; sensual; sexual. □□ **carnality** *n.*

**carnation** *n.* clove-scented pink; rosy-pink colour. **●** *adj.* rosy-pink.

**carnival** *n.* festivities or festival; merrymaking; series of sporting events.

**carnivore** *n.* animal or plant that feeds on animal flesh. □□ **carnivorous** *adj.*

**carob** *n.* seed pod of Mediterranean tree, used as chocolate substitute.

**carol ●** *n.* joyous song, esp. Christmas hymn. **●** *v.* (**carolled**) sing carols; sing joyfully.

**carotene** *n.* orange-coloured pigment in carrots etc.

**carotid ●** *n.* each of two main arteries carrying blood to head. **●** *adj.* of these arteries.

**carouse ●** *v.* have lively drinking party. **●** *n.* such party. □□ **carousal** *n.* **carouser** *n.*

**carousel** *n.* **1** merry-go-round. **2** rotating luggage delivery system at airport etc.

**carp ●** *n.* freshwater fish widely regarded as pest in Australia. **●** *v.* keep finding fault.

**carpel** *n.* part of flower in which seeds develop.

**carpenter** ● *n.* person skilled in woodwork. ● *v.* do or make by carpenter's work.□□ **carpentry** *n.*

**carpet** ● *n.* thick fabric for covering floor etc.; a covering. ● *v.* (**carpeted**) 1 cover (as) with carpet. 2 *colloq.* reprimand.

**carport** *n.* roofed open-sided shelter for car.

**carpus** *n.* (*pl.* **carpi**) group of small bones forming wrist in humans. □□ **carpal** *adj.*

**carrel** *n.* small cubicle for reader in library.

**carriage** *n.* 1 wheeled vehicle or support; a moving part; conveying of goods etc.; cost of this. 2 bearing, deportment.

**carriageway** *n.* part of the road on which vehicles travel.

**carrier** *n.* person or thing that carries; transport or freight company.

**carrion** *n.* dead decaying flesh; filth.

**carrot** *n.* 1 edible plant with tapering orange root; this root. 2 incentive. □ **carrot-and-stick** (of method of persuasion etc.) characterised by both offer of reward and threat of punishment.□□ **carroty** *adj.*

**carry** *v.* 1 support or hold up, esp. while moving; convey. 2 take (process etc.) to specified point. 3 involve. 4 transfer (figure) to column of higher value. 5 hold in specified way. 6 keep (goods) in stock. 7 (of sound) be audible at distance. 8 win victory or acceptance for; win acceptance from.□□ **carry on** 1 continue. 2 *colloq.* behave excitedly.

**cart** ● *n.* 1 wheeled vehicle for carrying loads. 2 facility on website that records items selected by customer for purchase until transaction is completed. ● *v.* carry, transport.

**carte blanche** *n.* full discretionary power.

**cartel** *n.* association of suppliers etc. to control prices.

**cartilage** *n.* firm flexible connective tissue in vertebrates. □□ **cartilaginous** *adj.*

**cartography** *n.* map-drawing. □□ **cartographer** *n.* **cartographic** *adj.*

**carton** *n.* light, esp. cardboard, container.

**cartoon** *n.* 1 humorous, esp. topical, drawing in newspaper etc. 2 sequence of drawings telling story; such sequence animated on film. 3 sketch for painting etc.□□ **cartoonist** *n.*

**cartridge** *n.* 1 case containing explosive charge or bullet. 2 sealed container of film, magnetic tape, etc. 3 component carrying stylus on record player. 4 ink container for insertion in pen, printer, etc.

**cartwheel** *n.* circular sideways handspring with arms and legs extended.

**carve** *v.* make or shape by cutting; cut pattern etc. in; cut (meat) into slices. □□ **carver** *n.*

**carving** *n.* carved object, esp. as work of art.

**cascade** ● *n.* waterfall, esp. one in series. ● *v.* fall in or like cascade.

**case** ● *n.* 1 instance of something occurring; situation. 2 lawsuit. 3 set of facts or arguments supporting something. 4 container or protective covering; this with its contents; suitcase. 5 *Gram.* relation of a word to other words in sentence; form of word expressing this. ● *v.* 1 enclose in a case. 2 *colloq.* inspect closely, esp. for criminal purpose. □ **case-sensitive** differentiating between upper and lower case letters. **in case** lest.

**casein** *n.* main protein in milk and cheese.

**casement** *n.* (part of) window hinged to open like door.

**cash** ● *n.* money in coins or notes. ● *v.* give or obtain cash for.

**cashew** ● *n.* evergreen tree bearing kidney-shaped edible nuts; this nut.

**cashier** ● *n.* person dealing with cash transactions in shop, bank, etc. ● *v.* dismiss from military service in disgrace.

**cashmere** *n.* fine soft (material of) wool, esp. of Kashmir goat.

**casing** *n.* enclosing material or cover.

**casino** *n.* public room etc. for gambling.

**cask** *n.* 1 barrel for liquids. 2 *Aust.* plastic or foil-lined container for wine etc., enclosed within cardboard pack.

**casket** *n.* 1 small box for valuables. 2 coffin.

**Cassandra** *n.* prophet of disaster, esp. one who is disregarded.

**cassava** *n.* plant with starchy roots; starch or flour from these.

**casserole** ● *n.* covered dish for cooking food in oven; food cooked in this. ● *v.* cook in casserole.

**cassette** *n.* sealed case containing magnetic tape, film, etc., ready for insertion in tape recorder, camera, etc.

**cassia** *n.* Sudanese tree whose leaves and pods yield senna; related Australian shrub or tree, having pinnate leaves and golden flowers.

**cassock** *n.* long usu. black or red garment worn by priests.

**cassowary** *n.* large flightless bird with heavy body, wattled neck, and bony crest on forehead.

**cast** ● *v.* (**cast**, **casting**) 1 throw; shed; direct (a glance). 2 register (one's vote). 3 shape (molten metal) in a mould. 4 select (actors) for play or film; assign role to. 5 calculate (horoscope). ● *n.* 1 throw of dice, fishing line, etc. 2 moulded mass of solidified material. 3 set of actors in a play etc. 4 form, type, or quality. 5 slight squint.

**castanets** *n.* pair of shell-shaped pieces of wood clicked in hand to accompany dancers.

**castaway** ● *n.* shipwrecked person. ● *adj.* shipwrecked.

**caste** *n.* social class, esp. in Hindu system.

**castellated** *adj.* built with battlements. □□ **castellation** *n.*

**caster** = CASTOR. □ **caster sugar** finely granulated white sugar.

**castigate** *v.* rebuke, punish severely. □□ **castigation** *n.*

**castle** ● *n.* 1 large fortified building with towers and battlements. 2 *Chess* rook. ● *v. Chess* combined move of king and rook.

**castor** *n.* (also **caster**) 1 small swivelled wheel enabling heavy furniture to be moved. 2 container perforated for sprinkling sugar etc. □ **castor sugar** = CASTER. **castor oil** vegetable oil used as laxative and lubricant.

**castrate** *v.* remove testicles of. □□ **castration** *n.*

**castrato** *n.* (*pl.* **castrati**) *hist.* male singer castrated in boyhood so as to retain soprano or alto voice.

**casual** ● *adj.* 1 chance. 2 not regular or permanent. 3 unconcerned. 4 careless. 5 (of clothes etc.) informal. ● *n.* casual worker. □□ **casually** *adv.* **casualness** *n.*

**casualty** *n.* 1 person killed or injured in war or accident; thing lost or destroyed. 2 (in full **casualty department**) part of hospital treating accident victims. 3 accident.

**casuarina** *n.* tree with tiny teeth-like leaves, native to Australia and SE Asia.

**casuist** *n.* 1 person who resolves cases of conscience etc., esp. cleverly but falsely. 2 sophist, quibbler. □□ **casuistic** *adj.* **casuistry** *n.*

**CAT** *abbr.* (in full **computerised axial tomography**) X-ray scanner providing series of cross-sectional pictures of internal organs.

**cat** *n.* small furry domestic quadruped; wild animal of same family.

**cataclysm** n. violent upheaval.
□□ **cataclysmic** adj.

**catacomb** n. underground gallery with recesses for tombs.

**catafalque** n. decorated coffin of distinguished person for funeral or lying in state.

**catalepsy** n. trance or seizure with rigidity of body.
□□ **cataleptic** adj. & n.

**catalogue** ● n. complete or extensive list, usu. in alphabetical or other systematic order. ● v. make catalogue of; enter in catalogue.

**catalysis** n. acceleration of chemical reaction by catalyst.□□ **catalyse** v.

**catalyst** n. 1 substance speeding chemical reaction without itself permanently changing. 2 person or thing that precipitates change.

**catalytic converter** n. part of exhaust system that reduces harmful effects of pollutant gases.

**catamaran** n. boat or raft with parallel twin hulls.

**catapult** ● n. 1 forked stick with elastic for shooting stones. 2 hist. military machine for hurling stones etc. 3 device for launching glider etc. ● v. launch with catapult; fling forcibly; leap or be hurled forcibly.

**cataract** n. 1 waterfall. 2 progressive opacity of eye lens.

**catarrh** n. inflammation of mucous membrane, air passages, etc.; mucus in nose caused by this.
□□ **catarrhal** adj.

**catastrophe** n. 1 great usu. sudden disaster. 2 denouement of drama.
□□ **catastrophic** adj. **catastrophically** adv.

**catatonia** n. schizophrenia with intervals of catalepsy and sometimes violence.□□ **catatonic** adj. & n.

**catcall** n. whistle of disapproval.

**catch** ● v. (**caught**, **catching**)
1 capture; seize; grasp and hold.
2 detect; surprise; trick. 3 overtake.

4 be in time for. 5 become infected with. ● n. 1 act of catching; something caught or worth catching.
2 unexpected difficulty or disadvantage. 3 fastener.□ **catch-22** dilemma in which either choice will cause suffering. **catch on** colloq. become popular. 2 understand. **catch out** detect in a mistake etc. **catch up** come abreast of; do arrears of work.

**catchment area** n. 1 area from which rainfall flows into river etc.
2 area served by school, hospital, etc.

**catchword** n. phrase or word in frequent use.

**catchy** adj. 1 (of tune) easily remembered. 2 attractive.

**catechise** v. (also -ize) instruct by question and answer.

**catechism** n. (book containing) principles of a religion in form of questions and answers; series of questions.

**categorical** adj. unconditional, absolute; explicit.
□□ **categorically** adv.

**categorise** v. (also -ize) place in category.□□ **categorisation** n.

**category** n. class or division of things, ideas, etc.)

**cater** v. supply food; provide what is needed or desired.□□ **caterer** n.

**caterpillar** n. 1 larva of butterfly or moth. 2 (in full Caterpillar track or tread) propr. steel band passing around wheels of vehicle for travel on rough ground.

**caterwaul** v. howl like cat.

**catfish** n. any of various fish having whisker-like barbels around mouth.

**catgut** n. thread made from intestines of sheep etc. used for strings of musical instruments, sutures, etc.

**catharsis** n. (pl. **catharses**) release of strong feeling or tension.
□□ **cathartic** adj.

**cathedral** n. principal church of diocese.

**catheter** n. tube inserted into body cavity for introducing or removing fluid.

**cathode** n. **1** negative electrode of cell. **2** positive terminal of battery etc.

**catholic** ● adj. **1** all-embracing; broad-minded; universal. **2** (Catholic) Roman Catholic. ● n. (Catholic) Roman Catholic. □□ **Catholicism** n. catholicity n.

**cation** n. positively charged ion. □□ **cationic** adj.

**catkin** n. spike of usu. hanging flowers of willow, hazel, etc.

**catmint** n. strong-smelling plant attractive to cats.

**catnap** n. short nap.

**catnip** n. catmint.

**cattle** n.pl. large ruminants bred esp. for milk or meat.

**catty** adj. spiteful. □□ **cattily** adv. cattiness n.

**catwalk** n. narrow platform extending into auditorium, used in fashion shows.

**Caucasian** ● adj. white-skinned; of European origin. ● n. Caucasian person.

**caucus** n. (pl. **caucuses**) meeting of parliamentary members of political party; those eligible to attend such meeting.

**caudal** adj. of, like, or at tail. □□ **caudate** adj.

**caught** see CATCH.

**caul** n. membrane enclosing foetus; part of this sometimes found on child's head at birth.

**cauldron** n. large deep vessel for boiling things in.

**cauliflower** n. cabbage with large white flower head.

**caulk** v. (also **calk**) stop up (ship's seams); make watertight.

**causal** adj. relating to cause (and effect). □□ **causality** n.

**cause** ● n. **1** thing producing effect. **2** reason or motive. **3** justification.

**4** principle, belief, or purpose. **5** matter to be settled, or case offered, at law. ● v. **1** be cause of. **2** produce. □□ **causation** n.

**cause célèbre** n. (pl. **causes célèbres**) issue arousing great interest.

**causeway** n. raised road across low or wet ground or water.

**caustic** ● adj. **1** corrosive, burning. **2** sarcastic, biting. ● n. caustic substance. □ **caustic soda** sodium hydroxide. □□ **caustically** adv.

**cauterise** v. (also -ize) burn (tissue), esp. to stop bleeding.

**caution** ● n. **1** attention to safety. **2** warning. ● v. warn, admonish.

**cautionary** adj. warning.

**cautious** adj. having or showing caution. □□ **cautiously** adv.

**cavalcade** n. procession of riders, vehicles, etc.

**cavalier** adj. offhand, arrogant, curt.

**cavalry** n. soldiers on horseback or in armoured vehicles.

**cave** ● n. large hollow in side of cliff, hill, etc., or underground. ● v. explore caves. □ **cave in** collapse; yield.

**caveat** n. **1** warning, proviso. **2** Law process in court to suspend proceedings.

**cavern** n. cave, esp. large or dark one. □□ **cavernous** adj.

**caviar** n. (also **caviare**) pickled sturgeon roe.

**cavil** ● v. make petty objections. ● n. a trivial objection.

**cavity** n. **1** hollow within solid body. **2** decayed part of tooth.

**cavort** v. caper.

**caw** ● n. cry of crow etc. ● v. utter this cry.

**cayenne** n. (in full **cayenne pepper**) powdered hot red pepper.

**cc** ● abbr. **1** carbon copy (used as an indication that a duplicate has been or should be sent to another person). **2** cubic centimetre(s).

● *v.* send copy of an email to (third party).

**CD** *abbr.* compact disc.

**CD-ROM** *n.* compact disc holding data for display on a computer screen.

**cease** *v.* stop; bring or come to an end.

**ceasefire** *n.* temporary suspension of fighting; a truce.

**ceaseless** *adj.* without end.
□□ **ceaselessly** *adv.*

**cedar** *n.* evergreen conifer of Europe etc.; its hard fragrant wood; any similar Australian tree.

**cede** *v.* give up one's rights to or possession of.

**cedilla** *n.* mark ( ҫ ) written under **c** (in French, to show it is pronounced *s*, not *k*).

**ceiling** *n.* upper interior surface of room or other compartment; upper limit.

**celebrant** *n.* person performing rite, esp. priest at Mass etc. or secular official authorised to conduct civil marriages.

**celebrate** *v.* mark or honour with festivities. □□ **celebration** *n.* **celebratory** *adj.*

**celebrity** *n.* well-known person; fame.

**celerity** *n. arch.* swiftness.

**celery** *n.* plant with crisp long stalks used as vegetable.

**celestial** *adj.* of sky or heavenly bodies; heavenly; divinely good.

**celibate** ● *adj.* unmarried, or abstaining from sexual relations.
● *n.* celibate person. □□ **celibacy** *n.*

**cell** *n.* **1** small room, esp. in prison or monastery; small compartment, e.g. in honeycomb. **2** small active political or terrorist group. **3** unit of structure of organic matter. **4** vessel containing electrodes for current generation or electrolysis.

**cellar** ● *n.* **1** underground storage room. **2** stock of wine in cellar.
● *v.* store in cellar.

**cello** *n.* bass instrument of violin family, held between legs of seated player. □□ **cellist** *n.*

**cellophane** *n. propr.* thin transparent wrapping material.

**cellphone** *n.* = *mobile phone.*

**cellular** *adj.* **1** consisting of cells. **2** of open texture, porous.
□□ **cellularity** *n.*

**cellulite** *n.* lumpy form of fat producing puckering of skin.

**celluloid** *n.* transparent plastic formerly used in cinematographic film; world of cinema, films.

**cellulose** *n.* carbohydrate forming plant cell walls, used in making plastics.

**Celsius** *adj.* of scale of temperature on which water freezes at 0° and boils at 100°.

**Celt** *n.* member of ancient European people or their descendants.
□□ **Celtic** *adj.*

**cement** ● *n.* substance made from lime and clay, mixed with water, sand, etc. to form mortar or concrete; similar substance that hardens and fastens on setting. ● *v.* unite firmly, strengthen; apply cement to.

**cemetery** *n.* public burial ground.

**cenotaph** *n.* tomblike monument to person(s) whose remains are elsewhere.

**censer** *n.* vessel for burning incense.

**censor** ● *n.* official with power to suppress or expurgate books, films, news, etc., on grounds of obscenity, threat to security, etc. ● *v.* act as censor of; make deletions or changes in. □□ **censorial** *adj.* **censorship** *n.*

---

**Usage** As a verb, *censor* is often confused with *censure*, which means 'to criticise harshly'.

---

**censorious** *adj.* severely critical.

**censure** ● v. criticise harshly; reprove. ● n. hostile criticism; disapproval.

**census** n. official count of population etc.

**cent** n. one hundredth of dollar or other decimal currency unit; coin of this value; *colloq.* very small amount.

**centaur** n. mythical creature, half man, half horse.

**centenarian** ● n. person 100 or more years old. ● adj. 100 or more years old.

**centenary** n. 100th anniversary.

**centennial** ● adj. of a centenary. ● n. centenary.

**centigrade** adj. Celsius.

> **Usage** *Celsius* is usually preferred to *centigrade* in technical contexts.

**centigram** n. (also **centigramme**) metric unit of mass, equal to 0.01 gram.

**centilitre** n. 0.01 litre.

**centimetre** n. 0.01 metre.

**centipede** n. arthropod with wormlike body and many legs.

**central** adj. 1 of, at, forming, or from centre. 2 essential, principal. □ **central nervous system** brain and spinal cord. □□ **centrality** n. **centrally** adv.

**centralise** v. (also **-ize**) concentrate (administration etc.) at single centre; subject (nation etc.) to this system. □□ **centralisation** n.

**centre** ● n. 1 middle point or part; place where a specified activity takes place. 2 point where something begins or is most intense. ● v. place in or at centre.

**centred** adj. 1 placed or situated in the centre. 2 (of a person) self balanced and confident or serene.

**centrefold** n. centre spread of magazine etc.

**centrifugal** adj. moving or tending to move from centre. □□ **centrifugally** adv.

**centrifuge** n. rapidly rotating machine for separating liquids from solids etc.

**centripetal** adj. moving or tending to move towards centre.

**centurion** n. commander in ancient Roman army.

**century** n. 100 years; *Cricket* score of 100 runs.

**cephalic** adj. of or in head.

**cephalopod** n. mollusc with tentacles on head, e.g. octopus.

**ceramic** ● adj. made of esp. baked clay; of ceramics. ● n. (**ceramics**) art of making pottery.

**cereal** ● n. edible grain; breakfast food made from cereal. ● adj. of edible grain.

**cerebellum** n. (pl. **cerebellums** or **cerebella**) part of brain at back of skull.

**cerebral** adj. of brain; intellectual. □ **cerebral palsy** paralysis resulting from brain damage at or before birth.

**cerebrum** n. (pl. **cerebra**) principal part of brain, located at front of skull.

**ceremonial** ● adj. of or with ceremony; formal. ● n. system of rites or ceremonies. □□ **ceremonially** adv.

**ceremonious** adj. fond of or characterised by ceremony; formal. □□ **ceremoniously** adv.

**ceremony** n. formal procedure; formalities, esp. ritualistic; excessively polite behaviour.

**cerise** n. light clear red.

**cerium** n. silvery metallic element (symbol **Ce**).

**certain** adj. 1 convinced; indisputable. 2 sure, destined. 3 reliable. 4 particular but not specified. 5 some.

**certainly** adv. 1 undoubtedly. 2 (in answer) yes.

**certainty** ● *n.* **1** undoubted fact; absolute conviction. **2** reliable thing or person.

**certifiable** *adj.* **1** able or needing to be certified. **2** officially recognised as needing treatment for mental disorder; *colloq.* mad; crazy.

**certificate** ● *n.* document attesting fact. ● *v.* (esp. as **certificated** *adj.*) provide with licence or attest by certificate.□□ **certification** *n.*

**certify** *v.* attest (to); declare by certificate; officially declare insane.

**certitude** *n.* feeling certain.

**cerulean** *adj.* & *n.* sky blue.

**cerumen** *n.* yellow-brown waxy substance in outer ear.

**cervix** *n.* (*pl.* **cervices**) neckline structure, esp. neck of uterus; neck. □□ **cervical** *adj.*

**cessation** *n.* ceasing or pause.

**cession** *n.* ceding; giving up.

**cesspit** *n.* (also **cesspool**) pit for liquid waste or sewage.

**cetacean** ● *n.* marine mammal with streamlined hairless body and dorsal blowhole for breathing, e.g. whale. ● *adj.* of cetaceans.

**cetane** *n.* liquid hydrocarbon used in standardising ratings of diesel fuel.

**cf.** *abbr.* compare.

**CFC** *abbr.* chlorofluorocarbon, usu. gaseous compound harmful to ozone layer.

**chablis** *n.* kind of dry white wine.

**chafe** ● *v.* **1** make or become sore or damaged by rubbing. **2** irritate; show irritation. **3** fret. **4** rub (esp. skin) to warm. ● *n.* sore caused by rubbing.

**chaff** ● *n.* **1** separated grain husks. **2** chopped hay or straw. **3** light-hearted teasing. **4** worthless stuff. ● *v.* tease, banter.

**chafing dish** *n.* vessel in which food is cooked or kept warm at table.

**chagrin** *n.* acute annoyance or disappointment.

**chain** ● *n.* **1** series of connected metal links; connected series or sequence. **2** (imperial) unit of length (66 ft, 20.1168 m). ● *v.* secure with chain; confine or restrict (person). □ **chain reaction** change causing further changes.

**chainsaw** ● *n.* motor-driven saw with teeth set on circular chain.

**chair** ● *n.* **1** seat usu. with back, for one person. **2** professorship. **3** (office of) chairperson. ● *v.* preside over (meeting).

**chairlift** *n.* series of chairs on a cable for carrying people up mountain.

**chairman** *n.* (*pl.* -**men**) chairperson.

**chairperson** *n.* person who presides over meeting or board of directors.

**chairwoman** *n.* (*pl.* -**women**) female chairperson.

**chaise longue** *n.* (*pl.* **chaise longues** or **chaises longues**) sofa with one arm rest.

**chalcedony** *n.* type of quartz.

**chalet** *n.* Swiss mountain hut or cottage; similar house; holiday house, esp. at ski resort.

**chalice** *n.* goblet.

**chalk** ● *n.* white soft limestone; (piece of) similar substance for writing or drawing. ● *v.* rub, mark, draw, or write with chalk.□□ **chalky** *adj.* **chalkiness** *n.*

**challenge** ● *n.* **1** call to take part in contest etc. or to prove or justify something. **2** demanding or difficult task. **3** objection or query. ● *v.* **1** issue challenge to. **2** dispute. **3** (as **challenging** *adj.*) stimulatingly difficult.□□ **challenger** *n.*

**challenged** *adj.* lacking a physical or mental attribute.

**chamber** *n.* hall used for meetings of council, parliament, etc.; *arch.* room, esp. bedroom; (**chambers**) set of rooms; rooms used by barrister; cavity or compartment. □ **chamber**

**music** music written for small group of players.

**chamberlain** *n.* officer managing royal or noble household.

**chameleon** *n.* small lizard able to change colour for camouflage.

**chamfer** ● *v.* bevel symmetrically. ● *n.* bevelled surface.

**chamois** *n.* **1** agile European and Asian mountain antelope. **2** (piece of) soft leather from sheep, goats, etc.

**champ** ● *v.* munch or chew noisily. ● *n.* chewing noise. □ **champ at the bit** show impatience.

**champagne** *n.* sparkling wine.

**champignon** *n.* button mushroom.

**champion** ● *n.* **1** person or thing that has defeated all rivals. **2** person who fights or argues for cause or another person. ● *v.* support cause of, defend. □□ **championship** *n.*

**chance** ● *n.* **1** probability; possibility. **2** unplanned occurrence; fate. ● *adj.* happening by chance. ● *v.* risk; happen.

**chancel** *n.* part of church near altar.

**chancellery** *n.* (also **chancelery**) chancellor's department, staff, or office.

**chancellor** *n.* **1** honorary head of university. **2** civil or legal official. **3** head of government in some European countries.

**chancre** *n.* painless ulcer developing in venereal disease etc.

**chancy** *adj.* uncertain; risky.

**chandelier** *n.* branched hanging support for lights.

**chandler** *n.* dealer in candles, oil, soap, paint, etc.

**change** ● *v.* make or become different; exchange; substitute; put fresh clothes or coverings on; go from one of two (sides, trains, etc.) to another; get or give small money or different currency for. ● *n.* **1** changing. **2** money in small units or returned as balance.

□ **change of heart** conversion to different view. **change one's mind** adopt different opinion or plan. □□ **changeable** *adj.*

**changeling** *n.* child believed to be substituted for another.

**channel** ● *n.* **1** stretch of water connecting two seas; passage for water. **2** medium of communication; band of frequencies used for radio and television transmission. **3** electric circuit that acts as a path for a signal. ● *v.* (**channelled**) guide, direct. □ **channel surf** flip rapidly between television channels using a remote control.

**chant** ● *n.* monotonous song; spoken singsong phrase, esp. performed in unison by crowd; melody for psalms. ● *v.* talk or repeat monotonously; sing or intone (psalm etc.)

**chaos** *n.* utter confusion. □□ **chaotic** *adj.*

**chap** ● *n.* colloq. man. ● *v.* (of the skin) split or crack.

**chapati** *n.* (also **chapatti**) flat cake of unleavened bread.

**chapel** *n.* place for private worship in cathedral or church, with its own altar; place of worship attached to school etc.

**chaperone** (also **chaperon**) ● *n.* person who accompanies and looks after another person or group of people. ● *v.* act as chaperone to.

**chaplain** *n.* member of clergy attached to private chapel, institution, ship, regiment, etc. □□ **chaplaincy** *n.*

**chaplet** *n.* garland or circlet for head; short string of beads; rosary.

**chapter** *n.* **1** division of book. **2** period of time. **3** canons of cathedral or meeting of these.

**char** *v.* (**charred**) blacken with fire; scorch; burn to charcoal.

**character** n. 1 distinguishing qualities or characteristics; moral strength; reputation. 2 person in novel, play, etc. 3 colloq. (esp. eccentric) person. 4 letter, symbol.

**characterise** v. (also **-ize**) describe character of; describe as; be characteristic of. □□ **characterisation** n.

**characteristic** ● adj. typical, distinctive. ● n. characteristic feature or quality. □□ **characteristically** adv.

**charade** n. 1 (**charades**) game involving guessing word from acted clues. 2 absurd pretence.

**charcoal** n. black residue of partly burnt wood etc.

**chardonnay** n. kind of white wine.

**charge** ● n. 1 price asked for goods or services. 2 quantity of explosive; electricity contained in substance. 3 task, duty. 4 custody; person or thing entrusted. 5 accusation. 6 rushing attack; (in sports) illegal push. ● v. 1 ask as price or from (person); record as debt. 2 load or fill with explosive; give electrical charge to. 3 give as task or duty; entrust. 4 accuse formally. 5 rush forward in attack; push (opposing player) illegally. □□ **chargeable** adj.

**chargé d'affaires** n. (pl. **chargés d'affaires**) ambassador's deputy.

**charger** n. 1 cavalry horse. 2 apparatus for charging battery.

**chariot** n. hist. two-wheeled horse-drawn vehicle, used in ancient warfare and racing.

**charioteer** n. chariot driver.

**charisma** n. power to inspire or attract others; great charm. □□ **charismatic** adj.

**charitable** adj. generous to those in need; of or connected with a charity; lenient in judging others. □□ **charitably** adv.

**charity** n. giving voluntarily to those in need; organisation for helping those in need; tolerance in judging others; love of fellow human beings.

**charlatan** n. person falsely claiming knowledge or skill. □□ **charlatanism** n.

**charm** ● n. power of delighting, attracting, or influencing; object, act, or word(s) supposedly having magic power; trinket on bracelet etc. ● v. delight, captivate; obtain or gain by charm; influence or protect (as) by magic. □□ **charmer** n.

**charming** adj. delightful.

**charnel house** n. place containing corpses or bones.

**chart** ● n. 1 map, esp. for navigation. 2 sheet of information in form of tables or diagrams. 3 (**the charts**) colloq. list of currently best-selling CDs etc. ● v. make chart of.

**charter** ● n. 1 official document granting rights. 2 contract to hire aircraft, ship, etc. for special purpose. ● v. 1 grant charter to. 2 hire (aircraft, ship, etc.)

**chartered** adj. qualified as member of professional body that has royal charter.

**chartreuse** n. green or yellow brandy liqueur.

**chary** adj. cautious, sparing.

**chase** ● v. 1 pursue; drive away; hurry in pursuit of. 2 colloq. pursue (thing overdue), try to locate. 3 colloq. try to attain. 4 court persistently. ● n. pursuit.

**chaser** n. drink taken after another of different kind.

**chasm** n. 1 deep cleft in earth, rock, etc. 2 wide difference in opinion etc.

**chassis** n. base frame of vehicle etc.

**chaste** adj. 1 abstaining from sexual intercourse. 2 pure, virtuous. 3 unadorned. □□ **chastely** adv.

**chasten** v. subdue, restrain; punish, discipline.

**chastise** v. rebuke severely; punish, beat.□□ **chastisement** n.

**chastity** n. being chaste.

**chat** ● v. (**chatted**) **1** talk in light familiar way. **2** exchange messages online. ● n. **1** informal talk. **2** online exchange of messages. **3** small colourful Australian bird with chattering call.

**chateau** n. (pl. **chateaux**) large French country house.

**chatelaine** n. hist. woman in charge of large house.

**chattel** n. a movable possession.

**chatter** ● v. talk quickly, incessantly, or indiscreetly. ● n. such talk.

**chatterbox** n. talkative person.

**chatty** adj. fond of or resembling chat; informal and lively.

**chauffeur** ● n. person employed to drive car. ● v. drive (car or person).

**chauvinism** n. **1** exaggerated or aggressive patriotism. **2** excessive or prejudiced support or loyalty for something.□□ **chauvinist** n. **chauvinistic** adj.

**cheap** adj. low in cost or value; of low quality.□□ **cheaply** adv.

**cheapen** v. make or become cheap; degrade.

**cheapskate** n. colloq. stingy person.

**cheat** ● v. **1** deceive; deprive of; gain unfair advantage. **2** avoid by luck. ● n. person who cheats; deception.

**check** ● v. **1** test, examine, verify. **2** stop or slow motion of. **3** agree or correspond when compared. ● n. **1** test for accuracy, quality, etc. **2** stopping or slowing of motion; rebuff, restraint. **3** pattern of small squares; fabric so patterned. **4** (also as int.) exposure of chess king to attack. □ **check in** register on arrival. **check out** register on departure; investigate.

**checkmate** ● n. situation in chess where capture of a king is inevitable. ● v. put into checkmate; defeat; foil.

**checkout** n. desk where goods are paid for in shop.

**cheddar** n. kind of firm smooth cheese.

**cheek** ● n. **1** side of face below eye. **2** impertinence; impertinent speech. **3** colloq. buttock. ● v. be impertinent to.

**cheeky** adj. impertinent.□□ **cheekily** adv. **cheekiness** n.

**cheer** ● n. a shout of encouragement or applause. ● v. **1** utter a cheer; applaud with a cheer. **2** gladden, comfort.

**cheerful** adj. in good spirits; bright, pleasant.□□ **cheerfully** adv. **cheerfulness** n.

**cheerless** adj. gloomy, dreary.

**cheese** n. **1** food made from pressed milk curds. **2** thick stiff cheese. □ **cheesed off** colloq. bored; exasperated.

**cheesecake** n. **1** open tart filled with flavoured cream cheese or curd cheese. **2** colloq. portrayal of women in sexually attractive manner.

**cheesecloth** n. thin loosely-woven cotton fabric.

**cheesy** adj. hackneyed and trite.

**cheetah** n. swift-running spotted feline resembling leopard.

**chef** n. (esp. chief) cook in restaurant etc.

**chemical** ● adj. of, made by, or employing chemistry. ● n. substance obtained or used in chemistry. □□ **chemically** adv.

**chemise** n. woman's loose-fitting undergarment or dress.

**chemist** n. **1** authorised dispenser of medicinal drugs; shop at which chemist operates. **2** expert in chemistry.

**chemistry** n. (pl. **-ies**) **1** study of substances and their reactions; its application in forming new substances; structure and properties of a substance. **2** attraction or interaction between people.

**chemotherapy** *n.* treatment of disease, esp. cancer, by chemical substances.

**chemurgy** *n.* chemical and industrial use of organic raw materials. □□ **chemurgic** *adj.*

**chenille** *n.* tufty velvety cord or yarn; fabric of this.

**cheque** *n.* written order to bank to pay sum of money; printed form for this.

**chequer** *n.* **1** pattern of squares often alternately coloured. **2** (in full **Chinese chequers**) game played with marbles or pegs in hollows on board.

**chequered** *adj.* **1** marked with chequer pattern. **2** having frequent changes of fortune.

**cherish** *v.* tend lovingly; hold dear, cling to.

**cheroot** *n.* cigar with both ends open.

**cherry** ● *n.* **1** small stone fruit; tree bearing it; wood of this. **2** bright red. ● *adj.* of bright red colour.

**cherub** *n.* (*pl.* **cherubs** or **cherubim**) **1** representation of winged child. **2** beautiful child. □□ **cherubic** *adj.*

**chess** *n.* game for two with 16 pieces each on chequered board.

**chest** *n.* **1** large strong box; small cabinet for medicines etc. **2** part of body enclosed by ribs; front surface of body from neck to bottom of ribs. □ **chest of drawers** piece of furniture with drawers for clothes etc.

**chestnut** ● *n.* **1** glossy hard brown edible nut; tree bearing it. **2** reddish-brown; horse of this colour. **3** *colloq.* stale joke etc. ● *adj.* reddish-brown.

**chevalier** *n.* member of certain orders of knighthood etc.

**chèvre** *n.* cheese made from goat's milk.

**chevron** *n.* V-shaped line or stripe.

**chew** ● *v.* work (food etc.) between the teeth. ● *n.* act of chewing. □ **chewing gum** flavoured gum for chewing.

**chewy** ● *adj.* tough; needing or suitable for chewing. ● *n.* chewing gum.

**chez** *prep.* at the home of.

**chia** *n.* plant whose seeds are used in various foods and drinks.

**chiack** (also **chyack**) *Aust.* ● *v.* taunt, tease. ● *n.* barracking. □□ **chiacking** *n.*

**chiaroscuro** *n.* treatment of light and shade in painting. **2** use of contrast in literature etc.

**chic** ● *adj.* stylish, elegant. ● *n.* stylishness, elegance.

**chicane** ● *n.* **1** artificial barrier or obstacle on motor-racing course etc. **2** chicanery. ● *v.* *arch.* use chicanery. **2** cheat (person).

**chicanery** *n.* trickery.

**chick** *n.* **1** young bird. **2** *colloq.* young woman.

**chicken** ● *n.* **1** domestic fowl; its flesh as food. **2** youthful person. **3** *colloq.* coward. ● *adj.* *colloq.* cowardly. □ **chicken feed** *colloq.* trifling amount of money. **chicken out** *colloq.* withdraw through cowardice.

**chickenpox** *n.* infectious illness with a rash of small red blisters.

**chickpea** *n.* pea-like seed of leguminous plant, used as vegetable.

**chicory** *n.* salad plant; its root, roasted and ground and used with or instead of coffee.

**chide** *v.* (chided or **chid**, **chidden**, **chiding**) scold, rebuke.

**chief** ● *n.* leader, ruler; person with highest rank. ● *adj.* first in position, importance or influence; prominent, leading.

**chiefly** *adv.* above all; mainly but not exclusively.

**chieftain** *n.* leader of a people or clan. □□ **chieftaincy** *n.*

**chiffon** n. diaphanous silky fabric.

**chignon** n. coil of hair at back of head.

**chihuahua** n. tiny smooth-haired dog.

**chilblain** n. itching swelling on hand, foot, etc., caused by exposure to cold.

**child** n. (pl. **children**) young human being; son or daughter; descendant, follower, or product of.

**childbirth** n. process of giving birth to child.

**childish** adj. of or like child; immature, silly. □□ **childishly** adv. **childishness** n.

**childlike** adj. innocent, frank, etc.

**chill** ● n. 1 cold sensation; unpleasant coldness. 2 feverish cold. 3 depressing influence. ● v. 1 make or become cold; cool (food or drink). 2 depress. 3 horrify. □ **chill out** colloq. calm down, relax. □□ **chilly** adj.

**chilli** n. (also **chili**) (pl. **chillies**) small hot-tasting pod of kind of capsicum, used fresh or dried as flavouring.

**chime** ● n. set of attuned bells; sounds made by this. ● v. 1 (of bells) ring; show (time) by chiming. 2 (of bell) be in agreement.

**chimera** n. 1 legendary monster with lion's head, goat's body, and serpent's tail. 2 wild impossible scheme or fancy. □□ **chimerical** adj.

**chimney** n. 1 channel conducting smoke etc. away from fire etc.; part of this above roof. 2 glass tube protecting flame of lamp.

**chimpanzee** n. small African ape.

**chin** n. front of lower jaw.

**china** ● n. fine white or translucent ceramic ware; things made of this. ● adj. made of china.

**chinchilla** n. 1 S. American rodent; its soft grey fur. 2 breed of cat or rabbit.

**chine** ● n. 1 backbone; joint of meat containing this. 2 ridge. ● v. cut (meat) through backbone.

**chink** ● n. 1 narrow opening. 2 sound of glasses or coins striking together. ● v. make this sound.

**chintz** n. glazed cotton fabric.

**chip** ● n. 1 small piece cut or broken off; place where piece has been broken off. 2 strip of potato, usu. fried. 3 potato crisp. 4 counter used as money in some games. 5 microchip. 6 Sports kick, pass, or shot, with ball to produce short lofted shot or pass. ● v. (**chipped**) 1 cut or break (piece) from hard material; break, flake. 2 Sports kick or strike (ball) with chip. □ **chip in** 1 make a contribution. 2 interrupt. **chip on one's shoulder** long-held grievance.

**chipboard** n. board made of compressed wood chips.

**chipmunk** n. N. American striped ground squirrel.

**chipolata** n. small sausage.

**chiropody** n. = PODIATRY.

**chiropractic** n. treatment of disease etc. by manipulation of spinal column. □□ **chiropractor** n.

**chirp** ● v. 1 (of small birds etc.) utter short thin note. 2 speak merrily. ● n. chirping sound.

**chirpy** adj. colloq. cheerful. □□ **chirpily** adv. **chirpiness** n.

**chisel** ● n. tool with bevelled blade for shaping wood, stone, or metal. ● v. (**chiselled**) 1 cut or shape with chisel. 2 colloq. cheat.

**chit** n. 1 young child. 2 written note.

**chitterlings** n.pl. small intestines of pig etc., cooked for food.

**chivalry** n. 1 medieval knightly system. 2 honour and courtesy, esp. to weak. □□ **chivalrous** adj. **chivalrously** adv.

**chive** n. herb related to onion.

**chivvy** v. urge persistently, nag.

**chlamydia** n. parasitic bacterium.

**chloral** n. compound used in making DDT, sedatives, etc.

**chloride** n. compound of chlorine and another element or group.

**chlorinate** v. impregnate or treat with chlorine. □□ **chlorination** n.

**chlorine** n. **1** chemical element (symbol Cl). **2** a poisonous gas.

**chlorofluorocarbon** see CFC.

**chloroform** ● n. colourless volatile liquid formerly used as general anaesthetic. ● v. render unconscious with this.

**chlorophyll** n. green pigment in most plants.

**chock** ● n. block of wood, wedge. ● v. make fast with chock(s).

**chock-a-block** adj. & adv. colloq. crammed close together; very full.

**chockers** adj. Aust. colloq. = CHOCK-A-BLOCK.

**chocolate** n. food made as paste, powder, or solid block from ground cacao seeds; sweet made of or covered with this; dark brown.

**choice** ● n. act of choosing; thing or person chosen; range to choose from; power to choose. ● adj. of superior quality.

**choir** n. **1** regular group of singers. **2** chancel in large church.

**choke** ● v. stop breathing of (person or animal); suffer such stoppage; block up; make or become speechless from emotion. ● n. **1** valve in carburettor controlling intake of air. **2** device for smoothing variations of alternating current.

**choker** n. close-fitting necklace.

**choko** n. succulent green pear-shaped vegetable.

**cholecalciferol** n. vitamin ($D_3$) produced by action of sunlight on skin.

**cholera** n. infectious often fatal bacterial disease of small intestine.

**choleric** adj. easily angered.

**cholesterol** n. fatty animal substance thought to cause hardening of arteries.

**chomp** v. munch noisily.

**chook** n. Aust. chicken.

**choose** v. (chose, chosen, choosing) select out of a number of things; take one or another; decide.

**choosy** adj. (choosier) colloq. fussy, hard to please.

**chop** ● v. (chopped) **1** cut by blow with axe or knife; cut into small pieces. **2** hit with short downward movement. **3** dispense with; shorten or curtail. ● n. **1** cutting blow. **2** thick slice of meat usu. including a rib.

**chopper** n. **1** cutting tool. **2** colloq. helicopter.

**choppy** adj. (of sea etc.) fairly rough.

**chopstick** n. each of pair of sticks held in one hand as eating utensils by Chinese, Japanese, etc.

**chop suey** n. Chinese-style dish of meat fried with vegetables.

**choral** adj. of, for, or sung by choir or chorus.

**chorale** n. simple stately hymn tune; choir.

**chord** n. **1** combination of notes sounded together. **2** straight line joining ends of arc. □□ **strike** (or **touch**) **a chord** appeal to the emotions of.

**chore** n. tedious or routine task, esp. domestic.

**choreography** n. design or arrangement of ballet etc. □□ **choreograph** v.

**chorister** n. member of choir.

**chortle** ● n. gleeful chuckle. ● v. chuckle gleefully.

**chorus** ● n. **1** group of singers; choir; music for this. **2** refrain of song. **3** simultaneous utterance; group of singers and dancers performing together. ● v. utter simultaneously.

**chose** see CHOOSE.

**chosen** see CHOOSE.

**chough** n. **1** Australian bird with black plumage and white wing markings. **2** European red-legged crow.

**choux pastry** n. very light pastry made with eggs.

**chowchilla** n. Aust. perching rainforest bird with distinctive call. Also called **log runner**.

**chowder** n. rich soup or stew, often containing seafood.

**chow mein** n. Chinese-style dish of fried noodles with shredded meat and vegetables.

**chrism** n. consecrated oil.

**christen** v. 1 baptise. 2 name. □□ **christening** n.

**Christendom** n. Christians worldwide.

**Christian** ● adj. 1 of Christ's teaching; believing in or following Christian religion. 2 colloq. kind, charitable, decent. ● n. adherent of Christianity.

**Christianity** n. Christian religion, quality, or character.

**Christmas** n. (period around) festival of Christ's birth, celebrated on 25 Dec. □□ **Christmassy** adj.

**chromatic** adj. 1 of colour, in colours. 2 Mus. of or having notes not belonging to prevailing key. □□ **chromatically** adv.

**chrome** n. chromium; yellow pigment got from compound of chromium.

**chroming** n. Aust. colloq. inhaling of fumes from chrome-based spray-paint.

**chromium** n. metallic element used as shiny decorative or protective coating (symbol **Cr**).

**chromosome** n. Biol. threadlike structure occurring in pairs in cell nucleus, carrying genes.

**chronic** adj. (of disease) long-lasting; (of patient) having chronic illness; colloq. bad, intense, severe. □□ **chronically** adv.

**chronicle** ● n. record of events in order of occurrence. ● v. record (events) thus.

**chronological** adj. according to order of occurrence. □□ **chronologically** adv.

**chronology** n. arrangement of events etc. in order of occurrence.

**chronometer** n. time-measuring instrument, esp. one used in navigation.

**chrysalis** n. (pl. **chrysalises** or **chrysalides**) pupa of butterfly or moth; case enclosing it.

**chrysanthemum** n. garden plant of daisy family.

**chubby** adj. plump, round.

**chuck¹** ● v. 1 colloq. fling or throw carelessly. 2 colloq. give up. 3 touch playfully, esp. under chin. 4 Aust. colloq. vomit. ● n. 1 a playful touch. 2 a toss.

**chuck²** n. 1 cut of beef from neck to ribs. 2 device for holding workpiece or bit. ● v. fix in chuck.

**chuckle** ● v. laugh quietly or inwardly. ● n. quiet or suppressed laugh.

**chuditch** n. Aust. western quoll.

**chuff** v. (of engine etc.) work with regular sharp puffing sound.

**chuffed** adj. colloq. 1 delighted. 2 displeased.

**chug** v. (chugged) make intermittent explosive sound; move with this.

**chum** n. close friend. □□ **chummy** adj.

**chump** n. 1 thick end of loin of lamb or mutton. 2 lump of wood. 3 colloq. foolish person.

**chunder** v. & n. Aust. colloq. vomit.

**chunk** n. lump cut or broken off.

**chunky** adj. 1 consisting of or resembling chunks. 2 small and sturdy. □□ **chunkiness** n.

**church** n. 1 building for public (usu. Christian) worship; religious service in this. 2 (**Church**) Christians collectively; particular group of these.

**churinga** n. Aust. (in Aboriginal ceremony) sacred object, normally carved or painted.

**churl** n. bad-mannered, surly person. □□ **churlish** adj.

**churn** ● n. machine for making butter, ice cream, etc.; large milk can. ● v. 1 agitate (milk etc.) in churn; make (butter) in churn. 2 upset, agitate.

**chute** n. 1 slide for sending things to lower level. 2 colloq. parachute.

**chutney** n. relish made of fruits, vinegar, spices, etc.

**chutzpah** n. colloq. extreme self-confidence or audacity.

**chyle** n. milky fluid into which chyme is converted.

**chyme** n. acid pulp formed from partly digested food.

**ciabatta** n. Italian bread made with olive oil.

**ciao** int. colloq. 1 goodbye. 2 hello.

**cicada** n. winged chirping insect.

**cicatrice** n. a scar.

**cider** n. drink of fermented apple juice.

**cigar** n. tight roll of tobacco leaves for smoking.

**cigarette** n. finely-cut tobacco rolled in paper for smoking.

**cilium** n. (pl. **cilia**) 1 hairlike structure on animal cells. 2 eyelash. □□ **ciliary** adj.

**cinch** n. colloq. certainty; easy task.

**cinder** n. residue of coal etc. after burning.

**cine-** comb. form cinematographic.

**cinema** n. theatre where films are shown; films collectively; art or industry of producing films. □□ **cinematic** adj.

**cinematography** n. art of making and projecting films. □□ **cinematographer** n. **cinematographic** adj.

**cineraria** n. plant with bright flowers.

**cinnabar** n. 1 red mercuric sulphide. 2 vermilion.

**cinnamon** n. 1 aromatic spice from dried bark of SE Asian tree; this tree. 2 yellowish-brown.

**cipher** (also **cypher**) n. 1 secret or disguised writing; key to this. 2 arithmetical symbol 0. 3 person or thing of no importance.

**circa** prep. about, approximately.

**circle** ● n. 1 perfectly round plane figure. 2 roundish enclosure, structure, or road. 3 curved upper tier of seats in theatre etc. 4 group with similar interests or shared acquaintances. ● v. move in or form circle.

**circlet** n. small circle; circular band, esp. as ornament.

**circuit** n. 1 line, route, or distance around a place. 2 path of electric current.

**circuitous** adj. indirect; roundabout.

**circuitry** n. system of electric circuits.

**circular** ● adj. shaped like or moving around a circle. ● n. leaflet sent to a circle of people. □□ **circularity** n.

**circulate** v. go or send around.

**circulation** n. 1 circulating; movement of blood from and to heart. 2 number of copies sold, esp. of a newspaper. □□ **circulatory** adj.

**circumcise** v. cut off foreskin. □□ **circumcision** n.

**circumference** n. line enclosing circle; distance around.

**circumflex** n. (in full **circumflex accent**) mark (^) over vowel indicating pronunciation.

**circumlocution** n. roundabout expression; evasive talk; verbosity. □□ **circumlocutory** adj.

**circumnavigate** v. sail around; go around or avoid (obstacle). □□ **circumnavigation** n.

**circumscribe** v. enclose or outline; lay down limits of; confine, restrict. □□ **circumscription** n.

**circumspect** adj. cautious; taking everything into account. □□ **circumspection** n.

**circumstance** n. occurrence or fact.

**circumstantial** adj. 1 (of evidence) suggesting but not proving something. 2 detailed.

**circumvent** v. evade; outwit.

**circus** n. 1 travelling show of performing acrobats, clowns, animals, etc. 2 colloq. scene of lively action.

**cirque** n. bowl-shaped hollow on mountain or valley.

**cirrhosis** n. chronic liver disease. □□ **cirrhotic** adj.

**cirrus** n. (pl. cirri) white wispy cloud.

**cisgender** adj. of a person whose sense of personal identity and gender corresponds with their birth sex.

**cistern** n. tank for storing water.

**citadel** n. fortress protecting or dominating city.

**citation** n. 1 citing or passage cited. 2 description of reasons for award.

**cite** v. 1 mention as example. 2 quote (book etc.) in support. 3 mention in official dispatch. 4 summon to lawcourt.

**citizen** n. 1 member of nation, either native or naturalised. 2 inhabitant of city. □□ **citizenship** n.

**citrate** n. salt of citric acid.

**citric acid** n. acid in juice of lemons, limes, etc.

**citron** n. tree bearing large lemon-like fruits; this fruit.

**citronella** n. a fragrant oil; grass from S. Asia yielding it.

**citrus** n. tree or fruit of group including lemon, orange, etc.

**city** n. 1 large town. 2 Aust. town qualified for city status; business part of city.

**civet** n. (in full **civet cat**) catlike animal of Central Africa; strong musky perfume obtained from it.

**civic** adj. of city or citizenship.

**civil** adj. 1 of or belonging to citizens; non-military. 2 polite, obliging. 3 Law concerning private rights and not criminal offences. □ **civil engineering** design and construction of roads, bridges, etc. **civil servant** = public servant. **civil war** war between citizens of same country. □□ **civilly** adv.

**civilian** n. person not in esp. armed forces. ● adj. of or for civilians.

**civilisation** n. (also **-ization**) 1 advanced stage of social development; progress towards this; comfort and convenience. 2 culture and way of life of particular area or period.

**civilise** v. (also **-ize**) cause to improve to developed stage of society; improve behaviour of.

**civility** n. politeness.

**clack** ● v. make sharp sound as of boards struck together. ● n. such sound.

**clad** adj. clothed; provided with cladding.

**cladding** n. covering or coating.

**claim** ● v. 1 assert. 2 demand as one's right. ● n. 1 demand or request. 2 application for compensation under terms of insurance policy. 3 right or title. 4 assertion. 5 thing claimed.

**claimant** n. person making claim, esp. in lawsuit.

**clairvoyance** n. supposed faculty of perceiving the future or the unseen. □□ **clairvoyant** n. & adj.

**clam** ● n. edible bivalve mollusc. ● v. (**clammed**) colloq. refuse to talk.

**clamber** v. climb using hands and feet or with difficulty.

**clammy** adj. damp and sticky.

**clamour** (also **clamor**) ● n. shouting, confused noise; protest, demand. ● v. make clamour; shout. □□ **clamorous** adj.

**clamp** ● n. device for holding things together tightly; device for immobilising illegally parked vehicle. ● v. strengthen or fasten with clamp; immobilise with clamp.

□ **clamp down on** become firmer about, put a stop to.

**clan** n. group of families with common ancestor, esp. among Aboriginal people and in Scotland; family as social group. □□ **clannish** adj.

**clandestine** adj. surreptitious, secret. □□ **clandestinely** adv.

**clang** ● n. loud resonant metallic sound. ● v. (cause) to make clang.

**clanger** n. colloq. mistake, blunder.

**clangour** n. continued clanging. □□ **clangorous** adj.

**clap** ● v. (clapped) strike palms loudly together, esp. in applause; strike or put quickly or vigorously. ● n. 1 act of clapping. 2 explosive sound, esp. of thunder. 3 slap. □□ **clapper** n.

**clapperboard** n. device in film-making for making sharp clap for synchronising picture and sound at start of scene.

**claptrap** n. pretentious talk; nonsense.

**claret** n. dry red wine; purplish-red.

**clarify** v. 1 make or become clear. 2 free from impurities. 3 make transparent. □□ **clarification** n.

**clarinet** n. woodwind instrument with single reed. □□ **clarinettist** n.

**clarion** n. clear rousing sound.

**clarity** n. clearness.

**clash** ● n. 1 loud jarring sound as of metal objects struck together; collision. 2 discord of colours etc. ● v. (cause to) make clash; coincide awkwardly; be at variance or discordant.

**clasp** ● n. device with interlocking parts for fastening; embrace; handshake. ● v. fasten (as) with clasp; embrace.

**class** ● n. set of people or things with characteristics in common; standard of quality; rank of society; set of students taught together. ● v. place in class. □ **class act** colloq. person or

thing displaying impressive and stylish excellence. **class action** lawsuit filed or defended by an individual acting on behalf of a group.

**classic** ● adj. 1 first-class; of lasting importance. 2 typical. 3 of ancient Greek and Latin culture etc. 4 (of style) simple and harmonious. ● n. 1 classic writer, artist, work, or example. 2 thing that is memorable and very good example of its kind. 3 (classics) study of ancient Greek and Latin. □□ **classicism** n. **classicist** n.

**classical** adj. 1 of ancient Greek or Latin literature etc. 2 traditional in form and style; serious or conventional.

**classified** adj. 1 arranged in classes. 2 (of information etc.) designated as officially secret. 3 (of newspaper advertisements) arranged according to categories.

**classify** v. 1 arrange systematically, class. 2 designate as officially secret. □□ **classification** n. **classificatory** adj.

**classless** adj. without distinctions of social class.

**classy** adj. colloq. superior, stylish. □□ **classiness** n.

**clatter** ● n. sound of hard objects struck together. ● v. (cause to) make clatter.

**clause** n. 1 part of sentence, including subject and predicate. 2 single statement in treaty, law, contract, etc.

**claustrophobia** n. abnormal fear of confined places. □□ **claustrophobic** adj.

**clavichord** n. small keyboard instrument with very soft tone.

**clavicle** n. collar bone.

**claw** ● n. pointed nail on animal's foot; foot armed with claws; pincers of shellfish; device for grappling, holding, etc. ● v. scratch, maul, or pull with claws or fingernails.

**clay** n. stiff sticky earth, used for making bricks, pottery, etc.

□ **clay pigeon** breakable disc thrown up as a target for shooting.
□□ **clayey** adj.

**Clayton's** n. propr. Aust. something that is largely illusory or exists in name only; imitation.

**clean** ● adj. **1** free from dirt; clear; pristine. **2** not obscene or indecent. **3** clear-cut. **4** without record of crime etc. **5** fair. ● adv. **1** completely. **2** in a clean way. ● n. make or become clean. ● n. process of cleaning.
□□ **cleaner** n.

**cleanliness** n. state of being personally clean, attentive to personal hygiene.

**cleanse** v. make clean or pure.
□□ **cleanser** n.

**clear** ● adj. **1** transparent. **2** free from doubt, difficulties, obstacles, etc. **3** easily seen, heard, or understood. ● v. **1** make or become clear. **2** prove innocent. **3** remove trees from (land). **4** get past or over. **5** make as net profit. □ **clear off** colloq. go away. **clear out 1** empty, tidy. **2** colloq. go away. □□ **clearly** adv. **clearness** n.

**clearance** n. **1** removal of obstructions, contents, etc. **2** space allowed for passing of two objects. **3** special authorisation. **4** clearing of cheque etc. **5** clearing out.

**clearing** n. open area in forest.
□ **clearing house** office at which banks exchange cheques; agency collecting and distributing information.

**cleat** n. projecting piece on sole of boot or device for fastening ropes etc.

**cleavage** n. **1** hollow between woman's breasts; division; line along which rocks etc. split.

**cleave** v. (cleaved, clove, or cleft; cleaved, cloven, or cleft; cleaving) literary split; divide.

**cleaver** n. butcher's heavy chopping tool.

**clef** n. Mus. symbol indicating the pitch of notes on staff.

**cleft** ● adj. split, partly divided. ● adj. a cleavage. □ **cleft palate** congenital split in roof of mouth.

**clematis** n. climbing flowering plant.

**clemency** n. mercy. □□ **clement** adj.

**clench** ● v. close tightly; grasp firmly. ● n. clenching action; clenched state.

**clerestory** n. upper row of windows in church etc.

**clergy** n. those ordained for religious duties. □□ **clergyman** n. **clergywoman** n.

**cleric** n. member of clergy.

**clerical** adj. **1** of or done by clerks. **2** of clergy or clergymen.

**clerk** ● n. person employed in office etc. to keep records, accounts, etc. ● v. work as clerk.

**clever** adj. **1** skilful, talented; quick to understand and learn; adroit, ingenious. **2** Aust. (in Aboriginal English) wise, learned in traditional lore, and spiritually powerful.
□□ **cleverly** adv. **cleverness** n.

**cliché** n. (also **cliche**) overused phrase or opinion. □□ **clichéd** adj.

**click** ● n. **1** slight sharp sound. **2** Computing act of pressing a button or touching a screen. **3** colloq. kilometre. ● v. **1** (cause to) make click. **2** (also **klick**) colloq. become clear, understood, or popular. **3** become friendly with. **4** Computing select by pressing a button or touching a screen.

**client** n. person using services of professional person; customer.

**clientele** n. clients collectively; customers.

**cliff** n. steep rock face, esp. on coast.

**cliffhanger** n. story or contest full of suspense.

**climate** n. prevailing weather conditions of area; region with particular weather conditions; prevailing trend of opinion etc.

☐ **climate change** change in global or regional climate patterns attributed largely to the increased levels of atmospheric carbon dioxide.
☐☐ **climatic** adj. **climatically** adv.

**climax** ● n. event or point of greatest intensity or interest; culmination. ● v. reach or bring to climax. ☐☐ **climactic** adj.

**climb** ● v. go up; rise. ● n. action of climbing; hill etc. (to be) climbed; an increase. ☐☐ **climber** n.

**clime** n. literary region; climate.

**clinch** ● v. confirm or settle conclusively; fasten; grapple. ● n. close hold or embrace.

**cline** n. Biol. graded sequence of differences within species etc.

**cling** v. adhere; be emotionally dependent on or unwilling to give up; maintain grasp. ☐☐ **clingy** adj.

**clinic** n. private or specialised hospital; place or occasion for giving medical treatment or specialist advice.

**clinical** adj. **1** of or for treatment of patients. **2** objective, coldly detached. **3** (of room etc.) bare, functional. ☐☐ **clinically** adv.

**clink** ● n. sharp ringing sound. ● v. make this sound.

**clinker** n. **1** mass of slag or lava. **2** stony residue from burnt coal. **3** (in full **clinker brick**) hard brick used esp. for paving.

**clip** ● n. **1** device for holding things tightly or together; act of clipping; piece clipped from something. **2** sharp blow. ● v. (**clipped**) **1** fix or fasten with clip. **2** cut with shears or scissors. **3** colloq. hit sharply.

**clipboard** n. **1** small board with spring clip for holding papers etc. **2** Computing temporary storage area where data copied from a file is kept until pasted into another file.

**clipper** n. **1** (**clippers**) instrument for clipping hair, hedges, etc. **2** fast sailing ship.

**clipping** n. piece clipped from newspaper.

**clique** n. small exclusive group of people. ☐☐ **cliquey** adj. **cliquish** adj.

**clitoris** n. small erectile part of female genitals.

**cloak** ● n. loose usu. sleeveless outdoor garment; covering.
● v. cover with cloak; conceal, disguise.

**clobber** ● v. colloq. hit repeatedly; defeat; criticise severely. ● n. colloq. clothing, belongings.

**clock** ● n. **1** instrument for measuring and showing time; any measuring device resembling this. **2** elapsed time as element in competitive sports etc. ● v. colloq. attain or register (distance etc.); time (race) with stopwatch. ☐ **clock in** (or **on**, **off**, or **out**) register one's time of arrival or departure. **round the clock** all day and (usu.) night.

**clockwise** adv. & adj. moving in direction of hands of clock.

**clockwork** n. mechanism with wheels and springs. ☐ **like clockwork** smoothly, regularly.

**clod** n. lump of earth or clay.

**clog** ● n. wooden-soled shoe.
● v. (**clogged**) (cause to) become obstructed; choke; impede.

**cloister** n. **1** covered walk, esp. in ecclesiastical building, college, etc. **2** monastic life, seclusion.

**cloistered** adj. shut away, sheltered, secluded.

**clone** ● n. **1** group of plants or organisms produced asexually from one ancestor. **2** person or thing regarded as identical with another; an identical copy. ● v. propagate as clone.

**close** ● adj. **1** near in space or time. **2** dear to each other. **3** dense, concentrated. **4** secretive; stingy. **5** stuffy, humid. ● adv. closely; in a near position. ● v. **1** shut; bring or come to an end. **2** bring or come nearer together. ● *n.* conclusion or end; street closed at one end; grounds surrounding cathedral. □ **close-up** photograph etc. taken at short range. □□ **closely** *adv.* **closeness** *n.*

**closet** ● *n.* small room; cupboard. ● *adj.* secret. ● *v.* (**closeted**) shut away in private conference or in study. □ **come out of the closet** make public what was previously concealed, esp. one's homosexuality.

**closure** *n.* closing; closed state; conclusion.

**clot** ● *n.* **1** thick lump formed from liquid, esp. blood. **2** *colloq.* foolish person. ● *v.* (**clotted**) form into clots.

**cloth** *n.* **1** woven or felted material; piece of this. **2** (**the cloth**) clergy.

**clothe** *v.* put clothes on; provide with clothes; cover as with clothes.

**clothes** *n.pl.* things worn to cover the body.

**clothing** *n.* clothes.

**cloud** ● *n.* **1** visible mass of condensed watery vapour floating in air; mass of smoke or dust; great number of (insects, birds, etc.) moving together. **2** state of gloom, trouble, or suspicion. **3** network of remote servers hosted on Internet and used to store, manage, and process data. ● *v.* **1** cover or darken with cloud(s); become overcast or gloomy. **2** make unclear. □□ **cloudless** *adj.*

**cloudy** *adj.* covered with clouds; not transparent; unclear. □□ **cloudiness** *n.*

**clout** ● *n.* **1** heavy blow. **2** influence, power of effective action. ● *v.* hit hard.

**clove** ● *n.* **1** dried bud of tropical plant, used as spice. **2** segment of compound bulb, esp. of garlic. ● *v.* see CLEAVE. □ **clove hitch** knot used to fasten rope around pole etc.

**clover** *n.* kind of trefoil fodder plant.

**clown** ● *n.* comic entertainer, esp. in circus; foolish or playful person. ● *v.* behave like clown.

**cloy** *v.* satiate or sicken by sweetness, richness, etc.

**club** ● *n.* **1** heavy stick used as weapon; stick with head used in golf. **2** association of people for social, sporting etc. purposes; premises of this. **3** playing card of suit marked with black trefoils. ● *v.* (**clubbed**) **1** beat (as) with club. **2** combine, esp. to raise sum of money. **3** *colloq.* go out to nightclub(s).

**cluck** ● *n.* chattering cry of hen. ● *v.* emit cluck(s).

**clucky** *adj. Aust. colloq.* (of woman) wanting to have a baby.

**clue** *n.* fact or idea giving guide to solution of problem.

**cluey** *adj. colloq.* knowledgeable; alert.

**clump** ● *n.* cluster, esp. of trees. ● *v.* **1** form clump; heap or plant together. **2** tread heavily.

**clumsy** *adj.* awkward in movement or shape; difficult to handle or use; tactless. □□ **clumsily** *adv.* **clumsiness** *n.*

**clung** see CLING.

**cluster** ● *n.* close group or bunch of similar people or things. ● *v.* be in or form into cluster(s); gather.

**clutch** ● *v.* seize eagerly; grasp tightly; snatch at. ● *n.* **1** a tight grasp. **2** (in vehicle) device for connecting engine to transmission. **3** set of eggs for hatching; chickens hatched from these. **4** small handbag without handles or strap.

**clutter** ● *n.* crowded and untidy collection of things. ● *v.* crowd untidily, fill with clutter.

**cm** *abbr.* centimetre(s).

**CO** *abbr.* Commanding Officer.

**Co.** *abbr.* company.

**c/o** *abbr.* (also **c/-**) care of.

**coach** ● *n.* **1** bus, usu. comfortably equipped for long journeys;

railway carriage; closed horse-drawn carriage. **2** trainer or private tutor.
● *v.* train or teach as coach; give hints to.

**coagulate** *v.* change from liquid to semi-solid; clot, curdle. □□ **coagulant** *n.* **coagulation** *n.*

**coal** *n.* hard black rock used as fuel.

**coalesce** *v.* come together and form a whole. □□ **coalescence** *n.* **coalescent** *adj.*

**coalition** *n.* temporary alliance, esp. of political parties; fusion into one whole.

**coarse** *adj.* **1** rough or loose in texture; of large particles. **2** lacking refinement; crude, obscene.
□□ **coarsely** *adv.* **coarsen** *v.* **coarseness** *n.*

**coast** ● *n.* border of land near sea; seashore. ● *v.* ride or move (usu. downhill) without use of power; make progress without exertion.
□□ **coastal** *adj.*

**coaster** *n.* **1** ship that sails along coast. **2** tray or mat for bottle or glass.

**coat** ● *n.* outer garment with sleeves; overcoat, jacket; covering layer; layer of paint etc. ● *v.* cover with coat or layer; form covering to. □ **coat of arms** design on shield as emblem of family, institution, etc.

**coating** *n.* layer of paint etc.

**coax** *v.* persuade gradually or by flattery; obtain (thing) from (person) thus; manipulate gently.

**coaxial** *adj.* **1** having common axis. **2** (of electric cable etc.) transmitting by means of two concentric conductors separated by insulator.

**cob** *n.* **1** roundish lump. **2** corn cob. **3** sturdy short-legged riding horse. **4** male swan.

**cobalt** *n.* **1** silvery-white metallic element (symbol **Co**). **2** (colour of) deep blue pigment made from it.

**cobber** *n. Aust. colloq.* companion, friend, mate.

**cobble** ● *n.* rounded stone used for paving. ● *v.* mend roughly.

**cobbler** *n.* mender of shoes.

**cobra** *n.* venomous hooded snake.

**cobweb** *n.* spider's network or thread. □□ **cobwebby** *adj.*

**coca** *n.* S. American shrub; its leaves, chewed as stimulant.

**cocaine** *n.* drug derived from coca, used as stimulant and sometimes as local anaesthetic.

**coccyx** *n.* (*pl.* **coccyges**) bone at base of spinal column.

**cochineal** *n.* scarlet dye; insects whose dried bodies yield this.

**cochlea** *n.* (*pl.* **cochleae**) spiral cavity of inner ear.

**cock** ● *n.* **1** male bird, esp. of domestic fowl. **2** *coarse colloq.* penis. **3** *colloq.* nonsense. **4** firing lever in gun, released by trigger. **5** tap or valve controlling flow. ● *v.* **1** raise or make upright. **2** turn or move (eye or ear) attentively or knowingly. **3** set (hat etc.) aslant. **4** raise cock of (gun).

**cockade** *n.* rosette etc. worn in hat.

**cockatiel** *n.* (also **cockateel**) *Aust.* small crested parrot.

**cockatoo** *n.* **1** any of several parrots having powerful beak and erectile crest. **2** *Aust.* lookout posted by those engaged in illegal activity.

**cockerel** *n.* young rooster.

**cockle** *n.* edible bivalve shellfish.

**cockney** ● *n.* native of East End of London; cockney dialect. ● *adj.* of cockneys.

**cockpit** *n.* compartment for pilot etc. in aircraft or spacecraft or for driver in racing car.

**cockroach** *n.* beetle-like insect.

**cockscomb** *n.* rooster's crest.

**cocksure** *adj.* arrogantly confident.

**cocktail** *n.* **1** drink of spirits, fruit juices, etc. **2** appetiser containing shellfish etc. **3** any hybrid mixture.

**cocky** ● *adj. colloq.* conceited, arrogant. ● *n. Aust. colloq.*

**1** cockatoo. **2** farmer with small holding; farm or rural interests generally.□□ **cockiness** n.

**cocoa** n. powder made from crushed cacao seeds; drink made from this.

**coconut** n. nut of tropical palm; its edible lining.

**cocoon** ● n. silky case spun by larva to protect it as pupa; protective covering. ● v. wrap (as) in cocoon.

**COD** abbr. cash on delivery.

**cod** n. **1** large sea fish. **2** Aust. Murray cod.

**coda** n. final passage of piece of music.

**coddle** v. **1** treat as invalid; pamper. **2** cook (egg) in water below boiling point.□□ **coddler** n.

**code** ● n. **1** system of signals or symbols etc., used for secrecy, brevity, or computer processing of information. **2** systematic set of laws etc.; standard of moral behaviour. ● v. put into code.

**codeine** n. alkaloid derived from morphine, used to relieve pain.

**codex** n. (pl. **codices**) **1** manuscript volume esp. of ancient texts. **2** collection of descriptions of drugs etc.

**codicil** n. addition to will.

**codify** v. arrange (laws etc.) into code. □□ **codification** n.

**codling** n. (also **codlin**) variety of apple; (in full **codling moth**) moth whose larva feeds on apples.

**co-education** n. education of both sexes together.□□ **co-educational** adj.

**coefficient** n. multiplier; quantity or expression placed before and multiplying another; factor by which a property is measured.

**coeliac disease** n. intestinal disease with symptoms including adverse reaction to gluten.

**coerce** v. persuade or restrain by force.□□ **coercion** n. **coercive** adj.

**coeval** formal ● adj. of the same age; contemporary. ● n. coeval person or thing.

**coexist** v. exist together, esp. in mutual tolerance.□□ **coexistence** n. **coexistent** adj.

**coffee** n. drink made from roasted and ground seeds of tropical shrub; cup of this; the shrub; its seeds; pale brown.

**coffer** n. large box for valuables; (**coffers**) financial resources.

**coffin** n. box in which corpse is buried or cremated.

**cog** n. each of series of projections on wheel etc. transferring motion by engaging with another series.

**cogent** adj. (of argument etc.) convincing, compelling.
□□ **cogency** n. **cogently** adv.

**cogitate** v. ponder, meditate.
□□ **cogitation** n.

**cognac** n. French brandy.

**cognate** ● adj. descended from same ancestor or root. ● n. cognate person or word.

**cognisant** adj. (also **cognizant**) having knowledge or being aware of.
□□ **cognisance** n.

**cognition** n. knowing, perceiving, or conceiving, as distinct from emotion and volition.□□ **cognitional** adj. **cognitive** adj.

**cohabit** v. live together.
□□ **cohabitation** n.

**cohere** v. stick together.

**coherent** adj. logical; articulate; forming consistent whole.
□□ **coherence** n. **coherently** adv.

**cohesion** n. sticking together; tendency to cohere.□□ **cohesive** adj.

**cohort** n. one tenth of Roman legion; group or set of people.

**coiffure** n. hairstyle.

**coil** ● v. **1** arrange or be arranged in concentric rings. **2** move sinuously. ● n. **1** coiled arrangement (of rope, electrical conductor, etc.);

single turn of something coiled.
**2** flexible contraceptive device placed in uterus.

**coin** ● *n.* piece of metal money.
● *v.* **1** make (coins) by stamping.
**2** invent (word, phrase).

**coinage** *n.* **1** coining; system of coins in use. **2** invention of word, invented word.

**coincide** *v.* occur at same time; agree or be identical.

**coincidence** *n.* remarkable concurrence of events, apparently by chance.□□ **coincident** *adj.*

**coincidental** *adj.* in the nature of or resulting from coincidence.
□□ **coincidentally** *adv.*

**coir** *n.* coconut fibre used for ropes, matting, etc.

**coitus** *n.* sexual intercourse.
□□ **coital** *adj.*

**coke** ● *n.* **1** solid left after gases have been extracted from coal. **2** *colloq.* cocaine. ● *v.* convert (coal) into coke.

**col** *n.* **1** depression in summit line of mountain chain. **2** *Meteorol.* low pressure region between anticyclones.

**Col.** *abbr.* Colonel.

**col.** *abbr.* column.

**cola** *n.* W. African tree with seeds containing caffeine; carbonated drink flavoured with these.

**colander** *n.* perforated vessel used as strainer in cookery.

**cold** ● *adj.* **1** at or having a low temperature. **2** not affectionate; not enthusiastic. ● *n.* **1** low temperature; cold weather. **2** infection of nose or throat causing catarrh and sneezing. ● *adv.* unrehearsed.
□ **cold-blooded 1** having blood temperature varying with that of surroundings. **2** unfeeling, ruthless.
**cold-call** unsolicited visit or telephone call made by someone trying to sell goods etc. **cold case** unsolved criminal investigation. **cold feet** *colloq.* loss of

nerve or confidence. **cold-shoulder** treat with deliberate unfriendliness.
**cold turkey** *colloq.* sudden withdrawal of drugs from addict. **cold war** hostility between nations without fighting.□□ **coldly** *adv.*
**coldness** *n.*

**coleslaw** *n.* salad of sliced raw cabbage etc.

**colic** *n.* spasmodic abdominal pain.
□□ **colicky** *adj.*

**colitis** *n.* inflammation of colon.

**collaborate** *v.* work together.
□□ **collaboration** *n.* **collaborative** *adj.* **collaborator** *n.*

**collage** *n.* picture made by glueing pieces of paper etc. on to backing.

**collagen** *n.* protein found in animal connective tissue, yielding gelatine on boiling.

**collapse** ● *n.* falling down of structure; sudden failure of plan etc.; physical or mental breakdown.
● *v.* **1** (cause to) undergo collapse.
**2** *colloq.* relax completely after effort.
**3** compress a displayed part of (electronic document).
□□ **collapsible** *adj.*

**collar** ● *n.* neckband, upright or turned over, of coat, shirt, dress, etc.; leather etc. band around animal's neck; band, ring, or pipe in machinery; marking resembling collar around neck of bird or animal.
● *v.* **1** capture, seize; gain control over. **2** *colloq.* accost.

**collate** *v.* collect and put in order.
□□ **collator** *n.*

**collateral** ● *n.* security pledged as guarantee for repayment of loan. ● *adj.* **1** side by side.
**2** additional but subordinate.
**3** descended from same ancestor but by different line.
□□ **collaterally** *adv.*

**collation** *n.* **1** collating. **2** light meal.

**colleague** *n.* fellow worker, esp. in profession or business.

**collect** v. bring or come together; obtain specimens of, esp. as hobby; fetch. □□ **collectable** adj. & n. (also **collectible**)

**collected** adj. calm and controlled.

**collection** n. collecting, being collected; things collected; money collected, esp. at church service etc.

**collective** ● adj. of or relating to group or society as a whole; joint; shared. ● n. cooperative enterprise; its members. □ **collective noun** Gram. noun (singular in any form) denoting a group, e.g. family. □□ **collectively** adv.

**collector** n. person who collects things.

**college** n. 1 establishment for further, higher, or professional education; college premises; students and teachers in college; organised body of persons with shared functions and privileges. 2 upper secondary school; private school.

**collegiate** adj. 1 of, or constituted as, college. 2 corporate.

**collide** v. come into collision or conflict.

**collie** n. sheepdog orig. of Scottish breed.

**colliery** n. coalmine and its buildings.

**collimate** v. adjust line of sight of (telescope etc.); make (rays etc.) accurately parallel.

**collision** n. violent impact of moving body against another or fixed object; clashing of interests etc.

**collocate** v. place (words) together. □□ **collocation** n.

**colloid** n. substance consisting of minute particles; mixture, esp. viscous solution of this and another substance. □□ **colloidal** adj.

**colloquial** adj. of ordinary or familiar conversation, informal. □□ **colloquially** adv.

**colloquium** n. (pl. **colloquiums** or **colloquia**) academic conference or seminar.

**collude** v. conspire. □□ **collusion** n. **collusive** adj.

**cologne** n. light perfume.

**colon** n. 1 punctuation mark (:), used between main clauses or before quotation or list. 2 lower and greater part of large intestine.

**colonel** n. army officer commanding regiment. □□ **colonelcy** n.

**colonial** ● adj. of colony or colonies; of colonialism. ● n. inhabitant of colony.

**colonialism** n. policy of acquiring or maintaining colonies.

**colonise** v. (also **-ize**) 1 establish colony in; join colony. 2 (of plants and animals) become established in an area. □□ **colonisation** n.

**colonnade** n. row of columns, esp. supporting roof. □□ **colonnaded** adj.

**colonoscopy** n. medical examination of colon.

**colony** n. 1 settlement or settlers in new territory remaining subject to mother country. 2 people of one nationality, occupation, etc. forming community in city etc. 3 group of animals etc. living close together. □□ **colonist** n.

**colophon** n. 1 publisher's emblem on title page. 2 hist. publisher's material at end of book.

**color** = COLOUR.

**coloration** n. (also **colouration**) colouring; arrangement of colours.

**coloratura** n. elaborate passages in vocal music; singer of these, esp. soprano.

**colossal** adj. 1 huge. 2 colloq. splendid. □□ **colossally** adv.

**colossus** n. (pl. **colossi** or **colossuses**) statue much bigger than life size; gigantic or remarkable person etc.

**colostomy** n. operation on colon to make opening in abdominal wall to provide artificial anus.

**colour** (also **color**) ● n. sensation produced by rays of light of particular wavelengths; pigment, paint; **(colours)** coloured ribbon, uniform etc. worn as symbol of school, club, etc.; flag of regiment or ship. ● v. put colour on; stain, dye; blush; give a special character or bias to.

**coloured** (also **colored**) ● adj. **1** having colour. **2** wholly or partly of non-White descent. ● n. coloured person.

**colourful** adj. (also **color-**) full of colour or interest. □□ **colourfully** adv.

**colouring** n. (also **color-**) appearance as regards colour, esp. facial complexion; application of colour; substance giving colour.

**colposcopy** n. examination of vagina and neck of uterus. □□ **colposcope** n.

**colt** n. **1** young male horse. **2** Sport inexperienced player.

**columbine** n. garden plant with purple-blue flowers.

**column** n. **1** pillar, usu. round and with base and capital; column-shaped thing. **2** series of numbers. **3** vertical division of printed page. **4** part of newspaper regularly devoted to particular subject or written by one writer. **5** long narrow arrangement of troops, vehicles, etc.

**columnist** n. journalist contributing regularly to newspaper etc.

**coma** n. prolonged deep unconsciousness.

**comatose** adj. in coma; lethargic; unconscious.

**comb** ● n. **1** toothed strip of rigid material for arranging hair; thing like comb. **2** red fleshy crest of fowl, esp. rooster. ● v. **1** draw comb through (hair). **2** colloq. search (place) thoroughly.

**combat** ● n. fight, struggle. ● v. do battle (with); oppose; strive against.

**combatant** ● n. fighter. ● adj. fighting.

**combative** adj. pugnacious.

**comber** n. long curling wave; breaker.

**combination** n. combining, being combined; combined set of things or people; sequence of numbers etc.

**combine** ● v. join together; unite; form into chemical compound. ● n. combination of esp. businesses.

**combustible** ● adj. capable of or used for burning. ● n. combustible substance. □□ **combustibility** n.

**combustion** n. burning; development of light and heat from combination of substance with oxygen.

**come** ● v. (**came**, **come**, **coming**) **1** move or be brought towards or reach a place, time, situation, or result. **2** be available. **3** occur. **4** become. **5** traverse. **6** colloq. behave like. ● n. coarse colloq. semen ejaculated. □ **come about** happen. **come across** meet or find unexpectedly. **come by** obtain. **come into** inherit. **come off** be successful. **come out** become visible; emerge; declare one's feelings openly. **come round** recover from fainting; be converted to the speaker's opinion.

**comeback** n. **1** return to success, former status, etc. **2** colloq. retort or retaliation.

**comedian** n. humorous entertainer or comedy actor.

**comedienne** n. female comedian.

**comedy** n. play or film of amusing character; humorous kind of drama etc.; amusing aspects. □□ **comedic** adj.

**comely** adj. literary handsome, good-looking. □□ **comeliness** n.

**comet** n. heavenly body with luminous tail of gas and dust.

**come-uppance** n. colloq. deserved punishment.

**comfort** ● *n.* state of ease and contentment; relief of suffering or grief; person or thing giving this. ● *v.* give comfort to.

**comfortable** *adj.* 1 giving ease; at ease. 2 having adequate standard of living. 3 appreciable. □□ **comfortably** *adv.*

**comfy** *adj. colloq.* comfortable.

**comic** ● *adj.* of or like comedy; funny. ● *n.* 1 comedian. 2 periodical in form of strip cartoons. □□ **comical** *adj.* **comically** *adv.*

**comma** *n.* punctuation mark ( , ) marking pause or break between parts of sentence.

**command** ● *v.* 1 give formal order to. 2 have authority or control over. 3 have at one's disposal. 4 deserve and get. 5 look down over. 6 dominate. ● *n.* 1 order; instruction. 2 mastery, control. 3 possess. 4 holding of authority, esp. in armed forces; body of troops or district under commander.

**commandant** *n.* commanding officer, esp. of military academy.

**commandeer** *v.* seize for use.

**commander** *n.* person who commands.

**commanding** *adj.* 1 impressive. 2 giving wide view. 3 substantial.

**commandment** *n.* divine command.

**commando** *n.* member of military unit specially trained for making raids and assaults.

**commemorate** *v.* preserve in memory by celebration or ceremony; be memorial of. □□ **commemoration** *n.* **commemorative** *adj.*

**commence** *v.* begin. □□ **commencement** *n.*

**commend** *v.* 1 praise. 2 recommend. 3 entrust. □□ **commendation** *n.*

**commendable** *adj.* praiseworthy.

**commensurable** *adj.* measurable by same standard; proportionate to. □□ **commensurability** *n.*

**commensurate** *adj.* extending over same space or time; proportionate.

**comment** ● *n.* brief critical or explanatory remark or note; opinion. ● *v.* make comment(s).

**commentariat** *n.* members of news media considered as a class.

**commentary** *n.* 1 broadcast description of event as it happens. 2 set of explanatory notes on book, performance, etc.

**commentate** *v.* act as commentator.

**commentator** *n.* writer or speaker of commentary.

**commerce** *n.* buying and selling; trading.

**commercial** ● *adj.* 1 of or engaged in commerce; done or run primarily for financial profit. 2 (of broadcasting) financed by advertising. ● *n.* television or radio advertisement. □□ **commercially** *adv.*

**commercialise** *v.* (also -ize) exploit or spoil for profit; make commercial. □□ **commercialisation** *n.*

**commingle** *v. literary* mix, unite.

**comminute** *v.* reduce to small fragments; divide (property) into small portions.

**commiserate** *v.* express or feel sympathy. □□ **commiseration** *n.*

**commissariat** *n.* department responsible for supply of food etc. for army; food supplied.

**commissary** *n.* deputy, delegate.

**commission** ● *n.* 1 committing. 2 authority to perform task; person(s) given such authority. 3 government utility. 4 warrant conferring rank of officer in armed forces; rank so conferred. 5 pay or percentage received by agent. ● *v.* 1 give commission to. 2 place order for. □ **in commission** ready for service. **out of commission** not in working order.

**commissionaire** *n.* uniformed door attendant.

**commissioner** n. person commissioned to perform specific task; member of government commission; representative of government in district.

**commit** v. (**committed**) 1 do; perform. 2 entrust, consign. 3 pledge to course of action. 4 order accused person to be tried by jury.

**commitment** n. 1 engagement or obligation; process or instance of committing or being committed. 2 dedication. 3 pledge or undertaking.

**committal** n. 1 act of committing, esp. to prison, etc. 2 (in full **committal hearing** or **proceedings**) proceedings before magistrate to determine whether there is sufficient evidence to warrant trial by jury.

**committee** n. group of people appointed for special function by (and usu. out of) larger body.

**commode** n. chamber pot in chair with cover.

**commodious** adj. roomy.

**commodity** n. article of trade.

**commodore** n. naval officer; commander of squadron or other division of fleet; president of yacht club.

**common** adj. 1 of or affecting all; occurring often. 2 ordinary; of inferior quality.□ **common law** unwritten law based on custom and former court decisions. **common room** room shared by students or workers for social purposes. **common sense** normal good sense in practical matters.

**commonalty** n. common people; general community.

**commonly** adv. usually, frequently.

**commonplace** ● adj. lacking originality; ordinary. ● n. event, topic, etc. that is ordinary or usual; trite remark.

**commonwealth** n. independent nation or community; (**the Commonwealth**) title of federated states and territories of Australia; the government of this federation; international association of nations previously part of the British Empire with the UK.

**commotion** n. noisy disturbance, uproar.

**communal** adj. shared among members of group or community. □□ **communally** adv.

**commune**[1] n. group of people sharing accommodation and goods.

**commune**[2] v. 1 speak intimately. 2 feel in close touch.

**communicable** adj. (esp. of disease) able to be passed on.

**communicant** n. receiver of Holy Communion.

**communicate** v. transmit or pass on by speaking or writing; exchange, convey (information, feelings, etc.) □□ **communicator** n.

**communication** n. sharing or imparting information; letter or message; (**communications**) means of communicating or of travelling.

**communicative** adj. ready to talk and impart information.

**communion** n. 1 sharing, esp. of thoughts, interests, etc. 2 fellowship. 3 group of Christians of same denomination; (**Holy Communion**) Eucharist.

**communiqué** n. official communication.

**communism** n. social system based on public ownership of property; political theory advocating this. □□ **communist** n. & adj.

**community** n. 1 group of people living in one place or having same religion, ethnic origin, profession, etc.; Ecol. group of animals or plants living or growing together. 2 similarity or identity.

**commute** v. 1 travel some distance to and from work. 2 Law change (punishment) to one less severe.

**commuter** *n.* person who commutes to and from work.

**compact** ● *adj.* closely or neatly packed together; concise. ● *v.* make compact. ● *n.* 1 small flat case for face powder. 2 agreement, contract. □ **compact disc** small disc from which sound etc. is reproduced by laser action. □□ **compaction** *n.* **compactly** *adv.* **compactness** *n.*

**companion** *n.* 1 person who accompanies or associates with another; thing that matches or accompanies another. 2 (**Companion**) member of the highest General or Military Division of the Order of Australia. □□ **companionship** *n.*

**companionable** *adj.* sociable, friendly. □□ **companionably** *adv.*

**company** *n.* 1 number of people assembled; guest(s); actors etc. working together. 2 commercial business. 3 subdivision of infantry battalion.

**comparable** *adj.* able to be compared. □□ **comparability** *n.* **comparably** *adv.*

**comparative** ● *adj.* 1 perceptible or estimated by comparison; relative; of or involving comparison. 2 *Gram.* (of adjective or adverb) expressing higher degree of a quality. ● *n. Gram.* comparative expression or word. □□ **comparatively** *adv.*

**compare** *v.* 1 estimate the similarity of. 2 declare to be similar. 3 be equal or equivalent to. □ **beyond compare** outstanding.

**comparison** *n.* comparing.

**compartment** *n.* space partitioned off within larger space.

**compass** *n.* 1 instrument showing direction of magnetic north and bearings from it. 2 range, scope. 3 (**compasses**) hinged instrument for taking measurements and drawing circles.

**compassion** *n.* pity.

**compassionate** *adj.* showing compassion, sympathetic. □□ **compassionately** *adv.*

**compatible** *adj.* able to exist or be used together; consistent. □□ **compatibility** *n.*

**compatriot** *n.* person from one's own country.

**compel** *v.* (**-ll-**) force.

**compelling** *adj.* arousing strong interest or attention.

**compendious** *adj.* comprehensive but brief.

**compendium** *n.* (*pl.* **compendiums** or **compendia**) summary, abridgement.

**compensate** *v.* recompense; make amends; counterbalance.

**compensation** *n.* 1 compensating, being compensated. 2 money etc. given as recompense. □□ **compensatory** *adj.*

**compère** ● *n.* person introducing variety show. ● *v.* act as compère (to).

**compete** *v.* take part in contest etc.; strive.

**competence** *n.* (also **competency**) ability; being competent; authority.

**competent** *adj.* 1 adequately qualified or capable; effective. 2 authorised to do something. □□ **competently** *adv.*

**competition** *n.* competing; event in which people compete; other people competing; opposition.

**competitive** *adj.* 1 of or involving competition; having strong urge to win. 2 (of prices etc.) comparing favourably with those of rivals. □□ **competitiveness** *n.*

**competitor** *n.* person who competes; rival, esp. in business.

**compile** *v.* 1 collect and arrange (material) into list, book, etc. 2 *Computing* translate (programming

language) into machine code.
□□ **compilation** n.

**complacent** adj. smugly self-satisfied; calmly content.

**complain** v. express dissatisfaction; say that one is suffering from (an ailment); state grievance concerning. □□ **complainant** n.

**complaint** n. 1 complaining; grievance, cause of dissatisfaction. 2 ailment.

**complaisant** adj. willing to please; acquiescent.□□ **complaisance** n.

**complement** ● n. 1 thing that completes or balances. 2 full number required. 3 word(s) added to verb to complete predicate of sentence. 4 amount by which angle is less than 90°. ● v. 1 complete. 2 form complement to.□□ **complementary** adj.

> **Usage** *Complement* is often confused with *compliment*.

**complete** ● adj. 1 having all its parts. 2 finished. 3 total. ● v. 1 finish. 2 make whole or perfect. 3 fill in (form etc.)□□ **completely** adv. **completeness** n. **completion** n.

**complex** ● adj. complicated; consisting of many parts. ● n. 1 buildings, rooms, etc. made up of related parts. 2 group of usu. repressed feelings or thoughts causing abnormal behaviour or mental states.□□ **complexity** n.

**complexion** n. natural colour, texture, and appearance of skin, esp. of face; aspect.

**compliant** adj. complying, obedient. □□ **compliance** n.

**complicate** v. make difficult or complex.□□ **complicated** adj. **complication** n.

**complicity** n. involvement in wrongdoing.□□ **complicit** adj.

**compliment** ● n. polite expression of praise. ● v. pay compliment to.

> **Usage** *Compliment* is often confused with *complement*.

**complimentary** adj. 1 expressing compliment. 2 given free of charge.

**comply** v. act in accordance (with request or command).

**component** ● n. part of larger whole. ● adj. being part of larger whole.

**componentry** n. parts of a machine or vehicle considered collectively.

**comport** v. literary conduct oneself; behave.□□ **comportment** n.

**compose** v. 1 create (a work of music or literature). 2 (of parts) make up (a whole). 3 calm; cause to appear calm. □□ **composer** n.

**composite** adj. made up of parts.

**composition** n. 1 act of putting together; thing composed. 2 arrangement of parts of picture. 3 constitution of substance. 4 compound artificial substance.

**compositor** n. person who sets up type for printing.

**compos mentis** adj. sane.

**compost** ● n. mixture of decayed organic matter used for enriching soil. ● v. make into compost.

**composure** n. tranquil manner.

**compote** n. fruit in syrup.

**compound** ● adj. 1 made up of two or more things; word made up of two or more existing words. 2 substance formed from two or more elements chemically united. ● n. 1 compound substance. 2 fenced-in enclosure. ● v. 1 combine; add to. 2 settle by agreement. 3 make worse.

**comprehend** v. 1 understand. 2 include.

**comprehensible** adj. intelligible.

**comprehension** n. **1** understanding. **2** text set as test of understanding. **3** inclusion.

**comprehensive** adj. **1** including all or nearly all. **2** (of motor insurance) providing protection against most risks. □□ **comprehensively** adv.

**compress** ● v. squeeze together; bring into smaller space or shorter time. ● n. pad pressed on part of body to relieve inflammation, stop bleeding, etc. □□ **compression** n. **compressor** n.

**comprise** v. consist of.

> **Usage** It is a mistake to use *comprise* to mean 'to compose or make up'.

**compromise** ● n. agreement reached by mutual concession; intermediate state between conflicting opinions etc. ● v. **1** settle dispute by mutual concession; modify one's opinions, demands, etc. **2** bring into disrepute or danger by indiscretion.

**comptroller** n. controller.

**compulsion** n. forcing or being forced; irresistible urge.

**compulsive** adj. **1** compelling; resulting or acting (as if) from compulsion. **2** irresistible. □□ **compulsively** adv.

**compulsory** adj. required by law or rule. □□ **compulsorily** adv.

**compunction** n. regret, scruple.

**compute** v. calculate; use computer. □□ **computation** n.

**computer** n. electronic device for storing and processing data, making calculations, or controlling machinery.

**computerise** v. (also **-ize**) equip with computer; store, perform, or produce by computer. □□ **computerisation** n.

**comrade** n. companion; friend, mate. □□ **comradeship** n.

**con** colloq. ● v. (**conned**) deceive or swindle after winning confidence. ● n. confidence trick. □ **pros and cons** reasons for and against.

**concatenate** ● v. link together (chain of events, computer data, etc.) ● adj. joined; linked. □□ **concatenation** n.

**concave** adj. curved like interior of circle or sphere. □□ **concavity** n.

**conceal** v. keep secret; hide. □□ **concealment** n.

**concede** v. admit to be true; admit defeat in; yield; grant.

**conceit** n. **1** personal vanity. **2** literary complex or surprising metaphor, far-fetched comparison.

**conceited** adj. vain, proud. □□ **conceitedly** adv.

**conceive** v. **1** become pregnant (with). **2** imagine; formulate (plan etc.) □□ **conceivable** adj. **conceivably** adv.

**concentrate** ● v. **1** focus one's attention. **2** bring together to one point. **3** increase strength of (liquid etc.) by removing water etc. **4** (as **concentrated** adj.) strong. ● n. concentrated solution.

**concentration** n. **1** concentrating, being concentrated. **2** mental attention. **3** weight of substance in given amount of mixture. □ **concentration camp** prison camp for political prisoners etc.

**concentric** adj. having common centre. □□ **concentrically** adv.

**concept** n. general notion; abstract idea. □□ **conceptual** adj.

**conception** n. **1** conceiving, conceived. **2** idea. **3** understanding.

**conceptualise** v. (also **-ize**) form concept or idea of. □□ **conceptualisation** n.

**concern** ● v. **1** be relevant or important to; relate to. **2** be about. **3** worry, affect. **4** (concern oneself) interest or involve oneself.
● n. **1** anxiety, worry. **2** matter of interest or importance to one. **3** business, firm.

**concerned** adj. **1** troubled, anxious. **2** involved, interested.

**concerning** ● prep. about, regarding. ● adj. causing anxiety; worrying.

**concert** n. **1** musical performance. **2** agreement.

**concerted** adj. jointly planned.

**concertina** ● n. musical instrument like accordion but smaller.
● v. compress or collapse in folds like those of concertina.

**concerto** n. (pl. concertos or concerti) composition for solo instrument(s) and orchestra.

**concession** n. **1** conceding; thing conceded. **2** reduction in price for certain category of people.
□□ **concessionary** adj.

**conch** n. large spiral shell.

**conchology** n. study of shells.

**concierge** n. door keeper or porter of hotel or block of flats.

**conciliate** v. **1** make calm; pacify. **2** reconcile; (esp. in industrial dispute) attempt to bring disputing parties to agreement. □□ **conciliation** n. **conciliator** n. **conciliatory** adj.

**concise** adj. brief but comprehensive.
□□ **concisely** adv. **conciseness** n. **concision** n.

**conclave** n. private meeting.

**conclude** v. **1** bring or come to end. **2** infer.

**conclusion** n. **1** ending; final result. **2** judgement reached by reasoning.

**conclusive** adj. decisive, convincing.
□□ **conclusively** adv.

**concoct** v. make by mixing ingredients; invent (story, lie, etc.)
□□ **concoction** n.

**concomitant** ● adj. accompanying.
● n. accompanying thing.
□□ **concomitance** n.

**concord** n. agreement, harmony.
□□ **concordant** adj.

**concordance** n. **1** agreement. **2** index of words used in book or by author.

**concourse** n. **1** crowd. **2** coming together. **3** open central area in large public building.

**concrete** ● adj. existing in material form; real; definite. ● n. mixture of gravel, sand, cement, and water, used for building. ● v. cover with or embed in concrete.

**concretion** n. hard solid mass; forming of this by coalescence.

**concubine** n. **1** arch. mistress. **2** (among polygamous peoples) secondary wife.

**concur** v. (concurred) **1** agree. **2** coincide.

**concurrent** adj. existing or in operation at the same.
□□ **concurrence** n. **concurrently** adv.

**concussion** n. **1** temporary unconsciousness or incapacity due to head injury. **2** violent shaking.

**condemn** v. **1** express utter disapproval of; pronounce unfit for use. **2** sentence (to punishment); doom (to something unpleasant).
□□ **condemnation** n.

**condensation** n. **1** condensing, being condensed. **2** condensed liquid. **3** abridgement.

**condense** v. **1** make denser or more concise. **2** reduce or be reduced from gas to liquid. □□ **condenser** n.

**condescend** v. **1** graciously consent to do a thing while showing superiority. **2** pretend to be on equal terms with (inferior). **3** (as condescending adj.) patronising.
□□ **condescendingly** adv. **condescension** n.

**condiment** n. seasoning or relish for food.

**condition** ● *n.* **1** something that must exist if something else is to exist or occur. **2** state of being. **3** (**conditions**) circumstances.
● *v.* **1** bring into desired state. **2** have strong effect on. **3** accustom.

**conditional** *adj.* subject to specified conditions.□□ **conditionally** *adv.*

**conditioner** *n.* substance that improves condition of hair, fabric, etc.

**condole** *v.* express sympathy with (person) over loss etc.
□□ **condolence** *n.*

**condom** *n.* contraceptive sheath worn on penis during sexual intercourse.

**condominium** *n.* **1** joint control of nation's affairs by other nations; joint rule or sovereignty. **2** building containing individually owned flats; such a flat.

**condone** *v.* forgive, overlook.

**conducive** *adj.* contributing or helping (towards something).

**conduct** ● *v.* **1** lead, guide; be conductor of; manage. **2** transmit (heat or electricity). ● *n.* behaviour; manner of directing or managing business etc.

**conduction** *n.* transmission of heat, electricity, etc. through substance.

**conductive** *adj.* transmitting heat, electricity, etc.□□ **conductivity** *n.*

**conductor** *n.* **1** person who controls orchestra's or choir's performance. **2** substance that conducts heat or electricity.

**conduit** *n.* channel or pipe conveying liquid or protecting insulated cable.

**cone** *n.* **1** solid figure with usu. circular base and tapering to point; cone-shaped object. **2** dry fruit of pine or fir. **3** minute cone-shaped structure in retina. **4** conical wafer for holding ice cream.

**coney** *n.* (also **cony**) rabbit; its fur.

**confection** *n.* sweet dish or delicacy.

**confectioner** *n.* maker or retailer of sweets or pastries.□□ **confectionery** *n.*

**confederacy** *n.* league or alliance.

**confederate** ● *adj.* allied. ● *n.* ally; accomplice. ● *v.* bring or come into alliance.

**confederation** *n.* union or alliance, esp. of nations.

**confer** *v.* (**conferred**) **1** grant, bestow. **2** discuss, consult.
□□ **conferrable** *adj.*

**conference** *n.* consultation; meeting for discussion.

**conferment** *n.* conferring of (degree, honour, etc.

**confess** *v.* **1** acknowledge, admit. **2** declare one's sins, esp. to priest.

**confessedly** *adv.* by one's own or general admission.

**confession** *n.* **1** act of confessing; thing confessed. **2** statement of principles.

**confessional** ● *n.* enclosed place where priest hears confessions. ● *adj.* of confession.

**confetti** *n.* small bits of coloured paper thrown by wedding guests at bride and groom.

**confidant** *n.* person in whom one confides.

**confidante** *n.* woman in whom one confides.

**confide** *v.* tell (secret) or entrust (task) to.

**confidence** *n.* firm trust; feeling of certainty; self reliance; boldness; something told as secret.
□ **confidence trick** swindle worked by gaining person's trust.

**confident** *adj.* feeling or showing confidence.□□ **confidently** *adv.*

**confidential** *adj.* spoken or written in confidence; entrusted with secrets; confiding.□□ **confidentiality** *n.* **confidentially** *adv.*

**configuration** *n.* manner of arrangement; shape; outline.
□□ **configure** *v.*

**confine** ● *v.* keep or restrict within certain limits; keep shut up.
● *n.* (**confines**) boundaries.

**confinement** *n.* **1** confining, being confined. **2** time of childbirth.

**confirm** *v.* **1** provide support for truth or correctness of; establish more firmly; make definite. **2** administer confirmation to.

**confirmation** *n.* **1** confirming circumstance or statement. **2** confirming baptised person as member of Christian Church; ceremony of confirming persons in Jewish faith.

**confirmed** *adj.* firmly settled in habit or condition.

**confiscate** *v.* take or seize by authority.□□ **confiscation** *n.*

**conflagration** *n.* large and destructive fire.

**conflate** *v.* fuse together; blend. □□ **conflation** *n.*

**conflict** ● *n.* opposition; fight, struggle; clashing of opposed interests etc. ● *v.* clash; be incompatible.

**confluence** *n.* **1** place where two rivers meet. **2** coming together; crowd of people.□□ **confluent** *adj.*

**conform** *v.* comply with rules or general custom; be in accordance with.

**conformation** *n.* thing's structure or shape.

**conformist** ● *n.* person who conforms to established practice. ● *adj.* conventional.
□□ **conformism** *n.*

**conformity** *n.* **1** accordance with established practice. **2** suitability.

**confound** *v.* **1** baffle; confuse. **2** *arch.* defeat. ● *int.* expressing annoyance.

**confront** *v.* **1** meet or stand facing, esp. in hostility or defiance, or to deal with. **2** (of difficulty etc.) present itself to. **3** bring face to face with.

□□ **confrontation** *n.* **confrontational** *adj.*

**confuse** *v.* **1** bewilder; destroy composure of. **2** make unclear. **3** throw into disorder.□□ **confusing** *adj.* **confusion** *n.*

**confute** *v.* prove to be false or wrong. □□ **confutation** *n.*

**conga** *n.* **1** Latin American dance, usu. performed in single file. **2** tall narrow drum beaten with hands.

**congeal** *v.* **1** make or become semi-solid by cooling. **2** (of blood etc.) coagulate.

**congenial** *adj.* pleasant, agreeable to oneself.□□ **congeniality** *n.* **congenially** *adv.*

**congenital** *adj.* existing or as such from birth.□□ **congenitally** *adv.*

**conger** *n.* large sea eel.

**congestion** *n.* abnormal accumulation or obstruction, esp. of traffic etc. or of mucus in nose etc.

**conglomerate** ● *adj.* **1** gathered into rounded mass. **2** (of rock) made up of small stones held together. ● *n.* **1** a number of different parts or items grouped together. **2** corporation of merged firms. **3** conglomerate rock.
● *v.* collect into coherent mass.
□□ **conglomeration** *n.*

**congratulate** *v.* express pleasure at the happiness, good fortune, or excellence of (person).
□□ **congratulation** *n.* **congratulatory** *adj.*

**congregate** *v.* collect or gather in crowd.

**congregation** *n.* **1** assembly of people, esp. for religious worship. **2** group of people regularly attending particular church etc.

**congress** *n.* formal meeting of delegates for discussion.
□□ **congressional** *adj.*

**congruent** *adj.* **1** suitable, agreeing. **2** *Geom.* (of figures) coinciding

exactly when superimposed.
□□ **congruence** n.

**conical** adj. cone-shaped.

**conifer** n. cone-bearing tree.
□□ **coniferous** adj.

**conjectural** adj. involving conjecture.

**conjecture** ● n. formation of opinion on incomplete information, guessing. ● v. guess.

**conjoined twins** n.pl. twins whose bodies are joined at birth.

**conjugal** adj. of marriage.

**conjugate** ● v. 1 give the different forms of (verb). 2 unite; become fused. ● adj. joined together.

**conjunct** adj. joined; combined; associated.

**conjunction** n. 1 joining, connection; word used to connect clauses, sentences, or words. 2 combination of events or circumstances.

**conjunctiva** n. mucous membrane covering front of eye and inside eyelid.

**conjunctivitis** n. inflammation of conjunctiva.

**conjure** v. perform seemingly magical tricks, esp. by movement of hands; summon, evoke.□□ **conjuror** n. (also **conjurer**)

**connect** v. 1 join. 2 be joined. 3 associate mentally or practically. 4 (of train etc.) arrive in time for passengers to transfer to another. 5 put into communication by telephone. 6 (usu. in passive) associate with (others) in relationships etc. 7 colloq. hit or strike effectively.□□ **connector** n.

**connection** n. 1 link, linking; place where things connect; connecting part; trains etc. timed to connect with one another. 2 (**connections**) influential relatives or associates.

**connective** adj. connecting.

**conning tower** n. superstructure of submarine containing periscope.

**connive** v. secretly allow.
□□ **connivance** n.

**connoisseur** n. expert judge in matters of taste.

**connote** v. imply in addition to literal meaning; mean, signify.
□□ **connotation** n. **connotative** adj.

**connubial** adj. conjugal.

**conquer** v. overcome in war or by effort.□□ **conqueror** n.

**conquest** n. conquering; something won.

**conscience** n. moral sense of right and wrong, esp. as affecting behaviour.

**conscientious** adj. diligent and scrupulous.□ **conscientious objector** person who refuses to serve in armed forces for moral reasons.
□□ **conscientiously** adv. **conscientiousness** n.

**conscious** adj. 1 awake and aware of one's surroundings etc.; aware, knowing. 2 intentional.
□□ **consciously** adv. **consciousness** n.

**conscript** ● v. summon for compulsory (esp. military) service. ● n. conscripted person.
□□ **conscription** n.

**consecrate** v. 1 make or declare sacred; dedicate formally to religious purpose. 2 colloq. devote to (purpose).□□ **consecration** n.

**consecutive** adj. following continuously; in unbroken or logical order.□□ **consecutively** adv.

**consensus** n. general agreement or opinion.

**consent** ● v. express willingness, give permission, agree.
● n. agreement, permission.

**consequence** n. 1 result of what has gone before. 2 importance.

**consequent** adj. that results; following as consequence.

**consequential** adj. 1 resulting, esp. indirectly. 2 important.

**consequently** adv. as a result.

**conservation** n. preservation esp. of natural environment or works of art etc. □□ **conservationist** n. **conservator** n.

**conservative** ● adj. 1 averse to (rapid) change. 2 (of estimate) purposely low. ● n. conservative person. □□ **conservatism** n.

**conservatorium** n. Aust. school of music.

**conservatory** n. greenhouse.

**conserve** ● v. preserve; keep from harm or damage. ● n. jam of fresh fruit.

**consider** v. 1 think about, esp. in order to decide. 2 believe; think. 3 take into account. 4 (as **considered** adj.) (esp. of opinion) formed after careful thought.

**considerable** adj. 1 lot of. 2 notable, important. □□ **considerably** adv.

**considerate** adj. giving thought to feelings or rights of others. □□ **considerately** adv.

**consideration** n. 1 careful thought. 2 being considerate. 3 fact or thing taken into account. 4 compensation; payment.

**considering** prep. in view of.

**consign** v. commit; deliver; send (goods). □□ **consignee** n. **consignor** n.

**consignment** n. consigning; goods consigned.

**consist** v. be composed of.

**consistency** n. 1 degree of density or firmness, esp. of thick liquids. 2 being consistent.

**consistent** adj. 1 unchanging. 2 not contradictory; compatible. □□ **consistently** adv.

**consolation** n. 1 alleviation of grief or disappointment. 2 consoling thing or person. □□ **consolatory** adj.

**console**[1] v. bring consolation to.

**console**[2] n. 1 panel holding controls for electronic equipment. 2 bracket supporting shelf etc.

**consolidate** v. 1 make or become strong or secure. 2 combine (territories, companies, debts, etc.) into one whole. □□ **consolidation** n.

**consommé** n. clear meat soup.

**consonance** n. agreement, harmony.

**consonant** ● n. speech sound in which breath is at least partly obstructed, sound other than a vowel; letter representing this. ● adj. consistent; in agreement or harmony. □□ **consonantal** adj.

**consort** ● n. 1 wife or husband, esp. of royalty. 2 Mus. group of players or instruments. ● v. keep company; harmonise.

**consortium** n. (pl. consortia or consortiums) association, esp. of several business companies.

**conspicuous** adj. clearly visible; attracting attention. □□ **conspicuously** adv.

**conspiracy** n. act of conspiring; plot.

**conspirator** n. person who takes part in conspiracy. □□ **conspiratorial** adj.

**conspire** v. 1 combine secretly for unlawful or harmful purpose. 2 (of events) seem to be working together.

**constable** n. police officer.

**constabulary** n. police force.

**constancy** n. dependability; faithfulness.

**constant** ● adj. continuous; occurring frequently; faithful, dependable. ● n. Math. & Physics unvarying quantity. □□ **constantly** adv.

**constellation** n. group of fixed stars.

**consternation** n. amazement or dismay.

**constipation** n. condition with hardened faeces and difficulty in emptying bowels.

**constituency** n. electorate.

**constituent** ● adj. 1 forming part of whole. 2 appointing or electing. ● n. 1 component part. 2 member of electorate.

**constitute** v. 1 be components or essence of; amount to. 2 establish.

**constitution** n. 1 composition. 2 set of principles by which nation etc. is governed. 3 person's inherent state of health, strength, etc.

**constitutional** ● adj. 1 of or in line with the constitution. 2 inherent. ● n. walk taken as exercise. □□ **constitutionally** adv.

**constrain** v. compel, oblige.

**constraint** n. restriction; limitation.

**constrict** v. make narrow or tight; compress. □□ **constriction** n. **constrictive** adj.

**constrictor** n. 1 snake (esp. boa) that kills by compressing. 2 muscle that contracts organ or part of body.

**construct** ● v. fit together; build. ● n. thing constructed, esp. by the mind. □□ **constructor** n.

**construction** n. 1 constructing; thing constructed. 2 interpretation, explanation. 3 syntactical arrangement. □□ **constructional** adj.

**constructive** adj. helpful, positive. □□ **constructively** adv.

**construe** v. 1 interpret. 2 combine (words) grammatically. 3 translate literally.

**consul** n. official appointed by nation to protect its citizens and interests in foreign city. □□ **consular** adj.

**consulate** n. offices or position of consul.

**consult** v. seek information or advice from; refer to; take into consideration. □□ **consultative** adj.

**consultant** n. specialist who gives professional advice. □□ **consultancy** n.

**consultation** n. 1 (meeting for) consulting. 2 lottery.

**consume** v. 1 eat or drink. 2 use up. 3 destroy. □□ **consumable** adj. & n.

**consumer** n. user of product or service.

**consummate** ● v. complete, esp. marriage by sexual intercourse.

● adj. 1 complete, perfect. 2 fully skilled. □□ **consummation** n.

**consumption** n. 1 consuming, being consumed. 2 purchase and use of goods. 3 arch. tuberculosis of the lungs.

**cont.** abbr. continued.

**contact** ● n. communication; person who is or may be contacted for information etc.; electrical connection. ● v. get in touch with. □ **contact lens** small lens worn directly on eyeball to correct vision.

**contagion** n. spreading of disease by contact. □□ **contagious** adj.

**contain** v. 1 hold or be capable of holding within itself; include; comprise. 2 control, restrain.

**container** n. box etc. for holding things.

**containment** n. action or policy of preventing expansion of hostile country or influence.

**contaminate** v. pollute; infect. □□ **contaminant** n. **contamination** n.

**contemplate** v. 1 survey with eyes or mind. 2 regard as possible; intend. □□ **contemplation** n. **contemplative** adj.

**contemporaneous** adj. existing or occurring at same time.

**contemporary** ● adj. 1 belonging to same time; of same age. 2 modern. ● n. contemporary person or thing.

**contempt** n. 1 feeling that person or thing deserves scorn or reproach; condition of being held in contempt. 2 (in full **contempt of court**) disobedience to or disrespect for court of law. □□ **contemptible** adj.

**contemptuous** adj. feeling or showing contempt; scornful. □□ **contemptuously** adv.

**contend** v. 1 compete; struggle. 2 assert, argue. □□ **contender** n.

**content**[1] ● adj. 1 satisfied. 2 willing. ● v. make content;

satisfy. ● *n.* contented state; satisfaction.□□ **contented** *adj.* **contentment** *n.*

**content**[2] *n.* what is contained in something. □ **content provider** organisation or individual that supplies information for use on website.

**contention** *n.* dispute, rivalry; point contended for in argument.

**contentious** *adj.* quarrelsome; likely to cause argument; controversial.

**contest** ● *n.* competition. ● *v.* dispute; contend or compete for; compete in. □□ **contestant** *n.*

**context** *n.* what precedes and follows word or passage; relevant circumstances. □□ **contextual** *adj.* **contextualise** *v.* (also **-ize**)

**contiguous** *adj.* touching, adjacent; in contact.

**continent**[1] *n.* any of the earth's main continuous bodies of land.

**continent**[2] *adj.* able to control bowels and bladder. □□ **continence** *n.*

**continental** *adj.* of or characteristic of a continent; (**Continental**) of or characteristic of Europe.

**contingency** *n.* event that may or may not occur. 2 something dependent on another uncertain event.

**contingent** ● *adj.* 1 conditional, dependent. 2 that may or may not occur. 3 fortuitous. ● *n.* group (of troops, ships, etc.) forming part of larger group; people sharing interest, origin, etc.

**continual** *adj.* constantly or frequently recurring. □□ **continually** *adv.*

**continue** *v.* 1 not cease; remain in existence; remain in a place or condition. 2 resume; extend. □□ **continuance** *n.* **continuation** *n.*

**continuous** *adj.* uninterrupted, connected without break. □□ **continuity** *n.* **continuously** *adv.*

**continuum** *n.* (*pl.* **continua**) thing with continuous structure.

**contort** *v.* twist or force out of normal shape. □□ **contortion** *n.*

**contortionist** *n.* entertainer who adopts contorted postures.

**contour** *n.* 1 outline. 2 (in full **contour line**) line on map joining points at same altitude.

**contra-** *comb. form* against.

**contraband** ● *n.* smuggled goods. ● *adj.* forbidden to be imported or exported.

**contraception** *n.* use of contraceptives.

**contraceptive** ● *adj.* preventing pregnancy. ● *n.* contraceptive device or drug.

**contract** ● *n.* written or spoken agreement, esp. one enforceable by law; document recording it. ● *v.* 1 make or become smaller. 2 make contract. 3 arrange (work) to be done by contract. 4 become affected by (disease). 5 incur (debt). □□ **contractor** *n.*

**contraction** *n.* 1 contracting. 2 shortening of uterine muscles during childbirth. 3 shrinking, diminution. 4 shortened word(s).

**contractual** *adj.* of or in the nature of a contract.

**contradict** *v.* deny; oppose verbally; be at variance with. □□ **contradiction** *n.* **contradictory** *adj.*

**contralto** *n.* lowest female singing voice; singer with this voice.

**contraption** *n.* machine or device, esp. strange one.

**contrapuntal** *adj. Mus.* of or in counterpoint.

**contrariwise** *adv.* on the other hand; in the opposite way.

**contrary** ● *adj.* **1** opposed in nature, tendency, or direction. **2** perverse, self-willed. ● *n.* (**the contrary**) the opposite. ● *adv.* in opposition or contrast.

**contrast** ● *n.* comparison showing differences; difference so revealed; thing or person having different qualities; degree of difference between tones in television picture or photograph etc. ● *v.* compare to reveal contrast; show contrast.

**contravene** *v.* break (rule etc.). □□ **contravention** *n.*

**contretemps** *n.* (*pl.* **contretemps**) disagreement.

**contribute** *v.* give to common fund or effort; help to cause something. □□ **contribution** *n.* **contributor** *n.* **contributory** *adj.*

**contrite** *adj.* penitent, feeling guilt. □□ **contrition** *n.*

**contrivance** *n.* something contrived, esp. plan or device; act of contriving.

**contrive** *v.* devise; manage.

**contrived** *adj.* artificial, forced.

**control** ● *n.* **1** power to give order or restrain something; means of restraining or regulating. **2** standard for checking results of experiment. ● *v.* (**controlled**) have control of; regulate; restrain.

**controller** *n.* input device for computer game console etc.

**controversial** *adj.* causing or subject to controversy.

**controversy** *n.* argument, dispute.

**controvert** *v.* dispute, deny. □□ **controvertible** *adj.*

**contumacy** *adj.* stubborn refusal to obey or comply.

**contuse** *v.* injure without breaking skin; bruise. □□ **contusion** *n.*

**conundrum** *n.* riddle; hard question.

**conurbation** *n.* group of towns united by urban expansion.

**convalesce** *v.* recover health after illness.

**convalescent** ● *adj.* recovering from illness. ● *n.* convalescent person. □□ **convalescence** *n.*

**convection** *n.* heat transfer by upward movement of heated medium.

**convene** *v.* summon; assemble. □□ **convenor** *n.* (also **convener**)

**convenience** *n.* **1** ease, lack of effort; something contributing to this. **2** public toilet.

**convenient** *adj.* involving little trouble or effort; easily accessible. □□ **conveniently** *adv.*

**convent** *n.* religious community, esp. of nuns; their residence.

**convention** *n.* **1** accepted custom; behaviour generally. **2** customary practice. **3** conference. **4** agreement, treaty.

**conventional** *adj.* **1** depending on or according with convention; bound by social conventions. **2** not spontaneous or sincere. **3** (of weapons etc.) not nuclear or biological. □□ **conventionally** *adv.*

**converge** *v.* come together or towards same point; approach from different directions. □□ **convergence** *n.* **convergent** *adj.*

**conversant** *adj.* well acquainted with.

**conversation** *n.* informal spoken communication; instance of this.

**conversational** *adj.* of or in conversation; colloquial. □□ **conversationally** *adv.*

**converse**[1] *v.* talk.

**converse**[2] ● *adj.* opposite, contrary, reversed. ● *n.* converse statement or proposition. □□ **conversely** *adv.*

**convert** ● *v.* **1** change; cause (person) to change belief etc.; change (money etc.) into different form or currency. **2** *Rugby* kick goal after (try). ● *n.* person converted, esp. to religious faith. □□ **conversion** *n.* **converter** *n.* **convertor** *n.*

**convertible** ● adj. able to be converted. ● n. car with folding or detachable roof.

**convex** adj. curved like outside of circle or sphere.

**convey** v. 1 transport, carry. 2 communicate (meaning etc.) 3 transfer by legal process. 4 transmit (sound etc.) □□ **conveyable** adj.

**conveyance** n. 1 conveying, being conveyed. 2 vehicle. 3 legal transfer of property; document effecting this.

**conveyancing** n. branch of law dealing with transfer of property.

**conveyor** n. person or thing that conveys.

**convict** ● v. prove or declare guilty. ● n. hist. person sentenced to term of penal servitude in Australian colony.

**conviction** n. 1 proving or finding guilty; being convicted. 2 being convinced; firm belief.

**convince** v. persuade (person) to believe or realise; (as **convinced** adj.) firmly persuaded.□□ **convincing** adj. **convincingly** adv.

**convivial** adj. fond of company; sociable, lively.□□ **conviviality** n.

**convoke** v. summon to assemble. □□ **convocation** n.

**convolution** n. coiling; coil; twist; complexity.□□ **convoluted** adj.

**convoy** n. group of ships, vehicles, etc. travelling together.

**convulse** v. affect with convulsions. □□ **convulsive** adj. **convulsively** adv.

**convulsion** n. violent involuntary movement of body; (**convulsions**) uncontrollable laughter.

**cony** var. of CONEY.

**cooee** Aust. colloq. ● n. long loud call used to attract attention. ● int. utterance of such call.

**cook** ● v. 1 prepare (food) by heating; undergo cooking. 2 colloq. falsify (accounts etc.) 3 (as **cooking**) colloq. happening or about to happen. ● n. person who cooks.

**cookery** n. art of cooking.

**cookie** n. 1 biscuit. 2 data sent to computer for future identification etc.

**cool** ● adj. 1 of or at fairly low temperature; suggesting or achieving coolness. 2 calm; lacking enthusiasm. 3 unfriendly. 4 colloq. stylish, fashionable. ● n. 1 coolness; cool place. 2 colloq. composure. ● v. make or become cool or calm. □□ **coolly** adv. **coolness** n.

**coolamon** n. Aust. basin-like vessel of wood or bark used by Aboriginal people to hold liquid, and for carrying etc.

**coolant** n. cooling agent, esp. fluid.

**coolibah** n. eucalypt of central and northern Australia.

**coolroom** n. Aust. refrigerated storeroom for perishable goods.

**coop** ● n. cage for keeping poultry. ● v. confine.

**co-op** n. colloq. cooperative society or shop.

**cooper** n. maker or repairer of casks and barrels.

**cooperate** v. (also **co-operate**) work or act together.□□ **cooperation** n.

**cooperative** (also **co-operative**) ● adj. 1 willing to cooperate. 2 (of business etc.) jointly owned and run by members, with profits shared. ● n. cooperative society, business, etc.

**co-opt** v. appoint to committee etc. by invitation of existing members. □□ **co-option** n.

**coordinate** ● adj. equal in importance. ● n. 1 Math. each of set of quantities used to fix position of point, line, or plane. 2 (**coordinates**) matching items of clothing. ● v. bring into proper relation; cause to function together efficiently. □□ **coordination** n. **coordinator** n.

**coot** n. black waterbird with white horny plate on head.

**coota** n. (also **couta**) *Aust. colloq.* = BARRACOUTA.

**cop** ● *colloq.* n. police officer.
● v. (**copped**) **1** catch or arrest.
**2** suffer; put up with. □ **cop it** get into trouble. **cop out** avoid doing something that one ought to.

**cope** ● v. deal effectively with; manage successfully.

**copernicium** n. radioactive element (symbol Cn).

**copier** n. machine that copies.

**coping** n. top (usu. sloping) course of masonry in wall.

**copious** adj. abundant; producing much. □□ **copiously** adv.

**copper** ● n. **1** red-brown metallic element (symbol Cu). **2** its colour.
**3** *colloq.* police officer. ● adj. made of or coloured like copper.

**coppice** ● n. area of undergrowth and small trees. ● v. cut back (trees) to stimulate growth; (of tree) put forth new growth.

**copra** n. dried coconut kernels.

**copulate** ● v. have sexual intercourse. □□ **copulation** n.

**copy** ● n. thing made to imitate or be identical to another; specimen of book etc.; material to be printed.
● v. **1** make copy of; imitate.
**2** transcribe.

**copyist** n. person who makes copies.

**copyright** ● n. exclusive right to print, publish, perform, etc. material.
● adj. protected by copyright.
● v. secure copyright for (material).

**coquette** n. woman who flirts.
□□ **coquetry** n. **coquettish** adj.

**coracle** n. small boat of wickerwork covered with watertight material.

**coral** ● n. hard substance built up by marine polyps. ● adj. of (red or pink colour of) coral.

**coralline** n. **1** seaweed with hard jointed stem. ● adj. of or like coral.

**cor anglais** n. (pl. **cors anglais**) woodwind instrument like oboe but lower in pitch.

**corbel** n. stone or timber projection from wall, acting as supporting bracket.

**cord** n. **1** long thin flexible material made from twisted strands etc.; piece of this; electric flex. **2** corduroy.

**cordate** adj. heart-shaped.

**cordial** ● adj. heartfelt; friendly. ● n. fruit-flavoured drink. □□ **cordiality** n. **cordially** adv.

**cordite** n. smokeless explosive.

**cordless** adj. (of hand-held electrical device) battery-powered.

**cordon** ● n. **1** line or circle of police etc. **2** ornamental cord or braid. **3** fruit tree trained to grow as single stem.
● v. enclose or separate with cordon of police etc.

**cordon bleu** adj. of highest class in cookery.

**cords** n.pl. *colloq.* corduroy trousers.

**corduroy** n. fabric with velvety ribs.

**core** ● n. **1** horny central part of certain fruits, containing seeds.
**2** central or most important part.
**3** part of nuclear reactor containing fissile material. **4** central part cut out.
**5** inner strand of electric cable.
**6** piece of soft iron forming centre of magnet etc. **7** muscles of the torso. ● v. remove core from.

**corella** n. white Australian parrot.

**corflute** n. *propr.* laminated plastic sheeting containing a corrugated layer; *Aust.* sign or poster made of this.

**corgi** n. dog of small breed with foxlike head.

**coriander** n. aromatic plant used as herb; its seed, used as flavouring.

**cork¹** ● n. **1** thick light-brown bark of S. European oak; bottle stopper of cork etc.; float of cork used in fishing etc. ● v. stop, confine; restrain (feelings etc.)

**ork²** v. Aust. bruise.☐☐ **corked** adj.

**orkage** n. charge made by restaurant etc. for serving customer's own wine etc.

**corked** adj. (of wine) spoilt by defective cork.

**orkscrew ●** n. spiral device for extracting corks from bottles.
● v. move spirally; twist.

**orm** n. swollen underground stem in certain plants.

**ormorant** n. diving waterbird having black or pied plumage.

**orn** n. **1** maize; cereal before or after harvesting, esp. chief crop of region; grain or seed of cereal plant. **2** small tender area of hard skin, esp. on toe. **3** colloq. something corny.

**ornea** n. transparent circular part of front of eyeball.☐☐ **corneal** adj.

**orned** adj. preserved in salt or brine.

**ornelian** n. (also **carnelian**) dull red variety of chalcedony.

**orner ●** n. **1** an angle or area where two lines, sides, edges, streets, etc. meet. **2** Soccer & Hockey free kick or hit from the corner of pitch.
● v. **1** force into difficult or inescapable position. **2** drive around corner. **3** obtain monopoly of (commodity).

**ornet** n. brass instrument resembling trumpet.

**ornice** n. ornamental moulding along top of internal wall.

**ornucopia** n. horn overflowing with flowers, fruit, etc. as symbol of plenty; abundant supply.

**orny** adj. colloq. banal; feebly humorous; sentimental.

**orolla** n. whorl of petals forming inner envelope of flower.

**orollary** n. proposition that follows from one proved; natural consequence.

**orona** n. (pl. **coronae**) ring of light around sun or moon.☐☐ **coronal** adj.

**coronary ●** adj. of arteries supplying blood to heart.
● n. (in full **coronary thrombosis**) blockage of (one of) these arteries by blood clot.

**coronation** n. ceremony of crowning sovereign.

**coroner** n. official holding inquest on death thought to be violent or accidental.☐☐ **coronial** adj.

**coronet** n. small crown.

**corporal** n. rank in army or air force, below sergeant.☐ **corporal punishment** whipping or beating.

**corporate** adj. being, or belonging to, corporation or group.

**corporation** n. group of people authorised to act as an individual, esp. in business.

**corporeal** adj. having a body, tangible.

**corps** n. (pl. **corps**) military unit with particular function; organised group of people.

**corpse** n. dead body.

**corpulent** adj. bulky; fat.
☐☐ **corpulence** n.

**corpus** n. (pl. **corpora**) body or collection of writings, texts, etc.
☐☐ **corpuscular** adj.

**corpuscle** n. blood cell.

**corpus delicti** n. Law facts and circumstances constituting breach of law.

**corral ●** n. pen for cattle, horses, etc.; enclosure for capturing wild animals. ● v. (**corralled**) put or keep in corral.

**correa** n. Australian shrub bearing tubular flowers.

**correct ●** adj. **1** true, accurate. **2** proper, in accordance with taste or standard. ● v. **1** set right. **2** admonish; counteract.☐☐ **correctly** adv. **correctness** n.

**correction** n. correcting; alteration correcting something.

**corrective** ● *adj.* serving to correct or counteract. ● *n.* corrective measure or thing.

**correlate** ● *v.* have or bring into mutual relation. ● *n.* either of two related or complementary things. □□ **correlation** *n.*

**correspond** *v.* 1 be similar or equivalent. 2 agree. 3 exchange letters.

**correspondence** *n.* 1 agreement or similarity. 2 (exchange of) letters.

**correspondent** *n.* 1 person who writes letter(s). 2 person employed to write or report for newspaper or broadcasting.

**corridor** *n.* passage giving access into rooms etc.; strip of territory of one nation passing through that of another; route for an aircraft over foreign country.

**corrigendum** *n.* (*pl.* **corrigenda**) error to be corrected.

**corroborate** *v.* confirm, give support to. □□ **corroboration** *n.* **corroborative** *adj.* **corroborator** *n.*

**corroboree** *n.* *Aust.* Aboriginal dance ceremony, incorporating song and rhythmical musical accompaniment.

**corrode** *v.* wear away, esp. by chemical action; decay; destroy gradually. □□ **corrosion** *n.* **corrosive** *adj.*

**corrugated** *adj.* shaped into alternate ridges and grooves. □□ **corrugation** *n.*

**corrupt** ● *adj.* 1 influenced by or using bribery. 2 immoral; wicked. 3 (of computer data etc.) made unreliable by errors or alterations. ● *v.* make or become corrupt. □□ **corruptible** *adj.* **corruption** *n.* **corruptly** *adv.*

**corsage** *n.* small bouquet worn by women.

**corsair** *n.* pirate ship; pirate.

**corset** *n.* closely-fitting undergarment worn to shape or support the body. □□ **corsetry** *n.*

**cortège** *n.* procession, esp. for funeral.

**cortex** *n.* (*pl.* **cortices**) outer part of organ, esp. brain or kidneys. □□ **cortical** *adj.*

**cortisone** *n.* hormone used in treating inflammation and allergy.

**corundum** *n.* hard crystallised alumina, used esp. as abrasive.

**corvette** *n.* small naval escort vessel.

**cos** *n.* lettuce with long narrow leaves.

**cosh** *colloq.* ● *n.* heavy blunt weapon. ● *v.* hit with cosh.

**cosine** *n.* ratio of side adjacent to an acute angle (in right-angled triangle) to hypotenuse.

**cosmetic** ● *adj.* beautifying; enhancing; superficially improving; (of surgery etc.) restoring or enhancing normal appearance. ● *n.* cosmetic preparation. □□ **cosmetically** *adv.*

**cosmic** *adj.* of the universe. □□ **cosmic rays** (or **radiation**) radiation from outer space.

**cosmology** *n.* science or theory of universe. □□ **cosmological** *adj.* **cosmologist** *n.*

**cosmonaut** *n.* Russian astronaut.

**cosmopolitan** ● *adj.* of or knowing many parts of world; free from national limitations or prejudices. ● *n.* cosmopolitan person. □□ **cosmopolitanism** *n.*

**cosmos** *n.* the universe as well-ordered whole.

**cosset** *v.* (**cosseted**) pamper.

**cost** ● *v.* 1 (**cost**, **costing**) have as price; involve loss or sacrifice of. 2 (**costed**, **costing**) fix or estimate cost of. ● *n.* what a thing costs.

**costal** *adj.* of ribs.

**costly** *adj.* costing much; expensive. □□ **costliness** *n.*

**costume** n. style of dress, esp. of particular place or time; set of clothes; actor's clothes for part.

**cosy** ● adj. **1** comfortable. **2** snug. ● n. cover to keep teapot etc. hot. □□ **cosily** adv. **cosiness** n.

**cot** n. **1** small high-sided bed for child etc. **2** small light bed. □□ **cot death** (also SIDS) unexplained death of sleeping baby.

**cote** n. shelter for animals or birds.

**coterie** n. exclusive group of people sharing interests.

**coterminous** adj. having same boundaries or extent.

**cottage** n. small house. □ **cottage cheese** soft white lumpy cheese made from curds.

**cotter** n. (also **cotter pin**) wedge or pin for securing machine part, e.g. bicycle pedal crank.

**cotton** n. soft white fibrous substance covering seeds of certain plants; such plant; thread or cloth from this. □ **cotton wool** fluffy wadding, orig. made from raw cotton, used to clean wounds etc.; colloq. excessive comfort or protection. □□ **cottony** adj.

**cotyledon** n. embryonic leaf in seed-bearing plants.

**couch**[1] ● n. upholstered piece of furniture for several people; sofa. ● v. **1** express in (language of specified kind). **2** Med. treat (cataract) by displacing lens of eye. □ **couch potato** person who likes lazing in front of television etc.

**couch**[2] n. (in full **couch grass**) kind of grass with long creeping roots.

**cougar** n. US puma.

**cough** ● v. expel air from lungs with sudden sharp sound. ● n. (sound of) coughing; condition of respiratory organs causing coughing.

**could** see CAN[1].

**couldn't** could not.

**coulomb** n. SI unit of electrical charge.

**council** n. (meeting of) advisory, deliberative, or administrative body; local administrative body of town etc. □□ **councillor** n.

**counsel** ● n. advice, esp. formal; consultation; legal adviser, esp. barrister. ● v. (**counselled**) advise, esp. on personal problems. □□ **counselling** n. **counsellor** n.

**count**[1] ● v. **1** find total of; say numbers in order; include or be included in reckoning. **2** be important. **3** regard as. ● n. **1** counting; number reached by this. **2** point being considered. **3** European nobleman. □ **count on** rely on; expect confidently.

**countdown** n. counting seconds etc. backwards to zero.

**countenance** ● n. **1** face or its expression; composure. **2** moral support. ● v. approve.

**counter**[1] n. **1** flat-topped bench in shop etc., across which business is conducted. **2** small disc for playing or scoring in board games, cards, etc.; device for counting.

**counter**[2] ● v. oppose, contradict; take opposing action. ● adv. in the opposite direction. ● adj. opposite. ● n. **1** parry. **2** countermove. □ **counter-attack** attack in reply to enemy's attack. **counter-intelligence** action against enemy spying. **counter-intuitive** contrary to intuition or to common-sense expectation.

**counter-** comb. form **1** retaliatory. **2** rival. **3** opposite. **4** corresponding.

**counteract** v. hinder or neutralise by contrary action. □□ **counteraction** n.

**counterbalance** ● n. weight or influence balancing another. ● v. act as counterbalance to.

**counterfeit** ● adj. imitation; not genuine; forged. ● n. forgery, imitation. ● v. imitate fraudulently.

**counterfoil** n. part of cheque, receipt, etc., retained as record.

**countermand** v. revoke, recall by contrary order.

**counterpane** n. bedspread.

**counterpart** n. person or thing complementing or equivalent to another; duplicate.

**counterpoint** n. **1** Mus. technique of combining melodies. **2** contrasting argument, plot, theme, etc.

**counterpoise** ● n. counterbalance; state of equilibrium.
● v. counterbalance.

**counterproductive** adj. having opposite of desired effect.

**countersign** v. add confirming signature to. ● n. password spoken to person on guard.

**countersink** v. (countersunk, countersinking) shape (screw hole) so that screw head lies level with surface; provide (screw) with countersink hole.

**counter tenor** n. male alto.

**countervailing** adj. (of influence) counterbalancing.

**countess** n. woman holding rank of count or earl; wife or widow of count or earl.

**countless** adj. too many to count.

**countrified** adj. rural, rustic.

**country** n. **1** nation's territory, sovereign State; land of person's birth or citizenship; region with regard to its aspect, associations, etc. **2** Aust. traditional territory of an Aboriginal people. **3** rural districts as opposed to towns. **4** national population, esp. as voters.

**county** n. territorial division of some countries forming chief unit of local administration.□ **county council** Aust. local government body performing specified function for group of other local government bodies.

**coup** n. successful stroke or move; coup d'état.

**coup de grâce** n. finishing stroke.

**coup d'état** n. (pl. **coups d'état**) sudden overthrow of government, esp. by force.

**coupé** n. two-door car with hard roof and sloping back.

**couple** ● n. two people or things; two people who are married or in sexual relationship. ● v. fasten, link, or associate together; copulate.

**couplet** n. two successive lines of rhyming verse.

**coupon** n. ticket or form entitling holder to something.

**courage** n. ability to disregard fear; bravery.□□ **courageous** adj. **courageously** adv.

**courgette** n. = ZUCCHINI.

**courier** n. company or person that transports commercial packages and documents.

**course** ● n. **1** continuous onward movement or progression; direction taken. **2** line of conduct. **3** area on which golf is played or a race takes place. **4** series of lectures, lessons, etc. **5** each successive part of meal. **6** sequence of medical treatment etc. **7** channel in which water flows.
● v. **1** move or flow freely. **2** use hounds to hunt.□ **in the course of** during. **in due course** at appropriate time. **of course 1** naturally. **2** as expected. **3** admittedly.

**court** ● n. **1** number of houses enclosing yard. **2** courtyard. **3** rectangular area for games. **4** (in full **court of law**) judicial body hearing legal cases. Also called **lawcourt**. **5** sovereign's establishment and retinue. ● v. **1** pay amorous attention to; seek to win (favour of). **2** try to win (fame etc.) **3** unwisely invite.□ **court martial** (pl. **courts martial**) court trying offences against military law; a trial by this.

**courteous** adj. polite, considerate.
□□ **courteously** adv. **courteousness** n.

**courtesan** n. prostitute, esp. one with wealthy or upper class clients.

**courtesy** n. courteous behaviour or act.

**courtier** n. person who attends sovereign's court.

**courtly** adj. dignified, refined. □□ **courtliness** n.

**courtship** n. courting, wooing.

**couscous** n. type of N. African semolina in granules.

**cousin** n. child of one's uncle or aunt.

**couture** n. design and manufacture of fashionable clothes.

**couturier** n. fashion designer.

**cove** n. small bay or inlet; sheltered recess.

**coven** n. assembly of witches.

**covenant** ● n. agreement, a contract. ● v. make a covenant.

**cover** ● v. 1 protect or conceal with cloth, lid, etc. 2 extend over. 3 include. 4 (of sum) be enough to meet (expense). 5 protect by insurance. 6 report on (subject) for newspaper, television, etc. 7 aim gun etc. at; protect by aiming gun. ● n. 1 thing that covers, esp. lid, binding, wrapper, etc.; protection, shelter. 2 pretence. 3 funds to meet liability or secure against loss.

**coverage** n. 1 area or amount covered. 2 publicity received by event etc.

**covering letter** n. explanatory letter with other documents.

**coverlet** n. bedspread.

**covert** ● adj. secret, disguised. ● n. shelter, hiding place. □□ **covertly** adv.

**covet** v. (**coveted**) desire greatly (esp. thing belonging to another person). □□ **covetous** adj.

**covey** n. 1 brood of partridges. 2 small group of people or things.

**cow** ● n. 1 fully-grown female of cattle and certain other large animals, e.g. elephant or whale. 2 colloq.

unpleasant person, esp. woman. ● v. intimidate.

**coward** n. person easily frightened. □□ **cowardly** adj.

**cowardice** n. lack of bravery.

**cowboy** n. 1 person who herds and tends cattle on ranch. 2 colloq. unscrupulous or reckless person in business.

**cower** v. crouch or shrink back in fear.

**cowl** n. (hood of) monk's cloak; hood-shaped covering of chimney or shaft.

**cowlick** n. projecting lock of hair.

**cowling** n. removable cover of vehicle or aircraft engine.

**cowrie** n. tropical mollusc with bright shell.

**cox** ● n. coxswain. ● v. act as cox (of).

**coxswain** n. person who steers, esp. rowing boat.

**coy** adj. affectedly shy; irritatingly reticent. □□ **coyly** adv.

**coyote** n. N. American wild dog.

**cozen** v. literary cheat, defraud; beguile.

**CPI** abbr. Consumer Price Index.

**CPU** n. Computing central processing unit.

**crab** n. ten-legged shellfish.

**crabbed** adj. 1 crabby. 2 (of handwriting) ill-formed; illegible.

**crabby** adj. irritable, morose. □□ **crabbily** adv.

**crabhole** n. 1 hole in ground made by land crab. 2 Aust. depression in heavy clay soils, esp. gilgai.

**crack** ● n. 1 sudden sharp noise; line where thing is broken but not separated; sharp blow. 2 colloq. a joke. 3 colloq. strong form of cocaine. ● adj. colloq. excellent; first-rate. ● v. 1 make or cause to make sound of a crack; break without parting completely; knock sharply. 2 (of voice) become harsh; give way under strain. 3 find solution to (problem). **4** open (bottle of beer etc.) **5** tell (joke). □ **crack down on** *colloq.* take severe measures against. **crack on** *Aust.* pursue with amorous intent. **crack up 1** *colloq.* have physical or mental breakdown. **2** burst into laughter.

**crackdown** *n. colloq.* severe measures against something.

**cracker** *n.* **1** paper cylinder pulled apart with sharp noise and releasing hat, joke, etc.; explosive firework. **2** crisp savoury biscuit. **3** *colloq.* exceptionally attractive or fine person or thing. **4** *Aust.* smallest imaginable amount of money.

**crackerjack** *n. colloq.* exceptionally fine or skilled person etc.

**crackers** *adj. colloq.* crazy.

**crackle** ● *v.* make repeated slight cracking sound. ● *n.* such sound. □□ **crackly** *adj.*

**crackling** *n.* crisp skin of roast pork.

**crackpot** ● *n. colloq.* eccentric person. ● *adj.* crazy, unworkable.

**cradle** ● *n.* **1** baby's bed, esp. on rockers. **2** place regarded as origin of something. **3** supporting framework or structure. **4** *Aust.* box-like apparatus for washing gold from gravel etc. ● *v.* **1** contain or shelter as in cradle. **2** *Aust.* wash (gravel etc.) in miner's cradle.

**craft** ● *n.* **1** special skill or technique; occupation needing this. **2** (*pl.* **craft**) boat, vessel, aircraft, or spacecraft. **3** cunning. ● *v.* make in skilful way.

**craftsman** *n.* (*pl.* **-men**) craftsperson. □□ **craftsmanship** *n.*

**craftsperson** *n.* worker skilled in a craft.

**craftswoman** *n.* (*pl.* **-women**) female craftsperson.

**crafty** *adj.* cunning, artful. □□ **craftily** *adv.*

**crag** *n.* steep rugged rock.

**craggy** *adj.* rugged; rough-textured.

**cram** *v.* (**crammed**) **1** fill to bursting; force. **2** prepare intensively for exam.

**cramp** ● *n.* **1** painful involuntary contraction of muscles. **2** (also **cramp iron**) metal bar with bent ends for holding masonry etc. together. ● *v.* **1** affect with cramp. **2** confine, restrict. **3** fasten with cramp.

**cramped** *adj.* **1** (of space) small. **2** (of handwriting) small and with letters close together.

**cranberry** *n.* (shrub bearing) small red acid berry.

**crane** ● *n.* **1** machine with projecting arm for moving heavy objects. **2** tall wading bird. ● *v.* stretch (one's neck) in order to see something.

**cranium** *n.* (*pl.* **craniums** or **crania**) skull; bones enclosing brain. □□ **cranial** *adj.*

**crank** ● *n.* **1** part of axle or shaft bent at right angles for converting rotary into reciprocal motion or vice versa. **2** eccentric person. ● *v.* turn with crank.

**cranky** *adj.* **1** irritable or ill-tempered. **2** eccentric. □□ **crankily** *adv.* **crankiness** *n.*

**cranny** *n.* chink, crevice.

**crapulent** *adj.* suffering the effects of drunkenness. □□ **crapulence** *n.* **crapulous** *adj.*

**crash** ● *v.* **1** (cause to) make loud smashing noise; (cause to) collide or fall violently. **2** fail, esp. financially. **3** *colloq.* gatecrash. **4** be heavily defeated. **5** (of computer, system, etc.) fail suddenly. **6** *colloq.* sleep, collapse into sleep. ● *n.* **1** sudden loud smashing noise; violent collision or fall, esp. of vehicle. **2** ruin, esp. financial. **3** sudden failure of computer system etc. ● *adj.* done rapidly or urgently. □ **crash helmet** helmet worn to protect head. **crash hot** *colloq.* excellent. **crash-land** (of aircraft) land hurriedly with crash.

**crass** adj. grossly stupid; insensitive. □□ **crassly** adv. **crassness** n.

**crate** ● n. slatted wooden case.
● v. pack in crate.

**crater** n. bowl-shaped cavity, esp. hollow on surface of moon etc.; mouth of volcano.

**cravat** n. man's scarf worn inside open-necked shirt.

**crave** v. long or beg for.

**craven** adj. cowardly, abject.

**craving** n. strong desire or longing.

**crawl** ● v. 1 move slowly, esp. on hands and knees or with body close to ground. 2 colloq. behave obsequiously. 3 be filled with moving things or people. 4 (esp. of skin) feel creepy sensation. ● n. 1 crawling motion; slow rate of movement. 2 high-speed overarm swimming stroke.

**crawler** n. colloq. person behaving obsequiously.

**crayfish** n. lobster-like freshwater crustacean; any of several Australian large marine crustaceans.

**crayon** ● n. stick or pencil of coloured chalk, wax, etc. ● v. draw or colour with crayons.

**craze** n. temporary enthusiasm.

**crazy** adj. insane, mad; foolish; colloq. extremely enthusiastic. □□ **crazily** adv.

**creak** ● n. harsh scraping or squeaking sound. ● v. 1 make creak. 2 move stiffly. □□ **creaky** adj.

**cream** ● n. 1 fatty part of milk; its yellowish-white colour; food or drink like or containing cream. 2 creamlike cosmetic. 3 best part of something. ● v. 1 take cream from. 2 make creamy; form cream or scum. 3 colloq. defeat thoroughly. ● adj. yellowish white. □ **cream cheese** soft rich cheese. **cream of tartar** compound of potassium used in baking powder. □□ **creamy** adj.

**crease** ● n. 1 line made by folding or crushing. 2 Cricket line marking

position of bowler or batter.
● v. make creases in; develop creases.

**create** v. 1 bring into existence; originate; invest with rank. 2 colloq. make fuss. □□ **creation** n.

**creative** adj. inventive, imaginative. □□ **creatively** adv. **creativity** n.

**creature** n. any living being, esp. animal.

**crèche** n. day nursery.

**credence** n. belief.

**credentials** n.pl. evidence of person's achievements, trustworthiness, etc., usu. in form of certificates or references; letter(s) of introduction.

**credible** adj. believable or worthy of belief. □□ **credibility** n.

> **Usage** *Credible* is sometimes confused with *credulous*.

**credit** ● n. 1 system of allowing payment to be deferred. 2 amount at person's disposal in bank; entry in account for sum received. 3 belief that a thing is true. 4 honour for achievement. 5 acknowledgement in book or film. ● v. (**credited**) 1 believe. 2 attribute. 3 enter as credit. □ **credit card** plastic card containing machine-readable magnetic code enabling holder to make purchases on credit. **on credit** with an arrangement to pay later.

**creditable** adj. praiseworthy. □□ **creditably** adv.

**creditor** n. person to whom debt is owing.

**credulous** adj. too ready to believe; gullible. □□ **credulity** n.

> **Usage** *Credulous* is sometimes confused with *credible*.

**creed** n. set of beliefs or principles.

**creek** *n.* watercourse, esp. stream or tributary of river.

**creel** *n.* fisherman's wicker basket.

**creep** ● *v.* (**crept, creeping**) **1** crawl; move stealthily, timidly, or slowly. **2** (of plant) grow along ground or up wall etc. **3** advance or develop gradually. **4** (of flesh) shudder with horror etc. ● *n.* **1** act of creeping. **2** (**the creeps**) *colloq.* feeling of revulsion or fear. **3** *colloq.* unpleasant person. **4** gradual change in shape of metal under stress.

**creeper** *n.* **1** climbing or creeping plant. **2** bird that climbs.

**creepy** *adj. colloq.* feeling or causing horror or fear. □□ **creepily** *adv.* **creepiness** *n.*

**cremate** *v.* burn (corpse) to ashes. □□ **cremation** *n.*

**crematorium** *n.* (*pl.* **crematoria** or **crematoriums**) place where corpses are cremated.

**crème de la crème** *n.* the best part; the elite.

**crenellated** *adj.* having battlements. □□ **crenellation** *n.*

**Creole** *n.* descendant of European settlers in W. Indies or Central or S. America, or French settlers in southern US; their dialect(s); (**creole**) former pidgin language that has developed into sole or native language of a community.

**creosote** ● *n.* oily wood preservative distilled from coal tar. ● *v.* treat with creosote.

**crêpe** *n.* (also **crepe**) **1** fine crinkled fabric. **2** thin pancake with savoury or sweet filling.

**crepitus** *n. Med.* grating noise from ends of fractured bone rubbing together; similar sound heard from chest in pneumonia etc.

**crept** see CREEP.

**crescendo** ● *n.* gradual increase in loudness. ● *adv. & adj.* increasing in loudness.

> **Usage** *Crescendo* is sometimes wrongly used to mean climax rather than progress towards it.

**crescent** ● *n.* sickle shape as of waxing or waning moon; thing of this shape, esp. curved street. ● *adj.* crescent-shaped.

**cress** *n.* plant with pungent edible leaves.

**crest** ● *n.* **1** comb or tuft on bird's or animal's head. **2** plume on helmet. **3** top of mountain, wave, etc. **4** *Heraldry* device above shield or on writing paper etc. ● *v.* reach crest of; crown; serve as crest to; form crest. □□ **crested** *adj.*

**crestfallen** *adj.* disappointed at failure.

**cretaceous** *adj.* chalky.

**cretin** *n.* **1** *colloq. derog.* **1** stupid person. **2** *dated* person who is physically deformed and has learning difficulties because of congenital thyroid deficiency. □□ **cretinism** *n.* **cretinous** *adj.*

**cretonne** *n.* heavy cotton usu. floral upholstery fabric.

**crevasse** *n.* deep open crack in glacier.

**crevice** *n.* narrow opening or fissure, esp. in rock.

**crew** *n.* people working ship or aircraft; group working together; gang. □ **crew cut** close-cropped hairstyle.

**crewel** *n.* thin worsted yarn for embroidery.

**crib** ● *n.* **1** baby's small bed or cot. **2** heavy crossed timbers used in foundations in loose soil etc. **3** light meal or refreshment, refreshment break. **4** *colloq.* translation of text for students. ● *v.* (**cribbed**) **1** copy unfairly. **2** confine in small space.

**cribbage** *n.* card game.

**rick** ● *n.* sudden painful stiffness, esp. in neck. ● *v.* produce crick in.

**ricket** *n.* **1** team game played on grass pitch with two teams of eleven players, in which ball is bowled at wicket defended with bat by player of other team. **2** grasshopper-like chirping insect. □□ **cricketer** *n.*

**rier** *n.* (also **cryer**) official making public announcements.

**rikey** *int. colloq.* expression of astonishment.

**rime** *n.* act punishable by law; such acts collectively; evil act; *colloq.* shameful act.

**riminal** ● *n.* person guilty of crime. ● *adj.* **1** of, involving, or concerning crime. **2** *colloq.* deplorable. □□ **criminality** *n.* **criminally** *adv.*

**riminology** *n.* study of crime. □□ **criminologist** *n.*

**rimp** *v.* press into small folds or waves; corrugate.

**rimson** *adj.* & *n.* rich deep red.

**ringe** *v.* cower; shrink in embarrassment or distaste; behave obsequiously.

**rinkle** ● *n.* wrinkle, crease. ● *v.* form crinkles (in). □□ **crinkly** *adj.*

**rinoline** *n.* hooped petticoat.

**ripple** ● *v.* make lame, damage seriously. ● *n. offens. dated* lame person.

**risis** *n.* (*pl.* **crises**) time of acute danger or difficulty; decisive moment.

**risp** ● *adj.* **1** hard but brittle; firm and fresh. **2** bracing. **3** brisk, decisive. **4** clear-cut. **5** crackling. **6** curly. ● *n.* potato chip. ● *v.* make or become crisp. □□ **crisply** *adv.* **crispness** *n.* **crispy** *adj.*

**criss-cross** ● *n.* pattern of crossing lines. ● *adj.* crossing; in crossing lines. ● *adv.* crosswise. ● *v.* intersect repeatedly; mark with criss-cross pattern.

**criterion** *n.* (*pl.* **criteria**) principle or standard by which thing is judged.

> **Usage** It is a mistake to use the plural form *criteria* when only one criterion is meant.

**critic** *n.* reviewer of literary, artistic, etc. works; person who criticises.

**critical** *adj.* **1** fault-finding; expressing criticism; providing textual criticism. **2** of the nature of a crisis, decisive. **3** marking transition from one state to another. □□ **critically** *adv.*

**criticise** *v.* (also -**ize**) **1** find fault with. **2** discuss critically.

**criticism** *n.* **1** fault-finding; censure. **2** work of critic; analytical article, essay, etc.

**critique** *n.* critical analysis.

**croak** ● *n.* deep hoarse sound, esp. of frog. ● *v.* **1** utter or speak with croak. **2** *colloq.* die. □□ **croaky** *adj.* **croakily** *adv.*

**crochet** ● *n.* needlework of hooked yarn producing patterned fabric. ● *v.* (**crocheted**) make using crochet.

**crockery** *n.* earthenware or china dishes, plates, etc.

**crocodile** *n.* large amphibious reptile with thick scaly skin, long tail, and long jaws. □ **crocodile tears** insincere sorrow.

**crocus** *n.* small plant with corm and white, yellow, or purple flowers.

**Crohn's disease** *n.* inflammatory disease of alimentary tract.

**croissant** *n.* light, crescent-shaped roll of rich yeast pastry.

**crone** *n.* withered old woman.

**cronk** *adj. Aust. colloq.* unfit; unsound.

**crony** n. usu. *derog.* friend, companion.

**crook** ● n. **1** hooked staff of shepherd or bishop. **2** bend, curve. **3** *colloq.* swindler. **4** criminal.
● v. bend, curve. ● adj. *Aust. colloq.* unwell, injured; unpleasant; out of order.

**crooked** adj. **1** not straight, bent. **2** *colloq.* dishonest.□□ **crookedly** adv. **crookedness** n.

**croon** ● v. sing or hum in low voice. ● n. such singing. □□ **crooner** n.

**crop** ● n. **1** produce of any cultivated plant or of land; group or amount produced at one time. **2** handle of whip. **3** very short haircut. **4** pouch in bird's gullet where food is prepared for digestion. ● v. (**cropped**) **1** cut off; bite off, eat down; cut (hair) short. **2** raise crop on (land); bear crop.

**croquet** n. lawn game with hoops, wooden balls, and mallets.

**croquette** n. fried breaded ball of potato, meat, etc.

**crosier** n. (also **crozier**) bishop's ceremonial hooked staff.

**cross** ● n. **1** mark made by drawing one line across another; something shaped like this; stake with transverse bar used in crucifixion. **2** heavy burden. **3** mixture of or compromise between two things; hybrid animal or plant. **4** crossing shot in soccer etc. **5** (**Cross**) *Aust.* Southern Cross constellation. ● v. **1** go or extend across; draw line(s) across; mark (cheque) in this way so that it must be paid into account. **2** cause to interbreed. **3** oppose the wishes of. ● adj. **1** passing from side to side. **2** reciprocal. **3** showing bad temper. **4** intersecting.□ **cross-bench** bench in parliament for members not belonging to government or main opposition. **cross-dressing** wearing clothes more usually associated with opposite sex. **cross-examine** question (witness in court) to check testimony already given. **cross-eyed** squinting. **cross-reference** reference to another place in same book. **cross-section 1** diagram showing internal structure **2** representative sample.□□ **crossly** adv. **crossness** n.

**crossbar** n. horizontal bar.

**crossfire** n. gunfire crossing another line of fire.

**crossing** n. **1** place where things (esp roads) meet; place for crossing street **2** journey across water.

**crossroads** n. place where roads intersect.

**crossword** n. puzzle in which intersecting words have to be inserted into diagram.

**crotch** n. fork, esp. between legs (of person, trousers, etc.)

**crotchet** n. *Mus.* note equal to quarter of semibreve and usu. one beat.

**crotchety** adj. peevish.

**crouch** ● v. stand, squat, etc. with legs bent close to body. ● n. this position.

**croup** n. childhood inflammation of larynx etc., with sharp cough and difficulty in breathing.

**croupier** n. person in charge of gaming table.

**crouton** n. small cube of fried or toasted bread.

**crow** ● n. any of various large black birds. ● v. (**crowed** or **crew**, **crowing**) (of rooster) utter loud cry; (of baby) utter happy sounds; gloat, boast.

**crowbar** n. iron bar used as lever and for digging holes.

**crowd** ● n. large gathering of people; *colloq.* particular set of people. ● v. **1** (cause to) come together in crowd. **2** force way into. **3** cram with. **4** *colloq.* come aggressively close to.□ **crowd surf** (esp. at rock concert) ride crowd by being passed over heads of crowd members.

**crowdfunding** n. funding a project etc. by raising money from a large number of people who each contribute a relatively small amount. □□ **crowdfund** v.

**crowdsourcing** n. obtaining input etc. into a task or project by enlisting the services of a large number of people. □□ **crowdsource** v.

**crowea** n. woody Australian shrub with flowers in white to deep rose.

**crown ●** n. 1 monarch's jewelled headdress; **(the Crown)** monarch as head of state, his or her authority. 2 top part of head, hill, etc. **●** v. 1 put crown on; make king or queen. 2 (often as **crowning** adj.) be consummation, reward, or finishing touch to. 3 colloq. hit on head.

**crozier** = CROSIER.

**cruces** SEE CRUX.

**crucial** adj. decisive, critical; very important. □□ **crucially** adv.

**crucible** n. melting pot for metals.

**crucifix** n. model of cross with figure of Christ on it.

**crucifixion** n. crucifying, esp. of Christ.

**cruciform** adj. cross-shaped.

**crucify** v. 1 put to death by fastening to cross; cause extreme pain to. 2 colloq. defeat thoroughly in argument, match, etc.

**ruddy** adj. colloq. dirty, unsavoury; shoddy.

**rude ●** adj. in natural or raw state; unpolished, lacking finish; rude, blunt; indecent. **●** n. natural mineral oil. □□ **crudely** adv. **crudeness** n.

**crudity** n.

**crudités** n.pl. dish of mixed raw vegetables, often served with dipping sauce.

**cruel** adj. causing pain or suffering, esp. deliberately; harsh, severe. □□ **cruelly** adv. **cruelty** n.

**cruet** n. set of small salt, pepper, etc. containers for use at table.

**cruise ●** v. 1 sail about, esp. travel by sea for pleasure; travel at relaxed or economical speed. 2 achieve objective with ease. 3 colloq. search for sexual partner in bars, streets, etc. **●** n. cruising voyage.

**cruiser** n. high-speed warship.

**cruisy** adj. (**cruisier**) Aust. colloq. relaxed; easy-going.

**crumb ●** n. 1 small fragment, esp. of bread. 2 AFL loose ball. **●** v. coat with breadcrumbs; crumble (bread).

**crumble ●** v. break or fall into fragments; disintegrate. **●** n. dish of stewed fruit with crumbly topping.

**crumbly** adj. (**crumblier**) colloq. easily crumbled.

**crummy** adj. (**crummier**) colloq. squalid; inferior.

**crumpet** n. soft flat yeast cake eaten toasted.

**crumple** v. crush or become crushed into creases; collapse, give way.

**crunch ●** v. crush noisily with teeth; make or emit crunch. **●** n. 1 crunching sound. 2 colloq. decisive event. □□ **crunchy** adj.

**crupper** n. strap looped under horse's tail to hold harness back.

**crusade ●** n. 1 hist. medieval Christian military expedition to recover Holy Land from Muslims. 2 vigorous campaign for cause. **●** v. engage in crusade. □□ **crusader** n.

**crush ●** v. compress violently so as to break, bruise, etc.; reduce to powder by pressure; crease, crumple; defeat or subdue completely. **●** n. 1 act of crushing. 2 crowded mass of people. 3 drink from juice of crushed fruit. 4 colloq. infatuation.

**crust ●** n. 1 hard outer layer, esp. of bread. 2 Aust. colloq. livelihood.

- *v.* cover with, form into, or become covered with crust. □□ **crusty** *adj.*

**crustacean** *n.* hard-shelled usu. aquatic animal, e.g. crab or yabby. ● *adj.* of crustaceans.

**crutch** *n.* 1 support for lame person, usu. with cross piece fitting under armpit. 2 support. 3 crotch. 4 hindquarters of sheep. ● *v. Aust.* remove wool from about the tail of sheep, esp. to prevent blowfly strike.

**crutchings** *n.pl. Aust.* wool clipped from hindquarters of sheep.

**crux** *n.* (*pl.* **cruxes** *or* **cruces**) decisive point at issue.

**cry** ● *v.* (**cries, cried, crying**) 1 shed tears. 2 call loudly; appeal for help. ● *n.* loud shout of grief, fear, pain, etc.; an appeal; rallying call; fit of weeping.

**cryer** = CRIER.

**cryogenics** *n.* branch of physics dealing with very low temperatures. □□ **cryogenic** *adj.*

**crypt** *n.* vault, esp. beneath church, used usu. as burial place.

**cryptic** *adj.* obscure in meaning; secret, mysterious. □□ **cryptically** *adv.*

**cryptocurrency** *n.* digital currency in which encryption techniques are used to regulate generation of units of currency and verify transfer of funds.

**cryptogram** *n.* text written in cipher.

**crystal** ● *n.* 1 (piece of) transparent colourless mineral; (articles of) highly transparent glass; substance solidified in definite geometrical form. ● *adj.* made of or as clear as crystal.

**crystalline** *adj.* of or as clear as crystal.

**crystallise** *v.* (also **-ize**) 1 form into crystals. 2 make or become definite. 3 preserve or be preserved in sugar. □□ **crystallisation** *n.*

**CS gas** *n.* gas causing tears and choking, used to control riots etc.

**CSIRO** *abbr. Aust.* Commonwealth Scientific and Industrial Research Organisation.

**CT scan** *see* CAT.

**cu.** *abbr.* cubic.

**cub** *n.* 1 young of fox, bear, lion, etc. 2 (**Cub Scout**) junior Scout.

**cubby hole** *n.* very small room; snug space.

**cubby house** *n.* child's playhouse.

**cube** *n.* 1 solid contained by six equal squares; cube-shaped block. 2 product of number multiplied by its square. ● *v.* 1 find cube of (number). 2 cut into small cubes. □ **cube root** number that produces given number when cubed.

**cubic** *adj.* 1 of three dimensions. 2 involving cube of a quantity. □ **cubic metre** volume of cube whose edge is one metre. □□ **cubical** *adj.*

**cubicle** *n.* small screened space.

**cubism** *n.* art style in which objects are represented geometrically. □□ **cubist** *n.* & *adj.*

**cubit** *n.* ancient measure of length, approximating length of forearm.

**cuckold** *dated* ● *n.* man whose wife is sexually unfaithful. ● *v.* make cuckold of.

**cuckoo** ● *n.* bird having characteristic cry, and often laying its eggs in nests of small birds. ● *adj. colloq.* crazy.

**cucumber** *n.* long green fleshy fruit used in salads.

**cud** *n.* half-digested food chewed by ruminant.

**cuddle** ● *v.* hug; fondle; nestle; lie close and snug. ● *n.* prolonged hug. □□ **cuddlesome** *adj.* **cuddly** *adj.*

**cudgel** ● *n.* thick stick used as weapon. ● *v.* (**cudgelled**) beat with cudgel.

**cue** ● *n.* 1 signal to do something. 2 long rod for striking balls in billiards etc. ● *v.* (**cued, cueing**) 1 give signal to (someone). 2 strike with cue. 3 set piece of audio or video equipment in readiness to play (a particular part of recorded material).

**cuff** ● n. 1 band of cloth around the end of sleeve; trouser turn up. 2 a blow with open hand. ● v. strike with open hand. □ **cuff link** device of two jointed studs etc. to fasten sides of cuff together. **off the cuff** colloq. without preparation.

**cuisine** n. style of cooking.

**cul-de-sac** n. (pl. **culs-de-sac** or **cul-de-sacs**) road etc. closed at one end.

**culinary** adj. of or for cooking.

**cull** ● v. select, gather; select and kill (surplus animals). ● n. 1 culling. 2 animal(s) culled.

**culminate** v. reach highest or final point. □□ **culmination** n.

**culottes** n.pl. women's trousers cut like skirt.

**culpable** adj. deserving blame. □□ **culpability** n.

**culprit** n. guilty person.

**cult** n. religious system, sect, etc.; devotion or homage to person or thing.

**cultivar** n. plant variety produced by cultivation.

**cultivate** v. 1 prepare and use (soil) for crops; raise (plant etc.) 2 (often as **cultivated** adj.) improve manners etc. 3 nurture (friendship). □□ **cultivation** n.

**cultivator** n. agricultural implement for breaking up ground etc.

**culture** ● n. 1 customs and civilisation of particular time or people; developed understanding of art, literature, music, etc. 2 artificial rearing of bacteria; quantity of bacteria grown for study. ● v. grow under artificial conditions. □□ **cultural** adj.

**culvert** n. underground channel carrying water under road etc.

**cum** ● prep. 1 with, combined with. 2 also used as. ● n. coarse colloq. = COME n.

**cumbersome** adj. (also **cumbrous**) inconveniently bulky; unwieldy.

**cumin** n. (also **cummin**) plant with aromatic seeds; these as flavouring.

**cummerbund** n. waist sash.

**cumquat** n. (also **kumquat**) small orange-like fruit.

**cumulative** adj. increasing in force etc. by successive additions. □□ **cumulatively** adv.

**cumulus** n. (pl. **cumuli**) cloud formation of heaped-up rounded masses.

**cuneiform** ● adj. wedge-shaped. ● n. wedge-shaped writing.

**cunjevoi** n. Aust. 1 sea squirt occurring on intertidal rocks in southern Australia; its flesh as bait. 2 rainforest plant with large leaves and greenish, lily-like flowers.

**cunnilingus** n. oral stimulation of the female genitals.

**cunning** ● adj. deceitful, crafty; ingenious. ● n. craftiness; ingenuity. □□ **cunningly** adv.

**cunt** n. coarse sl. 1 female genitals. 2 offens. unpleasant or stupid person or thing.

**cup** ● n. 1 small bowl-shaped drinking vessel; amount contained in this; cup-shaped thing; cup-shaped trophy as prize. 2 flavoured wine, cider, etc., usu. chilled. ● v. (**cupped**) make cup-shaped; hold as in cup. □□ **cupful** n.

**cupboard** n. recess or piece of furniture with door and (usu.) shelves.

**cupidity** n. greed; avarice.

**cupola** n. small dome.

**cupreous** adj. of or like copper.

**cupric** adj. of copper.

**cur** n. 1 mangy ill-tempered dog. 2 contemptible person.

**curable** *adj.* able to be cured.

**curaçao** *n.* orange-flavoured liqueur.

**curacy** *n.* curate's office or position.

**curare** *n.* poisonous extract of various plants.

**curate**¹ *n.* assistant to parish priest.
□ **curate's egg** something good in parts.

**curate**² *v.* select, organise, and look after items in (collection or exhibition); select, organise, and present (online content etc.)

**curative** ● *adj.* tending to cure. ● *n.* curative agent.

**curator** *n.* person in charge of museum or other collection; person who organises art exhibition etc.

**curb** ● *n.* **1** means of restraint. **2** kerb. ● *v.* **1** restrain. **2** put curb on.

**curdle** *v.* form or cause to form into curds.

**curds** *n.pl.* thick soft substance formed when milk turns sour.

**cure** ● *v.* **1** restore to health, relieve. **2** preserve (meat etc.) by salting etc. **3** vulcanise (rubber); harden (plastic). ● *n.* restoration to health; thing that cures; course of treatment.

**curette** ● *n.* surgeon's scraping instrument. ● *v.* scrape with this.
□□ **curettage** *n.*

**curfew** *n.* signal or time after which people must remain indoors.

**curie** *n.* unit of radioactivity.

**curio** *n.* rare or unusual object.

**curiosity** *n.* **1** desire to know; inquisitiveness. **2** strange or rare object.

**curious** *adj.* **1** eager to learn; inquisitive. **2** strange, surprising.
□□ **curiously** *adv.*

**curium** *n.* radioactive metallic element (symbol Cm).

**curl** ● *v.* bend or coil into spiral; move in curve; (of upper lip) be raised in contempt. ● *n.* lock of curled hair; anything spiral or curved inwards. □□ **curler** *n.* **curly** *adj.*

**curlew** *n.* long-billed wading bird; an similar Australian bird.

**curlicue** *n.* decorative curl or twist.

**curling** *n.* game like bowls played on ice with round flat stones.

**curmudgeon** *n.* bad-tempered person.

**currant** *n.* **1** small seedless dried grape. **2** (fruit of) any of various shrubs producing red, white, or black berries.

**currawong** *n.* Australian bird, havin predominantly black or grey plumage, yellow eyes, and loud, melodious, ringing call.

**currency** *n.* **1** money in use in a country. **2** being current; prevalence (of ideas etc.)

**current** ● *adj.* belonging to present time; happening now; in general circulation or use. ● *n.* **1** body of moving water, air, etc. passing through still water etc.; movement of electrically charged particles. **2** general tendency or course.
□□ **currently** *adv.*

**curriculum** *n.* (*pl.* **curricula**) course of study. □ **curriculum vitae** brief account of one's career.

**curry**¹ ● *n.* meat, vegetables, etc., cooked in spicy-hot sauce.

**curry**² ● *v.* groom (horse) with curry-comb. □ **curry-comb** metal device with serrated edge for grooming horses. **curry favour** win favour by flattery.

**curse** ● *n.* call for evil to come on person or thing; great evil; violent or profane exclamation. ● *v.* utter curse (against); afflict. □□ **cursed** *adj.*

**cursive** ● *adj.* (of writing) with joined characters. ● *n.* cursive writing.

**cursor** *n. Computing* movable indicator on display screen.

**cursory** *adj.* hasty, hurried.
□□ **cursorily** *adv.*

**curt** *adj.* noticeably or rudely brief.
□□ **curtly** *adv.* **curtness** *n.*

**curtail** v. cut short; reduce.
□□ **curtailment** n.

**curtain** n. piece of cloth etc. hung as screen, esp. at window.

**curtsy** (also **curtsey**) ● n. bending of knees by female in acknowledgement of applause or as greeting.
● v. make a curtsy.

**curvaceous** adj. colloq. (esp. of woman) shapely.

**curvature** n. curving, curved form; deviation of curve from plane.

**curve** ● n. line or surface of which no part is straight; curved line on graph. ● v. bend or shape so as to form curve. □□ **curvy** adj.

**cuscus** n. nocturnal, usu. arboreal, marsupial mammal.

**cushion** ● n. bag stuffed with soft material for sitting on etc.; protection against shock; padded rim of billiard table; air supporting hovercraft.
● v. provide or protect with cushion(s); mitigate effects of.

**cushy** adj. colloq. (of job etc.) easy, pleasant.

**cusp** n. 1 point at which two curves meet. 2 point of transition, esp. between astrological signs.
□□ **cuspate** adj. **cusped** adj. **cuspidal** adj.

**cuss** colloq. ● n. 1 curse. 2 awkward person. ● v. curse.

**custard** n. pudding or sweet sauce of eggs or flavoured cornflour and milk.

**custody** n. 1 guardianship.
2 imprisonment. □□ **custodial** adj.
**custodian** n.

**custom** n. 1 usual behaviour. 2 Law established usage. 3 business dealings, customers. 4 (customs) duty on imported goods.

**customary** adj. in accordance with custom, usual. □□ **customarily** adv.

**customer** n. person who buys goods or services.

**customise** v. (also **-ize**) make or modify to order; personalise.

**cut** ● v. 1 divide, wound, or shape by pressure with sharp-edged instrument. 2 reduce; intersect. 3 divide (pack of cards). 4 have (tooth) coming through gum. ● n. 1 wound or mark made by sharp edge. 2 piece cut off. 3 a stroke with knife, whip, etc. 4 style in which hair, garment, etc. is cut. 5 reduction; share. ● adj. 1 (of leaf) having margin deeply indented. 2 colloq. circumcised.

**cutaneous** adj. of the skin.

**cute** adj. 1 colloq. attractive, sexy.
2 sweet. 3 clever, ingenious. □□ **cutely** adv. **cuteness** n.

**cuticle** n. skin at base of fingernail or toenail.

**cutis** n. true skin, beneath epidermis.

**cutlass** n. hist. short broad-bladed curved sword.

**cutlery** n. knives, forks, and spoons for use at table.

**cutlet** n. neck chop of lamb, veal, etc.; fish steak.

**cutthroat** n. murderer.

**cutting** ● n. 1 piece cut from newspaper etc. 2 piece cut from plant for propagation. 3 excavated channel in hillside etc. for railway or road. ● adj. 1 that cuts. 2 hurtful.
□□ **cuttingly** adv.

**cuttlefish** n. ten-armed mollusc ejecting black fluid when threatened.

**cuvée** n. blend or batch of wine.

**cuz** n. Aust. colloq. (in Aboriginal English) familiar form of address to cousin or close friend.

**CV** abbr. curriculum vitae.

**cwt** abbr. hundredweight.

**cyanide** n. highly poisonous substance.

**cyanosis** n. bluish skin due to oxygen-deficient blood.

**cyber-** comb. form relating to electronic communication and virtual reality.

**cybernetics** n.pl. science of systems of control and communication in animals and machines.□□ **cybernetic** *adj.*

**cyberspace** *n.* notional environment in which electronic communication occurs.

**cycad** *n.* palmlike plant often growing to great height.

**cyclamen** *n.* plant with pink, red, or white flowers with backward-turned petals.

**cycle** ● *n.* **1** recurrent round or period (of events, phenomena, etc.) **2** series of related songs, poems, etc. **3** bicycle, tricycle, etc. ● *v.* **1** ride bicycle etc. **2** move in cycles. □□ **cyclist** *n.*

**cyclic** *adj.* (also **cyclical**) **1** recurring in cycles. **2** belonging to chronological cycle.

**cyclone** *n.* violent wind rotating around low-pressure region. □□ **cyclonic** *adj.*

**cyclotron** *n.* apparatus for acceleration of charged atomic particles revolving in magnetic field.

**cygnet** *n.* young swan.

**cylinder** *n.* solid or hollow roller-shaped body; container for liquefied gas etc.; piston chamber in engine.□□ **cylindrical** *adj.*

**cymbal** *n.* concave disc struck usu. with another to make ringing sound. □□ **cymbalist** *n.*

**cymbidium** *n.* tropical orchid.

**cynic** *n.* person with pessimistic view of human nature. □□ **cynical** *adj.* cynically *adv.* **cynicism** *n.*

**cypher** = CIPHER.

**cypress** *n.* conifer with dark foliage.

**Cyrillic** ● *adj.* of alphabet used esp. for Russian and Bulgarian. ● *n.* this alphabet.

**cyst** *n.* sac formed in body, containing liquid matter, parasitic larva, etc.

**cystic** *adj.* **1** of the bladder. **2** like a cyst □ **cystic fibrosis** hereditary disease usu. resulting in respiratory infections.

**cystitis** *n.* inflammation of bladder.

**cytology** *n.* study of cells.

**czar** = TSAR.

# Dd

**D** n. (also **d**) Roman numeral 500.

**d** abbr. (also **d.**) **1** died. **2** hist. (predecimal) penny.

**dab** ● v. (**dabbed**) strike or press lightly or feebly. ● n. small amount of something applied; light blow. □ **dab hand** expert.

**dabble** v. **1** engage (in activity etc.) superficially. **2** move about in shallow liquid.□□ **dabbler** n.

**da capo** adv. Mus. repeat from beginning.

**dachshund** n. short-legged long-bodied dog.

**dactyl** n. metrical foot of one long followed by two short syllables. □□ **dactylic** adj.

**dad** n. colloq. father.

**daddy** n. colloq. father.

**dado** n. lower, differently decorated, part of interior wall.

**daffodil** n. spring bulb with trumpet-shaped yellow flowers.

**daft** adj. colloq. silly, foolish, crazy.

**dag** n. Aust. **1** lump of matted wool and dung. **2** colloq. entertainingly eccentric character. **3** colloq. unfashionable, awkward, or untidy person.

**dagger** n. **1** short knifelike weapon. **2** obelus.

**daggy** adj. (**daggier**) Aust. **1** (of sheep) fouled with dags. **2** colloq. (of person) unkempt, unfashionable; eccentric.

**daguerreotype** n. early kind of photograph.

**dahlia** n. garden plant with large showy flowers.

**daily** ● adj. done, produced, or occurring every (week)day. ● adv. every day; constantly. ● n. colloq. daily newspaper.

**dainty** ● adj. delicately pretty or small; choice; fastidious. ● n. delicacy.□□ **daintily** adv. **daintiness** n.

**dairy** ● n. place for processing, distributing, or selling milk and milk products. ● adj. of, containing, or used for, dairy products. □□ **dairying** n.

**dais** n. low platform, esp. at upper end of hall.

**daisy** n. small plant bearing composite flowers with white radiating petals.

**dak** v. (**dakked**) Aust. colloq. pull down pants etc. of (person) as joke or punishment.

**Dalai Lama** n. spiritual head of Tibetan Buddhism.

**dale** n. chiefly Brit. valley.

**dally** v. delay; waste time; flirt, trifle. □□ **dalliance** n.

**Dalmatian** n. dog of large white breed with dark spots.

**dam** ● n. **1** barrier across river etc. **2** Aust. reservoir for storage of usu. run-off rainwater, esp. to provide water for stock. **3** mother of animal, esp. mammal. ● v. (**dammed**) provide or confine with dam; block up.

**damage** ● n. **1** harm, injury. **2** (**damages**) financial compensation for loss or injury. **3** (**the damage**) colloq. cost. ● v. inflict damage on.

**damask** n. **1** fabric with woven design made visible by reflection of light. ● adj. **1** made of damask. **2** velvety pink.

**dame** n. **1** (**Dame**) title given to woman with rank of knight; woman holding this title. **2** US colloq. woman.

**damn** ● v. condemn to hell; condemn, criticise; swear at.
● *int. colloq.* exclamation of annoyance. ● *adj. & adv.* (also **damned**) *colloq.* **1** annoying(ly). **2** extreme(ly).

**damnable** *adj.* hateful, annoying.

**damnation** ● n. eternal punishment in hell. ● *int.* expressing anger.

**damp** ● *adj.* slightly wet.
● n. slightly diffused or condensed moisture. ● v. **1** make damp. **2** take force or vigour out of, make burn less strongly. **3** *Mus.* stop vibration of (strings etc.) □□ **dampness** n.

**dampen** v. **1** make or become damp. **2** discourage.

**damper** n. **1** discouraging person or thing. **2** device that reduces shock, vibration, or noise. **3** metal plate in flue to control draught. **4** *Aust.* simple kind of unleavened bread.

**damsel** n. *arch.* young unmarried woman.

**dan** n. grade of proficiency in judo, karate, etc.

**dance** ● v. move rhythmically, usu. to music; skip or jump about; perform (dance, role, etc.). ● n. dancing as art; style or form of this; social gathering for dancing; lively motion.
□□ **dancer** n.

**d and c** *abbr.* dilatation and curettage, minor operation to clean uterus.

**dandelion** n. yellow-flowered weed.

**dandle** ● v. bounce (child) on one's knees etc.

**dandruff** n. flakes of dead skin in hair.

**dandy** ● n. man greatly devoted to style and fashion. ● *adj. colloq.* splendid.

**danger** n. liability or exposure to harm; thing causing harm.

**dangerous** *adj.* involving or causing danger. □□ **dangerously** *adv.*

**dangle** v. be loosely suspended and able to sway; hold or carry loosely suspended; hold out (hope, temptation, etc.) enticingly.

**dank** *adj.* damp and cold.

**daphne** n. flowering shrub.

**dapper** *adj.* **1** neat and precise, esp. in dress. **2** sprightly.

**dapple** ● v. mark with spots of colour or shade. ● n. dappled effect; dappled animal, esp. horse.

**dare** ● v. have the courage or impudence (to); defy, challenge.
● n. challenge.

**daredevil** n. recklessly daring person.

**daring** ● n. adventurous courage. ● *adj.* bold; prepared to take risks. □□ **daringly** *adv.*

**dark** ● *adj.* **1** with little or no light; of deep or sombre colour; (of person) with dark colouring. **2** gloomy; sinister; angry. **3** secret, mysterious.
● n. absence of light or knowledge; nightfall; unlit place. ● **dark horse** successful competitor of whom little is known. □ **darken** v. **darkly** *adv.* **darkness** n.

**darkroom** n. room for photographic work, with normal light excluded.

**darling** ● n. beloved or endearing person or animal. ● *adj.* beloved, lovable; *colloq.* charming.

**darmstadtium** n. radioactive element (symbol **Ds**).

**darn** v. mend by interweaving wool etc. across hole. ● n. darned area in material. ● *adj.* (also **darned**) *colloq.* damn.

**dart** ● n. **1** small pointed missile, esp. for throwing at target. **2** sudden rapid movement. **3** tapering tuck in garment. **4** fish of warmer waters. ● v. move, send, or go suddenly or rapidly.

**darter** n. large water bird with narrow head and long thin neck.

**darwinia** n. Australian shrub, having usu. red flowers.

**dash** ● v. 1 rush. 2 strike or fling forcefully so as to shatter. 3 frustrate, dispirit. ● n. 1 rush, onset. 2 punctuation mark ( — ) used to indicate break in sense. 3 (capacity for) impetuous vigour. 4 sprinting race. 5 longer signal of two in Morse code. 6 slight admixture. 7 dashboard.

**dashboard** n. 1 instrument panel of motor vehicle. 2 page on a website giving access to elements of the site's functionality.

**dashcam** n. video camera mounted on dashboard or windscreen of vehicle and used to record view of the road, traffic, etc.

**dashing** adj. spirited; showy.

**dastardly** adj. cowardly, despicable.

**data** n.pl. (also treated as *sing.*, as in *that is the only data we have*) 1 known facts used for inference or in reckoning. 2 quantities or characters operated on by a computer.

> **Usage** In Latin, *data* is the plural of *datum*. This singular form is now rarely heard in common usage.

**database** n. organised store of computerised data.

**date** ● n. 1 day, month, or year of thing's occurrence; period to which thing belongs. 2 *colloq.* social appointment; person to be met at this. 3 small brown edible fruit.
● v. 1 mark with date; assign date to; have its origins at particular time; appear or expose as old-fashioned. 2 *colloq.* make social appointment (with). □ **date line** imaginary north-south line through the Pacific Ocean, east of which the date is a day earlier than it is to the west. **to date** until now.

**dative** n. grammatical case expressing indirect object.

**datum** n. (pl. **data**) item of data.

**daub** v. paint or spread (plaster, paint, etc.) crudely or unskilfully; smear (surface) with paint etc.
● n. paint etc. daubed on surface; crude painting; clay etc. coating wattles to form wall.

**daughter** n. female child in relation to her parents. □ **daughter-in-law** (pl. **daughters-in-law**) one's child's wife.

**daunt** v. discourage, intimidate. □□ **daunting** adj.

**dauntless** adj. intrepid, persevering.

**davit** n. small crane on ship for holding lifeboat.

**dawdle** v. walk slowly and idly; waste time; procrastinate.

**dawn** ● n. daybreak; beginning.
● v. 1 (of day) begin; grow light. 2 become obvious (to).

**day** n. time while sun is above horizon; period of 24 hours; hours given to work during a day; a time, a period.

**daybreak** n. first light of day.

**daydream** ● n. pleasant idle thoughts. ● v. have daydreams.

**daze** ● v. stupefy, bewilder.
● n. dazed state.

**dazzle** ● v. blind or confuse temporarily with sudden bright light; impress or overpower with knowledge, ability, etc. ● n. bright confusing light. □□ **dazzler** n. **dazzling** adj.

**dB** abbr. decibel(s).

**DC** abbr. direct current.

**DDT** abbr. colourless chlorinated hydrocarbon used as insecticide.

**de-** prefix implying removal or reversal.

**deacon** n. member of clergy ranking below priest; lay officer in Nonconformist churches.

**dead** ● adj. 1 no longer alive. 2 lacking sensation or emotion;

lacking vigour; lacking resonance.
**3** no longer functioning; no longer relevant; extinct. **4** total, absolute.
● *adv.* absolutely; exactly; completely.□ **dead cat bounce** temporary recovery in share prices after substantial fall. **dead end 1** road closed at one end. **2** situation where no progress can be made. **dead heat** race in which two or more competitors finish exactly even.

**deaden** *v.* deprive of or lose vitality, force etc.; make insensitive.

**deadline** *n.* time limit.

**deadlock** ● *n.* **1** state where no progress can be made. **2** type of lock requiring a key to open or close it.
● *v.* bring or come to a standstill.

**deadly** ● *adj.* (**deadlier**) **1** causing death or serious damage; deathlike; very dreary. **2** *Aust. colloq.* fantastic; terrific. ● *adv.* **1** as if dead.
**2** extremely.

**deadpan** *n.* expressionless.

**deaf** *adj.* wholly or partly unable to hear; refusing to listen or comply.
□□ **deafness** *n.*

**deafen** *v.* (often as **deafening** *adj.*) overpower or make deaf by noise, esp. temporarily.□□ **deafeningly** *adv.*

**deal** ● *v.* (**dealt, dealing**) **1** distribute; hand out (cards) to players in a card game; give; inflict. **2** do business; trade. ● *n.* **1** player's turn to deal. **2** business transaction. **3** *colloq.* large amount.□ **deal with** take action about; be about or concerned with.

**dealer** *n.* **1** person who deals. **2** trader.

**dean** *n.* **1** university official. **2** head of ecclesiastical chapter.

**dear** ● *adj.* **1** beloved. **2** used before person's name, esp. at beginning of letter. **3** precious; expensive.
● *n.* dear person. ● *adv.* at great cost. ● *int.* expressing surprise, dismay, pity, etc.□□ **dearly** *adv.*

**dearth** *n.* scarcity, lack.

**death** *n.* dying, end of life; being dead; end; destruction.□ **death trap** unsafe place.□□ **deathlike** *adj.*

**deb** *n. colloq.* debutante.

**debacle** *n.* **1** utter collapse.
**2** confused rush.

**debar** *v.* (**debarred**) exclude.

**debase** *v.* lower in quality, value, or character; depreciate (coin) by alloying etc.□□ **debasement** *n.*

**debatable** *adj.* questionable.

**debate** ● *v.* discuss or dispute, esp. formally. ● *n.* formal discussion.

**debauchery** *n.* over-indulgence in harmful or immoral pleasures.
□□ **debauched** *adj.*

**debenture** *n.* certificate acknowledging a debt on which fixed interest is paid.

**debilitate** *v.* enfeeble.
□□ **debilitation** *n.*

**debility** *n.* feebleness, esp. of health.

**debit** ● *n.* entry in account recording sum owed. ● *v.* (**debited**) enter on debit side of account.

**debonair** *adj.* having carefree self-confident manner.

**debrief** *v. colloq.* question (diplomat etc.) about completed mission.
□□ **debriefing** *n.*

**debris** *n.* scattered fragments.

**debt** *n.* money etc. owing; obligation; state of owing.

**debtor** *n.* person owing money etc.

**debug** *v.* (**debugged**) remove bugs from.

**debunk** *v. colloq.* expose as spurious or false.

**debut** ● *n.* first public appearance.
● *v.* make debut.

**debutante** *n.* young woman making her social debut.

**Dec.** *abbr.* December.

**deca-** *comb. form* ten.

**decade** *n.* ten year period.

**decadence** *n.* moral or cultural decline; immoral behaviour.
□□ **decadent** *adj.*

**decaffeinated** *adj.* with caffeine removed.

**decagon** *n.* plane figure with ten sides and angles.□□ **decagonal** *adj.*

**decahedron** *n.* solid figure with ten faces.□□ **decahedral** *adj.*

**decamp** *v.* go away suddenly or secretly.

**decant** *v.* pour off (wine etc.) leaving sediment behind.

**decanter** *n.* stoppered glass container for decanted wine or spirit.

**decapitate** *v.* behead. □□ **decapitation** *n.*

**decarbonise** *v.* (also **-ize**) **1** reduce amount of gaseous carbon compounds in (process etc.) **2** remove carbon etc. from (engine of car etc.) □□ **decarbonisation** *n.*

**decathlon** *n.* athletic contest of ten events.□□ **decathlete** *n.*

**decay** ● *v.* **1** rot. **2** lose quality or strength. ● *n.* decaying, rot.

**decease** *n. Law* death.

**deceased** *formal* ● *adj.* dead. ● *n.* (**the deceased**) person who has died.

**deceit** *n.* deception; trick. □□ **deceitful** *adj.*

**deceive** *v.* make (person) believe what is false; mislead.□□ **deceiver** *n.*

**decelerate** *v.* (cause to) reduce speed.□□ **deceleration** *n.*

**December** *n.* twelfth month of year.

**decent** *adj.* **1** conforming to accepted standards of what is proper; respectable. **2** *colloq.* kind and obliging.□□ **decency** *n.* **decently** *adv.*

**decentralise** *v.* (also **-ize**) transfer from central to local control. □□ **decentralisation** *n.*

**deception** *n.* deceiving, being deceived; thing that deceives.

**deceptive** *adj.* likely to mislead.

**deci-** *comb. form* one tenth.

**decibel** *n.* unit used in comparison of sound etc.

**decide** *v.* resolve after consideration; settle (issue etc.); give judgement.

**decided** *adj.* definite, unquestionable; (of person) having clear opinions, positive, resolute.□□ **decidedly** *adv.*

**decider** *n.* game, race, etc. as tie-break.

**deciduous** *adj.* (of tree) shedding leaves annually; (of leaves etc.) shed periodically.

**decigram** *n.* (also **decigramme**) metric unit of mass, equal to 0.1 gram.

**decimal** ● *adj.* reckoned in tens or tenths. ● *n.* decimal fraction. □ **decimal currency** that with each unit 10 or 100 times the value of the one next below it. **decimal fraction** fraction based on powers of ten, shown as figures after a dot. **decimal point** dot used in decimal fraction.

**decimalise** *v.* (also **-ize**) express as decimal; convert to decimal system. □□ **decimalisation** *n.*

**decimate** *v.* destroy large proportion of.□□ **decimation** *n.*

**decipher** *v.* convert (coded information) into intelligible language; determine meaning of. □□ **decipherable** *adj.*

**decision** *n.* deciding; resolution after consideration; settlement; resoluteness.

**decisive** *adj.* **1** conclusive, settling an issue. **2** quick to decide.□□ **decisively** *adv.* **decisiveness** *n.*

**deck** ● *n.* **1** floor or storey of ship, bus, etc. **2** section for playing discs or tapes etc. in sound system. **3** pack of cards. ● *v.* **1** decorate. **2** *colloq.* floor (person) by hitting.

**decking** *n.* planks forming deck of ship or floor of verandah.

**declaim** *v.* speak or say as if addressing an audience. □□ **declamation** *n.* **declamatory** *adj.*

**declaration** *n.* declaring; formal, emphatic, or deliberate statement.

**declare** v. **1** announce openly or formally; assert emphatically. **2** *Cricket* close (innings) voluntarily.

**declassify** v. declare (information etc.) to be no longer secret. □□ **declassification** n.

**declension** n. *Gram.* class of nouns etc. having same inflectional forms.

**declination** n. **1** downward bend. **2** angular distance north or south of celestial equator. **3** deviation of compass needle from true north.

**decline** ● v. **1** deteriorate; lose strength or vigour; decrease. **2** refuse. **3** slope or bend downwards. **4** *Gram.* state case forms of (noun etc.) ● n. deterioration.

**declivity** n. downward slope.

**decoction** n. **1** boiling down to extract essence. **2** resulting liquid.

**decode** v. **1** decipher. **2** make (electronic signal) intelligible. □□ **decoder** n.

**decolonise** v. (also **-ize**) (of nation) withdraw from (colony) leaving it independent. □□ **decolonisation** n.

**decommission** v. close down (nuclear reactor etc.); take (ship) out of service.

**decompose** v. **1** rot. **2** separate into elements. □□ **decomposition** n.

**decompress** v. subject to decompression.

**decompression** n. **1** release from compression. **2** reduction of pressure on deep-sea diver etc.

**decongestant** n. medicine etc. that relieves nasal congestion.

**decontaminate** v. remove contamination from. □□ **decontamination** n.

**decor** n. (also **décor**) furnishing and decoration of room, stage, etc.

**decorate** v. **1** make attractive by adding ornaments etc.; paint, wallpaper, etc. (room etc.). **2** give medal or award to. □□ **decoration** n.

**decorative** adj. pleasing in appearance. □□ **decoratively** adv.

**decorator** n. person who decorates.

**decorous** adj. having or showing good decorum. □□ **decorously** adv.

**decorum** n. polite dignified behaviour.

**découpage** n. decoration of surfaces with paper cut-outs.

**decoy** ● n. person or thing used as lure; bait, enticement. ● v. lure by decoy.

**decrease** ● v. make or become smaller or fewer. ● n. decreasing; amount of this.

**decree** ● n. official legal order; legal decision. ● v. ordain by decree.

**decrepit** adj. weakened by age or infirmity; dilapidated. □□ **decrepitude** n.

**decriminalise** v. (also **-ize**) cease to treat as criminal.

**decry** v. disparage.

**dedicate** v. **1** devote to task or task. **2** address (book etc.) to friend etc. **3** (as **dedicated** adj.) serious in one's commitment to a task; exclusively set aside for particular purpose. □□ **dedicatory** adj. **dedication** n.

**deduce** v. infer logically. □□ **deducible** adj.

**deduct** v. subtract, take away, or withhold.

**deductible** adj. that may be deducted, esp. from tax or taxable income.

**deduction** n. **1** deducting; amount deducted. **2** inference from general to particular.

**deed** n. **1** thing done; action. **2** legal document.

**deejay** n. *colloq.* disc jockey.

**deem** v. *formal* consider, judge.

**deep** adj. **1** extending far down or in. **2** low-pitched. **3** intense. **4** profound. **5** fully absorbed, overwhelmed. □□ **deeply** adv. **deepness** n.

**deer** n. four-hoofed grazing animal, male of which usu. has antlers.

**deface** v. disfigure.□□ **defacement** n.

**de facto** ● adv. in fact. ● adj. existing in fact, whether by right or not. ● n. Aust. person living with another as if married.

**defame** v. attack good name or reputation of.□□ **defamation** n. **defamatory** adj.

**default** ● n. **1** failure to act, appear, or pay. **2** option adopted by computer program unless alternative instruction is selected. ● v. fail to fulfil obligations.□□ **defaulter** n.

**defeat** ● v. **1** overcome in battle, contest, etc. **2** frustrate, baffle. ● n. defeating, being defeated.

**defecate** v. evacuate bowels. □□ **defecation** n.

**defect** ● n. fault; shortcoming. ● v. abandon one's country or cause for another.□□ **defection** n. **defector** n.

**defence** n. (US **defense**) defending; protection; arguments against accusation.□□ **defenceless** adj.

**defend** v. protect from attack; uphold by argument; represent (defendant). □□ **defender** n.

**defendant** n. person etc. sued or accused in court of law.

**defensible** adj. able to be defended or justified.

**defensive** adj. **1** done or intended for defence. **2** over-reacting to criticism. □□ **defensively** adv. **defensiveness** n.

**defer** v. (**deferred**) **1** postpone. **2** yield or make concessions to. □□ **deferment** n. **deferral** n.

**deference** n. **1** respectful conduct. **2** compliance with another's wishes.

**deferential** adj. respectful. □□ **deferentially** adv.

**defiance** n. open disobedience; bold resistance.□□ **defiant** adj. **defiantly** adv.

**defibrillate** v. stop fibrillation of heart by administering controlled electric shock to restore normal rhythm.□□ **defibrillation** n. **defibrillator** n.

**deficient** adj. incomplete or insufficient.□□ **deficiency** n.

**deficit** n. amount by which total falls short; excess of liabilities over assets.

**defile** ● v. make dirty; pollute. ● n. narrow pass or gorge.

**define** v. give meaning of; describe scope of; outline; mark out boundary of.□□ **definable** adj.

**definite** adj. **1** certain. **2** clearly defined. **3** precise.□ **definite article** see ARTICLE.□□ **definitely** adv.

**definition** n. **1** defining; statement of meaning of word etc. **2** distinctness in outline.

**definitive** adj. **1** decisive, unconditional, final. **2** most authoritative.□□ **definitively** adv.

**deflate** v. **1** let air out of (tyre etc.) **2** (cause to) lose confidence. **3** subject (economy) to deflation.

**deflation** n. **1** deflating. **2** reduction of money in circulation to combat inflation.□□ **deflationary** adj.

**deflect** v. bend or turn aside from course or purpose; (cause to) deviate. □□ **deflection** n.

**deflower** v. literary deprive of virginity.

**defoliate** v. destroy leaves of. □□ **defoliant** n. **defoliation** n.

**deform** v. spoil the shape of. □□ **deformation** n.

**deformity** n. abnormality of shape, esp. of part of body.

**defraud** v. cheat by fraud.

**defray** v. provide money for (cost). □□ **defrayal** n.

**defriend** v. = UNFRIEND.

**defrost** v. remove frost or ice from; unfreeze; become unfrozen.

**deft** *adj.* skilful and quick.□□ **deftly** *adv.* **deftness** *n.*

**defunct** *adj.* no longer existing or in use; dead.

**defuse** *v.* 1 remove fuse from (bomb etc.) 2 reduce tension in (crisis etc.)

**defy** *v.* resist strongly; make difficult or impossible; challenge.

**degenerate** ● *adj.* having lost usual or good qualities; immoral.
● *n.* degenerate person etc.
● *v.* become degenerate; get worse.
□□ **degeneracy** *n.* **degeneration** *n.*

**degradable** *adj.* (of waste etc.) capable of being broken down by chemical or biological means.

**degrade** *v.* humiliate; dishonour; reduce to lower rank; (of soils) reduce to lower quality (by erosion, overuse, etc.) □□ **degradation** *n.*

**degree** *n.* 1 stage in scale, series, or process. 2 unit of measurement of angle or temperature. 3 extent of burns. 4 academic rank conferred by university etc.

**degustation** *n.* 1 tasting something carefully to appreciate it fully.
2 (of menu) providing wide variety of foods in small quantities.

**dehumanise** *v.* (also **-ize**) remove human qualities from; make impersonal. □□ **dehumanisation** *n.*

**dehydrate** *v.* 1 remove water from.
2 make dry. 3 (often as **dehydrated** *adj.*) deprive of fluids, make very thirsty. □□ **dehydration** *n.*

**deify** *v.* make a god or idol of.
□□ **deification** *n.*

**deign** *v.* condescend.

**deity** *n.* god or goddess; divine status or nature.

**déjàvu** *n.* illusion of having already experienced present situation.

**dejected** *adj.* sad, depressed.
□□ **dejectedly** *adv.* **dejection** *n.*

**de jure** *adj.* & *adv.* rightful, by right.

**delay** ● *v.* postpone; make or be late.
● *n.* delaying, being delayed; time lost by this.

**delectable** *adj.* delightful.

**delectation** *n.* enjoyment.

**delegate** ● *n.* elected representative sent to conference; member of delegation. ● *v.* commit (power etc.) to deputy etc.; entrust (task) to another; send or authorise as representative.

**delegation** *n.* group representing others; delegating, being delegated.

**delete** *v.* strike out (letter, word, etc.); *Computing* remove or overwrite data. □□ **deletion** *n.*

**deleterious** *adj.* harmful.

**deleverage** *v.* reduce level of one's debt by rapidly selling assets.

**deliberate** ● *adj.* 1 intentional, considered. 2 unhurried.
● *v.* 1 think carefully. 2 discuss.
□□ **deliberately** *adv.*

**deliberation** *n.* careful consideration or slowness.

**delicacy** *n.* 1 being delicate. 2 choice food.

**delicate** *adj.* 1 fine in texture, quality, etc. 2 subtle, hard to discern.
3 susceptible, tender. 4 requiring tact.
□□ **delicately** *adv.*

**delicatessen** *n.* shop or part of supermarket selling cooked meats, cheeses, etc.

**delicious** *adj.* highly enjoyable, esp. to taste or smell. □□ **deliciously** *adv.*

**delight** ● *v.* (often as **delighted** *adj.*) please greatly; take great pleasure in.
● *n.* great pleasure; thing that delights. □□ **delightful** *adj.*
**delightfully** *adv.*

**delimit** *v.* fix limits or boundary of.
□□ **delimitation** *n.*

**delineate** *v.* outline.
□□ **delineation** *n.*

**delinquent** ● *n.* offender.
● *adj.* guilty of misdeed; failing in a duty. □□ **delinquency** *n.*

**deliquesce** v. become liquid; dissolve in moisture from the air.
□□ **deliquescence** n. **deliquescent** adj.

**delirious** adj. affected with delirium; wildly excited.□□ **deliriously** adv.

**delirium** n. disordered state of mind, with incoherent speech etc.; wildly excited mood.

**deliver** v. **1** distribute (letters, goods) to destination(s); hand over. **2** save, rescue; set free. **3** give birth to; assist at birth of or in giving birth. **4** utter (speech). **5** (of judge etc.) pronounce (judgement). **6** launch or aim (blow etc.) **7** (in full **deliver the goods**) colloq. provide or carry out what is required.□□ **deliverer** n.
**delivery** n.

**delouse** v. rid of lice.

**dell** n. small wooded valley.

**delta** n. **1** triangular alluvial tract at mouth of river. **2** fourth letter of Greek alphabet (Δ, δ).

**deltoid** ● adj. triangular. ● n. (in full **deltoid muscle**) triangular muscle used for raising arm away from body.

**delude** v. deceive, mislead.

**deluge** ● n. flood; downpour of rain; overwhelming rush. ● v. flood or inundate.

**delusion** n. false belief or hope.
□□ **delusive** adj. **delusory** adj.

**deluxe** adj. luxurious; superior; sumptuous.

**delve** v. search or research deeply.

**demagogue** n. political agitator appealing to emotion and base instinct.□□ **demagogic** adj. **demagogy** n.

**demand** ● n. firm or official request; customers' desire for goods and services; a claim. ● v. **1** ask for insistently. **2** require.

**demanding** adj. making many demands; requiring great skill or effort.

**demarcation** n. marking of boundary or limits.□□ **demarcate** v.

**demean** v. lower the dignity of.

**demeanour** n. (also **demeanor**) outward behaviour, bearing.

**demented** adj. mad.

**dementia** n. chronic disorder of mental processes marked by poor memory, personality changes, etc.

**demerara** n. light brown cane sugar.

**demerit** n. fault, defect; mark given to an offender.

**demesne** n. landed property, estate.

**demilitarise** v. (also **-ize**) remove army etc. from (frontier, zone, etc.)

**demise** n. death; failure.

**demisemiquaver** n. Mus. note equal to half semiquaver.

**demist** v. clear mist from (windscreen etc.)□□ **demister** n.

**demo** n. colloq. demonstration.

**demobilise** v. (also **-ize**) disband (troops etc.)□□ **demobilisation** n.

**democracy** n. government by whole population, usu. through elected representatives; nation so governed.
□□ **democratic** adj. **democratically** adv.

**democrat** n. advocate of democracy.

**demography** n. statistical study of human populations.
□□ **demographic** adj.

**demolish** v. **1** pull down (building). **2** refute. **3** eat up voraciously.
□□ **demolition** n.

**demon** n. **1** evil spirit; devil. **2** cruel or destructive person. **3** energetic, forceful, or skilful person.
□□ **demonic** adj. **demoniac** adj. **demoniacal** adj.

**demonstrable** adj. able to be shown or proved.□□ **demonstrably** adv.

**demonstrate** v. **1** show (feelings etc.) **2** describe and explain by experiment etc. **3** prove truth or existence of. **4** take part in public demonstration.□□ **demonstrator** n.

**demonstration** n. **1** proving; exhibiting. **2** public protest.

**demonstrative** *adj.* **1** showing feelings readily; affectionate. **2** *Gram.* indicating person or thing referred to, e.g. this, that, those.
□□ **demonstratively** *adv.*
**demonstrativeness** *n.*

**demoralise** *v.* (also **-ize**) destroy morale of.□□ **demoralisation** *n.*

**demote** *v.* reduce to lower rank or class.□□ **demotion** *n.*

**demotivate** *v.* cause to lose motivation.□□ **demotivation** *n.*

**demur** ● *v.* **1** raise objections. **2** *Law* put in demurrer. ● *n.* (usu. in neg.) objection; objecting.

**demure** *adj.* quiet; modest; coy.
□□ **demurely** *adv.*

**demurrer** *n.* *Law* objection raised or exception taken.

**demystify** *v.* remove mystery from.

**den** *n.* **1** wild animal's lair. **2** place of crime or vice. **3** small private room.

**denature** *v.* change properties of; make (alcohol) unfit for drinking.

**dendrobium** *n.* any of various epiphytic or lithophytic orchids in SE Asia, India, and Australia.

**dendrochronology** *n.* dating of timber by study of annual growth rings.

**dendrology** *n.* study of trees.
□□ **dendrologist** *n.*

**dengue** *n.* viral disease with fever and acute joint pain.

**denial** *n.* denying or refusing.

**denigrate** *v.* disparage reputation of.□□ **denigration** *n.* **denigratory** *adj.*

**denim** *n.* twilled cotton fabric; (**denims**) *colloq.* jeans etc. made of this.

**denizen** *n.* *poet.* inhabitant or occupant.

**denominate** *v.* give name to, call, describe as.

**denomination** *n.* **1** Church or religious sect. **2** class of measurement or money. **3** name,

esp. for classification.
□□ **denominational** *adj.*

**denominator** *n.* number below line in vulgar fraction; divisor.

**denote** *v.* be sign of; indicate; be name for; signify.□□ **denotation** *n.*

**denouement** *n.* final resolution in play, novel, etc.

**denounce** *v.* accuse publicly; inform against.□□ **denunciation** *n.*

**dense** *adj.* **1** closely compacted; crowded together. **2** stupid.
□□ **densely** *adv.* **denseness** *n.*

**density** *n.* **1** denseness; quantity of mass per unit volume. **2** opacity of photographic image.

**dent** ● *n.* **1** depression in surface left by blow or pressure. **2** noticeable adverse effect. ● *v.* make dent in.

**dental** *adj.* **1** of teeth or dentistry. **2** (of sound) produced with tongue tip against front teeth. □ **dental floss** thread for cleaning between the teeth.

**dentate** *adj.* **1** toothed. **2** with toothlike notches.

**dentine** *n.* hard tissue forming teeth.

**dentist** *n.* person qualified to treat, extract, etc. teeth.□□ **dentistry** *n.*

**denture** *n.* artificial replacement for one or more teeth.

**denude** *v.* make naked or bare; strip of (covering etc.).□□ **denudation** *n.*

**deny** *v.* **1** declare untrue or non-existent. **2** repudiate. **3** withhold from.□□ **denier** *n.*

**deodorant** *n.* substance applied to body or sprayed into air to conceal smells.

**deodorise** *v.* (also **-ize**) remove smell from.□□ **deodorisation** *n.*

**deoxyribonucleic acid** see DNA.

**dep.** *abbr.* **1** departs. **2** deputy.

**depart** *v.* **1** go away; leave; set out. **2** deviate.□□ **departure** *n.*

**departed** ● *adj.* bygone. ● *n.* (**the departed**) *euphem.* dead person or people.

**department** n. separate part of complex whole, esp. branch of administration, division of school, etc.; section of large store; area of special expertise. □ **department store** large shop selling many kinds of goods. □□ **departmental** adj.

**depend** v. □ **depend on** be determined by; be unable to do without; trust confidently.

**dependable** adj. reliable. □□ **dependability** n.

**dependant** n. person supported, esp. financially, by another.

**dependence** n. being dependent; reliance; relation of subordinate thing to that from which it receives support etc.

**dependency** n. country etc. controlled by another; dependence (on drugs etc.).

**dependent** adj. **1** depending; unable to do without (esp. drug); maintained at another's cost. **2** (of clause etc.) subordinate to word etc.

**depict** v. **1** represent in painting etc. **2** describe. □□ **depiction** n.

**depilate** v. remove hair from. □□ **depilation** n.

**depilatory** adj. & n. (substance) removing hair.

**deplete** v. reduce by using quantities of. □□ **depletion** n.

**deplorable** adj. exceedingly bad. □□ **deplorably** adv.

**deplore** v. **1** regret. **2** be scandalised by; find deplorable.

**deploy** v. **1** spread out (troops) into line for action. **2** use (arguments etc.) effectively. □□ **deployment** n.

**deponent** n. person making deposition under oath.

**deport** v. remove forcibly or exile to another country. □□ **deportation** n.

**deportee** n. deported person.

**deportment** n. bearing, demeanour.

**depose** v. **1** remove from office; dethrone. **2** Law testify on oath.

**deposit** ● n. **1** money paid into bank account; thing stored for safe keeping. **2** payment as pledge or first instalment. **3** returnable sum paid on hire of item. **4** layer of accumulated matter. ● v. (**deposited**) **1** put or lay down. **2** entrust for keeping. **3** pay or leave as deposit.

**depositary** n. person to whom thing is entrusted.

**deposition** n. **1** deposing. **2** sworn evidence; giving of this. **3** depositing.

**depositor** n. person who deposits money, property, etc.

**depository** n. storehouse; store (of wisdom, knowledge, etc.); depositary.

**depot** n. **1** military storehouse or headquarters. **2** place where vehicles (e.g. buses) are kept.

**depraved** adj. morally bad; corrupt, wicked.

**depravity** n. moral corruption; wickedness.

**deprecate** v. express disapproval of. □□ **deprecation** n. **deprecatory** adj.

---

**Usage** *Deprecate* is often confused with *depreciate*.

---

**depreciate** v. diminish in value; belittle; reduce purchasing power of (money). □□ **depreciation** n.

**depredation** n. plundering, destruction.

**depress** v. **1** make dispirited. **2** push down. **3** reduce activity of (esp. trade). □□ **depressing** adj. **depressingly** adv.

**depressant** ● adj. reducing activity, esp. of body function. ● n. sedative drug.

**depression** n. **1** extreme dejection; mood of hopelessnesss and feeling of inadequacy. **2** long period of financial and industrial decline. **3** lowering of atmospheric pressure. **4** hollow on surface.

**depressive ●** *adj.* tending to depress. **●** *n.* chronically depressed person.

**deprive** *v.* **1** prevent from having or enjoying. **2** (as **deprived** *adj.*) lacking what is needed, underprivileged. □□ **deprival** *n.* **deprivation** *n.*

**Dept** *abbr.* Department.

**depth** *n.* **1** distance downwards or inwards from surface; deepest or most central part. **2** wisdom; intensity of emotion, colour, etc. □ **depth charge** bomb capable of exploding underwater. **in depth** thoroughly. **out of one's depth** in water over one's head; attempting something that is beyond one's ability.

**deputation** *n.* delegation.

**depute** *v.* delegate (task, authority); authorise as representative.

**deputise** *v.* (also **-ize**) act as deputy.

**deputy** *n.* person appointed to act for another; parliamentary representative in some countries.

**derail** *v.* cause (train etc.) to leave rails. □□ **derailment** *n.*

**derange** *v.* make insane. □□ **derangement** *n.*

**derby** *n.* major annual race for three-year-old horses; important sporting contest.

**deregulate** *v.* remove (esp. government) regulations from (industry etc.) □□ **deregulation** *n.*

**derelict ●** *adj.* dilapidated; abandoned. **●** *n.* vagrant; abandoned property.

**dereliction** *n.* neglect (of duty etc.)

**deride** *v.* mock. □□ **derision** *n.*

**de rigueur** *adj.* required by fashion or etiquette.

**derisive** *adj.* scoffing, ironical. □□ **derisively** *adv.*

**derisory** *adj.* (of sum offered etc.) ridiculously small, derisive.

**derivation** *n.* deriving, being derived; origin or formation of word; tracing of this.

**derive** *v.* get or trace from a source; arise from; assert origin or formation of (word etc.)

**dermatitis** *n.* inflammation of skin.

**dermatology** *n.* study of skin diseases. □□ **dermatological** *adj.* **dermatologist** *n.*

**dermis** *n.* **1** layer of living tissue below epidermis. **2** (in general use) the skin.

**derogatory** *adj.* disparaging; insulting.

**derrick** *n.* **1** crane. **2** framework over an oil well etc., for drilling machinery.

**dervish** *n.* member of Muslim fraternity vowed to poverty and austerity.

**desalinate** *v.* remove salt from (esp. sea water). □□ **desalination** *n.*

**descant** *n.* harmonising treble melody above hymn tune etc.

**descend** *v.* **1** go, come, or slope down; sink. **2** make sudden attack or visit. **3** be passed on by inheritance. **4** stoop (to unworthy act).

**descendant** *n.* person etc. descended from another.

**descent** *n.* **1** act or way of descending; downward slope. **2** lineage. **3** decline, fall. **4** sudden attack.

**describe** *v.* **1** state characteristics, appearance, etc. of. **2** assert to be. **3** draw or move in (curve etc.)

**description** *n.* **1** describing, being described. **2** sort, kind.

**descry** *v.* catch sight of; discern.

**desecrate** *v.* violate sanctity of. □□ **desecration** *n.* **desecrator** *n.*

**deselect** *v.* turn off (selected option) on electronic interface.

**desensitise** *v.* (also **-ize**) reduce or destroy sensitivity of. □□ **desensitisation** *n.*

**desert**[1] *v.* abandon; run away from military service. □□ **deserter** *n.* Mil. **desertion** *n.*

**desert**[2] **●** *n.* area of land, characteristically waterless and without vegetation; dry barren, esp. sandy, tract. ● *adj.* **1** of desert; uninhabited, desolate. **2** (of Australian flora) indigenous to arid areas.

**deserts** *n.pl.* deserved reward or punishment.

**deserve** *v.* be worthy of or entitled to. □□ **deservedly** *adv.*

**desex** *v.* castrate or spay (animal).

**desiccate** *v.* remove moisture from; dry completely. □□ **desiccation** *n.*

**design** ● *n.* **1** a drawing that shows how thing is to be made; general form or arrangement; lines or shapes as decoration. **2** mental plan; intention. ● *v.* **1** produce design for. **2** plan; intend. □ **have designs on** aim to acquire, esp. illicitly. □□ **designer** *n.* **designedly** *adv.*

**designate** ● *v.* **1** appoint to office or function. **2** specify. **3** describe as. ● *adj.* appointed but not yet installed.

**designation** *n.* **1** name or title. **2** designating.

**designing** *adj.* scheming; crafty.

**desirable** *adj.* **1** worth having or doing. **2** sexually attractive. □□ **desirability** *n.*

**desire** ● *n.* **1** unsatisfied longing; expression of this. **2** request. **3** sexual appetite. **4** thing desired. ● *v.* **1** long for. **2** request.

**desirous** *adj.* desiring, wanting; hoping.

**desist** *v.* cease.

**desk** *n.* piece of furniture with writing surface; counter in hotel, bank, etc.; section of newspaper office.

**desktop** *n.* **1** working surface of desk; working area of computer screen. **2** (in full **desktop computer**) computer for use on desk etc. □ **desktop publishing** producing documents etc. with personal computer and printer etc.

**desolate** *adj.* deserted, lonely; very unhappy. □□ **desolately** *adv.* **desolation** *n.*

**desolated** *adj.* feeling very distressed.

**despair** ● *n.* loss or absence of hope; cause of this. ● *v.* lose all hope.

**despatch** *v.* = DISPATCH.

**desperado** *n.* desperate or reckless criminal etc.

**desperate** *adj.* **1** reckless from despair; violent and lawless; extremely dangerous or serious. **2** needing or desiring very much. □□ **desperately** *adv.* **desperation** *n.*

**despicable** *adj.* contemptible. □□ **despicably** *adv.*

**despise** *v.* regard as inferior or contemptible.

**despite** *prep.* in spite of.

**despoil** *v. literary* plunder, rob. □□ **despoliation** *n.*

**despondent** *adj.* in low spirits, dejected. □□ **despondence** *n.* **despondency** *n.* **despondently** *adv.*

**despot** *n.* absolute ruler; tyrant. □□ **despotic** *adj.*

**dessert** *n.* sweet course of a meal.

**destabilise** *v.* (also **-ize**) make unstable or insecure. □□ **destabilisation** *n.*

**destination** *n.* place to which person or thing is going.

**destine** *v.* set apart for purpose; doom to particular fate.

**destiny** *n.* fate; this as power.

**destitute** *adj.* without food or shelter etc.; lacking. □□ **destitution** *n.*

**destroy** *v.* pull or break down; kill; make useless; ruin financially; defeat. □□ **destruction** *n.* **destructive** *adj.*

**destroyer** *n.* **1** person or thing that destroys. **2** fast warship.

**destruct** *v.* destroy or be destroyed deliberately.

**desultory** *adj.* constantly turning from one subject to another; unmethodical. □□

**detach** v. release and separate.
□□ **detachable** adj.

**detached** adj. **1** not joined to another. **2** free from bias or emotion.

**detachment** n. **1** indifference; impartiality. **2** detaching; being detached. **3** troops etc. detached for special duty.

**detail** ● n. **1** small separate item or particular; these collectively. **2** minor or intricate decoration. **3** small part of picture etc. shown alone. **4** small military detachment. ● v. **1** give particulars of, relate in detail. **2** (as **detailed** adj.) containing many details, itemised. **3** assign for special duty. **4** improve appearance of (motor vehicle), esp. before sale.

**detain** v. keep waiting, delay; keep in custody. □□ **detainment** n.

**detainee** n. person kept in custody.

**detect** v. discover; perceive. □□ **detectable** adj. **detection** adj. **detector** n.

**detective** n. person, esp. police officer, investigating crime etc.

**détente** n. (also **detente**) easing of strained esp. international relations.

**detention** n. detaining, being detained; being kept late in school as punishment.

**deter** v. (**deterred**) discourage or prevent, esp. through fear.

**detergent** n. cleansing agent used with water to remove dirt etc.

**deteriorate** v. become worse. □□ **deterioration** n.

**determinate** adj. limited; of definite scope or nature.

**determination** n. **1** resolute purpose. **2** deciding, determining. **3** conclusion of dispute by decision of arbitrator.

**determine** v. **1** control. **2** resolve firmly. **3** establish precisely.

**determined** adj. resolute. □□ **determinedly** adv.

**determinism** n. theory that action is determined by causes external to will. □□ **determinist** n. & adj. **deterministic** adj.

**deterrent** ● n. thing that deters. ● adj. deterring. □□ **deterrence** n.

**detest** v. hate, loathe. □□ **detestation** n.

**dethrone** v. remove from throne. □□ **dethronement** n.

**detonate** v. set off (explosive charge); be set off. □□ **detonation** n.

**detonator** n. device for detonating.

**detour** ● n. divergence from usual route; roundabout course. ● v. make or cause to make detour.

**detoxify** v. remove poison or harmful substances from. □□ **detoxification** n.

**detract** v. □ detract from reduce the credit due is due to; lessen. □□ **detraction** n.

**detractor** n. person who criticises unfairly.

**detriment** n. harm, damage; cause of this. □□ **detrimental** adj.

**detritus** n. gravel, sand, etc. produced by erosion; debris.

**de trop** adj. not wanted, unwelcome.

**deuce** n. **1** Tennis score of all 40. **2** two on dice or playing cards.

**deuterium** n. heavy isotope of hydrogen.

**devalue** v. reduce value of, esp. currency in relation to others or to gold. □□ **devaluation** n.

**devastate** v. **1** lay waste; cause great destruction to. **2** (often as **devastated** adj.) overwhelm with shock or grief. □□ **devastation** n.

**devastating** adj. **1** crushingly effective; overwhelming. **2** colloq. stunningly beautiful. □□ **devastatingly** adv.

**develop** v. (**developed**) **1** make or become bigger, fuller, or more elaborate. **2** bring or come to active, visible, or mature state. **3** begin to exhibit or suffer from. **4** make usable or profitable, build on (land). **5** treat (photographic film) to make image visible. □□ **developer** n.

**development** n.

**deviant** adj. **1** deviating from normal behaviour. **2** abnormal person or thing.

**deviate** v. turn aside; diverge. □□ **deviation** n.

**device** n. **1** thing made or adapted for special purpose. **2** scheme, trick. **3** heraldic design.

**devil** ● n. **1** demon; personified evil; (usu. **the Devil**) Satan. **2** mischievous clever person. **3** = *Tasmanian devil*. ● v. cook with hot seasoning. □ **devil's advocate** person who tests proposition by arguing against it.

**devilish** ● adj. of or like a devil; mischievous. ● adv. colloq. very. □□ **devilishly** adv.

**devilry** n. wickedness; reckless mischief; black magic.

**devious** adj. not straightforward; underhand; winding, circuitous. □□ **deviously** adv. **deviousness** n.

**devise** v. **1** plan or invent. **2** *Law* leave (real estate) by will.

**devoid** adj. □ **devoid of** lacking, free from.

**devolution** n. delegation of power, esp. from central to local administration. □□ **devolutionist** n. & adj.

**devolve** v. **1** (of duties etc.) pass or be passed to another. **2** (of property) descend to.

**devon** n. *Aust.* bland sausage.

**devonshire tea** n. *Aust.* scones with jam and cream served with tea etc.

**devote** v. give or use exclusively for particular purpose.

**devoted** adj. loving; loyal.

**devotee** n. **1** enthusiast, supporter. **2** pious person.

**devotion** n. great love or loyalty; worship; (**devotions**) prayers. □□ **devotional** adj.

**devour** v. eat hungrily or greedily; engulf, destroy; take in eagerly.

**devout** adj. earnestly religious or sincere. □□ **devoutly** adv. **devoutness** n.

**dew** n. condensed water vapour forming on cool surfaces at night; similar glistening moisture. □□ **dewy** adj.

**dewlap** n. loose fold of skin hanging from throat, esp. in cattle.

**dexterity** n. skill.

**dexterous** adj. (also **dextrous**) skilful at handling. □□ **dexterity** n. **dexterously** adv. **dexterousness** n.

**dhal** n. (also **dal**) kind of split pulse from India, Sri Lanka, etc.; dish made with this.

**di-** prefix two; double.

**dia.** abbr. diameter.

**diabetes** n. disease in which sugar and starch are not properly absorbed by body. □□ **diabetic** adj. & n.

**diabolical** adj. (also **diabolic**) of the Devil; inhumanly cruel or wicked; extremely bad. □□ **diabolically** adv.

**diachronic** adj. concerned with historical development of subject.

**diacritic** n. sign (e.g. accent) indicating sound or value of letter.

**diadem** n. crown.

**diaeresis** n. (also **dieresis**) (pl. **diaereses**) mark ( ¨ ) over vowel to show it is sounded separately, as in *Brontë*.

**diagnose** v. make diagnosis of.

**diagnosis** n. (pl. **diagnoses**) identification of disease or fault from symptoms. □□ **diagnostic** adj. **diagnostician** n.

**diagonal** ● adj. **1** crossing a straight-sided figure from corner to corner. **2** oblique. ● n. straight line joining two opposite corners. □□ **diagonally** adv.

**diagram** n. outline drawing, plan, etc. of thing or process. □□ **diagrammatic** adj.

**dial** ● n. 1 face of clock or watch; similar plate marked with scale for measuring. 2 numbered disc etc. on telephone for making connection. 3 disc etc. on radio etc. for selecting wavelength etc. 4 colloq. person's face. ● v. (**dialled**) select or operate by using dial or numbered buttons. □ **dial-up** (of computer system or service) used remotely via telephone line.

**dialect** n. local form of language.

**dialectic** n. investigation of truths, esp. by examining contradictions. □□ **dialectical** adj.

**dialogue** n. (US **dialog**) conversation, esp. in play, novel, etc.; discussion between representatives of two nations etc. with different opinions.

**dialysis** n. (pl. **dialyses**) separation of particles in liquid by differences in their ability to pass through membrane; purification of blood by this technique.

**diamanté** adj. decorated with synthetic diamonds etc.

**diameter** n. straight line passing through centre of circle or sphere to its edges; its length.

**diametrical** adj. (also **diametric**) 1 of or along diameter. 2 (of opposites) absolute. □□ **diametrically** adv.

**diamond** n. 1 very hard transparent precious stone. 2 rhombus. 3 playing card of suit marked with red rhombuses. 4 baseball field. □ **diamond wedding** 60th (or 75th) wedding anniversary.

**diaper** n. US nappy.

**diaphanous** adj. (of fabric etc.) light and almost transparent.

**diaphragm** n. 1 muscular partition between thorax and abdomen in mammals. 2 dome-shaped contraceptive device fitting over cervix. 3 vibrating disc in microphone, telephone, loudspeaker, etc. 4 device for varying aperture of camera lens.

**diarrhoea** n. condition of excessively frequent and loose bowel movements. □□ **diarrhoeic** adj.

**diary** n. daily record of events or thoughts; book for this or for noting future engagements. □□ **diarist** n.

**diastole** n. period between two contractions of heart when chambers fill with blood. □□ **diastolic** adj.

**diatribe** n. forceful verbal criticism.

**dice** ● n.pl. small cube marked on each face with 1–6 spots, used in games or gambling; game played with dice. ● v. 1 gamble, take risks. 2 cut into small cubes. 3 colloq. reject, abandon.

---

**Usage** The noun *dice* is properly the plural of *die*, but this singular form is now rarely used.

---

**dicey** adj. (**dicier, diciest**) colloq. risky, unreliable.

**dichotomy** n. division into two.

**dicky** ● adj. colloq. shaky, unsound. ● n. false shirt-front.

**dictate** ● v. 1 say or read aloud (material to be recorded). 2 state authoritatively. 3 order peremptorily. ● n. (**dictates**) authoritative requirement. □□ **dictation** n.

**dictator** n. usu. unelected absolute ruler; omnipotent or domineering person. □□ **dictatorship** n.

**dictatorial** adj. of or like dictator; overbearing. □□ **dictatorially** adv.

**diction** n. manner of uttering or pronouncing words.

**dictionary** n. book or electronic resource listing (usu. alphabetically) and explaining words of a language, or giving corresponding words in another language; similar book listing and explaining terms of particular subject.

**dictum** n. (pl. **dicta**) formal expression of opinion; a saying.

**did** see DO.

**didactic** adj. 1 meant to instruct. 2 (of person) tediously pedantic. □□ **didactically** adv. **didacticism** n.

**diddle** v. colloq. swindle.

**didgeridoo** n. Aust. long tubular Aboriginal wind instrument.

**die** ● v. (**died, dying**) 1 cease to be alive; cease to exist or function. 2 fade away. ● n. 1 device that stamps a design or that cuts or moulds material to shape. 2 see note at DICE.

**diehard** n. uncompromising or stubborn person.

**dielectric** ● adj. not conducting electricity. ● n. dielectric substance.

**dieresis** = DIAERESIS.

**diesel** n. (in full **diesel engine**) internal-combustion engine in which heat produced by compression of air in cylinder ignites fuel; vehicle driven by or fuel for diesel engine.

**diet** n. 1 person's usual food; special restricted course of food adopted to lose weight or for medical reasons. 2 parliamentary assembly in some countries. ● v. restrict what one eats. □□ **dietary** adj. **dieter** n.

**dietetic** ● n. (**dietetics**) study of diet and nutrition. ● adj. of diet and nutrition.

**dietitian** n. (also **dietician**) expert in dietetics.

**differ** v. be unlike; disagree.

**difference** n. 1 being different or unlike; degree of this; way in which things differ. 2 remainder after subtraction. 3 disagreement.

**different** adj. unlike, of another nature; distinct, separate; unusual. □□ **differently** adv.

**differential** ● adj. showing or depending on a difference. ● n. 1 difference, esp. between rates of interest or wages. 2 arrangement of gears allowing vehicle's wheels to revolve at different speeds when cornering.

**differentiate** v. be a difference between; distinguish between; become different. □□ **differentiation** n.

**difficult** adj. hard to do, deal with, or understand. □□ **difficulty** n.

**diffident** adj. lacking self confidence. □□ **diffidence** n. **diffidently** adv.

**diffract** v. break up (beam of light) into series of dark and light bands or coloured spectra. □□ **diffraction** n. **diffractive** adj.

**diffuse** ● adj. spread out, not concentrated; not concise. ● v. spread widely or thinly; intermingle. □□ **diffusible** adj. **diffusive** adj. **diffusion** n.

**dig** ● v. 1 break up or turn over (ground etc.); make (hole etc.) by digging; obtain by digging, find, discover; excavate. 2 colloq. like. 3 understand. 4 look at. 5 thrust, prod. ● n. 1 piece of digging. 2 thrust, poke. 3 colloq. pointed remark. 4 archaeological excavation. 5 (**digs**) colloq. lodgings.

**digest** ● v. assimilate (food, information, etc.). ● n. methodical summary. □□ **digestible** adj.

**digestion** n. digesting; capacity to digest food.

**digger** n. 1 person or machine that digs. 2 miner, esp. for gold. 3 Australian or New Zealand soldier. 4 Aust. (as form of address) mate.

**diggings** n.pl. goldfield.

**digit** n. 1 any numeral from 0 to 9. 2 finger or toe.

**digital** adj. 1 of or using signals or information represented by discrete values of a physical quantity such as voltage or magnetic polarisation; involving or relating to the use of computer technology. 2 of digits; (of clock etc.) giving reading by displayed digits. □□ **digitally** *adv.*

**digitalis** *n.* heart stimulant from foxglove leaves.

**digitise** *v.* (also **-ize**) convert (computer data etc.) into digital form.

**dignified** *adj.* having or showing dignity.

**dignify** *v.* give dignity to.

**dignitary** *n.* person of high rank or office.

**dignity** *n.* composed and serious manner; being worthy of respect; high rank or position.

**digress** *v.* depart from main subject. □□ **digression** *n.*

**dike** = DYKE.

**diktat** *n.* firm statement or order.

**dilapidated** *adj.* in disrepair. □□ **dilapidation** *n.*

**dilate** *v.* widen or expand; speak or write at length. □□ **dilatation** *n.* **dilation** *n.*

**dilatory** *adj.* given to or causing delay.

**dilemma** *n.* situation in which difficult choice has to be made.

**dilettante** *n.* (*pl.* **dilettanti** or **dilettantes**) dabbler in a subject. □□ **dilettantism** *n.*

**diligent** *adj.* hard-working; showing care and effort. □□ **diligence** *n.* **diligently** *adv.*

**dill** *n.* **1** herb with aromatic leaves and seeds. **2** *Aust. colloq.* fool, simpleton.

**dillybag** *n.* (also **dilly**) *Aust.* Aboriginal bag or basket of woven grass, fibre, etc.; any small bag.

**dilly-dally** *v. colloq.* dawdle; waste time by indecision.

**dilute** *v.* reduce strength of (fluid) by adding water etc.; weaken in effect. *adj.* (esp. of fluid) diluted. □□ **dilution** *n.*

**diluvial** *adj.* of flood, esp. Flood in Genesis.

**dim** • *adj.* **1** faintly luminous or visible; not bright; indistinctly perceived or remembered; (of eyes)

not seeing clearly. **2** *colloq.* stupid.
• *v.* (**dimmed**) make or become dim. □□ **dimly** *adv.* **dimness** *n.*

**dime** *n.* *US* 10-cent coin.

**dimension** *n.* measurable extent; scope. □□ **dimensional** *adj.*

**diminish** *v.* make or become smaller or less. □□ **diminution** *n.*

**diminuendo** *n.* (*pl.* **diminuendos** or **diminuendi**) *Mus.* gradual decrease in loudness.

**diminutive** • *adj.* tiny; (of word or suffix) implying smallness or affection. • *n.* diminutive word or suffix.

**dimmer** *n.* (in full **dimmer switch**) device for varying brightness of electric light.

**dimple** • *n.* small hollow, esp. in cheek or chin. • *v.* form dimples (in).

**dim sum** *n.* (also **dim sim**) **1** meal or course of savoury Cantonese-style snacks. **2** (usu. **dim sim**) *Aust.* small roll of seasoned meat etc. wrapped in thin dough and steamed or fried.

**din** • *n.* prolonged loud confused noise. • *v.* (**dinned**) force (information) into person by repetition.

**dine** *v.* eat dinner; (followed by *on*, *upon*) eat for dinner.

**diner** *n.* **1** person who dines. **2** small restaurant.

**ding** • *v.* **1** make ringing sound. **2** damage. • *n.* **1** ringing sound. **2** *Aust. colloq.* wild party. **3** *Aust. colloq.* minor collision, dent.

**dinghy** *n.* small, often inflatable, boat.

**dingo** *n.* wolf-like Australian dog, typically tawny yellow.

**dingy** *adj.* dirty-looking, drab. □□ **dinginess** *n.*

**dink** (also **double dink**) *Aust. colloq.* • *n.* lift on bicycle etc. ridden by another. • *v.* carry (passenger) on bicycle etc.

**dinkum** *Aust. colloq.* ● *adj.* reliable, genuine, honest, true. ● *adv.* really, truly.

**dinner** *n.* chief meal of day; formal evening meal.

**dinosaur** *n.* extinct, usu. large, reptile.

**dint** *n.* dent.

**diocese** *n.* district under bishop's pastoral care. □ **diocesan** *adj.*

**diode** *n.* **1** semiconductor allowing current in one direction only and having two terminals. **2** thermionic valve having two electrodes.

**diorama** *n.* **1** scenic painting lit to simulate sunrise etc. **2** small scene with three-dimensional figures. **3** small-scale model etc.

**dioxide** *n.* oxide with two atoms of oxygen.

**dioxin** *n.* any of several chemical derivatives used in herbicide.

**dip** ● *v.* (**dipped**) put briefly into liquid etc.; lower, go downwards. ● *n.* **1** dipping; short swim. **2** liquid or mixture into which something is dipped. **3** downward slope.

**diphtheria** *n.* infectious disease with inflammation of mucous membrane esp. of throat.

**diphthong** *n.* union of two vowels in one syllable (as *ay* in *day*).

**diplodocus** *n.* (*pl.* **diplodocuses**) giant long-necked herbivorous dinosaur.

**diploma** *n.* certificate of educational qualification; document conferring honour, privilege, etc.

**diplomacy** *n.* management of international relations; tact.

**diplomat** *n.* **1** member of diplomatic service. **2** tactful person. □□ **diplomatic** *adj.*

**dipper** *n.* ladle.

**diprotodon** *n.* extinct, large, herbivorous, quadruped marsupial.

**dipsomania** *n.* alcoholism. □□ **dipsomaniac** *n.*

**dipstick** *n.* **1** rod for measuring depth, esp. of oil in vehicle's engine. **2** *colloq. derog.* idiot.

**dipterous** *adj.* two-winged.

**diptych** *n.* painted altarpiece on two hinged panels.

**dire** *adj.* **1** dreadful; ominous; *colloq.* very bad. **2** urgent.

**direct** ● *adj.* extending or moving in straight line or by shortest route; not crooked or circuitous; straightforward, frank. ● *adv.* by a direct route. ● *v.* **1** tell how to do something or reach a place. **2** control; command; guide. **3** address (letter etc.) □ **direct debit** regular payment from bank account at request of payee. **direct object** *Gram.* primary object of transitive verb, person or thing directly affected. **direct speech** words actually spoken, not reported. □□ **directness** *n.*

**direction** *n.* **1** directing. **2** an instruction. **3** point to, from, or along which person or thing moves or looks.

**directional** *adj.* of or indicating direction; sending or receiving radio or sound waves in one direction only.

**directive** *n.* order from an authority.

**directly** ● *adv.* **1** at once, without delay; presently, shortly; exactly. **2** in a direct way. ● *conj. colloq.* as soon as.

**director** *n.* person who directs, esp. as member of board of company or for stage etc. □□ **directorship** *n.*

**directorate** *n.* board of directors; office of director.

**directory** *n.* book with list of telephone subscribers, inhabitants of district, or members of profession etc.

**dirge** *n.* lament for the dead; dreary piece of music.

**dirigible** *adj.* that can be steered. ● *n.* dirigible balloon or airship.

**dirk** *n.* short dagger.

**dirndl** *n.* full gathered skirt.

**dirt** n. unclean matter; earth; foul words; scandal.

**dirty** ● adj. **1** soiled; unclean; producing pollution. **2** dishonourable. **3** colloq. resentful, angry. ● v. make or become dirty.□□ **dirtily** adv. **dirtiness** n.

**dis** v. (also **diss**) (**dissed**) colloq. act or speak in disrespectful way towards.

**disability** n. physical incapacity, either congenital or caused by injury, disease, etc.; lack of some capacity etc. preventing action.

**disable** v. **1** render unable to function; deprive of an ability. **2** deprive of physical or mental ability, esp. through injury or disease. □□ **disablement** n.

**disabled** adj. (of a person) having mental or physical condition that limits their movements, senses, or activities; of or specifically designed for people with physical or metal disability.

**disabuse** v. disillusion.

**disadvantage** ● n. unfavourable circumstance or condition; damage. ● v. cause disadvantage to. □□ **disadvantaged** adj. **disadvantageous** adj.

**disaffected** adj. discontented, no longer feeling loyalty. □□ **disaffection** n.

**disagree** v. have different opinion; fail to agree.□□ **disagreement** n.

**disagreeable** adj. unpleasant, bad-tempered.□□ **disagreeably** adv.

**disallow** v. refuse to sanction.

**disappear** v. cease to be visible or in existence or circulation etc.; go missing.□□ **disappearance** n.

**disappoint** v. fail to fulfil desire or expectation of; frustrate. □□ **disappointment** n.

**disapprobation** n. disapproval.

**disapprove** v. consider bad or immoral.□□ **disapproval** n.

**disarm** v. deprive of weapons; reduce armed forces; defuse (bomb etc.); make less hostile, win over. □□ **disarmament** n. **disarmingly** adv.

**disarray** n. disorder.

**disassociate** v. dissociate. □□ **disassociation** n.

**disaster** n. great or sudden misfortune; complete failure. □□ **disastrous** adj. **disastrously** adv.

**disavow** v. disclaim knowledge or approval of or responsibility for. □□ **disavowal** n.

**disband** v. break up; disperse.

**disbelieve** v. refuse to believe; not believe; be sceptical.□□ **disbelief** n.

**disburse** v. pay out (money). □□ **disbursement** n.

**disc** n. (US **disk**) **1** flat thin circular object. **2** round flat or apparently flat surface or mark. **3** layer of cartilage between vertebrae. **4** disc containing recorded sound, images, etc. **5** (usu. **disk**) information storage device for computer. ● **disc jockey** person who introduces and plays music on radio or at club etc.

**discard** ● v. reject as unwanted; remove or put aside. ● n. discarded item.

**discern** v. perceive clearly with mind or senses; make out.□□ **discernible** adj. **discernment** n.

**discerning** adj. having good judgement.□□ **discernment** n.

**discharge** ● v. **1** send or flow out; release; dismiss. **2** pay (debt), perform (duty). ● n. discharging; substance discharged.

**disciple** n. follower or pupil of leader; one of the original followers of Christ.

**disciplinarian** n. enforcer of or believer in firm discipline.

**disciplinary** adj. of or enforcing discipline.

**discipline** ● n. **1** control or order exercised over people or animals;

system of rules for this; training or way of life aimed at self-control or conformity. **2** branch of learning. **3** punishment. ● v. punish; control by training in obedience.

**disclaim** v. deny, disown; renounce legal claim to.

**disclaimer** n. statement disclaiming something.

**disclose** v. expose, make known; reveal.□□ **disclosure** n.

**disco** n. (pl. **discos**) place where recorded music is played for dancing; equipment or music associated with this.

**discolour** v. (also **discolor**) cause to change from its normal colour; stain; tarnish.□□ **discoloration** n.

**discomfit** v. (**discomfited**) disconcert, baffle, frustrate.□□ **discomfiture** n.

Usage *Discomfit* is sometimes confused with *discomfort*.

**discomfort** ● n. lack of comfort; uneasiness of body or mind. ● v. make uncomfortable.

**disconcert** v. disturb composure of; fluster.□□ **disconcerted** adj. **disconcerting** adj.

**disconnect** v. break connection of or between; cut off power supply of. □□ **disconnection** n.

**disconnected** adj. incoherent and illogical.

**disconsolate** adj. forlorn, unhappy, disappointed.□□ **disconsolately** adv.

**discontent** ● n. lack of contentment; dissatisfaction, grievance. ● v. (esp. as **discontented** adj.) make dissatisfied.

**discontinue** v. **1** come or bring to an end. **2** give up.

**discord** n. **1** disagreement; strife; lack of harmony. **2** harsh noise; clashing sounds.□□ **discordant** adj.

**discothèque** n. disco.

**discount** ● n. amount deducted from normal price. ● v. **1** disregard as unreliable or unimportant. **2** deduct amount from (price etc.)

**discountenance** v. **1** disconcert. **2** refuse to approve of.

**discourage** v. deprive of courage or confidence; dissuade, deter; show disapproval of.□□ **discouragement** n.

**discourse** ● n. conversation; lecture, speech; a treatise. ● v. converse; speak or write at length.

**discourteous** adj. rude, uncivil. □□ **discourteously** adv. **discourtesy** n.

**discover** v. obtain sight or knowledge of.□□ **discovery** n.

**discredit** ● v. (**discredited**) cause to be disbelieved; harm good reputation of. ● n. (something causing) harm to reputation.

**discreditable** adj. bringing discredit; shameful.

**discreet** adj. circumspect in speech or action; tactful; prudent; unobtrusive.□□ **discreetly** adv. **discreetness** n.

**discrepancy** n. difference; inconsistency.

**discrete** adj. distinct; separate. □□ **discreteness** n.

**discretion** n. **1** being discreet; prudence; good judgement. **2** freedom or authority to act as one thinks fit.□□ **discretionary** adj.

**discriminate** v. make or see distinction; make unfair difference in one's treatment of people. □□ **discriminating** adj. **discriminatory** adj.

**discrimination** n. **1** unfavourable treatment based on racial, sexual, etc. prejudice. **2** good taste or judgement in artistic matters etc. **3** understanding the difference between one thing and another.

**discursive** adj. tending to digress, rambling.

**discus** n. (pl. **discuses**) heavy disc thrown in athletic events.

**discuss** v. talk about; talk or write about (subject) in detail.
□□ **discussion** n.

**disdain** ● n. scorn, contempt.
● v. regard with disdain; refrain or refuse out of disdain.
□□ **disdainful** adj.

**disease** n. unhealthy condition of organism or part of organism; (specific) disorder or illness.
□□ **diseased** adj.

**disembark** v. put or go ashore; get off aircraft, bus, etc.
□□ **disembarkation** n.

**disembodied** adj. (of soul etc.) separated from body or concrete form; without body.

**disembowel** v. (**disembowelled**) remove entrails of.
□□ **disembowelment** n.

**disenchant** v. disillusion.
□□ **disenchantment** n.

**disenfranchise** v. deprive of right to vote, of citizen's rights, or of franchise held. □□ **disenfranchisement** n.

**disengage** v. detach; release.
□□ **disengagement** n.

**disentangle** v. free or become free of tangles or complications.
□□ **disentanglement** n.

**disfavour** n. (also **disfavor**) disapproval; dislike.

**disfigure** v. spoil appearance of.
□□ **disfigurement** n.

**disgorge** v. eject from throat; pour forth.□□ **disgorgement** n.

**disgrace** ● n. shame; ignominy; shameful or very bad person or thing. ● v. bring shame or discredit on.

**disgraceful** adj. shameful; causing disgrace.□□ **disgracefully** adv.

**disgruntled** adj. discontented; sulky.

**disguise** ● v. conceal identity of; make unrecognisable; misrepresent

or cover up. ● n. costume, make-up, etc. used to disguise; action, manner, etc. used to deceive; disguised condition.

**disgust** ● n. strong aversion; repugnance. ● v. cause disgust in.
□□ **disgusting** adj. **disgustingly** adv.

**dish** n. shallow flat-bottomed container, esp. for food; food prepared according to recipe.□ **dish out** colloq. distribute. **dish up** serve out food.

**disharmony** n. lack of harmony; discord.

**dishearten** v. cause to lose courage or confidence.

**dishevelled** adj. untidy; ruffled.
□□ **dishevelment** n.

**dishonest** adj. fraudulent; insincere.
□□ **dishonestly** adv. **dishonesty** n.

**dishonour** n. (also **dishonor**) loss of honour; disgrace; cause of this.
● v. **1** disgrace (person, family, etc.) **2** refuse to pay (cheque etc.).

**dishonourable** adj. (also **dishonorable**) causing disgrace; ignominious; unprincipled.
□□ **dishonourably** adv.

**disillusion** ● v. free from illusion or mistaken belief, esp. disappointingly. ● n. disillusioned state. □□ **disillusionment** n.

**disincentive** n. thing discouraging action, effort, etc.

**disincline** v. make unwilling.
□□ **disinclination** n.

**disinfect** v. cleanse of infection.
□□ **disinfection** n.

**disinfectant** ● n. substance that destroys germs etc.
● adj. disinfecting.

**disinformation** n. false information, propaganda.

**disingenuous** adj. insincere, not candid. □□ **disingenuously** adv.

**disinherit** v. reject as one's heir; deprive of right to inherit.
□□ **disinheritance** n.

**disintegrate** v. separate into component parts; break up. □□ **disintegration** n.

**disinter** v. (disinterred) dig up; discover.

**disinterested** adj. **1** unbiased, impartial. **2** uninterested. □□ **disinterest** n. **disinterestedly** adv.

---

**Usage** The use of *disinterested* to mean 'uninterested' is common in informal use, but is widely regarded as incorrect.

---

**disjointed** adj. incoherent; disconnected.

**disjunction** n. separation.

**disk** n. = DISC.

**diskette** n. Computing = FLOPPY. n.

**dislike** ● v. have aversion to; not like. ● n. feeling of repugnance or not liking; object of this.

**dislocate** v. disturb normal connection of (esp. joint in body); disrupt. □□ **dislocation** n.

**dislodge** v. remove from established or fixed position. □□ **dislodgement** n.

**disloyal** adj. lacking loyalty; unfaithful. □□ **disloyalty** n.

**dismal** adj. **1** gloomy; miserable. **2** colloq. feeble, inept. □□ **dismally** adv.

**dismantle** v. take to pieces.

**dismay** ● v. fill with consternation or anxiety; reduce to despair. ● n. feeling of intense disappointment and discouragement.

**dismember** v. remove limbs from; partition (country etc.). □□ **dismemberment** n.

**dismiss** v. **1** send away; disband; allow to go; terminate employment of. **2** put out of one's thoughts. **3** Law refuse further hearing to. **4** Cricket put (batter, side) out. □□ **dismissal** n.

**dismissive** adj. dismissing rudely or casually; disdainful. □□ **dismissively** adv.

**dismount** v. **1** get off or down from horse or bicycle etc. **2** remove (thing) from mounting.

**disobedient** adj. disobeying; rebellious. □□ **disobedience** n. **disobediently** adv.

**disobey** v. refuse or fail to obey.

**disorder** n. **1** confusion; tumult; riot. **2** bodily or mental ailment. □□ **disordered** adj.

**disorderly** adj. untidy; confused; riotous.

**disorganise** v. (also -ize) throw into confusion or disorder; (as **disorganised** adj.) badly organised, untidy. □□ **disorganisation** n.

**disorientate** v. (also **disorient**) confuse (person) as to his or her bearings. □□ **disorientation** n.

**disown** v. deny or give up any connection with; repudiate, renounce.

**disparage** v. criticise; belittle. □□ **disparagement** n.

**disparate** adj. essentially different; unrelated.

**disparity** n. inequality; difference; incongruity.

**dispassionate** adj. free from emotion; impartial. □□ **dispassionately** adv.

**dispatch** (also **despatch**) ● v. **1** send off. **2** perform (task etc.) promptly. **3** kill. **4** colloq. eat (food) quickly. ● n. **1** dispatching, being dispatched. **2** official written message, esp. military or political. **3** promptness, efficiency.

**dispel** v. (dispelled) drive away; disperse.

**dispensable** adj. that can be done without.

**dispensary** n. place where medicines are dispensed.

**dispensation** n. **1** dispensing, distributing. **2** exemption from penalty, rule, etc. **3** system of government, organisation, etc.

**dispense** v. **1** distribute. **2** administer. **3** make up and give out (medicine). □ **dispense with** do without; make unnecessary.

**disperse** v. go or send widely or in different directions; scatter; station at different points; disseminate; separate (light) into coloured constituents. □□ **dispersion** n. **dispersal** n.

**dispirited** adj. dejected; despondent.

**displace** v. move from its place; remove from office; take the place of; oust. □□ **displacement** n.

**display** ● v. exhibit; show.
● n. displaying; exhibition; ostentation.

**displease** v. make upset or angry; offend. □□ **displeasure** n.

**disposable** adj. designed to be discarded after use; able to be disposed of.

**dispose** v. place, arrange; make willing or ready to do something. □ **be well disposed** be friendly or favourable. **dispose of** get rid of. □□ **disposal** adj.

**disposition** n. **1** natural tendency; temperament. **2** arrangement of parts.

**dispossess** v. deprive; dislodge; oust. □□ **dispossession** n.

**disproportion** n. lack of proportion. □□ **disproportional** adj. **disproportionally** adv.

**disproportionate** adj. out of proportion; relatively too large or small. □□ **disproportionately** adv.

**disprove** v. prove (theory etc.) false.

**disputable** adj. open to question.

**disputation** n. debate, esp. formal; argument; controversy.

**dispute** ● v. hold debate; quarrel; question truth or validity of; contend

for; resist. ● n. controversy, debate; quarrel.

**disqualify** v. make or pronounce (competitor, applicant, etc.) unfit or ineligible. □□ **disqualification** n.

**disquiet** ● v. make anxious.
● n. anxiety; uneasiness.
□□ **disquietude** n.

**disregard** ● v. ignore; treat as unimportant. ● n. **1** indifference. **2** neglect.

**disrepair** n. poor condition due to lack of repairs.

**disreputable** adj. having bad reputation; not respectable. □□ **disreputably** adv.

**disrepute** n. lack of good reputation; discredit.

**disrespect** n. lack of respect. □□ **disrespectful** adj.

**disrobe** v. literary undress.

**disrupt** v. interrupt continuity of; bring disorder to. □□ **disruption** n.

**disruptive** adj. **1** causing disruption. **2** innovative or groundbreaking.

**diss** = DIS.

**dissatisfied** adj. discontented. □□ **dissatisfaction** n.

**dissect** v. cut into pieces, esp. for examination or post-mortem; analyse or criticise in detail. □□ **dissection** n.

**dissemble** v. be hypocritical or insincere; disguise or conceal (feeling, intention, etc.)

**disseminate** v. scatter about, spread (esp. ideas) widely. □□ **dissemination** n.

**dissension** n. angry disagreement.

**dissent** ● v. disagree, esp. openly; differ, esp. from established or official opinion. ● n. difference of opinion; expression of this; nonconformity. □□ **dissenter** n.

**dissertation** n. lengthy essay.

**disservice** n. unhelpful or harmful action.

**dissident** ● *adj.* disagreeing, esp. with established government.
● *n.* dissident person.

**dissimilar** *adj.* unlike, not similar.
□□ **dissimilarity** *n.*

**dissipate** *v.* **1** disperse, dispel; squander. **2** (as **dissipated** *adj.*) dissolute.

**dissipation** *n.* **1** dissolute way of life. **2** being dissipated.

**dissociate** *v.* disconnect or separate; become disconnected.
□□ **dissociation** *n.*

**dissolute** *adj.* lax in morals; licentious.

**dissolution** *n.* dissolving of assembly or partnership.

**dissolve** *v.* **1** make or become liquid or dispersed in liquid; disappear gradually. **2** dismiss (assembly). **3** end (partnership).

**dissonant** *adj.* lacking harmony.
□□ **dissonance** *n.*

**dissuade** *v.* discourage; persuade against. □□ **dissuasion** *n.*

**distaff** *n.* cleft stick holding wool etc. for spinning by hand. □ **distaff side** mother's side of family.

**distance** ● *n.* length of space between two points; distant part; remoteness. ● *v.* separate.

**distant** *adj.* at specified or considerable distance away; aloof.
□□ **distantly** *adv.*

**distaste** *n.* dislike; aversion.
□□ **distasteful** *adj.*

**distemper** ● *n.* **1** paint for walls using glue etc. as base. **2** disease of dogs. ● *v.* paint with distemper.

**distend** *v.* swell out by pressure from within. □□ **distension** *n.*

**distil** *v.* (**distilled**) purify or extract essence from (substance) by vaporising and condensing it and collecting remaining liquid; make (whisky etc.) by distilling; extract essential meaning of (idea etc.).
□□ **distillation** *n.*

**distillery** *n.* factory etc. for distilling alcoholic liquor.

**distinct** *adj.* **1** separate, different in quality or kind. **2** clearly perceptible; definite, decided. □□ **distinctly** *adv.*

**distinction** *n.* **1** discriminating, distinguishing; difference between things; thing that differentiates. **2** excellence; mark of honour.

**distinctive** *adj.* distinguishing, characteristic. □□ **distinctively** *adv.* **distinctiveness** *n.*

**distinguish** *v.* **1** see or draw a difference between; discern. **2** make notable. □□ **distinguishable** *adj.*

**distinguished** *adj.* eminent; famous; dignified.

**distort** *v.* pull or twist out of shape; misrepresent (facts etc.); transmit (sound etc.) inaccurately.
□□ **distortion** *n.*

**distract** *v.* draw away attention of.

**distraction** *n.* **1** distracting, being distracted; thing that distracts; relaxation, amusement. **2** mental confusion; frenzy, madness.

**distraint** *n.* seizure of goods to enforce payment.

**distraught** *adj.* distracted with worry, fear, etc.; very agitated.

**distress** ● *n.* **1** suffering caused by pain, grief, worry, etc. **2** *Law* distraint.
● *v.* cause distress to; make unhappy.
□□ **distressed** *adj.* **distressing** *adj.*

**distribute** *v.* **1** give shares of; deal out; spread about. **2** put at different points; arrange; classify.
□□ **distribution** *n.* **distributive** *adj.*

**distributor** *n.* **1** person who markets goods. **2** device in an internal-combustion engine for passing current to each spark plug in turn. **3** main road carrying traffic away from busy centre.

**district** *n.* region; area of common characteristics; administrative division.

**distrust** ● *n.* lack of trust; suspicion. ● *v.* have no confidence in.□□ **distrustful** *adj.*

**disturb** *v.* break rest, quiet, or calm of; cause to move from settled position.

**disturbance** *n.* disturbing, being disturbed; tumult, disorder, agitation.

**disturbed** *adj.* emotionally or mentally unstable.

**disunite** *v.* separate; divide. □□ **disunity** *n.*

**disuse** *n.* state of no longer being used.

**ditch** ● *n.* long narrow excavation esp. for drainage or irrigation. ● *v.* **1** make or repair ditches. **2** *colloq.* abandon; discard.

**dither** ● *v.* hesitate; be indecisive. ● *n. colloq.* state of agitation or hesitation.□□ **ditherer** *n.* **dithery** *adj.*

**ditto** *n.* the aforesaid, the same.

**ditty** *n.* short simple song.

**ditzy** *adj. colloq.* silly or scatterbrained.□□ **ditz** *n.*

**diuretic** ● *adj.* causing increased output of urine. ● *n.* diuretic drug.

**diurnal** *adj.* in or of day; daily; occupying one day.□□ **diurnally** *adv.*

**diva** *n.* famous female singer.

**divan** *n.* low couch or bed without back or ends.

**dive** ● *v.* plunge head first into water; (of aircraft) descend fast and steeply; (of submarine or diver) submerge; go deeper. ● *n.* **1** act of diving; steep descent, fall. **2** *colloq.* disreputable nightclub, bar, etc.

> **Usage** In North America *dove* is acceptable as the past tense of *dive*. While it is often heard in Australia, it is non-standard.

**diver** *n.* person who dives, esp. one who works under water; diving bird.

**diverge** *v.* spread out from central point; depart from set course; (of opinions etc.) differ.□□ **divergence** *n.* **divergent** *adj.*

**diverse** *adj.* of differing kinds. □□ **diversity** *n.*

**diversify** *v.* make diverse; vary; spread (investment) over several enterprises; expand range of products.□□ **diversification** *n.*

**diversion** *n.* **1** diverting, being diverted; alternative route when road is temporarily closed. **2** recreation, pastime.□□ **diversionary** *adj.*

**divert** *v.* **1** turn aside; deflect; distract (attention). **2** (often as **diverting** *adj.*) entertain; amuse.

**divest** *v.* unclothe; strip; deprive, rid.

**divide** ● *v.* **1** separate into parts; split or break up; distribute, deal, share. **2** cause to disagree. **3** find how many times number contains another; be divisible by number without remainder. ● *n.* dividing line; watershed.

**dividend** *n.* **1** share of profit paid to shareholders. **2** a benefit from an action. **3** number to be divided.

**divider** *n.* **1** screen etc. dividing room. **2** (**dividers**) measuring compasses.

**divine** ● *adj.* **1** of, from, or like a god; sacred. **2** *colloq.* excellent. ● *v.* **1** discover by intuition or guessing. **2** foresee. **3** search for underground water etc. holding Y-shaped stick or rod that dips abruptly over right spot.□□ **divinely** *adv.*

**divinity** *n.* being divine; god; theology.

**divisible** *adj.* capable of being divided.□□ **divisibility** *n.*

**division** *n.* **1** dividing, being divided; dividing one number by another; separation of MPs for counting votes; one of parts into which thing is divided. **2** disagreement. **3** administrative unit, esp. group of teams in sporting competition or group of army units.□□ **divisional** *adj.*

**divisive** *adj.* causing disagreement. □□ **divisively** *adv.* **divisiveness** *n.*

**divisor** *n.* number by which another is to be divided.

**divorce** ● *n.* legal dissolution of marriage; separation. ● *v.* end marriage of (person) by divorce; separate.

**divorcee** *n.* divorced person.

**divot** *n.* piece of turf dislodged by head of golf club.

**divulge** *v.* disclose (secret).

**DIY** *abbr.* do-it-yourself.

**dizzy** ● *adj.* **1** giddy; dazed; causing giddiness. **2** *colloq.* empty-headed. ● *v.* **1** make dizzy. **2** bewilder.□□ **dizzily** *adv.* **dizziness** *n.*

**DJ** *n.* **1** disc jockey. **2** person who makes music with samples of recorded sounds.

**dl** *abbr.* decilitre(s).

**dm** *abbr.* decimetre(s).

**DNA** *abbr.* **1** deoxyribonucleic acid (substance carrying genetic information in chromosomes). **2** fundamental and distinctive characteristics or qualities of someone or something.

**do** ● *v.* (**does, did, done, doing**) **1** perform, complete; work at, deal with. **2** act, proceed; fare. **3** be suitable or acceptable. ● *v.aux.* used to form the present or past tense, in questions, for emphasis, or to avoid repeating verb just used. ● *n.* (*pl.* **dos** or **do's**) *colloq.* a party.□ **do away with** abolish; kill. **do in** *colloq.* kill; injure; tire out. **do out of** *colloq.* deprive of unfairly. **do without** manage without. **to do with** concerning; connected with.

**do.** *abbr.* ditto.

**dob** *v.* (**dobbed**) *Aust. colloq.* kick (esp. goal).□ **dob in 1** (also **dob on**)

inform on (person). **2** impose (responsibility etc.) on. **3** contribute (money).□□ **dobber** *n.*

**d.o.b.** *abbr.* date of birth.

**doc** *n.* **1** doctor. **2** documentary. **3** document.

**docile** *adj.* submissive, easily managed.□□ **docility** *n.*

**dock** ● *n.* **1** enclosed harbour for loading, unloading, and repair of ships. **2** enclosure in criminal court for accused. **3** weed with broad leaves. ● *v.* **1** (of ship) come into dock. **2** join (spacecraft) together in space; be joined thus. **3** cut short (tail); reduce or deduct (money etc.) □□ **docker** *n.*

**docket** ● *n.* document listing goods delivered, jobs done, contents of package, etc.; receipt. ● *v.* (**docketed**) label with or enter on docket.

**dockyard** *n.* area with docks and equipment for building and repairing ships.

**doctor** ● *n.* **1** qualified medical practitioner. **2** holder of doctorate. **3** *Aust.* cool sea breeze. ● *v. colloq.* **1** tamper with, falsify; adulterate. **2** castrate, spay.

**doctorate** *n.* highest university degree.□□ **doctoral** *adj.*

**doctrinaire** *adj.* applying theory or doctrine dogmatically.

**doctrine** *n.* principle or set of principles of religious or political etc. belief.□□ **doctrinal** *adj.*

**document** ● *n.* piece of written, printed, or electronic material giving information or evidence. ● *v.* **1** record. **2** prove by or support with documents. □□ **documentation** *n.*

**documentary** ● *adj.* **1** consisting of documents. **2** factual, based on real events. ● *n.* documentary film etc.

**dodder** *v.* tremble, totter, be feeble. □□ **dodderer** *n.* **doddery** *adj.*

**dodecagon** n. plane figure with twelve sides.

**dodecahedron** n. solid figure with twelve faces.

**dodge** ● v. 1 move quickly to elude pursuer, blow, etc.; evade by cunning or trickery. 2 colloq. acquire dishonestly. ● n. 1 quick evasive movement. 2 clever trick or expedient.

**dodgem** n. small electrically-driven car at funfair, bumped into others in enclosure.

**dodgy** adj. (dodgier) colloq. unreliable, risky.

**dodo** n. (pl. dodos) large extinct flightless bird.

**doe** n. female fallow deer, kangaroo, reindeer, hare, or rabbit.

**does** see DO.

**doff** v. remove (hat etc.)

**dog** ● n. 1 four-legged flesh-eating animal of many breeds akin to fox etc.; male of this, or of fox or wolf. 2 colloq. despicable person. 3 colloq. informer. 4 mechanical device for gripping. 5 (the dogs) colloq. greyhound racing. ● v. (dogged) follow closely; pursue, track. □ dog-eared (of pages) with bent or worn corners.

**dogged** adj. tenacious. □□ **doggedly** adv.

**dogger** n. Aust. dingo hunter.

**doggerel** n. poor or trivial verse.

**doghouse** n. dog's kennel. □ in the doghouse colloq. in disgrace or disfavour.

**dogma** n. principle, tenet; doctrinal system.

**dogmatic** adj. imposing personal opinions; authoritative; arrogant. □□ **dogmatically** adv. **dogmatism** n. **dogmatist** n.

**do-gooder** n. well-meaning but unrealistic promoter of social work or reform.

**dogsbody** n. colloq. a drudge.

**doh** n. Mus. first note of major scale, or the note C.

**doily** n. (also **doyley**) small lacy mat placed on plate for cakes etc.

**doldrums** n.pl. 1 (the doldrums) low spirits; feeling of boredom; period of inactivity. 2 equatorial ocean region with little or no wind.

**dole** ● n. colloq. 1 unemployment benefit. 2 charitable (esp. niggardly) gift or distribution. ● v. distribute sparingly. □ **dole bludger** Aust. colloq. person who exploits system of unemployment benefits by avoiding work.

**doleful** adj. 1 mournful. 2 dreary, dismal. □□ **dolefully** adv.

**doll** n. small model of human figure, esp. as child's toy. □ **doll up** colloq. dress smartly.

**dollar** n. chief monetary unit in Australia, US, and various other countries.

**dollop** n. a shapeless lump of food etc.

**dolly** n. 1 = DOLL. 2 small platform on wheels used for holding heavy objects. 3 easy catch in cricket.

**dolma** n. (pl. **dolmas** or **dolmades**) spiced rice or meat etc. wrapped in vine or cabbage leaves.

**dolomite** n. mineral or rock of calcium magnesium carbonate.

**dolour** n. (also **dolor**) sorrow, distress. □□ **dolorous** adj.

**dolphin** n. large porpoise-like sea mammal.

**dolt** n. stupid person. □□ **doltish** adj.

**domain** n. 1 area ruled over; realm; sphere of authority. 2 location on Internet. □ **domain name** Internet address.

**dome** n. rounded roof with a circular base; thing shaped like this. □□ **domed** adj.

**domestic** ● adj. 1 of home, household, or family affairs. 2 of one's own country. **3** (of animal) tamed. **4** fond of home life. ● *n.* **1** household servant. **2** argument or fight between members of household. □□ **domestically** *adv.*

**domesticate** *v.* **1** tame (animal) to live with humans. **2** accustom to housework etc. □□ **domestication** *n.*

**domesticity** *n.* being domestic; home life.

**domicile** ● *n.* dwelling place; place of permanent residence. ● *v.* (usu. as **domiciled** *adj.*) settle in a place. □□ **domiciliary** *adj.*

**dominant** *adj.* dominating, prevailing. □□ **dominance** *n.*

**dominate** *v.* command, control; be most influential or obvious; (of high place) overlook. □□ **domination** *n.*

**domineer** *v.* behave forcefully making others obey.

**dominion** *n.* **1** sovereignty; realm; domain. **2** *hist.* self-governing territory of British Commonwealth.

**domino** *n.* any of 28 small oblong pieces marked with 0–6 pips in each half, used in the game of **dominoes**.

**don** *v.* put on (garment).

**donate** *v.* give (money etc.), esp. to charity. □□ **donation** *n.*

**done** ● see **do**. ● *adj.* **1** completed; cooked. **2** *colloq.* socially acceptable.

**doner kebab** *n.* spiced lamb cooked on a spit and served in slices.

**donga** *n.* *Aust.* **1** shallow often circular depression in dry country. **2** the bush. **3** temporary dwelling.

**dongle** *n.* small device able to be connected to a computer to allow access to wireless broadband etc.

**donkey** *n.* (*pl.* **donkeys**) **1** domestic ass. **2** *colloq.* stupid or stubborn person. □ **donkey's years** *colloq.* a very long time.

**donnybrook** *n.* fight; uproar.

**donor** *n.* person who donates; person who provides blood for transfusion, organ for transplantation, etc.

**doodle** *v.* scribble or draw absent-mindedly.

**doof** *n.* *Aust. colloq.* dance music with very heavy beat.

**doom** ● *n.* terrible fate or destiny; death, ruin. ● *v.* condemn or destine; consign to ruin, destruction, etc.

**doona** *n. propr. Aust.* thick quilt with down filling.

**door** *n.* hinged or sliding barrier closing entrance to building, room, cupboard, etc.; doorway.

**doorstop** *n.* **1** device for keeping door open etc. **2** *Aust.* interview with politician etc. who is leaving or entering a building.

**doorway** *n.* opening filled by door; entrance.

**doover** *n.* (also **dooverlacky**) *Aust. colloq.* thingummy.

**dope** ● *n.* **1** *colloq.* drug, esp. narcotic. **2** *colloq.* stupid person. **3** *colloq.* information. ● *v.* give or add drug to.

**dopey** *adj.* (also **dopy**) **1** half asleep. **2** stupid.

**doppelganger** *n.* apparition or double of living person.

**Doppler effect** *n.* change in frequency of esp. sound waves when source and observer move closer or apart.

**dormant** *adj.* lying inactive; sleeping. □□ **dormancy** *n.*

**dormer** *n.* (in full **dormer window**) upright window in sloping roof.

**dormitory** *n.* sleeping room with several beds.

**dormouse** *n.* (*pl.* **dormice**) small mouselike hibernating rodent.

**Dorothy Dix** *n.* (also **Dorothy Dixer**) *Aust.* prearranged parliamentary question allowing minister to deliver prepared speech.

**dorsal** *adj.* of or on back.

**dory** *n.* edible marine fish.

**dosage** *n.* size of dose; giving of dose.

**dose** ● *n.* single portion of medicine; amount of radiation received.
● *v.* give medicine to; treat with.

**dossier** *n.* file containing information about person, event, etc.

**dot** ● *n.* small round mark; shorter signal of the two in Morse code.
● *v.* (dotted) 1 mark or scatter with dot(s). 2 *colloq.* hit. □ **dot ball** (in cricket match) bowled ball from which no runs are scored. **on the dot** exactly on time.

**dotage** *n.* old age, esp. as characterised by weakness.

**dote** *v.* □ **dote on** be excessively fond of. □ **dotingly** *adv.*

**dotterel** *n.* small plover.

**dotty** *adj.* (dottier) *colloq.* feeble minded.

**double** ● *adj.* consisting of two things or parts; twice as much or as many; designed for two people or things. ● *adv.* twice as much.
● *n.* 1 double quantity or thing. 2 (doubles) game with two players on each side. 3 person or thing very like another. ● *v.* 1 make or become twice as much or as many; fold in two; act two parts; have two uses. 2 turn back sharply. □ **double bass** largest and lowest-pitched instrument of violin family. **double-breasted** (of coat) with fronts overlapping. **double-cross** cheat, deceive. **double-dealing** deceit. **double Dutch** *colloq.* incomprehensible talk. **double entendre** phrase with two meanings, one of which is usu. indecent. **double figures** numbers from 10 to 99. **double negative** *Gram.* negative statement (incorrectly) containing two negative elements (*he didn't do nothing*). **double take** delayed reaction just after one's first reaction. **double whammy** situation in which two unwanted things happen together.

**doublet** *n.* 1 *hist.* man's close-fitting jacket. 2 one of pair of similar things.

**doubletalk** *n.* talk with deliberately ambiguous meaning.

**doubloon** *n. hist.* Spanish gold coin.

**doubt** ● *n.* feeling of uncertainty or disbelief. ● *v.* feel uncertain of the truth or existence of; disbelieve.

**doubtful** *adj.* feeling or causing doubt; unreliable. □ **doubtfully** *adv.*

**doubtless** *adv.* 1 certainly.
2 probably.

**douche** ● *n.* jet of liquid applied to part of body for cleansing or medicinal purposes; device for applying this. ● *v.* use douche (on).

**dough** *n.* 1 thick paste of flour mixed with liquid for baking. 2 *colloq.* money. □ **doughy** *adj.*

**doughnut** *n.* (also **donut**) 1 small cake of fried sweetened dough, usu. in shape of ring. 2 *colloq.* tight 360° turn in vehicle.

**doughty** *adj.* (doughtier) valiant. □ **doughtily** *adv.*

**dour** *adj.* severe, stern, obstinate. □ **dourly** *adv.* **dourness** *n.*

**douse** *v.* 1 throw water over; plunge into water. 2 extinguish (light).

**dove**[1] *n.* 1 bird of pigeon family, having short legs and full breast.
2 gentle or innocent person; advocate of peaceful policies.

**dove**[2] see note at DIVE.

**dovetail** ● *n.* mortise-and-tenon joint shaped like dove's spread tail. ● *v.* fit together; combine neatly; join with dovetails.

**dowager** *n.* widow with title or property from her late husband.

**dowdy** *adj.* (dowdier) unattractively dull. □ **dowdiness** *n.*

**dowel** *n.* cylindrical peg for holding parts of structure together.

**dowelling** *n.* rods for cutting into dowels.

**down** ● *adv.* 1 to, in, or at a lower place or state etc.; to a smaller size,

or lower price. **2** from an earlier to a later time. **3** recorded in writing. **4** to a source or place where a thing is. **5** paid as deposit or part. ● *prep.* downwards along, through, or into; at a lower part of. ● *adj.* **1** directed downwards. **2** travelling away from a central place. ● *v. colloq.* knock or bring or put down; swallow.
● *n.* **1** very fine soft furry feathers or short hairs. **2** area of open undulating land. □ **down and out** destitute. **down to** attributable to. **down-to-earth** sensible and practical. **down under** in the antipodes, esp. Australia.

**downcast** *adj.* dejected; (of eyes) looking downwards.

**downfall** *n.* fall from prosperity or power; something causing this.

**downgrade** *v.* reduce to a lower grade.

**download** ● *v.* copy (data) from one computer system to another. ● *n.* act or process of downloading data; file that has been downloaded.

**downmarket** *adj. & adv.* of or towards lower prices and quality.

**downpour** *n.* a great fall of rain.

**downright** ● *adj.* plain, straightforward; utter. ● *adv.* thoroughly.

**downsize** *v.* reduce number of staff employed by company etc.

**downstairs** *adv. & adj.* to or on a lower floor.

**Down syndrome** *n.* congenital disorder causing intellectual impairment and physical abnormalities.

**downtrodden** *adj.* oppressed.

**downward** ● *adj.* moving or leading down. ● *adv.* (also **downwards**) towards what is lower, less important, or later.

**downy** *adj.* (**downier**) of, like, or covered with down.

**dowry** *n.* property brought by bride to her husband.

**doyen** *n.* man who is the senior member of his group or profession.

**doyenne** *n.* woman who is the senior member of her group or profession.

**doz.** *abbr.* dozen.

**doze** ● *v.* sleep lightly; be half asleep. ● *n.* short light sleep.

**dozen** *n.* set of twelve; (**dozens**) very many.

**DPP** *abbr.* Director of Public Prosecutions.

**Dr** *abbr.* Doctor.

**drab** *adj.* (**drabber**) dull, uninteresting; not brightly coloured. □□ **drabness** *n.*

**drachma** *n.* (*pl.* **drachmas** or **drachmae**) (until 2002) chief monetary unit of Greece.

**draconian** *adj.* (of laws) harsh, cruel.

**draft** ● *n.* **1** preliminary written outline of scheme or version of speech, document, etc. **2** written order for payment of money by bank; drawing of money on this. **3** detachment from larger group. **4** conscription. ● *v.* **1** prepare draft of. **2** select for special duty or purpose. **3** conscript. **4** *Aust.* separate animal(s) from flock or herd.

**draftsman** *n.* **1** person who drafts documents. **2** person who makes drawings.

**drag** ● *v.* (**dragged**) **1** pull along; trail on the ground; bring or proceed with effort. **2** search water with hooks, nets, etc. **3** move (image or text) across computer screen using a mouse etc. **4** draw on (cigarette etc.) **5** *colloq.* take part in drag race. ● *n.* **1** something that slows progress. **2** *colloq.* boring or tiresome person, duty, etc. **3** *colloq.* a draw on a cigarette. **4** *colloq.* women's clothes worn by men. **5** (in full **drag race**) acceleration race between cars over a short distance.

**draggle** v. make dirty and wet by trailing; hang trailing.

**dragon** n. 1 mythical monster like reptile, usu. with wings and able to breathe fire. 2 any of various lizards, usu. having crests, spines, and neck frills.

**dragonet** n. spiny marine fish.

**dragonfly** n. large long-bodied gauzy-winged insect.

**dragoon** ● n. cavalryman.
● v. coerce or bully into.

**dragster** n. car built or modified to take part in drag races.

**drain** ● v. 1 draw off (liquid) by channels, pipes, etc.; flow away. 2 deprive gradually of strength or resources. 3 drink all of.
● n. 1 channel or pipe carrying off water, sewage, etc. 2 something that drains one's strength or resources.

**drainage** n. draining; system of drains; what is drained off.

**drake** n. male duck.

**dram** n. small drink of spirits, esp. whisky.

**drama** n. play for stage or broadcasting; art of writing, acting, and presenting plays; dramatic event or quality.□ **drama queen** person who responds to situations in a melodramatic way.□□ **dramatic** adj.

**dramatise** v. (also **-ize**) convert into play; make dramatic; behave dramatically.□□ **dramatisation** n. **dramatist** n.

**dramatis personae** n.pl. characters in a play.

**drank** SEE DRINK.

**drape** ● v. hang or cover or adorn with cloth etc.; arrange in graceful folds. ● n. (drapes) curtains.

**draper** n. retailer of textile fabrics.

**drapery** n. clothing or hangings arranged in folds; draper's trade or fabrics.

**drastic** adj. far-reaching in effect; severe.□□ **drastically** adv.

**drat** int. colloq. expression of annoyance.

**draught** ● n. 1 current of air indoors. 2 traction. 3 depth of water needed to float ship. 4 drawing of liquor from cask etc. 5 single act of drinking or inhaling; amount so drunk. 6 (draughts) game played with 24 round pieces on a chessboard.
● v. = DRAFT.

**draughtsman** n. (pl. **-men**) person who draws plans or sketches.

**draughty** adj. (draughtier) letting in sharp currents of air.

**draw** ● v. (drew, drawn, drawing) 1 produce (picture or diagram) by making marks. 2 pull; attract; take in (breath etc.); take from or out. 3 obtain by lottery. 4 finish (game) with equal scores. 5 require (specified depth) in which to float. 6 promote or allow draught of air (in). 7 make one's way, come. 8 infuse. ● n. 1 act of drawing. 2 person or thing attracting custom or attention. 3 drawing of lots, raffle. 4 drawn game. 5 inhalation of smoke etc.□ **draw on** use as resource. **draw out** 1 prolong. 2 encourage to talk.

**drawdown** n. 1 reduction in size of military force; withdrawal of water, oil, or gas from reservoir etc.; drawing on available funds or loan facilities. 2 decline in investment or fund.

**drawer** n. 1 person who draws. 2 storage compartment sliding in and out. 3 person who writes cheque. 4 (drawers) knickers, underpants.

**drawing** n. art of representing by line with pencil etc.; picture etc. made thus.□ **drawing pin** pin for fastening paper to surface. **drawing room** room in private house for sitting or entertaining in.

**drawl** ● v. speak with drawn-out vowel sounds. ● n. drawling utterance or way of speaking.

**dray | drink**

**dray** n. low cart without sides for heavy loads.

**dread** • v. fear greatly, esp. in advance. • n. great fear or apprehension. • adj. greatly feared.

**dreadful** adj. terrible; very annoying, very bad.□□ **dreadfully** adv.

**dream** • n. series of scenes in mind of sleeping person; a fantasy.
• v. (**dreamed** or **dreamt**, **dreaming**) have a dream; have an ambition; think of as a possibility.
□□ **dreamer** n.

**dreaming** n. Aust. = DREAMTIME, esp. as manifested in natural world and celebrated in Aboriginal ritual.

**dreamtime** n. Aust. (in Aboriginal belief) collection of events beyond living memory that shaped physical, spiritual, and moral world.

**dreamy** adj. (**dreamier**) 1 given to daydreaming; dreamlike; vague. 2 colloq. delightful.□□ **dreamily** adv.

**dreary** adj. dismal, dull, gloomy.
□□ **drearily** adv. **dreariness** n.

**dredge** • n. apparatus used to scoop up oysters etc., or to clear mud etc., from bottom of sea. • v. 1 remove (silt) from a river or channel; bring up (something forgotten). 2 sprinkle with flour, sugar, etc.

**dregs** n.pl. 1 sediment at bottom of drink. 2 small remnant. 3 least useful or valuable part; worthless part.

**drench** v. wet thoroughly.

**dress** • v. 1 put clothes on; have and wear clothes. 2 arrange or adorn. 3 put dressing on (wound). 4 prepare (poultry, crab, etc.) for cooking or eating. 5 add dressing to (salad etc.) 6 apply manure to. 7 finish surface of (leather, stone, etc.) • n. 1 woman's one-piece garment of bodice and skirt. 2 clothing, esp. whole outfit.
□ **dress circle** first gallery in theatre. **dress rehearsal** final rehearsal of play etc., in costume. **dress up** put on fancy dress; put on smart or formal clothes.

**dressage** n. training of horse in obedience and deportment.

**dresser** n. tall kitchen sideboard with shelves.

**dressing** n. 1 putting one's clothes on. 2 sauce, esp. of oil, vinegar, etc. 3 bandage, ointment, etc. for wound. 4 (also **top-dressing**) fertiliser, soil, etc. spread over land.□ **dressing down** scolding. **dressing table** table with mirror, for use while dressing etc.

**dressy** adj. (**dressier**) colloq. (of clothes or person) smart, elegant.
□□ **dressiness** n.

**drew** see DRAW.

**dribble** • v. 1 allow saliva to flow from mouth; flow or allow to flow in drops. 2 Soccer & Hockey move (ball) forward with slight touches of feet or stick. 3 Basketball bounce ball to advance or control it.
• n. 1 dribbling. 2 small trickling flow.

**dried** adj. (of food) preserved by the removal of moisture.

**drier** n. (also **dryer**) machine for drying hair, laundry, etc.

**drift** • v. be carried by or as if by current of water or air; progress casually or aimlessly; pass gradually into a particular state. • n. 1 drifting movement. 2 mass of snow etc. piled up by wind. 3 general meaning of what is said; gist.

**drill** • n. 1 tool or machine for boring holes or sinking wells. 2 training; routine procedure. 3 strong twilled cotton fabric. • v. 1 use drill; make (hole) with drill; sow (wheat) with drill. 2 train or be trained.

**drily** adv. (also **dryly**) in a dry way.

**drink** • v. (**drank**, **drunk**, **drinking**) swallow (liquid); take alcohol, esp. to excess; pledge good wishes (to) by drinking. • n. liquid for drinking; alcoholic liquor.□ **drink-driver** person who drives having drunk more than legal limit of alcohol. □□ **drinker** n.

**drip** • v. (**dripped**) fall or let fall in drops; be so wet as to shed drops. • n. 1 liquid falling in drops; drop of liquid; sound of dripping. 2 *colloq.* dull or ineffectual person. □ **drip-dry** dry or leave to dry crease-free when hung up. **drip-feed** 1 feed intravenously in drops. 2 apparatus for doing this.

**dripping** n. fat melted from roasted meat.

**drive** • v. (**drove**, **driven**, **driving**) 1 send or urge forward; propel. 2 operate (vehicle etc.) and direct its course; carry or be carried in vehicle. 3 cause; compel. 4 make (bargain). • n. 1 excursion in vehicle. 2 transmission of power to machinery, wheels, etc. 3 motivation and energy. 4 track for car leading to house, hotel, etc. 5 forceful stroke of bat etc. 6 organised group effort, esp. for fundraising. □□ **driver** n.

**drivel** • n. silly nonsense. • v. talk drivel.

**drizzle** • n. very fine rain. • v. fall in very fine drops. □□ **drizzly** adj.

**droid** n. 1 (in science fiction) robot. 2 *Computing* program that automatically collects information from remote systems.

**droll** adj. strange and amusing. □□ **drollery** n.

**dromedary** n. one-humped camel bred for riding.

**drone** • n. 1 deep humming sound; monotonous speaking tone. 2 non-working male of honeybee; idler. 3 remote-controlled pilotless aircraft or missile. • v. make deep humming sound; speak or utter monotonously.

**drongo** n. (pl. **drongos** or **drongoes**) 1 any of various black birds, having elongated tail feathers like fish's tail. 2 *Aust. colloq. derog.* fool, simpleton.

**drool** v. 1 slobber, dribble. 2 admire extravagantly.

**droop** • v. bend or hang down, esp. from weariness or lack of food, drink, etc.; sag; lose heart. • n. drooping position; loss of spirit. □□ **droopy** adj.

**drop** • n. 1 small rounded mass of liquid; (drops) medicine measured by drops; very small quantity. 2 a fall; a steep descent; distance of this. • v. (**dropped**) 1 fall, allow to fall; let go; make or become lower. 2 utter casually. 3 omit; reject; give up. □ **drop in pay** casual visit. **drop kick** 1 *AFL & Rugby* kick made by dropping ball and kicking it on the bounce. 2 *Aust. colloq. derog.* hopelessly inefficient or useless person. **drop off** fall asleep. **drop out** cease to participate. □□ **droplet** n.

**dropper** n. device for releasing liquid in drops.

**droppings** n.pl. dung.

**dropsy** n. oedema. □□ **dropsical** adj.

**dross** n. rubbish; scum of melted metals; impurities.

**drought** n. prolonged absence of rain.

**drove** • n. moving crowd or flock; (droves) *colloq.* great number. • v. 1 see **DRIVE**. 2 *Aust.* drive (herd, flock), esp. over great distance. □□ **drover** n.

**drown** v. 1 kill or die by submersion. 2 submerge; flood; drench. 3 deaden (grief etc.) by drinking. 4 overpower (sound) with louder sound.

**drowse** v. be lightly asleep.

**drowsy** adj. very sleepy, almost asleep. □□ **drowsily** adv. **drowsiness** n.

**drub** v. (**drubbed**) beat, thrash; defeat thoroughly. □□ **drubbing** n.

**drudge** • n. person who does dull, laborious, or menial work. • v. work laboriously; toil. □□ **drudgery** n.

**drug** • n. medicinal substance; (esp. addictive) narcotic, hallucinogen, or stimulant. ● v. (**drugged**) add or give drug to; stupefy.

**drum** ● n. **1** percussion instrument, round frame with skin etc. stretched across; cylindrical object. **2** (**the drum**) Aust. colloq. piece of reliable information. ● v. (**drummed**) beat or tap continuously.

**drummer** n. **1** player of drums. **2** marine fish.

**drumstick** n. **1** stick for beating drum. **2** lower part of fowl's leg.

**drunk** ● see DRINK. ● adj. **1** lacking control from drinking alcohol. **2** overcome with joy, success, power, etc. ● n. person who is drunk, esp. habitually.

**drunkard** n. person habitually drunk.

**drunken** adj. drunk; caused by or involving drunkenness; often drunk. □□ **drunkenly** adv. **drunkenness** n.

**druthers** n.pl. colloq. choice, preference.

**dry** ● adj. **1** without water, moisture, or rainfall; thirsty. **2** uninteresting; expressed with pretended seriousness. **3** (of a country) prohibiting sale of alcohol. **4** (of wine etc.) not sweet. ● v. make or become dry; preserve by removing moisture. ● n. dry ginger ale. □ **dry-clean** clean with solvents without using water. **dry rot** decay of wood that is not ventilated. □□ **dryness** n.

**dryad** n. wood nymph.

**dryandra** n. shrub or small tree of SW Australia, notable for its large flowers.

**DT** abbr. (also **DTs**) delirium tremens.

**dual** ● adj. in two parts; twofold; double. ● n. Gram. dual number or form. □□ **duality** n.

**dub** v. (**dubbed**) **1** replace soundtrack of film etc. **2** give name or nickname to.

**dubiety** n. literary doubt.

**dubious** adj. doubtful; questionable; unreliable. □□ **dubiously** adv. **dubiousness** n.

**dubnium** n. chemical element (symbol Db).

**ducal** adj. of or like duke.

**ducat** n. gold coin, formerly current in most of Europe.

**duchess** n. **1** woman holding rank of duke; duke's wife or widow. **2** (also **duchesse**) dressing table with pivoting mirror.

**duchy** n. territory of duke or duchess.

**duck** ● n. **1** swimming bird, esp. domesticated form of wild duck or mallard; female of this; its flesh as food. **2** score of 0 in cricket. ● v. **1** bob down, esp. to avoid being seen or hit; colloq. dodge (task etc.) **2** dip head briefly under water; plunge (person) briefly in water.

**duckling** n. young duck.

**duco** Aust. ● n. propr. kind of paint, used esp. on body of motor vehicle. ● v. paint (motor vehicle) with duco.

**duct** n. channel, tube; tube in body carrying secretions etc.

**ductile** adj. (of metal) capable of being drawn into wire; pliable; easily moulded. □□ **ductility** n.

**ductless** adj. (of gland) secreting directly into bloodstream.

**dud** colloq. ● n. **1** useless or broken thing; counterfeit article. **2** (**duds**) clothes. ● adj. useless, defective.

**dude** n. colloq. person, fellow; friend, mate.

**dudgeon** n. resentment, indignation.

**due** ● adj. **1** owing, payable. **2** merited. **3** appropriate. **4** expected or under obligation to do something or arrive at certain time. ● n. **1** what one owes or is owed. **2** (**dues**) fee or amount payable. ● adv. (of compass point) exactly, directly. □ **due diligence** reasonable steps taken by person to avoid committing an offence etc. **due process** fair treatment through normal judicial system.

**duel** • n. two-sided contest.
• v. (**duelled**) fight a duel. □□ **duellist** n.

**duet** n. musical composition for two performers.

**duff** v. *Aust.* steal and alter brands on (cattle etc.)

**duffer** n. 1 *Aust.* person who steals stock and alters brands. 2 *colloq.* inefficient or stupid person.

**duffle-coat** n. hooded overcoat fastened with toggles.

**dug**[1] see DIG.

**dug**[2] n. udder, teat.

**dugong** n. Asian sea mammal; sea cow.

**dugout** n. 1 underground shelter. 2 canoe made from hollowed tree trunk.

**duke** n. 1 person holding highest hereditary title of nobility; sovereign prince ruling duchy or small nation. 2 (usu. **dukes** or **dooks**) *colloq.* hand, fist. □□ **dukedom** n.

**dulcet** adj. sweet-sounding.

**dulcimer** n. metal stringed instrument struck with two hand-held hammers.

**dull** • adj. 1 tedious; not interesting. 2 (of weather) overcast. 3 (of colour, light, sound, etc.) not bright, vivid, or clear. 4 (of pain) indistinct; not acute. 5 slow-witted; stupid. 6 (of knife edge etc.) blunt. 7 listless; depressed.
• v. make or become dull.
□□ **dullness** n. **dully** adv.

**duly** adv. in due time or manner; rightly, properly.

**dumb** adj. 1 often *offens.* unable to speak. 2 *colloq.* stupid. □ **dumb-bell** short bar with weighted ends, lifted to exercise muscles. **dumb down** *colloq.* simplify, reduce intellectual content (of something).

**dumbfound** v. greatly astonish or amaze. □□ **dumbfounded** adj.

**dumdum** n. (in full **dumdum bullet**) soft-nosed bullet that expands on impact.

**dummy** • n. 1 sham article; model of human figure. 2 baby's rubber etc. teat. 3 *colloq.* sham; imitation.
• adj. sham; imitation.
• v. make pretended pass or swerve in rugby etc.

**dump** • n. 1 place for depositing rubbish; temporary store. 2 *colloq.* unpleasant or dreary place. 3 *Computing* copy of stored data. • v. 1 put down carelessly; deposit as rubbish. 2 sell (surplus goods) to foreign market at low price. 3 copy (contents of computer memory) to different location. 4 (of wave) break suddenly into shallow water.

**dumper** n. large wave that crashes down as it breaks.

**dumpling** n. ball of dough boiled in stew or containing apple etc.

**dumpy** adj. (**dumpier**) short and stout.

**dun** adj. & n. greyish brown.

**dunce** n. person slow at learning.

**dunderhead** n. stupid person.

**dune** n. drift of sand etc. formed by wind.

**dung** n. excrement of animals.

**dungarees** n.pl. overalls of coarse cotton cloth.

**dungeon** n. underground prison cell.

**dunk** v. dip food into liquid before eating; immerse.

**dunnart** n. *Aust.* narrow-footed marsupial mouse.

**duo** n. pair of performers; duet.

**duodecimal** adj. reckoned in twelves or twelfths.

**duodenum** n. part of small intestine next to stomach. □□ **duodenal** adj.

**dupe** • n. victim of deception.
• v. deceive, trick.

**duple** adj. of two parts.

**duplex** ● n. semi-detached house; building with flat on ground floor and flat above. ● adj. 1 having two parts. 2 (also **full-duplex**) Computing (of circuit) allowing simultaneous two-way transmission of signals.

**duplicate** ● adj. identical; doubled. ● n. identical thing, esp. copy. ● v. 1 double. 2 make or be exact copy of. 3 repeat (an action etc.), esp. unnecessarily. □□ **duplication** n.

**duplicity** n. double-dealing; deceitfulness.□□ **duplicitous** adj.

**durable** ● adj. lasting; hard-wearing. ● n. durable goods. □□ **durability** n.

**dura mater** n. tough outermost membrane enveloping brain and spinal cord.

**duration** n. time taken by event.

**duress** n. compulsion, esp. illegal use of threats or violence.

**during** prep. throughout or at some point in.

**durry** n. Aust. colloq. cigarette.

**dusk** n. darker stage of twilight.

**dusky** adj. (**duskier**) shadowy; dim; dark-coloured.

**dust** ● n. fine particles of earth or other matter. ● v. 1 wipe dust from (furniture etc.) 2 sprinkle with powder, sugar, etc.□ **dust jacket** paper etc. cover used to protect a book.

**duster** n. cloth for dusting furniture etc.

**dustpan** n. container into which dust is brushed from floor.

**dusty** adj. (**dustier**) 1 full of or covered with dust. 2 (of colour) dull or muted.

**Dutch courage** n. false courage obtained by drinking alcohol.

**dutiable** adj. requiring payment of duty.

**dutiful** adj. doing one's duty; obedient.□□ **dutifully** adv.

**duty** n. 1 moral or legal obligation; responsibility. 2 tax on certain goods, imports, etc. 3 job or function arising from business or office.

**duvet** n. = DOONA.

**dux** n. top pupil in class or in school.

**DVD** abbr. digital versatile (or video) disc, data storage medium for audio, video, etc.

**dwarf** ● n. (pl. **dwarfs** or **dwarves**) 1 person, animal, or plant much below normal size. 2 small mythological being, often with magical powers. 3 small usu. dense star. ● v. 1 stunt. 2 make look small by contrast.□□ **dwarfish** adj.

> **Usage** In sense 1, with regard to people, the term is often considered offensive.

**dwell** v. (**dwelt**, **dwelling**) live, reside.

**dwelling** n. house, residence.

**dwindle** v. become gradually less or smaller; lose importance.

**dye** ● n. substance used to change colour of hair, fabric, etc.; colour produced by this. ● v. (**dyed**, **dyeing**) colour with dye.□□ **dyer** n.

**dying** see DIE.

**dyke** (also **dike**) ● n. 1 embankment built to prevent flooding; low wall. 2 colloq. a lesbian. ● v. provide or protect with dyke(s).

**dynamic** adj. 1 energetic; active. 2 of motive force; of force in operation; of dynamics. 3 variations in volume in a musical work. □□ **dynamically** adv.

**dynamics** n.pl. mathematical study of motion and forces causing it.

**dynamite** ● n. high explosive mixture containing nitroglycerine. ● v. charge or blow up with this.

**dynamo** *n.* **1** machine converting mechanical into electrical energy. **2** *colloq.* energetic person.

**dynasty** *n.* line of hereditary rulers. □□ **dynastic** *adj.*

**dysentery** *n.* inflammation of intestines, causing severe diarrhoea.

**dyslexia** *n.* abnormal difficulty in reading and spelling. □□ **dyslectic** *adj. & n.* **dyslexic** *adj. & n.*

**dysmenorrhoea** *n.* painful or difficult menstruation.

**dyspepsia** *n.* indigestion. □□ **dyspeptic** *adj. & n.*

**dysphasia** *n.* lack of coordination in speech.

**dysprosium** *n.* metallic element (symbol Dy).

**dystrophy** *n.* wasting of part of body.

# Ee

**E** abbr. **1** east(ern). **2** colloq. drug ecstasy.

**e-** comb. form involving electronic communication.

**each** ● adj. every one of two or more, regarded separately.
● pron. each person or thing.
□ **each way** (of bet) backing horse to win or be placed.

**eager** adj. keen, enthusiastic.
□□ **eagerly** adv. **eagerness** n.

**eagle** n. **1** large bird of prey. **2** Golf score of two under par for hole.

**eaglet** n. young eagle.

**ear** n. **1** organ of hearing; external part of this; faculty of discriminating sound. **2** attention. **3** seed-bearing head of cereal plant.

**eardrum** n. membrane of middle ear.

**earl** n. British nobleman ranking between marquess and viscount.
□□ **earldom** n.

**early** adj. & adv. (earlier) **1** before the due, usual, or expected time. **2** not far on in day or night or in development etc. □ **early mark** Aust. approval to leave work, school, etc. early.

**earmark** ● n. distinguishing mark. ● v. set aside for special purpose.

**earn** v. obtain as reward for work or merit; bring in as income, interest, or profit. □□ **earner** n.

**earnest** adj. intensely serious.
□□ **earnestly** adv. **earnestness** n.

**earnings** n.pl. money earned.

**earphone** n. usu. pl. device worn on ear to listen to radio, recording, etc.

**earring** n. piece of jewellery worn on ear.

**earshot** n. distance over which something can be heard.

**earth** ● n. **1** (also **Earth**) one of planets of solar system orbiting around sun between Venus and Mars; planet on which we live. **2** land and sea as distinct from sky. **3** ground. **4** soil. **5** Electr. connection to earth as completion of circuit. **6** hole of fox etc. ● v. connect (electrical circuit) to earth. □□ **earthly** adj.

**earthen** adj. made of earth or baked clay.

**earthquake** n. violent shaking of earth's surface.

**earthy** adj. (earthier) **1** of or like earth or soil. **2** direct, uninhibited.

**earwig** n. insect with pincers at rear end.

**ease** ● n. **1** effortlessness. **2** freedom from pain, trouble, embarrassment, or constraint. ● v. **1** relieve from pain etc. **2** become less burdensome or severe; relax, slacken. **3** move or be moved by gentle force.

**easel** n. stand for paintings, blackboard, etc.

**easement** n. legal right of way over another's land.

**easily** adv. **1** without difficulty. **2** by far. **3** very probably.

**east** ● n. point of horizon where sun rises at equinoxes (cardinal point 90° to right of north); corresponding compass point; eastern part of country, town, etc. ● adj. towards, at, near, or facing east; (of wind) from east. ● adv. towards, at, or near east; further east than. □□ **eastward** adj., adv., & n. **eastwards** adv.

**Easter** n. festival of Christ's resurrection.

**easterly** ● adj. & adv. in an eastern position or direction; (of wind) from east. ● n. such wind.

**eastern** *adj.* of or in east.
□□ **easternmost** *adj.*

**easy** ● *adj.* (**easier**) **1** not difficult; free from pain, trouble, or anxiety; comfortably off, affluent; relaxed and pleasant. **2** compliant. **3** *colloq.* promiscuous. ● *adv.* with ease; in an effortless or relaxed manner.
□ **easy-going** relaxed in manner; not strict.

**eat** *v.* (**ate**, **eaten**, **eating**) **1** chew and swallow (food); have a meal. **2** destroy gradually by corrosion etc.

**eatable** ● *adj.* fit to be eaten. ● *n.* (**eatables**) food.

**eatery** *n.* restaurant or eating place.

**eau de Cologne** *n.* delicate perfume.

**eaves** *n.pl.* underside of projecting roof.

**eavesdrop** *v.* (**eavesdropped**) listen to private conversation.
□□ **eavesdropper** *n.*

**ebb** ● *n.* outflow of tide. ● *v.* **1** flow back. **2** decline. □ **at a low ebb** in poor or weak state.

**Ebola** *n.* virus that causes fever and severe internal bleeding.

**ebony** ● *n.* heavy hard black tropical wood. ● *adj.* made of or black as ebony.

**ebullient** *adj.* exuberant.
□□ **ebullience** *n.* **ebulliently** *adv.*

**ecad** *n.* *Ecology* organism modified by its environment.

**eccentric** ● *adj.* **1** unconventional and strange. **2** not concentric; not circular. ● *n.* eccentric person.
□□ **eccentrically** *adv.* **eccentricity** *n.*

**ecclesiastic** *n.* priest or clergyman.

**ecclesiastical** *adj.* of Church or clergy.

**ECG** *abbr.* electrocardiogram.

**echelon** *n.* **1** level in organisation, society, etc. **2** wedge-shaped formation of troops, aircraft, etc.

**echidna** *n.* monotreme with covering of spines, with long snout and long claws.

**echo** ● *n.* (*pl.* **echoes**) **1** repetition of sound by reflection of sound waves; reflected radio or radar beam. **2** close imitation. **3** circumstance or event reminiscent of earlier one. ● *v.* (**echoes**, **echoed**) **1** resound with echo. **2** repeat, imitate.

**éclair** *n.* finger-shaped iced cake of choux pastry filled with cream.

**eclampsia** *n.* convulsive condition occurring esp. in pregnant women.

**éclat** *n.* brilliant display; conspicuous success; prestige.

**eclectic** *adj.* choosing or accepting from various sources.
□□ **eclecticism** *n.*

**eclipse** ● *n.* **1** blocking of light from one heavenly body by another. **2** loss of influence or importance. ● *v.* **1** cause eclipse of; intercept (light). **2** outshine, surpass.

**eco** *adj.* *colloq.* not harming the environment; eco-friendly.

**eco-** *comb. form* ecological; ecological.

**eco-friendly** *adj.* not harmful to environment.

**E. coli** *n.* bacterium that can cause food poisoning.

**ecology** *n.* study of relations of organisms to one another and to their surroundings. □ **ecological footprint** amount of land required to sustain particular person or society.
□□ **ecological** *adj.* **ecologically** *adv.* **ecologist** *n.*

**economic** *adj.* of economics or the economy; profitable, not wasteful. □ **economic rationalism** *Aust.* theory or practice of government using narrow definitions of efficiency etc. as measures of economic success.
**economically** *adv.*

**economical** *adj.* sparing; avoiding waste. □□ **economically** *adv.*

**economics** *n.* science of the production and use of goods and services; (as *pl.*) financial aspects of something. □□ **economist** *n.*

**economise** v. (also **-ize**) reduce expenditure.

**economy** n. **1** wealth and resources of community, esp. in terms of production and consumption of goods and services. **2** frugality; sparing use.

**ecosystem** n. **1** biological community of interacting organisms and their physical environment. **2** complex network or interconnected system.

**ecotourism** n. tourism directed towards natural, often threatened, environments.

**ecru** n. light fawn colour.

**ecstasy** n. **1** overwhelming joy or rapture. **2** colloq. type of narcotic drug. □□ **ecstatic** adj.

**ECT** abbr. electroconvulsive therapy.

**ectopic** adj. Med. in abnormal place or position. □ **ectopic pregnancy** pregnancy occurring outside uterus.

**ecumenical** adj. of or representing whole Christian world; seeking worldwide Christian unity.
□□ **ecumenism** n.

**eczema** n. inflammation of skin, with itching and discharge.

**ed.** abbr. **1** edited by. **2** edition. **3** editor.

**eddy** ● n. circular movement of water, smoke, etc. ● v. swirl in eddies.

**edge** ● n. **1** boundary line or margin of area or surface; narrow surface of thin object; meeting line of surfaces. **2** sharpened side of blade; sharpness. **3** brink of precipice; crest of ridge. **4** effectiveness. ● v. **1** advance gradually or furtively. **2** give or form border to. **3** sharpen. **4** Cricket strike (ball) with edge of bat.

**edgeways** adv. (also **edgewise**) with edge foremost or uppermost.

**edging** n. thing forming edge or border.

**edgy** adj. (edgier) irritable; anxious.

**edible** adj. fit to be eaten.

**edict** n. order proclaimed by authority.

**edifice** n. building, esp. imposing one.

**edify** v. improve morally.
□□ **edification** n.

**edit** v. (edited) **1** prepare for publication or broadcast. **2** cut and collate (film etc.) to form unified sequence. **3** reword, modify.

**edition** n. **1** edited or published form of book etc. **2** copies of book or newspaper etc. issued at one time. **3** instance of regular broadcast.

**editor** n. **1** person who edits. **2** person who directs writing of newspaper or news program or section of one. **3** person who selects material for publication.

**editorial** ● adj. of editing or an editor. ● n. article giving newspaper's views on current topic.

**educate** v. train or instruct mentally and morally; provide systematic instruction for. □□ **educable** adj. **education** n. **educational** adj. **educative** adj. **educator** n.

**EEG** abbr. electroencephalogram.

**eel** n. snakelike fish.

**EEO** abbr. Equal Employment Opportunity.

**eerie** adj. (eerier) strange; weird.
□□ **eerily** adv.

**efface** v. rub out; obliterate.
□□ **effacement** n.

**effect** ● n. **1** result, consequence. **2** efficacy. **3** impression. **4** (**effects**) property. ● v. bring about.

> **Usage** As a verb, *effect* should not be confused with *affect*. *He effected an entrance* means 'He got in (somehow)'; but *This won't affect me* means 'My life won't be changed by this'.

**effective** adj. **1** producing intended result; operative. **2** fulfilling function

in fact though not officially.
□□ **effectively** adv. **effectiveness** n.

**effeminate** adj. feminine in appearance or manner.
□□ **effeminacy** n.

**effervesce** v. give off bubbles of gas.
□□ **effervescence** n. **effervescent** adj.

**effete** adj. feeble, languid.

**efficacious** adj. producing desired effect. □□ **efficacy** n.

**efficient** adj. productive with minimum waste or effort; capable, competent. □□ **efficiency** n. **efficiently** adv.

**effigy** n. sculpture or model of person.

**effloresce** v. **1** burst into flower. **2** (of substance) turn to powder.

**effluence** n. flowing out (of light, electricity, etc.); what flows out.

**effluent** n. outflow, sewage.

**effluvium** n. (pl. **effluvia**) unpleasant or noxious odour or exhaled substance.

**effort** n. **1** exertion; determined attempt; force exerted. **2** colloq. something accomplished.
□□ **effortless** adj. **effortlessly** adv.

**effrontery** n. impudence.

**effuse** v. pour forth.

**effusion** n. outpouring.

**effusive** adj. gushing; demonstrative, unrestrained. □□ **effusively** adv. **effusiveness** n.

**EFTPOS** abbr. electronic funds transfer at point of sale.

**e.g.** abbr. for example (Latin exempli gratia).

**egalitarian** ● adj. of or advocating equal rights for all. ● n. egalitarian person. □□ **egalitarianism** n.

**egg** n. oval or round object produced by females of birds etc., capable of developing into new individual; edible egg of domestic hen etc.; ovum. □ **egg on** colloq. urge on.

**egghead** n. colloq. derog. intellectual.

**eggplant** n. (plant bearing) purple or white egg-shaped fruit used as vegetable; aubergine.

**ego** n. the self; part of mind that has sense of individuality; self esteem; self conceit.

**egocentric** adj. self-centred.

**egoism** n. self-centredness; egotism. □□ **egoist** n. **egoistic** adj.

**egotism** n. self conceit; selfishness. □□ **egotist** n. **egotistic(al)** adj.

**egregious** adj. **1** extremely bad. **2** arch. remarkable.

**egress** n. exit; going out.

**egret** n. kind of heron having long white feathers in breeding season.

**eh** int. colloq. **1** expressing enquiry, surprise, etc. **2** inviting assent.

**eider** n. large duck of N. hemisphere.

**eiderdown** n. quilt stuffed with soft material, esp. down.

**eight** adj. & n. one more than seven (8, VIII). □□ **eighth** adj. & n.

**eighteen** adj. & n. one more than seventeen (18, XVIII).
□□ **eighteenth** adj. & n.

**eighty** adj. & n. eight times ten (80, LXXX). □□ **eightieth** adj. & n.

**einsteinium** n. radioactive metallic element (symbol **Es**).

**eisteddfod** n. congress of Welsh poets and musicians; festival for musical competitions etc.

**either** ● adj. & pron. one or other of two; each of two. ● adv. & conj. as the first alternative; likewise.

**ejaculate** v. **1** emit (semen) in orgasm. **2** exclaim. □□ **ejaculation** n.

**eject** v. throw out, expel; emit. □□ **ejection** n.

**eke** v. □ **eke out** make (supply etc.) last longer by careful use; make (a living) laboriously.

**elaborate** ● adj. minutely worked out; complicated. ● v. work out or explain in detail; likewise. □□ **elaborately** adv. **elaboration** n.

**élan** n. vivacity, vigour.

**elapse** v. (of time) pass by.

**elastic** ● adj. able to resume normal bulk or shape after being stretched or squeezed; springy; flexible. ● n. elastic cord or fabric, usu. woven with strips of rubber. □□ **elasticity** n.

**elated** adj. very happy and excited. □□ **elate** v. **elation** n.

**elbow** ● n. joint between forearm and upper arm; part of sleeve covering elbow; elbow-shaped bend etc. ● v. jostle or thrust (person, oneself); make (one's way) thus. □ **elbow grease** colloq. hard work. **elbow room** sufficient space to work in.

**elder** ● adj. senior; older. ● n. **1** older person; official in certain churches; person of recognised authority (in Aboriginal community). **2** tree with small dark berries.

**elderly** adj. rather old.

**eldest** adj. first born; oldest.

**eldorado** n. imaginary land of great wealth.

**elect** ● v. choose, decide; choose by voting. ● adj. chosen; chosen but not yet in office. □□ **elector** n.

**election** n. electing, being elected; occasion of this.

**electioneer** v. take part in election campaign.

**elective** ● adj. **1** chosen by or derived from election; having power to elect. **2** optional. ● n. elective course of study.

**electorate** n. **1** group of electors. **2** Aust. area represented by one member of parliament.

**electric** adj. **1** of, worked by, or charged with electricity. **2** causing or charged with excitement.

**electrical** adj. of or worked by electricity. □□ **electrically** adv.

**electrician** n. person who installs or maintains electrical equipment.

**electricity** n. form of energy present in electrons and protons; science of electricity; supply of electricity.

**electrify** v. charge with electricity; convert to use of electric power; startle, excite. □□ **electrification** n.

**electrocardiogram** n. record of electric currents generated by heartbeat.

**electroconvulsive** adj. (of therapy) using convulsive response to electric shocks.

**electrocute** v. kill by electric shock. □□ **electrocution** n.

**electrode** n. conductor through which electricity enters or leaves electrolyte, gas, vacuum, etc.

**electroencephalogram** n. record of electrical activity of brain.

**electrolysis** n. decomposition by application of an electric current; destruction of tumours, hair roots, etc. thus.

**electrolyte** n. substance that conducts electricity when molten or in solution.

**electromagnetism** n. magnetic forces produced by electricity; study of these.

**electrometer** n. instrument for measuring electrical potential without drawing current from circuit. □□ **electrometric** adj. **electrometry** n.

**electron** n. stable elementary particle with charge of negative electricity, found in all atoms and acting as primary carrier of electricity in solids.

**electronic** adj. **1** (of a device) having or operating with components such as microchips and transistors that control and direct electric currents; (of music) produced by electronic means; relating to electronics. **2** relating to electrons. **3** carried out or accessed by means of a computer etc. □□ **electronically** adv.

**electronics** n. **1** use of electronic devices. **2** (as pl.) electronic circuits.

**electroplate ●** v. coat with chromium, silver, etc., by electrolysis. **●** n. electroplated articles.

**elegant** adj. **1** tasteful, refined, graceful. **2** ingeniously simple. □□ **elegance** n. **elegantly** adv.

**elegy** n. sorrowful poem or song, esp. for the dead. □□ **elegiac** adj.

**element** n. **1** component part. **2** substance that cannot be broken down into other substances. **3** suitable or satisfying environment. **4** a trace. **5** wire that gives out heat in electrical appliance. **6** (**the elements**) atmospheric forces.

**elemental** adj. **1** of or like elements or forces of nature. **2** basic, essential.

**elementary** adj. **1** dealing with simplest facts of subject. **2** Chem. not decomposable.

**elephant** n. largest living land animal, with trunk and ivory tusks.

**elephantine** adj. huge.

**elevate** v. raise to higher position.

**elevation** n. **1** elevating, being elevated. **2** angle above horizontal. **3** height above sea level etc. **4** drawing showing one side of building.

**elevator** n. **1** lift. **2** movable part of tailplane for changing aircraft's altitude. **3** hoisting machine. **4** storage and handling place for grain.

**eleven** adj. & n. one more than ten (11, XI). □□ **eleventh** adj. & n.

**elf** n. (pl. **elves**) **1** mythological being, esp. small and mischievous one. **2** (in fantasy literature) human-sized being of great beauty, wisdom, etc.

**elfin** adj. (of face etc.) small and delicate; like an elf.

**elicit** v. (**elicited**) draw out (facts, response, etc.)

**elide** v. omit in pronunciation.

**eligible** adj. **1** fit or entitled to be chosen. **2** desirable or suitable, esp. for marriage. □□ **eligibility** n.

**eliminate** v. remove, get rid of; exclude. □□ **elimination** n. **eliminator** n.

**elision** n. omission of vowel or syllable in pronunciation.

**elite ●** n. group regarded as superior. **●** adj. of elite; first-class.

**elitism** n. advocacy of leadership or dominance by select group. □□ **elitist** n. & adj.

**elixir** n. magical or medicinal liquid.

**Elizabethan** adj. of the time of Queen Elizabeth I (1558–1603).

**elk** n. large type of deer.

**elkhorn** n. Aust. fern with large lobed fronds resembling horns of elk.

**ellipse** n. regular oval.

**ellipsis** n. (pl. **ellipses**) omission of words; dots indicating this.

**elliptical** adj. **1** of or like ellipse. **2** with word or words omitted.

**elm** n. tree with rough serrated leaves; its wood.

**El Niño** n. warming of central and eastern Pacific Ocean affecting global weather and ecology.

**elocution** n. art of clear and expressive speech.

**elongate** v. lengthen, extend. □□ **elongation** n.

**elope** v. run away to marry secretly. □□ **elopement** n.

**eloquence** n. fluent and effective use of language. □□ **eloquent** adj. **eloquently** adv.

**else** adv. **1** in addition. **2** instead, other. □ **or else** otherwise; if not.

**elsewhere** adv. somewhere else.

**elucidate** v. throw light on; explain. □□ **elucidation** n.

**elude** v. escape adroitly from; avoid; baffle.

**elusive** adj. **1** difficult to find, catch, or remember. **2** avoiding point raised. □□ **elusiveness** n.

**elven** adj. = ELFIN.

**emaciated** adj. thin from illness or starvation. □□ **emaciation** n.

**email** (also **e-mail**) ● *n.* messages distributed from one computer user to one or more recipients via a network. ● *v.* send email to.

**emanate** *v.* issue or originate (from source).☐☐ **emanation** *n.*

**emancipate** *v.* liberate; free from restraint.☐☐ **emancipation** *n.*

**emancipist** *n. Aust. hist.* convict who has been pardoned or whose sentence has expired.

**emasculate** ● *v.* **1** enfeeble. **2** castrate. ● *adj.* **1** deprived of force. **2** castrated. **3** effeminate. ☐☐ **emasculation** *n.*

**embalm** *v.* **1** preserve (corpse) from decay. **2** make fragrant.

**embankment** *n.* bank constructed to confine water or carry road, railway, etc.

**embargo** *n.* (embargoes) **1** order forbidding ships to enter or leave ports. **2** suspension of commerce or other activity.

**embark** *v.* put or go on board ship or aircraft.☐ **embark on** begin (enterprise).

**embarkation** *n.* embarking on ship.

**embarrass** *v.* make (person) feel awkward or ashamed. ☐☐ **embarrassment** *n.*

**embassy** *n.* ambassador's residence or offices; deputation to foreign government.

**embattled** *adj.* prepared for war; under heavy attack, in trying circumstances.

**embed** *v.* (also **imbed**) (**embedded**) fix firmly in surrounding mass.

**embellish** *v.* beautify, adorn; make fictitious additions to. ☐☐ **embellishment** *n.*

**ember** *n.* small piece of glowing coal etc. in dying fire.

**embezzle** *v.* divert (money) fraudulently to own use. ☐☐ **embezzlement** *n.* **embezzler** *n.*

**embitter** *v.* arouse bitter feelings in. ☐☐ **embitterment** *n.*

**emblem** *n.* symbol; type, embodiment; distinctive badge. ☐☐ **emblematic** *adj.*

**embody** *v.* **1** give concrete form to; be tangible expression of. **2** include, comprise.☐☐ **embodiment** *n.*

**embolism** *n.* obstruction of artery by clot, air bubble, etc.

**emboss** *v.* carve or decorate with design in relief.

**embrace** ● *v.* **1** hold closely in arms; enclose. **2** accept, adopt; include. ● *n.* act of embracing, clasp.

**embrocation** *n.* liquid for rubbing on body to relieve muscular pain.

**embroider** *v.* decorate with needlework; embellish. ☐☐ **embroiderer** *n.* **embroidery** *n.*

**embroil** *v.* involve (in conflict or difficulties).

**embryo** *n.* unborn or unhatched offspring; thing in rudimentary stage. ☐☐ **embryonic** *adj.*

**emend** *v.* correct, remove errors from (text etc.) ☐☐ **emendation** *n.*

**emerald** ● *n.* bright green gem; colour of this. ● *adj.* bright green.

**emerge** *v.* come up or out into view or notice; survive (ordeal etc.) usu. with specified result.☐☐ **emergence** *n.* **emergent** *adj.*

**emergency** *n.* serious situation needing prompt attention.

**emerita** *adj.* (of a woman) retired and holding honorary title.

**emeritus** *adj.* retired and holding honorary title.

**emery** *n.* coarse corundum for polishing metal etc.

**emetic** ● *adj.* that causes vomiting. ● *n.* emetic medicine.

**emigrate** *v.* leave own country to settle in another.☐☐ **emigrant** *n.* **emigration** *n.*

**émigré** *n.* emigrant, esp. political exile.

**eminence** n. 1 state of being eminent; (**Eminence**) title of cardinal. 2 piece of rising ground.

**eminent** adj. distinguished, notable.

**emir** n. Muslim ruler.

**emissary** n. person sent on diplomatic mission.

**emission** n. emitting; thing discharged.

**emit** v. (**emitted**) give or send out; discharge.

**emoji** n. small digital image or icon used to express an idea or emotion.

**emollient** ● adj. softening, soothing. ● n. emollient substance.

**emolument** n. fee from employment; salary.

**emote** v. portray emotion in theatrical manner.

**emoticon** n. representation using keyboard characters to convey emotion etc.

**emotion** n. strong instinctive feeling such as love or fear; emotional intensity or sensibility; feeling contrasted with reason.

**emotional** adj. of or expressing emotion(s); especially liable to emotion; arousing emotion. □□ **emotionalism** n. **emotionally** adv.

**emotive** adj. of or arousing emotion.

**empathy** n. ability to understand and share the feelings of another.

**emperor** n. 1 ruler of empire. 2 tropical fish.

**emphasis** n. (pl. **emphases**) importance attached to thing, fact, idea, etc.; significant stress on word(s); vigour of expression etc.

**emphasise** v. (also **-ize**) lay stress on.

**emphatic** adj. 1 forcibly expressive. 2 (of word) bearing emphasis, e.g. myself in I did it myself. □□ **emphatically** adv.

**emphysema** n. disease of lungs causing breathlessness.

**empire** n. large group of countries under single authority; supreme dominion; large commercial organisation etc. owned or directed by one person.

**empirical** adj. based on observation or experiment, not on theory. □□ **empiricism** n. **empiricist** n.

**employ** v. use services of (person) in return for payment; use (thing, time, energy, etc.); keep (person) occupied. □□ **employer** n. **employment** n.

**employee** n. person employed for wages.

**emporium** n. (pl. **emporiums** or **emporia**) large retail store; centre of commerce.

**empower** v. give power or authority to.

**empress** n. woman emperor; wife or widow of emperor.

**empty** ● adj. 1 containing nothing; vacant, unoccupied. 2 hollow, insincere. 3 without purpose. 4 vacuous; foolish. 5 colloq. hungry. ● v. remove contents of; transfer (contents of). ● n. colloq. emptied bottle etc. □□ **emptiness** n.

**emu** n. large flightless Australian bird able to run at high speed.

**emulate** v. try to equal or excel; imitate. □□ **emulation** n. **emulator** n.

**emulsifier** n. any substance that stabilises emulsion, esp. food additive used to stabilise processed foods; apparatus for producing emulsion.

**emulsify** v. make emulsion of.

**emulsion** n. fine dispersion of one liquid in another, esp. as paint, medicine, etc.

**enable** v. supply with means or authority; make possible; make (device) operational, switch on.

**enabler** n. person or thing that makes something possible; person who encourages negative behaviour in another.

**enact** v. 1 ordain, decree. 2 make (bill etc.) law. 3 play (part). □□ **enactment** n.

**enamel** ● *n.* **1** glasslike opaque coating on metal; smooth hard coating. **2** kind of hard gloss paint. **3** hard coating of teeth.
● *v.* (**enamelled**) inlay, coat, or portray with enamel.

**enamoured** *adj.* (also **enamored**) fond.

**en bloc** *adv.* as a whole; all at the same time.

**encamp** *v.* settle in (esp. military) camp. □□ **encampment** *n.*

**encapsulate** *v.* **1** enclose (as) in capsule. **2** summarise.

**encase** *v.* confine (as) in a case.

**encephalitis** *n.* inflammation of brain.

**enchant** *v.* delight; bewitch. □□ **enchanting** *adj.* **enchantment** *n.*

**encircle** *v.* surround. □□ **encirclement** *n.*

**enclave** *n.* part of territory of one nation surrounded by that of another; group of people who are culturally, intellectually, or socially distinct from those surrounding them.

**enclose** *v.* **1** shut in on all sides; seclude. **2** include with other contents.

**enclosure** *n.* enclosing; enclosed space or area; thing enclosed.

**encode** *v.* put into code.

**encomium** *n.* (*pl.* **encomiums** or **encomia**) formal or high-flown praise.

**encompass** *v.* contain, include; surround.

**encore** ● *n.* audience's demand for repetition of item, or for further item; such item. ● *v.* call for repetition of or by. ● *int.* again.

**encounter** ● *v.* meet by chance; meet as adversary. ● *n.* meeting by chance or in conflict.

**encourage** *v.* give courage to; urge; promote. □□ **encouragement** *n.*

**encroach** *v.* intrude on another's territory etc. □□ **encroachment** *n.*

**encrust** *v.* cover with or form crust; overlay with an ornamental crust of precious material etc.

**encrustation** *n.* = INCRUSTATION.

**encrypt** *v.* convert (data) into a code; conceal by this means. □□ **encryption** *n.*

**encumber** *v.* be burden to; hamper; burden with debts.

**encumbrance** *n.* burden; impediment; mortgage or other charge on property.

**encyclical** *n.* pope's letter for circulation to churches.

**encyclopedia** *n.* (also **encyclopaedia**) book of information on many subjects or on many aspects of one subject. □□ **encyclopedic** *adj.*

**end** ● *n.* **1** point after which something no longer exists or happens; furthest or final part or point; remnant. **2** death, destruction. **3** result. **4** goal, purpose. **5** part with which person is concerned.
● *v.* bring or come to an end. □ **end up** reach specified state or action eventually. **in the end** finally. **make ends meet** live within one's income.

**endanger** *v.* place in danger.

**endear** *v.* make dear to. □□ **endearing** *adj.*

**endearment** *n.* expression of affection.

**endeavour** (also **endeavor**) ● *v.* try, strive. ● *n.* attempt, effort.

**endemic** *adj.* regularly found among particular people or in particular region. □□ **endemically** *adv.*

**endive** *n.* curly-leaved plant used in salads.

**endless** *adj.* infinite; continual. □□ **endlessly** *adv.*

**endocrine** *adj.* (of gland) secreting directly into blood.

**endogenous** *adj.* growing or originating from within.

**endometrium** *n.* membrane lining uterus.

**endorphin** n. Biochem. any of group of peptide neurotransmitters occurring naturally in brain and having pain-relieving properties.

**endorse** v. 1 approve; declare. 2 select as candidate for election. 3 write on (document), esp. sign (cheque). □□ **endorsement** n.

**endoscope** n. instrument for viewing internal parts of body.

**endoskeleton** n. internal skeleton.

**endothelium** n. layer of cells lining blood vessels, heart, etc.

**endow** v. provide with a permanent income. □ **endowed with** possessing (desirable quality). □□ **endowment** n.

**endurance** n. power of enduring.

**endure** v. undergo; tolerate; last. □□ **endurable** adj.

**endways** adv. with an end facing forwards.

**enema** n. introduction of liquid etc. into rectum, esp. to expel its contents; liquid used for this.

**enemy** n. person actively hostile to another; adversary, opponent.

**energetic** adj. full of energy. □□ **energetically** adv.

**energise** v. (also **-ize**) give energy to.

**energy** n. force, vigour, activity; capacity of matter or radiation to do work.

**enervate** v. deprive of vigour. □□ **enervation** n.

**enfant terrible** n. (pl. **enfants terribles**) person whose behaviour is embarrassing or irresponsible.

**enfeeble** v. make feeble; weaken. □□ **enfeeblement** n.

**enfold** v. 1 wrap. 2 embrace.

**enforce** v. compel observance of; impose. □□ **enforceable** adj. **enforcement** n.

**enfranchise** v. give (person) right to vote. □□ **enfranchisement** n.

**engage** v. 1 employ (person). 2 reserve; occupy attention of. 3 begin battle with; interlock; establish contact. □ **engage in** occupy oneself with.

**engaged** adj. 1 having promised to marry a specified person. 2 occupied; in use.

**engagement** n. 1 engaging something. 2 promise to marry specified person. 3 appointment. 4 battle.

**engaging** adj. attractive, charming.

**engender** v. give rise to.

**engine** n. 1 mechanical contrivance of parts working together, esp. as source of power. 2 railway locomotive.

**engineer** ● n. person skilled in a branch of engineering; person who makes or is in charge of engines etc. ● v. 1 contrive, bring about. 2 act as engineer; construct or manage as engineer.

**engineering** n. application of science to design, building, and use of machines etc.

**English** ● n. 1 principal language of Australia, Britain, and several other countries. 2 (**the English**) people of England. ● adj. of England or its language.

**engraft** v. insert (scion of one tree into another); implant, incorporate.

**engrave** v. inscribe or cut (design) on hard surface; inscribe (surface) thus. 2 impress deeply (on memory etc.) □□ **engraver** n. **engraving** n.

**engross** v. absorb attention of; occupy fully. □□ **engrossment** n.

**engulf** v. flow over and swamp; overwhelm.

**enhance** v. 1 intensify. 2 improve. □□ **enhancement** n.

**enigma** n. puzzling thing or person; riddle. □□ **enigmatic** adj.

**enjoin** v. command, order; impose, prescribe.

**enjoy** v. **1** take pleasure in. **2** have use or benefit of.□□ **enjoyable** adj. **enjoyably** adv. **enjoyment** n.

**enlarge** v. make or become larger; reproduce on larger scale.● **enlarge upon** describe in greater detail. □□ **enlargement** n.

**enlighten** v. inform; free from ignorance.□□ **enlightenment** n.

**enlist** v. **1** enrol in armed services. **2** secure as means of help or support. □□ **enlistment** n.

**enliven** v. make lively or cheerful. □□ **enlivenment** n.

**en masse** adv. all together.

**enmesh** v. entangle (as) in net.

**enmity** n. **1** state of being an enemy. **2** hostility.

**ennui** n. boredom.

**enormity** n. great wickedness; monstrous crime.

**enormous** adj. extremely large. □□ **enormously** adv.

**enough** ● adj. as much or as many as required. ● n. sufficient amount or quantity. ● adv. **1** to required degree; adequately. **2** fairly. **3** quite.

**enquire** v. ask.□□ **enquirer** n. **enquiry** n.

**enrage** v. make furious.

**enrapture** v. delight intensely.

**enrich** v. enhance; make rich(er). □□ **enrichment** n.

**enrol** v. (enrolled) admit as or become a member.□□ **enrolment** n.

**en route** adv. on the way.

**ensconce** v. establish securely or comfortably.

**ensemble** n. **1** thing viewed as whole; an outfit. **2** group of performers working together.

**enshrine** v. preserve or cherish.

**ensign** n. banner, flag, esp. military or naval flag of nation.

**enslave** v. make (a person) a slave.

**ensnare** v. entrap.

**ensue** v. happen later or as result.

**ensuite** n. (also **en suite**) bathroom attached to bedroom.

**ensure** v. make certain or safe.

**ENT** abbr. ear, nose, and throat.

**entail** ● v. **1** necessitate or involve unavoidably. **2** Law bequeath (estate) to specified line of beneficiaries. ● n. Law entailed estate.

**entangle** v. catch or hold fast in snare etc.; involve in difficulties; complicate. □□ **entanglement** n.

**entente** n. friendly understanding between nations.

**enter** v. **1** go or come in or into; penetrate. **2** record (information) in book, computer, etc. **3** name, or name oneself, as competitor.

**enteric** adj. of intestines.

**enteritis** n. inflammation of intestines.

**enterprise** n. **1** bold undertaking; readiness to engage in this. **2** business firm or venture.

**enterprising** adj. full of initiative.

**entertain** v. **1** amuse. **2** receive as guest. **3** harbour (feelings). **4** consider (idea).□□ **entertainer** n. **entertaining** adj.

**entertainment** n. entertaining; thing that entertains; performance.

**enthral** v. (enthralled) captivate, please greatly.□□ **enthralment** n.

**enthrone** v. place (king, bishop, etc.) on throne; install in position of power. □□ **enthronement** n.

**enthuse** v. be or make enthusiastic.

**enthusiasm** n. great eagerness or admiration; object of this. □□ **enthusiast** n. **enthusiastic** adj. **enthusiastically** adv.

**entice** v. attract by offer of pleasure or reward.□□ **enticement** n. **enticing** adj. **enticingly** adv.

**entire** adj. complete; unbroken.

**entirely** adv. wholly.

**entirety** n. □ **in its entirety** as a whole.

**entitle** v. **1** give (person) claim or right. **2** give title to.

**entitlement** n. **1** having a right to something; amount to which a person has a right. **2** belief that one is inherently deserving of privileges.

**entity** n. thing with distinct existence; thing's existence.

**entomb** v. place in tomb; serve as tomb for.□□ **entombment** n.

**entomology** n. study of insects. □□ **entomological** adj. **entomologist** n.

**entourage** n. people attending important persons.

**entrails** n.pl. intestines; inner parts.

**entrance** v. fill with intense delight.

**entrance** n. **1** door or passage by which one enters. **2** right of admission. **3** fee for this. **4** coming in.

**entrant** n. person who enters (exam, profession, etc.)

**entreat** v. ask earnestly, beg.

**entreaty** n. earnest request.

**entrée** n. **1** dish served before main course of meal. **2** right to enter or join a particular sphere or group.

**entrench** v. **1** establish firmly; (as **entrenched** adj.) (of attitude etc.) not easily modified. **2** surround or fortify with trench.□□ **entrenchment** n.

**entrepreneur** n. person who undertakes commercial venture. □□ **entrepreneurial** adj.

**entropy** n. **1** measure of amount of system's thermal energy not available for conversion into mechanical work. **2** lack of order or predictability.

**entrust** v. give (person, thing) into care; assign responsibility for (person, thing) to.

**entry** n. **1** going or coming in; entering; place of entrance. **2** item entered. **3** person etc. competing in race etc.

**entwine** v. twine around, interweave.

**enumerate** v. mention (items) one by one.□□ **enumeration** n.

**enunciate** v. pronounce (words) clearly; state definitely. □□ **enunciation** n.

**envelop** v. (**enveloped**) wrap up, cover on all sides. □□ **envelopment** n.

**envelope** n. folded paper cover for letter, etc.

**enviable** adj. likely to excite envy. □□ **enviably** adv.

**envious** adj. feeling or showing envy □□ **enviously** adv.

**environment** n. **1** surroundings. **2** circumstances affecting person's life. **3** external conditions affecting growth of plants and animals; natural world.□□ **environmental** adj. environmentally adv.

**environmentalist** n. person concerned with protection of natural environment.

**environs** n.pl. district around town etc.

**envisage** v. visualise, imagine, contemplate.

**envoy** n. messenger or representative esp. to foreign government.

**envy** ● n. discontent aroused by another's better fortune etc.; object or cause of this. ● v. feel envy.

**enzyme** n. protein catalyst of specific biochemical reaction.

**eon** = AEON.

**epaulette** n. (also **epaulet**) ornamental shoulder piece, esp. on uniform.

**ephedrine** n. alkaloid drug used to relieve asthma etc.

**ephemera** n.pl. things of only short-lived relevance.

**ephemeral** adj. short-lived; transitory.

**epic** ● n. **1** long poem narrating adventures of heroic figure etc.; book or film based on this. **2** exceptionally long and arduous task or activity. ● adj. **1** like an epic. **2** grand heroic.

**epicentre** *n.* point on the earth's surface directly above the focus of an earthquake.

**epicure** *n.* person with refined taste in food and drink. □□ **epicurism** *n.*

**epicurean** ● *n.* person fond of pleasure and luxury. ● *adj.* characteristic of an epicurean. □□ **epicureanism** *n.*

**epidemic** ● *n.* widespread occurrence of particular disease in community at particular time. ● *adj.* in the nature of epidemic.

**epidemiology** *n.* study of incidence and distribution of epidemic diseases, and of their control. □□ **epidemiological** *n.*

**epidermis** *n.* outer layer of skin.

**epidural** ● *adj.* (of anaesthetic) introduced into space around dura mater of spinal cord. ● *n.* epidural anaesthetic, used esp. in childbirth.

**epiglottis** *n.* flap of cartilage at root of tongue, depressed during swallowing to cover windpipe. □□ **epiglottal** *adj.*

**epigram** *n.* short witty saying. □□ **epigrammatic** *adj.*

**epigraph** *n.* inscription.

**epilepsy** *n.* nervous disorder with convulsions and often loss of consciousness. □□ **epileptic** *adj. & n.*

**epilogue** *n.* short piece ending literary work; short speech at end of play.

**EpiPen** *n. propr.* hypodermic device that administers dose of adrenaline for treatment of acute allergic reaction.

**epiphyte** *n.* plant growing but not parasitic on another. □□ **epiphytic** *adj.*

**episcopacy** *n.* bishops collectively.

**episcopal** *adj.* of bishop or bishops; (of Church) governed by bishops. □□ **episcopally** *adv.*

**episiotomy** *n.* surgical cut made at vaginal opening during childbirth.

**episode** *n.* event as part of sequence; part of serial story; incident in narrative. □□ **episodic** *adj.*

**epistemology** *n.* philosophy of knowledge. □□ **epistemological** *adj.*

**epistle** *n.* letter; poem etc. in form of letter.

**epitaph** *n.* words in memory of dead person, esp. on tomb.

**epithet** *n.* adjective etc. expressing quality or attribute; this as term of abuse.

**epitome** *n.* person or thing embodying a quality etc.

**epitomise** *v.* (also **-ize**) make or be perfect example of (a quality etc.)

**epoch** *n.* **1** period marked by special events. **2** beginning of era.

**eponym** *n.* word etc. derived from person's name; person whose name is used in this way. □□ **eponymous** *adj.*

**epoxy resin** *n.* synthetic thermosetting resin, used esp. as glue.

**Epsom salts** *n.* magnesium sulphate used as purgative etc.

**equable** *adj.* not varying; moderate; calm. □□ **equably** *adv.*

**equal** ● *adj.* same in number, size, merit, etc.; having same rights or status. ● *n.* person or thing equal to another. ● *v.* (**equalled**) be same in size etc. as; do something equal to. □ **equal opportunity** opportunity to compete equally for jobs etc. regardless of race, sex, etc. □□ **equality** *n.* **equally** *adv.*

**equalise** *v.* (also **-ize**) make or become equal; (in sports) reach opponent's score. □□ **equalisation** *n.*

**equaliser** *n.* (also **-izer**) equalising goal etc.

**equanimity** *n.* composure, calm.

**equate** *v.* regard as equal or equivalent; be equal or equivalent to.

**equation** *n.* **1** making or being equal. **2** *Math.* statement that two expressions are equal. **3** *Chem.* symbolic representation of reaction.

**equator** n. imaginary line around earth or other body, equidistant from poles.

**equatorial** adj. of or near equator.

**equestrian** adj. horse riding; on horseback.□□ **equestrianism** n.

**equidistant** adj. at equal distances.

**equilateral** adj. having all sides equal.

**equilibrium** n. (pl. **equilibria** or **equilibriums**) state of balance; composure.

**equine** adj. of or like horse.

**equinox** n. time or date at which sun crosses equator, and day and night are of equal length.

**equip** v. (equipped) supply with what is needed.

**equipment** n. necessary tools, clothing, etc.; equipping, being equipped.

**equitable** adj. 1 fair, just. 2 Law valid in equity.□□ **equitably** adv.

**equity** n. 1 fairness; impartiality. 2 (equities) stocks and shares not bearing fixed interest. 3 net value of mortgaged property after deduction of charges.

**equivalent** ● adj. equal in value, meaning, etc.; corresponding. ● n. equivalent amount etc. □□ **equivalence** n.

**equivocal** adj. of double or doubtful meaning; (of person etc.) questionable.□□ **equivocally** adv.

**equivocate** v. use words ambiguously to conceal truth.□□ **equivocation** n.

**era** n. system of chronology starting from particular point; historical or other period.

**eradicate** v. root out; destroy. □□ **eradicable** adj. **eradication** n.

**erase** v. 1 rub out; obliterate. 2 remove recording from (disc etc.); delete (data) from computer's memory. □□ **erasure** n.

**eraser** n. piece of rubber etc. for removing esp. pencil etc. marks.

**erbium** n. soft metallic element (symbol Er).

**erect** ● adj. 1 upright, vertical. 2 (of part of body) enlarged and rigid, esp. from sexual excitement. ● v. 1 raise; set upright. 2 build; establish. □□ **erection** n.

**erectile** adj. capable of becoming erect.

**erg** n. unit of work or energy.

**ergo** adv. therefore.

**ergonomics** n. pl. study of work and its environment in order to improve efficiency.□□ **ergonomic** adj.

**ermine** n. stoat, esp. in its white winter fur; this fur.

**erode** v. wear away, destroy gradually. □□ **erosion** n. **erosive** adj.

**erogenous** adj. (of part of body) sexually sensitive.

**erotic** adj. arousing sexual desire or excitement.□□ **erotically** adv. **eroticism** n.

**err** v. be mistaken or incorrect; sin.

**errand** n. short journey, esp. on another's behalf, to take message etc.; object of such journey.

**errant** adj. 1 erring. 2 literary travelling in search of adventure.

**erratic** adj. inconsistent or uncertain in movement or conduct etc. □□ **erratically** adv.

**erratum** n. error in printing or writing.

**erroneous** adj. incorrect. □□ **erroneously** adv.

**error** n. mistake; condition of being morally wrong; degree of inaccuracy in calculation etc.

**ersatz** adj. used as substitute.

**erstwhile** adj. former.

**erudite** adj. learned.□□ **erudition** n.

**erupt** v. break out; (of volcano) shoot out lava etc.; (of rash) appear on skin. □□ **eruption** n.

**erysipelas** n. disease causing deep red inflammation of skin.

**erythrocyte** n. red blood cell.

**escalate** v. increase or develop by stages; intensify. □□ **escalation** n.

**escalator** n. moving staircase.

**escalope** n. thin slice of meat, esp. veal.

**escapade** n. piece of reckless behaviour.

**escape** ● v. get free of; avoid; elude; leak. ● n. escaping; means of escaping; leakage.

**escapee** n. person who has escaped.

**escapement** n. part of clock that regulates movement.

**escapism** n. pursuit of distraction and relief from reality. □□ **escapist** n. & adj.

**escapology** n. techniques of escaping from confinement, esp. as entertainment. □□ **escapologist** n.

**escarpment** n. long steep slope at edge of plateau etc.

**eschatology** n. doctrine of death and final destiny. □□ **eschatological** adj.

**eschew** v. formal abstain from.

**escort** ● n. 1 person(s) etc. accompanying another for protection or as courtesy; person accompanying person of opposite sex socially; person hired to accompany person socially. 2 euphem. prostitute. ● v. act as escort to.

**escritoire** n. writing desk with drawers etc.

**escutcheon** n. shield bearing coat of arms.

**esky** n. Aust. propr. portable insulated container for keeping food or drink cool.

**esophagus** = OESOPHAGUS.

**esoteric** adj. intelligible only to those with special knowledge.

**ESP** abbr. extrasensory perception.

**espadrille** n. light canvas shoe with plaited fibre sole.

**espalier** n. framework for training tree etc.; tree trained on espalier.

**especial** adj. special; particular.

**especially** adv. 1 more than any other; particularly, individually. 2 to a great extent.

**espionage** n. spying or using spies.

**esplanade** n. level space for walking on, esp. beside sea.

**espouse** v. 1 support (cause). 2 arch. marry. □□ **espousal** n.

**espresso** n. (also **expresso**) strong black coffee made under pressure.

**esprit de corps** n. devotion to and pride in one's group.

**espy** v. (**espied**, **espying**) catch sight of.

**essay** ● n. 1 short piece of writing on given subject. 2 formal attempt. ● v. attempt. □□ **essayist** n.

**essence** n. 1 fundamental nature; inherent characteristics. 2 extract got by distillation etc. 3 perfume.

**essential** ● adj. 1 necessary, indispensable. 2 of or constituting essence of person or thing. ● n. indispensable element or thing. □□ **essentially** adv.

**establish** v. set up; make permanent or secure; prove.

**establishment** n. 1 establishing, being established. 2 public institution. 3 place of business. 4 staff, household, etc. 5 (**the Establishment**) social group with authority or influence and seen as resisting change.

**estate** n. 1 landed property. 2 residential or industrial area with integrated design or purpose. 3 dead person's assets and liabilities.

**esteem** ● v. think highly of. ● n. favourable opinion; respect.

**ester** n. compound produced by replacing the hydrogen of an acid by an organic radical.

**estimable** adj. worthy of esteem.

**estimate** ● n. 1 approximate calculation or judgement of the value, number, quantity, or extent of something. 2 statement indicating likely price that will be charged for specified work etc. ● v. form estimate or opinion of.

**estimation** n. estimating; judgement of worth.

**estrange** v. **1** alienate, make hostile or indifferent. **2** (as **estranged** adj.) no longer living with spouse. □□ **estrangement** n.

**estrogen** = OESTROGEN.

**estuary** n. tidal mouth of river. □□ **estuarine** adj.

**ETA** abbr. estimated time of arrival.

**et al.** abbr. and others (Latin et alii).

**etc.** abbr. and other similar things (Latin et cetera).

**etch** v. **1** reproduce (picture etc.) by engraving metal plate with acid, esp. to print copies; engrave (plate) thus. **2** impress deeply.

**etching** n. print made from etched plate.

**eternal** adj. **1** existing always; without an end or beginning; unchanging. **2** colloq. constant, too frequent. □□ **eternally** adv.

**eternity** n. infinite time; endless life after death; (**an eternity**) colloq. very long time.

**ethane** n. gaseous hydrocarbon present in petroleum and natural gas.

**ethanol** n. alcohol.

**ether** n. **1** volatile liquid used as anaesthetic or solvent. **2** clear sky; upper air.

**ethereal** adj. **1** light, airy. **2** highly delicate, esp. in appearance. **3** heavenly. □□ **ethereally** adv.

**ethic** n. moral principle; (**ethics**) moral philosophy

**ethical** adj. relating to morals or ethics; morally correct; honourable. □□ **ethically** adv.

**ethnic** adj. of a group sharing common origin, culture, or language. □ **ethnic cleansing** mass expulsion or killing of people from an ethnic group. □□ **ethnically** adv.

**ethnology** n. comparative study of peoples. □□ **ethnological** adj.

**ethos** n. characteristic spirit of community, people, system, etc.

**ethylene** n. flammable hydrocarbon gas.

**etiolate** v. make pale by excluding light; give sickly colour to. □□ **etiolation** n.

**etiquette** n. conventional rules of social behaviour or professional conduct.

**et seq.** abbr. and following (pages etc.) (Latin et sequentia).

**étude** n. musical composition designed to develop player's skill.

**etymology** n. derivation and development of word in form and meaning; account of this. □□ **etymological** adj.

**EU** abbr. European Union.

**eucalyptus** n. (also **eucalypt**) Australian tree with leaves that yield strong-smelling oil.

**Eucharist** n. Christian sacrament commemorating the Last Supper, in which bread and wine are consumed; this bread and wine. □□ **Eucharistic** adj.

**eugenics** n.pl. science of improving human race by breeding. □□ **eugenic** adj. **eugenically** adv.

**eulogise** v. (also **-ize**) praise in speech or writing. □□ **eulogistic** adj.

**eulogy** n. speech or writing in praise or commendation.

**eunuch** n. castrated man.

**euphemism** n. mild expression substituted for blunt one. □□ **euphemistic** adj. **euphemistically** adv.

**euphonium** n. brass instrument of tuba family.

**euphony** n. pleasantness of sound, esp. in words. □□ **euphonious** adj.

**euphoria** n. intense feeling of well being and excitement. □□ **euphoric** adj.

**Eurasian** ● *adj.* of Europe and Asia; of mixed European and Asian parentage. ● *n.* Eurasian person.

**eureka** *int.* I have found it!

**euro**¹ *n.* chief monetary unit in European Union.

**euro**² *n.* reddish short-haired macropod of drier Australia.

**European** ● *adj.* of or in or extending over Europe. ● *n.* native or inhabitant of Europe.

**europium** *n.* metallic element (symbol **Eu**).

**Eustachian tube** *n.* passage between middle ear and back of throat.

**euthanasia** *n.* killing person painlessly, esp. one who has incurable painful disease.□□ **euthanase** *v.* (also **euthanise**)

**evacuate** *v.* **1** send away from a dangerous place. **2** empty. □□ **evacuation** *n.*

**evacuee** *n.* person evacuated.

**evade** *v.* escape from, avoid; avoid doing or answering directly.

**evaluate** *v.* assess, appraise; find or state number or amount of. □□ **evaluation** *n.*

**evaluative** *adj.* of an assessment to form an idea of the value of something.

**evanesce** *v. literary* fade from sight.

**evangelical** ● *adj.* of or according to teaching of gospel; of Protestant groups maintaining doctrine of salvation by faith. ● *n.* member of evangelical group. □□ **evangelicalism** *n.*

**evangelist** *n.* writer of one of four Gospels; preacher of gospel. □□ **evangelism** *n.* **evangelistic** *adj.*

**evaporate** *v.* turn into vapour; (cause to) lose moisture as vapour; (cause to) disappear. □□ **evaporation** *n.*

**evasion** *n.* evading; evasive answer.

**evasive** *adj.* seeking to evade. □□ **evasiveness** *n.*

**eve** *n.* evening or day before festival etc.; time just before an event.

**even** ● *adj.* **1** level, smooth; uniform; equal. **2** calm. **3** exactly divisible by two. ● *adv.* used for emphasis or in comparing things (*even faster*). ● *v.* make or become even. □□ **evenly** *adv.* **evenness** *n.*

**evening** *n.* end part of day, esp. late afternoon to bedtime.

**evens** *n.pl.* even money.

**evensong** *n.* evening service in Anglican Church.

**event** *n.* **1** thing that happens; fact of thing occurring. **2** item in (esp. sports) program.

**eventful** *adj.* marked by noteworthy events.

**eventual** *adj.* occurring in due course. □□ **eventually** *adv.*

**eventuality** *n.* possible event.

**ever** *adv.* at all times; always; at any time.

**evergreen** ● *adj.* **1** retaining green leaves all year round. **2** popular for long time. ● *n.* evergreen plant.

**everlasting** *adj.* lasting for ever or long time.

**every** *adj.* **1** each. **2** all.

**everybody** *pron.* every person.

**everyday** *adj.* worn or used on ordinary days; ordinary.

**everyone** *pron.* everybody.

**everything** *pron.* all things; all that is important.

**everywhere** *adv.* in every place.

**evict** *v.* expel (tenant) by legal process. □□ **eviction** *n.*

**evidence** ● *n.* **1** facts or information indicating whether a belief or proposition is true or valid. **2** statement etc. admissible in court of law. **3** indication, sign. ● *v.* be evidence of.

**evident** *adj.* obvious; manifest.

**evidential** *adj.* of or providing evidence.

**evidently** *adv.* **1** seemingly. **2** as shown by evidence.

**evil** ● *adj.* wicked; harmful.
● *n.* evil thing; wickedness.
□□ **evilly** *adv.*

**evince** *v.* indicate, display.

**evocative** *adj.* evoking (feelings etc.)

**evoke** *v.* inspire or draw forth (memories, response, etc.)
□□ **evocation** *n.*

**evolution** *n.* evolving; development of species from earlier forms; unfolding of events etc.
□□ **evolutionary** *adj.*

**evolve** *v.* develop gradually and naturally; develop from simple to more complex form; unfold; open out.

**ewe** *n.* female sheep.

**ewer** *n.* water jug with wide mouth.

**ex** ● *n. colloq.* former spouse or lover. ● *prep.* **1** (of goods) sold from. **2** (of stocks or shares) without, excluding.

**ex-** *prefix* **1** out, away. **2** thoroughly. **3** former.

**exabyte** *n. Computing* one thousand petabytes.

**exacerbate** *v.* make worse.
□□ **exacerbation** *n.*

**Usage** *Exacerbate* is sometimes confused with *exasperate*.

**exact** ● *adj.* accurate; correct in all details. ● *v.* demand and enforce payment of (fees etc.); demand, insist on.□□ **exactness** *n.*

**exacting** *adj.* making great demands; requiring much effort.

**exactitude** *n.* exactness.

**exactly** *adv.* **1** precisely. **2** I agree.

**exaggerate** *v.* make seem larger or greater than it really is; increase beyond normal or due proportions.
□□ **exaggeration** *n.*

**exalt** *v.* raise in rank, power, etc.; praise highly; (usu. as **exalted** *adj.*) make lofty or noble.
□□ **exaltation** *n.*

**Usage** Do not confuse *exalt* with *exult*.

**exam** *n.* examination.

**examination** *n.* examining, being examined; detailed inspection; testing of ability or knowledge by questions; formal questioning of witness etc. in court.

**examine** *v.* inquire into; test knowledge or ability of; check health of; question formally. □□ **examinee** *n.* **examiner** *n.*

**example** *n.* **1** thing illustrating general rule; model; pattern; specimen. **2** precedent. **3** warning to others.

**exasperate** *v.* irritate intensely.
□□ **exasperation** *n.*

**excavate** *v.* make (hole etc.) by digging; dig out material from (ground); reveal or extract by digging; dig systematically to explore (archaeological site).□□ **excavation** *n.* **excavator** *n.*

**exceed** *v.* **1** be more or greater than; go beyond, do more than is warranted by. **2** surpass.

**exceedingly** *adv.* extremely.

**excel** *v.* (**excelled**) surpass; be preeminent.

**excellence** *n.* outstanding merit.

**Excellency** *n.* title of ambassador, governor, etc.

**excellent** *adj.* extremely good.

**except** ● *prep.* not including; other than. ● *v.* exclude from general statement etc.

**excepting** *prep.* except.

**exception** *n.* excepting; something that does not follow the accepted rule; thing or case excepted.

**exceptionable** adj. open to objection.

Usage *Exceptionable* is sometimes confused with *exceptional*.

**exceptional** adj. forming an exception; unusual.
□□ **exceptionally** adv.

**excerpt** ● n. short extract from book, film, etc. ● v. take excerpts from.□□ **excerption** n.

**excess** ● n. **1** exceeding; amount by which thing exceeds; intemperance in eating or drinking. **2** part of an insurance claim to be paid by insured. ● adj. **1** that exceeds limited or given amount. **2** required as extra payment.

**excessive** adj. too much, too great.
□□ **excessively** adv.

**exchange** ● n. **1** giving one thing and receiving another in its place; exchanging of money for equivalent, esp. in other currency. **2** centre where telephone connections are made. **3** place where stockbrokers, bankers, etc. transact business. **4** short conversation. ● v. **1** give or receive in exchange. **2** interchange.
□□ **exchangeable** adj.

**excise** ● v. cut out or away. ● n. tax on goods produced or sold within country of origin; tax on certain licences.

**excitable** adj. easily excited.
□□ **excitability** n.

**excite** v. move to strong emotion; arouse (feelings etc.); arouse sexually; provoke (action etc.); stimulate to activity.□□ **excitement** n. **exciting** adj.

**exclaim** v. cry out suddenly; utter by exclaiming.

**exclamation** n. exclaiming; word(s) exclaimed.□ **exclamation mark**

punctuation mark ( ! ) placed after exclamation.□□ **exclamatory** adj.

**exclude** v. shut out, leave out; make impossible, preclude.□□ **exclusion** n.

**exclusive** ● adj. **1** excluding other things; not including; (of society etc.) tending to exclude outsiders. **2** high-class. **3** not obtainable or published elsewhere. ● n. exclusive item of news, film, etc.□□ **exclusively** adv. **exclusiveness** n. **exclusivity** n.

**excommunicate** v. deprive (person) from membership and sacraments of Church.□□ **excommunication** n.

**excoriate** v. **1** remove part of skin of by abrasion; strip off (skin). **2** censure severely.□□ **excoriation** n.

**excrement** n. waste discharged from body, esp. faeces.

**excrescence** n. **1** outgrowth on animal or plant. **2** unnecessary or unattractive addition.

**excreta** n.pl. matter (esp. faeces) excreted from body.

**excrete** v. (of animal or plant) expel (waste).□□ **excretion** n. **excretory** adj.

**excruciating** adj. acutely painful.
□□ **excruciatingly** adv.

**excursion** n. short journey, esp. for pleasure or education.

**excursive** adj. literary digressive.

**excuse** ● v. **1** try to lessen blame attaching to person; serve as reason to judge (person, act) less severely. **2** grant exemption to. **3** forgive.
● n. **1** reason put forward to mitigate or justify offence; apology. **2** poor or inadequate example of.
□□ **excusable** adj.

**execrable** adj. abominable.

**execute** v. **1** carry out, perform. **2** put to death. **3** make (legal instrument) valid.□□ **executable** adj.

**execution** n. **1** carrying out, performance. **2** putting to death.

**executioner** n. person carrying out death sentence.

**executive** ● *n.* **1** person or body with senior managerial or administrative responsibility. **2** branch of government responsible for putting decisions or laws into effect. ● *adj.* having power to put plans or actions into effect; relating to part of political administration with responsibility for putting into effect laws.

**executor** *n.* person appointed by testator to carry out terms of will. □□ **executorial** *adj.*

**exemplar** *n.* model; typical instance.

**exemplary** *adj.* **1** outstandingly good. **2** serving as example or warning.

**exemplify** *v.* give or be example of. □□ **exemplification** *n.*

**exempt** ● *adj.* free from obligation or liability imposed on others. ● *v.* make exempt. □□ **exemption** *n.*

**exercise** ● *n.* use of muscles, esp. for health; physical or other training; use or application of faculties etc.; practice. ● *v.* use; perform (function etc.) **2** take exercise; give exercise to. □ **exercise book** book for writing in.

**exert** *v.* **1** bring to bear, use. **2** (**exert oneself**) make effort. □□ **exertion** *n.*

**exeunt** *v.* (as stage direction) they (actors) leave the stage.

**exfoliate** *v.* **1** come off in scales or layers. **2** remove dead layers of skin from. □□ **exfoliation** *n.*

**ex gratia** ● *adv.* as favour; not from (esp. legal) obligation. ● *adj.* granted on this basis.

**exhale** *v.* breathe out; give off or be given off in vapour. □□ **exhalation** *n.*

**exhaust** ● *v.* use up completely; tire out. ● *n.* waste gases etc. expelled from engine after combustion; (also **exhaust pipe**) pipe or system by which these are expelled. □□ **exhaustible** *adj.* **exhaustion** *n.*

**exhaustive** *adj.* complete, comprehensive. □□ **exhaustively** *adv.*

**exhibit** *v.* show publicly; display. ● *n.* **1** thing(s) forming an exhibition. **2** document etc. produced in lawcourt as evidence. □□ **exhibitor** *n.*

**exhibition** *n.* display, esp. public show; exhibiting, being exhibited.

**exhibitionism** *n.* tendency towards attention-seeking behaviour. □□ **exhibitionist** *n.*

**exhilarate** *v.* make joyful or lively. □□ **exhilaration** *n.*

**exhort** *v.* urge strongly or earnestly. □□ **exhortation** *n.* **exhortative** *adj.* **exhortatory** *adj.*

**exhume** *v.* dig up. □□ **exhumation** *n.*

**exigency** *n.* (also **exigence**) urgent need; emergency. □□ **exigent** *adj.*

**exile** ● *n.* expulsion or long absence from one's country etc.; person in exile. ● *v.* send into exile.

**exist** *v.* be; have being; occur, be found; live; survive.

**existence** *n.* fact or manner of being or existing; all that exists. □□ **existent** *adj.*

**existential** *adj.* of or relating to existence.

**existentialism** *n.* philosophical theory emphasising existence of individual as free and self-determining agent. □□ **existentialist** *n.* & *adj.*

**exit** ● *n.* way out of building etc.; going out; place where vehicles can leave major road etc.; departure. ● *v.* make one's exit. □ **exit poll** poll of people leaving polling station, asking how they voted. **exit strategy** pre-planned means of extricating oneself from situation that is likely to become difficult etc.

**exocarp** *n.* outer layer of pericarp of a fruit.

**exodus** *n.* mass departure.

**ex officio** *adv.* & *adj.* by virtue of one's office.

**exonerate** *v.* free or declare free from blame. □□ **exoneration** *n.*

**exorbitant** *adj.* grossly excessive.

**exorcise** *v.* (also **-ize**) drive out (evil spirit) by prayers etc.; free (person, place) thus. □□ **exorcism** *n.* **exorcist** *n.*

**exoskeleton** *n.* external skeleton. □□ **exoskeletal** *adj.*

**exotic** ● *adj.* 1 introduced from foreign country; not native. 2 strange, unusual. ● *n.* exotic plant etc. □□ **exotically** *adv.*

**expand** *v.* 1 increase in size or importance. 2 stretch out, unfold; spread out; give fuller account. 3 become more genial. □□ **expandable** *adj.* **expansion** *n.*

**expanse** *n.* wide area or extent of land, space, etc.

**expansionism** *n.* advocacy of expansion, esp. of nation's territory. □□ **expansionist** *n.* & *adj.*

**expansive** *adj.* 1 able or tending to expand. 2 extensive. 3 genial. □□ **expansively** *adv.*

**expatiate** *v.* speak or write at length. □□ **expatiation** *n.*

**expatriate** ● *adj.* living abroad; exiled. ● *n.* expatriate person. ● *v.* expel from native country.

**expect** *v.* 1 regard as likely. 2 look for as one's due. □□ **expectation** *n.*

**expectant** *adj.* 1 expecting; expecting to become. 2 pregnant. □□ **expectancy** *n.* **expectantly** *adv.*

**expectorant** *adj.* causing coughing out of phlegm etc. ● *n.* expectorant medicine.

**expectorate** *v.* cough or spit out from chest or lungs. □□ **expectoration** *n.*

**expedient** ● *adj.* 1 advantageous. 2 advisable on practical rather than moral grounds. ● *n.* 1 means of achieving an end. 2 resource. □□ **expediency** *n.*

**expedite** *v.* 1 assist progress of. 2 accomplish quickly.

**expedition** *n.* 1 journey or voyage for particular purpose; people etc. undertaking this. 2 speed. □□ **expeditionary** *adj.*

**expeditious** *adj.* acting or done with speed and efficiency.

**expel** *v.* (**expelled**) 1 deprive of membership; force out, eject.

**expend** *v.* spend (money, time, etc.); use up. □□ **expendable** *adj.*

**expenditure** *n.* expending; amount expended.

**expense** *n.* 1 cost, charge. 2 (**expenses**) costs incurred in doing job etc.; amount paid to reimburse this.

**expensive** *adj.* costing or charging much. □□ **expensively** *adv.*

**experience** ● *n.* 1 personal observation or contact; knowledge or skill based on this. 2 event that affects one. ● *v.* 1 have experience of. 2 undergo. 3 feel. □□ **experiential** *adj.*

**experienced** *adj.* having had much experience; skilful through experience.

**experiment** ● *n.* 1 scientific procedure undertaken to make a discovery, test a hypothesis, or demonstrate a known fact. 2 course of action tentatively adopted without being sure of the outcome. ● *v.* make experiment(s). □□ **experimentation** *n.* **experimenter** *n.*

**experimental** *adj.* based on or done by way of experiment. □□ **experimentally** *adv.*

**expert** ● *adj.* well informed or skilful in subject. ● *n.* person with special knowledge or skill. □□ **expertly** *adv.*

**expertise** *n.* special skill or knowledge.

**expiate** *v.* pay penalty for or make amends for (wrong). □□ **expiation** *n.*

**expire** v. 1 come to an end; cease to be valid; die. 2 breathe out.
□□ **expiration** n.

**expiry** n. end of validity or duration.

**explain** v. 1 make intelligible; say by way of explanation. 2 account for.
□□ **explanation** n.

**explanatory** adj. serving to explain.

**expletive** n. swear word or exclamation.

**explicable** adj. that can be explained.

**explicit** adj. expressly stated; stated in detail; definite; outspoken; graphic; leaving nothing to imagination.
□□ **explicitly** adv. **explicitness** n.

**explode** v. 1 expand violently with loud noise; cause (bomb etc.) to do this. 2 give vent suddenly to emotion, esp. anger. 3 (of population etc.) increase suddenly. 4 discredit.

**exploit** ● n. daring feat. ● v. use or develop for one's own ends; take advantage of.□□ **exploitation** n. **exploitative** adj.

**explore** v. 1 travel through (country etc.) to learn about it. 2 inquire into; examine (part of body); probe (wound).□□ **exploration** n. **exploratory** adj.

**explosion** n. 1 exploding; loud noise caused by this. 2 outbreak; sudden increase.

**explosive** ● adj. 1 tending to explode. 2 likely to cause violent outburst etc. ● n. explosive substance.

**exponent** n. 1 person promoting idea etc. 2 practitioner of activity, profession, etc. 3 person who explains or interprets. 4 type, representative. 5 raised number or symbol showing how many of number are to be multiplied together, e.g. $2^3 = 2 \times 2 \times 2$.

**exponential** adj. (of increase) more and more rapid.

**export** ● v. 1 sell or send (goods or services) to another country; spread or introduce (ideas and beliefs) to another country. 2 Computing transfer (data) in format that can be used by other programs.
● n. exporting; thing exported.
□□ **exportation** n. **exporter** n.

**expose** v. 1 leave unprotected or uncovered; put at risk of, subject to (influence etc.) 2 Photog. subject (film) to light. 3 reveal; disclose; exhibit, display.□□ **exposure** n.

**exposé** n. 1 orderly statement of facts. 2 disclosure of discreditable thing.

**expostulate** v. protest, argue.
□□ **expostulation** n.

**expound** v. set out in detail; explain, interpret.□□ **exposition** n.

**express** ● v. 1 represent by symbols etc. or in language; put into words; (**express oneself**) communicate what one thinks, feels, or means. 2 squeeze out (juice, milk, etc.)
● adj. 1 operating at high speed; (of train etc.) not stopping at minor stations etc.; delivered by specially fast service. 2 definitely stated; explicit. ● adv. with speed; by express messenger or train.
● n. express train, bus, etc.; service for rapid transport of parcels etc.
□□ **expressible** adj.

**expression** n. 1 expressing, being expressed; wording, word, phrase. 2 appearance (of face) or intonation (of voice). 3 conveying or depiction of feeling. 4 Math. collection of symbols expressing quantity.
□□ **expressionless** adj.

**expressionism** n. style of painting etc. seeking to express emotion rather than depict external world.
□□ **expressionist** n. & adj.

**expressive** adj. full of expression; serving to express.
□□ **expressiveness** n.

**expressly** adv. explicitly.

**expresso** = ESPRESSO.

**expropriate** *v.* take away (property); dispossess. □□ **expropriation** *n.* **expropriator** *n.*

**expulsion** *n.* instance of expelling, being expelled.

**expunge** *v.* erase, remove. □□ **expunction** *n.*

**expurgate** *v.* remove objectionable matter from (book etc.); clear away (such matter). □□ **expurgation** *n.* **expurgator** *n.*

**exquisite** *adj.* **1** extremely beautiful or delicate. **2** acute, keen. □□ **exquisitely** *adv.*

**extant** *adj.* still existing, surviving.

**extempore** *adj. & adv.* without preparation.

**extemporise** *v.* (also **-ize**) improvise. □□ **extemporisation** *n.*

**extend** *v.* **1** lengthen in space or time; lay out at full length; reach or be or make continuous over specified area. **2** have certain scope. **3** offer or accord (invitation, kindness, etc.) **4** tax powers of. □□ **extendible** *adj.* **extensible** *adj.*

**extension** *n.* extending, enlargement; additional part of; subsidiary telephone on same line as main one; additional period of time.

**extensive** *adj.* large; far-reaching. □□ **extensively** *adv.* **extensiveness** *n.*

**extensor** *n.* muscle that extends part of body.

**extent** *n.* **1** space covered. **2** range, scope.

**extenuate** *v.* make (offence) seem less serious by providing partial excuse. □□ **extenuation** *n.*

**exterior** ● *adj.* outer; coming from outside. ● *n.* outward aspect or surface; outward demeanour.

**exterminate** *v.* destroy utterly; eliminate. □□ **extermination** *n.* **exterminator** *n.*

**external** *adj.* of or on the outside. □□ **externally** *adv.*

**extinct** *adj.* no longer existing; no longer burning; terminated, quenched; obsolete. □□ **extinction** *n.*

**extinguish** *v.* **1** put out (flame, light, etc.) **2** destroy, terminate. **3** wipe out (debt); make void (claim, right). □□ **extinguishable** *adj.* **extinguishment** *n.*

**extinguisher** *n.* = *fire extinguisher.*

**extirpate** *v.* root out; destroy. □□ **extirpation** *n.*

**extol** *v.* (**extolled**) praise enthusiastically.

**extort** *v.* obtain by force or threats.

**extortion** *n.* extorting, esp. money; illegal exaction.

**extortionate** *adj.* exorbitant.

**extra** ● *adj.* additional; more than usual or necessary. ● *adv.* more than usually; additionally. ● *n.* **1** extra thing; thing for which extra charge is made. **2** person engaged temporarily for minor part in film. **3** *Cricket* run scored other than from hit with bat.

**extra-** *comb. form* outside; beyond.

**extract** ● *v.* **1** take out. **2** obtain against person's will. **3** obtain from earth. **4** copy out, quote. **5** obtain (juice etc.) by pressure, distillation, etc. **6** derive (pleasure etc.) **7** *Math.* find (root of number). ● *n.* **1** passage from book etc. **2** preparation containing concentrated constituent of substance. □□ **extractor** *n.*

**extraction** *n.* **1** extracting. **2** removal of tooth. **3** lineage.

**extracurricular** *adj.* outside normal curriculum.

**extradite** *v.* hand over (person accused of crime) to country or state where crime was committed. □□ **extraditable** *n.* **extradition** *n.*

**extramarital** *adj.* (of sexual relationship) outside marriage.

**extramural** *adj.* additional to ordinary teaching or studies.

**extraneous** adj. 1 of external origin. 2 irrelevant, unrelated.

**extraordinary** adj. 1 unusual, remarkable; unusually great. 2 (of meeting etc.) additional. □□ **extraordinarily** adv.

**extrapolate** v. estimate (unknown facts or values) from known data; infer more widely from limited range of known factors. □□ **extrapolation** n.

**extrasensory** adj. derived by means other than known senses.

**extraterrestrial** ● adj. outside earth or its atmosphere. ● n. being from outer space.

**extravagant** adj. 1 spending (esp. money) excessively; excessive; costing much. 2 absurd. □□ **extravagance** n. **extravagantly** adv.

**extravaganza** n. 1 lavish, spectacular display. 2 fanciful composition.

**extreme** ● adj. 1 of high, or highest, degree. 2 severe, not moderate. 3 outermost. 4 utmost. ● n. 1 either of two things as remote or different as possible. 2 thing at either end. 3 highest degree. □□ **extremely** adv.

**extremist** n. person with extreme or fanatical political or religious views, esp. one who resorts to violence or extreme action. □□ **extremism** n.

**extremity** n. extreme point, end; (the extremities) hands and feet.

**extricate** v. disentangle, release. □□ **extrication** n.

**extrinsic** adj. not inherent or intrinsic; extraneous. □□ **extrinsically** adv.

**extrovert** ● n. outgoing or sociable person; person mainly concerned with external things. ● adj. typical or having nature of extrovert. □□ **extroversion** n. **extroverted** adj.

**extrude** v. thrust or squeeze out. □□ **extrusion** n.

**exuberant** adj. 1 lively, high-spirited; (of feelings etc.) abounding. 2 luxuriant, prolific. □□ **exuberance** n.

**exude** v. 1 ooze out; emit (smell). 2 display (emotion etc.) freely. □□ **exudation** n.

**exult** v. rejoice; have feeling of triumph (over person). □□ **exultant** adj. **exultation** n.

**eye** ● n. 1 organ or faculty of sight; region around eye; gaze, perception; eyelike thing. 2 leaf bud of potato. 3 centre of (cyclone). 4 hole of needle. ● v. (**eyed, eyeing**) watch, observe closely or suspiciously. □ **eye-opener** enlightening experience; unexpected revelation. **eye-tooth** canine tooth in upper jaw, below eye.

**eyeball** n. ball of eye within lids and socket.

**eyebrow** n. fringe of hair on ridge above eye socket.

**eyelash** n. any of hairs on edge of eyelid.

**eyelet** n. small hole for passing cord etc. through; metal ring strengthening this.

**eyelid** n. fold of skin that can cover eye.

**eyeliner** n. cosmetic applied as line around eye.

**eyepiece** n. lens to which eye is applied in telescope etc.

**eyeshadow** n. cosmetic applied to skin around eyes.

**eyesight** n. ability to see; range of vision.

**eyesore** n. ugly thing, esp. a building.

**eyewitness** n. person who actually saw something happen.

**eyrie** n. nest of bird of prey, esp. eagle, built high up.

# Ff

**F** *abbr.* Fahrenheit.

**f** *abbr.* (also **f.**) **1** female. **2** feminine. **3** *Mus.* forte.

**fable** *n.* fictional tale, esp. legendary or moral tale, often with animal characters.

**fabled** *adj.* celebrated; legendary.

**fabric** *n.* **1** woven material. **2** walls, floor, and roof of building. **3** structure.

**fabricate** *v.* **1** construct, esp. from components. **2** invent (story). **3** forge (document). □□ **fabrication** *n.*

**fabulous** *adj.* **1** marvellous; legendary. **2** *colloq.* very good. □□ **fabulously** *adv.*

**facade** *n.* (also **façade**) **1** front of building. **2** outward appearance.

**face** ● *n.* **1** front of head. **2** facial expression. **3** effrontery. **4** surface. **5** facade of building. **6** side of mountain. **7** dial of clock etc. **8** functional side of tool, bat, etc. **9** *Aust.* front of bushfire. **10** aspect. ● *v.* **1** look or be positioned towards. **2** be opposite. **3** meet resolutely, confront. **4** put facing on (garment, wall, etc.).

**faceless** *adj.* **1** without identity. **2** not identifiable.

**facet** *n.* **1** aspect. **2** side of cut gem etc.

**facetious** *adj.* treating serious issues with deliberately inappropriate humour; flippant. □□ **facetiously** *adv.*

**facia** = FASCIA.

**facial** ● *adj.* of or for the face. ● *n.* beauty treatment for face. □□ **facially** *adv.*

**facile** *adj.* easily achieved but of little value; glib; superficial.

**facilitate** *v.* **1** make easy or less difficult. **2** help progress (an action). □□ **facilitation** *n.*

**facility** *n.* absence of difficulty; a means for doing something.

**facing** *n.* material over part of garment etc. for contrast or strength; outer covering on wall etc.

**facsimile** *n.* exact copy of writing, picture, etc.

**fact** *n.* thing known to exist or be true; reality.

**faction** *n.* small dissenting group within larger one, esp. in politics. □□ **factional** *adj.*

**factious** *adj.* of or inclined to dissension.

**factor** *n.* **1** thing contributing to result. **2** whole number etc. that when multiplied produces given number, e.g. 2, 3, 4, and 6 are factors of 12.

**factory** *n.* building(s) for manufacture of goods.

**factotum** *n.* employee doing all kinds of work.

**factual** *adj.* based on or concerned with fact. □□ **factually** *adv.*

**faculty** *n.* **1** aptitude for particular activity; mental or physical power. **2** group of related university departments; academic staff of these departments.

**fad** *n.* craze; peculiar notion.

**fade** ● *v.* **1** (cause to) lose colour, light, or sound; slowly diminish; lose freshness or strength. **2** angle surfboard towards breaking part of wave. ● *n.* action of fading. □ **fade-up** instance of increasing brightness of image or volume of sound.

**faeces** *n.pl.* waste matter from bowels. □□ **faecal** *adj.*

**fag** *n.* **1** tedious task. **2** *colloq.* cigarette. **3** *colloq. offens.* male homosexual. ● *v.* exhaust.

**fah** n. (also **fa**) Mus. fourth note of tonic sol-fa.

**Fahrenheit** adj. of scale of temperature on which water freezes at 32° and boils at 212°.

**faience** n. decorated and glazed earthenware and porcelain.

**fail** ● v. 1 not succeed; be or judge to be unsuccessful in (exam etc.) 2 be unable, neglect. 3 disappoint. 4 be absent or insufficient. 5 become weaker. 6 cease functioning.
● n. 1 failure in exam. 2 colloq. mistake, failure, or instance of poor performance.

**failed** adj. unsuccessful, bankrupt.

**failing** ● n. fault, weakness.
● prep. in default of.

**failure** n. lack of success; unsuccessful person or thing; breaking down or ceasing to function.

**fain** adv. arch. willingly.

**faint** adj. 1 pale, dim. 2 weak; giddy. ● v. become faint; lose consciousness. ● n. act or state of fainting. □ **faint-hearted** timid.
□□ **faintly** adv. **faintness** n.

**fair** ● n. 1 stalls, amusements, etc. for public entertainment. 2 a gathering for a sale of goods, often with entertainments; exhibition of commercial goods. ● adj. 1 light in colour, having light-coloured hair. 2 (of weather) fine; (of wind) favourable. 3 just, unbiased. 4 of moderate quality or amount.
● adv. fairly.

**fairing** n. streamlining structure added to a ship, vehicle, etc.

**fairly** adv. 1 in a fair way. 2 moderately. 3 to a noticeable degree.

**fairway** n. 1 mown grass between golf tee and green. 2 navigable channel.

**fairy** n. imaginary small being with magical powers. □ **fairy godmother** benefactress providing a sudden unexpected gift. **fairy lights** strings of small coloured lights used as decoration. **fairy tale** (or **story**) tale about fairies or magic; falsehood.

**fait accompli** n. thing done and not capable of alteration.

**faith** n. reliance, trust; belief in a religious doctrine; loyalty, sincerity. □ **faith healing** a cure etc. dependent on faith.

**faithful** adj. loyal, trustworthy; true, accurate.

**faithfully** adv. in faithful way.

**faithless** adj. 1 disloyal. 2 without religious faith.

**fajitas** n.pl. tortilla wrapped around spiced meats, cheese, salad, etc.

**fake** ● n. false or counterfeit thing or person. ● adj. counterfeit; not genuine. ● v. make fake or imitation of; feign.

**falcon** n. small hawk.

**falconry** n. breeding and training of hawks.

**fall** ● v. (**fell**, **fallen**, **falling**) 1 go or come down freely; decrease. 2 pass into a specified state; occur. 3 (of the face) show dismay. 4 lose one's position or office; be captured or conquered; die in battle.
● n. 1 falling; the amount of this. 2 US autumn. 3 (**falls**) waterfall. □ **fall back** retreat. **fall back on** have recourse to. **fall for** 1 fall in love with. 2 be deceived by. **fall out** quarrel; happen. **fall short** be inadequate. **fall through** (of plan) fail.

**fallacy** n. mistaken belief; faulty reasoning; misleading argument.
□□ **fallacious** adj.

**fallback** n. 1 alternative plan. 2 reduction or decrease.

**fallible** adj. capable of making mistakes. □□ **fallibility** n.

**fallopian tube** n. either of two tubes along which ova travel from ovaries to uterus.

**fallow** adj. (of land) ploughed but left unsown; uncultivated.

**false** adj. 1 wrong, incorrect. 2 sham, artificial. 3 deceptive. 4 deceitful, treacherous.□ **false negative** test result that wrongly indicates that a particular condition etc. is absent. **false positive** test result that wrongly indicates that a particular condition is present. □□ **falsely** adv. **falseness** n.

**falsehood** n. untrue thing; lying; lie.

**falsetto** n. male voice above normal range.

**falsify** v. 1 fraudulently alter. 2 misrepresent. □□ **falsification** n.

**falter** v. stumble; go unsteadily; lose courage; speak hesitatingly.

**fame** n. renown; being famous; reputation.

**famed** adj. famous; much spoken of.

**familial** adj. of a family or its members.

**familiar** ● adj. 1 well known. 2 often encountered. 3 knowing (thing) well. 4 excessively informal. ● n. close friend. □□ **familiarity** n. **familiarly** adv.

**familiarise** v. (also **-ize**) make (person etc.) conversant. □□ **familiarisation** n.

**family** n. 1 set of relations, esp. parents and children; person's children; all the descendants of common ancestor. 2 group of related animals or things.

**famine** n. extreme scarcity, esp. of food.

**famished** adj. extremely hungry.

**famous** adj. 1 celebrated; well-known. 2 colloq. excellent. □□ **famously** adv.

**fan** ● n. 1 hand-held or mechanical device to create current of air for cooling etc.; fan-shaped thing. 2 devotee. ● v. (**fanned**) 1 blow air on (as) with fan. 2 spread out like fan.

□ **fan belt** belt driving fan that cools car engine.

**fanatic** ● n. person obsessively devoted to a belief, activity, etc. ● adj. excessively enthusiastic. □□ **fanatical** adj. **fanatically** adv. **fanaticism** n.

**fancier** n. connoisseur, enthusiast.

**fanciful** adj. imaginary; indulging in fancies. □□ **fancifully** adv.

**fancy** ● n. 1 imagination; something imagined, an unfounded idea. 2 a desire, a liking. ● adj. (**fancier**) ornamental, elaborate. ● v. 1 imagine, suppose. 2 colloq. find attractive. □ **fancy dress** costume representing animal, historical character, etc., worn for party. □□ **fancily** adv.

**fandango** n. (pl. **fandangos** or **fandangoes**) lively Spanish dance.

**fanfare** n. short showy sounding of trumpets etc.

**fang** ● n. long sharp tooth; canine tooth, esp. of dog or wolf; tooth of venomous snake. ● v. Aust. colloq. 1 borrow in pressurising way. 2 drive at high speed in car.

**fanlight** n. small window above door or larger window.

**fanny** n. 1 coarse colloq. female genitals. 2 US colloq. buttocks.

**fantasia** n. free or improvisatory musical etc. composition.

**fantasise** v. (also **-ize**) daydream; imagine; create fantasy about.

**fantastic** adj. 1 extravagantly fanciful. 2 eccentric; exotic. 3 colloq. excellent, extraordinary. □□ **fantastically** adv.

**fantasy** n. 1 imagination; daydream. 2 category of fiction concerned with magical worlds.

**FAQ** abbr. frequently asked question.

**far** ● adv. at, to, or by a great distance or time; by much. ● adj. 1 remote. 2 distant. 3 extreme. □ **far-fetched** unconvincing;

exaggerated; fanciful. **far-flung** widely scattered; remote. **far-out** colloq. unconventional; excellent. **far-sighted** long-sighted.

**farad** n. SI unit of electrical capacitance.

**farce** ● n. 1 comedy with ludicrously improbable plot. 2 absurdly futile proceedings. 3 pretence. □□ **farcical** adj.

**fare** ● n. 1 price charged for passenger to travel; passenger. 2 food. ● v. progress; get on; happen.

**farewell** ● int. goodbye. ● n. 1 leave taking. 2 function organised to mark person's departure. ● v. say goodbye to.

**farina** n. flour of corn, nuts, or starchy roots. □□ **farinaceous** adj.

**farm** ● n. land and its buildings used for growing crops, rearing animals, etc. ● v. 1 use (land) thus; be farmer; breed (fish etc.) commercially. 2 delegate or subcontract (work). □□ **farmer** n. **farming** n.

**farrago** n. medley, hotchpotch.

**farrier** n. smith who shoes horses.

**farrow** ● v. give birth to (piglets). ● n. litter of pigs.

**fart** v. colloq. send out wind from the anus.

**farther** = FURTHER.

**farthest** = FURTHEST.

**farthing** n. hist. coin worth quarter of a penny.

**fascia** n. (also **facia**) 1 stripe or band. 2 long flat surface of wood, covering ends of rafters. 3 Anat. thin sheath of fibrous tissue.

**fascinate** v. capture interest of; attract. □□ **fascination** n.

**fascinator** n. decorative woman's headpiece.

**fascism** n. authoritarian and nationalistic right-wing system of government. □□ **fascist** n.

**fashion** ● n. current popular custom or style, esp. in dress; manner of doing something. ● v. make or form.

**fashionable** adj. 1 of or conforming to current fashion. 2 of or favoured by high society. □□ **fashionably** adv.

**fast** ● adj. 1 moving or done quickly; allowing quick movement. 2 showing a time ahead of the correct time. 3 firmly fixed. ● adv. 1 quickly. 2 firmly, tightly. ● v. go without food. ● n. fasting; period of fasting. □ **fast food** food that is sold prepared for quick meal. **fast forward** move speedily forward in time.

**fasten** v. fix firmly; tie or join together; become fastened.

**fastening** n. (also **fastener**) device that fastens.

**fastidious** adj. 1 fussy. 2 easily disgusted. 3 squeamish.

**fat** ● n. oily substance, esp. in animal bodies; part of meat etc. containing this. ● adj. (**fatter**) plump; made plump for slaughter; fatted; containing much fat; thick; substantial. □ **fat chance** colloq. no chance. □□ **fatless** adj. **fatness** n. **fatten** v.

**fatal** adj. causing or ending in death or ruin. □□ **fatally** adv.

**fatalism** n. 1 belief in predetermination. 2 submissive acceptance. □□ **fatalist** n. **fatalistic** adj.

**fatality** n. death by accident or in war etc.

**fate** n. 1 power thought to control all events. 2 person's destiny.

**fated** adj. destined by fate; doomed.

**fateful** adj. 1 important, decisive. 2 controlled by fate. □□ **fatefully** adv.

**father** ● n. 1 male parent or ancestor. 2 founder, originator. 3 title of certain priests. ● v. 1 be father of. 2 originate. □□ **fatherhood** n. **fatherly** adj.

**father-in-law** n. (pl. **fathers-in-law**) father of one's wife or husband.

**fathom** ● n. measure of depth of water equal to six feet (1.8 m).
● v. 1 comprehend. 2 measure depth of (water). □□ **fathomable** adj.

**fatigue** ● n. 1 extreme tiredness. 2 weakness in metals etc. from repeated stress. 3 soldier's non-military task. ● v. cause fatigue in.

**fatuous** adj. vacantly silly; purposeless. □□ **fatuity** n. **fatuously** adv. **fatuousness** n.

**fatwa** n. ruling made by Islamic leader.

**faucet** n. US tap.

**fault** ● n. 1 defect, imperfection. 2 responsibility for wrongdoing, error, etc. 3 break in electric circuit. 4 Tennis etc. incorrect service. 5 break in rock strata. ● v. find fault with. □□ **faultless** adj. **faulty** adj.

**faun** n. Roman god of countryside with goat's legs and horns.

**fauna** n. animal life of region or period.

**faux pas** n. (pl. **faux pas**) tactless mistake.

**favour** (also **favor**) ● n. 1 liking; approval. 2 kindly or helpful act beyond what is due. 3 favouritism. ● v. 1 regard or treat with favour; oblige. 2 resemble (one parent etc.)

**favourable** adj. (also **favorable**) 1 well-disposed. 2 approving. 3 promising. 4 helpful, suitable. □□ **favourably** adv.

**favourite** (also **favorite**) ● adj. preferred to all others.
● n. favourite person or thing; competitor thought most likely to win; = BOOKMARK (n. 2).
● v. = BOOKMARK v.

**favouritism** n. (also **favoritism**) unfair favouring of one person etc.

**fawn** ● n. 1 deer in its first year. 2 light yellowish brown.
● adj. fawn-coloured. ● v. try to win favour by obsequiousness; (of dog) show extreme affection.

**fax** ● n. electronic transmission of exact copy of document etc.; such copy. ● v. transmit in this way.

**faze** v. fluster; daunt.

**fealty** n. allegiance.

**fear** ● n. panic etc. caused by impending danger, pain, etc.; cause of this; alarm; dread. ● v. be afraid of; feel anxiety about; dread; shrink from.

**fearful** adj. 1 afraid. 2 terrible, awful. 3 colloq. extremely unpleasant. □□ **fearfully** adv. **fearfulness** n.

**fearless** adj. not afraid, brave. □□ **fearlessly** adv. **fearlessness** n.

**fearsome** adj. frightening. □□ **fearsomely** adv.

**feasible** adj. practicable, possible. □□ **feasibility** n. **feasibly** adv.

> **Usage** Feasible should not be used to mean 'likely'. Possible or probable should be used instead.

**feast** ● n. 1 sumptuous meal. 2 religious festival. 3 sensual or mental pleasure. ● v. have feast; eat and drink sumptuously.

**feat** n. remarkable act or achievement.

**feather** ● n. one of structures forming bird's plumage, with horny stem and fine strands; these as material. ● v. 1 cover or line with feathers. 2 turn (oar) edgeways through air. □ **feather in one's cap** achievement to be proud of. **feather one's nest** enrich oneself. □□ **feathery** adj.

**featherweight** n. very lightweight thing or person; weight between bantamweight and lightweight.

**feature** ● *n.* **1** distinctive or characteristic part; part of face. **2** specialised article in newspaper etc. **3** (in full **feature film**) main film in cinema program. ● *v.* **1** make or be special feature. **2** emphasise. **3** take part in. □□ **featureless** *adj.*

**Feb.** *abbr.* February.

**febrile** *adj.* of fever; feverish; tense and excited.

**February** *n.* the second month.

**feckless** *adj.* feeble, ineffective; irresponsible.

**fecund** *adj.* fertile. □□ **fecundity** *n.*

**fed** see FEED. □ **fed up** *colloq.* bored, discontented.

**federal** *adj.* of system of government in which self-governing states unite for certain functions etc.; of such federation; of Commonwealth of Australia, as distinct from States. □□ **federalise** *v.* (also **-ize**) **federalism** *n.* **federalist** *n.* **federally** *adv.*

**federate** ● *v.* unite on federal basis. ● *adj.* federally organised. □□ **federative** *adj.*

**federation** *n.* **1** federal group; act of federating. **2** (**Federation**) association of six Australian colonies in federal union; formation of Commonwealth of Australia on 1 January 1901.

**fee** *n.* sum payable for professional services, or for a privilege.

**feeble** *adj.* weak; lacking strength, energy, or effectiveness. □□ **feebly** *adv.*

**feed** ● *v.* (**fed**, **feeding**) give food to; give as food; (of animals) take food; nourish; supply. ● *n.* a meal; food for animals.

**feedback** *n.* return of part of a system's output to its source; return of information about product, piece of work, etc. to producer.

**feeder** *n.* **1** person or thing that feeds; baby's feeding bottle; feeding apparatus in machine. **2** road or railway line etc. linking outlying areas to central system.

**feedlot** *n.* establishment for fattening cattle etc. for slaughter.

**feel** ● *v.* (**felt**, **feeling**) **1** examine, search, or perceive by touch. **2** experience. **3** be affected by; have sympathy or pity. **4** have impression. **5** consider, think. **6** seem. **7** be conscious. ● *n.* sense of touch; sensation produced by thing touched; act of feeling. □ **feel like** be in mood for.

**feeler** *n.* organ in certain animals for touching, foraging, etc.

**feeling** *n.* **1** capacity to feel; sense of touch; physical sensation. **2** sensitivity; emotional response. **3** opinion or notion. ● *adj.* sensitive, sympathetic. □□ **feelingly** *adv.*

**feet** see FOOT.

**feign** *v.* simulate; pretend.

**feint** *n.* sham attack or diversionary blow; pretence. ● *v.* make feint. ● *adj.* (of paper etc.) having faintly ruled lines.

**felafel** *n.* (also **falafel**) dish of patties of fried chickpea, spices, etc.

**feldspar** *n.* (also **felspar**) common aluminium silicate. □□ **feldspathic** *adj.*

**felicitate** *v.* congratulate. □□ **felicitation** *n.*

**felicity** *n.* intense happiness; capacity for apt expression.

**feline** ● *adj.* of cat family; catlike. ● *n.* animal of cat family.

**fell** *v.* strike or cut down. See also FALL.

**fellatio** *n.* oral stimulation of penis.

**fellow** *n.* **1** comrade, associate. **2** counterpart, equal. **3** graduate paid to do research. **4** *colloq.* man, boy. **5** (usu. **fella** or **feller**) (in Aboriginal English) person. **6** (usu. **Fellow**) member of learned society. ● *adj.* of same group etc.

**fellowship** *n.* **1** friendly association, companionship. **2** group of associates. **3** status or income of university fellow.

**felon** *n.* person who has committed felony.

**felony** *n.* serious, usu. violent, crime. □□ **felonious** *adj.*

**felt**[1] ● *n.* cloth of matted and pressed fibres of wool etc. ● *v.* **1** make into or cover with felt. **2** become matted.

**felt**[2] see FEEL.

**female** ● *adj.* **1** of the sex that can give birth or produce eggs. **2** (of plants) fruit-bearing. **3** of female people, animals, or plants. **4** (of screw, socket, etc.) hollow to receive inserted part. ● *n.* female person, animal, or plant.

**feminine** *adj.* **1** of women; womanly. **2** having the grammatical form of the female gender. □□ **femininity** *n.*

**feminism** *n.* advocacy of women's rights and sexual equality. □□ **feminist** *n.* & *adj.*

**femme fatale** *n.* (*pl.* **femmes fatales**) dangerously seductive woman.

**femur** *n.* (*pl.* **femurs** or **femora**) thigh bone. □□ **femoral** *adj.*

**fen** *n.* Brit. low marshy land.

**fence** ● *n.* **1** barrier or railing enclosing paddock, garden, etc. **2** jump for horses. **3** colloq. receiver of stolen goods. ● *v.* **1** surround (as) with fence. **2** practise swordplay. **3** be evasive. **4** colloq. deal in (stolen goods). □□ **fencer** *n.*

**fencing** *n.* **1** fences; material for fences. **2** sword fighting, esp. as sport.

**fend** *v.* □ **fend for** look after (esp. oneself). **fend off** ward off.

**fender** *n.* **1** low frame bordering fireplace. **2** US bumper or mudguard of car etc.

**fennel** *n.* fragrant herb used for flavouring.

**fenugreek** *n.* leguminous plant with aromatic seeds used for flavouring.

**feral** ● *adj.* **1** wild; (of domestic animal) escaped and living wild. **2** Aust. colloq. (of person) wild, uncontrolled; unconventional; dirty, scruffy. ● *n.* feral animal or person.

**ferment** ● *n.* **1** excitement. **2** fermentation; fermenting agent. ● *v.* **1** undergo or subject to fermentation. **2** excite.

**fermentation** *n.* **1** breakdown of substance by yeasts and bacteria etc. **2** excitement. □□ **fermentative** *adj.*

**fermium** *n.* radioactive metallic element (symbol Fm).

**fern** *n.* flowerless plant usu. having feathery fronds.

**ferocious** *adj.* fierce. □□ **ferociously** *adv.* **ferocity** *n.*

**ferret** ● *n.* small animal of weasel family. ● *v.* **1** hunt with ferrets. **2** rummage; search out.

**ferric** *adj.* (also **ferrous**) of or containing iron.

**Ferris wheel** *n.* giant revolving vertical wheel with passenger cars for fair rides.

**ferroconcrete** *n.* reinforced concrete.

**ferrule** *n.* ring or cap on end of stick, umbrella, etc.

**ferry** ● *n.* boat etc. for esp. regular transport across water; ferrying place or service. ● *v.* take or go in ferry; transport, esp. regularly, from place to place.

**fertile** *adj.* **1** (of soil) abundantly productive; fruitful; (of seed, egg, etc.) capable of growth; (of animal or plant) able to reproduce. **2** (of mind) inventive. **3** (of nuclear material) able to become fissile by capture of neutrons. □□ **fertility** *n.*

**fertilise** *v.* (also -**ize**) make fertile; cause (egg, female animal, etc.) to

develop new individual.
□□ **fertilisation** n.

**fertiliser** n. (also **-izer**) substance added to soil to make it more fertile.

**fervent** adj. ardent, intense.
□□ **fervency** n. **fervently** adv.

**fervid** adj. fervent. □□ **fervidly** adv.

**fervour** n. (also **fervor**) passion, zeal.

**fess** v. colloq. confess, own up.

**fester** v. 1 make or become septic. 2 cause continuing bitterness. 3 rot, stagnate.

**festival** n. 1 day or period of celebration. 2 series of cultural events in town etc.

**festive** adj. of or characteristic of festival; joyous.

**festivity** n. festive occasion; celebration.

**festoon** ● n. curved hanging chain of flowers, ribbons, etc. ● v. adorn with or form into festoons.

**festy** adj. (**festier**) colloq. 1 disgusting, revolting. 2 dirty.

**feta** n. white salty Greek cheese.

**fetch** v. 1 go for and bring back. 2 be sold for. 3 draw forth. 4 deal (blow).

**fetching** adj. attractive.
□□ **fetchingly** adv.

**fete** (also **fête**) ● n. outdoor fund-raising event. ● v. honour or entertain lavishly.

**fetid** adj. (also **foetid**) stinking.

**fetish** n. 1 abnormal object of sexual desire. 2 object of obsessive concern.
□□ **fetishism** n. **fetishist** n. **fetishistic** adj.

**fetlock** n. back of horse's leg where tuft of hair grows above hoof.

**fetter** ● n. shackle for ankles.
● v. put into fetters.

**fettle** n. condition, trim.

**fetus** n. = FOETUS.

**feud** ● n. prolonged hostility, esp. between families, tribes, etc.
● v. conduct feud.

**feudal** adj. 1 of, like, or according to feudal system. 2 reactionary. □ **feudal**

**system** medieval system of holding land by giving one's services to the owner. □□ **feudalism** n.

**feudalistic** adj.

**fever** n. 1 abnormally high body temperature; disease causing it. 2 nervous excitement.

**feverish** adj. 1 having symptoms of fever. 2 excited, restless.
□□ **feverishly** adv.

**few** adj. & n. not many.

> **Usage** Fewer, the comparative form of few, is usu. used with words denoting people or countable things (fewer members; fewer books). Less, on the other hand, is usu. used with mass nouns, denoting things that cannot be counted (less flour; less bother).

**fey** adj. 1 strange, other worldly. 2 whimsical.

**fez** n. (pl. **fezzes**) man's flat-topped conical red cap worn by some Muslims.

**ff.** abbr. following pages etc.

**fiancé** n. man one is engaged to marry.

**fiancée** n. woman one is engaged to marry.

**fiasco** n. ludicrous or humiliating failure.

**fiat** n. authorisation; decree.

**fib** ● n. trivial lie. ● v. (**fibbed**) tell fib. □□ **fibber** n.

**fibre** n. 1 threadlike strand; substance formed of fibres; fibrous material in food, roughage. 2 strength of character. □ **fibre optics** transmission of information by light along thin flexible glass fibres.
□□ **fibrous** adj.

**fibreglass** n. material made of or containing glass fibres.

**fibril** n. small fibre.

**fibrillate** *v.* **1** (of a muscle) make quivering movement due to uncoordinated contraction of individual fibrils. **2** (of a fibre) split up into fibrils. □□ **fibrillation** *n.*

**fibro** *Aust.* ● *n.* fibro-cement; house made of sheets of fibro. ● *adj.* made of fibro. □ **fibro-cement** mixture of various fibrous materials and cement, used in sheets for building etc.

**fibroid** ● *adj.* of, like, or containing fibrous tissue or fibres. ● *n.* benign fibrous tumour, esp. in uterus.

**fibrosis** *n.* thickening and scarring of connective tissue.

**fibrositis** *n.* rheumatic inflammation of fibrous tissue.

**fibula** *n.* (*pl.* **fibulae** or **fibulas**) bone on outer side of lower leg. □□ **fibular** *adj.*

**fiche** *n.* (*pl.* **fiche** or **fiches**) microfiche.

**fickle** *adj.* inconstant, changeable. □□ **fickleness** *n.*

**fiction** *n.* **1** non-factual literature, esp. novels; invented idea, thing, etc. **2** generally accepted falsehood. □□ **fictional** *adj.*

**fictitious** *adj.* imaginary, unreal; not genuine.

**fiddle** ● *n.* **1** violin or other stringed instrument, esp. when played as folk instrument. **2** illegal or fraudulent scheme. ● *v.* **1** play restlessly; move aimlessly. **2** tinker, tamper. **3** *colloq.* swindle, falsify, get by cheating. **4** play fiddle. □□ **fiddler** *n.*

**fiddling** *adj.* **1** petty, trivial. **2** *colloq.* fiddly.

**fiddly** *adj.* (**fiddlier**) *colloq.* awkward to do or use.

**fidelity** *n.* **1** faithfulness, loyalty. **2** accuracy; precision in sound reproduction.

**fidget** ● *v.* (**fidgeted**) move restlessly; be or make uneasy. ● *n.* **1** person who fidgets. **2** (the **fidgets**) restless state or mood. □□ **fidgety** *adj.*

**fief** *n. hist.* estate held by noble under feudalism.

**field** ● *n.* **1** area of esp. cultivated enclosed land; area rich in some natural product. **2** competitors. **3** expanse of snow, sea, sky, etc. **4** battlefield. **5** area of activity or study. **6** *Computing* part of record, representing item of data. ● *v.* **1** *Cricket etc.* act as fielder(s), stop and return (ball). **2** select (player, candidate). **3** deal with (questions etc.) □ **field day 1** wide scope for action or success. **2** *Aust.* day for display of agricultural machinery. **field events** athletic contests other than races.

**fielder** *n.* person who fields a ball; member of side not batting.

**fieldwork** *n.* practical work done outside libraries and laboratories by surveyors, social scientists, etc.

**fiend** *n.* **1** evil spirit, demon; wicked or cruel person; mischievous or annoying person. **2** *colloq.* devotee. **3** difficult or unpleasant thing. □□ **fiendish** *adj.* **fiendishly** *adv.*

**fierce** *adj.* **1** violently aggressive or frightening. **2** eager; intense. □□ **fiercely** *adv.* **fierceness** *n.*

**fiery** *adj.* (**fierier**) **1** consisting of or flaming with fire; bright red; burning hot. **2** spirited.

**fiesta** *n.* holiday, festival.

**fife** *n.* small shrill flute.

**fifteen** *adj. & n.* **1** one more than fourteen (15, XV). **2** *Rugby* team of fifteen players. □□ **fifteenth** *adj. & n.*

**fifth** *adj. & n.* next after fourth; any of five equal parts of thing. □□ **fifthly** *adv.*

**fifty** *adj. & n.* five times ten (50, L). □ **fifty-fifty** half and half, equal(ly). □□ **fiftieth** *adj. & n.*

**fig** *n.* soft fruit with many seeds; tree bearing it.

**fig.** *abbr.* figure.

**fight** ● v. (**fought**, **fighting**) struggle against, esp. in physical combat or war; contend; strive to obtain or accomplish something or to overcome. ● n. fighting; battle, contest; boxing match.

**fighter** n. person who fights; aircraft designed for attacking other aircraft.

**figment** n. imaginary thing.

**figurative** adj. metaphorical; not literal. □□ **figuratively** adv.

**figure** ● n. 1 written symbol of number. 2 a value, an amount of money. 3 (**figures**) arithmetic. ● v. 1 appear or be mentioned; form part of plan etc. 2 work out by arithmetic or logic. □ **figure of speech** expression used for effect rather than literally.

**figured** adj. woven pattern.

**figurehead** n. 1 carved figure on the prow of ship. 2 leader with only nominal power.

**figurine** n. small statue.

**filament** n. threadlike strand or fibre; conducting wire or thread in light bulb.

**filch** v. pilfer, steal.

**file** ● n. 1 folder, box, etc. for holding loose papers; papers kept in this. 2 collection of related computer data. 3 line of people or things one behind another. 4 tool with rough surface for smoothing things. ● v. 1 place in file or among records. 2 submit (petition for divorce etc.) 3 smooth or shape with file. 4 march in a long line. □ **file server** Computing device that controls access to one or more separately stored files.

**filial** adj. of or due from son or daughter. □□ **filially** adv.

**filibuster** n. 1 obstruction of progress in legislative assembly; US person who engages in this. ● v. act as filibuster.

**filigree** n. fine ornamental work in gold etc. wire; similar delicate work.

**filings** n.pl. particles rubbed off by file.

**fill** ● v. 1 make or become full; block. 2 occupy; appoint to (vacant office). ● n. enough to fill thing; enough to satisfy person's appetite or desire. 2 loose earth etc. used to level building site. □ **fill in** 1 complete (form etc.); fill completely. 2 act as substitute. 3 colloq. inform more fully. **fill out** 1 become or become enlarged, esp. to required size. 2 = **fill in** sense 1. **fill up** fill completely.

**filler** n. material used to fill cavity or increase bulk.

**fillet** ● n. 1 boneless piece of meat or fish; (in full **fillet steak**) undercut of sirloin. 2 ribbon etc. binding hair; thin narrow strip of anything. ● v. (**filleted**) 1 remove bones from (fish etc.) or divide into fillets. 2 bind or provide with fillet(s).

**filling** n. material that fills tooth, sandwich, pie, etc.

**fillip** n. stimulus, incentive.

**filly** n. young female horse.

**film** ● n. 1 thin coating or layer. 2 strip or sheet of light-sensitive material for taking photographs; motion picture. ● v. 1 make film of. 2 cover or become covered with thin layer.

**filmstrip** n. series of transparencies in a strip for projection.

**filmy** adj. (**filmier**) thin and almost transparent.

**filo pastry** n. pastry in very thin sheets.

**filter** ● n. porous device for removing impurities in liquid or gas passing through it; screen for absorbing or modifying light or electrical or sound waves. ● v. pass through filter, remove impurities in this way; pass gradually in or out.

**filth** n. 1 disgusting dirt. 2 obscenity.

**filthy** adj. 1 extremely dirty. 2 obscene. 3 colloq. excellent.

**filtrate** ● v. filter. ● n. filtered liquid.□□ **filtration** n.

**fin** n. organ esp. of fish, for propelling, steering, etc.; similar projection for stabilising aircraft, surfboard, etc.

**final** ● adj. at the end, coming last; conclusive, decisive. ● n. 1 last or deciding heat or game. 2 (**finals**) exams at end of degree course. □□ **finality** n. **finally** adv.

**finale** n. last movement or section of piece of music or drama etc.

**finalise** v. (also **-ize**) put into final form; complete.□□ **finalisation** n.

**finalist** n. competitor in final.

**finance** ● n. management of money; monetary support for enterprise; money resources.
● v. provide capital for.

**financial** adj. 1 of finance. 2 colloq. having ready money.□□ **financially** adv.

**financier** n. capitalist entrepreneur.

**finch** n. small seed-eating bird, often with brightly coloured plumage.

**find** ● v. (**found**, **finding**) discover, obtain; (of a jury) decide and declare. ● n. a discovery; thing found.□ **find out** find information about; detect, discover.□□ **finder** n.

**fine** ● n. money to be paid as penalty. ● v. punish by fine.
● adj. 1 of high quality; excellent; good, satisfactory. 2 pure, refined. 3 imposing. 4 bright and clear. 5 thin, small; in small particles. 6 subtle.
● adv. 1 finely. 2 very well.□□ **finely** adv. **fineness** n.

**finery** n. showy dress or decoration.

**finesse** n. delicate manipulation; tact.

**finger** ● n. any of terminal projections of hand (usu. excluding thumb); part of glove for finger; finger-like object. ● v. 1 touch, play, or turn about with fingers. 2 colloq. accuse.□□ **fingerless** adj.

**fingerboard** n. flat strip on stringed instrument against which strings are pressed with fingers to produce different notes.

**fingerling** n. any young or otherwise small fish, esp. trout or salmon.

**fingerprint** n. impression of the ridges on pad of finger; this used for identification.

**fingertip** n. tip of finger.

**finicky** adj. (also **finical**, **finicking**) over-particular, fastidious; detailed; fiddly.□□ **finickiness** n.

**finish** ● v. 1 bring or come to an end or end of; complete. 2 treat surface of. ● n. 1 last stage, completion; end of race etc. 2 method etc. of surface treatment.

**finite** adj. 1 limited; not infinite. 2 (of verb) having specific number and person.

**fiord** ● n. = FJORD.

**fir** n. evergreen conifer with needles growing singly on stems.

**fire** ● n. 1 combustion; heating device with a flame or glow; destructive burning. 2 the firing of guns. 3 angry or excited feeling.
● v. 1 shoot (gun etc. or missile from it). 2 dismiss (employee). 3 set fire to; catch fire. 4 bake or dry (pottery etc.) 5 excite.□ **fire brigade** organised body of people employed to extinguish fires. **fire escape** special staircase or apparatus for escape from a burning building. **fire extinguisher** apparatus discharging water, foam, etc. to extinguish fire.

**firearm** n. gun, esp. pistol or rifle.

**firebreak** n. strip of cleared land in forest etc. as obstacle to spread of fire.

**firecracker** n. explosive firework.

**firefighter** n. person whose task is to extinguish fires.

**firelighter** n. piece of flammable material to help start fire in barbecue etc.

**fireplace** n. recess with chimney for domestic fire.

**firewall** n. **1** wall etc. that inhibits or prevents spread of fire. **2** part of computer system or network that prevents unauthorised access.

**firework** n. device containing chemicals that burn or explode spectacularly.

**firie** n. Aust. colloq. firefighter.

**firing squad** n. group ordered to shoot condemned person.

**firm** ● adj. solid; fixed, steady; resolute; steadfast; (of offer etc.) definite. ● v. make or become firm or secure. ● n. business concern or its partners.

**firmament** n. sky with the stars etc.

**first** ● adj. earliest in time, order, or importance. ● n. first thing or occurrence; first day of month; first gear. ● adv. before all others or another; for the first time. □ **at first** in the beginning. **first aid** basic treatment given for injury etc. before doctor arrives. **First Australian** Aboriginal person. **first-class** of best quality; in best category of accommodation. **first-degree 1** of non-serious surface burns. **2** US of the most serious category of a crime. **first-hand** directly from original source. **first name** personal name. **first-rate** excellent.

**firth** n. inlet; estuary.

**fiscal** adj. of public revenue; financial.

**fish** ● n. **1** vertebrate cold-blooded animal living in water; its flesh as food. **2** colloq. person of specified kind. ● v. try to catch fish (in); search for; seek indirectly; retrieve with effort.

**fishery** n. place where fish are caught or reared; industry of fishing or breeding fish.

**fishmonger** n. dealer in fish.

**fishnet** n. open-meshed fabric.

**fishy** adj. (fishier) **1** of or like fish. **2** colloq. dubious, suspect.

**fissile** adj. capable of undergoing nuclear fission; tending to split.

**fission** ● n. **1** splitting of atomic nucleus. **2** cell division as mode of reproduction. ● v. (cause to) undergo fission.

**fissure** ● n. narrow crack or split. ● v. split.

**fist** n. clenched hand. □□ **fistful** n.

**fisticuffs** n.pl. fighting with fists.

**fistula** n. abnormal or artificial passage in body. □□ **fistular** adj. **fistulous** adj.

**fit** ● adj. (fitter) suitable; right and proper; in good health. ● v. (fitted) be or adjust to be right shape and size for; put into place; make or be suitable or competent. ● n. **1** way a thing fits. **2** sudden attack of convulsions or loss of consciousness. **3** sudden outburst of emotion, activity, etc. □□ **fitness** n.

**fitful** adj. spasmodic, intermittent. □□ **fitfully** adv.

**fitted** adj. made to fit closely; with built-in fittings; built-in.

**fitter** n. **1** mechanic who fits together and adjusts machinery. **2** supervisor of cutting, fitting, etc. of garments.

**fitting** ● n. **1** trying-on of garment etc. for adjustment before completion. **2** (fittings) fixtures and furnishings of a building. ● adj. proper, befitting. □□ **fittingly** adv.

**five** adj. & n. one more than four (5, V).

**fix** ● v. **1** make firm, stable, or permanent; fasten, secure. **2** settle, specify. **3** mend, repair. **4** direct (eyes etc.) steadily on; attract and hold (attention etc.) **5** identify, locate. **6** colloq. prepare (food or drink). **7** colloq. kill, deal with (person). **8** arrange result fraudulently.

● n. **1** *colloq.* dilemma, predicament. **2** position determined by bearings etc. **3** *colloq.* dose of addictive drug. **4** dishonest act, bribe.□□ **fixable** *adj.*

**fixated** *adj.* having an obsession.

**fixation** n. **1** fixing. **2** obsession.

**fixative** ● *adj.* tending to fix (colours etc.) ● n. fixative substance.

**fixedly** *adv.* intently.

**fixity** n. fixed state; stability; permanence.

**fixture** n. thing fixed in position; (date fixed for) sporting event; established person or thing.

**fizz** ● v. make hissing or spluttering sound; effervesce.
● n. effervescence; *colloq.* effervescent drink.

**fizzle** ● v. hiss or splutter feebly.
● n. fizzling sound.

**fjord** n. (also **fiord**) narrow sea inlet, as in Norway.

**fl.** *abbr.* **1** floruit. **2** fluid.

**flab** n. *colloq.* fat; flabbiness.

**flabbergast** v. *colloq.* astonish; dumbfound.□□ **flabbergasted** *adj.*

**flabby** *adj.* (**flabbier**) **1** (of flesh) limp, not firm. **2** feeble.□□ **flabbiness** n.

**flaccid** *adj.* soft, loose, and limp.
□□ **flaccidity** n.

**flag** ● n. **1** piece of cloth attached by one edge to pole or rope as country's emblem, standard, or signal; device used as symbol. **2** (**the flag**) *AFL* premiership. **3** plant with bladed leaf (esp. iris).
● v. (**flagged**) **1** grow tired; lag; droop. **2** mark out with flags. **3** give notice of.

**flagellant** ● n. person who scourges himself, herself, or others. ● *adj.* of flagellation.

**flagellate** v. whip or flog, esp. as religious discipline or sexual stimulus. □□ **flagellation** n.

**flageolet** n. small flute.

**flagon** n. large bottle or other vessel for wine.

**flagrant** *adj.* **1** blatant. **2** scandalous. □□ **flagrancy** n. **flagrantly** *adv.*

**flagship** n. **1** admiral's ship. **2** principal vessel, shop, product, etc.

**flagstone** n. flat paving stone.

**flail** ● n. staff with heavy stick swinging from it, used for threshing. ● v. **1** wave or swing wildly. **2** beat (as) with flail.

**flair** n. natural talent; style, finesse.

**flak** n. **1** anti-aircraft fire. **2** criticism; abuse.□ **flak jacket** protective jacket worn by soldiers etc.

**flake** ● n. **1** thin light piece of snow etc. **2** thin broad piece peeled or split off. **3** flesh of shark as food.
● v. **1** take off or come away in flakes; sprinkle with or fall in flakes; *colloq.* □ **flake out** fall asleep from exhaustion; faint. □□ **flaky** *adj.*

**flambé** *adj.* (of food) covered with alcohol and set alight briefly.

**flamboyant** *adj.* ostentatious; showy; florid.□□ **flamboyance** n. **flamboyantly** *adv.*

**flame** ● n. **1** ignited gas; portion of this; bright light; brilliant orange colour. **2** passion, esp. love; *colloq.* sweetheart. ● v. **1** burn; blaze; shine or glow like flame. **2** (of passion) break out; become angry. **3** send abusive message to newsgroup etc. on Internet.

**flamenco** n. Spanish gypsy guitar music with singing.

**flamingo** n. (*pl.* **flamingos** or **flamingoes**) tall long-necked wading bird with mainly pink plumage.

**flammable** *adj.* easily set on fire or excited.□□ **flammability** n.

> **Usage** *Flammable* is often used because *inflammable* could be taken to mean 'not flammable'. The negative is *non-flammable*.

**flan** *n.* pastry case with savoury or sweet filling; sponge base with sweet topping.

**flange** *n.* projecting flat rim, for strengthening etc.

**flank** ● *n.* side of body between ribs and hip; side of mountain, army, etc.; *AFL* outside position. ● *v.* (often as **flanked** *adj.*) be at or move alongside of.

**flannel** *n.* **1** woven woollen usu. napless fabric. **2** face washer. **3** (**flannels**) flannel trousers.

**flannelette** *n.* napped cotton fabric like flannel.

**flap** ● *v.* (**flapped**) **1** move or be moved loosely up and down. **2** beat, flutter. **3** *colloq.* be agitated or panicky. **4** *colloq.* (of ears) listen intently. ● *n.* **1** piece of cloth, wood, etc. attached by one side esp. to cover gap. **2** flapping. **3** *colloq.* agitation, panic. **4** aileron.

**flapjack** *n.* biscuit made with oats.

**flare** ● *v.* **1** blaze suddenly; burst into activity or anger. **2** widen outwards. ● *n.* sudden blaze; device producing flame as signal or illumination; flared shape.

**flash** ● *v.* **1** give out sudden bright light. **2** show suddenly or ostentatiously. **3** come suddenly into sight or mind. **4** move swiftly. **5** cause to shine briefly. **6** *colloq.* indecently expose oneself. ● *n.* **1** sudden burst of flame or light. **2** sudden show of wit or feeling. **3** very brief time; brief news item. **4** device producing brief bright light in photography.
● *adj.* gaudy, showy; vulgar. □ **flash drive** *Computing* data storage device containing flash memory.

**flash flood** sudden destructive flood.

**flash memory** *Computing* type of memory device that retains data in the absence of power. **flash mob** large public gathering at which people perform an unusual or seemingly random act and then disperse.

**flashback** *n.* change of scene in story or film to earlier period.

**flasher** *n.* *colloq.* man who indecently exposes himself.

**flashing** *n.* (usu. metal) strip used to prevent water penetration at roof joint etc.

**flashlight** *n.* electric torch.

**flashpoint** *n.* **1** temperature at which vapour ignites. **2** point at which violence often flares up.

**flask** *n.* narrow-necked bulbous bottle.

**flat** ● *adj.* (**flatter**) **1** horizontal, level; lying at full length. **2** absolute. **3** monotonous; dejected. **4** having lost effervescence or power to generate electric current. **5** below correct pitch in music. ● *adv.* **1** in a flat manner. **2** *colloq.* exactly. ● *n.* **1** flat surface, level ground. **2** set of rooms on one floor, used as a residence. **3** *Mus.* (sign indicating) note lowered by semitone. □ **flat out** at top speed; with maximum effort.

**flatfish** *n.* sea fish with flattened body and both eyes on one side.

**flatmate** *n.* person with whom one shares a flat.

**flatten** *v.* **1** make or become flat. **2** *colloq.* humiliate. **3** knock down.

**flatter** *v.* compliment insincerely; exaggerate the good looks of. □□ **flatterer** *n.* **flattering** *adj.* **flatteringly** *adv.* **flattery** *n.*

**flatulent** *adj.* **1** causing, caused by, or troubled by intestinal wind. **2** inflated, pretentious. □□ **flatulence** *n.*

**flaunt** *v.* display proudly; show off; parade.

> **Usage** *Flaunt* is often confused with *flout* which means 'to disobey contemptuously'.

**flautist** n. flute player.

**flavour** (also **flavor**) ● n. distinctive taste, characteristic quality. ● v. give flavour to; season. □□ **flavourless** adj. **flavoursome** adj.

**flavouring** n. (also **flavoring**) substance used to flavour food or drink.

**flaw** ● n. imperfection. ● v. spoil with flaw. □□ **flawless** adj. **flawlessly** adv.

**flax** n. blue-flowered plant cultivated for its oily seeds (linseed) and for making into linen.

**flaxen** adj. 1 of flax. 2 (of hair) pale yellow.

**flay** v. 1 strip skin or hide off; peel off. 2 criticise severely.

**flea** n. small wingless jumping parasitic insect. □ **flea market** market for second-hand goods.

**fleck** ● n. small patch of colour or light; speck. ● v. mark with fleck.

**fled** see FLEE.

**fledged** adj. (of young bird) able to fly.

**fledgling** (also **fledgeling**) ● n. young bird. ● adj. inexperienced.

**flee** v. (**fled**, **fleeing**) run away (from); leave abruptly.

**fleece** ● n. woolly coat of sheep etc.; this shorn from sheep; fleecy lining etc. ● v. 1 strip of money etc. 2 swindle. 3 shear. 4 cover as with fleece. □□ **fleecy** adj.

**fleet** ● n. 1 warships under one commander-in-chief; (**the fleet**) navy. 2 vehicles operating together or owned by one proprietor. ● adj. swift, nimble.

**fleeting** adj. transitory; brief. □□ **fleetingly** adv.

**flerovium** n. radioactive element (symbol Fl).

**flesh** n. 1 soft substance between skin and bones. 2 plumpness, fat. 3 body, as opposed to mind or soul, esp. as sinful. 4 pulpy substance of fruit etc. 5 (also **flesh-colour**) yellowish pink colour. □□ **fleshy** adj.

**fleshly** adj. worldly; carnal.

**fleur-de-lis** n. (also **fleur-de-lys**) (pl. **fleurs-de-lis**) heraldic design of lily with three petals.

**flew** see FLY.

**flex** ● n. 1 flexible insulated cable. 2 flexiday. ● v. bend; move (muscle) so that it bends a joint; tense (muscle). □ **flex off** take time off under a flexitime system.

**flexible** adj. able to bend without breaking; pliable; easily led; adaptable. □□ **flexibility** n. **flexibly** adv.

**flexiday** n. day off work under flexitime system.

**flexitime** n. system of flexible working hours.

**flibbertigibbet** n. gossiping, frivolous, or restless person.

**flick** ● n. 1 light sharp blow; sudden release of bent finger etc., esp. to propel thing. 2 jerk. 3 colloq. cinema film; (**the flicks**) cinema. ● v. strike or move with flick. □ **flick knife** knife with blade that springs out.

**flicker** ● v. shine or burn unsteadily; flutter; waver. ● n. 1 flickering movement or light. 2 brief feeling (of hope etc.).

**flier** = FLYER.

**flight** n. 1 flying; movement or path of a thing by air; group of birds or aircraft. 2 series of stairs. 3 tail of dart or arrow. 4 fleeing. □ **flight deck** cockpit of large aircraft; deck of aircraft carrier. **flight recorder** electronic device in aircraft recording details of its flight.

**flightless** adj. (of bird etc.) unable to fly.

**flighty** adj. (**flightier**) frivolous, fickle.

**flimsy** adj. (**flimsier**) insubstantial, rickety; unconvincing; (of clothing) thin. □□ **flimsily** adv.

**flinch** v. draw back in fear etc.; wince.

**fling** ● v. (flung, flinging) move or throw violently or hurriedly. ● n. spell of indulgence or wild behaviour.

**flint** n. **1** hard grey stone; piece of this, esp. as tool or weapon. **2** piece of hard alloy used to produce spark. □□ **flinty** adj.

**flintlock** n. old type of gun.

**flip** ● v. (flipped) flick; toss with sharp movement. ● n. **1** action of flipping. **2** somersault. ● adj. colloq. glib; flippant. □ **flip side** **1** less important side of a music single. **2** another aspect or version of something.

**flippant** adj. frivolous; disrespectful; offhand. □□ **flippancy** n. **flippantly** adv.

**flipper** n. **1** limb of turtle, penguin, etc., used in swimming; rubber foot attachment for underwater swimming. **2** Cricket top spinner given extra flip of the fingers.

**flirt** ● v. **1** behave in frivolously amorous or sexually enticing manner. **2** superficially interest oneself (in). **3** trifle. ● n. person who flirts. □□ **flirtation** n. **flirtatious** adj. **flirtatiously** adv. **flirtatiousness** n.

**flit** ● v. (flitted, flitting) **1** move lightly or rapidly; make short flights. **2** disappear secretly, esp. to escape creditors. ● n. act of flitting.

**flitch** n. side of bacon.

**float** ● v. **1** (cause to) rest or drift on surface of liquid; move or be suspended freely in liquid or gas. **2** offer (stocks, shares, etc.) on stock market. **3** (cause or allow to) have fluctuating exchange rate. **4** make (suggestion) to test reactions. ● n. **1** device or structure that floats. **2** decorated platform or tableau on truck in procession etc. **3** closed vehicle for transporting horse(s). **4** supply of loose change; petty cash.

**floaties** n.pl. inflatable arm bands for child learning to swim.

**floating** adj. not settled; variable.

**flocculent** adj. like tufts of wool.

**flock** ● n. **1** group of animals; large crowd of people. **2** people in care of priest etc. **3** shredded wool etc. used as stuffing. ● v. congregate; mass; troop.

**floe** n. sheet of floating ice.

**flog** v. (flogged) **1** beat with whip, stick, etc. **2** make work through violent effort. **3** colloq. steal. **4** colloq. sell.

**flood** ● n. overflow of water on place usually dry; great outpouring; inflow of tide. ● v. cover or fill with flood; overflow; come in great quantities.

**floodlight** ● n. lamp producing broad bright beam. ● v. (floodlit, floodlighting) illuminate with this.

**floor** ● n. **1** lower surface of room; bottom of sea, cave, etc. **2** storey. **3** part of legislative chamber where members sit and speak; right to speak in debate. **4** minimum of prices, wages, etc. **5** colloq. ground. ● v. **1** provide with floor. **2** knock down. **3** baffle. **4** overcome. □ **floor show** cabaret.

**floozie** n. (also **floozy**) colloq. derog. woman, esp. promiscuous one.

**flop** ● v. (flopped) **1** sway about heavily or loosely; move, fall, sit, etc. awkwardly or suddenly. **2** colloq. fail, collapse. **3** make dull soft thud or splash. ● n. **1** flopping movement or sound. **2** colloq. failure. ● adv. with a flop.

**floppy** ● adj. tending to flop; flaccid. ● n. (in full **floppy disk**) flexible disc for storage of computer data. □□ **floppiness** n.

**flora** n. plant life of region or period.

**floral** adj. of or decorated with flowers. □□ **florally** adv.

**floret** n. **1** each of small flowers of flower head. **2** each stem of head of cauliflower, broccoli, etc.

**florid** adj. **1** ruddy. **2** ornate; showy. □□ **floridly** adv. **floridness** n.

**florin** n. hist. silver two shilling coin.

**florist** n. person who deals in or sells flowers.

**floruit** n. & v. (period at which person) was alive and working.

**floss** ● n. **1** rough silk of silkworm's cocoon. **2** silk embroidery thread. **3** dental floss. ● v. clean (teeth) with dental floss. □□ **flossy** adj.

**flotilla** n. small fleet; fleet of small ships.

**flotsam** n. wreckage found floating. □ **flotsam and jetsam** odds and ends.

**flounce** ● v. go or move angrily or impatiently. ● n. **1** flouncing movement. **2** frill on dress etc.

**flounder** ● v. struggle helplessly. ● n. small edible flatfish.

**flour** ● n. meal or powder from ground wheat etc. ● v. sprinkle with flour. □□ **floury** adj.

**flourish** ● v. **1** grow vigorously; thrive, prosper; be in good health. **2** wave; brandish. ● n. showy gesture; ornamental curve in handwriting; Mus. ornate passage or fanfare.

**flout** v. disobey (law etc.) contemptuously.

> **Usage** Flout is often confused with flaunt which means 'to display proudly or show off'.

**flow** ● v. **1** glide along, move smoothly. **2** gush out. **3** hang gracefully. **4** be plentiful or in flood. **5** result. ● n. flowing movement or liquid; stream; rise of tide. □ **flow chart** diagram showing the sequence of events in a process. **go with the**

**flow** be relaxed and not resist the tide of events. ●

**flower** ● n. part of plant from which fruit or seed is developed; plant bearing blossom. ● v. **1** bloom. **2** reach peak. □□ **flowered** adj. **flowery** adj.

**flowerpot** n. pot in which plants are grown.

**flown** SEE FLY.

**flu** n. colloq. influenza.

**fluctuate** ● v. vary; rise and fall. □□ **fluctuation** n.

**flue** n. smoke duct in chimney; channel for conveying heat.

**fluent** adj. expressing oneself easily and naturally, esp. in foreign language. □□ **fluency** n. **fluently** adv.

**fluff** ● n. **1** soft fur, feathers, fabric particles, etc. **2** colloq. mistake in performance etc. ● v. **1** shake into or become soft mass. **2** colloq. make mistake; bungle. □□ **fluffy** adj.

**fluid** ● n. substance, esp. gas or liquid, capable of flowing freely; liquid secretion. ● adj. **1** able to flow freely; constantly changing. □□ **fluidity** n.

**fluke** ● n. **1** lucky accident. **2** parasitic flatworm. ● v. achieve by fluke. □□ **fluky** adj. (also **flukey**)

**flum** n. & v. Aust. colloq. fluke.

**flummery** n. **1** nonsense, flattery. **2** sweet dish of beaten eggs, sugar, etc.

**flummox** v. colloq. bewilder.

**flung** SEE FLING.

**fluorescence** n. light radiation from certain substances; property of absorbing invisible light and emitting visible light. □□ **fluoresce** v. **fluorescent** adj.

**fluoridate** v. add fluoride to (water etc.) □□ **fluoridation** n.

**fluoride** n. compound of fluorine with metal, esp. used to prevent tooth decay. ● adj. containing fluoride.

**fluorinate** v. fluoridate; introduce fluorine into (compound). □□ **fluorination** n.

**fluorine** n. poisonous pale-yellow gaseous element (symbol F).

**fluorocarbon** n. compound of hydrocarbon with fluorine atoms.

**flurry** ● n. 1 gust, squall; burst of activity, excitement, etc. ● v. confuse; agitate.

**flush** ● v. 1 become red in the face. 2 cleanse or dispose of with a flow of water. 3 drive out from cover. ● n. 1 a blush. 2 rush of emotion. 3 rush of water. ● adj. 1 level, in same plane. 2 colloq. having plenty of money.

**fluster** ● v. make agitated and confused. ● n. confused or agitated state. □□ **flustered** adj.

**flute** n. 1 wind instrument consisting of pipe with holes along it and a mouth hole at the side. 2 ornamental groove. 3 tall narrow wine glass.

**flutter** ● v. flap (wings) in flying or trying to fly; wave or flap quickly; move about restlessly; (of pulse etc.) beat feebly or irregularly. ● n. 1 fluttering; tremulous excitement. 2 colloq. small bet on horse. 3 abnormally rapid heartbeat; rapid variation of pitch, esp. of recorded sound.

**fluvial** adj. of or found in rivers.

**flux** n. 1 flowing, flowing out; discharge. 2 continuous change. 3 substance mixed with metal etc. to aid fusion.

**fly** ● v. (flew, flown, flying) 1 move or travel through air with wings or in aircraft; control flight of (aircraft). 2 display (flag). 3 go quickly; flee. ● n. 1 flying. 2 two-winged insect. 3 fastening down the front of trousers. □ **with flying colours** with great credit or success.

**flyblown** adj. tainted by flies' eggs.

**flycatcher** n. bird that catches flying insects.

**flyer** n. (also **flier**) colloq. 1 airman or airwoman; thing that flies in specified way; fast-moving animal etc. 2 small handbill.

**flying** adj. able to fly. □ **flying buttress** buttress based on a structure separate from wall it supports. **flying fox** 1 large fruit-eating bat. 2 Aust. overhead cable and apparatus for transport of material etc. over rough terrain; similar device used for military training, in playgrounds, etc. **flying saucer** alien spacecraft, esp. circular.

**flyleaf** n. blank page at beginning or end of book.

**flysheet** n. outer cover for a tent.

**flyweight** n. weight below bantamweight, in amateur boxing between 48 and 51 kg.

**flywheel** n. heavy wheel revolving on a shaft to regulate machinery.

**FM** abbr. frequency modulation.

**foal** ● n. young of horse or related animal. ● v. give birth to (foal).

**foam** ● n. 1 mass of small bubbles. 2 spongy rubber or plastic. ● v. emit with foam; froth. □□ **foamy** adj.

**fob** n. 1 chain of pocket watch. 2 small pocket for watch etc. 3 tab on key ring. □ **fob off** palm off; get person to accept something inferior.

**focaccia** n. kind of flat Italian bread.

**fo'c's'le** = FORECASTLE.

**focus** n. (pl. **focuses** or **foci**) 1 centre of interest or activity. 2 point at which rays etc. meet after reflection or refraction or from which rays etc. appear to proceed. 3 point at which object must be situated to give well-defined image; adjustment of eye or lens to give clear image; state of clear definition. 4 principal site of infection or disease. ● v. (**focused** or focussed) **1** bring into focus; adjust focus of (lens, eye). **2** concentrate or be concentrated on.

**fodder** n. hay, straw, etc. as animal food.

**foe** n. enemy.

**foetid** = FETID.

**foetus** n. (also **fetus**) (pl. **foetuses**) developed embryo in uterus or egg. □□ **foetal** adj.

**fog** ● n. thick mist. ● v. (**fogged**) cover or become covered with fog or condensed vapour.

**fogey** n. (also **fogy**) (pl. **fogeys** or **fogies**) old-fashioned person.

**foggy** adj. (**foggier**) full of fog; or of like fog; vague.

**foible** n. minor weakness or idiosyncrasy.

**foil** ● n. **1** very thin sheet of metal. **2** person or thing that enhances qualities of another by contrast. **3** long thin sword with a button at the end. ● v. frustrate, defeat.

**foist** v. force (thing, oneself) on to (unwilling person); introduce surreptitiously or unwarrantably.

**fold** ● v. **1** bend so one part lies on another. **2** clasp, envelop. **3** cease to function. **4** enclose (sheep) in a fold. ● n. **1** folded part; line or hollow made by folding. **2** enclosure for sheep.

**folder** n. **1** folding cover or holder for loose papers. **2** Computing directory containing related files or documents.

**foliage** n. leaves, leafage.

**foliate** ● adj. leaflike; having leaves. ● v. split into thin layers. □□ **foliation** n.

**folic acid** n. vitamin of B complex, deficiency of which causes pernicious anaemia.

**folio** ● n. leaf of paper etc. numbered here on front; sheet of paper folded once; book of such sheets. ● adj. (of book) made of folios.

**folk** ● n. (pl. **folk** or **folks**) people; one's relatives. ● adj. (of music, song, etc.) in the traditional style of a country.

**folklore** n. traditional beliefs and tales of community.

**folksy** adj. **1** of or like folk art. **2** friendly, unpretentious. □□ **folksiness** n.

**follicle** n. **1** small sac or vesicle, esp. for hair root. **2** single-carpelled dry fruit opening on one side only to release its seeds. □□ **follicular** adj.

**follow** v. **1** go or come after; go along (route); come next in order or time. **2** act according to (instructions etc.); accept ideas of. **3** take interest in; track (person, group, etc.) by subscribing to their account on social media. **4** be a consequence or conclusion. □ **follow suit** follow person's example. **follow up** pursue; supplement.

**follower** n. **1** supporter, devotee. **2** someone who is tracking particular person, group, etc. on social media. **3** AFL either of two players without fixed position, ruckman.

**following** ● prep. after in time; as sequel to. ● n. group of supporters. ● adj. that follows.

**folly** n. **1** foolishness; foolish act, idea, etc. **2** building for display only.

**foment** v. stir up (trouble).

**fond** adj. **1** liking; affectionate; doting. **2** foolishly optimistic. □□ **fondly** adv. **fondness** n.

**fondant** n. soft sugary sweet.

**fondle** v. stroke lovingly; caress.

**fondue** n. dish of melted cheese.

**font** n. **1** receptacle for baptismal water. **2** (also **fount**) set of printing type of same face and size.

**fontanelle** n. space in infant's skull at angles of parietal bones.

**food** n. substance (esp. solid) that can be taken into the body of animal or plant to maintain its life. □ **food chain** **1** series of organisms each dependent

**foodstuff** *n.* substance used as food.

**fool** ● *n.* foolish person. ● *v.* joke; tease; play about idly; trick.

**foolery** *n.* foolish behaviour.

**foolhardy** *adj.* foolishly bold; reckless. □□ **foolhardily** *adv.* **foolhardiness** *n.*

**foolish** *adj.* lacking good sense or judgement. □□ **foolishly** *adv.* **foolishness** *n.*

**foolscap** *n.* large size of paper, about 330 x 200 mm.

**foot** ● *n.* 1 part of leg below ankle. 2 lowest part or end. (*pl.* **feet** or **foot**) 3 linear measure (in imperial system) of 12 in. (30.48 cm). 4 metrical unit of verse forming part of line. ● *v.* 1 pay (bill). 2 (usu. as **foot it**) go on foot. □ **foot-and-mouth disease** viral disease of cattle etc. □□ **footless** *adj.*

**footage** *n.* a length of TV or cinema film etc.

**football** *n.* large inflated usu. leather ball; team game played with this. □□ **footballer** *n.*

**footer** *n.* 1 person or thing of so many feet in length or height. 2 line or block of text appearing at bottom of each page of a book or document.

**foothills** *n.pl.* low hills near the bottom of a mountain or range.

**foothold** *n.* a place just wide enough for one's foot; a small but secure position gained.

**footing** *n.* 1 foothold; secure position. 2 operational basis. 3 relative position or status. 4 (**footings**) foundation of wall.

**footlights** *n.pl.* row of lights along front of stage floor.

**footloose** *adj.* independent, without responsibilities.

**footnote** *n.* note printed at bottom of page.

**footpath** *n.* path for pedestrians; pavement.

**footprint** *n.* impression left by foot or shoe.

**footsie** *n. colloq.* flirtatious touching of another's feet with one's own.

**footsore** *adj.* with feet sore from walking.

**footstep** *n.* a step; sound of this.

**fop** *n.* man obsessed with fashion, appearance, etc. □□ **foppery** *n.* **foppish** *adj.*

**for** ● *prep.* 1 in place of. 2 as the price or penalty of. 3 in defence or favour of. 4 with a view to. 5 in the direction of. 6 intended to be received or used by. 7 because of. 8 during. ● *conj.* because, since.

**forage** ● *n.* 1 food for horses or cattle. 2 searching for food. ● *v.* search for food; rummage; collect food from.

**foray** ● *n.* sudden attack; raid. ● *v.* make foray.

**forbade** see FORBID.

**forbear** *v.* (**forbore**, **forborne**, **forbearing**) refrain (from).

**forbearance** *n.* patience; tolerance.

**forbid** *v.* (**forbade**, **forbidden**, **forbidding**) order not to; refuse to allow.

**forbidding** *adj.* stern, threatening. □□ **forbiddingly** *adv.*

**force** ● *n.* 1 power, strength, intense effort. 2 coercion, compulsion. 3 group of soldiers, police, etc. 4 influence. 5 person etc. with moral power. ● *v.* 1 compel, coerce. 2 make way, break into, or open by force. 3 drive, propel. 4 cause, produce, or attain by effort; strain. 5 artificially hasten maturity of; accelerate process.

**forceful** *adj.* powerful, impressive. □□ **forcefully** *adv.* **forcefulness** *n.*

**forcemeat** *n.* minced seasoned meat for stuffing or garnish.

**forceps** n. (pl. **forceps**) surgical pincers.

**forcible** adj. done by or involving force; forceful. □□ **forcibly** adv.

**ford** ● n. shallow place where river etc. may be crossed. ● v. cross (water) at ford. □□ **fordable** adj.

**fore** ● adj. situated in front. ● n. front part; bow of ship.

**forearm** n. arm from elbow to wrist or fingertips.

**forebears** n.pl. ancestors.

**foreboding** n. expectation of trouble.

**forecast** ● v. (**forecast, forecasting**) predict; estimate beforehand. ● n. prediction, esp. of weather. □□ **forecaster** n.

**forecastle** n. (also **fo'c's'le**) forward part of ship, formerly living quarters.

**foreclose** v. **1** stop (mortgage) from being redeemable; repossess mortgaged property of (person) when loan is not duly repaid. **2** exclude, prevent. □□ **foreclosure** n.

**forecourt** n. enclosed space in front of building.

**forefathers** n.pl. ancestors.

**forefinger** n. finger next to thumb.

**forefront** n. leading position; foremost part.

**forego** = FORGO.

**foregoing** adj. preceding; previously mentioned.

**foregone conclusion** n. easily predictable result.

**foreground** n. part of view or picture nearest observer.

**forehand** Tennis etc. ● adj. (of stroke) played with palm of hand facing forward. ● n. forehand stroke.

**forehead** n. part of face above eyebrows.

**foreign** adj. **1** of, from, in, or characteristic of, country or language other than one's own; dealing with other countries; of another district, society, etc. **2** unfamiliar, alien; coming from outside. □□ **foreignness** n.

**foreigner** n. person born in or coming from another country.

**foreknowledge** n. knowledge of a thing before it occurs.

**foreleg** n. front leg of animal.

**forelock** n. lock of hair just above forehead.

**foreman** n. worker supervising others; member of jury presiding over its deliberations and speaking on its behalf.

**foremost** ● adj. **1** most notable, best. **2** first, front. ● adv. most importantly.

**forename** n. first name.

**forensic** adj. of or used in law courts. □ **forensic medicine** medical knowledge used in police investigations etc. □□ **forensically** adv.

**foreplay** n. stimulation preceding sexual intercourse.

**forerunner** n. predecessor.

**foresee** v. (**foresaw, foreseen, foreseeing**) see or be aware of beforehand. □□ **foreseeable** adj.

**foreshadow** v. be warning or indication of (future event).

**foreshore** n. shore between high and low water marks.

**foreshorten** v. portray (object) with apparent shortening due to perspective.

**foresight** n. care or provision for future; foreseeing.

**foreskin** n. fold of skin covering end of penis.

**forest** ● n. **1** large area of trees. **2** large number, dense mass. ● v. **1** plant with trees. **2** convert into forest. □□ **forested** adj.

**forestall** v. prevent by advance action; deal with beforehand.

**forester** n. manager of forest; expert in forestry.

**forestry** *n.* science or management of forests.

**foretaste** *n.* small preliminary experience of something.

**foretell** *v.* (foretold, foretelling) predict, prophesy; indicate approach of.

**forethought** *n.* 1 care or provision for future. 2 previous thinking or devising. 3 deliberate intention.

**forever** *adv.* always, constantly.

**forewarn** *v.* warn beforehand.

**foreword** *n.* introductory remarks in book, often not by author.

**forfeit** ● *n.* (thing surrendered as) penalty. ● *adj.* lost or surrendered as penalty. ● *v.* (forfeited) lose right to, or surrender as penalty. □□ **forfeiture** *n.*

**forgather** *v.* assemble; associate.

**forgave** see FORGIVE.

**forge** *v.* 1 make or write in fraudulent imitation. 2 shape by heating and hammering. 3 advance gradually or steadily. ● *n.* furnace etc. for refining metal; blacksmith's workshop. □□ **forger** *n.*

**forgery** *n.* (making of) forged document etc.

**forget** *v.* (forgot, forgotten, forgetting) cease to remember or think about. □□ **forgettable** *adj.*

**forgetful** *adj.* apt to forget; neglectful. □□ **forgetfully** *adv.* **forgetfulness** *n.*

**forgive** *v.* (forgave, forgiven, forgiving) 1 cease to feel angry or bitter towards or about. 2 cancel (a debt). □□ **forgivable** *adj.* **forgiveness** *n.* **forgiving** *adj.*

**forgo** *v.* (also **forego**) (forwent, forgone, forgoing) go without; give up.

**fork** ● *n.* 1 pronged item of cutlery. 2 similar large tool for digging etc. 3 forked part, esp. support for bicycle wheel. 4 (place of) divergence of road etc. ● *v.* 1 form fork or branch. 2 take one road at fork. 3 dig with fork. □ **fork out** *colloq.* pay money (reluctantly).

**forklift** *n.* (in full **forklift truck**) truck with forked device for lifting and carrying loads.

**forlorn** *adj.* sad and abandoned. □ **forlorn hope** only faint hope left; desperate enterprise. □□ **forlornly** *adv.*

**form** ● *n.* 1 shape, appearance; the way in which a thing exists. 2 school class. 3 etiquette. 4 document with blanks to be filled in. 5 a bench. 6 (of athlete, horse, etc.) condition of health and training. 7 reputation or record. ● *v.* shape; produce; constitute; take shape, develop.

**formal** ● *adj.* 1 in accordance with rules, convention, or ceremony. 2 of form. 3 regular in design. ● *n.* official dance etc., esp. to mark graduation from school etc. □□ **formally** *adv.*

**formaldehyde** *n.* colourless gas used as disinfectant and preservative.

**formalin** *n.* solution of formaldehyde in water.

**formalise** *v.* (also **-ize**) 1 give definite (esp. legal) form to. 2 make formal. □□ **formalisation** *n.*

**formalism** *n.* strict adherence to external form without regard to content. □□ **formalist** *n.* **formalistic** *adj.*

**formality** *n.* formal act, regulation, etc., esp. with implied lack of real significance; rigid observance of rules or convention.

**format** ● *n.* 1 shape and size (of book, etc.) 2 style or manner of procedure etc. 3 *Computing* defined structure for holding data etc. in record for processing or storage. ● *v.* (formatted) 1 arrange in format. 2 *Computing* prepare (storage medium) to receive data.

**formation** n. forming; thing formed; particular arrangement, e.g. of troops; rocks or strata with common characteristic.

**formative** adj. serving to form; of formation.

**former** adj. **1** of the past, earlier, previous. **2** (**the former**) first or first-mentioned of two.

**formerly** adv. in former times; previously.

**formic acid** n. colourless irritant volatile acid contained in fluid emitted by ants.

**formidable** adj. **1** inspiring dread, awe, or respect. **2** hard to deal with. □□ **formidably** adv.

**formless** adj. without definite or regular form. □□ **formlessness** n.

**formula** n. (pl. **formulas** or **formulae**) **1** chemical symbols showing constituents of substance. **2** mathematical rule expressed in symbols. **3** fixed form of words. **4** list of ingredients. **5** classification of racing car, esp. by engine capacity. □□ **formulaic** adj.

**formulate** v. **1** express in formula. **2** express clearly and precisely. □□ **formulation** n.

**fornicate** v. arch. or joc. have sexual intercourse outside marriage. □□ **fornication** n. **fornicator** n.

**forsake** v. (**forsook**, **forsaken**, **forsaking**) withdraw one's help or companionship from; abandon.

**forswear** v. (**forswore**, **forsworn**, **forswearing**) renounce on oath.

**fort** n. fortified building or position.

**forte** ● n. person's strong point or speciality. ● adv. Mus. loudly.

**fortescue** n. Aust. fish with venomous spines.

**forth** adv. **1** forward(s). **2** onwards in time. **3** out.

**forthright** adj. outspoken; straightforward; decisive.

**forthwith** adv. at once; without delay.

**fortification** n. fortifying; defensive wall or building etc.

**fortify** v. **1** strengthen against attack. **2** increase vigour, alcohol content, or food value of.

**fortitude** n. courage in pain or adversity.

**fortnight** n. two weeks.

**fortnightly** ● adj. done, produced, or occurring once a fortnight. ● adv. every fortnight.

**fortress** n. fortified building or town.

**fortuitous** adj. happening by chance. □□ **fortuitously** adv. **fortuitousness** n. **fortuity** n.

**fortunate** adj. **1** lucky. **2** auspicious. □□ **fortunately** adv.

**fortune** n. **1** chance or luck in human affairs; person's destiny; good luck. **2** prosperity. **3** colloq. large sum of money. □ **fortune teller** person who claims to foretell future events in people's lives.

**forty** adj. & n. four times ten (40, XL). □ **forty winks** colloq. short sleep. □□ **fortieth** adj. & n.

**forum** n. **1** place of or meeting for public discussion; website where users can post comments about a particular issue and reply to other users' postings. **2** court or tribunal.

**forward** ● adj. **1** onward. **2** towards front. **3** precocious; bold; presumptuous. **4** relating to the future. **5** approaching maturity or completion. ● n. attacking player in football, hockey, etc. ● adv. to front; into prominence; so as to make progress; towards future; forwards. ● v. **1** send (letter etc.) on; dispatch. **2** help to advance; promote.

**forwards** adv. in direction one is facing.

**fossick** v. Aust. **1** rummage, search. **2** search for gold etc. in abandoned workings. □□ **fossicker** n. **fossicking** n.

**fossil** ● n. **1** remains or impression of (usu. pre-historic) plant or animal

**foster** v. **1** promote growth of. **2** bring up (another's child). □ **foster child** child brought up by parents other than its own. **foster home** home in which foster child is reared. **foster parent** person who fosters child.

**fought** SEE FIGHT.

**foul** ● adj. **1** causing disgust. **2** against the rules of a game. ● n. an action that breaks rules. ● adv. unfairly. ● v. **1** make or become foul. **2** entangle or collide with; obstruct. **3** commit a foul against. □□ **foully** adv. **foulness** n.

**found** v. **1** establish (institution etc.); base. **2** melt and mould (metal or glass); make object in this way. See also FIND. □□ **founder** n.

**foundation** n. **1** founding; institution or fund founded. **2** base, first layer; underlying principle.

**founder** v. **1** (of ship) fill with water and sink. **2** (of plan) fail. **3** (of horse) stumble, fall lame.

**foundling** n. abandoned infant of unknown parentage.

**foundry** n. workshop for casting metal.

**fount** n. **1** literary fountain. **2** source. **3** var. of FONT.

**fountain** n. **1** spring or jet of water; structure provided for this. **2** source. □ **fountain pen** pen that can be filled with supply of ink.

**four** adj. & n. one more than three (4, IV). □ **four-wheel drive** motive power acting on all four wheels of vehicle.

**fourfold** adj. & adv. four times as much or many.

**foursome** n. **1** group of four people. **2** golf match between two pairs.

**fourteen** adj. & n. one more than thirteen (14, XIV). □□ **fourteenth** adj. & n.

**fourth** n. **1** next after third. **2** any of four equal parts of thing. □ **fourth estate** the media; journalism. □□ **fourthly** adv.

**fowl** n. chicken kept for eggs and meat; poultry as food.

**fox** n. **1** wild animal of dog family with bushy tail; its fur. **2** cunning person. ● v. deceive or puzzle by acting cunningly.

**foxtrot** n. dance with slow and quick steps; music for this.

**foyer** n. entrance hall in hotel, theatre, etc.

**fracas** n. (pl. fracas) noisy quarrel.

**fracking** n. injecting liquid at high pressure into subterranean rocks so as to force open existing fissures and extract oil or gas.

**fraction** n. part of whole number; small part, amount, etc.; portion of mixture obtained by distillation etc. □□ **fractional** adj. **fractionally** adv.

**fractious** adj. irritable, peevish; unruly.

**fracture** ● n. breakage, esp. of bone. ● v. cause fracture in; suffer fracture.

**fragile** adj. **1** easily broken. **2** delicate. □□ **fragility** n.

**fragment** ● n. part broken off; isolated part. ● v. break into fragments. □□ **fragmentary** adj. **fragmentation** n.

**fragrant** adj. having a pleasant smell. □□ **fragrance** n.

**frail** adj. **1** fragile, delicate. **2** morally weak.

**frailty** n. frail quality; weakness, foible.

**frame** ● n. **1** rigid structure supporting other parts; open case or border enclosing picture or pane of glass etc. **2** single complete picture in a series forming a cinema, television,

---

hardened in rock etc. **2** colloq. antiquated or unchanging person or thing. ● adj. of or like fossil. □ **fossil fuel** fuel such as coal or gas, formed from remains of living organisms. □□ **fossilise** v. (also -ize) **fossilisation** n.

or video film; *Computing* graphic panel in a display window. ● *v.* **1** put or form frame around. **2** construct. **3** *colloq.* concoct false charge etc. against.□ **frame of mind** temporary state of mind.

**framework** *n.* supporting frame.

**franc** *n.* unit of currency in Switzerland; (until 2002) unit of currency of France, Belgium, etc.

**franchise** *n.* **1** right to vote; citizenship. **2** authorisation to sell company's goods etc. in particular area; business or service given a franchise to operate; general title or concept used for creating or marketing a series of products. **3** right granted to person or corporation. ● *v.* grant franchise to.

**francium** *n.* radioactive metallic element (symbol **Fr**).

**frangipani** *n.* tropical American tree with clusters of fragrant flowers; unrelated small Australian rainforest tree.

**frank** ● *adj.* candid, outspoken; undisguised; ingenuous; open. ● *v.* mark (letter) to record payment of postage. ● *n.* franking signature or mark.□ **frankly** *adv.* **frankness** *n.*

**frankfurt** *n.* (also **frankfurter**) seasoned smoked sausage.

**frankincense** *n.* aromatic gum resin burnt as incense.

**frantic** *adj.* **1** wildly excited; frenzied; hurried, anxious; desperate, violent. **2** *colloq.* extreme.□□ **frantically** *adv.*

**fraternal** *adj.* **1** of brothers, brotherly. **2** comradely.□□ **fraternally** *adv.*

**fraternise** *v.* (also **-ize**) **1** associate. **2** make friends, esp. with enemy etc. □□ **fraternisation** *n.*

**fraternity** *n.* **1** religious brotherhood. **2** group with common interests, or of same professional class. **3** brotherhood.

**fratricide** *n.* killing of one's brother or sister.□□ **fratricidal** *adj.*

**Frau** *n.* title of German married woman.

**fraud** *n.* criminal deception; dishonest trick; impostor. □□ **fraudulence** *n.* **fraudulent** *adj.* **fraudulently** *adv.*

**fraught** *adj.* causing or suffering anxiety.□ **fraught with** filled with, involving.

**Fräulein** *n.* title of German unmarried woman.

**fray** ● *v.* **1** make or become worn, esp. producing loose threads in woven material. **2** strain (nerves or temper). ● *n.* a conflict, a fight. □□ **frayed** *adj.*

**frazzle** ● *colloq. n.* exhausted state. ● *v.* wear out; exhaust.

**freak** ● *n.* **1** monstrosity; abnormal person or thing. **2** *colloq.* unconventional person. **3** fanatic of specified kind. ● *v. colloq.* **1** experience or cause to experience strong emotions, whether good or bad. **2** get into panic or rage. **3** (cause to) undergo drug hallucinations etc. □ **freak out** experience strong emotions; behave wildly and irrationally.□□ **freakish** *adj.* **freaky** *adj.*

**freckle** ● *n.* light brown spot on skin. ● *v.* spot or become spotted with freckles.□□ **freckly** *adj.*

**free** ● *adj.* (**freer**) **1** not in the power of another, not a slave; having freedom. **2** not fixed. **3** without; not subject to. **4** costing nothing. **5** not occupied; not in use. **6** lavish. ● *adv.* freely; without cost. ● *v.* (**frees**, **freed**) make free; rid of; clear, disentangle.□ **free fall** unrestricted falling under force of gravity, esp. part of skydive before parachute opens. **free from** not containing. **free market** market governed by unrestricted competition. **free-range** (of hens) allowed to range freely in search of

food; (of eggs) from such hens.
□□ **freely** adv.

**freebie** n. colloq. something provided free of charge.

**freebooter** n. pirate.

**freedom** n. 1 being free; independence. 2 frankness. 3 unrestricted use. 4 honorary membership or citizenship.

**freehand** adj. (of drawing or plan) done by hand without special instruments or guides.

**freehold** n. complete ownership of property for unlimited period; such land or property. □□ **freeholder** n.

**freelance** ● n. person working for no fixed employer. ● v. work as freelance. ● adv. as freelance.

**Freemason** n. member of fraternity for mutual help with secret rituals. □□ **Freemasonry** n.

**freesia** n. African bulb with fragrant flowers.

**freestyle** ● adj. (of race or contest) in which all styles are allowed. ● n. swimming race allowing any stroke.

**freeway** n. motorway.

**freewheel** v. 1 ride a bicycle without pedalling. 2 act without constraint.

**freeze** ● v. (froze, frozen, freezing) 1 change from liquid to solid by extreme cold; be so cold that water turns to ice; preserve by refrigeration; chill or be chilled by extreme cold or fear. 2 make (assets) unable to be realised; hold (prices or wages) at a fixed level. 3 stop, stand very still. ● n. 1 period of freezing weather. 2 freezing of prices etc.

**freezer** n. refrigerated container for preserving food in frozen state.

**freight** ● n. transport of goods; goods transported; charge for transport of goods. ● v. transport as or load with freight.

**freighter** n. ship or aircraft for carrying freight.

**Fremantle doctor** see DOCTOR 3.

**French** adj. & n. (a native, the language) of France. □ **French bread** white bread in a long crisp loaf. **French dressing** salad dressing of oil and vinegar. **French fries** = CHIP n. **French horn** brass wind instrument with a coiled tube. **French polish** polish (wood) with shellac polish. **French window** window reaching to ground, used also as door.

**frenetic** adj. frantic, frenzied. □□ **frenetically** adv.

**frenzy** n. 1 mental derangement. 2 wild excitement or fury. □□ **frenzied** adj.

**frequency** n. commonness of occurrence; frequent occurrence; rate of recurrence (of vibration etc.)

**frequent** ● adj. occurring often or in close succession; habitual. ● v. go to habitually. □□ **frequently** adv.

**fresco** n. (pl. **frescos** or **frescoes**) painting on fresh plaster.

**fresh** ● adj. 1 newly made or obtained. 2 other, different. 3 new. 4 additional. 5 lately arrived from. 6 not stale or faded. 7 (of food) not preserved. 8 (of water) not salty. 9 pure, refreshing. 10 (of wind) brisk. 11 colloq. cheeky. 12 amorously impudent. 13 inexperienced. ● adv. newly, recently. □□ **freshly** adv. **freshness** n.

**freshen** v. 1 make or become fresh. 2 wash, tidy oneself, etc. 3 revive.

**freshwater** adj. of fresh water, not of sea.

**fret** ● v. (**fretted**) be worried or distressed. ● n. bar or ridge on finger board of guitar etc.

**fretful** adj. constantly worrying or crying. □□ **fretfully** adv.

**Fri.** abbr. Friday.

**friable** adj. easily crumbled. □□ **friability** n.

**friand** *n.* Aust. small cake made from almond meal.

**friar** *n.* member of certain male religious orders.

**friary** *n.* monastery for friars.

**fricassee** ● *n.* pieces of meat in thick sauce. ● *v.* make a fricassee of.

**friction** *n.* 1 rubbing of one object against another; resistance so encountered. 2 clash of wills, opinions, etc. □□ **frictional** *adj.*

**Friday** *n.* day of week following Thursday.

**fridge** *abbr.* refrigerator.

**friend** *n.* 1 supportive and respected associate, esp. one for whom affection is felt; ally; kind person. 2 contact on social networking website. 3 supporter of institution etc. □□ **friendship** *n.*

**friendly** *adj.* (**friendlier**) outgoing, kindly; on amicable terms; not hostile; user-friendly. □□ **friendliness** *n.*

**Friesian** *n.* breed of black and white dairy cattle.

**frieze** *n.* part of entablature, often filled with sculpture, between architrave and cornice; band of decoration, esp. at top of wall.

**frigate** *n.* naval escort vessel.

**fright** *n.* 1 (instance of) sudden or extreme fear. 2 grotesque-looking person or thing.

**frighten** *v.* fill with fright; drive by fright. □□ **frightening** *adj.* **frighteningly** *adv.*

**frightful** *adj.* 1 dreadful, shocking, revolting; *colloq.* extremely bad. 2 *colloq.* extreme. □□ **frightfully** *adv.*

**frigid** *adj.* 1 unfriendly, cold. 2 *derog.* (of woman) sexually unresponsive. 3 (of climate) cold. □□ **frigidity** *n.*

**frill** *n.* ornamental edging of gathered or pleated material; unnecessary embellishments, affectations. □□ **frilly** *adj.*

**fringe** ● *n.* 1 border of tassels or loose threads; any border or edging; front hair cut to hang over forehead; outer limit. 2 unimportant area or part; area of sparse settlement bordering arid inland. ● *v.* adorn with fringe; serve as fringe to. ● *adj.* (of theatre etc.) unconventional. □ **fringe benefit** one provided in addition to wages.

**frippery** *n.* showy unnecessary finery or ornament.

**frisbee** *n.* propr. concave plastic disc for skimming through air as outdoor game.

**frisk** ● *v.* 1 leap or skip playfully. 2 *colloq.* search (person). ● *n.* playful leap or skip.

**frisky** *adj.* (**friskier**) lively, playful; *colloq.* sexually aroused.

**frisson** *n.* emotional thrill.

**frittata** *n.* kind of omelette with herbs, vegetables, etc.

**fritter** ● *v.* waste triflingly. ● *n.* fruit, meat, etc. coated in batter and fried.

**fritz** *n.* (also **devon**, German sausage) bland sausage usu. sliced and eaten cold.

**frivolous** *adj.* not serious, silly, shallow; trifling. □□ **frivolity** *n.*

**frizz** *v.* form (hair) into tight curls. ● *n.* frizzed hair or state. □□ **frizzy** *adj.*

**frizzle** *v.* 1 fry until crisp. 2 form (hair) into tight curls.

**frock** *n.* 1 woman's or girl's dress. 2 monk's or priest's gown.

**frog** *n.* 1 tailless leaping amphibian. 2 ornamental coat fastening of button and loop. □ **frog in one's throat** *colloq.* hoarseness.

**frogman** *n.* (*pl.* **-men**) swimmer with rubber suit and oxygen supply for working under water.

**frogmarch** *v.* hustle (person) forcibly, holding the arms.

**frogmouth** n. nocturnal bird with a wide frog-like beak and mottled plumage.

**frolic** ● v. (**frolicked, frolicking**) play about cheerfully. ● n. cheerful play.

**from** prep. expressing separation or origin.

**fromage frais** n. type of soft cheese.

**frond** n. leaflike part of fern, palm, seaweed, etc.

**frons** n. (pl. **frontes**) Zool. forehead or equivalent part of animal.

**front** ● n. 1 side or part normally nearer to or towards the spectator or line of motion. 2 outward appearance; cover for secret activities. 3 boundary between warm and cold air masses. 4 battle line; forward edge of advancing bushfire. ● adj. of or at the front. ● v. 1 face, have the front forwards. 2 colloq. serve as cover for secret activities. 3 colloq. turn up, make an appearance. □ **front runner** favourite in race, election, etc. **in front** at the front.

**frontage** n. 1 front of building. 2 land next to street, water, etc. 3 extent of front.

**frontal** adj. of or on front; of forehead.

**frontbencher** n. MP entitled to sit on front benches in Parliament, reserved for ministers and the shadow cabinet.

**frontier** n. 1 border between countries; district on each side of this. 2 limits of attainment or knowledge in subject. □□ **frontiersman** n.

**frontispiece** n. illustration facing title page of book.

**frost** ● n. frozen dew or vapour; temperature below freezing point. ● v. 1 become covered with frost; cover (as) with frost. 2 roughen surface of (glass) to make opaque.

**frostbite** n. injury to body tissues due to freezing. □□ **frostbitten** adj.

**frosting** n. icing.

**frosty** adj. (**frostier**) 1 cold or covered with frost. 2 unfriendly. □□ **frostiness** n.

**froth** ● n. 1 foam. 2 idle talk. ● v. 1 emit or gather froth. 2 cause (beer etc.) to foam. □□ **frothy** adj.

**frown** ● v. wrinkle one's brows in thought or disapproval. ● n. frowning movement or look. □ **frown on** disapprove of.

**frowzy** adj. (also **frowsy**) fusty; slatternly, dingy.

**froze** see FREEZE.

**frozen** see FREEZE.

**fructose** n. sugar in honey, fruits, etc.

**frugal** adj. sparing; meagre. □□ **frugality** n. **frugally** adv.

**fruit** ● n. 1 seed-bearing part of plant or tree; this as food. 2 (**fruits**) the product of labour. ● v. bear fruit.

**fruiterer** n. dealer in fruit.

**fruitful** adj. 1 productive. 2 successful. □□ **fruitfully** adv.

**fruition** n. realisation of aims or hopes.

**fruitless** adj. 1 not bearing fruit. 2 useless, unsuccessful. □□ **fruitlessly** adv.

**fruity** adj. (**fruitier**) 1 of or resembling fruit. 2 (of voice etc.) deep and rich. 3 colloq. slightly indecent.

**frump** n. offens. dowdy woman. □□ **frumpish** adj. **frumpy** adj.

**frustrate** v. prevent from achieving something; prevent something being achieved. □□ **frustrating** adj. **frustratingly** adv. **frustration** n.

**fry** ● v. (**fried, frying**) cook or be cooked in hot oil or fat. ● n. 1 lamb's liver as food. (pl. **fry**) 2 young fish. 3 (**fries**) oblong strips of potato fried in oil. □ **small fry** people of little importance. □□ **fryer** n.

**frypan** n. (electric) frying pan.

**ft** abbr. foot, feet.

**FTA** abbr. Free Trade Agreement.

**fuchsia** *n.* shrub with drooping flowers.

**fuck** *coarse colloq.* ● *v.* have sexual intercourse (with). ● *n.* sexual intercourse; partner in this. ● *int.* 1 expressing anger or annoyance. 2 expressing amazement or delight. □ **fuck off** go away.

**fuddle** *v.* confuse, esp. with alcohol.

**fuddy-duddy** *colloq.* ● *adj.* old-fashioned or quaintly fussy. ● *n.* such person.

**fudge** ● *n.* 1 soft toffee-like sweet. 2 faking. ● *v.* 1 make or do clumsily or dishonestly. 2 fake.

**fuel** ● *n.* 1 material for burning or as source of heat, power, or nuclear energy. 2 thing that sustains or inflames passion etc. ● *v.* (fuelled) 1 supply with fuel. 2 inflame.

**fug** *n. colloq.* stuffy atmosphere. □□ **fuggy** *adj.*

**fugitive** ● *n.* person who flees. ● *adj.* fleeing; transient, fleeting.

**fugue** *n.* piece of music in which short melody or phrase is introduced by one part and taken up and developed by others.□□ **fugal** *adj.*

**führer** *n.* (also **fuehrer**) leader, esp. a tyrannical one.

**fulcrum** *n.* (*pl.* **fulcrums** or **fulcra**) point on which lever is supported.

**fulfil** *v.* (**fulfilled**) accomplish, carry out (task); satisfy, do what is required by (contract etc.) □□ **fulfilment** *n.*

**full** ● *adj.* 1 holding or having as much as is possible; copious. 2 complete. 3 plump. 4 made with material hanging in folds. 5 (of tone) deep and mellow. 6 *colloq.* drunk. ● *adv.* completely; exactly. □ **full back** (in some sports) defensive player near goal.

**full-blooded** vigorous, hearty.

**full-blown** fully developed. **full moon** moon with the whole disc illuminated. **full-scale** of actual size, not reduced. **full stop** dot used as punctuation mark at end of sentence or abbreviation; complete stop. □□ **fully** *adv.*

**fulminate** *v.* 1 criticise loudly and forcefully. 2 explode, flash. □□ **fulmination** *n.*

**fulsome** *adj.* 1 complimentary or flattering to an excessive degree. 2 generous or abundant. □□ **fulsomely** *adv.*

**fumble** ● *v.* grope about; handle clumsily or nervously. ● *n.* act of fumbling.

**fume** ● *n.* exuded gas, smoke, or vapour. ● *v.* 1 emit fumes; subject to fumes. 2 be very angry.

**fumigate** *v.* disinfect or purify with chemical fumes.□□ **fumigation** *n.* **fumigator** *n.*

**fun** *n.* 1 playful amusement; source of this. 2 mockery.□ **make fun of** mock; ridicule.

**function** ● *n.* 1 proper role etc.; official duty; public or social occasion. 2 *Math.* quantity whose value depends on varying values of others. 3 *Computing* program unit that computes single value. ● *v.* fulfil function, operate; be in working order; perform role of (another person or thing).

**functional** *adj.* of or serving a function; practical rather than attractive; in working order. □□ **functionally** *adv.*

**functionary** *n.* an official.

**fund** ● *n.* sum of money for special purpose; (**funds**) monetary resources. ● *v.* provide with money.

**fundamental** ● *adj.* of or being base or foundation; essential, primary. ● *n.* fundamental fact or principle.□□ **fundamentally** *adv.*

**fundamentalist** *n.* person who upholds strict or literal interpretation

of religious beliefs.
□□ **fundamentalism** n.

**funeral** ● n. ceremonial burial or cremation of dead. ● adj. of or used at funerals.

**funerary** adj. of or used at funerals.

**funereal** adj. of or appropriate to funeral; dismal, dark.
□□ **funereally** adv.

**fungicide** n. substance that kills fungi.□□ **fungicidal** adj.

**fungus** n. (pl. **fungi**) plant without green colouring matter, e.g. mushroom.□□ **fungal** adj. **fungoid** adj. **fungous** adj.

**funicular** n. cable railway with ascending and descending cars counterbalanced.

**funk** n. colloq. dance music with heavy rhythmical beat.

**funky** adj. 1 of funk. 2 fashionable; exciting, excellent.

**funnel** n. tube widening at top, for pouring liquid etc. into small opening; chimney of steam engine or ship. ● v. (**funnelled**) guide or move (as) through funnel.

**funny** ● adj. (**funnier**) 1 amusing, comical. 2 strange, perplexing, hard to account for. 3 impertinent.
● n. colloq. joke.□ **funny bone** part of elbow over which very sensitive nerve passes.□□ **funnily** adv.

**fur** ● n. 1 short fine animal hair; hide with fur on it; garment of or lined with fur. 2 coating on tongue, in kettle, etc. ● v. (**furred**) cover or become covered in fur.

**furbish** v. refurbish.

**furious** adj. very angry; raging, frantic.□□ **furiously** adv.

**furl** v. roll up (sail, umbrella, etc.); become furled.

**furlong** n. (in imperial system) eighth of mile (201.168 m).

**furlough** n. leave of absence.

**furnace** n. chamber for intense heating by fire; very hot place.

**furnish** v. equip with furniture; provide, supply.

**furnishings** n.pl. furniture and fitments.

**furniture** n. movable contents of house, room, etc.; equipment; accessories, e.g. handles and locks.

**furore** n. uproar; enthusiasm.

**furphy** n. Aust. false report or rumour; absurd story.

**furrier** n. dealer in or dresser of furs.

**furrow** ● n. narrow trench made by plough; rut; wrinkle. ● v. plough; make furrows in.

**furry** adj. (**furrier**) like or covered with fur.

**further** ● adv. & adj. (also **farther**) at or to greater distance; more distant; to greater extent; in addition.
□□ **furtherance** n.

**furthest** ● adj. most distant.
● adv. to or at the greatest distance.

**furtive** adj. sly, stealthy.□□ **furtively** adv.

**fury** n. wild anger, rage; violence.

**fuse** ● v. 1 blend (metals etc.); become blended; unite. 2 fit with fuse; stop functioning because of melting of fuse. ● n. strip of wire placed in electric circuit to melt and interrupt current when circuit is overloaded; (also **fuze**) a length of easily burnt material for igniting bomb or explosive.

**fuselage** n. body of an aeroplane.

**fusible** adj. that can be melted.
□□ **fusibility** n.

**fusillade** n. continuous discharge of firearms or outburst of criticism etc.

**fusion** n. fusing; blending; union of atomic nuclei with release of energy.

**fuss** ● n. 1 excited commotion; bustle. 2 excessive concern about trivial things. 3 sustained protest.
● v. behave with nervous concern; agitate, worry.□□ **fusser** n.

**fussed** adj. worried, concerned, bothered.

**fussy** *adj.* (**fussier**) inclined to fuss; over-elaborate; fastidious.

**fustian** *n.* **1** thick twilled cotton. **2** pompous language.

**fusty** *adj.* (**fustier**) musty, stuffy; antiquated. □□ **fustiness** *n.*

**futile** *adj.* useless, ineffectual. □□ **futility** *n.*

**futon** *n.* Japanese mattress used as bed; this with frame.

**future** ● *adj.* about to happen, be, or become; of time to come; *Gram.* (of tense) describing event yet to happen. ● *n.* **1** time to come; future events or condition etc. **2** prospect of success etc. **3** *Gram.* future tense. **4** (**futures**) *Stock Exch.* goods etc. sold for future delivery.

**futuristic** *adj.* suitable for the future; ultra-modern.

**fuzz** *n.* fluff; fluffy or frizzy thing.

**fuzzy** *adj.* (**fuzzier**) fluffy; blurred, indistinct.

**FYI** *abbr.* for your information.

# Gg

**G** *abbr.* **1** giga-; gauss. **2** (of film or video game) classified as 'for general audiences'.

**g** *abbr.* gram(s); gravity; generation.

**gab** *colloq.* • *n.* **1** talk, idle chitchat. **2** smooth eloquence. • *v.* talk idly, chitchat.

**gabble** • *v.* talk or utter unintelligibly or too fast. • *n.* rapid talk.□□ **gabbler** *n.*

**gaberdine** *n.* (also **gabardine**) twill-woven cloth; raincoat etc. made of this.

**gable** *n.* triangular upper part of wall at end of ridged roof; gable-topped wall.□□ **gabled** *adj.*

**gad** *v.* (**gadded**)□ **gad about** go about idly or in search of pleasure.

**gadabout** *n.* person who gads about.

**gadfly** *n.* **1** fly that bites cattle etc. **2** stingingly critical or irritating person.

**gadget** *n.* small mechanical device or tool.□□ **gadgetry** *n.*

**gadolinium** *n.* soft silvery white element (symbol Gd).

**Gaelic** • *n.* Celtic language of Ireland and Scotland. • *adj.* of the Celts or the Celtic languages.

**gaff** • *n.* stick with hook for landing fish; barbed fishing spear. • *v.* seize (a fish) with gaff.

**gaffe** *n.* blunder; indiscreet act or remark.

**gaffer** *n.* chief electrician in film unit.

**gag** • *n.* **1** thing thrust into or tied across mouth to prevent speaking or crying out; closure of debate in parliament; thing restricting free speech. **2** joke or comic scene. • *v.* (**gagged**) **1** apply gag to; silence; deprive of free speech; apply gag in parliament. **2** choke, retch.

**gage** *n.* **1** pledge, thing deposited as security. **2** symbol of challenge to fight.

**gaggle** *n.* **1** flock of geese. **2** *colloq.* disorganised group of people.

**gaiety** *n. dated* being merry; mirth; merrymaking; bright appearance.

**gain** • *v.* **1** obtain, win; acquire, earn; get more of, improve. **2** benefit, profit. **3** (of clock etc.) become fast. **4** come closer to person or thing pursued. **5** reach (desired place). • *n.* **1** increase (of wealth), profit; improvement. **2** *Electronics* factor by which power etc. is increased; logarithm of this. **3** volume of amplifier.

**gainful** *adj.* **1** (of employment) paid. **2** lucrative.□□ **gainfully** *adv.*

**gainsay** *v.* deny, contradict.

**gait** *n.* manner of walking or proceeding.

**gaiter** *n.* covering for lower leg.

**gala** • *n.* festive occasion. • *adj.* festive, celebratory.

**galah** *n. Aust.* **1** grey-backed, pink-breasted cockatoo. **2** *colloq.* fool, idiot.

**galaxy** *n.* independent system of stars, gas, dust, etc., in space; (**the Galaxy**) Milky Way.□□ **galactic** *adj.*

**gale** *n.* **1** very strong wind; storm. **2** outburst, esp. of laughter.

**gall** • *n.* **1** impudence, boldness. **2** something very hurtful. **3** bile. **4** sore made by chafing; place rubbed bare. **5** abnormal growth produced by insects etc. on plants. • *v.* **1** rub sore. **2** vex, humiliate.□ **gall bladder** organ attached to the liver, storing bile.

**gallant** *adj.* **1** brave; fine, stately. **2** very attentive to women. □□ **gallantly** *adv.* **gallantry** *n.*

**galleon** *n.* large Spanish sailing ship of the 15th–17th centuries.

**gallery** *n.* **1** room or building for showing works of art. **2** balcony in theatre or hall. **3** covered walk. **4** long narrow room or passage. **5** group of spectators at golf match etc.

**galley** *n.* **1** *hist.* long flat single-decked vessel usu. rowed by slaves. **2** ship's or aircraft's kitchen. **3** (in full **galley proof**) *Printing* proof in continuous form before division into pages.

**gallinaceous** *adj.* of the order of birds including domestic poultry.

**galling** *adj.* annoying.

**gallium** *n.* soft bluish-white metallic element (symbol Ga).

**gallivant** *v.* gad about, flirt.

**gallon** *n.* **1** measure of capacity, equal to eight pints (approximately 4.5 litres). **2** (in *pl.*) *colloq.* large amount.

**gallop** ● *n.* fastest pace of horse; a ride at this pace. ● *v.* (**galloped**) go at gallop; go fast.

**gallows** *n.* framework with noose for hanging criminals.

**gallstone** *n.* small hard mass forming in gall bladder.

**Gallup poll** *n. propr.* assessment of public opinion by questioning sample group.

**galore** *adj.* in abundance.

**galoshes** *n.pl.* (also **goloshes**) waterproof overshoes.

**galvanic** *adj.* **1** producing an electric current by chemical action; (of electricity) produced thus. **2** stimulating; full of energy.

**galvanise** *v.* (also **-ize**) **1** stimulate into activity. **2** coat (iron) with zinc. □□ **galvanisation** *n.*

**galvanometer** *n.* instrument for detecting and measuring small electric currents.

**gambit** *n.* **1** opening move. **2** *Chess* opening with sacrifice of pawn etc.

**gamble** ● *v.* play games of chance for money; bet (money); lose by gambling; act in the hope of.
● *n.* risky undertaking; spell of gambling. □□ **gambler** *n.*

**gambol** ● *v.* (**gambolled**) skip or jump about playfully. ● *n.* frolic.

**game** ● *n.* **1** activity that one engages in for amusement or fun; form of play or sport; section of this as scoring unit. **2** a scheme. **3** wild animals or birds hunted for sport or food; their flesh as food. ● *adj.* brave; willing. ● *v.* **1** manipulate (a situation). **2** gamble for money. **3** play video games. □□ **gamely** *adv.*

**gamer** *n.* person who plays video games etc.

**gamete** *n.* mature germ cell able to unite with another in sexual reproduction. □□ **gametic** *adj.*

**gaming** *n.* **1** playing gambling games. **2** playing video games.

**gamma radiation** *n.* (also **gamma rays**) electromagnetic radiation of shorter wavelength than X-rays.

**gammon** *n.* bottom piece of flitch of bacon including hind leg; ham of pig cured like bacon.

**gammy** *adj. colloq.* lame, crippled.

**gamut** *n.* entire range or scope.

**gander** *n.* **1** male goose. **2** *colloq.* look, glance.

**gang** *n.* **1** band of people associating for some (usu. antisocial or criminal) purpose. **2** set of workers, slaves, or prisoners. □ **gang rape** rape of one person by several people. **gang up (on)** combine in group (against person).

**gang-gang** *n. Aust.* grey cockatoo.

**gangling** *adj.* (of person) loosely built; lanky.

**ganglion** *n.* (*pl.* **ganglia** or **ganglions**) group of nerve cells; cyst on tendon.

**gangplank** *n.* movable plank for boarding or disembarking from ship etc.

**gangrene** n. death of body tissue, usu. resulting from obstructed circulation. □□ **gangrenous** adj.

**gangster** n. member of gang of violent criminals.

**gangway** n. 1 passage, esp. between rows of seats. 2 opening in ship's bulwarks. 3 bridge from ship to shore.

**gannet** n. large diving sea bird.

**gantry** n. structure supporting travelling crane, road signals, rocket-launching equipment, etc.

**gaol** = JAIL.

**gap** n. 1 empty space, interval. 2 deficiency. 3 breach in hedge, fence, etc. 4 wide divergence in views etc. 5 gorge, pass. □ **gap insurance** Aust. private health insurance taken to cover difference between scheduled fee and Medicare pay-out. □□ **gappy** adj.

**gape** • v. 1 open one's mouth wide; be or become wide open; split. 2 stare at. • n. 1 open-mouthed stare. 2 opening.

**garage** • n. building for housing vehicle(s); establishment selling petrol, repairing vehicles, etc. • v. put or keep in garage. □ **garage sale** sale of miscellaneous household goods.

**garam masala** n. fragrant mixture of spices.

**garb** • n. clothing, esp. of distinctive kind. • v. dress.

**garbage** n. 1 refuse, esp. kitchen waste; trash, worthless stuff. 2 colloq. nonsense.

**garble** v. (esp. as **garbled** adj.) distort or confuse (facts, messages, etc.)

**garden** • n. piece of ground for growing flowers, vegetables, etc.; (**gardens**) ornamental public grounds. • v. cultivate or tend garden. □□ **gardening** n.

**gardener** n. person who gardens, esp. for living.

**gardenia** n. tree or shrub with fragrant flowers.

**garfish** n. marine fish with long spearlike snout.

**gargantuan** adj. gigantic.

**gargle** • v. wash (throat) with liquid kept in motion by breathing out through it. • n. liquid for gargling.

**gargoyle** n. grotesque carved spout projecting from gutter of building.

**garish** adj. obtrusively bright; showy; gaudy. □□ **garishly** adv. **garishness** n.

**garland** • n. wreath of flowers etc. • v. adorn or crown with garland(s).

**garlic** n. plant of onion family with pungent bulb used in cookery. □□ **garlicky** adj.

**garment** n. article of clothing.

**garner** • v. collect; store. • n. storehouse or granary.

**garnet** n. glassy silicate mineral, esp. red kind used as gem.

**garnish** • v. decorate (esp. food). • n. decoration, esp. to food.

**garret** n. attic or room in roof.

**garrison** • n. troops stationed in town; building they occupy. • v. provide with or occupy as garrison.

**garrotte** (also **garote**) • v. kill by strangulation, esp. with wire collar. • n. device used for this.

**garrulous** adj. talkative, esp. on trivial matters; wordy. □□ **garrulity** n. **garrulousness** n.

**garter** n. band worn to keep sock or stocking up. □ **garter stitch** plain knitting stitch.

**gas** • n. (pl. **gases**) any airlike substance (i.e. not solid or liquid); such substance used as fuel or as anaesthetic. • v. (**gassed**) 1 kill or overcome by poisonous gas. 2 colloq. talk idly or boastfully. □ **gas chamber** room filled with poisonous gas to kill people. **gas mask** device worn over face as protection against poisonous gas.

**gaseous** adj. of or like gas.

**gash** ● n. long deep slash, cut, or wound. ● v. make gash in.

**gasket** n. sheet or ring of rubber etc., shaped to seal the junction of metal surfaces.

**gasoline** n. (also **gasolene**) US petrol.

**gasometer** n. large tank from which gas is distributed.

**gasp** ● v. catch one's breath with an open mouth as in exhaustion or astonishment; utter with gasps. 2 be filled with desire for, crave. ● n. convulsive catching of breath.

**gassy** adj. of or like gas; full of gas.

**gastric** adj. of the stomach. □ **gastric flu** colloq. intestinal disorder of unknown cause.

**gastro** n. Aust. colloq. gastroenteritis; similar gastric disorder.

**gastroenteritis** n. inflammation of stomach and intestines.

**gastronomy** n. science or art of good eating and drinking. □□ **gastronomic** adj. **gastronomically** adv.

**gastropod** n. mollusc that moves by means of ventral muscular organ, e.g. snail.

**gate** n. 1 hinged barrier used to close opening through wall, fence, etc.; such opening; means of entrance or exit; numbered place of access to aircraft at airport. 2 device regulating passage of water in lock etc. 3 number of people paying to enter sports ground etc.; (in full **gate money**) money taken thus.

**gateau** n. (pl. **gateaus** or **gateaux**) large rich cake.

**gatecrash** v. go to (party etc.) without being invited. □□ **gatecrasher** n.

**gateway** n. 1 opening closed by gate. 2 means of access. 3 device interconnecting two computer networks.

**gather** ● v. 1 bring or come together; accumulate; collect (harvest, dust, etc.) 2 infer, deduce. 3 increase (speed). 4 summon up (energy etc.) 5 draw together in folds or wrinkles. ● n. fold or pleat.

**gathering** n. assembly.

**gauche** adj. socially awkward; tactless. □□ **gauchely** adv. **gaucheness** n.

**gaucho** n. (pl. **gauchos**) S. American cowboy.

**gaudy** adj. tastelessly showy. □□ **gaudily** adv. **gaudiness** n.

**gauge** ● n. 1 standard measure; instrument for measuring. 2 distance between rails or opposite wheels; capacity, extent. 3 criterion, test. ● v. measure exactly; measure the capacity or content of; estimate.

**gaunt** adj. lean, haggard; grim, desolate. □□ **gauntness** n.

**gauntlet** n. 1 stout glove with long loose wrist. 2 hist. armoured glove. □ **run the gauntlet** undergo harsh criticism. **throw down the gauntlet** issue challenge.

**gauss** n. (pl. **gauss** or **gausses**) unit of magnetic induction.

**gauze** n. thin transparent fabric of silk, cotton, etc.; fine mesh of wire etc. □□ **gauzy** adj.

**gave** past of GIVE.

**gavel** n. auctioneer's, chairperson's, or judge's hammer.

**gavotte** n. old French dance; music for this.

**gawk** ● v. colloq. gawp. ● n. awkward or bashful person.

**gawky** adj. awkward or ungainly.

**gawp** v. colloq. stare stupidly or obtrusively.

**gay** adj. 1 homosexual. 2 dated light-hearted, cheerful; brightly coloured. ● n. homosexual. □□ **gaily** adv.

**gaze** ● v. look fixedly. ● n. intent look.

**gazebo** n. free-standing garden structure with wide view.

**gazelle** n. small antelope.

**gazette** • n. newspaper; official government publication.
• v. publish in a gazette.

**gazetteer** n. geographical index.

**gazillion** n. colloq. very large number or quantity.

**gazump** v. colloq. raise price of property after accepting offer (from buyer); swindle.

**Gb** abbr. gigabyte.

**GBH** abbr. **1** grievous bodily harm. **2** = GHB.

**g'day** int. Aust. colloq. good-day.

**GDP** abbr. gross domestic product.

**gear** • n. **1** (often in pl.) set of toothed wheels that work together, esp. those connecting engine to road wheels; particular setting of these. **2** equipment; personal belongings. **3** colloq. clothing. • v. **1** adjust or adapt to. **2** equip with gears, make ready.

**gearbox** n. (case enclosing) set of gears, esp. in vehicle.

**gearing** n. **1** set or arrangement of gears. **2** Finance proportion of capital existing in form of debt.

**gearstick** n. (also **gearshift**) lever used to engage or change gear.

**gecko** n. tropical lizard.

**geebung** n. fruit of an Australian shrub, having an edible fleshy layer around the stone.

**geek** n. colloq. **1** Aust. look. **2** socially inept or studious person.

**geese** see GOOSE.

**geezer** n. colloq. peculiar person; person, bloke, etc.; old man.

**Geiger counter** n. device for detecting and measuring radioactivity.

**geisha** n. Japanese hostess trained to entertain men.

**gel** n. a jelly-like substance.

**gelatine** n. (also **gelatin**) transparent tasteless substance used in cookery, photography, etc. □□ **gelatinous** adj.

**gelato** n. (pl. **gelati** or **gelatos**) kind of Italian ice cream made with water.

**geld** v. castrate.

**gelding** n. castrated animal, esp. horse.

**gelignite** n. nitroglycerine explosive.

**gem** n. precious stone; thing or person of great beauty or worth.

**gemfish** n. marine fish valued as food.

**geminate** • adj. combined in pairs. • v. **1** double, repeat. **2** arrange in pairs. □□ **gemination** n.

**Gemini** n. third sign of zodiac, the Twins. □□ **Geminian** adj. & n.

**gen** abbr. colloq. general.

**gender** n. **1** state of being or identifying as male or female. **2** class of noun (masculine, feminine, or neuter).

**gene** n. unit in chromosome determining heredity.

**genealogy** n. line of descent traced continuously from ancestor; study of lines of descent; organism's line of development from earlier forms. □□ **genealogical** adj. **genealogist** n.

**genera** pl. of GENUS.

**general** • adj. **1** of or involving all or most parts, things, or people; not detailed or specific. **2** (in titles) chief. • n. high ranking army officer. □ **general election** election of parliamentary representatives from the whole country. **general practitioner** community doctor treating cases of all kinds. □□ **generally** adv.

**generalise** v. (also **-ize**) draw a general conclusion; speak in general terms. □□ **generalisation** n.

**generality** n. being general; statement without details.

**generate** v. bring into existence; produce.

**generation** n. **1** all people born at about the same time; period of about 30 years. **2** single stage in development of a type of product or technology. **3** production or creation of something.

**generative** *adj.* **1** of procreation. **2** productive.

**generator** *n.* machine converting mechanical energy into electricity.

**generic** *adj.* **1** general, not specific or special. **2** characteristic of or relating to class or genus. **3** (of goods, esp. medicinal drugs) having no brand name.□□ **generically** *adv.*

**generous** *adj.* giving or given freely; magnanimous; abundant.
□□ **generosity** *n.* **generously** *adv.*

**genesis** *n.* **1** origin; mode of formation. **2** (**Genesis**) first book of Old Testament.

**genetic** *adj.* **1** of genetics or genes. **2** of or in origin. **3** (**genetics**) study of heredity and variation of inherited characteristics.□□ **genetically modified** (of an organism) with a change of genetic structure to improve yield, taste, etc. **genetic engineering** manipulation of DNA to modify hereditary features. **genetic fingerprinting** (or **profiling**) identifying individuals by DNA patterns.□□ **genetically** *adv.*

**genial** *adj.* sociable, kindly; mild and warm; cheering.□□ **geniality** *n.* **genially** *adv.*

**genie** *n.* (*pl.* **genii**) spirit or goblin of Arabian tales.

**genital** ● *adj.* of animal reproduction or reproductive organs. ● *n.pl.* (**genitals** (also **genitalia**)) external reproductive organs.

**genitive** *n.* grammatical case expressing possession or source.

**genius** *n.* (*pl.* **geniuses**) **1** exceptional natural ability; person with this. **2** guardian spirit.

**genocide** *n.* deliberate extermination of people or nation.□□ **genocidal** *adj.*

**genome** *n.* complete set of genetic material of organism.

**genotype** *n.* genetic constitution of individual.

**genre** *n.* style of art or literature.

**genteel** *adj.* affectedly polite and refined.

**Gentile** *n.* non-Jewish person.

**gentility** *n.* **1** social superiority. **2** genteel habits.

**gentle** *adj.* **1** not rough or severe; mild, kind; moderate; well-bred. **2** quiet.□□ **gentleness** *n.* **gently** *adv.*

**gentleman** *n.* man; chivalrous man; man of good social position.

**gentrify** *v.* alter (an area) to conform to middle-class tastes.

**gentry** *n.pl.* people in upper levels of society.

**genuflect** *v.* bend the right knee (or both knees), esp. in worship.
□□ **genuflection** *n.* (also **genuflexion**.)

**genuine** *adj.* really what it is said to be; not sham; sincere.□□ **genuinely** *adv.* **genuineness** *n.*

**genus** *n.* (*pl.* **genera**) group of animals or plants with common structural characteristics, usu. containing several species; kind, class.

● **geoblocking** *n.* restricting access to Internet content according to user's location.

● **geocaching** *n.* activity in which an item is hidden at a particular location for GPS users to find by means of coordinates.

**geocentric** *adj.* considered as viewed from earth's centre; having earth as centre.

**geode** *n.* cavity lined with crystals; rock containing this.

**geodesic** *adj.* (also **geodetic**) of geodesy.

**geodesy** *n.* study of shape and area of earth.

**geographical** *adj.* (also **geographic**) of geography.□□ **geographically** *adv.*

**geography** n. science of earth's physical features, resources, etc.; features of place. □□ **geographer** n.

**geology** n. science of earth's crust, strata, etc. □□ **geological** adj. **geologically** adv. **geologist** n.

**geometric** adj. (also **geometrical**) of geometry; (of design etc.) with regular lines and shapes. □□ **geometrically** adv.

**geometry** n. science of properties and relations of lines, surfaces, and solids. □□ **geometrician** n.

**Georgian** adj. of the time of kings of England George I–IV or of George V and VI.

**geosequestration** n. underground storage of carbon dioxide.

**geranium** n. cultivated flowering plant.

**gerbil** n. rodent with long hind legs.

**geriatric** ● adj. of geriatrics; of old people. ● n. 1 old person under geriatric care. 2 offens. any elderly person.

**geriatrics** n.pl. (usu. treated as sing.) branch of medicine or social science dealing with health and care of old people. □□ **geriatrician** n.

**germ** n. 1 microbe. 2 portion of organism capable of developing into new one; rudiment of animal or plant in seed. 3 idea etc. from which something may develop; elementary principle.

**German** adj. & n. (a native, the language) of Germany. □ **German measles** = RUBELLA. **German sausage** = DEVON. **German shepherd** large wolf-like dog.

**german** adj. having same two parents or grandparents.

**germane** adj. relevant.

**germanium** n. semi-metallic element (symbol Ge).

**germicide** n. substance that destroys germs. □□ **germicidal** adj.

**germinal** adj. 1 of germs. 2 in earliest stage of development.

**germinate** v. (cause to) sprout, bud, or develop. □□ **germination** n. **germinator** n.

**gerontology** n. study of old age and ageing.

**gerrymander** v. manipulate boundaries of electorate etc. to gain unfair electoral advantage.

**Gestapo** n. hist. Nazi secret police.

**gestation** n. 1 carrying or being carried in uterus between conception and birth; this period. 2 development of plan etc. □□ **gestate** v. **gestational** adj.

**gesticulate** v. use gestures instead of, or with, speech. □□ **gesticulation** n.

**gesture** ● n. 1 meaningful movement of limb or body etc. 2 action performed as courtesy or to indicate intention. 3 token or not very committed response.
● v. gesticulate.

**get** v. (**got**, **getting**) 1 come into possession of; receive. 2 fetch; capture, catch. 3 prepare (a meal). 4 bring or come into certain state. 5 colloq. understand. 6 colloq. annoy. □ **get off** be acquitted. **get on** make progress; be on harmonious terms; advance in age. **get out of** evade. **get over** recover from. **get round** persuade; evade, avoid. **get-together** social gathering. **get up** stand up; get out of bed; prepare, organise. **get-up** an outfit.

> **Usage** In North America **gotten** is acceptable as the past participle of **get**. Except in the adjective **ill-gotten**, this form is non-standard in Australian English.

**getaway** n. 1 an escape after a crime. 2 holiday.

**geyser** n. intermittent hot spring.
**ghastly** adj. horrible; frightful; deathlike, pallid. □□ **ghastliness** n.
**GHB** abbr. (also **GBH**) drug (gamma hydroxybutyrate) related to ecstasy.
**ghee** n. Indian clarified butter.
**gherkin** n. small pickled cucumber.
**ghetto** n. (pl. **ghettos**) part of city occupied by particular group (often a minority or socially disadvantaged one). □ **ghetto blaster** large portable stereo radio etc.
**ghost** n. 1 apparition of dead person etc.; disembodied spirit. 2 shadow or semblance. 3 secondary image in defective telescope or television picture. □ **ghost writer** person who writes book etc. for another to pass off as his or her own. □□ **ghostly** adj.
**ghoul** n. 1 person morbidly interested in death etc. 2 evil spirit; (in Arabic mythology) spirit preying on corpses. □□ **ghoulish** adj. **ghoulishly** adv.
**GI** n. soldier in the US army.
**giant** ● n. mythical being of human form but superhuman size; person, animal, or thing of extraordinary size, ability, etc. ● adj. gigantic.
**gibber**[1] v. make meaningless sounds in shock or terror.
**gibber**[2] n. Aust. stone, rock, boulder.
**gibberish** n. unintelligible or meaningless speech or sounds.
**gibbet** n. hist. gallows.
**gibbon** n. long-armed ape.
**gibbous** adj. 1 convex. 2 (of moon etc.) with bright part greater than semicircle.
**gibe** (also **jibe**) ● v. jeer, mock. ● n. jeering remark, taunt.
**giblets** n.pl. gizzard, liver, etc. of bird removed and usu. cooked separately.
**giddy** adj. dizzy, tending to fall or stagger; mentally intoxicated; excitable, frivolous, flighty; making dizzy. □□ **giddily** adv. **giddiness** n.
**gift** n. 1 thing given; present. 2 talent. 3 colloq. easy task.

**gifted** adj. talented; intelligent.
**gig** n. 1 engagement to play music etc., usu. for one night. 2 gigabyte. 3 light two-wheeled one-horse carriage. 4 small boat. 5 Aust. inquisitive look.
**giga-** comb. form one thousand million.
**gigabit** n. one thousand megabits.
**gigabyte** n. one thousand megabytes.
**gigantic** adj. huge, giant-like.
**giggle** ● v. laugh in half-suppressed spasms. ● n. such laugh. □□ **giggler** n. **giggly** adj.
**gigolo** n. man hired as escort; male prostitute.
**gild** v. cover thinly with gold; tinge with golden colour; give false brilliance to.
**gilgai** n. Aust. landscape with hollows and mounds.
**gills** n. 1 organ with which fish breathes. 2 vertical plates on underside of mushroom etc.
**gilt** adj. overlaid (as) with gold. ● n. gold.
**gimbals** n.pl. contrivance of rings to keep instruments horizontal on ship.
**gimlet** n. small boring tool.
**gimmick** n. trick or device, esp. to attract attention or deceive. □□ **gimmickry** n. **gimmicky** adj.
**gin** n. 1 alcoholic spirit flavoured with juniper berries. 2 machine separating cotton from seeds. ● v. (ginned) treat (cotton) in gin.
**ginger** n. 1 hot spicy root of tropical plant; this plant. 2 light reddish-yellow. ● adj. ginger-coloured. □ **ginger beer** (or **ale**) ginger-flavoured fizzy drink. **ginger group** a group urging a more active policy. □□ **gingery** adj.
**gingerbread** n. ginger-flavoured cake.
**gingerly** ● adv. in careful or cautious manner. ● adj. showing extreme care or caution.
**gingham** n. plain-woven usu. checked cotton cloth.

**gingivitis** n. inflammation of the gums.

**ginkgo** n. tree with fan-shaped leaves and yellow flowers.

**ginseng** n. medicinal plant with fragrant root.

**gipsy** = GYPSY.

**giraffe** n. large four-legged African animal with long neck.

**gird** v. encircle or attach with waistband, belt, etc.

**girder** n. iron or steel beam or compound structure for bridge, building etc.

**girdle** ● n. 1 belt or cord worn around waist. 2 corset. 3 ring of bones in body. ● v. surround with girdle.

**girl** n. female child; young woman. □□ **girlhood** n. **girlish** adj.

**girlfriend** n. regular female companion or lover.

**girth** n. 1 distance around thing. 2 band around body of horse securing saddle etc.

**gist** n. substance or essence of matter.

**git** n. silly or contemptible person.

**give** ● v. (**gave**, **given**, **giving**) 1 cause to receive or have. 2 utter; make or perform (an action or effort). 3 yield as a product or result. 4 be flexible. ● n. springiness; elasticity. □ **give away** give as a gift; reveal (a secret etc.) unintentionally. **give in** acknowledge defeat. **give off** emit. **give out** announce; become exhausted or used up. **give up** cease; part with, hand over; abandon hope or an attempt. **give way** yield. □□ **giver** n.

**giveaway** n. 1 free gift. 2 colloq. an unintentional disclosure.

**given** see GIVE. ● adj. 1 specified. 2 having a tendency (given to swearing). □ **given name** first name (given in addition to family name).

**gizmo** n. colloq. gadget.

**gizzard** n. bird's second stomach, for grinding food.

**glacé** adj. 1 (of fruit) preserved in sugar. 2 (of cloth etc.) smooth; polished.

**glacial** adj. of ice in masses; Geol. characterised or produced by ice; icy cold; Chem. forming ice-like crystals on freezing.

**glaciated** adj. marked or polished by moving ice; covered with glaciers. □□ **glaciation** n.

**glacier** n. slowly moving mass of ice formed on land.

**glad** adj. pleased; joyful. □□ **gladly** adv. **gladness** n.

**gladden** v. make glad.

**glade** n. open space in forest.

**gladiator** n. hist. trained fighter in ancient Roman shows. □□ **gladiatorial** adj.

**gladiolus** n. (pl. **gladioli**) garden plant with bright flower spikes.

**gladwrap** n. propr. thin transparent plastic sheeting for wrapping food etc.

**glamorise** v. (also **-ize**) make glamorous or attractive.

**glamour** n. (also **glamor**) physical, esp. cosmetic, attractiveness; alluring or exciting beauty or charm. □□ **glamorous** adj. **glamorously** adv.

**glance** ● v. 1 look or refer briefly. 2 hit at fine angle and bounce off. ● n. 1 brief look. 2 flash, gleam. 3 swift oblique stroke in cricket. □□ **glancingly** adv.

**gland** n. organ etc. secreting substances for use in body; similar organ in plant.

**glandular** adj. of gland('s).

**glans** n. (pl. **glandes**) rounded part forming end of penis or clitoris.

**glare** ● v. 1 look fiercely. 2 shine oppressively. ● n. 1 oppressive light or public attention. 2 fierce look. 3 tawdry brilliance. □□ **glaringly** adv.

**glasnost** n. (in former USSR) policy of more open government.

**glass** ● n. 1 hard brittle transparent substance; things made of this.

**2** drinking vessel; contents of this. **3** (**glasses**) spectacles; binoculars. ● *adj.* of or made from glass. ● *v. colloq.* hit (someone) in face with beer glass etc.□ **glass ceiling** unacknowledged barrier to advancement in a career. □□ **glassy** *adj.*

**glasshouse** *n.* greenhouse.

**glaucoma** *n.* eye disease with pressure in eyeball and gradual loss of sight.

**glaze** ● *v.* **1** fit with glass or windows. **2** cover (pottery etc.) with vitreous substance or (surface) with smooth shiny coating. **3** (of eyes) become glassy. ● *n.* substance used for or surface produced by glazing.

**glazier** *n.* person who glazes windows etc.

**gleam** ● *n.* **1** faint or brief light. **2** show. ● *v.* emit gleam(s).

**glean** *v.* **1** acquire (facts etc.) **2** gather (corn left by reapers).

**glee** *n.* **1** mirth; delight. **2** musical composition for several voices.

**gleeful** *adj.* joyful. □□ **gleefully** *adv.* **gleefulness** *n.*

**glib** *adj.* (**glibber**) speaking or spoken fluently but insincerely. □□ **glibly** *adv.* **glibness** *n.*

**glide** ● *v.* **1** move smoothly or continuously. **2** (of aircraft or pilot) fly without engine power. **3** go stealthily. ● *n.* gliding motion.

**glider** *n.* thing that glides; light aircraft without engine; tree-dwelling marsupial able to glide through the air.

**glimmer** ● *v.* shine faintly or intermittently. ● *n.* **1** feeble or wavering light. **2** (also **glimmering**) small sign.

**glimpse** ● *n.* **1** brief view, look. **2** faint transient appearance. ● *v.* have brief view of.

**glint** *v.* flash, glitter.

**glisten** ● *v.* shine like wet or polished surface. ● *n.* glitter.

**glitch** *n. colloq.* **1** malfunction (of equipment). **2** a difficulty.

**glitter** ● *v.* shine with brilliant reflected light; sparkle; be showy or splendid. ● *n.* sparkle; showiness; tiny pieces of sparkling material.

**glitz** *n. colloq.* showy glamour. □□ **glitzy** *adj.*

**gloaming** *n. poet.* twilight.

**gloat** *v.* look or ponder with greedy or malicious pleasure.

**global** *adj.* **1** worldwide; all-embracing. **2** *Computing* relating to an entire program, set of data, etc. □ **global warming** an increase in the temperature of the earth's atmosphere.□□ **globally** *adv.*

**globe** *n.* ball-shaped object; spherical map of the earth; light bulb.

**globetrotter** *n.* person who travels widely.□□ **globetrotting** *n.* & *adj.*

**globular** *adj.* globe-shaped; composed of globules.

**globule** *n.* small globe, round particle, or drop.

**globulin** *n.* molecule-transporting protein in plant and animal tissues.

**glockenspiel** *n.* musical instrument of bells, metal bars, or tubes played with hammers.

**gloom** ● *n.* **1** darkness. **2** melancholy; depression. ● *v.* **1** become dark or threatening. **2** be melancholy. **3** frown.

**gloomy** *adj.* **1** dark. **2** depressed, depressing.

**glorify** *v.* **1** make glorious. **2** make seem more splendid than is the case; (as **glorified** *adj.*) treated as more important than it is. □□ **glorification** *n.*

**glorious** *adj.* possessing or conferring glory; splendid, excellent. □□ **gloriously** *adv.*

**glory** ● *n.* **1** (thing bringing) renown, honourable fame, etc.;

adoring praise. **2** resplendent majesty, beauty, etc. **3** halo of saint. ● *v.* take pride. □ **glory box** *Aust.* accumulation of linen, household goods, etc. in anticipation of marriage.

**gloss** ● *n.* **1** surface lustre. **2** deceptively attractive appearance. **3** (in full **gloss paint**) paint giving glossy finish. ● *v.* make glossy. □ **gloss over** try to conceal.

**glossary** *n.* dictionary of technical or special words.

**glossy** *adj.* (**glossier**) smooth and shiny; printed on such paper.

**glottis** *n.* opening at upper end of windpipe and between vocal cords. □□ **glottal** *adj.*

**glove** ● *n.* hand covering for protection, warmth, etc. ● *v.* cover or provide with gloves.

**glovebox** *n.* recess for small articles in car dashboard.

**glow** ● *v.* **1** emit flameless light and heat. **2** feel bodily heat or strong emotion. **3** show warm colour. **4** (as **glowing** *adj.*) expressing pride or satisfaction. ● *n.* glowing state, appearance, or feeling.

**glower** *v.* scowl.

**glucose** *n.* kind of sugar found in blood, fruits, etc.

**glue** ● *n.* any adhesive substance. ● *v.* (**glued, gluing**) fasten with glue; attach closely. □ **glue-sniffing** inhaling glue fumes for their narcotic effect. □□ **gluey** *adj.*

**gluggy** *adj. colloq.* gluey, sticky.

**glum** *adj.* (**glummer**) sad and gloomy. □□ **glumly** *adv.* **glumness** *n.*

**glut** ● *v.* (**glutted**) supply with more than is needed; satisfy. ● *n.* an excessive supply.

**gluten** *n.* sticky part of flour.

**gluteus** *n.* (*pl.* **glutei**) buttock muscle that moves the thigh.

**glutinous** *adj.* sticky; like glue.

**glutton** *n.* **1** excessive eater. **2** *colloq.* insatiably eager person. □□ **gluttony** *n.* gluttonous *adj.* **gluttonously** *adv.*

**glycerine** *n.* (also **glycerol**) sweet colourless viscous liquid used in medicines, explosives, etc.

**glycerol** *n.* = GLYCERINE.

**glyphosate** *n.* type of herbicide.

**GM** *abbr.* genetically modified.

**gm** *abbr.* gram(s).

**GMT** *abbr.* Greenwich Mean Time.

**gnarled** *adj.* knobbly, twisted, rugged.

**gnash** *v.* grind (one's teeth); (of teeth) strike together.

**gnat** *n.* small biting fly.

**gnaw** *v.* **1** wear away by biting; bite persistently. **2** corrode. **3** torment.

**gnome** *n.* dwarf in fairy tales.

**gnomon** *n.* rod etc. on sundial, showing time by its shadow.

**GNP** *abbr.* gross national product.

**gnu** *n.* an ox-like antelope.

**go** ● *v.* (**goes, went, gone, going**) **1** move; depart; travel. **2** be functioning; make (a specified movement or sound); (of time) pass. **3** belong in a specified place. **4** become; proceed. **5** be sold; be spent or used up. **6** collapse, fail, die. **7** *colloq.* say. ● *n.* (*pl.* **goes**) **1** a turn or try. **2** energy. **3** Japanese board game. □ **go-ahead** *colloq.* permission to proceed. **go back on** fail to keep (a promise). **go-between** messenger or negotiator. **go for** **1** like, choose. **2** *colloq.* attack. **go-getter** *colloq.* aggressively enterprising person. **go-kart** (also **go-cart**) miniature racing car. **go off** **1** explode. **2** (of foodstuffs) deteriorate. **go round** be enough for everyone. **go slow** work at a deliberately slow pace as a protest. **go under** succumb; fail. **go with** match; harmonise. **on the go** in constant motion; active.

**goad** ● *n.* spiked stick used for urging cattle; anything that torments or incites. ● v. **1** urge with goad; irritate. **2** stimulate.

**goal** ● n. **1** object of effort; destination. **2** structure into or through which ball is driven in certain games; point(s) so won. ● v. score goal. □□ **goalless** adj.

**goalie** n. colloq. goalkeeper.

**goalkeeper** n. player protecting goal.

**goalpost** n. either of two posts of goal. □ **move the goalposts** unfairly alter conditions or rules of a procedure once it has started.

**goanna** n. Australian monitor lizard.

**goat** n. **1** hardy domesticated cud-chewing mammal, with horns and (in male) beard. **2** colloq. foolish person.

**goatee** n. small pointed beard.

**gob** n. colloq. **1** mouth. **2** clot of slimy matter.

**gobble** v. **1** eat hurriedly and noisily. **2** (of turkey) make guttural sound. **3** take over, seize control of. **4** read eagerly, devour (book etc.)

**gobbledegook** n. (also **gobbledygook**) colloq. pompous or unintelligible jargon.

**goblet** n. drinking vessel with foot and stem.

**goblin** n. mischievous dwarflike creature.

**goby** n. small fish with sucker on underside.

**god** n. **1** superhuman being or spirit worshipped as possessing power over nature, human fortunes, etc. **2** (God) (in Christian and other monotheistic religions) creator and ruler of the universe. **3** adored person. **4** (the gods) (occupant of) gallery in theatre. **5** (God!) exclamation of surprise, anger, etc.□ **god-forsaken 1** dismal. **2** inaccessible, remote.

**godchild** n. person in relation to godparent.

**god-daughter** n. female godchild.

**goddess** n. **1** female deity. **2** adored woman.

**godfather** n. **1** male godparent. **2** person directing illegal organisation, esp. the Mafia.

**godhead** n. divine nature; deity.

**godless** adj. **1** impious. **2** wicked. **3** not believing in God. □□ **godlessness** n.

**godly** adj. pious, devout. □□ **godliness** n.

**godmother** n. female godparent.

**godparent** n. person who presents child at baptism and responds on child's behalf.

**godsend** n. unexpected welcome event or acquisition.

**godson** n. male godchild.

**goer** n. **1** person or thing that goes. **2** colloq. lively person. **3** project likely to succeed. **4** thing that goes very fast.

**gofer** n. colloq. person who does menial jobs, runs errands, etc. for others; toady, crawler.

**goggle** ● v. look with wide-open eyes; (of eyes) be rolled, project; roll (eyes). ● adj. (of eyes) protuberant, rolling. ● n. (in pl.) spectacles for protecting eyes.

**going** ● n. condition of ground as affecting riding etc. ● adj. **1** in action. **2** existing, available; current, prevalent.

**goitre** n. abnormal enlargement of thyroid gland.

**gold** ● n. chemical element (symbol Au) yellow metal of high value; coins or articles made of this; its colour; gold medal (awarded as first prize). ● adj. of or coloured like gold.□ **gold leaf** gold beaten into a very thin sheet. **gold rush** a rush to a newly discovered goldfield.

**golden** adj. **1** gold. **2** precious; excellent.□ **golden handshake** cash payment etc. given on redundancy or early retirement. **golden wedding** 50th anniversary of wedding.

**goldfield** n. area where gold is found.

**goldfish** n. (pl. **goldfish** or **goldfishes**) small reddish carp kept in a bowl or pond.

**goldsmith** n. person who makes gold articles.

**golf** ● n. game in which small hard ball is struck with clubs into series of small holes. ● v. play golf. □ **golf course** (or **links**) area of land on which golf is played. □□ **golfer** n.

**golliwog** n. black-faced soft doll with fuzzy hair.

**gonad** n. animal organ producing gametes, e.g. testis or ovary.

**gondola** n. light Venetian canal boat.

**gondolier** n. oarsman of gondola.

**gone** ● see GO. ● adj. 1 (of time) past. 2 lost, hopeless, dead. 3 colloq. pregnant for specified time. 4 consumed, used up.

**goner** n. colloq. person or thing that is doomed or irrevocably lost.

**gong** n. metal disc giving resonant note when struck; colloq. medal, award, etc.

**gonorrhoea** n. (also **gonorrhea**) type of venereal disease.

**goo** n. colloq. 1 sticky or slimy substance. 2 sickly sentiment.

**good** ● adj. (**better**, **best**) 1 having the right or desirable qualities; proper, expedient; morally correct, kindly; well-behaved. 2 enjoyable, beneficial. 3 efficient; thorough. 4 considerable, full. ● n. 1 that which is morally right. 2 profit, benefit. 3 (**goods**) movable property; articles of trade; things to be carried by road or rail. 4 (**the goods**) colloq. incriminating evidence. □ **as good as** practically, almost. **good for nothing** worthless. **Good Friday** Friday before Easter, commemorating crucifixion of Christ.

**goodbye** int. & n. expression used when parting.

**goodness** n. 1 virtue; excellence; kindness. 2 nutriment.

**goodwill** n. friendly feeling; established popularity of a business, treated as saleable asset.

**gooey** adj. (**gooier**) colloq. wet and sticky.

**goof** colloq. ● n. foolish or stupid person or mistake. ● v. bungle; blunder. □□ **goofy** adj.

**goog** n. (also **googie**) Aust. colloq. egg.

**google** v. search for (something) on Internet with search engine.

**googly** n. Cricket ball bowled so as to bounce in unexpected direction.

**goon¹** n. colloq. 1 stupid person. 2 US hired ruffian.

**goon²** n. Aust. colloq. cheap wine, esp. when sold in cask.

**goose** n. (pl. **geese**) web-footed bird larger than duck; female of this. □ **goose step** way of marching without bending knees.

**gooseberry** n. yellowish-green berry with juicy flesh; thorny shrub bearing this.

**goosebumps** n.pl. (also **goose pimples**, **goose flesh**) bristling bumpy skin produced by cold or fright.

**gopher** n. 1 American burrowing rodent. 2 colloq. = GOFER.

**gore** ● n. 1 clotted blood. 2 wedge-shaped piece in garment. 3 triangular or tapering piece in sail etc. ● v. pierce with horn, tusk, etc.

**gorge** ● n. 1 narrow opening between hills. 2 surfeit. 3 contents of stomach. ● v. feed greedily; satiate.

**gorgeous** adj. 1 richly coloured. 2 colloq. splendid, strikingly beautiful. □□ **gorgeously** adv.

**gorgon** n. (in Greek mythology) any of three snake-haired sisters able to turn people to stone.

**gorilla** n. largest anthropoid ape.

**gormandise** v. (also **-ize**) devour voraciously.

**gormless** *adj. colloq.* foolish, lacking sense. □□ **gormlessly** *adv.*

**gorse** *n.* spiny yellow-flowered shrub.

**gory** *adj.* involving bloodshed; bloodstained; *colloq.* nasty, unpleasant.

**goshawk** *n.* large short-winged and long-tailed hawk.

**gosling** *n.* young goose.

**gospel** *n.* **1** teaching or revelation of Christ; (**Gospel**) (each of four books giving) account of Christ's life in New Testament. **2** thing regarded as absolutely true.

**gossamer** ● *n.* filmy substance of small spiders' webs; delicate filmy material. ● *adj.* light and flimsy as gossamer.

**gossip** ● *n.* casual talk about other people's affairs; person fond of such talk. ● *v.* (**gossiped**) talk or write gossip. □□ **gossipy** *adj.*

**got** see GET.

**Gothic** *adj.* **1** of an architectural style of the 12th–16th centuries, with pointed arches. **2** (of a novel etc.) in a horrific style popular in the 18th–19th centuries.

**gotten** see note at GET.

**gouache** *n.* painting with opaque water colour; pigments used for this.

**gouge** ● *n.* concave-bladed chisel; groove etc. made with this. ● *v.* **1** cut with gouge; force out (as) with gouge. **2** *Aust.* dig for opal.

**gouging** *n.* (in football etc.) poking finger into opponent's eye.

**goulash** *n.* stew of meat and vegetables seasoned with paprika.

**gourd** *n.* fleshy fruit of trailing cucumber-like plant; this plant; dried rind of this fruit used as bottle etc.

**gourmand** *n.* **1** glutton. **2** gourmet.

**gourmet** *n.* connoisseur of good food.

**gout** *n.* disease with inflammation of small joints. □□ **gouty** *adj.*

**govern** *v.* rule with authority; conduct policy and affairs of; influence or determine; curb, control.

**governance** *n.* act, manner, or function of governing.

**governess** *n.* woman employed to teach children in private household.

**government** *n.* manner or system of governing; group of people governing nation etc. □□ **governmental** *adj.*

**governor** *n.* anyone who governs; representative of the Crown in each Australian state; member of governing body of institution. □ **governor-general** (*pl.* **governors-general** or **governor-generals**) representative of the Crown in the Commonwealth of Australia or in any other country regarding the British monarch as Head of State. □□ **governorship** *n.*

**gown** *n.* loose flowing garment; woman's long dress; official robe.

**GP** *abbr.* general practitioner.

**GPO** *abbr.* General Post Office.

**GPS** *abbr.* Global Positioning System, worldwide navigational and surveying system based on reception of satellite signals.

**gr** *abbr.* (also **gr.**) **1** gram(s). **2** grain(s). **3** gross.

**grab** ● *v.* (**grabbed**) **1** seize suddenly; snatch at. **2** take greedily. **3** impress. ● *n.* sudden clutch or attempt to seize; device for clutching. □□ **grabber** *n.*

**grace** ● *n.* **1** elegance of proportions, manner, or movement; courteous good will; attractive feature; goodwill. **2** delay granted. **3** thanksgiving at meals. ● *v.* **1** add grace to. **2** bestow honour on. □ **grace note** *Mus.* extra note as an embellishment.

**graceful** *adj.* full of grace or elegance. □□ **gracefully** *adv.*

**graceless** *adj.* lacking grace or charm; boorish.

**gracious** adj. kindly, esp. to inferiors; merciful. □□ **graciously** adv. **graciousness** n.

**gradation** n. stage in process of gradual change.

**grade** ● n. 1 degree in rank, merit, etc.; mark indicating quality of student's work. 2 class in school. ● v. 1 arrange in grades; pass between grades; give grade to. 2 reduce to easy gradients. ● adj. (of sports) organised in grades according to ability.

**grader** n. 1 person etc. that grades. 2 machine for levelling the ground, esp. in roadmaking.

**gradient** n. 1 sloping road etc.; amount of such slope. 2 rate of rise or fall of temperature, pressure, etc. in passing from one region to another.

**gradual** adj. happening by degrees; not rapid or abrupt. □□ **gradually** adv.

**graduate** ● n. holder of an academic degree. ● v. 1 obtain academic degree. 2 move up to. 3 mark in degrees or portions; arrange in gradations. □□ **graduation** n.

**graffiti** n.pl. writing or drawing on wall etc.

**graft** ● n. 1 plant shoot fixed into cut in another plant to form new growth. 2 piece of transplanted living tissue. 3 colloq. hard work. 4 colloq. bribery, corrupt practice. ● v. 1 insert (graft). 2 transplant (living tissue). 3 insert or fix (thing) permanently to another. 4 colloq. work hard.

**grain** ● n. 1 fruit or seed of cereal; wheat or allied food grass. 2 particle of sand, salt, etc. 3 unit of weight (about 65 mg). 4 least possible amount. 5 texture in skin, wood, stone, etc.; arrangement of lines in wood. ● v. 1 paint in imitation of grain of wood. 2 form into grains. □□ **grainy** adj.

**gram** n. (also **gramme**) 1 one thousandth of a kilogram. 2 any of various pulses used as food.

**grammar** n. system and structure of language(s), including morphology and syntax; set of actual or presumed prescriptive notions about correct use of a language.

**grammatical** adj. of or according to grammar. □□ **grammatically** adv.

**gramophone** n. record player.

**grampus** n. dolphin-like sea creature.

**gran** n. colloq. grandmother.

**granary** n. storehouse for grain; region producing much grain.

**grand** ● adj. great; splendid; imposing; colloq. excellent. ● n. colloq. thousand dollars; grand piano. □ **grand piano** large piano with horizontal strings. **grand slam** winning of all of group of matches. □□ **grandly** adv. **grandness** n.

**grandad** n. colloq. grandfather.

**grandchild** n. child of one's son or daughter.

**granddaughter** n. female grandchild.

**grandeur** n. majesty, splendour; dignity; high rank, eminence.

**grandfather** n. male grandparent. □ **grandfather clock** clock in tall wooden case.

**grandiloquent** adj. pompous or inflated in language. □□ **grandiloquence** n.

**grandiose** adj. 1 imposing. 2 planned on a large scale. 3 pretentiously grand. □□ **grandiosity** n.

**grandma** n. colloq. grandmother.

**grandmother** n. female grandparent.

**grandpa** n. colloq. grandfather.

**grandparent** n. parent of one's father or mother.

**grand prix** 1 highest award in competition etc. 2 (usu. **Grand Prix**) any of several important international motor racing events.

**grandson** n. male grandchild.

**grandstand** ● n. main stand for spectators at racecourse etc. ● v. act in an ostentatious, self-important manner. ● adj. advantageous for observing.

**granite** n. granular crystalline rock of quartz, mica, etc.

**granny** n. (also **grannie**) **1** colloq. grandmother. **2** (in Aboriginal English) elderly relative, community elder. □ **granny flat** part of house made into self-contained accommodation.

**Granny Smith** n. green variety of apple.

**grant** ● v. **1** consent to fulfil. **2** allow to have; give formally, transfer legally. **3** admit, concede. ● n. granting; thing, esp. money, granted. □□ **grantor** n.

**granular** adj. of or like grains or granules.

**granulate** v. **1** form into grains. **2** roughen surface of. □□ **granulation** n.

**granule** n. small grain.

**grape** n. usu. green or purple berry growing in clusters on vine; vine bearing such berries.

**grapefruit** n. (pl. **same**) large round usu. yellow citrus fruit; tree bearing this fruit.

**grapevine** n. vine bearing grapes. □ **on the grapevine** colloq. by means of rumour.

**graph** ● n. symbolic diagram representing relation between two or more variables. ● v. plot on graph.

**graphic** ● adj. **1** of writing, drawing, etc. **2** vividly descriptive. ● n. (**graphics**) diagrams used in calculation and design; drawings; computer images. □□ **graphically** adv.

**graphical** adj. using diagrams or graphs.

**graphite** n. crystalline form of carbon used as lubricant, in pencils, etc. □□ **graphitic** adj.

**graphology** n. study of handwriting. □□ **graphologist** n.

**grapnel** n. **1** iron-clawed instrument for dragging or grasping. **2** small many-fluked anchor.

**grapple** ● v. **1** fight at close quarters. **2** try to manage (problem etc.) **3** grip with hands, come to close quarters with. **4** seize. ● n. **1** hold (as) of wrestler. **2** contest at close quarters. **3** clutching instrument. □ **grappling iron** (or **hook**) grapnel.

**grasp** ● v. **1** clutch at; seize greedily; hold firmly. **2** understand, realise. ● n. **1** firm hold; grip. **2** mastery, mental hold.

**grasping** adj. avaricious.

**grass** ● n. **1** plant with green blades; pasture land; grass-covered ground. **2** colloq. marijuana. **3** colloq. informer. ● v. **1** cover with turf; pasture. **2** colloq. betray, inform the police. □ **grass tree** Aust. xanthorrhoea. □□ **grassy** adj.

**grasshopper** n. jumping and chirping plant-eating insect.

**grassroots** ● n.pl. **1** fundamental level or source. **2** ordinary members of organisation. ● adj. pertaining to or deriving from ordinary people etc.

**grate** ● v. **1** reduce to small particles by rubbing on rough surface. **2** make harsh sound by rubbing. **3** have irritating effect. ● n. frame holding fuel in fireplace etc.; grating.

**grateful** adj. thankful; feeling or showing gratitude. □□ **gratefully** adv.

**grater** n. device for grating food.

**gratify** v. please, delight; indulge. □□ **gratification** n.

**grating** n. framework of parallel or crossed metal bars.

**gratis** adv. & adj. free, without charge.

**gratitude** n. being thankful.

**gratuitous** *adj.* **1** without reason, uncalled for. **2** free of charge. □□ **gratuitously** *adv.*

**gratuity** *n.* small present of money given esp. for service.

**grave** ● *n.* hole dug for burial of corpse. ● *adj.* serious, causing great anxiety, solemn. □□ **gravely** *adv.*

**grave accent** *n.* mark (`); over letter, indicating pronunciation.

**gravel** *n.* coarse sand and small stones used for paths etc.

**gravelly** *adj.* **1** of or like gravel. **2** deep and rough-sounding.

**graveyard** *n.* burial ground.

**gravid** *adj.* pregnant.

**gravitate** *v.* move or be attracted (towards).

**gravitation** *n.* attraction between each particle of matter and every other; effect of this, esp. falling of bodies to earth. □□ **gravitational** *adj.*

**gravity** *n.* **1** force that attracts body to centre of earth etc.; intensity of this. **2** weight. **3** importance, seriousness; solemnity.

**gravy** *n.* (sauce made from) juices exuding from meat in cooking. □ **gravy train** source of easy money.

**graze** *v.* **1** feed on growing grass; pasture cattle in (a paddock). **2** injure by scraping the skin. **3** touch or scrape lightly in passing.

**grazier** *n. Aust.* owner of large-scale property on which sheep or cattle are raised.

**grease** ● *n.* oily or fatty matter, esp. as lubricant; melted fat of dead animal. ● *v.* smear or lubricate with grease. □□ **greasy** *adj.*

**greasepaint** *n.* actor's make-up.

**greaseproof** *adj.* impervious to grease.

**great** ● *adj.* above average in bulk, number, extent, or intensity; important, pre-eminent; imposing, distinguished; of remarkable ability

etc. ● *n.* great person or thing. □ **great white shark** large aggressive shark. □□ **greatness** *n.*

**great-** *comb. form* (of family relationships) one degree more remote (*great-grandfather, great niece*).

**greatly** *adv.* very much.

**grebe** *n.* diving bird.

**Grecian** *adj.* Greek. □ **Grecian nose** straight nose.

**greed** *n.* excessive desire, esp. for food or wealth. □□ **greedy** *adj.* **greedily** *adv.*

**green** ● *adj.* **1** of the colour of growing grass. **2** concerned with protecting the environment. **3** unripe; inexperienced, easily deceived. ● *n.* **1** green colour n. **2** (**greens**) green vegetables. **3** (often **greenie**) supporter of protection of environment. □ **green ban** *Aust.* prohibition preventing demolition of building of historical etc. significance; similar prohibition against development of site in a green belt. **green belt** area of open land within or around a city, designated for preservation. **green fingers** = *green thumb*. **green light** *colloq.* signal or permission to proceed. **Green Paper** preliminary report of government proposals. **green room** room used by actors etc. when not performing. **green thumb** skill in growing plants. □□ **greenness** *n.*

**greenery** *n.* green foliage or growing plants.

**greenfly** *n.* green aphid.

**greengage** *n.* round green plum.

**greengrocer** *n.* **1** retailer of fruit and vegetables. **2** *Aust.* kind of large cicada.

**greenhorn** *n.* novice; new recruit.

**greenhouse** *n.* light structure with sides and roof mainly of glass for rearing plants.

□ **greenhouse effect** trapping of sun's radiation by pollution in atmosphere, causing rise in temperature.

**greenhouse gas** gas contributing to greenhouse effect.

**greet** v. **1** address on meeting or arrival. **2** receive or acknowledge in specified way. **3** become apparent to (eye, ear, etc.).

**greeting** n. act, words, etc. used to greet.

**gregarious** adj. **1** fond of company. **2** living in flocks etc. □□ **gregariousness** n.

**gremlin** n. colloq. mischievous sprite said to cause mechanical faults etc.

**grenade** n. small bomb thrown by hand (hand grenade) or shot from rifle.

**grevillea** n. shrub or tree with showy flowers.

**grew** past of GROW.

**grey** ● adj. of the colour between black and white. ● n. grey colour or thing. □ **grey area** situation not clearly defined. **grey matter** brain. **grey nomad** Aust. colloq. retired person who travels extensively. **grey water** used household water recycled for use in garden. □□ **greyish** adj. **greyness** n.

**greyhound** n. slender swift dog used in racing.

**grid** n. grating; system of numbered squares for map references; network of lines, electric power connections, etc.; pattern of lines marking starting place on motor racing track.

**griddle** n. circular iron plate placed over heat for baking etc.

**gridiron** n. **1** barred metal frame for broiling or grilling. **2** American football field; the game itself.

**gridlock** n. **1** traffic jam affecting whole network of streets.
**2** = DEADLOCK.

**grief** n. (cause of) intense sorrow.

**grievance** n. real or imagined cause for complaint.

**grieve** v. (cause to) feel grief.

**grievous** adj. **1** severe. **2** causing grief; injurious; flagrant, heinous. □□ **grievously** adv.

**griffin** n. (also **gryphon**) mythical creature with eagle's head and wings and lion's body.

**grill** ● n. device on cooker for radiating heat downwards; gridiron; grilled food. ● v. **1** cook under grill or on gridiron; subject to or experience extreme heat. **2** subject to severe questioning.

**grille** n. (also **grill**) grating, latticed screen; metal grid protecting vehicle radiator.

**grim** adj. (**grimmer**) stern, severe; without cheerfulness, unattractive. □□ **grimly** adv. **grimness** n.

**grimace** n. distortion of face made in disgust etc. or to amuse. ● v. make grimace.

**grime** ● n. deeply ingrained dirt. ● v. blacken; befoul. □□ **grimy** adj.

**grin** v. (**grinned**) smile broadly. ● n. broad smile.

**grind** ● v. (**ground**, **grinding**) **1** crush into grains or powder; crush or oppress by cruelty. **2** sharpen or smooth by friction; rub harshly together. ● n. grinding process; hard dull work. □□ **grinder** n.

**grindstone** n. thick revolving abrasive disc for grinding, sharpening, etc.

**grip** ● v. (**gripped**) take firm hold of; compel the attention of. ● n. **1** firm hold or grasp; method of holding. **2** intellectual mastery. **3** travelling bag.

**gripe** ● v. colloq. complain. ● n. **1** colic. **2** colloq. complaint.

**grisly** adj. (**grislier**) causing horror, disgust, or fear.

**grist** n. corn for grinding.□ **grist to the mill** source of profit or advantage.

**gristle** n. tough flexible tissue; cartilage.□□ **gristly** adj.

**grit** • n. 1 particles of sand etc.; coarse sandstone. 2 colloq. pluck, endurance. • v. 1 clench (the teeth). 2 make grating sound.□□ **gritty** adj.

**grizzle** v. colloq. cry fretfully. □□ **grizzly** adj.

**grizzled** adj. grey-haired.

**grizzly** n. large brown bear of N. America.

**groan** • v. 1 make deep sound expressing pain, grief, or disapproval; utter with groans. 2 be loaded or oppressed. • n. 1 sound made in groaning. 2 colloq. boring person or thing.

**grocer** n. dealer in food and household provisions.

**grocery** n. grocer's trade, shop, or goods.

**grog** n. 1 Aust. colloq. beer, alcoholic drink. 2 hist. drink of rum (or other spirit) and water.

**groggy** adj. incapable, unsteady; colloq. drunk.□□ **groggily** adv.

**groin** • n. 1 depression between belly and thigh. 2 (in architecture) edge formed by intersecting vaults; arch supporting vault. • v. (in architecture) build with groins.

**grommet** n. 1 eyelet placed in hole to protect or insulate rope or cable passed through it. 2 tube passed through eardrum to middle ear. 3 colloq. young inexperienced surfer.

**groom** • n. 1 person employed to tend horses. 2 bridegroom. • v. 1 tend (horse). 2 give neat or attractive appearance to. 3 prepare or train (someone) for a particular purpose or activity; (of paedophile) prepare (child) for meeting, esp. via Internet, with intention of committing sexual offence.

**groove** • n. 1 channel, elongated hollow. 2 habitual pattern. 3 colloq. established rhythmic pattern. • v. 1 make groove(s) in. 2 colloq. enjoy oneself.

**groovy** adj. colloq. excellent; trendy.

**grope** • v. 1 feel about or search blindly. 2 search mentally. 3 colloq. fondle clumsily for sexual pleasure. • n. act of groping.

**groper** n. large sea fish.

**gross** • adj. 1 overfed, bloated. 2 coarse, unrefined, indecent. 3 flagrant. 4 total; not net. • v. produce as gross profit. • n. (pl. **gross**) twelve dozen. • int. colloq. exclamation indicating revulsion etc. □□ **grossly** adv.

**grotesque** • adj. comically or repulsively distorted; incongruous, absurd. • n. decoration interweaving human and animal features; comically distorted figure or design.□□ **grotesquely** adv.

**grotto** n. (pl. **grottoes** or **grottos**) picturesque cave.

**grotty** adj. colloq. unpleasant, dirty, ugly.

**grouch** colloq. • v. grumble. • n. discontented grumbler; complaint; sulky grumbling mood. □□ **grouchy** adj.

**ground** • v. 1 see GRIND. 2 prevent (aircraft or pilot) from flying. 3 give a basis to. 4 give basic training to. 5 colloq. withdraw privileges etc. • n. 1 solid surface of earth; area, position, or distance on this; (**grounds**) land belonging to large house. 2 (**grounds**) reason for a belief or action. 3 (**grounds**) coffee dregs.

**grounding** n. basic instruction.

**groundless** adj. without motive or foundation.

**groundsman** n. person who maintains sports ground.

**groundswell** n. **1** heavy sea. **2** increasingly forceful public opinion.

**groundwork** n. preliminary or basic work.

**group** ● n. a number of people or things near, categorised, or working together. ● v. form into group(s); place in group(s).

**grouse** ● n. game bird with feathered feet. ● v. colloq. grumble. ● adj. Aust. colloq. very good of its kind.

**grout** ● n. thin fluid mortar. ● v. apply grout to.

**grove** n. group of trees.

**grovel** v. (**grovelled**) **1** behave obsequiously. **2** lie prone.

**grow** v. (**grew, grown, growing**) **1** increase in size, height, amount, etc. **2** develop or exist as living plant or natural product; cultivate (crops etc.) **3** develop specified characteristic, become. □ **grow on** become gradually more favoured by. **grow up** become adult or mature. □□ **grower** n.

**growl** ● v. **1** make low guttural sound, usu. of anger. **2** rumble. ● n. growling sound; angry murmur.

**grown** see GROW.

**growth** n. **1** process of growing; increase; what has grown or is growing. **2** Med. tumour.

**groyne** n. (also **groin**) wall built out into sea to stop beach erosion.

**grub** ● n. **1** worm-like larva of certain insects. **2** Aust. = WITCHETTY. **3** colloq. food. **4** colloq. dirty or untidy child. ● v. (**grubbed**) dig superficially; extract by digging.

**grubber** n. **1** thing that grubs. **2** Cricket ball bowled underarm along ground. **3** (also **grubber kick**) Rugby forward kick of ball along ground.

**grubby** adj. dirty.

**grudge** ● n. persistent feeling of resentment or ill will.

● v. be unwilling to give or allow; feel resentful about (doing something).

**gruel** n. liquid food of oatmeal etc. boiled in milk or water.

**gruelling** adj. exhausting, punishing.

**gruesome** adj. grisly, disgusting.

**gruff** adj. **1** rough-voiced. **2** surly. □□ **gruffly** adv.

**grumble** v. **1** complain peevishly. **2** rumble. ● n. **1** complaint. **2** rumble. □□ **grumbler** n.

**grump** colloq. ● n. **1** irritable person. (in pl.) **2** fit of sulks. ● v. grumble, complain.

**grumpy** adj. ill-tempered.

**grunge** n. **1** style of rock music characterised by heavy guitar and low-fi production. **2** grime, dirt.

**grunt** ● n. low guttural sound characteristic of pig. ● v. utter with grunt.

**gryphon** = GRIFFIN.

**GST** abbr. goods and services tax.

**G-string** n. narrow strip of cloth covering genitals, attached to string around waist.

**guacamole** n. dish of mashed avocado mixed with onion, tomatoes, chilli etc.

**guano** n. excrement of sea birds, used as manure.

**guarantee** ● n. formal promise to do something or that a thing is of a specified quality; something offered as security; a guarantor. ● v. give or be a guarantee of or to.

**guarantor** n. the giver of a guarantee.

**guard** ● v. **1** defend, protect; keep watch; prevent from escaping; keep in check. **2** take precautions against. ● n. **1** vigilant state. **2** protector. **3** soldiers etc. protecting place or person. **4** official in charge of train. **5** device to prevent injury or accident.

**guarded** adj. (of remark etc.) cautious. □□ **guardedly** adv.

**guardian** n. protector, keeper; person having custody of another, esp. a minor.□□ **guardianship** n.

**guava** n. edible orange acid fruit; tropical tree bearing this.

**gubba** n. (also **gub**) Aust. colloq. name given by Aboriginal people to white person.

**gudgeon** ● n. 1 small freshwater fish. 2 credulous person. ● v. fool, dupe.

**Guernsey** n. 1 one of breed of cattle from Guernsey. 2 (guernsey) type of thick knitted woollen sweater. 3 (guernsey) Aust. football jumper. □ **get a guernsey** Aust. colloq. gain approval or recognition.

**guerrilla** n. (also **guerilla**) member of one of several independent groups fighting against regular forces.

**guess** ● v. estimate without calculation or measurement; conjecture, think likely; conjecture rightly. ● n. estimate, conjecture.

**guest** n. person invited to visit another's house or have meal etc. at another's expense; person lodging at hotel etc.□ **guest house** private house offering paid accommodation.

**guestbook** n. book at hotel, museum, etc., where visitors can record their personal details, comments, etc.; similar facility on website.

**guffaw** ● n. coarse or boisterous laugh. ● v. utter guffaw.

**guidance** n. 1 advice. 2 guiding.

**guide** ● n. 1 person who shows the way; conductor of tours. 2 adviser. 3 directing principle. 4 guidebook. 5 (Guide) member of girls' organisation similar to the Scouts. ● v. act as guide to; lead, direct.

**guideline** n. principle directing action.

**guild** n. 1 society for mutual aid or with common object. 2 medieval association of craftsmen.

**guile** n. sly behaviour; treachery, deceit.□□ **guileless** adj.

**guillotine** ● n. 1 beheading machine. 2 machine for cutting paper. 3 method of shortening debate in parliament by fixing time of vote. ● v. use guillotine on.

**guilt** n. fact of having committed offence; (feeling of) culpability.

**guilty** adj. having, feeling, or causing feeling of guilt.□□ **guiltily** adv.

**guinea** n. hist. (coin worth) 21 shillings.□ **guinea fowl** domestic fowl with white-spotted grey plumage. **guinea pig** 1 domesticated S. American rodent. 2 person used in experiment.

**guise** n. external, esp. assumed, appearance; pretence.

**guitar** n. usu. six-stringed musical instrument played with fingers or plectrum.□□ **guitarist** n.

**gulf** ● n. 1 large area of sea with narrow-mouthed inlet. 2 deep hollow; chasm. 3 wide difference of opinion etc. ● v. engulf.

**gull** n. long-winged web-footed sea bird.

**gullet** n. food passage from mouth to stomach; throat.

**gullible** adj. easily persuaded or deceived.□□ **gullibility** n.

**gully** n. 1 water-worn ravine. 2 Aust. eroded watercourse; (small) river valley. 3 gutter or drain. 4 Cricket fielding position between point and slips.□ **gully trap** (also **gulley trap**) Aust. water-sealed trap through which household drainage flows to outside drains.

**gulp** ● v. 1 swallow hastily or with effort. 2 choke. 3 suppress. ● n. 1 gulping. 2 large mouthful.

**gum** n. 1 firm flesh around roots of teeth. 2 sticky secretion of some trees and shrubs. 3 = GUMTREE. 4 chewing gum. 5 glue. ● v. fasten with gum; apply gum to.

**gumboot** n. rubber boot, wellington.

**gumption** n. colloq. resourcefulness; enterprise; common sense.

**gumtree** n. (also **gum**) **1** any tree of genus *Eucalyptus*, esp. those eucalypts that have smooth trunk. **2** any other tree that exudes gum.

**gun** ● n. **1** weapon that fires shells or bullets from metal tube; device forcing out a substance through tube. **2** (in full **gun shearer**) *Aust.* shearer with high daily tally of sheep shorn. ● v. (**gunned**) **1** shoot with gun. **2** search for determinedly to attack or rebuke (*he's gunning for you*). **3** colloq. accelerate engine etc. ● adj. pre-eminent (in occupation etc.); exceptionally skilled.

**gunboat** n. small warship with heavy guns.□ **gunboat diplomacy** diplomacy backed by the threat of force.

**gunfire** n. firing of guns.

**gunge** n. colloq. unpleasantly sticky and messy substance.

**gung-ho** adj. (arrogantly) eager.

**gunman** n. armed lawbreaker.

**gunmetal** n. **1** bluish-grey colour. **2** alloy of copper, tin, and usu. zinc.

**gunnery** n. construction and management, or firing, of large guns.

**gunny** n. coarse material used for making sacks; a sack.

**gunpowder** n. explosive of saltpetre, sulphur, and charcoal.

**gunrunner** n. person selling or importing guns illegally.

**gunshot** n. shot from gun; range of gun.

**gunsmith** n. maker and repairer of small firearms.

**gunwale** n. upper edge of ship's or boat's side.

**gunyah** n. *Aust.* Aboriginal shelter.

**guppy** n. small brightly coloured tropical fresh-water fish.

**gurgle** ● v. make bubbling sound as of water; utter with such sound. ● n. bubbling sound.

**guru** n. Hindu spiritual teacher; influential or revered teacher.

**gush** ● v. **1** flow in sudden or copious stream. **2** speak or behave effusively. ● n. **1** sudden or copious stream. **2** effusiveness.□□ **gushing** adj.

**gusher** n. **1** oil well emitting unpumped oil. **2** effusive person.

**gushy** adj. (**gushier, gushiest**) excessively emotional, effusive.

**gusset** n. piece let into garment etc. to strengthen or enlarge it.

**gust** ● n. sudden violent rush of wind; burst of rain, smoke, anger, etc. ● v. blow in gusts.□□ **gusty** adj.

**gusto** n. zest; enjoyment.

**gut** ● n. **1** intestines; thread made from animal intestines; (**guts**) abdominal organs. **2** (**guts**) courage and determination. ● adj. colloq. instinctive, fundamental. ● v. (**gutted**) remove (guts) from fish etc.; remove or destroy the internal fittings or parts of.

**gutful** n. colloq. = BELLYFUL.

**gutless** adj. colloq. lacking courage or energy.

**gutsy** adj. (**gutsier**) colloq. **1** courageous. **2** greedy.

**gutter** ● n. **1** shallow trough below eaves, or channel at side of street, for carrying off rainwater; (gutter) groove. **2** (**the gutter**) poor or degraded environment. ● v. **1** furrow, channel (as water does). **2** (of candle) burn unsteadily and melt away.

**guttering** n. (material for) gutters.

**guttural** ● adj. throaty, harsh-sounding; (of sound) produced in throat. ● n. guttural consonant.

**gutzer** n. (also **gutser**) *Aust.* colloq. **1** heavy fall. **2** failure.

**guy** n. **1** colloq. a man. **2** (**guys**) colloq. people of either sex. **3** rope or chain to keep a thing steady or secured.

**guzzle** v. eat or drink greedily.
□□ **guzzler** n.

**gybe** v. (also **jibe**) (of a sail or boom) swing across; (of a boat) change course in this way.

**gym** ● n. gymnasium; gymnastics. ● adj. pertaining to gymnastics.

**gymkhana** n. sporting competition, esp. for horse-riding.

**gymnasium** n. (pl. **gymnasiums** or **gymnasia**) room etc. equipped for physical training, gymnastics, etc.

**gymnast** n. expert in gymnastics.

**gymnastics** n. & n.pl. exercises to develop the muscles or demonstrate agility. □□ **gymnastic** adj.

**gymnosperm** n. plant having seeds unprotected by an ovary, including conifers, cycads, and ginkgos.

**gynaecology** n. (also **gynecology**) science of physiological functions and diseases of women. □□ **gynaecological** adj. **gynaecologist** n.

**gyp** colloq. ● v. (**gypped, gypping**) defraud, cheat. ● n. swindle; swindler.

**gypsum** n. chalk-like substance.

**gypsy** (also **gipsy**) ● n. 1 member of dark-skinned nomadic people of Europe. 2 one whose looks, lifestyle, etc. suggest a gypsy. ● adj. of or pertaining to gypsies.

**gyrate** v. move in circle or spiral. □□ **gyration** n. **gyratory** adj.

**gyro** n. colloq. gyroscope.

**gyroscope** n. rotating wheel whose axis is free to turn but maintains fixed direction unless perturbed. used for stabilisation. □□ **gyroscopic** adj.

# Hh

**H** *abbr.* **1** hard (pencil lead). **2** *colloq.* heroin.

**ha** ● *abbr.* hectare(s).
● *int.* exclamation of triumph.

**habeas corpus** *n.* writ requiring person to be brought before judge etc., esp. to investigate lawfulness of his or her detention.

**haberdasher** *n.* dealer in dress accessories and sewing goods.
□□ **haberdashery** *n.*

**habit** *n.* **1** settled or regular tendency or practice; practice that is hard to give up; mental constitution or attitude. **2** clothes, esp. of religious order.

**habitable** *adj.* suitable for living in.
□□ **habitability** *n.*

**habitat** *n.* natural home of plant or animal.

**habitation** *n.* inhabiting; house, home.

**habitual** *adj.* done regularly or constantly; usual. □□ **habitually** *adv.*

**habituate** *v.* accustom.
□□ **habituation** *n.*

**hack** ● *v.* **1** cut, chop or hit roughly. **2** gain unauthorised access to computer files; program quickly and roughly. **3** *colloq.* manage; cope with. **4** ride on horseback on road at ordinary pace. ● *n.* **1** rough cut, blow, or stroke. **2** *colloq.* act of computer hacking; piece of computer code providing a quick solution to a particular problem. **3** person doing routine work esp. as writer. **4** strategy etc. for managing one's time or activities more efficiently. **5** horse for ordinary riding.

**hacker** *n.* *colloq.* computer enthusiast, esp. one who gains unauthorised access to files.

**hacking** *adj.* (of cough) short, dry, and frequent.

**hackles** *n.pl.* hairs on animal's neck that rise when it is angry or alarmed.

**hackneyed** *adj.* overused, trite.

**hacksaw** *n.* saw for metal.

**had** see HAVE.

**haddock** *n.* (*pl.* **haddock**) edible sea fish.

**haem-** *prefix* (also **hem-**) of the blood.

**haematology** *n.* study of blood.
□□ **haematologist** *n.*

**haemoglobin** *n.* oxygen-carrying substance in red blood cells.

**haemophilia** *n.* hereditary tendency to bleed severely from even slight injury through failure of blood to clot.

**haemorrhage** ● *n.* profuse bleeding. ● *v.* bleed heavily.

**haemorrhoids** *n.pl.* varicose veins at or near the anus.

**hafnium** *n.* silvery metallic element (symbol Hf).

**haft** ● *n.* handle of knife etc.
● *v.* provide with haft.

**hag** *n.* **1** ugly old woman. **2** witch.

**haggard** *adj.* looking exhausted and distraught.

**haggis** *n.* Scottish dish of offal boiled in bag with oatmeal etc.

**haggle** ● *v.* bargain persistently. ● *n.* haggling.

**ha-ha** *n.* boundary consisting of ditch with sunken wall in it.

**hahnium** *n.* radioactive element (symbol Ha).

**haiku** *n.* (*pl.* **haiku**) Japanese three-line poem of usu. seventeen syllables.

**hail** *n.* **1** pellets of frozen rain. **2** shower of blows, questions, etc.
● *v.* **1** pour down as or like hail. **2** greet, call to; signal.

**hailstone** n. pellet of frozen rain.

**hair** n. any of the fine filaments growing from skin of mammals, esp. of human head. □ **hair-raising** terrifying.

**haircut** n. cutting of the hair; style in which the hair is cut.

**hairdo** n. (pl. **hairdos**) arrangement of hair.

**hairdresser** n. person who cuts and arranges hair.

**hairline** n. edge of hair on the forehead etc.; very narrow crack or line.

**hairpin bend** n. a sharp U-shaped bend.

**hairy** adj. 1 covered with hair. 2 colloq. frightening, dangerous. □□ **hairiness** n.

**haj** n. (also **hajj**) Islamic pilgrimage to Mecca.

**haka** n. Maori ceremonial war dance; similar dance by sports team before match.

**hake** n. (pl. **hake**) 1 codlike sea fish. 2 gemfish.

**hakea** n. Australian shrub with spiny flower heads and woody fruits.

**halal** adj. (of food or food shop) fulfilling requirements of Islamic law.

**halberd** n. hist. combined spear and battleaxe.

**halcyon** adj. calm, peaceful, happy.

**hale** adj. strong and healthy.

**half** ● n. (pl. **halves**) 1 either of two (esp. equal) parts into which a thing is divided. 2 Sport either of two equal periods of play. 3 colloq. **half-back.** ● adj. 1 forming a half. 2 incomplete. ● adv. partly. □ **half-back** Rugby player between forwards and full back(s). **half-caste** offens. person whose parents are of different races. **half-forward** AFL (player in) position between forward and centre lines. **half-hearted** not very enthusiastic. **half-life** time after which radioactivity etc. is half its original

level. **half-mast** (of flag) lowered in mourning.

**halfway** ● adv. 1 at point midway between two others. 2 to some extent. ● adj. situated halfway.

**halfwit** n. colloq. derog. stupid person. □□ **half-witted** adj.

**halibut** n. large edible fish.

**halitosis** n. bad breath.

**hall** n. 1 entrance area of house; corridor. 2 large room or building for meetings, concerts, etc. 3 (in full **hall of residence**) residence for students.

**hallelujah** = ALLELUIA.

**hallmark** n. mark used to show standard of gold, silver, and platinum; distinctive feature.

**halloumi** n. firm white cheese made from goats' or ewes' milk.

**hallowed** adj. holy or honoured as holy.

**Halloween** n. (also **Hallowe'en**) eve of All Saints' Day, 31 Oct.

**hallucinate** v. experience hallucinations.

**hallucination** n. illusion of seeing or hearing something. □□ **hallucinatory** adj.

**hallucinogenic** adj. causing hallucinations.

**halo** ● n. 1 disc of light shown around head of sacred person. 2 glory associated with idealised person etc. 3 circle of light around sun or moon etc. ● v. surround with halo.

**halogen** n. any of the non-metallic elements (fluorine, chlorine, etc.) that form a salt when combined with metal.

**halon** n. gaseous halogen used to extinguish fires.

**halt** ● n. stop (usu. temporary). ● v. (cause to) make a halt.

**halter** n. 1 strap around head of horse for holding or leading it; strap passing behind back of neck holding dress etc. up.

**2** (also **halter-neck**) dress etc. held by this.

**halva** n. (also **halwa**) confection of sesame flour, honey, etc.

**halve** v. divide into halves; reduce by half.

**halyard** n. rope or tackle for raising or lowering sail etc.

**ham** ● n. **1** (meat from) pig's thigh, salted or smoked. **2** bad actor; amateur radio operator.
● v. (**hammed**) colloq. overact.
□ **ham-fisted** clumsy.

**hamburger** n. flat round cake of minced beef.

**hamlet** n. small village.

**hammer** ● n. **1** tool with heavy metal head at right angles to its handle, used for driving nails etc.; similar device, as for exploding charge in gun, striking strings of piano, etc.; auctioneer's mallet. **2** metal ball attached to wire for throwing as athletic contest.
● v. **1** strike or drive (as) with hammer. **2** colloq. defeat utterly.
□□ **hammering** n.

**hammerlock** n. wrestling hold in which twisted arm is bent behind back.

**hammock** n. bed of canvas or netting suspended by cords at ends.

**hamper** ● n. large basket, usu. with hinged lid, and containing food; selection of food etc. for special occasion. ● v. **1** obstruct movement of. **2** hinder.

**hamster** n. mouselike rodent often kept as pet.

**hamstring** ● n. tendon at the back of knee or hock. ● v. (**hamstrung**, **hamstringing**) cripple by cutting hamstrings; cripple the activity of.

**hand** ● n. **1** part of arm below wrist. **2** control, influence, or help. **3** manual worker. **4** person's handwriting. **5** pointer on dial etc. **6** side or direction. **7** round of card game;

player's cards. **8** measure of horse's height, 10.16 cm (4 in.). **9** bunch (of bananas etc.) ● v. give or pass. □ **at hand** close by. **hands down** easily. **on hand** available. **out of hand** out of control. **to hand** within reach.

**handbag** n. bag to hold purse and personal articles.

**handball** n. **1** game with ball thrown or hit by hand. **2** Soccer intentional touching of ball with hand or arm (a foul). **3** AFL = HANDPASS.

**handbill** n. printed note circulated by hand.

**handbook** n. book giving useful facts.

**handcuff** ● n. metal ring linked to another, for securing prisoner's wrists. ● v. put handcuffs on.

**handful** n. **1** enough to fill the hand; small number or amount. **2** colloq. troublesome person or task.

**handicap** ● n. **1** circumstance that makes progress or success difficult. **2** dated offens. condition that restricts person's ability to function physically etc. **3** disadvantage imposed on superior competitor to equalise chances; race etc. in which this is imposed. ● v. (**handicapped**) impose handicap on; place at disadvantage.

**handicraft** n. work requiring manual and artistic skill.

**handiwork** n. work done or thing made by hand, or by particular person.

**handkerchief** n. (pl. **handkerchiefs** or **handkerchieves**) square of cloth used to wipe nose etc.

**handle** ● n. **1** part by which thing is held, carried, or controlled. **2** colloq. person's title or name. ● v. touch, feel, operate, etc. with hands; manage, deal with.

**handlebar** n. steering bar of bicycle etc.

**handler** n. person in charge of trained dog etc.

**handout** n. something distributed free of charge.

**handpass** AFL ● n. pass (to teammate) in which ball is held in one hand and struck with the other. ● v. deliver handpass.

**handrail** n. rail beside stairs etc.

**handset** n. mobile phone; part of a telephone that is held up to speak into and listen to.

**handshake** n. clasping of person's hand as greeting etc.

**handsome** adj. 1 good-looking. 2 generous; (of a price etc.) very large. □□ **handsomely** adv.

**handspring** n. somersault in which one lands first on hands and then on feet.

**handstand** n. balancing on one's hands with feet in air.

**handwriting** n. (style of) writing by hand. □□ **handwritten** adj.

**handy** adj. (**handier**) 1 convenient. 2 clever with one's hands.

**hang** ● v. (**hung, hanging**) 1 support or be supported from above. 2 droop; be present oppressively; remain. 3 (**hanged, hanging**) kill or be killed by suspension from a rope around neck. ● n. way thing hangs. □ **get the hang of** colloq. learn how to do. **hang back** hesitate; remain behind.

**hang-gliding** sport of gliding in an airborne frame using holding one person. **hang on** 1 hold tightly. 2 colloq. wait. 3 depend on. **hang out** colloq. spend time relaxing.

**hangar** n. building for housing aircraft etc.

**hanger** n. loop or hook by which a thing is hung; shaped piece of wood etc. to hang garment on.

**hangings** n.pl. draperies hung on walls.

**hangover** n. unpleasant after-effects from drinking too much alcohol.

**hank** n. coil of yarn.

**hanker** v. long for; crave. □□ **hankering** n.

**hanky** n. (also **hankie**) colloq. handkerchief.

**hanky-panky** n. colloq. misbehaviour; trickery.

**Hansard** n. record of parliamentary debates and proceedings.

**Hanukkah** n. Jewish festival of lights, beginning in December.

**haphazard** adj. casual; random. □□ **haphazardly** adv.

**hapless** adj. unlucky.

**happen** v. occur; chance. □ **happen to** be the fate or experience of.

**happy** adj. 1 feeling or showing pleasure or contentment; fortunate; apt, pleasing. 2 colloq. inclined to use excessively or at random. □ **happy medium** satisfactory compromise. □□ **happily** adv. **happiness** n.

**harangue** v. lecture earnestly and at length.

**harass** v. trouble, annoy; attack repeatedly. □□ **harassment** n.

**harbinger** n. person or thing announcing another's approach; forerunner.

**harbour** (also **harbor**) ● n. place of shelter for ships; shelter.
● v. 1 give shelter to. 2 entertain (thoughts etc.)

**hard** ● adj. 1 firm, not easily cut. 2 difficult; not easy to bear; harsh; strenuous. 3 (of drugs) strong and addictive; (of currency) not likely to drop suddenly in value; (of drinks) strongly alcoholic; (of water) containing minerals that prevent soap from lathering freely.
● adv. intensively; with difficulty; so as to be hard. □ **hard-boiled** 1 (of eggs) boiled until yolk and white are set. 2 (of people) callous. **hard copy** material produced in printed form from computer. **hard-headed** shrewd and practical. **hard-hearted** unfeeling. **hard of hearing** slightly deaf.

**hard sell** aggressive salesmanship.

**hard up** short of money. □□ **hardness** n.

**hardbitten** adj. tough and tenacious.

**hardboard** n. stiff board made of compressed wood pulp.

**harden** v. make or become hard or unyielding.

**hardly** adv. **1** scarcely. **2** with difficulty.

**hardship** n. severe suffering or privation.

**hardware** n. **1** tools and household implements sold by these. **2** weapons. **3** mechanical and electronic components of computer.

**hardwood** n. hard heavy wood of eucalypts and deciduous broad-leaved trees.

**hardy** adj. robust; capable of endurance; (of plant) able to grow in open air all year. □□ **hardiness** n.

**hare** ● n. mammal like large rabbit. ● v. run rapidly. □ **hare-brained** wild and foolish; rash.

**harelip** n. congenital cleft in upper lip.

**harem** n. **1** women's quarters in Muslim household. **2** wives etc. of polygamous man.

**haricot** n. (in full **haricot bean**) French bean with small white seeds.

**hark** v. listen. □ **hark back** return to earlier subject.

**harlequin** ● n. masked pantomime character in diamond-patterned costume. ● adj. in varied colours.

**harlot** n. arch. prostitute. □□ **harlotry** n.

**harm** ● n. hurt, damage. ● v. cause harm to.

**harmful** adj. causing or likely to cause harm. □□ **harmfully** adv.

**harmless** adj. not able or likely to harm. □□ **harmlessly** adv.

**harmonica** n. small rectangular instrument played by blowing and sucking air through it.

**harmonise** v. (also **-ize**) add notes to (melody) to produce harmony; bring into or be in harmony. □□ **harmonisation** n.

**harmonium** n. keyboard instrument with bellows and metal reeds.

**harmony** n. combination of musical notes to form chords; melodious sound; agreement, concord. □□ **harmonic** adj. **harmonious** adj. **harmoniously** adv.

**harness** ● n. straps etc. by which horse is fastened to cart etc. and controlled; similar arrangement for fastening thing to person. ● v. **1** put harness on. **2** utilise (natural resources), esp. to produce energy.

**harp** n. musical instrument with strings in triangular frame. □ **harp on** talk repeatedly about. □□ **harpist** n.

**harpoon** ● n. spearlike missile for shooting whales etc. ● v. spear with harpoon.

**harpsichord** n. keyboard instrument with strings plucked mechanically. □□ **harpsichordist** n.

**harpy** n. **1** mythological monster with woman's face and bird's wings and claws. **2** grasping unscrupulous person.

**harridan** n. bad-tempered old woman.

**harrier** n. **1** hound used for hunting hares. **2** cross-country runner. **3** kind of falcon.

**harrow** ● n. frame with metal teeth and discs for breaking up clods of earth. ● v. **1** draw harrow over. **2** (usu. as **harrowing** adj.) distress greatly.

**harry** v. ravage, despoil. **2** harass.

**harsh** adj. **1** rough to hearing, taste, etc. **2** severe, cruel. □□ **harshly** adv. **harshness** n.

**hart** n. adult male deer.

**harum-scarum** adj. colloq. wild, reckless.

**harvest** ● n. **1** gathering in crops etc.; season for this; season's yield.

**2** product of any action. • *v.* reap and gather in.

**harvester** *n.* reaper; reaping machine.

**has** see HAVE. □ **has-been** *colloq.* person or thing that has lost former importance or popularity.

**hash** *n.* **1** dish of reheated pieces of cooked meat. **2** mixture; jumble; recycled material. **3** the symbol #. **4** *colloq.* hashish. *colloq.* □ **make a hash of** make a mess of; bungle.

**hashish** *n.* cannabis resin.

**hashtag** *n.* hash sign (#); word or phrase preceded by this sign.

**hasp** *n.* hinged metal clasp passing over staple and secured by padlock.

**hassium** *n.* chemical element (symbol **Hs**).

**hassle** *colloq.* • *n.* trouble, problem; argument. • *v.* harass.

**hassock** *n.* **1** kneeling cushion. **2** tuft of matted grass.

**haste** *n.* urgency of movement; hurry.

**hasten** *v.* (cause to) proceed or go quickly.

**hasty** *adj.* hurried; said, made, or done too quickly; quick-tempered. □□ **hastily** *adv.* **hastiness** *n.*

**hat** *n.* (esp. outdoor) head covering. □ **hat trick** three successes in a row, esp. in sport.

**hatch** • *n.* **1** opening in wall, floor, ship's deck, etc.; its cover. **2** act of hatching; brood hatched. • *v.* **1** emerge from egg or produce (young) from egg. **2** devise (plot). **3** mark with parallel lines.

**hatchback** *n.* car with rear door that opens upwards.

**hatchery** *n.* place for hatching eggs.

**hatchet** *n.* light short axe. □ **hatchet-faced** sharp-featured; grim looking. **hatchet job** fierce attack on person, esp. in print.

**hate** • *v.* dislike intensely. • *n.* hatred. • *adj.* expressing hate.

**hateful** *adj.* arousing hatred; detestable.

**hatred** *n.* intense dislike, ill will.

**haughty** *adj.* proud, arrogant. □□ **haughtily** *adv.* **haughtiness** *n.*

**haul** • *v.* **1** pull or drag forcibly. **2** transport by truck, cart, etc. • *n.* **1** hauling. **2** amount gained or acquired. **3** distance to be traversed.

**haulage** *n.* (charge for) commercial transport of goods.

**haulier** *n.* person or firm engaged in transport of goods.

**haunch** *n.* fleshy part of buttock and thigh; leg and loin of animal as food; hindquarter.

**haunt** • *v.* **1** (of ghost etc.) visit regularly. **2** frequent (place). **3** linger in mind of. **4** distress, torment, be often in company of person. • *n.* place frequented by person.

**haunting** *adj.* **1** (of memory, melody, etc.) lingering. **2** poignant, evocative.

**haute couture** *n.* high fashion.

**have** • *v.* (**has, had, having**) **1** possess; contain. **2** experience, undergo; give birth to. **3** cause to be or do or be done; allow; be compelled (to do). **4** *colloq.* cheat, deceive. • *v.aux.* used with past participle to form past tenses (*he has gone*). □ **have it out** settle problem by frank discussion. **haves and have-nots** people with and without wealth or privilege. **have up** bring (person) to trial.

**haven** *n.* refuge.

**haversack** *n.* canvas bag carried on back or over shoulder.

**havoc** *n.* devastation, confusion.

**hawk** • *n.* **1** bird of prey with rounded wings. **2** *Polit.* person who advocates aggressive policy. • *v.* carry (goods) for sale.

**hawker** *n.* person who hawks goods.

**hawser** *n.* thick rope or cable for mooring ship.

**hawthorn** *n.* thorny shrub with red berries.

**hay** *n.* grass cut and dried for fodder. □ **hay fever** allergy caused by pollen and dust.

**haywire** *adj.* badly disorganised.

**hazard** ● *n.* danger; risk; chance; obstacle. ● *v.* venture; risk.

**hazardous** *adj.* risky.

**haze** *n.* 1 slight mist. 2 mental obscurity, confusion.

**hazel** ● *n.* nut-bearing shrub or small tree; shrub resembling hazel. ● *adj.* greenish-brown.

**hazmat** *n.* dangerous substances; hazardous material.

**hazy** *adj.* 1 misty. 2 vague; confused. □□ **hazily** *adv.* **haziness** *n.*

**HB** *abbr.* hard black (pencil lead).

**HDMI** *abbr. propr.* high-definition multimedia interface, a standard for connecting video devices .

**he** *pron.* (as subject of verb) the male person or animal in question; person of unspecified sex.

> **Usage** The use of *he* to refer to a person of unspecified sex is now generally regarded as old-fashioned or sexist.

**head** ● *n.* 1 part of the body containing eyes, nose, mouth, and brain; the intellect. 2 individual person or animal. 3 something like the head in form or position, top or leading part of position; foam on beer etc.; chief person. 4 (**heads**) side of coin showing a head, turned upwards after being tossed. 5 body of water or steam confined for exerting pressure. ● *v.* 1 be at the front or in charge of. 2 move or send in specified direction. 3 provide with heading. 4 strike (ball) with one's head. □ **head job** *coarse colloq.* act of fellatio. **head off** get ahead of so as to intercept and turn aside; forestall. **head-on** with the head or front foremost. **head over heels** (or **head over turkey**) so as to turn completely over; utterly. **heads-up** *colloq.* advance warning of something.

**headache** *n.* continuous pain in head; worrying problem.

**headdress** *n.* ornamental covering worn on head.

**header** *n.* 1 *Soccer* shot or pass made with head. 2 *colloq.* headlong fall or dive. 3 line or block of text appearing at top of each page of a book or document.

**headgear** *n.* something worn on head as a hat, protective covering, etc.

**headhunt** *v.* seek to recruit (senior staff) from another firm.

**heading** *n.* title at head of page etc.

**headland** *n.* promontory.

**headlight** *n.* powerful light on front of vehicle etc.; its beam.

**headline** *n.* heading in newspaper; (**headlines**) summary of broadcast news.

**headlong** *adj. & adv.* falling or plunging with head first; in hasty and rash way.

**headphones** *n.pl.* set of earphones for listening to audio equipment.

**headquarters** *n.pl.* place from which organisation is controlled.

**headspace** *n.* 1 space left above contents in sealed container. 2 *colloq.* person's state of mind; time to think clearly.

**headstone** *n.* stone set up at head of grave.

**headstrong** *adj.* self-willed and obstinate.

**headway** *n.* progress.

**headwind** *n.* wind blowing from directly in front.

**heady** *adj.* exciting, intoxicating; impetuous; (of liquor) potent. □□ **headily** *adv.* **headiness** *n.*

**heal** v. become healthy again; cure; put right (differences). □□ **healer** n.

**health** n. state of being well and free from illness; condition of the body.

**healthy** adj. (**healthier**) having, showing, or producing good health; functioning well. □□ **healthily** adv. **healthiness** n.

**heap** ● n. **1** disorderly pile. **2** (**heaps**) colloq. plenty. ● v. pile or become piled in a heap; load with large quantities.

**hear** v. (**heard**, **hearing**) perceive (sounds) with the ear; pay attention to; receive information. □ **hear! hear!** I agree. □□ **hearer** n.

**hearing** n. **1** faculty of perceiving sounds; range within which sounds may be heard; opportunity to be heard. **2** trial of case before court. □ **hearing aid** small sound amplifier worn to improve hearing.

**hearse** n. vehicle for carrying coffin.

**heart** n. **1** organ in body keeping up circulation of blood by contraction and dilation; region of heart, breast. **2** seat of thought, feeling, or emotion (esp. love); courage; mood. **3** central or innermost part, essence. **4** (conventionally) heart-shaped thing. **5** playing card of suit marked with red hearts. □ **break a person's heart** cause someone overwhelming grief. **by heart** memorised thoroughly. **heart attack** (also **heart failure**) sudden failure of heart to function normally. **heart-rending** very distressing. **heart-searching** examination of one's own feelings and motives. **heart-throb** colloq. attractive person, esp. one inspiring amorous feelings. **heart-to-heart** frank and personal. **heart-warming** emotionally moving and encouraging.

**heartbeat** n. pulsation of heart.

**heartburn** n. burning sensation in lower part of chest from indigestion.

**hearten** v. make or become more cheerful. □□ **heartening** adj.

**heartfelt** adj. felt deeply, sincere.

**hearth** n. floor of fireplace; this as symbol of home.

**heartless** adj. unfeeling, pitiless. □□ **heartlessly** adv.

**hearty** adj. (**heartier**) **1** strong, vigorous. **2** (of meal or appetite) large. **3** warm, friendly. □□ **heartily** adv. **heartiness** n.

**heat** ● n. **1** condition or sensation of being hot; hot weather. **2** energy arising from motion of molecules. **3** warmth of feeling; anger. **4** most intense part or period of activity. **5** preliminary contest before final(s). ● v. make or become hot; inflame. □ **on heat** (of female mammals) ready to mate.

**heated** adj. angry; impassioned. □□ **heatedly** adv.

**heater** n. device for heating room, water, etc.

**heath** n. flattish tract of uncultivated land with low shrubs; plant growing on heath or in the bush.

**heathen** ● n. person who does not believe in an established religion. ● adj. of heathens; having no religion; unenlightened.

**heather** n. purple-flowered plant of moors and heaths. □ **heathing** n. equipment used to heat building etc.

**heatstroke** n. illness caused by overexposure to sun.

**heatwave** n. long period of hot weather.

**heave** ● v. **1** lift or haul with great effort. **2** colloq. throw. **3** utter (a sigh). **4** rise and fall like waves. **5** pant, retch. ● n. act of heaving. □ **heave to** (**hove**, **heaving**) bring ship to standstill with its head to the wind.

**heaven** n. **1** home of God, home of blessed after death; place or state of bliss. **2** colloq. delightful thing.

**3 (the heavens)** sky as seen from earth. □ **heavenly bodies** sun, stars, planets, etc. □□ **heavenly** adj.

**heavy** ● adj. (**heavier, heaviest**) **1** having great weight, force, or intensity. **2** dense; stodgy. **3** serious. ● v. put pressure on, harass. □ **heavy industry** industry producing metal or heavy machines etc. **heavy metal** type of loud rock music. □□ **heavily** adv. **heaviness** n.

**heavyweight** ● adj. having great weight or influence. ● n. heavyweight person; highest weight class in boxing etc.

**Hebrew** ● n. member of a Semitic people in ancient Palestine; their language; modern form of this, used esp. in Israel. ● adj. of or in Hebrew; of Jewish people. □□ **Hebraic** adj.

**heckle** ● v. interrupt or harass. ● n. act of heckling. □□ **heckler** n.

**hectare** n. metric unit of square measure (10,000 sq. metres or 2.471 acres).

**hectic** adj. busy and confused; excited; feverish. □□ **hectically** adv.

**hecto-** comb. form one hundred.

**hector** ● v. bluster, bully. ● n. bully.

**hedge** ● n. **1** fence of bushes or low trees. **2** protection against possible loss. ● v. **1** surround with hedge; enclose. **2** secure oneself against loss (on bet etc.) **3** avoid committing oneself. □ **hedge fund** investment fund that engages in speculation using credit or borrowed capital.

**hedgehog** n. small animal covered in stiff spines.

**hedonism** n. (behaviour based on) belief in pleasure as humankind's proper aim. □□ **hedonist** n. **hedonistic** adj.

**heed** ● v. attend to; take notice of. ● n. care, attention. □□ **heedless** adj. **heedlessly** adv.

**heel** ● n. back of foot below ankle; part of sock or shoe covering this. **2** colloq. scoundrel. ● v. **1** fit or renew heel on (shoe). **2** (of a boat) tilt to one side.

**heeler** n. Australian sheep or cattle dog trained to work stock by nipping at animals' heels.

**heft** ● v. lift (something heavy), esp. to judge its weight.

**hefty** adj. (of person) big, strong; (of thing) heavy, powerful.

**hegemony** n. leadership; domination; predominance. □□ **hegemonic** adj.

**Hegira** n. (also **Hejira**) Muhammad's departure from Mecca to Medina (AD 622), from which the Muslim era is reckoned.

**heifer** n. young cow, esp. one that has not had more than one calf.

**height** n. **1** measurement from base to top; elevation above ground or other level. **2** being tall; high place; highest degree of something.

**heighten** v. make or become higher or more intense.

**heinous** adj. atrocious.

**heir** n. person entitled to property or rank as legal successor of former holder; person, group etc. deriving continuing tradition from predecessors.

**heiress** n. female heir.

**heist** ● v. colloq. steal, shoplift. ● n. colloq. theft.

**held** SEE HOLD.

**helical** adj. spiral.

**helicopter** n. wingless aircraft lifted and propelled by blades revolving horizontally.

**heliotrope** n. **1** European plant with fragrant purple flowers. **2** light purple colour.

**heliport** n. place where helicopters take off and land.

**helium** n. light non-flammable gaseous element (symbol He).

**helix** n. (pl. **helices**) spiral or coiled curve.

**hell** ● n. home of damned after death; place or state of misery. ● int. exclamation of surprise or annoyance.□ **hell-bent** recklessly determined. **hell for leather** very fast.

**hellish** ● adj. of or like hell; colloq. extremely difficult or unpleasant. ● adv. colloq. extremely. □□ **hellishly** adv.

**hello** (also **hallo, hullo**) ● int. expressing informal greeting or surprise, or calling attention. ● n. cry of 'hello'.

**helm** n. tiller or wheel for managing rudder.□ **at the helm** in control.

**helmet** n. protective head covering worn by construction workers, cyclists, etc.

**helmsman** n. person who steers ship.

**help** ● v. do part of another's work; be useful (to); make easier; serve with food; assist. ● n. act of helping; person or thing that helps. □□ **helper** n.

**helpful** adj. giving help; useful. □□ **helpfully** adv. **helpfulness** n.

**helping** ● n. portion of food. ● adj. providing support etc.

**helpless** adj. lacking help, defenceless; unable to act without help.□□ **helplessly** adv. **helplessness** n.

**helpline** n. telephone service providing help with problems.

**helter-skelter** adv. & adj. in disorderly haste.

**hem** ● n. edge (of cloth) turned under and sewn down. ● v. (hemmed) sew hem on.

**hemisphere** n. half sphere; half earth, esp. as divided by equator or by line passing through the poles; each half of brain.□□ **hemispherical** adj.

**hemlock** n. poisonous plant with small white flowers; poison made from it.

**hemp** n. Asian herbaceous plant with coarse fibres used in making rope and cloth.

**hen** n. female bird, esp. of domestic fowl.□ **hen's night** (or **hen's party**) party for women only.

**hence** adv. **1** from this time; for this reason. **2** arch. from here.

**henceforth** adv. (also **henceforward**) from this time on, in future.

**henchman** n. trusted supporter.

**henna** n. reddish dye used to colour hair.

**henry** n. SI unit of electric inductance.

**hepatic** adj. of the liver.

**hepatitis** n. inflammation of liver.

**heptagon** n. plane figure with seven sides and angles.□□ **heptagonal** adj.

**heptathlon** n. athletic contest of seven events for all competitors. □□ **heptathlete** n.

**her** ● pron. (as object of verb) female person or thing in question. ● adj. belonging to her.

**herald** ● n. messenger; forerunner; official. ● v. proclaim approach of; usher in.□□ **heraldic** adj.

**heraldry** n. (science or art of) armorial bearings.

**herb** n. plant used as flavouring or in medicine.

**herbaceous** adj. soft-stemmed.

**herbage** n. vegetation collectively, esp. pasturage.

**herbal** ● adj. of herbs. ● n. book about herbs.

**herbalist** n. dealer in medicinal herbs; writer on herbs.

**herbarium** n. (pl. **herbaria**) collection of dried plants.

**herbicide** n. poison used to destroy unwanted vegetation.

**herbivore** n. plant-eating animal. □□ **herbivorous** adj.

**herculean** adj. having or requiring great strength or effort.

**herd** n. **1** number of cattle etc. feeding or travelling together.

**2 (the herd)** *derog.* large number of people. ● *v.* **1** (cause to) go in herd. **2** tend.

**here** ● *adv.* **1** in or to this place. **2** indicating person or thing. **3** at this point. ● *n.* this place.

**hereafter** *adv.* from now on. □ **the hereafter** life after death.

**hereby** *adv.* by this means; as a result of this.

**hereditary** *adj.* transmitted genetically from one generation to another; descending by inheritance, holding position by inheritance.

**heredity** *n.* genetic transmission of physical or mental characteristics; these characteristics.

**herein** *adv.* in this matter, book, etc.

**heresy** *n.* religious belief contrary to orthodox doctrine; opinion contrary to what is normally accepted.

**heretic** *n.* believer in heresy. □□ **heretical** *adj.*

**heritable** *adj.* that can be inherited.

**heritage** *n.* **1** what is or may be inherited; inherited circumstances, benefits, etc. **2** nation's historic buildings, countryside, etc.

**hermaphrodite** ● *n.* person, animal, or plant with organs of both sexes. ● *adj.* combining both sexes. □□ **hermaphroditic** *adj.*

**hermetic** *adj.* **1** with airtight seal. **2** relating to alchemy, magic, etc. □□ **hermetically** *adv.*

**hermit** *n.* person living in solitude.

**hernia** *n.* protrusion of part of organ through wall of cavity containing it.

**hero** *n.* (*pl.* **heroes**) person admired for courage, outstanding achievements, etc.; chief male character in story.

**heroic** ● *adj.* very brave. ● *n.pl.* (**heroics**) over-dramatic behaviour. □□ **heroically** *adv.*

**heroin** *n.* powerful addictive drug prepared from morphine.

**heroine** *n.* woman admired for courage, outstanding achievements etc.; chief female character in story.

**heroism** *n.* heroic conduct.

**heron** *n.* long-necked long-legged wading bird.

**herpes** *n.* viral disease causing skin blisters.

**herpetology** *n.* study of reptiles. □□ **herpetological** *adj.* **herpetologist** *n.*

**Herr** *n.* (*pl.* **Herren**) title of German man, corresponding to Mr.

**herring** *n.* edible N. Atlantic fish.

**herringbone** *n.* zigzag pattern or arrangement.

**hers** *pron.poss.* belonging to her.

**herself** *pron.* emphatic and reflexive form of SHE and HER.

**hertz** *n.* (*pl.* **hertz**) SI unit of frequency of electromagnetic waves.

**hesitant** *adj.* hesitating. □□ **hesitance** *n.* **hesitancy** *n.* **hesitantly** *adv.*

**hesitate** *v.* show or feel indecision; pause; be reluctant. □□ **hesitation** *n.*

**hessian** *n.* strong coarse hemp or jute sacking.

**heterodox** *adj.* not orthodox. □□ **heterodoxy** *n.*

**heterogeneous** *adj.* diverse; varied in content. □□ **heterogeneity** *n.*

**heterosexual** *adj.* & *n.* (person) sexually attracted to people of opposite sex. □□ **heterosexuality** *n.*

**heuristic** *adj.* serving to discover; using trial and error.

**hew** *v.* (**hewed**, **hewn** or **hewed**, **hewing**) chop or cut with axe, sword, etc.; cut into shape.

**hex** ● *v.* practise witchcraft; bewitch. ● *n.* magic spell.

**hexa-** *comb. form* six.

**hexadecimal** *adj.* Computing of a number system using sixteen rather than ten as a base.

**hexagon** *n.* plane figure with six sides and angles. □□ **hexagonal** *adj.*

**hexagram** n. six-pointed star formed by two intersecting equilateral triangles; figure of six lines.

**hexahedron** n. solid figure with six faces.

**hexameter** n. verse line of six metrical feet.

**hey** int. calling attention or expressing joy, surprise, enquiry, enthusiasm, etc.

**heyday** n. time of greatest success, prime.

**hiatus** n. (pl. **hiatuses**) break or gap in a sequence.

**hibbertia** n. shrub of temperate Australia, with masses of gold or orange flowers.

**hibernate** v. (of animal) spend winter in dormant state; remain inactive or secluded. □□ **hibernation** n.

**Hibernian** adj. & n. (a native) of Ireland.

**hibiscus** n. shrub with large brightly coloured flowers.

**hiccup** (also **hiccough**) ● n. 1 involuntary audible spasm of respiratory organs. 2 temporary or minor stoppage or difficulty. ● v. (**hiccuped**, **hiccuping**) make hiccup.

**hick** n. colloq. yokel.

**hickory** n. N. American tree related to walnut; any similar tree.

**hide** ● v. (**hid**, **hidden**, **hiding**) put or keep out of sight; keep secret; conceal (oneself). ● n. 1 camouflaged shelter for observing birds etc. 2 animal's skin. 3 colloq. impertinence, effrontery.

**hidebound** adj. rigidly conventional.

**hideous** adj. repulsive, revolting. □□ **hideously** adv. **hideousness** n.

**hiding** n. thrashing, belting; sound defeat.

**hierarchy** n. system of grades of authority ranked one above the other. □□ **hierarchical** adj.

**hieroglyph** n. picture representing word or syllable, esp. in ancient Egyptian; secret or enigmatic symbol. □□ **hieroglyphic** adj. **hieroglyphics** n. pl.

**hi-fi** ● adj. high fidelity. ● n. high-quality amplifier, etc., reproducing original sounds with little distortion.

**higgledy-piggledy** adv. & adj. in disorder.

**high** ● adj. 1 extending far upwards or a specified distance high; far above ground or sea level. 2 ranking above others; greater than normal; (of sound or voice) not deep or low. 3 (of meat) slightly decomposed. 4 colloq. intoxicated; under influence of drugs. ● n. 1 high level; area of high barometric pressure. 2 colloq. euphoric state, esp. drug-induced. ● adv. in, at, or to a high level. □ **high definition** high degree of detail in an image or screen. **higher education** education continued beyond completed secondary schooling, esp. at university. **high-handed** using authority arrogantly. **high-rise** with many storeys. **high road** main road. **high school** secondary school. **high-spirited** lively. **high-tech** (also **hi-tech**) involving advanced technology and electronics. **high tide** tide at its highest level. **high time** a time that is late or overdue. **high water** high tide.

**highbrow** adj. very intellectual, cultured.

**High Court** n. (in full **High Court of Australia**) supreme Federal Court and final court of appeal from the Supreme Courts of the states and from Federal Courts.

**highfalutin** adj. (also **highfaluting**) colloq. pompous, pretentious.

**highlands** n. pl. mountainous region. □□ **highland** adj.

**highlight** ● *n.* **1** moment or detail of vivid interest. **2** bright part of picture; bleached streak in hair.
● *v.* **1** bring into prominence. **2** mark with highlighter.

**highlighter** *n.* coloured marker pen for emphasising printed word.

**highly** *adv.* **1** in high degree. **2** favourably. □ **highly-strung** nervous, easily upset.

**highness** *n.* **1** state of being high. **2** (**Highness**) title of prince, princess, etc.

**highway** *n.* public road, main route.

**highwayman** *n. hist.* robber of passengers, travellers, etc.

**hijack** ● *v.* illegally seize control of (vehicle or aircraft etc. in transit).
● *n.* hijacking. □□ **hijacker** *n.*

**hike** ● *n.* **1** long walk, esp. in country for pleasure. **2** rise in prices etc.
● *v.* go on hike. □□ **hiker** *n.*

**hilarious** *adj.* extremely funny; boisterously merry. □□ **hilariously** *adv.* **hilarity** *n.*

**hill** *n.* natural elevation of ground, lower than mountain; heap, mound. □□ **hilly** *adj.*

**hillbilly** *n. US colloq.* unsophisticated country person.

**hillock** *n.* small hill, mound.

**hilt** *n.* handle of sword, dagger, etc. □ **to the hilt** completely.

**him** *pron.* (as object of verb) male person or animal in question, person of unspecified sex.

**himself** *pron.* emphatic and reflexive form of HE and HIM.

**hind** *n.* female deer.
● *adj.* situated at back.

**hinder** *v.* impede; delay.

**Hindi** *n.* **1** group of spoken languages in N. India. **2** literary form of Hindustani. **3** official language of India.

**hindrance** *n.* obstruction.

**Hindu** ● *n.* follower of Hinduism.
● *adj.* of Hindus or Hinduism.

**Hinduism** *n.* main religious and social system of India.

**Hindustani** *n.* language based on Hindi, used in much of India.

**hinge** ● *n.* **1** movable joint on which door, lid, etc. swings. **2** principle on which all depends. ● *v.* attach or be attached by hinge. □ **hinge on** depend on.

**hinny** *n.* offspring of female donkey and male horse.

**hint** ● *n.* **1** indirect suggestion; slight indication; small piece of practical information. **2** faint trace.
● *v.* suggest indirectly.

**hinterland** *n.* district behind that lying along coast etc.

**hip** *n.* **1** projection of pelvis on each side of body. **2** fruit of rose. □ **hip pocket** *colloq.* state of one's finances.

**hip hop** *n.* style of music featuring rap with electronic backing; culture associated with this.

**hippie** var. of HIPPY.

**hippopotamus** *n.* (*pl.* **hippopotamuses** or **hippopotami**) large African river mammal with thick skin.

**hippy** *n.* (also **hippie**) (*pl.* **hippies**) person of unconventional appearance, rejecting mainstream values etc.

**hipster** *n. colloq.* person who follows latest trends, esp. those regarded as being outside the cultural mainstream.

**hire** ● *v.* obtain use of (thing) or services of (person) for payment. ● *n.* hiring, being hired; payment for this. □ **hire out** grant temporary use of for payment. **hire purchase** system of purchase by payment in instalments.

**hireling** *n. derog.* person who does anything (only) for money.

**hirsute** *adj.* hairy. □□ **hirsuteness** *n.*

**his** *adj.* of or belonging to him.

**Hispanic** ● *adj. & n.* (native) of Spain or a Spanish-speaking country.

**hiss** ● *v.* make sharp sibilant sound, as of letter **s**; express disapproval of thus; whisper urgently or angrily.
● *n.* sharp sibilant sound.

**histamine** *n.* chemical compound in body tissues, associated with allergic reactions.

**histology** *n.* study of tissue structure.

**historian** *n.* writer of history; person learned in history.

**historic** *adj.* famous in history or potentially so.

**historical** *adj.* of history; belonging to or dealing with the past; not legendary.□□ **historically** *adv.*

**history** *n.* continuous record of events; study of past events; total accumulation of these; (esp. eventful) past or record.□ **make history** do something important and memorable.

**histrionic** ● *adj.* of acting; theatrical in manner. ● *n.* (**histrionics**) theatrical behaviour.

**hit** ● *v.* (**hit, hitting**) **1** strike with blow or missile; come forcefully against. **2** affect badly. **3** reach; find. ● *n.* **1** a blow; a stroke; shot that hits its target. **2** *colloq.* a murder; dose of a drug. **3** *colloq.* popular success. □ **hit it off** *colloq.* like one another.

**hitch** ● *v.* **1** fasten with loop etc. **2** move (thing) with jerk. **3** *colloq.* hitch-hike, obtain (ride).
● *n.* **1** temporary difficulty, snag. **2** jerk. **3** kind of noose or knot. **4** *colloq.* free ride in vehicle. □ **get hitched** *colloq.* marry. **hitch-hike** travel by seeking free lifts in passing vehicles.

**hither** *adv. formal* to this place.

**HIV** *abbr.* human immunodeficiency virus (causing AIDS).

**hive** *n.* **1** structure in which bees live; bees in it; busy swarming place;

swarming multitude. **2** (**hives**) skin eruption esp. nettle rash.

**HMAS** *abbr.* Her (or His) Majesty's Australian Ship.

**hoard** ● *n.* store (esp. of money or food). ● *v.* amass and store.
□□ **hoarder** *n.*

**hoarding** *n.* **1** structure erected to carry advertisements. **2** temporary fence around building site etc.

**hoarse** *adj.* (of voice) rough, husky; having hoarse voice.□□ **hoarsely** *adv.* **hoarseness** *n.*

**hoary** *adj.* grey or white with age; aged; old and trite.

**hoax** ● *n.* humorous or malicious deception; practical joke.
● *v.* deceive with hoax.□□ **hoaxer** *n.*

**hob** *n.* cooking surface with hotplates.

**hobble** ● *v.* **1** walk lamely, limp; proceed haltingly. **2** tie together legs of (horse etc.) to limit movement. ● *n.* **1** limping gait. **2** rope etc. used to hobble horse.

**hobby** *n.* something done for pleasure in one's spare time. □ **hobby farm** farm maintained as hobby, not as main source of income. **hobby horse 1** child's toy consisting of stick with horse's head. **2** preoccupation; favourite topic of conversation.

**hobgoblin** *n.* mischievous imp.

**hobnob** *v.* (**hobnobbed**) mix socially or informally.

**Hobson's choice** *n.* no alternative to thing offered.

**hock** ● *n.* **1** joint of quadruped's hind leg between knee and fetlock. **2** kind of dry white wine. ● *v. colloq.* pawn; sell, esp. illegally.

**hockey** *n.* team game played with ball and hooked sticks.

**hocus-pocus** *n.* trickery; supposed magical formula in conjuring.

**hod** *n.* trough on pole for carrying bricks etc.

**hoe** ● *n.* long-handled tool for weeding etc. ● *v.* (**hoed, hoeing**) weed (crops), loosen (soil), or dig up etc. with hoe.□ **hoe into** attack with vigour.

**hog** ● n. 1 castrated male pig. 2 colloq. greedy person.
● v. (**hogged**) colloq. take greedily; hoard selfishly.□ **go the whole hog** colloq. do something thoroughly.

**hogget** n. (meat of) yearling sheep.

**hoick** v. colloq. lift or jerk.

**hoi polloi** n. ordinary people.

**hoist** ● v. 1 raise or haul up; raise with ropes and pulleys etc. 2 colloq. steal; shoplift. 3 colloq. throw.
● n. 1 hoisting; apparatus for hoisting. 2 Aust. rotary clothes-hoist. 3 colloq. theft.

**hokum** n. colloq. bunkum; rubbish; sentimental or unreal material in film etc.

**hold** ● v. (**held, holding**) 1 keep in one's arms or hands etc. or in one's possession or control; keep in position or condition; contain; bear weight of. 2 remain unbroken under strain; continue, remain valid. 3 possess (qualifications etc.) 4 cause to take place. 5 believe. ● n. 1 act, manner, or means of holding; means of exerting influence. 2 storage cavity in lower part of ship or aircraft.
□ **hold on** 1 keep one's grasp on something. 2 wait a moment. **hold out** resist; survive; last; continue to make demand. **hold up** hinder; stop and rob. **hold-up** a delay; robbery. **hold with** agree with.

**holdall** n. large soft travel bag.

**holding** n. something held or owned; land held by owner or tenant.

**hole** ● n. 1 hollow place; burrow; opening. 2 wretched place; awkward situation. ● v. make hole(s) in; put into hole.□□ **holey** adj.

**holiday** ● n. period of recreation.
● v. spend a holiday.

**holiness** n. sanctity; being holy or sacred; (**His, Your Holiness**) title of pope.

**holism** n. (also **wholism**) theory that certain wholes are greater than the sum of their parts; Med. treating of whole person rather than symptoms of disease.□□ **holistic** adj.

**holland** n. smooth, durable, linen fabric.

**hollow** ● adj. 1 having cavity; not solid, sunken. 2 echoing. 3 empty. 4 hungry. 5 meaningless. 6 insincere. ● n. hollow place; hole; valley. ● v. make hollow; excavate.

**holly** n. evergreen prickly-leaved European shrub with red berries.

**hollyhock** n. tall plant with showy flowers.

**holmium** n. metallic element (symbol Ho).

**holocaust** n. destruction or slaughter on mass scale.

**hologram** n. photographic pattern having three-dimensional effect.

**holograph** ● adj. wholly in handwriting of person named as author. ● n. such document.

**holography** n. study or production of holograms.

**holster** n. leather case for pistol or revolver on belt etc.

**holus-bolus** adv. all at once; altogether.

**holy** adj. dedicated to a deity; pious, virtuous; consecrated, sacred.

**homage** n. tribute, expression of reverence.

**home** ● n. 1 place where one lives; dwelling house. 2 institution caring for people or animals. ● adj. of one's home or country; played on one's own ground. ● adv. at or to one's home; to the point aimed at. ● v. make its way home or to a target.□ **home truth** unpleasant truth about oneself.□□ **homeward** adj. & adv. **homewards** adv.

**homeland** n. one's native land.

**homeless** adj. lacking a home. □□ **homelessness** n.

**homely** adj. (**homelier**) simple and informal; plain, not beautiful. □□ **homeliness** n.

**homeopathy** = HOMOEOPATHY.

**homepage** n. person's or organisation's introductory document on World Wide Web.

**homesick** adj. longing for home.

**homeward** adj. & adv. going towards home. □□ **homewards** adv.

**homework** n. work set for pupil to do away from school.

**homicide** n. killing of person by another. □□ **homicidal** adj.

**homily** n. short sermon; moralising lecture. □□ **homiletic** adj.

**homing** adj.attrib. **1** (of pigeon) trained to fly home. **2** (of device) for guiding to target etc.

**hominid** ● adj. of family of existing and fossil humans. ● n. member of this.

**hominoid** ● adj. like a human. ● n. animal resembling human.

**homoeopathy** n. (also **homeopathy**) treatment of disease by minute doses of drugs that in healthy person would produce symptoms of the disease. □□ **homoeopath** n. **homoeopathic** adj.

**homogeneous** adj. (also **homogenous**) (having parts) of same kind or nature; uniform. □□ **homogeneity** n. **homogeneously** adv.

**homogenise** v. (also **-ize**) **1** make homogeneous. **2** treat (milk) so that cream does not separate.

**homograph** n. word spelt the same way as another.

**homologous** adj. having same relation, relative position, etc.; corresponding.

**homonym** n. word spelt or pronounced like another but of different meaning.

**homophobia** n. hatred or fear of homosexuals. □□ **homophobe** n. **homophobic** adj.

**homophone** n. word with same sounds as another.

**Homo sapiens** n. modern humans.

**homosexual** adj. & n. (person) sexually attracted to people of same sex. □□ **homosexuality** n.

**hone** ● n. whetstone, esp. for razors. ● v. sharpen (as) on hone.

**honest** ● adj. not lying, cheating, or stealing; sincere; fairly earned. ● adv. colloq. genuinely, really. □□ **honestly** adv.

**honesty** n. being honest; truthfulness.

**honey** n. **1** sweet sticky yellowish fluid made by bees from nectar; colour of this; sweetness. **2** colloq. darling; person etc. exciting admiration. □ **honey ant** Australian ant able to store honey-like liquid in its crop. **honey-bag** Aust. honeycomb of wild bee.

**honeybee** n. common hive bee.

**honeycomb** n. **1** structure of hexagonal cells of wax, made by bees to store honey and eggs; pattern of six-sided sections. **2** brittle golden sweet made by aerating boiling sugar and water etc.

**honeydew** n. **1** sweet substance excreted by aphids. **2** variety of melon with smooth green flesh.

**honeyeater** n. Australian bird with brush-tipped tongue for feeding on flower nectar etc.

**honeyed** adj. sweet, sweet-sounding.

**honeymoon** ● n. holiday of newly married couple; initial period of enthusiasm or goodwill. ● v. spend honeymoon.

**honeysuckle** n. **1** exotic climbing shrub with fragrant flowers.

2 Australian shrub with nectar-rich flowers.

**hongi** *n.* NZ Maori greeting in which people press their noses together.

**honk** ● *n.* sound of car horn; cry of wild goose. ● *v.* make this noise.

**honky-tonk** *n.* ragtime piano music.

**honorarium** *n.* (*pl.* honorariums or honoraria) voluntary payment made where no fee is legally required.

**honorary** *adj.* 1 conferred as honour. 2 unpaid.

**honorific** *adj.* conferring honour; implying respect; title of formal respect, as Doctor, Professor, etc.

**honour** (also honor) ● *n.* high respect, public regard; mark of this, privilege; good personal character or reputation. ● *v.* feel honour for; confer an honour on; pay (cheque) or fulfil (promise etc.) □ **honours degree** degree of higher standard than pass.

**honourable** *adj.* (also honorable) deserving, bringing, or showing honour; (**Honourable**) courtesy title of MPs and certain high officials. □□ **honourably** *adv.*

**hood** ● *n.* 1 covering for head and neck, esp. as part of garment; hoodlike part or thing. 2 = BONNET. 3 *colloq.* hoodlum. ● *v.* cover with hood. □□ **hooded** *adj.*

**hoodlum** *n.* hooligan, young thug; gangster.

**hoodoo** ● *n.* bad luck, thing or person that brings this. ● *v.* make unlucky; bewitch.

**hoodwink** *v.* deceive, delude.

**hoof** *n.* (*pl.* hoofs or hooves) horny part of horse's foot. □ **hoof it** *colloq.* travel on foot; run away.

**hook** ● *n.* 1 bent piece of metal etc. for catching hold of or hanging things on. 2 short blow made with elbow bent. ● *v.* 1 grasp, secure, fasten, or catch with a hook. 2 (in sports) send (ball) in curving or deviating path.

3 *Rugby* secure (ball) in scrum with foot. □ **hook up** 1 link or be linked to electronic equipment. 2 *colloq.* (of two people) meet or form relationship. **off the hook** 1 (of telephone receiver) off its rest. 2 *colloq.* no longer in difficulty.

**hookah** *n.* tobacco pipe with long tube passing through water to cool smoke.

**hooked** *adj.* 1 hook-shaped; furnished with hook(s). 2 *colloq.* stolen. 3 *colloq.* addicted or captivated.

**hooker** *n.* 1 *Rugby* player in front row of scrum who tries to hook ball. 2 *colloq.* prostitute.

**hooligan** *n.* young ruffian. □□ **hooliganism** *n.*

**hoon** *Aust. colloq.* ● *n.* 1 hooligan. 2 show-off, exhibitionist. ● *v.* (also **hoon around**) drive dangerously or at reckless speed.

**hoop** ● *n.* circular band of metal, wood, etc. ● *v.* bind with hoop(s).

**hooray** = HURRAH.

**hooroo** *int. & n.* (also **hooray**) *Aust. colloq.* conventional form of farewell, goodbye.

**hoot** ● *n.* 1 owl's cry; sound of car's horn etc.; shout of derision. 2 *colloq.* (cause of) laughter. 3 (also **two hoots**) *colloq.* anything, not the slightest. ● *v.* utter or make a hoot.

**hooter** *n.* 1 thing that hoots, esp. car's horn or siren. 2 *colloq.* nose.

**hoover** ● *n. propr.* vacuum cleaner. ● *v.* suck up with vacuum cleaner.

**hop** ● *v.* (hopped) 1 jump on one foot; jump with all feet together. 2 *colloq.* make short quick trip. ● *n.* 1 hopping movement; informal dance; short flight. 2 climbing plant cultivated for its bitter cones, used to flavour beer etc. □ **on the hop** *colloq.* unprepared.

**hope** ● n. expectation and desire; person or thing giving cause for hope; what is hoped for. ● v. feel hope; expect and desire.

**hopeful** adj. feeling or inspiring hope; promising.□□ **hopefully** adv.

**hopeless** adj. **1** feeling or admitting no hope. **2** inadequate, incompetent. **3** impossible to resolve.
□□ **hopelessly** adv. **hopelessness** n.

**hopper** n. **1** hopping insect, esp. young locust. **2** funnel-like device for feeding grain into mill etc.

**hopscotch** n. game involving hopping over marked squares.

**horde** n. large group or crowd.

**horizon** n. **1** line at which earth and sky appear to meet. **2** limit of mental perception, interest, etc.

**horizontal** adj. **1** parallel to plane of horizon, going across rather than up and down. **2** level, flat.
□□ **horizontally** adv.

**hormone** n. substance produced by body and transported in tissue fluids to stimulate cells or tissues to growth etc.; similar synthetic substance.
□□ **hormonal** adj.

**horn** n. **1** hard outgrowth, often curved and pointed, on head of animal; hornlike projection; substance of horns. **2** brass wind instrument. **3** instrument giving warning.□□ **horned** adj.

**hornblende** n. dark brown etc. mineral constituent of granite.

**hornet** n. large wasp.

**hornpipe** n. (music for) lively dance associated esp. with sailors.

**horny** adj. (**hornier**) **1** of or like horn. **2** hard. **3** colloq. sexually excited.
□□ **horniness** n.

**horology** n. measurement of time; clock making.□□ **horological** adj.

**horoscope** n. forecast of events based on position of stars, planets, etc.

**horrendous** adj. horrifying.
□□ **horrendously** adv.

**horrible** adj. causing horror; very unpleasant.□□ **horribly** adv.

**horrid** adj. horrible.

**horrific** adj. horrifying.
□□ **horrifically** adv.

**horrify** v. **1** arouse horror in. **2** shock, scandalise.□□ **horrifying** adj.

**horror** ● n. intense fear or loathing; deep dislike. ● adj. (of films etc.) designed to arouse feelings of horror.

**hors-d'oeuvre** n. appetiser served at start of meal.

**horse** n. **1** large four-legged hoofed mammal with mane, used for riding etc. **2** vaulting block. **3** supporting frame.□ **horse around** fool around.

**horseplay** n. boisterous play.

**horsepower** n. unit for measuring power of engine etc.

**horseradish** n. plant with pungent root used to make sauce.

**horseshoe** n. U-shaped iron shoe for horse; thing of this shape.

**horsy** adj. of or like horse; concerned with horses.

**hortatory** adj. (also **hortative**) tending to encourage, exhort.

**horticulture** n. art or practice of gardening.□□ **horticultural** adj. **horticulturist** n.

**hosanna** n. & int. cry of adoration.

**hose** ● n. **1** (also **hosepipe**) flexible tube for conveying liquids. **2** stockings and socks collectively. ● v. water or spray with a hose.

**hosiery** n. stockings, socks, etc.

**hospice** n. **1** home for (esp. terminally) ill people. **2** arch. travellers' lodging kept by religious order etc.

**hospitable** adj. giving hospitality; open or receptive, esp. to ideas etc.
□□ **hospitably** adv.

**hospital** n. **1** institution providing medical and surgical treatment and nursing for ill and injured people. **2** hist. hospice.

**hospitalise** v. (also **-ize**) send or admit to hospital.
□□ **hospitalisation** n.

**hospitality** n. friendly and generous reception of guests or strangers.

**host** ● n. **1** large number of people or things. **2** person who entertains another as guest; compère. **3** animal or plant having parasite. **4** recipient of transplanted organ. **5** computer that stores data, provides services, etc. that can be accessed over Internet.
● v. **1** be host to (party or event). **2** store (data etc.) on a server so that it can be accessed over Internet.

**hostage** n. person seized or held as security for fulfilment of condition.

**hostel** n. house of residence or lodging for students, homeless people, etc.

**hostess** n. woman who entertains guests or nightclub customers.

**hostile** adj. **1** unfriendly, opposed. **2** of an enemy. **3** colloq. angry.

**hostility** n. being hostile; enmity; state of warfare; (**hostilities**) acts of warfare.

**hot** adj. **1** at or having a high temperature. **2** producing burning sensation to tongue; spicy. **3** eager; angry; excited, excitable.□ **hot air** excited or boastful talk. **hot dog** hot sausage in bread roll. **hot key** key providing quick access to a particular function within a computer program. **hot up** (**hotted**) make or become hot or exciting. **in hot water** in trouble or disgrace.

**hotbed** n. place encouraging vice, intrigue, etc.

**hotchpotch** n. (also **hodgepodge**) confused mixture, jumble.

**hotel** n. **1** place providing accommodation for payment. **2** Aust. pub.

**hotelier** n. hotel-keeper.

**hothead** n. impetuous person.

**hothouse** n. heated greenhouse.

**hotline** n. direct telephone line for speedy communication.

**hotplate** n. heated surface on a cooker or hob.

**hotshot** colloq. ● n. important or exceptionally able person.
● adj. important; able; expert; suddenly prominent.

**hotspot** n. **1** small area that is relatively hot. **2** lively or dangerous place. **3** place where wireless signal is made available so that Internet can be accessed.

**houmous** = HUMMUS.

**hound** ● n. **1** (hunting) dog. **2** colloq. despicable man. ● v. harass or pursue.

**hour** n. one twenty-fourth part of a day and night; a point in time; (**hours**) time fixed or set aside for work or activity.

**hourglass** n. two vertically connected glass bulbs containing sand taking an hour to pass from upper to lower bulb.

**houri** n. beautiful young woman in Muslim Paradise.

**hourly** ● adj. done or occurring once an hour; continual.
● adv. every hour; frequently.

**house** ● n. **1** building for people to live in, or for a specific purpose; household. **2** legislative assembly; business firm; theatre audience or performance; family or dynasty. **3** section of boarding school etc.; division of school for sports etc. **4** (**house music**) type of electronic music with vocal loops and fast beats. ● v. provide accommodation or storage space for; encase.□ **house arrest** detention in one's own home. **House of Representatives** lower house of Australian Federal Parliament. **house-proud** giving great attention to appearance of one's home. **house-trained** (of animals)

trained to be clean in house.
**house-warming** party to celebrate
occupation of new home. **on the
house** (of drinks in bar etc.) provided
free of charge.

**houseboat** n. boat fitted up as
dwelling.

**housebound** adj. unable to leave one's
house, esp. through illness.

**housebreaker** n. burglar.

**household** n. occupants of house
living as group. □ **household word**
familiar saying or name.

**householder** n. person who owns or
rents house or flat.

**housekeeper** n. person employed to
look after household.

**housekeeping** n. management of
household affairs; money used for
this.

**housewife** n. (pl. **-wives**) woman
managing household.

**housework** n. cleaning and cooking
etc. in a house.

**housing** n. 1 accommodation. 2 rigid
case enclosing machinery.

**hove** see HEAVE.

**hovea** n. Australian shrub bearing
purple or blue pea flowers in spring.

**hovel** n. small miserable dwelling.

**hover** v. (of bird etc.) remain in one
place in air; linger.

**hovercraft** n. vehicle supported
by air thrust downwards from its
engines.

**how** adv. 1 by what means, in what
way; to what extent or amount etc.
2 in what condition.

**howdah** n. (usu. canopied) seat for
riding elephant or camel.

**however** adv. in whatever way, to
whatever extent; nevertheless.

**howitzer** n. short gun firing shells at
high elevation.

**howl** ● n. long doleful cry of dog
etc.; prolonged wailing cry; loud cry
of pain, rage, derision, or laughter.
● v. make howl; weep loudly.

**howler** n. colloq. glaring mistake.

**hoy** n. game of chance resembling
bingo, using playing cards.

**h.p.** abbr. (also **hp**) **1** horsepower.
**2** hire purchase.

**HQ** abbr. headquarters.

**HRH** abbr. His or Her Royal Highness.

**HTML** abbr. hypertext markup
language.

**HTTP** abbr. hypertext transfer (or
transport) protocol.

**hub** n. **1** central part of wheel, rotating
on or with axle. **2** centre of interest,
activity, etc.; focal point.

**hubbub** n. **1** confused noise of
talking. **2** disturbance.

**hubcap** n. cover for the hub of car
wheel.

**hubris** n. arrogant pride,
presumption.

**huckster** ● n. aggressive salesman;
hawker. ● v. haggle; hawk (goods).

**huddle** ● v. **1** crowd together; nestle
closely; curl one's body up.
● n. close mass or group.

**hue** n. colour, tint. □ **hue and cry** an
outcry.

**huff** ● n. colloq. fit of
annoyance. ● v. **1** blow air, steam,
etc. **2** (esp. **huff and puff**) bluster.
□□ **huffy** adj.

**hug** ● v. (**hugged**) squeeze tightly in
one's arms; keep close to. ● n. an
embrace.

**huge** adj. very large or great.
□□ **hugely** adv.

**Hughie** n. (also **Huey**) Aust. joc. the
water god, as controlling rain, good
waves for surfers, etc.

**hula** n. (also **hula-hula**) Polynesian
women's dance. □ **hula hoop** propr.
large hoop for spinning around body.

**hulk** n. **1** body of dismantled ship.
**2** large clumsy-looking person or
thing.

**hulking** adj. bulky; clumsy.

**hull** ● n. **1** body of ship etc. **2** pod of
pea or bean; cluster of leaves on

strawberry. ● v. remove hulls of (beans, strawberries, etc.)

**hullabaloo** n. uproar.

**hullo** = HELLO.

**hum** ● v. (**hummed**) **1** sing with closed lips; make similar sound. **2** be in state of activity. ● n. humming sound.

**human** ● adj. of humankind; of people; not impersonal or insensitive. ● n. human being. □ **human being** any man, woman, or child.

**humane** adj. benevolent, compassionate; inflicting minimum pain. □□ **humanely** adv.

**humanise** v. (also **-ize**) make human; make humane.

**humanism** n. system of thought concerned with human affairs and ethics (not theology). □□ **humanisation** n.

**humanitarian** ● adj. **1** seeking to promote human welfare. **2** of an event etc. that causes or involves widespread human suffering. ● n. humanitarian person. □□ **humanitarianism** n.

**humanity** n. **1** human nature or qualities; kindness; the human race. **2** (**humanities**) arts subjects such as history, philosophy, etc.

**humankind** n. human beings collectively.

**humanly** adv. **1** within human capabilities. **2** in a human way.

**humble** ● adj. meek; without pride; having or showing low estimate of one's own importance; lowly, modest. ● v. make humble. □□ **humbly** adv.

**humbug** ● n. **1** misleading behaviour or talk. **2** hist. (in Aboriginal English) trouble, difficulty. ● v. **1** deceive; trick. **2** Aust. (in Aboriginal English) impose upon or harass (someone). □□ **humbugger** n. **humbuggery** n.

**humdinger** n. colloq. remarkable person or thing.

**humdrum** adj. commonplace, dull.

**humerus** n. (pl. **humeri**) bone in upper arm. □□ **humeral** adj.

**humid** adj. (of air or climate) warm and damp.

**humidify** v. keep air moist in room etc. □□ **humidifier** n.

**humidity** n. dampness; degree of moisture, esp. in atmosphere.

**humiliate** v. injure dignity or self-respect of. □□ **humiliating** adj. **humiliation** n.

**humility** n. humbleness, meekness.

**hummock** n. hillock, hump.

**hummus** n. (also **houmous**) paste of chickpeas, tahini, lemon juice, and garlic.

**humorist** n. humorous writer, talker, or actor.

**humorous** adj. showing humour, comic. □□ **humorously** adv.

**humour** (also **humor**) ● n. **1** quality of being amusing; expression of humour in literature etc.; (in full **sense of humour**) ability to perceive or express humour or take joke. **2** state of mind, mood. **3** hist. each of four bodily fluids formerly held to determine physical and mental qualities. ● v. gratify or indulge (person, taste, etc.) □□ **humourless** adj.

**hump** ● n. rounded lump, esp. on back; rounded raised mass of earth etc. ● v. colloq. **1** lift or carry with difficulty; hoist up, shoulder (one's pack etc.) **2** make hump-shaped.

**humpback** n. whale with hump on its back.

**humpy** n. Aust. gunyah; any rough-and-ready hut etc.

**humus** n. organic constituent of soil formed by decomposition of plants.

**hunch** ● v. bend or arch into hump; sit with body hunched. ● n. **1** intuitive feeling. **2** hump.

**hundred** adj. & n. **1** ten times ten (100, C). **2** (**hundreds**) large number. □□ **hundredth** adj. & n.

**hundredfold** adj. & adv. hundred times as much or many.

**hundredweight** n. unit of weight in imperial system equal to 112 lb (about 50.8 kg.); (in full **metric hundredweight**) unit of weight equal to 50 kg.

**hung** ● see HANG. ● adj. (of a council, parliament, etc.) with no party having clear majority. □ **hung-over** suffering from hangover.

**hunger** n. pain or discomfort felt when one has not eaten for some time; strong desire. ● v. feel hunger. □ **hunger strike** refusal of food as form of protest.

**hungry** adj. (**hungrier**) feeling, showing, or inducing hunger; craving. □□ **hungrily** adv.

**hunk** n. **1** large piece cut off. **2** colloq. sexually attractive man. □□ **hunky** adj.

**hunt** ● v. **1** pursue (wild animals) for food or sport; (of animal) pursue prey; search. **2** (as **hunted** adj.) (of look) frightened. ● n. hunting; search; pursuit.

**hunter** n. person or animal that hunts.

**hunting** n. practice of pursuing wild animals, esp. for sport.

**huntsman** n. (in full **huntsman spider**) large flat-bodied hairy spider.

**huon pine** n. tall Tasmanian conifer with weeping foliage and valuable pale yellow wood.

**hurdle** n. portable fencing panel; frame to be jumped over in a race; obstacle, difficulty. □□ **hurdler** n.

**hurdy-gurdy** n. droning musical instrument played by turning handle; colloq. barrel organ.

**hurl** ● v. throw violently. ● n. violent throw.

**hurly-burly** n. boisterous activity; commotion.

**hurrah** int. & n. exclamation of joy or approval.

**hurricane** n. storm with violent wind. □ **hurricane lamp** lamp with flame protected from wind.

**hurry** ● v. act or move with eagerness or too quickly; cause to do this. ● n. hurrying. □ **hurry-up** spur to action. □□ **hurriedly** adv.

**hurt** ● v. cause pain, harm, or injury (to); feel pain. ● n. injury; harm. □□ **hurtful** adj.

**hurtle** v. move or hurl rapidly.

**husband** ● n. married man in relation to his spouse. ● v. use (resources) economically, try to save.

**husbandry** n. **1** farming. **2** management of resources.

**hush** ● v. make, become, or be silent. ● int. calling for silence. ● n. silence. □ **hush up** suppress discussion of or information about.

**husk** ● n. dry outer covering of fruit or seed. ● v. remove husk from.

**husky** ● adj. **1** dry, hoarse. **2** strong, hefty. ● n. Arctic sled dog. □□ **huskily** adv.

**hussar** n. light-cavalry soldier.

**hussy** n. dated or joc. impudent or immoral girl or woman.

**hustings** n. election campaign or proceedings.

**hustle** ● v. **1** jostle; force or hurry. **2** colloq. solicit business. ● n. act or instance of hustling. □□ **hustler** n.

**hut** n. small simple or crude house or shelter.

**hutch** n. box or cage for rabbits etc.

**hyacinth** n. bulbous plant with bell-shaped fragrant flowers.

**hybrid** ● n. offspring of two animals or plants of different species etc.; thing of mixed origins. ● adj. **1** bred as hybrid. **2** heterogeneous. □□ **hybridise** v. (also **-ize**) **hybridisation** n. **hybridism** n.

**hydra** n. **1** freshwater polyp. **2** something hard to destroy.

**hydrangea** *n.* shrub with globular clusters of white, pink, or blue flowers.

**hydrant** *n.* outlet for drawing water from main.

**hydrate** ● *n.* chemical compound of water with another compound etc. ● *v.* (cause to) combine with water. □□ **hydration** *n.*

**hydraulic** ● *adj.* (of water etc.) conveyed through pipes etc.; operated by movement of liquid. ● *n.* (**hydraulics**) science of hydraulic operations. □□ **hydraulically** *adv.*

**hydro** *n.* hydroelectric power plant.

**hydro-** *comb. form* **1** water. **2** combined with hydrogen.

**hydrocarbon** *n.* compound of hydrogen and carbon.

**hydrocephalus** *n.* accumulated fluid in brain, esp. in young children. □□ **hydrocephalic** *adj.*

**hydrochloric acid** *n.* solution of hydrogen chloride in water.

**hydrodynamic** *adj.* of forces exerted by liquid in motion.

**hydroelectric** *adj.* generating electricity by water power; (of electricity) so generated. □□ **hydroelectricity** *n.*

**hydrofoil** *n.* boat with structure that raises its hull out of the water when in motion.

**hydrogen** *n.* light colourless, odourless, gaseous element, combining with oxygen to form water (symbol **H**). □ **hydrogen bomb** powerful bomb releasing energy by fusion of hydrogen nuclei. □□ **hydrogenous** *adj.*

**hydrogenate** *v.* charge with or cause to combine with hydrogen. □□ **hydrogenation** *n.*

**hydrography** *n.* science of surveying and charting seas, lakes, rivers, etc. □□ **hydrographer** *n.* **hydrographic** *adj.*

**hydrology** *n.* science of relationship between water and land. □□ **hydrologist** *n.*

**hydrolysis** *n.* decomposition by chemical reaction with water.

**hydrometer** *n.* instrument for measuring density of liquids.

**hydropathy** *n.* (medically unorthodox) treatment of disease by water. □□ **hydropathic** *adj.*

**hydrophobia** *n.* **1** aversion to water, esp. as symptom of rabies in humans. **2** rabies. □□ **hydrophobic** *adj.*

**hydroponics** *n.* growing plants without soil, in sand, water, etc. with added nutrients.

**hydrostatic** *adj.* of the equilibrium of liquids and the pressure exerted by liquids at rest.

**hydrotherapy** *n.* use of water in treatment of disease or injury.

**hydrous** *adj.* containing water.

**hyena** *n.* wolf-like mammal with howl that sounds like laughter.

**hygiene** *n.* conditions or practices conducive to maintaining health; cleanliness; sanitary science. □□ **hygienic** *adj.* **hygienically** *adv.* **hygienist** *n.*

**hygrometer** *n.* instrument for measuring humidity of air etc.

**hygroscopic** *adj.* tending to absorb moisture from the air.

**hymen** *n.* membrane at opening of vagina, usu. broken at first sexual intercourse.

**hymenopterous** *adj.* of order of insects with four membranous wings, including bees and wasps.

**hymn** ● *n.* song of esp. Christian praise. ● *v.* praise or celebrate in hymns.

**hymnal** *n.* book of hymns.

**hyoscine** *n.* alkaloid used to prevent motion sickness etc.

**hype** *colloq.* ● *n.* **1** intensive promotion of product etc. **2** cheating; swindle. ● *v.* promote with hype.

**hyper-** *prefix* **1** over, above. **2** too.

**hyperactive** *adj.* (of person) abnormally active.

**hyperbola** *n.* (pl. **hyperbolas** or **hyperbolae**) curve produced when cone is cut by plane making larger angle with base side of cone makes.□□ **hyperbolic** *adj.*

**hyperbole** *n.* exaggeration, esp. for effect.□□ **hyperbolical** *adj.*

**hyperglycaemia** *n.* (also **hyperglycemia**) excess of glucose in bloodstream.

**hyperlink** *n.* Computing link from hypertext document to another location, activated by clicking on highlighted word etc.

**hypersensitive** *adj.* excessively sensitive.

**hypersonic** *adj.* of speeds of more than five times that of sound.

**hypertension** *n.* **1** abnormally high blood pressure. **2** extreme tension.

**hypertext** *n.* Computing system allowing simultaneous use of, and cross-reference between, several texts.

**hyperventilation** *n.* abnormally rapid breathing.□□ **hyperventilate** *v.*

**hyphen** ● *n.* punctuation mark ( - ) used to join or divide words. ● *v.* hyphenate.

**hyphenate** *v.* join or divide with hyphen.□□ **hyphenation** *n.*

**hypnosis** *n.* sleep-like condition produced in a person who then obeys suggestions.

**hypnotherapy** *n.* treatment of disease etc. by hypnosis.

**hypnotic** ● *adj.* **1** of or causing hypnosis. **2** sleep-inducing. ● *n.* hypnotic drug or influence. □□ **hypnotically** *adv.*

**hypnotise** *v.* (also **-ize**) **1** produce hypnosis in. **2** fascinate.

**hypnotism** *n.* study or practice of hypnosis.□□ **hypnotist** *n.*

**hypo** *n.* sodium thiosulphate used as photographic fixer.

**hypo-** *prefix* **1** under. **2** below normal. **3** slightly.

**hypochondria** *n.* abnormal anxiety about one's health. □□ **hypochondriac** *n.* & *adj.*

**hypocrisy** *n.* simulation of virtue; insincerity.

**hypocrite** *n.* person guilty of hypocrisy.□□ **hypocritical** *adj.* hypocritically *adv.*

**hypodermic** ● *adj.* (of drug, syringe, etc.) introduced under the skin. ● *n.* hypodermic injection or syringe.

**hypotension** *n.* abnormally low blood pressure.

**hypotenuse** *n.* longest side of right-angled triangle.

**hypothalamus** *n.* (pl. **hypothalami**) region of brain controlling body temperature, thirst, hunger, etc.

**hypothermia** *n.* abnormally low body temperature.

**hypothesis** *n.* supposition made as basis for reasoning.□□ **hypothesise** *v.* (also **-ize**)

**hypothetical** *adj.* of or resting on hypothesis.□□ **hypothetically** *adv.*

**hypoventilation** *n.* abnormally slow breathing.

**hyssop** *n.* small bushy aromatic herb.

**hysterectomy** *n.* surgical removal of uterus.

**hysteria** *n.* wild uncontrollable emotion.□□ **hysterical** *adj.* hysterically *adv.*

**hysterics** *n.pl.* hysterical outburst; *colloq.* uncontrollable laughter.

**Hz** *abbr.* hertz.

# Ii

**I¹** *n.* (also **i**) (Roman numeral) 1.

**I²** *pron.* used by speaker or writer to refer to himself or herself as subject of verb.

**iambic** *adj. & n. poet.* using iambuses, metrical feet of one short and one long syllable.

**ibid.** *abbr.* in same book or passage etc.

**ibis** *n.* wading bird with long curved bill.

**ibuprofen** *n.* analgesic and anti-inflammatory drug.

**ice** ● *n.* **1** frozen water. **2** ice cream. **3** *colloq.* form of methamphetamine that can be smoked. ● *v.* **1** mix with or cool in ice; (cause or become covered (as) with ice; freeze. **2** cover (cake etc.) with icing. □□ **break the ice** start conversation, relieve shyness. **ice cream** sweet creamy frozen food.

**iceberg** *n.* **1** mass of floating ice at sea. **2** *colloq.* cold unemotional person.

**iceblock** *n. Aust.* confection of frozen fruit juice, flavoured with water, etc.

**ichthyology** *n.* study of fishes. □□ **ichthyological** *adj.* **ichthyologist** *n.*

**ichthyosaur** *n.* large extinct reptile-like animal.

**icicle** *n.* hanging spike of ice, formed from dripping water.

**icing** *n.* coating of sugar etc. on cakes or biscuits.

**icon** *n.* **1** sacred painting, mosaic, etc.; image, statue. **2** person or thing regarded as a representative symbol or as worthy of veneration. **3** *Computing* symbol etc. on a screen of program, option, or window.

**iconic** *adj.* **1** of the nature of an icon. **2** of person or thing regarded as representative of a culture or movement; important or influential in a particular context.

**iconoclast** *n.* person who attacks cherished beliefs; *hist.* breaker of religious images. □□ **iconoclasm** *n.* **iconoclastic** *adj.*

**iconography** *n.* illustration of subject by drawings etc.; study of portraits, esp. of one person, or of artistic images or symbols.

**icy** *adj.* **1** very cold; covered with or abounding in ice. **2** (of manner) unfriendly.

**ID** *abbr.* identification, identity.

**id** *n. Psychol.* part of mind comprising instinctive impulses of individual etc.

**I'd 1** I had. **2** I should. **3** I would.

**idea** *n.* plan etc. formed by mental effort; mental impression or concept; vague belief or fancy; intention, purpose.

**ideal** ● *adj.* perfect; existing only in idea; visionary. ● *n.* perfect type, thing, principle, etc. as standard for imitation.

**idealise** *v.* (also **-ize**) regard or represent as ideal; regard or represent (esp. person) as better than he or she really is. □□ **idealism** *n.* **idealistic** *adj.*

**identical** *adj.* absolutely alike, same; (of twins) developed from single ovum. □□ **identically** *adv.*

**identifier** *n.* person etc. that identifies; *Computing* sequence of characters used to identify etc. element of program.

**identify** *v.* establish identity of; select, discover; closely associate with; treat as identical to; regard oneself as sharing basic characteristics with. □□ **identification** *n.*

**identikit** n. set of pictures or features that can be put together to form likeness of person.

**identity** n. **1** being specified person or thing; individuality; identification or the result of it. **2** absolute sameness. **3** colloq. outstanding or well-known person.

**ideogram** n. (also **ideograph**) symbol representing thing or idea without indicating sounds in its name, e.g. Chinese characters, or '=' for 'equals').

**ideology** n. scheme of ideas at basis of political etc. theory or system; characteristic thinking of class etc. □□ **ideological** adj.

**idiocy** n. utter foolishness; foolish act.

**idiom** n. phrase etc. established by usage and not immediately comprehensible from the words used; form of expression peculiar to language; characteristic mode of expression.

**idiomatic** adj. using idioms; sounding natural. □□ **idiomatically** adv.

**idiosyncrasy** n. attitude or form of behaviour peculiar to person. □□ **idiosyncratic** adj.

**idiot** n. very stupid person. □□ **idiotic** adj.

**idle** ● adj. **1** lazy, indolent. **2** not in use. **3** unoccupied. **4** useless, purposeless. ● v. **1** be idle; pass (time) in idleness. **2** (of engine) run slowly without doing any work. □□ **idleness** n. **idler** n. **idly** adv.

**idol** n. image as object of worship; object of devotion.

**idolatry** n. worship of idols. □□ **idolater** n. **idolatrous** adj. **idolatry** n.

**idolise** v. (also **-ize**) venerate or love to excess; treat as idol. □□ **idolisation** n.

**idyll** n. account of picturesque scene or incident etc.; such scene etc. □□ **idyllic** adj.

**i.e.** abbr. that is to say.

**if** ● conj. on condition or supposition that; whether. ● n. condition or supposition.

**iffy** adj. colloq. uncertain; of doubtful quality.

**igloo** n. Inuit dome-shaped snow house.

**igneous** adj. of fire; (esp. of rocks) produced by volcanic action.

**ignite** v. **1** set fire to; catch fire. **2** provoke or excite (feelings etc.)

**ignition** n. mechanism for starting combustion in cylinder of motor engine; igniting.

**ignoble** adj. **1** dishonourable. **2** of low birth or position. □□ **ignobly** adv.

**ignominy** n. disgrace, humiliation. □□ **ignominious** adj. **ignominiously** adv.

**ignoramus** n. (pl. **ignoramuses**) ignorant person.

**ignorant** adj. **1** lacking knowledge; uninformed. **2** colloq. uncouth. □□ **ignorance** n.

**ignore** v. refuse to take notice of.

**iguana** n. large Central and S. American lizard.

**iguanodon** n. large herbivorous dinosaur.

**ileum** n. part of small intestine.

**iliac** adj. of flank or hip bone.

**ilk** n. sort, kind.

**ill** ● adj. **1** in bad health; sick. **2** unfavourable, harmful; hostile, unkind. **3** faulty, defective. ● adv. badly; unfavourably. ● n. harm; evil. □□ **ill-advised** unwise. **ill at ease** uncomfortable, embarrassed. **ill-gotten** gained by evil or unlawful means. **ill-mannered** having bad manners. **ill-treat** treat badly or cruelly. **ill will** hostility, unkind feeling.

**illegal** adj. contrary to law. □□ **illegality** n. **illegally** adv.

**illegible** adj. not legible; unreadable. □□ **illegibility** n. **illegibly** adv.

**illegitimate** *adj.* **1** born of parents not married to each other. **2** contrary to law or rule.□□ **illegitimacy** *n.*

**illiberal** *adj.* **1** narrow-minded. **2** stingy.□□ **illiberality** *n.*

**illicit** *adj.* unlawful, forbidden; unlicensed.□□ **illicitly** *adv.*

**illiterate** ● *adj.* unable to read; uneducated. ● *n.* illiterate person. □□ **illiteracy** *n.*

**illness** *n.* disease, sickness.

**illogical** *adj.* devoid of or contrary to logic.□□ **illogicality** *n.* **illogically** *adv.*

**illuminate** *v.* **1** light up; decorate with lights. **2** decorate (manuscript etc.) with gold, colour, etc. **3** help to explain (subject etc.); enlighten spiritually or intellectually. □□ **illuminating** *adj.* **illumination** *n.*

**illusion** *n.* false belief; something wrongly supposed to exist.

**illusionist** *n.* conjuror.

**illusory** *adj.* (also **illusive**) based on illusion, deceptive.

**illustrate** *v.* provide with pictures; make clear, esp. by drawings; serve as example of.□□ **illustration** *n.* **illustrative** *adj.* **illustrator** *n.*

**illustrious** *adj.* distinguished, renowned.

**illywhacker** *n. Aust. colloq.* confidence trickster.

**image** ● *n.* **1** representation of object; visible impression obtained by camera, telescope, or other device, or displayed on computer screen etc.; appearance as seen in mirror or through lens. **2** reputation or persona of person, company, etc. **3** idea, conception. **4** simile, metaphor. ● *v.* **1** make image of. **2** mirror; reflect. **3** picture.

**imagery** *n.* figurative illustration; use of images in literature etc.; images, statuary; mental images collectively.

**imaginary** *adj.* existing only in the imagination.

**imagination** *n.* mental faculty of forming images of objects not present to senses; creative faculty of mind.

**imaginative** *adj.* having or showing high degree of imagination. □□ **imaginatively** *adv.*

**imagine** *v.* form mental image, conceive; guess; suppose, think.

**imago** *n.* (*pl.* **imagos** or **imagines**) fully developed stage of insect.

**imam** *n.* leader of prayers in mosque.

**imbalance** *n.* lack of balance; disproportion.

**imbecile** *n. colloq. derog.* stupid person.

**imbed** = EMBED.

**imbibe** *v.* drink; absorb; inhale.

**imbroglio** *n.* confused or complicated situation.

**imbue** *v.* **1** inspire. **2** saturate. **3** dye.

**IMF** *abbr.* International Monetary Fund.

**imitate** *v.* follow example of; mimic; make copy of; be like.□□ **imitable** *adj.* **imitative** *adj.* **imitator** *n.*

**imitation** *n.* act of imitating, being imitated; copy; counterfeit.

**immaculate** *adj.* pure, spotless; perfectly clean; faultless; innocent, sinless.□□ **immaculately** *adv.* **immaculateness** *n.*

**immanent** *adj.* **1** inherent. **2** (of God) omnipresent.□□ **immanence** *n.*

**immaterial** *adj.* **1** unimportant; irrelevant. **2** not material. □□ **immateriality** *n.*

**immature** *adj.* not mature; undeveloped, esp. emotionally. □□ **immaturity** *n.*

**immeasurable** *adj.* **1** not measurable. **2** immense. □□ **immeasurably** *adv.*

**immediate** *adj.* **1** occurring at once. **2** direct. **3** nearest. **4** having priority. □□ **immediacy** *n.* **immediately** *adv.*

**immemorial** *adj.* ancient, beyond memory.

**immense** adj. **1** vast; huge. **2** colloq. excellent. □□ **immensity** n.

**immensely** adv. colloq. vastly, very much.

**immerse** v. put completely into liquid; involve deeply.

**immersion** n. immersing, being immersed.

**immigrant** ● n. person who immigrates. ● adj. immigrating; of immigrants.

**immigrate** v. enter country to settle permanently. □□ **immigration** n.

**imminent** adj. soon to happen. □□ **imminence** n. **imminently** adv.

**immobile** adj. motionless; immovable. □□ **immobility** n.

**immobilise** v. (also -**ize**) prevent from being moved. □□ **immobilisation** n.

**immoderate** adj. excessive. □□ **immoderately** adv.

**immolate** v. kill as sacrifice. □□ **immolation** n.

**immoral** adj. opposed to, or not conforming to, (esp. sexual) morality; dissolute. □□ **immorality** n. **immorally** adv.

**immortal** adj. living for ever, not mortal; famous for all time. □□ **immortalise** v. (also -**ize**) **immortality** n.

**immovable** adj. not movable; unyielding. □□ **immovability** n.

**immune** adj. having immunity; relating to immunity; exempt.

**immunise** v. (also -**ize**) make immune. □□ **immunisation** n.

**immunity** n. **1** living organism's power of resisting and overcoming infection. **2** freedom, exemption.

**immunodeficiency** n. reduction in normal immune defences.

**immunology** n. scientific study of immunity. □□ **immunological** adj. **immunologist** n.

**immure** v. imprison.

**immutable** adj. unchangeable. □□ **immutability** n.

**imp** n. mischievous child; little devil.

**impact** ● n. collision, force of this; strong effect. ● v. **1** collide forcefully with something. **2** press firmly. □□ **impaction** n.

**impair** v. damage, weaken. □□ **impairment** n.

**impaired** adj. **1** weakened or damaged; adversely affected by alcohol or drugs. **2** having disability of specified kind.

**impale** v. fix or pierce with pointed object. □□ **impalement** n.

**impalpable** adj. not easily grasped; imperceptible to touch.

**impart** v. communicate (news etc.); give share of.

**impartial** adj. fair, not partial. □□ **impartiality** n. **impartially** adv.

**impassable** adj. that cannot be traversed. □□ **impassability** n.

**impasse** n. deadlock.

**impassioned** adj. filled with passion; ardent.

**impassive** adj. not feeling or showing emotion. □□ **impassively** adv. **impassivity** n.

**impasto** n. technique of laying on paint thickly.

**impatiens** n. any of several plants including busy Lizzie.

**impatient** adj. not patient; intolerant; restlessly eager. □□ **impatience** n. **impatiently** adv.

**impeach** v. charge with crime against nation etc.; charge (holder of public office) with misconduct; call in question, disparage. □□ **impeachment** n.

**impeccable** adj. faultless, exemplary. □□ **impeccability** n. **impeccably** adv.

**impecunious** adj. having little or no money.

**impedance** n. total effective resistance of electric circuit etc. to alternating current.

**impede** v. obstruct; hinder.

**impediment** n. hindrance; speech defect, esp. stammer.

**impel** v. (impelled) drive, force; propel.

**impend** v. 1 be imminent. 2 hang; overhang. □□ **impending** adj.

**impenetrable** adj. not penetrable; inscrutable; unfathomable. □□ **impenetrability** n.

**imperative** ● adj. 1 urgent, obligatory; peremptory. 2 Gram. (of mood) expressing command. ● n. 1 Gram. imperative mood. 2 command. 3 essential or urgent thing.

**imperceptible** adj. not perceptible; very slight or gradual. □□ **imperceptibility** n. **imperceptibly** adv.

**imperfect** adj. 1 not perfect; faulty; incomplete. 2 Gram. (of past tense) implying action in progress but not completed. ● n. imperfect tense. □□ **imperfectly** adv.

**imperfection** n. imperfectness; fault, blemish.

**imperial** adj. 1 of empire or sovereign state; majestic. 2 (of non-metric weights and measures) used in UK.

**imperialism** n. policy of having or extending empire. □□ **imperialist** n. **imperialistic** adj.

**imperil** v. (imperilled) endanger.

**imperious** adj. overbearing, domineering. □□ **imperiousness** n.

**impermeable** adj. not permeable. □□ **impermeability** n.

**impersonal** adj. 1 having no personality or personal feeling or reference; unfeeling. 2 impartial. □□ **impersonality** n.

**impersonate** v. pretend to be, play part of. □□ **impersonation** n. **impersonator** n.

**impertinent** adj. insolent, saucy. □□ **impertinence** n. **impertinently** adv.

**imperturbable** adj. not excitable; calm. □□ **imperturbability** n. **imperturbably** adv.

**impervious** adj. 1 impermeable. 2 not responsive.

**impetigo** n. contagious skin disease.

**impetuous** adj. acting or done rashly or suddenly; moving violently. □□ **impetuosity** n. **impetuously** adv.

**impetus** n. moving force; momentum; impulse.

**impinge** v. 1 make impact. 2 encroach.

**impish** adj. of or like imp; mischievous. □□ **impishly** adv.

**implacable** adj. not able to be appeased; relentless. □□ **implacability** n. **implacably** adv.

**implant** ● v. insert, fix; instil; plant; (of fertilised ovum) become attached to wall of uterus. ● n. thing implanted. □□ **implantation** n.

**implausible** adj. not plausible. □□ **implausibly** adv.

**implement** ● n. tool, utensil. ● v. carry into effect. □□ **implementation** n.

**implicate** v. show (person) to be involved (in crime etc.); imply.

**implication** n. thing implied; implicating or implying.

**implicit** adj. 1 implied though not expressed. 2 unquestioning. □□ **implicitly** adv.

**implode** v. (cause to) burst inwards. □□ **implosion** n.

**implore** v. beg earnestly.

**imply** v. insinuate; hint; mean.

**impolite** adj. uncivil, rude. □□ **impolitely** adv. **impoliteness** n.

**impolitic** adj. risky, unwise.
□□ **impoliticly** adv.

**imponderable** ● adj. **1** that cannot be estimated. **2** very light.
● n. imponderable thing.
□□ **imponderability** n.
**imponderably** adv.

**import** ● v. **1** bring (goods or services) into a country from abroad for sale; introduce (idea) from a different place or context.
**2** Computing transfer (data) into file or document. **3** imply, mean.
● n. **1** importing; something imported. **2** meaning; importance.
□□ **importation** n. **importer** n.

**important** adj. **1** of great consequence; momentous.
**2** (of person) having position of authority or rank. **3** pompous.
□□ **importance** n. **importantly** adv.

**importunate** adj. making persistent requests.
□□ **importunity** n.

**importune** v. make insistent requests to; solicit.

**impose** v. enforce compliance with; inflict, lay (tax etc.) □ **impose on** take advantage of.

**imposing** adj. impressive, esp. in appearance.

**imposition** n. imposing, being imposed; unfair demand or burden; tax, duty.

**impossible** adj. **1** not possible.
**2** colloq. outrageous, intolerable.
□□ **impossibility** n. **impossibly** adv.

**impost** n. tax, duty.

**impostor** n. (also **imposter**) person who assumes false character; swindler.

**impotent** adj. **1** powerless. **2** (of male) unable to achieve erection of penis or have sexual intercourse.
□□ **impotence** n.

**impound** v. confiscate; shut up in pound.

**impoverish** v. make poor; exhaust strength or fertility of.
□□ **impoverishment** n.

**impracticable** adj. not possible in practice. □□ **impracticability** n.
**impracticably** adv.

---

**Usage** *Impracticable* is sometimes confused with *impractical*.

---

**impractical** adj. not adapted for use or action; not sensible or realistic.
□□ **impracticality** n.

**imprecation** n. formal spoken curse.

**imprecise** adj. not precise.

**impregnable** adj. safe against attack
□□ **impregnability** n.

**impregnate** v. **1** fill, saturate. **2** make pregnant. □□ **impregnation** n.

**impresario** n. organiser of public entertainments.

**impress** ● v. **1** affect or influence deeply; arouse admiration or respect in. **2** emphasise. **3** imprint, stamp.
● n. **1** mark impressed.
**2** characteristic quality.
□□ **impressible** adj.

**impression** n. **1** effect produced on mind; belief. **2** imitation of person or sound, esp. as entertainment.
**3** impressing, mark impressed.
**4** unaltered reprint of book etc.; issue of book or newspaper etc.

**impressionable** adj. easily influenced.

**impressive** adj. arousing respect, approval, or admiration.
□□ **impressively** adv.

**imprimatur** n. licence to print; official approval.

**imprint** ● v. **1** impress firmly, esp. on mind; make impression of (figure etc.) on thing; make impression on (thing) with stamp etc.
● n. **1** impression. **2** printer's

or publisher's name printed in book etc.

**imprison** v. put in prison; confine. □□ **imprisonment** n.

**improbable** adj. unlikely; difficult to believe. □□ **improbability** n. **improbably** adv.

**improbity** n. dishonesty.

**impromptu** adj. & adv. without preparation or rehearsal.

**improper** adj. unseemly, indecent; inaccurate, wrong. □□ **improperly** adv.

**impropriety** n. indecency; instance of this; incorrectness, unfitness.

**improve** v. make or become better; produce something better than. □□ **improvement** n.

**improvident** adj. **1** lacking foresight. **2** wasteful. □□ **improvidence** n. **improvidently** adv.

**improvise** v. compose extempore; provide or construct from materials etc. not intended for the purpose; invent, esp. on spur of the moment. □□ **improvisation** n. **improvisational** adj. **improvisatory** adj.

**impudent** adj. impertinent; shamelessly presumptuous. □□ **impudence** n. **impudently** adv.

**impugn** v. challenge, call in question.

**impulse** n. sudden urge; tendency to follow such urges; impelling; impetus.

**impulsive** adj. apt to act on impulse; done on impulse; tending to impel. □□ **impulsively** adv. **impulsiveness** n.

**impunity** n. exemption from punishment or bad consequences.

**impure** adj. adulterated; dirty; unchaste.

**impurity** n. being impure; substance that makes another impure.

**impute** v. ● attribute (fault etc.); blame. □□ **imputation** n.

**in** ● prep. **1** enclosed or surrounded by; having as a position or state within (limits of space, time,

surroundings, etc.) **2** having as state or manner. **3** into; towards.
   ● adv. **1** in or to position bounded by limits; inside. **2** in fashion, season, or office. ● adj. **1** internal; living etc. inside. **2** fashionable. **3** (of joke etc.) confined to small group. □ **in for** about to experience; competing in. **ins and outs** details. **in so far as** to the extent that. **in tray** tray holding documents needing attention.

**inability** n. being unable.

**inaccessible** adj. not accessible; unapproachable. □□ **inaccessibility** n.

**inaccurate** adj. not accurate. □□ **inaccuracy** n. **inaccurately** adv.

**inaction** n. absence of action.

**inactive** adj. not active; not operating. □□ **inactivity** n.

**inadequate** adj. insufficient; incompetent. □□ **inadequacy** n. **inadequately** adv.

**inadmissible** adj. not allowable. □□ **inadmissibility** n. **inadmissibly** adv.

**inadvertent** adj. **1** unintentional. **2** inattentive. □□ **inadvertence** n. **inadvertently** adv.

**inadvisable** adj. not advisable. □□ **inadvisability** n.

**inalienable** adj. that cannot be transferred to another or taken away.

**inane** adj. silly, senseless; empty. □□ **inanely** adv. **inanity** n.

**inanimate** adj. not endowed with animal life; spiritless, dull.

**inappropriate** adj. not appropriate. □□ **inappropriately** adv. **inappropriateness** n.

**inarticulate** adj. **1** unable to express oneself clearly; not articulate; indistinct; not able to speak. **2** not jointed. □□ **inarticulately** adv.

**inasmuch** □ **inasmuch as** since, because; to the extent that.

**inattentive** adj. not paying attention; neglecting to show courtesy.
  □□ **inattention** n. **inattentively** adv.

**inaudible** adj. that cannot be heard.
  □□ **inaudibly** adv.

**inaugurate** v. admit (person) to office; initiate use of or begin with ceremony; begin, introduce.
  □□ **inaugural** adj. **inauguration** n.

**inauspicious** adj. not of good omen; unlucky. □□ **inauspiciously** adv. **inauspiciousness** n.

**inboard** adj. & adv. (of engine) inside boat.

**inborn** adj. existing from birth; innate.

**inbox** n. **1** folder in which emails received are held. **2** in tray.

**inbred** adj. inborn; produced by inbreeding.

**inbreeding** n. breeding from closely related animals or persons.

**inbuilt** adj. essentially and naturally part of something.

**Inc.** abbr. incorporated.

**incalculable** adj. too great for calculation; not calculable beforehand; uncertain.
  □□ **incalculability** n. **incalculably** adv.

**incandescent** adj. glowing with heat; shining; (of artificial light) produced by glowing filament etc.
  □□ **incandescence** n.

**incantation** n. spell, charm.
  □□ **incantational** adj.

**incapable** adj. unable to do something; helpless.
  □□ **incapability** n.

**incapacitate** v. make incapable or unfit.

**incapacity** n. inability; legal disqualification.

**incarcerate** v. imprison.
  □□ **incarceration** n.

**incarnate** adj. embodied esp. in human form.

**incarnation** n. embodiment, esp. in human form; (**the Incarnation**) embodiment of God in Christ.

**incautious** adj. rash.

**incendiary** ● adj. **1** designed to cause fire. **2** tending to provoke conflict. **3** inflammatory.
  ● n. **1** incendiary bomb. **2** arsonist.

**incense¹** n. gum or spice giving sweet smell when burned; smoke of this, esp. in religious ceremonial.

**incense²** v. make angry.

**incentive** n. **1** motive, incitement. **2** payment etc. encouraging effort in work. ● adj. serving to motivate or incite.

**inception** n. beginning.

**incessant** adj. unceasing, continual, repeated. □□ **incessantly** adv.

**incest** n. sexual intercourse between very closely related people.
  □□ **incestuous** adj.

**inch** ● n. twelfth of linear foot (2.54 cm); small amount. ● v. move gradually.

**inchoate** adj. just begun; undeveloped; rudimentary.
  □□ **inchoation** n.

**incidence** n. **1** rate at which a thing occurs. **2** *Physics* the falling of line, ray, etc. on surface.

**incident** n. event esp. one causing trouble.

**incidental** adj. occurring in connection with something else; minor, not essential. □ **incidental music** background music composed for film etc.

**incidentally** adv. **1** by the way. **2** in an incidental way.

**incinerate** v. burn to ashes.
  □□ **incineration** n.

**incinerator** n. furnace or device for incineration.

**incipient** adj. beginning; in early stage.

**incise** v. make cut in; engrave.
  □□ **incision** n.

**incisive** adj. clear and decisive.
  □□ **incisively** adv. **incisiveness** n.

**incisor** n. sharp-edged front tooth.

**incite** v. urge on to action, stir up. □□ **incitement** n.

**incivility** n. rudeness; impolite act.

**inclement** adj. unpleasant.

**inclination** n. 1 tendency; liking or preference. 2 a slope.

**incline** ● v. 1 slope; bend. 2 have or cause a certain tendency; influence. ● n. slope.

**include** v. comprise, regard, or treat as part of whole. □□ **inclusion** n.

**inclusive** adj. including; including the limits stated; comprehensive; including all charges, services, etc. □□ **inclusively** adv.

**incognito** adj. & adv. with one's name or identity concealed. ● n. person who is incognito.

**incoherent** adj. unintelligible; lacking logic or consistency; not clear. □□ **incoherence** n. **incoherently** adv.

**incombustible** adj. that cannot be burnt.

**income** n. money received, esp. periodically, from work, investments, etc.

**incoming** adj. 1 coming in. 2 succeeding another.

**incommunicado** adj. 1 without means of communication. 2 in solitary confinement.

**incomparable** adj. without equal; matchless.

**incompatible** adj. 1 opposed in character. 2 discordant. □□ **incompatibility** n.

**incompetent** adj. inept; lacking the necessary skill; not legally qualified. □□ **incompetence** n.

**incomplete** adj. not complete.

**incomprehensible** adj. not able to be understood. □□ **incomprehension** n.

**inconceivable** adj. unable to be imagined; most unlikely. □□ **inconceivably** adv.

**inconclusive** adj. (of argument etc.) not decisive or convincing. □□ **inconclusively** adv.

**incongruous** adj. out of place; absurd; out of keeping. □□ **incongruity** n. **incongruously** adv.

**inconsequential** adj. unimportant. □□ **inconsequentially** adv.

**inconsiderable** adj. 1 of small size, value, etc. 2 not worth considering. □□ **inconsiderably** adv.

**inconsiderate** adj. not considerate of others; thoughtless.

**inconsistent** adj. not consistent. □□ **inconsistency** n.

**inconsolable** adj. that cannot be consoled. □□ **inconsolably** adv.

**inconspicuous** adj. not conspicuous; not easily noticed.

**inconstant** adj. fickle; variable. □□ **inconstancy** n.

**incontestable** adj. that cannot be disputed. □□ **incontestably** adv.

**incontinent** adj. 1 unable to control bowels or bladder. 2 lacking self-restraint. □□ **incontinence** n.

**incontrovertible** adj. indisputable; undeniable. □□ **incontrovertibly** adv.

**inconvenience** ● n. lack of ease or comfort; trouble; cause or instance of this. ● v. cause inconvenience to.

**inconvenient** adj. causing trouble, difficulty, or discomfort; awkward. □□ **inconveniently** adv.

**incorporate** ● v. 1 include as part or ingredient; unite (in one body); admit as member of company etc. 2 (esp. as **incorporated** adj.) constitute as legal corporation. ● adj. incorporated. □□ **incorporation** n.

**incorrect** adj. 1 untrue, inaccurate. 2 improper, unsuitable. □□ **incorrectly** adv.

**incorrigible** adj. that cannot be corrected or improved. □□ **incorrigibility** n. **incorrigibly** adv.

**incorruptible** adj. that cannot decay or be corrupted. □□ **incorruptibility** n. **incorruptibly** adv.

**increase** ● v. make or become greater or more numerous. ● n. growth, enlargement; (of people, animals, or plants) multiplication; increased amount.

**increasingly** adv. more and more.

**incredible** adj. **1** that cannot be believed. **2** colloq. amazing, extremely good. □□ **incredibly** n. **incredibly** adv.

**incredulous** adj. unwilling to believe; showing disbelief. □□ **incredulity** n. **incredulously** adv.

**increment** n. amount of increase; added amount. □□ **incremental** adj.

**incriminate** v. indicate as guilty; charge with crime. □□ **incrimination** n. **incriminatory** adj.

**incrustation** n. (also **encrustation**) encrusting, being encrusted; crust or deposit formed on surface.

**incubate** v. hatch (eggs) by sitting on them or by artificial heat; cause (bacteria etc.) to develop; develop slowly. □□ **incubation** n.

**incubator** n. apparatus providing warmth for hatching eggs, rearing premature babies, or developing bacteria.

**inculcate** v. urge, impress persistently. □□ **inculcation** n.

**incumbent** ● adj. forming an obligation or duty. ● n. the holder of office or post.

**incur** v. (**incurred**) bring on oneself.

**incurable** ● adj. that cannot be cured. ● n. incurable person.

**incursion** n. invasion, sudden attack. □□ **incursive** adj.

**indebted** adj. owing gratitude or money. □□ **indebtedness** n.

**indecent** adj. offending against decency; unbecoming; unsuitable. □ **indecent assault** sexual assault not involving rape. **indecent exposure**

exposing one's genitals in public. □□ **indecency** n. **indecently** adv.

**indecipherable** adj. that cannot be deciphered.

**indecision** n. inability to decide; hesitation.

**indecorous** adj. improper, undignified; in bad taste. □□ **indecorously** adv.

**indeed** ● adv. in truth; really; admittedly. ● int. expressing irony, incredulity, etc.

**indefatigable** adj. unwearying, unremitting. □□ **indefatigably** adv.

**indefeasible** adj. Law (esp. of claim, rights, etc.) that cannot be forfeited or annulled. □□ **indefeasibly** adv.

**indefensible** adj. that cannot be defended. □□ **indefensibility** n. **indefensibly** adv.

**indefinable** adj. that cannot be defined; mysterious. □□ **indefinably** adv.

**indefinite** adj. **1** vague, undefined; unlimited. **2** (of adjectives, adverbs, and pronouns) not determining person etc. referred to. □ **indefinite article** see ARTICLE.

**indefinitely** adv. **1** for unlimited time. **2** in indefinite manner.

**indelible** adj. that cannot be rubbed out; permanent. □□ **indelibly** adv.

**indelicate** adj. coarse, unrefined; tending to indecency; tactless. □□ **indelicacy** n. **indelicately** adv.

**indemnify** v. **1** secure against loss or legal responsibility; exempt from penalty. **2** compensate. □□ **indemnification** n.

**indemnity** n. compensation for damage; sum exacted by victor in war; security against damage or loss; exemption from penalties.

**indent** v. **1** set back (beginning of line) inwards from margin; form recesses in (surface). **2** place official order (for goods etc.) □□ **indentation** n.

**indenture** ● n. written contract, esp. of apprenticeship. ● v. bind by this.

**independent** ● adj. **1** not depending on authority; self-governing. **2** not depending on another person for one's opinions or livelihood. **3** (of income) making it unnecessary to earn one's livelihood. **4** unwilling to be under obligation to others. **5** not belonging to or supported by a political party. ● n. politician etc. independent of any political party.□□ **independence** n. **independently** adv.

**indescribable** adj. beyond description; that cannot be described. □□ **indescribably** adv.

**indestructible** adj. that cannot be destroyed.□□ **indestructibility** n. **indestructibly** adv.

**indeterminable** adj. that cannot be ascertained.

**indeterminate** adj. not fixed in extent, character, etc.; vague. □□ **indeterminacy** n.

**index** ● n. (pl. **indexes** or **indices**) **1** alphabetical list of subjects etc. with references, usu. at end of book; indicator of something; measure of prices or wages compared with previous month, year, etc. **2** Math. exponent. ● v. (**indexed**) **1** furnish (book etc.) with index; enter in index. **2** relate (wages, investment income, etc.) to a price index.□ **index finger** finger next to thumb.

**indexation** n. practice of linking wages and benefits to the cost of living.

**indicate** v. **1** point out, make known; show. **2** be sign of. **3** call for, require. **4** state briefly; give as reading or measurement. **5** point by hand; use vehicle's indicator.□□ **indication** n. **indicative** adj.

**indicator** n. **1** flashing light on vehicle showing intended direction of turn. **2** person or thing that indicates.

**3** device indicating condition of machine etc.

**indices** pl. of INDEX.

**indict** v. accuse formally by legal process.□□ **indictable** adj. **indictment** n.

**indifferent** adj. **1** showing no interest or sympathy. **2** neither good nor bad. **3** of poor quality and ability.□□ **indifference** n. **indifferently** adv.

**indigenous** adj. native or belonging naturally to a place.

**indigent** adj. formal needy, poor. □□ **indigence** n.

**indigestible** adj. difficult or impossible to digest. □□ **indigestibility** n.

**indigestion** n. difficulty in digesting food; pain caused by this.

**indignant** adj. feeling or showing indignation.□□ **indignantly** adv.

**indignation** n. anger at supposed injustice etc.

**indignity** n. humiliating treatment; insult.

**indigo** n. deep violet-blue; dye of this colour.

**indirect** adj. not going straight to the point; (of route etc.) not straight. □ **indirect object** Gram. person or thing indirectly affected by verb. **indirect speech** reported speech. **indirect taxes** taxes paid on goods and services, not on income or capital. □□ **indirectly** adv.

**indiscernible** adj. that cannot be discerned.

**indiscreet** adj. not discreet; injudicious, unwary.□□ **indiscreetly** adv. **indiscretion** n.

**indiscriminate** adj. making no distinctions; done or acting at random.□□ **indiscriminately** adv.

**indispensable** adj. that cannot be dispensed with; necessary; (of law etc.) that is not to be set aside. □□ **indispensably** adv.

**indisposed** adj. 1 slightly unwell. 2 unwilling. □□ **indisposition** n.

**indisputable** adj. that cannot be disputed; unquestionable. □□ **indisputably** adv.

**indissoluble** adj. 1 that cannot be dissolved. 2 lasting, stable. □□ **indissolubly** adv.

**indistinct** adj. not distinct; confused, obscure. □□ **indistinctly** adv.

**indistinguishable** adj. not distinguishable.

**indium** n. soft silvery-white metallic element (symbol In).

**individual** ● adj. of, for, or characteristic of single person or thing; having distinct character; single; particular. ● n. single member of class; single human being; distinctive person. □□ **individually** adv. **individuality** n.

**individualist** n. person who is very independent in their thought and action.

**indivisible** adj. not divisible.

**indoctrinate** v. teach to accept a particular view uncritically. □□ **indoctrination** n.

**indolent** adj. lazy; averse to exertion. □□ **indolence** n. **indolently** adv.

**indomitable** adj. unconquerable, unyielding. □□ **indomitably** adv.

**indoor** ● adj. done etc. in building or under cover. ● adv. (**indoors**) inside a building.

**indubitable** adj. that cannot be doubted. □□ **indubitably** adv.

**induce** v. 1 prevail on; persuade. 2 bring on (labour) artificially. 3 produce by induction. 4 infer. □□ **inducible** adj.

**inducement** n. attractive offer; incentive; bribe.

**induct** v. introduce into office.

**inductance** n. property of electric circuit in which variation in current produces electromotive force.

**induction** n. 1 inducting, inducing. 2 act of bringing on (esp. labour) artificially. 3 general inference from particular instances. 4 formal introduction to new job etc. 5 production of electric or magnetic state by proximity to electric circuit or magnetic field. □□ **inductive** adj.

**indulge** v. take one's pleasure freely; yield freely to (desire etc.); gratify by compliance with wishes. □ **indulge in** allow oneself (something pleasant).

**indulgence** n. 1 indulging; thing indulged in. 2 privilege granted.

**indulgent** adj. lenient; willing to overlook faults etc.; indulging. □□ **indulgently** adv.

**industrial** adj. of, engaged in, for use in, or serving the needs of industry; having highly developed industries. □ **industrial action** strike or similar protest. **industrial relations** relations between management and workers. □□ **industrially** adv.

**industrialised** adj. (also **-ized**) full of industries.

**industrialism** n. system in which manufacturing industries predominate.

**industrialist** n. owner or manager in industry.

**industrious** adj. hard-working. □□ **industriously** adv.

**industry** n. 1 branch of trade or manufacture; commercial enterprise; trade or manufacture collectively. 2 concerted activity; diligence.

**inebriated** adj. drunk.

**inedible** adj. not suitable for eating.

**ineducable** adj. incapable of being educated.

**ineffable** adj. too great for description in words. □□ **ineffability** n. **ineffably** adv.

**ineffective** adj. not achieving the desired effect or results. □□ **ineffectively** adv. **ineffectiveness** n.

**ineffectual** *adj.* ineffective, feeble. □□ **ineffectually** *adv.*

**inefficient** *adj.* not efficient or fully capable; (of machine etc.) wasteful. □□ **inefficiency** *n.* **inefficiently** *adv.*

**inelegant** *adj.* ungraceful; unrefined. □□ **inelegance** *n.* **inelegantly** *adv.*

**ineligible** *adj.* not eligible or qualified. □□ **ineligibility** *n.*

**ineluctable** *adj.* inescapable, unavoidable.

**inept** *adj.* **1** unskilful. **2** absurd; out of place. □□ **ineptitude** *n.* **ineptly** *adv.*

**inequality** *n.* difference in size, degree, circumstances, etc.; lack of equality.

**inequitable** *adj.* unfair, unjust.

**inequity** *n.* unfairness, injustice.

**inert** *adj.* without inherent power of action etc.; chemically inactive; sluggish; slow; lifeless.

**inertia** *n.* **1** property by which matter continues in existing state of rest or motion unless acted on by external force. **2** inertness, tendency to remain unchanged. □ **inertia reel** reel holding one end of a seatbelt, allowing free movement unless it is pulled suddenly.

**inescapable** *adj.* that cannot be escaped or avoided.

**inestimable** *adj.* too great etc. to be estimated. □□ **inestimably** *adv.*

**inevitable** *adj.* unavoidable; sure to happen. □□ **inevitability** *n.* **inevitably** *adv.*

**inexact** *adj.* not exact. □□ **inexactitude** *n.*

**inexcusable** *adj.* that cannot be justified. □□ **inexcusably** *adv.*

**inexhaustible** *adj.* that cannot be used up.

**inexorable** *adj.* relentless. □□ **inexorably** *adv.*

**inexpensive** *adj.* cheap; good value.

**inexperience** *n.* lack of experience. □□ **inexperienced** *adj.*

**inexpert** *adj.* unskilful.

**inexplicable** *adj.* that cannot be explained. □□ **inexplicably** *adv.*

**inexpressible** *adj.* that cannot be expressed. □□ **inexpressibly** *adv.*

**in extremis** *adj.* at the point of death; in great difficulties.

**inextricable** *adj.* from which one cannot get free. □□ **inextricably** *adv.*

**infallible** *adj.* incapable of error; unfailing; sure. □□ **infallibility** *n.* **infallibly** *adv.*

**infamous** *adj.* notoriously vile; evil; abominable. □□ **infamously** *adv.* **infamy** *n.*

**infant** *n.* child during earliest period of life; thing in early stage of development. □□ **infancy** *n.*

**infanticide** *n.* killing of an infant, esp. soon after birth.

**infantile** *adj.* of or like infants; very childish.

**infantry** *n.* (group of) foot soldiers.

**infarct** *n.* small area of dead tissue caused by inadequate blood supply. □□ **infarction** *n.*

**infatuated** *adj.* filled with intense unreasoning love. □□ **infatuation** *n.*

**infect** *v.* affect or contaminate with germ, virus, or disease; imbue; taint.

**infection** *n.* infecting, being infected; disease; communication of disease.

**infectious** *adj.* infecting; transmissible by infection; apt to spread. □□ **infectiously** *adv.*

**infer** *v.* (**inferred**) deduce, conclude.

> **Usage** It is a mistake to use *infer* to mean 'imply' as in *Are you inferring that I am a liar?*

**inference** *n.* **1** act of inferring. **2** thing inferred. **3** *colloq.* something implied. □□ **inferential** *adj.*

**inferior** *adj.* • lower in rank etc.; of poor quality; situated below.
• *n.* inferior person. □□ **inferiority** *n.*

**infernal** adj. **1** of hell; hellish. **2** colloq. detestable, tiresome. □□ **infernally** adv.

**inferno** n. **1** raging fire. **2** scene of horror or distress; hell.

**infertile** adj. not fertile. □□ **infertility** n.

**infest** v. overrun in large numbers. □□ **infestation** n.

**infidel** n. person who does not believe in (particular) religion.

**infidelity** n. being unfaithful.

**infighting** n. conflict or competitiveness in organisation.

**infill** ● n. material used to fill hole, gap, etc. ● v. fill in (cavity etc.)

**infiltrate** v. **1** enter (territory, political party, etc.) gradually and secretly; cause to do this. **2** permeate by filtration; introduce (fluid) by filtration. □□ **infiltration** n. **infiltrator** n.

**infinite** adj. boundless; endless; very great, many.

**infinitesimal** adj. very small. □□ **infinitesimally** adv.

**infinitive** n. verb form not indicating tense, number, or person, e.g. to go.

**infinity** n. infinite number or extent; being infinite; very great distance.

**infirm** adj. weak from age or illness. □□ **infirmity** n.

**infirmary** n. hospital; sick quarters in school etc.

**inflame** v. **1** provoke to strong feeling. **2** cause inflammation in; make hot. **3** aggravate. **4** (cause to) catch fire.

**inflammable** adj. flammable. □□ **inflammability** n.

> **Usage** see note at *flammable*.

**inflammation** n. redness and heat in part of body.

**inflammatory** adj. tending to inflame; of inflammation.

**inflatable** ● adj. that can be inflated. ● n. inflatable object.

**inflate** v. **1** fill with air or gas so as to swell. **2** increase artificially; exaggerate.

**inflation** n. **1** inflating, being inflated. **2** general rise in prices and a fall in the purchasing power of money. □□ **inflationary** adj.

**inflect** v. **1** change or vary pitch of (voice). **2** modify (word) to express grammatical relation; undergo such change. □□ **inflection** n.

**inflexible** adj. **1** unbendable. **2** unwilling to yield or compromise; unable to be changed. □□ **inflexibility** n. **inflexibly** adv.

**inflict** v. **1** deal (blow etc.) **2** impose. □□ **infliction** n.

**inflight** adj. occurring or provided during a flight.

**inflorescence** n. collective flower head of plant; arrangement of flowers on plant; flowering.

**inflow** n. flowing in; that which flows in.

**influence** ● n. **1** effect person or thing has on another. **2** ascendancy, moral power; thing or person exercising this. ● v. exert influence on; affect.

**influential** adj. having great influence.

**influenza** n. infectious viral disease with fever, aching, and catarrh.

**influx** n. arrival of large number of people or things.

**infographic** n. visual representation of information or data.

**infomercial** n. (also **informercial**) advertising program, esp. on television.

**inform** v. **1** tell. **2** give incriminating information about person to authorities.

**informal** adj. **1** without formality; everyday, not formal; (of language) colloquial. **2** *Aust.* (of vote) not

valid.□□ **informality** *n.*
informally *adv.*

**informant** *n.* giver of information.

**information** *n.* what is told;
knowledge; news.□ **information
superhighway** electronic network
for rapid transfer of information.
**information technology** (also
**information science**) study and use
of computers, microelectronics, etc.
for storing and transferring
information.

**informed** *adj.* **1** knowing the facts.
**2** instructed.

**infra dig** *adj. colloq.* beneath one's
dignity.

**infrared** *adj.* of or using radiation just
beyond red end of spectrum.

**infrastructure** *n.* **1** basic structural
parts of something. **2** roads, bridges,
sewers, etc., regarded as country's
basic facilities.

**infrequent** *adj.* not frequent.
□□ **infrequently** *adv.*

**infringe** *v.* break or violate (law,
another's rights, etc.); encroach;
trespass.□□ **infringement** *n.*

**infuriate** *v.* enrage; irritate greatly.
□□ **infuriating** *adj.*

**infuse** *v.* **1** fill (with a quality). **2** steep
or be steeped in liquid to extract
properties.

**infusion** *n.* **1** infusing; liquid extract
so obtained. **2** infused element.

**ingenious** *adj.* clever at contriving;
cleverly contrived.□□ **ingeniously**
*adv.* **ingenuity** *n.*

**ingenuous** *adj.* artless.
□□ **ingenuously** *adv.*

**ingest** *v.* take in (food etc.); absorb
(knowledge etc.)□□ **ingestion** *n.*

**inglorious** *adj.* **1** shameful. **2** not
famous.

**ingot** *n.* (usu. oblong) piece of cast
metal, esp. gold.

**ingrained** *adj.* **1** deeply rooted.
**2** inveterate. **3** (of dirt etc.) deeply
embedded.

**ingratiate** *v.* bring (oneself) into a
person's favour, esp. to gain
advantage.□□ **ingratiating** *adj.*

**ingratitude** *n.* lack of due gratitude.

**ingredient** *n.* component part in
mixture.

**ingress** *n.* going in; right to go in;
place where one goes in.

**ingrowing** *adj.* (of toenail) growing
into the flesh.

**inhabit** *v.* dwell in, occupy.
□□ **inhabitable** *adj.* **inhabitant** *n.*

**inhalant** *n.* medicinal substance to be
inhaled.

**inhale** *v.* breathe in.□□ **inhalation** *n.*

**inhaler** *n.* device for administering
inhalant, esp. to relieve asthma.

**inherent** *adj.* existing in something as
essential or permanent attribute.
□□ **inherently** *adv.*

**inherit** *v.* **1** receive as heir. **2** derive
(characteristic) from ancestors.
**3** derive or take over (situation) from
predecessor.□□ **inheritance** *n.*

**inhibit** *v.* **1** hinder, restrain, prevent;
(as **inhibited** *adj.*) suffering from
inhibition. **2** prohibit.□□ **inhibitor** *n.*

**inhibition** *n.* restraint of direct
expression of instinct; emotional
resistance to thought or action;
inhibiting, being inhibited.

**inhospitable** *adj.* not hospitable;
affording no shelter.

**in-house** *adj. & adv.* within an
organisation.

**inhuman** *adj.* brutal; unfeeling;
barbarous.□□ **inhumanity** *n.*
inhumanly *adv.*

**inhumane** *adj.* not humane; callous.
□□ **inimically** *adv.*

**inimical** *adj.* hostile; harmful.
□□ **inimically** *adv.*

**inimitable** *adj.* impossible to imitate.
□□ **inimitably** *adv.*

**iniquity** *n.* wickedness; gross
injustice.□□ **iniquitous** *adj.*

**initial** ● *adj.* of or at the
beginning. ● *n.* first letter, esp. of
person's name. ● *v.* (**initialled**) mark

or sign with one's initials. □□ **initially** adv.

**initialise** v. (also **-ize**) Computing set variable value etc. at start of operation.

**initiate** ● v. **1** originate, set going. **2** admit into society, office, etc., esp. with ritual. **3** instruct in subject. ● n. (esp. newly) initiated person. □□ **initiation** n. **initiatory** adj.

**initiative** n. **1** ability to initiate. **2** enterprise. **3** first step. **4** (the initiative) power or right to begin.

**inject** v. **1** force liquid into body with syringe; administer medicine etc. to (person) by injection. **2** introduce (new element) into situation etc. □□ **injection** n.

**injudicious** adj. unwise; ill-judged.

**injunction** n. authoritative order; judicial order restraining from specified act, or compelling restitution.

**injure** v. hurt, harm, impair; do wrong to.

**injurious** adj. hurtful; defamatory; wrongful.

**injury** n. physical harm or damage; offence to feelings etc.; unjust treatment.

**injustice** n. unfairness; unjust act.

**ink** ● n. **1** coloured fluid for writing or printing. **2** black liquid ejected by cuttlefish etc. **3** tattoo(s). ● v. mark, cover, or smear with ink. □□ **inky** adj.

**inkling** n. slight knowledge or suspicion.

**inland** ● adj. & adv. in or towards interior of a country. ● n. (the inland) interior of a country.

**in-laws** n.pl. relatives by marriage.

**inlay** ● v. (**inlaid**, **inlaying**) embed (thing in another); decorate (thing thus; (as **inlaid** adj.) (of furniture etc.) ornamented by inlaying. ● n. inlaid material or work.

**inlet** n. **1** small arm of sea etc. **2** piece inserted. **3** way of entry.

**in-line skate** n. = ROLLERBLADE.

**in loco parentis** adv. acting in place of parent.

**inmate** n. occupant of hospital, prison, institution, etc.

**in memoriam** ● prep. in memory of. ● n. obituary.

**inmost** adj. most inward.

**inn** n. small hotel providing liquor, food, accommodation, etc.

**innards** n.pl. colloq. **1** entrails. **2** works (of engine etc.)

**innate** adj. inborn; natural. □□ **innately** adv.

**inner** adj. nearer to centre or inside; interior, internal.

**innermost** adj. furthest inward.

**innings** n. Sport batter's or team's turn at batting.

**innocent** ● adj. free from moral wrong; not guilty; guileless; harmless. ● n. innocent person, esp. young child. □□ **innocence** n. **innocently** adv.

**innocuous** adj. harmless; inoffensive.

**innovate** v. bring in new ideas etc.; make changes. □□ **innovation** n. **innovative** adj. **innovator** n.

**innuendo** n. (pl. **innuendoes** or **innuendos**) allusive (usu. depreciatory or sexually suggestive) remark.

**innumerable** adj. countless.

**innumerate** adj. not knowing basic mathematics. □□ **innumeracy** n.

**inoculate** v. treat with vaccine or serum to promote immunity against disease. □□ **inoculation** n.

**inoperable** adj. **1** that cannot be cured by surgical solution. **2** unable to be operated or used.

**inoperative** adj. not working or taking effect.

**inopportune** adj. not appropriate, esp. not timely.

**inordinate** adj. excessive. □□ **inordinately** adv.

**inorganic** adj. **1** *Chem.* not organic. **2** without organised physical structure. **3** extraneous.

**inpatient** n. patient staying in hospital during treatment.

**input** ● n. **1** what is put in or taken in. **2** energy supplied to device or system; electrical signal; information put into a computer. ● v. (**input** or **inputted**, **inputting**) put in; supply (data, programs, etc.) to a computer.

**inquest** n. inquiry held by coroner into cause of death; judicial inquiry to ascertain facts of incident etc.

**inquire** v. make investigation.

**inquiry** n. investigation.

**inquisition** n. **1** act of detailed or relentless questioning. **2** (**the Inquisition**) *RC Ch.* ecclesiastical tribunal for suppression of heresy. □□ **inquisitional** adj. **inquisitor** n. **inquisitorial** adj.

**inquisitive** adj. curious, prying; seeking knowledge. □□ **inquisitively** adv. **inquisitiveness** n.

**inroad** n. hostile attack. □ **make inroads into** encroach on; use up; destroy.

**insalubrious** adj. unhealthy, unwholesome.

**insane** adj. **1** seriously mentally ill. **2** *colloq.* extremely foolish. **3** *colloq.* wonderful. □□ **insanely** adv. **insanity** n.

**insanitary** adj. dirty and unhygienic.

**insatiable** adj. that cannot be satisfied. □□ **insatiability** n. **insatiably** adv.

**inscribe** v. write or engrave.

**inscription** n. words inscribed.

**inscrutable** adj. mysterious, impenetrable. □□ **inscrutability** n. **inscrutably** adv.

**insect** n. small invertebrate animal with segmented body and six legs.

**insecticide** n. substance for killing insects.

**insectivorous** adj. insect-eating.

**insecure** adj. **1** not secure or safe. **2** lacking confidence. □□ **insecurity** n.

**inseminate** v. introduce semen into; sow (seed etc.) □□ **insemination** n.

**insensible** adj. **1** unconscious; unaware. **2** callous. **3** imperceptible. □□ **insensibility** n. **insensibly** adv.

**insensitive** adj. not sensitive. □□ **insensitively** adv. **insensitiveness** n. **insensitivity** n.

**inseparable** adj. that cannot be separated; (of friends) reluctant to part. □□ **inseparability** n. **inseparably** adv.

**insert** ● v. place or put (thing into another). ● n. thing inserted. □□ **insertion** n.

**in-service** adj. (of training) for people working in the profession concerned.

**inset** ● n. extra piece inserted in book, garment, etc.; small map etc. within border of larger one. ● v. (**inset**, **insetting**) put in as inset; decorate with inset.

**inshore** adv. & adj. at sea but close to shore.

**inside** ● n. inner side, surface, or part. ● adj. **1** on, in, or to the inside. **2** nearer to centre of sports field. ● adv. **1** on, in, or to the inside. **2** *colloq.* in prison. ● prep. on, in, or to the inside of; within. □ **inside out** with inner side outwards; thoroughly.

**insider** n. **1** person within organisation etc. **2** person privy to secret. □ **insider trading** illegal practice of using confidential information to gain advantage in buying stocks and shares.

**insidious** adj. proceeding inconspicuously but harmfully. □□ **insidiously** adv.

**insight** n. capacity for understanding hidden truths etc.; instance of this.

**insignia** n. badges or marks of office etc.

**insignificant** *adj.* unimportant; trivial.☐☐ **insignificance** *n.*

**insinuate** *v.* hint obliquely, esp. unpleasantly; introduce subtly or deviously.☐☐ **insinuation** *n.*

**insipid** *adj.* dull, lifeless; tasteless. ☐☐ **insipidity** *n.* **insipidly** *adv.*

**insist** *v.* maintain or demand assertively.☐☐ **insistent** *adj.* **insistence** *n.* **insistently** *adv.*

**in situ** *adv.* in its original place.

**insole** *n.* removable inner sole for use in shoe.

**insolent** *adj.* impertinently insulting. ☐☐ **insolence** *n.* **insolently** *adv.*

**insoluble** *adj.* that cannot be solved or dissolved.☐☐ **insolubility** *n.* **insolubly** *adv.*

**insolvent** ● *adj.* unable to pay debts. ● *n.* insolvent debtor. ☐☐ **insolvency** *n.*

**insomnia** *n.* inability to sleep. ☐☐ **insomniac** *n.*

**insouciant** *adj.* carefree; unconcerned.☐☐ **insouciance** *n.*

**inspect** *v.* look closely at; examine officially.☐☐ **inspection** *n.*

**inspector** *n.* **1** official employed to inspect or supervise. **2** police officer next above sergeant in rank.

**inspiration** *n.* **1** creative force or influence; person etc. stimulating creativity etc. **2** breathing in. ☐☐ **inspirational** *adj.*

**inspire** *v.* **1** stimulate (person) to esp. creative activity; animate; instil thought or feeling. **2** inhale. ☐☐ **inspiring** *adj.*

**inst.** *abbr.* instant, or current month.

**instability** *n.* lack of stability.

**install** *v.* place (person) into office ceremonially; set in position and ready for use; establish. ☐☐ **installation** *n.*

**instalment** *n.* any of several usu. equal payments for something; one part of a serial.

**instance** ● *n.* example; particular case. ● *v.* cite as an instance.

**instant** ● *adj.* **1** occurring immediately; (of food etc.) processed for quick preparation. **2** pressing. ● *n.* precise moment; short space of time.☐☐ **instantly** *adv.*

**instantaneous** *adj.* occurring or done in an instant. ☐☐ **instantaneously** *adv.*

**instead** *adv.* in place of; as substitute.

**instep** *n.* inner arch of foot between toes and ankle; part of shoe etc. fitting this.

**instigate** *v.* bring about by persuasion; incite.☐☐ **instigation** *n.* **instigator** *n.*

**instil** *v.* (instilled) **1** put (idea etc.) into mind etc. gradually. **2** put in by drops. ☐☐ **instillation** *n.* **instilment** *n.*

**instinct** *n.* innate pattern of behaviour; unconscious skill; intuition.

**institute** ● *n.* organisation for promotion of science, education, etc. ● *v.* establish; found; initiate (inquiry etc.).

**institution** *n.* **1** organisation or society. **2** established law or custom. **3** well-known person. **4** instituting, being instituted. ☐☐ **institutional** *adj.*

**institutionalise** *v.* (also **-ize**) **1** place or keep in an institution. **2** make institutional. **3** (as **institutionalised** *adj.*) made dependent by long period in institution.

**instruct** *v.* **1** teach. **2** direct, command. **3** employ (lawyer). **4** inform. ☐☐ **instructor** *n.*

**instruction** *n.* teaching; statement telling a person what to do. ☐☐ **instructional** *adj.*

**instructive** *adj.* tending to instruct; enlightening.

**instrument** *n.* **1** tool, implement. **2** device for producing musical sounds. **3** thing used in performing

action. **4** person made use of.
**5** measuring device, esp. in aircraft.

**instrumental** adj. **1** serving as instrument or means. **2** (of music) performed on instruments.

**instrumentalist** n. performer on musical instrument.

**instrumentation** n. arrangement of music for instruments; orchestration.

**insubordinate** adj. disobedient; rebellious.☐☐ **insubordination** n.

**insubstantial** adj. **1** lacking solidity or substance. **2** not real.

**insufferable** adj. intolerable; unbearably conceited etc.
☐☐ **insufferably** adv.

**insufficient** adj. not enough; inadequate.☐☐ **insufficiency** n. **insufficiently** adv.

**insular** adj. **1** of or like an island. **2** separated, remote; narrow-minded.
☐☐ **insularity** n.

**insulate** v. **1** cover with substance that prevents passage of electricity, sound, or heat, etc. **2** protect from outside influences, pressures, etc.
☐☐ **insulation** n. **insulator** n.

**insulin** n. hormone regulating amount of glucose in blood.

**insult** ● v. abuse scornfully.
● n. insulting remark or action; thing so worthless etc. as to be offensive.
☐☐ **insulting** adj. **insultingly** adv.

**insuperable** adj. impossible to surmount; impossible to overcome.
☐☐ **insuperability** n. **insuperably** adv.

**insupportable** adj. **1** unable to be endured. **2** unjustifiable.

**insurance** n. procedure or contract securing compensation for loss, damage, death, etc. on payment of premium; sum paid to effect insurance.

**insure** v. **1** protect by insurance. **2** US ensure.

**insurgent** ● adj. in revolt; rebellious. ● n. rebel.
☐☐ **insurgency** n.

**insurmountable** adj. insuperable.

**insurrection** n. usu. armed rising in resistance to authority; rebellion.
☐☐ **insurrectionist** n.

**intact** adj. undamaged; entire; untouched.

**intake** n. action of taking in; people, things, or quantity taken in; place where water is taken into pipe, or fuel or air into engine.

**intangible** adj. that cannot be touched or mentally grasped.
☐☐ **intangibility** n. **intangibly** adv.

**integer** n. whole number.

**integral** ● adj. **1** of or essential to a whole; complete. **2** of or denoted by an integer. ● n. Math. quantity of which given function is the derivative.
☐☐ **integrally** adv.

**integrate** v. **1** combine (parts) into whole, complete by adding parts. **2** bring or come into equal membership of society.☐☐ **integration** n.

**integrity** n. **1** honesty. **2** wholeness. **3** soundness.

**intellect** n. faculty of knowing and reasoning; understanding.

**intellectual** ● adj. of, requiring, or using the intellect; having highly developed intellect. ● n. intellectual person.☐☐ **intellectualise** v. (also -ize) **intellectually** adv.

**intelligence** n. **1** intellect; quickness of understanding. **2** collecting of information, esp. secretly for military or political purposes; information so collected, people employed in this.

**intelligent** adj. having or showing good intelligence, clever.
☐☐ **intelligently** adv.

**intelligentsia** n. class of intellectuals regarded as cultured and politically enterprising.

**intelligible** adj. that can be understood.☐☐ **intelligibility** n. **intelligibly** adv.

**intend** v. have as one's purpose; design, destine.

**intense** adj. 1 existing in high degree. 2 violent; forceful; extreme. 3 very emotional. □□ **intensely** adv. **intensity** n.

**intensifier** n. 1 thing that makes something more intense. 2 word or prefix used to give force or emphasis.

**intensify** v. make or become (more) intense. □□ **intensification** n.

**intensive** adj. 1 thorough, vigorous. 2 concentrated. 3 of or relating to intensity. 4 increasing production relative to costs. □ **intensive care** medical treatment with constant attention for seriously ill patient. □□ **intensively** adv. **intensiveness** n.

**intent** ● n. intention; purpose. ● adj. resolved, bent; attentively occupied; eager. □□ **intently** adv.

**intention** n. aim, purpose; intending.

**intentional** adj. done on purpose. □□ **intentionally** adv.

**inter** v. (interred) bury (corpse etc.)

**inter-** prefix 1 between, among. 2 mutually, reciprocally.

**interact** v. have an effect upon each other. □□ **interaction** n. **interactive** adj.

**inter alia** adv. among other things.

**inter alios** adv. among other people.

**interbreed** v. (interbred, interbreeding) (cause to) breed to produce hybrid individual.

**intercede** v. intervene on behalf of another; plead.

**intercept** v. seize, catch, stop, etc. in transit; cut off. □□ **interception** n. **interceptor** n.

**intercession** n. interceding. □□ **intercessor** n.

**interchange** ● v. 1 (of two people) exchange (things) with each other; make exchange of (two things). 2 alternate. ● n. 1 reciprocal exchange. 2 departure and arrival point for buses etc. 3 major road junction, esp. where freeways converge. 4 *Sport* player not on field who may be substituted for active player in same team. □□ **interchangeable** adj.

**intercom** n. colloq. system of intercommunication by radio or telephone.

**intercourse** n. 1 dealings between people or countries. 2 sexual intercourse.

**interdependent** adj. mutually dependent.

**interdict** n. formal prohibition.

**interdisciplinary** adj. of or involving different branches of learning.

**interest** ● n. 1 feeling of wanting to know or learn about something or someone; quality causing this; activity or subject that one enjoys doing or studying. 2 advantage. 3 money paid for use of money borrowed etc. 4 thing in which one has stake or concern; legal concern, title, or right. ● v. 1 arouse interest of. 2 cause to take interest. 3 (as **interested** adj.) having private interest, not impartial.

**interesting** adj. causing curiosity; holding the attention. □□ **interestingly** adv.

**interface** ● n. 1 point where two systems, subjects, organisations, etc. meet and interact; surface forming common boundary between two regions etc. 2 device or program enabling user to communicate with computer. ● v. 1 connect by means of interface. ● v. 2 interact.

**interfere** v. meddle; be obstacle; intervene.

**interference** n. interfering; fading or disturbing of received radio signals etc.

**interferon** n. protein inhibiting development of virus in cell.

**interim** ● *n.* intervening time.
● *adj.* provisional, temporary.

**interior** ● *adj.* **1** inner; inland.
**2** internal, domestic. ● *n.* **1** inner
part. **2** inside; inland region. **3** home
affairs of country.

**interject** *v.* make remark abruptly or
parenthetically; interrupt; heckle.

**interjection** *n.* exclamation.

**interlace** *v.* bind intricately together;
interweave. □□ **interlacement** *n.*

**interlink** *v.* link together.

**interlock** *v.* engage with each
other by overlapping; lock
together. ● *n.* machine-knitted
fabric with fine stitches.

**interloper** *n.* intruder; person who
interferes in others' affairs.
□□ **interlope** *v.*

**interlude** *n.* interval (between acts of
play etc.); performance filling this.

**intermarry** *v.* (of races, castes,
families, etc.) become connected by
marriage; marry near relation.
□□ **intermarriage** *n.*

**intermediary** ● *n.* mediator.
● *adj.* **1** acting as mediator.
**2** intermediate.

**intermediate** ● *adj.* coming
between in time, place, order,
etc. ● *n.* intermediate thing.

**interment** *n.* burial.

**intermezzo** *n.* short piece of music.

**interminable** *adj.* endless; tediously
long. □□ **interminably** *adv.*

**intermingle** *v.* mix together;
mingle.

**intermission** *n.* pause, cessation;
interval in cinema etc.

**intermittent** *adj.* occurring at
intervals; not continuous.
□□ **intermittently** *adv.*

**intern** ● *n.* student etc. who works in
order to gain experience or satisfy
requirements for a qualification;
junior doctor working in hospital
while completing further
training. ● *v.* confine within
prescribed limits. □□ **internee** *n.*
**internment** *n.*

**internal** *adj.* **1** of or in the inside of
thing; inside the body. **2** of nation's
domestic affairs. **3** used or applying
within an organisation. **4** intrinsic, of
mind or soul. □ **internal-combustion
engine** engine producing power from
fuel exploded within a cylinder.
□□ **internally** *adj.*

**internalise** *v.* (also **-ize**) learn, absorb
into the mind.

**international** ● *adj.* existing or
carried on between nations; agreed
on by many nations. ● *n.* contest,
esp. in sport, between representatives
of different nations; one of these
representatives. □ **international date
line** = *date line.* □□ **internationality** *n.*
**internationally** *adv.*

**internationalise** *v.* (also **-ize**) make
international; bring under joint
protection etc. of different nations.

**internecine** *adj.* mutually
destructive.

**Internet** *n.* global computer network
providing information and
communication facilities.

**interpersonal** *adj.* between people.

**interplay** *n.* interaction.

**interpolate** *v.* **1** insert or introduce
between other things. **2** make (esp.
misleading) insertions in.
□□ **interpolation** *n.*

**interpose** *v.* **1** place between one
thing and another. **2** interrupt.
**3** intervene. □□ **interposition** *n.*

**interpret** *v.* **1** explain the meaning of.
**2** render, represent. **3** act as
interpreter. □□ **interpretation** *n.*

**interpreter** *n.* person who translates
orally.

**interracial** *adj.* involving different
races.

**interregnum** *n.* interval with
suspension of normal government
between successive reigns or regimes;
interval, pause.

**interrelated** v. related to each other.□□ **interrelation** n. **interrelationship** n.

**interrogate** v. question closely or formally.□□ **interrogation** n. **interrogator** n.

**interrogative** adj. forming or in the form of question.

**interrupt** v. break continuity of (action, speech, etc.); obstruct (view etc.)□□ **interruption** n.

**inter se** adv. between or among themselves.

**intersect** v. divide by passing or lying across; cross or cut each other.

**intersection** n. intersecting; place where roads intersect.

**intersex** adj. of a person or animal that both have male and female sex organs or other sexual characteristics.

**intersperse** v. scatter; vary (thing) by scattering others among it. □□ **interspersion** n.

**interstate** adj. existing or carried on between States.

**interstellar** adj. between stars.

**interstice** n. gap, chink, crevice.

**intertwine** v. twine closely together.

**interval** n. 1 intervening time or space. 2 pause; break. 3 Mus. difference of pitch between two sounds.

**intervene** v. 1 interfere; prevent or modify events. 2 come between people or things; mediate. □□ **intervention** n.

**interview** ● n. oral examination of applicant; conversation with reporter, for broadcast or publication; meeting of people, esp. for discussion.
● v. hold interview with. □□ **interviewee** n. **interviewer** n.

**interweave** v. (interwove, interwoven, interweaving) weave together; blend.

**intestate** ● adj. not having made a will before death. ● n. person who has died intestate.□□ **intestacy** n.

**intestine** n. lower part of alimentary canal.□□ **intestinal** adj.

**intimate²** v. state or make known; imply.□□ **intimation** n.

**intimate²** ● adj. 1 closely acquainted; familiar; closely personal; having sexual relations. 2 (of knowledge) thorough.
● n. close friend.□□ **intimacy** n. **intimately** adv.

**intimidate** v. frighten or overawe, esp. in order to influence conduct. □□ **intimidation** n.

**into** prep. 1 to the inside of, to a point within. 2 to a particular state or occupation. 3 so as to touch. 4 dividing (a number) mathematically. 5 colloq. interested in; knowledgeable about.

**intolerable** adj. that cannot be endured.□□ **intolerably** adv.

**intolerant** adj. not tolerant. □□ **intolerance** n.

**intonation** n. modulation of voice; accent; intoning.

**intone** v. recite with prolonged sounds, esp. in monotone.

**intoxicant** ● adj. causing intoxication. ● n. intoxicating substance.

**intoxicate** v. make drunk; excite or elate beyond self-control. □□ **intoxication** n.

**intra-** prefix within.

**intractable** adj. not easily dealt with; stubborn.□□ **intractability** n.

**intramural** adj. 1 within the walls of an institution. 2 part of ordinary university work.

**intransigent** ● adj. uncompromising. ● n. such person. □□ **intransigence** n.

**intransitive** adj. Gram. (of verb) not taking direct object.

**intrauterine** adj. within uterus.

**intravenous** adj. in or administered into vein.□□ **intravenously** adv.

**intrepid** adj. fearless; brave.

**intricate** adj. complicated; perplexingly detailed. □□ **intricacy** n. **intricately** adv.

**intrigue** ● v. 1 carry on an underhand plot, use secret influence. 2 arouse the curiosity of, fascinate. ● n. underhand plot or plotting; secret arrangement. □□ **intriguing** adv. **intriguingly** adv.

**intrinsic** adj. inherent, essential. □□ **intrinsically** adv.

**introduce** v. 1 make (person) known by name to another; present to audience. 2 bring into use. 3 bring (legislation) before parliament. 4 initiate (person) in subject. 5 insert. 6 occur at the start of. □□ **introducible** adj.

**introduction** n. 1 introducing, being introduced. 2 formal presentation. 3 preliminary section in book. □□ **introductory** adj.

**introspection** n. examination of one's own thoughts. □□ **introspective** adj.

**introvert** n. introspective and shy person. □□ **introverted** adj.

**intrude** v. come uninvited or unwanted; force on person. □□ **intruder** n. **intrusion** n. **intrusive** adj.

**intuition** n. immediate understanding without reasoning. □□ **intuit** v. **intuitive** adj. **intuitively** adv.

**Inuit** n. (pl. **Inuit** or **Inuits**) any of several indigenous peoples of Canada, Alaska, and Greenland.

**inundate** v. 1 flood. 2 overwhelm. □□ **inundation** n.

**inure** v. habituate, accustom. □□ **inurement** n.

**invade** v. 1 enter (country etc.) with arms to control or subdue it; enter, permeate, etc. as enemy. 2 (of disease) attack. 3 encroach upon (person's privacy etc.) □□ **invader** n.

**invalid**[1] n. person suffering from ill health.

**invalid**[2] adj. not valid. □□ **invalidity** n.

**invalidate** v. make invalid. □□ **invalidation** n.

**invaluable** adj. having value too great to be measured.

**invariable** adj. unchangeable; always the same. □□ **invariably** adv.

**invasion** n. invading, being invaded. □□ **invasive** adj.

**invective** n. strong verbal attack.

**inveigle** v. entice, persuade by guile.

**invent** v. 1 create by thought. 2 originate. 3 fabricate. □□ **inventor** n.

**invention** n. inventing, being invented; thing invented.

**inventive** adj. 1 able to invent. 2 imaginative. □□ **inventiveness** n.

**inventory** n. detailed list of goods or furniture.

**inverse** adj. inverted in position, order, or relation. □□ **inversely** adv.

**invert** v. turn upside down; reverse position, order, or relation of. □□ **inverted commas** quotation marks. □□ **inversion** n.

**invertebrate** adj. & n. (animal) having no backbone.

**invest** v. 1 apply or use (money) for profit. 2 devote (time etc.) to an enterprise. 3 buy (something useful or rewarding). 4 provide with qualities etc. 5 clothe with insignia of office. □□ **investor** n.

**investigate** v. inquire into; examine. □□ **investigation** n. **investigative** adj. **investigator** n.

**investiture** n. formal investing of person with honours etc.

**investment** n. investing; money invested; property etc. in which money is invested.

**inveterate** adj. (of person) confirmed in (usu. undesirable) habit etc.; (of habit etc.) long-established. □□ **inveteracy** n.

**invidious** adj. likely to cause resentment or anger.

**invigilate** v. supervise examination candidates.□□ **invigilation** n. **invigilator** n.

**invigorate** v. give vigour to. □□ **invigorating** adj.

**invincible** adj. unconquerable. □□ **invincibility** n. **invincibly** adv.

**inviolable** adj. not to be violated. □□ **inviolability** n.

**inviolate** adj. 1 not violated. 2 safe (from harm).□□ **inviolacy** n.

**invisible** adj. that cannot be seen. □□ **invisibility** n. **invisibly** adv.

**invite** ● v. 1 request courteously to come, to do, etc.; solicit courteously. 2 tend to evoke unintentionally. 3 attract. ● n. invitation. □□ **invitation** n.

**inviting** adj. attractive.□□ **invitingly** adv.

**in vitro** adv. in test tube or other laboratory environment.□ **in vitro fertilisation** (also **IVF**) fertilisation of esp. human egg in test tube and implanting of resultant embryo in uterus.

**invocation** n. invoking; calling on, esp. in prayer or for inspiration etc.

**invoice** ● n. bill for usu. itemised goods etc. ● v. send invoice to; make invoice of.

**invoke** v. call for help or protection of; summon (spirit).

**involuntary** adj. done without intention.□□ **involuntarily** adv.

**involution** n. 1 involving. 2 intricacy. 3 curling inwards, part so curled.

**involve** v. 1 cause (person, thing) to share experience or effect. 2 imply, make necessary. 3 implicate (person) in charge, crime, etc. 4 include or affect in its operation. 5 (as **involved** adj.) complicated. □□ **involvement** n.

**invulnerable** adj. that cannot be harmed.

**inward** adj. 1 directed towards inside; going in; situated within. 2 mental, spiritual.□□ **inwardly** adv. **inwards** adj.

**iodine** n. 1 black solid halogen element forming violet vapour (symbol I). 2 solution of this used as antiseptic.

**iodise** v. (also **-ize**) treat or impregnate with iodine.

**ion** n. atom or group of atoms that has lost or gained one or more electrons.

**ionise** v. (also **-ize**) convert or be converted into ion(s). □□ **ionisation** n.

**ionosphere** n. ionised region in upper atmosphere.□□ **ionospheric** adj.

**iota** n. 1 ninth letter of the Greek alphabet (I, ι). 2 (usu. with neg.) a jot.

**IOU** n. signed document acknowledging debt.

**ipso facto** adv. by that very fact.

**IQ** abbr. intelligence quotient; number showing how person's intelligence compares with average.

**irascible** adj. irritable; hot-tempered. □□ **irascibility** n.

**irate** adj. angry, enraged.

**ire** n. literary anger.

**iridescent** adj. showing rainbow-like luminous colours; changing colour with position.□□ **iridescence** n.

**iridium** n. metallic element (symbol Ir).

**iris** n. 1 circular coloured membrane surrounding pupil of eye. 2 bulbous or tuberous plant with sword-shaped leaves and showy flowers.

**irk** v. irritate, annoy.

**irksome** adj. annoying, tiresome.

**iron** n. 1 metallic element (symbol Fe). 2 strong hard metal. 3 implement with flat base heated to smooth clothes etc. 4 golf club with iron or steel head. 5 (**irons**) fetters.

● adj. made of iron; strong as

iron. ● v. smooth (clothes etc.) with an iron.

**ironbark** n. Aust. eucalypt with thick hard bark and hard, dense timber.

**ironic** adj. (also **ironical**) using or displaying irony.□□ **ironically** adv.

**irony** n. **1** expression of one's meaning by using language that normally signifies the opposite. **2** state of affairs etc. that seems deliberately contrary to what one expects and is often amusing as a result.

**irradiate** v. **1** subject to radiation. **2** shine on; throw light on; light up. □□ **irradiation** n.

**irrational** adj. **1** illogical; unreasonable; not endowed with reason. **2** Math. not expressible as ordinary fraction.

**irrecoverable** adj. that cannot be recovered or remedied.

**irredeemable** adj. **1** that cannot be redeemed. **2** hopeless. □□ **irredeemably** adv.

**irrefutable** adj. that cannot be refuted.□□ **irrefutably** adv.

**irregular** adj. **1** not even or smooth. **2** contrary to rules or custom. **3** (of verb, noun, etc.) not inflected according to usual rules. □□ **irregularity** n. **irregularly** adv.

**irrelevant** adj. not relevant. □□ **irrelevance** n. **irrelevancy** n.

**irreligious** adj. lacking or hostile to religion; irreverent.

**irreparable** adj. that cannot be rectified or made good. □□ **irreparably** adv.

**irreplaceable** adj. that cannot be replaced.

**irrepressible** adj. impossible to control or subdue.□□ **irrepressibly** adv.

**irreproachable** adj. faultless, blameless.□□ **irreproachably** adv.

**irresistible** adj. too strong, convincing, charming, etc. to be resisted.□□ **irresistibly** adv.

**irresolute** adj. hesitating; lacking in resolution.□□ **irresolutely** adv. **irresoluteness** n. **irresolution** n.

**irrespective** adj. □ **irrespective of** not taking (a thing) into account.

**irresponsible** adj. acting or done without due sense of responsibility; not responsible.□□ **irresponsibility** n. **irresponsibly** adv.

**irretrievable** adj. that cannot be retrieved or restored. □□ **irretrievably** adv.

**irreverent** adj. lacking in reverence. □□ **irreverence** n. **irreverently** adv.

**irreversible** adj. that cannot be reversed or altered.□□ **irreversibly** adv.

**irrevocable** adj. **1** unalterable. **2** gone beyond recall.□□ **irrevocably** adv.

**irrigate** v. **1** water (land) by means of channels, pipes, etc. **2** Med. moisten (wound etc.) with constant flow of liquid.□□ **irrigable** adj. **irrigation** n. **irrigator** n.

**irritable** adj. **1** easily annoyed. **2** very sensitive to contact. □□ **irritability** n. **irritably** adv.

**irritant** ● adj. causing irritation. ● n. irritant substance.

**irritate** v. **1** excite to anger; annoy. **2** stimulate discomfort in (part of body).□□ **irritation** n.

**ISBN** abbr. international standard book number.

**-ish** comb. form approximately, roughly; rather, somewhat.

**isinglass** n. gelatine obtained from fish.

**Islam** n. religion of Muslims, proclaimed by Prophet Muhammad; the Muslim world.□□ **Islamic** adj.

**island** n. **1** piece of land surrounded by water. **2** traffic island. **3** detached or isolated thing.

**islander** n. native or inhabitant of island; (**Islander**) Aust. indigenous inhabitant of Torres Strait Islands.

**isle** n. island.

**islet** *n.* small island.

**ism** *n. colloq.* set of ideas; a movement.

**isobar** *n.* line on map connecting places with same atmospheric pressure.□□ **isobaric** *adj.*

**isolate** *v.* **1** place apart or alone; separate (esp. infectious patient from others). **2** insulate (electrical apparatus), esp. by gap. **3** disconnect. □□ **isolation** *n.*

**isolationism** *n.* policy of holding aloof from affairs of other countries or groups.□□ **isolationist** *n.*

**isomer** *n.* one of two or more compounds with same molecular formula but different arrangement of atoms.□□ **isomeric** *adj.* **isomerism** *n.*

**isopogon** *n.* Australian shrub with large globe-shaped fruit cones.

**isosceles** *adj.* (of triangle) having two sides equal.

**isotherm** *n.* line on map connecting places with same temperature. □□ **isothermal** *adj.*

**isotope** *n.* one of two or more forms of chemical element with different relative atomic mass and different nuclear but not chemical properties. □□ **isotopic** *adj.*

**issue** ● *n.* **1** important topic. **2** one edition, e.g. of magazine. **3** an outflow; issuing; quantity issued. **4** offspring. ● *v.* **1** flow out. **2** supply for use; send out. **3** publish.

**isthmus** *n.* (*pl.* **isthmuses**) narrow strip of land connecting two larger land masses.

**IT** *abbr.* information technology.

**it** *pron.* **1** the thing mentioned or being discussed. **2** used as a subject of an impersonal verb (*it is raining*).

**italic** ● *adj.* (of type etc.) of sloping kind. ● *n.* italic type.

**italicise** *v.* (also **-ize**) print in italics.

**itch** ● *n.* **1** irritation in skin. **2** restless desire. ● *v.* feel irritation or restless desire.□□ **itchy** *adj.*

**item** *n.* single thing in list or collection; separate or distinct piece of news etc.

**itemise** *v.* (also **-ize**) state by items. □□ **itemisation** *n.*

**iterate** *v.* repeat; state repeatedly. □□ **iterative** *adj.*

**itinerant** ● *adj.* travelling from place to place. ● *n.* itinerant person.

**itinerary** *n.* route; record of travel; guidebook.

**its** *adj.* of or belonging to it.

**it's** it is; it has.

**itself** *pron.* emphatic and reflexive form of IT.

**IUD** *abbr.* intrauterine (contraceptive) device.

**IVF** *abbr.* in vitro fertilisation.

**ivory** *n.* hard creamy-white substance forming tusks of elephant etc.; object made of this; its colour.□ **ivory tower** place providing seclusion from harsh realities of life.

**ivy** *n.* climbing evergreen plant with shiny five-angled leaves.

# Jj

**J** *abbr.* joule(s).

**jab** ● *v.* (jabbed) poke roughly; stab; thrust (thing) hard or abruptly.
● *n.* **1** abrupt blow or thrust. **2** *colloq.* hypodermic injection.

**jabber** ● *v.* chatter rapidly and/or indistinctly. ● *n.* chatter; gabble.

**jabiru** *n.* Australian stork with greenish-black and white plumage and red legs.

**jacaranda** *n.* tropical American tree with trumpet-shaped blue flowers.

**jack** ● *n.* **1** device for lifting heavy objects, esp. vehicles. **2** lowest-ranking court card. **3** ship's flag, esp. showing nationality. **4** device using single-pronged plug to connect electrical circuit. **5** small white target ball in bowls. ● *v.* raise (as) with jack.

**jackal** *n.* African or Asian wild animal of the dog family.

**jackass** *n.* **1** male ass. **2** stupid person. **3** (in full **laughing jackass**) *Aust.* = KOOKABURRA.

**jackboot** *n.* military boot reaching above the knee.

**jackdaw** *n.* grey-headed bird of the crow family.

**jackeroo** *Aust.* (also **jackaroo**)
● *n.* trainee on cattle or sheep station. ● *v.* work as jackeroo.

**jacket** *n.* short coat with sleeves; outer covering; skin of potato.

**jackhammer** *n.* pneumatic drill.

**jackknife** ● *n.* large knife with folding blade. ● *v.* (of semitrailer) fold against itself in accident.

**jackpot** ● *n.* large prize, esp. accumulated in poker machine, lottery, etc. ● *v.* (**jackpotted**) (of prize money) accumulate (if not won). □ **hit the jackpot** have great and sudden success.

**Jacky Howe** *n. Aust.* navy sleeveless singlet worn esp. by shearers etc.

**jacky winter** *n.* small Australian flycatcher.

**jacuzzi** *n. propr.* spa bath.

**jade** *n.* hard green, blue, or white stone for ornaments; green colour of jade.

**jaded** *adj.* **1** tired out. **2** surfeited.

**jaffle** *n. Aust.* sandwich toasted in jaffle iron or similar electrical appliance. □ **jaffle iron** long-handled hinged mould for toasting sandwiches over fire.

**jagged** *adj.* unevenly cut or torn.
□□ **jaggedly** *adv.* **jaggedness** *n.*

**jaggery** *n.* dark brown palm sugar.

**jaguar** *n.* large American spotted animal of cat family.

**jail** ● *n.* prison; imprisonment.
● *v.* put in jail. □□ **jailer** *n.*

**jailbird** *n.* prisoner or habitual criminal.

**Jainism** *n.* a religion of India.
□□ **Jain** *n.*

**jalapeño** *n.* (*pl.* **jalapeños**) very hot green chilli pepper, used in Mexican style cookery.

**jalopy** *n. colloq.* dilapidated old vehicle.

**jam** ● *n.* **1** thick sweet substance made by boiling fruit with sugar. **2** a squeeze, a crush, a crowded mass making movement difficult. **3** *colloq.* difficult situation. ● *v.* (**jammed**) **1** squeeze or cram into space; block, crowd, jam. **2** apply (brakes) suddenly. **3** make (a broadcast) unintelligible by interference.

**jamb** *n.* side post or side face of doorway or window.

**jamboree** *n.* **1** celebration. **2** large rally of Scouts.

**Jan.** *abbr.* January.

**jangle** ● *v.* (cause to) make harsh metallic sound. ● *n.* such sound.

**janitor** *n.* doorkeeper; caretaker.

**January** *n.* first month of year.

**Janus-faced** *adj.* 1 having two sharply contrasting aspects or characteristics. 2 insincere or deceitful.

**japan** ● *n.* hard usu. black varnish. ● *v.* (**japanned**) make black and glossy (as) with japan.

**japonica** *n.* shrub with red flowers and edible fruits.

**jar** *n.* container, usu. of glass and cylindrical. ● *v.* jolt; have a harsh or disagreeable effect on.

**jargon** *n.* 1 words used by particular group or profession. 2 debased or pretentious language; gibberish.

**jarrah** *n.* tall Western Australian eucalypt with valuable durable red wood.

**jasmine** *n.* shrub with perfumed flowers.

**jasper** *n.* red, yellow, or brown opaque quartz.

**jaundice** *n.* yellowing of skin caused by liver disease, bile disorder, etc.

**jaundiced** *adj.* 1 affected by jaundice. 2 filled with resentment.

**jaunt** *n.* short pleasure trip. ● *v.* take a jaunt.

**jaunty** *adj.* (**jauntier**) cheerful and self-confident; sprightly. □□ **jauntily** *adv.* **jauntiness** *n.*

**Java** *n. propr.* general purpose computer programming language.

**javelin** *n.* light spear thrown in sport or, formerly, as weapon.

**jaw** *n.* 1 bone(s) forming framework of mouth. 2 *colloq.* lengthy talk. 3 (**jaws**) gripping parts of tool; mouth of valley, channel, etc. ● *v. colloq.* speak at tedious length. □ **jaw-dropping** *colloq.* amazing.

**jay** *n.* 1 Australian bird with loud call. 2 European bird of crow family.

**jaywalking** *n.* crossing road carelessly.

**jazz** *n.* type of music with strong rhythm, improvisation, and syncopation.

**jealous** *adj.* 1 resentful of rivalry in love. 2 envious (of person etc.) 3 protective (of rights etc.) □□ **jealousy** *n.*

**jeans** *n.pl.* casual esp. denim trousers.

**jeep** *n. propr.* small sturdy esp. military vehicle with four-wheel drive. 2 *Aust.* shopping trolley.

**jeer** ● *v.* scoff; deride. ● *n.* taunt.

**Jehovah** *n.* (in Old Testament) God.

**jejune** *adj.* 1 (of ideas, writing, etc.) naive, or dry and uninteresting. 2 meagre.

**jell** *v. colloq.* 1 set as jelly. 2 (of ideas etc.) take definite form; cohere.

**jelly** *n.* 1 (usu. fruit-flavoured) translucent dessert set with gelatine; similar preparation as jam or condiment. 2 *colloq.* gelignite. □□ **jelly-like** *adj.*

**jellyfish** *n.* marine animal with jelly-like body and stinging tentacles.

**jemmy** ● *n.* burglar's crowbar. ● *v.* force open with jemmy.

**jenny** *n.* female donkey.

**jeopardise** *v.* (also **-ize**) endanger.

**jeopardy** *n.* danger, esp. severe.

**jerboa** *n.* 1 small jumping desert rodent. 2 *Aust.* = KULTARR.

**jerk** *n.* 1 sharp sudden pull, twist, etc. 2 spasmodic muscular twitch. 3 *colloq. derog.* a fool, obnoxious person. ● *v.* 1 move, pull, throw, etc. with jerk. 2 speak in halting way.

**jerkin** *n.* sleeveless jacket.

**jerky** *adj.* (**jerkier**) moving suddenly or abruptly; spasmodic. □□ **jerkily** *adv.* **jerkiness** *n.*

**jerry-built** *adj.* poorly built.

**jerrycan** *n.* can for carrying petrol or water.

**jersey** n. **1** knitted usu. woollen pullover; knitted fabric. **2** (Jersey) dairy cow from Jersey.

**jest** ● n. a joke. ● v. make jokes.

**jester** n. clown at medieval court.

**Jesuit** n. member of Society of Jesus, a Roman Catholic religious order.

**jet** ● n. **1** stream of water, steam, gas, flame, etc. shot esp. from small opening; spout or nozzle for this; jet engine or plane. **2** hard black lignite often carved and highly polished. ● v. spurt out in jet(s). □ **jet lag** delayed tiredness etc. after a long flight. **jet set** wealthy people who travel widely, esp. for pleasure. **jet ski** small jet-propelled vehicle that skims across the surface of water.

**jetsam** n. objects washed ashore, esp. jettisoned from ship.

**jettison** v. throw (cargo, fuel, etc.) from ship or aircraft to lighten it; abandon; get rid of.

**jetty** n. pier or breakwater protecting or defending harbour etc.; landing pier.

**Jew** n. person of Hebrew descent or whose religion is Judaism. □□ **Jewish** adj.

**jewel** n. **1** precious stone cut or set as ornament. **2** precious person or thing. □□ **jewelled** adj.

**jeweller** n. maker of or dealer in jewels or jewellery.

**jewellery** n. rings, brooches, necklaces, etc. collectively.

**jewfish** n. (also **dhufish**) **1** large edible marine fish found off Western Australia. **2** = MULLOWAY.

**Jewry** n. Jewish people collectively.

**jezebel** n. offens. shameless or immoral woman.

**jib** ● n. **1** projecting arm of crane. **2** triangular staysail. ● v. (**jibbed**) refuse to proceed. □ **jib at** show aversion to.

**jiffy** n. colloq. a moment. □ **jiffy bag** padded envelope.

**jig** ● n. **1** lively dance; music for this. **2** device that holds piece of work and guides tools operating on it. ● v. (**jigged**) **1** dance a jig. **2** move quickly up and down; fidget.

**jigger** n. **1** colloq. name for tool, device, etc., the correct name for which eludes one. **2** small glass for measure of spirits etc.

**jiggery-pokery** n. colloq. trickery; swindling.

**jiggle** ● v. rock or jerk lightly; fidget. ● n. light shake.

**jigsaw** n. **1** (in full **jigsaw puzzle**) picture on board etc. cut into irregular interlocking pieces to be reassembled as pastime. **2** mechanical fine-bladed fretsaw.

**jihad** n. Islam **1** struggle or fight against enemies of Islam. **2** spiritual struggle within oneself against sin. □□ **Jihadi** n. **Jihadist** n.

**jillaroo** n. Aust. (also **jilleroo**) ● n. female trainee on cattle or sheep station. ● v. work as jillaroo.

**jilt** v. abruptly reject or abandon (esp. lover).

**jingera** n. Aust. remote and mountainous bush-covered country.

**jingle** ● n. **1** mixed ringing or clinking noise. **2** repetition of sounds in phrase. **3** short catchy verse in advertising etc. ● v. (cause to) make jingling sound.

**jingoism** n. blustering, excessive patriotism. □□ **jingoist** n. **jingoistic** adj.

**jinnee** n. (pl. **jinn** or **djinn**) (in Muslim mythology) spirit of supernatural power in human or animal form.

**jinx** n. colloq. influence causing bad luck.

**jitters** n.pl. colloq. extreme nervousness. □□ **jittery** adj.

**jive** ● n. lively dance of 1950s; music for this. ● v. dance to or play jive music.

**Jnr** abbr. junior.

**job**[1] *n.* **1** piece of work; paid employment. **2** *colloq.* difficult task.

**job**[2] *v.* (jobbed) prod; *colloq.* punch.

**jobber** *n.* principal or wholesaler dealing on the Stock Exchange.

**jobbing** *adj.* doing single pieces of work for payment.

**jobless** *adj.* unemployed.
□□ **joblessness** *n.*

**jock** *n. colloq.* **1** male athlete or sports fan, esp. one with few other interests. **2** (jocks) men's brief underpants.

**jockey** ● *n.* rider in horserace.
● *v.* trick, cheat. □ **jockey shorts** men's brief underpants.

**jockstrap** *n.* support for male genitals, worn esp. in sport.

**jocular** *adj.* fond of joking; humorous.
□□ **jocularity** *n.* **jocularly** *adv.*

**jocund** *adj. literary* merry, cheerful.
□□ **jocundity** *n.* **jocundly** *adv.*

**jodhpurs** *n.pl.* riding breeches fitting closely from ankle to knee.

**joey** *n. Aust.* young kangaroo or other marsupial, esp. one in its mother's pouch.

**jog** ● *v.* (jogged) **1** run slowly, esp. as exercise. **2** nudge, esp. to alert. **3** stimulate (person's memory). ● *n.* **1** slow run. **2** a nudge.
□□ **jogger** *n.*

**joggle** ● *v.* move in jerks. ● *n.* slight shake.

**jogtrot** *n.* slow regular trot.

**john** *n. colloq.* toilet.

**John Dory** *n.* marine fish with thin deep body.

**joie de vivre** *n.* **1** exuberance. **2** high spirits.

**join** ● *v.* **1** unite; connect. **2** come into company of; take one's place in; become member of. ● *n.* place where things join.

**joiner** *n.* maker of wooden doors, windows, etc. □□ **joinery** *n.*

**joint** ● *n.* **1** place at which two or more things are joined; device for

doing this; point at which two bones fit together. **2** division of an animal carcass as meat. **3** *colloq.* place. **4** *colloq.* marijuana cigarette.
● *adj.* held by, done by, or belonging to two or more people. ● *v.* connect by joint(s); divide at joint or into joints. □□ **jointly** *adv.*

**jointure** *n.* estate settled on a widow for her lifetime.

**joist** *n.* supporting beam in floor, ceiling, etc.

**jojoba** *n.* plant with seeds yielding oil used in cosmetics etc.

**joke** ● *n.* **1** thing said or done to cause laughter; witticism. **2** ridiculous person or thing. ● *v.* make jokes.
□□ **jokily** *adv.* **jokiness** *n.* **jokingly** *adv.* **jokey** *adj.* **joky** *adj.*

**joker** *n.* **1** person who jokes. **2** playing card used in some games. **3** *Aust. colloq.* person, fellow.

**jollification** *n.* merrymaking.

**jollity** *n.* being jolly; merrymaking.

**jolly** ● *adj.* (jollier) cheerful; festive; pleasant. ● *adv. colloq.* very.

**jolt** ● *v.* **1** shake or dislodge with jerk; move jerkily; surprise or shock into action. ● *n.* jolting movement; shock.

**jonquil** *n.* narcissus with fragrant yellow or white flowers.

**josh** ● *colloq. v.* tease, make fun of. ● *n.* good-natured joke.

**joss stick** *n.* thin stick that burns with the smell of incense.

**jostle** *v.* push roughly.

**jot** ● *v.* (jotted) write briefly or hastily. ● *n.* very small amount.

**joule** *n.* SI unit of work and energy (symbol J).

**journal** *n.* newspaper or periodical; daily record of events; account book.

**journalist** *n.* person who writes for newspapers, magazines, or news websites, or prepares news to be broadcast. □□ **journalism** *n.*

**journey** ● *n.* act of going from one place to another; distance travelled, time taken. ● *v.* make journey.

**journeyman** *n.* qualified mechanic or artisan working for another.

**joust** *hist.* ● *n.* combat with lances between two mounted knights. ● *v.* engage in joust. □□ **jouster** *n.*

**jovial** *adj.* merry, convivial, hearty. □□ **joviality** *n.* **jovially** *adv.*

**jowl** *n.* loose skin on throat.

**joy** *n.* gladness, pleasure; thing causing delight.

**joyful** *adj.* full of joy. □□ **joyfully** *adv.* **joyfulness** *n.*

**joyous** *adj.* joyful. □□ **joyously** *adv.*

**joyride** *n. colloq.* fast and dangerous drive in stolen car.

**joystick** *n. colloq.* **1** control column of aircraft. **2** lever controlling movement of image on screen, used esp. in computer games.

**JP** *abbr.* Justice of the Peace.

**Jr** *abbr.* Junior.

**jubilant** *adj.* exultant, rejoicing. □□ **jubilantly** *adv.* **jubilation** *n.*

**jubilee** *n.* special anniversary.

**Judaic** *adj.* of or characteristic of Jewish people.

**Judaism** *n.* religion of Jewish people.

**judas** *n.* traitor.

**judder** ● *v.* shake noisily or violently. ● *n.* this movement.

**judge** ● *n.* **1** public official appointed to hear and try cases in law courts. **2** person who decides who has won a contest; person able to give an authoritative opinion. ● *v.* try (case) in law court; act as judge of.

**judgement** *n.* (also **judgment**, esp. in legal contexts) **1** ability to make considered decisions or come to sensible conclusions; opinion or conclusion. **2** decision of law court or judge.

**judgemental** *adj.* (also **judgmental**) of judgement; severe, critical.

**judicial** *adj.* **1** of, done by, or proper to court of law; having function of judge. **2** impartial. □□ **judicially** *adv.*

**judiciary** *n.* judges collectively.

**judicious** *adj.* sensible, prudent. □□ **judiciously** *adv.*

**judo** *n.* sport derived from ju jitsu.

**jug** *n.* **1** container with handle and shaped lip, for holding and pouring liquids. **2** *colloq.* prison. □□ **jugful** *n.*

**juggernaut** *n.* **1** large heavy semitrailer etc. **2** overwhelming force or object.

**juggle** ● *v.* **1** keep several objects in air at once by throwing and catching. **2** manipulate or rearrange (facts etc.) **3** deal with (several activities) simultaneously. ● *n.* **1** juggling. **2** fraud. □□ **juggler** *n.*

**jugular** ● *adj.* of the neck or throat. ● *n.* jugular vein. □ **jugular vein** either of the two large veins in the neck.

**juice** ● *n.* **1** liquid part of vegetable, fruit, or meat. **2** fluid secreted by an organ of the body. **3** *colloq.* petrol. ● *v.* extract juice from. □□ **juicy** *adj.*

**ju jitsu** *n.* Japanese system of unarmed combat.

**jukebox** *n.* coin-operated machine that plays recorded music.

**Jul.** *abbr.* July.

**julienne** ● *n.* vegetables cut into thin strips. ● *adj.* cut into thin strips.

**July** *n.* seventh month of year.

**jumble** ● *v.* confuse; mix; muddle. ● *n.* confused heap etc.; muddle. □ **jumble sale** sale of second-hand articles, esp. for charity.

**jumbo** ● *n.* (*pl.* **jumbos**) something very large of its kind; (in full **jumbo jet**) very large jet aircraft.

**jumbuck** *n. Aust.* sheep.

**jump** ● *v.* **1** move up off the ground etc. by movement of the legs; rise or move suddenly; jerk or twitch from shock or excitement; pass over (obstacle) by jumping. **2** reach (conclusion) hastily. **3** (of train etc.) leave (rails). **4** pass (red traffic light). **5** get on or off (train etc.) quickly, esp. illegally. **6** attack (person) unexpectedly. ● *n.* **1** act of jumping. **2** sudden movement caused by shock etc. **3** abrupt rise in price, status, etc. **4** obstacle to be jumped. **5** gap in series. **6** descent by parachute.

**jumper** *n.* **1** knitted pullover. **2** short wire making or breaking electrical circuit. □ **jumper leads** *Aust.* pair of cables for carrying current from vehicle's battery to that of another.

**jumpsuit** *n.* one-piece garment for whole body.

**jumpy** *adj.* (**jumpier**) nervous; easily startled. □□ **jumpiness** *n.*

**Jun.** *abbr.* June.

**junction** *n.* joining point; place where railway lines or roads meet; act or instance of joining. □ **junction box** box containing a junction of electric cables.

**juncture** *n.* **1** point of time, esp. critical one. **2** joining point.

**June** *n.* sixth month of year.

**jungle** *n.* **1** land overgrown with tangled vegetation, esp. in tropics. **2** wild tangled mass. **3** place of bewildering complexity or struggle.

**junior** ● *adj.* lower in age, standing, or position; the younger (esp. after name); (of school) for younger pupils. ● *n.* junior person.

**juniper** *n.* prickly evergreen shrub or tree with purple berry-like cones.

**junk** *n.* **1** discarded articles, rubbish; anything regarded as of little value. **2** *colloq.* narcotic drug, esp. heroin. **3** flat-bottomed sailing vessel in China seas. □ **junk food** food with low nutritional value. **junk mail** unrequested advertising material sent by post or email.

**junket** *n.* **1** official's tour at public expense. **2** sweetened and flavoured milk curds.

**junkie** *n.* (also **junky**) *colloq.* drug addict.

**junta** *n.* (usu. *military*) clique taking power in coup d'état.

**jurisdiction** *n.* administration of justice; legal or other authority; extent of this.

**jurisprudence** *n.* science or philosophy of law.

**jurist** *n.* expert in law.

**juror** *n.* member of jury.

**jury** *n.* group of people giving verdict in court of justice; judges of competition.

**just** ● *adj.* **1** morally right, fair. **2** deserved; justified. **3** well-grounded. ● *adv.* exactly; by only a short amount etc.; only a moment ago; merely; positively. □ **just now** a very short time ago. □□ **justly** *adv.*

**justice** *n.* **1** just treatment, fairness; legal proceedings. **2** a judge. □ **Justice of the Peace** non-professional magistrate who can witness oaths etc.

**justify** *v.* **1** to be right or reasonable; be sufficient reason for. **2** *Printing* adjust (line of type or piece of text) to fill space evenly or form straight edge at margin. □□ **justification** *n.*

**jut** *v.* (**jutted**) □ jut out protrude over.

**jute** *n.* fibre from bark of tropical plant, used for sacking, mats, etc.; plant yielding this; sacking woven from jute.

**juvenile** ● *adj.* **1** youthful; childish. **2** of or for young people. ● *n.* young person. □ **juvenile court** court of law for the trial of defendants under the age of eighteen.

**juxtapose** *v.* place side by side; put (thing) beside another. □□ **juxtaposition** *n.*

# Kk

**K** *abbr.* (also **K.**) **1** kelvin(s).
**2** *Computing* kilobyte(s).
**3** (also **k**) 1000.

**kadaitcha** *n. Aust.* **1** malignant spirit of Aboriginal lore. **2** mission of vengeance.

**kaffir lime** *n.* citrus tree with fragrant leaves used esp. in Thai cookery.

**kaftan** *n.* (also **caftan**) long tunic worn by men in SW Asia; long loose dress.

**kaiser** *n. hist.* emperor, esp. of Germany or Austria.

**kale** *n.* (also **kail**) green vegetable.

**kaleidoscope** *n.* **1** tube containing mirrors and coloured glass producing reflected patterns when shaken. **2** constantly changing scene, group, etc. □□ **kaleidoscopic** *adj.*

**kamikaze** ● *n. hist.* explosive-laden Japanese aircraft deliberately crashed on to target in Second World War; pilot of this. ● *adj.* reckless, suicidal.

**Kanaka** *n. Aust. hist.* Pacific Islander forced to serve as indentured labourer in Queensland.

**kangaroo** ● *n.* plant-eating Australian marsupial with short forelimbs, large thick tail, long feet, and swift bounding motion.
● *v.* hunt kangaroos; move like a kangaroo. □ **kangaroo court** unofficial court that has little regard for legal principles etc. **kangaroo grass** tussocky Australian perennial grass. **kangaroo paw** Australian plant with straplike leaves and flowers shaped like paws on tall stems.

**kaolin** *n.* fine white clay used esp. for porcelain and in medicines.

**kapok** *n.* cotton-like substance from tropical tree, used for padding.

□ **kapok tree** small deciduous Australian tree bearing seeds embedded in cottony fibre.

**kaput** *adj. colloq.* broken; ruined.

**karabiner** *n.* = CARABINER.

**karak** *n. Aust.* red-tailed black cockatoo.

**karaoke** *n.* entertainment in which people sing popular songs to pre-recorded backing tracks.

**karate** *n.* Japanese system of unarmed combat.

**kark** *v.* var. of CARK (sense 3).

**karma** *n. Buddhism & Hinduism* person's actions in one life, believed to decide fate in next.

**karri** *n.* tall eucalypt of Western Australia yielding valuable hard red wood.

**kauri** *n.* New Zealand conifer valued for its timber.

**kayak** *n.* canoe for one person.

**kebab** *n.* pieces of meat, vegetables, etc. cooked on skewer.

**kedgeree** *n.* dish of rice, split peas, fish, onions, etc.

**keel** ● *n.* main lengthwise structure along base of ship etc. ● *v.* (cause to) fall down or over; turn keel upwards. □ **keel over** capsize; collapse, fall over.

**keen** *adj.* **1** intense; very eager. **2** sharp; penetrating; piercingly cold. □ **keen on** *colloq.* liking greatly. □□ **keenly** *adv.* **keenness** *n.*

**keep** *v.* (**kept**, **keeping**) **1** have charge of; retain possession of; maintain or remain in specified state or condition; detain; put aside for future time. **2** provide with food and other necessities; own and look after (animals); manage (a shop etc.). **3** continue doing something;

remain in good condition.
● *n.* **1** maintenance, food. **2** strongly fortified structure in a castle. □ **keep off** avoid; abstain from. **keep on** continue. **keep up** progress at the same pace as others; continue; maintain.

**keeper** *n.* **1** person who looks after or is in charge of an animal, person, or thing. **2** wicketkeeper; goalkeeper. **3** ring holding another on finger.

**keeping** *n.* custody, charge. □ **in keeping with** suited to.

**keepsake** *n.* souvenir, esp. of person.

**keg** *n.* small barrel.

**kelp** *n.* large seaweed suitable for manure.

**kelpie** *n.* Australian short-haired sheepdog.

**kelvin** *n.* SI unit of temperature.

**ken** *n.* range of knowledge or sight.

**kennedia** *n. Aust.* trailing perennial with trifoliate leaves and bright pea flowers.

**kennel** *n.* shelter for a dog; (**kennels**) breeding or boarding place for dogs.

**kept** see KEEP.

**keratin** *n.* fibrous protein in hair, hoofs, claws, etc.

**kerb** *n.* concrete etc. edging to street etc.

**kerfuffle** *n. colloq.* fuss, commotion.

**kg** *abbr.* kilogram(s).

**KGB** *n. hist.* secret police of former USSR.

**khaki** ● *adj.* dull brownish-yellow. ● *n.* khaki cloth; khaki colour.

**khan** *n.* title of rulers and officials in central Asia.

**kHz** *abbr.* kilohertz.

**kibble** *v.* grind coarsely.

**kibbutz** *n.* (*pl.* **kibbutzim**) communal settlement in Israel.

**kibosh** *n.* (also **kybosh**) *colloq.* nonsense. □ **put the kibosh on** put an end to.

**kernel** *n.* **1** (usu. soft) edible centre within hard shell of nut, fruit stone, seed, etc. **2** central or essential part.

**kerosene** *n.* fuel distilled from petroleum. □ **kerosene bush** small aromatic Australian shrub.

**kestrel** *n.* small falcon.

**ketch** *n.* small two-masted sailing boat.

**ketchup** *n.* thick sauce made esp. from tomatoes.

**kettle** *n.* vessel for boiling water.

**kettledrum** *n.* drum with parchment stretched over large metal bowl.

**key** ● *n.* **1** instrument for moving bolt of lock, winding clock, etc. **2** something giving access, control, or insight; explanatory list of symbols used in map, table, etc. **3** finger-operated button or lever on typewriter, piano, computer keyboard, etc. **4** system of related notes in music. ● *adj.* of crucial importance. ● *v.* enter or operate on (data) by means of computer keyboard etc. □ **keyed up** stimulated, nervously tense.

**keyboard** ● *n.* set of keys on typewriter, computer, piano, etc. ● *v.* enter (data) by means of keyboard. □□ **keyboarder** *n.* **keyboardist** *n.*

**keyhole** *n.* hole for key in a lock. □ **keyhole surgery** surgery carried out through very small incision.

**keynote** *n.* **1** prevailing theme or idea. **2** person who delivers keynote address. □ **keynote address** speech intended to set out or summarise central theme of conference etc.; main or most prestigious speech at conference etc.

**keystone** *n.* central stone at top of arch locking the whole together.

**keyword** *n.* **1** key to a cipher. **2** significant word used in indexing, information retrieval, etc.

**kick** ● *v.* **1** strike or propel forcibly with foot or hoof. **2** (of gun) recoil when fired. **3** *colloq.* give up (habit). ● *n.* **1** an act of kicking; a blow with the foot. **2** *colloq.* a thrill. □ **kick-off** start of football game. **kick on** *Aust.* continue to play well; continue (party etc.) **kick out** *colloq.* drive out forcibly; dismiss. **kick-start 1** lever pressed with foot to start motorcycle etc.; start engine using this. **2** provide initial impetus for. **kick up** *colloq.* create (a fuss etc.).

**kickback** *n.* **1** recoil. **2** payment for collaboration.

**kid** ● *n.* **1** young goat; leather from this. **2** *colloq.* child. ● *v.* (**kidded**) *colloq.* deceive, tease.

**kidnap** *v.* (**kidnapped**) carry off (person) illegally, esp. to obtain ransom. □□ **kidnapper** *n.*

**kidney** *n.* either of two organs serving to excrete urine; animal's kidney as food. □ **kidney bean** red-skinned bean.

**kill** ● *v.* **1** cause the death of; put an end to. **2** *colloq.* cause pain or discomfort to. **3** pass (time) while waiting. ● *n.* a killing, an animal killed.

**killjoy** *n.* person who casts gloom over other people's enjoyment.

**kiln** *n.* oven for burning, baking, or drying, esp. for pottery.

**kilo** *n.* kilogram.

**kilo-** *comb. form* one thousand.

**kilobit** *n. Computing* unit of memory or data equal to 1024 bits.

**kilobyte** *n. Computing* unit of memory or data equal to 1024 bytes.

**kilocalorie** *n.* large calorie.

**kilogram** *n.* SI unit of mass equal to 1000 grams.

**kilohertz** *n.* 1000 hertz.

**kilojoule** *n.* 1000 joules.

**kilolitre** *n.* 1000 litres.

**kilometre** *n.* 1000 metres.

**kiloton** *n.* (also **kilotonne**) unit of explosive power equivalent to that of 1000 tons of TNT.

**kilovolt** *n.* 1000 volts.

**kilowatt** *n.* 1000 watts.

**kilt** *n.* pleated usu. tartan skirt, traditionally worn by Scottish Highland men.

**kilter** *n.* (also **kelter**) good working order.

**kimono** *n.* (*pl.* **kimonos**) wide-sleeved Japanese robe; similar dressing gown.

**kin** ● *n.* one's relatives or family. ● *adj.* related.

**kind** ● *n.* species, natural group of animals, plants, etc.; class, type, variety. ● *adj.* friendly, benevolent. □ **in kind** (of payment) in goods etc., not money. **kind-hearted** of kind disposition.

**kindergarten** *n.* class or school for young children.

**kindle** *v.* **1** set on fire, light. **2** inspire; become aroused or animated.

**kindling** *n.* small sticks etc. for lighting fires.

**kindly** ● *adv.* **1** in a kind way. **2** please. ● *adj.* (**kindlier**) **1** kind. **2** (of climate etc.) pleasant, mild.

**kindred** ● *adj.* related, allied, similar. ● *n.* blood relationship; one's relatives.

**kinetic** *adj.* of or due to motion. □□ **kinetically** *adv.*

**king** *n.* **1** male ruler of a country, esp. by right of birth; man or thing regarded as supreme. **2** chess piece; playing card next above queen. □ **king parrot** scarlet and green Australian parrot. **king tide** *Aust.* unusually high spring tide.

**kingdom** *n.* **1** territory or country ruled by king or queen. **2** division of natural world.

**kingfish** *n.* large food fish of Australian waters.

**kingfisher** *n.* small brightly coloured river bird, diving for fish etc.

**kingpin** *n.* essential person or thing.

**kink** ● *n.* **1** twist or bend in wire etc. **2** tight wave in hair. **3** mental peculiarity. **4** flaw, weak spot. ● *v.* (cause to) form kink.

**kinky** *adj.* **1** having kinks. **2** given to or involving unusual sexual behaviour.

**kinsfolk** *n.* person's relatives. □□ **kinsman** *n.* **kinswoman** *n.*

**kinship** *n.* blood relationship; similarity.

**kiosk** *n.* open-fronted booth selling food, newspapers, tickets, etc.

**kip** *n.* **1** *colloq.* a sleep. **2** *Aust.* piece of wood from which coins are spun in two-up.

**kipper** *n.* fish, esp. herring, split, salted, dried, and usu. smoked.

**kirk** *n. Scot. & N.Engl.* church.

**kirsch** *n.* spirit distilled from cherries.

**kismet** *n.* destiny, fate.

**kiss** *n. & v.* touch or caress with the lips.

**kit** ● *n.* equipment, clothing, etc. for specific purpose; set of parts needed to assemble furniture, model, etc. ● *v.* (**kitted**) equip with kit.

**kitbag** *n.* bag for holding kit.

**kitchen** *n.* room where meals are prepared. □ **kitchen garden** garden for fruit, vegetables, and herbs. **kitchen tea** *Aust.* party held for a bride before her wedding, usu. attended by female guests bringing gifts of kitchen equipment.

**kite** *n.* **1** light framework with thin covering flown on long string. **2** large hawk.

**kith and kin** *n.* relatives.

**kitsch** *n.* art, objects, or design considered to be in poor taste because of excessive garishness or sentimentality.

**kitten** *n.* young cat, ferret, etc.

**kittenish** *adj.* playful, flirtatious.

**kitty** *n.* **1** joint fund; pool in some card games. **2** jack in lawn bowls.

**kiwi** *n.* **1** flightless NZ bird. **2** (**Kiwi**) *colloq.* New Zealander. □ **kiwi fruit** soft fruit with brown hairy skin and green flesh.

**kleptomania** *n.* irresistible urge to steal. □□ **kleptomaniac** *n. & adj.*

**klick** = CLICK[?].

**km** *abbr.* kilometre(s).

**knack** *n.* ability to do something skilfully.

**knacker** ● *n.* buyer of useless horses for slaughter. ● *v. colloq.* exhaust, wear out; damage.

**knapsack** *n.* bag carried on back.

**knave** *n.* **1** rogue, scoundrel. **2** jack (in playing cards). □□ **knavery** *n.* **knavish** *adj.*

**knead** *v.* work into dough, paste, etc., esp. by hand; make (bread, pottery, etc.) thus; massage.

**knee** ● *n.* joint between thigh and lower leg; area around this; lap of sitting person; part of garment covering knee. ● *v.* (**kneed**, **kneeing**) touch or strike with the knee. □ **knee-jerk** (of a reaction) automatic and predictable.

**kneecap** ● *n.* small bone over front of knee. ● *v.* (**kneecapped**) shoot in knee as punishment.

**kneel** *v.* (**knelt** or **kneeled**, **kneeling**) rest on knees.

**knell** *n.* sound of bell, esp. for death or funeral; event etc. seen as bad omen.

**knelt** SEE KNEEL.

**knew** SEE KNOW.

**knickerbockers** *n.pl.* loose-fitting breeches gathered at knee.

**knickers** *n.pl.* underpants.

**knick-knack** *n.* (also **nick-nack**) trinket, small ornament.

**knife** ● *n.* (*pl.* **knives**) cutting or spreading instrument with blade and handle. ● *v.* stab with knife.

**knight** ● *n.* **1** man awarded non-hereditary title (Sir) by sovereign. **2** *hist.* man raised to honourable military rank. **3** lady's champion in tournament. **4** chess piece usu. shaped like horse's

head. ● *v.* confer knighthood on.
□□ **knighthood** *n.*

**knit** *v.* (**knitted** or **knit, knitting**)
1 make (garment etc.) by interlocking loops of esp. wool with knitting needles or knitting machine; make (plain stitch) in knitting. 2 wrinkle (brow). 3 make or become close; (of broken bone) become joined; heal.

**knitting** *n.* work being knitted.

**knob** *n.* rounded protuberance, e.g. door handle, radio control, etc.; small piece (of butter etc.) □□ **knobbly** *adj.*

**knock** ● *v.* 1 strike with audible sharp knock; strike (door etc.) for admittance; make (hole) by knocking; drive by striking. 2 *colloq.* criticise. 3 (of engine) make thumping etc. noise. ● *n.* the act or sound of knocking; a sharp blow. □ **knock about** treat roughly; wander casually. **knock-kneed** having knees that bend inwards. **knock off** *colloq.* cease work; complete quickly; steal. **knock out** 1 strike unconscious. 2 eliminate from competition. **knock up** *colloq.* 1 make or arrange hastily. 2 make pregnant.

**knockabout** *adj.* suitable for rough use; casual.

**knocker** *n.* 1 hinged device on door for knocking with. 2 carping critic.

**knockout** *n.* 1 striking someone unconscious. 2 tournament in which loser in each round is eliminated. 3 *colloq.* outstanding person or thing.

**knoll** *n.* small hill, mound.

**knot** ● *n.* 1 intertwining of rope, string, etc. so as to fasten; set method of this; tangle in hair, knitting, etc. 2 unit of ship's or aircraft's speed, equal to one nautical mile per hour. 3 hard mass formed in tree trunk where branch grows out; round cross-grained piece in timber caused by this. 4 cluster. ● *v.* (**knotted**) tie in knot; entangle.

**knotty** *adj.* (**knottier**) 1 full of knots. 2 puzzling.

**know** *v.* (**knew, known, knowing**)
1 have in one's mind or memory. 2 feel certain. 3 recognise; be familiar with. 4 understand. □ **in the know** *colloq.* having inside information.
**know-how** practical knowledge or skill.

**knowing** *adj.* cunning; showing knowledge, shrewd.

**knowingly** *adv.* consciously, intentionally; in knowing way.

**knowledge** *n.* awareness, familiarity; person's range of information; understanding (of subject); sum of what is known.

**knowledgeable** *adj.* (also **knowledgable**) well-informed; intelligent. □□ **knowledgeably** *adv.*

**knuckle** ● *n.* 1 bone at finger joint. 2 knee or ankle joint of quadruped; this as joint of meat. ● *v.* strike, rub, etc. with knuckles. □ **knuckle down** apply oneself seriously (to task etc.)

**knuckleduster** *n.* metal guard worn over knuckles in fighting.

**KO** *abbr.* knockout.

**koala** *n.* tree-dwelling Australian marsupial with small stout body, thick grey-brown fur, large rounded ears, leathery nose, and strong claws.

**koel** *n.* large black cuckoo.

**kofta** *n.* savoury ball made with minced meat, paneer, or vegetables.

**kohlrabi** *n.* cabbage with an edible turnip-like stem.

**kookaburra** *n.* Australian kingfisher with distinctive laughing call.

**Koori** *n. Aust.* Aboriginal person of esp. SE Australia.

**koradji** *n. Aust.* Aboriginal person with traditional medicine skills and ceremonial role.

**Koran** *n.* (also **Quran**) Islamic sacred book. □□ **Koranic** *adj.*

**kosher** *adj.* 1 (of food or food shop) fulfilling requirements of Jewish law. 2 *colloq.* correct, genuine. ● *n.* kosher food or shop.

**kowari** *n. Aust.* small yellow-brown carnivorous marsupial with black brush on tail.

**kowtow** ● *n. hist.* Chinese custom of touching ground with forehead, esp. in submission. ● *v.* **1** act obsequiously. **2** *hist.* perform kowtow.

**krill** *n.* tiny plankton crustaceans.

**Kriol** *n.* creole spoken by Aboriginal people in northern Australia.

**krypton** *n.* gaseous element used in lamps etc. (symbol **Kr**).

**kudos** *n. colloq.* glory; renown.

**kultarr** *n. Aust.* long-legged bounding marsupial mouse.

**kumanjayi** *n.* (with many spelling variants) *Aust.* (in Aboriginal society) substitute name for person who has recently died.

**kumarl** *n.* (also **goomal**) *Aust.* common brushtail possum.

**kumquat** = CUMQUAT.

**kung fu** *n.* Chinese form of unarmed combat.

**kunzea** *n.* Australian shrub with bottlebrush or ball flowers.

**kurrajong** *n.* evergreen Australian tree with glossy leaves and cream bell flowers.

**kV** *abbr.* kilovolt(s).

**kW** *abbr.* kilowatt(s).

**kWh** *abbr.* kilowatt hour(s).

**kylie** *n. Aust.* boomerang.

---

**L** abbr. **1** large. **2** learner driver. **3** (Roman numeral) 50.

**l** abbr. **1** left. **2** line. **3** litre(s).

**lab** n. colloq. laboratory.

**label** ● n. note fixed on an object to show its nature, destination, etc. ● v. (**labelled**) **1** attach a label to. **2** describe as.

**labia** n.pl. lips of female genitals.

**labial** adj. of the lips.

**laboratory** n. place used for scientific experiments and research.

**laborious** adj. needing or showing much effort. □□ **laboriously** adv.

**labour** (also **labor**) n. ● **1** physical or mental work; exertion; workers, esp. as economic or political force. **2** (**Labor**) Australian Labor Party. **3** process of childbirth. **4** task. ● v. **1** work hard; exert oneself. **2** elaborate needlessly. **3** proceed with difficulty. (as **laboured** adj.) done with great effort. **4** suffer because of.

**labourer** n. person doing paid manual work.

**Labrador** n. dog of retriever breed with black or golden coat.

**labyrinth** n. complicated network of passages; intricate or tangled arrangement. □□ **labyrinthine** adj.

**lac** n. resinous substance from SE Asian insect, used to make varnish and shellac.

**lace** ● n. **1** open patterned fabric or trimming made by twisting, knotting, or looping threads in patterns. **2** cord etc. passed through eyelets or hooks for fastening shoes etc. ● v. **1** fasten with a lace or laces; intertwine. **2** add spirits etc. to (drink).

**lacerate** v. **1** tear (esp. flesh etc.) roughly. **2** wound (feelings etc.) □□ **laceration** n.

**lachrymal** adj. (also **lacrimal**) of tears.

**lachrymose** adj. given to weeping; tearful.

**lack** ● n. deficiency, want. ● v. be without.

**lackadaisical** adj. unenthusiastic; listless; idle. □□ **lackadaisically** adv.

**lackey** n. servile follower.

**lacking** adj. undesirably absent; without.

**lacklustre** adj. lacking brightness, enthusiasm, or conviction.

**laconic** adj. using few words.

**lacquer** ● n. hard shiny shellac or synthetic varnish. ● v. coat with lacquer.

**lacrosse** n. hockey-like game played with ball carried in long-handled racquet.

**lactate** v. (of mammals) secrete milk. □□ **lactation** n.

**lactic** adj. of milk. □ **lactic acid** found in sour milk and produced in muscles during exercise.

**lactose** n. sugar present in milk.

**lacuna** n. (pl. **lacunas** or **lacunae**) a gap.

**lacy** adj. (**lacier**) like lace fabric.

**lad** n. boy, youth; colloq. any male.

**ladder** ● n. **1** set of horizontal bars fixed between two uprights for climbing up and down. **2** unravelled stitching in stocking etc. **3** means of advancement in career etc. ● v. cause or develop a ladder (in).

**laden** adj. loaded.

**ladle** ● n. deep long-handled spoon used for serving liquids. ● v. transfer with a ladle.

**lady** n. **1** woman; well-mannered woman. **2** (**Our Lady**) Virgin Mary. **3** (**Lady**) (in the British system) title of peeresses, and of wives, widows, and daughters of certain noblemen. **4 (the ladies)** women's public toilet.

**ladybird** n. small flying beetle, usu. red with black spots.

**lag** ● v. (**lagged**) **1** go too slow, not keep up. **2** enclose in material that prevents loss of heat. ● n. **1** a delay. **2** hist. convict transported to Australia.

**lager** n. kind of light-coloured beer.

**lagoon** n. expanse of shallow fresh water; salt water lake separated from sea by sandbank, reef, etc.

**lah** n. Mus. sixth note of a major scale, or the note A.

**laid** see LAY¹.□ **laid-back** colloq. easygoing, relaxed.

**lain** see LIE¹.

**lair** n. **1** place where an animal rests. **2** hiding place.

**laissez-faire** n. policy of non-interference, esp. in politics or economics.

**laity** n. lay people, as distinct from the clergy.

**lake** n. **1** large body of water surrounded by land. **2** reddish pigment.

**laksa** n. Asian dish of rice noodles served in spicy sauce or curry.

**lam** v. (**lammed**) colloq. hit hard; thrash.

**lama** n. Tibetan or Mongolian Buddhist monk.

**lamb** ● n. **1** young sheep; its flesh as food. **2** gentle, innocent, or weak person. ● v. (of sheep) give birth.

**lambaste** v. reprimand severely.

**lambertia** n. Western Australian shrub with woody fruits.

**lame** ● adj. **1** disabled in foot or leg. **2** (of excuse etc.) unconvincing. □ **lamely** adv. **lameness** n.

**lamé** n. fabric with metallic thread woven in.

**lament** ● n. passionate expression of grief; song etc. of mourning etc. ● v. **1** express or feel grief for or about; utter lament. **2** regret. □□ **lamentation** n.

**lamentable** adj. deplorable, regrettable. □□ **lamentably** adv.

**laminate** n. laminated material.

**laminated** adj. made of layers joined one upon another.

**laminex** n. Aust. propr. durable plastic laminate used as table surface etc.

**lamington** n. Aust. square of sponge cake coated with chocolate icing and desiccated coconut.

**lamp** n. device for giving light.

**lampoon** ● n. satirical attack on person etc. ● v. satirise. □□ **lampoonist** n.

**lamprey** n. eel-like aquatic animal with sucker mouth.

**lampshade** n. shade on lamp screening its light.

**LAN** abbr. Computing local area network.

**lance** ● n. long spear, esp. one used by horseman. ● v. prick or open with a needle. □ **lance corporal** army rank below corporal.

**lancet** n. small broad two-edged surgical knife with sharp point.

**land** ● n. **1** part of earth's surface not covered by water; ground, soil. **2** region, country, or nation. ● v. **1** set or go ashore; come or bring to the ground. **2** bring to or reach place or situation. **3** colloq. deal (person) a blow. **4** obtain (prize, job, etc.) □□ **landless** adj.

**landed** adj. owning or consisting of land.

**landfall** n. the approach to land after journey by sea or air.

**landfill** n. waste material used in landscaping or reclaiming ground; the use of this.

**landing** n. **1** platform at top of or part way up stairs. **2** coming to land.

**landline** n. telephone connection by cable laid across land.

**landlocked** adj. surrounded by land.

**landlord** n. person who rents a building etc. to a tenant.

**landlubber** n. person unfamiliar with the sea or sailing.

**landmark** n. conspicuous feature of landscape etc.; event marking important stage or turning point.

**landscape** ● n. scenery in area of land; painting etc. of it. ● v. improve (a piece of land) by laying out the grounds, planting, etc., so as to create a pleasing effect.

**landslide** n. **1** a sliding down of a mass of land on a slope. **2** overwhelming majority of votes.

**lane** n. **1** narrow road; division of road for one line of traffic. **2** strip of track or water for competitor in race. **3** regular course followed by ship or aircraft.

**language** n. **1** words and their use; system of this used by a nation or group. **2** gestures or symbols used for communication. **3** system of symbols and rules for computer programs.

**languid** adj. lacking vigour; idle. □□ **languidly** adv.

**languish** v. lose or lack vitality.

**languor** n. **1** lack of energy; idleness. **2** soft or tender mood or effect. □□ **languorous** adj.

**lank** adj. tall and lean; (of hair) straight and limp. □□ **lanky** adj.

**lanolin** n. fat from sheep's wool used in cosmetics etc.

**lantana** n. shrub with usu. yellow or orange flowers.

**lantern** n. **1** lamp with transparent case protecting flame etc. **2** glazed structure on top of dome or room. **3** light chamber of lighthouse.

**lanthanum** n. a metallic element (symbol La).

**lanyard** n. short rope for securing things on a ship; cord for hanging a whistle etc. round the neck or shoulder.

**lap** ● n. **1** flat area over thighs of seated person. **2** single circuit of racecourse; section of journey. ● v. (**lapped**) **1** take up (liquid) by movements of tongue; flow (against) with ripples. **2** wrap around; be one or more laps ahead of (a competitor). □ **lap up** take or accept eagerly.

**laparoscope** n. fibre optic instrument inserted through abdomen to view internal organs. □□ **laparoscopy** n.

**lapel** n. part of coat front folded back.

**lapidary** adj. **1** of stones. **2** (of language) dignified and concise.

**lapis lazuli** n. blue semi-precious stone.

**lapse** ● n. **1** temporary failure of concentration, memory, etc. **2** decline in standard. **3** interval or passage of time. ● v. **1** fail to maintain one's position or standard. **2** become void or no longer valid.

**laptop** n. portable computer.

**lapwing** n. plover.

**larceny** n. theft of personal property. □□ **larcenous** adj.

**lard** ● n. pig fat used in cooking etc. ● v. **1** insert strips of fat in (meat etc.) before cooking. **2** embellish (talk etc.) with (strange terms etc.)

**larder** n. room or cupboard for storing food.

**large** adj. **1** of relatively great size or extent; of larger kind. **2** comprehensive. □□ **largeness** n. **largish** adj.

**largely** adv. to a great extent.

**largess** n. (also **largesse**) money or gifts generously given.

**lariat** n. lasso.

**lark** n. **1** small bird with tuneful song, esp. skylark. **2** colloq. something done for fun.

**larrikin** n. Aust. person who is unsophisticated but likeable and good-hearted; person who acts with apparent disregard for social conventions.□□ **larrikinism** n.

**larva** n. (pl. **larvae**) insect in first stage of its life after coming out of egg. □□ **larval** adj.

**laryngitis** n. inflammation of larynx.

**larynx** n. part of throat holding vocal cords.

**lasagne** n. pasta sheets; a dish of these layered with sauces of meat, cheese, etc.

**lascivious** adj. lustful. □□ **lasciviously** adv.

**laser** ● n. device producing intense beam of light, or other electromagnetic radiation. ● v. treat or remove (something) using a laser.

**lash** ● v. **1** make sudden violent movement; beat with a whip; strike violently. **2** fasten with a rope etc. ● n. **1** flexible part of a whip; a stroke with this. **2** eyelash.□ **lash out** attack with blows or words; spend lavishly.

**lashings** n.pl. a lot.

**lass** n. girl.

**lassa fever** n. serious viral disease of tropical Africa.

**lassitude** n. languor; disinclination to exert oneself.

**lasso** ● n. (pl. **lassos** or **lassoes**) rope with running noose used esp. for catching cattle, brumbies, etc. ● v. (**lassoed**, **lassoing**) catch with lasso.

**last** ● adj. & adv. after all others; coming at or belonging to the end; most recent(ly). ● n. **1** last person or thing. **2** foot-shaped block used in making and repairing shoes. ● v. remain unexhausted, adequate, or alive for specified or long time. □ **at last** (or **at long last**) after much delay. **last post** military bugle call sounded at sunset or military funerals. **last resort** final course of action, used only when all else has failed. **last straw** an addition to existing difficulties, making them unbearable. **last word** final statement in dispute; latest fashion.

**lastly** adv. finally.

**lat.** abbr. latitude.

**latch** ● n. bar with catch as fastening for gate etc.; spring lock as fastening of outer door. ● v. fasten with latch.

**latchet** n. edible marine fish with large pectoral fins and reddish skin.

**latchkey** n. key of an outer door.

**late** ● adj. **1** after due or usual time. **2** far on in day or night etc. **3** flowering, ripening, etc. towards end of season. **4** no longer alive or having specified status. **5** of recent date. ● adv. **1** after due or usual time; far on in time; at or till late hour; at late stage of development. **2** formerly but not now.□ **of late** lately. □□ **lateness** n.

**lately** adv. not long ago; recently.

**latent** adj. existing but not developed or manifest; concealed, dormant. □□ **latency** n.

**lateral** ● adj. of, at, towards, or from side(s). ● n. lateral shoot or branch. □□ **laterally** adv.

**latex** n. milky fluid of esp. rubber tree; synthetic product like this.

**lath** n. (pl. **laths**) thin flat strip of wood.

**lathe** n. machine for shaping wood, metal, etc. by rotating article against cutting tools.

**lather** ● n. **1** froth made by agitating soap etc. and water. **2** frothy sweat. **3** state of agitation. ● v. (of soap) form lather; cover with lather.

**Latin** ● n. language of ancient Romans. ● adj. **1** of or in Latin. **2** of countries or peoples speaking languages descended from Latin.

**latitude** *n.* **1** angular distance N. or S. of equator. **2** region. **3** freedom from restriction in action or opinion.
□□ **latitudinal** *adj.*

**latrine** *n.* communal toilet, esp. in camp.

**latter** ● *adj.* **1** second mentioned of two. **2** nearer the end. ● *n.* (**the latter**) latter person or thing.
□ **latter-day** modern, recent.

**lattice** *n.* structure of crossed laths or bars with spaces between, used as screen, fence, etc.; arrangement resembling this.□□ **latticed** *adj.*

**laudable** *adj.* commendable.
□□ **laudably** *adv.*

**laudanum** *n.* opium prepared for use as sedative.

**laudatory** *adj.* praising.

**laugh** ● *v.* make sounds and facial movements expressing amusement or scorn. ● *n.* act or manner of laughing; *colloq.* amusing incident.
□ **laughing stock** person or thing that is ridiculed.

**laughable** *adj.* amusing, ridiculous.
□□ **laughably** *adv.*

**laughter** *n.* act or sound of laughing.

**launch** ● *v.* **1** set (vessel) afloat. **2** hurl or send forth (rocket etc.) **3** start or set in motion (enterprise, person, etc.) **4** formally introduce (new product) with publicity. **5** make start on. ● *n.* **1** launching. **2** large motor boat.

**launder** *v.* **1** wash and iron (clothes etc.) **2** *colloq.* transfer (money) to conceal origin.

**laundromat** *n.* (also **launderette**) establishment with coin-operated washing machines and driers for public use.

**laundry** *n.* place where clothes etc. are laundered; clothes etc. that have been or need to be laundered.

**laurel** *n.* **1** shrub with dark green glossy leaves. **2** (**laurels**) wreath of bay leaves as emblem of victory or poetic merit.

**lava** *n.* matter flowing from volcano and solidifying as it cools.

**lavage** *n. Med.* washing out of a body cavity.

**lavatorial** *adj.* of or like lavatories; (esp. of humour) relating to excretion.

**lavatory** *n.* toilet.

**lavender** *n.* **1** evergreen fragrant-flowered shrub. **2** pale mauve colour.

**lavish** ● *adj.* profuse; abundant; generous. ● *v.* bestow or spend (money, praise, etc.) abundantly.
□□ **lavishly** *adv.* **lavishness** *n.*

**law** *n.* **1** rule or set of rules established in community demanding or prohibiting certain actions; influence or operation of such rules. **2** statement of what always happens in certain circumstances. **3** (in Aboriginal society) body of religious belief and social customs arising from it. □ **law-abiding** obeying the law.

**lawcourt** *n.* **1** room or building in which legal trials are held. **2** court of law.

**lawful** *adj.* permitted, appointed, or recognised by law; not illegal.
□□ **lawfully** *adv.* **lawfulness** *n.*

**lawless** *adj.* having no laws; disregarding laws; unbridled, uncontrolled. □□ **lawlessness** *n.*

**lawn** *n.* **1** piece of close-mown grass in garden etc. **2** fine linen or cotton cloth. □ **lawn tennis** played with a soft ball on a grass or hard court.

**lawrencium** *n.* radioactive metallic element (symbol Lw).

**lawsuit** *n.* process of bringing dispute before lawcourt for settlement.

**lawyer** *n.* person practising law, esp. solicitor or barrister.

**lax** adj. lacking care or precision; not strict. □□ **laxity** n. **laxly** adv. **laxness** n.

**laxative** ● adj. helping evacuation of bowels. ● n. laxative medicine.

**lay**[1] ● v. (**laid, laying**) **1** place on a surface; arrange ready for use. **2** cause to be in a certain condition. **3** (of hen) produce eggs. ● n. way a thing lies. □ **lay-by** Aust. system of paying deposit on article that is then reserved by retailer until full price is paid. **lay off** discharge workers (temporarily); stop. **lay on** provide. **lay out** 1 arrange; prepare body for burial. **2** spend (money) for a purpose. **3** knock unconscious. **lay up** store; cause (person) to be ill. **lay waste** devastate (area).

> **Usage** See note at LIE[1].

**lay**[2] adj. not professionally qualified; not ordained into the clergy; of or done by such persons.

**lay**[3] see LIE[1].

**layer** ● n. **1** thickness of matter, esp. one of several, covering surface. **2** hen that lays eggs. ● v. **1** arrange in layers; cut (hair) in layers. **2** propagate (plant) by fastening shoot down to take root.

**layette** n. clothes etc. prepared for newborn child.

**layman** n. (pl. **laymen**) non-professional person.

**layout** n. arrangement of parts etc. according to a plan.

**laze** ● v. spend time idly. ● n. spell of lazing.

**lazy** adj. (**lazier**) unwilling to work; doing little work; showing little energy. □□ **lazily** adv. **laziness** n.

**lb** abbr. pound(s) (weight).

**lbw** abbr. Cricket leg before wicket.

**l.c.** abbr. **1** = LOC. CIT. **2** lower case.

**LCD** abbr. liquid crystal display.

**lea** n. poet. piece of meadow or arable land.

**leach** v. make (liquid) percolate through soil etc.; remove (soluble matter) or be removed in this way.

**lead**[1] ● v. (**led, leading**) **1** guide; influence into an action, opinion or state. **2** be a route or means of access. **3** pass (one's life). **4** go or be first; be ahead. ● n. **1** guidance; clue. **2** leading place; amount by which competitor is ahead of others. **3** wire conveying electric current. **4** strap or cord for leading animal. **5** chief part in play etc. **6** Mining vein of metal ore.

**lead**[2] n. **1** chemical element (symbol Pb). **2** heavy grey metal. **3** graphite used in pencils. **4** lump of lead used in sounding.

**leaden** adj. made of lead; heavy, slow; (of the sky) dark grey.

**leader** n. **1** person or thing that leads; principal performer in orchestra, quartet, etc. **2** = EDITORIAL. □□ **leadership** n.

**leading question** adj. question worded to prompt the right answer.

**leaf** n. **1** flat usu. green organ growing from stem or root of plant. **2** a single thickness of paper; a page; very thin sheet of metal. **3** hinged flap or extra section of table. □ **leaf mould** soil or compost consisting of decayed leaves. **leaf through** turn over leaves of (book).

**leaflet** n. **1** sheet of paper, pamphlet, etc., giving information. **2** young leaf; Bot. division of compound leaf.

**leafy** adj. (**leafier**) having many leaves.

**league** n. people, countries, groups, etc., joining together for particular purpose; group of sports clubs which compete for championship; a class of contestants. □ **in league with** conspiring with.

**leak** ● n. **1** hole through which liquid or gas escapes accidentally; liquid etc.

passing through this; similar escape of electrical charge. **2** disclosure of secret information. **3** *colloq.* urination. ● *v.* escape or let out from container; disclose. □□ **leakage** *n.* **leaky** *adj.*

**lean** ● *v.* (**leaned** or **leant, leaning**) **1** be or place in sloping position. **2** (cause to) rest for support against. **3** rely, depend. **4** be inclined or partial. ● *adj.* **1** (of person etc.) without much flesh; (of meat) containing little fat. **2** meagre. ● *n.* lean part of meat. □ **lean on 1** depend on for help. **2** *colloq.* influence by intimidating. □□ **leanness** *n.*

**leaning** *n.* tendency or inclination.

**leap** ● *v.* (**leaped** or **leapt, leaping**) **1** jump, spring forcefully. **2** (of prices etc.) increase dramatically. ● *n.* forceful jump. □ **leap year** year with extra day (29 Feb.), occurring once every four years.

**leapfrog** ● *v.* game in which each player vaults over another who is bending down. ● *v.* (**leapfrogged**) perform this vault (over); overtake alternately.

**learn** *v.* (**learned** or **learnt, learning**) get knowledge of or skill in by study, experience, or being taught; commit to memory; be told about, find out. □□ **learner** *n.*

**learned** *adj.* having much knowledge from studying; showing or requiring learning.

**learning** *n.* knowledge got by study.

**lease** ● *n.* contract by which owner of land, building, etc., allows another to use it for specified time, usu. for rent. ● *v.* grant or take on lease. □□ **leasehold** *n.* **leaseholder** *n.*

**leash** ● *n.* strap for holding dog(s). ● *v.* put leash on; restrain.

**least** ● *adj.* smallest, slightest. ● *n.* least amount. ● *adv.* in the least degree.

**leather** ● *n.* material made from the skin of animal by tanning etc. ● *v.* cover with leather.

**leathery** *adj.* **1** like leather. **2** tough.

**leave** ● *v.* (**left, leaving**) **1** go away (from); go away finally or permanently. **2** let remain; deposit; entrust to others; abandon. ● *n.* permission; permission to be absent from duty; period for which this lasts. □ **leave out** not insert or include.

**leaven** ● *n.* **1** substance (e.g. yeast) causing dough to ferment and rise. **2** transforming influence. ● *v.* **1** ferment (dough) with leaven. **2** permeate, transform.

**lecherous** *adj.* lustful. □□ **lecherously** *adv.* **lechery** *n.*

**lecithin** *n.* compound found in plants and animals used as food emulsifier and stabiliser.

**lectern** *n.* stand for holding Bible etc. in church; similar stand for lecturer etc.

**lecture** ● *n.* **1** talk giving information to class etc. **2** admonition, reprimand. ● *v.* **1** deliver lecture(s). **2** admonish, reprimand. □□ **lectureship** *n.*

**lecturer** *n.* person who lectures, esp. as teacher in higher education.

**LED** *abbr.* light-emitting diode.

**led** see LEAD¹.

**ledge** *n.* narrow shelf or projection from vertical surface.

**ledger** *n.* book used for keeping accounts.

**lee** *n.* shelter given by neighbouring object; side away from wind.

**leech** *n.* **1** bloodsucking worm. **2** person who sponges on others.

**leek** *n.* vegetable of onion family with long cylindrical white bulb.

**leer** ● *v.* look slyly, lasciviously, or maliciously. ● *n.* leering look.

**lees** *n.pl.* sediment of wine etc.; dregs.

**leet** *n.* informal language or code used on the Internet.

**leeward** ● *adj. & adv.* on or towards sheltered side. ● *n.* this direction.

**left**[1] ● *adj.* of, on, or towards west side of person or thing facing north. ● *n.* 1 left side or region; left hand or foot. 2 = *left wing*.□ **left field** unconventional or unusual position or experience. **left-handed** using left hand. **left wing** radical, progressive, or socialist section of society, political party, etc.

**left**[2] see LEAVE.

**leftovers** *n.pl.* things remaining when the rest is finished.

**leg** *n.* 1 each of limbs on which person or animal walks and stands; leg of animal as food; part of garment covering leg. 2 support of chair, table, etc. 3 *Cricket* half of field behind batter's back. 4 section of journey or competition.

**legacy** *n.* something left to someone in a will, or handed down by a predecessor.

**legal** *adj.* of, based on, or concerned with law; appointed, required, or permitted by law.□□ **legality** *n.* **legally** *adv.*

**legalise** *v.* (also **-ize**) make legal. □□ **legalisation** *n.*

**legate** *n.* envoy.

**legatee** *n.* recipient of legacy.

**legation** *n.* diplomatic minister and his or her staff; this minister's official residence.

**legato** *Mus.* ● *adv. & adj.* in smooth flowing manner. ● *n.* legato passage.

**legend** *n.* 1 story handed down from the past; such stories collectively. 2 very famous person. 3 inscription on coin or medal. 4 explanation of symbols on map.

**legendary** *adj.* 1 existing in legend. 2 *colloq.* remarkable.

**legerdemain** *n.* sleight of hand; trickery, sophistry.

**leggings** *n.* close-fitting trousers.

**legible** *adj.* clear enough to read. □□ **legibility** *n.* **legibly** *adv.*

**legion** ● *n.* division of 3000–6000 men in ancient Roman army; large organised body. ● *adj.* great in number.

**legionnaire** *n.* member of legion. □ **legionnaire's disease** form of bacterial pneumonia.

**legislate** *v.* make laws.□□ **legislator** *n.*

**legislation** *n.* making laws; laws made.

**legislative** *adj.* making laws. □ **Legislative Assembly** lower house of parliaments of Victoria, New South Wales, and Western Australia, and sole house of parliaments of Queensland, Australian Capital Territory, and Northern Territory. **Legislative Council** upper house of parliaments of all Australian states except Queensland.

**legislature** *n.* legislative body of state, nation, etc.

**legitimate** ● *adj.* 1 lawful, proper, regular. 2 (of child) born of parents married to each other. 3 logically admissible. ● *v.* = LEGITIMISE. □□ **legitimacy** *n.* **legitimately** *adv.*

**legitimise** *v.* (also **-ize**) 1 make legitimate. 2 serve as justification for. □□ **legitimisation** *n.*

**legless** *adj.* 1 without legs. 2 *colloq.* drunk.

**Lego** *n. propr.* construction toy consisting of interlocking plastic building blocks.

**legume** *n.* plant of family bearing seeds in pods; a pod of this. □□ **leguminous** *adj.*

**leisure** *n.* free time; time at one's own disposal.□ **at one's leisure** when one has time.□□ **leisured** *adj.*

**leisurely** ● *adj.* unhurried, relaxed. ● *adv.* without hurry.

**leitmotif** *n.* (also **leitmotiv**) recurrent theme in musical, literary etc.

composition representing particular person, idea, etc.

**lemming** n. 1 Arctic rodent reputed to rush into sea and drown during migration. 2 person who unthinkingly joins a mass movement.

**lemon** n. 1 yellow fruit with acid juice; tree bearing it; pale yellow colour. 2 *colloq.* thing regarded as failure. 3 (**lemons**) *AFL* break at three-quarter time.□□ **lemony** adj.

**lemonade** n. drink made from lemons; synthetic substitute for this.

**lemur** n. tree-dwelling primate of Madagascar.

**lend** v. (**lent, lending**) 1 give or allow to use temporarily; provide (money) temporarily in return for payment of interest. 2 contribute as a help or effect.□ **lend itself to** be suitable for. □□ **lender** n.

**length** n. 1 measurement from end to end; extent in or of time; length of horse, boat, etc. as measure of lead in race; long stretch or extent. 2 degree of thoroughness in action.□ **at length** after or taking a long time. □□ **lengthways** adv. **lengthwise** adj. & adv.

**lengthen** v. make or become longer.

**lengthy** adj. (**lengthier**) very long; long and boring.□□ **lengthily** adv.

**lenient** adj. merciful, not severe. □□ **lenience** n. **leniency** n. **leniently** adv.

**lens** n. 1 piece of transparent substance with one or (usu.) both sides curved, used in spectacles, telescopes, cameras, etc. 2 transparent part of eye, behind pupil.

**Lent** n. Christian period of fasting and penitence before Easter.□□ **Lenten** adj.

**lent** see LEND.

**lentil** n. leguminous plant yielding edible seeds; these seeds.

**Leo** n. fifth sign of Zodiac, the Lion. □□ **Leonian** adj. & n.

**leonine** adj. of or like a lion.

**leopard** n. 1 large animal of the cat family, with dark-spotted yellowish or all black coat. 2 panther.

**leotard** n. close-fitting stretchy garment worn by dancers, gymnasts, etc.

**leper** n. person with leprosy.

**leprechaun** n. (in Irish folklore) elf resembling little old man.

**leprosy** n. contagious disease of skin and nerves.□□ **leprous** adj.

**lerp** n. 1 whitish, sweet, waxy secretion produced by insect larvae on leaves of certain eucalypts. 2 manna.

**lesbian** ● n. homosexual woman. ● adj. of female homosexuality.□□ **lesbianism** n.

**lesion** n. damage; injury; change in part of body due to injury or disease.

**less** ● adj. not so much of; smaller in amount or degree. ● adv. to a smaller extent. ● n. a smaller amount. ● prep. minus.

---

**Usage** See note at FEW.

---

**lessee** n. person holding property by lease.

**lessen** v. diminish.

**lesser** adj. not so great as the other(s).

**lesson** n. amount of teaching given at one time; something to be learnt by pupil; experience by which one can learn.

**lessor** n. person who lets property by lease.

**lest** conj. for fear that.

**let** ● v. (**let, letting**) 1 allow, enable, or cause to. 2 allow use of (rooms, land, etc.) in return for payment. ● v.aux. used in requests, commands, assumptions, or challenges. ● n. (in tennis) an obstruction of the ball. □ **let alone** not to mention. **let down** 1 fail to support; disappoint. 2 let out air from (a tyre etc.) **let off 1** excuse from. **2** fire or explode (a weapon etc.) **let on** colloq. reveal a secret. **let up** colloq. relax.

**-let** comb. form small; young.

**lethal** adj. causing death. □□ **lethally** adv.

**lethargy** n. lack of energy; unnatural sleepiness. □□ **lethargic** adj. **lethargically** adv.

**letter** ● n. **1** character representing one or more sounds used in speech. **2** written or printed message, usu. sent in envelope by post. **3** precise terms of statement. **4** (letters) literature. ● v. inscribe letters (on).

**letterbox** n. receptacle for receiving regular deliveries of mail.

**letterhead** n. printed heading on stationery.

**lettuce** n. plant with crisp leaves used in salad.

**leuco-** comb. form white.

**leucocyte** n. white blood cell.

**leukaemia** n. (also **leukemia**) malignant progressive disease in which too many white blood cells are produced.

**levee** n. embankment against river floods.

**level** ● n. **1** horizontal line or plane; device for testing this; level surface or area; floor within multistorey building. **2** measured height or value; relative position; intellectual, social, or moral standard; position in a hierarchy. **3** (in a video game) each of series of stages of increasing difficulty through which player may progress. ● adj. **1** horizontal. **2** without projections or hollows. **3** on a level with. **4** steady; uniform. ● v. (**levelled**) **1** make or become level; knock down (a building). **2** aim (a gun etc.) □ **level crossing** place where a road and railway cross at the same level. **level pegging**

equality in score. **on the level** honest(ly).

**lever** ● n. **1** bar pivoted about fulcrum to transfer force; bar used on pivot to prise or lift. **2** projecting handle used to operate mechanism. **3** means of exerting moral pressure. ● v. use lever; lift, move, etc. (as with lever.

**leverage** ● n. **1** action or power of lever. **2** means of accomplishing purpose. ● v. use (something) to maximum advantage.

**leveret** n. young hare.

**leviathan** n. **1** Bibl. sea monster. **2** very large or powerful thing.

**levitate** v. (cause to) rise and float in air. □□ **levitation** n.

**levity** n. lack of serious thought, frivolity.

**levy** ● v. impose or collect (a payment etc.) by authority or force. ● n. levying; payment levied.

**lewd** adj. lascivious; indecent.

**lexical** adj. of the words of a language; (as) of a lexicon.

**lexicography** n. compiling of dictionaries. □□ **lexicographer** n.

**lexicon** n. dictionary.

**LF** abbr. low frequency.

**LGBTQIA** abbr. lesbian, gay, bisexual, transgender, queer (or questioning), intersex, and asexual (or allies).

**liability** n. **1** being liable. **2** colloq. handicap. **3** (liabilities) debts for which one is liable.

**liable** adj. **1** legally bound; subject to. **2** exposed or open to (something undesirable). **3** under an obligation. **4** answerable for.

**liaise** v. colloq. establish cooperation, act as link.

**liaison** n. **1** communication, cooperation. **2** illicit sexual relationship.

**liana** n. (also **liane**) climbing plant of tropical forests.

**liar | lieutenant**

**liar** *n.* person who tells lies.

**lib** *n. colloq.* **1** (also **Lib**) Liberal. **2** liberation.

**libation** *n.* **1** (pouring out of) drink offering to god. **2** *joc.* celebratory drink.

**libel** ● *n. Law* published unjustified statement damaging to person's reputation; publishing of this; false defamatory statement. ● *v.* (**libelled**) *Law* publish a libel against. □□ **libellous** *adj.*

**liberal** ● *adj.* **1** abundant. **2** giving freely, generous. **3** open-minded. **4** not rigorous. **5** (of studies) for general broadening of mind. **6** *Polit.* favouring moderate reforms. ● *n.* person of liberal views. □□ **liberalism** *n.* **liberality** *n.* **liberally** *adv.*

**liberalise** *v.* (also **-ize**) make or become more liberal or less strict. □□ **liberalisation** *n.*

**liberate** *v.* set free. □□ **liberation** *n.* **liberator** *n.*

**libertine** *n.* licentious person.

**liberty** *n.* freedom. □ **take liberties** behave with undue freedom or familiarity.

**libidinous** *adj.* lustful.

**libido** *n.* psychic impulse or drive, esp. that associated with sex instinct. □□ **libidinal** *adj.*

**Libra** *n.* seventh sign of Zodiac, the Scales. □□ **Libran** *adj.* & *n.*

**librarian** *n.* person in charge of, or assistant in, library. □□ **librarianship** *n.*

**library** *n.* collection of books, films, records, etc.; room or building where these are kept.

**libretto** *n.* (*pl.* **librettos** or **libretti**) text of opera etc. □□ **librettist** *n.*

**lice** see LOUSE.

**licence** *n.* **1** official permit to own, use, or do something, or carry on trade; permission. **2** excessive liberty of action. **3** writer's etc. deliberate deviation from fact.

**license** *v.* **1** grant licence to. **2** authorise use of (premises) for certain purpose. □□ **licensed** *adj.*

**licensee** *n.* holder of licence, esp. to sell alcoholic liquor.

**licentiate** *n.* holder of certificate of professional competence.

**licentious** *adj.* sexually promiscuous.

**lichen** *n.* plant composed of fungus and alga in association, growing on rocks, trees, etc.

**lick** ● *v.* **1** pass tongue over; bring into specified condition by licking. **2** (of flame etc.) play lightly over. **3** *colloq.* defeat, thrash. ● *n.* **1** act of licking with tongue. **2** small amount of something. **3** *colloq.* smart blow. **4** *colloq.* short phrase or solo in jazz or popular music.

**licorice** = LIQUORICE.

**lid** *n.* **1** hinged or removable cover, esp. at top of container. **2** eyelid. □□ **lidded** *adj.*

**lie**[1] ● *v.* (**lay**, **lain**, **lying**) **1** have or put one's body in flat or resting position; be at rest on something. **2** be in specified state; be situated. ● *n.* way a thing lies. □ **lie in** lie in bed late in the morning. **lie low** conceal oneself or one's intentions.

> **Usage** The verb *lie* is often confused with the verb *lay*, giving rise to incorrect uses such as *he is laying on the bed* (correct use is *he is lying on the bed*).

**lie**[2] ● *n.* statement speaker knows to be untrue. ● *v.* (**lied**, **lying**) tell a lie.

**liege** *n. hist.* one's feudal superior; one's king.

**lieu** *n.* □ **in lieu** instead.

**lieutenant** *n.* **1** army officer; naval officer. **2** deputy. □□ **lieutenancy** *n.*

**life** *n.* (*pl.* **lives**) **1** capacity for growth, functional activity, and continual change until death; living things and their activity; period during which life lasts; period from birth to present time or from present time to death. **2** duration of thing's existence or ability to function. **3** person's state of existence. **4** living person. **5** business and pleasures of the world. **6** energy, liveliness. **7** biography. **8** *colloq.* imprisonment for life. **9** living (esp. nude) form or model. □ **life cycle** series of forms into which a living thing changes. **life jacket** buoyant or inflatable jacket for keeping person afloat in water. **life sciences** biology and related subjects. **life support** use of specialised equipment to maintain person's essential physical functions when they are very ill etc.

**lifebelt** *n.* belt of buoyant material to keep person afloat.

**lifebuoy** *n.* buoyant device for keeping person afloat.

**lifeless** *adj.* **1** dead. **2** unconscious; lacking movement or vitality. □□ **lifelessly** *adv.*

**lifelike** *adj.* closely resembling life or person or thing represented.

**lifeline** *n.* **1** rope used in rescue. **2** vital means of communication.

**lifelong** *adj.* for all one's life.

**lifer** *n. colloq.* person serving life sentence.

**lifesaver** *n. Aust.* expert swimmer who supervises surfing beaches etc.; person or thing that is of great help.

**lifestyle** *n.* way of spending one's life.

**lifetime** *n.* duration of person's life.

**lift** *v.* **1** raise to higher position, go up, be raised. **2** yield to upward force. **3** give upward direction to (eyes or face). **4** add interest to. **5** (of the sky) rise, disperse. **6** remove (barrier etc.) **7** transport supplies, troops, etc. by air. **8** *colloq.* steal; plagiarise.

● *n.* **1** lifting. **2** a ride in another person's vehicle. **3** apparatus for raising and lowering people or things to different floors, levels, etc. **4** transport by air. **5** upward pressure on aerofoil. **6** supporting or elevating influence. **7** elated feeling. □ **lift-off** vertical take-off of aircraft etc.

**ligament** *n.* band of tough fibrous tissue linking bones.

**ligature** *n.* **1** thing used for tying. **2** *Printing* two or more letters joined, e.g. æ.

**light**¹ ● *n.* **1** electromagnetic radiation that stimulates sight and makes things visible; brightness; source of light, electric lamp; flame or spark. **2** enlightenment. **3** an aspect; way something appears to mind. ● *adj.* full of light, not in darkness; pale. ● *v.* (**lit** or **lighted**, **lighting**) **1** set burning; begin to burn. **2** provide with light; brighten. ● *adj.* **1** full of light; not in darkness. **2** pale. □ **bring to light** reveal. **come to light** be revealed. **light on** find accidentally. **light pen** light-emitting device for reading bar codes; pen-shaped device for drawing on computer screen. **light up** put lights on at dusk; brighten; begin to smoke cigarette etc. **light year** distance light travels in one year, $9.4607 \times 10^{12}$ km (nearly 9.5 million million kilometres).

**light**² ● *adj.* **1** having little weight; not heavy; easy to lift, carry, or do; of less than average weight, force, or intensity. **2** cheerful; not profound or serious. **3** (of food) easy to digest. ● *adv.* lightly, with little load. ● *n. Aust. colloq.* beer with low alcohol content. □ **light-fingered** apt to steal. **light-headed** feeling slightly faint; delirious. **light-hearted** cheerful, not serious. **light industry** industry producing small or light articles. **make light of** treat as unimportant. □□ **lightly** *adv.* **lightness** *n.*

**lighten**[1] *v.* **1** shed light on. **2** make or grow bright.

**lighten**[2] *v.* make or become less heavy.

**lighter** *adj.* **1** device for lighting cigarettes etc. **2** flat-bottomed boat for unloading ships.

**lighthouse** *n.* tower with beacon light to warn or guide ships.

**lightning** ● *n.* flash of light produced by electric discharge between clouds or between clouds and ground. ● *adj.* very quick.

**lights** *n.pl.* the lungs of certain animals, used as animal food.

**lightweight** ● *adj.* not having great weight or influence. ● *n.* lightweight person; boxing weight between featherweight and welterweight.

**lignite** *n.* brown coal of woody texture.

**lignum** *n.* Australian plant forming tangled, impenetrable thickets.

**like**[1] ● *adj.* having the qualities or appearance of; characteristic of. ● *prep.* in manner of; to same degree as. ● *adv. colloq.* likely. ● *n.* person or thing like another.

**like**[2] ● *v.* **1** find pleasant or satisfactory; wish for. **2** (in social media) indicate one's approval etc. for (someone or something) by means of particular icon etc. ● *n.* (**likes**) things one likes or prefers.

**likeable** *adj.* (also **likable**) pleasant, easy to like. □□ **likeably** *adv.*

**likelihood** *n.* probability.

**likely** ● *adj.* (**likelier**) such as may reasonably be expected to occur or be true; seeming to be suitable or have a chance of success. ● *adv.* probably.

**liken** *v.* point out resemblance between (person, thing) and (another).

**likeness** *n.* resemblance; semblance; guise; portrait, representation.

**likewise** *adv.* **1** also, moreover. **2** similarly.

**liking** *n.* what one likes; one's taste; fondness, fancy.

**lilac** ● *n.* **1** shrub with fragrant pinkish-violet or white flowers. **2** pale pinkish-violet colour. ● *adj.* of this colour.

**lilly-pilly** *n.* (also **lilli-pilli**) Australian rainforest tree with glossy dark-green foliage, white flowers, and pink edible fruits.

**lilt** *n.* **1** rise and fall of voice when speaking. **2** light pleasant rhythm in a tune. □□ **lilting** *adj.*

**lily** *n.* **1** tall bulbous plant with large trumpet-shaped flowers. **2** heraldic fleur-de-lis.

**lily-trotter** *n.* = *lotus bird.*

**limb** *n.* arm, leg, wing; large branch of tree; branch of cross.

**limber** ● *adj.* lithe, flexible; agile. ● *v.* make oneself supple; warm up for athletic etc. activity.

**limbo**[1] *n.* state of waiting or being unable to act or make decision.

**limbo**[2] *n.* (*pl.* **limbos**) W. Indian dance in which dancer bends backwards to pass under bar.

**lime**[1] *n.* **1** white caustic substance used in making cement. **2** round yellowish-green fruit like lemon; tree bearing this; the fruit's bright pale green colour.

**limelight** *n.* glare of publicity.

**limerick** *n.* humorous five-line verse.

**limestone** *n.* rock composed mainly of calcium carbonate.

**limewood** *n.* Australian eucalypt with white bark yielding chalky powder when touched.

**limit** ● *n.* **1** point beyond which something does not continue. **2** greatest or smallest amount permitted. ● *v.* set or serve as limit; keep within limits. □ **off limits** out of bounds; not allowed. □□ **limitation** *n.*

**limousine** *n.* large luxurious car.

**limp** ● *v.* walk or proceed lamely or awkwardly. ● *n.* a limping walk. ● *adj.* **1** not stiff or firm. **2** without energy or will.☐☐ **limply** *adv.* **limpness** *n.*

**limpet** *n.* mollusc with conical shell sticking tightly to rocks.

**limpid** *adj.* **1** clear, transparent. **2** (of writing) easily understood. ☐☐ **limpidity** *n.*

**linchpin** *n.* **1** pin passed through axle end to keep wheel on. **2** person or thing vital to organisation etc.

**linctus** *n.* syrupy medicine, esp. soothing cough mixture.

**line** ● *n.* **1** long narrow mark; outline; boundary; row of people or things; row of words; brief letter; (**lines**) words of actor's part. **2** a series, several generations of families. **3** direction, course; railway track; type of activity, business, or goods; service of ships, buses, or aircraft. **4** piece of cord for particular purpose; electrical or telephone cable; connection by this. **5** each of a set of military fieldworks. ● *v.* **1** mark with lines; arrange in lines. **2** cover inside surface of.☐ **line-ball** borderline; liable to go one way or the other. **line up** arranged or be arranged in a row. **line up** arranged or be arranged in a row.

**lineage** *n.* lineal descent; ancestry.

**lineal** *adj.* **1** in direct line of descent or ancestry. **2** linear.☐☐ **lineally** *adv.*

**linear** *adj.* **1** of or in lines; long and narrow and of uniform breadth. **2** sequential.

**linen** ● *n.* cloth woven from flax; articles made or orig. made of linen, as sheets, shirts, underwear, etc. ● *adj.* made of linen.

**liner** *n.* **1** ship or aircraft carrying passengers on regular line. **2** removable lining.

**linesman** *n.* **1** umpire's assistant at the boundary line. **2** person who maintains railway, electrical, or telephone lines.

**ling** *n.* (*pl.* **ling**) **1** long slender marine food fish. **2** heather.

**linger** *v.* be slow or reluctant to depart; stay about; dally.

**lingerie** *n.* women's underwear and nightclothes.

**lingo** *n.* **1** *colloq.* a foreign language. **2** vocabulary of special subject or group of people.

**lingua franca** *n.* (*pl.* **lingua francas**) common language used among people whose native languages are different.

**lingual** *adj.* of the tongue; of speech or languages.

**linguist** *n.* person skilled in languages or linguistics.

**linguistic** ● *adj.* of language or study of languages. ● *n.* (**linguistics**) study of language.☐☐ **linguistically** *adv.*

**liniment** *n.* embrocation.

**lining** *n.* material used to cover surface.

**link** ● *n.* **1** one loop or ring of chain etc. **2** one in series. **3** means of connection. **4** connection from one site to other sites on World Wide Web. ● *v.* **1** connect, join. **2** clasp or intertwine (hands etc.)☐☐ **linkage** *n.*

**links** *n.pl.* golf course.

**lino** *n.* linoleum.

**linoleum** *n.* canvas-backed material coated with linseed oil, cork, etc.

**linseed** *n.* seed of flax.

**lint** *n.* linen or cotton with one side made fluffy; fluff.

**lintel** *n.* horizontal timber, stone, etc. over top of door or window.

**lion** *n.* large carnivorous animal of cat family.

**lionise** *v.* (also **-ize**) treat as a celebrity.

**lip** *n.* **1** either edge of opening of mouth. **2** edge of cup, vessel, etc., esp. part shaped for pouring from.

**3** *colloq.* impudent talk. □ **lip service** insincere expression of support etc.

**lipectomy** *n.* (*pl.* **lipectomies**) surgical procedure to remove unwanted body fat.

**lipid** *n.* any of group of fatlike substances including oils, waxes, and steroids.

**lipo-** *comb. form* relating to fat or other lipids.

**lipstick** *n.* cosmetic for colouring lips.

**liquefy** *v.* make or become liquid. □□ **liquefaction** *n.*

**liqueur** *n.* strong sweet alcoholic spirit.

**liquid** ● *n.* flowing substance like water or oil. ● *adj.* **1** in form of liquid. **2** (of assets) easy to convert into cash.

**liquidate** *v.* **1** close down (a business) and divide its assets between creditors. **2** pay (a debt). **3** *colloq.* get rid of, esp. by killing. □□ **liquidation** *n.* **liquidator** *n.*

**liquidise** *v.* (also **-ize**) reduce to liquid state.

**liquor** *n.* alcoholic (esp. distilled) drink.

**liquorice** *n.* (also **licorice**) black substance used in medicine and as a sweet, made from a plant root.

**lisp** ● *n.* speech defect in which *s* and *z* are pronounced like *th*. ● *v.* speak or utter with lisp.

**lissom** *adj.* lithe, agile.

**list**[1] ● *n.* written or printed series of names, items, figures, etc. ● *v.* make list of; enter in list.

**list**[2] ● *v.* (of ship etc.) lean over to one side. ● *n.* listing position.

**listen** *v.* make effort to hear; pay attention; take notice of. □ **listen in** overhear conversation; listen to broadcast.

**listless** *adj.* lacking energy or enthusiasm. □□ **listlessly** *adv.* **listlessness** *n.*

**lit** see LIGHT[1].

**litany** *n.* **1** series of supplications to God used in church services. **2** *colloq.* tedious recital.

**literacy** *n.* ability to read and write.

**literal** *adj.* **1** taking words in their basic sense without metaphor etc. **2** corresponding exactly to original words. **3** prosaic; matter-of-fact. □□ **literalism** *n.* **literally** *adv.*

**literary** *adj.* of or concerned with or interested in literature.

**literate** ● *adj.* able to read and write. ● *n.* literate person.

**literature** *n.* written works, esp. those valued for form and style; writings of country or period on any subject; *colloq.* printed matter, leaflets, etc.

**lithe** *adj.* flexible, supple.

**lithium** *n.* soft silver-white metallic element (symbol Li).

**lithograph** ● *n.* lithographic print. ● *v.* print by lithography.

**lithography** *n.* process of printing from plate so treated that ink sticks only to design to be printed. □□ **lithographer** *n.* **lithographic** *adj.*

**lithophyte** *n.* plant that grows on rock or stone. □□ **lithophytic** *adj.*

**litigant** ● *n.* party to lawsuit. ● *adj.* engaged in lawsuit.

**litigate** *v.* go to law; contest (point) at law. □□ **litigation** *n.* **litigator** *n.*

**litigious** *adj.* fond of litigation; contentious.

**litmus** *n.* dye turned red by acid and blue by alkali. □ **litmus test** real or ultimate test.

**litotes** *n.* ironic understatement.

**litre** *n.* metric unit of capacity equal to 1000 cubic centimetres.

**litter** ● *n.* **1** refuse, esp. paper, discarded in public place. **2** odds and ends lying about. **3** leaves etc. accumulated on forest floor. **4** young animals brought forth at one birth.

**5** kind of stretcher for sick and wounded. **6** straw etc. as bedding for animals; material for animal's, esp. cat's, indoor toilet. **7** *hist.* vehicle containing couch and carried on men's shoulders or by animals.
● *v.* **1** make (place) untidy. **2** give birth to (puppies etc.). **3** provide (horse etc.) with bedding.

**little** ● *adj.* small in size, amount, or intensity etc. ● *n.* small amount, time, or distance. ● *adv.* to a small extent, not at all.

**littoral** *adj.* of or by the shore.

**liturgy** *n.* fixed form of public worship. □□ **liturgical** *adj.*

**live**[1] *adj.* **1** alive. **2** burning; unexploded; charged with electricity. **3** (of broadcasts) transmitted while actually happening. ● *v.* **live down** live so as to cause (scandal etc.) to be forgotten. **live on** **1** eat (a type of food) as one's regular diet. **2** (have an amount of money) to buy necessities.

**live**[2] *v.* **1** be or remain alive. **2** have one's home in particular place. **3** spend one's life in particular way; live life to the full.

**livelihood** *n.* means of living; job, income.

**lively** *adj.* (**livelier**) full of energy or action. □□ **liveliness** *n.*

**liven** *v.* make or become lively, cheer up.

**liver** ● *n.* large glandular organ in abdomen of vertebrates; liver of some animals as food. ● *adj.* reddish brown colour.

**liverish** *adj.* **1** suffering from liver disorder. **2** peevish, glum.

**livermorium** *n.* chemical element (symbol Lv).

**livery** *n.* distinctive uniform of servant etc.; distinctive guise or marking; distinctive colour scheme for company's vehicles etc.

**livestream** (also **live stream**)
● *v.* transmit or receive live video and audio coverage of (an event) over Internet. ● *n.* livestream transmission.

**livid** *adj.* **1** *colloq.* furious. **2** bluish-grey.

**living** *n.* **1** being alive. **2** livelihood. ● *adj.* **1** contemporary; now alive. **2** (of likeness) exact. **3** (of language) still in vernacular use.

**lizard** *n.* reptile with usu. long body and tail, four legs, and scaly hide.

**ll.** *abbr.* lines.

**llama** *n.* S. American ruminant kept as beast of burden and for its woolly fleece.

**LNG** *abbr.* liquefied natural gas.

**load** ● *n.* **1** thing or quantity carried; burden or responsibility or worry. **2** amount of electric current supplied. **3** (**loads**) *colloq.* plenty. ● *v.* **1** put a load in or on; receive a load. **2** fill heavily. **3** put ammunition into (a gun) or film into (a camera); put (data) into a computer).

**loaded** *adj.* **1** *colloq.* rich. **2** *colloq.* drunk. **3** (of dice etc.) weighted. **4** (of question or statement) carrying hidden implication.

**loading** *n.* **1** additional payment to employees in acknowledgement of special skills, or as holiday bonus, etc. **2** increase in insurance premium due to increased risk.

**loaf** ● *n.* (*pl.* **loaves**) **1** quantity of bread shaped in one piece. **2** *colloq.* head. ● *v.* spend time idly, stand or saunter about.

**loam** *n.* rich soil of clay, sand, and humus. □□ **loamer** *n.* **loamy** *adj.*

**loan** ● *n.* thing lent, esp. money; lending, being lent. ● *v.* lend (money, works of art, etc.) □ **loan shark** person lending money at very high rates of interest.

**loath** *adj.* (also **loth**) disinclined, reluctant.

**loathe** *v.* detest, hate. □□ **loathing** *n.* **loathsome** *adj.*

**lob** ● v. (**lobbed**) **1** hit or throw (ball etc.) slowly or in high arc. **2** *colloq.* arrive without ceremony, turn up.
● n. ball struck in high arc.

**lobar** adj. of lobe, esp. of lung.

**lobby** ● n. **1** porch, ante-room, entrance hall, corridor. **2** group seeking to influence legislators on behalf of particular interest; organised rally of lobbying members of public; cause supported by such rally. ● v. solicit support of (influential person); inform (legislators etc.) in order to influence them.

**lobbyist** n. person who lobbies MP etc.

**lobe** n. lower soft pendulous part of outer ear; similar part of other organs. □□ **lobed** adj.

**lobotomy** n. incision into frontal lobe of brain to relieve mental disorder.

**lobster** n. **1** *Aust.* = CRAYFISH. **2** N. Atlantic marine crustacean with two pincer-like claws; its flesh as food.

**local** ● adj. of or affecting particular place or small area. ● n. **1** inhabitant of particular place. **2** *colloq.* one's nearest hotel, pub, etc.□ **local anaesthetic** anaesthetic that affects restricted area of body. **local area network** communication network linking a number of computers in the same locality. **local government** administration of a district by representatives elected locally. □□ **locally** adv.

**locale** n. scene or locality of event or occurrence.

**localise** v. (also **-ize**) restrict or assign to particular place; invest with characteristics of place.

**locality** n. district; thing's site or scene; thing's position.

**locate** v. discover exact place of; establish in a place, situate; state locality of.

**location** n. **1** particular place; natural, not studio, setting for film etc. **2** locating.

**loc. cit.** abbr. in the passage cited.

**loch** n. *Scot.* lake or narrow inlet of the sea.

**loci** see LOCUS.

**lock** n. **1** mechanism for fastening door etc. with bolt requiring key of particular shape. **2** section of canal or river confined within sluice gates, for moving boats from one level to another. **3** turning of vehicle's front wheels. **4** interlocked or jammed state; wrestling hold. **5** portion of hair that hangs together. **6** (**locks**) hair.
● v. **1** fasten with lock; shut (house etc.) thus; enclose (person, thing) by locking. **2** store inaccessibly. **3** make or become rigidly fixed. **4** (cause to) jam or catch. □□ **lockable** adj.

**lockdown** n. *US* confining of prisoners to their cells.

**locker** n. lockable cupboard where things can be stored securely.

**locket** n. small ornamental case for portrait etc., usu. on chain around neck.

**lockout** n. exclusion of employees from workplace during dispute.

**locksmith** n. maker and mender of locks.

**locomotion** n. motion or power of motion from place to place.

**locomotive** ● n. engine for pulling trains. ● adj. of, having, or bringing about locomotion.

**locum** n. temporary stand-in for doctor, clergyman, etc.

**locus** n. (pl. **loci**) thing's exact place. **2** *Math.* line or curve etc. formed by certain points or by movement of point or line.

**locust** n. grasshopper that devours vegetation.

**lode** n. vein of metal ore.

**lodestar** n. star (esp. the pole star) used as guide for navigation.

**lodestone** n. oxide of iron used as magnet.

**lodge** ● n. 1 cabin for use by skiers, hunters, etc. 2 (**the Lodge**) official Canberra residence of the Australian Prime Minister. 3 gatekeeper's house; porter's room at entrance to building. 4 members or meeting place of branch of certain societies.
● v. 1 provide with sleeping quarters or temporary accommodation; live as lodger. 2 submit (complaint); deposit; be or become embedded.

**lodger** n. person paying for accommodation in another's house.

**lodging** n. 1 place where one lodges. 2 (**lodgings**) room or rooms rented for living in.

**loft** ● n. space under roof; attic; room over stable; gallery in church.
● v. send (ball) in high arc.

**lofty** adj. (**loftier**) very tall; noble; haughty. □□ **loftily** adv. **loftiness** n.

**log** ● n. 1 piece cut from trunk or branch of tree. 2 device for gauging ship's speed; logbook, entry in this. 3 logarithm. ● v. (**logged**) enter (facts) in logbook. □ **log on** (or **off**), **log in** (or **out**) go through procedures to begin (or conclude) use of computer system; enter (or exit) secure website etc.

**loganberry** n. large dark red fruit resembling blackberry.

**logarithm** n. arithmetic exponent used in computation.
□□ **logarithmic** adj.

**logbook** n. book for recording details of journey.

**logger** n. person employed to fell etc. forest etc. trees for timber.

**loggerheads** n.pl. □ **at loggerheads** disagreeing or quarrelling.

**loggia** n. open-sided gallery or arcade.

**logging** n. work of cutting and preparing forest timber.

**logic** n. 1 science or method of reasoning. 2 inexorable force.
□□ **logician** n.

**logical** adj. of or according to logic; correctly reasoned; consistent; capable of correct reasoning.
□□ **logicality** n. **logically** adv.

**logistics** n.pl. detailed organisation and implementation of a plan or operation. □□ **logistic** adj. **logistical** adj. **logistically** adv.

**logjam** n. crowded mass of logs in river; a deadlock; backlog.

**logo** n. (pl. **logos**) organisation's emblem used in display material etc.

**-logy** comb. form science or study of particular subject.

**loin** n. side and back of the body between ribs and hip bones.

**loiter** v. stand about idly; linger.

**LOL** abbr. colloq. laughing out loud.

**loll** v. 1 stand, sit, or recline in lazy attitude. 2 hang loosely.

**lollipop** n. hard sweet on stick.

**lollop** v. (**lolloped**) colloq. flop about; move in ungainly bounds.

**lolly** n. 1 Aust. any sweet. 2 colloq. money. 3 colloq. head.

**lone** adj. solitary; isolated.

**lonely** adj. (**lonelier**) 1 solitary; sad because one lacks friends. 2 not much frequented. □□ **loneliness** n.

**loner** n. person or animal preferring to be alone.

**lonesome** adj. lonely; causing loneliness.

**long** ● adj. of great or specified length. ● adv. for a long time; throughout a specified time. ● v. feel a longing. □ **long black** Aust. espresso coffee made with additional hot water. **long face** dismal expression. **long johns** close-fitting underpants with long legs. **long-life** (of milk etc.) treated to prolong its shelf life. **long-range** having a relatively long range; relating to a long period of future time. **long shot** wild guess or venture. **long-sighted** able to see clearly only what is comparatively distant. **long standing** that has long existed. **long term** for or of a long period. **long wave** radio wave of frequency less than 300 kHz. **long winded** talking or writing at tedious length.□□ **longish** adj.

**longevity** n. long life.

**longhand** n. ordinary writing, not shorthand or typing etc.

**longing** n. intense wish.

**longitude** n. distance east or west (measured in degrees on map) from Greenwich meridian.

**longitudinal** adj. of or in length; running lengthwise; of longitude. □□ **longitudinally** adv.

**loo** n. colloq. toilet.

**loofah** n. rough bath sponge made from dried pod of type of gourd.

**look** ● v. 1 use or direct one's eyes in order to see, search, or examine; face. 2 seem. ● n. act of looking; inspection, search; appearance of something. □ **look after** take care of; attend. **look down on** detest; despise. **look forward to** await eagerly. **look into** investigate. **look out** be vigilant. **look up** search for information about; improve in prospects; go to visit. **look up to** admire and respect.

**lookout** n. 1 observation post. 2 person keeping watch.

**loom** ● n. apparatus for weaving. ● v. appear dimly, esp. as vague and often threatening shape.

**loop** ● n. 1 figure produced by curve or doubled thread etc. crossing itself; thing, path, etc. forming this figure; similarly shaped attachment used as fastening. 2 contraceptive coil. 3 endless band of tape or film etc. allowing continuous repetition; repeated sequence of sound, image, etc. ● v. form or bend into loop;

fasten or join with loop(s); enclose in a loop. □ **loop the loop** fly in a vertical circle.

**loophole** n. 1 means of evading rule etc. without infringing it. 2 narrow vertical slit in wall of fort etc.

**loose** ● adj. 1 not tightly held. 2 free from bonds or restraint. 3 not held together. 4 not compact or dense. 5 inexact. 6 morally lax. ● v. 1 free. 2 untie, detach. 3 release. 4 relax (hold etc.) □ **at a loose end** without a definite occupation. **loose-leaf** with each page removable. **on the loose** having escaped from confinement. □□ **loosely** adv.

**loosen** v. make or become loose or looser.

**loot** ● n. spoil, booty; colloq. money. ● v. rob or steal; esp. after rioting etc.; plunder.

**lop** v. (lopped) cut off, esp. branches. □ **lop-eared** with drooping ears.

**lope** ● v. run with long bounding stride. ● n. such stride.

**lopsided** adj. unevenly balanced.

**loquacious** adj. talkative. □□ **loquacity** n.

**lord** n. a master, a ruler; a nobleman; title of certain British peers or high officials; (**Lord**) God or Christ.

**lore** n. body of tradition and information on a subject or held by particular group.

**lorgnette** n. pair of eyeglasses or opera glasses on long handle.

**lorikeet** n. Aust. small brightly-coloured parrot.

**lorry** n. Brit. = TRUCK.

**lory** n. Aust. brightly-coloured parrot.

**lose** v. (lost, losing) 1 cease to have or maintain; become unable to find. 2 fail to get; get rid of. 3 be defeated in a contest etc. 4 suffer loss (of); cause the loss of. □ **lose heart** be discouraged. **lose oneself** be engrossed in. **lose one's way** become lost. **lose out** be unsuccessful or disadvantaged. □□ **loser** n.

**loss** n. losing; being lost; what is lost; detriment resulting from losing. □ **be at a loss** be puzzled or uncertain.

**lost** adj. strayed or separated from its owner. See also **LOSE**.

**lot** n. 1 (**a lot** or **lots**) colloq. large number or amount. 2 each of set of objects used to make chance selection; this method of deciding, share or responsibility resulting from it. 3 destiny, fortune, condition. 4 plot, allotment. 5 article or set of articles for sale at auction etc. 6 group of associated people or things.

> **Usage** *A lot of* is somewhat informal, but acceptable in serious writing, whereas *lots of* is not.

**lotion** n. medicinal or cosmetic liquid preparation applied externally.

**lottery** n. means of raising money by selling numbered tickets and giving prizes to holders of numbers drawn at random; something where outcome is governed by luck.

**lotto** n. game of chance like bingo; lottery.

**lotus** n. 1 legendary plant inducing luxurious languor when eaten. 2 kind of water lily. □ **lotus bird** Australian waterbird, able to walk on waterweeds.

**loud** ● adj. 1 strongly audible; noisy. 2 (of behaviour) aggressive; coarse. 3 (of colours etc.) gaudy, obtrusive. ● adv. loudly. □□ **loudly** adv. **loudness** n.

**loudspeaker** n. apparatus that converts electrical impulses into sound.

**lounge** ● v. recline comfortably; loll; stand or move about idly. ● n. place for lounging, esp. sitting room in

house, public room (in hotel), or place in airport etc. with seats for waiting passengers; sofa. □ **lounge suit** man's ordinary suit for daywear.

**lour** v. (also **lower**) 1 frown; look sullen. 2 (of sky etc.) look dark and threatening.

**louse** ● n. (pl. **lice**) 1 parasitic insect. 2 colloq. contemptible person. ● v. 1 delouse. 2 (**louse up**) spoil or ruin (something).

**lousy** adj. (**lousier**) colloq. 1 very bad; disgusting; ill. 2 Aust. mean, stingy. 3 well supplied, teeming (with). 4 infested with lice. □□ **lousily** adv. **lousiness** n.

**lout** n. crude or ill-mannered person. □□ **loutish** adj.

**louvre** n. (also **louver**) each of set of overlapping slats designed to admit air and some light and exclude rain.

**lovable** adj. easy to love.

**love** ● n. 1 deep, intense affection; sexual passion; a loved person. 2 (in games) no score, nil. ● v. feel love for; like very much. □ **love affair** romantic or sexual relationship between people who are in love. **make love** have sexual intercourse.

**lovebird** n. small parakeet that shows great affection for its mate.

**lovelorn** adj. pining with love.

**lovely** adj. (**lovelier**) beautiful; attractive; delightful. □□ **loveliness** n.

**lover** n. person in love with another, or having love affair; person who likes or enjoys something.

**loving** ● adj. feeling or showing love; affectionate. ● n. affection. □□ **lovingly** adv.

**low** ● adj. 1 not high or tall. 2 not elevated in position. 3 (of the sun) near horizon. 4 of humble rank. 5 of small or less than normal amount, extent, or intensity. 6 dejected. 7 lacking vigour. 8 (of sound) not shrill or loud. 9 commonplace. 10 (of opinion) unfavourable. 11 mean,

**lowbrow | luminous**

vulgar. • n. 1 low or lowest level or number. 2 area of low pressure. 3 deep sound made by cattle. • adv. in, at, or to a low level. • v. (of cattle) make a deep mooing sound. □ **low-down** n. colloq. relevant information. 2 mean, dishonourable.

**low-fi** (of sound recording, transmission, etc.) having low fidelity.

**low-key** lacking intensity or prominence; restrained. **low-tech** using relatively simple technology. □□ **lowish** adj. **lowness** n.

**lowbrow** adj. not intellectual or cultured.

**lower** v. let or haul down; make or become lower; degrade. □ **lower case** small letters.

**lowly** adj. (lowlier) of humble origins. □□ **lowliness** n.

**loyal** adj. faithful; steadfast in allegiance etc. □□ **loyalist** n. **loyally** adv. **loyalty** n.

**lozenge** n. 1 rhombus; four-sided diamond-shaped figure. 2 small sweet or medicinal tablet to be dissolved in mouth.

**LP** abbr. long-playing (record).

**LPG** abbr. liquefied petroleum gas.

**LSD** abbr. lysergic acid diethylamide, a powerful hallucinogenic drug.

**Ltd** abbr. Limited.

**lubra** n. Aust. offens. Aboriginal woman.

**lubricant** n. lubricating substance.

**lubricate** v. 1 apply oil or grease etc. to. 2 make slippery. □□ **lubrication** n.

**lubricious** adj. 1 slippery, evasive. 2 lewd. □□ **lubricity** n.

**lucerne** n. alfalfa.

**lucid** adj. 1 expressing or expressed clearly. 2 sane. □□ **lucidity** n. **lucidly** adv.

**luck** n. good or bad fortune; circumstances brought by this; success due to chance.

**luckless** adj. unlucky; ending in failure.

**lucky** adj. (**luckier**) having, bringing, or resulting from good luck. □□ **luckily** adv.

**lucrative** adj. profitable. □□ **lucratively** adv.

**lucre** n. derog. financial gain.

**Luddite** n. person opposed to new technology.

**lug** • v. (**lugged**) drag or carry with effort. • n. 1 hard or rough pull. 2 colloq. ear. 3 projection on object by which it may be carried, fixed in place, etc.

**luggage** n. suitcases, bags, etc., for traveller's belongings.

**lugger** n. small ship with four-cornered sails (lugsails).

**lugubrious** adj. doleful; mournful. □□ **lugubriously** adv. **lugubriousness** n.

**lukewarm** adj. 1 moderately warm; tepid. 2 unenthusiastic.

**lull** • v. 1 soothe, send to sleep. 2 deceive (person) into undue confidence. 3 allay (suspicions etc.) 4 (of noise, storm, etc.) lessen, fall quiet. • n. temporary quiet period.

**lullaby** n. soothing song to send child to sleep.

**lumbago** n. rheumatic pain in muscles of lower back.

**lumbar** adj. of lower back.

**lumber** • n. 1 disused and cumbersome articles. 2 partly prepared timber. • v. 1 encumber (person). 2 move in slow clumsy way. 3 cut and prepare forest timber. 4 colloq. arrest; imprison.

**luminary** n. 1 literary natural light-giving body. 2 wise person; celebrated member of group.

**luminescence** n. emission of light without heat. □□ **luminescent** adj.

**luminous** adj. 1 shedding light; phosphorescent, visible in darkness. 2 throwing light on subject. □□ **luminosity** n.

**lump** ● *n.* **1** compact shapeless mass; tumour; swelling, bruise. **2** heavy or ungainly person. ● *v.* class; mass.

**lumpy** *adj.* (lumpier) full of or covered with lumps. □□ **lumpily** *adv.* **lumpiness** *n.*

**lunacy** *n.* insanity; great folly.

**lunar** *adj.* of, like, concerned with, or determined by the moon. □ **lunar month** period between new moons (29 ½ days), four weeks.

**lunate** *adj.* crescent-shaped.

**lunatic** ● *n.* insane person; wildly foolish person. ● *adj.* insane; very reckless or foolish.

**lunch** ● *n.* midday meal. ● *v.* take lunch; provide lunch for.

**luncheon** *n.* lunch.

**lung** *n.* either of pair of respiratory organs in humans and many other vertebrates.

**lunge** ● *n.* sudden movement forward; attacking move in fencing. ● *v.* deliver or make lunge.

**lupine** *adj.* like a wolf.

**lupus** *n.* skin disease producing ulcers.

**lurch** *n.* make an unsteady swaying movement, stagger. □ **leave in the lurch** leave (a person) in difficulties.

**lure** ● *v.* entice, usu. with reward, bait, etc. ● *n.* thing used to entice; enticing quality (of chase etc.)

**lurid** *adj.* **1** bright and glaring in colour. **2** sensational, shocking. □□ **luridly** *adv.*

**lurk** ● *v.* wait furtively or out of sight; be latent or lingering. ● *n. colloq.* a dodge, racket, or scheme.

**luscious** *adj.* delicious; voluptuously attractive.

**lush** *adj.* **1** growing thickly and strongly. **2** luxurious. **3** *colloq.* excellent.

**lust** ● *n.* intense sexual desire; any intense desire. ● *v.* feel lust. □□ **lustful** *adj.* **lustfully** *adv.*

**lustre** *n.* (*US* luster) **1** gloss, shining surface. **2** radiance, splendour. **3** iridescent glaze on pottery and porcelain. □□ **lustrous** *adj.*

**lusty** *adj.* (lustier) healthy and strong; vigorous, lively. □□ **lustily** *adv.* **lustiness** *n.*

**lute** *n.* guitar-like instrument with long neck and pear-shaped body. □□ **lutenist** *n.*

**lutetium** *n.* silvery metallic element (symbol Lu).

**Lutheran** *n.* follower of Martin Luther; member of Lutheran Church. □□ **Lutheranism** *n.*

**lux** *n.* SI unit of illumination.

**luxuriant** *adj.* growing profusely. □□ **luxuriance** *n.* **luxuriantly** *adv.*

**luxuriate** *v.* feel great enjoyment in something.

**luxurious** *adj.* supplied with luxuries; very comfortable. □□ **luxuriously** *adv.*

**luxury** ● *n.* choice and costly surroundings, possessions, etc.; thing giving comfort or enjoyment but not essential. ● *adj.* comfortable, expensive, etc.

**lx** *abbr.* lux.

**lychee** *n.* sweet white juicy brown-skinned fruit; tree bearing this.

**lycra** *n. propr.* elastic polyurethane fabric.

**lye** *n.* water made alkaline with wood ashes; any alkaline solution for washing.

**lying** see LIE¹.

**lymph** *n.* colourless fluid containing white blood cells.

**lymphatic system** *n.* network of vessels carrying lymph, protecting against infection.

**lymphoma** *n.* (*pl.* lymphomas or lymphomata) tumour of the lymph glands.

**lynch** *v.* put (person) to death by mob action without legal trial. □□ **lynching** *n.*

**lynx** *n.* (*pl.* **lynx** or **lynxes**) wild cat with short tail, spotted fur, and proverbially keen sight.

**lyre** *n.* ancient U-shaped stringed instrument.

**lyrebird** *n.* ground-dwelling Australian bird, the male of which has a long lyre-shaped tail.

**lyric** ● *adj.* **1** (of poetry) expressing writer's emotions, usu. briefly; (of poet) writing in this way. **2** meant or fit to be sung, songlike. **3** (of voice) light in timbre. ● *n.* **1** lyric poem. **2** (**lyrics**) words of a song.

**lyrical** *adj.* **1** lyric. **2** resembling, or using language appropriate to, lyric poetry. **3** *colloq.* highly enthusiastic. □□ **lyrically** *adv.*

**lyricist** *n.* writer of lyrics.

# Mm

**M** ● *abbr.* **1** (of film or computer game) Mature; not recommended for persons under 15 years of age. **2** Monsieur. ● *n.* (Roman numeral) 1000.

**m** *abbr.* **1** male; masculine. **2** married. **3** mile(s); metre(s); million(s).

**m-** *prefix* denoting commercial activity conducted via mobile phones.

**MA** *abbr.* **1** Master of Arts. **2** (of film or computer game) Mature Accompanied; restricted to persons 15 years and over.

**macabre** *adj.* grim, gruesome.

**macadam** *n.* **1** broken stone as material for roadmaking. **2** tarmac. □□ **macadamise** *v.* (also **-ize**)

**macadamia** *n.* Australian rainforest tree cultivated for its large edible nut; this nut.

**macaroni** *n.* **1** pasta tubes. **2** *colloq.* nonsense, baloney.

**macaw** *n.* kind of American parrot.

**macchiato** *n.* short black coffee with small amount of milk or cream.

**mace** *n.* **1** staff of office, esp. symbol of Speaker's authority in House of Representatives. **2** dried outer covering of nutmeg as spice. **3** (**Mace**) chemical aerosol spray used to immobilise an aggressor temporarily.

**macerate** *v.* soften by soaking.

**Mach** *n.* (in full **Mach number**) ratio of speed of moving body to speed of sound.

**machete** *n.* broad heavy knife.

**machiavellian** *adj.* cunning; unscrupulous. □□ **machiavellianism** *n.*

**machinations** *n.pl.* plot, intrigue.

**machine** ● *n.* **1** apparatus for applying mechanical power, having several interrelated parts. **2** bicycle, motorcycle, etc. **3** computer. **4** controlling system of organisation. ● *v.* make, operate on, or finish with machine. □ **machine code** computer language that controls computer directly, interpreting instructions passing between software and machine. **machine gun** automatic gun giving continuous fire. **machine-readable** in form that computer can process.

**machinery** *n.* machines; a mechanism; a system.

**machinist** *n.* person who works machine.

**machismo** *n.* being macho; masculine pride.

**macho** *adj.* aggressively masculine.

**mackerel** *n.* (*pl.* **mackerel** or **mackerels**) marine food fish.

**mackintosh** *n.* (also **macintosh**) waterproof coat or cloak; cloth waterproofed with rubber.

**macramé** *n.* art of knotting cord or string in patterns; work so made.

**macro** *n. Computing* single instruction that expands automatically into set of instructions for particular task.

**macro-** *comb. form* long; large; large-scale.

**macrobiotic** *adj.* of or following a dietary system comprising wholefoods.

**macrocosm** *n.* **1** universe. **2** whole of a complex structure.

**macroeconomics** *n.* study of the economy as whole. □□ **macroeconomic** *adj.*

**macropod** *n.* herbivorous marsupial, e.g. kangaroo.

**macula** n. (pl. **maculae**) **1** region of greatest visual acuity in retina. **2** area of skin discolouration. □□ **macular** adj.

**mad** adj. (**madder**) **1** insane; frenzied; wildly foolish. **2** colloq. annoyed. **3** colloq. great. □□ **madly** adv.

**madam** n. polite or formal address to woman.

**Madame** n. (pl. **Mesdames**) title of French-speaking woman.

**madcap** adj. wildly impulsive.

**madden** v. make mad; irritate. □□ **maddening** adj.

**madder** n. red dye.

**made** SEE MAKE.

**Madeira** n. **1** fortified wine from Madeira. **2** rich sponge cake.

**Mademoiselle** n. (pl. **Mesdemoiselles**) title of unmarried French-speaking woman.

**madonna** n. picture or statue of the Virgin Mary.

**madrigal** n. part-song for unaccompanied voices.

**maelstrom** n. great whirlpool.

**maestro** n. (pl. **maestri** or **maestros**) great musical conductor or composer; master of any art.

**Mafia** n. organised group of criminals originating in Sicily; (**mafia**) group regarded as exerting hidden sinister influence.

**magazine** n. **1** periodical publication containing contributions by various writers. **2** chamber holding cartridges fed automatically to breech of gun; similar device in slide projector etc. **3** store for explosives, arms etc.

**magenta** adj. & n. mauvish-crimson shade.

**maggot** n. larva, esp. of blowfly. □□ **maggoty** adj.

**magic** ● n. **1** art of influencing events supernaturally. **2** conjuring tricks. **3** inexplicable influence.
● adj. **1** of magic. **2** colloq. wonderful. □□ **magical** adj. **magically** adv.

**magician** n. **1** person skilled in magic. **2** conjuror.

**magisterial** adj. **1** imperious; authoritative. **2** of magistrate.

**magistrate** n. civil officer administering law; official conducting court for minor cases and preliminary hearings.

**magma** n. molten rock under earth's crust.

**magnanimous** adj. nobly generous; not petty in feelings or conduct. □□ **magnanimity** n.

**magnate** n. person of wealth, authority, etc.

**magnesia** n. **1** magnesium oxide. **2** hydrated magnesium carbonate, used as antacid and laxative.

**magnesium** n. white metallic element that burns with an intensely bright flame (symbol **Mg**).

**magnet** n. **1** piece of iron, steel, etc., having properties of attracting iron and pointing approximately north when suspended. **2** lodestone. **3** person or thing that attracts.

**magnetic** adj. **1** having properties of magnet; produced or acting by magnetism; capable of being attracted by or acquiring properties of magnet. **2** very attractive. □ **magnetic tape** strip of plastic coated with magnetic particles, used in recording, computers, etc.

**magnetise** v. (also **-ize**) make into magnet; attract like magnet.

**magnetism** n. **1** magnetic phenomena; science of these. **2** personal charm.

**magneto** n. electric generator using permanent magnets (esp. for ignition in internal-combustion engine).

**magnificent** adj. **1** splendid; sumptuously constructed or adorned. **2** excellent. □□ **magnificence** n. **magnificently** adv.

**magnify** v. **1** make (thing) appear larger than it is, as with lens;

exaggerate. **2** intensify. **3** *arch.* glorify. □□ **magnifiable** *adj.* **magnifier** *n.*

**magnitude** *n.* **1** largeness; size. **2** importance.

**magnolia** *n.* **1** tree with waxy scented flowers. **2** creamy-pink colour.

**magnum** *n.* wine bottle twice normal size.

**magpie** *n.* **1** black and white bird with melodious, carolling call. **2** idle chatterer. **3** indiscriminate collector.

**maharaja** *n.* (also **maharajah**) *hist.* title of some Indian princes.

**maharani** *n.* *hist.* maharaja's wife or widow.

**maharishi** *n.* great Hindu sage.

**mahatma** *n.* (in India etc.) revered person.

**mah-jong** *n.* (also **mah-jongg**) Chinese game played with 136 or 144 tiles.

**mahogany** *n.* very hard reddish-brown wood; *Aust.* eucalypt yielding similar wood; reddish-brown colour.

**mahout** *n.* elephant driver.

**maid** *n.* **1** female servant. **2** *arch.* girl, young woman.

**maiden** ● *n.* *arch.* young unmarried woman; virgin. ● *adj.* **1** first. **2** unmarried. **maiden name** Your woman's family name before she married. **maiden over** in cricket with no runs scored. □□ **maidenly** *adj.*

**maidenhair** *n.* delicate kind of fern.

**mail** ● *n.* **1** letters etc. conveyed by post; the post; email. **2** armour made of metal rings or chains. ● *v.* send by mail. □ **mail order** purchase of goods by post.

**maim** *v.* cripple, mutilate.

**main** ● *adj.* chief, principal. ● *n.* (usu. **mains**) principal channel for conveying water, sewage, gas, or electricity. □ **in the main** for the most part; on the whole. □□ **mainly** *adv.*

**mainframe** *n.* central processing unit and primary memory of computer; powerful computer system.

**mainland** *n.* country or continent without its adjacent islands.

**mainline** *v.* *colloq.* take drugs intravenously.

**mainmast** *n.* ship's principal mast.

**mainsail** *n.* lowest sail or sail set on after part of mainmast.

**mainspring** *n.* **1** chief spring of watch or clock. **2** chief motivating force.

**mainstay** *n.* cable supporting mainmast; chief support.

**mainstream** *n.* dominant trend of opinion or style etc.

**maintain** *v.* **1** keep up; keep going. **2** assert as true. **3** keep in good repair.

**maintenance** *n.* **1** maintaining, being maintained. **2** provision of enough to support life. **3** alimony.

**maisonette** *n.* **1** *Aust.* semi-detached house. **2** a flat on more than one floor.

**maize** *n.* cereal plant bearing large grains set in rows on a cob; grain of this.

**majestic** *adj.* stately and dignified; imposing. □□ **majestically** *adv.*

**majesty** *n.* **1** stateliness of aspect, language, etc. **2** (His, Her, Your Majesty) title used of or to king or queen.

**major** ● *adj.* **1** greater or relatively great in size etc. **2** unusually serious or significant. **3** *Mus.* of or based on scale having semitone next above third and seventh notes. **4** of full legal age. ● *n.* **1** army officer. **2** person of full legal age. **3** student's main subject or course. **4** *AFL* goal. ● *v.* study or qualify in (subject) as one's main subject.

**majority** *n.* **1** greater number or part. **2** number by which winning vote exceeds next. **3** full legal age.

**makarrata** *n.* *Aust.* (in Aboriginal ceremony) ritual symbolising restoration of peace after dispute; agreement.

**make** ● *v.* (**made, making**) **1** form, prepare, produce; cause to exist, be, or become. **2** succeed in arriving at or achieving; gain, acquire. **3** reckon to be. **4** compel. **5** perform (an action etc.) ● *n.* brand of goods.□ **make believe** pretence. **make do** manage with something not satisfactory. **make for** try to reach; tend to bring about. **make good** become successful; repair or pay compensation for. **make off** leave quickly. **make out 1** decipher; interpret, understand. **2** write out. **3** pretend, claim. **make over** transfer ownership of; refashion (garment etc.) **make up 1** constitute. **2** invent. **3** compensate for; complete (an amount). **4** be reconciled. **5** apply cosmetics (to). **make-up 1** cosmetics applied to face. **2** composition of something; person's character. **on the make** *colloq.* intent on gain.

**makeover** *n.* complete transformation or remodelling.

**makeshift** *adj. & n.* (something) used as improvised substitute.

**makings** *n.pl.* **1** earnings, profit. **2** essential qualities for becoming.

**mal-** *comb. form* bad, badly; faulty.

**malachite** *n.* green mineral used for ornament.

**maladjusted** *adj.* (of person) unable to cope with demands of social environment.□□ **maladjustment** *n.*

**maladminister** *v.* manage badly or improperly.□□ **maladministration** *n.*

**maladroit** *adj.* clumsy; bungling.

**malady** *n.* ailment, disease.

**malaise** *n.* feeling of unease or illness.

**malapropism** *n.* comical confusion between words.

**malaria** *n.* disease transmitted by mosquitoes.□□ **malarial** *adj.*

**malcontent** ● *n.* discontented person. ● *adj.* discontented.

**male** ● *adj.* **1** of the sex that can fertilise egg cells produced by female. **2** (of plants) producing pollen, not seeds. **3** (of parts of machinery) designed to enter or fill corresponding hollow part. ● *n.* male person, animal, or plant.

**malediction** *n.* curse.□□ **maledictory** *adj.*

**malefactor** *n.* criminal; evil-doer.□□ **malefaction** *n.*

**malevolent** *adj.* wishing evil to others.□□ **malevolence** *n.*

**malfeasance** *n.* misconduct.

**malformation** *n.* faulty formation.□□ **malformed** *adj.*

**malfunction** ● *n.* failure to function normally. ● *v.* function abnormally.

**malice** *n.* ill will; desire to do harm.□□ **malicious** *adj.* **maliciously** *adv.*

**malign** ● *adj.* injurious; malignant; malevolent. ● *v.* speak ill of; slander.

**malignant** *adj.* **1** (of tumour) growing harmfully and uncontrollably. **2** feeling or showing intense ill will.□□ **malignancy** *n.*

**malinger** *v.* pretend to be ill, esp. to escape work.□□ **malingerer** *n.*

**mall** *n.* **1** sheltered walk. **2** shopping precinct.

**mallard** *n.* kind of wild duck.

**malleable** *adj.* that can be shaped by hammering etc.; pliable.□□ **malleability** *n.*

**mallee** *n. Aust.* small eucalypt with several trunks or stems arising from common base; (also **mallee scrub**) vegetation community characterised by presence of such trees.□ **mallee fowl** turkey-like Australian megapode.

**mallet** *n.* hammer, usu. of wood; implement for striking croquet or polo ball.

**malnutrition** *n.* lack of foods necessary for health.

**malodorous** *adj.* evil-smelling.

**malpractice** *n.* improper, negligent, or criminal professional conduct.

**malt** *n.* barley or other grain prepared for brewing etc.; malt whisky. □□ **malty** *adj.*

**maltreat** *v.* ill-treat. □□ **maltreatment** *n.*

**maluka** *n.* (also **maluga**) *Aust.* person in charge.

**malware** *n.* software designed to damage or gain unauthorised access to computer.

**mammal** *n.* animal of class secreting milk to feed young. □□ **mammalian** *adj. & n.*

**mammary** *adj.* of breasts.

**mammogram** *n.* image obtained by mammography.

**mammography** *n.* X-ray technique for screening breasts.

**mammoth** ● *n.* large extinct elephant. ● *adj.* huge.

**man** ● *n.* (*pl.* **men**) adult male person; human being; humankind; male servant or employee; ordinary soldier etc., not officer; one of the small objects used in board games. ● *v.* (**manned**) supply with people to do something. □ **man-made** artificial, not produced or occurring naturally. **man to man** with frankness.

> **Usage** The use of *man* to refer to a human being (regardless of sex) is now generally regarded as old-fashioned or sexist.

**manacle** ● *n.* handcuff. ● *v.* put manacles on.

**manage** *v.* **1** organise, regulate. **2** succeed in achieving, contrive; succeed with limited resources; cope; succeed in controlling. □□ **manageable** *adj.*

**management** *n.* managing, being managed; administration; people managing a business.

**manager** *n.* person controlling or administering business etc. □□ **managerial** *adj.*

**manatee** *n.* large tropical aquatic mammal.

**manchester** *n. Aust.* household linen.

**mandarin** *n.* **1** (**Mandarin**) official language of China. **2** *hist.* Chinese official. **3** influential person, esp. bureaucrat. **4** small flattish orange with loose skin.

**mandate** ● *n.* official command; authority given by electors to government etc.; authority to act for another. ● *v.* instruct (delegate) how to act or vote.

**mandatory** *adj.* compulsory; of or conveying command.

**mandible** *n.* jaw or jaw-like part.

**mandolin** *n.* kind of lute with paired metal strings plucked with plectrum.

**mandrake** *n.* poisonous plant with forked root.

**mandrill** *n.* large W. African baboon.

**mane** *n.* long hair on horse's or lion's neck; *colloq.* person's long hair.

**manful** *adj.* brave; resolute. □□ **manfully** *adv.*

**manga** *n.* Japanese cartoons, comic books, and animated films, often intended for mature audience.

**manganese** *n.* **1** grey brittle metallic element (**Mn**). **2** black oxide of this.

**mange** *n.* skin disease of dogs etc.

**manger** *n.* eating trough in stable.

**mangle** ● *n.* clothes wringer. ● *v.* damage by cutting or crushing roughly; mutilate.

**mango** *n.* (*pl.* **mangoes** or **mangos**) tropical fruit with sweet yellowish juicy flesh.

**mangrove** n. tree or shrub growing in shore mud with many tangled roots above ground.

**mangy** adj. (**mangier**) having mange; shabby.

**manhandle** v. 1 colloq. handle roughly. 2 move by human effort.

**manhole** n. opening through which person can enter ditch etc. to inspect it.

**manhood** n. 1 state of being a man; manliness; men collectively. 2 colloq. penis.

**manhunt** n. organised search for person, esp. a criminal.

**mania** n. 1 mental illness marked by excitement and violence. 2 excessive enthusiasm; obsession.

**maniac** ● n. 1 colloq. person behaving wildly; obsessive enthusiast. 2 person suffering from mania. ● adj. of or behaving like a maniac. □□ **maniacal** adj.

**manic** adj. of or affected by mania. □ **manic depression** older term for bipolar disorder.

**manicure** ● n. cosmetic treatment of hands. ● v. give manicure to. □□ **manicurist** n.

**manifest** ● adj. clear and unmistakable. ● v. show clearly; give signs of. ● n. list of cargo or passengers carried by a ship or aircraft. □□ **manifestation** n.

**manifesto** n. declaration of policies.

**manifold** ● adj. many and various; having various forms, parts, applications, etc. ● n. 1 manifold thing. 2 pipe etc. with several outlets.

**manikin** n. 1 model of human body. 2 little man; dwarf.

**manila** n. strong fibre of Philippine tree; brown paper made of this or other material.

**manipulate** v. 1 handle, esp. with skill. 2 manage to one's own advantage, esp. unfairly. □□ **manipulation** n. **manipulator** n.

**mankind** n. the human species.

> **Usage** Many people consider the use of *mankind* to be sexist and prefer where possible to use *humankind* or the *human race* instead.

**manly** adj. (**manlier**) of those qualities traditionally associated with men, such as courage, strength, and spirit. □□ **manliness** n.

**manna** n. 1 food miraculously supplied to Israelites in wilderness. 2 Aust. = LERP.

**mannequin** n. dummy for display of clothes; fashion model.

**manner** n. 1 way a thing is done or happens; person's way of behaving towards others; (**manners**) polite social behaviour. 2 kind, sort.

**mannered** adj. behaving in specified way; showing mannerisms.

**mannerism** n. distinctive gesture or feature of style; excessive use of this in art etc.

**manoeuvre** (also **maneuver**) ● n. a planned movement of vehicle or troops; skilful or crafty move or plan. ● v. perform manoeuvres; move or guide skilfully or craftily. □□ **manoeuvrable** adj.

**manor** n. Brit. large country house usu. with lands.

**manpower** n. number of people working or available for work or service.

**manse** n. (esp. Presbyterian) minister's house.

**mansion** n. large grand house.

**manslaughter** n. unintentional (but not accidental) culpable killing of human being.

**mantelpiece** n. shelf above fireplace.

**mantilla** n. Spanish lace scarf worn over head and shoulders.

**mantis** n. (pl. **mantis** or **mantises**) kind of predatory insect.

**mantle** n. loose cloak; covering.

**mantra** n. **1** Hindu or Buddhist devotional incantation. **2** Vedic hymn. **3** statement or slogan frequently repeated.

**manual** • adj. of or done with hands. • n. **1** reference book. **2** colloq. vehicle with manual transmission.□□ **manually** adv.

**manufacture** • n. making of articles, esp. in factory etc.; branch of industry. • v. make, esp. on industrial scale; invent, fabricate. □□ **manufacturer** n.

**manure** • n. fertiliser, esp. dung. • v. apply manure to.

**manuscript** • n. book or document written by hand; author's copy of work prepared for printing and publication. • adj. written by hand.

**many** • adj. numerous. • n. many people or things.

**mañana** adv. & n. some time in the future.

**Maori** • n. (pl. **Maori** or **Maoris**) member of indigenous people of New Zealand; their language. • adj. of or concerning the Maori or their language.

**map** • n. flat representation of (part of) earth's surface, or of sky; diagram. • v. (**mapped**) represent on map.□ **map out** plan in detail.

**maple** n. Northern hemisphere tree with broad leaves; (in full **Queensland maple**) unrelated Australian tree yielding, usu. pinkish, cabinet timber.

**mar** v. (**marred**) spoil, damage.

**Mar.** abbr. March.

**maraca** n. clublike bean-filled gourd etc., shaken as percussion instrument.

**marathon** n. long-distance foot race; long-lasting, esp. difficult undertaking.

**maraud** v. make raid; pillage. □□ **marauder** n.

**marble** • n. **1** crystallised limestone that can be polished; sculpture in this. **2** small ball of glass etc. used in children's games **3** (**marbles**) colloq. one's mental faculties. • v. give veined or mottled appearance to.

**marcasite** n. crystalline iron sulphide; crystals of this used in jewellery.

**March** n. third month of year.

**march** • v. walk in military manner or with regular paces; proceed steadily; cause to march or walk. • n. act of marching; uniform military step; long difficult walk; procession as demonstration; progress; piece of music suitable for marching to.□□ **marcher** n.

**marches** n.pl. border regions.

**marchioness** n. woman holding rank of marquess; wife or widow of marquess.

**mardo** n. Aust. yellow-footed marsupial mouse.

**mare** n. female equine animal, esp. horse.

**margarine** n. substance made from animal or vegetable fats and used like butter.

**margin** n. **1** edge or border of surface; plain space around printed page etc. **2** amount by which thing exceeds, falls short, etc. **3** increment to basic wage, paid for particular skill etc.

**marginal** adj. **1** of or in a margin; near a limit. **2** (of electorate) held by small majority.□□ **marginally** adv.

**marginalise** v. (also -**ize**) make or treat as insignificant; exclude (person or group) from mainstream of interest, power, etc. □□ **marginalisation** n.

**marguerite** n. flower of the daisy family.

**marigold** n. plant with golden or bright yellow flowers.

**marijuana** n. dried leaves etc. of hemp smoked as drug.

**marimba** n. African and Central American xylophone; orchestral instrument developed from this.

**marina** n. harbour for pleasure boats.

**marinade** ● n. mixture of wine, vinegar, oil, spices, etc. for soaking meat or fish. ● v. soak in marinade.

**marinate** v. marinade.

**marine** ● adj. of, found in, or produced by the sea; for use at sea; of shipping. ● n. **1** soldier trained to serve on land or at sea. **2** country's shipping, fleet, or navy.

**mariner** n. seaman.

**marionette** n. puppet worked by strings.

**marital** adj. of marriage.

**maritime** adj. connected with the sea or seafaring; living or found near the sea.

**marjoram** n. aromatic herb used in cookery.

**mark** ● n. **1** thing that visibly breaks uniformity of a surface; distinguishing feature; something indicating presence of a quality or feeling; symbol. **2** point given for merit; (in AFL) the fair catching of ball kicked at least fifteen metres; a target; line or object serving to indicate position; numbered design on piece of equipment etc. **3** (until 2002) unit of money in Germany. ● v. **1** make mark on; characterise; brand, castrate, and dock tails of (livestock). **2** assign marks of merit to. **3** notice, watch carefully; keep close to and ready to hamper (opponent in football etc.) **4** AFL take ball in fair catch. □ **mark time** move feet as if marching but without advancing. **quick off the mark** reacting quickly.

**marked** adj. clearly noticeable. □□ **markedly** adv.

**marker** n. person or thing that marks; pen with broad felt tip.

**market** ● n. **1** gathering for sale of commodities, livestock, etc.; space for this. **2** demand for commodity etc.; place or group providing such demand; conditions for buying or selling; rate of purchase or sale. ● v. **1** offer for sale. **2** buy or sell goods in market. □ **market garden** farm producing vegetables. **on the market** offered for sale.

□□ **marketable** adj.

**marking** n. mark(s); colouring of animal's skin, fur, or feathers.

**marksman** n. person who is skilled shot. □□ **marksmanship** n.

**markup** n. **1** amount added to price by retailer for profit. **2** process or result of correcting text in preparation for printing. **3** Computing set of tags assigned to elements of text to indicate their relation to rest of text or dictate how they should be displayed.

**marl** n. soil of clay and lime, used as fertiliser.

**marlin** n. (pl. **marlin** or **marlins**) long-nosed marine fish.

**marmalade** n. jam of oranges or other citrus fruit.

**marmoset** n. small bushy-tailed monkey.

**marmot** n. burrowing rodent with short bushy tail.

**maroon** ● adj. & n. brownish-crimson. ● v. put and leave ashore on desolate island or coast; leave stranded.

**marquee** n. large tent.

**marquess** n. British nobleman ranking between duke and earl.

**marquetry** n. inlaid work in wood etc.

**marquis** n. French nobleman ranking between duke and count.

**marquise** n. woman holding rank of marquis; wife or widow of marquis.

**marri** n. Western Australian eucalypt with profuse cream, pink, or red flowers.

**marriage** n. **1** legally or formally recognised union of two people as

partners in a personal relationship; act or ceremony marking this.
**2** intimate union; combination, blend. □ **marriage celebrant** person empowered to perform marriage, esp. in non-religious ceremony.

**marriageable** adj. suitable or old enough for marriage.

**marron** n. Aust. large freshwater crayfish.

**marrow** n. **1** large fleshy gourd eaten as vegetable. **2** soft fatty substance in cavities of bones.

**marry** v. unite or give or take in marriage; unite (things).

**marsh** n. low watery land. □□ **marshy** adj.

**marshal** ● n. **1** officer arranging ceremonies, controlling racecourses, crowds, etc. **2** (in some countries) military or law enforcement officer. ● v. (**marshalled**) arrange in proper order, assemble; conduct (person) ceremoniously.

**marshmallow** n. soft sweet made from sugar, egg white, gelatine, etc.

**marsupial** ● n. mammal giving birth to underdeveloped young subsequently carried in pouch. ● adj. of or like marsupial.

**mart** n. market.

**martial** adj. **1** of warfare; warlike. **2** brave. □ **martial law** military government suspending ordinary law.

**martin** n. kind of European swallow; any similar migratory bird.

**martinet** n. strict disciplinarian.

**martini** n. cocktail of gin and vermouth.

**martyr** ● n. **1** person who undergoes death or suffering for great cause. **2** person who suffers or pretends to suffer to obtain sympathy. ● v. put to death as martyr; torment. □□ **martyrdom** n.

**marvel** ● n. wonderful thing. ● v. (**marvelled**) feel surprise or wonder.

**marvellous** adj. astonishing; excellent. □□ **marvellously** adv.

**Marxism** n. political and economic theories of Karl Marx. □□ **Marxist** n. & adj.

**marzipan** n. paste of ground almonds, sugar, etc.

**masala** n. mixture of spices ground together for use in Indian cookery.

**mascara** n. cosmetic for darkening eyelashes.

**mascot** n. person, animal, or thing supposed to bring luck.

**masculine** adj. of, like, or traditionally considered suitable for men; having grammatical form of male gender. □□ **masculinity** n.

**mash** ● n. **1** soft mixture of grain or bran. **2** mashed potatoes etc. ● v. beat into soft mass. □ **mash-up** mixture or fusion of disparate elements. □□ **masher** n.

**mask** ● n. **1** covering for all or part of face, worn as disguise or for protection. **2** respirator. **3** likeness of person's face, esp. one made by taking mould. **4** disguise. ● v. cover with mask; conceal, disguise, screen.

**masochism** n. pleasure in suffering physical or mental pain, esp. as sexual perversion; colloq. enjoyment of what appears to be painful or tiresome. □□ **masochist** n. **masochistic** adj.

**mason** n. person who builds or works with stone.

**masonry** n. stonework; work of mason.

**masque** n. musical drama with mime.

**masquerade** ● n. false show, pretence. ● v. pretend to be what one is not.

**mass** ● n. **1** coherent unit of matter; large quantity, heap, or expanse; quantity of matter a body contains. **2** (**the masses**) ordinary people. **3** (usu. **Mass**) celebration, esp. in RC Church, of Eucharist; form of liturgy used in this. ● *v.* gather or assemble into a mass. □ **mass-produce** manufacture in large quantities by standardized process.

**massacre** ● *n.* great slaughter.
● *v.* slaughter in large numbers; *colloq.* defeat heavily.

**massage** ● *n.* rubbing and kneading of muscles etc. to reduce pain or stiffness. ● *v.* treat thus.

**masseur** *n.* person who practises massage professionally.

**masseuse** *n.* woman who practises massage professionally.

**massif** *n.* compact group of mountain heights.

**massive** *adj.* large and heavy or solid; unusually large or severe; substantial. □□ **massively** *adv.* **massiveness** *n.*

**mast** *n.* upright post on ship's keel to support sails; tall structure supporting radio or television aerial; flag pole.

**mastectomy** *n.* surgical removal of breast.

**master** ● *n.* **1** man who has control of people or things; male teacher. **2** person with great skill, great artist. **3** something from which series of copies is made. **4** (**Master**) title of boy not old enough to be called *Mr.* ● *adj.* superior; principal; controlling others. ● *v.* bring under control; acquire knowledge or skill in. □ **master key** that opens several different locks. **master stroke** very skilful act of policy etc.

**masterclass** *n.* class given by famous musician, artist, etc.

**masterful** *adj.* **1** powerful and able to control others. **2** masterly.

**masterly** *adj.* very skilful.

**mastermind** ● *n.* person of outstanding mental ability; person directing an enterprise. ● *v.* plan and direct.

**masterpiece** *n.* outstanding piece of work.

**mastery** *n.* **1** control, dominance. **2** comprehensive knowledge or skill.

**mastic** *n.* **1** gum or resin from certain trees. **2** waterproof filler and sealant.

**masticate** *v.* chew.

**mastiff** *n.* large strong breed of dog.

**mastitis** *n.* inflammation of breast or udder.

**mastodon** *n.* extinct mammal resembling elephant.

**mastoid** *n.* projecting piece of bone behind ear.

**masturbate** *v.* stimulate genitals with hand etc. □□ **masturbation** *n.*

**mat** ● *n.* **1** piece of coarse fabric on floor, esp. for wiping shoes on; piece of material laid on table etc. to protect surface. **2** var. of MATT. ● *v.* (**matted**) bring or come into thickly entangled state.

**matador** *n.* bullfighter.

**match** ● *n.* **1** short thin piece of wood etc. with combustible tip. **2** contest, game. **3** person or thing equal to, exactly resembling, or corresponding to another; marriage; person viewed as marriage prospect. ● *v.* **1** be equal, correspond. **2** be or find match for. **3** place in conflict or competition with.

**matcha** *n.* powdered green tea leaves.

**matchmaker** *n.* person who arranges marriages, or schemes to bring couples together.

**mate** ● *n.* **1** very close friend; acquaintance or fellow worker. **2** each of pair of mated animals. **3** merchant ship's officer. **4** checkmate. ● *v.* put or come together as pair; come or bring (animals) together to breed.

**material** ● *n.* **1** that from which thing is or can be made. **2** cloth, fabric. ● *adj.* **1** of matter; of the physical (not spiritual) world. **2** significant.

**materialise** v. (also **-ize**) become a fact; happen; appear, become visible. □□ **materialisation** n.

**materialism** n. **1** greater interest in material possessions and comfort than in spiritual values. **2** *Philos.* theory that nothing exists but matter. □□ **materialist** n. **materialistic** adj.

**maternal** adj. of or like a mother; motherly; related through one's mother.□□ **maternally** adv.

**maternity** ● n. motherhood; motherliness. ● adj. for women during pregnancy and childbirth.

**mateship** n. comradeship.

**mathematics** n. (as *sing.*) science of numbers, quantities, and measurement; (as *pl.*) use of this. □□ **mathematical** adj. **mathematician** n.

**maths** n. *colloq.* mathematics.

**matilda** n. *Aust. hist.* bushman's bundle; swag.

**matinée** n. (also **matinee**) afternoon performance in theatre, cinema, etc. □ **matinée jacket** baby's jacket.

**matins** n. (also **mattins**) morning prayer.

**matriarch** n. female head of family or community.□□ **matriarchal** adj.

**matriarchy** n. female-dominated system of society.

**matrices** see MATRIX.

**matricide** n. killing of one's mother.

**matriculate** v. admit (student) to university.□□ **matriculation** n.

**matrimony** n. rite, state, or sacrament of marriage. □□ **matrimonial** adj.

**matrix** n. (pl. **matrices** or **matrixes**) **1** environment in which something develops; mould in which thing is cast or shaped. **2** *Math.* rectangular array of quantities treated as single element. **3** *Computing* gridlike array of interconnected circuit elements.

**matron** n. **1** married woman. **2** woman nurse and housekeeper at school etc.; (formerly) woman in charge of nursing in hospital.

**matronly** adj. like a matron, esp. portly or staid.

**matt** adj. (also **mat**) dull, not shiny or glossy.

**matter** ● n. that which occupies space in visible world; specified substance or material; specified things; situation or business being considered. ● v. be of importance.

**mattock** n. tool like pickaxe with adze and chisel edge.

**mattress** n. fabric case for sleeping on, filled with soft or firm material, air, water, or springs.

**mature** ● adj. **1** fully grown or developed. **2** (of life insurance policy, investment, etc.) be due for payment. ● v. make or become mature.□□ **maturity** n.

**maudlin** adj. weakly sentimental.

**maul** ● v. tear and mutilate; handle roughly; damage. ● n. **1** *Rugby* loose scrum. **2** brawl. **3** heavy hammer.

**maunder** v. talk ramblingly.

**mausoleum** n. magnificent tomb.

**mauve** n. & adj. pale purple.

**maverick** n. & adj. (someone) unorthodox and independent-minded.

**mawkish** adj. feebly sentimental.

**maxillary** adj. of the jaw.

**maxim** n. general truth or rule of conduct briefly expressed.

**maximise** v. (also **-ize**) **1** make as large or great as possible. **2** make the best use of.□□ **maximisation** n.

**maximum** ● n. (pl. **maxima**) highest possible amount, size, etc. ● adj. greatest in amount, size, etc. □□ **maximal** adj.

**May** n. fifth month.

**may** v.aux. used to express wish, possibility, or permission.

**maya** n. (in Hinduism) illusion, magic.

**maybe** adv. perhaps.

**mayday** n. international radio distress signal.

**mayonnaise** n. creamy dressing of oil, egg yolk, vinegar, etc.; dish dressed with this.

**mayor** n. head of local council of city or town etc. □□ **mayoral** adj. **mayoralty** n.

**mayoress** n. woman mayor; wife of mayor.

**maze** n. network of paths etc. designed as puzzle; labyrinth; confused network etc.

**MB** abbr. **1** Bachelor of Medicine. **2** Computing (also **Mb**) megabyte(s).

**MBA** abbr. Master of Business Administration.

**MC** abbr. **1** Master of Ceremonies. **2** musician who performs rap.

**MD** abbr. Doctor of Medicine.

**ME** abbr. myalgic encephalomyelitis, condition with prolonged flu-like symptoms and depression.

**me¹** pron. the objective case of I.

**me²** n. Mus. third note of major scale, or the note E.

**mea culpa** int. acknowledgement of guilt or error.

**mead** n. alcoholic drink of fermented honey and water.

**meadow** n. field of grass.

**meagre** adj. scant in amount or quality.

**meal¹** n. **1** occasion when food is eaten; the food itself. **2** coarsely ground grain.

**mealy** adj. of, like, or containing meal. □ **mealy-mouthed** trying excessively to avoid offending people.

**mean¹** v. (**meant**, **meaning**) have as one's purpose; intend; convey; express; be likely to result in; be of specified purpose.

**mean²** adj. miserly; selfish; unkind; poor in quality of appearance;

vicious; low in rank. □□ **meanly** adv. **meanness** n.

**mean³** ● n. a value arrived at by adding several quantities together and dividing by the number of these. ● adj. calculated as a mean.

**meander** ● v. follow winding course; wander in leisurely way. ● n. winding course.

**meaning** n. what is meant. ● adj. expressive. □□ **meaningful** adj. **meaningless** adj.

**means** n. (as sing. or pl.) that by which result is brought about. **2** (as pl.) resources. □ **by all means** certainly. **means test** official inquiry to establish need before giving financial help from public funds.

**meantime** ● adv. meanwhile. ● n. intervening period.

**meanwhile** adv. **1** in intervening time. **2** at same time.

**measles** n.pl. infectious viral disease producing red rash on body.

**measly** adj. (**measlier**) colloq. meagre.

**measurable** adj. able to be measured.

**measure** ● n. **1** size or quantity found by measuring; unit, system, standard, or device used in measuring. **2** action taken for a purpose, a law. **3** rhythm. ● v. **1** find size, quantity, proportions, etc. of by comparison with known standard. **2** be of specified size. **3** mark or deal (measured amount). □ **measure up to** reach standard required by. □□ **measurement** n.

**measured** adj. **1** rhythmical; regular. **2** (of language) carefully considered.

**meat** n. animal flesh as food. □□ **meaty** adj.

**meaty** adj. (**meatier**) **1** like meat; full of meat. **2** full of subject matter. □□ **meatiness** n.

**mechanic** n. person skilled in using or repairing machinery.

**mechanical** adj. **1** working, or produced by, machines or mechanism. **2** automatic. **3** lacking originality. **4** of mechanics as science. □□ **mechanically** adv.

**mechanics** n.pl. **1** study of motion and force; science of machinery. **2** way a thing works.

**mechanise** v. (also **-ize**) introduce machines in; make mechanical; equip with tanks, armoured cars, etc. □□ **mechanisation** n.

**mechanism** n. **1** way a machine works, its parts. **2** a process.

**medal** n. commemorative metal disc etc., esp. awarded for military or sporting prowess.

**medallion** n. large medal; circular ornamental design.

**medallist** n. winner of (specified) medal.

**meddle** v. interfere in others' concerns.

**meddlesome** adj. interfering.

**media** n.pl. **1** see MEDIUM. **2** (**the media**) mass communication (broadcasting, publishing, and Internet) regarded collectively.

**mediaeval** = MEDIEVAL.

**medial** adj. situated in middle.

**median** adj. in or passing through middle. ● n. **1** straight line drawn from angle of triangle to middle of opposite side. **2** middle value of series.

**mediate** v. act as go-between or peacemaker. □□ **mediation** n. **mediator** n.

**medical** ● adj. of medicine. ● n. medical examination. □□ **medically** adv.

**medicament** n. substance used in curative treatment.

**Medicare** n. Aust. Federal system of basic health care.

**medicate** v. treat medically; impregnate with medicine etc. □□ **medication** n.

**medicine** n. **1** science or practice of diagnosis, treatment, and prevention of disease or illness. **2** substance used to treat disease or illness.

**medieval** adj. (also **mediaeval**) of Middle Ages.

**mediocre** adj. **1** of indifferent quality. **2** second-rate. □□ **mediocrity** n.

**meditate** v. **1** think deeply; focus one's mind for relaxation or spiritual purposes. **2** plan mentally. □□ **meditation** n. **meditative** adj.

**medium** n. (pl. **media** or **mediums**) **1** middle size, quality, etc. **2** substance or surroundings in which thing exists. **3** agency or means; means of communication. **4** person claiming to communicate with the dead.

**medley** n. (pl. **medleys**) assortment; excerpts of music from various sources; swimming race of set distances in different strokes.

**medulla** n. **1** inner part of certain bodily organs etc. **2** soft internal tissue of plants. □□ **medullary** adj.

**meek** adj. humble and submissive or gentle. □□ **meekly** adv. **meekness** n.

**meet** ● v. (**met**, **meeting**) **1** come into contact (with). **2** be present at arrival of (person, train, etc.) **3** make the acquaintance of. **4** experience. **5** satisfy (requirement etc.) ● n. **1** assembly for athletics. **2** colloq. assignation, date. □ **meet with** receive (particular reaction or response).

**meeting** n. coming together; assembly for discussion.

**meg** n. one megabyte.

**mega-** comb. form **1** large. **2** one million. **3** colloq. extremely.

**megabit** n. Computing unit of data size or network speed, equal to roughly 1,000,000 bits (per second).

**megabyte** n. Computing $2^{20}$ bytes (loosely 1,000,000) as unit of computer storage.

**megahertz** n. one million hertz, esp. as measure of frequency of radio transmissions.

**megalith** n. large stone, esp. as prehistoric monument.
□□ **megalithic** adj.

**megalomania** n. **1** mental disorder producing delusions of grandeur. **2** passion for grandiose schemes.
□□ **megalomaniac** adj. & n.

**megaphone** n. large funnel-shaped device for amplifying voice.

**megapode** n. Australian bird that builds mound for incubation of eggs.

**megaton** n. unit of explosive power equal to one million tons of TNT.

**meitnerium** n. chemical element (symbol **Mt**).

**melaleuca** n. large, essentially Australian genus of trees and shrubs with bottlebrush or ball flowers.

**melamine** n. resilient plastic used for laminated coatings.

**melancholy** ● n. pensive sadness; depression; tendency to this. ● adj. sad; depressing.
□□ **melancholic** adj.

**melanin** n. dark pigment in the hair, skin, etc.

**melanoma** n. malignant skin tumour.

**meld** v. merge, blend.

**melee** n. (also **mêlée**) confused fight or scuffle; muddle.

**mellifluous** adj. (of voice etc.) pleasing, musical.

**mellow** ● adj. **1** (of sound, colour, light, or flavour) soft and rich, free from harshness. **2** (of character) gentle; mature; genial. ● v. make or become mellow. □□ **mellowly** adv. **mellowness** n.

**melodeon** n. (also **melodion**) small organ or harmonium.

**melodic** adj. **1** of melody. **2** melodious. □□ **melodically** adv.

**melodious** adj. of, producing, or having melody; sweet-sounding.
□□ **melodiously** adv.

**melodrama** n. sensational play etc. appealing blatantly to the emotions; this type of drama.
□□ **melodramatic** adj.

**melody** n. arrangement of notes to make distinctive pattern; tune; principal part in harmonised music; tunefulness.

**melon** n. sweet fleshy fruit of various climbers of gourd family.

**melt** v. **1** make into or become liquid, esp. by heat. **2** soften through pity or love. **3** fade away.

**meltdown** n. **1** disastrous collapse or breakdown; colloq. uncontrolled emotional outburst or mental collapse. **2** accident in nuclear reactor in which the fuel overheats and melts reactor core etc.

**member** n. **1** person etc. belonging to society, team, group, etc. **2** (**Member**) person elected to certain assemblies etc. **3** part of larger structure. **4** part or organ of body, esp. limb.
□□ **membership** n.

**membrane** n. pliable tissue connecting or lining organs in plants and animals; pliable sheet or skin.
□□ **membranous** adj.

**meme** n. **1** image, video, etc., that is copied and spread rapidly by Internet users, often with slight variations. **2** element of culture etc. passed from one individual to another by imitation alone.

**memento** n. (pl. **mementoes** or **mementos**) souvenir of person or event.

**memo** n. memorandum.

**memoir** n. written account of events etc. that one remembers.

**memorable** adj. worth remembering; easily remembered.
□□ **memorably** adv.

**memorandum** n. (pl. **memoranda** or **memorandums**) **1** note written as reminder. **2** written message from one colleague to another.

**memorial** ● n. object etc. established in memory of person or event. ● adj. commemorating.

**memorise** v. (also **-ize**) commit to memory.

**memory** n. **1** faculty by which things are recalled to or kept in mind; store of things remembered; remembrance, esp. of person etc. **2** storage capacity of computer etc. **3** posthumous reputation. □ **memory stick** propr. = flash drive.

**men** see MAN.

**menace** ● n. **1** threat. **2** annoying or troublesome person or thing. ● v. threaten. □□ **menacingly** adv.

**ménage** n. household.

**menagerie** n. small zoo.

**menarche** n. onset of first menstruation.

**mend** ● v. restore to good condition; repair; regain health; improve. ● n. darn or repair in material etc.

**mendacious** adj. lying, untruthful. □□ **mendacity** n.

**mendelevium** n. radioactive metallic element (symbol **Md**).

**mendicant** adj. & n. (person) living by begging.

**menfolk** n.pl. men in general; men of a family.

**menial** ● adj. (of esp. work) degrading, servile. ● n. domestic servant; lowly worker.

**meningitis** n. (esp. viral) infection and inflammation of membranes enclosing brain and spinal cord.

**meningococcus** n. (pl. **meningococci**) bacterium involved in some forms of meningitis etc. □□ **meningococcal** adj.

**meniscus** n. curved surface of liquid; lens convex on one side and concave on the other.

**menopause** n. time of life when woman ceases to menstruate. □□ **menopausal** adj.

**menorah** n. seven-branched Jewish candelabrum.

**menstrual** adj. of menstruation.

**menstruate** v. experience monthly discharge of blood from uterus. □□ **menstruation** n.

**mensuration** n. measuring; mathematical rules for this.

**mental** adj. **1** of, in, or done by mind. **2** caring for mentally ill. **3** colloq. insane. □□ **mentally** adv.

**mentality** n. mental character or disposition.

**menthol** n. mint-tasting organic alcohol found in oil of peppermint etc., used as flavouring and to relieve local pain.

**mentholated** adj. treated with or containing menthol.

**mention** ● v. refer to briefly or by name; disclose. ● n. reference, esp. by name.

**mentor** n. experienced and trusted adviser.

**menu** n. **1** list of dishes available in restaurant etc., or to be served at meal. **2** Computing list of available commands or facilities.

**meow** (also **miaow**) = MEW.

**mephedrone** n. mood-altering drug with stimulant properties.

**mercantile** adj. of trade, trading; commercial.

**mercenary** ● adj. primarily concerned with or working for money etc. ● n. hired soldier in foreign service.

**mercerised** adj. (also **-ized**) (of cotton) treated with slightly glossy substance that adds strength.

**merchandise** ● n. goods for sale. ● v. trade (in); promote (goods, ideas, etc.)

**merchant** n. wholesale trader, esp. with foreign countries; retail trader.

□ **merchant bank** bank dealing in commercial loans and financing of businesses.

**merciful** *adj.* showing mercy.
□□ **mercifulness** *n.*

**mercifully** *adv.* **1** in merciful way. **2** fortunately.

**merciless** *adj.* showing no mercy.
□□ **mercilessly** *adv.*

**mercurial** *adj.* **1** liable to sudden changes of mood; lively; volatile. **2** of or containing mercury.

**mercury** *n.* silvery usu. heavy liquid metallic element (symbol **Hg**).
□□ **mercuric** *adj.*

**mercy** *n.* **1** compassion towards someone in one's power. **2** act of mercy. **3** thing to be thankful for.

**mere**[1] *adj.* no more or no better than.
□□ **merely** *adv.*

**mere**[2] *n. poetic* lake.

**meretricious** *adj.* showily but falsely attractive.

**merge** *v.* combine into whole; blend gradually.

**merger** *n.* combining, esp. of two commercial companies etc., into one.

**meridian** *n.* circle of constant longitude, passing through given place and N. & S. poles; corresponding line on map.
□□ **meridional** *adj.*

**meringue** *n.* sugar, whipped egg whites, etc. baked crisp; cake of this.

**merino** *n.* breed of sheep with long fine wool.

**merit** ● *n.* quality of deserving well; excellence, worth; thing that entitles one to reward or gratitude.
● *v.* (**merited**) deserve.

**meritocracy** *n.* government by people selected for merit.

**meritorious** *adj.* praiseworthy.

**mermaid** *n.* legendary creature with woman's head and trunk and fish's tail.

**merry** *adj.* (**merrier**) **1** joyous; full of laughter or gaiety. **2** *colloq.* slightly drunk. □ **merry-go-round** fairground ride with revolving model horses, cars, etc.; cycle of activities.
□□ **merrily** *adv.* **merriment** *n.*

**mescaline** *n.* (also **mescalin**) hallucinogenic drug.

**mesclun** *n.* Provençal green salad made from mixture of edible leaves and flowers.

**mesh** ● *n.* network fabric or structure; space between threads in net or sieve etc. ● *v.* **1** (of toothed wheel) engage with another. **2** make or become entangled; be in harmony.

**mesmerise** *v.* (also **-ize**) hypnotise; fascinate.

**meso-** *comb. form* middle, intermediate.

**mesolithic** *adj.* period between palaeolithic and neolithic.

**meson** *n.* elementary particle with mass between that of electron and proton.

**mess** ● *n.* **1** dirty or untidy condition; untidy collection of things; something spilt; difficult or confused situation, trouble. **2** (in armed forces) group who eat together; their dining room. ● *v.* **1** make untidy or dirty; muddle, bungle. **2** (in armed forces) eat with group. □ **mess about** potter; fool about.

**message** ● *n.* **1** communication sent by one person to another. **2** moral of book etc. **3** (**messages**) errand, esp. shopping. ● *v.* send message to, esp. by electronic means.

**messenger** *n.* person who carries message.

**Messiah** *n.* promised deliverer of Jewish people; Christ regarded as this.
□□ **Messianic** *adj.*

**Messrs** see **Mr.**

**messy** *adj.* (**messier**) **1** untidy or dirty; slovenly. **2** complicated and difficult.
□□ **messily** *adv.*

**met** see **MEET.**

**metabolise** v. (also -ize) process (food) in metabolism.

**metabolism** n. all the chemical processes in living organism producing energy and growth. □□ **metabolic** adj.

**metacarpus** n. (pl. metacarpi) set of bones forming part of hand between wrist and fingers. □□ **metacarpal** adj.

**metadata** n. set of data that describes and gives information about other data.

**metal** ● n. 1 any of class of workable elements such as gold, silver, iron, or tin; alloy of any of these. 2 blue metal. ● adj. made of metal. ● v. (metalled) make or mend (road) with blue metal.

**metalanguage** n. form of language or set of terms used for the description or analysis of another language.

**metallic** adj. of or like metal(s); sounding like struck metal. □□ **metallically** adv.

**metallurgy** n. science of metals and their application: extraction and purification of metals. □□ **metallurgist** n.

**metamorphic** adj. of metamorphosis; (of rock) transformed naturally. □□ **metamorphism** n.

**metamorphose** v. change by metamorphosis.

**metamorphosis** n. (pl. metamorphoses) change of form or character.

**metaphor** n. application of name or description to something to which it is not literally applicable. □□ **metaphorical** adj. **metaphorically** adv.

**metaphysics** n.pl. branch of philosophy dealing with nature of existence, truth, and knowledge. □□ **metaphysical** adj.

**metastasis** n. (pl. metastases) transference of bodily function, disease, etc. from one part or organ to another.

**metatarsus** n. (pl. metatarsi) set of bones forming part of foot between ankle and toes. □□ **metatarsal** adj.

**meteor** n. small solid body from outer space becoming incandescent when entering earth's atmosphere.

**meteoric** adj. 1 rapid; dazzling. 2 of meteors.

**meteorite** n. fallen meteor; fragment of rock or metal from outer space.

**meteorology** n. study of atmospheric phenomena, esp. for forecasting weather. □□ **meteorological** adj. **meteorologist** n.

**mete out** v. give what is due.

**meter** ● n. instrument that measures or records, esp. gas, electricity, etc. used, distance travelled, etc.; parking meter. ● v. measure or record by meter.

**methadone** n. narcotic drug used esp. as substitute for heroin etc.

**methamphetamine** n. amphetamine derivative used as stimulant.

**methane** n. colourless odourless flammable gaseous hydrocarbon, the main constituent of natural gas.

**methanol** n. colourless flammable organic liquid used as solvent.

**method** n. 1 way of doing something; procedure; orderliness. 2 scheme of classification.

**methodical** adj. characterised by method or order. □□ **methodically** adv.

**Methodist** ● n. member of Protestant denomination originating in 18th-c. evangelistic movement. ● adj. of Methodists or Methodism. □□ **Methodism** n.

**methodology** n. system of methods used in activity or study.

**methyl** n. hydrocarbon radical CH₃.

**methylate** v. mix or impregnate with methanol; introduce methyl group into (molecule). □ **methylated spirit** alcohol impregnated with methanol, used for cleaning etc.

**meticulous** adj. **1** giving great attention to detail. **2** very careful and precise. □□ **meticulously** adv.

**métier** n. **1** one's trade, profession, or field of activity. **2** one's speciality.

**metonymy** n. substitution of name of attribute etc. for that of thing meant, e.g. *Crown* for *king*.

**metre** n. (*US* **meter**) **1** SI unit of length (100 cm; 39.4 in.). **2** poetic rhythm. **3** basic rhythm of music.

**metric** adj. of or based on the metre. □ **metric system** decimal system of weights and measures, using metre, litre, and gram as units.

**metrical** adj. **1** of or composed in rhythmic metre. **2** of or involving measurement. □□ **metrically** adv.

**metricate** v. convert to metric system. □□ **metrication** n.

**metro** n. underground railway.

**metronome** n. device ticking at selected rate to mark musical time.

**metropolis** n. chief city; capital. □□ **metropolitan** adj.

**mettle** n. quality or strength of character; spirit, courage. □□ **mettlesome** adj.

**mew** ● n. cat's cry. ● v. utter this sound.

**mews** n. *Brit.* set of stables converted into houses.

**mezzanine** n. storey between two others (usu. ground and first floors).

**mezzo** ● adv. (in music) half; moderately. ● n. mezzo-soprano, voice between soprano and contralto.

**mezzotint** n. method of printing or engraving; print so produced.

**mf** abbr. mezzo forte.

**mg** abbr. milligram(s).

**MHA** abbr. Member of the House of Assembly.

**MHR** abbr. Member of the House of Representatives.

**MHz** abbr. megahertz.

**mia-mia** n. *Aust.* gunyah; traveller's temporary shelter.

**miaow** (also **meow**) n. = MEW.

**miasma** n. **1** unpleasant or unwholesome air.

**mic** n. *colloq.* microphone.

**mica** n. silicate mineral used as electrical insulator.

**mice** SEE MOUSE.

**micro-** *comb. form* **1** extremely small. **2** one millionth.

**microbe** n. microorganism (esp. bacterium) causing disease or fermentation. □□ **microbial** adj.

**microbiology** n. study of microorganisms. □□ **microbiologist** n.

**microchip** n. small piece of semiconductor used to carry integrated circuits.

**microclimate** n. climate of very small or restricted area.

**microcosm** n. **1** community, place, or situation regarded as encapsulating in miniature the characteristics of something much larger. **2** miniature representation. □□ **microcosmic** adj.

**microeconomics** n. branch of economics dealing with individual commodities, producers, etc.

**microfiche** n. (*pl.* **microfiche** or **microfiches**) small flat piece of film bearing microphotographs of documents etc.

**microfilm** ● n. length of film bearing microphotographs of documents etc. ● v. photograph on microfilm.

**micrometer** n. gauge for accurate small-scale measurement.

**micron** n. millionth of a metre.

**microorganism** n. microscopic organism.

**microphone** n. instrument for converting sound waves into electrical energy for transmitting or amplifying.

**microprocessor** n. data processor using integrated circuits contained on microchip(s).

**microscope** n. instrument with lenses for magnifying objects or details invisible to naked eye.

**microscopic** adj. tiny; visible only with microscope; of or using microscope. □□ **microscopically** adv. **microscopy** n.

**microsurgery** n. intricate surgery using microscopes.

**microwave** • n. electromagnetic wave of length between 1 mm and 30 cm; oven using microwaves to cook or heat food quickly. • v. cook in microwave oven.

**mid-** comb. form middle of.

**midday** n. noon.

**midden** n. dunghill; refuse heap; mirrnyong.

**middle** • adj. at an equal distance, time, or number from extremities; central; intermediate in rank, quality, etc.; average. • n. 1 middle point, position, or part. 2 waist.
• v. place in middle. □□ **middle age** part of life between youth and old age. **Middle Ages** 5th c.–1453, or c.1000–1453, as period of European history. **middle class** class of society between upper and working classes. **Middle East** area from Egypt to Iran inclusive.

**middleman** n. trader handling commodity between producer and consumer.

**middleweight** n. weight above welterweight, in amateur boxing between 71 and 75 kg.

**middling** • adj. moderately good. • adv. fairly, moderately.

**middy** n. medium-sized measure of beer.

**midfield** n. part of football field away from goals.

**midge** n. small biting insect.

**midget** n. extremely small person or thing.

**MIDI** n. (also **midi**) interface allowing electronic musical instruments and computers to be connected.

**midnight** n. 12 o'clock at night.

**midriff** n. front of body just above waist.

**midshipman** n. naval officer ranking next above cadet.

**midst** n. middle.

**midwife** n. (pl. **midwives**) person trained to assist at childbirth. □□ **midwifery** n.

**mien** n. literary person's manner or bearing.

**migaloo** n. Aust. (in Aboriginal English) white person.

**might** v.aux. used to request permission or to express possibility.

**might** n. great strength or power.

**mighty** adj. (**mightier**) very powerful or strong; very great. □□ **mightily** adv.

**migraine** n. recurrent throbbing headache often accompanied by nausea and visual disturbance.

**migrant** • n. person leaving his or her own country to take up permanent residence in another; migrating animal or bird.
• adj. migrating.

**migrate** v. move from one place, etc. one country, to settle in another; (of bird etc.) change habitation seasonally. □□ **migration** n. **migratory** adj.

**mike** n. colloq. microphone.

**mild** adj. 1 (esp. of person) gentle; not severe or harsh. 2 (of weather) moderately warm. 3 (of flavour etc.) not sharp or strong. □□ **mildly** adv. **mildness** n.

**mildew** • n. destructive growth of minute fungi on plants, damp paper, leather, etc. ● v. taint or be tainted with mildew.

**mile** n. (in imperial system) measure of length (1760 yds, approx. 1.6 km).

**mileage** n. **1** number of miles travelled. **2** colloq. profit, advantage.

**milestone** n. stone showing the distance to a certain place; significant event or stage reached.

**milieu** n. (pl. milieux or milieus) environment, social surroundings.

**militant** ● adj. **1** combative; engaged in warfare. **2** aggressively active in support of cause.
● n. militant person. □□ militancy n. militantly adv.

**militarism** n. aggressively military policy etc.; military spirit.
□□ militarist n. militaristic adj.

**military** adj. of soldiers or army or all armed forces.

**militate** v. have force or effect.

> **Usage** Militate is often confused with mitigate which means 'to make less intense or severe'.

**militia** n. military force, esp. one conscripted in emergency.
□□ militiaman n.

**milk** ● n. opaque white fluid secreted by female mammals for nourishing young; milk of cows, goats, etc. as food; milky juice of coconut etc.
● v. **1** draw milk from (cow etc.) **2** extract venom or sap from (snake, tree, etc.) **3** exploit (person, situation) to utmost. □ **milk teeth** first (temporary) teeth in young mammals.

**milkshake** n. drink of milk whisked with ice cream and flavoured syrup etc.

**milksop** n. weak or timid man.

**milky** adj. (milkier) **1** of, like, or mixed with milk. **2** (of gem or liquid) cloudy.

□ **Milky Way** faint band of stars crossing night sky; part of our galaxy.

**mill** ● n. machinery for grinding or processing specified material; building containing this. ● v. **1** grind or treat in mill. **2** produce grooves in (metal). **3** move in a confused mass. □□ miller n.

**millennial** ● adj. **1** of a period or anniversary of a thousand years. **2** of people reaching adulthood in early 21st century. ● n. millennial person.

**millennium** n. (pl. millenniums or millennia) **1** thousand-year period. **2** (esp. future) period of happiness on earth.

**millet** n. cereal plant bearing small nutritious seeds; seed of this.

**milli-** comb. form one-thousandth part of (as in milligram; millilitre; millimetre.).

**millibar** n. unit of atmospheric pressure equivalent to 100 pascals.

**milliner** n. maker or seller of women's hats. □□ millinery n.

**million** n. & adj. one thousand thousand (1,000,000); (millions) colloq. very large number.
□□ millionth adj. & n.

**millionaire** n. person who has over a million dollars etc.

**millipede** n. (also millepede) small crawling invertebrate with long segmented body with many legs.

**milt** n. sperm-filled reproductive gland or sperm of male fish.

**mime** ● n. acting without words, using only gestures; performance using mime. ● v. express or represent by mime. □□ mimer n.

**mimic** ● v. (mimicked, mimicking) imitate (person, gesture, etc.), esp. to entertain or ridicule; copy minutely or servilely; resemble closely.
● n. person who is clever at mimicking others. □□ mimicry n.

**mimosa** n. 1 shrub with globular flowers. 2 acacia plant with yellow flowers.

**minaret** n. slender turret next to mosque used by the muezzin.

**mince** ● v. 1 cut into small pieces in mincer. 2 speak or walk with affected refinement. ● n. minced beef etc.

**mincemeat** n. 1 mixture of dried fruit, sugar, spices, etc. used in pies. 2 minced meat.

**mincer** n. machine with revolving blades for cutting food into very small pieces.

**mind** ● n. 1 seat of consciousness, thought, volition, and feeling; intellect; sanity. 2 attention, concentration; memory. 3 opinion. ● v. 1 be distressed or worried by, object to. 2 remember; take care to. 3 have charge of temporarily. □ **be of one mind** share opinion. **have in mind** intend. **mind out for** guard against; avoid.

**minded** adj. disposed, inclined.

**minder** n. person employed to look after person or thing.

**mindful** adj. taking heed or care. □□ **mindfully** adv.

**mindless** adj. lacking intelligence; brutish; not requiring thought or skill. □□ **mindlessness** n.

**mine**[1] adj. & pron. poss. belonging to me.

**mine**[2] ● n. 1 excavation for extracting metal or coal etc.; abundant source. 2 explosive device laid in or on ground or in water. ● v. 1 dig for minerals; extract in this way. 2 lay explosive mines under or in. 3 search (books etc.) for information. □□ **mining** n.

**minefield** n. 1 area where explosive mines have been laid. 2 situation full of difficulties.

**miner** n. 1 worker in mine. 2 Australian honeyeater with yellow bill and legs.

**mineral** ● n. any inorganic substance; substance obtained by mining. ● adj. of or containing mineral(s); obtained by mining. □ **mineral turpentine** liquid distilled from petroleum and used as solvent etc. **mineral water** water naturally or artificially impregnated with dissolved salts.

**mineralogy** n. study of minerals. □□ **mineralogical** adj. **mineralogist** n.

**minestrone** n. soup containing vegetables and pasta, beans, or rice, etc.

**mingle** v. mix, blend.

**mingy** adj. (**mingier**) colloq. stingy.

**mini-** comb. form miniature; small of its kind.

**miniature** ● adj. much smaller than normal; represented on small scale. ● n. miniature object; detailed small-scale portrait.

**miniaturise** v. (also -**ize**) produce in smaller version; make small. □□ **miniaturisation** n.

**minibus** n. small bus.

**minim** n. Mus. note equal to two crotchets or half a semibreve.

**minimal** adj. very minute or slight; being a minimum. □□ **minimally** adv.

**minimalism** n. the use of simple basic design forms; including only the minimum. □□ **minimalist** n.

**minimise** v. (also -**ize**) reduce to, or estimate at, minimum; estimate or represent at less than true value etc. □□ **minimisation** n.

**minimum** ● n. (pl. **minima**) least possible or attainable amount. ● adj. that is minimum.

**minion** n. derog. servile subordinate.

**miniseries** n. short series of television programs on common theme.

**miniskirt** n. very short skirt.

**minister** • n. 1 head of government department. 2 member of clergy, esp. in Protestant Churches. 3 senior diplomatic representative. • v. help, serve, look after.□□ **ministerial** adj.

**ministration** n. help, service.

**ministry** n. 1 government department headed by minister. 2 (**the ministry**) body of ministers of government or religion. 3 vocation, office, or profession of religious minister.

**mink** n. small semi-aquatic stoatlike animal; its valuable fur.

**min-min** n. Aust. will-o'-the-wisp.

**minnow** n. small fish.

**minor** • adj. 1 lesser or comparatively small in size or importance. 2 Mus. (of scale) having semitone above its second, fifth, and seventh notes; (of key) based on minor scale. • n. 1 person under full legal age. 2 student's subsidiary subject or course. 3 Mus. minor key. 4 AFL behind.

**minority** n. 1 smaller number or part, esp. in politics; smaller group of people differing from larger in race, religion, language, etc. 2 being under full legal age; period of this.

**minstrel** n. 1 hist. medieval singer or musician. 2 musical entertainer with blacked face.

**mint¹** n. aromatic herb used in cooking; peppermint; a sweet flavoured with this.□□ **minty** adj.

**mint²** • n. place authorised to make country's coins. • v. make (coins).

**minuet** n. slow stately dance in triple time; music for this.

**minus** • prep. with subtraction of; below zero; colloq. lacking. • adj. negative. • n. 1 minus sign (−). 2 negative quantity. 3 colloq. disadvantage.

**minuscule** adj. (also **miniscule**) extremely small or unimportant.

> **Usage** The variant miniscule should not be used in formal contexts.

**minute¹** • n. 1 sixtieth part of hour; distance covered in minute; moment. 2 sixtieth part of angular degree. 3 summary of proceedings of meeting; official memorandum. • v. record in minutes; send minutes to.

**minute²** adj. very small; accurate, detailed.□□ **minutely** adv.

**minutiae** n.pl. very small, precise, or minor details.

**minx** n. mischievous girl.

**MIPS** abbr. (also **mips**) Computing million instructions per second.

**miracle** n. extraordinary supposedly supernatural event; remarkable happening.□□ **miraculous** adj. **miraculously** adv.

**mirage** n. optical illusion caused by atmospheric conditions, esp. appearance of water in desert or on hot road; illusory thing.

**mire** • n. area of swampy ground; mud. • v. sink in mire; bespatter with mud.

**mirrnyong** n. (also **mirnyong**) Aust. archaeologically significant mound of ashes, shells, and other debris.

**mirror** • n. polished surface, usu. of coated glass, reflecting image; anything reflecting state of affairs etc. • v. reflect in mirror; correspond to; be image of.

**mirth** n. merriment, laughter. □□ **mirthful** adj.

**mis-** prefix badly; wrongly.

**misadventure** n. 1 Law accident without crime or negligence. 2 bad luck.

**misanthrope** *n.* (also **misanthropist**) person who dislikes people in general.□□ **misanthropic** *adj.* **misanthropy** *n.*

**misapprehend** *v.* misunderstand (words, person).
□□ **misapprehension** *n.*

**misappropriate** *v.* take dishonestly.
□□ **misappropriation** *n.*

**misbehave** *v.* behave badly.
□□ **misbehaviour** *n.*

**miscalculate** *v.* calculate wrongly.
□□ **miscalculation** *n.*

**miscarriage** *n.* abortion occurring naturally.

**miscarry** *v.* **1** (of woman) have miscarriage. **2** (of plan etc.) fail.

**miscegenation** *n.* interbreeding of races.

**miscellaneous** *adj.* of mixed composition or character; of various kinds.□□ **miscellaneously** *adv.*

**miscellany** *n.* mixture, medley.

**mischief** *n.* troublesome, but not malicious, conduct, esp. of children.

**mischievous** *adj.* full of mischief.
□□ **mischievously** *adv.*

**misconception** *n.* wrong interpretation.

**misconduct** *n.* improper or unprofessional behaviour.

**misconstrue** *v.* interpret wrongly.
□□ **misconstruction** *n.*

**miscreant** *n.* vile wretch, villain.

**misdeed** *n.* evil deed, wrongdoing.

**misdemeanour** *n.* (also **misdemeanor**) **1** misdeed. **2** offence less serious than felony.

**miser** *n.* person who hoards wealth and lives miserably.□□ **miserly** *adj.*

**miserable** *adj.* wretchedly unhappy or uncomfortable; contemptible; mean, causing discomfort.
□□ **miserably** *adv.*

**misery** *n.* condition or feeling of wretchedness; cause of this.

**misfire** ● *v.* (of gun, motor engine, etc.) fail to go off, start, or function

smoothly; (of plan etc.) go wrong.
● *n.* such failure.

**misfit** *n.* person unsuited to surroundings, occupation, etc.

**misfortune** *n.* bad luck; instance of this.

**misgiving** *n.* feeling of mistrust or apprehension.

**misguided** *adj.* mistaken in thought or action.□□ **misguidedly** *adv.*

**mishandle** *v.* deal with incorrectly or inefficiently; handle roughly.

**mishap** *n.* unlucky accident.

**mishmash** *n.* confused mixture.

**misinform** *v.* give wrong information to, mislead.
□□ **misinformation** *n.*

**misinterpret** *v.* interpret wrongly; draw wrong inference from.
□□ **misinterpretation** *n.*

**misjudge** *v.* judge wrongly; have wrong opinion of.□□ **misjudgement** *n.* (also **misjudgment**)

**mislay** *v.* (**mislaid**, **mislaying**) lose temporarily.

**mislead** *v.* (**misled**, **misleading**) cause to infer what is not true; deceive.

**mismanage** *v.* manage badly or wrongly.□□ **mismanagement** *n.*

**misnomer** *n.* wrongly used name or term.

**misogyny** *n.* dislike of, contempt for, or prejudice against women.
□□ **misogynist** *n.* & *adj.*

**misplace** *v.* put in wrong place; bestow (affections, confidence, etc.) on inappropriate object.
□□ **misplacement** *n.*

**misprint** *n.* error in printing.

**misquote** *v.* quote inaccurately.
□□ **misquotation** *n.*

**misread** *v.* (**misread**) read or interpret wrongly.

**misrepresent** *v.* represent wrongly; give false account.
□□ **misrepresentation** *n.*

**misrule** ● *n.* bad government.
● *v.* govern badly.

**Miss** n. (pl. **Misses**) title of girl or unmarried woman.

**miss** ● v. **1** fail to hit, reach, find, catch, or perceive; fail to seize (opportunity etc.); avoid. **2** regret absence of. ● n. failure. □ **miss out** omit, leave out. **miss out on** colloq. be deprived of.

**misshapen** adj. deformed, distorted.

**missile** n. object thrown or fired at target.

**missing** adj. not present; not in its place, lost.

**mission** n. **1** task or goal assigned to person or group; journey etc. undertaken as part of this. **2** group of people sent to conduct negotiations or to evangelise. **3** missionaries' headquarters.

**missionary** ● adj. of or concerned with religious missions. ● n. person doing missionary work.

**misspell** v. (**misspelt** or **misspelled**, **misspelling**) spell wrongly.

**mist** ● n. **1** water vapour in minute drops; condensed vapour obscuring glass etc. **2** dimness or blurring of sight caused by tears etc. ● v. cover or be covered (as) with mist.

**mistake** ● n. incorrect idea or opinion; thing incorrectly done, thought, or judged. ● v. (**mistook**, **mistaken**, **mistaking**) misunderstand meaning or intention of; choose or identify wrongly.

**mistletoe** n. parasitic Australian plant, usu. seen on eucalypts; parasitic white-berried European plant.

**mistreat** v. treat badly. □□ **mistreatment** n.

**mistress** n. **1** female head of household; woman in authority; female teacher. **2** woman having illicit sexual relationship with (usu. married) man.

**mistrial** n. trial made invalid by error in proceedings.

**mistrust** ● v. be suspicious of; feel no confidence in. ● n. suspicion; lack of confidence. □□ **mistrustful** adj.

**misty** adj. (**mistier**) full of mist; indistinct. □□ **mistily** adv.

**misunderstand** v. (**misunderstood**, **misunderstanding**) understand incorrectly; misinterpret. □□ **misunderstanding** n.

**misuse** ● v. use wrongly; ill treat. ● n. wrong or improper use.

**Mitchell** n. (in full **Mitchell grass**) Aust. hardy tussock-forming perennial grass valued as fodder.

**mite** n. **1** small spider-like animal. **2** small creature esp. child. **3** small amount.

**mitigate** v. make less intense or severe. □□ **mitigation** n.

**mitre** n. **1** bishop's or abbot's tall deeply-cleft headdress. **2** joint of two pieces of wood at angle of 90°, such that line of junction bisects this angle. ● v. join this way.

**mitt** n. mitten; baseball glove.

**mitten** n. glove with no partitions between fingers.

**mix** ● v. **1** combine (different things) or be combined; blend; prepare by doing this. **2** be compatible; be sociable. ● n. mixture; proportion of materials in mixture. □ **mix up** mix thoroughly; confuse. □□ **mixer** n.

**mixed** adj. of diverse qualities or elements; containing persons from various backgrounds, of both sexes, etc. □ **mixed-up** colloq. confused; not well adjusted emotionally.

**mixture** n. process or result of mixing; combination of ingredients, qualities, etc.

**mizzenmast** n. mast that is next aft of mainmast.

**ml** abbr. **1** millilitre(s). **2** mile(s).

**MLA** abbr. Member of the Legislative Assembly.

**MLC** abbr. Member of the Legislative Council.

**mm** *abbr.* millimetre(s).

**MMS** *abbr.* Multimedia Messaging Service, system that enables mobile phones to receive audio and video, as well as text messages.

**mnemonic** *adj. & n.* (verse etc.) aiding memory.

**moan** ● *n.* 1 low murmur expressing physical or mental suffering or pleasure. 2 *colloq.* complaint; grievance. ● *v.* 1 make moan or moans. 2 *colloq.* complain, grumble. □□ **moaner** *n.*

**moat** *n.* defensive ditch around castle etc., usu. filled with water.

**mob** ● *n.* 1 large disorderly crowd; *colloq.* a group. 2 friends one usu. associates with. 3 *Aust.* flock (of sheep etc.) ● *v.* (**mobbed**) crowd around to attack or admire.

**mobile** ● *adj.* 1 movable; able to move easily. 2 of mobile phones, handheld computers, and similar technology. ● *n.* 1 decoration that may be hung so as to turn freely. 2 mobile phone.□ **mobile phone** portable phone without physical connection to network.
□□ **mobility** *n.*

**mobilise** *v.* (also **-ize**) make or become ready for (esp. military) service or action.□□ **mobilisation** *n.*

**moccasin** *n.* soft flat-soled leather shoe.

**mocha** *n.* kind of coffee.

**mock** ● *v.* ridicule, scoff (at); treat with scorn or contempt; mimic contemptuously. ● *adj.* sham, imitation.□ **mock-up** model for testing or study.□□ **mockingly** *adv.*

**mockery** *n.* derision, ridicule; counterfeit or absurdly inadequate representation; travesty.

**mod cons** *n.pl. colloq.* modern conveniences.

**mode** *n.* 1 way in which thing is done; prevailing fashion or custom. 2 *Mus.* any of several types of scale. 3 value

that occurs most frequently in given set of data.

**model** ● *n.* 1 representation in three dimensions of person or thing or of proposed structure, esp. on smaller scale; pattern. 2 simplified description of system or process, to assist calculations and predictions. 3 exemplary person or thing. 4 person employed to pose for artist or display clothes by wearing them. ● *adj.* exemplary; ideally perfect.
● *v.* (**modelled**) 1 make model of; fashion or shape in clay, wax, etc. 2 work as artist's or fashion model; display (clothes) in this way.

**modem** *n.* device for sending and receiving computer data by means of telephone line.

**moderate** ● *adj.* medium; not extreme or excessive. ● *n.* person of moderate views. ● *v.* 1 make or become less violent, intense, rigorous, etc. 2 act as moderator of or to. □□ **moderately** *adv.*

**moderation** *n.* moderating; avoidance of extremes.□ **in moderation** in moderate amounts.

**moderator** *n.* 1 arbitrator, mediator. 2 presiding officer. 3 Presbyterian or Uniting Church minister presiding over ecclesiastical body.

**modern** *adj.* of present and recent times; in current fashion.
□□ **modernity** *n.*

**modernise** *v.* (also **-ize**) make modern; adapt to modern needs or habits.□□ **modernisation** *n.*

**modernism** *n.* modern ideas or methods, esp. in art. □□ **modernist** *n. & adj.*

**modest** *adj.* 1 having humble estimate of one's own merits; not vain; not ostentatious. 2 small, moderate in size, amount, etc. 3 avoiding indecency.□□ **modestly** *adv.* **modesty** *n.*

**modicum** *n.* small quantity.

**modify** v. **1** make partial changes. **2** make less severe.
□□ **modification** n.

**modish** adj. fashionable.
□□ **modishly** adv.

**modulate** v. regulate; adjust; moderate; vary in tone or pitch.
□□ **modulation** n.

**module** n. **1** standardised part or independent unit forming part of complex structure. **2** unit or period of training or education.
□□ **modular** adj.

**modus operandi** n. (pl. **modi operandi**) method of working.

**modus vivendi** n. (pl. **modi vivendi**) way of living or coping; compromise between people agreeing to differ.

**mogul** n. colloq. important or influential person.

**mohair** n. hair of angora goat; yarn or fabric from this.

**moiety** n. half; each of two parts of thing; Anthropology division of a people on basis of lineal descent.

**moist** adj. slightly wet; damp.

**moisten** v. make or become moist.

**moisture** n. water or other liquid diffused as vapour or within solid, or condensed on surface.

**moisturise** v. (also **-ize**) make less dry (esp. the skin by use of cosmetic).
□□ **moisturiser** n.

**mojo** n. **1** magic charm or spell. **2** influence, power.

**molar** ● adj. (usu. of mammal's back teeth) serving to grind. ● n. molar tooth.

**molasses** n.pl. syrup extracted from raw sugar.

**mole** n. **1** small burrowing mammal with dark velvety fur and very small eyes. **2** colloq. spy established in position of trust in organisation. **3** small permanent dark spot on skin. **4** pier or breakwater.

**molecule** n. group of atoms forming smallest fundamental unit of chemical compound.
□□ **molecular** adj.

**molest** v. **1** assault or abuse (person) sexually. **2** dated annoy or pester (person).□□ **molestation** n. **molester** n.

**mollify** v. soften, appease.
□□ **mollification** n.

**mollusc** n. invertebrate with soft body and usu. hard shell, e.g. snail, oyster.

**mollycoddle** v. pamper.

**molly-dook** n. Aust. colloq. left-handed person.

**Molotov cocktail** n. improvised bomb; bottle filled with flammable liquid.

**molten** adj. melted, esp. made liquid by heat.

**molto** adv. Mus. very.

**molybdenum** n. silver-white metallic element added to steel to give strength and resistance to corrosion (symbol **Mo**).

**moment** n. **1** very brief portion of time; exact point of time. **2** importance.

**momentary** adj. lasting only a moment; transitory.□□ **momentarily** adv.

**momentous** adj. very important.

**momentum** n. impetus gained by movement or initial effort.

**Mon.** abbr. Monday.

**monarch** n. sovereign with title of king, queen, emperor, empress, etc.
□□ **monarchic** adj. **monarchical** adj.

**monarchist** n. advocate of monarchy.

**monarchy** n. government headed by monarch; nation with this.

**monastery** n. residence of community of monks.

**monastic** adj. of or like monasteries or monks, nuns, etc.□□ **monastically** adv. **monasticism** n.

**Monday** n. day of week following Sunday.

**monetarist** n. person who advocates control of money supply to curb inflation.□□ **monetarism** n.

**monetary** adj. of currency in use; of or consisting of money.

**money** n. 1 current coins and banknotes. 2 (pl. **moneys**) any form of currency. 3 wealth.

**moneyed** adj. rich.

**mongoose** n. (pl. **mongooses**) small flesh-eating civet-like mammal.

**mongrel** ● n. 1 dog of no definable type or breed; any animal or plant resulting from crossing of different breeds or types. 2 colloq. derog. despicable person or exasperating thing. 3 colloq. fighting spirit, 'guts'. ● adj. 1 of mixed origin or character. 2 colloq. derog. (of a person) worthless, contemptible.

**moniker** n. colloq. nickname.

**monitor** ● n. 1 person or device for observing or testing operation of something. 2 school pupil with special duties. 3 VDU, computer screen. 4 large lizard. ● v. keep watch over; record and report or control.

**monk** n. member of religious community of men living under vows. □□ **monkish** adj.

**monkey** n. (pl. **monkeys**) 1 any of various primates, e.g. marmosets, baboons. 2 mischievous person.
● v. (**monkeyed, monkeying**) tamper mischievously.

**mono** adj. colloq. monophonic.

**mono-** comb. form (usu. **mon-** before vowel) one, alone, single.

**monochrome** n. photograph or picture done in one colour, or in black and white only. ● adj. having or using one colour or black and white only.

**monocle** n. single eyeglass. □□ **monocled** adj.

**monocular** adj. with or for one eye.

**monoculture** n. cultivation of only one crop in area.

**monogamy** n. practice or state of being married to one person at a time.□□ **monogamous** adj.

**monogram** n. two or more letters, esp. initials, interwoven. □□ **monogrammed** adj.

**monograph** n. treatise on single subject.

**monolith** n. 1 single block of stone, esp. shaped into pillar etc. 2 person or thing like monolith in being massive, immovable, or solidly uniform. □□ **monolithic** adj.

**monologue** n. scene in drama in which person speaks alone; long speech by one person in conversation etc.

**monomania** n. obsession by single idea or interest.□□ **monomaniac** n. & adj.

**monophonic** adj. (of sound-reproduction) using only one channel of transmission.

**monopolise** v. (also **-ize**) 1 obtain exclusive possession or control of (trade etc.) 2 dominate (conversation etc.) □□ **monopolisation** n.

**monopoly** n. exclusive possession or control of trade in commodity or service; sole possession or control.

**monorail** n. railway with single-rail track.

**monosodium glutamate** n. sodium salt of glutamic acid used to enhance flavour of food.

**monosyllable** n. word of one syllable.□□ **monosyllabic** adj.

**monotheism** n. doctrine that there is only one god.□□ **monotheist** n. **monotheistic** adj.

**monotone** n. sound continuing or repeated on one note or without change of pitch.

**monotonous** adj. lacking in variety; tedious through sameness. □□ **monotonously** adv. **monotony** n.

**monotreme** n. mammal (e.g. platypus, echidna) found only in

Australia and New Guinea, that lays eggs through common opening for urine, faeces, etc.

**monoxide** n. oxide containing one oxygen atom.

**Monsieur** n. (pl. **Messieurs**) title of a French-speaking man.

**monsoon** n. wind in S. Asia, esp. in Indian Ocean; rainy season accompanying summer monsoon.

**monster** n. imaginary creature, usu. large and frightening; inhumanly wicked person; something very large; something abnormal in shape.

**monstrosity** n. huge or outrageous thing.

**monstrous** adj. like a monster; abnormally formed; huge; outrageously wrong; atrocious. □□ **monstrously** adv.

**montage** n. making of composite picture from pieces of others; composite whole made from juxtaposed photographs etc.

**monte** n. Aust. colloq. certainty.

**month** n. (in full **calendar month**) each of 12 divisions of year; period of time between same dates in successive calendar months; period of 28 days.

**monthly** ● adj. done, produced, or occurring once every month. ● adv. every month. ● n. monthly periodical.

**monument** n. anything enduring that serves to commemorate, esp. structure, building, or memorial stone.

**monumental** adj. extremely great; stupendous; massive and permanent; of or serving as monument.

**moo** ● n. cow's deep low cry. ● v. make this sound.

**mooch** v. colloq. 1 wander aimlessly around. 2 cadge.

**mood** n. 1 temporary state of mind or feeling. 2 fit of bad temper or depression.

**moody** adj. (**moodier**) given to changes of mood; sulky, gloomy.

**mook-mook** n. (also **muk-muk**) Aust. kind of owl.

**moon** ● n. natural satellite of the earth, orbiting it monthly, illuminated by and reflecting sun; satellite of any planet. ● v. behave dreamily or listlessly. □□ **moonless** adj.

**moonshine** n. colloq. 1 foolish talk or ideas. 2 illicitly distilled alcoholic liquor.

**Moor** n. member of Muslim people of NW Africa.

**moor**[1] n. Brit. open uncultivated land with low shrubs.

**moor**[2] v. attach (boat etc.) to fixed object; attach or fix securely.

**moorhen** n. small waterbird.

**moorings** n. cables or place for mooring boat.

**moose** n. 1 N. American deer. 2 elk.

**moot point** n. debatable or undecided issue.

**mop** ● n. bundle of yarn or cloth or a sponge on end of stick for cleaning floors etc.; thick mass of hair. ● v. (**mopped**) wipe or clean (as) with mop.

**mope** v. feel dejected and apathetic. □□ **mopy** adj.

**mopoke** n. 1 = BOOBOOK. 2 = FROGMOUTH.

**moraine** n. area of debris carried down and deposited by glacier.

**moral** ● adj. 1 concerned with goodness or badness of human character or behaviour, or with difference between right and wrong. 2 virtuous in conduct. ● n. moral lesson or principle; (**morals**) person's moral habits. □ **moral hazard** lack of incentive to guard against risk when one is protected from its consequences. **moral support** encouragement. **moral victory** a triumph although without concrete gain. □□ **morally** adv.

**morale** n. state of person's or group's spirits and confidence.

**moralise** v. (also **-ize**) indulge in moral reflection or talk. □□ **moralisation** n.

**moralist** n. person who practises or teaches morality. □□ **moralistic** adj.

**morality** n. degree of conformity to moral principles; moral conduct; science of morals; system of morals.

**morass** n. 1 entanglement. 2 literary boggy area.

**moratorium** n. (pl. **moratoriums** or **moratoria**) temporary prohibition or suspension of (activity, penalty, etc.).

**morbid** adj. 1 given to preoccupation with unwholesome or gloomy things. 2 of or indicative of disease. □□ **morbidity** n. **morbidly** adv.

**morbillivirus** n. any of group of viruses causing diseases such as measles and canine distemper.

**mordant** ● adj. (of sarcasm etc.) caustic, biting. ● n. substance that fixes dye.

**more** ● adj. greater in quantity, or intensity etc. ● n. & pron. greater amount or number. ● adv. to a greater extent; again. □ **more or less** approximately.

**moreish** n. (also **morish**) colloq. so tasty you want more.

**moreover** adv. besides, in addition to.

**mores** n.pl. customs or conventions.

**morgue** n. room or building in which dead bodies are kept until burial or cremation.

**moribund** adj. 1 at point of death. 2 lacking vitality.

**Mormon** n. member of Church of Jesus Christ of Latter-Day Saints. □□ **Mormonism** n.

**mornay** n. cheese-flavoured white sauce.

**morning** n. early part of day till noon or lunchtime. □ **morning sickness** nausea felt in early pregnancy.

**moron** n. colloq. derog. very stupid person. □□ **moronic** adj.

**morose** adj. sullen, gloomy. □□ **morosely** adv. **moroseness** n.

**morph** v. change smoothly and gradually from one image to another.

**morpheme** n. meaningful unit of language that cannot be further divided.

**morphine** n. narcotic drug from opium.

**morphology** n. study of forms of things, esp. of animals and plants and of words and their structure. □□ **morphological** adj.

**morse** n. (in full **morse code**) code in which letters are represented by combinations of long and short light or sound signals.

**morsel** n. small amount; small piece of food.

**mortal** ● adj. 1 subject to or causing death; (of combat) fought to the death. 2 (of enemy) implacable. ● n. human being. □□ **mortally** adv.

**mortality** n. being subject to death; loss of life on large scale; (in full **mortality rate**) death rate.

**mortar** n. 1 mixture of lime or cement, sand, and water, for bonding bricks or stones. 2 short cannon for firing shells at high angles. 3 vessel in which ingredients are pounded with pestle.

**mortarboard** n. stiff square cap worn as part of academic dress.

**mortgage** ● n. loan for purchase of property, in which the property itself is pledged as security; agreement effecting this. ● v. pledge (property) as security in this way.

**mortgagee** n. creditor in mortgage.

**mortgagor** n. (also **mortgager**) debtor in mortgage.

**mortify** v. 1 humiliate, wound (person's feelings). 2 bring (body etc.) into subjection by self-discipline.

**3** (of flesh) become gangrenous. □□ **mortification** n. **mortifying** adj.

**mortise** (also **mortice**) ● n. hole in framework to receive end of another part. ● v. join securely, esp. by mortise and tenon; cut mortise in.

**mortuary** ● n. morgue. ● adj. of death or burial.

**morwong** n. Aust. marine food fish.

**mosaic** n. **1** picture or pattern made with small variously coloured pieces of glass, stone etc. **2** diversified thing. **3** viral disease causing leaf-mottling in plants.

**moscovium** n. chemical element (symbol Mc).

**moselle** n. kind of light medium dry white wine.

**Moslem** = MUSLIM.

**mosque** n. Muslim place of worship.

**mosquito** n. (pl. **mosquitoes**) biting insect, esp. with long proboscis to suck blood.

**moss** n. small flowerless plant growing in dense clumps in moist places.

**mossie** n. = MOZZIE.

**most** ● adj. & pron. existing in the greatest quantity or degree; the majority. ● n. greatest amount or number. ● adv. to greatest extent; very.

**mostly** adv. mainly; usually.

**mote** n. speck of dust.

**motel** n. roadside hotel for motorists etc.

**moth** n. nocturnal insect like butterfly; similar insect breeding in cloth etc., on which its larva feeds.

**mothball** n. small ball of naphthalene etc. for keeping moths away from clothes.

**mother** ● n. **1** female parent. **2** origin of something. **3** main ship etc. in fleet or mission. **4** (in full **Mother Superior**) head of female religious community. ● v. treat as mother does. □ **mother-in-law**

(pl. **mothers-in-law**) mother of one's wife or husband. **mother-of-pearl** smooth iridescent substance forming inner layer of shell of some molluscs. **mother tongue** one's native language. □□ **motherhood** n. **motherly** adj.

**motherboard** n. printed circuit board containing principal components of computer etc.

**motherland** n. one's native country.

**motif** n. **1** theme repeated and developed in artistic etc. work. **2** decorative design or pattern.

**motion** ● n. **1** moving; movement; changing position. **2** formal proposal put to committee etc. **3** application to court for order. **4** evacuation of bowels. ● v. direct (person) by gesture. □□ **motionless** adj.

**motivate** v. **1** supply motive to; be motive of. **2** cause (person) to act in particular way. **3** stimulate the interest of, inspire. □□ **motivation** n.

**motive** ● n. what induces person to act. ● adj. producing movement; causing or being the reason for something.

**mot juste** n. (pl. **mots justes**) the most appropriate word.

**motley** ● adj. **1** diversified in colour. **2** of varied character. ● n. hist. jester's particoloured costume.

**motocross** n. cross-country racing on motorcycles.

**motor** ● n. thing that imparts motion; machine (esp. using electricity or internal combustion) supplying motive power for vehicle or other machine. ● adj. giving, imparting, or producing motion; driven by motor; of or for motor vehicles. □ v. go or convey by motor vehicle. □ **motor neurone** nerve cell forming part of a pathway along which impulses pass from brain or spinal cord to a muscle or gland.

**motorbike** n. a motorcycle.

**motorcade** n. procession of motor vehicles.

**motorcycle** n. two-wheeled motor-driven vehicle.

**motorise** v. (also **-ize**) equip with motor transport; provide with motor.

**motorist** n. driver of car.

**mottled** adj. patterned with irregular patches of colour.

**motto** n. (pl. **mottoes**) maxim adopted as rule of conduct; words accompanying coat of arms; appropriate inscription.

**motza** n. (also **motser** or **motzer**) Aust. colloq. **1** large sum of money. **2** certainty.

**mould** (also **mold**) ● n. **1** hollow container into which substance is poured or pressed to harden into required shape; something made in this. **2** furry growth of tiny fungi on damp surface. **3** soft fine earth rich in organic matter. ● v. **1** shape (as) in mould; give shape to. **2** influence development of.

**moulder** v. decay, rot, crumble.

**moulding** n. ornamental strip of plaster etc. as architectural feature, esp. in cornice.

**mouldy** adj. (**mouldier**) **1** covered with mould; stale. **2** colloq. dull, miserable.

**moult** ● v. shed (feathers, hair, shell, etc.) in renewing plumage, coat, etc. ● n. moulting.

**mound** n. raised mass of earth, stones, etc.; heap, pile; hillock. ● v. heap up in mound(s).

**mount** ● v. **1** ascend; climb on to; get up on (horse etc.); (as **mounted** adj.) serving on horseback. **2** increase, accumulate. **3** (of male animal) get on to (female) to copulate. **4** set in frame etc., esp. for viewing. **5** organise, arrange (exhibition, attack, etc.) ● n. **1** backing etc. on which picture etc. is set for display. **2** horse for

riding. **3** setting for gem etc. **4** mountain or hill.

**mountain** n. large abrupt elevation of ground; large heap or pile; huge quantity.

**mountaineer** ● n. person who climbs mountains. ● v. climb mountains as sport.
□□ **mountaineering** n.

**mountainous** adj. **1** having many mountains. **2** huge.

**mountebank** n. swindler; charlatan.

**mourn** v. feel or show sorrow or regret; grieve for loss of (dead person etc.) □□ **mourner** n.

**mournful** adj. doleful, sad, sorrowing. □□ **mournfully** adv.

**mourning** n. expressing of sorrow for dead, esp. by wearing black clothes; such clothes.

**mouse** n. (pl. **mice**) **1** small rodent with a long tail. **2** timid or shy person. **3** (pl. also **mouses**) small hand-held device controlling cursor on computer screen.

**moussaka** n. (also **mousaka**) Greek dish of minced meat and eggplant.

**mousse** n. **1** frothy, creamy dish. **2** foamy preparation used as aid to hair styling.

**moustache** n. hair on upper lip.

**mousy** adj. **1** of or like mouse; dark grey. **2** shy and timid.

**mouth** ● n. **1** opening in head for taking in food and emitting sound; cavity behind it containing teeth and vocal organs. **2** opening of container, cave, trumpet, etc. **3** place where river enters sea. **4** colloq. impudent talk, cheek. ● v. form (words) soundlessly with lips. □ **mouth organ** = HARMONICA.

**mouthpiece** n. part of instrument placed between or near lips; spokesperson.

**mouthwash** n. liquid for cleansing mouth.

**move** ● v. **1** change in place, position, or attitude; change one's residence. **2** provoke emotion in; take action. **3** put to meeting for discussion. ● n. act or process of moving; moving of a piece in chess etc.; calculated action. □□ **movable** adj.

**movement** n. **1** moving; a move; moving parts. **2** group with common cause. **3** section of long piece of music.

**movie** n. film for viewing in cinema or on DVD, television, etc.

**moving** adj. emotionally affecting.

**mow** v. (**mowed** or **mown**, **mowing**) cut down (grass or grain etc.); cut grass etc. from. □ **mow down** kill or destroy in great numbers. □□ **mower** n.

**mozz** n. Aust. (also **maz**) jinx, malign influence (put the mozz on him).

**mozzarella** n. soft Italian cheese.

**mozzie** n. (also **mossie**) Aust. colloq. mosquito.

**MP** abbr. Member of Parliament.

**mph** abbr. miles per hour.

**MP3** n. means of compressing sound sequence etc. into very small file, for downloading from Internet etc.

**Mr** n. (pl. **Messrs**) title prefixed to man's name.

**Mrs** n. (pl. **Mrs**) title prefixed to married woman's name.

**MS** abbr. **1** multiple sclerosis. **2** (pl. **MSS**) manuscript.

**Ms** n. title prefixed to woman's name.

**Mt** abbr. Mount.

**much** ● adj. existing in great quantity. ● pron. large amount, great quantity. ● adv. to a great extent.

**mucilage** n. **1** viscous substance obtained from plants. **2** adhesive substance.

**muck** n. **1** dirt, filth. **2** anything disgusting. **3** manure. □ **muck out** clean (stable). **muck up** colloq. **1** spoil, bungle. **2** Aust. misbehave. □□ **mucky** adj.

**mucous** adj. of or covered with mucus. □□ **mucosity** n.

**mucus** n. slimy substance coating inner surface of hollow organs of body.

**mud** n. soft wet earth. □□ **muddy** adj.

**muddle** ● v. bring into disorder; bewilder, confuse. ● n. disorder; confusion. □□ **muddler** n.

**muesli** n. breakfast food of crushed cereals, dried fruit, nuts, etc.

**muezzin** n. Muslim crier who proclaims hours of prayer.

**muff** ● n. covering, esp. of fur, for keeping hands or ears warm. ● v. colloq. bungle.

**muffin** n. **1** cup-shaped cake made from batter of egg, flour, etc. **2** small flat round yeast cake, eaten toasted and buttered.

**muffle** v. wrap for warmth or to deaden sound; make sound less loud or less distinct.

**muffler** n. **1** wrap or scarf worn for warmth. **2** thing used to deaden sound. **3** silencer of vehicle.

**mufti** n. **1** plain clothes worn by person who also wears uniform. **2** Muslim legal expert.

**mug** ● n. **1** drinking vessel, usu. cylindrical with handle; its contents. **2** colloq. gullible person. **3** colloq. the face. ● adj. colloq. stupid. ● v. (**mugged**) attack and rob (person), esp. in public. □□ **mugger** n. **mugging** n.

**mugga** n. Aust. medium-sized eucalypt with deeply-furrowed black bark.

**muggy** adj. (**muggier**) (of weather etc.) oppressively humid. □□ **mugginess** n.

**mulberry** n. **1** tree bearing edible purple or white berries; its fruit. **2** dark red, purple.

**mulch** ● n. layer of straw, leaves, compost, etc. spread around plant to insulate or enrich soil. ● v. treat with mulch.

**mule** n. 1 offspring of donkey and horse. 2 obstinate person. 3 *colloq.* courier for illegal drugs.□□ **mulish** adj.

**mulga** n. *Aust.* 1 wattle yielding distinctive brown and yellowish timber. 2 (**the mulga**) the outback; remote or sparsely populated country.

**mull**[1] v. heat (wine etc.) with sugar and spices, as a drink.□ **mull over** think over.

**mull**[2] *Aust. colloq.* ● n. chopped blend of marijuana. ● v. chop up (marijuana) for smoking.

**mullah** n. Muslim learned in Islamic theology and sacred law.

**mullet** n. 1 small edible sea fish. 2 haircut with hair short at top and front and long at back.

**mullion** n. vertical bar between panes in window.□□ **mullioned** adj.

**mullock** n. *Aust.* mining refuse; rubbish; nonsense.

**mulloway** n. *Aust.* large marine and estuarine food fish.

**mullygrub** n. *Aust.* grub, esp. witchetty grub.

**mullygrubber** n. (also **grubber**) *Aust. Cricket* ball bowled along ground.

**multi-** *comb. form* many.

**multicultural** adj. of, relating to, or consisting of several cultural or ethnic groups within a society. □□ **multiculturalism** n.

**multifarious** adj. many and various; of great variety.

**multilateral** adj. 1 (of agreement etc.) in which three or more parties participate. 2 having many sides. □□ **multilaterally** adv.

**multimedia** adj. using more than one medium of expression etc.; (of computer applications) incorporating audio and video.

**multinational** ● adj. operating in several countries; of several nationalities. ● n. multinational company.

**multiplatform** adj. compatible with or involving more than one type of computer or operating system.

**multiplayer** adj. denoting computer game etc. for or involving more than one player.

**multiple** ● adj. having several parts, elements, or components; many and various. ● n. quantity exactly divisible by another.

**multiplicand** n. quantity to be multiplied.

**multiplication** n. multiplying.

**multiplicity** n. 1 manifold variety. 2 great number.

**multiplier** n. quantity by which number is multiplied.

**multiply** v. add a number to itself a specified number of times; increase in number, esp. by procreation.

**multiracial** adj. of several races.

**multitasking** n. concurrent execution of a number of tasks or jobs.

**multitude** n. great number of things or people.□□ **multitudinous** adj.

**mum** *colloq.* ● n. mother. ● adj. silent (keep mum).

**mumble** ● v. speak or utter indistinctly. ● n. indistinct utterance.

**mumbo-jumbo** n. 1 meaningless ritual. 2 meaningless or unnecessarily complicated language. 3 nonsense.

**mummer** n. actor in traditional mime.

**mummify** v. preserve (body) as mummy.□□ **mummification** n.

**mummy** n. 1 *colloq.* mother. 2 dead body preserved by embalming, esp. in ancient Egypt.

**mumps** n. viral disease with painful swelling of neck and face.

**munch** v. chew steadily.

**mundane** adj. **1** dull, routine. **2** of this world.□□ **mundanely** adv.

**munga** n. (also **munger**) Aust. colloq. food.

**mung bean** n. edible seed of leguminous Indian plant.

**municipal** adj. of municipality or its self-government.

**municipality** n. town or district with local self-government; its governing body.

**munificent** adj. (of giver or gift) splendidly generous.□□ **munificence** n.

**munitions** n.pl. military weapons, ammunition, etc.

**muntries** n. Aust. edible fruit of prostrate kunzea.

**muon** n. unstable elementary particle.

**mural** ● n. painting executed directly on wall. ● adj. of or on a wall.

**murder** ● n. **1** intentional unlawful killing of human being by another. **2** colloq. unpleasant or dangerous state of affairs. ● v. **1** kill (human being) intentionally and unlawfully. **2** colloq. utterly defeat. **3** spoil by bad performance etc.□□ **murderer** n. **murderess** n.

**murderous** adj. involving or capable of murder.

**murky** adj. (**murkier**) dark, gloomy.

**murmur** ● n. **1** subdued continuous sound; softly spoken utterance. **2** subdued expression of discontent. ● v. make murmur; utter in low voice.

**murnong** n. (also **myrrnong**) milky coconut-flavoured tuber of Australian perennial herb.

**murrain** n. infectious disease of cattle.

**Murri** n. Aboriginal person, esp. one from Queensland.

**muscatel** n. **1** muscat wine or grape. **2** raisin from muscat grape.

**muscle** n. **1** fibrous tissue producing movement in or maintaining position of animal body; part of body composed of muscles. **2** strength, power.□ **muscle in** colloq. force oneself on others.

**muscular** adj. **1** of or affecting muscles; having well-developed muscles. **2** robust.□ **muscular dystrophy** progressive weakening and wasting of muscles.□□ **muscularity** n.

**muse** ● v. ponder, reflect. ● n. poet's source of inspiration.

**museum** n. building for storing and exhibiting objects of historical, scientific, or cultural interest.

**mush** ● n. **1** soft pulp. **2** feeble sentimentality. ● v. crush to make soft pulp.

**mushroom** ● n. **1** edible fungus with stem and domed cap. **2** pinkish-brown colour. **3** colloq. person deliberately kept ignorant of facts etc. ● v. **1** gather mushrooms. **2** develop rapidly. **3** spread out in mushroom shape.

**music** n. art of combining vocal or instrumental sounds in harmonious or expressive way; sounds so produced; musical composition; written or printed score of this; pleasant sound.

**musical** ● adj. of music; (of sounds etc.) melodious, harmonious; fond of or skilled in music; set to or accompanied by music. ● n. musical film or play.□□ **musicality** n. **musically** adv.

**musician** n. person skilled in practice of music.□□ **musicianship** n.

**musicology** n. study of history and forms of music.□□ **musicological** adj. **musicologist** n.

**musk** n. substance secreted by male musk deer and used in perfumes.□□ **musky** adj. **muskiness** n.

**musket** n. hist. infantryman's (esp. smooth-bored) light gun.

**Muslim** ● n. follower of Islamic religion. ● adj. of Muslims or their religion.

**muslin** n. fine delicately woven cotton fabric.

**muss** v. colloq. disarrange, dishevel.

**mussel** n. edible bivalve mollusc.

**must**[1] ● v.aux. used to express necessity or obligation, certainty, or insistence. ● n. colloq. something that must be done or visited etc.

> **Usage** The negative I must not go means 'I am not allowed to go'. To express a lack of obligation, use I need not go, or I don't have to go.

**must**[2] n. grape juice before fermentation is complete.

**mustang** n. small wild horse of Mexico and California.

**mustard** n. **1** plant with yellow flowers; seeds of this crushed into paste and used as spicy condiment. **2** brownish-yellow colour.

**muster** ● v. **1** collect (orig. soldiers) for inspection. **2** come together. **3** summon (courage etc.) **4** Aust. gather (livestock) for branding, counting, etc. ● n. assembly of people etc. for inspection. □□ **mustering** n.

**musty** adj. (**mustier**) smelling mouldy; stale. □□ **mustiness** n.

**mutable** adj. liable to change. □□ **mutability** n.

**mutagen** n. something causing genetic mutation.

**mutant** ● adj. resulting from mutation. ● n. mutant organism or gene.

**mutate** v. (cause to) undergo mutation.

**mutation** n. change; genetic change that when transmitted to offspring gives rise to heritable variations.

**mute** ● adj. silent, refraining from or temporarily bereft of speech; dated offens. (of a person) lacking faculty of speech. ● n. **1** dated offens. person who is unable to speak. **2** device for damping sound of musical instrument. ● v. deaden or muffle sound of. □□ **mutely** adv.

**mutilate** v. injure or disfigure by cutting off a part or by some other act of destruction. □□ **mutilation** n.

**mutineer** n. person who mutinies.

**mutinous** adj. rebellious.

**mutiny** ● n. open revolt, esp. by soldiers or sailors against officers. ● v. engage in mutiny.

**mutt** n. colloq. **1** dog. **2** derog. stupid person.

**mutter** ● v. speak in barely audible manner; grumble. ● n. muttered words etc.; muttering.

**mutton** n. flesh of (esp. older) sheep as food.

**muttonbird** n. Aust. brownish-black petrel.

**mutual** adj. (of feelings, actions, etc.) experienced or done by each of two or more parties to the other(s); common to two or more people; having same (specified) relationship to each other. □□ **mutuality** n. mutually adv.

**muzak** n. propr. recorded music played in public places.

**muzzle** ● n. **1** projecting part of animal's face, including nose and mouth; guard put over animal's nose and mouth. **2** open end of firearm. ● v. **1** put muzzle on. **2** impose silence on.

**my** adj. of or belonging to me.

**myalgia** n. muscular pain. □□ **myalgic** adj.

**myall**[1] Aust. ● n. Aboriginal person living in traditional manner. ● adj. **1** (of Aboriginal people) living in traditional manner. **2** (of animal etc.) wild.

**myall²** *n. Aust.* wattle with silvery foliage.

**mycelium** *n.* microscopic threadlike parts of fungus.

**mycology** *n.* study of fungi; fungi of particular region.

**myelin** *n.* substance forming protective sheath around nerve fibres.

**mynah** *n.* (also **myna**) bird of starling family that can mimic sounds.

**myopia** *n.* **1** short-sightedness. **2** lack of imagination.□□ **myopic** *adj.*

**myriad** *literary* ● *n.* indefinitely great number. ● *adj.* innumerable.

**myrrh** *n.* gum resin used in perfume, medicine, incense, etc.

**myrtle** *n.* evergreen European shrub with shiny leaves and white scented flowers; any of various shrubs and trees resembling myrtle.

**myself** *pron.* emphatic and reflexive form of I² and ME.

**mysterious** *adj.* full of or wrapped in mystery.□□ **mysteriously** *adv.*

**mystery** *n.* matter that remains unexplained; quality of being unexplained or obscure; story dealing with puzzling crime.

**mystic** ● *adj.* mysterious and awe-inspiring; having symbolic spiritual meaning. ● *n.* person who seeks unity with deity through contemplation etc., or who believes in spiritual apprehension of truths beyond understanding.□□ **mysticism** *n.*

**mystical** *adj.* of mystics or mysticism; of hidden meaning; spiritually symbolic.□□ **mystically** *adv.*

**mystify** *v.* bewilder, confuse.□□ **mystification** *n.*

**mystique** *n.* atmosphere of mystery and veneration attending some activity, person, profession, etc.

**myth** *n.* **1** traditional story usu. involving supernatural or imaginary persons and embodying popular ideas on natural or social phenomena. **2** widely held but false idea. **3** fictitious person, thing, or idea.□□ **mythical** *adj.* **mythically** *adv.*

**mythology** *n.* body or study of myths.□□ **mythological** *adj.* **mythologise** *v.*

**myxomatosis** *n.* infectious and usu. fatal viral disease of rabbits.

# Nn

**N** *abbr.* **1** north, northern. **2** newton(s). **3** *Chess* knight.

**n/a** *abbr.* (also **n.a.**) **1** not applicable. **2** not available.

**naan** *abbr.* (also **nan**) flat leavened Indian bread.

**nab** *v.* (**nabbed**) *colloq.* arrest; catch in wrongdoing; seize.

**nabarlek** *n.* small wallaby of Western Australia and Arnhem Land.

**nacre** *n.* mother-of-pearl from any shelled mollusc.□□ **nacreous** *adj.*

**nadir** *n.* **1** lowest point. **2** time of despair.

**naevus** *n.* (*pl.* **naevi**) raised red birthmark.

**nag** ● *v.* (**nagged**) persistently criticise or scold; find fault or urge, esp. persistently; (of pain etc.) be persistent. ● *n.* *colloq.* horse.

**nail** ● *n.* **1** small metal spike hammered in to fasten things. **2** horny covering on upper surface of tip of human finger or toe. ● *v.* **1** fasten with nail(s). **2** *colloq.* catch, arrest. **3** *colloq.* perform (task or action) perfectly.

**naive** *adj.* showing lack of experience or judgement.□□ **naively** *adv.* **naivety** *n.*

**naked** *adj.* **1** unclothed, nude; without usual covering. **2** undisguised. **3** (of light, flame, sword, etc.) unprotected. **4** defenceless.□ **naked eye** unassisted vision, e.g. without telescope or microscope.□□ **nakedly** *adv.* **nakedness** *n.*

**naltrexone** *n.* synthetic drug, similar to morphine, used in treatment of heroin addiction.

**namby-pamby** *adj.* **1** insipidly pretty or sentimental. **2** weak.

**name** ● *n.* **1** word by which individual person, animal, place, or thing is spoken of. **2** (usu. abusive) term used of person. **3** word denoting object or class of objects. **4** reputation, esp. good. ● *v.* **1** give name to. **2** state name of. **3** mention. **4** specify. **5** cite.

**namely** *adv.* that is to say; in other words.

**namesake** *n.* person or thing with the same name as another.

**nan** *n.* (also **nana, nanna**) *colloq.* grandmother.

**nanny** *n.* **1** child's nurse. **2** *colloq.* grandmother. **3** (in full **nanny goat**) female goat.□ **nanny state** government regarded as overprotective or as interfering unduly with personal choice.

**nannygai** *n.* *Aust.* short-bodied, reddish, marine food fish.

**nano-** *comb. form* one thousand-millionth.

**nanosecond** *n.* **1** one thousand-millionth of a second. **2** *colloq.* very short time; moment.

**nanotechnology** *n.* branch of technology that deals with extremely small dimensions.

**nap** ● *n.* **1** short sleep, esp. during the day. **2** short raised fibres on surface of cloth or leather. ● *v.* (**napped**) have a short sleep.

**napalm** *n.* thick jellied hydrocarbon mixture used in bombs.

**nape** *n.* back of the neck.

**naphtha** *n.* a flammable oil.

**naphthalene** *n.* white crystalline substance produced by distilling tar.

**napkin** *n.* **1** piece of linen etc. for wiping lips, fingers, etc. at table. **2** baby's nappy.

**nappy** *n.* piece of towelling etc. wrapped around baby to absorb or retain urine and faeces.

**narcissism** *n.* excessive or erotic interest in oneself. □□ **narcissistic** *adj.*

**narcissus** *n.* (*pl.* **narcissi**) flower of group including daffodil.

**narcosis** *n.* state of drowsiness.

**narcotic** ● *adj.* **1** (of substance) inducing drowsiness etc. **2** (of drug) affecting the mind. ● *n.* narcotic substance or drug.

**nardoo** *n. Aust.* clover-like perennial fern, the pea-sized spores of which may be ground and used as food.

**narrate** *v.* give continuous story or account of; provide spoken accompaniment for (film etc.) □□ **narration** *n.* **narrator** *n.*

**narrative** ● *n.* ordered account of connected events; story. ● *adj.* of or by narration.

**narrow** ● *adj.* **1** small across, not wide. **2** with little margin or scope. ● *n.* (**narrows**) narrow part of strait, river, etc. ● *v.* become or make narrower. □ **narrow-minded** intolerant. □□ **narrowly** *adv.* **narrowness** *n.*

**nasal** *adj.* of the nose; sounding as if breath came out through nose.

**nascent** *adj.* just coming into existence. □□ **nascency** *n.*

**nashi** *n.* type of apple-like Japanese pear.

**nasturtium** *n.* trailing plant with edible leaves and bright orange, yellow, or red flowers.

**nasty** *adj.* unpleasant; unkind; difficult. □□ **nastily** *adv.* **nastiness** *n.*

**natal** *adj.* of or from one's birth.

**nation** *n.* community of people having mainly common descent, history, language, etc. or forming sovereign state or inhabiting territory.

**national** ● *adj.* of nation; characteristic of particular nation. ● *n.* citizen of specified country. □ **national anthem** song adopted by a nation, intended to inspire patriotism. **national park** area of natural significance set aside for conservation and recreational purposes, and protected by law. □□ **nationally** *adv.*

**nationalise** *v.* (also **-ize**) take (industry etc.) into government ownership; make national. □□ **nationalisation** *n.*

**nationalism** *n.* **1** patriotic feeling, principles, etc. **2** policy of national independence. □□ **nationalist** *n.* **nationalistic** *adj.*

**nationality** *n.* **1** membership of nation; being national. **2** ethnic group within one or more political nations.

**native** ● *n.* **1** person born in specified place; local inhabitant. **2** indigenous animal or plant. ● *adj.* **1** inherent; innate. **2** of one's birth. **3** belonging to specified place. **4** of the indigenous people of a place. □ **native title** *Aust.* right of indigenous people to own their traditional land.

**nativity** *n.* **1** (esp. **the Nativity**) Christ's birth. **2** birth.

**NATO** *abbr.* North Atlantic Treaty Organisation.

**natter** *colloq.* ● *v.* chatter idly. ● *n.* aimless chatter.

**natural** ● *adj.* **1** existing in or caused by nature; not artificial. **2** spontaneous. **3** not surprising; to be expected. **4** unaffected. **5** innate. **6** physically existing. **7** *Mus.* not flat or sharp. ● *n.* **1** *colloq.* adept, person, or thing naturally suitable, adept, etc. **2** *Mus.* sign showing return to natural pitch, natural note. □ **natural history** study of animal and plant life.

**naturalise** *v.* (also **-ize**) **1** admit (foreigner) to citizenship. **2** introduce (animal, plant, etc.) into another region. **3** adopt (foreign word, custom, etc.) □□ **naturalisation** n.

**naturalism** n. realistic representation in art and literature. □□ **naturalistic** adj.

**naturalist** n. student of natural history.

**naturally** adv. **1** in natural way. **2** as might be expected. **3** of course.

**nature** n. **1** physical power producing all phenomena of material world; these phenomena, including plants, animals, landscape, etc. **2** thing's or person's essential qualities or character. **3** kind, class. **4** heredity as influencing or determining character. □ **nature strip** Aust. strip of land between front boundary of property and road; cultivated median strip between two traffic lanes.

**naturist** n. nudist.

**naturopathy** n. treatment of illness etc. without drugs, usu. involving diet, exercise, massage, etc. □□ **naturopath** n.

**naught** ● n. nothing. ● adj. worthless.

**naughty** adj. (**naughtier**) **1** disobedient; badly behaved. **2** slightly indecent. □□ **naughtily** adv. **naughtiness** n.

**nausea** n. **1** inclination to vomit. **2** revulsion.

**nauseate** v. affect with nausea. □□ **nauseating** adj.

**nauseous** adj. **1** causing or inclined to vomit. **2** disgusting.

**nautical** adj. of sailors or navigation. □ **nautical mile** unit of 1852 metres.

**nautilus** n. (pl. **nautiluses** or **nautili**) kind of mollusc with spiral shell.

**naval** adj. of navy; of ships.

**nave** n. central part of church excluding chancel and side aisles.

**navel** n. depression in belly marking site of attachment of umbilical cord; central point of place.

**navigable** adj. (of river etc.) suitable for ships; (of boat) able to be steered and sailed. □□ **navigability** n.

**navigate** v. direct course of (ship, vehicle, etc.); sail in or through (sea, river, etc.) □□ **navigation** n. **navigator** n.

**navvy** n. labourer employed in building roads etc.

**navy** n. **1** branch of armed services of a state that conducts military operations at sea; ships of navy. **2** (in full **navy blue**) dark blue colour.

**Nazi** n. **1** hist. member of National Socialist German Workers' Party. **2** derog. person with extreme racist or authoritarian views; person who seeks to impose their views on others in a very autocratic or inflexible way.

**NB** abbr. (Latin nota bene) note well.

**NBN** abbr. Aust. National Broadband Network.

**NCO** abbr. non-commissioned officer.

**NE** abbr. north-east(ern).

**neap** n. (in full **neap tide**) tide with smallest rise and fall.

**near** ● adv. at, to, or within short distance or interval; nearly. ● prep. near to. ● adj. **1** with only short distance or interval between; closely related; with little margin. **2** of side of vehicle that is normally nearest kerb. ● v. draw near. □ **near-sighted** short-sighted. □□ **nearness** n.

**nearby** ● adj. near in position. ● adv. close.

**nearly** adv. almost; closely.

**neat** adj. **1** tidy, methodical. **2** elegantly simple. **3** brief and clear. **4** cleverly done. **5** undiluted. **6** colloq. good, pleasing. □□ **neaten** v. **neatly** adv. **neatness** n.

**nebula** n. (pl. **nebulae**) cloud of gas and dust in space. □□ **nebular** adj.

**nebulous** adj. cloudlike; indistinct, vague.

**necessarily** adv. as necessary result, inevitably.

**necessary** ● adj. essential in order to achieve something; happening or existing by necessity.
● n. (necessaries) essential items.

**necessitate** v. make necessary (esp. result).

**necessitous** adj. poor, needy.

**necessity** n. **1** indispensable thing. **2** pressure of circumstances. **3** imperative need. **4** poverty. **5** constraint or compulsion seen as natural law governing human action.

**neck** ● n. **1** part of body connecting head to shoulders; part of garment around neck. **2** narrow part of anything; length of horse's head and neck as measure of its lead in race. ● v. colloq. kiss and caress amorously. □ neck and neck running level in race etc.

**necklace** n. piece of jewellery worn around neck.

**necromancy** n. divination by communication with the dead; magic. □□ **necromancer** n.

**necropolis** n. cemetery.

**necrosis** n. death of tissue. □□ **necrotic** adj.

**nectar** n. **1** sugary substance produced by plants and made into honey by bees. **2** Mythol. drink of gods.

**nectarine** n. smooth-skinned variety of peach.

**née** adj. born (used in stating married woman's maiden name).

**need** ● v. **1** require (something) as essential, not as luxury. **2** be under necessity or obligation.
● n. **1** requirement; circumstances requiring action. **2** destitution, poverty. **3** emergency.

**needful** adj. requisite; necessary.

**needle** ● n. small thin pointed piece of steel used in sewing; something

shaped like this; pointer of compass or gauge; end of hypodermic syringe. ● v. colloq. annoy; provoke.

**needless** adj. unnecessary. □□ **needlessly** adv.

**needy** adj. (needier) very poor.

**nefarious** adj. wicked.

**negate** v. **1** nullify. **2** deny existence of. □□ **negation** n.

**negative** ● adj. **1** expressing or implying denial, prohibition, or refusal. **2** lacking positive attributes; pessimistic; opposite to positive. **3** (of quantity) less than zero, to be subtracted. **4** Electr. of, containing, or producing, kind of charge carried by electrons. ● n. **1** negative statement or word. **2** Photog. image with black and white reversed or colours replaced by complementary ones. □ **negative equity** situation in which value of property falls below debt outstanding on it. **negative gearing** Aust. practice of investing borrowed money in such a way as to result in loss that can be claimed as tax deduction. □□ **negatively** adv.

**neglect** ● v. fail to care for or do; fail; pay no attention to; disregard. ● n. negligence; neglecting; being neglected. □□ **neglectful** adj. **neglectfully** adv.

**negligee** n. woman's flimsy dressing gown.

**negligence** n. lack of reasonable care and attention; culpable carelessness. □□ **negligent** adj.

**negligible** adj. not worth considering; insignificant.

**negotiate** v. **1** confer in order to reach agreement; obtain (result) by negotiating; deal successfully with (obstacle etc.) **2** convert (cheque etc.) into money. □□ **negotiable** adj. **negotiation** n. **negotiator** n.

**Negress** n. female Negro.

**Negro** n. (pl. **Negroes**) member of dark-skinned group of peoples orig. native to Africa.

> **Usage** The terms *Negro* and *Negress* are considered offensive, *black* is usually preferred.

**neigh** ● n. cry of horse. ● v. make a neigh.

**neighbour** (also **neighbor**)
● n. 1 person living next door or nearby. 2 fellow human being. ● v. border on; adjoin.

**neighbourhood** n. (also **neighborhood**) district; vicinity; people of district. □ **neighbourhood watch** systematic vigilance by residents to deter crime in their area.

**neighbourly** adj. (also **neighborly**) like a good neighbour; friendly; helpful. □□ **neighbourliness** n.

**neither** ● adj. & pron. not either. ● adv. not (either).

**nematode** n. worm with slender unsegmented cylindrical shape.

**nem. con.** abbr. unanimously, with no one disagreeing.

**nemesis** n. 1 inescapable agent of someone's or something's downfall; justice bringing deserved punishment. 2 long-standing rival; arch-enemy.

**neo-** comb. form new.

**neodymium** n. metallic element (symbol Nd).

**neolithic** adj. of later part of Stone Age.

**neologism** n. new word.

**neon** n. 1 inert gaseous element (symbol Ne). 2 this used in illuminated signs etc.

**neonatal** adj. of the newly born.

**neophyte** n. new convert; novice.

**nephew** n. son of one's brother or sister or of one's spouse's brother or sister.

**nephritis** n. inflammation of kidneys.

**nepotism** n. favouritism to relatives or friends in giving jobs.

**neptunium** n. radioactive metallic element (symbol Np).

**nerd** n. colloq. person who is socially inept or boringly studious.

**nerve** ● n. 1 fibre carrying impulses of sensation or movement between brain and part of the body. 2 courage. 3 colloq. impudence. 4 (**nerves**) nervousness; effect of mental stress. ● v. give courage to.

**nervous** adj. 1 easily upset, timid, highly strung; anxious. 2 affecting nerves. 3 afraid. □□ **nervously** adv. **nervousness** n.

**nervy** adj. (**nervier**) nervous; easily excited.

**nest** ● n. 1 structure or place where bird lays eggs and shelters young; breeding place, lair; snug place. 2 group or set of similar objects. ● v. 1 use or build nest. 2 (of objects) fit one inside another. □ **nest egg** sum of money saved for future use.

**nestle** v. 1 settle oneself comfortably. 2 press oneself against another in affection etc. 3 lie half hidden or embedded.

**nestling** n. bird too young to leave nest.

**net**[1] ● n. 1 open-meshed fabric of cord, rope, etc.; this used for particular purpose. 2 (also **Net**) Internet. ● v. (**netted**) 1 cover, confine, or catch with net. 2 hit (ball) into net.

**net**[2] (also **nett**) ● adj. 1 remaining after necessary deductions. 2 (of price) not reducible. 3 (of weight) excluding packaging etc. 4 (of effect, result, etc.) ultimate, actual. ● v. (**netted**) obtain as net profit.

**netball** n. team game in which ball has to be thrown into high net.

**nether** adj. lower.

**netting** n. meshed fabric of cord or wire.

**nettle** ● n. plant covered with stinging hairs. ● v. irritate, provoke.

**network** ● n. 1 arrangement of intersecting lines. 2 complex system of railways etc. 3 people connected by exchange of information etc. 4 group of broadcasting stations connected for simultaneous broadcast of program. 5 system of interconnected computers. ● v. 1 broadcast on network. 2 establish contact with others for exchange of ideas, information, etc.

**networking** n. interacting with others to exchange information and develop useful contacts.

**neural** adj. of nerve or central nervous system.

**neuralgia** n. intense pain along nerve, esp. in face or head. □□ **neuralgic** adj.

**neuritis** n. inflammation of nerve(s).

**neurology** n. study of nerve systems. □□ **neurological** adj. **neurologist** n.

**neuron** n. (also **neurone**) nerve cell.

**neurosis** n. (pl. **neuroses**) disturbed behaviour pattern associated with nervous distress.

**neurotic** adj. 1 caused by or relating to neurosis; suffering from neurosis. 2 abnormally sensitive or obsessive. □□ **neurotically** adv.

**neuter** ● adj. neither masculine nor feminine. ● v. castrate or spay.

**neutral** ● adj. 1 supporting neither of two opposing sides, impartial. 2 vague, indeterminate. 3 (of a gear) in which engine is disconnected from driven parts. 4 (of colours) not strong or positive. 5 Chem. neither acid nor alkaline. 6 Electr. neither positive nor negative. ● n. 1 neutral nation or person. 2 neutral gear. □□ **neutrality** n.

**neutralise** v. (also **-ize**) 1 make neutral. 2 make ineffective by opposite force. □□ **neutralisation** n.

**neutrino** n. elementary particle with zero electric charge and probably zero mass.

**neutron** n. elementary particle of about same mass as proton but without electric charge.

**never** adv. 1 at no time; on no occasion. 2 not ever; not at all. 3 colloq. surely not. □ **never mind** 1 do not worry. 2 do not bother.

**nevermore** adv. at no future time.

**nevertheless** adv. in spite of that; notwithstanding; all the same.

**new** ● adj. not existing before, recently made, discovered, experienced, etc. ● adv. newly, recently. □ **new moon** moon seen as a crescent.

**New Age** n. set of beliefs including alternative approaches to religion, medicine, etc.

**newel** n. top or bottom post of handrail of stair; central pillar of winding stair.

**newfangled** adj. different from what one is used to.

**newly** adv. recently; afresh, anew.

**news** n.pl. information about important or interesting recent events, esp. when published or broadcast; (**the news**) broadcast report of news.

**newsagent** n. shopkeeper who sells newspapers, magazines, etc.

**newsgroup** n. topic-based group on Internet to which users subscribe and then receive all mail on particular topic.

**newsletter** n. informal report containing news of interest to members of club etc.

**newspaper** n. printed daily or weekly publication containing news reports; paper forming this.

**newsprint** n. type of paper on which newspapers are printed.

**newsreader** n. person who reads broadcast news reports.

**newsworthy** adj. worth reporting as news. □□ **newsworthiness** n.

**newt** n. small tailed amphibian.

**newton** n. SI unit of force.

**next** ● adj. being, placed, or living nearest; nearest in time.
● adv. nearest in place or degree; on first or soonest occasion. ● n. next person or thing. □ **next door** in or to the next house or room. **next of kin** closest living relative. **next to**
**1** beside. **2** in comparison with. **3** apart from. **4** almost.

**nexus** n. (pl. **nexus**) **1** connected group or series. **2** central or most important point.

**NGO** abbr. non-governmental organisation.

**niacin** n. nicotinic acid.

**nib** n. **1** pen point. **2** crushed coffee or cocoa beans.

**nibble** ● v. take small bites at; eat in small amounts; bite gently or playfully. ● n. **1** act of nibbling. **2** very small amount of food.

**nibblies** n.pl. colloq. snacks.

**nice** adj. **1** pleasant, satisfactory; kind, good-natured. **2** (of distinctions) subtle; fastidious. □□ **nicely** adv. **niceness** n.

**nicety** n. subtle distinction or detail; precision.

**niche** n. **1** shallow recess, esp. in wall. **2** comfortable or apt position in life or employment; profitable corner of the market.

**nick** ● n. **1** small cut or notch. **2** colloq. prison. ● v. **1** make nick in. **2** colloq. steal; arrest. □ **in good nick** in good condition. **in the nick of time** only just in time. **nick off** slip (away etc.); depart.

**nickel** n. **1** silver-white metallic element (symbol Ni). **2** used esp. in magnetic alloys. **3** US 5-cent coin.

**nickname** ● n. familiar or humorous name added to or substituted for real name of person or thing. ● v. give nickname to.

**nicotine** n. poisonous alkaloid present in tobacco.

**nicotinic acid** n. vitamin of B group.

**niece** n. daughter of one's brother or sister, or of one's spouse's brother or sister.

**nifty** adj. (**niftier**) colloq. **1** clever, adroit. **2** smart, stylish.

**niggardly** adj. stingy. □□ **niggard** n.

**nigger** n. offens. black person.

**niggle** ● v. **1** fuss over details; find fault in petty way. **2** colloq. irritate, nag. ● n. **1** trifling complaint or criticism. **2** worry. **3** twinge of pain. □□ **niggling** adj.

**nigh** adv. & prep. arch. near.

**night** n. period of darkness from one day to next; time from sunset to sunrise; nightfall; darkness of night; evening.

**nightcap** n. alcoholic or hot drink taken at bedtime.

**nightclub** n. club open at night, providing drinks and entertainment.

**nightdress** n. woman's or child's loose garment worn in bed.

**nightie** n. colloq. nightdress.

**nightingale** n. small reddish-brown European bird.

**nightjar** n. night-flying bird with harsh cry.

**nightly** ● adj. happening, done, or existing in the night; recurring every night. ● adv. every night.

**nightmare** n. unpleasant dream or experience.

**nightshade** n. plant with poisonous berries.

**nightshirt** n. long shirt worn in bed.

**nightwatchman** n. 1 person whose job is to keep watch by night. 2 *Cricket* inferior batter sent in when wicket falls near close of day's play.

**nihilism** n. rejection of all religious and moral principles. □□ **nihilist** n. **nihilistic** adj.

**nihonium** n. chemical element (symbol Nh).

**nil** n. nothing.

**nimble** adj. able to move quickly; agile. □□ **nimbly** adv.

**nimbus** n. (pl. **nimbi** or **nimbuses**) 1 halo. 2 rain cloud.

**nimby** n. & adj. (person) objecting to siting of unpleasant developments in one's own locality (from the phrase *not in my back yard*).

**nincompoop** n. foolish person.

**nine** adj. & n. one more than eight (9, IX). □□ **ninth** adj. & n.

**ninepins** n. game of skittles played with nine objects.

**nineteen** adj. & n. one more than eighteen (19, XIX). □□ **nineteenth** adj. & n.

**ninety** adj. & n. nine times ten (90, XC). □□ **ninetieth** adj. & n.

**ning nong** n. fool.

**ninja** n. 1 person skilled in ninjutsu. 2 *colloq.* person who excels in a particular skill or activity.

**ninjutsu** n. Japanese martial art of stealth, camouflage, etc.

**ninny** n. foolish person.

**niobium** n. metallic element (symbol Nb).

**nip** ● v. (**nipped**) 1 pinch, squeeze sharply, bite. 2 *colloq.* go quickly. 3 *colloq.* cadge. ● n. 1 sharp pinch, squeeze, or bite. 2 sharp coldness. 3 small drink of spirits.

**nipper** n. 1 person or thing that nips; claw of crab etc. 2 *colloq.* child; *Aust.* (in sport) a junior. 3 *Aust.* marine crustacean used as bait.

**nipple** n. small projection in mammals from which in females milk for young is secreted; teat of feeding bottle; device like nipple in function; nipple-like protuberance.

**nippy** adj. (**nippier**) 1 *colloq.* quick, nimble. 2 chilly.

**nirvana** n. (in Buddhism and Hinduism) perfect bliss attained by the extinction of individuality.

**nit** n. 1 egg or young of louse or other parasitic insect. 2 *colloq.* stupid person. □ **nit-picking** n. petty fault-finding.

**nitrate** n. salt of nitric acid; potassium or sodium nitrate as fertiliser.

**nitric acid** n. colourless corrosive poisonous liquid.

**nitrogen** n. gaseous element forming four-fifths of atmosphere (symbol N). □□ **nitrogenous** adj.

**nitroglycerine** n. explosive yellow liquid.

**nitrous oxide** n. colourless gas used as anaesthetic.

**nitty-gritty** n. *colloq.* realities or practical details of a matter.

**nitwit** n. *colloq.* stupid person.

**nix** *colloq.* ● n. 1 nothing. 2 denial or refusal. ● v. cancel; reject.

**Nn**

**NNE** abbr. north-north-east.

**NNW** abbr. north-north-west.

**no** ● adj. not any. ● adv. (used as a denial or refusal of something); not at all. ● n. (pl. **noes**) a negative reply; a vote against a proposal. □ **no-hoper** *colloq.* incompetent or ineffectual person.

**No.** abbr. (also **no.**) number.

**nobble** v. *colloq.* 1 try to influence, esp. unfairly; tamper with (racehorse etc.). 2 steal; seize, catch.

**nobelium** n. radioactive metallic element (symbol No).

**nobility** n. 1 nobleness of character or of rank; titled people.

**noble** ● *adj.* aristocratic; possessing excellent qualities, esp. of character; generous, not petty; imposing. ● *n.* member of the nobility. □□ **nobleness** *n.* **nobly** *adv.*

**nobleman** *n.* (*pl.* **noblemen**) male member of the nobility.

**noblesse oblige** *n.* privilege entails responsibility.

**noblewoman** *n.* (*pl.* **noblewomen**) female member of the nobility.

**nobody** ● *pron.* no person. ● *n.* person of no importance.

**nocturnal** *adj.* of or in the night; done or active by night.

**nocturne** *n. Mus.* short romantic composition.

**nod** ● *v.* (**nodded**) move head down and up quickly; indicate (agreement or casual greeting) in this way; let head droop, be drowsy; (of flowers etc.) bend and sway. ● *n.* nodding movement, esp. in agreement or greeting. □ **nod off** *colloq.* fall asleep.

**node** *n.* **1** point in network where lines intersect. **2** small mass of tissue. **3** point on stem where leaf or bud grows out. □□ **nodal** *adj.*

**nodule** *n.* small rounded lump of anything; small node. □□ **nodular** *adj.*

**noise** *n.* **1** sound, esp. loud, harsh, or unwanted. **2** extraneous signal in electronic system. □□ **noiseless** *adj.*

**noisome** *adj.* harmful; evil-smelling; disgusting.

**noisy** *adj.* (**noisier**) making much noise; full of noise. □□ **noisily** *adv.*

**nomad** *n.* member of people that travels from place to place to find pasture for its animals and has no permanent home; wanderer. □□ **nomadic** *adj.*

**nom de plume** *n.* (*pl.* **noms de plume**) writer's pseudonym.

**nomenclature** *n.* system of names for things; terminology of a science etc.

**nominal** *adj.* **1** existing in name only; not real or actual. **2** (of sum of money etc.) very small. **3** of, as, or like noun. □ **nominal value** face value of coin etc. **nominally** *adv.*

**nominate** *v.* put oneself forward for election; propose (candidate) for election; appoint to office; appoint (date or place). □□ **nomination** *n.* **nominator** *n.*

**nominative** *Gram.* ● *n.* case expressing subject of verb. ● *adj.* of or in this case.

**nominee** *n.* person who is nominated.

**non-** *prefix* not; an absence of.

> **Usage** For words starting with *non-* that are not found below, the root words should be consulted.

**nonagenarian** *n.* person from 90 to 99 years old.

**non-aligned** *adj.* (of nation etc.) not aligned with major power. □□ **non-alignment** *n.*

**nonchalant** *adj.* calm and casual. □□ **nonchalance** *n.* **nonchalantly** *adv.*

**non-committal** *adj.* avoiding commitment to definite opinion or course of action.

**nonconformist** *n.* person who does not conform to established practices; (**Nonconformist**) member of Protestant sect dissenting from Anglican Church.

**non-contributory** *adj.* not involving contributions.

**nonda** *n.* Australian tree yielding edible, plum-like, yellow fruit.

**nondescript** ● *adj.* lacking distinctive characteristics, not easily classified. ● *n.* such a person or thing.

**none** ● *pron.* **1** not any. **2** no person(s). ● *adv.* by no amount; not at all.

> **Usage** The verb following *none* can be singular or plural when it means 'not any of several', e.g. *None of us knows* or *None of us know*.

**nonentity** *n.* **1** person or thing of no importance. **2** non-existence; non-existent thing.

**nonetheless** *adv.* nevertheless.

**non-event** *n.* insignificant event, esp. contrary to hopes or expectations.

**non-fiction** *n.* literary work other than fiction.

**nong** *n. Aust. colloq. derog.* foolish or stupid person.

**nonpareil** ● *adj.* unrivalled, unique. ● *n.* such a person or thing.

**nonplussed** *adj.* **1** completely puzzled. **2** *colloq.* not disconcerted; unperturbed.

**non-proliferation** *n.* prevention of an increase in something, esp. possession of nuclear weapons.

**nonsense** *n.* absurd or meaningless words or ideas; foolish conduct. □□ **nonsensical** *adj.* **nonsensically** *adv.*

**non sequitur** *n.* conclusion that does not logically follow from premises.

**non-starter** *n. colloq.* person or scheme not worth considering.

**non-stick** *adj.* that does not allow things to stick to it.

**non-stop** ● *adj.* done without stopping. ● *adv.* without stopping.

**noodle** *n.* **1** strip or ring of pasta. **2** *colloq.* head.

**nook** *n.* corner or recess; secluded place.

**noolbenger** *n. Aust.* honey possum with long snout.

**noon** *n.* 12 o'clock in day, midday.

**noose** ● *n.* **1** loop of rope etc. with knot that tightens when pulled. **2** snare. ● *v.* catch with or enclose in noose.

**nor** *conj.* **1** and not. **2** (and) neither.

**norm** *n.* standard, type; customary behaviour.

**normal** ● *adj.* conforming to standard or usual; free from mental or emotional disorders. ● *n.* normal value of temperature etc.; usual state, level, etc. □□ **normalcy** *n.* **normalise** *v.* **normality** *n.* **normally** *adv.*

**north** ● *n.* point or direction to left of person facing east; northern part or region. ● *adj.* towards, at, near, or facing north; (of wind) from north. ● *adv.* towards, at, or near north; further north than.
□ **north-east** in or towards point or direction midway between north and east. **north-west** in or towards point or direction midway between north and west. □□ **northward** *adj., adv., & n.* **northwards** *adv.*

**northerly** ● *adj. & adv.* in northern position or direction; (of wind) from north. ● *n.* such wind.

**northern** *adj.* of or in the north. □□ **northernmost** *adj.*

**northerner** *n.* native or inhabitant of the north.

**nose** ● *n.* **1** organ above mouth, used for smelling and breathing; sense of smell. **2** talent for detecting something. **3** projecting part or front end of car, aircraft, etc. ● *v.* **1** push nose against something, esp. to smell; sniff (something). **2** pry or search. **3** move forward cautiously.

**nosebag** *n.* bag of fodder for hanging on horse's head.

**nosedive** ● *n.* steep downward plunge, esp. of aeroplane. ● *v.* make this plunge.

**nosegay** *n.* small bunch of flowers.

**nosh** *colloq.* ● *n.* meal. ● *v.* eat.

**nostalgia** n. **1** yearning for past period. **2** homesickness. □□ **nostalgic** adj.

**nostril** n. either of two openings in nose.

**nostrum** n. **1** quack remedy. **2** pet scheme.

**nosy** adj. (**nosier**) colloq. inquisitive, prying.

**not** adv. expressing negation, refusal, or denial. □ **not at all 1** definitely not. **2** polite response to thanks.

**notable** ● adj. worthy of note; remarkable, eminent. ● n. eminent person. □□ **notability** n. **notably** adv.

**notary** n. person authorised to perform certain legal formalities, e.g. drawing up and certifying contracts. □□ **notarial** adj.

**notation** n. representation of numbers, quantities, musical notes, etc. by symbols; set of such symbols.

**notch** ● n. **1** V-shaped indentation on edge or surface. **2** step or degree. ● v. **1** make notches in. **2** score, win, achieve (esp. amount or quantity).

**note** ● n. **1** brief written record as memory aid; short or informal letter; short written comment. **2** banknote. **3** musical tone of definite pitch; symbol representing pitch and duration of a musical sound; each of keys on piano etc. **4** eminence; notice, attention. **5** quality or tone expressing mood (a note of anger.). ● v. notice, pay attention to; write down.

**notebook** n. **1** book with blank pages on which to write notes. **2** laptop.

**notecase** n. wallet for banknotes.

**noted** adj. famous, well known.

**notelet** n. small folded card for short informal letter.

**noteworthy** adj. worthy of attention; remarkable.

**nothing** ● n. **1** no thing. **2** not anything. **3** person or thing of no importance. **4** non-existence. **5** no

amount. **6** nought. ● adv. **1** not at all. **2** in no way.

**notice** ● n. **1** attention. **2** displayed sheet etc. with announcement. **3** intimation, warning. **4** formal declaration of intention to end agreement or employment at specified time. **5** short published review of new play, book, etc. ● v. perceive, observe; remark upon; speak of. □ **take notice** show interest.

**noticeable** adj. easily seen or noticed. □□ **noticeably** adv.

**notifiable** adj. (esp. of disease) that must be notified to authorities.

**notify** v. inform, give notice to (person); make known. □□ **notification** n.

**notion** n. concept, idea; opinion; vague understanding; intention.

**notional** adj. hypothetical, imaginary. □□ **notionally** adv.

**notorious** adj. well known, esp. unfavourably. □□ **notoriety** n. **notoriously** adv.

**notwithstanding** ● prep. in spite of. ● adv. nevertheless. ● conj. although.

**nougat** n. sweet made from sugar or honey, nuts, and egg white.

**nought** n. digit 0; nothing.

**noun** n. word used as the name of person, place, or thing.

**nourish** v. sustain with food; foster, cherish (feeling etc.) □□ **nourishing** adj.

**nourishment** n. sustenance, food.

**nous** n. colloq. common sense.

**Nov.** abbr. November.

**nova** n. (pl. **novae** or **novas**) star that suddenly becomes much brighter for short time.

**novel** ● n. fictitious prose story of book length. ● adj. of new kind or nature; strange; previously unknown.

**novelette** n. short (esp. romantic) novel.

**novelist** n. writer of novels.

**novelty** ● *n.* **1** newness; new or unusual thing or occurrence. **2** small toy. ● *adj.* having novelty.

**November** *n.* eleventh month of year.

**novice** *n.* person new to and inexperienced in an activity; probationary member of religious order.

**now** ● *adv.* **1** at the present time; immediately. **2** (with no reference to time) I wonder, surely, I insist (*now why didn't I think of that?*). ● *conj.* as a consequence of or simultaneously with the fact that. ● *n.* the present time.

**nowadays** ● *adv.* at present time or age. ● *n.* the present time.

**nowhere** ● *adv.* in or to no place. ● *pron.* no place.

**noxious** *adj.* harmful, unwholesome.

**nozzle** *n.* spout on hose etc.

**NSW** *abbr.* New South Wales.

**NT** *abbr.* **1** Northern Territory. **2** New Testament.

**nuance** *n.* subtle shade of meaning, feeling, colour, etc.

**nub** *n.* point or gist (of matter or story).

**nubile** *adj.* (of woman) marriageable, sexually attractive. □□ **nubility** *n.*

**nuclear** *adj.* of, relating to, or constituting a nucleus; using nuclear energy. □ **nuclear family** a couple and their children.

**nucleic acid** *n.* either of two complex organic molecules (DNA and RNA), present in all living cells.

**nucleon** *n.* proton or neutron.

**nucleus** *n.* (*pl.* **nuclei**) **1** central part or thing around which others collect; central portion of atom, seed, or cell. **2** initial part.

**nuddy** *n.* □ **in the nuddy** *colloq.* naked.

**nude** ● *adj.* **1** naked, unclothed. **2** of clothing or make-up that is of colour resembling that of wearer's skin; of pale pinkish-beige colour. ● *n.* **1** nude person; painting etc. of nude human figure. **2** nude colour. □□ **nudity** *n.*

**nudge** ● *v.* prod gently with elbow to attract attention; push gradually. ● *n.* gentle push.

**nudist** *n.* person who advocates or practises going unclothed. □□ **nudism** *n.*

**nugget** *n.* **1** lump of gold etc. as found in earth; lump of anything. **2** *Aust.* stocky animal or person.

**nuisance** *n.* person, thing, or circumstance causing annoyance.

**nuke** *colloq.* ● *n.* nuclear weapon. ● *v.* attack or destroy (as if) with nuclear weapon(s).

**null** *adj.* **1** having no legal force. **2** *Computing* empty. □□ **nullity** *n.*

**nulla-nulla** *n. Aust.* (in traditional Aboriginal use) club used in fighting and hunting.

**nullify** *v.* neutralise, invalidate. □□ **nullification** *n.*

**numb** ● *adj.* deprived of feeling or power of motion. ● *v.* make numb; stupefy, paralyse. □□ **numbness** *n.*

**numbat** *n. Aust.* small termite-eating marsupial with long, pointed snout and striped red to grey-brown fur.

**number** ● *n.* **1** symbol or word indicating how many; a total, a quantity; numeral assigned to person or thing. **2** single issue of magazine; item. ● *v.* count; amount to; mark or distinguish with number. □ **number one** *colloq.* oneself. **number plate** plate on motor vehicle, bearing its registration number.

**numberless** *adj.* innumerable.

**numeral** ● *n.* symbol or group of symbols denoting a number. ● *adj.* of or denoting a number.

**numerate** *adj.* acquainted with basic principles of mathematics; able to do basic arithmetic etc. □□ **numeracy** *n.*

**numerator** *n.* number above line in vulgar fraction.

**numerical** *adj.* of or relating to number(s).□□ **numerically** *adv.*

**numerology** *n.* study of supposed occult significance of numbers.

**numerous** *adj.* many; consisting of many.

**numinous** *adj.* 1 indicating presence of a divinity. 2 awe-inspiring.

**numismatics** *n.pl.* study of coins and medals.□□ **numismatist** *n.*

**nun** *n.* member of community of women living under religious vows.

**nuncio** *n.* papal ambassador.

**nunnery** *n.* religious house of nuns.

**nuptial** ● *adj.* of marriage or weddings. ● *n.* (**nuptials**) wedding ceremony.

**nurse** ● *n.* person trained to care for sick or infirm. ● *v.* 1 work as nurse; attend to (sick person). 2 feed or be fed at breast. 3 hold or treat carefully; foster; harbour (grievance etc.); pay special attention to.□ **nursing home** privately run hospital or home for invalids.

**nursery** *n.* 1 room or place equipped for young children; creche. 2 place where plants are reared for sale. □ **nursery rhyme** traditional verse for children.

**nurture** ● *n.* bringing up, fostering care; nourishment; sociological factors as influencing or determining personality. ● *v.* 1 bring up. 2 rear.

**nut** *n.* 1 fruit with hard shell around edible kernel; this kernel. 2 small threaded metal ring for use with bolt. 3 *colloq.* head. 4 *colloq.* eccentric person.

**nutcase** *n. colloq.* crazy person.

**nutmeg** *n.* hard fragrant tropical seed, ground or grated as spice etc.

**nutrient** ● *n.* substance providing essential nourishment. ● *adj.* serving as or providing nourishment.

**nutriment** *n.* nourishing food.

**nutrition** *n.* food, nourishment; study of nutrients and nutrition. □□ **nutritional** *adj.* **nutritionist** *n.*

**nutritious** *adj.* nourishing.

**nutshell** *n.* hard covering of nut. □ **in a nutshell** expressed very briefly.

**nutter** *n. colloq.* crazy person.

**nutty** *adj.* (**nuttier**) 1 full of nuts; tasting like nuts. 2 *colloq.* crazy.

**nuytsia** *n. Aust.* parasitic tree with profuse golden flowers.

**nuzzle** *v.* 1 prod or rub gently with the nose. 2 nestle, lie snug.

**NW** *abbr.* north-west(ern).

**nylon** *n.* tough light synthetic fibre; fabric made from it.

**nymph** *n.* 1 mythological semi-divine female spirit associated with rivers, woods, etc. 2 immature form of some insects.

**nymphomania** *n.* excessive sexual desire in woman.□□ **nymphomaniac** *n. & adj.*

**NZ** *abbr.* New Zealand.

# Oo

**oaf** *n.* awkward lout.□□ **oafish** *adj.* **oafishly** *adv.* **oafishness** *n.*

**oak** *n.* deciduous European hardwood tree bearing acorns; its wood; any similar native tree.□□ **oaken** *adj.*

**OAM** *abbr.* Medal of Order of Australia.

**oar** *n.* 1 pole with blade used to row boat. 2 rower.

**oasis** *n.* (*pl.* **oases**) 1 fertile place in desert. 2 area or period of calm in midst of turbulence.

**oat** *n.* cereal plant; (**oats**) its grain.

**oath** *n.* 1 solemn promise. 2 curse.

**oatmeal** *n.* 1 meal ground from oats. 2 greyish-fawn colour flecked with brown.

**obdurate** *adj.* stubborn. □□ **obduracy** *n.*

**obedient** *adj.* obeying or ready to obey; submissive to another's will. □□ **obedience** *n.* **obediently** *adv.*

**obeisance** *n.* gesture expressing submission, respect, etc.□□ **obeisant** *adj.*

**obelisk** *n.* tall pillar set up as monument.

**obese** *adj.* very fat.□□ **obesity** *n.*

**obey** *v.* carry out command of; do what one is told to do.

**obfuscate** *v.* obscure, confuse, bewilder.□□ **obfuscation** *n.* **obfuscatory** *adj.*

**obituary** *n.* notice of death(s); brief biography of deceased person.

**object** ● *n.* 1 something solid that can be seen or touched. 2 person or thing to which action or feeling is directed. 3 purpose, intention. 4 *Gram.* noun etc. acted upon by transitive verb or preposition. ● *v.* state that one is opposed to, protest.□ **no object** not a limiting factor. **object lesson** striking practical example of a principle. □□ **objector** *n.*

**objection** *n.* disapproval, opposition; statement of this; reason for objecting.

**objectionable** *adj.* 1 unpleasant, offensive. 2 open to objection. □□ **objectionably** *adv.*

**objective** ● *adj.* 1 external to mind; actually existing. 2 not influenced by personal feelings or opinions. 3 *Gram.* of form of word used when it is object of verb or preposition. ● *n.* 1 object or purpose. 2 *Gram.* objective case.□□ **objectively** *adv.* **objectivity** *n.*

**objet d'art** *n.* (*pl.* **objets d'art**) small decorative object.

**oblation** *n.* thing offered to divine being.

**obligate** *v.* bind (person) legally or morally.

**obligation** *n.* compelling power of law, duty, etc.; duty; binding agreement; indebtedness for service or benefit.

**obligatory** *adj.* binding; compulsory. □□ **obligatorily** *adv.*

**oblige** *v.* 1 compel. 2 help or gratify by small service.

**obliged** *adj.* indebted.

**obliging** *adj.* polite and helpful. □□ **obligingly** *adv.*

**oblique** ● *adj.* 1 slanting; at an angle. 2 not going straight to the point, indirect. ● *n.* oblique stroke ( / ). □□ **obliquely** *adv.* **obliqueness** *n.* **obliquity** *n.*

**obliterate** *v.* blot out, leave no clear trace of.□□ **obliteration** *n.*

**oblivion** *n.* state of having or being forgotten; state of being unconscious or unaware.

**oblivious** adj. unaware. □□ **obliviously** adv. **obliviousness** n.

**oblong** n. & adj. (having) rectangular shape with adjacent sides unequal.

**obloquy** n. verbal abuse, criticism; disgrace.

**obnoxious** adj. offensive, objectionable. □□ **obnoxiously** adv. **obnoxiousness** n.

**oboe** n. double-reeded woodwind instrument. □□ **oboist** n.

**obscene** adj. offensive in repulsive way. □□ **obscenely** adv. **obscenity** n.

**obscure** ● adj. 1 not clearly expressed or easily understood; unexplained. 2 dark; indistinct.
● v. make obscure; conceal.
□□ **obscurity** n.

**obsequies** n.pl. funeral rites.

**obsequious** adj. fawning, servile. □□ **obsequiously** adv. **obsequiousness** n.

**observance** n. keeping or performing of law, duty, etc.; rite, ceremony.

**observant** adj. good at observing. □□ **observantly** adv.

**observation** n. 1 taking notice; careful watching. 2 remark or statement. 3 perception. □□ **observational** adj.

**observatory** n. building for astronomical or other observation.

**observe** v. 1 perceive, become aware of; watch. 2 keep (rules etc.) 3 remark (rite etc.) 4 remark; take note of scientifically. □□ **observer** n. **observable** adj.

**obsess** v. occupy thoughts of (some one) persistently. □□ **obsession** n.

**obsessive** adj. & n. **obsessively** adv. **obsessiveness** n.

**obsolescent** adj. becoming obsolete. □□ **obsolescence** n.

**obsolete** adj. no longer used or of use.

**obstacle** n. thing obstructing progress.

**obstetrics** n. branch of medicine and surgery dealing with childbirth. □□ **obstetric** adj. **obstetrician** n.

**obstinate** adj. stubborn, intractable; inflexible, unyielding. □□ **obstinacy** n. **obstinately** adv.

**obstreperous** adj. noisy, unruly. □□ **obstreperously** adv. **obstreperousness** n.

**obstruct** v. block; prevent or retard progress of. □□ **obstruction** n. **obstructive** adj.

**obtain** v. 1 acquire, come into possession of. 2 be prevalent or established.

**obtrude** v. be obtrusive; persistently push forward (oneself, one's opinion, etc.) □□ **obtrusion** n.

**obtrusive** adj. unpleasantly noticeable; obtruding oneself. □□ **obtrusively** adv. **obtrusiveness** n.

**obtuse** adj. 1 blunt in shape. 2 (of angle) more than 90° but less than 180°. 3 slow at understanding. □□ **obtuseness** n.

**obverse** n. counterpart, opposite; side of coin or medal bearing head or principal design; front or top side.

**obviate** v. get round or do away with (need, inconvenience, etc.)

**obvious** adj. easily seen, recognised, or understood. □□ **obviously** adv. **obviousness** n.

**occasion** ● n. 1 time at which event happens; special event. 2 reason, need. 3 suitable time or opportunity.
● v. cause, esp. incidentally.

**occasional** adj. 1 happening infrequently. 2 for particular occasion. □□ **occasionally** adv.

**Occident** n. the West, the western world. □□ **occidental** adj.

**occlude** v. 1 stop up; obstruct. 2 Chem. absorb (gases). □ **occluded front** upward movement of mass of warm air caused by cold front overtaking it, producing prolonged rainfall. □□ **occlusion** n.

**occult** adj. **1** involving the supernatural or magic. **2** esoteric; secret.

**occupant** n. person occupying dwelling, office, or position. □□ **occupancy** n.

**occupation** n. **1** profession or employment. **2** pastime. **3** occupying, being occupied.

**occupational** adj. of or connected with one's occupation. □ **occupational health (and safety)** programs maintaining health and safety of workers in their place of employment. **occupational therapy** program of mental or physical activity to assist recovery from disease or injury.

**occupy** v. be in, live in; fill. □□ **occupier** n.

**occur** v. (**occurred**) come into being as event or process; happen; exist.

**occurrence** n. happening; incident or event.

**ocean** n. sea surrounding continents of the earth. □□ **oceanic** adj.

**oceanography** n. study of oceans. □□ **oceanographer** n.

**ocelot** n. S. American leopard-like cat.

**ochre** n. **1** earth used as pigment. **2** pale brownish yellow. □□ **ochreous** adj.

**ocker** Aust. ● n. uncouth, uncultured, or boorish Australian. ● adj. characteristic of such a person.

**o'clock** adv. of the clock (used to specify hour) (6 o'clock).

**Oct.** abbr. October.

**octagon** n. plane figure with eight sides. □□ **octagonal** adj.

**octahedron** n. solid figure with eight sides. □□ **octahedral** adj.

**octane** n. colourless flammable hydrocarbon occurring in petrol.

**octave** n. interval of eight notes between one musical note and next note of same name above or below it.

**octavo** n. (pl. **octavos**) size of book formed by folding a standard sheet three times to form eight leaves.

**octet** n. group of eight voices or instruments; music for these.

**October** n. tenth month of year.

**octogenarian** n. person from 80 to 89 years old.

**octopus** n. (pl. **octopuses**) mollusc with eight suckered tentacles. □ **octopus strap** Aust. rubber strap with metal hooks at each end, used to secure luggage, surfboards, etc.

**ocular** adj. of, for, or by the eyes.

**oculist** n. specialist in treatment of eyes.

**OD** colloq. ● n. drug overdose. ● v. (**Od'd, Od'ing**) take overdose.

**odd** adj. **1** unusual; occasional. **2** not part of a set. **3** (of number) not exactly divisible by two. **4** strange, weird. □□ **oddly** adv. **oddness** n.

**oddity** n. unusual person, thing, or occurrence; strangeness.

**oddment** n. thing left over; isolated article.

**odds** n.pl. a probability; ratio between amounts staked by parties to a bet. □ **at odds** in conflict with. **odds and ends** oddments. **odds-on** with success more likely than failure.

**ode** n. lyric poem addressed to person or celebrating event.

**odious** adj. hateful, repulsive. □□ **odiously** adv. **odiousness** n.

**odium** n. general dislike or disapproval.

**odometer** n. instrument measuring distance travelled by wheeled vehicle.

**odoriferous** adj. diffusing (usu. pleasant) odours.

**odour** n. (also **odor**) smell or fragrance; lasting quality or trace attaching to something. □□ **odorous** adj. **odourless** adj.

**odyssey** n. (pl. **odysseys**) long adventurous journey.

**OECD** *abbr.* Organisation for Economic Cooperation and Development.

**oedema** *n.* accumulation of excess fluid in body tissues, causing swelling.
□□ **oedematose** *adj.* **oedematous** *adj.*

**oesophagus** *n.* (also **esophagus**) tube from mouth to stomach.
□□ **oesophageal** *adj.*

**oestrogen** *n.* (also **estrogen**) sex hormone responsible for controlling female bodily characteristics.

**of** *prep.* belonging to; from; composed or made from; concerning; for, involving.

**off** ● *adv.* **1** away; out of position, disconnected. **2** not operating, cancelled. ● *prep.* away from; below normal standard of. ● *adj.* **1** (of food) decayed. **2** of side of vehicle furthest from kerb. **3** *colloq.* annoying; not acceptable. **4** *Cricket* of, in, or into half of field which batter faces. □ **off-air** not being broadcast on radio or television. **off colour 1** unwell. **2** indecent; indelicate. **off-white** not quite pure white. **on the off chance** in case of remote possibility that.

**offal** *n.* **1** edible organs of animals, esp. heart, liver, etc. **2** refuse, scraps.

**offbeat** *adj.* unusual, unconventional.

**offcourse** *adj.* (of betting) taking place away from racecourse.

**offcut** *n.* piece of waste material left after cutting off a larger piece.

**offence** *n.* **1** illegal act; transgression. **2** feeling of annoyance or resentment. **3** insult. **4** aggressive action.

**offend** *v.* cause offence to; upset; displease, anger; do wrong.
□□ **offender** *n.* **offending** *adj.*

**offensive** ● *adj.* **1** causing offence; insulting; disgusting. **2** aggressive. ● *n.* aggressive attitude, action, or

campaign. □□ **offensively** *adv.* **offensiveness** *n.*

**offer** ● *v.* **1** present for acceptance, refusal, or consideration. **2** express readiness, show intention; attempt. ● *n.* expression of readiness to do or give if desired, or to buy or sell; amount offered; proposal, esp. of marriage; bid.

**offering** *n.* contribution, gift; thing offered.

**offertory** *n.* **1** offering of bread and wine at Eucharist. **2** collection of money at religious service.

**offhand** ● *adj.* unceremonious, casual. ● *adv.* in offhand way.

**office** *n.* **1** room or building used for clerical and similar work. **2** position of authority or trust; tenure of official position.

**officer** *n.* **1** person holding position of authority or trust, esp. one with commission in armed forces; policeman or policewoman; president, treasurer, etc. of society. **2** (**Officer**) member of grade below Companion in Order of Australia.

**official** ● *adj.* properly authorised by authority etc. ● *n.* person holding office or engaged in official duties.
□□ **officialdom** *n.* **officially** *adv.*

**officialese** *n.* *colloq.* official's jargon.

**officiate** *v.* act in official capacity; conduct religious service.

**officious** *adj.* domineering; intrusive in correcting etc.□□ **officiously** *adv.* **officiousness** *n.*

**offline** *adj.* & *adv.* not controlled by or not connected to computer; unavailable on or not connected to Internet.

**offset** ● *v.* (**offset, offsetting**) **1** counterbalance, compensate for. **2** print by offset process.
● *n.* **1** something that counterbalances or compensates for. **2** side shoot of plant used for propagation. **3** sloping

ledge. **4** printing method using inked rubber surface.

**offshoot** n. **1** side shoot. **2** subsidiary product.

**offshore** ● adj. at sea; (of wind) blowing from land to sea. ● adv. move (some of a company's processes etc.) overseas.

**offsider** n. Aust. assistant; colleague.

**offspring** n. (pl. offspring) person's child, children, or descendants; animal's young or descendants.

**often** adv. frequently; many times; at short intervals; in many instances.

**oganesson** n. chemical element (symbol Og).

**ogee** n. S-shaped curve or moulding.

**ogle** ● v. look lecherously or flirtatiously (at). ● n. flirtatious glance.

**ogre** n. human-eating giant; terrifying person.

**oh** int. (also O) expressing surprise, pain, etc.

**ohm** n. SI unit of electrical resistance.

**oil** ● n. **1** viscous, usu. flammable liquid insoluble in water. **2** petroleum. **3** (oils) oil paint. ● v. lubricate or treat with oil. □□ oily adj.

**oilfield** n. place where oil is found in ground.

**oilskin** n. cloth waterproofed by treatment with oil; waterproof clothing made with this.

**ointment** n. smooth greasy healing or cosmetic preparation for skin.

**OK** (also okay) colloq. ● int. used to express agreement or acceptance. ● adj. & adv. all right.

**okra** n. African plant with edible seed pods used as vegetable.

**old** adj. having lived, existed, or been known for long time; of specified age; shabby from age or wear; former; not recent or modern. □ **old wives' tale** foolish or unscientific tradition or belief. □□ oldish adj. oldness n.

**oleaginous** adj. **1** like or producing oil; oily. **2** obsequious, ingratiating.

**oleander** n. evergreen poisonous shrub.

**olfactory** adj. of sense of smell.

**oligarch** n. member of oligarchy.

**oligarchy** n. government, or nation governed, by small group of people; members of such government. □□ oligarchic adj.

**olive** ● n. **1** oval hard-stoned fruit yielding oil; tree bearing this. **2** dull yellowish green. ● adj. **1** olive green. **2** (of complexion) yellowish-brown. □ **olive branch** gesture of reconciliation or friendship.

**ombudsman** n. official appointed to investigate complaints against public authorities.

**omega** n. last letter of Greek alphabet (Ω, ω).

**omelette** n. beaten eggs fried and often folded over filling.

**omen** n. event regarded as warning of good or evil.

**OMG** abbr. colloq. oh my God!

**ominous** adj. threatening; inauspicious. □□ ominously adv.

**omit** v. (omitted) leave out; not include; neglect (to do something). □□ omission n.

**omnibus** ● n. **1** volume containing several novels etc. previously published separately. **2** formal bus. ● adj. serving several purposes at once; comprising several items.

**omnipotent** adj. all-powerful. □□ omnipotence n.

**omnipresent** adj. present everywhere. □□ omnipresence n.

**omniscient** adj. knowing everything. □□ omniscience n.

**omnium** n. track cycling competition including races and time trials.

**omnivorous** adj. **1** feeding on both plant and animal material. **2** making

use of everything available.
□□ **omnivore** n. **omnivorousness** n.

**on** ● *prep.* **1** supported by, attached to, covering, on top. **2** close to, near, at; towards. **3** (of time) exactly at, during. **4** concerning, about. **5** added to. ● *adv.* **1** so as to be on or covering something. **2** further forward, towards something. **3** with continued movement or action; operating; taking place. ● *adj.* Cricket of, in, or into half of field behind batsman's back. □ **on-air** being broadcast on radio or television. **on and off** from time to time.

**once** ● *adv.* **1** on one occasion or for one time only. **2** formerly. ● *conj.* as soon as. ● *n.* one time or occasion.

**oncogene** n. gene that transforms cell into cancer cell.

**oncology** n. study of tumours.

**oncoming** *adj.* approaching.

**one** ● *n.* smallest whole number (1, I); single person or thing. ● *adj.* single, individual, forming unity. ● *pron.* any person. □ **one another** each other. **one day** at some unspecified date. **one-eyed** colloq. strongly biased towards (person or thing). **one-night stand** colloq. casual sexual encounter. **one-sided** favouring or dealing with only one side in a dispute etc. **one-upmanship** maintaining advantage over others. **one-way** allowing movement in one direction only.

**onerous** *adj.* burdensome.
□□ **onerousness** n.

**oneself** *pron.* emphatic and reflexive form of ONE.

**onesie** n. one-piece leisure garment covering torso and legs.

**ongoing** *adj.* continuing; in progress.

**onion** n. **1** vegetable with edible bulb of pungent smell and flavour. **2** colloq. head. □□ **oniony** adj.

**onkus** *adj.* Aust. colloq. disagreeable; distasteful; out of order.

**online** *adj. & adv.* controlled by or connected to computer; available on or performed using Internet or other computer network.

**onlooker** n. spectator. □□ **onlooking** adj.

**only** ● *adv.* solely, merely, exclusively. ● *adj.* existing alone of its or their kind. ● *conj.* colloq. except that; but.

**o.n.o.** *abbr.* or nearest offer.

**onomatopoeia** n. formation of word from sound associated with thing named, e.g. *cuckoo*, *sizzle*.
□□ **onomatopoeic** adj.

**onset** n. **1** a beginning. **2** an attack.

**onshore** ● *adj.* on land; (of wind) blowing from sea to land. ● *v.* (of a company) transfer (business operation) back to the country from which it was originally relocated.

**onslaught** n. fierce attack.

**onto** *prep.* = on to.

**onus** n. (*pl.* **onuses**) burden, duty, responsibility.

**onward** *adj. & adv.* **1** with advancing motion. **2** further on. □□ **onwards** adv.

**onyx** n. semiprecious variety of agate with coloured layers.

**oodles** n.pl. colloq. very great amount.

**oolite** n. granular limestone.
□□ **oolitic** adj.

**oomph** n. colloq. **1** energy, enthusiasm. **2** attractiveness, esp. sex appeal.

**ooze** ● *v.* **1** trickle or leak slowly out. **2** exude. ● *n.* wet mud. □□ **oozy** adj.

**op.** n. opus.

**opacity** n. opaqueness.

**opal** n. semiprecious milky or bluish stone with iridescent reflections.

**opalescent** *adj.* iridescent.
□□ **opalescence** n.

**opaline** *adj.* opal-like, opalescent.

**opaque** *adj.* not transmitting light; impenetrable to sight; unintelligible.
□□ **opaquely** adv. **opaqueness** n.

**op. cit.** abbr. in the work already quoted.

**OPEC** abbr. Organisation of Petroleum Exporting Countries.

**open** ● adj. **1** able to be entered, not closed or sealed or locked; not covered or concealed or restricted. **2** unfolded. **3** frank; undisguised. **4** not yet decided. **5** (**open to**) willing to receive. ● v. make or become open or more open; begin, establish. □ **in the open air** not in house or building etc. **open-ended** with no fixed limit. **open-handed** generous. **open house** hospitality to all comers. **open letter** one addressed to person but printed in newspaper. **open-plan** having large rooms with few or no internal dividing walls. **open-source** software for which original source code is made freely available. **open verdict** one not specifying whether a crime is involved. □□ **openness** n.

**opencast** adj. (of mining) on surface of ground.

**opener** n. **1** device for opening tins, bottles, etc. **2** Cricket opening batter.

**opening** n. **1** gap, aperture. **2** opportunity. **3** job vacancy. **4** beginning; initial part. ● adj. initial, first.

**openly** adv. frankly; publicly.

**opera** n. musical drama with sung or spoken dialogue. □ **opera glasses** small binoculars used in theatre.

**operable** adj. that can be operated; suitable for treatment by surgical operation.

**operate** v. **1** work, control (machine etc.); be in action. **2** perform surgical operation(s). □ **operating system** basic software allowing computer program to run. **operating theatre** room for surgical operations.

**operatic** adj. of or like opera.

**operation** n. **1** action, working. **2** performance of surgery on patient. **3** military manoeuvre. **4** financial transaction. □□ **operational** adj. **operationally** adv.

**operative** ● adj. **1** in operation. **2** having principal relevance. **3** of or by surgery. ● n. worker, artisan.

**operator** n. **1** person operating machine, esp. connecting lines in telephone exchange. **2** person engaging in business.

**ophidian** ● n. member of suborder of reptiles including snakes. ● adj. of this order.

**ophthalmic** adj. of or relating to the eye and its diseases.

**ophthalmology** n. study of the eye. □□ **ophthalmologist** n.

**ophthalmoscope** n. instrument for examining the eye.

**opiate** ● adj. **1** containing opium. **2** soporific. ● n. **1** drug containing opium, usu. to ease pain or induce sleep. **2** soothing influence.

**opine** v. hold or express as opinion.

**opinion** n. **1** unproven belief; view held as probable. **2** piece of professional advice. **3** estimation.

**opinionated** adj. dogmatic in one's opinions.

**opium** n. drug made from juice of certain poppy, used as analgesic and narcotic.

**opossum** n. tree-living American marsupial.

**opponent** n. person who opposes.

**opportune** adj. well-chosen, specially favourable; (of action, event) well-timed.

**opportunist** n. person who grasps opportunities. □□ **opportunism** n. **opportunistic** adj.

**opportunity** n. favourable chance or opening offered by circumstances. □ **opportunity shop** Aust. shop selling second-hand clothes etc., usu. run by a charitable organisation.

**oppose** v. set oneself against; resist; argue against; place in opposition or contrast. □□ **opposer** n.

**opposite** ● *adj.* 1 facing, on other side. 2 contrary. 3 diametrically different. ● *n.* opposite thing, person, or term. ● *adv. & prep.* in opposite position (to).

**opposition** *n.* 1 antagonism, resistance; being in conflict or disagreement. 2 contrast. 3 group or party of opponents; chief parliamentary party opposed to party in office. 4 act of placing opposite.

**oppress** *v.* 1 govern tyrannically; treat with gross harshness or injustice. 2 weigh down. □□ **oppression** *n.* **oppressor** *n.*

**oppressive** *adj.* oppressing; hard to endure; (of weather) sultry and tiring. □□ **oppressively** *adv.* **oppressiveness** *n.*

**opprobrious** *adj.* (of language) severely scornful; abusive.

**opprobrium** *n.* disgrace; cause of this.

**opt** *v.* make a choice, decide. □ **opt out** choose not to participate.

**optic** *adj.* of eye or sight.

**optical** *adj.* visual; of or according to optics; aiding sight. □ **optical fibre** (also **optic fibre**) thin glass fibre through which signals are transmitted. □□ **optically** *adv.*

**optician** *n.* = OPTOMETRY.

**optics** *n.pl.* 1 study of sight and light as its medium. 2 way in which an event or course of action is perceived by the public.

**optimal** *adj.* best, most favourable.

**optimise** *v.* (also **-ize**) make best or most effective use of. □□ **optimisation** *n.*

**optimism** *n.* inclination to hopefulness and confidence. □□ **optimist** *n.* **optimistic** *adj.* **optimistically** *adv.*

**optimum** ● *n.* most favourable conditions; best practical solution. ● *adj.* optimal.

**option** *n.* 1 choice; choosing; right to choose. 2 right to buy, sell, etc. on specified conditions at specified time.

**optional** *adj.* not obligatory. □□ **optionally** *adv.*

**optometry** *n.* occupation of measuring eyesight, prescribing corrective lenses, detecting eye disease, etc. □□ **optometrist** *n.*

**opulent** *adj.* 1 wealthy; luxurious. 2 abundant. □□ **opulence** *n.*

**opus** *n.* (*pl.* **opera**) musical composition numbered as one of composer's works; any artistic work.

**or** *conj.* introducing alternatives; also known as; otherwise; if not.

**oracle** *n.* person or thing regarded as infallible guide; (in ancient times) place where gods answered questions. □□ **oracular** *adj.*

**oral** ● *adj.* spoken, verbal; not written; by word of mouth; done or taken by mouth. ● *n.* spoken examination. □□ **orally** *adv.*

**orange** ● *n.* round juicy citrus fruit with reddish-yellow peel; this colour. ● *adj.* orange-coloured.

**orang-utan** *n.* large reddish-haired anthropoid ape.

**oration** *n.* formal or ceremonial speech.

**orator** *n.* maker of public speech; skilful speaker.

**oratorio** *n.* semi-dramatic work for orchestra and voices esp. on sacred theme.

**oratory** *n.* 1 art of or skill in public speaking. 2 small private chapel. □□ **oratorical** *adj.*

**orb** *n.* sphere, globe.

**orbit** ● *n.* 1 curved course of planet, satellite, etc.; one complete passage around another body. 2 range or sphere of action. ● *v.* (**orbited**) go around in an orbit. □□ **orbital** *adj.* **orbiter** *n.*

**orchard** *n.* piece of enclosed land with fruit trees. □□ **orchardist** *n.*

**orchestra** n. large group of instrumental performers.
□□ **orchestral** adj.

**orchestrate** v. arrange or compose for orchestral performance; arrange (elements) for desired effect.
□□ **orchestration** n.

**orchid** n. any of various plants bearing flowers in fantastic shapes and brilliant colours.

**orchitis** n. inflammation of testicles.

**ordain** v. 1 confer holy orders on. 2 decree, order; destine.

**ordeal** n. 1 painful or horrific experience. 2 severe trial.

**order** ● n. 1 way in which things are placed in relation to each other; the proper or usual sequence. 2 efficient or law-abiding state. 3 a command; request to supply goods etc., things supplied; written instruction or permission. 4 a rank, kind, or quality; group of plants or animals classified as similar. 5 monastic organisation.
● v. 1 arrange in order. 2 command; give an order for (goods etc.)
□ **in order 1** properly arranged. 2 in accordance with the rules. 3 able to function. **Order of Australia** the Australian order of honour, consisting of four levels. These, from highest to lowest, are AC, AO, AM, OAM.

**orderly** ● adj. 1 methodically arranged; tidy. 2 well-behaved.
● n. 1 hospital attendant. 2 soldier in attendance on officer etc.
□□ **orderliness** n.

**ordinal** n. (in full **ordinal number**) number defining position in series, e.g. 1st, 2nd, etc. (compare *cardinal number*.)

**ordinance** n. authoritative order; decree.

**ordinand** n. candidate for ordination.

**ordinary** adj. normal; not exceptional; commonplace.
□□ **ordinarily** adv. **ordinariness** n.

**ordination** n. conferring of holy orders.

**ordnance** n. artillery and military supplies.

**ordure** n. dung.

**ore** n. naturally occurring mineral yielding metal or other valuable minerals.

**oregano** n. herb used in cooking.

**organ** n. 1 keyboard instrument with pipes supplied with wind by bellows; similar instrument producing sounds electronically. 2 part of body serving specific function. 3 medium of communication, esp. a newspaper.

**organdie** n. fine translucent muslin, usu. stiffened.

**organic** adj. 1 of or formed from living things. 2 of bodily organs. 3 using no artificial fertilisers or pesticides. 4 organised as a system.
□□ **organically** adv.

**organisation** n. (also **-ization**) organised body, business, charity, etc.; organising, being organised; systematic arrangement; tidiness.
□□ **organisational** adj.

**organise** v. (also **-ize**) arrange systematically; make arrangements for; form (people) into association for common purpose. □ **organised crime** criminal activity carried out by coordinated organisation, esp. on large or widespread scale.
□□ **organiser** n.

**organism** n. living being; individual plant or animal; system made up of interdependent parts.

**organist** n. organ player.

**organza** n. thin stiff transparent fabric.

**orgasm** ● n. climax of sexual excitement. ● v. have sexual orgasm.
□□ **orgasmic** adj.

**orgy** n. 1 wild festivity with indiscriminate sexual activity. 2 excessive indulgence in an activity.
□□ **orgiastic** adj.

**orient** ● v. place or determine
position of with aid of compass; find
bearings of; direct; place (building
etc.) to face specified direction.
● n. (the Orient) the East, countries
east of Mediterranean, esp. E. Asia.
□ **orient oneself** determine how one
stands in relation to one's
surroundings.□□ **orientation** n.

**oriental** (often **Oriental**) ● adj. of
the Orient. ● n. native of the Orient.

**orientate** v. orient.

**orienteering** n. competitive sport of
running across country using map
and compass.

**orifice** n. opening, esp. in body.

**origami** n. Japanese art of folding
paper into decorative shapes.

**origin** n. point, source, or cause from
which thing begins its existence;
person's ancestry or parentage.

**original** ● adj. 1 existing from the
first; earliest; being the first form of
something; new in character or
design. 2 inventive; creative.
● n. first form; thing from which
another is copied.□□ **originality** n.
**originally** adv.

**originate** v. bring or come into being.
□□ **origination** n. **originator** n.

**oriole** n. kind of bird with striking
plumage.

**ormolu** n. gold-coloured alloy of
copper; articles made of this.

**ornament** ● n. thing used to make
something more attractive;
decoration. ● v. adorn; beautify.
□□ **ornamentation** n.

**ornamental** adj. serving as ornament;
decorative.□□ **ornamentally** adv.

**ornate** adj. elaborately adorned;
(of literary style) flowery.
□□ **ornately** adv.

**ornithology** n. study of birds.
□□ **ornithological** adj. **ornithologist** n.

**ornithorhynchus** n. = PLATYPUS.

**orphan** ● n. child whose parents are
dead. ● v. bereave of parents.

**orphanage** n. home for orphans.

**orthodontics** n. correction of
irregularities in teeth and jaws.
□□ **orthodontic** adj. **orthodontist** n.

**orthodox** adj. holding usual or
accepted views, esp. on religion,
morals, etc.; conventional.
□□ **orthodoxy** n.

**orthography** n. spelling, esp. with
reference to its correctness.
□□ **orthographic** adj.

**orthopaedics** n. (also **orthopedics**)
surgical correction of deformities in
bones or muscles.□□ **orthopaedic**
adj. **orthopaedist** n.

**OS** abbr. Computing operating system.

**oscillate** v. 1 (cause to) swing to and
fro. 2 vacillate. 3 Electr. (of current)
undergo high-frequency alternations.
□□ **oscillation** n. **oscillator** n.

**oscilloscope** n. device for viewing
oscillations usu. on screen of
cathode-ray tube.

**osier** n. willow used in basketwork;
twig of this.

**osmium** n. hard metallic element
(symbol Os).

**osmosis** n. passage of solvent
through semi-permeable partition
into another solution; process by
which something is acquired by
absorption.□□ **osmotic** adj.

**osprey** n. (pl. **ospreys**) large bird
preying on fish.

**osseous** adj. of bone; bony.

**ossify** v. turn into bone; harden; make
or become rigid or unprogressive.
□□ **ossification** n.

**ostensible** adj. 1 professed. 2 used to
conceal real purpose or nature.
□□ **ostensibly** adv.

**ostentation** n. pretentious display of
wealth; showing off.□□ **ostentatious**
adj.

**osteoarthritis** n. degenerative
disease of joints.□□ **osteoarthritic** adj.

**osteopath** n. practitioner who treats
certain conditions by manipulating

bones and muscles. □□ **osteopathic** *adj.* **osteopathy** *n.*

**osteoporosis** *n.* condition of brittle and fragile bones caused by loss of bony tissue.

**ostracise** *v.* (also **-ize**) exclude from society; refuse to associate with.

**ostrich** *n.* large flightless swift-running African bird.

**other** ● *adj.* alternative, additional, being the remaining one of a set of two or more; not the same. ● *n. & pron.* the other person or thing. ● *adv.* otherwise. □ **other than** apart from; differently from. the **other day** (or **week**) a few days (or weeks) ago.

**otherwise** ● *adv.* 1 or else. 2 in different circumstances. 3 in other respects. 4 in a different way. 5 as an alternative. ● *adj.* different.

**otiose** *adj.* serving no practical purpose.

**otitis** *n.* inflammation of ear.

**otter** *n.* furred aquatic fish-eating mammal.

**ottoman** *n.* storage box with padded top used as seat.

**ouch** *int.* expressing sharp or sudden pain.

**ought** *v.aux.* expressing duty, rightness, probability etc.

**ouija board** *n. propr.* board marked with letters or signs used with movable pointer to try to obtain messages at seance.

**ounce** *n.* unit of weight (one sixteenth of pound or approx. 28 g); very small amount.

**our** *adj.* of or belonging to us.

**ours** *pron.poss.* belonging to us.

**ourselves** *pron.* emphatic or reflexive form of WE or US.

**oust** *v.* drive out or expel, esp. by seizing place of.

**out** ● *adv.* 1 away from or not in a place; not at home. 2 not in effective action; in error; not possible; unconscious. 3 into the open, so as to be heard or seen. ● *prep.* out of. □ **out** 1 way of escape. 2 an excuse. ● *v.* reveal homosexuality of. □ **be out to** be intending to. **out of** from inside or among; having no more of. **out of date** no longer fashionable, current, or valid.

**out-take** scene, sequence, or song filmed or recorded for a film, program, or album but not included in final version. **out tray** tray for documents that have been dealt with.

**out-** *prefix* more than, so as to exceed.

**outback** *Aust.* ● *n.* (also the **Outback**) remote sparsely inhabited inland areas. ● *adv.* out, in, or to areas remote from major centre of population. ● *adj.* of or relating to remote area.

**outboard** *adj.* (of motor) attached to outside of boat.

**outbox** *n.* 1 folder in which emails are held before being sent. 2 out tray.

**outbreak** *n.* sudden eruption of emotion, war, disease, fire, etc.

**outbuilding** *n.* shed, barn, etc. detached from main building.

**outburst** *n.* bursting out, esp. of emotion in vehement words.

**outcast** ● *n.* person rejected by family or society. ● *adj.* 1 rejected. 2 homeless.

**outclass** *v.* surpass in quality.

**outcome** *n.* result; consequence.

**outcrop** *n.* rock etc. emerging at surface; noticeable manifestation.

**outcry** *n.* uproar; loud public protest.

**outdated** *adj.* out of date; obsolete.

**outdistance** *v.* leave (competitor) behind completely.

**outdo** *v.* (outdid, outdone, outdoing) be or do better than.

**outdoor** *adj.* done, existing, or used out of doors; fond of open air. □□ **outdoors** *adv.*

**outer** ● *adj.* outside; external; farther from centre or inside.

● *n. Aust.* uncovered area for non-members at sports ground etc.
□□ **outermost** *adj.*

**outface** *v.* disconcert by staring or by confident manner.

**outfall** *n.* outlet of river, drain, etc.

**outfit** *n.* 1 set of equipment or clothes; equipment etc. for specific purpose. 2 *colloq.* (organised) group or company.

**outflank** *v.* get around flank of (enemy); outmanoeuvre.

**outgoing** ● *adj.* 1 friendly. 2 retiring from office; going out.
● *n.* (outgoings) expenditure.

**outgrow** *v.* (**outgrew**, **outgrown**, **outgrowing**) 1 grow faster than; grow larger than. 2 leave aside as one develops.

**outhouse** *n.* outdoor toilet, shed, barn, etc.

**outing** *n.* excursion.

**outlandish** *adj.* strange, bizarre.
□□ **outlandishly** *adv.*
**outlandishness** *n.*

**outlast** *v.* last longer than.

**outlaw** ● *n.* fugitive from law; *hist.* person deprived of protection of law. ● *v.* make illegal; *hist.* make (someone) outlaw.

**outlay** *n.* expenditure.

**outlet** *n.* means of exit; means of expressing feelings; market for goods.

**outlier** *n.* 1 outlying part or member. 2 (in statistics) result differing greatly from others in same sample. 3 younger rock formation isolated in older rocks.

**outline** ● *n.* 1 line showing thing's shape or boundary. 2 summary or rough draft. ● *v.* draw or describe in outline; mark outline of.

**outlive** *v.* live longer than, beyond, or through.

**outlook** *n.* 1 prospect. 2 mental attitude; view.

**outlying** *adj.* far from centre; remote.

**outmoded** *adj.* outdated; out of fashion.

**outnumber** *v.* exceed in number.

**outpace** *v.* go faster than; outdo in contest.

**outpatient** *n.* person visiting hospital for treatment but not staying overnight.

**outpost** *n.* 1 detachment on guard at distance from army. 2 remote settlement.

**output** ● *n.* 1 amount produced (by machine, worker, etc.) 2 electrical power etc. supplied by apparatus. 3 place where energy, information, etc., leaves a system. ● *v.* (**output** or **outputted**, **outputting**) (of computer) supply (results etc.)

**outrage** ● *n.* extreme shock and anger; something that provokes this. ● *v.* subject to outrage; insult; shock and anger.

**outrageous** *adj.* immoderate; shocking; immoral; offensive.
□□ **outrageously** *adv.*

**outrider** *n.* motorcyclist or mounted guard riding ahead of car(s).

**outrigger** *n.* spar or framework projecting from or over side of ship, canoe, etc. to give stability; boat with this.

**outright** ● *adv.* 1 altogether, entirely; not gradually. 2 without reservation. ● *adj.* 1 downright, complete. 2 undisputed.

**outrun** *v.* (**outran**, **outrun**, **outrunning**) run faster or farther than; go beyond.

**outset** *n.* □ **at (or from) the outset** at or from the beginning.

**outside** ● *n.* 1 outer side, surface, or part; external appearance. 2 *Aust.* (also **Outside**) area remote from major city; outback. ● *adj.* of, on, or nearer the outside; outer. ● *adv.* on, at, or to the outside; outdoors.
● *prep.* on, at, or to the outside of; other than; beyond the limits of.

□ **outside chance** remote possibility.

**outsider** n. 1 non-member of group, organisation, profession, etc. 2 competitor thought to have little chance.

**outsize** adj. much larger than average.

**outskirts** n.pl. outer area of town etc.

**outsmart** v. outwit, be too clever for.

**outsource** v. 1 obtain (goods) from outside source. 2 (of organisation, company, etc.) contract (some of its functions or work) out to another organisation.

**outspoken** adj. saying openly what one thinks; frank. □□ **outspokenly** adv. **outspokenness** n.

**outstanding** adj. 1 conspicuous because of excellence. 2 still to be dealt with. □□ **outstandingly** adv.

**outstation** n. Aust. 1 subordinate grazing property at some distance from main establishment. 2 autonomous Aboriginal community distant from centre on which it depends for services etc.

**outstrip** v. (**outstripped**) run faster or further than; surpass.

**outvote** v. defeat by majority of votes.

**outward** • adj. 1 of or on outside. 2 (of journey) going out. • adv. in outward direction. □□ **outwardly** adv. **outwards** adv.

**outweigh** v. exceed in weight, value, influence, etc.

**outwit** v. (**outwitted**) be too clever for; overcome by greater ingenuity.

**outwork** n. work done away from employer's premises. □□ **outworker** n.

**ouzo** n. Greek aniseed-flavoured spirit.

**ova** see OVUM.

**oval** • adj. egg-shaped; elliptical. • n. 1 elliptical closed curve; thing with oval outline. 2 sports ground.

**ovary** n. either of two ova-producing organs in female; seed vessel in plant. □□ **ovarian** adj.

**ovate** adj. egg-shaped.

**ovation** n. enthusiastic applause or reception.

**oven** n. enclosed chamber for cooking food etc.

**ovenware** n. dishes for use in oven.

**over** • prep. 1 in or to a position higher than; above and across; more than. 2 throughout; during. • adv. 1 outwards and downwards from the brink or an upright position etc. 2 from one side or end etc. to the other; across space or distance. 3 besides, in addition. 4 with repetition. 5 finished, at an end. • n. Cricket sequence of six balls bowled from one end of pitch; play resulting from this. □ **over and over** again and again. **over the top** colloq. excessive.

**over-** prefix 1 excessively. 2 upper, outer. 3 over. 4 completely.

**overall** • adj. taking everything into account; inclusive, total. • adv. 1 including everything. 2 on the whole. • n. garment worn to protect other clothing; (**overalls**) one-piece garment of this kind covering body and legs.

**overarm** adj. & adv. with arm raised above shoulder.

**overawe** v. overcome with awe.

**overbalance** v. lose balance and fall; cause to do this.

**overbearing** adj. domineering, oppressive.

**overblown** adj. 1 inflated or pretentious. 2 (of flower) past its prime.

**overboard** adv. from ship into water. □ **go overboard** colloq. be highly enthusiastic; behave immoderately, go too far.

**overcast** adj. 1 (of sky) covered with cloud. 2 (in sewing) edged with stitching.

**overcharge** ● v. **1** charge too high a price to. **2** put too much charge into (battery, gun, etc.) ● n. excessive charge (of money etc.)

**overcoat** n. warm outdoor coat.

**overcome** v. **1** win victory over; succeed in subduing or dealing; be victorious. **2** make weak or helpless.

**overdo** v. (overdid, overdone, overdoing) do too much; cook for too long.

**overdose** ● n. excessive dose of drug etc. ● v. take overdose.

**overdraft** n. overdrawing of bank account; amount by which account is overdrawn.

**overdraw** v. (overdrew, overdrawn, overdrawing) draw more from (bank account) than amount in credit.

**overdrive** ● n. **1** mechanism in vehicle providing gear above top gear for economy at high speeds. **2** state of high activity. ● v. overwork.

**overdue** adj. past time when due or ready; late, in arrears.

**overestimate** ● v. form too high an estimate of. ● n. too high an estimate. □□ overestimation n.

**overflow** ● v. **1** flow over edge or limits (of); (of crowd etc.) extend beyond limits or capacity of. **2** (of kindness, harvest, etc.) be very abundant. ● n. what overflows or is superfluous; outlet for excess liquid.

**overgraze** v. damage land by allowing stock to graze land too extensively.

**overgrown** adj. **1** grown too big. **2** covered with weeds etc. □□ overgrowth n.

**overhaul** ● v. **1** check over thoroughly and make repairs if necessary. **2** overtake. ● n. thorough examination, with repairs if necessary.

**overhead** ● adv. above one's head; in sky. ● adj. placed overhead. ● n. routine administrative or maintenance expense of business.

□ **overhead projector** projector producing image from transparency placed flat on light source.

**overhear** v. (overheard, overhearing) hear as hidden or unintentional listener.

**overjoyed** adj. filled with great joy.

**overkill** n. amount by which capacity for destruction exceeds what is necessary for victory; use of more resources than necessary to achieve aim; excess.

**overland** ● adj. & adv. by land and not by sea. ● v. Aust. drive (livestock) overland, esp. a great distance. □□ overlanding n.

**overlap** ● v. (overlapped) **1** extend beyond edge of. **2** partly coincide. ● n. overlapping; overlapping part or amount.

**overleaf** adv. on other side of page of book.

**overload** ● v. **1** load too heavily (with baggage, work, etc.). **2** put too great a demand on (electrical circuit etc.) ● n. excessive quantity or demand.

**overlook** v. **1** fail to observe. **2** tolerate. **3** have view of from above.

**overly** adv. excessively.

**overnight** ● adv. **1** for or during night. **2** instantly, suddenly. ● adj. **1** done or for use etc. overnight. **2** instant.

**overpass** n. road crossing another by means of bridge.

**overpower** v. **1** subdue, reduce to submission. **2** (of heat or feelings) extremely intense.

**overrate** v. have too high an opinion of.

**overreach** v. □ **overreach oneself** fail through being too ambitious.

**overreact** v. respond more forcibly than is justified. □□ overreaction n.

**override** v. (overrode, overridden, overriding) overrule; prevail over; intervene and cancel the operation of.

**overrule** v. set aside (decision etc.) by using one's authority.

**overrun** v. (overran, overrun, overrunning) **1** spread over and occupy or injure. **2** exceed (limit).

**overseas** adj. & adv. across or beyond the sea, abroad.

**oversee** v. (oversaw, overseen, overseeing) supervise (workers etc.) □□ overseer n.

**overshadow** v. **1** appear much more prominent or important than. **2** cast into shade.

**overshoot** v. (overshot, overshooting) pass or send beyond (target or limit etc.)

**oversight** n. **1** failure to notice. **2** inadvertent mistake. **3** supervision.

**overstay** v. stay longer than (one's welcome etc.)

**oversteer** ● v. (of car) tend to turn more sharply than was intended. ● n. this tendency.

**overstep** v. (overstepped) pass beyond.

**overstock** v. stock excessively.

**overt** adj. done openly; unconcealed. □□ **overtly** adv.

**overtake** v. (overtook, overtaken, overtaking) **1** catch up and pass. **2** (of bad luck etc.) come suddenly upon.

**overtax** v. make excessive demands on.

**overthrow** ● v. (overthrew, overthrown, overthrowing) cause downfall of. ● n. **1** defeat or downfall. **2** Cricket fielder's inaccurate return of ball allowing further runs.

**overtime** ● n. time worked in addition to regular hours; payment for this. ● adv. in addition to regular hours.

**overtone** n. subtle extra quality or implication.

**overture** n. **1** orchestral composition forming prelude to performance.

**2** (overtures) initial approach or proposal.

**overturn** v. **1** (cause to) fall down or over. **2** reverse, cancel (decision etc.)

**overview** n. general review or summary of a subject.

**overweight** adj. above weight allowed or desirable.

**overwhelm** v. **1** overpower with emotion. **2** overcome by force of numbers. **3** bury, submerge utterly.

**overwhelming** adj. **1** too great to resist or overcome. **2** by a great number. □□ **overwhelmingly** adv.

**overwrought** adj. **1** overexcited, nervous, distraught. **2** too elaborate.

**oviduct** n. tube through which ova pass from ovary.

**ovine** adj. of or like sheep.

**oviparous** adj. egg-laying.

**ovoid** adj. (of solid) egg-shaped.

**ovulate** v. produce ova or ovules, or discharge them from ovary. □□ **ovulation** n.

**ovule** n. structure containing germ cell in female plant.

**ovum** n. (pl. **ova**) female egg cell from which young develop after fertilisation.

**owe** v. be under obligation to (re)pay or render; be in debt; be indebted to person, thing, etc. for.

**owing** adj. owed and not yet paid. □ **owing to** caused by; because of.

**owl** n. **1** nocturnal bird of prey. **2** solemn or wise-looking person. □□ **owlish** adj.

**own** ● adj. belonging to myself or yourself etc.; not another's; individual, peculiar, particular. ● v. **1** have as property, possess. **2** Aust. (in Aboriginal English) have spiritual responsibility for (place). **3** acknowledge as true or belonging to one. **4** colloq. completely get the better of. □ **own up** confess. □□ **owner** n. **ownership** n.

**ox** *n.* (*pl.* **oxen**) animal of kind kept as domestic cattle; castrated male of domestic species of cattle.

**oxalis** *n.* clover-like exotic plant.

**oxidation** *n.* process of being combined with oxygen.

**oxide** *n.* compound of oxygen with another element.

**oxidise** *v.* (also **-ize**) **1** combine with oxygen. **2** rust. **3** coat (metal) with oxide. □□ **oxidisation** *n.*

**oxtail** *n.* tail of ox, used in soups etc.

**oxyacetylene** *adj.* of or using mixture of oxygen and acetylene, esp. in cutting or welding metals.

**oxygen** *n.* colourless tasteless odourless gaseous element essential to life and combustion (symbol **O**).

**oxygenate** *v.* supply, treat, or mix with oxygen; oxidise.

**oyster** *n.* **1** bivalve mollusc, esp. edible kind, sometimes producing pearl. **2** greyish-white. □ **oyster blade** lean cut of beef from shoulder.

**oz.** *abbr.* ounce(s).

**ozone** *n.* colourless toxic gas with pungent odour. □ **ozone layer** layer in stratosphere containing high concentration of ozone, absorbing most of sun's ultraviolet radiation.

**p** *abbr.* (also **p.**) **1** page. **2** piano (softly).

**PA** *abbr.* **1** public address (system). **2** personal assistant.

**pa** *n. colloq.* father.

**p.a.** *abbr.* per annum, yearly.

**pace** ● *n.* **1** single step in walking or running; distance covered in this. **2** rate of progress. ● *v.* walk, esp. with slow or regular step; measure (distance) by pacing.

**pacemaker** *n.* **1** runner etc. who sets pace for another. **2** device regulating heart contractions.

**pachyderm** *n.* thick-skinned mammal, esp. elephant or rhinoceros. □□ **pachydermatous** *adj.*

**pacific** ● *adj.* **1** tending to peace; peaceful. **2** (**Pacific**) of or adjoining Pacific. ● *n.* (**the Pacific**) ocean between America to the east and Asia to the west.

**pacifist** *n.* person opposed to war. □□ **pacifism** *n.*

**pacify** *v.* appease (person, anger, etc.); soothe (baby); bring (country etc.) to state of peace. □□ **pacification** *n.*

**pack** ● *n.* **1** collection of things wrapped or tied together for carrying. **2** backpack. **3** set of packaged items. **4** set of playing cards. **5** group of wild animals, hounds, etc. **6** forwards in rugby team. **7** *AFL* group of players contesting ball. **8** crowded floating ice in sea. ● *v.* **1** put into or fill container. **2** press or crowd together; fill (space) in this way. **3** cover or protect with something packed tightly. **4** select (jury etc.) to secure decision in one's favour. □ **send packing** dismiss abruptly.

**package** ● *n.* **1** parcel; box etc. in which goods are packed. **2** (in full **package deal**) set of proposals or items offered or agreed to as a whole. ● *v.* make up into or enclose in package. □□ **packager** *n.* **packaging** *n.*

**packet** *n.* **1** small package. **2** *colloq.* large sum of money.

**pact** *n.* agreement; treaty.

**pad** *n.* **1** piece of soft material used to diminish jarring, raise surface, absorb fluid, etc.; sanitary towel. **2** sheets of blank paper fastened together at one edge. **3** fleshy underpart of animal's foot. **4** leg guard in sports. **5** flat surface for helicopter take-off or rocket-launching. **6** *colloq.* lodging. ● *v.* (**padded**) **1** provide with pad or padding, stuff. **2** fill out (book etc.) with superfluous matter. **3** walk softly or steadily.

**padding** *n.* **1** material used to pad. **2** superfluous material used to lengthen (book etc.).

**paddle** ● *n.* **1** short oar with broad blade at one or each end. **2** paddle-shaped instrument. **3** fin, flipper. **4** board on paddle wheel or mill wheel. **5** action or spell of paddling. ● *v.* **1** move on water or propel (boat etc.) with paddle(s). **2** row gently. **3** wade about with bare feet in shallow water.

**paddock** *n.* **1** *Aust.* piece of land fenced, defined by natural boundaries, or otherwise considered distinct; playing field. **2** small field, esp. for keeping horses in; enclosure where horses are saddled before race. ● *v.* confine (livestock) in paddock.

**paddy**[1] *n.* (in full **paddy field**) field where rice is grown; rice before threshing or in the husk.

**paddy²** *n. colloq.* rage; temper.

**paddymelon** *n.* (also **pademelon**) *Aust.* plant bearing bristly, melon-like fruit.

**paddy wagon** *n.* secure van used by police for transporting prisoners.

**pademelon** *n.* (also **paddymelon**) small, compact-bodied wallaby of eastern Australia.

**padlock** ● *n.* detachable lock hanging by pivoted hook. ● *v.* secure with padlock.

**padre** *n.* chaplain in army etc.

**paean** *n.* (also **pean**) song of praise or triumph.

**paediatrics** *n.pl.* (also **pediatrics**) study of children's diseases. □□ **paediatric** *adj.* **paediatrician** *n.*

**paedophile** *n.* (also **pedophile**) person feeling sexual attraction towards children.

**paella** *n.* Spanish dish of rice, saffron, chicken, seafood, etc.

**pagan** *adj. & n.* (person) holding religious beliefs other than those of established religion. □□ **paganism** *n.*

**page¹** ● *n.* 1 leaf of book etc.; one side of this; webpage. 2 boy attendant of a bride etc. ● *v.* summon by announcement, messenger, or pager.

**pageant** *n.* public show or procession, esp. with people in costume. □□ **pageantry** *n.*

**pager** *n.* radio device with a bleeper for summoning the bearer.

**pagoda** *n.* temple or sacred tower in India and E. Asia; ornamental imitation of this.

**paid** see PAY.

**pail** *n.* bucket.

**pain** ● *n.* 1 bodily suffering caused by injury, pressure, etc.; mental suffering; *colloq.* troublesome person or thing. 2 (**pains**) careful effort. ● *v.* cause pain to.

**painful** *adj.* 1 causing or suffering pain. 2 laborious. □□ **painfully** *adv.*

**painkiller** *n.* drug for reducing pain.

**painless** *adj.* not causing pain. □□ **painlessly** *adv.*

**painstaking** *adj.* careful, industrious, thorough. □□ **painstakingly** *adv.*

**paint** ● *n.* colouring matter, esp. in liquid form, for applying to surface. ● *v.* 1 cover (surface) with paint or liquid. 2 portray or make pictures in colours. 3 describe vividly. □ **paint-up** (in Aboriginal English) decoration of body for ceremonial purposes.

**paintball** *n.* game in which participants use airguns to shoot capsules of paint at each other.

**painter¹** *n.* 1 person who paints, esp. as artist or decorator. 2 rope at bow of boat for tying it up.

**painting** *n.* painted picture.

**pair** ● *n.* 1 set of two people or things; thing with two joined or corresponding parts. 2 couple in relationship etc. ● *v.* arrange or unite as pair, in pairs, or in marriage; mate.

**paisley** *n.* pattern of curved feather-shaped figures.

**pakeha** *n. NZ* white person, not Maori.

**pal** *n. colloq.* friend.

**palace** *n.* official residence of sovereign, president, archbishop, or bishop; splendid or spacious building.

**palaeography** *n.* study of ancient writing and documents.

**palaeolithic** *adj.* of earlier Stone Age.

**palaeontology** *n.* study of life in geological past. □□ **palaeontologist** *n.*

**palatable** *adj.* pleasant to taste; (of idea etc.) acceptable, satisfactory.

**palate** *n.* 1 roof of mouth in vertebrates. 2 sense of taste. 3 liking.

**palatial** *adj.* like palace; splendid.

**palaver** *n.* 1 tedious fuss and bother. 2 idle talk. 3 cajolery. 4 *colloq.* an affair or business.

**pale¹** ● *adj.* 1 light in colour. 2 (of light) dim. ● *v.* 1 grow or make pale.

**2** seem feeble in comparison (with). □ **beyond the pale** outside bounds of acceptable behaviour. □□ **palely** adv.

**palette** n. artist's thin board for mixing colours on; range of colours used by artist.

**palimpsest** n. writing material reused after original writing has been erased.

**palindrome** n. word or phrase that reads same backwards as forwards. □□ **palindromic** adj.

**paling** n. pointed piece of wood used as fencing material.

**pall** ● n. **1** cloth spread over coffin etc. **2** ecclesiastical vestment. **3** dark covering. ● v. become uninteresting.

**palladium** n. rare metallic element (symbol Pd).

**pallbearer** n. person helping to carry or walking beside coffin at funeral.

**pallet** n. **1** straw mattress; makeshift bed. **2** portable platform for transporting and storing loads.

**palliate** v. alleviate without curing; excuse, extenuate. □ **palliative care** care of terminally ill, esp. in hospice etc. □□ **palliative** adj. & n.

**pallid** adj. pale, sickly-looking.

**pallor** n. paleness.

**palm** ● n. **1** (usu. tropical) treelike plant with unbranched stem and crown of large esp. fan-shaped leaves. **2** inner surface of hand between wrist and fingers. ● v. conceal in hand. □ **palm off** persuaded to accept fraudulently or unwillingly.

**palmistry** n. fortune telling from lines etc. in palm of hand. □□ **palmist** n.

**palomino** n. golden or cream coloured horse with light coloured mane and tail.

**palpable** adj. that can be touched or felt; readily perceived. □□ **palpably** adv.

**palpate** v. examine (esp. medically) by touch. □□ **palpation** n.

**palpitate** v. pulsate, throb, tremble. □□ **palpitation** n.

**palsy** n. paralysis, esp. with involuntary tremors. □□ **palsied** adj.

**paltry** adj. worthless, contemptible, trifling.

**pampas** n.pl. large treeless S. American plains.

**pamper** v. overindulge.

**pamphlet** n. small unbound booklet or information leaflet.

**pamphleteer** n. writer of (esp. political) pamphlets.

**pan**[1] ● n. **1** flat-bottomed usu. metal vessel used in cooking etc.; contents of this. **2** shallow container or tray. **3** toilet bowl. ● v. (**panned**) **1** colloq. criticise harshly. **2** wash (gold-bearing gravel) in pan; search for gold thus.

**pan**[2] ● v. (**panned**) swing (film camera) horizontally to give panoramic effect or follow moving object; (of camera) be moved thus. ● n. panning movement.

**pan-** comb. form **1** all. **2** the whole of.

**panacea** n. universal remedy.

**panache** n. assertively flamboyant or confident style.

**panama** n. straw hat.

**pancake** n. thin flat cake of fried batter.

**pancetta** n. kind of Italian bacon.

**pancreas** n. gland near stomach supplying digestive fluid and secreting insulin. □□ **pancreatic** adj.

**panda** n. large bearlike black and white mammal native to China and Tibet.

**pandanny** n. palm-like Tasmanian tree.

**pandanus** n. tropical tree with spined leaves and large fruits resembling pineapple.

**pandemic** adj. (of disease) prevalent over whole country or world.

**pandemonium** n. uproar; utter confusion.

**pander** v. □ pander to gratify by satisfying weakness or vulgar taste.

**pane** n. single sheet of glass in window or door.

**paneer** n. type of milk curd cheese used in Indian and Middle Eastern cooking.

**panegyric** n. eulogy; speech or essay of praise.

**panel** ● n. 1 distinct, usu. rectangular, section of surface, esp. of wall, door, or vehicle. 2 strip of material in garment. 3 group or team of people assembled for discussion, consultation, etc. 4 list of available jurors; jury. ● v. (**panelled**) fit with panels. □ **panel beater** person repairing metal panels of motor vehicles. □□ **panelling** n.

**panellist** n. member of panel.

**pang** n. sudden sharp pain or distressing emotion.

**panic** ● n. sudden alarm; infectious fright. ● adj. characterised or caused by panic. ● v. (**panicked**) affect or be affected with panic. □□ **panicky** adj.

**panicle** n. loose branching cluster of flowers.

**pannier** n. one of pair of baskets or bags carried on bicycle or motorcycle or by beast of burden.

**pannikin** n. small metal drinking vessel.

**panoply** n. 1 complete or splendid array. 2 full armour.

**panorama** n. unbroken view of surrounding region; picture or photograph containing wide view. □□ **panoramic** adj.

**pan pipes** n.pl. musical instrument made of series of short pipes graduated in length.

**pansy** n. 1 garden plant with richly-coloured flowers. 2 colloq. offens. effeminate or homosexual man.

**pant** ● v. 1 breathe with quick breaths. 2 yearn. ● n. panting breath.

**pantaloons** n.pl. baggy trousers gathered at the ankles.

**pantheism** n. 1 doctrine that God is in everything. 2 worship or toleration of many gods. □□ **pantheist** n. **pantheistic** adj.

**pantheon** n. 1 building with memorials of illustrious dead. 2 deities of a people collectively. 3 temple of all gods.

**panther** n. leopard.

**panties** n.pl. colloq. short-legged or legless knickers.

**pantile** n. curved roof tile.

**pantograph** n. instrument for copying plan etc. on any scale.

**pantomime** n. 1 theatrical entertainment based on fairy tale. 2 gestures and facial expression conveying meaning, esp. in drama and dance.

**pantry** n. room or cupboard for storing food, crockery, cutlery, etc.

**pants** n.pl. trousers; underpants.

**pantyhose** n. women's tights.

**pap** n. 1 soft or semi-liquid food. 2 trivial reading matter.

**papa** n. father.

**papacy** n. position or authority of pope.

**papal** adj. of pope or papacy.

**paparazzi** n.pl. freelance photographers who pursue celebrities.

**papaya** = PAWPAW.

**paper** ● n. 1 substance manufactured in thin sheets from wood fibre, rags, etc., used for writing on, wrapping, etc. 2 newspaper; set of examination questions; document; dissertation. ● v. decorate or cover (wall etc.) with paper.

**paperback** adj. & n. (a book) bound in stiff paper, not boards.

**paperweight** n. small heavy object for holding loose papers down.

**paperwork** n. routine clerical or administrative work.

**papier mâché** n. moulded paper pulp used for making models etc.

**papilla** n. (pl. **papillae**) small nipple-like protuberance.
□□ **papillary** adj.

**papilloma** n. wart-like usu. benign tumour.

**pappadam** n. crisp, fried lentil wafer.

**paprika** n. red pepper; condiment made from this.

**pap smear** n. cervical smear test used to detect cancer in early stage.

**papyrus** n. (pl. **papyri**) aquatic plant of N. Africa; writing material made from this.

**par** n. **1** average or normal value, degree, condition, etc. **2** equality; equal footing. **3** Golf number of strokes made by first-class player for hole or course. **4** face value.

**parable** n. story used to illustrate moral or spiritual truth.

**parabola** n. plane curve formed by intersection of cone with plane parallel to its side. □□ **parabolic** adj.

**paracetamol** n. drug used to relieve pain and reduce fever.

**parachute** ● n. usu. umbrella-shaped apparatus allowing person or heavy object to descend safely from a height, esp. from aircraft, or used to retard forward motion etc.
● v. convey or descend by parachute.
□□ **parachutist** n.

**parade** ● n. public procession; muster of troops etc. for inspection; ostentatious display; public square, promenade. ● v. march ceremonially; assemble for parade; display ostentatiously.

**paradigm** n. example or pattern; model.

**paradise** n. **1** heaven. **2** place or state of complete happiness.

**paradox** n. seemingly absurd or self-contradictory though often true statement. □□ **paradoxical** adj. **paradoxically** adv.

**paraffin** n. flammable waxy or oily hydrocarbon distilled from petroleum etc., used as fuel.

**paragon** n. model of excellence or virtue.

**paragraph** n. distinct passage in writing usu. marked by indentation of first line; mark of reference (¶).

**parakeet** n. small usu. long-tailed parrot.

**parallax** n. apparent difference in position or direction of object caused by change in observer's position; angular amount of this.
□□ **parallactic** adj.

**parallel** ● adj. **1** (of lines) continuously equidistant. **2** precisely similar, analogous, or corresponding. **3** (of processes etc.) occurring or performed simultaneously.
● n. **1** person or thing analogous to another; a comparison. **2** line of latitude. ● v. (**paralleled**, **paralleling**) be parallel or correspond, to; represent as similar; compare.
□□ **parallelism** n.

**parallelogram** n. four-sided rectilinear figure with opposite sides parallel.

**paralyse** v. affect with paralysis; bring (work, system, etc.) to halt.

**paralysis** n. impairment or loss of esp. motor function of nerves, causing immobility; powerlessness.

**paralytic** ● adj. **1** affected by paralysis. **2** colloq. very drunk.
● n. person affected with paralysis.

**paramedic** n. skilled person working in support of medical staff.
□□ **paramedical** adj.

**parameter** n. **1** (esp. measurable or quantifiable) characteristic or feature; Math. quantity constant in case considered but varying in different cases. **2** limit or boundary that defines the scope of a particular process or activity.

**paramilitary** *adj.* organised like military force.

**paramount** *adj.* supreme; most important or powerful.

**paranoia** *n.* mental disorder with delusions of persecution or grandeur; abnormal suspicion and mistrust. □□ **paranoiac** *adj.* & *n.* **paranoid** *adj.* & *n.*

**paranormal** *adj.* beyond scope of normal scientific investigation etc.

**parapet** *n.* **1** low wall at edge of roof, balcony, bridge, etc. **2** mound along front of trench.

**paraphernalia** *n.pl.* (also treated as *sing.*) **1** personal belongings. **2** miscellaneous accessories, etc.

**paraphrase** ● *n.* restatement of sense of passage etc. in other words. ● *v.* express meaning in other words.

**paraplegia** *n.* paralysis of legs and part or all of trunk. □□ **paraplegic** *adj.* & *n.*

**parapsychology** *n.* study of mental phenomena outside sphere of ordinary psychology.

**parasailing** *n.* (also **parascending**) sport in which person wearing parachute is towed behind motor boat or vehicle.

**parasite** *n.* animal or plant living in or on another and feeding on it; person exploiting another or others. □□ **parasitic** *adj.* **parasitism** *n.*

**parasol** *n.* light umbrella giving shade from sun.

**paratroops** *n.pl.* airborne troops landing by parachute. □□ **paratrooper** *n.*

**parboil** *v.* partly cook by boiling.

**parcel** ● *n.* **1** goods etc. packed up in single wrapping. **2** something considered as unit. ● *v.* (**parcelled**) **1** wrap into parcel. **2** divide into portions.

**parch** *v.* make or become hot and dry.

**parchment** *n.* skin, esp. of sheep or goat, prepared for writing etc.; manuscript written on this.

**pardalote** *n.* small spotted finch-like Australian bird.

**pardon** ● *n.* forgiveness. ● *v.* (**pardoned**) forgive or excuse. □□ **pardonable** *adj.*

**pare** *v.* trim or reduce by cutting away surface or edge; whittle away.

**parent** ● *n.* **1** person who has had or adopted a child; father or mother. **2** initiating organisation or enterprise. **3** source, origin, etc. ● *v.* be the parent of. □□ **parental** *adj.* **parenthood** *n.*

**parentage** *n.* ancestry; origin.

**parenthesis** *n.* (*pl.* **parentheses**) word or phrase inserted into a passage; brackets (like these) placed around this. □□ **parenthetic** *adj.*

**parenting** *n.* being parent.

**par excellence** *adv.* being supreme example of its kind.

**pariah** *n.* social outcast.

**parietal** *adj.* of wall of body or any of its cavities. □ **parietal bone** each of a pair of bones forming part of skull.

**paring** *n.* strip pared off.

**parish** *n.* **1** area having its own church and clergyman. **2** local government district.

**parishioner** *n.* inhabitant of parish.

**parity** *n.* equality.

**park** ● *n.* **1** public garden or recreation ground. **2** large area of land kept in its natural state for public benefit. **3** area for specified purpose (*science park*); area for vehicles to be parked. ● *v.* place and leave (vehicle) temporarily.

**parka** *n.* hooded jacket.

**Parkinson's disease** *n.* progressive disease of nervous system with tremor, muscular rigidity, and emaciation.

**Parkinson's law** *n.* notion that work expands to fill the time available.

**parlance** *n.* way of speaking.

**parley** ● n. meeting between disputants, esp. to discuss peace terms etc. ● v. (**parleyed, parleying**) hold parley.

**parliament** n. assembly that makes laws of country or state.
□□ **parliamentarian** n. **parliamentary** adj.

**parlour** n. (also **parlor**) **1** arch. sitting room in private house, convent, etc. **2** shop providing specified goods or services.

**parlous** adj. difficult; dangerous.

**parma wallaby** n. Aust. greyish-brown wallaby, having white throat and white cheek stripe.

**parmesan** n. hard Italian cheese.

**parochial** adj. **1** of parish. **2** of narrow range, merely local.
□□ **parochialism** n.

**parody** ● n. humorous exaggerated imitation of author, style, etc.; travesty. ● v. write parody of; mimic humorously. □□ **parodist** n.

**parole** ● n. temporary or permanent release of prisoner before end of sentence, on promise of good behaviour; such promise.
● v. put (prisoner) on parole.

**paroxysm** n. fit (of pain, rage, coughing, etc.).

**parquet** n. flooring of wooden blocks arranged in pattern. □□ **parquetry** n.

**parricide** n. killing of one's own parent. □□ **parricidal** adj.

**parrot** n. **1** bird with short hooked bill, often vivid plumage, and the ability to mimic human voice. **2** unintelligent imitator or chatterer.
● v. (**parroted**) repeat mechanically.

**parry** v. avert, ward off. ● n. act of parrying.

**parse** v. describe (word) or analyse (sentence) in terms of grammar; Computing analyse (string or text) into logical syntactic components.

**parsec** n. unit of stellar distance, about 3.25 light years.

**parsimony** n. carefulness in use of money etc.; meanness.
□□ **parsimonious** adj.

**parsley** n. herb used to season and garnish food.

**parsnip** n. plant with pale yellow tapering root used as vegetable.

**parson** n. any (esp. Protestant) clergyman or minister.

**parsonage** n. parson's house.

**part** ● n. **1** some but not all; distinct portion; portion allotted; component. **2** character assigned to actor in a play etc. ● v. separate, divide.
● adv. partly. □ **part of speech** grammatical class of word (noun, verb, adjective, preposition, etc.). **part-time** occupying or using only part of one's working time. **part with** give up possession of. **take part** join in; participate.

**partake** v. (**partook, partaken, partaking**) **1** participate. **2** take portion of, esp. food.

**partial** adj. **1** not total or complete. **2** biased, unfair. □ **be partial to** have liking for. □□ **partiality** n. **partially** adv.

**participate** v. have share or take part. □□ **participant** n. **participation** n.

**participle** n. word formed from verb as past participle (e.g. written; burnt) or a present participle (e.g. writing; burning). □□ **participial** adj.

**particle** n. minute portion of matter; minor esp. indeclinable part of speech.

**particoloured** adj. of more than one colour.

**particular** ● adj. **1** relating to or considered as one as distinct from others. **2** special. **3** scrupulously exact; fastidious. ● n. a detail; piece of information. □ **in particular** specifically. □□ **particularly** adv.

**parting** n. **1** leaving, being separated. **2** dividing line of combed hair.

**partisan** ● *n.* **1** strong supporter of party, cause, etc. **2** guerrilla.
● *adj.* **1** of partisans. **2** biased.
□□ **partisanship** *n.*

**partition** ● *n.* division into parts; structure dividing a space, esp. light interior wall. ● *v.* **1** divide into parts. **2** separate with partition.

**partitive** ● *adj. Gram.* (of word etc.) denoting part of or by a collective whole. ● *n.* group or quantity.

**partly** *adv.* not completely; to some extent.

**partner** ● *n.* person who shares or takes part with another or others, esp. in a business; each of a pair; either member of a couple. ● *v.* be partner of; put together as partners.
□□ **partnership** *n.*

**partridge** *n.* kind of game bird.

**parturition** *n.* process of giving birth to young.

**party** ● *n.* **1** social gathering. **2** group of people travelling or working together. **3** group of people united in a cause, opinion, etc., esp. political party. **4** each side in agreement or dispute. **5** *colloq.* person. ● *v.* attend party; celebrate. □ **party wall** wall common to two buildings or rooms.

**pascal** *n.* SI unit of pressure.

**paschal** *adj.* of Passover; of Easter.

**pash** *colloq.* ● *n.* an infatuation; *Aust.* passionate kiss. ● *v. Aust.* kiss passionately.

**pashmina** *n.* shawl made from goat's wool.

**paspalum** *n.* robust kind of pasture grass.

**pass** ● *v.* **1** move onward or go past; (cause) to be transferred from one person or place to another; go beyond. **2** discharge from body as or with excreta. **3** change from one state into another; happen; occupy (time). **4** be accepted; examine and declare satisfactory; achieve required standard in test. **5** (in a game) refuse one's turn. **6** allow (bill in parliament) to proceed. ● *n.* **1** passing. **2** movement made with hands or thing held. **3** written permission, ticket, or order. **4** narrow way through mountains. □ **pass away** die. **pass out** become unconscious. **pass over** disregard. **pass up** refuse to accept.

**passable** *adj.* **1** adequate; fairly good. **2** (of road etc.) that can be traversed. □□ **passably** *adv.*

**passage** *n.* **1** process or means of passing; transit. **2** passageway. **3** right to pass through. **4** journey by sea or air. **5** transition from one state to another. **6** short part of book or piece of music etc. **7** duct etc. in body.

**passcode** *n.* string of characters used as a password.

**passé** *adj.* old-fashioned.

**passenger** *n.* **1** traveller in or on vehicle (other than driver, pilot, crew, etc.) **2** *colloq.* idle member of team etc.

**passer-by** *n.* (*pl.* **passers-by**) person who happens to be going past.

**passim** *adv.* throughout.

**passion** *n.* **1** strong emotion; intense sexual love; strong enthusiasm; object arousing this. **2** (**the Passion**) sufferings of Christ during his last days. □□ **passionless** *adj.*

**passionate** *adj.* dominated, displaying, or caused by strong emotion. □□ **passionately** *adv.*

**passive** *adj.* **1** acted upon, not active; not resisting; lacking initiative or forceful qualities. **2** *Gram.* (of verb) of which the subject undergoes the action, e.g. *was written* in *it was written by me*. □□ **passively** *adv.* **passivity** *n.*

**Passover** *n.* Jewish spring festival commemorating escape of Israelites from Egypt.

**passport** *n.* official document showing holder's identity and nationality etc. and authorising travel abroad; thing that ensures achieving something (*passport to success*).

**password** n. string of characters that allows access to computer system or service; secret word or phrase used to gain admission.

**past** ● adj. 1 gone by in time; no longer existing. 2 *Gram.* expressing past action or state. ● n. 1 past time or events. 2 person's past life or career. 3 past tense. ● prep. beyond. ● adv. so as to pass by.

**pasta** n. dried flour paste in various shapes; cooked dish made with this.

**paste** ● n. 1 thick, moist substance. 2 adhesive. 3 meat, fish, or tomato etc. spread. 4 hard glasslike material used for imitation gems. ● v. 1 fasten or coat with paste. 2 *colloq.* beat. □□ **pasting** n.

**pasteboard** n. cardboard.

**pastel** ● n. light shade of colour; crayon of dry pigment paste; drawing in pastel. ● adj. of pale shade of colour.

**pasteurise** v. (also **-ize**) partially sterilise (milk etc.) by heating. □□ **pasteurisation** n.

**pastiche** n. picture or musical composition made up from or imitating various sources; literary or other work imitating style of author or period etc.

**pastille** n. small sweet or lozenge.

**pastime** n. recreation, hobby.

**pastor** n. minister in charge of church or congregation.

**pastoral** ● adj. 1 of, pertaining to, or engaged in, stock-raising as distinct from crop-raising; (of land) used for pasture; of (esp. romanticised) rural life. 2 of shepherds. 3 of spiritual guidance; of pastor. ● n. pastoral poem, play, picture, etc. □ **pastoral company** *Aust.* commercial enterprise engaged in large-scale stock-raising. **pastoral lease** *Aust.* agreement under which area of Crown land is held on condition that it is used for stock-raising; land so held.

**pastoralist** n. owner of substantial stock-raising establishment(s).

**pastrami** n. seasoned smoked beef.

**pastry** n. dough of flour, fat, and water; (item of) food made with this.

**pasturage** n. pasture land.

**pasture** ● n. 1 land covered with grass etc. for grazing animals. 2 herbage for animals. ● v. put (animals) to pasture.

**pasty**¹ n. pastry with sweet or savoury filling, baked without dish.

**pasty**² adj. 1 of or like paste. 2 pallid.

**pat** ● v. (**patted**) strike gently with hand or flat surface; flatten by patting. ● n. 1 light stroke or tap, esp. with hand in affection etc.; patting sound. 2 small mass, esp. of butter, made (as) by patting. ● adv. & adj. unconvincingly quick and simple. □ **pat-down** searching person for concealed items such as weapons or drugs, by passing hands over their clothing.

**patch** ● n. 1 piece put on in mending or as reinforcement. 2 cover protecting injured eye. 3 large or irregular spot on surface. 4 distinct area or period. 5 small plot of ground. ● v. 1 mend with patch(es). 2 piece together. 3 settle (quarrel etc.), esp. hastily.

**patchwork** n. stitching together of small pieces of variegated cloth to form pattern; something made of assorted pieces.

**patchy** adj. uneven in quality; having or existing in patches. □□ **patchily** adv.

**pâté** n. paste of meat, fish, etc.

**patella** n. (pl. **patellae**) kneecap.

**patent** ● n. government document conferring right, title, etc.; esp. sole right to make, use, or sell some invention; invention or process so protected. ● adj. 1 obvious, plain. 2 conferred or protected by patent. ● v. obtain patent for (invention). □ **patent leather** glossy varnished leather. □□ **patently** adv.

**patentee** *n.* holder of a patent.

**paternal** *adj.* of father; fatherly; related through one's father.

**paternalism** *n.* policy of restricting freedom and responsibility by well-meant regulations. □□ **paternalistic** *adj.*

**paternity** *n.* fatherhood; one's paternal origin.

**Paterson's curse** *n. Aust.* European herb with bluish-purple flowers, esp. regarded as noxious weed.

**path** *n.* (*pl.* **paths**) **1** footpath, track. **2** line along which person or thing moves; course of action.

**pathetic** *adj.* exciting pity, sadness, or contempt. □□ **pathetically** *adv.*

**pathogen** *n.* agent causing disease. □□ **pathogenic** *adj.*

**pathology** *n.* study of disease. □□ **pathological** *adj.* **pathologist** *n.*

**pathos** *n.* quality that excites pity or sadness.

**pathway** *n.* path; its course.

**patience** *n.* **1** ability to endure delay, hardship, provocation, pain, etc.; perseverance. **2** solo card game.

**patient** ● *adj.* having or showing patience. ● *n.* person receiving medical etc. treatment. □□ **patiently** *adv.*

**patina** *n.* green film on surface of old bronze; similar film on other surfaces.

**patio** *n.* paved outdoor area adjoining house.

**patisserie** *n.* shop where pastries are made and sold; pastries collectively.

**patka** *n.* man's head covering consisting of small piece of cloth wrapped around the head, worn esp. by young Sikhs.

**patriarch** *n.* **1** male head of family or community. **2** chief bishop in certain churches. □□ **patriarchal** *adj.*

**patriarchy** *n.* male-dominated social system with descent reckoned through male line.

**patrician** ● *n. hist.* person of noble birth, esp. in ancient Rome. ● *adj.* noble; aristocratic.

**patricide** *n.* killing of one's father. □□ **patricidal** *adj.*

**patrimony** *n.* property inherited from father or ancestors; heritage.

**patriot** *n.* person devoted to and ready to support his or her country. □□ **patriotic** *adj.* **patriotism** *n.*

**patrol** ● *n.* act of walking or travelling around area etc. to protect or supervise it; person(s) or vehicle(s) sent out on patrol. ● *v.* (**patrolled**) carry out patrol of; act as patrol.

**patron** *n.* **1** person who gives financial or other support. **2** customer.

**patronage** *n.* **1** patron's or customer's support. **2** control of appointments to office, privileges, etc. **3** patronising or condescending manner.

**patronise** *v.* (also **-ize**) **1** treat condescendingly. **2** act as patron. **3** be customer of. □□ **patronising** *adj.*

**patronymic** *n.* name derived from that of father or ancestor.

**patter** ● *v.* **1** make a series of quick tapping sounds; run with quick short steps. **2** talk or say glibly. ● *n.* **1** a pattering. **2** rapid speech.

**pattern** ● *n.* **1** decorative design on surface. **2** regular or logical form, order, etc. **3** model, design, or instructions from which thing is to be made. **4** excellent example. ● *v.* **1** model (thing) on design etc. **2** decorate with pattern.

**patty** *n.* little pie; small flat cake of minced meat etc.

**paucity** *n.* smallness of number or quantity.

**paunch** *n.* belly, stomach.

**pauper** *n.* very poor person. □□ **pauperism** *n.*

**pause** ● *n.* temporary stop or silence. ● *v.* make a pause.

**pave** v. cover (street, floor, etc.) with flat stones, bricks, etc. □□ **paving** n.

**pavement** n. path at side of road.

**pavilion** n. 1 building on sportsground for spectators or players. 2 large tent. 3 ornamental building.

**pavlova** n. dessert of large, soft-centred meringue cake topped with whipped cream and fruit.

**paw** ● n. 1 foot of animal with claws. 2 colloq. person's hand. ● v. 1 touch with paw. 2 colloq. fondle indecently or awkwardly.

**pawn** ● n. 1 chess piece of smallest size and value. 2 person subservient to another's plans. ● v. deposit with pawnbroker as security for money borrowed.

**pawnbroker** n. person licensed to lend money on the security of personal property deposited.

**pawpaw** n. melon-shaped tropical fruit with orange flesh; tree bearing this.

**pay** ● v. (paid, paying) 1 discharge debt to. 2 give as due. 3 render. 4 bestow (attention etc.) 5 yield adequate return. 6 make (visit). 7 reward or punish. ● n. wages; payment. □ **pay-off** act of payment, esp. a bribe; final outcome.

**payable** adj. that must or may be paid.

**PAYE** abbr. pay-as-you-earn.

**payee** n. person to whom money is paid or to be paid.

**PAYG** abbr. pay-as-you-go.

**payload** n. 1 part of vehicle's load from which revenue is derived. 2 explosive device carried by rocket etc.

**paymaster** n. official who pays troops, workers, etc.

**payment** n. act or instance of paying; amount paid; reward, recompense.

**payroll** n. list of employees receiving regular pay. □ **payroll tax** payable by employer on all wages and salaries paid or payable in excess of a general exemption.

**paywall** n. (on website) system that restricts access to paid subscribers.

**paywave** n. propr. = **tap and go**.

**PB** abbr. personal best.

**PC** abbr. 1 personal computer. 2 politically correct.

**PDA** n. personal digital assistant, small portable computer.

**PE** abbr. physical education.

**pea** n. 1 climbing plant bearing round edible seeds in pods; one of its seeds; similar Australian plant that can cause stock-poisoning. 2 Aust. colloq. person expected to win job etc. over other applicants; (in horseracing) favourite.

**peace** n. 1 freedom from war or civil disorder. 2 mental calm.

**peaceable** adj. avoiding conflict; peaceful.

**peaceful** adj. characterised by peace; tranquil. □□ **peacefully** adv. **peacefulness** n.

**peach** n. 1 round juicy stone fruit with downy yellow or rosy skin; tree bearing it; its yellowish-pink colour. 2 colloq. someone or something attractive or of the best quality.

**peacock** n. male bird with brilliant plumage and erectile fanlike tail.

**peahen** n. female peacock.

**peak** ● n. 1 pointed top, esp. of mountain. 2 stiff projecting brim in front of cap. 3 highest point of achievement, intensity, etc. ● v. reach highest value, quality, etc. ● adj. maximum. □□ **peaked** adj.

**peaky** adj. (peakier) looking pale and sickly.

**peal** ● n. 1 loud ringing of bell(s); set of bells. 2 burst of thunder or laughter. ● v. (cause to) sound in a peal.

**peanut** n. 1 plant bearing underground pods containing seeds used as food and yielding oil; this seed. **2** (**peanuts**) trivial amount, esp. of money.

**pear** *n.* fleshy fruit tapering towards stalk; tree bearing it.

**pearl** ● *n.* **1** rounded lustrous usu. white solid formed in shell of certain oysters and prized as gem; imitation of this. **2** mother-of-pearl. **3** precious thing. **4** finest example. ● *v.* **1** form drops on. **2** fish for pearls. □ **pearl barley** barley rubbed into small rounded grains. □□ **pearly** *adj.*

**peasant** *n.* **1** farm labourer; small farmer; agricultural worker. **2** *derog.* lout. □□ **peasantry** *n.*

**peat** *n.* vegetable matter decomposed by water and partly carbonised. □□ **peaty** *adj.*

**peatmoss** *n.* any of various mosses that grow in damp conditions and form peat as they decay.

**pebble** *n.* small smooth round stone. □□ **pebbly** *adj.*

**pecan** *n.* pinkish-brown smooth nut; type of hickory producing this.

**peck** ● *v.* **1** strike, pick up, pluck out, or make (hole) with beak. **2** kiss hastily or perfunctorily. **3** *colloq.* eat listlessly or fastidiously. ● *n.* **1** stroke or mark made with beak. **2** hasty or perfunctory kiss.

**pecker** *n. colloq.* penis.

**peckish** *adj. colloq.* hungry.

**pectin** *n.* soluble gelatinous substance in ripe fruits, causing jam etc. to set.

**pectoral** ● *adj.* of or relating to chest or breast. ● *n.* pectoral muscle or fin.

**peculiar** *adj.* **1** odd. **2** belonging exclusively to one person or place or thing; particular, special. □□ **peculiarity** *n.* **peculiarly** *adv.*

**pecuniary** *adj.* of or in money.

**pedagogue** *n.* strict or pedantic teacher.

**pedagogy** *n.* science of teaching. □□ **pedagogical** *adj.*

**pedal** ● *n.* lever or key operated by foot, esp. on bicycle, motor vehicle, or musical instrument. ● *v.* (**pedalled**) operate by pedals; ride (bicycle). ● *adj.* of foot or feet.

**pedant** *n.* person who insists on strict adherence to literal meaning or formal rules. □□ **pedantic** *adj.*

**peddle** *v.* sell as pedlar; advocate; sell (drugs etc.) illegally.

**peddler** *n.* person who sells drugs illegally.

**pedestal** *n.* **1** base of column. **2** block on which something stands.

**pedestrian** ● *n.* walker, esp. in town. ● *adj.* prosaic; dull.

**pediatrics** = PAEDIATRICS.

**pedicure** *n.* care or treatment of feet and toenails.

**pedigree** *n.* recorded (esp. distinguished) line of descent of person or animal; genealogical table; *colloq.* thing's history.

**pediment** *n.* triangular part crowning front of building, esp. over portico.

**pedlar** *n.* travelling seller of small wares; seller of illegal drugs; retailer of gossip etc.

**pedometer** *n.* instrument for estimating distance travelled on foot.

**peduncle** *n.* stalk of flower, fruit, etc.

**pee** *colloq.* ● *v.* urinate. ● *n.* act of urination; urine.

**peek** ● *v.* peep, glance.

**peel** ● *v.* **1** remove rind etc. from; strip off (outer covering). **2** become bare of bark, skin, etc.; flake off. ● *n.* rind or outer covering of fruit, vegetable, etc. □□ **peeler** *n.* **peelings** *n.pl.*

**peep** ● *v.* look furtively or through narrow aperture; come cautiously or partly into view; emerge. ● *n.* **1** furtive or peering glance. **2** first light of dawn. □ **peeping Tom** furtive voyeur.

**peer**[1] *v.* **1** look closely or with difficulty. **2** appear. **3** peep out.

peer | penicillin

**peer²** ● *n.* equal (in ability, standing, rank, or value). **2** contemporary. **3** duke, marquess, earl, viscount, or baron. □ **peer-to-peer** denoting a network in which each computer can act as a server for the others.

**peerage** *n.* peers as a class; rank of peer or peeress.

**peeress** *n.* female peer; peer's wife.

**peerless** *adj.* unequalled.

**peeved** *adj. colloq.* irritated, annoyed.

**peevish** *adj.* irritable. □□ **peevishly** *adv.*

**peg** ● *n.* wooden or metal etc. pin or bolt for holding things together, hanging things on, etc.; each of the pins used to tighten or loosen strings of violin etc.; wooden or plastic clip etc. for hanging washing on line.
● *v.* (**pegged**) **1** fix, mark, or hang out (as) with peg(s). **2** keep (prices etc.) stable. □ **off the peg** (of clothes) ready-made.

**pejorative** *adj.* expressing disapproval.

**pelican** *n.* large water bird with pouch below bill for storing fish.

**pellagra** *n.* disease involving cracking of skin, caused by deficiencies in diet.

**pellet** *n.* **1** small compressed ball of a substance. **2** small shot.

**pell-mell** *adv.* **1** headlong. **2** in disorder.

**pellucid** *adj.* transparent; clear.

**pelmet** *n.* hanging border concealing curtain rod etc.

**peloton** *n.* main field or group of cyclists in race.

**pelt** ● *v.* **1** assail with missiles, abuse, etc. **2** (of rain) come down hard. **3** run at full speed. ● *n.* skin of animal.

**pelvis** *n.* basin-shaped cavity formed from hip bones with sacrum and coccyx. □□ **pelvic** *adj.*

**pen** ● *n.* **1** implement for writing with ink. **2** small enclosure for cows,

sheep, poultry, etc. **3** *Aust.* division in shearing shed. **4** female swan.
● *v.* (**penned**) **1** write (a letter etc.). **2** put or keep in confined space. □ **pen name** author's pseudonym.
**pen-pushing** *colloq. derog.* clerical work.

**penal** *adj.* **1** of or involving punishment. **2** punishable.

**penalise** *v.* (**-ize**) subject to penalty or disadvantage; make punishable.

**penalty** *n.* punishment for breach of law, rule, contract, etc.

**penance** *n.* act of self-punishment as reparation for guilt.

**pence** SEE PENNY.

**penchant** *n.* inclination or liking for.

**pencil** ● *n.* instrument for writing or drawing, usu. of graphite etc. enclosed in wooden cylinder or metal case with tapering end; something used or shaped like this.
● *v.* (**pencilled**) **1** write, draw, or mark with pencil. **2** note or arrange provisionally.

**penda** *n.* Australian tree valued for its hard brown wood.

**pendant** *n.* **1** ornament hung from necklace etc. **2** light fitting etc. hanging from ceiling.

**pendent** *adj.* (also **pendant**) hanging.

**pending** ● *adj.* awaiting decision or settlement. ● *prep.* **1** during. **2** until.

**pendulous** *adj.* **1** hanging down. **2** swinging.

**pendulum** *n.* weight suspended so as to be free to swing, esp. movement of clock's works.

**penetrate** *v.* make way into or through; pierce; permeate; see into or through; be absorbed by mind. □□ **penetrable** *adj.* **penetration** *n.*

**penetrating** *adj.* **1** showing or having insight. **2** (of sound) piercing.

**penguin** *n.* flightless sea bird of S. hemisphere.

**penicillin** *n.* antibiotic obtained from mould.

**peninsula** n. piece of land almost surrounded by water or projecting far into sea etc. □□ **peninsular** adj.

**penis** n. organ by which male mammal copulates and urinates.

**penitent** • adj. repentant.
• n. 1 penitent person. 2 person doing penance. □□ **penitence** n. penitently adv.

**penitential** adj. of penitence or penance.

**penitentiary** • n. US prison. • adj. of penance or reformatory treatment.

**pennant** n. 1 tapering flag, esp. that at masthead of ship in commission. 2 victory symbol in sports etc.

**penniless** adj. having no money; destitute.

**pennon** n. long narrow triangular or swallow-tailed flag; long pointed streamer on ship.

**penny** n.pl. (pl. **pennies** for separate coins, **pence** for sum of money) 1 British unit worth one-hundredth of pound. 2 hist. Australian etc. coin worth one two-hundred-and-fortieth of pound.

**penology** n. study of punishment and prison management.

**pension** • n. periodic payment made by government, superannuation fund, etc. to person above specified age, or to retired, widowed, or disabled person. • v. grant pension to. □ **pension off** dismiss.

**pensionable** adj. entitled or entitling person to pension.

**pensioner** n. recipient of (esp. retirement) pension.

**pensive** adj. deep in thought. □□ **pensively** adv.

**pentagon** n. plane figure with five sides and angles. □□ **pentagonal** adj.

**pentagram** n. five-pointed star.

**Pentateuch** n. first five books of Old Testament.

**pentathlon** n. athletic contest of five events. □□ **pentathlete** n.

**Pentecost** n. 1 Whit Sunday. 2 Jewish harvest festival, 50 days after second day of Passover.

**pentecostal** adj. (of Christian sect) emphasising divine gifts, esp. healing, and often fundamentalist in outlook.

**penthouse** n. flat on roof or top floor of tall building.

**penultimate** adj. & n. last but one.

**penumbra** n. (pl. **penumbrae** or **penumbras**) 1 partly shaded region around shadow of opaque body. 2 partial shadow. □□ **penumbral** adj.

**penury** n. destitution; poverty. □□ **penurious** adj.

**people** • n.pl. 1 persons in general. 2 race or nation. 3 (**the people**) ordinary people, esp. as electorate. • v. fill with people; populate.

**pep** colloq. • n. vigour; spirit. • v. (**pepped**) fill with vigour. □ **pep talk** talk designed to encourage confidence and effort.

**pepper** • n. 1 hot aromatic condiment from dried berries of some plants. 2 capsicum. • v. 1 sprinkle or flavour with pepper. 2 scatter large amount of something on or over; pelt with missiles. □□ **peppery** adj.

**peppercorn** n. dried black berry from which pepper is made. □ **peppercorn rent** very low rent.

**peppermint** n. 1 species of mint grown for its strong-flavoured oil; sweet flavoured with this oil. 2 eucalypt with leaves yielding aromatic, peppermint-like oils.

**pepperoni** n. sausage seasoned with pepper.

**pepsin** n. enzyme contained in gastric juice.

**peptic** adj. digestive.

**per** prep. 1 for each. 2 by. 3 by means of. 4 through.

**perambulate** v. formal walk. □□ **perambulation** n.

**per annum** adv. for each year.

**per capita** *adv. & adj.* for each person.

**perceive** *v.* become aware of by one of senses; apprehend; understand. □□ **perceivable** *adj.*

**per cent** (also **percent**) • *adv.* in every hundred. • *n.* **1** percentage. **2** one part in every hundred.

**percentage** • *n.* rate, number, or amount in each hundred; proportion; a part. • *adj. Sports* (of style of play) orthodox, not taking risks.

**perceptible** *adj.* that can be perceived. □□ **perceptibility** *n.* **perceptibly** *adv.*

**perception** *n.* act or faculty of perceiving. □□ **perceptual** *adj.*

**perceptive** *adj.* sensitive; discerning; capable of perceiving. □□ **perceptively** *adv.* **perceptiveness** *n.*

**perch**¹ • *n.* bird's resting place above ground; high place for person or thing to rest on. • *v.* rest or place on perch.

**perch**² *n.* edible spiny-finned freshwater fish.

**percipient** *adj.* perceptive. □□ **percipience** *n.*

**percolate** *v.* filter gradually; (of idea etc.) permeate gradually; prepare (coffee) in percolator. □□ **percolation** *n.*

**percolator** *n.* apparatus for making coffee by circulating boiling water through ground beans.

**percussion** *n.* **1** playing of music by striking instruments with sticks etc.; such instruments collectively. **2** gentle tapping of body in medical diagnosis. **3** forcible striking of one body against another. □□ **percussionist** *n.* **percussive** *adj.*

**perdition** *n.* damnation.

**peregrine** *n.* falcon.

**peremptory** *adj.* admitting no denial or refusal; imperious. □□ **peremptorily** *adv.*

**perennial** • *adj.* lasting through the year; (of plant) living several years;

lasting long or for ever. • *n.* perennial plant. □□ **perennially** *adv.*

**perentie** *n.* giant monitor lizard.

**perestroika** *n.* (in former USSR) reform of economic and political system.

**perfect** • *adj.* **1** faultless; excellent. **2** very enjoyable. **3** exact, precise. **4** entire, unqualified. **5** *Gram.* (of tense) expressing completed action. • *v.* **1** make perfect. **2** complete. • *n. Gram.* perfect tense. □□ **perfectly** *adv.* **perfection** *n.*

**perfectionist** *n.* person who seeks perfection. □□ **perfectionism** *n.*

**perfidious** *adj.* treacherous; disloyal. □□ **perfidy** *n.*

**perforate** *v.* pierce; make hole(s) through; make row of small holes in (paper etc.). □□ **perforation** *n.*

**perforce** *adv. arch.* unavoidably, necessarily.

**perform** *v.* **1** carry out (task etc.); function. **2** act, sing, etc., esp. in public. □□ **performance** *n.* **performer** *n.*

**perfume** • *n.* sweet smell; fragrant liquid, esp. for application to body; scent. • *v.* impart perfume to. □□ **perfumery** *n.*

**perfunctory** *adj.* done merely out of duty; superficial. □□ **perfunctorily** *adv.*

**pergola** *n.* arbour or covered walk; *Aust.* horizontal wooden framework with vertical supports, attached to house.

**perhaps** *adv.* it may be; possibly.

**pericardium** *n.* (*pl.* pericardia) membranous sac enclosing heart.

**pericarp** *n.* seed vessel such as a pea pod.

**perigee** *n.* point nearest to earth in orbit of moon etc.

**perihelion** *n.* (*pl.* perihelia) point nearest to sun in orbit of comet etc. around it.

**peril** *n.* serious and immediate danger.

**perilous** adj. full of risk, dangerous. □□ **perilously** adv.

**perimeter** n. circumference or outline of closed figure; length of this; outer boundary.

**perinatal** adj. of the time immediately before and after birth.

**perineum** n. (pl. **perinea**) region of body between anus and scrotum or vulva. □□ **perineal** adj.

**period** ● n. **1** amount of time during which something runs its course; distinct portion of history, life, etc. **2** occurrence of menstruation; time of this. **3** complete sentence; full stop in punctuation. ● adj. characteristic of past period.

**periodic** adj. appearing or recurring at intervals.

**periodical** ● n. newspaper, magazine, etc., issued at regular intervals. ● adj. periodic. □□ **periodically** adv.

**peripatetic** adj. going from place to place.

**peripheral** ● adj. **1** of minor importance. **2** of periphery. **3** near surface of body. ● n. input, output, or storage device connected to computer.

**periphery** n. boundary; outer or surrounding area.

**periphrasis** n. (pl. **periphrases**) roundabout phrase or way of speaking.

**periscope** n. apparatus with tube and mirrors or prisms for viewing things otherwise out of sight.

**perish** v. suffer destruction; die; (cause to) rot or deteriorate.

**perishable** ● adj. subject to speedy decay; liable to perish. ● n. perishable thing (esp. food).

**peristalsis** n. involuntary wavelike movement propelling contents of digestive tract.

**peritoneum** n. (pl. **peritoneums** or **peritonea**) membrane lining abdominal cavity. □□ **peritoneal** adj.

**peritonitis** n. inflammation of peritoneum.

**perjure** v.refl. Law wilfully tell lie when on oath. □□ **perjury** n.

**perk** n. colloq. perquisite.

**perky** adj. lively; cheerful.

**perm** ● n. long-lasting artificial wave in hair. ● v. treat (hair) with perm.

**permafrost** n. permanently frozen subsoil.

**permanent** adj. lasting, or intended to last, indefinitely. □□ **permanence** n. **permanency** n. **permanently** adv.

**permeable** adj. capable of being permeated. □□ **permeability** n.

**permeate** v. penetrate, saturate; pervade; be diffused. □□ **permeation** n.

**permissible** adj. allowable. □□ **permissibility** n.

**permission** n. consent; authorisation.

**permissive** adj. tolerant, liberal; giving permission. □□ **permissiveness** n.

**permit** ● v. (**permitted**) give permission to or for; allow as possible. ● n. written order giving permission or allowing entry.

**permutation** n. **1** one of possible ordered arrangements of set of things. **2** combination or selection of specified number of items from larger group.

**pernicious** adj. destructive, harmful.

**pernickety** adj. colloq. fastidious; over-precise.

**peroration** n. concluding part of speech.

**peroxide** ● n. (in full **hydrogen peroxide**) colourless liquid used in water solution esp. to bleach hair. ● v. bleach (hair) with peroxide.

**perpendicular** ● adj. at right angles; upright; very steep. ● n. perpendicular line etc. □□ **perpendicularity** n.

**perpetrate** v. commit. □□ **perpetration** n. **perpetrator** n.

**perpetual** adj. lasting for ever or indefinitely; continuous; frequent. □□ **perpetually** adv.

**perpetuate** v. make perpetual; cause to be always present. □□ **perpetuation** n.

**perpetuity** n. perpetual continuance or possession.

**perplex** v. puzzle, bewilder; complicate, tangle. □□ **perplexing** adj. **perplexity** n.

**per pro** abbr. through the agency of (indicating that a person is signing on behalf of another).

**perquisite** n. (also **perk**) privilege given in addition to wages; an extra profit or right.

**per se** adv. by or in itself; intrinsically.

**persecute** v. subject to constant hostility or ill treatment; harass, worry. □□ **persecution** n. **persecutor** n.

**persevere** v. continue steadfastly. □□ **perseverance** n.

**persimmon** n. tree bearing edible tomato-like fruit; this fruit.

**persist** v. continue to exist or do something in spite of obstacles. □□ **persistence** n. **persistent** adj. **persistently** adv.

**person** n. (pl. **people** or **persons**) 1 individual human being. 2 Gram. one of three classes of pronouns, verb forms, etc. denoting respectively person etc. speaking, spoken to, or spoken of. □ **in person** oneself, physically present.

**Usage** The plural form *people* is used in most ordinary contexts, while *persons* tends to be restricted to official or formal contexts.

**persona** n. (pl. **personae**) aspect of personality as perceived by or shown to others; role adopted by someone.

**personable** adj. pleasing in appearance or behaviour.

**personage** n. person, esp. an important one.

**personal** adj. 1 one's own; individual, private; done etc. in person; directed to or concerning individual. 2 referring (esp. in hostile way) to individual's private life. 3 of or denoting grammatical person. □ **personal computer** one designed for use by single individual. **personal organiser** looseleaf folder or pocket-sized computer for keeping details of meetings, phone numbers, addresses, etc. □□ **personally** adv.

**personalise** v. (also **-ize**) identify as belonging to particular person.

**personality** n. 1 distinctive personal character. 2 well-known person.

**personify** v. 1 attribute human characteristics to; symbolise by human figure. 2 (usu. as **personified** adj.) be typical example of. 3 embody. □□ **personification** n.

**personnel** n. employees, staff.

**perspective ●** n. 1 art of drawing so as to give effect of solidity and relative position and size. 2 relation as to position and distance, or proportion between visible objects, parts of subject, etc. 3 mental view of relative importance of things. 4 view, prospect. **●** adj. of or in perspective.

**perspex** n. propr. tough light transparent plastic.

**perspicacious** adj. having great insight or discernment. □□ **perspicacity** n.

**perspicuous** adj. clearly expressed; lucid. □□ **perspicuity** n.

**perspire** v. sweat. □□ **perspiration** n.

**persuade** v. cause (person) by argument etc. to believe or do something; convince.

**persuasion** n. 1 persuading; persuasive argument. 2 religious etc. beliefs.

**persuasive** adj. able or tending to persuade.□□ **persuasively** adv. **persuasiveness** n.

**pert** adj. **1** saucy, impudent. **2** jaunty. □□ **pertly** adv. **pertness** n.

**pertain** v. belong, relate.

**pertinacious** adj. persistent; obstinate.□□ **pertinacity** n.

**pertinent** adj. relevant. □□ **pertinence** n.

**perturb** v. agitate; throw into confusion.□□ **perturbation** n.

**pertussis** n. = whooping cough.

**peruse** v. **1** read. **2** scan.□□ **perusal** n.

**perv** (also **perve**) colloq. ● n. sexual pervert; voyeur; voyeurism. ● v. observe, esp. with erotic or sexual interest.

**pervade** v. spread through, permeate. □□ **pervasion** n. **pervasive** adj.

**perverse** adj. stubbornly or wilfully in the wrong; contrary to reason. □□ **perversely** adv. **perversity** n.

**pervert** ● v. turn aside from proper or normal use; lead astray from right behaviour or belief. ● n. person who is perverted, esp. sexually. □□ **perversion** n.

**pervious** adj. permeable; allowing passage or access.

**pessimism** n. tendency to take worst view or expect worst outcome. □□ **pessimist** n. **pessimistic** adj.

**pest** n. troublesome or destructive person, animal, or thing.

**pester** v. trouble or annoy, esp. with persistent requests.

**pesticide** n. substance for destroying harmful insects etc.

**pestilence** n. deadly epidemic disease.□□ **pestilential** adj.

**pestilent** n. deadly; harmful or morally destructive.

**pestle** n. instrument for pounding substances in mortar.

**pesto** n. Italian sauce of crushed basil, parmesan, olive oil, pine nuts, and garlic, used on pasta etc.

**pet** ● n. domestic animal kept for pleasure and company; a favourite. ● adj. as, of, or for a pet; favourite. ● v. (**petted**) fondle, esp. erotically; treat as pet.

**petabyte** n. one thousand terabytes.

**petal** n. each division of flower corolla.

**peter** v. peter out diminish gradually.

**pethidine** n. synthetic soluble analgesic, chemically similar to morphine.

**petite** adj. of small dainty build.

**petition** ● n. formal written request signed by many people. ● v. make petition to.

**petrel** n. seabird.

**petrify** v. **1** paralyse with terror or astonishment etc. **2** turn or be turned into stone.□□ **petrifaction** n.

**petrochemical** n. substance obtained from petroleum or natural gas.

**petrol** n. refined petroleum used as fuel in motor vehicles, aircraft, etc.

**petroleum** n. hydrocarbon oil found in upper strata of earth, refined for use as fuel etc.

**petrolhead** n. Aust. colloq. person who is a motor car fanatic.

**petticoat** n. woman's or girl's undergarment hanging from waist or shoulders.

**pettish** adj. peevish, fretful.

**petty** adj. unimportant, trivial; of relatively low rank; mean, small-minded.□ **petty cash** money kept by an office etc. for small payments.□□ **pettiness** n.

**petulant** adj. peevishly impatient or irritable.□□ **petulance** n. **petulantly** adv.

**petunia** n. cultivated plant with white, purple, red, etc. funnel-shaped flowers.

**pew** n. (in church) long bench with back.

**pewter** n. grey alloy of tin, antimony, and copper.

**PG** *abbr.* (of film or computer game) classified as suitable for children subject to parental guidance.

**pH** *n.* measure of acidity or alkalinity.

**phablet** *n. propr.* smartphone with large screen.

**phagocyte** *n.* blood corpuscle capable of absorbing foreign matter.

**phalanger** *n.* tree-dwelling marsupial with thick woolly fur.

**phalanx** *n.* (*pl.* **phalanxes** or **phalanges**) **1** *hist.* group of infantry in close formation. **2** united or organised party or company.

**phallocentric** *adj.* centred on phallus or male attitudes.

**phallus** *n.* (*pl.* **phalli** or **phalluses**) (image etc. of) penis.□□ **phallic** *adj.*

**phantom ● ** *n.* **1** spectre, apparition. **2** mental illusion. ● *adj.* illusory.

**pharaoh** *n.* ruler of ancient Egypt.

**pharmaceutical** *adj.* of or engaged in pharmacy.□□ **pharmaceutics** *n.pl.*

**pharmacist** *n.* person qualified to practise pharmacy, chemist.

**pharmacology** *n.* study of action of drugs on the body.
□□ **pharmacological** *adj.* **pharmacologist** *n.*

**pharmacopoeia** *n.* book with list of drugs and directions for use; stock of drugs.

**pharmacy** *n.* preparation and dispensing of drugs; chemist's shop.

**pharynx** *n.* cavity behind nose and mouth.□□ **pharyngeal** *adj.*

**phascogale** *n.* tree-dwelling carnivorous marsupial.

**phase ● ** *n.* distinct period or stage in process of change or development. ● *v.* carry out (a program etc.) in stages.

**PhD** *abbr.* Doctor of Philosophy.

**pheasant** *n.* long-tailed game bird.

**phenome** *n.* phenotypic counterpart or expression of genome; complete set of phenotypic characteristics of organism.□□ **phenomic** *adj.*

**phenomenal** *adj.* **1** extraordinary, remarkable. **2** of or concerned with phenomena.□□ **phenomenally** *adv.*

**phenomenon** *n.* (*pl.* **phenomena**) **1** observed or apparent object, fact, or occurrence. **2** remarkable person or thing.

**phenomics** *n.pl.* branch of science concerned with phenomic characteristics of organisms.

**phenotype** *n.* set of observable characteristics of individual or group as determined by its genotype and environment.□□ **phenotypic** *adj.*

**pheromone** *n.* chemical secreted by animal for detection and response by others of same species.

**phial** *n.* small glass bottle.

**philander** *v.* flirt or have casual love affairs.□□ **philanderer** *n.*

**philanthropy** *n.* desire to promote the welfare of others, expressed esp. by the generous donation of money to good causes.□□ **philanthropic** *adj.* **philanthropist** *n.*

**philately** *n.* stamp collecting.
□□ **philatelist** *n.*

**philistine** *n.* uncultured person.
□□ **philistinism** *n.*

**philology** *n.* study of language.
□□ **philological** *adj.* **philologist** *n.*

**philosopher** *n.* person who engages in philosophy.

**philosophical** *adj.* (also **philosophic**) **1** of or according to philosophy. **2** calm under adverse circumstances.□□ **philosophically** *adv.*

**philosophise** *v.* (also **-ize**) reason like philosopher; theorise.

**philosophy** *n.* use of reason and argument in seeking truth and knowledge, esp. of ultimate reality or of general causes and principles; philosophical system; system for conduct of life.

**philtre** *n.* love potion.

**phishing** n. illegally acquiring person's bank account details etc. via bogus email etc.

**phlebitis** n. inflammation of vein. □□ **phlebitic** adj.

**phlegm** n. bronchial mucus ejected by coughing.

**phlegmatic** adj. calm; apathetic. □□ **phlegmatically** adv.

**phobia** n. abnormal fear or aversion. □□ **phobic** adj. & n.

**phoenix** n. mythical bird said to burn itself on funeral pyre and rise with renewed youth from its ashes.

**phone** n. & v. telephone.

**phonetic** adj. **1** of or representing vocal sounds. **2** (of spelling etc.) corresponding to pronunciation. **3** (**phonetics**) study or representation of vocal sounds. □□ **phonetically** adv. **phonetician** n.

**phoney** (also **phony**) colloq. • adj. false, sham; counterfeit. • n. phoney person or thing. □□ **phoniness** n.

**phonic** • adj. of speech sounds. • n. (**phonics**) method of teaching reading based on sounds.

**phono-** comb. form of sound.

**phosphate** n. salt of phosphoric acid, esp. used as fertiliser.

**phosphorescent** adj. luminous. □□ **phosphorescence** n.

**phosphorus** n. **1** chemical element (symbol P). **2** occurring esp. as waxlike substance appearing luminous in dark. □□ **phosphoric** adj. **phosphorous** adj.

**photo** n. photograph. □ **photo finish** close finish of race or contest.

**photo-** comb. form of light; of photography.

**photobomb** v. colloq. spoil (photograph) by unexpectedly appearing in camera's field of view as picture is taken.

**photocopier** n. machine for photocopying documents.

**photocopy** • n. photographic copy of document. • v. make photocopy of.

**photoelectric cell** n. electronic device emitting electric current when light falls on it.

**photofit** n. likeness of person made up of separate photographs of features.

**photogenic** adj. looking attractive in photographs.

**photograph** • n. picture made with digital camera; picture formed by chemical action of light on sensitive film. • v. take photograph of. □□ **photographer** n. **photography** n.

**photogravure** n. picture produced from photographic negative transferred to metal plate and etched in; this process.

**photojournalism** n. reporting of news by photographs in magazines etc.

**photon** n. quantum of electromagnetic radiation energy.

**photoshop** v. edit or alter (image) digitally using computer software.

**photosynthesis** n. process in which energy of sunlight is used by green plants to form carbohydrates from carbon dioxide and water. □□ **photosynthesise** v. (also **-ize**) **photosynthetic** adj.

**photovoltaic** adj. of production of electric current at junction of two substances exposed to light.

**phrase** • n. **1** group of words forming conceptual unit but usu. not a sentence; short idiomatic expression. **2** Mus. short sequence of notes. • v. **1** express in words. **2** divide (music) into phrases.

**phraseology** n. choice or arrangement of words. □□ **phraseological** adj.

**phrenology** n. hist. study of external form of cranium as supposed indication of mental faculties. □□ **phrenologist** n.

**phyllode** *n.* flattened leaf stalk resembling, and functioning as, true leaf.

**phylum** *n.pl.* (*pl.* **phyla**) major division of plant or animal kingdom.

**physical** ● *adj.* **1** of the body; of thing perceived by the senses. **2** of nature or according to its laws; of physics. ● *n.* (in full **physical examination**) medical examination. □ **physical education** instruction in exercises and games, esp. in schools. □□ **physically** *adv.*

**physician** *n.* doctor, esp. specialist in medical diagnosis and treatment.

**physics** *n.* science of properties and interaction of matter and energy. □□ **physicist** *n.*

**physio** *n. colloq.* physiotherapy; physiotherapist.

**physiognomy** *n.* features of person's face.

**physiology** *n.* science of functioning of living organisms. □□ **physiological** *adj.* **physiologist** *n.*

**physiotherapy** *n.* treatment of injury or disease by exercise, heat, or other physical agencies. □□ **physiotherapist** *n.*

**physique** *n.* bodily structure and development.

**pi** *n.* Greek letter (π) used as symbol of ratio of circumference of circle to diameter (approx. 3.14).

**pia mater** *n.* inner membrane enveloping brain and spinal cord.

**pianissimo** *adv. Mus.* very softly.

**pianist** *n.* piano player.

**piano** ● *n.* (*pl.* **pianos**) keyboard instrument with metal strings struck by hammers. ● *adv. Mus.* softly.

**pianoforte** *n. arch.* piano.

**piazza** *n.* public square or market place.

**pica¹** *n.* unit of type size; size of letters in typewriting.

**pica²** *n.* eating of substances other than normal food.

**picaresque** *adj.* (of style of fiction) dealing with episodic adventures of rogues.

**piccaninny** *n. offens.* small Black or Aboriginal child.

**piccolo** *n.* small high-pitched flute.

**pick** ● *v.* **1** select. **2** use a pointed instrument or the fingers or beak etc. to make (hole) or in or remove bits from (thing). **3** detach (flower or fruit) from plant bearing it. **4** eat (food, meal, etc.) in small bits. **5** *colloq.* victimise; pick on. ● *n.* **1** picking; a selection; best part. **2** pickaxe. **3** plectrum. □ **pick holes in** criticise. **pick on** find fault with; victimise. **pick up** lift or take up; collect; acquire, obtain; become acquainted with casually; recover health, improve; gather (speed). □□ **picker** *n.*

**pickaxe** long-handled tool having curved iron bar pointed at one or both ends, used for breaking up hard ground, masonry, etc.

**picket** ● *n.* **1** one or more people stationed to dissuade workers from entering workplace during strike etc. **2** pointed stake driven into ground. **3** small body of troops sent to watch for enemy. ● *v.* (**picketed**) **1** place or act as picket. **2** post as military picket. **3** secure with stakes.

**pickings** *n.pl.* profits or gains acquired easily or dishonestly.

**pickle** ● *n.* **1** vegetables etc. preserved in vinegar or brine; liquid used for this. **2** *colloq.* difficult or embarrassing situation. ● *v.* preserve in or treat with pickle.

**pickpocket** *n.* thief who steals from people's pockets.

**pickup** *n.* **1** small van with low sides. **2** device producing an electric signal in response to change; device on musical instrument that converts sound vibrations into electrical signals for amplification.

**picky** adj. colloq. highly fastidious; choosy.

**picnic** ● n. 1 outing including outdoor meal; such a meal. 2 something pleasantly or easily accomplished. ● v. (**picnicked**, **picnicking**) eat meal outdoors.

**pictograph** n. pictorial symbol used as form of writing.

**pictorial** adj. of, expressed in, or illustrated with picture(s). □□ **pictorially** adv.

**picture** ● n. 1 representation made by painting, drawing, or photography etc.; scene; description; idea, mental image. 2 cinema film. 3 (**the pictures**) cinema. ● v. 1 imagine. 2 depict.

**picturesque** adj. striking and pleasant to look at; (of language etc.) strikingly graphic.

**piddle** v. colloq. 1 urinate. 2 (as **piddling**) trivial. 3 work or act in trifling way.

**pide** n. flat Turkish bread.

**pidgin** n. simplified language, esp. used between speakers of different languages.

**pie** n. dish of meat, fruit, etc., encased in or covered with pastry etc. and baked.

**piebald** adj. having irregular patches of two colours, esp. black and white.

**piece** ● n. 1 distinct portion forming part of or broken off from larger object. 2 literary or musical composition. 3 object used to make moves in board game. ● v. 1 form into whole; put together; join. 2 eke out. 3 form (a theory etc.) by combining separate parts etc.

**pièce de résistance** n. (pl. **pièces de résistance**) most important or remarkable item.

**piecemeal** ● adv. 1 piece by piece. 2 gradually. ● adj. 1 gradual. 2 unsystematic.

**pied** adj. of mixed colours.

**pier** n. 1 structure built out into sea etc., as promenade and landing stage or breakwater. 2 support of arch or of span of bridge. 3 pillar. 4 solid part of wall between windows etc.

**pierce** v. 1 go through or into like spear or needle; make hole in. 2 force a way through; penetrate.

**piercing** ● adj. 1 having or showing shrewdness or keen intelligence. 2 (of cold or wind) penetrating sharply; (of sound) shrilly audible; (of a feeling) intense. ● n. small hole in part of the body made so as to insert a ring, stud, etc.; ring, stud, etc. worn in pierced part of body. □□ **piercingly** adv.

**pierrot** n. white-faced French pantomime character with clown's costume.

**piety** n. piousness.

**piffle** colloq. ● n. nonsense. ● v. talk or act feebly.

**pig** n. 1 mammal with broad snout and stout bristly body. 2 colloq. derog. greedy, dirty, obstinate, or annoying person. 3 oblong mass of smelted iron or other metal.

**pigeon** n. 1 bird of dove family. 2 person who is easily duped or swindled.

**pigeonhole** ● n. small compartment in desk or cabinet. ● v. 1 put away for future consideration or indefinitely. 2 classify.

**pigface** n. succulent, perennial Australian plant with daisy-like flowers.

**piggery** n. pig farm; pigsty.

**piggy** adj. like pig. □ **piggy bank** money box shaped like pig.

**piggyback** ● n. a ride on the back and shoulders of another person. ● v. 1 carry by or as if by means of piggyback. 2 link to or take advantage of (existing system or body of work).

**pigheaded** adj. obstinate.

**piglet** n. young pig.

**pigment** ● n. coloured substance used as paint etc., or occurring naturally in plant or animal tissue. ● v. colour (as) with natural pigment. □□ **pigmentary** adj. **pigmentation** n.

**pigmy** = PYGMY.

**pigsty** n. pen for pigs; filthy room, house, etc.

**pigtail** n. plait of hair hanging from the back or each side of the head.

**pigweed** n. Aust. prostrate plant with edible stems and leaves.

**pike** n. (pl. **pike** or **pikes**) 1 large voracious freshwater fish of the N. hemisphere. 2 spear formerly used by infantry.

**pikelet** n. Aust. small pancake.

**pilaf** n. (also **pilau**) Middle Eastern or Indian dish of rice with meat, spices, etc.

**pilaster** n. rectangular column, esp. one fastened into wall.

**pilchard** n. small marine fish related to herring.

**pilchers** n.pl. Aust. waterproof cover worn over baby's nappy.

**pile** ● n. 1 heap of things laid on one another; colloq. large amount. 2 heavy beam driven vertically into ground as support for building or bridge. 3 cut or uncut loops on the surface of fabric. 4 (**piles**) haemorrhoids. ● v. heap, stack, load. □ **pile up** accumulate.

**pilfer** v. steal or thieve in petty way.

**pilgrim** n. person who journeys to sacred place etc. □□ **pilgrimage** n.

**pill** n. ball or flat piece of medicinal substance to be swallowed whole; (usu. **the pill**) colloq. contraceptive pill.

**pillage** n. & v. plunder.

**pillar** n. 1 slender upright structure used as support or ornament. 2 person regarded as mainstay. 3 upright mass.

**pillion** n. seating for passenger behind motorcyclist.

**pillory** ● n. hist. frame with holes for hands and head, allowing offender to be publicly ridiculed. ● v. 1 expose to ridicule. 2 hist. set in pillory.

**pillow** ● n. 1 cushion as support for head, esp. in bed. 2 pillow-shaped support. ● v. rest (as) on pillow.

**pilot** ● n. 1 person operating controls of aircraft; person in charge of ships entering or leaving harbour etc.; a guide. 2 experimental or preliminary study or undertaking. ● adj. experimental, preliminary. ● v. (**piloted**) act as pilot to. □ **pilot light** 1 small gas burner kept alight to light another. 2 electric indicator light or control light.

**pimelea** n. Australian shrub with heads of white or pink flowers.

**pimento** n. 1 allspice. 2 (also **pimiento**) sweet pepper.

**pimp** ● n. 1 man who lives off earnings of prostitute or brothel. 2 informer, sneak. ● v. act as pimp.

**pimple** n. small hard inflamed spot on skin; pustule. □□ **pimply** adj.

**PIN** abbr. personal identification number (as issued by banks etc.) to validate electronic transactions).

**pin** ● n. 1 small thin pointed piece of metal with head used as fastening. 2 small brooch. 3 wooden or metal peg. ● v. (**pinned**) fasten with pin(s); transfix with pin, lance, etc.; fix (blame, responsibility, etc.); seize and hold fast. □ **pins and needles** tingling sensation. **pin-up** photograph of popular or attractive person, for hanging on wall; such person.

**pinafore** n. 1 apron. 2 (in full **pinafore dress**) dress without collar or sleeves, worn over blouse or jumper.

**piñata** n. figure of animal etc. containing toys and sweets that is suspended from a height and broken open by blindfolded children as part of celebration.

**pinball** *n.* game in which balls are propelled across a sloping board to strike targets.

**pince-nez** *n.* pair of eyeglasses with spring that clips on nose.

**pincers** *n.pl.* gripping tool forming pair of jaws; pincer-shaped claw in crustaceans.

**pinch** ● *v.* **1** squeeze between two surfaces, esp. between finger and thumb. **2** *colloq.* steal; arrest. ● *n.* **1** pinching. **2** the stress of circumstances. **3** very small amount. □ **at a pinch** if really necessary.

**pine** ● *n.* **1** evergreen needle-leaved coniferous tree; any similar Australian tree; wood of these. ● *v.* **1** waste away with grief, disease, etc. **2** feel intense longing. □ **pine nut** edible seed of various pine trees.

**pineapple** *n.* large juicy tropical fruit with yellow flesh and tough skin.

**ping** ● *n.* **1** abrupt single ringing sound. **2** *Aust.* a try, an attempt. ● *v.* **1** (cause to) make ping; (of vehicle engine) emit high-pitched explosive sound caused by faulty combustion. **2** query (another computer on network) to determine whether there is a connection to it; send electronic message to (someone). **3** *Aust.* (in sport) penalise (player).

**ping-pong** *n.* table tennis.

**pinion** *n.* **1** bird's wing. **2** small cogwheel. ● *v.* **1** cut off pinion of (wing or bird) to prevent flight. **2** restrain by binding arms to sides.

**pink** ● *adj.* pale red. ● *n.* **1** pink colour. **2** garden plant with fragrant flowers. ● *v.* cut zigzag edge on; pierce slightly. □ **in the pink** in very good health. □□ **pinkish** *adj.*
**pinkness** *n.*

**pinky** *n.* (also **pinkie**) little finger.

**pinnace** *n.* ship's small boat.

**pinnacle** *n.* culmination, climax; natural peak; small ornamental turret crowning buttress, roof, etc.

**pinot** *n.* variety of black or white grape; wine made from this.

**pinpoint** *v.* locate precisely.

**pinstripe** *n.* very narrow stripe in cloth fabric.

**pint** *n.* imperial measure of capacity (one eighth of gallon, 0.568 litre).

**pioneer** ● *n.* initiator of new enterprise etc.; explorer or settler. ● *v.* **1** be first to explore, use, or develop. **2** act as pioneer.

**pious** *adj.* devout; religious; sanctimonious; dutiful. □□ **piously** *adv.*

**pip** ● *n.* **1** small seed in fruit. **2** short high-pitched sound. **3** star showing rank on army officer's uniform. ● *v.* (**pipped**) (also **pip at the post**) *colloq.* defeat narrowly.

**pipe** ● *n.* **1** tube through which something can flow. **2** wind instrument. **3** (pipes) bagpipes. **4** narrow tube with bowl at one end for smoking tobacco etc. ● *v.* **1** convey (as) through pipes. **2** play (music) on pipe. **3** *Computing* use output from one process as input for another. **4** utter in a shrill voice. □ **pipe down** *colloq.* be quiet. **pipe dream** unrealistic hope or scheme. □□ **pipeful** *n.*

**pipeline** *n.* long pipe for conveying petroleum, gas, etc. over a distance; channel of supply or information. □ **in the pipeline** on the way; in preparation.

**piper** *n.* player of pipes.

**pipette** *n.* slender tube for transferring or measuring small quantities of liquid.

**pipi** *n.* *Aust.* edible marine bivalve, often used as bait.

**piping** *n.* ornamentation of dress, upholstery, etc. by means of cord enclosed in pipelike fold; ornamental lines of cream, icing, etc. on cake or other dish; length or system of pipes.

**pipit** *n.* small bird resembling lark.

**piquant** *adj.* agreeably pungent, sharp, appetising, stimulating. □□ **piquancy** *n.*

**pique** ● *v.* 1 hurt the pride of. 2 arouse (curiosity, interest etc.) ● *n.* resentment; hurt pride.

**piquet** *n.* card game for two players.

**piranha** *n.* voracious S. American freshwater fish.

**pirate** ● *n.* 1 seafaring robber attacking ships. 2 person who infringes copyright or regulations or encroaches on rights of others etc. ● *v.* copy (book, CD, etc.) or trade (goods) without permission. □□ **piratical** *adj.* **piracy** *n.*

**pirouette** *n.* dancer's spin on one foot or point of toe.

**Pisces** *n.* twelfth sign of zodiac, the Fishes. □□ **Piscean** *adj.* & *n.*

**pisonia** *n.* Aust. rainforest tree.

**piss** *colloq.* ● *v.* urinate. ● *n.* 1 urine, urinating. 2 alcoholic drink, esp. beer. ● *adj.* (as **pissed**) drunk.

**pisser** *n.* colloq. 1 men's urinal or toilet. 2 Aust. hotel.

**pistachio** *n.* kind of nut with green kernel.

**piste** *n.* ski run.

**pistil** *n.* seed-producing part of flower. □□ **pistillate** *adj.*

**pistol** *n.* small gun.

**piston** *n.* sliding cylinder fitting closely in tube and moving up and down in it, used in steam or petrol engine to impart motion; sliding valve in trumpet etc.

**pit** ● *n.* 1 large hole in ground; coalmine; sunken area. 2 stone of fruit. 3 (**the pits**) colloq. worst imaginable place, situation, person, etc. 4 area to side of track where racing cars are refuelled etc. during race. ● *v.* (**pitted**) 1 set against in competition. 2 make pit or depression in. 3 remove stones from olives etc.

**pita** *n.* (also **pitta**) flat unleavened bread that can be split and filled.

**pitch** ● *v.* 1 set up (esp. tent, camp, etc.) in chosen position. 2 throw. 3 express in particular style or at particular level. 4 fall heavily. 5 (of ship etc.) plunge in lengthwise direction. 6 *Mus.* set at particular point. ● *n.* 1 act of pitching. 2 playing field. 3 steepness. 4 intensity. 5 gradient esp. of roof. 6 *Mus.* degree of highness or lowness of tone. 7 place where street trader or performer is stationed; place where tent is pitched. 8 dark tarry substance. 9 *colloq.* persuasive sales talk. 10 distance between successive points, lines, etc. □ **pitch-black** (also **pitch-dark**) very or completely dark. **pitch in** *colloq.* join in task.

**pitchblende** *n.* uranium oxide occurring in pitchlike masses and yielding radium.

**pitcher** *n.* 1 large jug; ewer. 2 player who delivers ball in baseball and softball.

**piteous** *adj.* deserving of or arousing pity. □□ **piteously** *adv.*

**pith** *n.* 1 spongy tissue in stems or fruits. 2 essential part.

**pithy** *adj.* 1 condensed and forcible. 2 terse. □□ **pithily** *adv.* **pithiness** *n.*

**pitiful** *adj.* 1 causing pity. 2 contemptible. □□ **pitifully** *adv.*

**piton** *n.* peg driven in to support climber or rope.

**pitta**[1] *n.* vividly-coloured bird of Australia, India, etc.

**pitta**[2] = PITA.

**pittance** *n.* scanty allowance; small amount.

**pittosporum** *n.* tree with fragrant flowers and orange fruit.

**pituitary gland** *n.* small ductless gland at base of brain, influencing bodily growth and function.

**pituri** *n.* shrub widespread in central Australia, the leaves being traditionally chewed by Aboriginal people for their powerful narcotic effect.

**pity** ● *n.* sorrow for another's suffering; cause for regret. ● *v.* feel pity for.□□ **pitying** *adj.*

**pivot** ● *n.* shaft or pin on which something turns; crucial person or point. ● *v.* (**pivoted**) **1** turn (as) on pivot. **2** provide with pivot. □□ **pivotal** *adj.*

**pixel** *n.* any of the minute areas of illumination of which image on display screen is composed.

**pixelate** *v.* display as or divide into pixels.

**pixie** *n.* (also **pixy**) fairy-like being.

**pizza** *n.* flat piece of dough baked with topping of tomatoes, cheese, etc.

**pizzeria** *n.* pizza restaurant.

**pizzicato** *adv. Mus.* plucking the strings of a violin etc, instead of using the bow.

**pizzle** *n. Aust.* penis of animal.

**pizzling** *n. Aust.* a thrashing or heavy defeat.

**pl.** *abbr.* **1** plural. **2** place.

**placard** ● *n.* large notice for public display. ● *v.* advertise by placards.

**placate** *v.* pacify; conciliate. □□ **placatory** *adj.*

**place** ● *n.* **1** particular portion of space or of area; particular town, district, building, etc. **2** a position; (duty appropriate to) one's rank. ● *v.* **1** put into a place, find a place for. **2** locate, identify. **3** put or give (order for goods etc.) □ **be placed** (in race) be among first three. **take place** occur.

**placebo** *n.* **1** medicine with no physiological effects prescribed for psychological reasons. **2** dummy pill etc. used in controlled trial.

**placement** *n.* putting someone or something in place or home; posting someone temporarily in workplace for experience.

**placenta** *n.* (*pl.* **placentae** or **placentas**) organ in uterus of pregnant mammal that nourishes foetus.□□ **placental** *adj.*

**placid** *adj.* calm; unruffled; not easily disturbed.□□ **placidity** *n.* **placidly** *adv.*

**plagiarise** *v.* (also **-ize**) take and use (another's writings etc.) as one's own. □□ **plagiarism** *n.* **plagiarist** *n.*

**plague** *n.* deadly contagious disease; infestation; great trouble or affliction. ● *v. colloq.* annoy, pester.

**plaid** *n.* chequered or tartan, esp. woollen, cloth.

**plain** ● *adj.* **1** clear, evident. **2** readily understood. **3** simple. **4** not beautiful or distinguished-looking. ● *adv.* **1** clearly. **2** simply. ● *n.* **1** level tract of country. **2** ordinary stitch in knitting. □ **plain clothes** civilian clothes, not a uniform. **plain sailing** period or activity that is free from difficulties.□□ **plainly** *adv.*

**plainsong** *n.* (also **plain chant**) medieval church music for voices, without regular rhythm.

**plaintiff** *n.* person who brings case against another into court.

**plaintive** *adj.* mournful-sounding. □□ **plaintively** *adv.*

**plait** ● *n.* length of hair, straw, etc. in three or more interlaced strands. ● *v.* form into plait.

**plan** ● *n.* **1** method or procedure for doing something. **2** drawing exhibiting relative position and size of parts of building etc.; diagram, map. ● *v.* (**planned**) make a plan (of).□□ **planning** *n.*

**plane** ● *n.* **1** level surface; level of thought or development. **2** aeroplane. **3** tool for smoothing surface of wood by paring shavings from it. **4** tall spreading tree with broad leaves. ● *v.* smooth or pare with plane. ● *adj.* level.

**planet** *n.* heavenly body orbiting star. □□ **planetary** *adj.*

**planetarium** *n.* (*pl.* **planetariums** or **planetaria**) building in which image of night sky, as seen at various times and places, is projected.

**plangent** adj. **1** loud and resonant. **2** sad and mournful.

**plank** ● n. **1** long flat piece of timber. **2** item in political or other program. ● v. provide or cover with planks.

**plankton** n. chiefly microscopic organisms drifting in sea or fresh water.

**plant** ● n. **1** organism such as tree, grass, etc., capable of living wholly on inorganic substances, and lacking power of movement. **2** equipment for industrial process; factory. **3** Aust. animals, equipment, personnel, etc. employed by stockman etc., on the move. **4** colloq. thing deliberately placed for discovery, esp. to incriminate another. ● v. **1** place (seeds etc.) in soil to grow. **2** fix firmly. **3** establish. **4** cause (idea etc.) to be established, esp. in another person's mind. **5** deliver (blow, kiss, etc.). **6** colloq. place (something incriminating) for later discovery.

**plantain** n. plant related to banana; banana-like fruit of this.

**plantation** n. estate for cultivation of bananas, coffee, etc.; number of growing plants, esp. trees, planted together.

**planter** n. **1** manager or owner of plantation. **2** container for house plants.

**plaque** n. **1** commemorative plate, usu. fixed on wall. **2** deposit on teeth where bacteria proliferate.

**plasma** n. (also **plasm**) **1** colourless fluid part of blood etc. in which corpuscles etc. float. **2** protoplasm. **3** gas of positive ions and free electrons in about equal numbers. □□ **plasmic** adj.

**plaster** n. **1** mixture of lime, sand, and water, etc. used for covering walls. ● v. cover with plaster; coat, daub.□ **plaster of Paris** white paste made from gypsum, for making moulds or casts.□□ **plasterer** n.

**plasterboard** n. board with a core of plaster, for making internal walls, partitions, etc.

**plastered** adj. colloq. drunk.

**plastic** ● n. **1** synthetic resinous substance that can be given any shape. **2** colloq. credit card(s). ● adj. **1** made of plastic. **2** capable of being moulded. **3** (of people) artificial in manner, false. **4** giving form to clay, wax, etc.□ **plastic bullet** solid plastic cylinder etc. fired as riot control device etc. rather than to kill. **plastic surgery** operation to replace or repair injured or defective external tissue. □□ **plasticise** v. (also **-ize**) **plasticity** n. **plasticky** adj.

**plasticine** n. propr. pliant substance used for modelling.

**plate** ● n. **1** almost flat, usu. circular utensil for holding food. **2** Aust. contribution of cakes, sandwiches, etc. brought by guests to party. **3** articles of gold, silver, or other metal. **4** thin flat sheet of metal, glass, or other material. **5** illustration on special paper in book. **6** denture. **7** each of several sheets of rock thought to form earth's crust. ● v. **1** cover or coat with metal. **2** serve or arrange on plate.□□ **plateful** n.

**plateau** ● n. (pl. **plateaux** or **plateaus**) **1** area of level high ground. **2** state of little variation following an increase. ● v. reach level or static state after period of increase.

**platelet** n. small disc in blood, involved in clotting.

**platen** n. **1** plate in printing press by which paper is pressed against type; roller of typewriter or printer.

**platform** n. **1** raised level surface, esp. one from which speaker addresses audience, or one along side of line at railway station; thick sole of shoe. **2** declared policy of political party; opportunity to voice one's views or initiate action.

**platinum** n. **1** white heavy metallic element (symbol Pt). **2** that does not tarnish.

**platitude** n. commonplace remark. □□ **platitudinous** adj.

**platonic** adj. (of love or friendship) not sexual.

**platoon** n. subdivision of infantry company.

**platter** n. large plate for serving food.

**platypus** n. (pl. **platypuses**) amphibious, burrowing, egg-laying Australian mammal with thick brown fur and ducklike bill.

**plaudits** n.pl. round of applause; praise.

**plausible** adj. reasonable, probable; persuasive but deceptive. □□ **plausibility** n. **plausibly** adv.

**play** ● v. **1** occupy oneself in (game) or in other recreational activity; compete against in game; move (piece, ball, etc.) in a game. **2** act the part of. **3** perform on (musical instrument). **4** cause (radio, recording, etc.) to produce sound. **5** move lightly; touch gently. ● n. **1** playing. **2** activity, operation. **3** dramatic work. **4** freedom of movement. □ **play along** pretend to cooperate. **play at** perform in a half-hearted way. **play down** minimise the importance of. **play the game** behave honourably. **play on** exploit (weakness). **play up** fail to work properly; cause trouble; be unruly.

**playboy** n. pleasure-loving usu. rich man.

**player** n. **1** participant in game. **2** person who plays musical instrument; device for playing recorded music or video. **3** actor.

**playful** adj. fond of or inclined to play; done in fun. □□ **playfully** adv. **playfulness** n.

**playing card** n. each of a set of usu. 52 oblong pieces of card etc. used in games.

**playlist** n. list of recorded music etc. to be played.

**playmate** n. child's companion in play.

**playwright** n. person who writes plays.

**plaza** n. public square in city or town; Aust. shopping mall.

**plea** n. **1** appeal, entreaty. **2** Law formal statement by or on behalf of defendant. **3** excuse.

**plead** v. **1** make earnest appeal to. **2** address court as advocate or party. **3** allege as excuse. **4** declare oneself to be (guilty or not guilty of charge). **5** make appeal or entreaty.

**pleasant** adj. agreeable; giving pleasure. □□ **pleasantly** adv.

**pleasantry** n. pleasant or amusing remark.

**please** ● v. **1** give pleasure to. **2** think fit, have the desire. ● adv. polite word of request. □□ **pleased** adj. **pleasing** adj.

**pleasurable** adj. causing pleasure. □□ **pleasurably** adv.

**pleasure** n. feeling of satisfaction or joy; source of pleasure.

**pleat** ● n. flattened fold in cloth. ● v. make pleat(s) in.

**pleb** n. colloq. rough uncultured person.

**plebeian** adj. of the common people; uncultured, coarse.

**plebiscite** n. referendum.

**plectrum** n. (pl. **plectrums** or **plectra**) thin flat piece of plastic etc. for plucking strings of musical instrument.

**pledge** ● n. **1** solemn promise; thing given as security for payment of debt etc. **2** token. ● v. **1** deposit as security. **2** promise solemnly by pledge; bind by solemn promise.

**plenary** adj. (of assembly) to be attended by all members; entire, unqualified.

**plenipotentiary** ● n. person (esp. diplomat) having full authority to act. ● adj. having such power.

**plenitude** n. completeness; abundance.

**plentiful** adj. abundant, copious. □□ **plentifully** adv.

**plenty** n. abundance, quite enough.

**plethora** n. large or excessive amount of something.

**pleurisy** n. inflammation of membrane enclosing lungs. □□ **pleuritic** adj.

**pliable** adj. easily bent or influenced; supple; compliant. □□ **pliability** n.

**pliant** adj. pliable. □□ **pliancy** n.

**pliers** n.pl. pincers with parallel flat surfaces for holding small objects, bending wire, etc.

**plight** n. unfortunate condition or state.

**Plimsoll line** n. marking on ship's side showing limit of legal submersion under various conditions.

**plinth** n. base supporting column, vase, statue, etc.

**plod** v. (plodded) walk or work laboriously. □□ **plodder** n.

**plonk** n. colloq. Aust. cheap or inferior wine.

**plop** ● n. sound as of smooth object dropping into water. ● v. (plopped) (cause to) fall with plop. ● adv. with a plop.

**plot** ● n. 1 small piece of land. 2 plan or interrelationship of main events of play, film, etc. 3 secret plan, conspiracy. ● v. (plotted) 1 make chart, diagram, graph, etc. of. 2 hatch secret plans. 3 devise secretly. 4 mark on chart or diagram. □□ **plotter** n.

**plough** ● n. implement for furrowing and turning up soil. ● v. 1 cut or turn up (soil etc.) with plough. 2 (plough

through) make one's way laboriously. □ **ploughman's lunch** meal of bread, cheese, and pickle.

**plover** n. plump-breasted wading bird.

**ploy** n. a cunning manoeuvre.

**pluck** ● v. 1 pick or pull out or away. 2 strip (bird) of feathers. 3 pull at, twitch. 4 tug or snatch at. 5 sound (string of musical instrument) with finger or plectrum. ● n. 1 plucking movement. 2 courage.

**plucky** adj. brave, spirited.

**plug** ● n. 1 something fitting into hole or filling cavity. 2 device of metal pins etc. for making electrical connection. 3 colloq. piece of free publicity. 4 cake or stick of tobacco. ● v. (plugged) 1 stop with plug. 2 colloq. shoot. 3 colloq. seek to popularise by frequent recommendation.

**plum** n. 1 roundish fleshy stone fruit; tree bearing this. 2 Australian tree or shrub bearing edible plum-like fruit. 3 reddish-purple. 4 colloq. prized thing.

**plumage** n. bird's feathers.

**plumb** ● n. lead weight attached to line for testing water's depth or whether wall etc. is vertical. ● adv. 1 exactly. 2 vertically. ● adj. vertical. ● v. 1 test with plumb. 2 experience (extreme feelings). 3 learn detailed facts about.

**plumber** n. person who fits and repairs apparatus of water supply etc.

**plumbing** n. system or apparatus of water supply, drainage, etc.

**plume** ● n. feather, esp. large and showy one; feathery ornament in hat, hair, etc.; feather-like formation, esp. of smoke. ● v. furnish with plume(s).

**plummet** v. (plummeted, plummeting) fall or plunge.

**plump** ● adj. having full rounded shape; fleshy. ● v. 1 make or become plump. 2 put down heavily. □ **plump for** choose, decide on. □□ **plumpness** n.

**plunder** ● v. 1 rob or steal, esp. in war. 2 embezzle. ● n. 1 plundering. 2 property plundered.

**plunge** ● v. 1 thrust forcefully, dive; (cause to) become or enter into impetuously. 2 move suddenly downward. ● n. 1 plunging, a dive. 2 decisive step. □ **take the plunge** *colloq.* commit oneself to course of action.

**plunger** n. 1 part of mechanism that works with plunging or thrusting motion. 2 rubber cup on handle for removing blockages by plunging action.

**pluperfect** *Gram.* ● adj. expressing action completed prior to some past point of time. ● n. pluperfect tense.

**plural** ● adj. more than one in number; *Gram.* (of word or form) denoting more than one. ● n. plural number; *Gram.* plural word or form. □□ **plurality** n.

**pluralism** n. form of society in which minority groups retain independent traditions; multiculturalism. □□ **pluralist** n. **pluralistic** adj.

**plus** ● *prep.* 1 with addition of. 2 (of temperature) above zero. ● adj. 1 more than zero. 2 more than the amount indicated. 3 *Math.* positive. 4 additional, extra. ● n. 1 sign (+). 2 advantage.

**plush** ● n. cloth of silk, cotton, etc., with long soft pile. ● adj. 1 made of plush. 2 *colloq.* luxurious. □□ **plushy** adj.

**plutocracy** n. government or control by the wealthy; wealthy elite. □□ **plutocrat** n. **plutocratic** adj.

**plutonium** n. 1 chemical element (symbol Pu). 2 radioactive substance used in nuclear weapons and reactors.

**pluvial** adj. of or caused by rain.

**ply**[1] n. 1 thickness, layer. 2 plywood.

**ply**[2] v. 1 wield; work at. 2 supply continuously or approach repeatedly with. 3 (of vehicle etc.) go to and fro.

**plywood** n. strong thin board made by gluing layers of wood with the direction of the grain alternating.

**PM** *abbr.* prime minister.

**p.m.** *abbr.* after noon (Latin *post meridiem*).

**pneumatic** adj. filled with air or wind; operated by compressed air. □□ **pneumatically** adv.

**pneumonia** n. inflammation of lung(s).

**PO** *abbr.* Post Office.

**poach** v. 1 cook (an egg without shell) in or over boiling water; simmer in small amount of liquid. 2 take (game or fish) illegally; trespass, encroach. □□ **poacher** n.

**pocket** ● n. 1 small bag sewn into or on garment, for carrying small articles; pouch-like compartment. 2 financial resources. 3 isolated group or area. 4 cavity in earth etc. containing ore. 5 AFL side position. ● adj. small, esp. small enough for carrying in pocket. ● v. (pocketed) 1 put into pocket. 2 appropriate. □ **in (or out of) pocket** having made a profit (or loss). **pocket money** for minor expenses; allowance given regularly to child.

**pocketbook** n. 1 notebook. 2 small folding case for money or papers.

**pock-marked** adj. marked by scars or pits.

**pod**[1] n. long seed vessel, esp. of pea or bean.

**pod**[2] n. small herd of whales or seals.

**podcast** ● n. digital audio file made available on Internet for downloading to computer etc. ● v. make (file) available as podcast.

**poddy** *Aust.* ● n. calf old enough to wean and fatten; unbranded calf; hand-fed calf or lamb. ● adj. hand-fed.

**podgy** adj. short and fat.

**podium** n. (pl. **podiums** or **podia**) pedestal or platform.

**poem** n. literary composition with attention to diction, imagery, rhythm, and metre (and sometimes rhyme).

**poet** n. writer of poems.

**poetic** adj. (also **poetical**) of or like poetry or poets. □□ **poetically** adv.

**poetry** n. 1 poems; poet's work. 2 poetic or tenderly pleasing quality.

**po-faced** adj. colloq. solemn.

**pogo** n. (also **pogo stick**) stilt-like toy with spring, used to jump about on.

**pogrom** n. organised massacre (orig. of Jewish people in Russia).

**poignant** adj. painfully sharp; deeply moving; arousing sympathy; pleasantly piquant. □□ **poignance** n. **poignancy** n. **poignantly** adv.

**poinsettia** n. plant with large scarlet or pink bracts surrounding small yellow flowers.

**point** ● n. 1 tapered or sharp end, a tip; promontory. 2 particular place, moment, or stage; (in cricket) fielding position near batter. 3 unit of measurement or scoring; (AFL) a behind. 4 item, detail; characteristic; chief or important feature. 5 effectiveness. 6 electrical socket. 7 movable rail for directing train from one line to another. ● v. 1 aim, direct (finger, weapon, etc.); have a certain direction; indicate. 2 fill in (joints of brickwork) with mortar. □ **on the point of** on the verge of (an action). **point blank** at very close range. **point duty** traffic control by police officer at road junction. **pointing the bone** (in Aboriginal ritual practice) ceremony of pointing bone at person whose death is willed. **point of view** way of looking at things. **point out** draw attention to. **to the point** relevant.

**pointed** adj. 1 having point. 2 (of remark etc.) cutting. 3 emphasised. □□ **pointedly** adv.

**pointless** adj. purposeless; meaningless; ineffective. □□ **pointlessly** adv. **pointlessness** n.

**poise** ● n. dignified self-assured manner. ● v. balance; hold suspended or supported; be balanced or suspended.

**poison** ● n. 1 substance that when absorbed by living organism kills or injures it. 2 colloq. harmful influence etc. ● v. 1 administer poison to; kill or injure with poison. 2 corrupt, pervert; spoil. □□ **poisoner** n. **poisonous** adj.

**poke** ● v. 1 push with (end of) finger, stick, etc.; push forward or into something. 2 search, pry. ● n. poking; a thrust, a nudge.

**poker** n. 1 metal rod for stirring fire. 2 gambling game. □ **poker face** expression concealing one's thoughts or feelings. **poker machine** gaming machine that pays according to the combination of symbols appearing on edges of wheels etc. operated by player.

**poky** adj. small and cramped.

**polar** adj. 1 of or near South or North Pole. 2 having magnetic or electric polarity. 3 directly opposite in character etc. □ **polar bear** white bear of Arctic regions.

**polarise** v. (also **-ize**) 1 restrict vibrations of (light waves etc.) to one direction. 2 give polarity to. 3 divide into two opposing groups. □□ **polarisation** n.

**polaroid** n. propr. 1 material in thin sheets polarising light passing through it. 2 camera that produces print immediately after each exposure.

**pole** ● n. 1 long slender rounded piece of wood, metal, etc., esp. as support etc. 2 north (**North Pole**) or south (**South Pole**) end of earth's axis. 3 each of two opposite points on surface of magnet at which magnetic forces are strongest. 4 positive or

negative terminal of battery etc.
• *v.* push off or propel with pole.
□ **pole position** most favourable starting position in motor race. **poles apart** having nothing in common.

**polecat** *n.* small dark brown European mammal of weasel family.

**polemic** • *n.* verbal attack; controversy. • *adj.* (also **polemical**) involving dispute; controversial.
□□ **polemicist** *n.*

**polenta** *n.* maize flour as used in Italian cookery; paste or dough made from this and fried etc.

**police** • *n.* civil force responsible for maintaining public order. • *v.* control or provide with police; keep in order, administer, control.

**policeman** *n.* (*pl.* **policemen**) male member of police force.

**policewoman** *n.* (*pl.* **policewomen**) female member of police force.

**policy** *n.* **1** general course of action adopted by government, business, etc. **2** insurance contract.

**polio** *n.* poliomyelitis.

**poliomyelitis** *n.* infectious viral disease of grey matter of central nervous system with temporary or permanent paralysis.

**polish** • *v.* make or become smooth or glossy by rubbing; refine, perfect.
• *n.* substance used for polishing; smoothness, glossiness; elegance.

**polished** *adj.* (of manner or performance) elegant, perfected.

**polite** *adj.* having good manners; courteous; cultivated, refined.
□□ **politely** *adv.* **politeness** *n.*

**politic** *adj.* showing prudent judgement.

**political** *adj.* of nation or its government; of public affairs; of, engaged in, or taking a side in, politics; relating to pursuit of power, status, etc. □ **political correctness** avoidance of any expressions or behaviour that may be considered discriminatory.
□□ **politically** *adv.*

**politician** *n.* person involved in politics.

**politics** *n.* art and science of government; political life, affairs, principles, etc.; activities relating to pursuit of power, status, etc.

**polity** *n.* form of civil administration; society.

**polka** *n.* lively dance for couples.
□ **polka dots** round evenly spaced dots on fabric.

**poll** • *n.* votes cast in election; place for this; estimate of public opinion made by questioning people.
• *v.* **1** take or receive vote(s) of; vote; record opinion of (person, group). **2** cut off top of (tree etc.).

**pollard** • *n.* **1** hornless animal. **2** tree polled to produce dense head of young branches. **3** fine bran.
• *v.* make pollard of (tree).

**pollen** *n.* fertilising powder discharged from flower's anther.

**pollie** *n.* (also **polly**) *Aust. colloq.* politician.

**pollinate** *v.* fertilise with pollen.
□□ **pollination** *n.*

**pollster** *n.* person conducting opinion poll.

**pollute** *v.* contaminate; make impure or dirty. □□ **pollutant** *n.* **polluter** *n.* **pollution** *n.*

**Pollyanna** *n.* excessively cheerful or optimistic person.

**polo** *n.* game like hockey played on horseback. □ **polo neck** high turned-over collar.

**polonaise** *n.* slow processional dance.

**polonium** *n.* radioactive metallic element (symbol **Po**).

**poltergeist** *n.* noisy mischievous ghost.

**poly-** *comb. form* **1** many. **2** polymerised.

**polyandry** n. polygamy in which woman has more than one husband.

**polychrome** adj. in many colours. □□ **polychromatic** adj.

**polyester** n. synthetic fibre or resin.

**polygamy** n. practice of having more than one wife or husband at once. □□ **polygamist** n. **polygamous** adj.

**polyglot** n. & adj. (person) knowing several languages.

**polygon** n. figure with many sides. □□ **polygonal** adj.

**polygraph** n. machine for reading physiological characteristics (e.g. pulse rate), used as lie detector.

**polyhedron** n. (pl. **polyhedra** or **polyhedrons**) solid figure with many faces. □□ **polyhedral** adj.

**polymath** n. person of great or varied learning.

**polymer** n. compound molecule(s) formed from repeated units of smaller molecules.

**polymerise** n. (also **-ize**) combine into a polymer. □□ **polymerisation** n.

**polyp** n. **1** simple organism with tube-shaped body. **2** small growth on mucous membrane.

**polyphony** n. contrapuntal music. □□ **polyphonic** adj.

**polystyrene** n. polymer of styrene used to make hard plastic or expanded with gas to produce lightweight white material for packaging etc.

**polytheism** n. belief in or worship of more than one god. □□ **polytheistic** adj.

**polythene** n. tough light plastic.

**polyunsaturated** adj. (of fat) containing several double or triple bonds in each molecule and therefore capable of combining with hydrogen and not associated with accumulation of cholesterol.

**polyurethane** n. synthetic resin or plastic used esp. in paints or foam.

**pom** n. Aust. colloq. often offens. = POMMY.

**pomander** n. ball of mixed aromatic substances.

**pomegranate** n. tropical tough-rinded, many-seeded fruit; tree bearing this.

**pommel** n. knob of sword hilt; projecting front of saddle.

**pommy** (also **pommie**) Aust. colloq. often offens. • n. inhabitant of, or person from, British Isles (esp. England). • adj. of or pertaining to England; English; British.

**pomp** n. splendid display; splendour; specious glory.

**pompom** n. (also **pompon**) decorative tuft or ball on hat, shoe, etc.

**pompous** n. self-important, affectedly grand or solemn. □□ **pomposity** n. **pompously** adv. **pompousness** n.

**ponce** colloq. • n. **1** a pimp. **2** offens. homosexual or effeminate man. • v. act as ponce. □□ **poncy** adj.

**poncho** n. cloak of rectangular piece of material with slit in middle for head.

**pond** n. small body of still water.

**ponder** v. think over; muse.

**ponderous** adj. heavy and unwieldy; laborious; dull. □□ **ponderously** adv. **ponderousness** n.

**pong** n. & v. colloq. stink. □□ **pongy** adj.

**pontiff** n. the Pope.

**pontificate** v. be pompously dogmatic.

**pontoon** n. **1** flat-bottomed boat; floating platform. **2** card game.

**pony** n. horse of any small breed.

**ponytail** n. long hair drawn back and tied to hang down.

**poo** colloq. • n. faeces. • v. defecate.

**poodle** n. dog of breed with thick curly coat.

**poof** n. (also **poofter**) colloq. offens. male homosexual; man whose manner etc. does not conform to that of conventional masculinity.

**pooh** int. exclamation of contempt.

**pool ●** n. **1** small body of still water; small shallow body of any liquid; swimming pool; deep place in river. **2** a shared fund or supply. **3** game resembling snooker. **●** v. put into common fund or supply; share.

**poop** n. stern of ship; raised deck at stern.

**pooped** adj. colloq. exhausted.

**poor** adj. having little money or means; not abundant; not very good; pitiable.

**poorly ●** adv. in poor manner, badly. **●** adj. unwell.

**pop ●** n. **1** abrupt explosive sound. **2** colloq. effervescent drink. **3** popular music. **●** v. (**popped**) **1** (cause to) make pop. **2** move, come, or put unexpectedly or suddenly. **3** colloq. (cause to) burst. **●** adj. in a popular modern style. □ **pop-up 1** (of book etc.) containing folded cut-out pictures that rise up when page is turned. **2** Computing (of menu etc.) able to be superimposed on screen being worked on and suppressed rapidly. **3** of shop etc. that opens quickly in a temporary location and operates for short period of time.

**popcorn** n. corn that bursts open when heated.

**pope** n. head of the RC Church.

**poplar** n. slender tree with straight trunk and often tremulous leaves.

**poplin** n. closely-woven corded fabric.

**popper** n. propr. small plastic box of soft drink etc. with drinking straw attached.

**poppet** n. colloq. (esp. as term of endearment) small child.

**poppy** n. plant with bright flowers and milky narcotic sap.

**poppycock** n. colloq. nonsense.

**populace** n. general public.

**popular** adj. generally liked or admired; of, for, or prevalent among the general public. □□ **popularity** n. **popularly** adv.

**popularise** v. (also **-ize**) **1** make generally liked. **2** present in popular non-technical form.

**populate** v. **1** fill with population. **2** Computing fill in (data).

**population** n. inhabitants of town, country, etc.; total number of these.

**populist** n. politician claiming to represent ordinary people. ● adj. concerned with ordinary people.

**populous** adj. thickly inhabited.

**porcelain** n. fine translucent ceramic; things made of this.

**porch** n. covered entrance to building.

**porcine** adj. of or like pigs.

**porcupine** n. large rodent with body and tail covered with erectile spines.

**pore** n. minute opening in surface through which fluids may pass. □ **pore over** study closely.

**pork** n. flesh of pig used as food.

**porn** colloq. ● n. pornography. ● adj. pornographic.

**pornography** n. explicit presentation of sexual activity in literature, films, etc., to stimulate erotic feelings. □□ **pornographer** n. **pornographic** adj.

**porous** adj. having pores; permeable. □□ **porosity** n.

**porphyry** n. hard rock with feldspar crystals in fine-grained red mass.

**porpoise** n. sea mammal of whale family.

**porridge** n. oatmeal or other cereal boiled in water or milk.

**port** n. **1** harbour; town with harbour. **2** opening in ship's side, a porthole. **3** left-hand side of ship or aircraft. **4** strong sweet wine. **5** Computing socket etc. in electronic circuit for connection of peripheral equipment. **6** (esp. in Queensland) suitcase; school satchel.

**portable** *adj.* easily movable, convenient for carrying.
□□ **portability** *n.*

**portal** *n.* doorway, gate.

**portcullis** *n.* strong heavy grating lowered in defence of fortress gateway.

**portend** *v.* foreshadow.

**portent** *n.* **1** omen, significant sign. **2** marvellous thing. □□ **portentous** *adj.*

**porter** *n.* **1** person employed to carry luggage etc. **2** doorkeeper of large building etc.

**portfolio** *n.* **1** folder for loose sheets of paper, drawings, etc. **2** samples of artist's work. **3** list of investments held by investor. **4** office of government minister.

**portico** *n.* (pl. **porticoes** or **porticos**) **1** colonnade. **2** roof supported by columns serving as porch to building.

**portion** ● *n.* part, share; amount of food for one person. ● *v.* **1** divide. **2** (portion out) distribute.

**portly** *adj.* corpulent, stout.

**portmanteau** *n.* (pl. **portmanteaus** or **portmanteaux**) case for clothes etc., opening into two equal parts.

**portrait** *n.* drawing, painting, photograph, etc. of person or animal; description.

**portray** *v.* make likeness of; describe; represent in film etc. □□ **portrayal** *n.*

**Portuguese man-of-war** = BLUEBOTTLE.

**pose** ● *v.* **1** assume attitude, esp. for artistic purpose; pretend to be. **2** constitute or present (problem). **3** arrange in required attitude. ● *n.* **1** attitude of body or mind. **2** affectation, pretence.

**poser** *n.* **1** poseur. **2** *colloq.* puzzling question or problem.

**poseur** *n.* person who behaves affectedly.

**posh** *colloq.* ● *adj.* luxurious; supposedly upper-class. ● *adv.* in supposedly upper-class way.
□□ **poshly** *adv.* poshness *n.*

**posit** *v.* assume as fact, postulate.

**position** ● *n.* **1** place occupied by person or thing. **2** way thing is placed. **3** advantage. **4** mental attitude. **5** situation. **6** rank, status, job. **7** point of view; opinion about issue. ● *v.* place in position.
□□ **positional** *adj.*

**positive** ● *adj.* **1** explicit, definite. **2** constructive; affirmative, asserting. **3** (of a quantity) greater than zero. **4** (of battery terminal) through which electric current enters. **5** (of photograph) with lights, shades, or colours as in the subject, not reversed. ● *n.* positive quality, quantity, or photograph. □ **positive pole** north-seeking pole of magnet.
□□ **positively** *adv.*

**positron** *n.* elementary particle with same mass as but opposite charge to electron.

**posse** *n.* strong force or company.

**possess** *v.* hold as property, own; have; occupy; dominate mind of.
□□ **possessor** *n.*

**possession** *n.* **1** owning, something owned. **2** *Football etc.* control of ball by player or team. □ **take possession of** become possessor of.

**possessive** ● *adj.* **1** wanting to retain what one possesses; jealous and domineering. **2** *Gram.* indicating possession. ● *n.* *Gram.* possessive word or case.
□□ **possessiveness** *n.*

**possible** ● *adj.* **1** capable of existing, happening, being done, etc. **2** potential. ● *n.* possible candidate, member of team, etc. □□ **possibility** *n.* possibly *adv.*

**possum** *n.* *Aust.* chiefly herbivorous, long-tailed, tree-dwelling marsupial. □ **play possum** pretend to be asleep. **stir the possum** *Aust.* excite interest or controversy.

**post** ● *n.* **1** official conveying of parcels, letters, etc.; the letters conveyed. **2** piece of timber, metal, etc. set upright to support or mark something. **3** place of duty; job; outpost of soldiers; trading post. **4** piece of writing, image, or other item of content published online. ● *v.* **1** send (letters etc.) by post. **2** put up (notice); announce in this way; publish (content) online. **3** place, station. □ keep me posted keep me informed.

**post-** *prefix* after.

**postage** *n.* charge for sending letter etc. by post.

**postal** *adj.* of or by post.

**postcard** *n.* card for sending messages by post without envelope.

**postcode** *n.* group of numbers etc. in a postal address to assist sorting; area denoted by particular postcode.

**postdate** *v.* give later than true date to; occur later than.

**postdoctorate** ● *n.* period of research undertaken after completion of doctoral research; person engaged in this research. ● *adj.* of postdoctoral research. □□ **postdoctoral** *adj.*

**poster** ● *n.* **1** placard in public place; large printed picture. **2** *AFL* kick for goal that hits goal post and hence scores only a point.

**posterior** ● *adj.* later in time or order; at the back. ● *n.* buttocks.

**posterity** *n.* future generations.

**postern** *n.* back or side entrance.

**postgraduate** ● *n.* person on course of study after taking first degree. ● *adj.* relating to post-graduates.

**post-haste** *adv.* with great haste.

**posthumous** *adj.* occurring after death; published after author's death. □□ **posthumously** *adv.*

**postmodern** *adj.* of movement reacting to modernism, esp. by

drawing attention to former conventions. □□ **postmodernism** *n.*

**post-mortem** *n.* examination of body made after death; analysis of something that has happened. ● *adv.* & *adj.* after death.

**post-natal** *adj.* after childbirth.

**postpone** *v.* cause to take place at later time. □□ **postponement** *n.*

**postprandial** *adj. formal* after lunch or dinner.

**postscript** *n.* addition at end of letter etc. after signature.

**post-traumatic stress disorder** *n.* condition of persistent mental or emotional stress occurring as result of injury or severe psychological shock.

**postulant** *n.* candidate, esp. for admission to religious order.

**postulate** *v.* assume to be true as basis for reasoning. □□ **postulation** *n.*

**posture** ● *n.* **1** way person stands, walks, etc. **2** mental attitude. **3** condition or state (of affairs etc.). ● *v.* assume posture, esp. for effect.

**posy** *n.* small bunch of flowers.

**pot** ● *n.* **1** vessel for holding liquids or solids, or for cooking in. **2** *colloq.* marijuana. ● *v.* (**potted**) **1** put into pot. **2** pocket (ball) in billiards etc. □ go to pot *colloq.* fall into bad state.

**pot belly 1** protruding stomach; person with this. **2** bulbous stove or heater.

**pot luck** whatever (hospitality etc.) is available.

**potable** *adj.* drinkable.

**potash** *n.* potassium carbonate.

**potassium** *n.* soft silver-white metallic element (symbol **K**).

**potato** *n.* (*pl.* **potatoes**) edible plant tuber; plant bearing this.

**potboiler** *n.* a book, painting, etc. produced merely to make money.

**potch** *n. Aust.* valueless opal with little or no play of colour; material found in association with precious opal.

**poteen** *n.* illegally distilled whisky.

**potent** adj. **1** powerful; strong. **2** (of a man) capable of sexual erection. □□ **potency** n.

**potentate** n. monarch, ruler.

**potential** ● adj. capable of coming into being; latent. ● n. **1** capacity for use or development. **2** quantity determining energy of mass in gravitational field or of charge in electric field. □□ **potentiality** n. **potentially** adv.

**potion** n. liquid dose of medicine, poison, etc.

**potoroo** n. (also **rat-kangaroo**) Aust. small nocturnal macropod.

**pot-pourri** n. scented mixture of dried petals and spices; medley or mixture.

**potted** ● v. see POT. ● adj. **1** preserved in a pot. **2** abridged.

**potter**[1] v. work on trivial tasks in a leisurely way.

**potter**[2] n. maker of pottery.

**pottery** n. vessels etc. made of baked clay; potter's work or workshop.

**potty** colloq. ● adj. foolish, crazy. ● n. chamber pot, esp. for child.

**pouch** ● n. small bag, detachable pocket; baggy area of skin under eyes etc.; bag-like receptacle in which marsupials carry undeveloped young. ● v. put or make into pouch.

**pouffe** n. firm cushion as low seat or footstool.

**poultice** n. soft usu. hot dressing applied to sore or inflamed part of body.

**poultry** n. domestic fowls.

**pounce** ● v. spring, swoop; make sudden attack; seize eagerly. ● n. act of pouncing.

**pound**[1] n. **1** unit of weight equal to 16 oz. (0.454 kg). **2** (in full **pound sterling**) monetary unit of UK etc.

**pound**[2] v. crush or beat with repeated strokes; deliver heavy blows or gunfire; walk, run, etc. heavily.

**pound**[3] n. enclosure where stray animals or officially removed vehicles are kept until claimed.

**pour** v. **1** (cause to) flow in stream or shower; dispense (drink). **2** rain heavily; come or go in profusion or in a rush.

**pout** ● v. push one's lips forward. ● n. pouting expression.

**poverty** n. **1** lack of necessities of life; scarcity. **2** inferiority, poorness.

**POW** abbr. prisoner of war.

**powder** ● n. mass of fine dry particles; medicine or cosmetic in this form; gunpowder. ● v. apply powder to. □ **powder room** women's toilet. □□ **powdery** adj.

**power** ● n. **1** ability to do or act. **2** vigour, strength. **3** control, influence, authority; influential person or country etc. **4** a product of a number multiplied by itself a given number of times. **5** mechanical or electrical energy; the electricity supply. ● v. supply with mechanical or electrical energy. □ **power of attorney** legal authority to act for another person. **power station** building where electricity is generated for distribution.

**powerful** adj. having great power or influence. □□ **powerfully** adv. **powerfulness** n.

**powerless** adj. without power, wholly unable. □□ **powerlessness** n.

**pp** abbr. Mus. pianissimo.

**pp.** abbr. pages.

**p.p.** abbr. (also **pp**) = PER PRO.

**P-plate** n. Aust. sign bearing the letter P attached to vehicle, indicating driver has provisional licence. □□ **P-plater** n.

**PPS** abbr. **1** Parliamentary Private Secretary. **2** post-postscript, additional postscript.

**PR** abbr. **1** public relations. **2** proportional representation.

**practicable** *adj.* that can be done or used. □□ **practicability** *n.*

**practical** ● *adj.* **1** of or concerned with practice rather than theory. **2** functional. **3** good at making, organising, or mending things. **4** realistic. **5** that is such in effect, virtual. ● *n.* practical examination or lesson. □ **practical joke** humorous trick played on person. □□ **practicality** *adj.*

**practically** *adv.* **1** virtually, almost. **2** in practical way.

**practice** *n.* **1** habitual action; repeated exercise to improve skill. **2** action as opposed to theory. **3** doctor's or lawyer's etc. professional business. **4** procedure, esp. of specified kind.

> **Usage** The spelling *practice* is a noun, *practise* is a verb.

**practise** *v.* **1** carry out in action; do repeatedly to improve skill; exercise oneself in or on. **2** engage in (profession, religion, etc.).

**practised** *adj.* experienced.

**practitioner** *n.* professional worker, esp. in medicine or law.

**pragmatic** *adj.* dealing with matters from a practical point of view. □□ **pragmatically** *adv.* **pragmatism** *n.*

**prairie** *n.* large area of treeless grassland, esp. in N. America.

**praise** ● *v.* express warm approval or admiration of; glorify. ● *n.* praising; commendation.

**praiseworthy** *adj.* deserving praise.

**pram** *n.* carriage for baby, pushed by person on foot.

**prance** *v.* move springily.

**prang** *v. colloq.* crash (car).

**prank** *n.* practical joke.

**prankster** *n.* person fond of playing pranks.

**praseodymium** *n.* metallic element (symbol Pr).

**prat** *n. colloq. derog.* silly or foolish person.

**prattle** ● *v.* talk in childish or inconsequential way. ● *n.* prattling talk.

**prawn** ● *n.* **1** marine crustacean prized as food. **2** *colloq.* fool. ● *v.* fish for prawns.

**pray** *v.* say prayers; make devout supplication; entreat.

**prayer** *n.* request or thanksgiving to one's god or object of worship; formula used in praying; entreaty.

**pre-** *prefix* before (in time, place, order, degree, or importance).

**preach** *v.* deliver (sermon); proclaim or teach (religious belief); give moral advice obtrusively; advocate, inculcate. □□ **preacher** *n.*

**preamble** *n.* preliminary statement; introductory part of statute, deed, etc.

**prearrange** *v.* arrange beforehand. □□ **prearrangement** *n.*

**prebiotic** ● *adj.* **1** occurring before emergence of life. **2** promoting growth of beneficial intestinal microorganisms. ● *n.* food that promotes growth of beneficial microorganisms in intestines.

**precarious** *adj.* uncertain; dependent on chance; perilous. □□ **precariously** *adv.* **precariousness** *n.*

**precast** *adj.* (of concrete) cast in shape before use.

**precaution** *n.* action taken beforehand to avoid risk or ensure good result. □□ **precautionary** *adj.*

**precede** *v.* come or go before in time, order, importance, etc.; cause to be preceded by.

**precedence** *n.* priority; right of preceding others.

**precedent** ● *n.* previous case etc. taken as guide or justification etc. ● *adj.* preceding.

**precept** n. rule for action or conduct.

**precinct** n. **1** enclosed area, esp. around building. **2** district in town, esp. where traffic is excluded. **3** (precincts) surrounding area.

**precious** adj. **1** of great value, beloved. **2** affectedly refined.

**precipice** n. **1** vertical or steep face of rock, cliff, mountain, etc. **2** dangerous situation.

**precipitate** ● v. **1** hasten occurrence of; cause to go into (war etc.) hurriedly or violently; throw down headlong. **2** Chem. cause (substance) to be deposited in solid form from solution. **3** Physics condense (vapour) into drops. ● adj. **1** headlong; hasty, rash. **2** inconsiderate. ● n. solid matter precipitated; moisture condensed from vapour.

**precipitation** n. rain or snow; precipitating; being precipitated.

**precipitous** adj. very steep.

**précis** (also precis) ● n. (pl. précis) summary, abstract. ● v. make précis of.

**precise** adj. accurately worded; definite, exact; punctilious. □□ **precisely** adv. **precision** n.

**preclude** v. prevent; make impossible.

**precocious** adj. prematurely developed in some respect. □□ **precociously** adv. **precociousness** n. **precocity** n.

**precognition** n. (esp. supernatural) foreknowledge. □□ **precognitive** adj.

**preconceived** adj. (of an idea) formed beforehand. □□ **preconception** n.

**precondition** n. condition that must be fulfilled beforehand.

**precursor** n. forerunner; person who precedes in office etc.; harbinger.

**predate** v. precede in time.

**predator** n. predatory animal.

**predatory** adj. (of animal) preying naturally on others; plundering or exploiting others.

**predecessor** n. previous holder of office or position; ancestor; thing to which another has succeeded.

**predestination** n. doctrine that everything has been determined in advance.

**predicament** n. difficult or unpleasant situation.

**predicate** n. Gram. part of sentence that says something about the subject, e.g. is blue in the dress is blue. □□ **predicative** adj.

**predict** v. forecast, prophesy.

**predictable** adj. able to be predicted. □□ **predictably** adv.

**predilection** n. preference, special liking.

**predispose** v. influence favourably in advance; render liable or inclined beforehand. □□ **predisposition** n.

**predominate** v. have control over; prevail; preponderate. □□ **predominant** adj.

**pre-eminent** adj. excelling others; outstanding. □□ **pre-eminence** n. **pre-eminently** adv.

**pre-empt** v. forestall; acquire or appropriate in advance; prevent (attack) by disabling enemy. □□ **pre-emption** n. **pre-emptive** adj.

**preen** v. (of bird) smooth (feathers) with beak. □ **preen oneself** groom oneself; show self-satisfaction.

**prefab** n. colloq. prefabricated building.

**prefabricate** v. manufacture sections of (building etc.) prior to assembly on site. □□ **prefabrication** n.

**preface** ● n. introduction to book, speech, etc. ● v. **1** introduce or begin (as) with preface. **2** (of event etc.) lead up to (another).

**prefect** n. **1** senior pupil in school, helping to maintain order. **2** chief administrative official in certain countries.

**prefer** v. (preferred) **1** like better. **2** submit (information, accusation, etc.) **3** promote (person).

**preferable** adj. more desirable. □□ **preferably** adv.

**preference** n. **1** preferring, being preferred; thing preferred; favouring of one person etc. before others; (in system of preferential voting) numerical ranking given to candidate on ballot paper. **2** prior right.
● v. Aust. direct preferences to (candidate or party).

**preferential** adj. giving or receiving preference.□□ **preferentially** adv.

**preferment** n. promotion.

**prefix** ● n. word or syllable placed in front of word to change its meaning. ● v. add as prefix or introduction.

**pregnant** adj. **1** having child or young developing in uterus. **2** full of meaning.□□ **pregnancy** n.

**prehensile** adj. (of tail, limb, etc.) capable of grasping.

**prehistoric** adj. of period before written records; colloq. utterly out of date.□□ **prehistory** n.

**prejudge** v. form premature judgement on (person etc.)

**prejudice** ● n. **1** preconceived opinion; bias. **2** harm (possibly) resulting from action or judgement.
● v. **1** harm the rights of. **2** cause to have prejudice.□□ **prejudiced** adj.

**prejudicial** adj. harmful to rights or interests.

**prelate** n. high ranking church dignitary.

**preliminary** ● adj. introductory, preparatory. ● n. preliminary action or event.□ **preliminary to** preparatory to; in advance of.

**prelude** n. action or event leading up to another; introductory part or piece of music.

**premarital** adj. occurring before marriage.

**premature** adj. **1** occurring or done before usual or right time. **2** too hasty **3** (of baby) born three or more weeks before expected time.
□□ **prematurely** adv.

**premedication** n. medication in preparation for an operation.

**premeditated** adj. planned beforehand.□□ **premeditation** n.

**premenstrual** adj. of the time immediately before menstruation.

**premier** ● n. **1** (Premier) prime minister, head of government; chief minister of state government in Australia. **2** (premiers) sporting team that wins premiership. ● adj. first in importance, order, or time.

**premiere** ● n. first performance or showing of play or film. ● v. give premiere of.

**premiership** n. **1** the office of Premier. **2** organised sporting competition among sporting clubs; the winning of this.

**premise** n. statement from which another is inferred.

**premises** n.pl. house or other building with its grounds etc.

**premium** n. **1** amount to be paid for contract of insurance. **2** sum added to interest, wages etc.; bonus; reward or prize.□ **at a premium 1** above the normal or usual price. **2** scarce and in demand.

**premonition** n. forewarning; presentiment.□□ **premonitory** adj.

**prenatal** adj. existing or occurring before birth.

**preoccupation** n. being preoccupied; something that fills one's thoughts.

**preoccupied** adj. mentally engrossed and inattentive to other things.

**preparation** n. preparing; something done to make ready; substance prepared for use.

**preparatory** ● adj. serving to prepare; introductory. ● adv. as preparation.

**prepare** v. make or get ready; get oneself ready.

**prepay** v. (prepaid, prepaying) pay in advance for.

**preponderate** v. be superior in influence, quantity, or number; predominate.□□ **preponderance** n. **preponderant** adj.

**preposition** n. Gram. word used before noun or pronoun to indicate its relationship to another word, e.g. at home, by car.□□ **prepositional** adj.

**prepossessing** adj. attractive.

**preposterous** adj. utterly absurd; contrary to nature or reason. □□ **preposterously** adv.

**prepubescent** ● adj. of period preceding puberty. ● n. prepubescent child.

**prepuce** n. foreskin.

**prerequisite** ● adj. required as precondition. ● n. prerequisite thing.

**prerogative** n. right or privilege.

**presage** ● n. omen; presentiment. ● v. portend; indicate (future event etc.); foretell, foresee.

**Presbyterian** ● adj. (of a church) governed by elders all of equal rank. ● n. member of Presbyterian Church.□□ **Presbyterianism** n.

**preschool** ● adj. of time before child is old enough to go to school. ● n. place of learning for children usu. aged between 4 and 5.

**prescient** adj. having foreknowledge or foresight.□□ **prescience** n.

**prescribe** v. 1 advise use of (medicine etc.) 2 lay down authoritatively.

> **Usage** Prescribe is sometimes confused with proscribe, which means 'to forbid.'

**prescription** n. 1 prescribing. 2 doctor's written instructions for preparation and use of medicine.

**prescriptive** adj. 1 prescribing, laying down rules. 2 arising from custom.

**preselect** v. select in advance.

**preselection** n. choosing of candidate for forthcoming election by (local) members of political party.

**presence** n. being present; place where person is; person's appearance; person or spirit that is present.

**present**[1] ● adj. 1 being in the place in question. 2 now existing, occurring, or being dealt with etc. 3 Gram. expressing present action or state. ● n. 1 (the present) now. 2 Gram. present tense.

**present**[2] ● n. gift. ● v. 1 give as gift or reward. 2 introduce. 3 bring to public.

**presentable** adj. of good appearance; fit to be shown. □□ **presentability** n. **presentably** adv.

**presentation** n. presenting, being presented; thing presented; manner or quality of presenting; demonstration of materials etc.; lecture.

**presentiment** n. vague expectation; foreboding.

**presently** adv. 1 before long. 2 at present.

**preservative** n. substance for preserving food etc. ● adj. tending to preserve.

**preserve** ● v. keep safe or free from decay; maintain, retain; treat (food) to prevent decomposition or fermentation. ● n. 1 (also **preserves**) preserved fruit, jam. 2 sphere of activity regarded by person as his or hers alone.□□ **preservation** n.

**preside** v. exercise control or authority.

**president** n. head of republic; head of society or group etc.; person in charge of meeting.□□ **presidency** n. **presidential** adj.

**press** ● v. 1 apply weight or force against; squeeze; flatten, smooth; iron (clothes). 2 urge. 3 throng closely. 4 bring into use as a makeshift. ● n. 1 pressing. 2 device for compressing, flattening, extracting juice, etc. **3 (the press)** newspapers and periodicals; people involved in producing these. □ **be pressed for** have barely enough of. **press conference** interview given to journalists to make announcement or answer questions. **press-gang** force into service. **press on** go forward doggedly. **press-up** = *push-up*.

**pressing** *adj.* urgent.

**pressure** ● *n.* **1** exertion of continuous force; force so exerted, amount of this. **2** urgency. **3** affliction or difficulty; stress. ● *v.* apply pressure to, coerce, persuade. □ **pressure cooker 1** airtight pan for cooking food quickly under steam pressure. **2** highly stressful situation etc.

**pressurise** *v.* (also **-ize**) **1** (esp. as **pressurised** *adj.*) maintain normal atmospheric pressure in (aircraft cabin etc.) at high altitude. **2** raise to high pressure. **3** pressure (person).

**prestige** *n.* respect resulting from good reputation or achievements. □□ **prestigious** *adj.*

**presto** *adv. Mus.* very quickly.

**prestressed** *adj.* (of concrete) strengthened by stretched wires in it.

**presumably** *adv.* as may reasonably be presumed.

**presume** *v.* **1** suppose to be true. **2** be presumptuous. □□ **presumption** *n.*

**presumptuous** *adj.* unduly confident; arrogant. □□ **presumptuously** *adv.*

**presuppose** *v.* **1** assume beforehand. **2** imply. □□ **presupposition** *n.*

**pre-tax** *adj.* (of income) before deduction of taxes.

**pretence** *n.* **1** pretending, make-believe; pretext. **2** (esp. false) claim. **3** ostentation.

**pretend** *v.* **1** create a false impression (in play or deception). **2** claim falsely that one has or is something. □□ **pretender** *n.*

**pretension** *n.* **1** assertion of claim. **2** pretentiousness.

**pretentious** *adj.* **1** making excessive claim to merit or importance. **2** ostentatious. □□ **pretentiously** *adv.* **pretentiousness** *n.*

**preterm** *adj. & adv.* born or occurring prematurely.

**preternatural** *adj.* extraordinary; supernatural.

**pretext** *n.* ostensible reason; an excuse.

**prettify** *v.* make (something) look superficially attractive.

**pretty** ● *adj.* **1** attractive in delicate way. **2** fine, good. **3** considerable. ● *adv.* fairly, moderately; very. ● *v.* make pretty. □□ **prettily** *adv.* **prettiness** *n.*

**pretzel** *n.* crisp salted biscuit.

**prevail** *v.* **1** be victorious. **2** be the more usual or predominant. **3** exist or occur in general use. **4** persuade. □ **prevail on** (or **upon**) persuade.

**prevalent** *adj.* generally existing or occurring. □□ **prevalence** *n.*

**prevaricate** *v.* speak or act evasively or misleadingly. □□ **prevarication** *n.*

**prevent** *v.* **1** stop. **2** hinder. □□ **preventable** *adj.* **prevention** *n.*

**preventative** *adj. & n.* preventive.

**preventive** ● *adj.* serving to prevent, esp. disease. ● *n.* preventive agent, measure, drug, etc.

**preview** ● *n.* **1** the act of seeing in advance. **2** showing of film, play, etc., before seen by general public; film trailer. ● *v.* see or show in advance.

**previous** ● *adj.* **1** coming before in time or order. **2** *colloq.* hasty, premature. □□ **previously** *adv.*

**prey** *n.* animal hunted or killed by another for food; victim.□ **bird of prey** one that kills and eats animals. **prey on 1** seek or take as prey. **2** cause worry to.

**price** ● *n.* amount of money for which thing is bought or sold; what must be given, done, etc. to obtain thing. ● v. fix or find price of; estimate value for.

**priceless** adj. **1** invaluable. **2** colloq. very amusing or absurd.

**prick** ● v. **1** pierce slightly; make small hole in; mark with pricks or dots. **2** trouble mentally. **3** erect (the ears). ● n. **1** act of pricking; sensation of being pricked. **2** colloq. penis. □ **prick up one's ears** listen alertly.

**prickle** ● n. small thorn or spine; prickling sensation. ● v. cause or feel prickling sensation.

**prickly** adj. (pricklier) **1** having prickles. **2** irritable. □□ **prickliness** n.

**pride** ● n. **1** elation or satisfaction at one's achievements, possessions, etc.; object of this; unduly high opinion of oneself; proper sense of one's own worth, position, etc. **2** group of lions. ● v. (**pride oneself on**) be proud of. □ **pride of place** most prominent position.

**priest** n. member of clergy; religious official. □□ **priesthood** n. **priestly** adj.

**priestess** n. female priest.

**prig** n. self-righteous or moralistic person. □□ **priggish** adj. **priggishness** n.

**prim** adj. (**primmer**) stiffly formal and precise; prudish. □□ **primly** adv. **primness** n.

**primacy** n. pre-eminence.

**prima donna** n. **1** chief female singer in an opera. **2** colloq. temperamentally self-important person.

**prima facie** ● adv. at first sight. ● adj. (of evidence) based on first impression.

**primal** adj. **1** primitive, primeval. **2** fundamental.

**primary** ● adj. **1** chief, most important; fundamental; original; initial. ● n. primary colour, feather, school, etc. □ **primary colour** colour not made by mixing others, i.e. (for light) red, green, or blue, (for paint) red, blue, or yellow. **primary industry** agriculture, sheep and cattle raising, fishing, forestry, etc. as opposed to manufacturing industry. **primary source** first-hand account or other source that constitutes direct evidence of an object of study. □□ **primarily** adv.

**primate** n. **1** member of highest order of mammals, including apes, humans, etc. **2** chief bishop of country; archbishop.

**prime** ● adj. **1** chief, most important. **2** of highest quality. **3** primary, fundamental. **4** (of number etc.) divisible only by itself and unity. ● n. a state of greatest perfection. ● v. **1** prepare for use or action. **2** provide with information in preparation for something. □ **prime minister** head of parliamentary government. **prime number** number that can be divided exactly only by itself and one.

**primed** adj. colloq. drunk.

**primer** n. **1** substance applied to bare wood, metal, etc. before painting; cosmetic applied to face before another product. **2** cap, cylinder, etc. used to ignite the powder of a cartridge etc. **3** pump for pumping fuel to prime an internal combustion engine. **4** elementary textbook.

**primeval** adj. (also **primaeval**) of first age of world; ancient, primitive.

**primitive** adj. **1** at early stage of evolution or civilisation; of preliterate, non-industrial society or culture. **2** crude, simple. □□ **primitively** adv. **primitiveness** n.

**primogeniture** n. being first-born; first-born's right to inheritance.

**primordial** adj. primeval.

**primrose** n. European plant bearing pale yellow spring flower; this flower; pale yellow.

**primula** n. cultivated plant bearing flowers of various colours.

**prince** n. male member of royal family; sovereign's son or grandson.

**princely** adj. of or worthy of a prince; sumptuous, splendid.

**princess** n. female member of royal family; sovereign's daughter or granddaughter; prince's wife.

**principal** ● adj. first in rank or importance. ● n. **1** chief person; head of some schools; leading performer in concert, play, etc. **2** capital sum lent or invested. **3** person for whom another is agent etc.

> **Usage** *Principal* is often confused with *principle*.

**principality** n. nation ruled by prince.

**principally** adv. mainly.

**principle** n. **1** fundamental truth or law as basis of reasoning or action. **2** personal code of conduct. **3** fundamental source or element. □ **in principle 1** as general idea. **2** as regards fundamentals but not necessarily in detail. **on principle** because of one's moral beliefs.

**print** ● v. **1** press (a mark) on surface, mark (surface) in this way; produce by applying inked type to paper. **2** write in unjoined letters. **3** produce positive picture from (photographic negative). **4** produce computer output in printed form. ● n. **1** mark left on surface by pressure; printed lettering or words; printed design, picture, or fabric. **2** fingerprint.

**printer** n. **1** person who prints books etc.; owner of printing business. **2** device that prints, esp. computer output.

**printout** n. printed material produced from computer printer etc.

**prior** ● adj. earlier; coming before in time, order, or importance. ● adv.

before. ● n. superior of religious house; deputy of abbot.

**prioress** n. female prior.

**priority** n. thing considered more important than others; right to do something before other people. □□ **prioritise** v. (also **-ize**)

**priory** n. religious house governed by prior or prioress.

**prise** v. (also **prize**) force open or out by leverage.

**prism** n. solid figure whose two ends are equal parallel rectilinear figures, and whose sides are parallelograms; transparent body of this form with refracting surfaces.

**prismatic** adj. of, like, or using prism; (of colours) distributed (as if) by transparent prism.

**prison** n. place of captivity, esp. building to which persons are consigned while awaiting trial or for punishment.

**prisoner** n. person kept in prison; person or thing confined by illness, another's grasp, etc.; (in full **prisoner of war**) person captured in war.

**prissy** adj. prim, prudish. □□ **prissily** adv. **prissiness** n.

**pristine** adj. in its original condition; unspoilt.

**privacy** n. **1** (right to) being private. **2** freedom from intrusion or publicity.

**private** ● adj. **1** belonging to person or group, not public; confidential; secluded. **2** not supported, managed, or provided by government. ● n. soldier of lowest rank. □ **in private** privately. **private parts** colloq. genitals. □□ **privately** adv.

**privation** n. lack of comforts or necessities.

**privatise** v. (also **-ize**) transfer from government to private ownership. □□ **privatisation** n.

**privet** n. bushy evergreen European shrub used for hedges.

**privilege** n. **1** right, advantage, or immunity, belonging to person, class, or office; (in full **parliamentary privilege**) special right of members of parliament to speak freely in parliament without risk of prosecution. **2** special benefit or honour.□□ **privileged** adj.

**privy** adj. ● **be privy to** share in the secret of, know about.

**prize** ● n. **1** reward in competition, lottery, etc.; reward given as symbol of victory or superiority; thing (to be) striven for. ● adj. **1** to which prize is awarded. **2** excellent of its kind. ● v. value highly.

**pro** n. colloq. a professional.

**pro-** prefix in favour of.

**proactive** adj. taking the initiative.

**probability** n. **1** quality or state of being probable; likelihood of something happening. **2** Math. extent to which an event is likely to occur, measured by ratio of favourable cases to whole number of cases possible.

**probable** ● adj. that may be expected to happen or prove true; likely. ● n. probable candidate, member of team, etc.
□□ **probably** adv.

**probate** n. official proving of will; verified copy of will.

**probation** n. **1** Law system of supervising the behaviour of offenders as alternative to prison. **2** period of testing character and abilities of esp. new employee.
□□ **probationary** adj.

**probationer** n. person undergoing probationary period.

**probe** ● n. blunt surgical instrument for exploring wound; unmanned exploratory spacecraft; an investigation. ● v. examine closely; explore with probe.

**probiotic** ● adj. of substance that stimulates the growth of microorganisms. ● n. probiotic substance; microorganism introduced into the body for its beneficial qualities.

**probity** n. uprightness, honesty.

**problem** n. doubtful or uncertain question; thing hard to understand or deal with.□□ **problematic** adj. (also **problematical**)

**proboscis** n. **1** long flexible trunk or snout, e.g. of elephant. **2** elongated mouth parts of some insects.

**procedure** n. way of conducting business etc.; performing task; set series of actions.□□ **procedural** adj.

**proceed** v. **1** go forward or on further; make one's way; continue or resume. **2** adopt course of action. **3** go on to say. **4** start lawsuit against. **5** originate.

**proceedings** n.pl. **1** what takes place. **2** lawsuit. **3** published report of discussions or conference.

**proceeds** n.pl. profits from sale etc.

**process** ● n. series of operations used in making something; procedure; series of changes or events. ● v. subject to a process; deal with.

**procession** n. people etc. advancing in orderly succession, esp. at ceremony, demonstration, or festivity.

**processor** n. machine that processes things; machine for chopping, blending, etc. food.

**pro-choice** adj. favouring right of woman to choose to have abortion.

**proclaim** v. announce publicly.
□□ **proclamation** n.

**proclivity** n. natural tendency.

**procrastinate** v. defer action; delay.
□□ **procrastination** n.

**procreate** v. produce young, reproduce.□□ **procreation** n. **procreative** adj.

**procure** v. obtain by care or effort, acquire.□□ **procurement** n.

**procurer** n. person who obtains prostitute for someone else.

**prod** ● v. (prodded) 1 poke. 2 stimulate to action. ● n. 1 prodding action; instrument for prodding things. 2 stimulus to action.

**prodigal** ● adj. wasteful. ● n. spendthrift. □□ prodigality n.

**prodigious** adj. marvellous; enormous.

**prodigy** n. exceptionally gifted person, esp. precocious child; marvellous thing; wonderful example (of).

**produce** ● v. 1 manufacture or prepare. 2 bring forward for inspection etc. 3 bear, yield, or bring into existence; cause or bring about. 4 administer or supervise production etc. of (film, play, etc.) ● n. what is produced, esp. agricultural products; amount produced; result. □□ production n.

**producer** n. 1 person who produces goods etc. 2 person who supervises production of play, film, broadcast, etc.

**product** n. 1 thing or substance produced, esp. by manufacture; result. 2 number obtained by multiplying.

**productive** adj. producing, esp. abundantly. □□ productively adv. productiveness n.

**productivity** n. capacity to produce; effectiveness of industry, workforce, etc.

**profane** ● adj. 1 irreverent, blasphemous. 2 obscene. 3 not sacred. ● v. treat irreverently; violate, debase. □□ profanely adv. profanity n.

**profess** v. 1 claim openly to have. 2 pretend. 3 declare. 4 affirm one's faith in or allegiance to.

**professed** adj. 1 self-acknowledged. 2 alleged, ostensible. □□ professedly adv.

**profession** n. 1 occupation or calling, esp. learned or scientific; people in profession. 2 declaration, avowal.

**professional** ● adj. 1 of, belonging to, or connected with a profession. 2 skilful and conscientious. 3 doing something for payment, not as a pastime. ● n. professional worker or player. □□ professionalism n. professionally adv.

**professor** n. highest-ranking academic in university department; (in US) university lecturer. □□ professorial adj.

**proffer** v. offer.

**proficient** adj. adept, expert. □□ proficiency n. proficiently adv.

**profile** ● n. 1 side view or outline, esp. of human face. 2 short article giving description of person or organisation. 3 extent to which person or organisation attracts public notice. 4 Statistics representation by graph etc. of information recorded in quantified form. 5 vertical cross section of structure. ● v. represent by profile.

**profit** ● n. advantage, benefit; financial gain; excess of returns over outlay. ● v. (profited) be beneficial to; obtain advantage.

**profitable** adj. yielding profit; beneficial. □□ profitability n. profitably adv.

**profiteer** ● v. make or seek excessive profits, esp. illegally. ● n. person who profiteers.

**profiterole** n. small hollow cake of choux pastry with creamy filling.

**profligate** ● adj. recklessly extravagant; licentious, dissolute. ● n. profligate person. □□ profligacy n. profligately adv.

**profound** adj. 1 having or demanding great knowledge, study, or insight. 2 intense, thorough; deep. □□ profoundly adv. profundity n.

**profuse** adj. lavish; extravagant; copious. □□ profusely adv. profusion n.

**progenitor** n. ancestor.

**progeny** n. offspring.

**progesterone** n. sex hormone that stimulates uterus to prepare for pregnancy.

**prognosis** n. (pl. prognoses) forecast, esp. of course of disease. □□ **prognostic** adj.

**prognosticate** v. foretell, betoken. □□ **prognostication** n.

**program** (also **programme**, except in computing) ● n. 1 list of events, performers, etc.; plan of action. 2 radio or television broadcast. 3 series of coded instructions for computer. ● v. 1 (**programmed**) make a program. 2 instruct (computer) by means of a program. □□ **programmer** n. **programmable** adj.

**progress** ● n. forward movement; advance, development; improvement. ● v. move forward or onward; advance, develop, improve. □□ **progression** n.

**progressive** ● adj. 1 moving forward; proceeding step by step; cumulative. 2 favouring rapid reform. 3 modern. 4 efficient. 5 (of disease etc.) increasing in severity or extent. 6 (of taxation) increasing with sum taxed. ● n. advocate of progressive policy. □□ **progressively** adv.

**prohibit** v. (**prohibited**) forbid; prevent. □□ **prohibition** n.

**prohibitive** adj. 1 (of prices, taxes, etc.) so high as to prevent purchase etc. 2 forbidding something. □□ **prohibitively** adv.

**project** ● n. plan, scheme; extensive essay, piece of research, etc. by student(s). ● v. 1 protrude, jut out. 2 throw. 3 impel. 4 forecast. 5 plan. 6 cause (light, image, etc.) to fall on surface. 7 cause (voice etc.) to be heard at distance. □□ **projective** adj.

**projectile** n. missile.

**projection** n. 1 projecting, being projected. 2 thing that protrudes.

3 presentation of image(s) etc. on surface. 4 forecast, estimate. 5 mental image viewed as objective reality. 6 transfer of feelings to other people etc.

**projector** n. apparatus for projecting image or film on screen.

**prolapse** n. (also **prolapsus**) slipping forward or downward of part or organ.

**proletariat** n. working-class people. □□ **proletarian** n. & adj.

**pro-life** adj. in favour of preserving life, esp. in opposing abortion.

**proliferate** v. reproduce rapidly; multiply. □□ **proliferation** n.

**prolific** adj. producing many offspring or much output; abundantly productive; copious. □□ **prolifically** adv.

**prologue** n. introduction to play, poem, etc.

**prolong** v. extend. □□ **prolongation** n.

**prolonged** adj. continuing for long time.

**prom** adj. 1 promenade concert. 2 US formal dance, esp. one held at end of high school or college.

**promenade** n. paved public walk, esp. along sea front. □ **promenade concert** concert where part of the audience is not seated and can move about.

**promethium** n. radioactive element (symbol Pm).

**prominent** adj. jutting out; conspicuous; well known; distinguished. □□ **prominence** n. **prominently** adv.

**promiscuous** adj. 1 having frequent casual sexual relationships. 2 indiscriminate. 3 colloq. casual. □□ **promiscuity** n. **promiscuously** adv.

**promise** ● n. 1 explicit undertaking to do or not to do something. 2 favourable indications. ● v. 1 make promise. 2 seem likely. 3 colloq. assure.

**promising** adj. likely to turn out well. □□ **promisingly** adv.

**promissory** adj. expressing or implying promise.

**promo** n. colloq. publicity, advertising.

**promontory** n. point of high land jutting out into sea etc.; headland.

**promote** v. 1 advance (person) to higher office or position. 2 help forward; encourage. 3 publicise and sell. □□ **promoter** n. **promotion** n. **promotional** adj.

**prompt** ● adj. acting, made, or done immediately. ● adv. punctually. ● v. 1 incite. 2 supply (actor, speaker) with next words or with suggestion. 3 inspire. ● n. 1 prompting. 2 thing said to prompt actor etc. 3 sign on computer screen inviting input. □□ **promptly** adv. **promptness** n.

**prompter** n. person seated out of sight of the audience who prompts the actors.

**promulgate** v. make known to public; proclaim. □□ **promulgation** n.

**prone** adj. 1 lying face downwards. 2 disposed, liable. □□ **proneness** n.

**prong** n. spike of fork.

**pronoun** n. word used as substitute for noun or noun phrase usu. already mentioned or known. □□ **pronominal** adj.

**pronounce** v. 1 utter (sound or word) distinctly or in certain way. 2 declare. □□ **pronunciation** n.

**pronounced** adj. strongly marked.

**pronto** adv. colloq. promptly, quickly.

**proof** ● n. 1 fact, evidence, reasoning, or demonstration that proves something. 2 test, trial. 3 standard of strength of distilled alcohol. 4 copy of printed matter for correction. 5 photographic print made for selection etc. ● adj. impervious to penetration, damage, etc., esp. by specified thing.

● v. make proof, esp. against water or bullets.

**proofread** v. read and correct (printed proofs). □□ **proofreader** n.

**prop** ● n. 1 support to prevent something from falling, sagging, or failing. 2 Rugby forward at either end of front row of scrum. 3 colloq. stage property. 4 colloq. propeller. ● v. (**propped**) support (as) with prop. 2 Aust. (of galloping horse) stop suddenly with forelegs rigid; (of person) stop, remain.

**propaganda** n. information, esp. of biased or misleading character, used to promote cause. □□ **propagandist** n. & adj.

**propagate** v. 1 breed or reproduce (plant) from parent stock. 2 disseminate, transmit. □□ **propagation** n. **propagator** n.

**propane** n. gaseous hydrocarbon used as fuel.

**propel** v. (**propelled**) drive or push forward; urge on. □□ **propellant** n. & adj.

**propeller** n. revolving shaft with blades, esp. for propelling ship or aircraft.

**propensity** n. inclination, tendency.

**proper** adj. 1 suitable; correct; conforming to social conventions. 2 colloq. thorough. □ **proper noun** (or **name**) name of individual person, place, animal, title, etc., and spelt with capital letter. □□ **properly** adv.

**property** n. 1 thing(s) owned. 2 Aust. farm, station. 3 quality, characteristic. 4 movable object used on theatre stage or in film.

**prophecy** n. prediction of future events.

**prophesy** v. 1 foretell. 2 speak as prophet.

**prophet** n. 1 person who foretells events. 2 religious leader inspired by God.

**prophetic** adj. containing prediction; predicting; of prophet.

**prophylactic** ● adj. tending to prevent disease etc. ● n.
1 preventive medicine or action.
2 condom. □□ **prophylaxis** n.

**propinquity** n. nearness.

**propitiate** v. appease. □□ **propitiation** n. **propitiatory** adj.

**propitious** adj. 1 favourable, auspicious. 2 suitable.

**proponent** n. person advocating proposal etc.

**proportion** ● n. 1 fraction or share of a whole. 2 ratio; correct relation in size or degree. 3 (proportions) dimensions. ● v. make proportionate. □ **proportional representation** electoral system in which each party receives seats in proportion to number of votes cast for its candidates. □□ **proportional** adj. **proportionally** adv.

**proportionate** adj. proportional. □□ **proportionately** adv.

**proposal** n. 1 proposing; scheme etc. proposed. 2 offer of marriage.

**propose** v. 1 put forward for consideration; declare as one's plan; nominate. 2 make proposal of marriage. □□ **proposer** n.

**proposition** n. 1 statement; proposal, scheme proposed. 2 colloq. problem or undertaking. ● v. put proposal to, esp. of sexual nature.

**propound** v. offer for consideration.

**proprietary** adj. made and sold by particular firm, usu. under patent; of owner or ownership.

**proprietor** n. owner. □□ **proprietorial** adj.

**propriety** n. correctness of behaviour.

**propulsion** n. driving or pushing forward; force causing this. □□ **propulsive** adj.

**propylene** n. gaseous hydrocarbon used in manufacture of chemicals.

**pro rata** ● adj. proportional. ● adv. proportionally.

**prorogue** v. (prorogued, proroguing) discontinue meetings of (parliament etc.) without dissolving it. □□ **prorogation** n.

**prosaic** adj. 1 like prose. 2 unromantic; commonplace. □□ **prosaically** adv.

**pros and cons** n.pl. arguments for and against something.

**proscenium** n. (pl. **prosceniums** or **proscenia**) part of theatre stage in front of curtain and enclosing arch.

**proscribe** v. forbid. □□ **proscription** n. **proscriptive** adj.

> **Usage** Proscribe is sometimes confused with prescribe.

**prose** n. 1 ordinary language, not in verse. 2 dullness.

**prosecute** v. 1 institute legal proceedings against. 2 continue with, carry on (course of action). □□ **prosecution** n. **prosecutor** n.

**proselyte** n. convert, esp. recent. □□ **proselytism** n.

**proselytise** v. (also -ize) (seek to) convert.

**prosody** n. 1 patterns of rhythm and sound used in poetry; study of this. 2 patterns of stress and intonation in a language.

**prospect** n. 1 what one is to expect. 2 chance of advancement. ● v. explore (for gold etc.) □□ **prospector** n.

**prospective** adj. some day to be; expected; future.

**prospectus** n. printed document advertising or describing commercial enterprise, school, etc.

**prosper** v. succeed, thrive.

**prosperous** adj. successful, rich; thriving. □□ **prosperity** n.

**prostanthera** n. Aust. mint bush.

**prostate** *n.* (in full **prostate gland**) large gland round neck of male mammal's bladder.

**prosthesis** *n.* (*pl.* **prostheses**) artificial body part.

**prostitute** ● *n.* person who offers sexual intercourse for payment. ● *v.* **1** make prostitute of. **2** misuse, offer for sale unworthily. □□ **prostitution** *n.*

**prostrate** ● *adj.* **1** lying face downwards, esp. in submission; lying horizontally. **2** overcome, esp. exhausted. **3** growing along the ground. ● *v.* **1** lay or throw flat. **2** overcome, make weak. □□ **prostration** *n.*

**protactinium** *n.* radioactive metallic element (symbol **Pa**).

**protagonist** *n.* **1** chief person in drama, story, etc.; main figure in contest, situation, etc. **2** supporter of cause.

**protean** *adj.* variable; versatile.

**protect** *v.* keep (person etc.) safe; shield. □□ **protection** *n.* **protector** *n.*

**protectionism** *n.* policy of protecting home industries from competition by tariffs etc. □□ **protectionist** *n.*

**protective** *adj.* protecting; intended for or giving protection. □□ **protectively** *adv.* **protectiveness** *n.*

**protectorate** *n.* nation controlled and protected by another.

**protégé** *n.* person who is helped and protected by another.

**protein** *n.* any of class of organic compounds essential in all living organisms.

**pro tem** *adj.* & *adv.* for the time being.

**protest** ● *n.* expression of dissent or disapproval. ● *v.* **1** make protest. **2** affirm (innocence etc.) □□ **protester** *n.*

**Protestant** ● *n.* member or adherent of any of the Churches separated from RC Church in Reformation. ● *adj.* of Protestant Churches or Protestants. □□ **Protestantism** *n.*

**protestation** *n.* strong affirmation; protest.

**proto-** *comb. form* first.

**protocol** *n.* **1** etiquette applying to rank and status. **2** draft of treaty.

**proton** *n.* elementary particle with positive electric charge equal to electron's, and occurring in all atomic nuclei.

**protoplasm** *n.* viscous translucent substance comprising the living part of cell in organism. □□ **protoplasmic** *adj.*

**prototype** *n.* original thing or person from which copies, improvements, etc., are made. □□ **prototypic** *adj.* **prototypical** *adj.*

**protozoan** *n.* (*pl.* **protozoa**) (also **protozoon**) one-celled microscopic animal.

**protract** *v.* prolong, lengthen. □□ **protraction** *n.*

**protractor** *n.* instrument for measuring angles, usu. in form of graduated semicircle.

**protrude** *v.* thrust forward; stick out. □□ **protrusion** *n.* **protrusive** *adj.*

**protuberance** *n.* bulging part.

**protuberant** *adj.* bulging out; prominent.

**proud** *adj.* **1** haughty, arrogant. **2** feeling greatly honoured or pleased; giving cause for pride. **3** imposing, splendid. □□ **proudly** *adv.*

**prove** *v.* (**proved** or **proving**) **1** demonstrate to be true by evidence or argument. **2** (**prove oneself**) show one's abilities etc. **3** test accuracy of. **4** (of dough) rise. □□ **provable** *adj.*

**provenance** *n.* **1** (place of) origin. **2** history.

**provender** n. fodder.

**proverb** n. short pithy saying in general use.

**proverbial** adj. **1** notorious. **2** of or referred to in proverbs. □□ **proverbially** adv.

**provide** v. **1** supply, make available; supply the necessities of life. **2** stipulate in legal document. **3** make preparations. □□ **provider** n.

**provided** conj. on condition (that).

**providence** n. **1** protective care of God or nature. **2** foresight. **3** thrift.

**provident** adj. **1** having or showing foresight. **2** thrifty.

**providential** adj. **1** of or by divine foresight or intervention. **2** opportune, lucky. □□ **providentially** adv.

**province** n. **1** principal administrative division of country etc.; **(the provinces)** whole of country outside capital. **2** sphere of action. **3** branch of learning.

**provincial** ● adj. **1** of province(s). **2** unsophisticated or uncultured. ● n. **1** inhabitant of province or the provinces. **2** unsophisticated or uncultured person. □□ **provincialism** n.

**provision** ● n. **1** process of providing things. **2** (**provisions**) food and drink. **3** stipulation in treaty or contract etc. ● v. supply with provisions.

**provisional** adj. **1** providing for immediate needs only. **2** temporary. □ **provisional licence** Aust. initial licence to drive motor vehicle. **provisional tax** advance payment anticipating tax on income not taxed at source. □□ **provisionally** adv.

**proviso** n. (pl. **provisos**) stipulation; limiting clause. □□ **provisory** adj.

**provoke** v. **1** incite to anger. **2** rouse; produce as a reaction. □□ **provocation** n. **provocative** adj.

**provost** n. **1** head of college etc. **2** member of military police.

**prow** n. **1** bow of ship. **2** pointed or projecting front part.

**prowess** n. **1** skill, expertise. **2** valour, gallantry.

**prowl** ● v. roam, esp. stealthily in search of prey, plunder, etc. ● n. prowling. □□ **prowler** n.

**proximate** adj. nearest, next before or after.

**proximity** n. nearness.

**proxy** n. authorisation given to deputy; person authorised to deputise; written authorisation to vote on another's behalf; vote so given.

**prude** n. excessively squeamish or sexually modest person. □□ **prudery** n.

**prudent** adj. **1** cautious. **2** politic. □□ **prudence** n. **prudently** adv.

**prudential** adj. of or showing prudence.

**prudish** adj. showing prudery. □□ **prudishly** adv. **prudishness** n.

**prune** ● n. dried plum. ● v. trim by cutting away dead or overgrown parts.

**prunus** n. ornamental tree of plum family.

**prurient** adj. having or encouraging lustful thoughts. □□ **prurience** n.

**pry** v. (**pried**, **prying**) inquire impertinently; snoop; look inquisitively.

**PS** abbr. postscript.

**psalm** n. sacred song; **(the Book of Psalms)** book of these in Old Testament.

**psalter** n. copy of Book of Psalms.

**psaltery** n. ancient and medieval plucked stringed instrument.

**psephology** n. statistical study of voting etc. □□ **psephologist** n.

**pseudo-** comb. form false.

**pseudoephedrine** n. drug used as nasal decongestant.

**pseudonym** n. fictitious name, esp. of author.

**psoriasis** n. skin disease with red scaly patches.

**psyche** n. soul, spirit, or mind.

**psychedelic** adj. **1** expanding the mind's awareness, hallucinatory. **2** vivid in colour, design, etc.

**psychiatry** n. study and treatment of mental disease. □□ **psychiatric** adj. **psychiatrist** n.

**psychic** ● adj. (of person) considered to exercise occult powers; supernatural; of the soul or mind. ● n. psychic person; medium.

**psycho-** comb. form of the mind or psychology.

**psychoanalysis** n. treating mental disorders by investigating interaction of conscious and unconscious elements in the mind. □□ **psychoanalyse** v. **psychoanalyst** n. **psychoanalytical** adj.

**psychokinesis** n. telekinesis.

**psychology** n. **1** study of human mind. **2** mental characteristics; mental factors governing a situation or activity. □□ **psychological** adj. **psychologist** n.

**psychopath** n. person suffering from severe mental disorder, esp. with abnormal or violent social behaviour. □□ **psychopathic** adj.

**psychosis** n. (pl. **psychoses**) severe mental derangement involving loss of contact with reality.

**psychosomatic** adj. **1** (of disease) mental, not physical, in origin. **2** of both mind and body.

**psychotherapy** n. treatment of mental disorder by psychological means. □□ **psychotherapist** n.

**psychotic** ● adj. of or suffering from psychosis. ● n. psychotic person.

**pt** abbr. **1** part. **2** pint. **3** point. **4** port.

**pterodactyl** n. large extinct flying reptile.

**PTO** abbr. please turn over.

**Pty** abbr. proprietary.

**pub** n. colloq. hotel.

**puberty** n. period of sexual maturing. □□ **pubertal** adj.

**pubic** adj. of the abdomen at the lower front part of pelvis.

**public** ● adj. **1** of, for, or known to people in general. **2** provided by or belonging to government. **3** involved in community affairs. ● n. members of community in general. □ **public relations** promotion (by company etc.) of favourable public image. **public sector** part of economy controlled by government. **public servant** Aust. member of public service. **public service** Aust. permanent professional branches of government administration; civil service. □□ **publicly** adv.

**publican** n. keeper of hotel.

**publication** n. preparation and issuing of book, newspaper, etc., to the public; book etc. so issued; act or instance of making something publicly known.

**publicise** v. (also **-ize**) advertise; make publicly known. □□ **publicist** n.

**publicity** n. (means of attracting) public attention; (material used for) advertising.

**publish** v. prepare and issue (book, newspaper, etc.) for public sale; make (content) available online; make generally known; formally announce. □□ **publisher** n.

**puce** adj. & n. brownish purple.

**puck** n. rubber disc used in ice hockey.

**pucker** ● v. gather into wrinkles, folds, or bulges. ● n. such wrinkle etc.

**pudding** n. **1** sweet cooked dish. **2** dessert. **3** savoury dish containing flour, suet, etc. **4** kind of sausage. **5** colloq. plump or lazy person.

**puddle** ● n. **1** small pool of rainwater or other liquid. **2** clay made into watertight coating. ● v. knead (clay and sand) into puddle.

**pudenda** n.pl. genitals.

**puerile** adj. childish, immature. □□ **puerility** n.

**puerperal** adj. of or due to childbirth.

**puff** • n. **1** short light blowing of breath, wind, smoke, etc. **2** soft pad for applying powder to the skin. **3** light pastry cake. **4** gathered material in dress etc. • v. **1** send (air etc.) or come out in puffs; breathe hard. **2** swell.

**puffin** n. N. Atlantic and N. Pacific sea bird with large head and brightly coloured triangular bill.

**puffy** adj. swollen, puffed out.

**pug** n. dog of small breed with flat nose.

**puggle** n. Aust. colloq. young echidna.

**pugilist** n. boxer. □□ **pugilism** n. **pugilistic** adj.

**pugnacious** adj. quarrelsome; disposed to fight. □□ **pugnaciously** adv. **pugnacity** n.

**puke** v. & n. colloq. vomit.

**pukka** adj. colloq. genuine; reliable.

**pull** • v. **1** exert force on (thing etc.) to move it to oneself or origin of force; attract. **2** extract by pulling. **3** damage (muscle etc.) by abnormal strain. **4** proceed with effort. **5** draw (liquor) from barrel etc. **6** inhale or drink deeply, suck. **7** Cricket strike (ball) to leg side. **8** Golf strike (ball) widely to left. **9** colloq. achieve or accomplish. • n. **1** act of pulling. **2** influence; advantage; attraction. **3** deep draught of liquor. **4** prolonged effort. **5** suck at cigarette etc. □ **pull in** move towards side of road or into stopping place. **pull off** colloq. succeed in achieving. **pull out** withdraw; move away from side of road or stopping place. **pull through** come or bring successfully through illness or difficulty.

**pullet** n. young hen, esp. less than one year old.

**pulley** n. **1** grooved wheel(s) for cord etc. to run over, mounted in block and used to lift weight etc. **2** wheel or drum mounted on shaft and turned by belt, used to increase speed or power.

**pullover** n. garment covering top half of body.

**pulmonary** adj. of lungs.

**pulp** • n. **1** fleshy part of fruit etc. **2** soft shapeless mass. **3** poor quality writing. • v. reduce to or become pulp. □□ **pulpy** adj. **pulpiness** n.

**pulpit** n. raised enclosed platform for preaching from.

**pulsar** n. cosmic source of regular rapid pulses of radiation.

**pulsate** v. expand and contract rhythmically; throb; vibrate, quiver. □□ **pulsation** n.

**pulse** • n. **1** rhythmical throbbing of arteries as blood is propelled along them, as felt in the wrists or temples; each beat of arteries or heart. **2** throb or thrill of life or emotion. **3** general feeling. **4** single vibration of sound, electric current, etc. **5** rhythmical (esp. musical) beat. **6** (plant producing) edible seeds of peas, lentils, beans, etc. • v. pulsate.

**pulverise** v. (also **-ize**) **1** reduce or crumble to powder or dust. **2** colloq. defeat utterly. □□ **pulverisation** n.

**puma** n. large tawny American feline.

**pumice** n. (in full **pumice stone**) light porous lava used as abrasive; piece of this.

**pummel** v. (**pummelled**) strike repeatedly, esp. with fists.

**pump** • n. machine or device for raising or moving liquids or gases; act of pumping. • v. **1** raise, remove, inflate, empty, etc. (as) with pump; work pump. **2** persistently question (person) to elicit information. **3** move vigorously up and down.

**pumpernickel** n. wholemeal rye bread.

**pumpkin** n. kind of yellow or orange fruit, used as vegetable etc.; plant bearing this.

**pun** n. humorous use of word(s) with two or more meanings; a play on words. □□ **punning** adj. & n.

**punch** v. 1 strike with fist; make hole (as) with punch; pierce (hole) thus. ● n. 1 blow with fist; instrument or machine for piercing holes or impressing design in leather, metal etc. 2 mixture of wine or spirit with fruit juices etc. □□ **puncher** n.

**punchline** n. words bringing point of joke or story.

**punctilious** adj. attentive to formality or etiquette; precise in behaviour. □□ **punctiliously** adv. **punctiliousness** n.

**punctual** adj. observing appointed time; prompt. □□ **punctuality** n. **punctually** adv.

**punctuate** v. insert punctuation marks in; interrupt at intervals. □□ **punctuation** n.

**puncture** ● n. small hole caused by sharp object, esp. in tyre. ● v. make puncture in; suffer puncture; deflate.

**pundit** n. expert.

**pungent** adj. having sharp or strong taste or smell. □□ **pungency** n.

**punish** v. 1 inflict penalty on (offender) or for (offence). 2 tax, abuse, or treat severely. 3 make heavy demands on. □□ **punishable** adj. **punishing** adj. **punishment** n.

**punitive** adj. inflicting or intended to inflict punishment; extremely severe.

**punk** n. 1 deliberately outrageous style of rock music, emerging in 1970s; follower of this. 2 colloq. hooligan; lout.

**punnet** n. small basket for small fruit; container for seedlings.

**punt¹** ● v. kick (football dropped from hands) before it reaches ground. ● n. (in full **punt kick**) this kick.

**punt²** ● n. square-ended flat-bottomed boat propelled by long pole. ● v. travel or carry in punt.

**punter** n. colloq. person who gambles or bets.

**puny** adj. small and weak.

**pup** ● n. young dog, seal, rat, etc. ● v. (**pupped**) give birth to (pups).

**pupa** n. (pl. **pupae**) insect in stage between larva and imago.

**pupate** v. become a pupa.

**pupil** n. 1 person being taught. 2 opening in centre of iris of eye.

**puppet** n. 1 small figure moved esp. by strings as entertainment. 2 person controlled by another. □□ **puppetry** n.

**puppy** n. young dog.

**purchase** ● v. 1 buying; thing bought. 2 firm hold on thing. 3 leverage. 4 equipment for moving heavy objects. □□ **purchaser** n.

**purdah** n. screening of Muslim or Hindu women from strangers or men.

**pure** adj. 1 not mixed with any other substances. 2 mere; utter. 3 innocent; chaste. 4 (of mathematics or sciences) dealing with theory not practical applications. □□ **pureness** n. **purity** n.

**purée** ● n. smooth pulp of vegetables or fruit etc. ● v. make purée of.

**purely** adv. 1 in a pure way. 2 merely, solely, exclusively.

**purgative** ● adj. 1 serving to purify. 2 strongly laxative. ● n. purgative thing.

**purgatory** n. place or state of spiritual cleansing, esp. after death and before entering heaven; place or state of temporary suffering or expiation. □□ **purgatorial** adj.

**purge** ● v. 1 make physically or spiritually clean. 2 remove by cleansing. 3 rid of unacceptable members. 4 empty (bowels). 5 Law atone for (offence). ● n. 1 purging. 2 purgative.

**purify** v. make pure. □□ **purification** n. **purificatory** adj.

**purist** n. stickler for correctness.

**puritan** *n.* person who is strict in morals and regards certain pleasures as sinful.

**purl** ● *n.* knitting stitch. ● *v.* knit with purl stitch.

**purler** *n. colloq.* heavy fall.

**purlieu** *n.* (*pl.* **purlieus**) person's limits or usual haunts.

**purloin** *v.* steal, pilfer.

**purple** ● *n.* colour between red and blue. ● *adj.* of purple. □□ **purplish** *adj.*

**purport** ● *v.* 1 profess. 2 be intended to seem. 3 have as its meaning. ● *n.* 1 ostensible meaning. 2 tenor of document or statement. □□ **purportedly** *adv.*

**purpose** ● *n.* aim to be attained; thing intended; intention to act; resolution, determination. ● *v.* intend. □ **on purpose** by intention.

**purposeful** *adj.* having or indicating purpose; intentional. □□ **purposefully** *adv.*

**purposely** *adv.* on purpose.

**purr** ● *v.* 1 make low vibratory sound of cat expressing pleasure. 2 (of machinery etc.) run smoothly and quietly. ● *n.* purring sound.

**purse** ● *n.* 1 small pouch for carrying money in. 2 funds, money. ● *v.* pucker or contract (lips etc.); become wrinkled.

**purser** *n.* ship's officer who keeps accounts.

**pursuance** *n.* performance (of duties etc.)

**pursue** *v.* (**pursued**, **pursuing**) 1 follow with intent to overtake, capture, or harm. 2 proceed along; engage in (study etc.); carry out (plan etc.) 3 seek after; continue to investigate etc.; persistently importune or assail. □□ **pursuer** *n.*

**pursuit** *n.* pursuing; occupation or activity pursued.

**purulent** *adj.* of, containing, or discharging pus. □□ **purulence** *n.*

**purvey** *v.* provide or supply food etc. as one's business. □□ **purveyor** *n.*

**pus** *n.* thick yellowish liquid produced from infected tissue.

**push** ● *v.* 1 move away by exerting force. 2 thrust forward or upward. 3 make demands on the abilities or tolerance of. 4 urge, impel. 5 *colloq.* sell (drugs) illegally. ● *n.* 1 act or force of pushing. 2 vigorous effort. □ **push ahead** carry on, proceed. **push off** *colloq.* go away. **push-up** exercise of pressing on hands to raise body while lying face down. □□ **pusher** *n.*

**pushbike** *n.* bicycle.

**pushchair** *n.* folding chair on wheels, in which a child can be pushed along.

**pushy** *adj. colloq.* excessively self-assertive. □□ **pushily** *adv.* **pushiness** *n.*

**pusillanimous** *adj.* cowardly, timid.

**puss** *n.* (also **pussy**) *colloq.* cat.

**pustule** *n.* pimple containing pus. □□ **pustular** *adj.*

**put** ● *v.* (**put**, **putting**) 1 cause to be in specified place, position, state, or relationship. 2 express, phrase. 3 throw (shot or weight) as athletic exercise. ● *n.* throw of the shot etc. □ **put by** save for future use. **put down** suppress; snub; have (animal) killed; record in writing. **put off** postpone; dissuade, repel. **put out** disconcert; inconvenience; extinguish; dislocate. **put up** construct; raise the price of; provide (money etc.); give temporary accommodation to. **put upon** *colloq.* unfairly burdened. **put up with** endure, tolerate.

**putative** *adj.* reputed, supposed. □□ **putatively** *adv.*

**putrefy** *v.* 1 become or make putrid. 2 go bad. □□ **putrefaction** *n.* **putrescence** *n.* **putrescent** *adj.*

**putrid** *adj.* decomposed, rotten; noxious; corrupt. □□ **putridity** *n.*

**putt** ● *v.* (**putted**) strike (golf ball) on putting green. ● *n.* putting stroke.

**putter** *n.* golf club for putting.

**putty** ● *n.* paste of chalk, linseed oil, etc. for fixing panes of glass, filling holes, etc. ● *v.* fix, fill, etc. with putty.

**puzzle** ● *n.* difficult or confusing problem; problem or toy designed to test ingenuity. ● *v.* (cause to) think hard. □□ **puzzlement** *n.*

**PVC** *abbr.* polyvinyl chloride, a type of plastic.

**pygmy** (also **pigmy**) ● *n.* member of dwarf people of esp. equatorial Africa; very small person, animal, or thing. ● *adj.* very small.

**pyjamas** *n.pl.* suit of trousers and top for sleeping in.

**pylon** *n.* tall structure, esp. as support for electric cables etc.

**pyorrhoea** *n.* (also **pyorrhea**) disease causing discharge of pus from the tooth sockets.

**pyramid** *n.* **1** structure with triangular sloping sides that meet at top. **2** organisation etc. that is structured with fewer people or things at each level as one approaches the top. □□ **pyramidal** *adj.*

**pyre** *n.* heap of combustible material, esp. for burning corpse.

**pyrethrum** *n.* aromatic chrysanthemum; insecticide from its dried flowers.

**pyretic** *adj.* of or producing fever.

**pyrex** *n. propr.* hard heat-resistant glass.

**pyrites** *n.* (in full **iron pyrites**) yellow sulphide of iron.

**pyromania** *n.* obsessive desire to start fires. □□ **pyromaniac** *n. & adj.*

**pyrotechnics** *n.pl.* art of making fireworks; display of fireworks. □□ **pyrotechnic** *adj.*

**pyrrhic victory** *n.* one gained at too great a cost.

**python** *n.* large snake that crushes its prey.

**Q** abbr. Question.

**QC** abbr. Queen's Counsel.

**QED** abbr. which was to be proved (*quod erat demonstrandum*).

**Qld** abbr. Queensland.

**qua** conj. in the capacity of, as.

**quack** ● n. **1** harsh sound made by ducks. **2** unqualified practitioner, esp. of medicine. ● v. (of duck) make its harsh cry.

**quad** ● colloq. ● n. **1** quadrangle. **2** quadruplet. **3** quadraphonics. ● adj. quadraphonic. □ **quad bike** four-wheeled motorcycle.

**quadrangle** n. **1** four-sided plane figure, esp. square or rectangle. **2** four-sided courtyard.

**quadrant** n. **1** quarter of a circle or its circumference. **2** *hist.* optical instrument for measuring angle between distant objects.

**quadraphonic** adj. (also **quadrophonic**) (of sound reproduction) using four transmission channels. □□ **quadraphonically** adv. **quadraphonics** n.pl.

**quadratic equation** n. one involving the square (and no higher power) of unknown quantity or variable.

**quadrella** n. *Aust.* form of gambling in which the better must select winners of four specified horse races.

**quadriceps** n. four-headed muscle at front of thigh.

**quadrilateral** ● adj. having four sides. ● n. four-sided figure.

**quadrille** n. square dance; music for this.

**quadriplegia** n. paralysis of both arms and legs. □□ **quadriplegic** adj. & n.

**quadruped** n. four-footed animal, esp. mammal.

**quadruple** ● adj. fourfold; having four parts; (of time in music) having four beats in bar. ● n. fourfold number or amount. ● v. multiply by four.

**quadruplet** n. each of four children born at one birth.

**quaff** v. *literary* drink deeply; drain (cup etc.) in long draughts. □□ **quaffable** adj.

**quagmire** n. muddy or boggy area; hazardous situation.

**quail** ● n. small European game bird reared for its flesh and eggs; any similar ground-dwelling bird. ● v. flinch; show fear.

**quaint** adj. attractively odd or old-fashioned. □□ **quaintly** adv. **quaintness** n.

**quake** ● v. shake, tremble. ● n. earthquake.

**Quaker** n. member of Society of Friends, Christian sect with no written creed or ordained ministers.

**qualification** n. **1** accomplishment fitting person for position or purpose. **2** thing that modifies or limits. **3** qualifying, being qualified.

**qualify** v. **1** (often as **qualified** adj.) make competent or fit for position or purpose; make legally entitled. **2** satisfy conditions. **3** modify, limit. **4** *Gram.* (of word) attribute quality to (esp. noun). **5** moderate, mitigate. **6** be describable as. □□ **qualifier** n.

**qualitative** adj. of or concerned with quality.

**quality** ● n. **1** degree of excellence. **2** attribute, faculty; relative nature or character. ● adj. of high degree of excellence. □ **quality time** time devoted exclusively to another person in order to strengthen a relationship.

**qualm** *n.* uneasy feeling of worry or fear.

**quamby** ● *v.* 1 *Aust. hist.* lie down. 2 stop. 3 die. ● *n.* camp; temporary shelter.

**quandary** *n.* perplexed state; difficult situation.

**quandong** *n.* Australian shrub or tree bearing globular fruit with wrinkled stone.

**quango** *n.* semi-public administrative body appointed by government.

**quantify** *v.* determine quantity of; express as quantity. □□ **quantifiable** *adj.*

**quantitative** *adj.* of or concerned with quantity. □ **quantitative easing** introduction of new money into money supply by central bank.

**quantity** *n.* 1 amount or number of substance or thing. 2 (**quantities**) large amounts. 3 *Math.* value, component, etc. that may be expressed in numbers. □ **quantity surveyor** person who measures and prices building work.

**quantum** *n.* (*pl.* **quanta**) *Physics* discrete quantity of energy; discrete amount of any other substance. □ **quantum leap** sudden great advance. **quantum theory** theory of physics based on the assumption that energy exists in indivisible units.

**quarantine** *n.* 1 isolation imposed on person, animal, or plant to prevent infection, contagion, or introduction to country of plant disease or pest; period of this. ● *v.* put in quarantine.

**quark** *n.* 1 *Physics* component of elementary particles. 2 kind of low-fat curd cheese.

**quarrel** ● *n.* severe or angry dispute; cause of complaint. ● *v.* (**quarrelled**)

engage in a quarrel. □□ **quarrelsome** *adj.*

**quarry** ● *n.* 1 intended victim or prey; object of pursuit. 2 place from which stone etc. is extracted. ● *v.* extract (stone) from quarry.

**quart** *n.* imperial liquid measure equal to quarter of gallon; two pints (0.946 litre).

**quarter** ● *n.* 1 each of four equal parts. 2 period of three months. 3 point of time 15 minutes before or after any hour. 4 25 US or Canadian cents, coin for this. 5 part of town, esp. as occupied by particular class. 6 point of the compass, region at this. 7 direction, district. 8 source of supply. 9 accommodation of troops etc. 10 one-fourth of lunar month. 11 mercy towards enemy etc. on condition of surrender. 12 *Sport* each of four equal periods of play. 13 (**quarters**) lodgings. ● *v.* 1 divide into quarters. 2 put into lodgings. □ **quarter final** match or round preceding semifinal.

**quarterdeck** *n.* part of ship's upper deck nearest stern.

**quarterly** ● *adj.* & *adv.* produced or occurring once every quarter of year. ● *n.* quarterly journal.

**quartermaster** *n.* regimental officer in charge of stores etc.; naval petty officer in charge of steering and signals.

**quartet** *n.* musical composition for four performers; the performers; any group of four.

**quarto** *n.* size of book or page made by folding sheet of standard size twice to form four leaves.

**quartz** ● *n.* silica in various mineral forms. ● *adj.* (of clock or watch) operated by vibrations of electrically driven quartz crystal.

**quasar** *n.* starlike object with large red shift.

**quash** v. annul; reject as not valid; suppress.

**quasi-** comb. form **1** seeming to be but not really so. **2** almost.

**quatrain** n. stanza or poem having four lines.

**quaver** ● v. vibrate, shake, tremble; sing or say with quavering voice. ● n. **1** Mus. note half as long as crotchet. **2** trill in singing. **3** tremble in speech. □□ **quavery** adj.

**quay** n. artificial landing place for loading and unloading ships.

**queasy** adj. **1** (of person) nauseous; (of stomach) easily upset; (of conscience etc.) over-scrupulous. □□ **queasily** adv. **queasiness** n.

**queen** n. **1** female ruler of country, esp. by right of birth; king's wife; woman or thing regarded as supreme in some way. **2** fertile female ant, bee, etc. **3** most powerful piece in chess; court card depicting queen. **4** offens. effeminate male homosexual. □□ **queenly** adj.

**queenfish** n. marine fish valued as game.

**queer** ● adj. **1** strange, odd, eccentric. **2** colloq. often offens. homosexual. **3** of sexual or gender identity that does not correspond to established norms. **4** dated slightly ill; faint. ● n. colloq. often offens. homosexual.

**quell** v. suppress, crush.

**quench** v. **1** satisfy (thirst) by drinking. **2** extinguish (fire or light); cool, esp. with water. **3** stifle, suppress.

**quenda** n. small marsupial of southern Australia.

**quern** n. handmill for grinding corn or pepper.

**querulous** adj. complaining, peevish. □□ **querulously** adv.

**query** ● n. question; question mark. ● v. ask, inquire; call in question; dispute accuracy of.

**quesadilla** n. heated cheese-filled tortilla.

**quest** ● n. long search. ● v. go about in search of something.

**question** ● n. sentence worded or expressed so as to seek information or answer; doubt or dispute about matter; raising of such doubt etc.; matter to be discussed or decided; problem requiring solution. ● v. ask questions of; subject (person) to examination; throw doubt on. □ **in question** being discussed or disputed. **no question of** no possibility of. **out of the question** completely impracticable. **question mark** punctuation mark ( ? ) placed after question.

**questionable** adj. open to doubt.

**questionnaire** n. list of questions for obtaining information.

**queue** ● n. line or sequence of people, computer processes, vehicles, etc. waiting their turn. ● v. (**queued**, **queuing** or **queueing**) form or join queue.

**quibble** ● n. petty objection; trivial point of criticism; evasion. ● v. use quibbles.

**quiche** n. savoury flan.

**quick** ● adj. **1** taking only a short time. **2** able to learn or think quickly. **3** (of temper) easily roused. ● adv. quickly. ● n. **1** sensitive flesh below the nails. **2** Cricket fast bowler. □□ **quickly** adv.

**quicken** v. make or become quicker; accelerate; give life or vigour to; rouse.

**quicksand** n. area of loose wet deep sand into which heavy objects will sink.

**quicksilver** n. mercury.

**quickstep** n. ballroom dance.

**quid** n. (pl. **quids**) colloq. (formerly) one Australian pound. □ **not the full quid** Aust. mentally deficient; crazy. **quids in** *colloq.* in a position of profit.

**quid pro quo** *n.* (*pl.* **quid pro quos**) favour etc. exchanged for another.

**quiescent** *adj.* inert, inactive. □□ **quiescence** *n.*

**quiet** ● *adj.* with little or no sound or motion; of gentle or peaceful disposition; unobtrusive, not showy; not overt, disguised; undisturbed, uninterrupted; not busy. ● *n.* silence; stillness; undisturbed state; tranquillity. ● *v.* make or become quiet, calm. □ **on the quiet** unobtrusively; secretly. □□ **quietly** *adv.* **quietness** *n.*

**quieten** *v.* make or become quiet or calm.

**quiff** *n.* upright tuft of hair.

**quill** *n.* **1** large feather; pen made of this. **2** each of the spines of an echidna or porcupine.

**quilt**[1] ● *n.* coverlet, esp. of quilted material. ● *v.* line bedspread or garment with padding enclosed between layers of fabric by lines of stitching. □□ **quilter** *n.* **quilting** *n.*

**quilt**[2] *v. colloq.* beat soundly; thrash. □□ **quilting** *n.*

**quin** *n. colloq.* quintuplet.

**quince** *n.* (tree bearing) acid pear-shaped fruit used in jams etc.

**quinella** *n.* form of gambling in which better must select the first two place getters in horserace.

**quinine** *n.* bitter drug used as tonic and to reduce fever.

**quinoa** *n.* seeds of S. American plant used as food.

**quintessence** *n.* purest and most perfect form, manifestation, or embodiment of quality etc.; highly refined extract. □□ **quintessential** *adj.* **quintessentially** *adv.*

**quintet** *n.* musical composition for five performers; the performers; any group of five.

**quintuple** ● *adj.* fivefold; having five parts. ● *n.* fivefold number or amount. ● *v.* multiply five.

**quintuplet** *n.* each of five children born at one birth.

**quip** ● *n.* clever saying; epigram. ● *v.* (**quipped**) make quips.

**quire** *n.* 25 (formerly 24) sheets of paper.

**quirk** *n.* peculiar feature; trick of fate. □□ **quirky** *adj.*

**quisling** *n.* collaborator, traitor.

**quit** *v.* (**quitted** or **quit**, **quitting**) **1** leave, abandon. **2** cease, stop.

**quitch** *n.* (in full **quitch-grass**) couch grass.

**quite** *adv.* **1** completely; exactly (expressing agreement). **2** somewhat; really, actually. □ **quite a few** a considerable number.

**quits** *adj.* on even terms by retaliation or repayment.

**quiver** ● *v.* tremble or vibrate with slight rapid motion. ● *n.* **1** quivering motion or sound. **2** case for arrows.

**quixotic** *adj.* idealistic; impractical. □□ **quixotically** *adv.*

**quiz** ● *n.* series of questions testing knowledge, esp. as entertainment. ● *v.* (**quizzed**) interrogate.

**quizzical** *adj.* mocking, gently amused. □□ **quizzically** *adv.*

**quod** *n. colloq.* prison.

**quoit** *n.* ring thrown to encircle peg in the game of *quoits*.

**quokka** *n.* small short-tailed wallaby of Western Australia.

**quoll** *n.* long-tailed spotted Australian marsupial.

**quorate** *adj.* having a quorum present.

**quorum** *n.* minimum number of people that must be present to constitute valid meeting.

**quota** *n.* share to be contributed to or received from total; number of goods, people, etc. stipulated or permitted.

**quotable** *adj.* worth quoting.

**quotation** n. passage or remark quoted; quoting, being quoted. □ **quotation marks** punctuation marks (' or "") enclosing words quoted.

**quote** v. **1** cite or appeal to as example, authority, etc.; repeat or copy out passage from; cite (author, book, etc.); cite (author etc.) as proof, evidence, etc. **2** state price of; state (price) for job.

**quotidian** adj. daily.

**quotient** n. result of division sum.

**Quran** n. = KORAN.

**q.v.** abbr. which see (indicating that the reader should look at the reference given).

**qwerty** adj. denoting standard keyboard on English-language keyboards.

**qy** abbr. query.

# Rr

**R** *abbr.* (also **R.**) **1** Regina, Rex (*Elizabeth R*). **2** river. **3** (of film) Restricted; classified as not suitable for persons under eighteen. **4** registered as trademark. **5** *Chess* rook.

**rabbi** *n.* Jewish religious leader; Jewish scholar or teacher, esp. of law. □□ **rabbinical** *adj.*

**rabbit** ● *n.* burrowing mammal of hare family. ● *v.* (**rabbited**) talk pointlessly, chatter. □□ **rabbiter** *n.*

**rabble** *n.* disorderly crowd; mob; contemptible or inferior set of people.

**rabid** *adj.* affected with rabies, mad; violent, fanatical. □□ **rabidity** *n.*

**rabies** *n.* contagious viral disease of esp. dogs.

**raccoon** (also **racoon**) (*pl.* **raccoon** or **raccoons**) N. American mammal with bushy tail.

**race** ● *n.* **1** contest of speed or to be first to achieve something; (**races**) series of races for horses etc. **2** large group of people with common ancestry and inherited physical characteristics; a genus, species, breed, or variety of animal or plant. ● *v.* take part in race (with); move or operate at full or excess speed.

**racecourse** *n.* ground where horse races are held.

**racehorse** *n.* horse kept for racing.

**raceme** *n.* flower cluster with flowers attached by short stalks at equal distances along stem.

**racial** *adj.* of or concerning race; on grounds of or connected with difference in race. □□ **racially** *adv.*

**racism** *n.* belief in superiority of particular race; theory that human abilities are determined by race; antagonism between races. □□ **racist** *n.* & *adj.*

**rack** ● *n.* **1** framework, usu. with rails, bars, etc., for holding things. **2** cogged or toothed bar or rail engaging with wheel, pinion etc. **3** *hist.* instrument of torture stretching victim's joints. ● *v.* (also **wrack**) inflict suffering on. □ **rack and ruin** destruction. **rack off!** *Aust.* get lost! **rack** (or **wrack**) **one's brains** make great mental effort.

**racket**¹ *n.* **1** uproar, din. **2** *colloq.* scheme for obtaining money etc. by dishonest means, dodge, sly game. **3** *colloq.* line of business.

**racket**² *n.* = RACQUET.

**racketeer** *n.* person who operates dishonest business. □□ **racketeering** *n.*

**raconteur** *n.* teller of anecdotes.

**racoon** *n.* = RACCOON.

**racquet** *n.* (also **racket**) a bat with round or oval frame strung with catgut, nylon, etc., used in tennis etc.

**racy** *adj.* lively and vigorous in style; risqué; of distinctive quality. □□ **raciness** *n.*

**rad** ● *n.* unit of absorbed dose of ionising radiation. ● *adj. colloq.* radical, excellent.

**radar** *n.* radio system for detecting direction, range, or presence of objects; apparatus for this.

**raddle** ● *n.* red ochre. ● *v.* **1** colour with raddle or rouge. **2** *Aust.* mark (sheep) with red dye.

**radial** ● *adj.* **1** of or arranged like rays or radii, having spokes or radiating lines; acting or moving along such lines. **2** (in full **radial ply**) (of tyre) having fabric layers arranged radially. ● *n.* radial ply tyre. □□ **radially** *adv.*

**radian** n. SI unit of plane angle (about 57°); angle at centre of circle formed by arc equal in length to the radius.

**radiant** ● adj. **1** emitting or issuing in rays. **2** beaming with joy etc.; splendid, dazzling. ● n. point or object from which light or heat radiates.□□ **radiance** n. **radiantly** adv.

**radiata pine** n. conifer cultivated in plantations for its valuable soft wood.

**radiate** v. emit rays of light, heat, etc.; be emitted in rays; emit or spread from centre; transmit or demonstrate.

**radiation** n. radiating; emission of energy as electromagnetic waves; energy thus transmitted, esp. invisibly. □ **radiation therapy** = RADIOTHERAPY.

**radiator** n. **1** device for heating room etc. **2** engine-cooling device in motor vehicle or aircraft.

**radical** ● adj. fundamental; drastic, thorough; holding extremist views. ● n. person desiring radical reforms or holding radical views. □□ **radicalism** n. **radically** adv.

**radicchio** n. salad plant with bitter red leaves.

**radicle** n. embryo root.

**radii** see RADIUS.

**radio** ● n. transmission and reception of messages etc. by electromagnetic waves of radio frequency; apparatus for receiving, broadcasting, or transmitting radio signals; sound broadcasting (station or channel). ● v. communicate or broadcast by radio. ● adj. of or involving radio.

**radioactive** adj. emitting radiation caused by the decay of atomic nuclei. □□ **radioactivity** n.

**radiocarbon** n. radioactive isotope of carbon.

**radiography** n. production of X-ray photographs.□□ **radiographer** n.

**radiology** n. Med. study of X-rays and other high-energy radiation. □□ **radiological** adj. **radiologist** n.

**radiophonic** adj. electronically produced sound, esp. music.

**radiotherapy** n. treatment of disease by X-rays or other forms of radiation.

**radish** n. plant with crisp pungent root; this root.

**radium** n. radioactive metallic element obtained from pitchblende (symbol Ra).

**radius** n. (pl. **radii** or **radiuses**) **1** straight line from centre to circumference of circle or sphere, its length. **2** bone of forearm, on same side as thumb.

**radon** n. **1** gaseous radioactive inert element (symbol Rn). **2** arising from disintegration of radium.

**raffia** n. strips of fibre from the leaves of a palm tree native to Madagascar.

**raffish** adj. disreputable, rakish.

**raffle** ● n. fund-raising lottery with prizes. ● v. sell by raffle.

**raft** n. **1** flat floating structure of wood etc. used for transport. **2** large collection.

**rafter** n. any of sloping beams forming framework of roof.

**rag** ● n. **1** torn, frayed, or worn piece of woven material. **2** (**rags**) old or worn clothes. **3** colloq. newspaper. **4** prank, esp. one performed by students. ● v. (**ragged**) tease.

**ragamuffin** n. person in ragged dirty clothes.

**rage** ● n. **1** violent anger; a fit of this. **2** widespread temporary fashion; fad. **3** Aust. colloq. lively party. ● v. **1** show violent anger. **2** (of storm or battle) continue furiously.

**ragged** adj. torn; frayed; in ragged clothes; with a broken or jagged outline or surface.

**raglan** adj. sleeve that continues to the neck, joined by sloping seams.

**ragout** *n.* highly seasoned stew of meat and vegetables.

**ragtime** *n.* form of highly syncopated early jazz.

**raid** ● *n.* rapid surprise attack; surprise visit by police etc., to arrest suspects or seize illicit goods. ● *v.* make raid on. □□ **raider** *n.*

**rail** ● *n.* bar used to hang things on or as protection, part of fence, top of banisters, etc.; steel bar(s) making railway track; railway. ● *v.* 1 provide or enclose with rail(s). 2 complain or protest strongly; rant.

**railing** *n.* fence made of rails supported on upright metal bars.

**railroad** ● *n.* railway. ● *v.* 1 coerce. 2 rush.

**railway** *n.* track or set of tracks of steel rails on which trains run; organisation and personnel required to work such a system.

**rain** ● *n.* condensed atmospheric moisture falling in drops, fall of these; falling liquid or objects. ● *v.* send down or fall as or like rain. □ **rain check** 1 promise to supply out-of-stock goods at marked-down price. 2 *US* ticket given for later use when outdoor event is interrupted or postponed by rain.

**rainbow** ● *n.* arch of colours formed in sky by reflection, refraction, and dispersion of sun's rays in falling rain etc. ● *adj.* many-coloured.

**raincoat** *n.* waterproof or water-resistant coat.

**rainforest** *n.* dense wet tropical forest.

**rainy** *adj.* (rainier) (of weather, climate, day, etc.) in or on which rain is falling or much rain usually falls.

**raise** ● *v.* 1 bring to higher level or upright position. 2 breed, grow; bring up (child). 3 procure. ● *n.* an increase in salary.

**raisin** *n.* dried grape.

**raison d'être** *n.* (*pl.* raisons d'être) purpose that accounts for, justifies, or originally caused thing's existence.

**rajah** *n.* (also raja) *hist.* Indian king or prince.

**rake** ● *n.* 1 implement with long handle and toothed crossbar for drawing together hay, smoothing loose soil, etc. 2 backward slope of an object. 3 man who leads an irresponsible and immoral life. ● *v.* 1 collect or gather (as) with rake. 2 search thoroughly. 3 direct gunfire along (line) from end to end.

**rakish** *adj.* of or like rake; dashing; jaunty.

**rallentando** *adv. Mus.* with gradual decrease of speed.

**rally** ● *v.* 1 bring or come (back) together for a united effort. 2 revive; recover strength. ● *n.* 1 act of rallying, recovery. 2 mass meeting or protest. 3 driving competition over public roads. 4 extended exchange of strokes in tennis.

**RAM** *abbr.* random access memory.

**ram** ● *n.* 1 uncastrated male sheep. 2 falling weight of pile-driving machine. 3 hydraulic water pump. ● *v.* (rammed) force into place; beat down or drive in by heavy blows; (of ship, vehicle, etc.) strike, crash against. □ **ram raid** robbery in which vehicle is crashed into shop etc.

**Ramadan** *n.* ninth month of Muslim year, with strict fasting from sunrise to sunset.

**ramble** ● *v.* 1 walk for pleasure. 2 talk or write incoherently. ● *n.* walk taken for pleasure. □□ **rambler** *n.*

**ramekin** *n.* small dish.

**ramification** *n.* 1 consequence, esp. when complex or unwelcome. 2 subdivision of complex structure.

**ramify** *v.* form branches or subdivisions.

**ramp** n. **1** slope joining two levels of ground, floor, etc. **2** stairs for entering or leaving aircraft. **3** transverse ridge in road, making vehicles slow down; speed hump.

**rampage** • v. **1** rush wildly. **2** rage, storm. • n. wild or violent behaviour.

**rampant** adj. **1** unchecked, flourishing excessively. **2** rank, luxuriant. **3** fanatical. **4** Heraldry (of lion etc.) standing on left hind foot with forepaws in the air. □□ **rampancy** n.

**rampart** n. defensive broad-topped wall; defence, protection.

**ramrod** n. **1** rod for ramming down charge of muzzle-loading firearm. **2** thing that is very straight or rigid.

**ramshackle** adj. tumbledown, rickety.

**ran** see RUN.

**ranch** n. cattle-breeding establishment, esp. in N. America; farm where certain other animals are bred. □□ **rancher** n.

**rancid** adj. smelling or tasting like stale fat. □□ **rancidity** n.

**rancour** n. (also **rancor**) feeling of bitterness or hate. □□ **rancorous** adj.

**rand** n. unit of money in South Africa.

**R&B** abbr. rhythm and blues.

**R&D** abbr. research and development.

**random** adj. made, done, etc. without method or conscious choice. colloq. strange, inexplicable, unexpected. □□ **randomly** adv. **randomness** n.

**randy** adj. colloq. eager for sexual gratification.

**rang** see RING².

**ranga** n. Aust. colloq. derog. person with red hair.

**range** • n. **1** line or series of things; series of mountains or hills. **2** limits between which something operates or varies. **3** distance over which things can travel or be effective; distance to objective. **4** large open area for grazing or hunting. **5** place with targets for shooting practice. **6** stove. • v. **1** arrange in rows etc. **2** extend. **3** vary between limits. **4** go about a place.

**rangefinder** n. device for calculating distance to target.

**ranger** n. **1** keeper of national park etc. **2** (**Ranger**) senior Guide.

**rangy** adj. tall and thin.

**rank¹** • n. **1** place in scale; position in hierarchy; grade of advancement; distinct social class, grade of dignity or achievement. **2** row or line; single line of soldiers drawn up abreast. **3** place where taxis await customers. • v. have rank or place; classify, give certain grade to; arrange in rank; have value as specified. • adj. **1** luxuriant, coarse. **2** choked with weeds etc. **3** foul-smelling; loathsome; flagrant, gross, complete. □ **rank and file** ordinary people.

**rankle** v. cause persistent annoyance or resentment.

**ransack** v. pillage, plunder; thoroughly search.

**ransom** • n. sum demanded or paid for release of prisoner. • v. buy freedom or restoration of; hold (prisoner) to ransom; release for ransom.

**ransomware** n. malicious software designed to block access to computer system until sum of money is paid.

**rant** v. speak loudly, bombastically, or violently.

**rap¹** • n. **1** smart slight blow; sound of this; a tap. **2** colloq. blame, punishment. **3** style of music in which words are recited rapidly and rhythmically over instrumental backing. • v. (**rapped**) **1** strike smartly. **2** make sharp tapping sound. **3** criticise adversely. **4** Mus. perform rap. **5** (also **rap on**) colloq. talk, chat. □ **take the rap** suffer the consequences. □□ **rapper** n.

**rap²** *n. Aust.* praise, commendation.

**rapacious** *adj.* grasping, extortionate, predatory. □□ **rapacity** *v.*

**rape¹** ● *n.* have sexual intercourse with (person) without consent.
● *n.* this act or crime; destruction of place or thing.

**rape²** *n.* **1** plant grown as fodder, and for oil from its seed. **2** canola.

**rapid** ● *adj.* quick, swift.
● *n.* (**rapids**) swift current where river bed slopes steeply. □□ **rapidity** *n.* **rapidly** *adv.* **rapidness** *n.*

**rapier** *n.* light slender sword for thrusting.

**rapist** *n.* person who commits rape.

**rapport** *n.* harmonious communication or relationship.

**rapprochement** *n.* resumption of harmonious relations, esp. between nations.

**rapt** *adj.* very intent and absorbed, enraptured.

**rapture** *n.* intense delight.
□□ **rapturous** *adj.* **rapturously** *adv.*

**rare** *adj.* **1** seldom done, found, or occurring; uncommon.
**2** exceptionally good. **3** of less than usual density. **4** (of meat) underdone.
□□ **rarely** *adv.* **rareness** *n.*

**rarefied** *adj.* **1** (of atmosphere) of low density, thin. **2** (of idea etc.) very subtle. □□ **rarefaction** *n.*

**raring** *adj.* *colloq.* eager.

**rarity** *n.* rareness; uncommon thing.

**rascal** *n.* dishonest or mischievous person. □□ **rascally** *adj.*

**rase** = RAZE.

**rash** ● *n.* skin eruption in spots or patches. ● *adj.* reckless, impetuous, hasty.

**rasher** *n.* slice of bacon or ham.

**rasp** ● *n.* **1** coarse file. **2** grating noise or utterance. ● *v.* **1** scrape roughly or with rasp. **2** make grating sound; say gratingly.

**raspberry** *n.* **1** red fruit like blackberry; plant bearing this.

**2** *colloq.* sound made by blowing through lips, expressing derision or disapproval.

**rasterise** *v.* (also **-ize**) convert (image) into pixels that can be displayed on computer screen.

**rat** ● *n.* **1** large mouselike rodent; any similar rat-like Australian animal.
**2** *colloq.* treacherous person.
● *v.* (**ratted**) **1** hunt or kill rats.
**2** *Aust. colloq.* rob (person); steal (money etc.) □ **rat on** *colloq.* desert or betray. **rat race** *colloq.* fiercely competitive struggle for position, power, etc.

**ratable** = RATEABLE.

**ratatouille** *n.* dish of zucchinis, tomatoes, eggplant, etc. stewed in olive oil.

**ratbag** *n. Aust. colloq.* obnoxious person; trouble maker; unconventional person; holder of rigid political views etc.
□□ **ratbaggery** *n.*

**ratchet** *n.* set of teeth on edge of bar or wheel with catch ensuring motion in one direction only.

**rate** ● *n.* **1** ratio of one amount etc. to another. **2** fixed price or charge.
**3** (**rates**) tax on land and buildings levied by local government. **4** a speed.
● *v.* **1** estimate worth or value of; consider, regard as. **2** deserve. □ **at any rate** no matter what happens; at least.

**rateable** *adj.* (also **ratable**) liable to rates.

**ratepayer** *n.* person paying rates.

**rather** *adv.* **1** by preference (*I'd rather not*). **2** as a more likely alternative. **3** more precisely. **4** slightly, to some extent.

**ratify** *v.* confirm or accept by formal consent, signature, etc.
□□ **ratification** *n.*

**rating** *n.* **1** level at which thing is rated. **2** (**ratings**) a measurement of popularity of broadcast program determined by estimating size of its audience.

**ratio** n. quantitative relation between similar magnitudes.

**ratiocinate** v. reason logically.
□□ **ratiocination** n.

**ration** ● n. fixed allowance of food etc. ● v. limit to a ration.

**rational** adj. of or based on reason; sensible; endowed with reason.
□□ **rationality** n. **rationally** adv.

**rationale** n. fundamental reason, logical basis.

**rationalise** v. **1** invent rational explanation for. **2** make more efficient by reorganising.
□□ **rationalisation** n.

**rationalism** n. treating reason as basis of belief and knowledge.
□□ **rationalist** n. & adj. **rationalistic** adj.

**rattan** n. palm with long, thin, many-jointed stems; cane of this.

**rattle** ● v. **1** (cause to) give out rapid succession of short sharp hard sounds. **2** colloq. make nervous or annoyed. ● n. rattling sound; device or plaything made to rattle. □ **rattle off** utter rapidly. □□ **rattly** adj.

**rattlesnake** n. venomous American snake with rattling tail.

**raucous** adj. harsh sounding and loud.
□□ **raucously** adv. **raucousness** n.

**raunchy** adj. colloq. sexually boisterous.

**ravage** ● v. devastate, plunder.
● n. (ravages) damage.

**rave** ● v. talk wildly or deliriously; speak with rapturous enthusiasm. ● n. **1** large party or event with dancing to loud fast electronic music, often associated with drugs. **2** colloq. rage. **3** colloq. highly enthusiastic review.

**ravel** v. (ravelled) **1** entangle, become entangled. **2** fray out.

**raven** ● n. large glossy black crow with hoarse cry. ● adj. glossy black.

## ratio | reach

**ravenous** adj. **1** very hungry.
**2** voracious. **3** rapacious.
□□ **ravenously** adv.

**ravine** n. deep narrow gorge.

**raving** adj. **1** delirious; mad. **2** colloq. utter.

**ravioli** n. small pasta envelopes containing meat, spinach, etc.

**ravish** v. **1** rape. **2** enrapture.

**ravishing** adj. entrancing, delightful.

**raw** adj. **1** not cooked; not yet processed. **2** inexperienced, untrained. **3** stripped of skin; sensitive because of this. **4** (of emotion or quality) strong and undisguised.
□ **raw deal** harsh or unfair treatment.

**ray** n. **1** single line or narrow beam of light or other radiation; a radiating line. **2** large marine fish with flat body. **3** Mus. second note of scale in tonic sol-fa.

**rayon** n. textile fibre or fabric made from cellulose.

**raze** v. (also **rase**) tear down (a building).

**razoo** n. Aust. imaginary coin of trivial value. □ **not have a (brass) razoo** have no money at all.

**razor** n. instrument for shaving.

**razzmatazz** n. extravagant publicity and display.

**RC** abbr. Roman Catholic.

**Rd** abbr. Road.

**re** prep. concerning.

**re-** prefix again; back again.

---

**Usage** For words starting with re- that are not listed below, the root words should be consulted.

---

**reach** ● v. **1** extend, go as far as; arrive at. **2** stretch out hand in order to touch or take. **3** establish communication with. **4** achieve, attain. ● n. **1** distance over which person or thing can reach. **2** section of river. □ **out of reach** not able to be reached or obtained. □□ **reachable** adj.

**react** v. cause or undergo reaction. □□ **reactive** adj.

**reaction** n. response to stimulus or act or situation etc.; chemical change produced by substances acting upon each other; occurrence of one condition after period of the opposite; bad physical response to drug etc.

**reactionary** adj. & n. (person) opposed to progress and reform.

**reactor** n. (in full **nuclear reactor**) device in which nuclear reaction is used to produce energy.

**read** ● v. (read, **read**, read) 1 look at and understand meaning of (written or printed words or symbols); speak (such words etc.) aloud; study or discover by reading; have a certain wording. 2 (of instrument) indicate measurement. 3 interpret mentally. 4 (of computer) copy, extract, or transfer (data). ● n. spell of reading.

**readable** adj. able to be read; interesting to read. □□ **readability** n.

**reader** n. 1 person who reads; book intended for reading practice. 2 device for producing image that can be read from microfilm etc.; device or software used for reading or obtaining data stored on cards or other media. 3 (**Reader**) university lecturer below grade of professor.

**readership** n. readers of newspaper etc.

**readily** adv. 1 willingly. 2 easily.

**reading** n. 1 act of reading; matter to be read; literary knowledge; entertainment at which something is read. 2 figure etc. shown by recording instrument. 3 interpretation or view taken. 4 presentation of bill to legislature.

**readjust** v. adjust again or to former state; adapt oneself again. □□ **readjustment** n.

**ready** ● adj. 1 fit or available for action or use. 2 willing; about or inclined to (do something). 3 quick. ● adv. beforehand. ● v. prepare. □□ **readiness** n.

**reagent** n. substance used to cause chemical reaction.

**real** ● adj. actually existing or occurring; genuine; not artificial. ● adv. colloq. really, very. □ **real estate** land or housing etc.

**realise** v. (also **-ize**) 1 be or become aware of; understand clearly. 2 convert into actuality. 3 convert into money. 4 be sold for. □□ **realisation** n.

**realism** n. representing or viewing things in their true nature; showing life as it is in fact. □□ **realist** n.

**realistic** adj. regarding things as they are; based on facts rather than ideals. □□ **realistically** adv.

**reality** n. what is real or existent or underlies appearances; real nature of; real existence; being real; likeness to original. □ **reality television** television programming that follows real people in their everyday lives or in artificial environment.

**really** adv. 1 in fact. 2 very. 3 indeed; I assure you; I protest.

**realm** n. 1 kingdom. 2 field of activity or interest.

**realty** n. real estate.

**ream** n. 1 500 sheets of paper etc. 2 (**reams**) large quantity of writing etc.

**reap** v. 1 cut (grain etc.) as harvest. 2 receive as consequence of actions. □□ **reaper** n.

**rear** ● n. the back part. ● adj. at the back. ● v. 1 bring up and educate; breed and care for. 2 cultivate. 3 (of horse etc.) raise itself on hind legs. 4 raise, build.

**rearguard** n. 1 troops detached to protect rear, esp. in retreat. 2 defensive or conservative element in organisation etc. □ **rearguard**

**action 1** engagement undertaken by rearguard. **2** defensive stand in argument etc., esp. when losing.

**rearm** v. arm again, esp. with improved weapons.
□□ **rearmament** n.

**rearrange** v. arrange in a different way.

**rearward** adj., adv., & n. (towards or at) the rear.□□ **rearwards** adv.

**reason** ● n. **1** motive, cause, or justification. **2** ability to think and draw conclusions; sanity; good sense or judgement. ● v. form or try to reach conclusions by connected thought; use argument with person by way of persuasion; conclude or assert in argument; think out.

**reasonable** adj. **1** having sound judgement. **2** moderate. **3** ready to listen to reason. **4** inexpensive. **5** tolerable.□□ **reasonableness** n. **reasonably** adv.

**reassure** v. **1** restore confidence to. **2** confirm in opinion.
□□ **reassurance** n.

**rebate**[1] ● n. **1** partial refund. **2** deduction from sum to be paid, discount. ● v. pay back as rebate.
□□ **rebatable** adj.

**rebate**[2] n. step-shaped channel cut along edge or face of wood etc., usu. to receive edge or tongue of another piece. ● v. (**rebated**) join with rebate; make rebate in.

**rebel** ● n. person who rebels.
● v. (**rebelled**) fight against or refuse allegiance to established government or conventions; resist.□□ **rebellion** n. **rebellious** adj.

**reboot** v. start up (computer) again.

**rebound** v. **1** spring back after impact. **2** have adverse effect on (doer). ● n. **1** rebounding; recoil. **2** reaction.

**rebuff** ● n. rejection of person who makes advances, offers help, etc.; snub. ● v. give rebuff to.

**rebuke** ● v. express sharp disapproval to (person) for fault; censure. ● n. rebuking, being rebuked.

**rebus** n. representation of word (esp. name) by pictures etc. suggesting its parts.

**rebut** v. (**rebutted**) refute, disprove.
□□ **rebuttal** n.

**recalcitrant** adj. obstinately disobedient; objecting to restraint.
□□ **recalcitrance** n.

**recall** ● v. **1** summon to return. **2** remember. ● n. recalling; being recalled.

**recant** v. withdraw and renounce (belief or statement) as erroneous or heretical.□□ **recantation** n.

**recap** colloq. ● v. (**recapped**) recapitulate. ● n. recapitulation.

**recapitulate** v. restate briefly; summarise.□□ **recapitulation** n.

**recede** v. go or shrink back; be left at an increasing distance; slope backwards; decline in force or value; (of hair) cease to grow at the front etc.

**receipt** n. act of receiving; written acknowledgement that something has been received or money paid.

**receive** v. **1** acquire, accept or take in. **2** experience, be treated with. **3** greet on arrival. **4** Tennis be player to whom ball is served.

**receiver** n. **1** part of telephone that contains earpiece. **2** person appointed to administer property of bankrupt person etc. or property under litigation. **3** device that receives electrical signals and converts them into sound or images.

**receivership** n. office of official receiver; state of being dealt with by receiver.

**recent** adj. happening in time shortly before the present.□□ **recently** adv.

**receptacle** n. object or space used to contain something.

**reception** n. an act, process, or way of receiving; social occasion for receiving guests; place where visitors register on arriving at hotel, office, etc.

**receptionist** n. person employed to receive guests, clients, etc.

**receptive** adj. able or quick to receive ideas. □□ **receptiveness** n.

**recess** n. 1 part or space set back from the line of a wall or room etc. 2 temporary cessation of business; break between school classes.
● v. make recess in or of.

**recession** n. 1 temporary decline in economic activity or prosperity. 2 receding, withdrawal.

**recessive** adj. tending to recede. 2 (of inherited characteristic) appearing in offspring only when not masked by inherited dominant characteristic.

**recidivist** n. person who relapses into crime. □□ **recidivism** n.

**recipe** n. statement of ingredients and procedure for preparing cooked dish; way of achieving something.

**recipient** n. person who receives something.

**reciprocal** ● adj. 1 in return. 2 mutual. ● n. Math. expression or function so related to another that their product is unity. □□ **reciprocally** adv. **reciprocity** n.

**reciprocate** v. 1 requite, return; give in return. 2 (of machine part) move backwards and forwards. □□ **reciprocation** n.

**recital** n. reciting, being recited; concert of classical music by soloist or small group. 2 detailed account of (facts etc.); narrative.

**recitation** n. 1 act or instance of reciting. 2 piece recited.

**recitative** n. passage of singing in speech rhythm of opera or oratorio.

**recite** v. repeat aloud or declaim from memory; enumerate.

**reckless** adj. disregarding consequences or danger etc. □□ **recklessly** adv. **recklessness** n.

**reckon** v. 1 think; consider. 2 count; calculate. 3 rely or base plans on.

**reclaim** v. 1 seek return of (one's property etc.) 2 bring (land) into use, esp. from state of being underwater. 3 win back from vice, error, etc. □□ **reclamation** n.

**recline** v. assume or be in horizontal or leaning position.

**recluse** n. person given to or living in seclusion. □□ **reclusive** adj.

**recognisance** n. Law bond with which person undertakes to observe some condition; sum pledged as surety for this.

**recognise** v. (also **-ize**) 1 identify as already known; realise or discover nature of. 2 acknowledge existence, validity, character, or claims of. 3 show appreciation of; reward; treat. □□ **recognisable** adj.

**recognition** n. recognising, being recognised.

**recoil** ● v. jerk or spring back in horror, disgust, or fear; shrink mentally in this way; rebound; (of gun) be driven backwards by discharge. ● n. act or sensation of recoiling.

**recollect** v. remember; call to mind. □□ **recollection** n.

**recommend** v. suggest as fit for purpose or use; advise (course of action etc.); (of qualities etc.) make acceptable or desirable; commend or entrust. □□ **recommendation** n.

**recompense** ● v. make amends to; compensate; reward or punish (person or action). ● n. reward, requital; retribution.

**reconcile** v. make friendly after estrangement; induce to tolerate something unwelcome; make compatible. □□ **reconcilable** adj.

**reconciliation** n. reconciling; *Aust.* unity between indigenous and non-indigenous Australians.

**recondite** adj. obscure, dealing with an obscure subject.

**recondition** v. overhaul, renovate, make usable again.

**reconnaissance** n. survey of region to locate enemy or ascertain strategic features; preliminary survey.

**reconnoitre** v. make reconnaissance (of).

**reconsider** v. consider again, esp. for possible change of decision.
□□ **reconsideration** n.

**reconstitute** v. reconstruct; reorganise; rehydrate (dried food etc.) □□ **reconstitution** n.

**reconstruct** v. build again; form impression of (past events) by assembling evidence; re-enact (crime); reorganise.
□□ **reconstruction** n.

**record** ● v. **1** put in writing or other permanent form. **2** preserve (sound) on disc etc. for later reproduction. **3** (of measuring instrument) indicate, register. **4** register (vote etc.)
● n. **1** information set down in writing etc.; document bearing this. **2** disc bearing recorded sound. **3** facts known about person's past. **4** best performance or most remarkable event of its kind. □ **off the record** unofficially or not for publication.

**recorder** n. **1** apparatus for recording. **2** woodwind instrument. **3** keeper of records.

**recount** v. narrate, tell in detail.

**re-count** ● v. count again.
● n. re-counting, esp. of votes.

**recoup** v. recover or regain (loss); reimburse.

**recourse** n. source of help to which one may turn. □ **have recourse to** turn to for help.

**recover** v. regain possession, use, or control of; return to health, consciousness, or normal state or position. □□ **recovery** n.

**recreation** n. pastime; relaxation.
□□ **recreational** adj.

**recriminate** v. make mutual or counter accusations.
□□ **recrimination** n. **recriminatory** adj.

**recruit** ● n. new member of armed forces etc. ● v. enlist (person) as recruit; form (army etc.) by enlisting recruits; seek recruits.
□□ **recruitment** n.

**rectal** adj. of the rectum.

**rectangle** n. plane figure with four straight sides and four right angles, esp. with adjacent sides unequal in length. □□ **rectangular** adj.

**rectify** v. **1** adjust or make right. **2** purify esp. by repeated distillation. **3** convert (alternating current) to direct current. □□ **rectifiable** adj. **rectification** n.

**rectilinear** adj. bounded or characterised by straight lines.

**rectitude** n. moral uprightness.

**recto** n. right-hand page of open book.

**rector** n. **1** incumbent in charge of parish. **2** *RC Ch.* head priest of church or religious institution. **3** head of university or college. □□ **rectorship** n.

**rectory** n. rector's house.

**rectum** n. final section of large intestine, between colon and anus.

**recumbent** adj. lying down, reclining.

**recuperate** v. recover from illness, exhaustion, loss, etc.; regain.
□□ **recuperation** n. **recuperative** adj.

**recur** v. (**recurred**) occur again or repeatedly.

**recurrent** adj. recurring.
□□ **recurrence** n.

**recusant** n. person refusing submission or compliance.
□□ **recusancy** n.

**recuse** v. US (of a judge) excuse oneself from a case because of a potential conflict of interest or lack of impartiality.

**recycle** v. convert (waste) to reusable material.□□ **recyclable** n.

**red** ● adj. 1 of or like the colour of blood; (of hair) reddish-brown. 2 colloq. communist, favouring communism. ● n. 1 red colour or thing. 2 colloq. communist. □ **in the red** in debt. **red carpet** privileged treatment for important person. **red-handed** in the act of or just after committing crime. **red herring** misleading clue or diversion. **red-hot** 1 glowing red from heat. 2 highly exciting. **red-letter day** memorable day because of success or happy event. **red light** signal to stop; danger signal. **red-light district** district containing many brothels. **red tape** excessive formalities in official transactions. **see red** colloq. become very angry.□□ **redness** n.

**redact** v. edit (text) for publication; censor or obscure (part of text) for legal or security purposes.□□ **redaction** n.

**redcurrant** n. small edible red berry; bush bearing this.

**redden** v. make or become red.

**redeem** v. 1 buy back; convert (tokens or bonds) into goods or cash. 2 reclaim. 3 deliver from sin and damnation.□□ **redemption** n. **redemptive** adj.

**redeploy** v. send (troops, workers, etc.) to new place or task. □□ **redeployment** n.

**redhead** n. person with red hair.

**redistribute** v. 1 distribute again or differently. 2 change electoral boundaries to even out the number of voters in all electorates. □□ **redistribution** n.

**redolent** adj. strongly smelling; reminiscent (of).□□ **redolence** n.

**redouble** v. increase, intensify.

**redoubtable** adj. formidable.

**redress** ● v. remedy; put right again. ● n. reparation for wrong; redressing (grievance etc.)

**reduce** v. 1 make or become smaller or less; lose weight. 2 convert to another (esp. simpler) form. 3 bring lower in status, rank, or price. 4 bring to weaker or worse state. □□ **reducible** adj. **reduction** n.

**redundant** adj. superfluous; no longer needed; no longer needed at work and therefore unemployed. □□ **redundancy** n.

**reed** n. 1 water or marsh plant with firm stems; its stem. 2 vibrating part of some wind instruments.

**reedy** adj. (**reedier**) (of voice) having high thin tone.□□ **reediness** n.

**reef** n. 1 ridge of rock or coral etc. at or near surface of sea. 2 part of a sail that can be drawn in if there is a high wind. ● v. shorten (a sail).

**reefer** n. 1 thick double-breasted jacket. 2 colloq. marijuana cigarette.

**reek** ● v. smell strongly. ● n. foul or stale smell.

**reel** ● n. 1 cylindrical device on which thread, film, wire, etc. are wound. 2 lively folk or Scottish dance. ● v. 1 wind on or off reel. 2 stagger. □ **reel off** say rapidly without apparent effort.

**re-enact** v. act out (past event). □□ **re-enactment** n.

**ref** n. colloq. referee.

**refectory** n. dining room, esp. in monastery or college.

**refer** v. (**referred**) □ **refer to** 1 mention. 2 send to (authority) for decision; send to specialist. 3 turn to for information.□□ **referable** adj.

**referee** ● n. 1 umpire; person referred to for decision in dispute etc. 2 person willing to testify to character of applicant for employment etc.

● *v.* (refereed, refereeing) act as referee (for).

**reference** *n.* 1 an act of referring; a mention. 2 source of information. 3 testimonial. 4 person willing to testify to another's character, ability, etc. □ **in** (or **with**) **reference to** in connection with; about. **reference book** book providing information. **reference library** one containing books that can be consulted but not taken away. □□ **referential** *adj.*

**referendum** *n.* (*pl.* **referendums** or **referenda**) referring of question to the people for decision by general vote.

**referral** *n.* referring of person to medical specialist etc.

**refill** ● *v.* fill again. ● *n.* thing that refills; refilling. □□ **refillable** *adj.*

**refine** *v.* free from impurities or defects; make elegant or cultured. □□ **refined** *adj.*

**refinement** *n.* 1 refining, being refined. 2 fineness of feeling or taste; elegance. 3 added development or improvement. 4 subtle reasoning. 5 fine distinction.

**refinery** *n.* place where oil, sugar, etc. is refined.

**refit** *v.* (**refitted**) renew or repair the fittings of.

**reflate** *v.* restore (financial system) after deflation. □□ **reflation** *n.* **reflationary** *adj.*

**reflect** *v.* 1 throw back (heat, light, sound, etc.); show image of. 2 bring (credit or discredit, etc.) 3 think deeply.

**reflection** *n.* 1 reflecting, being reflected. 2 reflected light, heat, colour, or image. 3 reconsideration. □ **reflection on** 1 source of discredit to. 2 idea arising in mind; a comment.

**reflective** *adj.* 1 reflecting (light etc.) 2 thoughtful. □□ **reflectively** *adv.*

**reflector** *n.* something that reflects heat or light.

**reflex** *n.* (also **reflex action**) involuntary or instinctive movement in response to a stimulus. □ **reflex angle** angle of more than 180°.

**reflexive** *Gram.* ● *adj.* 1 (of word or form) referring back to subject, e.g. *myself* in I *hurt myself*. 2 (of verb) having reflexive pronoun as object. ● *n.* reflexive word or form.

**reflexology** *n.* massaging of points on the feet as a treatment for stress and other conditions. □□ **reflexologist** *n.*

**reflux** *n.* the flowing back of a bodily fluid.

**reform** ● *v.* make or become better; abolish or cure (abuse etc.) ● *n.* removal of abuses, esp. political; improvement. □□ **reformation** *n.* **reformer** *n.* **reformist** *adj.*

**refract** *v.* deflect (light) at certain angle when it enters obliquely from another medium. □□ **refraction** *n.* **refractive** *adj.* **refractor** *n.*

**refractory** *adj.* stubborn, unmanageable, rebellious; resistant to treatment; hard to fuse or work.

**refrain** ● *v.* avoid doing (action). ● *n.* recurring lines of song; music for these.

**refresh** *v.* 1 give fresh spirit or vigour to. 2 revive (memory). 3 *Computing* update display on (screen). □□ **refreshing** *adj.* **refreshingly** *adv.*

**refreshment** *n.* 1 refreshing, being refreshed. 2 (**refreshments**) food or drink.

**refrigerate** *v.* cool or freeze (esp. food). □□ **refrigeration** *n.*

**refrigerator** *n.* cabinet or room in which food etc. is refrigerated.

**refuge** *n.* shelter from pursuit, danger, or trouble; person or place offering this.

**refugee** *n.* person taking refuge, esp. in foreign country from war, persecution, etc.

**refulgent** *adj. literary* shining, gloriously bright.□□ **refulgence** *n.*

**refund** ● *v.* pay back (money etc.); reimburse. ● *n.* act of refunding; sum refunded.□□ **refundable** *adj.*

**refurbish** *v.* brighten up; redecorate. □□ **refurbishment** *n.*

**refuse**¹ *v.* say or show that one is unwilling to accept or do (what is asked).□□ **refusal** *n.*

**refuse**² *n.* waste material.

**refute** *v.* **1** prove falsity or error of. **2** rebut by argument. **3** deny or contradict (without argument). □□ **refutation** *n.*

---

**Usage** The use of *refute* to mean 'deny, contradict' is considered incorrect by some people. *Repudiate* can be used instead.

---

**regain** *v.* obtain possession or use of after loss.

**regal** *adj.* like or fit for a monarch. □□ **regality** *n.* **regally** *adv.*

**regale** *v.* feed or entertain well.

**regalia** *n.pl.* insignia of royalty or of an order, mayor, etc.

**regard** ● *v.* **1** heed, take into account. **2** gaze on. **3** look upon or think of in specified way. ● *n.* **1** gaze; steady look. **2** attention, care. **3** esteem. **4** (**regards**) kindly greetings conveyed in a message.□ **as regards** (or **with regard to**) concerning.

**regarding** *prep.* concerning; in respect of.

**regardless** *adj. & adv.* without regard or consideration (for).

**regatta** *n.* event consisting of rowing or yacht races.

**regency** *n.* office of regent; commission acting as regent; regent's period of office.

**regenerate** *v.* give new life or vigour to.□□ **regeneration** *n.* **regenerative** *adj.*

**regent** *n.* person acting as head of state because monarch is absent, ill, or a child.

**reggae** *n.* W. Indian style of music with strongly accented subsidiary beat.

**regicide** *n.* killing of king.

**regime** *n.* (also **régime**) **1** method of government. **2** usu. *derog.* particular government. **3** prevailing system. **4** regimen.

**regimen** *n.* prescribed course of exercise, way of life, and diet.

**regiment** ● *n.* permanent unit of army. ● *v.* organise rigidly. □□ **regimentation** *n.*

**regimental** *adj.* of an army regiment.

**Regina** *n.* reigning queen, e.g. Elizabeth Regina.

**region** *n.* geographical area or division, having definable boundaries or characteristics; administrative area of country; part of body; sphere or realm.□ **regional** *adj.*

**register** ● *n.* **1** official list. **2** range of voice or musical instrument; level of formality in language. ● *v.* **1** enter in register; record in writing. **2** notice and remember. **3** pay annual fee on motor vehicle etc. **4** indicate; record; make an impression.

**registrar** *n.* **1** official keeping register. **2** chief administrator in university etc. **3** hospital doctor training as specialist.

**registration** *n.* **1** registering, being registered. **2** annual fee payable by owner of motor vehicle etc.

**registry** *n.* **1** registration. **2** place where written records are kept. □ **registry office** place where records of births, marriages, and deaths are kept, and where civil marriages may be performed.

**rego** *n. Aust. colloq.* motor vehicle registration.

**regress** ● *v.* **1** move backwards. **2** return to former stage or state.

● n. act of regressing. □□ **regression** n. **regressive** adj.

**regret** ● v. (**regretted**) **1** feel or express sorrow, repentance, or distress over (action or loss). **2** say with sorrow or remorse. ● n. sorrow, repentance, etc., over action or loss. □□ **regretful** adj. **regretfully** adv.

**regrettable** adj. (of events or conduct) undesirable, unwelcome; deserving censure. □□ **regrettably** adv.

**regular** ● adj. **1** acting, occurring, or done in uniform manner or at a fixed time or interval; conforming to a rule or habit; even; symmetrical. **2** forming country's permanent armed forces. ● n. **1** regular soldier. **2** colloq. regular customer, visitor, etc. □ **regular expression** Computing sequence of characters etc. expressing string or pattern to be searched for within longer piece of text. □□ **regularity** n. **regularly** adv.

**regularise** v. (also **-ize**) make regular; make lawful or correct. □□ **regularisation** n.

**regulate** v. control by rule; subject to restrictions; adapt to requirements; adjust (clock etc.) to work accurately. □□ **regulator** n.

**regulation** n. prescribed rule; regulating.

**regurgitate** v. **1** bring (swallowed food) up again to mouth. **2** reproduce (information etc.). □□ **regurgitation** n.

**rehab** n. colloq. rehabilitation; course of treatment for drug or alcohol dependence.

**rehabilitate** v. restore to normal life by training etc., esp. after imprisonment or illness; restore to former privileges or reputation or to proper condition. □□ **rehabilitation** n.

**rehash** ● v. put into new form without significant change or improvement. ● n. material rehashed; rehashing.

**rehearse** v. **1** practise before performing in public. **2** recite or say over. □□ **rehearsal** n.

**reign** ● n. sovereign's (period of) rule. ● v. be king or queen; hold sway; prevail.

**reimburse** v. repay (person); refund. □□ **reimbursement** n.

**rein** n. **1** long narrow strap used to guide horse. **2** means of control. ● v. control with reins; restrain.

**reincarnation** n. rebirth of soul in new body. □□ **reincarnate** v.

**reindeer** n. (pl. **reindeer** or **reindeers**) subarctic deer with large antlers.

**reinforce** v. strengthen or support, esp. with additional personnel or material. □□ **reinforcement** n.

**reinstate** v. replace in former position; restore to former privileges. □□ **reinstatement** n.

**reiterate** v. say or do again or repeatedly. □□ **reiteration** n.

**reject** v. **1** refuse to accept or believe in; put aside or send back as not to be used, done, or complied with. ● n. rejected thing or person. □□ **rejection** n.

**rejig** v. (**rejigged**) re-equip for new work; rearrange.

**rejoice** v. feel joy, be glad; take delight.

**rejoin** v. **1** join again. **2** say in answer, retort.

**rejoinder** n. a reply; a retort.

**rejuvenate** v. make (as if) young again. □□ **rejuvenation** n. **rejuvenator** n.

**relapse** ● v. fall back (into worse state after improvement). ● n. relapsing, esp. deterioration in patient's condition after partial recovery.

**relate** v. **1** narrate, recount. **2** connect in thought or meaning. **3** have reference to. **4** feel connected or sympathetic to.

**related** adj. having a common descent or origin.

**relation** n. **1** similarity connecting people or things. **2** a relative. **3** narrating. **4** (**relations**) dealings (with others). □ **in relation to** as regards. □□ **relationship** n.

**relative** ● adj. considered in relation or proportion to something else; having a connection. ● n. person related to another by descent or marriage. □□ **relatively** adv.

**relativity** n. **1** being relative. **2** Physics Einstein's theory of the universe, showing that all motion is relative and treating time as a fourth dimension related to space.

**relax** v. make or become less stiff, rigid, tense, formal, or strict; rest from work or effort. □□ **relaxation** n.

**relay** ● n. **1** fresh set of workers relieving others. **2** relay race. **3** relayed transmission. **4** device transmitting things or activating an electrical circuit. ● v. receive and transmit to others. □ **relay race** a race between teams in which each person in turn covers part of the total distance.

**release** ● v. **1** set free; remove from a fixed position. **2** make (information, a film or recording) available to the public. ● n. **1** releasing; handle, catch, etc. that unfastens something. **2** information or film etc. released.

**relegate** v. consign or dismiss to inferior position. □□ **relegation** n.

**relent** v. relax severity.

**relentless** adj. unrelenting. □□ **relentlessly** adv.

**relevant** adj. closely connected or appropriate to what is being done or considered; of contemporary interest. □□ **relevance** n.

**reliable** adj. that may be relied on. □□ **reliability** n. **reliably** adv.

**reliance** n. trust, confidence. □□ **reliant** adj.

**relic** n. something that survives from earlier times.

**relief** n. **1** (feeling accompanying) alleviation of or deliverance from pain, distress, etc. **2** feature etc. that breaks up monotony or relaxes tension. **3** assistance given to people in special need; replacing of person(s) on duty by another or others. **4** a carving etc., in which design projects from surface; similar effect given by colour or shading.

**relieve** v. bring or give relief to; release from a task or duty; raise the siege of. □ **relieve oneself** urinate or defecate. □□ **relieved** adj.

**religion** n. belief in superhuman controlling power, esp. in personal God or gods entitled to obedience; system of this; thing person is devoted to.

**religious** adj. **1** of religion; devout, pious. **2** very conscientious. □□ **religiously** adv.

**relinquish** v. give up, let go, resign, surrender. □□ **relinquishment** n.

**reliquary** n. receptacle for relics of holy person.

**relish** ● n. **1** liking or enjoyment. **2** appetising flavour, attractive quality. **3** condiment eaten with food to add flavour. ● v. get pleasure out of; enjoy greatly; anticipate with pleasure.

**relocate** v. move to different place.

**reluctant** adj. unwilling, disinclined. □□ **reluctance** n.

**rely** v. (**relied**) □ **rely on 1** depend on with confidence. **2** be dependent on.

**REM** abbr. rapid eye movement, jerky eye movements during dreaming.

**remain** v. **1** be left over. **2** stay in same place or condition. **3** be left behind. **4** continue to be.

**remainder** ● n. residue; remaining people or things; number left after division or subtraction; (any of) copies of book left unsold. ● v. dispose of remainder of (book) at reduced prices.

**remains** *n.pl.* what remains after other parts have been removed or used; dead body.

**remand** ● *v.* return (prisoner) to custody, esp. to allow further inquiry. ● *n.* recommittal to custody.

**remark** ● *v.* say by way of comment; make comment; notice. ● *n.* comment, anything said; noticing, commenting.

**remarkable** *adj.* worth notice; exceptional; striking. □□ **remarkably** *adv.*

**remedial** *adj.* 1 affording or intended as remedy. 2 (of teaching) for pupils with special learning difficulties.

**remedy** ● *n.* treatment (for disease etc.); thing that puts a matter right. ● *v.* rectify; make good.

**remember** *v.* keep in one's mind and recall at will. □□ **remembrance** *adv.*

**remind** *v.* cause to remember or think of.

**reminder** *n.* thing that reminds; memento.

**reminisce** *v.* think or talk about past events.

**reminiscence** *n.* reminiscing; account of things remembered.

**reminiscent** *adj.* having characteristics that remind one (of something).

**remiss** *adj.* negligent.

**remission** *n.* 1 cancellation of debt or penalty. 2 diminution of force, degree, etc. (esp. of disease or pain).

**remit** *v.* (remitted) 1 refrain from exacting or inflicting (debt, punishment, etc.) 2 abate, slacken. 3 send (esp. money). 4 refer (matter for decision) to some authority.

**remittance** *n.* money sent; sending of money.

**remix** ● *v.* 1 mix again. 2 (of recording) alter relative sound levels of performers etc. ● *n.* remixed recording.

**remnant** *n.* small remaining quantity; surviving piece or trace.

**remonstrate** *v.* make protest. □□ **remonstrance** *n.*

**remorse** *n.* deep regret for wrong committed. □□ **remorseful** *adj.* **remorsefully** *adv.*

**remorseless** *adj.* relentless. □□ **remorselessly** *adv.*

**remote** *adj.* 1 distant in place or time; secluded. 2 slight. □□ **remotely** *adv.* **remoteness** *n.*

**removalist** *n. Aust.* person etc. who transfers furniture etc. for those moving house.

**remove** ● *v.* take off or away; dismiss from office; get rid of. ● *n.* degree of remoteness or difference. □□ **removable** *adj.*

**remunerate** *v.* pay for service rendered. □□ **remuneration** *n.*

**Renaissance** *n.* 1 revival of classical art and literature in Europe in 14th–16th centuries. 2 (renaissance) a revival.

**renal** *adj.* of the kidneys.

**renascent** *adj.* springing up anew; being reborn. □□ **renascence** *n.*

**rend** *v.* (rent, rending) tear or wrench forcibly.

**render** *v.* 1 provide, give (assistance or service); submit (bill etc.) 2 cause to become; make. 3 represent or portray. 4 *Computing* process (image) using colour and shading in order to make it appear solid and three-dimensional. 5 translate. 6 melt down (fat). 7 cover (stone or brick) with plaster. □□ **rendering** *n.*

**rendezvous** ● *n.* (*pl.* same) prearranged meeting or meeting place. ● *v.* meet at rendezvous.

**rendition** *n.* interpretation or rendering of artistic piece.

**renegade** *n.* deserter of party or principles.

**renege** *v.* go back on promise or agreement.

**renew** v. restore to original state; revive; replace with fresh thing; get, make, or give again.□□ **renewal** n.

**renewable** adj. able to be renewed; (of a natural resource etc.) not depleted when used.

**rennet** n. curdled milk from calf's stomach, or artificial preparation, used in making cheese etc.

**renounce** v. formally abandon or give up; reject.

**renovate** v. restore to good condition; repair.□□ **renovation** n. **renovator** n.

**renown** n. fame.

**renowned** adj. famous.

**rent** • n. 1 periodical payment for use of land, rooms, machinery, etc. 2 payment for hire of machinery etc. 3 a tear; a gap. • v. 1 pay or receive rent for. 2 see REND.

**rental** n. rent; renting; something rented.

**renunciation** n. renouncing.

**rep** n. colloq. 1 representative, esp. commercial traveller or elected representative of employees. 2 repertory theatre. 3 reputation.

**repair** • v. restore to good condition after damage or wear; set right or make amends for. • n. (result of) restoring to sound condition; good or relative condition for working or using.□□ **repairer** n.

**repartee** n. exchange of witty retorts.

**repast** n. formal a meal.

**repatriate** v. send (someone) back to their own country; send or bring (money) back to one's own country. □□ **repatriation** n.

**repay** v. (**repaid**, **repaying**) pay back. □□ **repayable** adj. **repayment** n.

**repeal** • v. revoke, annul. • n. repealing.

**repeat** • v. say, do, produce, or occur again; tell (a thing told to oneself) to another person. • n. repeating; something repeated.

**repeatedly** adv. again and again.

**repeater** n. 1 firearm that fires several shots without reloading. 2 device for retransmitting broadcast etc. message.

**repel** v. (**repelled**) 1 drive back. 2 be impossible for (substance) to penetrate. 3 be repulsive or distasteful to.

**repellent** • adj. that repels. 2 disgusting, repulsive. • n. substance that repels esp. insects etc.

**repent** v. feel deep sorrow about one's actions etc.; wish one had not done; resolve not to continue (wrongdoing etc.).□□ **repentance** n. **repentant** adj.

**repercussion** n. 1 indirect effect or reaction following event etc. 2 recoil after impact.

**repertoire** n. stock of works that performer etc. knows or is prepared to perform.

**repertory** n. 1 performance of various plays for short periods by one company. 2 repertoire.

**repetition** n. repeating, being repeated; thing repeated.

**repetitious** adj. repetitive.

**repetitive** adj. characterised by repetition.□□ **repetitively** adv.

**repine** v. literary 1 fret. 2 be discontented.

**replace** v. 1 put back in place. 2 be or provide substitute for. □□ **replacement** n.

**replay** • v. play (match, recording, etc.) again. • n. replaying of match, recorded incident in game, etc.

**replenish** v. refill; renew (supply etc.) □□ **replenishment** n.

**replete** adj. full or well-supplied. □□ **repletion** n.

**replica** n. exact copy.

**replicate** v. make replica of. □□ **replication** n.

**reply** • v. answer, respond. • n. an answer.

**report** ● v. 1 give account of; tell as news. 2 make formal complaint about. 3 present oneself on arrival. ● n. 1 spoken or written account; written statement about pupil's work etc.; a rumour. 2 explosive sound. □ **reported speech** speaker's words as reported by another person.

**reporter** n. person employed to report news etc. for media.

**repose** ● n. rest; sleep; tranquillity. ● v. rest; lie, esp. when dead.

**repository** n. place where things are stored or may be found.

**repossess** v. regain possession of (esp. goods on which payment is in arrears). □□ **repossession** n.

**reprehend** v. rebuke; blame.

**reprehensible** adj. blameworthy.

**represent** v. 1 stand for, correspond to; describe or depict; symbolise. 2 be specimen of. 3 present likeness of to mind or senses. 4 declare. 5 allege. 6 show or play part of; be substitute or deputy for. 7 be elected by as member of legislature etc.

**representation** n. 1 representing, being represented; picture, diagram, etc. 2 (**representations**) statements made as appeal, protest, or allegation.

**representative** ● adj. 1 typical of group or class. 2 (of government etc.) of elected members or based on representation. ● n. 1 sample, specimen, or typical embodiment of. 2 agent. 3 commercial traveller. 4 delegate or member, esp. in representative assembly.

**repress** v. suppress; keep (emotions) from finding an outlet. □□ **repression** n. **repressive** adj.

**reprieve** ● v. 1 remit or postpone execution of. 2 give respite to. ● n. reprieving, being reprieved.

**reprimand** ● n. official rebuke. ● v. rebuke officially.

**reprint** ● v. print again. ● n. reprinting of book etc.; quantity reprinted.

**reprisal** n. act of retaliation.

**reproach** ● v. express disapproval to (person) for fault. ● n. 1 rebuke, censure. 2 thing that brings discredit. □□ **reproachful** adj. **reproachfully** adv.

**reprobate** n. unprincipled or immoral person.

**reproduce** v. produce copy or representation of; produce further members of same species. □□ **reproducible** adj. **reproduction** n.

**reproductive** adj. of reproduction.

**reproof** n. blame; rebuke.

**reprove** v. give reproof to.

**Reps** n. (the Reps) Aust. colloq. = House of Representatives.

**reptile** n. cold-blooded scaly animal of class including snakes, lizards, etc. □□ **reptilian** adj.

**republic** n. nation in which supreme power is held by the people or their elected representatives.

**republican** ● adj. 1 of or characterising republic(s); advocating or supporting republican government. ● n. supporter or advocate of republican government. □□ **republicanism** n.

**repudiate** v. disown, disavow, deny; refuse to recognise or obey (authority) or discharge (obligation or debt). □□ **repudiation** n.

**repugnant** adj. distasteful; objectionable. □□ **repugnance** n.

**repulse** ● v. drive back; rebuff, reject. ● n. driving back; rejection, rebuff.

**repulsion** n. 1 aversion, disgust. 2 Physics tendency of bodies to repel each other.

**repulsive** adj. causing aversion or loathing. □□ **repulsively** adv.

**repurpose** v. adapt for use in a different purpose.

**reputable** *adj.* of good reputation; respectable.

**reputation** *n.* what is generally said or believed about character of person or thing.

**repute** *n.* reputation.

**reputed** *adj.* said or thought to be.

**request** ● *n.* asking for something, thing asked for; state of being sought after; demand. ● *v.* ask to be given, allowed, etc.; ask (person) to do something; ask that.

**requiem** *n.* special Mass for the repose of souls of the dead; music for this. **2** memorial.

**require** *v.* need; depend on for success etc. **2** lay down as imperative; command, instruct; demand, insist on.

**requirement** *n.* a need.

**requisite** ● *adj.* required; necessary. ● *n.* thing needed.

**requisition** ● *n.* official order laying claim to use of property or materials; formal written demand. ● *v.* demand use or supply of.

**requite** *v.* make return for (a service etc.)

**resale** *n.* a sale to another person of something one has bought.

**rescind** *v.* abrogate, revoke, cancel. □□ **rescission** *n.*

**rescue** ● *v.* save or set free from danger or harm. ● *n.* rescuing, being rescued. □□ **rescuer** *n.*

**research** ● *n.* systematic investigation of materials, sources, etc. to establish facts. ● *v.* do research into or for. □□ **researcher** *n.*

**resemble** *v.* be like. □□ **resemblance** *n.*

**resent** *v.* feel indignation at; be aggrieved by. □□ **resentful** *adj.* resentfully *adv.* **resentment** *n.*

**reservation** *n.* **1** reserving, being reserved; thing reserved, e.g. room in hotel. **2** doubt. **3** land set aside for special use.

**reserve** ● *v.* put aside or keep back for later occasion or special use; order to be retained or allocated for person at particular time; retain.
● *n.* **1** something reserved, extra stock available. **2** (also **reserves**) forces outside the regular armed services; extra player chosen as possible substitute in team; (**reserves**) reserve-grade team. **3** land set aside for special use. **4** lowest acceptable price for item to be auctioned. **5** tendency to avoid showing feelings or friendliness. □ **reserve grade** *Aust.* (in sport) second grade.

**reserved** *adj.* reticent; slow to reveal emotions or opinions; uncommunicative.

**reservoir** *n.* large natural or artificial lake as source of water supply; receptacle for fluid.

**reshuffle** ● *v.* interchange; reorganise. ● *n.* reshuffling.

**reside** *v.* dwell permanently.

**residence** *n.* residing; place where person lives. □ **in residence** living in specified place to perform one's work.

**resident** ● *n.* **1** permanent inhabitant. **2** guest staying at hotel.
● *adj.* residing, in residence.

**residential** *adj.* designed for living in; lived in; providing accommodation.

**residue** *n.* what is left over. □□ **residual** *adj.*

**resign** *v.* **1** give up job, position, etc.; relinquish, surrender. **2** (**resign oneself to**) accept (situation etc.) reluctantly. □□ **resignation** *n.*

**resilient** *adj.* resuming original form after compression etc.; readily recovering from shock etc.; buoyant. □□ **resilience** *n.*

**resin** *n.* sticky substance from plants and certain trees; similar substance made synthetically, used in plastics. □□ **resinous** *adj.*

**resist** v. **1** withstand action or effect of. **2** abstain from (pleasure etc.) **3** strive against; oppose; offer opposition.□□ **resistance** n. **resistant** adj.

**resistible** adj. able to be resisted.

**resistor** n. device having resistance to passage of electric current.

**reskill** v. teach or equip with new skills.

**resolute** adj. determined, decided; purposeful.□□ **resolutely** adv.

**resolution** n. **1** resolute character or temper. **2** thing resolved; intention. **3** formal expression of opinion of public meeting. **4** solving of problem etc.; resolving, being resolved. **5** smallest interval measurable by (esp. optical) instrument; amount of graphic material able to be shown on computer display; degree of detail visible in photographic etc. image.

**resolve** ● v. **1** make up one's mind, decide firmly; solve; settle; pass resolution by vote; (cause to) separate into constituent parts. **2** analyse. **3** Mus. convert or be converted into concord. ● n. determination.

**resonant** adj. echoing, resounding; continuing to sound; causing reinforcement or prolongation of sound, esp. by vibration. □□ **resonance** n.

**resonate** v. produce or show resonance; resound; be able to evoke images and memories. □□ **resonator** n.

**resort** n. **1** popular holiday place. **2** recourse.□ **resort to** to turn to for help; adopt as a measure.

**resound** v. **1** ring or echo; fill place with sound. **2** be much talked of, produce sensation.

**resource** n. **1** something to which one can turn for help. **2** ingenuity. **3** (**resources**) available assets.

**resourceful** adj. clever at finding ways of doing things.□□ **resourcefully** adv. **resourcefulness** n.

**respect** ● n. **1** admiration or esteem; politeness arising from this; consideration. **2** aspect of situation etc. ● v. feel or show respect for. □□ **respectful** adj. **respectfully** adv.

**respectable** adj. **1** of acceptable social standing; decent in appearance or behaviour. **2** reasonably good in condition, appearance, size, etc. □□ **respectability** n. **respectably** adv.

**respective** adj. of or relating to each of several individually.

**respectively** adv. for each separately or in turn, and in the order mentioned.

**respiration** n. **1** breathing. **2** plant's absorption of oxygen and emission of carbon dioxide.

**respirator** n. apparatus worn over mouth and nose to filter inhaled air; apparatus for maintaining artificial respiration.

**respiratory** adj. of respiration.

**respire** v. breathe.

**respite** n. interval of rest or relief; delay permitted before discharge of obligation or suffering of penalty.

**resplendent** adj. brilliant, dazzlingly or gloriously bright. □□ **resplendence** n.

**respond** v. answer, reply; react.

**respondent** ● n. defendant, esp. in appeal case. ● adj. in position of defendant.

**response** n. **1** answer, reply. **2** action, feeling, etc. caused by stimulus etc.

**responsibility** n. being responsible; person or thing for which one is responsible.

**responsible** adj. **1** being the cause (of); liable to be called to account; morally accountable for actions. **2** of good credit and repute; trustworthy.

3 involving responsibility.
□□ **responsibly** adv.

**responsive** ● adj. 1 responding readily (to some influence). 2 sympathetic. 3 answering, by way of answer.
□□ **responsiveness** n.

**rest** ● v. 1 be still; (cause or allow to) cease from motion or tiring activity. 2 (of a matter) be left without further discussion. 3 place or be placed for support. 4 rely. 5 remain in a specified state. ● n. 1 (period of) inactivity or sleep. 2 prop or support for steadying something.□ **the rest** remaining parts; the others.

**restaurant** n. public premises where meals can be bought and eaten.

**restaurateur** n. restaurant keeper.

**restful** adj. quiet, soothing.

**restitution** n. 1 restoring of property etc. to its owner. 2 reparation.

**restive** adj. restless; unmanageable.
□□ **restiveness** n.

**restless** adj. 1 without rest. 2 uneasy, agitated, fidgeting.□□ **restlessly** adv. **restlessness** n.

**restorative** ● adj. tending to restore health or strength. ● n. restorative food, medicine, etc.

**restore** v. 1 bring back to former condition, place, state, or use. 2 give back. 3 reinstate.□□ **restorer** n.

**restrain** v. check or hold in; keep under control; repress; confine.

**restraint** n. restraining, being restrained; restraining agency or influence; moderation, self-control.

**restrict** v. 1 confine, limit. 2 withhold from general disclosure.
□□ **restriction** n. **restrictive** adj.

**result** ● n. 1 product of an activity, operation, or calculation. 2 score, marks, or name of winner in contest. ● v. occur or have as result.

**resultant** adj. occurring as result.

**resume** v. begin again; recommence; take again, return to using.
□□ **resumption** n. **resumptive** adj.

**resumé** n. (also **resume**) 1 summary. 2 curriculum vitae.

**resurface** v. 1 put new surface on. 2 return to surface.

**resurgent** adj. rising or arising again.
□□ **resurgence** n.

**resurrect** v. bring back to life or into use.

**resurrection** n. 1 rising from the dead. 2 colloq. revival from disuse or decay etc.

**resuscitate** v. revive from unconsciousness or apparent death; revive, restore.□□ **resuscitation** n.

**retail** ● n. selling of goods to the public in relatively small quantities, and usu. not for resale. ● adj. & adv. by retail; at retail price. ● v. 1 sell or be sold by retail. 2 recount; relate details of.□□ **retailer** n.

**retain** v. 1 keep possession of, continue to have, use, etc. 2 keep in mind. 3 keep in place. 4 hold fixed. 5 secure services of (esp. barrister) with preliminary fee.

**retainer** n. 1 fee for securing person's services. 2 faithful servant. 3 person or thing that retains.

**retaliate** v. repay in kind; attack in return.□□ **retaliation** n. **retaliatory** adj.

**retard** v. make slow or late; delay progress or accomplishment of.
□□ **retardation** n.

**retarded** adj. less advanced in mental or physical development.

**retch** v. strain one's throat as if vomiting.

**retention** n. retaining, being retained.

**retentive** adj. able to retain things.

**rethink** ● v. (rethought, rethinking) consider again, esp. with view to making changes. ● n. reassessment; rethinking.

**reticence** n. avoidance of saying all one knows or feels; taciturnity.
□□ **reticent** adj.

**reticulate** ● v. divide or be divided in fact or appearance into network; supply (water etc.) through network of pipes. ● adj. reticulated.
□□ **reticulation** n.

**retina** n. (pl. **retinas** or **retinae**) light-sensitive layer at back of eyeball.

**retinue** n. group of people attending important person.

**retire** v. 1 leave office or employment, esp. because of age; cause (employee) to retire. 2 withdraw, retreat, seek seclusion or shelter; go to bed. 3 Cricket (of batter) suspend one's innings.□□ **retirement** n.

**retiring** adj. shy; fond of seclusion.

**retort** ● n. 1 incisive, witty, or angry reply. 2 vessel for carrying out chemical process on large scale, e.g. heating coal to generate gas. 3 hist. long-necked glass container used in distilling. ● v. 1 say by way of retort. 2 repay in kind.

**retouch** v. improve (esp. photograph) by minor alterations.

**retrace** v. 1 go back over (one's steps etc.) 2 trace back to source or beginning.

**retract** v. withdraw (statement etc.); draw or be drawn back or in.
□□ **retractable** adj. **retraction** n.

**retractile** adj. able to be retracted.

**retreat** ● v. go back, retire; recede.
● n. 1 act or instance of retreating; military signal for this. 2 place of seclusion or shelter.

**retrench** v. 1 Aust. sack employee(s) to reduce costs. 2 cut down expenses; economise.□□ **retrenchment** n.

**retrial** n. retrying of a case.

**retribution** n. 1 recompense, usu. for evil. 2 vengeance.
□□ **retributive** adj.

**retrieve** v. 1 regain possession of. 2 find again. 3 extract (information) from computer. 4 rescue. 5 restore to good state. 6 repair, set right.

**retriever** n. dog of breed used for retrieving game.

**retro** colloq. ● adj. imitating styles in dress, music, etc., from recent past. ● n. retro fashion or style.

**retroactive** adj. having retrospective effect.

**retrograde** ● adj. directed backwards; reverting, esp. to inferior state. ● v. move backwards; decline, revert.

**retrogress** v. 1 move backwards. 2 deteriorate.□□ **retrogression** n. **retrogressive** adj.

**retrospect** n. survey of past time or events.

**retrospective** ● adj. looking back on or dealing with past; (of law etc.) applying to past as well as future. ● n. exhibition etc. showing artist's lifetime development.
□□ **retrospectively** adv.

**retroussé** adj. (of the nose) turned up at the tip.

**retroverted** adj. inclining backwards.
□□ **retroversion** n.

**retrovirus** n. any of group of RNA viruses which transfer genetic material into DNA of host cells.

**retry** v. try (defendant, law case) again.

**retsina** n. Greek resin-flavoured wine.

**return** ● v. come or go back; bring, give, put, or send back. ● n. 1 returning. 2 (in full **return ticket**) ticket for journey to place and back again. 3 profit. 4 (in full **return match**) second game between same opponents. 5 formal report submitted by order.□□ **returnable** adj.

**reunion** n. gathering of people who were formerly associated.

**reunite** v. (cause to) come together again.

**reusable** adj. able to be used again.

**rev** colloq. ● n. a revolution of an engine. ● v. (revved) cause (engine) to run quickly; (of engine) revolve.

**Rev.** *abbr.* (also **Revd**) Reverend.

**revalue** *v.* give different, esp. higher, value to.□□ **revaluation** *n.*

**revamp** *v.* renovate, revise, patch up. ● *n.* revamping.

**reveal** *v.* 1 display, show; allow to appear. 2 (often as **revealing** *adj.*) disclose, divulge.

**reveille** *n.* military waking signal.

**revel** ● *v.* make merry; be riotously festive; take keen delight (in). ● *n.* revelling.□□ **reveller** *n.* **revelry** *n.*

**revelation** *n.* revealing; surprising thing revealed.

**revenge** ● *n.* injury inflicted in return for what one has suffered; opportunity to defeat victorious opponent. ● *v.* avenge.

**revenue** *n.* income, esp. nation's annual income from which public expenses are met.

**reverberate** *v.* (of sound, light, heat, etc.) be returned or reflected repeatedly; return (sound etc.) thus; (of event) produce continuing effect.□□ **reverberation** *n.*

**revere** *v.* regard with deep and affectionate or religious respect.

**reverence** *n.* revering, being revered; deep respect. ● *v.* treat with reverence.

**reverend** *adj.* (esp. as title of member of clergy) deserving reverence.

**reverent** ● *n.* (Reverend) member of clergy. ● *adj.* deserving reverence.

**reverie** *n.* fit of musing, daydream.

**revers** *n.* (*pl.* **revers**) (material of) turned-back front edge of garment.

**reverse** ● *v.* turn other way round, upside down, or inside out; move backwards or in opposite direction; convert to its opposite; undo, cancel. ● *adj.* opposite in character or order; upside down. ● *n.* 1 reverse side or effect. 2 piece of misfortune.□□ **reversely** *adv.* **reversible** *adj.*

**revert** *v.* return to (former condition, practice, opinion, etc.); (of property etc.) return or pass to another holder.□□ **reversion** *n.*

**revhead** *n. Aust. colloq.* person passionately interested in cars.

**review** ● *n.* 1 general survey of events or subject; revision or reconsideration; published criticism of book, play, etc. 2 ceremonial inspection of troops etc. ● *v.* make or write review of.□□ **reviewer** *n.*

**revile** *v.* abuse verbally.

**revise** *v.* 1 examine and improve or amend. 2 reconsider and alter (opinion etc.); go over (work etc.) again, esp. for examination.□□ **revisory** *adj.* **revision** *n.*

**revivalist** *n.* person who seeks to promote religious fervour.□□ **revivalism** *n.*

**revive** *v.* come or bring back to consciousness, life, vigour, use, or notice.□□ **revival** *n.*

**revivify** *v.* restore to life, strength, or activity.□□ **revivification** *n.*

**revoke** *v.* 1 rescind, withdraw, or cancel. 2 *Cards* fail to follow suit though able to.□□ **revocable** *adj.* **revocation** *n.*

**revolt** ● *v.* 1 rise in rebellion against authority. 2 cause strong disgust in; nauseate. ● *n.* insurrection; rebellious mood.

**revolting** *adj.* 1 disgusting, horrible. 2 in revolt.□□ **revoltingly** *adv.*

**revolution** *n.* 1 forcible overthrow of government or social order; fundamental change. 2 revolving; single completion of orbit or rotation.

**revolutionary** ● *adj.* involving great change; of political revolution. ● *n.* instigator or supporter of political revolution.

**revolutionise** *v.* (also **-ize**) change fundamentally.

**revolve** *v.* turn around; rotate; move in orbit.

**revolver** n. pistol with revolving chambers enabling several shots to be fired without reloading.

**revue** n. theatrical entertainment of usu. comic sketches and songs.

**revulsion** n. abhorrence; sudden violent change of feeling.

**reward** ● n. recompense for service or merit; sum offered for detection of criminal, return of lost property, etc. ● v. give or serve as reward to. □□ **rewarding** adj.

**rewire** v. provide with new electrical wiring.

**Rex** n. reigning king.

**Rh** abbr. rhesus.□ **Rh-negative** not having rhesus factor. **Rh-positive** having rhesus factor.

**rhapsodise** v. (also **-ize**) speak or write rhapsodies.

**rhapsody** n. **1** enthusiastic extravagant speech or composition. **2** melodic musical piece, often based on folk culture. □□ **rhapsodic** adj.

**rhenium** n. rare metallic element (symbol **Re**).

**rheostat** n. instrument used to control electric current by varying resistance.

**rhesus** n. small monkey common in northern India. □ **rhesus factor** substance usu. present in human blood (see also **Rh**).

**rhetoric** n. art of persuasive speaking or writing; language intended to impress, esp. seen as inflated and meaningless.

**rhetorical** adj. expressed artificially or extravagantly; of the nature of rhetoric. □ **rhetorical question** one used for dramatic effect, not seeking answer. □□ **rhetorically** adv.

**rheumatism** n. disease marked by inflammation and pain in joints, muscles, or fibrous tissue. □□ **rheumatic** adj. **rheumaticky** adj.

**rheumatoid** adj. having the character of rheumatism.

**rhinestone** n. imitation diamond.

**rhino** n. (pl. **rhino** or **rhinos**) colloq. rhinoceros.

**rhinoceros** n. (pl. **rhinoceros** or **rhinoceroses**) large thick-skinned mammal with usu. one horn on nose.

**rhizome** n. underground rootlike stem bearing both roots and shoots.

**rhodium** n. **1** metallic element (symbol **Rh**). **2** used in alloys to increase hardness.

**rhododendron** n. evergreen shrub with large clusters of flowers.

**rhomboid** ● adj. like a rhombus. ● n. quadrilateral of which only opposite sides and angles are equal.

**rhombus** n. quadrilateral all of whose sides have same length.

**rhubarb** n. **1** (stalks of) plant with long fleshy leaf stalks cooked and eaten as dessert. **2** colloq. indistinct conversation or noise, from repeated use of word 'rhubarb' by stage crowd.

**rhyme** ● n. similarity of sound between words or syllables; word providing rhyme to another; poem with line-endings that rhyme. ● v. form a rhyme.

**rhythm** n. **1** periodical ascent and duration of notes in music; type of structure formed by this; measured flow of words in verse or prose; *Physiol.* pattern of successive strong and weak movements. **2** recurring sequence of events. □ **rhythm method** contraception by avoiding sexual intercourse near time of ovulation. □□ **rhythmic** adj. **rhythmical** adj. **rhythmically** adv.

**rib** ● n. **1** each of the curved bones joined to spine in pairs and protecting organs of chest; structural part resembling this. **2** combination of plain and purl stitches producing ribbed design. ● v. (**ribbed**) **1** provide or mark (as) with ribs. **2** colloq. tease. □□ **ribbed** adj. **ribbing** n.

**ribald** *adj.* irreverent, coarsely humorous. □□ **ribaldry** *n.*

**riband** *n.* ribbon.

**ribbon** *n.* narrow band of silky material; strip resembling this.

**riboflavin** *n.* (also **riboflavine**) vitamin of B complex, found in liver, milk, and eggs.

**ribonucleic acid** *n.* substance controlling protein synthesis in cells.

**rice** *n.* cereal plant grown in wetlands or irrigated fields; its seeds used as food.

**rich** *adj.* **1** having much wealth. **2** abundant; containing a large proportion of something, e.g. fat or fuel. **3** (of soil) fertile. **4** (of colour, sound, or smell) pleasantly deep and strong. □□ **richness** *n.*

**riches** *n.pl.* wealth.

**richly** *adv.* in a rich way; fully, thoroughly.

**Richter scale** *n.* scale of 0–10 for representing strength of earthquake.

**rick** • *n.* **1** stack of hay etc. **2** slight sprain or strain. • *v.* slightly sprain or strain.

**rickets** *n.* bone disease caused by vitamin D deficiency.

**rickety** *adj.* shaky, insecure.

**rickshaw** *n.* (also **ricksha**) light two-wheeled hooded vehicle drawn by one or more people.

**ricochet** • *v.* (**ricocheted**) rebound from surface after striking it with glancing blow. • *n.* rebound of this kind.

**ricotta** *n.* soft Italian cheese.

**rid** *v.* (**rid**, **ridding**) make (person, place) free of.

**ridden** SEE RIDE.

**riddle** • *n.* **1** verbal puzzle or test, often with trick answer; puzzling fact, thing, or person. **2** a coarse sieve. • *v.* **1** speak in riddles. **2** pass through a coarse sieve; permeate thoroughly.

**ride** • *v.* (**rode, ridden, riding**) sit on and be carried by (horse or bicycle etc.); travel in vehicle; float on. • *n.* spell of riding; a journey in vehicle; roller-coaster or similar fairground amusement.

**rider** *n.* **1** person riding. **2** additional remark following statement, verdict, etc.

**ridge** *n.* line of junction of two surfaces sloping upwards towards each other; long narrow hilltop; mountain range; any narrow elevation across surface. □□ **ridged** *adj.*

**ridgy-didge** *adj.* Aust. colloq. all right, genuine.

**ridicule** *n.* derision, mockery. • *v.* make fun of; mock; laugh at.

**ridiculous** *adj.* **1** deserving to be laughed at. **2** unreasonable. □□ **ridiculously** *adv.*

**riding** *n.* Aust. electoral division of shire.

**riesling** *n.* kind of dry white wine.

**rife** *adj.* widespread. □ **rife in** abounding in.

**riff** • *n.* **1** short repeated phrase in jazz etc. **2** monologue or spoken improvisation. • *v.* play or perform riff.

**riffle** • *v.* leaf quickly through (pages); shuffle (cards). • *n.* riffling.

**riff-raff** *n.* rabble; disreputable people.

**rifle** • *n.* gun with long grooved barrel. • *v.* **1** search and rob. **2** make spiral grooves in (gun etc.) to make projectile spin.

**rift** *n.* crack, split; cleft; disagreement, dispute. □ **rift valley** steep-sided valley caused by subsidence.

**rig** • *v.* (**rigged**) **1** provide (ship) with rigging etc.; fit with clothes or equipment. **2** set up hastily or as makeshift. **3** manage or fix fraudulently. • *n.* **1** arrangement of ship's masts, sails, etc. **2** equipment for special purposes. **3** oil rig. **4** large truck, semitrailer. **5** colloq. style of dress, uniform. □□ **rigger** *n.*

**rigging** n. ship's spars, ropes, etc.

**right ●** adj. **1** morally good; in accordance with justice; proper; correct, true. **2** in good condition. **3** on or towards east side of person or thing facing north. **4** of the political Right. **5** (of side of fabric etc.) meant to show. **6** (as **are you right?** or **you right?**) (in shopping) are you being served?, may I help you? **●** n. **1** what is just; something one is entitled to. **2** right hand side or region; the right hand or foot. **3** (often **Right**) Polit. people supporting more conservative policies than others in their group. **●** v. **1** restore to correct or upright position. **2** set right. **●** adv. **1** on or towards right hand side. **2** directly. **□ in the right** having truth or justice on one's side. **right angle** angle of 90°. **right away** immediately. **right-hand man** indispensable or chief assistant. **right of way** right to proceed while another vehicle must wait; right to pass over another's land. **right-to-life** of or pertaining to movement opposing legal abortion. **□□ rightness** n.

**righteous** adj. doing what is morally right; making a show of this; morally justifiable.

**rightful** adj. just, proper, legal. **□□ rightfully** adv.

**rigid** adj. unbendable; inflexible, harsh. **□□ rigidity** n. **rigidly** adv.

**rigmarole** n. **1** complicated procedure. **2** rambling tale etc.

**rigor mortis** n. stiffening of body after death.

**rigour** n. severity, strictness; harshness of weather or conditions. **□□ rigorous** adj.

**rile** v. colloq. anger, irritate.

**rill** n. small stream.

**rim** n. edge or border, esp. of something circular; outer ring of wheel, holding the tyre; part of

spectacle frames around lens. **□□ rimless** adj. **rimmed** adj.

**rime** n. frost.

**rind** n. tough outer layer or covering of fruit and vegetables, cheese, bacon, etc.

**ring¹ ●** n. **1** outline of circle; circular metal band usu. worn on finger. **2** enclosure for sporting events etc. **3** group of people acting together dishonestly. **●** v. **1** put ring on; encircle. **2** Aust. ringbark.

**ring² ●** v. (**rang**, **rung**, **ringing**) **1** give out loud clear resonant sound; cause (bell) to do this; signal by ringing; be filled with sound. **2** call by telephone. **●** n. **1** act or sound of ringing. **2** specified tone or feeling conveyed by words etc. **3** colloq. telephone call. **□ ring off** end telephone call. **ring the changes** vary things. **ring up** make telephone call to.

**ringbark** v. kill (tree) by cutting ring of bark from around trunk.

**ringer** n. Aust. colloq. **1** fastest shearer in shed. **2** stockman or station hand. **3** person who excels (at an activity etc.)

**ring-in** n. Aust. **1** fraudulent substitution, esp. of one horse for another in race, horse etc. so substituted. **2** person or thing that is not of kind with others in group or set.

**ringleader** n. person who leads others in wrongdoing.

**ringlet** n. curly lock of esp. long hair.

**ringside** n. area beside boxing ring. **□ ringside seat** position from which one has clear view of scene of action.

**ringtone** n. musical tone or sound mobile phone makes when it rings.

**ringworm** n. fungal infection producing round scaly patches on skin.

**rink** n. area of ice for skating, curling etc.; enclosed area for roller-skating; building containing either of these;

strip of bowling green; team in bowls etc.

**rinse** ● v. wash or treat with clean water etc.; wash lightly; remove by rinsing. ● n. 1 rinsing. 2 temporary hair tint.

**riot** ● n. 1 disturbance of peace by crowd; loud revelry. 2 lavish display. 3 colloq. very amusing thing or person. ● v. make or engage in riot. □□ **rioter** n.

**riotous** adj. disorderly, unruly, boisterous. □□ **riotously** adv.

**RIP** abbr. may he, she, or they rest in peace (requiesca(n)t in pace).

**rip** ● v. (**ripped**) 1 tear or cut quickly or forcibly away or apart; make (hole etc.) thus; make long tear or cut in; come violently apart, split. 2 rush along. 3 Computing copy (sound etc.) to computer. ● n. 1 long tear or cut; act of ripping. 2 stretch of rough water caused by meeting currents. □ **rip off** colloq. a swindle.

**ripcord** n. cord for releasing parachute from its pack.

**ripe** adj. ready to be reaped, picked, or eaten; mature; fit, ready. □□ **ripeness** n.

**ripen** v. make or become ripe.

**riposte** ● n. 1 quick retort. 2 quick return thrust in fencing. ● v. deliver riposte.

**ripped** adj. 1 torn. 2 colloq. intoxicated by drug. 3 (foll. by off) robbed, exploited, stolen. 4 colloq. having prominent muscles.

**ripper** ● colloq. n. person or thing exciting admiration, enthusiasm, etc. ● adj. excellent, admirable.

**ripple** ● n. 1 ruffling of water's surface; small wave(s). 2 gentle lively sound, e.g. of laughter or applause. 3 slight variation in strength of current etc. ● v. form ripples. □□ **ripply** adj.

**rise** ● v. (**rose, risen, rising**) 1 come, go, or extend upwards; get up from

lying or sitting, get out of bed. 2 become higher; increase. 3 rebel. 4 have its origin or source. ● n. 1 an act or amount of rising, an increase. 2 upward slope. 3 an increase in salary. □ **give rise to** cause.

**risible** adj. laughable, ludicrous.

**risk** ● n. chance of danger, loss, injury, etc.; person or thing causing risk. ● v. expose to risk; venture on, take chance of.

**risky** adj. (**riskier**) full of risk. □□ **riskily** adv. **riskiness** n.

**risotto** n. Italian savoury rice dish.

**risqué** adj. (of story etc.) slightly indecent.

**rissole** n. fried cake of minced meat, spices, breadcrumbs, etc.

**rite** n. religious or solemn ceremony or observance.

**ritual** ● n. prescribed order, esp. of religious ceremony; solemn or colourful pageantry etc.; procedure regularly followed. ● adj. of or done as ritual or rite. □□ **ritually** adv.

**rival** ● n. person or thing that competes with another or equals another in quality. ● v. (**rivalled**) be rival of or comparable to. □□ **rivalry** n.

**river** n. large natural stream of water; copious flow.

**rivet** ● n. nail or bolt for joining metal plates etc. ● v. 1 join or fasten with rivets. 2 fix, make immovable. 3 direct intently. 4 engross.

**rivulet** n. small stream.

**RNA** abbr. ribonucleic acid.

**roach** n. (pl. **roach**) 1 small freshwater fish of carp family. 2 colloq. cockroach.

**road** n. 1 prepared track along which people and vehicles may travel; way of reaching something. 2 (**roads**) water near shore in which ships can ride at anchor. □ **road hog** reckless or inconsiderate driver. **road metal** broken stone for making foundation of road or railway. **road rage** hostility or violence directed at driver of vehicle by another driver etc.

**roadblock** n. barrier or barricade on a road; hindrance or obstruction.

**roadie** n. colloq. assistant of touring band etc., responsible for equipment.

**roadkill** n. animal killed on the road by vehicle.

**roadshow** n. **1** (performance given by) touring company of pop musician etc. **2** television program etc. done on location.

**roadster** n. open car without rear seats.

**roadway** n. road, esp. as distinct from footpath beside it.

**roadworks** n.pl. construction or repair of roads.

**roadworthy** adj. (of vehicle) fit to be used on road. □□ **roadworthiness** n.

**roam** v. wander. □□ **roamer** n.

**roaming** n. use or ability to use mobile phone etc. on different network, overseas, etc.

**roan** ● adj. (esp. of horse) having coat thickly interspersed with hairs of another colour. ● n. roan animal.

**roar** ● n. loud deep hoarse sound as of lion; loud laugh. ● v. utter loudly, or make roar, roaring laugh.

**roaring** adj. **1** noisy, giving a roar, very loud. **2** colloq. great (a roaring success).

**roast** ● v. **1** cook or be cooked by exposure to open heat or in oven. **2** criticise severely. ● adj. roasted. ● n. roast joint of meat.

**roasting** ● adj. very hot. ● n. severe criticism or denunciation.

**rob** v. (robbed) steal from. □□ **robber** n. **robbery** n.

**robe** ● n. long loose esp. ceremonial garment. ● v. dress in robe.

**robin** n. red-breasted bird; any of many small, active, Australian etc. birds, some having brightly coloured breast.

**robocall** n. automated telephone call that delivers recorded message.

**robot** n. machine able to carry out a complex series of actions automatically; machine-like person. □□ **robotic** adj.

**robotics** n. science or study of robot design and operation.

**robust** adj. strong, esp. in health and physique; (of exercise etc.) vigorous, straightforward; (of statement etc.) bold. □□ **robustly** adv. **robustness** n.

**rock**[1] n. **1** solid part of earth's crust; material or projecting mass of this. **2** large detached stone; stone of any size. **3** colloq. precious stone, esp. diamond. □ **on the rocks 1** (of drink) served with ice cubes. **2** colloq. in difficulties. **rock plant** alpine plant that grows among rocks. **rock wallaby** small wallaby inhabiting rocky ranges of mainland Australia.

**rock**[2] ● v. move gently to and fro; set, keep, or be in such motion; (cause to) sway; oscillate, shake, reel. ● n. **1** rocking movement. **2** modern popular music with heavy beat. □ **rock and roll** rock music often with elements of blues.

**rocker** n. **1** device for rocking, esp. curved bar etc. on which something rocks; rocking chair. **2** rock music devotee.

**rockery** n. pile of rough stones with soil between them for growing rock plants on.

**rocket** ● n. **1** firework or signal propelled to great height after ignition; engine operating on same principle. **2** rocket propelled missile, spacecraft, etc. **3** plant used as salad vegetable. ● v. (rocketed) move rapidly upwards or away.

**rocketry** n. science or practice of rocket propulsion.

**rockmelon** n. edible melon with fragrant orange flesh; cantaloupe.

**rocky** adj. (**rockier**) **1** of, like, or full of rock(s). **2** unsteady, tottering.

**rococo** ● adj. of ornate style of art, music, and literature in 18th-c. Europe. ● n. this style.

**rod** n. slender straight round stick or bar; fishing rod.

**rode** see RIDE.

**rodent** n. mammal with strong incisors and no canine teeth, e.g. rat, mouse, etc.

**rodeo** n. (pl. **rodeos**) competition or exhibition of cowboy-type skills.

**roe**[1] n. mass of eggs in female fish.

**roe**[2] n. (pl. **roe** or **roes**) small kind of deer.

**roentgen** n. unit of ionising radiation.

**roentgenium** n. radioactive element (symbol **Rg**).

**rogaining** n. Aust. sport similar to orienteering, held over greater time and distance. □□ **rogaine** n. **rogainer** n.

**roger** int. (in signalling) message received and understood.

**rogue** n. **1** dishonest or unprincipled person; mischievous person. **2** wild fierce animal driven or living apart from herd. **3** inferior or defective specimen.

**roguish** adj. mischievous, playful.

**role** n. actor's part; person's or thing's function. □ **role playing** exercise in which participants act the part of another character; participation in role-playing game. **role-playing game** game in which players take on roles of imaginary characters who take part in adventures etc.

**roll** ● v. **1** move (on surface) on wheels or by turning over and over. **2** turn on axis or over and over. **3** form into cylindrical or spherical shape. **4** flatten with roller. **5** flatten with roller. **6** rock from side to side. **7** undulate. **8** move or pass steadily. **9** colloq. soundly defeat, rob.

● n. **1** cylinder of flexible material turned over and upon itself. **2** small loaf of bread for one person. **3** undulation. **4** official list or register. **5** long deep sound. □ **on a roll** colloq. be experiencing bout of success or progress; engaged in period of intense activity. **roll-call** calling of list of names to establish who is present.

**roller** n. **1** revolving cylinder for smoothing, flattening, crushing, spreading, etc.; small cylinder on which hair is rolled for setting; long swelling wave. □ **roller derby** contact sport in which two teams compete on roller skates. **roller skate** boot or frame fitted with small wheels, for gliding across hard surface.

**rollerblade** n. propr. boot with four wheels fitted underneath in line, designed for skating on hard surfaces.

**rollicking** adj. jovial, exuberant.

**rollmop** n. rolled uncooked pickled herring fillet.

**ROM** abbr. Computing read only memory.

**roman** adj. **1** (of type) plain and upright, used in ordinary print. **2** (of alphabet etc.) based on ancient Roman system with letters A–Z. □ **Roman Catholic** (member) of church that acknowledges Pope as its head. □ **Roman numerals** letters representing numbers (I = 1, V = 5, etc.)

**romance** ● n. **1** idealised, poetic, or unworldly atmosphere or tendency. **2** love affair. **3** (work of) literature concerning romantic love. **4** exaggeration. **5** picturesque falsehood. ● adj. (**Romance**) (of a language) descended from Latin. ● v. **1** exaggerate, fantasise. **2** woo.

**Romanesque** adj. & n. (of or in) style of European architecture c. 900–1200, with massive vaulting and round arches.

**romantic** ● *adj.* **1** of, characterised by, or suggestive of romance. **2** imaginative, visionary. **3** (of literature or music etc.) concerned more with emotion than with form. **4** (also **Romantic**) of the 18th–19th-c. romantic movement or style in European arts. ● *n.* romantic person. □□ **romantically** *adv.*

**romanticise** *v.* (also **-ize**) make romantic; indulge in romance.

**romanticism** *n.* adherence to romantic style in literature, art, etc.

**romeo** *n.* passionate male lover or seducer.

**romp** *v.* **1** play roughly and energetically. **2** *colloq.* proceed without effort.

**rondeau** *n.* (*pl.* **rondeaux**) short poem with two rhymes only and opening words used as refrains.

**rondo** *n.* (*pl.* **rondos**) musical form with recurring leading theme.

**roo** (also **'roo**) ● *n.* kangaroo. ● *adj.* pertaining to kangaroo.

**rood screen** *n.* screen separating nave from chancel in church.

**roof** ● *n.* (*pl.* **roofs**) upper covering of building, covered vehicle, etc.; top interior surface of cave, oven, etc. ● *v.* cover with roof; be roof of. □ **roof rack** framework for carrying luggage etc. on roof of vehicle.

**rook**¹ ● *n.* **1** European black bird of crow family. **2** chess piece with battlement-shaped top. ● *v. colloq.* defraud.

**rookery** *n.* colony of rooks, penguins, or seals.

**rookie** *n. colloq.* recruit.

**room** *n.* enclosed part of building; space that is or could be occupied; scope to allow something. ● *v.* lodge, board, or share room (with). □ **room service** provision of food etc. in hotel bedroom.

**roomy** *adj.* (**roomier**) having much room, spacious. □□ **roominess** *n.*

**roost** ● *n.* bird's perch. ● *v.* (of bird) settle for rest or sleep.

**rooster** *n.* male domestic fowl.

**root** ● *n.* **1** part of plant below ground conveying nourishment from soil; embedded part of hair, tooth, etc. **2** a source, basis. **3** a number in relation to another that it produces when multiplied by itself a specified number of times. **4** (**roots**) emotional attachment to place. **5** *Aust. coarse colloq.* act of sexual intercourse; sexual partner. ● *v.* **1** (cause to) take root; cause to stand fixed and unmoving. **2** (of animal) turn up ground with snout or beak in search of food; rummage; extract. **3** *Aust. coarse colloq.* have sexual intercourse with; ruin; exhaust; frustrate. □ **root for** *colloq.* support, cheer on. **root out** drag or dig up by the roots; get rid of. **take root** send down roots; become established. □□ **rootless** *adj.*

**rope** ● *n.* strong thick cord. ● *v.* fasten or secure with rope; enclose with rope. □ **on the ropes** near to defeat or collapse.

**ropeable** *adj.* **1** capable of being roped. **2** *Aust. colloq.* angry, furious.

**rorqual** *n.* whale with dorsal fin.

**rort** *Aust. colloq.* ● *n.* a trick, a fraud; dishonest practice. ● *v.* defraud, manipulate. □□ **rorter** *n.*

**rosary** *n. RC Ch.* repeated sequence of prayers; string of beads for keeping count in this.

**rose**¹ ● *n.* **1** prickly shrub bearing fragrant flowers; this flower. **2** pinkish-red colour or complexion. ● *adj.* rose-coloured.

**rose**² *see* RISE.

**rosé** *n.* light pink wine.

**rosella** *n.* any of several brightly coloured Australian parrots, with white or blue cheek patches.

**rosemary** *n.* evergreen fragrant shrub used as herb.

**rosette** n. rose-shaped ornament made of ribbons etc.

**rosewood** n. dark fragrant wood used for making furniture.

**rosin** n. resin.

**Ross River virus** n. mosquito-borne virus causing non-fatal disease characterised by rash, and joint and muscle pain.

**roster** ● n. list or plan of turns of duty etc. ● v. place on roster.

**rostrum** n. (pl. rostra or rostrums) platform for public speaking etc.

**rosy** adj. (rosier) **1** pink, red. **2** optimistic, hopeful.

**rot** ● v. **1** (rotted) undergo decay by putrefaction; perish, waste away; cause to rot, make rotten. ● n. **1** decay. **2** colloq. nonsense.

**rota** n. list of duties to be done or people to do them in rotation.

**rotary** adj. acting by rotation. □ **rotary hoe** machine with rotating blades for breaking up uncultivated ground.

**rotate** v. **1** move around axis or centre, revolve. **2** arrange or take in rotation. □□ **rotatable** adj. **rotation** n.

**rote** n. □ **by rote** by memory without thought of meaning; by fixed procedure.

**rotisserie** n. revolving spit for roasting food.

**rotor** n. rotary part of machine; rotating aerofoil on helicopter.

**rotten** adj. **1** rotting or rotted. **2** fragile from age etc. **3** morally or politically corrupt. **4** colloq. disagreeable, worthless. **5** colloq. ill, very drunk. □□ **rottenness** n.

**rotund** adj. rounded, plump. □□ **rotundity** n.

**rotunda** n. circular building, esp. domed.

**rouble** n. (also **ruble**) chief monetary unit of Russia and some other former republics of the USSR.

**rouge** ● n. **1** red cosmetic used to colour cheeks. **2** powdered ferric oxide. ● v. colour with or apply rouge.

**rough** ● adj. **1** having uneven or irregular surface. **2** not gentle or careful, violent; (of weather) stormy. **3** not perfected or detailed; approximate. ● adv. in a rough way. ● n. **1** rough thing or state; rough ground. **2** rough person. ● v. make rough. □ **rough diamond** person of good nature but lacking polished manners. **rough it** do without comforts. **rough out** plan or sketch roughly. **rough trot** Aust. period of misfortune. **rough up** colloq. fight; brawl. □□ **roughly** adv. **roughness** n.

**roughage** n. fibrous material in food, stimulating intestinal action.

**roughie** n. Aust. colloq. **1** outsider with slight chance of winning. **2** unfair act. **3** a rough person.

**roughshod** adj. □ **ride roughshod over** treat inconsiderately or arrogantly.

**roughy** n. Aust. small reef-dwelling food fish.

**roulade** n. light sweet or savoury mixture baked in flat tin, spread with filling and rolled while hot.

**roulette** n. gambling game with ball dropped on revolving numbered wheel.

**round** ● adj. **1** curved, circular, spherical, or cylindrical. **2** complete. **3** (of a number) altered for convenience, e.g. to nearest multiple of ten. ● n. **1** round object; circular or recurring course or series. **2** song for several voices that start same tune at different times. **3** a shot from firearm; ammunition for this. **4** a drink etc. for each member of group. **5** one section of a competition. ● adv. & prep. = AROUND. ● v. **1** make or become round. **2** make into a round figure. **3** travel around. □ **in the round** with all sides visible.

**round off** complete. **round the clock** continuously through day and night. **round trip** circular tour; outward and return journey. **round up** gather into one place.

**roundabout** ● *n.* **1** road junction with traffic passing in one direction round central island. **2** revolving device in children's playground. **3** merry-go-round. ● *adj.* circuitous. ● *adv.* approximately.

**roundel** *n.* small disc.

**rounders** *n.* team game in which players hit ball and run through round of bases.

**roundly** *adv.* **1** emphatically; thoroughly; bluntly, severely. **2** in rounded shape.

**roundsman** *n. Aust.* journalist covering specific subject.

**roundworm** *n.* parasitic worm with a rounded body.

**rouse¹** *v.* wake; cause to become active or excited.

**rouse²** *v. Aust.* scold.

**rouseabout** ● *Aust. n.* labourer or odd jobber on farm, in shearing shed, etc. ● *v.* work as rouseabout.

**rousing** *adj.* vigorous, stirring.

**roust** *v. Aust.* = ROUSE². □□ **rousting** *n.*

**roustabout** *n.* rouseabout.

**rout** ● *n.* disorderly retreat of defeated troops; overthrow, defeat. ● *v.* **1** put to flight, defeat. **2** use router.

**route** *n.* course or way taken from one place to another. □ **route march** training march for troops.

**router** *n.* **1** type of plane with two handles used for cutting grooves etc. into wood. **2** device forwarding computer messages to correct part of network.

**routine** ● *n.* regular course or procedure, unvarying performance of certain acts; set sequence in dance, comedy act, etc. ● *adj.* performed as

routine; of customary or standard kind. □□ **routinely** *adv.*

**roux** *n.* mixture of fat and flour used in sauces etc.

**rove** *v.* wander.

**rover** *n.* **1** wanderer. **2** *AFL* one of three players making up ruck.

**row¹** *n.* line of people or things.

**row²** ● *v.* propel (boat) with oars; convey thus. ● *n.* spell of rowing. □□ **rower** *n.*

**row³** ● *n.* loud noise, commotion; quarrel, dispute; reprimand. ● *v.* make or engage in row.

**rowdy** ● *adj.* (**rowdier**) noisy and disorderly. ● *n.* rowdy person. □□ **rowdily** *adv.* **rowdiness** *n.*

**rowlock** *n.* device holding oar in place.

**royal** ● *adj.* **1** of, suited to, or worthy of king or queen; of the family or in the service of royalty. **2** splendid; on great scale. ● *n. colloq.* member of (esp. British) royal family. □ **royal blue** bright blue. □□ **royally** *adv.*

**royalist** *n.* supporter of monarchy.

**royalty** *n.* **1** being royal; royal people. **2** percentage of profit from book, public performance, patent, etc. paid to author etc.; payment made by producer of minerals etc. to owner of mine site.

**RPG** *abbr.* role-playing game.

**RPI** *abbr.* retail price index.

**rpm** *abbr.* revolutions per minute.

**RSI** *abbr.* repetitive strain injury.

**RSL** *abbr.* Returned and Services League of Australia.

**RSPCA** *abbr.* Royal Society for the Prevention of Cruelty to Animals.

**RSVP** *abbr.* please answer (French *répondez s'il vous plaît*).

**rub** ● *v.* (**rubbed**) press against surface and slide to and fro; clean, polish, chafe, or make dry, sore, or bare by rubbing. ● *n.* **1** act or process of rubbing. **2** difficulty.

□ **rub it in** emphasise or remind person constantly of unpleasant fact.

**rubber** n. 1 elastic substance made from latex of plants or synthetically; piece of this or other substance for erasing pencil marks. 2 colloq. condom. 3 series of games between same sides or people at whist, bridge, tennis, etc. □ **rubber-stamp** approve automatically without proper consideration. □□ **rubberise** v. (also **-ize**) **rubbery** adj.

**rubbish** ● n. waste or worthless material; nonsense. ● v. colloq. denigrate; disparage. □□ **rubbishy** adj.

**rubble** n. waste or rough fragments of stone, brick, etc.

**rubella** n. contagious viral disease resembling measles.

**rubidium** n. soft silvery metallic element (symbol **Rb**).

**rubric** n. 1 words put as heading or note of explanation; category. 2 statement of purpose or function.

**ruby** ● n. crimson or rose-coloured precious stone; deep red colour. ● adj. deep red. □ **ruby wedding** 40th wedding anniversary.

**ruche** n. fabric gathered as a trimming.

**ruck** ● n. 1 (**the ruck**) main group of competitors not likely to overtake leaders. 2 undistinguished crowd or people or things. 3 AFL group of three players without fixed positions who follow the play; a ruckman. 4 Rugby loose scrum. ● v. AFL play as follower.

**ruckman** n. AFL player without fixed position.

**rucksack** n. bag carried on back.

**ruckus** n. row, commotion.

**ructions** n.pl. colloq. unpleasant arguments or protests.

**rudder** n. flat device hinged to vessel's stern or rear of aeroplane for steering.

**ruddy** adj. (**ruddier**) 1 freshly or healthily red; reddish. 2 colloq. bloody, damnable.

**rude** adj. 1 impolite, offensive. 2 roughly made; primitive. 3 abrupt, sudden. 4 colloq. indecent, lewd. □□ **rudely** adv. **rudeness** n.

**rudiment** n. 1 rudimentary part. 2 (**rudiments**) elements or first principles of subject. □□ **rudimental** adj.

**rudimentary** adj. incompletely developed; basic, elementary.

**rue** ● n. evergreen European shrub with bitter strong-scented leaves. ● v. repent, regret.

**rueful** adj. genuinely or humorously sorrowful. □□ **ruefully** adv.

**ruff** n. 1 projecting starched frill worn around neck. 2 projecting or coloured ring of feathers or hair around bird's or animal's neck.

**ruffian** n. violent lawless person.

**ruffle** ● v. 1 disturb smoothness or tranquillity of; annoy. 2 gather (lace etc.) into ruffle. 3 (of bird) erect (feathers) in anger, display, etc. ● n. frill of lace etc.

**rufous** adj. reddish-brown.

**rug** n. floor mat; thick woollen coverlet or wrap.

**rugby** n. (in full **rugby football**) team game played with oval ball that may be kicked or carried.

**rugged** adj. 1 (esp. of ground) rough, uneven; (of features) furrowed, irregular. 2 harsh, severe. 3 robust, hardy. □□ **ruggedly** adv. **ruggedness** n.

**rugger** n. colloq. rugby.

**ruin** ● n. destruction; complete loss of one's fortune or prospects; broken remains; cause of ruin. ● v. cause ruin to; reduce to ruins. □□ **ruination** n.

**ruinous** adj. bringing ruin, disastrous; dilapidated.

**rule** ● n. 1 statement of what can or should be done; dominant custom;

governing, control. **2** straight measuring device, ruler. **3** (**Rules**) *colloq.* Australian Rules. **4** (usu. **Rules** or **Old Rule**) (in Aboriginal English) body of religious belief and social custom. ● *v.* **1** govern; keep under control; give authoritative decision. **2** draw (a line) using ruler. □ **as a rule** usually. **rule of law** restriction of arbitrary exercise of power by subordinating it to well-defined and established laws. **rule of thumb** rule for general guidance, based on experience. **rule out** exclude.

**ruler** *n.* **1** person exercising government or dominion. **2** straight strip of plastic etc. used to draw or measure.

**ruling** *n.* authoritative pronouncement.

**rum** ● *n.* spirit distilled from sugar cane or molasses. ● *adj. colloq.* odd, strange, queer.

**rumba** *n.* a ballroom dance.

**rumble** ● *v.* make continuous deep sound as of thunder; (esp. of vehicle) move with such sound. ● *n.* **1** rumbling sound. **2** *colloq.* fight; argument.

**rumbustious** *adj. colloq.* boisterous, uproarious.

**ruminant** ● *n.* animal that chews the cud. ● *adj.* **1** of ruminants. **2** meditative.

**ruminate** *v.* **1** meditate, ponder. **2** chew the cud. □□ **rumination** *n.* **ruminative** *adj.*

**rummage** ● *v.* search, esp. unsystematically. ● *n.* untidy search through a number of things.

**rummy** *n.* card game, played usu. with two packs.

**rumour** *n.* (also **rumor**) general talk, assertion, or hearsay of doubtful accuracy. □ **be rumoured that** be spread as rumour.

**rump** *n.* hind part of mammal or bird, esp. the buttocks.

**rumple** *v.* crease, ruffle.

**rumpus** *n. colloq.* row, uproar.

**run** ● *v.* (**ran**, **run**, **running**) **1** move with quick steps with always at least one foot off the ground; go smoothly or swiftly; compete in a race. **2** (of liquid etc.) flow, exude liquid. **3** function. **4** travel or convey from one point to another; extend. **5** be current or valid. **6** manage, organise; own and use (vehicle etc.) **7** seek election. **8** (of stockings etc.) ladder. **9** *Aust.* provide pasture for (sheep etc.); raise (livestock). ● *n.* **1** spell of running. **2** point scored in cricket or baseball. **3** ladder in fabric. **4** continuous stretch or sequence; (in Australia) uninterrupted session of shearing; a regular route. **5** enclosure where domestic animals can range. **6** *Aust.* tract of land used as pasture or for raising livestock. **7** permission to make unrestricted use of something. □ **in the long run** in the end; over a long period. **on the run** escaping; running away. **run across** happen to meet or find. **run away** flee; leave secretly. **run down** reduce the numbers of; disparage; knock down or over. **run into** collide with; happen to meet. **run-of-the-mill** ordinary. **run out** become used up. **run over** knock down or crush with a vehicle. **run through 1** rehearse briefly; peruse. **2** traverse. **3** consume. **run up** allow (a bill) to mount. **run-up** period preceding important event.

**rundown** ● *n.* detailed analysis. ● *adj.* (**run-down**) weak or exhausted.

**rune** *n.* letter of earliest Germanic alphabet. □□ **runic** *adj.*

**rung**[1] *n.* step of ladder. **2** strengthening crosspiece of chair etc.

**rung**[2] see RING[2].

**runner** *n.* **1** person who runs, esp. in race. **2** creeping plant stem that can take root. **3** rod, groove, etc. for thing to slide along or on. **4** messenger. **5** long narrow strip of cloth or ornamental cloth. **6** (in full **runner bean**) kind of climbing bean. **7** (**runners**) running shoes, sneakers.

**runny** adj. (**runnier**) semi-liquid, tending to flow or exude fluid.

**runt** n. undersized person or animal.

**runway** n. prepared surface on which aircraft may take off and land.

**rupee** n. chief monetary unit of India, Pakistan, Sri Lanka, Nepal, etc.

**rupiah** n. chief monetary unit of Indonesia.

**rupture** ● n. **1** breaking. **2** breach. **3** abdominal hernia. ● v. **1** burst; break. **2** affect with or suffer hernia.

**rural** adj. in, of, or suggesting the country; pastoral or agricultural.

**ruse** n. stratagem, trick.

**rush** ● v. go or convey with great speed; act hastily; force into hasty action; attack with a sudden assault. ● n. **1** rushing; instance of this; period of great activity; sudden flow or surge. **2** marsh plant with slender pithy stem. □ **rush hour** time each day when traffic is at its heaviest.

**rusk** n. slice of bread rebaked as light biscuit, esp. for infants.

**russet** ● adj. reddish-brown. ● n. russet colour.

**rust** ● n. **1** reddish corrosive coating formed on iron etc. by oxidation. **2** plant disease with rust-coloured spots. **3** reddish-brown. ● v. **1** affect or be affected with rust. **2** become impaired through disuse.

**rustic** ● adj. of or like country people or country life; unsophisticated; of rough workmanship; made of untrimmed branches or rough timber. ● n. country person. □□ **rusticity** n.

**rustle** ● v. **1** (cause to) make sound as of dry blown leaves. **2** steal (cattle or horses). ● n. rustling sound. □□ **rustler** n.

**rusty** adj. **1** rusted, affected by rust. **2** stiff with age or disuse. **3** (of knowledge etc.) impaired by neglect. **4** rust-coloured. **5** discoloured by age.

**rut**[1] ● n. **1** deep track made by passage of wheels. **2** fixed (esp. tedious) practice or routine. ● v. (**rutted**) esp. as **rutted** mark with ruts.

**rut**[2] ● n. periodic sexual excitement of male deer etc. ● v. (**rutted**) be affected with rut.

**ruthenium** n. rare metallic element (symbol **Ru**).

**rutherfordium** n. unstable element (symbol **Rf**).

**ruthless** adj. having no pity or compassion. □□ **ruthlessly** adv. **ruthlessness** n.

**rye** n. cereal plant; grain of this; whisky from this.

**ryegrass** n. forage or coarse lawn grass.

# Ss

**S** abbr. (also **S.**) **1** south; southern. **2** siemens.

**s** abbr. (also **s.**) second(s).

**SA** abbr. South Australia.

**sabbath** n. religious day of rest (Friday for Muslims, Saturday for Jews, Sunday for Christians).

**sabbatical** ● adj. (of leave) granted at intervals to university teacher for study or travel. ● n. period of sabbatical leave.

**sable** ● n. small dark-furred mammal of N. Europe and N. Asia; its skin or fur. ● adj. black.

**sabotage** ● n. deliberate destruction or damage, esp. for political purpose. ● v. commit sabotage on. □□ **saboteur** n.

**sabre** n. curved cavalry sword; light fencing sword.

**sac** n. membranous bag in animal or plant.

**saccharin** n. sugar substitute.

**saccharine** adj. sickly sentimental or sweet.

**sachet** n. small bag or sealed pack.

**sack** ● n. **1** large strong bag for storage or conveyance. **2** (**the sack**) colloq. dismissal. ● v. **1** colloq. dismiss from employment. **2** plunder and destroy (town etc.).

**sackcloth** n. coarse fabric for making sacks.

**sacking** n. sackcloth.

**sacral** adj. of sacrum.

**sacrament** n. symbolic religious ceremonies of Christianity; sacred thing. □□ **sacramental** adj.

**sacred** adj. venerated as connected with a god or religion; holy; safeguarded or required, esp. by tradition; inviolable; reverently dedicated. □ **sacred cow** colloq. idea

which its supporters will not allow to be criticised.

**sacrifice** ● n. voluntary relinquishing of something valued; thing so relinquished; loss entailed; slaughter of animal or person, or surrender of possession, as offering to deity; animal, person, or thing so offered. ● v. give up; devote to; offer or kill (as) sacrifice. □□ **sacrificial** adj.

**sacrilege** n. violation of what is sacred. □□ **sacrilegious** adj.

**sacristy** n. room in church for vestments, vessels, etc.

**sacrosanct** adj. most sacred; inviolable. □□ **sacrosanctity** n.

**sacrum** n. (pl. **sacra** or **sacrums**) triangular bone between hip bones.

**sad** adj. (**sadder**) showing or causing sorrow; regrettable. □□ **sadly** adv. **sadness** n.

**sadden** v. make sad.

**saddle** ● n. **1** seat of leather etc. strapped on horse etc.; bicycle etc. seat. **2** joint of meat consisting of the two loins. **3** ridge rising to summit at each end. ● v. put saddle on (horse etc.); burden with task etc.

**saddler** n. maker of or dealer in saddles etc. □□ **saddlery** n.

**sadism** n. enjoyment of cruelty to others; sexual perversion characterised by this. □□ **sadist** n. **sadistic** adj. **sadistically** adv.

**s.a.e.** abbr. stamped addressed envelope.

**safari** n. expedition, esp. in Africa, to observe or hunt animals.

**safe** ● adj. not subject to risk or danger; not harmed; providing security. ● n. strong lockable cabinet etc. for valuables. □ **safe conduct** immunity or protection from arrest or harm. **safe deposit** building containing safes and strongrooms for hire. **safe sex** sexual activity in which people take precautions to protect themselves against sexually transmitted diseases. □□ **safely** *adv.*

**safeguard** ● *n.* a means of protection. ● *v.* protect.

**safety** *n.* being safe; freedom from risk or danger. □ **safety net** welfare measures etc. that protect the disadvantaged. **safety pin** brooch-like pin with guard protecting point. **safety valve 1** valve that opens automatically to relieve excessive pressure in steam boiler etc. **2** harmless outlet for emotion.

**safflower** *n.* thistle-like European plant yielding red dye and edible oil.

**saffron** ● *n.* deep yellow colouring and flavouring from dried crocus stigmas; colour of this. ● *adj.* deep yellow.

**sag** ● *v.* (**sagged**) drop or curve down in the middle. ● *n.* state or amount of sagging. □□ **saggy** *adj.*

**saga** *n.* long story.

**sagacious** *adj.* showing insight or good judgement; wise. □□ **sagacity** *n.*

**sage** ● *n.* **1** culinary herb with dull greyish-green leaves. **2** old wise man. ● *adj.* wise. □□ **sagely** *adv.*

**Sagittarius** *n.* ninth sign of zodiac, the Archer. □□ **Sagittarian** *adj.* & *n.*

**sago** *n.* starch made from powdered pith of sago palm, used in puddings etc.

**said** see SAY.

**sail** ● *n.* piece of material extended on rigging to catch wind and propel vessel; ship's sails collectively; voyage or excursion in sailing boat; wind-catching apparatus of windmill. ● *v.* **1** travel by water; begin voyage; navigate (ship etc.) **2** glide or move smoothly or with dignity. **3** *colloq.* succeed easily.

**sailboard** *n.* board with a mast and sail, used in windsurfing. □□ **sailboarder** *n.* **sailboarding** *n.*

**sailcloth** *n.* canvas for sails; canvas-like dress material.

**sailor** *n.* member of ship's crew.

**saint** *n.* holy or canonised person, regarded as deserving special veneration; very virtuous person. ● *v.* (as **sainted** *adj.*) holy, virtuous. □□ **sainthood** *n.* **saintlike** *adj.* **saintliness** *n.* **saintly** *adj.*

**sake** □ **for the sake of** in order to please or honour (person) or to get or keep (thing).

**sake** *n.* Japanese rice wine.

**salaam** *n.* Indian etc. greeting meaning 'Peace'; Muslim greeting consisting of low bow.

**salacious** *adj.* tending to cause sexual desire; erotic; lecherous. □□ **salaciousness** *n.* **salacity** *n.*

**salad** *n.* cold mixture of usu. raw vegetables, often with dressing. □ **salad days** period of youthful inexperience.

**salamander** *n.* tailed lizard-like amphibian formerly supposed to live in fire.

**salami** *n.* highly-seasoned orig. Italian sausage.

**salaried** *adj.* receiving salary.

**salary** *n.* fixed regular payment by employer to employee.

**sale** *n.* exchange of commodity for money etc.; act or instance of selling; amount sold; temporary offering of goods at reduced prices; event at which goods are sold.

**saleable** *adj.* fit or likely to be sold. □□ **saleability** *n.*

**salesman** *n.* (*pl.* **-men**) man employed to sell goods.

**salesmanship** *n.* skill in selling.

**salesperson** *n.* (*pl.* **-persons**) person employed to sell goods.

**saleswoman** *n.* (*pl.* **-women**) woman employed to sell goods.

**saleyards** *n.pl. Aust.* market for livestock.

**salient** *adj.* prominent; conspicuous; most pertinent; (of angle) pointing outwards.□□ **salience** *n.* **saliency** *n.*

**salination** *n.* increase in salt content of soil, resulting in progressive infertility of land.

**saline** ● *adj.* salty, containing salt(s). ● *n.* saline solution.□□ **salinity** *n.*

**saliva** *n.* colourless liquid produced by glands in mouth.

**salivate** *v.* secrete saliva, esp. in excess or in greedy anticipation.

**sallow** ● *adj.* (esp. of complexion) yellowish. ● *n.* low-growing willow.

**sally¹** *n.* sudden swift attack; lively or witty remark. □ **sally forth** rush out in attack; set out on journey.

**sally²** *n.* (also **sallee**) *Aust.* any of several eucalypts and wattles resembling willow.

**salmon** ● *n.* (*pl.* **salmon**) large fish with pinkish flesh. ● *adj.* orange-pink.

**salmonella** *n.* bacterium causing food poisoning; such food poisoning.

**salon** *n.* **1** room or establishment of hairdresser, beautician, etc. **2** *hist.* meeting of eminent people at fashionable home.

**saloon** *n.* **1** large room or hall on ship, in hotel, etc., or for specified purpose. **2** (**saloon bar**) comfortable bar in hotel etc. **3** (**saloon car**) car with a separate boot, not a hatchback.

**salsa** *n.* **1** dance music of Cuban origin. **2** kind of spicy sauce.

**salsify** *n.* plant with long fleshy root used as vegetable.

**salt** ● *n.* **1** sodium chloride, esp. mined or evaporated from sea water, and used for seasoning or preserving food. **2** (**salts**) substance resembling salt in form, esp. a laxative. **3** chemical compound of a metal and an acid. **4** sting; piquancy; pungency; wit.

● *adj.* containing, tasting of, or preserved with salt. ● *v.* cure, preserve, or season with salt. □ **take with a grain** (or **pinch**) **of salt** regard sceptically; believe only part of. **worth one's salt** efficient, capable. □□ **saltiness** *n.* **salty** *adj.*

**saltbush** *n.* any of various herbs and shrubs of drier Australia.

**saltpetre** *n.* white crystalline salty substance used in preserving meat and in gunpowder.

**saltwater** *n.* sea water.

**salubrious** *adj.* health-giving. □□ **salubrity** *n.*

**salutary** *adj.* producing good effect.

**salutation** *n.* a greeting.

**salute** ● *n.* gesture of respect, homage, greeting etc.; *Mil. & Naut.* prescribed gesture or use of weapons or flags as sign of respect etc. ● *v.* make salute (to); greet, commend.

**salvage** ● *n.* rescue of property from sea, fire, etc.; saving and use of waste materials; property or materials salvaged. ● *v.* save from wreck etc.□□ **salvageable** *adj.*

**salvation** *n.* saving, being saved; deliverance from sin and damnation; person or thing that saves.

**salve** ● *n.* healing ointment; thing that soothes. ● *v.* soothe.

**salver** *n.* a small tray.

**salvo** *n.* (*pl.* **salvoes** or **salvos**) **1** simultaneous discharge of guns etc.; series of actions performed in quick succession. **2** (**Salvo;** *pl.* **Salvos**) *Aust.* member of Salvation Army.

**sal volatile** *n.* solution of ammonium carbonate used as smelling salts.

**samarium** *n.* metallic element (symbol Sm).

**samba** *n.* ballroom dance of Brazilian origin.

**same** ● *adj.* identical; unvarying. ● *pron.* the one already mentioned.

● *adv.* in the same way. □ **all the same** nevertheless. □□ **sameness** *n.*

**samosa** *n.* fried triangular pastry containing spiced vegetables or meat.

**sampan** *n.* small boat used in China etc.

**sample** ● *n.* small representative part or quantity; specimen; typical example; part of audio recording etc., esp. as used in new recording.
● *v.* **1** test by taking sample of. **2** use (part of audio recording etc.) in new recording.

**sampler** *n.* **1** piece of embroidery worked to show proficiency. **2** thing that contains sample(s). **3** person who samples.

**samurai** *n. hist.* member of Japanese military caste.

**sanatorium** *n.* (*pl.* **sanatoriums** or **sanatoria**) residential clinic esp. for convalescents and chronically sick.

**sanctify** *v.* consecrate; treat as holy; purify from sin. □□ **sanctification** *n.*

**sanctimonious** *adj.* ostentatiously pious. □□ **sanctimoniously** *adv.* **sanctimony** *n.*

**sanction** ● *n.* **1** permission, approval. **2** penalty imposed on a country or organisation.
● *v.* give sanction to; authorise.

**sanctity** *n.* holiness, sacredness; inviolability.

**sanctuary** *n.* **1** place of refuge or safety; place where wildlife is protected. **2** sacred place.

**sanctum** *n.* holy place; private place.

**sand** ● *n.* **1** fine grains resulting from erosion of esp. siliceous rocks. **2** (**sands**) expanse of sand; sandbank. ● *v.* smooth or treat with sandpaper, sander, or sand.

**sandal** *n.* shoe with openwork upper or no upper, fastened by straps.

**sandalwood** *n.* scented wood of sandal tree.

**sandbag** ● *n.* bag filled with sand, used in fortification, defence, etc.

● *v.* (**sandbagged**) protect with sandbags.

**sandbank** *n.* underwater deposit of sand.

**sander** *n.* power tool for smoothing surfaces.

**sandpaper** ● *n.* paper with coating of sand or other abrasive substance, used for smoothing surfaces. ● *v.* smooth with this.

**sandshoe** *n.* canvas shoe with rubber sole.

**sandstone** *n.* rock formed of compressed sand.

**sandwich** ● *n.* two or more slices of bread with filling between them; something arranged like this. ● *v.* put between two other people or things.

**sandy** *adj.* **1** like sand; covered with sand. **2** (of hair) yellowish-red.

**sane** *adj.* of sound mind; not mad; (of views etc.) moderate, sensible.

**sang** see SING.

**sangfroid** *n.* calmness in danger or difficulty.

**sanguinary** *adj.* bloody; bloodthirsty.

**sanguine** *adj.* optimistic.

**sanitary** *adj.* **1** (of conditions etc.) affecting health. **2** hygienic.
□ **sanitary towel** (or **napkin**) absorbent pad worn during menstruation. □□ **sanitariness** *n.*

**sanitation** *n.* sanitary conditions; maintenance or improving of these; drainage and disposal of waste.

**sanitise** *v.* (also **-ize**) clean, make hygienic; make more palatable by removing controversial elements from.

**sanity** *n.* condition of being sane.

**sank** see SINK.

**sans serif** *n.* style of type without serifs.

**sap** ● *n.* **1** food-carrying liquid in plants. **2** *colloq.* foolish person.
● *v.* (**sapped**) exhaust gradually.

**sapling** *n.* young tree.

**sapphire** ● n. transparent blue precious stone; its colour.

● adj. (also **sapphire blue**) bright blue.

**saprophyte** n. plant or microorganism living on dead or decayed organic matter.

**sarcasm** n. ironically scornful language. □□ **sarcastic** adj. **sarcastically** adv.

**sarcoma** n. malignant tumour of connective tissue.

**sarcophagus** n. (pl. sarcophagi) stone coffin.

**sardine** n. young pilchard etc. sold fresh or closely packed in tins.

**sardonic** adj. bitterly mocking; cynical. □□ **sardonically** adv.

**sari** n. length of cloth draped around body, traditionally worn by Indian women.

**sarong** n. garment of long strip of cloth tucked around waist or under armpits; ankle-length tube of cloth worn tucked around waist.

**SARS** n. sudden acute respiratory syndrome, contagious viral illness.

**sarsaparilla** n. dried roots of smilax etc., used to flavour drinks and medicines and formerly as tonic; plant yielding this.

**sartorial** adj. of or relating to clothes, esp. fashionable, elegant, or well-tailored. □□ **sartorially** adv.

**SAS** abbr. Special Air Service, armed regiment trained in commando techniques.

**sash** n. strip or loop of cloth worn over one shoulder or around waist. □ **sash window** window opened and shut by sliding up and down in grooves.

**sashimi** n. Japanese dish of garnished raw fish in thin slices.

**sat** see SIT.

**Sat.** abbr. Saturday.

**Satan** n. (in some religions) supreme spirit of evil.

**satanic** adj. **1** of or like Satan. **2** evil or wicked.

**Satanism** n. worship of Satan. □□ **Satanist** n.

**satay** n. dish of small pieces of spiced meat grilled on skewer and served with spiced sauce.

**satchel** n. small bag, esp. for carrying school books.

**sate** v. **1** satisfy (desire etc.) **2** supply with as much or more than is desired.

**satellite** ● n. heavenly or artificial body orbiting earth or another planet. ● adj. transmitted by satellite; receiving signal from satellite.

**satiate** v. satisfy fully; glut. □□ **satiation** n. **satiety** n.

**satin** ● n. silky material that is glossy on one side. ● adj. smooth as satin. □□ **satiny** adj.

**satire** n. criticism through ridicule, irony, or sarcasm; creative work using satire. □□ **satirical** adj. **satirically** adv.

**satirise** v. (also **-ize**) attack or describe with satire. □□ **satirist** n.

**satisfactory** adj. adequate; giving satisfaction. □□ **satisfactorily** adv.

**satisfy** v. **1** meet expectations or wishes of; be adequate; meet (appetite or want). **2** rid (person) of appetite or want. **3** pay. **4** fulfil, comply with. **5** convince. □□ **satisfaction** n.

**satsuma** n. **1** kind of red-skinned plum. **2** small variety of orange.

**saturate** v. **1** fill with moisture; soak thoroughly; fill to capacity or to excess. □□ **saturation** n.

**Saturday** n. day of week following Friday.

**saturnine** adj. of gloomy temperament or appearance.

**satyr** n. (in classical mythology) woodland god with goat's ears, tail, and legs.

**sauce** ● n. **1** liquid food added for flavour; something adding piquancy to. **2** *colloq.* impudence. ● *v.* **1** give piquancy. **2** *colloq.* be impudent to.

**saucepan** *n.* cooking pot with long handle.

**saucer** *n.* shallow circular dish, esp. for standing cup or pot plant on.

**saucy** *adj.* **1** impudent, cheeky. **2** *colloq.* bold, lively, stylish. □□ **saucily** *adv.* **sauciness** *n.*

**sauerkraut** *n.* German dish of pickled cabbage.

**sauna** *n.* specially designed hot room for cleaning and refreshing body.

**saunter** ● *v.* stroll. ● *n.* leisurely walk.

**saurian** *adj.* of or like lizard.

**sausage** *n.* **1** seasoned minced meat etc. in edible cylindrical case; sausage-shaped object. **2** *colloq.* penis. □ **sausage sizzle** *Aust.* fundraising or social event at which barbecued sausages etc. are sold or provided.

**sauté** *v.* fry quickly in shallow oil.

**sauternes** *n.* sweet white wine.

**sauvignon blanc** *n.* variety of white grape; wine made from this.

**savage** ● *adj.* **1** fierce, cruel. **2** wild, primitive. ● *n.* **1** *offens. hist.* member of people regarded as primitive and uncivilised. **2** very cruel person. ● *v.* attack and maul; attack verbally. □□ **savagely** *adv.* **savagery** *n.*

**savannah** *n.* (also **savanna**) grassy plain in tropical or subtropical region.

**save** ● *v.* **1** rescue or preserve from danger or harm. **2** keep for future use; avoid wasting; keep money in this way. **3** prevent (goal) from being scored. **4** *Computing* keep (data) by moving copy to storage location. ● *n.* *Soccer etc.* prevention of goal etc.□□ **saver** *n.*

**saveloy** *n.* seasoned red pork sausage; thick frankfurt.

**savings** *n.pl.* money put aside for future use.

**saviour** *n.* (also **savior**) person who rescues others from harm.

**savoir faire** *n.* ability to behave appropriately; tact.

**savory** *n.* herb.

**savour** ● *n.* **1** characteristic taste, flavour, etc. **2** tinge or hint. **3** attractiveness. **4** interest. ● *v.* **1** appreciate, enjoy. **2** imply, suggest.

**savoury** ● *adj.* having appetising taste or smell; (of food) salty or piquant, not sweet; pleasant. ● *n.* bite-sized salty or spicy snack; canapé; savoury dish served esp. at end of dinner.

**savoy** *n.* cabbage with wrinkled leaves.

**savvy** *colloq.* ● *v.* know. ● *n.* understanding; shrewdness.

**saw** ● *n.* implement with toothed blade etc. for cutting wood etc. ● *v.* cut or make with saw; use saw; make to-and-fro sawing motion.

**saw** see SEE.

**sawdust** *n.* powdery fragments of wood, made in sawing timber.

**sawtoothed** *adj.* serrated.

**sax** *n. colloq.* saxophone.

**saxophone** *n.* keyed brass wind instrument.□□ **saxophonist** *n.*

**say** ● *v.* (**says, said**) **1** utter, remark; express; state; indicate. (in *passive*) **2** be asserted. **3** *colloq.* state, order. **4** convey (information). **5** adduce, plead. **6** decide. **7** take as example or as near enough. ● *n.* opportunity to express view; share in decision.

**saying** *n.* maxim, proverb, etc.

**s.c.** *abbr.* small capitals.

**scab** ● *n.* **1** crust over healing cut, sore, etc.; skin disease or plant disease causing similar roughness. **2** *colloq.* contemptible person; *derog.* blackleg; strikebreaker. ● *v.* (**scabbed**) **1** form scab. **2** *Aust. colloq.* cadge, borrow money. **3** *derog.* break strike.□ **scab duty** *Aust. colloq.* picking up litter.

**scabbard** *n.* sheath of sword etc.

**scabies** *n.* contagious skin disease causing itching.

**scabrous** *adj.* **1** rough-surfaced. **2** indecent.

**scaffold** *n.* **1** scaffolding. **2** *hist.* platform for execution of criminals.

**scaffolding** *n.* temporary structure of poles, planks, etc. for building work; materials for this.

**scald** ● *v.* burn (skin etc.) with hot liquid or steam; heat (esp. milk) to near boiling point. ● *n.* **1** burn etc. caused by scalding. **2** plant disease that produces an effect similar to that of scalding. **3** *Aust.* area of land that is bare of vegetation due to soil erosion, salinity, etc.

**scale** ● *n.* **1** ordered series of units or quantities etc. for measuring or classifying things. **2** fixed series of notes in a system of music. **3** relative size or extent. **4** (scales) instrument for weighing things. **5** each of thin horny plates protecting skin of fish and reptiles; thing resembling this. **6** incrustation inside kettle etc. or forming on teeth. ● *v.* **1** climb. **2** represent in proportion to the size of the original. **3** remove scale from. □□ **scaly** *adj.*

**scalene** *adj.* (of triangle) having unequal sides.

**scallion** *n.* shallot or spring onion.

**scallop** *n.* (also **scollop**) **1** edible bivalve with fan-shaped ridged shells. **2** ornamental edging of semicircular curves. **3** *Aust.* thin slice of potato, battered and fried. □□ **scalloped** *adj.*

**scallywag** *n.* scamp, rascal.

**scalp** ● *n.* skin and hair on head; *hist.* this taken as trophy or to obtain bounty etc.; trophy or symbol of conquest. ● *v.* **1** take scalp of. **2** resell (shares, tickets, etc.) at high or quick profit. □□ **scalper** *n.*

**scalpel** *n.* small surgical knife.

**scam** *n.* *colloq.* trick, fraud; illegal business racket.

**scamp** *n.* *colloq.* rascal; rogue.

**scamper** ● *v.* run hastily or in play. ● *n.* a scampering run.

**scan** ● *v.* (**scanned**) **1** look at intently or quickly. **2** (of verse etc.) have regular rhythm; analyse rhythm of. **3** pass radar or electronic beam over; resolve (picture) into elements of light and shade for transmission or reproduction; read barcode on packaging etc.; electronically reproduce document etc. in computer-readable form etc.
● *n.* scanning; image obtained by scanning.

**scandal** *n.* disgraceful event; outrage; malicious gossip. □□ **scandalous** *adj.* **scandalously** *adv.*

**scandalise** *v.* (also **-ize**) offend morally; shock.

**scandalmonger** *n.* person who spreads scandal.

**scandium** *n.* metallic element (symbol Sc).

**scanner** *n.* device for scanning.

**scansion** *n.* metrical scanning of verse.

**scant** *adj.* barely sufficient; deficient.

**scanty** *adj.* of small extent or amount; barely sufficient. □□ **scantily** *adv.* **scantiness** *n.*

**scapegoat** *n.* person bearing blame that should fall on others.

**scapula** *n.* (*pl.* **scapulae** or **scapulas**) shoulder blade. □□ **scapular** *adj.*

**scar** ● *n.* mark where wound has healed. ● *v.* (**scarred**) mark with or form scar(s).

**scarab** *n.* **1** sacred dung beetle of ancient Egypt. **2** any of various beetles.

**scarce** *adj.* in short supply; rare.

**scarcely** *adv.* hardly, only just.

**scarcity** *n.* lack or shortage.

**scare** ● *v.* frighten; be frightened. ● *n.* a fright; widespread alarm.

**scarecrow** n. figure dressed in old clothes and set up to scare birds away from crops.

**scarf** n. (pl. **scarves** or **scarfs**) piece of material worn around neck or over head for warmth or ornament.

**scarify** v. 1 make slight incisions in. 2 hurt by severe criticism etc. 3 loosen (soil). □□ **scarification** n.

**scarlet** adj. & n. brilliant red tinged with orange. □ **scarlet fever** infectious fever producing scarlet rash.

**scarp** ● n. steep slope; inner side of ditch in fortification. ● v. make perpendicular or steep.

**scary** adj. colloq. frightening.

**scathing** adj. (of criticism) very severe; scornful. □□ **scathingly** adv.

**scatology** n. preoccupation with excrement or obscenity. □□ **scatological** adj.

**scatter** ● v. 1 throw about; strew; cover by scattering. 2 (cause to) flee or disperse. 3 (as **scattered** adj.) wide apart, sporadic. 4 Physics deflect or diffuse (light, particles, etc.) ● n. act of scattering; small amount scattered; extent of distribution.

**scatterbrain** n. careless or forgetful person. □□ **scatterbrained** adj.

**scatty** adj. colloq. lacking concentration. □□ **scattily** adv. **scattiness** n.

**scavenge** v. search for and collect (discarded items). □□ **scavenger** n.

**scenario** n. 1 outline of plot of play, film, etc.; a setting. 2 imagined sequence of future events.

**scene** n. 1 place of actual or fictitious occurrence; incident; public display of emotion, temper, etc. 2 piece of continuous action in play, film, book, etc. 3 landscape, view. 4 colloq. area of interest or activity. ● **behind the scenes** hidden from public view.

**scenery** n. 1 features (esp. picturesque) of landscape. 2 painted

backcloths, props, etc. used as background in play etc.

**scenic** adj. picturesque; of scenery. □□ **scenically** adv.

**scent** ● n. 1 characteristic, esp. pleasant, smell; liquid perfume; smell left by animal; power of detecting smells. 2 clues etc. leading to discovery. ● v. 1 discern by smell. 2 sense. 3 apply scent to; make fragrant.

**sceptic** n. 1 sceptical person. 2 cynic. 3 person who doubts truth of religions or possibility of knowledge.

**sceptical** adj. inclined to doubt accepted opinions; critical; incredulous. □□ **sceptically** adv. **scepticism** n.

**sceptre** n. staff as symbol of sovereignty.

**schadenfreude** n. enjoyment of another's misfortune.

**schedule** ● n. a timetable; plan of work; list, esp. of rates or prices. ● v. include in schedule; make schedule of. □ **schedule fee** (also **scheduled fee**) Aust. government approved fee for medical service.

**schema** n. (pl. **schemata** or **schemas**) synopsis, outline, diagram.

**schematic** ● adj. of or as scheme or diagram; simplified or simplistic. ● n. diagram, esp. of electronic circuit.

**schematise** v. (also **-ize**) put in schematic form.

**scheme** ● n. systematic arrangement; plan of work or action. ● v. plan, esp. secretly or deceitfully. □□ **scheming** adj.

**scherzo** n. Mus. vigorous and lively movement or composition.

**schism** n. division of esp. religious group into sects etc. □□ **schismatic** adj. & n.

**schist** n. layered crystalline rock.

**schizoid** ● adj. tending to schizophrenia. ● n. schizoid person.

**schizophrenia** n. mental disorder marked by disconnection between thoughts, feelings, and actions. □□ **schizophrenic** adj. & n.

**schmaltz** n. colloq. sugary sentimentality. □□ **schmaltzy** adj.

**schmick** adj. (also **smick**) Aust. colloq. stylish, excellent.

**schnapps** n. alcoholic spirit.

**schnitzel** n. escalope of veal.

**scholar** n. learned person; holder of scholarship; student. □□ **scholarly** adj.

**scholarship** n. **1** learning, erudition. **2** financial award etc. towards education.

**scholastic** adj. of universities, schools, education, etc.; academic.

**school** ● n. **1** educational institution. **2** group of artists, philosophers, etc. following or holding similar principles, etc. **3** shoal of fish, sea mammals, etc. **4** Aust. group of drinkers. ● v. train, discipline.

**schoolie** n. Aust. colloq. schoolteacher; secondary school student. □ **schoolies' week** post-exam celebration for year twelve students.

**schooling** n. education.

**schooner** n. **1** two-masted fore-and-aft rigged ship. **2** large beer glass.

**sciatica** n. condition causing pain in hip and thigh.

**science** n. branch of knowledge involving systematised observation, experiment, and induction; knowledge so gained; pursuit or principles of this. □□ **scientific** adj.

**scientist** n. expert in science.

**scimitar** n. curved oriental sword.

**scintilla** n. a trace.

**scintillating** adj. lively, witty.

**scion** n. **1** plant shoot cut for grafting. **2** descendant.

**scissors** n.pl. cutting instrument with pair of pivoted blades.

**sclerosis** n. **1** abnormal hardening of tissue. **2** (in full **multiple sclerosis**) serious progressive disease of nervous system. □□ **sclerotic** adj.

**scoff** ● v. **1** speak scornfully; jeer. **2** colloq. eat greedily. ● n. mocking words; taunt.

**scold** v. rebuke; find fault noisily. □□ **scolding** n.

**sconce** n. wall bracket holding candlestick or light fitting.

**scone** n. **1** small cake of flour, milk, etc. baked quickly. **2** Aust. colloq. head.

**scoop** ● n. **1** short-handled deep shovel; long-handled ladle; excavating part of digging machine etc.; quantity taken up by scoop; scooping movement. **2** exclusive news item. **3** large profit made quickly. ● v. **1** hollow out. **2** lift (as) with scoop. **3** forestall (rival newspaper etc.) with scoop. **4** secure (large profit etc.), esp. suddenly.

**scoot** v. colloq. run or dart away, esp. hastily.

**scooter** n. **1** child's toy with footboard on two wheels and long steering handle. **2** low-powered motorcycle.

**scope** n. range, opportunity; extent of ability, outlook, etc.

**scorch** v. burn or discolour surface of with heat; become so discoloured etc.

**scorcher** n. colloq. very hot day.

**scorching** adj. very hot.

**score** ● n. **1** number of points, goals, etc. made by player or side in game; respective scores at end of game; mark gained in test or exam; act of gaining esp. goal. **2** (set of) 20. **3** a great many. **4** reason, motive. **5** Mus. copy of composition with parts arranged one below another. **6** music for film or play. **7** notch, line, etc. made on surface. **8** record of money owing. **9** present situation. ● v. **1** win, gain;

make (points etc.) in game; keep score; mark with notches etc. **2** have an advantage. **3** *Mus.* orchestrate or arrange (piece of music). **4** *colloq.* obtain drugs illegally, make sexual conquest. □□ **scorer** *n.*

**scorn** ● *n.* disdain, contempt, derision. ● *v.* hold in contempt; reject or refuse to do as unworthy. □□ **scornful** *adj.* **scornfully** *adv.*

**Scorpio** *n.* eighth sign of zodiac, the Scorpion. □□ **Scorpian** *adj.* & *n.*

**scorpion** *n.* arachnid with jointed stinging tail and lobster-like claws.

**scotch** ● *v.* decisively put an end to. ● *n.* (**Scotch**) type of whisky.

**scot-free** *adv.* unharmed, unpunished.

**scotty** *adj. colloq.* irritable, bad-tempered.

**scoundrel** *n.* unscrupulous villain; rogue.

**scour** ● *v.* **1** rub clean; clear out (pipe etc.) by flushing through; remove grease, dirt, etc. from (wool etc.) by washing. **2** search thoroughly. ● *n.* **1** scouring, being scoured. **2** (also **scours**) diarrhoea in livestock. □□ **scourer** *n.*

**scourge** ● *n.* **1** person or thing regarded as causing suffering. **2** *hist.* whip. ● *v.* **1** *hist.* whip. **2** punish, oppress.

**scout** ● *n.* **1** person sent out to get information or reconnoitre. **2** (also **Scout**) member of (orig. boys') association intended to develop character. ● *v.* seek information etc.; make search; explore. □□ **scouting** *n.*

**scowl** ● *n.* sullen or bad-tempered expression. ● *v.* wear scowl.

**scrabble** ● *v.* scratch or grope busily about. ● *n.* scrabbling.

**scraggy** *adj.* thin and bony. □□ **scragginess** *n.*

**scram** *v.* (**scrammed**) *colloq.* go away.

**scramble** ● *v.* **1** clamber, crawl, climb, etc. **2** struggle with competitors (for thing or share). **3** mix indiscriminately. **4** cook (eggs) by stirring them in heated pan. **5** alter sound frequencies of (broadcast or telephone conversation) so as to make it unintelligible without decoding device. **6** (of fighter aircraft or pilot) take off rapidly. ● *n.* **1** scrambling. **2** difficult climb or walk. **3** eager struggle or competition. **4** emergency take-off by fighter aircraft. □□ **scrambler** *n.*

**scrap** ● *n.* **1** fragment, esp. one left after use, eating, etc. **2** discarded metal for reprocessing. **3** *colloq.* a fight, a quarrel. ● *v.* (**scrapped**) **1** discard as useless. **2** fight, quarrel.

**scrapbook** *n.* book for newspaper cuttings or similar souvenirs.

**scrape** ● *v.* **1** move hard edge across (surface), esp. to smooth or clean; remove by scraping; rub (surface) harshly against another; scratch, damage, or make by scraping; make harsh sound doing this. **2** narrowly achieve; barely manage. **3** be economical. ● *n.* **1** act or sound of scraping. **2** scraped place. **3** *colloq.* predicament caused by unwise behaviour. **4** *colloq.* a fight, a quarrel. □□ **scraper** *n.*

**scrapie** *n.* disease of sheep causing loss of coordination.

**scrappy** *adj.* (**scrappier**) made up of scraps or disconnected elements. □□ **scrappily** *adv.* **scrappiness** *n.*

**scratch** ● *v.* **1** score or wound superficially, esp. with sharp object; scrape with claws or fingernails; make thin scraping sound by doing this. **2** obtain with difficulty. **3** cancel; withdraw from competition. ● *n.* **1** mark, wound, or sound made by scratching. **2** act of scratching oneself. ● *adj.* collected or made from whatever is available. □ **from scratch 1** from beginning. **2** without advantage. **up to scratch**

meeting required standard.
□□ **scratchy** adj.

**scratchie** n. (also **scratchy**) Aust. colloq. instant lottery ticket with removable surface concealing symbols indicating prize etc.

**scrawl** ● v. write in hurried untidy way. ● n. hurried writing; scrawled note.□□ **scrawly** adj.

**scrawny** adj. lean, scraggy.

**scream** ● n. 1 piercing cry (as) of terror, pain, etc. 2 colloq. hilarious occurrence or person. ● v. emit scream; utter in or with scream; berate loudly; laugh uncontrollably; be blatantly obvious.

**screamer** n. colloq. 1 (in full **two-pot screamer**) Aust. person with low tolerance of alcohol. 2 AFL spectacular overhead mark.

**scree** n. small loose stones; mountain slope covered with these.

**screech** ● n. harsh scream.
● v. utter with or make screech.
□□ **screechy** adj.

**screed** n. 1 long usu. tiresome letter or harangue. 2 layer of cement etc. applied to level a surface.

**screen** ● n. 1 fixed or movable upright partition for separating, concealing, or protecting from heat etc.; thing used to conceal or shelter; windscreen; flyscreen. 2 flat panel or area on electronic device on which images and data are displayed; blank surface on which images are projected; (**the screen**) cinema industry, films collectively. 3 system for detecting disease, ability, attribute, etc. ● v. 1 shelter, hide; protect from detection, censure, etc.; conceal behind screen; fit flyscreen to. 2 show (film etc.) 3 prevent from causing, or protect from, electrical interference. 4 test (person or group) for disease, reliability, loyalty, etc.□ **screen saver** Computing program that, after set time, replaces unchanging screen display with moving image to prevent damage.

**screenplay** n. script of a film.

**screw** ● n. 1 metal pin with spiral ridge running around its length, fastened by turning; thing twisted to tighten or press something; act of twisting or tightening. 2 propeller. 3 colloq. prison warder. 4 coarse colloq. sexual intercourse. ● v. 1 fasten or tighten with screw(s); turn (a screw); twist, become twisted. 2 oppress, extort. 3 coarse colloq. have sexual intercourse with.□ **screw up 1** summon up (courage). 2 colloq. bungle; cause (someone) to be emotionally disturbed.

**screwdriver** n. tool for turning screws.

**scribble** ● v. write or draw carelessly or hurriedly. ● n. something scribbled.

**scribbly gum** n. smooth-barked Australian eucalypt having characteristic scribbles on bark formed by burrowing moth larvae.

**scribe** n. 1 ancient or medieval copyist of manuscripts. 2 person who writes out document.

**scrim** n. open-weave fabric for lining, upholstery etc.

**scrimmage** ● n. tussle; brawl.
● v. engage in scrimmage.

**scrimp** v. skimp.

**scrip** n. 1 provisional certificate of money subscribed to company etc. 2 extra share(s) instead of dividend. 3 colloq. doctor's prescription.

**script** ● n. 1 text of play, film, or broadcast. 2 handwriting; typeface imitating handwriting; alphabet or system of writing. 3 colloq. doctor's prescription. 4 Computing automated series of instructions carried out in a specific order. ● v. write script for (film etc.)

**scripture** n. sacred writings; (Scripture, the Scriptures) Bible. □□ **scriptural** adj.

**scroll** ● n. roll of parchment or paper; ornamental design imitating roll of parchment. ● v. move (display on computer screen) to view earlier or later material.

**scrotum** n. (pl. **scrota** or **scrotums**) pouch of skin enclosing testicles. □□ **scrotal** adj.

**scrounge** v. obtain things by cadging; collect by foraging. □□ **scrounger** n.

**scrub¹** ● v. (**scrubbed**) 1 clean by hard rubbing, esp. with brush. 2 colloq. cancel. ● n. process of scrubbing.

**scrub²** ● n. 1 generally low, apparently stunted forms of vegetation, frequently growing in poor soil; land covered with this. 2 (the scrub) country areas in general. ● adj. of small or dwarf variety; (of livestock) of inferior breed or physique; (of Australian flora and fauna) indigenous to scrub-covered land.□ **scrub itch** Aust. skin irritation caused by the parasitic larvae of mites. □□ **scrubby** adj.

**scruff** n. back of neck.

**scruffy** adj. colloq. shabby, slovenly, untidy.□□ **scruffily** adv. **scruffiness** n.

**scrum** n. Rugby massed forwards on each side pushing to gain possession of ball thrown on ground between them.

**scrummage** n. Rugby scrum.

**scrumptious** adj. colloq. delicious.

**scrunch** ● v. crumple; crunch. ● n. crunching sound.

**scruple** ● n. doubt about doing something, produced by one's conscience. ● v. hesitate because of scruples.

**scrupulous** adj. conscientious, thorough; careful to avoid doing wrong; over-attentive to details. □□ **scrupulously** adv.

**scrutineer** n. person who scrutinises or examines something, esp. conduct and result of ballot.

**scrutinise** v. (also -ize) subject to scrutiny.

**scrutiny** n. critical gaze; close investigation.

**scuba** n. portable underwater breathing apparatus (acronym from self-contained underwater breathing apparatus).

**scud** v. (**scudded**) move along fast and smoothly.

**scuff** ● v. graze or brush against; mark (shoes, furniture, etc.) in this way; shuffle or drag feet. ● n. mark of scuffing.

**scuffle** ● n. confused struggle or fight. ● v. engage in scuffle.

**scull** ● n. one of pair of small oars; oar that rests on boat's stern, worked with screw-like movement. ● v. 1 row with sculls 2 = SKOL.

**sculpt** v. sculpture.

**sculptor** n. artist who sculptures.

**sculpture** ● n. art of making three-dimensional forms by chiselling, carving, modelling, casting, etc.; work of sculpture. ● v. represent in or adorn with sculpture. □□ **sculptural** adj.

**scum** ● n. 1 layer of dirt etc. at surface of liquid. 2 derog. worst part, person, or group. ● v. remove scum from; form scum (on). □□ **scummy** adj.

**scungies** n.pl. Aust. colloq. stretch sports briefs worn under netball skirt, board shorts, etc.

**scupper** ● n. hole in ship's side to drain water from deck. ● v. colloq. sink (ship, crew); defeat or ruin (plan etc.)

**scurf** n. dandruff.

**scurrilous** adj. grossly or obscenely abusive.□□ **scurrility** n. **scurrilously** adv. **scurrilousness** n.

**scurry** • v. run hurriedly, scamper. • n. 1 scurrying sound or movement. 2 flurry of rain or snow.

**scurvy** n. disease resulting from deficiency of vitamin C.

**scuttle** • n. box or bucket for holding coal. • v. 1 scurry. 2 sink (ship) by letting in water.

**scythe** n. implement with curved blade on long handle, for cutting long grass.

**SD card** n. type of memory card used in cameras and other portable devices.

**SE** abbr. south-east(ern).

**sea** n. expanse of salt water covering most of earth; area of this; large inland lake; (motion or state of) waves of sea; vast quantity or expanse.□ **at sea** in a ship on the sea; perplexed. **sea horse** small fish with horse-like head. **sea lion** large seal. **sea urchin** sea animal with round spiky shell.

**seaboard** n. the coast.

**seaborgium** n. chemical element (symbol Sg).

**seachange** n. notable or unexpected transformation; Aust. significant change in lifestyle.

**seafaring** adj. & n. working or travelling on the sea.□□ **seafarer** n.

**seafood** n. fish or shellfish from sea eaten as food.

**seagull** n. gull.

**seal¹** • v. 1 close or coat so as to prevent penetration. 2 stick down; affix a seal to. 3 settle (e.g. a bargain). • n. 1 engraved piece of metal used to stamp a design; its impression. 2 action etc. serving to confirm or guarantee something. 3 something used to close opening very tightly.

**seal²** n. amphibious sea animal with thick fur or bristles.

**sealant** n. material for sealing, esp. to make watertight.

**seam** • n. 1 line where two edges join. 2 layer of coal etc. • v. join with seam.□□ **seamless** adj.

**seaman** n. (pl. **seamen**) sailor; person skilled in seafaring.

**seamy** adj. sordid and disreputable.

**seance** n. meeting where people try to make contact with spirits of the dead.

**sear** v. 1 scorch, cauterise. 2 cause anguish to. 3 brown (meat) quickly.

**search** • v. examine thoroughly to find something; make investigation; look for, seek out; (as **searching** adj.) keenly questioning. • n. act of searching; investigation.□ **search engine** computer program that searches for items on Internet etc. **search warrant** official authorisation to enter and search building etc. □□ **searcher** n. **searchingly** adv.

**searching** adj. thorough.

**season** • n. 1 each of climatic divisions of year; time of year characterised by climatic features; fixed time in year when a particular sporting activity is pursued. 2 proper or suitable time; time when something is plentiful, active, etc. 3 set or sequence of related television programs; a series. • v. 1 flavour with salt, herbs, etc. 2 enhance with wit etc. 3 moderate.□ **season ticket** ticket valid for any number of journeys or performances or visits in specified period.

**seasonable** adj. suitable or usual to season.

> **Usage** Seasonable is sometimes confused with seasonal.

**seasonal** adj. of, depending on, or varying with season.□□ **seasonally** adv.

**seasoned** adj. experienced.

**seasoning** n. salt, herbs, etc. as flavouring for food.

**seat** ● n. 1 thing made or used for sitting on. 2 buttocks, part of garment covering them. 3 a place as member of committee or parliament etc.; place where something is based.
● v. cause to sit; provide sitting accommodation for.

**seatbelt** n. strap securing person to seat in vehicle or aircraft.

**seaweed** n. plant growing in the sea.

**seaworthy** adj. fit to put to sea.

**sebaceous** adj. fatty; secreting oily matter.

**secateurs** n.pl. pruning clippers.

**secede** v. withdraw formally from political or religious body. □□ **secession** n.

**seclude** v. 1 keep (person, place) apart from others. 2 (esp. as **secluded** adj.) screen from view.

**seclusion** n. secluded state or place.

**second**[1] ● adj. 1 next after first. 2 additional. 3 subordinate. 4 inferior. 5 comparable to. 6 alternate.
● n. 1 runner-up. 2 person or thing coming second. 3 inferior goods. 4 colloq. second helping. 5 assistant to duellist, boxer, etc. 6 (**seconds**) reserve or second-grade team in sporting clubs. ● v. 1 support, back up. 2 formally support (nomination, proposal, etc.) □ **second-degree 1** of burns that cause blistering but not permanent scars. 2 US of less serious category of crime than that of first-degree. **second-hand** (also **secondhand**) bought after use by previous owner. **second nature** habit or characteristic that has become automatic. **second-rate** of mediocre quality; inferior. **second sight** supposed power to foresee future events. **second thoughts** a change of mind after reconsideration. **second wind** renewed capacity for effort. □□ **secondly** adv.

**second**[2] n. SI unit of time (one sixtieth of minute); one sixtieth of minute of angle; colloq. very short time.

**second**[3] v. transfer (person) temporarily to another department etc. □□ **secondment** n.

**secondary** ● adj. 1 coming after or derived from what is primary. 2 (of education etc.) following primary. ● n. secondary thing. □ **secondary colour** result of mixing two primary colours. **secondary source** book, article, or other source that provides information about an object of study but does not constitute direct, first-hand evidence.

**secret** ● adj. kept from knowledge of most people. ● n. thing (to be) kept secret; mystery; effective but not widely known method. □ **in secret** secretly. □□ **secrecy** n. **secretly** adv.

**secretariat** n. administrative office or department; its members or premises.

**secretary** n. employee who assists with correspondence, records, making appointments, etc.; official of society etc. who keeps minutes, writes letters, organises meeting, etc.; head of public service department. □ **secretary-general** principal administrative officer. □□ **secretarial** adj.

**secrete** v. 1 (of cell, organ, etc.) produce and discharge (substance). 2 conceal. □□ **secretory** adj.

**secretion** n. 1 process or act of secreting. 2 secreted substance.

**secretive** adj. concealing information etc. □□ **secretively** adv. **secretiveness** n.

**secretory** adj. of physiological secretion.

**sect** n. group with beliefs, esp. religious ones, that differ from those generally accepted.

**sectarian** ● adj. of sect(s); bigoted in following one's sect. ● n. member of sect; bigot. □□ **sectarianism** n.

**section** ● n. distinct part; cross-section; subdivision. ● v. arrange in or divide into sections.

**sectional** adj. of a social group; partisan; made in sections; local rather than general. □□ **sectionally** adv.

**sector** n. part of an area; plane figure enclosed between two radii of circle etc.; branch of enterprise, society, economy, etc.

**secular** adj. of worldly (not religious or spiritual) matters. □□ **secularise** v. (also **-ize**) **secularisation** n. **secularism** n.

**secure** ● adj. untroubled by danger or fear; safe; reliable; stable; fixed; certain to achieve. ● v. make secure or safe; fasten or close securely; obtain; guarantee (loan) against loss. □□ **securely** adv.

**security** n. 1 secure condition or feeling; thing that guards or guarantees; safety against espionage, theft, etc.; organisation for ensuring this. 2 thing deposited as guarantee for undertaking or loan. 3 (often in pl.) document as evidence of loan, certificate of stock, bonds, etc.

**sedan** n. four-door car with body closed off from luggage compartment.

**sedate** ● adj. calm and dignified. ● v. put under sedation. □□ **sedately** adv. **sedateness** n.

**sedation** n. treatment with sedatives.

**sedative** ● n. calming drug or influence. ● adj. calming, soothing.

**sedentary** adj. 1 seated; (of work etc.) done while sitting. 2 (of person) disinclined to exercise.

**sedge** n. grasslike waterside or marsh plant. □□ **sedgy** adj.

**sediment** n. matter that settles to bottom of liquid; dregs; matter

deposited on land by water or wind. □□ **sedimentary** adj. **sedimentation** n.

**sedition** n. conduct or speech inciting rebellion. □□ **seditious** adj.

**seduce** v. entice into sexual activity; tempt, lure; lead astray. □□ **seducer** n. **seduction** n. **seductive** adj.

**sedulous** adj. persevering, diligent; painstaking. □□ **sedulity** n. **sedulously** adv.

**see** ● v. (**saw, seen, seeing**) 1 perceive with eyes or mind; watch; understand. 2 consider. 3 experience. 4 meet; interview. 5 escort. 6 ensure. ● n. district of bishop or archbishop. □ **see about** attend to. **seeing that** in view of the fact that.

**seed** ● n. 1 part of plant (esp. in form of grain) capable of developing into another such plant; semen; prime cause; beginning; offspring. 2 Tennis etc. seeded player. ● v. 1 plant with seeds; produce seeds. 2 remove seeds from (fruit etc.) 3 Tennis etc. designate (competitor in knockout competition) so that strong competitors do not meet each other until later rounds; arrange (order of play) thus.

**seedless** adj. not containing seeds.

**seedling** n. young plant.

**seedy** adj. 1 shabby, disreputable. 2 colloq. unwell. 3 full of seed. □□ **seediness** n.

**seek** v. (**sought, seeking**) search, inquire; try (to do something); request; endeavour. □□ **seeker** n.

**seem** v. appear, give the impression. □□ **seemingly** adv.

**seemly** adj. in good taste; decorous. □□ **seemliness** n.

**seen** see SEE.

**seep** v. ooze out; percolate. □□ **seepage** n.

**seer** n. prophet, visionary.

**see-saw** ● n. long board balanced on central support, for children to sit

on at each end and move up and down alternately; up-and-down or to-and-fro motion. ● v. play or move (as) on see-saw; vacillate.
● *adj.* & *adv.* with up-and-down or to-and-fro motion.

**seethe** v. bubble as if boiling; be very agitated or excited.

**segment** ● *n.* part cut off, marked off, or separable from other parts; part of circle or sphere cut off by intersecting line or plane. ● v. divide into segments.□□ **segmental** *adj.* **segmentation** n.

**segregate** v. separate from others, isolate.□□ **segregation** n.

**seine** n. fishing net that hangs from floats.

**seismic** *adj.* of earthquake(s).

**seismograph** n. instrument for recording details of earthquakes.
□□ **seismographic** *adj.*

**seismology** n. study of earthquakes.
□□ **seismological** *adj.* **seismologist** n.

**seize** v. 1 take hold or possession of, esp. forcibly, suddenly, or by legal power; take advantage of. 2 affect suddenly and strongly.

**seizure** n. 1 seizing, being seized. 2 sudden attack of epilepsy, apoplexy, etc.

**seldom** *adv.* rarely, not often.

**select** v. choose, esp. with care. ● *adj.* 1 chosen for excellence or suitability. 2 (of society etc.) exclusive.□□ **selector** n.

**selection** n. selecting, being selected; selected person or thing; things from which choice may be made.

**selective** *adj.* of or using selection; able to select; selecting what is convenient.□□ **selectively** *adv.* **selectivity** n.

**selenium** n. chemical element (symbol Se).

**self** n. (*pl.* **selves**) individuality, essence; object of introspection or reflexive action; one's own interests or pleasure, concentration on these.

**self-** *comb. form* of or to be done by oneself or itself.

**self-conscious** *adj.* embarrassed from knowing that one is observed.

**self-determination** n. nation's choice of its own form of government, allegiances, etc.

**self-evident** *adj.* obvious, needing no argument or proof.

**selfie** n. *colloq.* photograph that one has taken of oneself.

**selfish** *adj.* concerned chiefly with one's own interests or pleasure; actuated by or appealing to self-interest.□□ **selfishness** n.

**selfless** *adj.* unselfish.

**self-possessed** *adj.* calm, controlled.
□□ **self-possession** n.

**selfsame** *adj.* the very same.

**sell** ● v. (**sold**, **selling**) 1 exchange or be exchanged for money; stock for sale; have specified price; betray or prostitute for money etc.; advertise, publicise; cause to be sold. 2 make (person) enthusiastic about (idea etc.) ● n. act of selling or promoting. □ **sell off** dispose of by selling, esp. at reduced price. **sell out** 1 sell all of one's stock. 2 betray. **sell** (someone or something) **short** fail to recognise or state the true value of. **sell up** sell one's house or business.□□ **seller** n.

**sellotape** n. *propr.* adhesive usu. transparent cellulose tape.

**selvedge** n. (also **salvage**) edge of cloth woven to prevent fraying.

**semantic** ● *adj.* of meaning in language. ● *n.pl.* (**semantics**) study of meaning.

**semaphore** ● n. 1 system of signalling with arms or two flags.

2 railway signalling apparatus with arm(s) etc. ● v. signal or send by semaphore.

**semblance** n. outward appearance or form.

**semen** n. reproductive fluid of male animals.

**semester** n. half-year term in universities, schools, etc.

**semi-** prefix half; partly.

**semibreve** n. Mus. note equal to four crotchets.

**semicircle** n. half of circle or its circumference.□□ **semicircular** adj.

**semicolon** n. punctuation mark (;) of intermediate value between comma and full stop.

**semiconductor** n. substance that is poor electrical conductor when either pure or cold and good conductor when either impure or hot.

**semi-detached** ● adj. (of house) joined to another on one side. ● n. such house.

**semi-final** n. match or round preceding final.□□ **semi-finalist** n.

**semillon** n. variety of white grape; white wine made from it.

**seminal** adj. of seed, semen, or reproduction; germinal; (of idea etc.) providing basis for future development.

**seminar** n. small class for discussion and research.

**seminary** n. training college for priests etc.□□ **seminarist** n.

**semi-precious** adj. (of gem) less valuable than precious stone.

**semiquaver** n. Mus. note equal to half a quaver.

**Semite** n. member of peoples said to be descended from Shem, including Jews and Arabs. □□ **Semitic** adj.

**semitone** n. half a tone in musical scale.

**semitrailer** n. articulated vehicle consisting of long trailer supported at front by prime mover.

**semolina** n. hard round grains of wheat used for puddings, pasta, etc.; pudding of this.

**senate** n. upper house of Australian Federal Parliament; legislative body, esp. upper and smaller assembly in some countries; governing body of university.

**senator** n. member of senate. □□ **senatorial** adj.

**send** v. (**sent**, **sending**) order or cause to go to or reach destination; send message, cause to move or go or become.□ **send for** order to come or be brought. **send up** colloq. make fun of by imitating. □□ **sender** n.

**senile** adj. of old age; mentally or physically infirm because of old age. □□ **senility** n.

**senior** ● adj. higher in age or standing; (placed after person's name) senior to relative of same name. ● n. senior person; one's elder or superior.□ **senior citizen** elderly person. □□ **seniority** n.

**senna** n. cassia; laxative from dried leaves and pods of this.

**sensation** n. 1 awareness or feeling produced by stimulation of sense organ or of mind; ability to feel such stimulation. 2 excited interest; person or thing producing this.

**sensational** adj. causing or intended to cause public excitement etc.; wonderful.□□ **sensationally** adv.

**sensationalism** n. use of or interest in sensational matters. □□ **sensationalist** n.

**sense** ● n. 1 any of faculties (sight, hearing, smell, taste, touch) by which a living thing becomes aware of external world; ability to perceive or be conscious of a thing. 2 practical wisdom. **3** meaning. **4** (**senses**) consciousness, sanity. ● *v.* perceive by sense or mental impression. □ **make sense** have meaning; be sensible idea. **make sense of** find meaning in.

**senseless** *adj.* **1** pointless. **2** foolish. **3** unconscious. □□ **senselessly** *adv.* **senselessness** *n.*

**sensibility** *n.* sensitiveness.

> **Usage** *Sensibility* should not be used to mean 'possession of good sense'.

**sensible** *adj.* **1** having or showing good sense. **2** aware. □□ **sensibly** *adv.*

**sensitise** *v.* (also **-ize**) make sensitive. □□ **sensitisation** *n.*

**sensitive** *adj.* **1** acutely affected by external impressions, having sensibility; easily offended or hurt; responsive to or recording slight changes of condition. **2** (of topic etc.) requiring tact or secrecy. □□ **sensitively** *adv.* **sensitiveness** *n.* **sensitivity** *n.*

**sensor** *n.* device to detect or measure physical property.

**sensory** *adj.* of sensation or senses.

**sensual** *adj.* of physical, esp. sexual, pleasure. □□ **sensuality** *n.* **sensually** *adv.*

**sensuous** *adj.* of or affecting senses; physically attractive, esp. sexually. □□ **sensuously** *adv.* **sensuousness** *n.*

**sent** see SEND.

**sentence** ● *n.* **1** series of words making single complete statement. **2** punishment decided by law court. ● *v.* **1** declare sentence of. **2** condemn.

**sentential** *adj.* pompously moralising; affectedly formal; using maxims. □□ **sententiously** *n.*

**sentient** *adj.* capable of perception and feeling. □□ **sentience** *n.* **sentiently** *adv.*

**sentiment** *n.* **1** mental feeling; opinion. **2** sentimentality.

**sentimental** *adj.* of or showing sentiment; showing or affected by emotion rather than reason; appealing to sentiment. □□ **sentimentalism** *n.* **sentimentality** *n.* **sentimentally** *adv.*

**sentinel** *n.* sentry.

**sentry** *n.* soldier etc. stationed to keep guard.

**sepal** *n.* division or leaf of calyx.

**separable** *adj.* able to be separated. □□ **separability** *n.*

**separate** ● *adj.* forming unit by itself, existing apart; disconnected, distinct, or individual. ● *n.* (in *pl.*) trousers, skirts, etc. that are not parts of suits. ● *v.* make separate, sever; prevent union or contact of; go different ways; (esp. as **separated** *adj.*) cease to live together as married or de facto couple; secede; divide or sort into parts or sizes; extract or remove (ingredient etc.). □□ **separately** *adv.* **separation** *n.* **separator** *n.*

**separatist** *n.* person who favours separation, esp. political independence. □□ **separatism** *n.*

**sepia** *n.* dark reddish-brown colour or paint; brown tint used in photography.

**sepsis** *n.* septic condition.

**Sept.** *abbr.* September.

**September** *n.* ninth month of year.

**septennial** *adj.* lasting for seven years; recurring every seven years.

**septet** *n.* **1** *Mus.* composition for seven performers; the performers. **2** any group of seven.

**septic** *adj.* contaminated with bacteria, putrefying. □ **septic tank** tank in which sewage is liquefied by bacterial action.

**septicaemia** *n.* (also **septicemia**) blood poisoning.

**septuagenarian** *n.* person from 70 to 79 years old.

**sepulchre** n. tomb, esp. cut in rock or built of stone or brick.

**sequel** n. what follows; novel, film, etc. that continues story of earlier one.

**sequence** n. **1** succession; order of succession; set of things belonging next to one another; unbroken series. **2** episode or incident in film etc.

**sequential** adj. forming sequence or consequence.□□ **sequentially** adv.

**sequester** v. **1** (esp. as **sequestered** adj.) seclude, isolate. **2** sequestrate.

**sequestrate** v. confiscate; take temporary possession of (debtor's estate etc.)□□ **sequestration** n. **sequestrator** n.

**sequin** n. circular spangle, esp. sewn on to clothing.□□ **sequinned** adj. (also **sequined**)

**seraglio** n. harem.

**serang** n. Aust. person in authority.

**seraph** n. (pl. **seraphim** or **seraphs**) member of highest of nine orders of angels.□□ **seraphic** adj.

**serenade** ● n. music played for lover, or suitable for this. ● v. perform serenade to.

**serendipity** n. faculty of making happy discoveries by accident. □□ **serendipitous** adj.

**serene** adj. clear and calm; tranquil, unperturbed.□□ **serenely** adv. **serenity** n.

**serf** n. hist. labourer who was not allowed to leave land on which he worked.□□ **serfdom** n.

**serge** n. durable woollen fabric.

**sergeant** n. non-commissioned military rank; rank in police. □ **sergeant baker** Aust. large brightly-coloured marine fish.

**serial** ● n. story published, broadcast, or shown in instalments. ● adj. of, in, or forming series.□ **serial killer** person who murders repeatedly. □□ **serially** adv.

**serialise** v. (also **-ize**) publish or produce in instalments. □□ **serialisation** n.

**series** n. (pl. **series**) number of similar or related things, events, etc.; succession, row, or set; set of related television or radio programs.

**serif** n. slight projection finishing off stroke of letter in certain typefaces.

**serious** adj. **1** thoughtful, solemn; sincere, in earnest. **2** important, demanding consideration, significant, not negligible; dangerous. □□ **seriously** adv. **seriousness** n.

**serjeant-at-arms** n. (pl. **serjeants-at-arms**) official of parliament, court, etc., with ceremonial duties.

**sermon** n. discourse on religion or morals, esp. delivered in church; admonition, reproof.

**sermonise** v. (also **-ize**) moralise (to).

**serpent** n. large snake.

**serpentine** ● adj. **1** of or like serpent; coiling, meandering. **2** cunning, treacherous. ● n. soft usu. dark green rock, sometimes mottled.

**serrated** adj. with sawlike edge. □□ **serration** n.

**serried** adj. close together.

**serum** n. (pl. **sera** or **serums**) fluid left when blood has clotted; this used for inoculation; watery fluid from animal tissue.

**servant** n. **1** person employed for domestic work. **2** devoted follower or helper.

**serve** ● v. **1** do service for; be servant to; carry out duty; be employed in (esp. armed forces). **2** be useful to or serviceable for; meet requirements. **3** perform function. **4** present (food) to eat. **5** act as waiter; attend to (customer etc.) **6** supply (with goods). **7** treat (person) in specified way. **8** Law deliver (writ etc.) **9** set (ball) in play at tennis etc. **10** spend (period)

at a post or prison. ● n. 1 service.
2 colloq. severe reprimand, rebuke.

**server** n. 1 person who serves or attends. 2 computer or program managing access to resource or service on network.

**servery** n. room or counter from which meals etc. are served.

**service** ● n. 1 work done or doing of work for employer or for community etc.; work done by machine etc.; assistance or benefit given.
2 provision of some public need, e.g. transport, or water, electricity, etc.
3 employment as servant; state or period of employment. 4 public or Crown department or organisation.
5 (**the services**) armed forces.
6 ceremony of worship; form of liturgy for this. 7 (routine) maintenance and repair of machine etc., quality of this. 8 assistance given to customers. 9 serving of food etc., quality of this. 10 set of dishes etc. for serving meals. 11 act of serving in tennis etc.; person's turn to serve; game in which one player serves.
● v. 1 maintain or repair (car, machine, etc.) 2 provide with service for. 3 pay interest etc. on (debt).
□ **service station** place beside road selling petrol etc.

**serviceable** adj. 1 useful. 2 durable but plain. □□ **serviceability** n.

**serviette** n. table napkin.

**servile** adj. excessively submissive.
□□ **servility** n.

**servitude** n. slavery, subjection.

**sesame** n. plant with seeds used as food and yielding edible oil; its seeds.

**sesqui-** comb. form one and a half (sesquicentenary.)

**session** n. 1 period devoted to an activity. 2 assembly of parliament, court, etc.; single meeting for this; period during which such meetings

are regularly held. 3 colloq. period spent drinking or using drugs.
□□ **sessional** adj.

**set** ● v. (**set, setting**) 1 put, place, or fix in position or readiness; fix or appoint (date etc.); assign as something to be done; put into specified state. 2 make or become hard, firm, or established.
3 have certain movement. 4 (of sun etc.) be brought below horizon by earth's movement. ● n. 1 way a thing sets or is set. 2 people or things grouped as similar or forming unit.
3 games forming part of match in tennis. 4 Surfing series of waves followed by lull. 5 radio or television receiver. 6 setting, stage furniture, etc. for play, film, etc. 7 Aust. colloq. a grudge. □ **set about** begin (a task); attack. **set back** halt or slow progress of; cost (person) specified amount. **set eyes on** catch sight of. **set fire to** cause to burn. **set forth** set out. **set in** become established. **set off** begin journey; cause to explode; improve appearance of by contrast. **set out** declare, make known; begin journey. **set piece** formal or elaborate construction. **set sail** begin sea journey. **set square** right-angled triangular drawing instrument. **set up** 1 establish; erect.
2 colloq. make (innocent person) to appear guilty. **set-up** organisation or arrangement.

**setback** n. delay in progress; problem.

**settee** n. sofa.

**setter** n. dog of long-haired breed.

**setting** n. 1 position or manner in which thing is set. 2 surroundings; period, place, etc. of story, film, etc.
3 frame etc. for jewel. 4 music to which words are set. 5 cutlery, plates, etc. for one person at table.
6 operating level of machine.

**settle** v. 1 establish or become established in way of life or lifestyle.
2 regain calm after disturbance.

**3** adopt regular or secure way of life. **4** apply oneself. **5** (cause to) sit down or come to rest. **6** become or make composed etc. **7** determine, decide, agree on; resolve (dispute etc.); agree to terminate (lawsuit). **8** pay (bill). **9** establish; colonise. **10** subside, sink. □□ **settler** n.

**settlement** n. **1** settling, being settled; place occupied by settlers; small community. **2** Aust. Aboriginal community. **3** political or financial etc. agreement. **4** arrangement ending dispute. **5** terms on which property is given to person; deed stating these; amount or property given.

**seven** adj. & n. one more than six (7, VII). □□ **seventh** adj. & n.

**seventeen** adj. & n. one more than sixteen (17, XVII). □□ **seventeenth** adj. & n.

**seventy** adj. & n. seven times ten (70, LXX). □□ **seventieth** adj. & n.

**sever** v. divide, break, or make separate, esp. by cutting; end employment contract (of person). □□ **severance** n.

**several** ● pron. more than two but not many; a few. ● adj. **1** a few. **2** quite a large number of. **3** formal separate or respective. □□ **severally** adv.

**severe** adj. **1** rigorous and harsh; serious; forceful; extreme; exacting. **2** plain in style. □□ **severely** adv. **severity** n.

**sew** v. (sewed, sewn or sewed, sewing) fasten, join, etc. with needle and thread or sewing machine; make (garment etc.) thus.

**sewage** n. waste matter carried in sewers.

**sewer** n. (usu. underground) conduit for carrying off drainage water and waste matter.

**sewerage** n. system of or drainage by sewers.

**sewing** n. material or work to be sewn.

**sewn** see SEW.

**sex** ● n. **1** of males or females collectively; fact of belonging to either group. **2** sexual instincts, desires, activity, etc. **3** sexual intercourse, sexual activity.
● v. **1** determine sex of. **2** (as **sexed** adj.) having specified sexual appetite. ● adj. of or relating to sex or sexual difference.

**sexagenarian** n. person from 60 to 69 years old.

**sexist** adj. discriminating in favour of one sex; assuming person's abilities and social functions are predetermined by his or her sex. □□ **sexism** n.

**sexless** adj. **1** neither male nor female. **2** lacking sexual desire or attractiveness.

**sext** ● v. (usu. as n. **sexting** ) send (someone) sexually explicit images or messages via mobile phone.
● n. such an image or message.

**sextant** n. optical instrument for measuring angle between distant objects, esp. sun and horizon.

**sextet** n. group of six instruments or voices; music for these.

**sexton** n. person who looks after church and churchyard.

**sextuplet** n. each of six children born at one birth.

**sexual** adj. of sex, the sexes, or relations between them.
□ **sexual intercourse** sexual contact involving penetration, esp. insertion of penis into vagina. □□ **sexuality** n. **sexually** adv.

**sexy** adj. **1** sexually attractive or provocative. **2** colloq. (of project etc.) exciting. □□ **sexily** adv. **sexiness** n.

**Sgt** abbr. Sergeant.

**shabby** adj. **1** faded and worn, dingy, dilapidated. **2** contemptible. □□ **shabbily** adv. **shabbiness** n.

**shack** *n.* roughly built hut or cabin; small holiday house. □ **shack up** *colloq.* cohabit.

**shackle** ● *n.* metal loop or link closed by bolt; coupling link; fetter; restraint. ● *v.* fetter, impede, restrain.

**shade** ● *n.* 1 comparative darkness; place sheltered from the sun; screen or cover used to block or moderate light; (**shades**) sunglasses. 2 degree or depth of colour. 3 a differing variety. 4 a small amount. ● *v.* 1 block rays of; give shade to; darken (parts of a drawing). 2 pass or change gradually into another colour or variety.

**shadecloth** *n.* heavy knitted fibreglass etc. fabric, used over pergola, in shadehouse, etc. to moderate sunlight.

**shadehouse** *n.* roofed structure to protect sensitive plants from summer sun.

**shadow** ● *n.* 1 shade or patch of shade. 2 dark shape projected by body blocking out light. 3 inseparable attendant or companion. 4 person secretly following another. 5 slightest trace; insubstantial remnant. 6 gloom, sadness. ● *v.* 1 cast shadow over. 2 secretly follow and watch. □ **Shadow Cabinet** members of the main opposition party in parliament holding posts parallel to those of the government Cabinet. □□ **shadowy** *adj.*

**shady** *adj.* 1 giving or situated in shade. 2 disreputable; of doubtful honesty.

**shaft** ● *n.* 1 narrow usu. vertical space for access to mine or (in building) for lift, ventilation, etc. 2 ray (of light). 3 bolt (of lightning). 4 handle of tool etc. 5 long narrow part supporting, connecting, or driving (thicker part(s) etc. 6 arrow, spear, its long slender stem. 7 hurtful or provocative remark. 8 each of pair of poles between which horse is harnessed to vehicle. 9 central part of feather. 10 column, esp. between base and capital. ● *v.* treat harshly or unfairly.

**shag**¹ ● *n.* 1 coarse tobacco. 2 rough mass of hair. 3 carpet with long rough pile. 4 cormorant. ● *adj.* (of carpet) with long rough pile. □ **shag on a rock** *Aust.* emblem of isolation, deprivation, etc.

**shag**² *colloq.* ● *v.* 1 have sexual intercourse with. 2 exhaust; tire out. ● *n.* act of sexual intercourse.

**shaggy** *adj.* 1 hairy, rough-haired. 2 unkempt. □□ **shagginess** *n.*

**shagreen** *n.* kind of untanned granulated leather. 2 sharkskin.

**shah** *n. hist.* ruler of Iran.

**shake** ● *v.* (**shook**, **shaken**, **shaking**) 1 move quickly up and down or to and fro; dislodge by doing this. 2 shock. 3 make less firm. 4 (of voice) become uneven. 5 shake hands. ● *n.* 1 shaking, being shaken. 2 a shock. 3 (**the shakes**) *colloq.* fit of trembling. 4 milkshake. □ **shake-up** upheaval, reorganisation. □□ **shaker** *n.*

**shaky** *adj.* unsteady; trembling; unsound, infirm; unreliable. □□ **shakily** *adv.* **shakiness** *n.*

**shale** *n.* soft rock that splits easily. □□ **shaly** *adj.*

**shall** *v.aux.* used with *I* and *we* to express future tense, and with other words in promises or statements of obligation.

**shallot** *n.* onion-like plant with cluster of small bulbs.

**shallow** ● *adj.* of little depth; superficial, trivial. ● *n.* shallow place. □□ **shallowness** *n.*

**shalom** *n. & int.* Jewish salutation at meeting or parting.

**sham** ● *v.* (**shammed**) pretend; pretend (to be). ● *n.* a pretence; something that is not genuine. ● *adj.* pretended, counterfeit.

**shaman** ● *n.* person regarded as having access to, and influence in, the world of good and evil spirits.
□□ **shamanism** *n.*

**shamble** ● *v.* walk or run awkwardly, dragging feet. ● *n.* shambling gait.

**shambles** *n. colloq.* mess, muddle; scene of carnage.

**shame** ● *n.* humiliation caused by consciousness of guilt or folly; capacity for feeling this; state of disgrace or discredit; person or thing that brings disgrace etc.; wrong or regrettable thing. ● *v.* bring disgrace on, make ashamed; force by shame.

**shamefaced** *adj.* looking ashamed.

**shameful** *adj.* disgraceful, scandalous. □□ **shamefully** *adv.* **shamefulness** *n.*

**shameless** *adj.* having or showing no shame; impudent. □□ **shamelessly** *adv.*

**shammy** *n. colloq.* chamois leather.

**shampoo** ● *n.* **1** liquid for washing hair. **2** similar substance for washing upholstery, carpets, etc. ● *v.* wash with shampoo.

**shamrock** *n.* clover-like plant as national emblem of Ireland.

**shandy** *n.* beer with lemonade or ginger beer.

**shanghai** ● *v.* **1** *hist.* trick or force (person) to do something, esp. be a sailor. **2** *Aust.* shoot with catapult. **3** *colloq.* steal. ● *n. Aust.* child's catapult.

**shank** *n.* leg; lower part of leg; shaft or stem, esp. part of tool etc. joining handle to working end.

**shantung** *n.* soft undressed Chinese silk.

**shanty** *n.* **1** hut, cabin. **2** sailors' work song.

**shape** ● *n.* **1** outline; form; specific form or guise. **2** good or specified condition. **3** person or thing seen indistinctly. **4** mould, pattern.
● *v.* give certain form to; fashion, create; influence; make conform.
□□ **shapeless** *adj.*

**shapely** *adj.* of pleasing shape, well-proportioned. □□ **shapeliness** *n.*

**shard** *n.* broken fragment of pottery, glass, etc.

**share** *n.* **1** portion of whole given to or taken from person. **2** each of equal parts into which company's capital is divided, entitling owner to proportion of profits. **3** instance of posting or reposting something on social media. ● *v.* **1** have or use with another or others. **2** get, have, or give share of. **3** participate. **4** divide and distribute. **5** have in common. **6** post or repost (something) on social media. □ **share farmer** *Aust.* tenant farmer who receives an agreed share of the profits from the land.

**shareholder** *n.* owner of shares in company.

**sharemarket** *n. Aust.* stock exchange.

**shareware** *n.* computer programs freely available for trial, paid for by fee to author if used regularly.

**shark** *n.* **1** large voracious sea fish. **2** *colloq.* swindler, profiteer. ● *v. AFL* intercept ball passed between two members of opposing team.

**sharkskin** *n.* fabric with slightly lustrous textured weave.

**sharp** ● *adj.* **1** having edge or point able to cut or pierce; tapering to point or edge. **2** abrupt, steep, angular. **3** well-defined. **4** severe, intense. **5** pungent, acid. **6** shrill, piercing. **7** harsh. **8** acute, sensitive, clever. **9** unscrupulous. **10** vigorous, brisk. **11** *Mus.* above true pitch, semitone higher than note named. ● *n.* **1** *Mus.* sharp note; sign ( # ) indicating this. **2** (usu. in *pl.*) syringe. **3** *colloq.* swindler, cheat. ● *adv.* **1** punctually, exactly. **2** suddenly. **3** at sharp angle.

**4** *Mus.* above true pitch. □□ **sharply** *adv.* **sharpness** *n.*

**sharpen** *v.* make or become sharp or sharper.

**shatter** *v.* break suddenly in pieces; severely damage, destroy; upset calmness of.

**shave** ● *v.* **1** remove (bristles, hair) with razor. **2** reduce by small amount. **3** pare (wood etc.) to shape it. **4** miss or pass narrowly. ● *n.* **1** shaving, being shaved. **2** narrow miss or escape. □□ **shaver** *n.*

**shaven** *adj.* shaved.

**shaving** *n.* thin paring of wood, cheese, etc.

**shawl** *n.* large usu. rectangular piece of fabric worn over shoulders etc. or wrapped around baby.

**she** *pron.* **1** female person or animal in question. **2** thing in question.

**s/he** *pron.* written representation of 'he or she'.

**sheaf** ● *n.* (*pl.* **sheaves**) bundle of things laid lengthwise together and usu. tied, esp. reaped wheat or collection of papers. ● *v.* make into sheaves.

**shear** ● *v.* (**sheared**, **shorn**) **1** clip wool off (sheep etc.); remove by cutting; cut with scissors, shears, etc. **2** strip bare, deprive. **3** distort, be distorted, or break. ● *n.* **1** strain produced by pressure in structure of substance. **2** (**shears**) scissor-shaped clipping or cutting instrument. □ **shears** *Aust.* (of sheep) newly shorn. □□ **shearer** *n.* **shearing** *n.*

**shearwater** *n.* long-winged seabird.

**sheath** *n.* close-fitting cover, esp. for blade; condom.

**sheathe** *v.* put into a case; encase in a covering.

**shebang** *n. colloq.* matter or affair.

**shed** ● *n.* **1** building for storage or shelter, or as workshop. **2** *Aust.* shearing shed; gang of shearers working in it. ● *v.* (**shed**, **shedding**) **1** lose by natural falling off; take off; allow to fall or flow. **2** put (animals) into shed. □ **shed hand** *Aust.* semi-skilled or unskilled worker in shearing shed.

**sheen** *n.* lustre; brightness.

**sheep** *n.* (*pl.* **sheep**) **1** mammal with thick woolly coat, esp. kept for its wool or meat. **2** timid, silly, or easily-led person. □ **sheep dip** preparation for cleansing sheep of vermin; deep trough where sheep are dipped in this.

**sheepdog** *n.* dog trained to herd sheep.

**sheepish** *adj.* embarrassed or shy; ashamed. □□ **sheepishly** *adv.*

**sheepskin** *n.* sheep's skin with wool on; coat etc. made of this.

**sheer** ● *adj.* **1** pure, not mixed or qualified. **2** very steep. **3** (of textile) diaphanous. ● *adv.* directly, straight up or down. ● *v.* swerve or change course.

**sheet** ● *n.* **1** large rectangle of cotton etc. as part of bedclothes. **2** broad thin flat piece of paper, metal, etc. **3** wide expanse of water, ice, flame, etc. **4** rope at lower corner of sail to control it. ● *v.* **1** cover (as) with sheets. **2** (of rain etc.) fall in sheets.

**sheikh** *n.* **1** chief or head of Arab community, family, or village. **2** Muslim leader. □□ **sheikhdom** *n.*

**sheila** *n. Aust. colloq.* girl or woman; girlfriend.

**shelf** *n.* (*pl.* **shelves**) wooden etc. board projecting from wall, or forming part of bookcase, cupboard, etc.; ledge on cliff face etc.; reef or sandbank. □ **shelf life** time for which stored item of food etc. remains usable.

**shell** ● *n.* **1** hard outer case of many molluscs, tortoise, egg, nut kernel, seed, etc. **2** explosive artillery projectile. **3** hollow container for fireworks, cartridges, etc.; outer structure of something, esp. when hollow. **4** *Computing* interface program mediating access to server etc. ● v. **1** remove shell or pod from. **2** bombard with shells. □ **shell out** *colloq.* pay (sum of money). **shell shock** psychological disturbance from exposure to battle conditions; state or feeling of severe shock or surprise.

**shellac** ● n. resin used for making varnish. ● v. (**shellacked**) varnish with shellac.

**shellfish** n. edible water animal that has a shell.

**shelter** ● n. protection from danger, bad weather, etc.; placing providing this. ● v. act or serve as shelter to; shield; take shelter.

**shelve** v. **1** put aside, esp. temporarily. **2** put on shelf. **3** (of ground) slope.

**shelving** n. shelves.

**shepherd** ● n. **1** person who tends sheep; pastor. ● v. **1** tend (sheep); marshal or guide like sheep. **2** (in football etc.) guard teammate in possession of ball by blocking opponents etc.

**sherbet** n. **1** flavoured effervescent powder or drink. **2** *Aust. colloq.* beer.

**sheriff** n. **1** *Aust.* officer of Supreme Court enforcing judgments and execution of writs, and attending to administrative matters. **2** *US* elected chief law-enforcing officer in county. **3** *Brit.* Crown's chief executive officer in county.

**sherry** n. fortified wine orig. from Spain.

**shiatsu** n. Japanese therapy involving pressure on specific points of body.

**shibboleth** n. **1** custom, mode of dress, etc., distinguishing particular class etc. of people; catchword, formula, etc. adopted by party or sect by which its followers may be discerned. **2** long-standing doctrine held to be true by party or sect.

**shickered** adj. (also **shicker**) *Aust. colloq.* drunk.

**shield** ● n. **1** piece of armour held in front of body when fighting; person or thing giving protection; protective plate or screen in machinery etc.; shieldlike part of animal, esp. shell. **2** shield-shaped trophy. ● v. protect or screen.

**shift** ● v. (cause to) change or move from one position to another; remove, esp. with effort; *colloq.* hurry; *colloq.* sell. ● n. **1** shifting. **2** relay of workers; period for which they work. **3** woman's loose straight dress. **4** key on keyboard for switching between lower and upper case etc.

**shiftless** adj. lazy and inefficient.

**shifty** adj. *colloq.* evasive; deceitful.

**Shi'ite** (also **Shiite**) ● n. adherent of branch of Islam rejecting first three Sunni caliphs. ● adj. of this branch.

**shilling** n. *hist.* former coin and monetary unit of Australia, Britain, etc., worth one-twentieth of pound.

**shilly-shally** v. be indecisive.

**shimmer** ● v. shine tremulously or faintly. ● n. tremulous or faint light.

**shimmy** n. dance involving shaking of whole body.

**shin** ● n. front of leg below knee; cut of beef from this part. ● v. (**shinned**) (**shin up**) climb quickly using arms and legs.

**shindig** n. *colloq.* **1** lively noisy party. **2** brawl, disturbance.

**shine** ● v. (**shone**, **shining**) **1** emit or reflect light, be bright, glow; cause to shine. **2** (of sun, star, etc.) be visible. **3** be brilliant, excel. (**shined**, **shining**) **4** polish. ● n. light; brightness; polish; lustre.

**shiner** n. *colloq.* black eye.

**shingle** n. **1** small smooth pebbles on seashore. **2** rectangular wooden tile used on roofs etc. **3** (**shingles**) disease with rash of small blisters. □□ **shingly** adj.

**shingleback** n. Aust. slow-moving lizard with short rounded tail.

**Shinto** n. Japanese religion with worship of ancestors and nature spirits. □□ **Shintoism** n.

**shiny** adj. **1** having shine. **2** (of clothing) with nap worn off.

**ship** ● n. large seagoing vessel. ● v. (**shipped**) put or take on board a ship; transport.

**shipment** n. goods shipped; act of shipping goods etc.

**shipping** n. transport of goods etc.; cost of this; ships collectively.

**shipshape** adv. & adj. in good order, tidy.

**shipwreck** n. destruction of ship by storm or striking rocks etc. □□ **shipwrecked** adj.

**shipyard** n. establishment where ships are built.

**shiralee** n. Aust. dated swag.

**shire** n. **1** Aust. local government administrative unit, esp. in rural areas. **2** Brit. county.

**shirk** v. avoid (duty, work, etc.) □□ **shirker** n.

**shirr** n. elasticated gathered threads forming smocking.

**shirt** n. lightweight garment for upper part of body. □ **shirt-front** Aust. **1** esp. AFL deliver fierce tackle on (opponent). **2** colloq. confront (someone) in an aggressive way.

**shirty** adj. colloq. angry; annoyed. □□ **shirtily** adv. **shirtiness** n.

**shish kebab** n. pieces of meat and vegetables grilled on skewer.

**shit** coarse colloq. ● n. **1** faeces. **2** defecating. **3** contemptible person. **4** nonsense. ● v. (**shitted** or **shat** or **shit, shitting**) defecate.

**shiver** v. **1** tremble slightly, esp. with cold or fear. **2** shatter. ● n. shivering movement. □□ **shivery** adj.

**shivoo** n. Aust. colloq. party or celebration.

**shoal** ● n. **1** multitude, esp. of fish swimming together. **2** area of shallow water. ● v. form shoal(s).

**shock** ● n. **1** violent collision, impact, etc. **2** sudden and disturbing emotional effect. **3** acute prostration following wound, pain, etc. **4** electric shock. **5** disturbance in stability of organisation etc. **6** unkempt or shaggy mass of hair. ● v. **1** horrify; outrage. **2** cause shock; experience shock. □ **shock jock** presenter on radio program who expresses opinions in deliberately offensive or provocative way.

**shocker** n. colloq. shocking person or thing; extremely bad or disappointing thing.

**shocking** adj. causing shock; scandalous; colloq. very bad. □□ **shockingly** adv.

**shod** see SHOE.

**shoddy** adj. poorly made; base, mean. □□ **shoddily** adv. **shoddiness** n.

**shoe** ● n. protective foot covering of leather etc., esp. one not reaching above ankle; protective metal rim for horse's hoof; thing like shoe in shape or use. ● v. (**shod, shoeing**) fit with shoe(s).

**shoehorn** n. curved implement for easing one's heel into shoe.

**shoelace** n. cord for lacing up shoes.

**shoestring** n. **1** shoelace. **2** colloq. barely adequate amount of money.

**shonky** adj. Aust. colloq. unreliable; unsound; dishonest.

**shoo** ● int. sound uttered to frighten animals etc. away. ● v. (**shoos, shooed**) drive away by this.

**shook** see SHAKE.

**shoot** ● v. (**shot, shooting**) **1** cause (weapon) to discharge missile; kill or wound with bullet, arrow, etc.; send out or discharge rapidly. **2** come or go swiftly or suddenly. **3** (of plant) put forth buds etc. **4** film, photograph.

**shop | shove**

5 *Football etc.* score or take shot at (goal). 6 *Surfing* ride (wave). 7 *colloq.* inject (drug). ● *n.* 1 young branch or sucker. 2 hunting party or expedition. □ **shooting gallery** *colloq.* place where intravenous drug users may inject (heroin etc.) in safety. **shooting star** small meteor.

**shop** ● *n.* 1 place for retail sale of goods or services; act of shopping. 2 workshop. ● *v.* (**shopped**) go to shop or shops to buy goods. □ **shop around** look for best bargain. **shop floor** workers as distinct from management. **shop-soiled** soiled from being on display in shop. **shop steward** trade union official elected by workers as their spokesperson. □□ **shopper** *n.*

**shoplifter** *n.* person who steals goods from shop. □□ **shoplifting** *n.*

**shopping** *n.* buying goods in shops; goods bought.

**shore** ● *n.* land adjoining sea, lake, etc. ● *v.* prop or support with length of timber.

**shorn** see SHEAR.

**short** ● *adj.* 1 measuring little from end to end in space or time, or from head to foot. 2 deficient; scanty. 3 concise, brief. 4 curt; uncivil. 5 *colloq.* lacking in money. 6 (of memory) unable to remember distant events. 7 (of vowel or syllable) having the lesser of two recognised durations. 8 (of pastry) easily crumbled. 9 (of odds) nearly even. ● *adv.* 1 before the natural or expected time or place. 2 abruptly. 3 rudely. ● *n.* 1 short circuit. 2 short film. ● (**shorts**) trousers that do not reach ankle. ● *v.* short-circuit. □ **short-sighted** unable to see clearly only what is close; lacking foresight. **short wave** radio wave of frequency greater than 3 MHz. □□ **shorten** *v.*

**shortage** *n.* deficiency; lack.

**shortbread** *n.* rich sweet biscuit.

**short circuit** ● *n.* fault in electrical circuit when current flows by shorter route than normal. ● *v.* (**short-circuit**) cause short circuit in; bypass.

**shortcoming** *n.* failure to reach required standard; a fault.

**shortening** *n.* fat used to make pastry etc.

**shortfall** *n.* deficit.

**shorthand** *n.* method of writing rapidly with system of symbols.

**shortlist** ● *n.* list of selected candidates from which final choice will be made. ● *v.* put on shortlist.

**shortly** *adv.* 1 soon. 2 curtly.

**shot** ● *v.* see SHOOT. ● *n.* 1 firing of gun etc.; sound of this; person of specified skill in shooting; missiles for cannon, gun, etc. 2 an attempt to hit something or reach target; a stroke in certain ball games; an attempt. 3 heavy ball thrown as a sport. 4 a photograph. 5 injection. 6 *colloq.* measure of spirits. □ **like a shot** *colloq.* without hesitation.

**should** *v.aux.* used to express duty or obligation, a possible or expected future action, or (with *I* or *we*) a polite statement or a conditional or indefinite clause.

**shoulder** ● *n.* 1 part of body where arm or foreleg is attached; animal's upper foreleg as joint of meat. 2 strip of land next to road. ● *v.* 1 push with one's shoulder. 2 take (blame or responsibility etc.) on oneself.

**shout** ● *v.* 1 speak or cry loudly. 2 *Aust.* buy drink(s) for person(s). 3 *Aust.* give as treat etc. ● *n.* 1 loud cry of joy or call to attention. 2 *Aust.* round of drinks; person's turn to buy round of drinks etc. □ **shout down** silence by shouting.

**shove** ● *v.* 1 push vigorously. 2 *colloq.* put casually. ● *n.* act of shoving. □ **shove off** 1 push away from shore in boat. 2 *colloq.* go away.

**shovel** ● *n.* spadelike scoop for shifting earth etc. ● *v.* (**shovelled**) move (as) with shovel.

**show** ● *v.* (**showed, shown, showing**) 1 allow or cause to be seen, offer for inspection or viewing; be able to be seen; present an image of. 2 demonstrate, point out, prove; cause to understand. 3 conduct. ● *n.* 1 process of showing; display, public exhibition or performance; outward appearance. 2 *Med.* discharge of blood etc. at onset of childbirth. 3 *colloq.* chance. □ **show business** entertainment profession. **show off** display well, proudly, or ostentatiously; try to impress people. **show up** 1 make or be clearly visible; reveal (fault etc.) 2 *colloq.* arrive.

**showdown** *n.* confrontation that settles argument.

**shower** ● *n.* 1 brief fall of rain, snow, etc. 2 brisk flurry of bullets, dust, etc. 3 sudden copious arrival of gifts, honours, etc. 4 cubicle, bath, etc. in which one stands under spray of water; act of bathing in shower. 5 (in full **shower party** or **shower tea**) party for giving presents to prospective bride, newborn baby, etc. ● *v.* 1 take shower. 2 lavishly bestow. 3 descend, send, or give in shower.

**showery** *adj.* with showers of rain.

**showjumping** *n.* competitive sport of riding horses to jump over obstacles. □□ **showjumper** *n.*

**showman** *n.* (*pl.* **showmen**) organiser of circuses or theatrical entertainments.

**showmanship** *n.* skill in presenting entertainment or goods etc. well.

**shown** SEE SHOW.

**showroom** *n.* room where goods are displayed for inspection.

**showy** *adj.* (**showier**) striking; ostentatious or gaudy. □□ **showily** *adv.* **showiness** *n.*

**shoyu** *n.* type of Japanese soy sauce.

**shrank** SEE SHRINK.

**shrapnel** *n.* 1 fragments of exploded bomb etc. 2 *Aust. colloq.* small change.

**shred** ● *n.* scrap, fragment; least amount. ● *v.* (**shredded**) tear or cut into shreds. □□ **shredder** *n.*

**shrew** *n.* small mouselike long-nosed European mammal.

**shrewd** *adj.* astute; clever. □□ **shrewdly** *adv.* **shrewdness** *n.*

**shriek** ● *n.* shrill scream or sound. ● *v.* make shriek; say in shrill tones.

**shrike** *n.* bird with strong hooked and toothed bill.

**shrill** ● *adj.* piercing and high-pitched. ● *v.* sound or utter shrilly. □□ **shrillness** *n.* **shrilly** *adv.*

**shrimp** *n.* 1 small edible shellfish. 2 *colloq.* very small person.

**shrine** *n.* sacred or revered place; casket or tomb holding sacred relics.

**shrink** ● *v.* (**shrank, shrunk, shrinking**) 1 make or become smaller. 2 recoil, flinch. ● *n.* 1 shrinking. 2 *colloq.* psychiatrist.

**shrinkage** *n.* 1 shrinking of textile fabric. 2 loss by theft or wastage.

**shrivel** *v.* (**shrivelled**) contract into wrinkled or dried-up state.

**shroud** ● *n.* 1 wrapping for corpse; thing that conceals. 2 rope supporting mast. ● *v.* clothe (corpse) for burial; cover, conceal.

**shrub** *n.* woody plant smaller than tree and usu. branching from near ground. □□ **shrubby** *adj.*

**shrubbery** *n.* area planted with shrubs.

**shrug** ● *v.* (**shrugged**) draw up (shoulders) momentarily as gesture of indifference, ignorance, etc. ● *n.* shrugging movement.

**shrunk** SEE SHRINK.

**shudder** ● *v.* 1 shiver from fear, cold, etc. 2 feel strong repugnance, fear, etc. 3 vibrate. ● *n.* act of shuddering.

**shuffle** ● v. 1 drag or slide (feet) in walking. 2 re-arrange or mix up (esp. cards); play or arrange (tracks on music player) in a random order. 3 keep shifting one's position. ● n. 1 shuffling action or movement. 2 change of relative positions.

**shun** v. (shunned) avoid.

**shunt** ● v. 1 move (train etc.) to another track. 2 redirect. ● n. 1 shunting, being shunted. 2 conductor joining two points of electric circuit for diversion of current. 3 *Surgery* alternative path for circulation of blood.

**shush** int. & v. colloq. hush!

**shut** v. (**shut, shutting**) 1 move (door, window, lid, etc.) into position to block opening; become or be capable of being closed or sealed. 2 become or make closed for trade. 3 fold or contract (book, telescope, etc.) 4 bar access to (place). □ **shut down** stop or cease working or business. **shut-eye** colloq. sleep. **shut off** supply of. **shut out** exclude (person, light, etc.) from a place; block from the mind. 2 prevent (a possibility etc.) **shut up** 1 shut securely. 2 colloq. stop talking or making noise.

**shutter** n. 1 movable hinged cover for window. 2 device for exposing film in camera.

**shuttle** ● n. 1 part of loom which carries weft thread between warp threads; thread carrier carrying lower thread in sewing machine. 2 train, bus, etc. used in shuttle service. 3 spacecraft for repeated use. ● v. (cause to) move to and fro like shuttle.

**shuttlecock** n. small cone-shaped feathered object struck to and fro in badminton.

**shy** ● adj. 1 timid and nervous in company; self-conscious; easily startled. 2 colloq. having lost. 3 short of. ● v. (**shies, shied**) jump in alarm; avoid something through

nervousness. ● n. sudden startled movement. □□ **shyly** adv. shyness n.

**shyster** n. colloq. derog. unscrupulous or unprofessional person.

**SI** abbr. Système International, international system of units of measurement.

**Siamese** adj. of Siam, former name of Thailand. □ **Siamese cat** cat of cream-coloured short-haired breed. **Siamese twins** = CONJOINED TWINS.

**sibilant** adj. 1 sounded with hiss. 2 hissing. □□ **sibilance** n.

**sibling** n. brother or sister.

**sibyl** n. prophetess.

**sic** adv. used or spelt thus (confirming form of quoted words).

**sick**[1] ● adj. 1 unwell; ill; vomiting or likely to vomit. 2 colloq. disgusted; surfeited. 3 colloq. (of joke) cruel, morbid, perverted, offensive. 4 colloq. excellent. ● n. colloq. vomit. ● v. colloq. vomit.

**sick**[2] v. (also **sic**) set upon; attack.

**sicken** v. 1 make or become sick, disgusted, etc.; show symptoms of illness. 2 (as **sickening** adj.) disgusting. □□ **sickeningly** adv.

**sickie** n. Aust. colloq. day's sick leave, esp. taken without sufficient medical reason.

**sickle** n. short-handled tool with semicircular blade. □ **sickle cell** sickle-shaped blood cell, esp. as found in type of severe hereditary anaemia.

**sickly** adj. 1 weak. 2 liable to be ill. 3 faint, pale. 4 causing sickness. 5 mawkish, weakly sentimental.

**sickness** n. being ill; disease; vomiting, nausea. □ **sickness country** (in Australian Aboriginal belief) area of spiritual significance where mythological beings may cause illness, esp. to those disturbing or profaning area.

**side** ● *n.* **1** each of inner or outer surfaces of object, esp. as distinct from top and bottom or front and back or ends; bounding line of plane figure; slope of hill or ridge. **2** part near an edge; region next to person or thing. **3** either of two halves into which something is divided; aspect of a problem etc.; one of two opposing groups or teams etc. ● *v.* join forces with person in a dispute. ● *adj.* at or on the side. □ **on the side** as a sideline; as surreptitious activity. **side by side** close together. **side effect** secondary (usu. bad) effect.

**sideboard** *n.* **1** piece of dining-room furniture with drawers and cupboards for china etc. **2** (**sideboards**) sideburns.

**sideburns** *n.pl.* hair grown by man down side of face.

**sideline** *n.* **1** something done in addition to one's main activity. **2** (**sidelines**) lines bounding the sides of football field etc.; place for spectators; position etc. apart from main action.

**sidelong** ● *adj.* **1** directed to the side. **2** oblique. ● *adv.* to the side.

**sidereal** *adj.* of or measured or determined by stars.

**sideshow** *n.* small show or attraction forming part of large one.

**sidestep** *v.* (**sidestepped**) avoid by stepping sideways; evade.

**sidetrack** *v.* divert.

**sidewalk** *n.* US pavement.

**sideways** *adj. & adv.* **1** to or from a side. **2** with one side facing forward.

**siding** *n.* short track at side of railway line for shunting etc.

**sidle** *v.* walk timidly or furtively.

**SIDS** *abbr.* sudden infant death syndrome; cot death.

**siege** *n.* surrounding and blockading of place by armed forces in order to capture it.

**sienna** *n.* kind of earth used as pigment; its colour of reddish- or yellowish-brown.

**sierra** *n.* long jagged mountain chain, esp. in Spain or Spanish America.

**siesta** *n.* afternoon sleep or rest, esp. in hot countries.

**sieve** ● *n.* perforated or meshed utensil for separating solids or coarse material from liquids or fine particles. ● *v.* sift.

**sift** *v.* **1** separate with or cause to pass through sieve. **2** closely examine details of, analyse. **3** (of snow, light, etc.) fall as if from sieve.

**sigh** ● *v.* **1** emit long deep audible breath in sadness, weariness, relief, etc. **2** yearn. ● *n.* act of sighing; sound (like that) made in sighing.

**sight** ● *n.* **1** ability to see; seeing, being seen. **2** something seen or worth seeing; unsightly thing. **3** device looked through to aim or observe with gun or telescope etc. ● *v.* get sight of; aim or observe with sight etc. □ **sight-read** play or sing (music) without preliminary study of score.

**sightseeing** *n.* visiting places of interest. □□ **sightseer** *n.*

**sign** ● *n.* **1** indication of quality, state, future event, etc. **2** mark, symbol, etc. **3** gesture or motion used to convey order, information, etc. **4** signpost. **5** each of twelve divisions of zodiac. ● *v.* **1** write one's name on (document etc.) as authorisation. **2** communicate by sign or gesture. □ **sign in** sign a register on arrival. **sign on 1** agree to contract, employment, etc. **2** begin work. **sign up** commit oneself to period of employment, education, etc.

**signal** ● *n.* **1** sign, esp. prearranged one, conveying information etc.; message of such signs; device on railway giving instructions or warnings to train drivers etc. **2** event which causes immediate activity. **3** electrical

impulses or radio waves transmitted as signal; sequence of these. ● *v.* (**signalled**) make signal(s); transmit, announce, or direct by signal.
● *adj.* remarkable, noteworthy.
□□ **signaller** *n.* **signally** *adv.*

**signalman** *n.* railway employee responsible for operating signals and points.

**signatory** *n.* party or esp. nation that has signed agreement etc.

**signature** *n.* **1** person's name or initials used in signing; act of signing. **2** *Mus.* indication of key or tempo at beginning of musical score.
□ **signature tune** tune used to announce particular performer or program.

**signet** *n.* small seal.

**significance** *n.* **1** importance. **2** meaning. **3** being significant.
□□ **significant** *adj.* **significantly** *adv.*

**signification** *n.* meaning.

**signify** *v.* be sign or symbol of; mean, represent; communicate; make known; be of importance, matter.

**Sikh** *n.* member of Indian religion.

**silage** *n.* **1** green fodder stored in silo. **2** storage in silo.

**silence** ● *n.* **1** absence of sound; abstinence from speech or noise. **2** withholding of information.
● *v.* make silent, esp. by force or superior argument.

**silencer** *n.* device for reducing sound.

**silent** *adj.* without sound; not speaking; not giving information.
□□ **silently** *adv.*

**silhouette** ● *n.* dark shadow or outline against lighter background; contour, outline, profile; portrait in profile showing outline only, usu. cut from paper or in black on white.
● *v.* represent or show in silhouette.

**silica** *n.* silicon dioxide, occurring as quartz and as main constituent of sand etc. □□ **siliceous** *adj.*

**silicate** *n.* compound of metal(s), silicon, and oxygen.

**silicon** *n.* **1** chemical element (symbol Si). **2** found in earth's crust in its compound forms. □ **silicon chip** silicon microchip.

**silicone** *n.* any organic compound of silicon with high resistance to cold, heat, water, etc.

**silicosis** *n.* lung disease caused by inhaling dust containing silica.

**silk** *n.* **1** fine soft lustrous fibre produced by silkworms; thread or cloth made from this. **2** *colloq.* senior counsel. □□ **silky** *adj.*

**silken** *adj.* of or resembling silk; soft, smooth, lustrous.

**silkworm** *n.* caterpillar that spins its cocoon of silk.

**sill** *n.* slab of stone, wood, etc. at base of window or doorway.

**silly** *adj.* foolish, imprudent; lacking good sense. □□ **silliness** *n.*

**silo** *n.* **1** pit or tower for storing grain, cement, etc. **2** underground storage chamber for guided missile.

**silt** ● *n.* sediment in channel, harbour, etc. ● *v.* choke or be choked with silt.

**silvan** = SYLVAN.

**silver** ● *n.* **1** chemical element (symbol Ag). **2** a white precious metal; coins or articles made of or looking like this; colour of silver. ● *adj.* of or coloured like silver. ● *v.* **1** coat or plate with silver. **2** provide (mirror glass) with backing of tin amalgam etc. **3** make silvery. **4** turn grey or white. □ **silver anniversary** 25th anniversary of a wedding etc.

**silverbeet** *n.* green leafy vegetable similar to spinach.

**silverfish** *n.* small wingless insect with fish-like body.

**silverside** *n.* joint of beef cut from haunch, below topside.

**silvery** adj. 1 like silver in colour or appearance. 2 having clear gentle ringing sound.

**SIM** n. (also **SIM card**) card inside mobile phone, carrying a unique identification number, storing personal data, and preventing operation if removed.

**simian** adj. resembling ape or monkey. ● n. ape or monkey.

**similar** adj. like, alike; having resemblance.□□ **similarity** n. **similarly** adv.

**simile** n. (esp. poetical) comparison of two things using words like or as.

**similitude** n. similarity.

**simmer** ● v. 1 be or keep just below boiling point. 2 be in state of suppressed anger or excitement. ● n. simmering condition.□ **simmer down** become calm or less agitated.

**simper** ● v. smile in silly affected way; utter with simpering. ● n. simpering smile.

**simple** adj. 1 of one element or kind; not complicated or showy. 2 foolish, feeble-minded.□□ **simplicity** n. **simply** adv.

**simplify** v. make simple or simpler. □□ **simplification** n.

**simplistic** adj. excessively or affectedly simple.□□ **simplistically** adv.

**simulate** v. pretend to be, have, or feel; counterfeit; reproduce conditions of (situation etc.), e.g. for training; produce computer model of. □□ **simulation** n. **simulator** n.

**simultaneous** adj. occurring or operating at same time. □□ **simultaneity** n. **simultaneously** adv.

**sin** ● n. breaking of religious or moral law; act which does this. ● v. (**sinned**) commit a sin. □□ **sinner** n.

**since** ● prep. throughout or during period after. ● conj. 1 during or in time after. 2 because. ● adv. from that time or event until now.

**sincere** adj. free from pretence; genuine, honest, frank.□□ **sincerity** n.

**sincerely** adv. in sincere way.

**sine** n. ratio of side opposite angle (in right-angled triangle) to hypotenuse.

**sinecure** n. profitable or prestigious position requiring little or no work.

**sine qua non** n. indispensable condition or qualification.

**sinew** n. tough fibrous tissue joining muscle to bone; tendon; (**sinews**) muscles; strength.□□ **sinewy** adj.

**sinful** adj. committing or involving sin.□□ **sinfully** adv. **sinfulness** n.

**sing** v. (**sang, sung, singing**) 1 utter musical sounds, esp. words in set tune; perform (song, tune); (of wind, kettle, etc.) hum, buzz, or whistle. 2 colloq. become informer. 3 celebrate. 4 bring to specified state by singing. □□ **singer** n.

**singe** ● v. (**singeing**) burn superficially; burn ends or edges of. ● n. slight burn.

**single** ● adj. one only, not double or multiple; designed for one person or thing; unmarried; (of ticket) valid for outward journey only. ● n. 1 single person or thing; room etc. for one person; single ticket; short record or CD featuring one main song or track. 2 (**singles**) game with one player on each side.□ **single figures** numbers from 1 to 9. **single-handed** without help. **single-minded** with one's mind set on single purpose. **single out** choose or distinguish from others. **single parent** person bringing up child or children without partner. □□ **singly** adv.

**singlet** n. sleeveless vest.

**singleton** n. player's only card of particular suit.

**singsong** ● adj. with monotonous rise and fall of voice. ● n. informal singing by group of people.

**singular** ● *adj.* **1** unique. **2** outstanding. **3** extraordinary. **4** strange. **5** *Gram.* denoting one person or thing. ● *n. Gram.* singular word or form. □□ **singularity** *n.* **singularly** *adv.*

**sinister** *adj.* **1** suggestive of evil. **2** wicked, criminal. **3** ominous. **4** *Heraldry* on left of shield etc. (i.e. to observer's right).

**sink** ● *v.* (**sank**, **sunk**, **sinking**) **1** fall or come slowly downwards; make or become submerged; lose value or strength. **2** send (ball) into pocket or hole. **3** invest (money). ● *n.* fixed basin with drainage pipe. □□ **sink in** become understood. **sinking fund** money set aside regularly for repayment of debt etc.

**sinker** *n.* weight used to sink fishing or sounding line.

**sinology** *n.* study of China and its language, history, etc. □□ **sinologist** *n.*

**sinuous** *adj.* **1** with many curves. **2** undulating. **3** lithe, slinky. □□ **sinuosity** *n.*

**sinus** *n.* either of cavities in skull connecting with nostrils.

**sinusitis** *n.* inflammation of sinus.

**sip** ● *v.* (**sipped**) drink in small mouthfuls. ● *n.* **1** small mouthful of liquid. **2** act of taking this.

**siphon** ● *n.* **1** tube used to convey liquid upwards from a reservoir and then down to a lower level of its own accord. **2** bottle from which fizzy water is forced by pressure of gas. ● *v.* **1** conduct or flow through siphon. **2** divert or set aside (funds etc.).

**sir** *n.* polite form of address or reference to man; (**Sir**) title of knight or baronet.

**sire** ● *n.* male parent. ● *v.* be the sire of.

**siren** *n.* **1** device for making loud prolonged signal or warning sound. **2** dangerously fascinating woman.

**sirloin** *n.* upper (best) part of loin of beef.

**sirocco** *n.* (*pl.* **siroccos**) hot wind blowing from N. Africa to s. Europe.

**sisal** *n.* fibre from leaves of agave.

**sissy** (also **cissy**) ● *n. derog.* effeminate or cowardly person. ● *adj.* effeminate; cowardly.

**sister** *n.* **1** daughter of same parents as another person. **2** (in Aboriginal English) female relative of same generation as speaker. **3** female fellow member of group. **4** member of female religious order. □ **sister-in-law** (*pl.* **sisters-in-law**) sister of one's husband or wife; wife of one's brother. □□ **sisterly** *adj.*

**sisterhood** *n.* **1** relationship (as) of sisters. **2** society of esp. religious or charitable women. **3** community of feeling among women.

**sit** *v.* (**sat**, **sitting**) **1** support body by resting buttocks on ground, seat, etc.; cause to sit; place in sitting position; (of bird) perch or remain on nest to hatch eggs; (of animal) rest with hind legs bent and buttocks on ground. **2** (of parliament, committee, etc.) be in session. **3** pose (for portrait). **4** be MP for (electorate). **5** take (exam).

**sitar** *n.* long-necked Indian lute.

**sitcom** *n. colloq.* situation comedy.

**site** ● *n.* ground chosen or used for town, building, etc.; place where some activity is or has been conducted; address on Internet. ● *v.* locate, place.

**sittella** *n.* (also **sitella**) small Australian tree-living bird.

**sitter** *n.* **1** person who sits, esp. for portrait. **2** babysitter. **3** *colloq.* easy catch or shot.

**sitting** *n.* **1** continuous period spent engaged in an activity. **2** time during which assembly is engaged in business. **3** session in which meal is served.

**situate** v. place or put in position, situation, etc.

**situation** n. **1** place and its surroundings; circumstances. **2** position. **3** state of affairs. **4** formal paid job. □□ **situational** adj.

**six** adj. & n. one more than five (6, VI). □□ **sixth** adj. & n.

**sixteen** adj. & n. one more than fifteen (16, XVI). □□ **sixteenth** adj. & n.

**sixty** adj. & n. six times ten (60, LX). □□ **sixtieth** adj. & n.

**size** ● n. **1** relative bigness or extent of thing; dimensions, magnitude; each of classes into which things are divided by size. **2** sticky solution used for glazing paper and stiffening textiles etc. ● v. sort in sizes or by size. □ **size up** colloq. form judgement of.

**sizeable** adj. (also **sizable**) fairly large.

**sizzle** ● v. sputter or hiss, esp. in frying. ● n. **1** sizzling sound. **2** Aust. sausage sizzle. □□ **sizzling** adj. & adv.

**skanky** adj. colloq. very unpleasant; dirty; unattractive.

**skate** ● n. **1** boot with blade or wheels attached for gliding over ice or hard surface. **2** large edible marine flatfish. ● v. move, glide, or perform (as) on skates; skateboard. □ **skate over** make only passing reference to. □□ **skater** n.

**skateboard** ● n. small board with wheels for riding on while standing. ● v. ride on skateboard. □□ **skateboarder** n.

**skedaddle** v. colloq. run away, depart quickly.

**skeg** n. **1** fin underneath rear of surfboard. **2** Aust. colloq. surfer; skateboarder.

**skein** n. **1** loosely-coiled bundle of yarn or thread. **2** flock of wild geese etc. in flight.

**skeleton** n. hard supporting structure of animal body; any supporting

structure; framework. □ **skeleton key** key made so as to fit many locks. **skeleton service** one reduced to a minimum. □□ **skeletal** adj.

**sketch** ● n. **1** rough or unfinished drawing or painting; rough draft or general outline. **2** short usu. humorous play. ● v. make or give sketch of; draw sketches.

**sketchy** adj. rough and not detailed or substantial. □□ **sketchily** adv.

**skew** ● adj. oblique, slanting, set askew. ● n. slant. ● v. make skew; distort; move obliquely.

**skewbald** adj. (of animal) with irregular patches of white and another colour.

**skewer** ● n. long pin for holding meat together while cooking. ● v. pierce (as) with skewer.

**ski** ● n. each of pair of long narrow pieces of wood etc. fastened under feet etc. for travelling over snow. ● v. (**skis**, **skied**, **skiing**) travel on skis. □□ **skier** n.

**skid** ● v. (**skidded**) (of vehicle etc.) slide, esp. sideways or obliquely on slippery road etc.; cause (vehicle) to skid. ● n. **1** act of skidding. **2** runner beneath aircraft for use when landing.

**skiff** n. light rowing or sculling boat.

**skilful** adj. having or showing skill. □□ **skilfully** adv.

**skill** n. ability to do something well. □□ **skilled** adj.

**skillet** n. frying pan.

**skillion** n. (also **skilling**) Aust. a lean-to attached to dwelling, esp. used as kitchen.

**skim** v. (**skimmed**) **1** take matter from surface of liquid. **2** glide. **3** read quickly. □ **skim milk** (also **skimmed milk**) milk from which cream has been skimmed.

**skimp** v. economise; use too little of; supply meagerly; do hastily or carelessly.

**skimpy** adj. meagre; insufficient.

**skin** ● n. **1** flexible covering of human or other animal body; material made from animal skin; complexion; outer layer; film like skin on liquid etc. **2** unit into which an Australian Aboriginal people is divided, usu. on basis of lineal descent. ● v. (**skinned**) **1** strip skin from. **2** colloq. swindle. □ **skin diving** sport of swimming underwater without diving suit.

**skinflint** n. miserly person.

**skinhead** n. youth with shaven head, esp. one of aggressive gang.

**skink** n. small lizard.

**skinny** adj. very thin.

**skint** adj. colloq. having little money.

**skip** ● v. (**skipped**) **1** move along lightly, esp. with alternate hops; jump lightly, esp. over skipping rope. **2** move quickly from one subject etc. to another. **3** omit; miss; colloq. not attend etc. **4** colloq. leave hurriedly. ● n. **1** skipping movement or action. **2** large container for refuse etc.; container for transporting or raising materials in mining etc.

**skipper** n. captain of ship or aircraft, team, etc.

**skirmish** ● n. minor battle, short argument, etc. ● v. engage in skirmish.

**skirt** ● n. **1** woman's garment hanging from waist; this part of a garment; any similar part. **2** cut of beef from the flank. ● v. go or be along or round edge of; avoid.

**skirting** n. **1** (in full **skirting board**) narrow board around bottom of room. **2** (**skirtings**) Aust. trimmings or inferior parts of fleece.

**skit** n. light piece of satire, burlesque.

**skitch** v. Aust. colloq. incite dog to attack.

**skite** Aust. colloq. ● v. boast, brag. ● n. **1** braggart, boaster. **2** boasting. □□ **skiter** n.

**skittish** adj. lively and unpredictable.

**skittle** n. pin used in game of skittles in which number of wooden pins are set up to be bowled or knocked down.

**skivvy** n. long-sleeved usu. cotton top with roll neck.

**skol** v. (also **scull**, **skull**) Aust. colloq. drink (glass etc. of alcoholic liquor) in a single draught; finish (one's drink) quickly.

**skua** n. large predatory sea bird.

**skulduggery** n. trickery; unscrupulous behaviour.

**skulk** v. move stealthily; lurk, hide.

**skull** n. bony framework of head.

**skunk** n. **1** black and white bushy-tailed mammal, emitting powerful stench when attacked. **2** colloq. derog. contemptible person.

**sky** n. region of the clouds or upper air.

**skydiving** n. sport of jumping from aircraft and performing acrobatic movements in sky before opening parachute.

**skylark** ● n. lark that sings while hovering in flight. ● v. play mischievously.

**skylight** n. window in roof or ceiling.

**skyscraper** n. very tall building.

**slab** n. broad flat piece of something solid; Aust. colloq. carton of 24 cans of beer.

**slack** ● adj. **1** (of rope etc.) not taut. **2** inactive or sluggish. **3** negligent, remiss. **4** (of tide etc.) neither ebbing nor flowing. ● n. **1** slack part of rope. **2** slack period. ● v. **1** slacken. **2** colloq. take a rest, be lazy. □□ **slackness** n.

**slacken** v. make or become slack.

**slacker** n. shirker.

**slacks** n.pl. trousers for casual wear.

**slag**¹ ● n. **1** solid waste left after ore has been smelted etc. **2** derog. promiscuous woman. ● v. (**slagged**) (also **slag off**) colloq. criticise; insult.

**slag**² v. & n. colloq. spit.

**slain** see SLAY.

**slake** v. **1** satisfy (thirst). **2** cause (lime) to heat and crumble by action of water.

**slalom** n. downhill ski race on zigzag course between artificial obstacles; obstacle race in canoes etc.

**slam** ● v. (**slammed**) **1** shut, throw, or put down forcefully or with bang. **2** colloq. criticise severely. **3** colloq. hit. ● n. slamming noise.

**slander** ● n. false and damaging utterance about person. ● v. utter slander about.□□ **slanderous** adj.

**slang** n. very informal words, phrases, or meanings, not regarded as standard and often peculiar to profession, age group, etc.□□ **slangy** adj.

**slant** ● v. **1** slope. **2** present (news etc.) from particular point of view. ● n. **1** slope, oblique position. **2** point of view, esp. biased one. ● adj. sloping, oblique.□□ **slantwise** adv.

**slap** ● v. (**slapped**) strike with open hand or something flat; place forcefully or carelessly. ● n. slapping sound or stroke. ● adv. suddenly, directly.□□ **slap-happy** colloq. cheerfully casual. **slap-up** colloq. first-class, lavish.

**slapdash** adj. hasty and careless.

**slapstick** n. boisterous comedy.

**slash** ● v. **1** cut or gash with knife etc.; deliver or aim cutting blows. **2** reduce (prices etc.) drastically. ● n. **1** slashing cut. **2** Printing oblique stroke (/) used between alternatives, in fractions, etc.

**slat** n. narrow strip of wood, metal, etc.

**slate** ● n. fine-grained bluish-grey rock easily split into smooth plates; piece of this as tile or for writing on; colour of slate. ● v. **1** cover with slates. **2** colloq. criticise severely. ● adj. of (colour of) slate.□□ **slating** n. **slaty** adj.

**slaughter** ● v. kill (animals) for food etc.; kill ruthlessly or in large numbers; colloq. defeat utterly. ● n. act of slaughtering.□□ **slaughterer** n.

**Slav** adj. & n. (member) of any of the peoples of Europe who speak a Slavonic language.

**slave** ● n. person who is owned by and has to serve another; drudge; hard worker; obsessive devotee. ● v. work extremely hard.

**slaver** v. dribble; drool.

**slavery** n. condition of slave; drudgery; practice of having slaves.

**slavish** adj. excessively submissive or imitative.□□ **slavishly** adv.

**Slavonic** adj. & n. (of) group of languages including Russian and Polish.

**slay** v. (**slew**, **slain**, **slaying**) kill. □□ **slayer** n.

**sleazy** adj. squalid; corrupt, immoral; promiscuous.□□ **sleaze** n. **sleaziness** n.

**sled** n. & v. sledge.

**sledge¹** ● n. vehicle on runners for use on snow. ● v. travel or carry by sledge.

**sledge²** v. Sport verbally taunt opponent on field of play. □□ **sledging** n.

**sledgehammer** n. large heavy hammer.

**sleek** ● adj. (of hair, skin, etc.) smooth and glossy; looking well-fed and comfortable. ● v. make sleek. □□ **sleekness** n.

**sleep** ● n. natural condition of rest with unconsciousness and relaxation of muscles; spell of this. ● v. (**slept**, **sleeping**) **1** be or spend (time) in state of sleep. **2** provide with sleeping accommodation. **3** colloq. have sexual intercourse. □ **sleeping bag** padded bag for sleeping in. □□ **sleepless** adj. **sleeplessness** n.

**sleeper** n. 1 sleeping person or animal. 2 beam supporting railway track. 3 sleeping car. 4 ring worn in pierced ear to keep hole open.

**sleepout** n. *Aust.* verandah or porch etc. providing sleeping accommodation.

**sleepwalk** v. walk about while asleep.

**sleepy** adj. drowsy; quiet, inactive. □□ **sleepily** adv. **sleepiness** n.

**sleet** ● n. snow and rain together; hail or snow melting as it falls. ● v. fall as sleet. □□ **sleety** adj.

**sleeve** n. 1 part of garment covering arm; tattooing that wholly or partly covers an arm. 2 cover for record; tube enclosing rod etc. □ **up one's sleeve** concealed but ready for use, in reserve. □□ **sleeved** adj. **sleeveless** adj.

**sleigh** ● n. sledge, esp. for riding on. ● v. travel on sleigh.

**sleight of hand** n. dexterity, esp. in conjuring.

**slender** adj. slim and graceful; small in amount.

**slept** see SLEEP.

**sleuth** n. colloq. detective.

**slew¹** (also **slue**) ● v. turn or swing to new position. ● n. such turn.

**slew²** see SLAY.

**slice** ● n. 1 thin flat piece or wedge cut from something; kitchen utensil with broad blade; *Aust.* sweet cake-like biscuit. 2 share; part. 3 *Sport* stroke sending ball obliquely. ● v. 1 cut, esp. into slices. 2 strike (ball) with slice.

**slick** ● adj. 1 skilful, efficient. 2 superficially dexterous. 3 glib. 4 sleek, smooth. ● n. 1 patch of oil etc., esp. on sea. 2 *Motor Racing* smooth tyre. ● v. colloq. make smooth or sleek. □□ **slickly** adv. **slickness** n.

**slide** ● v. (**slid**, **sliding**) (cause to) move along smooth surface touching it always with same part; move quietly or smoothly; glide. ● n. 1 act of sliding. 2 rapid decline. 3 smooth slope down which people or things slide. 4 part of machine or instrument that slides. 5 mounted transparency viewed with projector. 6 piece of glass holding object for microscope. □ **sliding scale** scale of fees or taxes etc. that varies according to the variation of some standard.

**slight** ● adj. small; insignificant; inadequate; slender, frail-looking. ● v. treat disrespectfully; ignore. ● n. snub. □□ **slightly** adv. **slightness** n.

**slim** ● adj. (**slimmer**) not fat, slender; small, insufficient. ● v. (**slimmed**) become slimmer by dieting, exercise, etc.; make smaller. □□ **slimmer** n. **slimming** n.

**slime** n. thick slippery mud or sticky substance.

**slimy** adj. 1 like, covered with, or full of slime. 2 colloq. disgustingly obsequious. □□ **sliminess** n.

**sling** ● n. 1 strap etc. used to support or raise thing; bandage supporting injured arm; strap etc. used to throw missile. 2 *Aust.* colloq. a tip or bribe. ● v. (**slung**, **slinging**) 1 suspend with sling. 2 colloq. throw. 3 *Aust.* colloq. tip, bribe.

**slingshot** n. shanghai, catapult.

**slink** v. (**slunk**, **slinking**) move in stealthy or guilty manner.

**slinky** adj. (**slinkier**) (of garment) close-fitting and sinuous.

**slip** ● v. (**slipped**) slide accidentally; lose one's balance in this way; go or put smoothly; escape hold or capture; detach, release; become detached from. ● n. 1 act of slipping. 2 slight mistake. 3 small piece of paper. 4 pillowcase. 5 petticoat. 6 slipway. 7 *Cricket* (fielder in) position behind wicket on off side. □ **slipped disc** between vertebrae that has become displaced. **slip road** road for entering or leaving freeway etc. □□ **slippage** *n.*

**slipper** *n.* light loose indoor shoe.

**slippery** *adj.* difficult to grasp, stand on, etc., because smooth or wet; unreliable, unscrupulous. □□ **slipperiness** *n.*

**slipshod** *adj.* careless, slovenly.

**slipstream** *n.* current of air driven backward as something is propelled forward.

**slit** ● *n.* straight narrow incision or opening. ● *v.* (**slit**, **slitting**) make slit in; cut in strips.

**slither** *v.* slide unsteadily. □□ **slithery** *adj.*

**sliver** ● *n.* long thin slice or piece. ● *v.* cut or split into slivers.

**slob** *n. colloq.* lazy, untidy, or fat person.

**slobber** *v. & n.* slaver, dribble.

**slog** ● *v.* (**slogged**) **1** hard and usu. wildly. **2** work or walk doggedly. ● *n.* **1** hard random hit. **2** hard steady work or walk; spell of this.

**slogan** *n.* catchy phrase used in advertising etc.; motto of political party etc.

**sloop** *n.* small one-masted fore-and-aft-rigged vessel.

**slop** ● *v.* spill over edge of vessel; spill or splash liquid on. ● *n.* **1** liquid spilled or splashed; (**slops**) liquid refuse. **2** (**slops**) *Aust. colloq.* beer.

**slope** ● *n.* inclined position, direction, or state; piece of rising or falling ground; difference in level between two ends or sides of a thing. ● *v.* have or take slope, slant; cause to slope.

**sloppy** *adj.* **1** wet, watery, too liquid. **2** careless, untidy. **3** foolishly sentimental. **4** ill-fitting. □□ **sloppily** *adv.* **sloppiness** *n.*

**slosh** *v.* **1** splash or flounder. **2** *colloq.* hit. **3** *colloq.* pour (liquid)

clumsily. ● *n.* **1** splashing sound. **2** *colloq.* heavy blow.

**sloshed** *adj. colloq.* drunk.

**slot** ● *n.* **1** slit or other opening in machine etc. for something (esp. coin) to be inserted. **2** allotted place in schedule. **3** *Aust. colloq.* prison cell. ● *v.* (**slotted**) fit into slot.

**sloth** *n.* **1** laziness, indolence. **2** slow-moving arboreal S. American mammal.

**slothful** *adj.* lazy. □□ **slothfully** *adv.*

**slouch** ● *v.* stand, move, or sit in drooping fashion. ● *n.* **1** slouching posture or movement. **2** *colloq.* incompetent or slovenly worker etc.

**slough¹** *n.* **1** swamp. **2** muddy place.

**slough²** *n.* part that animal (esp. snake) casts or moults. ● *v.* cast or drop off as slough.

**slovenly** ● *adj.* careless and untidy; unmethodical. ● *adv.* in a slovenly way. □□ **slovenliness** *n.*

**slow** ● *adj.* **1** taking relatively long time to do thing(s); acting, moving, or done without speed; not conducive to speed; reluctant; (of clock etc.) showing earlier than correct time. **2** dull-witted, stupid. ● *adv.* slowly. ● *v.* reduce speed (of). □□ **slowly** *adv.* **slowness** *n.*

**slowcoach** *n. colloq.* slow or lazy person.

**sludge** *n.* **1** thick greasy mud or sediment. **2** sewage. □□ **sludgy** *adj.*

**slug** *n.* **1** small shell-less mollusc. **2** small lump of metal; bullet. ● *v.* (**slugged**) *colloq.* hit hard.

**sluggish** *adj.* slow-moving, not lively. □□ **sluggishly** *adv.* **sluggishness** *n.*

**sluice** ● *n.* sliding gate or other contrivance for regulating volume or flow of water; water so regulated; artificial water channel; place for or act of rinsing. ● *v.* provide or wash with sluice(s); rinse; (of water) rush out (as if) from sluice.

**slum** n. squalid house or district. □□ **slummy** adj.

**slumber** v. & n. sleep.

**slump** ● n. sudden severe or prolonged fall in prices and trade. ● v. 1 undergo slump. 2 sit or fall heavily or limply.

**slung** SEE SLING.

**slunk** SEE SLINK.

**slur** ● v. (slurred) 1 sound (words, musical notes, etc.) so that they run into one another. 2 make insinuations against (person, character). 3 pass over lightly. ● n. 1 slurred sound; curved line marking notes to be slurred in music. 2 a discredit.

**slurp** colloq. ● v. eat or drink noisily. ● n. sound of this.

**slurry** n. thin semi-liquid cement, mud, manure, etc.

**slush** n. 1 thawing snow. 2 colloq. silly sentimentality. □ **slush fund** fund of money for bribes etc. □□ **slushy** adj.

**slut** n. derog. slovenly or promiscuous woman. □□ **sluttish** adj.

**sly** adj. 1 crafty, wily; secretive. 2 knowing. 3 insinuating. 4 Aust. colloq. (esp. of liquor) illicit. □□ **slyly** adv. **slyness** n.

**smack** ● n. 1 sharp slap or blow; hard hit. 2 loud kiss. 3 a flavour, a trace. 4 single-masted sailing boat. 5 colloq. heroin. ● v. 1 slap. 2 part (lips) noisily in anticipation of food. 3 have slight flavour or trace. ● adv. colloq. 1 with a smack. 2 suddenly. 3 violently. 4 exactly.

**small** ● adj. 1 not large or big; not great in importance, amount, number, etc.; not much. 2 insignificant. ● n. slenderest part, esp. of back. ● adv. into small pieces; in a small size. □ **small talk** light social conversation. **small-time** colloq. unimportant or petty. □□ **smallish** adj. **smallness** n.

**smallholding** n. small farm. □□ **smallholder** n.

**smallpox** n. contagious viral disease, with fever and pustules.

**smarmy** adj. 1 colloq. ingratiating. 2 obsequious. □□ **smarmily** adv. **smarminess** n.

**smart** ● adj. 1 well-groomed, neat; well dressed; bright and fresh in appearance. 2 clever, ingenious, quickwitted. 3 quick, brisk. 4 painfully severe, sharp, vigorous. ● v. 1 feel or give pain. 2 rankle. ● n. sharp pain; stinging sensation. □□ **smartish** adj. & adv. **smartly** adv. **smartness** n.

**smarten** v. make or become smart.

**smartphone** n. mobile phone that performs many of the functions of computer.

**smash** ● v. break into pieces; bring or come to destruction, defeat, or disaster; move forcefully; break with crushing blow; hit (ball) hard, esp. downwards. ● n. 1 act or sound of smashing; collision. 2 (in full **smash hit**) very successful play, song, etc.

**smashed** adj. colloq. affected by alcohol or other drugs.

**smattering** n. slight knowledge.

**smear** ● v. 1 daub or mark with grease etc.; smudge. 2 defame. ● n. 1 action of smearing. 2 a slander. □□ **smeary** adj.

**smell** ● n. ability to perceive things with sense organs of nose; a quality perceived in this way; act of smelling. ● v. (smelt or smelled, smelling) perceive smell of; give off smell. □□ **smelly** adj.

**smelt** v. melt (ore) to extract metal; obtain (metal) in this way. □□ **smelter** n.

**smidgen** n. (also **smidgin**) colloq. small bit or amount.

**smile** ● n. facial expression indicating pleasure or amusement, with lips upturned. ● v. give a smile; look favourable.

**smirch** v. & n. stain, smear.

**smirk** ● n. conceited or silly smile.
● v. give smirk.

**smite** v. (**smote, smitten**) *literary* hit hard; affect suddenly.

**smith** n. blacksmith; worker in metal.

**smithereens** n.pl. small fragments.

**smithy** n. blacksmith's workshop, forge.

**smitten** see SMITE.

**smock** ● n. loose shirtlike garment often ornamented with smocking. ● v. adorn with smocking.

**smocking** n. ornamentation on cloth made by gathering it tightly with stitches.

**smog** n. dense smoky fog. □□ **smoggy** adj.

**smoke** n. 1 visible vapour from burning substance. 2 act of smoking tobacco etc.; colloq. cigarette, cigar. 3 (**the** (**big**) **Smoke**) colloq. large city. ● v. 1 inhale and exhale smoke of (cigarette etc.); do this habitually; emit smoke or visible vapour. 2 darken or preserve with smoke. 3 (in Aboriginal English) ritually cleanse (person, place) of unwelcome spirits. □□ **smoky** adj.

**smoker** n. 1 person who habitually smokes cigarettes etc. 2 *Aust.* yellow parrot with long dark tail.

**smokescreen** n. something intended to disguise or conceal activities.

**smoko** n. *Aust. colloq.* brief rest from work.

**smooch** colloq. ● v. kiss and caress. ● n. smooching. □□ **smoochy** adj.

**smoodge** (also **smooge**) *Aust. colloq.* ● v. 1 behave amorously. 2 behave in ingratiating manner. ● n. 1 display of amorous behaviour. 2 flattery, ingratiating behaviour. □□ **smoodger** n.

**smooth** ● adj. 1 having even surface; free from projections and roughness. 2 that can be traversed uninterrupted; (of journey etc.) easy.

3 not harsh in sound or taste. 4 suave, conciliatory; slick. ● v. 1 make or become smooth. 2 get rid of (differences, faults, etc.) □□ **smoothly** adv. **smoothness** n.

**smoothie** n. thick drink of fruit purée, milk, yoghurt, etc.

**smorgasbord** n. buffet meal with various esp. savoury dishes; wide variety or choice.

**smote** see SMITE.

**smother** v. suffocate, stifle; overwhelm or cover with; extinguish (fire) by covering it; suppress, conceal.

**smoulder** ● v. 1 burn internally or without flame. 2 (of person) show silent or suppressed emotion. ● n. smouldering.

**SMS** abbr. Short Message (or Messaging) Service.

**smudge** ● n. blurred or smeared line, mark, etc. ● v. make smudge on or with; become smeared or blurred. □□ **smudgy** adj.

**smug** adj. (**smugger**) self-satisfied. □□ **smugly** adv. **smugness** n.

**smuggle** v. import or export illegally, esp. without paying duties; convey secretly. □□ **smuggler** n. **smuggling** n.

**smut** ● n. 1 small flake of soot etc.; small black mark. 2 indecent talk, pictures, or stories. 3 fungous disease of cereals. ● v. mark with smut(s). □□ **smutty** adj.

**snack** n. 1 light, casual, or hurried meal. 2 *Aust. colloq.* something easily accomplished.

**snaffle** ● n. (in full **snaffle-bit**) simple bridle-bit without curb. ● v. steal.

**snag¹** ● n. unexpected obstacle or drawback; jagged projection; tear in material etc. ● v. (**snagged**) catch or tear on snag.

**snag²** n. *Aust. colloq.* sausage.

**snail** n. slow-moving mollusc with spiral shell.

**snake** ● *n.* long limbless reptile.
● *v.* move in winding course.
□□ **snaky** *adj.*

**snap** ● *v.* (**snapped**) 1 break suddenly, esp. with sharp sound; (cause to) emit sudden sharp sound; open or close with snapping sound; speak irritably. 2 move quickly. 3 photograph. ● *n.* 1 act or sound of snapping. 2 (in full **cold snap**) sudden brief spell of cold weather. 3 snapshot. 4 *colloq.* easy task. 5 *AFL* quick kick at goal. ● *adj.* with snapping sound. ● *adj.* done without forethought. □ **snap up** take eagerly.

**snapper** *n.* (also **schnapper**) marine fish valued as food.

**snappy** *adj. colloq.* 1 brisk, lively. 2 neat and elegant. 3 irritable. □□ **snappily** *adv.*

**snapshot** *n.* 1 informal photograph taken quickly. 2 brief look or summary.

**snare** ● *n.* 1 trap, esp. with noose; trap, trick, or temptation. 2 twisted strings of gut, hide, or wire, stretched across lower head of side drum to produce rattle. 3 (in full **snare drum**) drum fitted with snares. ● *v.* catch in snare; trap.

**snarl** ● *v.* 1 growl with bared teeth. 2 speak angrily. 3 become entangled. ● *n.* 1 act or sound of snarling. 2 a tangle. □ **snarl-up** *colloq.* traffic jam.

**snatch** ● *v.* seize quickly or eagerly. ● *n.* 1 act of snatching. 2 fragment of song, talk, etc. 3 (in weightlifting) rapid raising of weight from floor to above head. 4 short spell of activity etc.

**snazzy** *adj. colloq.* smart, stylish, showy.

**sneak** ● *v.* 1 go or convey furtively; achieve or obtain furtively. 2 *colloq.* tell tales. ● *n.* 1 mean-spirited

underhand person. 2 *colloq.* tell-tale.
□□ **sneaky** *adj.*

> **Usage** In North America *snuck* is acceptable as the past form of *sneak*. While it is often heard in Australia, it is non-standard.

**sneaker** *n. colloq.* soft-soled shoe.

**sneaking** *adj.* (of a feeling) persistent but not openly acknowledged.

**sneer** ● *n.* derisive smile or remark.
● *v.* smile or speak derisively.
□□ **sneering** *adj.* **sneeringly** *adv.*

**sneeze** ● *n.* sudden involuntary explosive expulsion of air through nose and mouth. ● *v.* make sneeze.

**snicker** *n. & v.* snigger.

**snide** *adj.* sneering; slyly derogatory.

**sniff** ● *v.* inhale audibly through nose; draw in through nose; smell scent by sniffing. ● *n.* act or sound of sniffing.

**sniffle** ● *v.* sniff slightly or repeatedly. ● *n.* act of sniffling; a slight cold.

**snigger** ● *n.* sly giggle. ● *v.* utter this.

**snip** ● *v.* (**snipped**) cut with scissors etc., esp. in small quick strokes.
● *n.* 1 act or sound of snipping. 2 *colloq.* a bargain, a certainty.

**snipe** ● *n.* wading bird with long straight bill. ● *v.* 1 fire shots from hiding, usu. at long range. 2 make sly critical attack. □□ **sniper** *n.*

**snippet** *n.* small piece.

**snitch** *colloq.* ● *v.* 1 steal. 2 inform on person. ● *n.* informer.

**snivel** *v.* (**snivelled**) weep with sniffling; show weak or tearful sentiment.

**snob** *n.* person who despises people with inferior social position, wealth, intellect, taste, etc. □□ **snobbery** *n.* **snobbish** *adj.* **snobby** *adj.*

**snooker** • *n.* game played on oblong cloth-covered table with 1 white, 15 red, and 6 other coloured balls; position in this game where direct shot would lose points. • *v.* 1 subject (player) to snooker. 2 (esp. as **snookered** *adj.*) *colloq.* thwart, defeat.

**snoop** *v. colloq.* pry.□□ **snooper** *n.*

**snooty** *adj. colloq.* supercilious; snobbish.□□ **snootily** *adv.*

**snooze** *colloq.* • *n.* short sleep, nap. • *v.* take snooze.

**snore** • *n.* snorting or grunting sound of breathing during sleep. • *v.* make this sound.

**snorkel** • *n.* breathing tube for underwater swimmer. • *v.* (**snorkelled**) swim using snorkel.

**snort** • *n.* 1 explosive sound made by driving breath violently through nose, esp. by horses, or by humans to show contempt, incredulity, etc. 2 *colloq.* small drink of liquor. • *v.* 1 make snort; express or utter with snort. 2 *colloq.* inhale (esp. cocaine).

**snout** *n.* projecting nose (and mouth) of animal; pointed front of thing.

**snow** • *n.* frozen vapour falling to earth in light white flakes; fall or layer of this; thing resembling snow in whiteness or texture etc. • *v.* fall as or like snow.□□ **snowy** *adj.*

**snowball** • *n.* snow pressed into ball for throwing. • *v.* increase rapidly.

**snowboarding** *n.* sport of sliding downhill over snow while standing on single wide ski.

**snub** • *v.* (**snubbed**) rebuff or humiliate in a sharp or cutting way. • *n.* snubbing, rebuff. • *adj.* (of nose) short and turned up.

**snuck** see note at SNEAK.

**snuff** • *n.* powdered tobacco for sniffing. • *v.* put out (candle). □ **snuff it** *colloq.* die.

**snuffle** • *v.* 1 make sniffing sounds. 2 speak nasally; breathe noisily, esp. with blocked nose. • *n.* snuffling sound or tone.

**snug** *adj.* (**snugger**) cosy, comfortable, sheltered; close-fitting; (of income etc.) allowing comfort.□□ **snugly** *adv.*

**snuggle** *v.* settle or move into warm comfortable position.

**so** • *adv.* 1 to such an extent. 2 in that manner or state. 3 also. 4 indeed, actually. 5 very. 6 thus. • *conj.* 1 consequently. 2 in order that. 3 and then. 4 (introducing question) after that. □ **so-and-so** 1 person or thing that need not be named. 2 *colloq.* person one dislikes. **so as to** in order to. **so-called** commonly known as, often incorrectly. **so that** with the aim or result that.

**soak** • *v.* make or become thoroughly wet through saturation; (of rain etc.) drench; absorb (liquid, knowledge, etc.); penetrate by saturation. • *n.* 1 soaking. 2 *Aust.* hollow where water collects, on or below surface of ground; waterhole. □ **soak up** absorb.

**soap** • *n.* 1 cleansing agent that is compound of fatty acid with soda etc. 2 *colloq.* soap opera. • *v.* apply soap to. □ **soap opera** television etc. serial usu. dealing with domestic issues.

**soapbox** *n.* 1 box for holding soap. 2 makeshift stand for public speaker.

**soapie** *n. colloq.* soap opera. 2 *Aust.* young fish, esp. jewfish.

**soapy** *adj.* 1 of or like soap; containing or smeared with soap. 2 unctuous, flattering.

**soar** *v.* fly or rise high; reach high level or standard; fly without flapping wings or using motor power.

**sob** • *n.* uneven drawing of breath when weeping or gasping. • *v.* (**sobbed**) weep, breathe, or utter with sobs.

**sober** ● adj. **1** not drunk; serious. **2** (of colour etc.) not bright, dull. ● v. make or become sober. □□ **soberly** adv. **sobriety** n.

**sobriquet** n. (also **soubriquet**) nickname.

**soccer** n. football played with round ball that may be handled only by goalkeeper.

**sociable** adj. liking company, gregarious; friendly. □□ **sociability** n. **sociably** adv.

**social** ● adj. **1** of society or its organisation. **2** living in communities; gregarious. ● n. social gathering. □ **social media** websites and applications that enable users to create and share content or to participate in social networking. **social networking** use of dedicated websites and applications to interact with other users, or to connect people with similar interests. **social security** government financial assistance for those in need. □□ **socially** adv.

**socialise** v. (also **-ize**) **1** mix socially; make social. **2** organise on socialistic principles.

**socialism** n. political and economic theory of social organisation advocating community ownership and control of means of production, distribution, and exchange; social system based on this. □□ **socialist** n. & adj. **socialistic** adj.

**socialite** n. person moving in fashionable society.

**society** n. **1** organised and interdependent community; system and organisation of this. **2** socially advantaged members of community. **3** mixing with other people. **4** companionship, company. **5** club, association. □□ **societal** adj.

**sociology** n. study of development, structure, and functioning of human society. □□ **sociological** adj. **sociologist** n.

**sock** ● n. **1** knitted covering for foot and lower leg. **2** colloq. a hard blow. ● v. colloq. hit hard.

**socket** n. hollow thing to fit into etc.; device receiving electric plug, light bulb, etc.

**sod** n. **1** turf, piece of turf. **2** colloq. unpleasant or awkward person or thing.

**soda** n. **1** any of various compounds of sodium in common use. **2** (in full **soda water**) water made fizzy by charging with carbon dioxide under pressure.

**sodden** adj. **1** saturated; soaked through. **2** stupid or dull etc. with drunkenness.

**sodium** n. soft silver-white metallic element (symbol Na).

**sodomy** n. anal intercourse. □□ **sodomite** n.

**sofa** n. long upholstered seat with raised back and ends.

**soft** ● adj. **1** not hard or firm or rough. **2** not loud. **3** gentle, tender-hearted. **4** flabby, feeble. **5** (of drinks) non-alcoholic. **6** (of drugs) unlikely to cause addiction. **7** (of currency) likely to fall suddenly in value. ● adv. softly. □ **soft option** easy alternative. **soft spot** colloq. feeling of affection. □□ **softish** adj. **softly** adv. **softness** n.

**softball** n. form of baseball using large soft ball.

**soften** v. **1** make or become soft(er). **2** reduce strength, resistance, etc. □□ **softener** n.

**software** n. computer programs.

**softwood** n. wood of pine, spruce, or other conifers, easily sawn.

**soggy** adj. sodden, waterlogged. □□ **sogginess** n.

**soh** n. (also **so**) Mus. fifth note of major scale.

**soignée** adj. well-groomed and sophisticated.

**soil** ● *n.* upper layer of earth in which plants grow; ground, territory. ● *v.* make dirty, smear, stain; defile; discredit.

**soirée** *n.* evening party.

**sojourn** *n.* temporary stay. ● *v.* stay temporarily.

**solace** ● *n.* comfort in sadness or disappointment. ● *v.* give solace to.

**solar** *adj.* of or reckoned by sun; using sun's energy.□ **solar cell** device converting solar radiation into electricity. **solar panel** panel for collecting sun's rays as source of energy. **solar plexus** network of nerves at pit of stomach. **solar system** sun with planets etc. that revolve around it.

**solarium** *n.* (*pl.* **solaria**) room with sun lamps or glass roof etc.

**sold** see SELL.

**solder** ● *n.* fusible alloy used for joining metals, wires, etc. ● *v.* join with solder.□ **soldering iron** tool for melting and applying solder.

**soldier** ● *n.* member of army. ● *v.* serve as soldier.□ **soldier on** *colloq.* persevere doggedly. □□ **soldierly** *adj.*

**sole** ● *n.* **1** undersurface of foot; part of shoe, sock, etc. under foot, esp. part other than heel. **2** type of flatfish. ● *adj.* one and only; single, exclusive. ● *v.* provide with sole. □□ **solely** *adv.*

**solemn** *adj.* serious and dignified; formal; awe-inspiring; of cheerless manner; grave.□□ **solemnity** *n.* **solemnly** *adv.* **solemness** *n.*

**solemnise** *v.* (also **-ize**) duly perform (esp. marriage ceremony); make solemn.□□ **solemnisation** *n.*

**solenoid** *n.* cylindrical coil of wire acting as magnet when carrying electric current.

**sol-fa** *n.* system of syllables representing musical notes.

**solicit** *v.* seek repeatedly or earnestly; accost as prostitute. □□ **solicitation** *n.*

**solicitor** *n.* lawyer qualified to advise clients, represent them in lower courts, and instruct barristers.

**solicitous** *adj.* showing concern; eager, anxious.□□ **solicitously** *adv.* **solicitude** *n.*

**solid** ● *adj.* **1** keeping its shape, firm; not liquid or gas. **2** not hollow; of same substance throughout; continuous. **3** three-dimensional. **4** sound and reliable. **5** uninterrupted. **6** unanimous. ● *n.* a solid substance, body, or food. ● *adv.* solidly. □□ **solidly** *adv.* **solidity** *n.*

**solidarity** *n.* unity, esp. political or in industrial dispute; mutual dependence.

**solidify** *v.* make or become solid.

**solidus** *n.* (*pl.* **solidi**) oblique stroke (/) used in writing fractions, to denote alternatives, etc.

**soliloquy** *n.* talking without or regardless of hearers; this part of play. □□ **soliloquise** *v.* (also **-ize**)

**solitaire** *n.* **1** jewel set by itself; ring etc. with this. **2** game for one person played on board with pegs. **3** *US* = PATIENCE (sense 2).

**solitary** ● *adj.* **1** living or being alone; not gregarious; lonely; secluded. **2** single. ● *n.* recluse.

**solitude** *n.* being solitary; solitary place.

**solo** ● *n.* (*pl.* **solos**) music for single performer; unaccompanied performance etc. ● *adj. & adv.* unaccompanied, alone.

**soloist** *n.* performer of solo.

**solstice** *n.* either of times (about 22 December and 21 June) when sun is furthest from equator.

**soluble** *adj.* that can be dissolved or solved.□□ **solubility** *n.*

**solution** n. **1** act of solving or means of solving problem. **2** conversion of solid or gas into liquid by mixture with liquid; state resulting from this; act of dissolving or state of being dissolved. □□ **solvable** adj.

**solve** v. answer, remove, or deal with (problem). □□ **solvable** adj.

**solvent** ● adj. **1** able to pay one's debts. **2** able to dissolve or form solution. ● n. solvent liquid etc., esp. one able to dissolve grease etc. □□ **solvency** n.

**somatic** adj. of body, not of mind.

**sombre** adj. dark, gloomy; dismal; forbidding. □□ **sombrely** adv. **sombreness** n.

**sombrero** n. broad-brimmed hat worn esp. in Latin America.

**some** ● adj. **1** unspecified amount or number; approximate. **2** that is unknown or unnamed. **3** considerable. **4** colloq. remarkable. ● pron. some people or things, some number or amount. ● adv. colloq. to some extent.

**somebody** n. & pron. **1** unspecified person. **2** person of importance.

**somehow** adv. in unspecified or unexplained manner.

**someone** n. & pron. somebody.

**somersault** ● n. leap or roll in which one turns head over heels. ● v. perform somersault.

**something** n. & pron. **1** unspecified thing or extent. **2** notable thing. □ **something like** rather like; approximately.

**sometime** ● adj. former. ● adv. at some unspecified time.

**sometimes** adv. at some times but not all the time.

**somewhat** adv. to some extent.

**somewhere** adv. at, in, or to an unspecified place.

**somnambulist** n. sleepwalker. □□ **somnambulism** n.

**somnolent** adj. sleepy, drowsy; inducing drowsiness. □□ **somnolence** n.

**son** n. male in relation to his parents. □ **son-in-law** (pl. **sons-in-law**) one's child's husband.

**sonar** n. system for detecting objects under water by reflected sound; apparatus for this.

**sonata** n. composition for one or two instruments in several related movements.

**song** n. words set to music or for singing; vocal music; composition suggestive of song; cry of some birds. □ **going for a song** colloq. being sold very cheaply.

**songbird** n. bird with musical cry.

**songline** n. Aust. (in traditional Aboriginal culture) route taken by ancestral being on journey through particular landscape and recorded in song.

**songman** n. Aust. Aboriginal man who memorises and performs traditional songs of community.

**songster** n. **1** singer. **2** songbird.

**songwoman** n. Aust. Aboriginal woman who memorises and performs traditional songs of community.

**sonic** adj. of or using sound or sound waves. □ **sonic boom** explosive noise caused by shock wave from vehicle when it passes speed of sound.

**sonky** adj. Aust. colloq. foolish; gawky.

**sonnet** n. poem of 14 lines with fixed rhyme scheme.

**sonorous** adj. **1** having loud, full, or deep sound. **2** (of speech etc.) imposing. □□ **sonority** n.

**sook** n. Aust. colloq. often derog. timid, bashful person; person who sheds tears frequently. □□ **sooky** adj.

**sool** v. Aust. colloq. (of dog) attack or worry; incite dog to attack; urge.

**soon** adv. **1** in a short time. **2** relatively early. **3** readily, willingly. □ **sooner or**

later at some future time, eventually. □□ **soonish** adv.

**soot** n. black powdery deposit from smoke.

**soothe** v. calm; soften or mitigate.

**soothsayer** n. seer, prophet.

**sooty** adj. covered with soot; black or brownish-black.

**sop** ● n. 1 thing given or done to pacify or bribe. 2 piece of bread etc. dipped in gravy etc. ● v. (**sopped**) dip in liquid; soak up (liquid).

**sophisticated** adj. 1 worldly-wise; cultured; elegant. 2 highly developed and complex. □□ **sophistication** n.

**sophistry** n. (also **sophism**) clever and subtle but perhaps misleading reasoning. □□ **sophist** n.

**soporific** ● adj. inducing sleep. ● n. soporific drug or influence.

**sopping** adj. drenched.

**soppy** adj. colloq. mawkishly sentimental; silly.

**soprano** n. highest singing voice; singer with this.

**sorbet** n. flavoured water ice.

**sorcerer** n. 1 magician, wizard. 2 koradji. □□ **sorcery** n.

**sordid** adj. 1 dirty, squalid. 2 ignoble, mercenary. □□ **sordidly** adv. **sordidness** n.

**sore** ● adj. 1 painful; suffering pain. 2 colloq. aggrieved, vexed. ● n. sore place; source of distress etc. ● adv. severely. □□ **soreness** n.

**sorely** adv. very much, severely.

**sorghum** n. tropical cereal grass.

**sorrel** ● n. sour-leaved herb. ● adj. reddish brown.

**sorrow** ● n. mental distress caused by loss or disappointment etc.; cause of sorrow. ● v. feel sorrow, mourn. □□ **sorrowful** adj.

**sorry** adj. 1 pained, regretful, penitent. 2 feeling pity for. 3 wretched. 4 (in Aboriginal English) of or relating to mourning. □ **sorry business** (in Aboriginal English) mourning rites.

**sort** ● n. class, kind; colloq. person of specified kind. ● v. arrange systematically. □ **sort out** solve (problems).

**sortie** n. sally, esp. from besieged garrison; operational military flight.

**SOS** n. international code signal of extreme distress; urgent appeal for help.

**sot** n. habitual drunkard. □□ **sottish** adj.

**sotto voce** adv. in an undertone.

**soubriquet** n. = SOBRIQUET.

**soufflé** n. light spongy dish usu. made with stiffly beaten egg white.

**sough** v. 1 moan or whisper like wind in trees etc. n. 2 this sound.

**sought** see SEEK.

**soul** n. 1 spiritual or immaterial part of person; moral, emotional, or intellectual nature of person. 2 personification, pattern. 3 an individual. 4 animating or essential part. 5 energy, intensity. 6 (also **soul music**) African-American music with elements of rhythm and blues, rock, and gospel.

**soulful** adj. having, expressing, or evoking deep feeling. □□ **soulfully** adv.

**soulless** adj. 1 lacking sensitivity or noble qualities. 2 undistinguished, uninteresting.

**sound**[1] ● n. 1 sensation caused in ear by vibration of surrounding air etc.; vibrations causing this; what is or may be heard. ● v. 1 produce or cause to produce sound; utter, pronounce; seem when heard. 2 test depth of (river or sea etc.); examine with probe. ● adj. 1 healthy; not diseased or damaged; secure. 2 correct, well-founded; thorough. ● **sound barrier** high resistance of air to objects moving at speeds near that of sound. **sound bite** short extract from recorded interview, chosen for its pungency or aptness. **sounding board**

**1** board to reflect sound or increase resonance. **2** person used to test opinion. **sound off** express one's opinions loudly. □□ **soundless** *adj.*

**sound**[2] *n.* narrow stretch of water; a strait.

**soundproof** ● *adj.* not able to be penetrated by sound. ● *v.* make soundproof.

**soup** ● *n.* liquid food made by boiling meat, fish, or vegetables. ● *v.* (**soup up**) *colloq.* make more powerful or impressive. □ **soup kitchen** place dispensing soup etc. to disadvantaged. □□ **soupy** *adj.*

**soupçon** *n.* very small quantity.

**sour** ● *adj.* **1** having acid taste like lemon or vinegar, esp. due to unripeness. **2** (of food) bad because of fermentation. **3** bad tempered, morose. ● *v.* make or become sour. □ **sour grapes** resentful disparagement of something one cannot personally acquire. □□ **sourly** *adv.* **sourness** *n.*

**source** *n.* place from which river or stream issues; place of origination; person, book, etc. providing information.

**sourdough** *n.* fermenting dough, esp. that left over from a previous baking, used as leaven; bread made from this.

**sourpuss** *n. colloq.* bad-tempered or habitually sullen person.

**souse** ● *v.* **1** immerse in pickle or other liquid; drench. **2** (as **soused** *adj.*) *colloq.* drunk. ● *n.* **1** pickle made with salt. **2** plunge or drench in water.

**south** ● *n.* point or direction to right of person facing east; southern part. ● *adj.* in the south; (of wind) from south. ● *adv.* towards south. □□ **southward** *adj.*, *adv.*, & *n.* **southwards** *adv.*

**southerly** *adj.* & *adv.* in southern position or direction; (of wind) from south.

**southern** *adj.* of or in south. □ **southern lights** *Aust.* aurora australis. **southern oscillation** climate phenomenon related to fluctuations in air pressure in eastern and western Pacific, where increase in pressure in one region corresponds to decrease in the other.

**southerner** *n.* native or inhabitant of south.

**southernmost** *adj.* furthest south.

**souvenir** *n.* memento of occasion, place, etc.

**souvlaki** *n.* Greek dish of pieces of lamb etc. grilled on skewer.

**sou'wester** *n.* **1** waterproof hat with broad flap at back. **3** SW wind.

**sovereign** ● *n.* **1** supreme ruler, esp. monarch. **2** *hist.* British gold coin nominally worth £1. ● *adj.* supreme; (of a state) independent. □□ **sovereignty** *n.*

**sow**[1] *v.* (**sowed**, **sown** or **sowed**, **sowing**) scatter (seed) on or in earth; plant with seed; initiate.

**sow**[2] *n.* adult female pig.

**soy** *n.* (also **soya**) (in full **soybean** or **soya bean**) leguminous plant yielding edible oil and flour; seed of this.

**sozzled** *adj. colloq.* very drunk.

**SP** *abbr. Aust. Racing* starting price.

**spa** *n.* **1** curative mineral spring; resort with this. **2** (in full **spa bath**) large bath with underwater jets of water to massage body.

**space** ● *n.* boundless expanse in which all objects exist and move; portion of this; empty area or extent; universe beyond earth's atmosphere; interval. ● *v.* arrange with spaces between. □ **spaced out** *colloq.* dazed; under influence of drugs; tired or sluggish. □□ **spacer** *n.*

**spacecraft** *n.* vehicle for travelling in outer space.

**spaceship** *n.* spacecraft.

**spacious** *adj.* having ample space; roomy. □□ **spaciously** *adv.* **spaciousness** *n.*

**spade** *n.* **1** long-handled digging tool with broad sharp-edged metal blade. **2** playing card of suit denoted by black inverted heart-shaped figures with short stalks. □□ **spadeful** *n.*

**spadework** *n.* hard preparatory work.

**spaghetti** *n.* pasta in long thin strands.

**spam** *n.* **1** irrelevant or unsolicited messages sent over Internet etc. for purposes of advertising etc. **2** *propr.* tinned meat product made mainly from ham.

**span** ● *n.* extent from end to end; distance or part between uprights of arch or bridge. ● *v.* (**spanned**) extend across.

**spangle** ● *n.* small piece of glittering material, esp. one of many used to ornament dress etc. ● *v.* (esp. as **spangled** *adj.*) cover (as) with spangles.

**spaniel** *n.* dog of breed with long silky coat and drooping ears.

**spank** *v. & n.* slap, esp. on buttocks.

**spanking** ● *adj.* **1** brisk. **2** *colloq.* striking. **3** *colloq.* excellent. ● *adv. colloq.* very. ● *n.* slapping on buttocks.

**spanner** *n.* tool for turning nut on bolt etc.

**spar** ● *n.* stout pole, esp. as ship's mast etc. ● *v.* (**sparred**) box, esp. for practice; quarrel, argue.

**spare** ● *adj.* **1** not required for normal or immediate use; extra; for emergency or occasional use. **2** lean; thin. **3** frugal. ● *n.* extra thing kept in reserve. ● *v.* **1** afford to give. **2** dispense with. **3** refrain from killing, hurting, etc.; not inflict. **4** be frugal or

grudging of. □□ **sparely** *adv.* **spareness** *n.*

**sparing** *adj.* frugal; economical; restrained. □□ **sparingly** *adv.*

**spark** ● *n.* **1** fiery particle of burning substance. **2** small amount. **3** flash of light between electric conductors etc. **4** flash of wit etc. **5** (also **bright spark**) witty or lively person. ● *v.* **1** emit spark(s). **2** stir into activity; initiate. □ **spark plug** device for firing explosive mixture in internal combustion engine. □□ **sparky** *adj.*

**sparkle** ● *v.* emit or seem to emit sparks; glisten. **2** be lively or witty. ● *n.* **1** glitter. **2** lively quality. □□ **sparkly** *adj.*

**sparkler** *n.* hand-held sparkling firework.

**sparkling** *adj.* (of wine or mineral water) effervescent, fizzy.

**sparrow** *n.* small brownish-grey bird.

**sparse** *adj.* thinly scattered. □□ **sparsely** *adv.* **sparseness** *n.*

**spartan** *adj.* (of conditions) austere, rigorous.

**spasm** *n.* **1** sudden involuntary muscular contraction. **2** convulsive movement or emotion etc. **3** *colloq.* brief spell.

**spasmodic** *adj.* **1** of or in spasms. **2** intermittent. □□ **spasmodically** *adv.*

**spastic** ● *adj.* **1** of or affected by muscle spasm; of a form of muscular weakness typical of cerebral palsy. **2** *offens.* (of person) having cerebral palsy. ● *n. offens.* **1** person who has cerebral palsy. **2** *colloq.* stupid or incompetent person. □□ **spasticity** *n.*

**Usage** The use of the word *spastic* is often considered offensive.

**spat** ● *n.* **1** short gaiter. **2** slight quarrel. ● *v.* see SPIT.

**patchcock** n. very small chicken or game bird.

**pate** n. **1** river flood. **2** large amount or number (of similar events etc.)

**patial** adj. of space. □□ **spatially** adv.

**patter** ● v. scatter or splash in drips. ● n. splash; pattering. □□ **spattering** n.

**spatula** n. broad-bladed implement used esp. by artists and in cookery.

**spawn** ● v. (of fish, frog, etc.) produce (eggs); be produced as eggs or young; produce or generate in large numbers. ● n. **1** eggs of fish, frogs, etc. **2** white fibrous matter from which mushrooms or other fungi grow.

**spay** v. sterilise (female animal) by removing ovaries.

**speak** v. (**spoke**, **spoken**, **speaking**) utter (words) in ordinary voice; say something, converse; express something by speaking. ● **speak out** speak loudly or freely, give one's opinion. **speak up** = *speak out*.

**speaker** n. **1** person who speaks, esp. in public; person who speaks specified language. **2** (**Speaker**) presiding officer in legislative assembly. **3** loudspeaker.

**speakerphone** n. telephone with a loudspeaker and microphone, that does not need to be held in the hand.

**spear** ● n. thrusting or throwing weapon with long shaft and sharp-pointed head; tip and stem of asparagus, broccoli, etc. ● v. pierce or strike (as) with spear.

**spearhead** ● n. foremost part of advancing force. ● v. be spearhead of.

**spec** n. colloq. **1** specification. **2** speculation. □ **on spec** as a gamble, on the off chance.

**special** ● adj. **1** exceptional, out of the ordinary. **2** peculiar, specific. **3** for particular purpose. ● n. **1** special

train, edition of newspaper, dish on menu, etc. **2** item offered for sale or purchased at reduced price. □ **special effects** illusions created for films etc. by props, computer graphics, etc. □□ **specially** adv.

**specialise** v. (also **-ize**) **1** be or become a specialist. **2** adapt for a particular purpose. □□ **specialisation** n.

**specialist** n. person trained in particular branch of subject.

**speciality** n. special subject, product, activity, etc.; special feature or skill.

**species** n. (pl. **species**) class of things having common characteristics; group of animals or plants within genus; kind, sort.

**specific** ● adj. **1** clearly defined. **2** relating to particular subject. **3** peculiar. **4** exact, giving full details. ● n. specific aspect. □□ **specifically** adv.

**specification** n. specifying; detailed description of work (to be) done or of invention, patent, etc.

**specify** v. **1** name or mention expressly or as condition. **2** include in specifications.

**specimen** n. **1** individual or sample taken as example of class or whole, esp. in experiments etc. **2** sample of urine etc. for testing.

**specious** adj. plausible but wrong.

**speck** ● n. small spot or particle. ● v. **1** (esp. as **specked** adj.) marked with specks, (of gold etc.) found on surface. **2** Aust. search for surface gold, opal, etc. □□ **specker** n.

**speckle** n. small spot, esp. as natural marking.

**specs** n.pl. colloq. spectacles.

**spectacle** n. **1** striking, impressive, or ridiculous sight. **2** public show. **3** (**spectacles**) pair of lenses in frame supported on nose and ears, to correct defective eyesight.

**spectacular ●** adj. striking, impressive, lavish. ● n. spectacular performance. □□ **spectacularly** adv.

**spectator** n. person who watches a show, game, incident, etc. □□ **spectate** v.

**spectral** adj. 1 of or like spectre. 2 of or like spectrum.

**spectre** n. ghost; haunting presentiment.

**spectrum** n. (pl. spectra) 1 band of colours as seen in rainbow etc.; arrangement of electromagnetic radiation by wavelength. 2 entire or wide range of ideas etc.

**speculate** v. 1 theorise, conjecture. 2 deal in commodities etc. in expectation of profiting from fluctuating prices. □□ **speculation** n. **speculative** adj. **speculator** n.

**sped** see SPEED.

**speech** n. 1 faculty, act, or manner of speaking. 2 formal public address. 3 language, dialect.

**speechless** adj. temporarily silenced by emotion etc.

**speed** ● n. 1 rate of progress or motion; a fast rate, rapidity. 2 colloq. amphetamine drug. ● v. (sped, speeding) 1 move, pass, or send quickly. (speeded, speeding) 2 travel at illegal speed.

**speedometer** n. instrument on vehicle indicating its speed.

**speedwell** n. small blue-flowered herbaceous plant.

**speedy** adj. (speedier) rapid; prompt. □□ **speedily** adv.

**speleology** n. exploration and study of caves. □□ **speleologist** n.

**spell** ● v. (spelt or spelled, spelling) 1 give in correct order letters that form (word). 2 produce result. ● n. 1 words supposed to have magic power; their influence; a fascination, an attraction. 2 a period of time, weather, or activity. □□ **speller** n. **spelling** n.

**spellbound** adj. entranced.

**spencer** n. woman's thin singlet with sleeves.

**spend** v. (spent, spending) 1 pay out (money) in buying something. 2 use up; pass (time etc.) □□ **spender** n.

**spendthrift** n. wasteful spender.

**sperm** n. (pl. sperms or sperm) male reproductive cell; semen.

**spermatozoon** n. (pl. spermatozoa) fertilising cell of male organism.

**spermicidal** adj. killing sperm.

**spew** ● v. 1 vomit; (cause to) gush out. 2 Aust. colloq. be very angry. ● n. vomit.

**SPF** abbr. sun protection factor.

**sphagnum** n. (in full sphagnum moss) moss growing in bogs and peat, widely used in horticulture.

**sphere** ● n. 1 solid figure with every point on its surface equidistant from centre; ball, globe. 2 field of action, influence, etc.

**spherical** adj. shaped like sphere. □□ **spherically** adv.

**sphincter** n. ring of muscle closing and opening orifice.

**sphinx** n. 1 ancient Egyptian stone figure with lion's body and human or ram's head. 2 enigmatic or inscrutable person.

**sphygmomanometer** n. instrument for measuring blood pressure.

**spice** ● n. flavouring substance with strong taste or smell; something that adds zest. ● v. flavour with spice. □□ **spicy** adj.

**spick and span** adj. neat and clean.

**spider** n. 1 eight-legged arthropod, many species of which spin webs. 2 Aust. carbonated soft drink to which ice cream has been added. □□ **spidery** adj.

**spiel** n. colloq. glib speech or story; sales pitch. □□ **spieler** n.

**spigot** n. small peg or plug; device for controlling flow of liquid in tap.

.47

**pike** ● *n.* **1** sharp point. **2** forceful attacking hit over net in volleyball. **3** large nail. ● *v.* **1** impale on a spike; form into spikes. **2** *colloq.* add alcohol etc. to (drink), contaminate. **3** *Volleyball* hit ball forcefully over net with overarm action. □□ **spiky** *adj.*

**spill** ● *v.* (spilt or spilled, spilling) **1** cause or allow to run over edge of container; overflow; be spilt. **2** throw from vehicle, saddle, etc. **3** *colloq.* make known (information etc.) ● *n.* **1** spilling, being spilt. **2** tumble, esp. from horse or vehicle. **3** *Aust.* vacating of all or several posts of parliamentary party. **4** thin strip of wood, paper, etc. for lighting candle etc. □□ **spillage** *n.* **spiller** *n.*

**spin** ● *v.* (spun, spinning) **1** turn rapidly on its axis. **2** draw out and twist into threads; make (yarn etc.) in this way. ● *n.* **1** spinning motion. **2** *colloq.* short drive for pleasure. **3** *Aust.* (in two-up) act of tossing coins. □ **spin doctor** *colloq.* political spokesperson employed to give favourable interpretation of events to media. **spin out** prolong.

**spina bifida** *n.* congenital defect of spine, in which part of spinal cord is exposed.

**spinach** *n.* green vegetable with edible leaves; *Aust.* silverbeet.

**spinal** *adj.* of spine.

**spindle** *n.* slender rod for twisting and winding thread in spinning; pin or axis on which something revolves; turned piece of wood used as chair leg etc.

**spindly** *adj.* (spindlier) long or tall and thin.

**spindrift** *n.* spray on surface of sea.

**spine** *n.* **1** series of vertebrae extending from skull, backbone. **2** needle-like outgrowth of animal or plant. **3** part of book enclosing page fastening. **4** ridge, sharp projection.

**spinebill** *n.* *Aust.* small honeyeater.

**spinel** *n.* hard crystalline mineral of various colours.

**spineless** *adj.* lacking resolve.

**spinet** *n.* *hist.* small harpsichord with oblique strings.

**spinifex** *n.* *Aust.* any of many tussocky perennial grasses of arid areas or sand dunes.

**spinnaker** *n.* large three-cornered sail of racing yacht.

**spinner** *n.* **1** person or thing that spins. **2** *Cricket* spin bowler; spun ball. **3** *Aust.* player tossing coins in two-up. **4** revolving bait or lure. **5** spinneret.

**spinneret** *n.* spinning organ in spider etc.

**spinster** *n.* often *derog.* unmarried woman.

**spiny** *adj.* (spinier) having (many) spines.

**spiracle** *n.* external respiratory opening in insects, whales, etc.

**spiral** ● *adj.* winding about centre in an enlarging or decreasing continuous circular motion, either on flat plane or rising in cone. ● *n.* **1** spiral curve. **2** progressive rise or fall. ● *v.* (spiralled) **1** move in spiral course. **2** (of prices etc.) rise or fall continuously.

**spire** *n.* tapering structure, esp. on church tower; any tapering thing.

**spirit** ● *n.* **1** mind as distinct from body; soul; person's nature. **2** ghost. **3** characteristic quality; intended meaning of law etc. **4** liveliness, boldness. **5** (spirits) feeling of cheerfulness or depression. **6** strong distilled alcoholic drink. ● *v.* carry off swiftly and mysteriously. □ **spirit level** sealed glass tube containing a bubble in liquid, used to test that things are horizontal.

**spirited** *adj.* lively, bold. □□ **spiritedly** *adv.*

**spiritual** *adj.* **1** of spirit. **2** religious, divine, inspired. **3** refined, sensitive. □□ **spirituality** *n.* **spiritually** *adv.*

**spiritualism** n. belief in, and practice of, communication with dead, esp. through mediums. □□ **spiritualist** n. **spiritualistic** adj.

**spit** ● v. (**spat** or **spit**, **spitting**) **1** eject from mouth; eject saliva. **2** (of rain) fall lightly. ● n. **1** spittle, spitting. **2** foamy liquid secretion of some insects. **3** rod for skewering meat for roasting over fire etc. **4** point of land projecting into sea. □ **spit the dummy** Aust. colloq. be very angry.

**spite** ● n. malicious desire to hurt or annoy someone. ● v. hurt, thwart.

**spiteful** adj. malicious. □□ **spitefully** adv.

**spitfire** n. **1** fiery-tempered person. **2** Aust. larva of sawfly.

**spittle** n. saliva.

**splash** ● v. **1** (cause to) scatter in drops; wet or stain by splashing; move with splashing. **2** display (news) prominently. **3** spend (money) ostentatiously. ● n. **1** act or noise of splashing. **2** prominent news feature, sensation, etc. **3** patch of colour.

**splatter** ● v. splash esp. with continuous noisy action; spatter.

**splay** v. spread apart; become wider or more separate.

**splayd** n. propr. Aust. fork with spoon-shaped bowl and cutting edge.

**spleen** n. **1** abdominal organ regulating quality of blood. **2** moroseness, irritability.

**splendid** adj. magnificent; glorious, dignified; excellent. □□ **splendidly** adv.

**splendour** n. (also **splendor**) dazzling brightness; magnificence.

**splenetic** adj. bad-tempered; peevish.

**splice** ● v. join by interweaving or overlapping the ends. ● n. join made by splicing.

**splint** ● n. strip of rigid material bound to broken limb while it heals. ● v. secure with splint.

**splinter** ● n. small sharp fragment of wood, stone, glass, etc. ● v. break into splinters; shatter. □ **splinter group** small group that has broken away from larger one.

**split** ● v. (**split**, **splitting**) **1** break or come apart, esp. lengthwise; divide, share. **2** colloq. leave, esp. suddenly. ● n. **1** splitting; a split thing or place. **2** (**splits**) acrobatic position with legs stretched fully apart. □ **split infinitive** infinitive with word placed between to and verb.

**splodge** colloq. ● n. daub, blot, or smear. ● v. make splodge on. □□ **splodgy** adj.

**splotch** n. & v. splodge. □□ **splotchy** adj.

**splurge** colloq. ● n. instance of sudden extravagance, esp. in spending money; ostentatious display or effort. ● v. make splurge.

**splutter** ● v. speak or express in choking manner; emit spitting sounds; speak rapidly or incoherently. ● n. spluttering speech or sound.

**spoil** ● v. (**spoilt** or **spoiled**, **spoiling**) **1** make or become useless or unsatisfactory; decay, go bad. **2** reduce enjoyment etc. of. **3** ruin character of by over-indulgence. ● n. (**spoils**) plunder, stolen goods. □ **be spoiling for** desire (fight etc.).

**spoilsport** n. person who spoils others' enjoyment.

**spoke¹** n. each of rods running from hub to rim of wheel.

**spoke²** see SPEAK.

**spoken** see SPEAK.

**spokesman** n. (pl. **-men**) spokesperson.

**spokesperson** n. (pl. **-persons** or **-people**) person who speaks on behalf of group.

**spokeswoman** n. (pl. **-women**) female spokesperson.

**sponge** ● n. **1** sea animal with porous body wall and tough elastic skeleton; this skeleton or piece of porous rubber etc. used in bathing, cleaning, etc.; thing like sponge in consistency etc., esp. sponge cake. **2** act of sponging. ● *v.* **1** wipe or clean with sponge; absorb (as) with sponge. **2** live as parasite; obtain (drink etc.) by cadging. □□ **spongy** *adj.*

**sponger** *n.* parasitic person.

**spongiform** *adj.* of or like a sponge.

**sponsor** ● *n.* **1** person who pledges money to charity in return for specified activity by someone; patron of artistic or sporting activity etc.; company etc. financing broadcast in return for advertising. **2** person introducing legislation. **3** godparent. ● *v.* be sponsor for. □□ **sponsorship** *n.*

**spontaneous** *adj.* acting, done, or occurring without external cause; instinctive, automatic, natural. □□ **spontaneity** *n.* **spontaneously** *adv.*

**spoof** *n.* & *v. colloq.* parody; hoax.

**spook** *colloq.* ● *n.* **1** ghost. **2** spy. ● *v.* frighten, unnerve. □□ **spooked** *adj.* **spooky** *adj.*

**spool** ● *n.* reel on which something is wound. ● *v.* **1** wind on spool. **2** *Computing* send (data for printing etc.) to intermediate store.

**spoon** ● *n.* utensil with bowl and handle for putting food in mouth, or for stirring etc.; spoonful; spoon-shaped thing. ● *v.* **1** take or lift with spoon. **2** hit (ball) feebly upwards. □□ **spoonful** *n.*

**spoonbill** *n.* wading bird with broad flat-tipped bill.

**spoonerism** *n.* (usu. accidental) transposition of initial sounds of two or more words (*he's a boiled sprat*).

**spoonfeed** *v.* (**spoonfed**, **spoonfeeding**) **1** feed from spoon. **2** give excessive help to.

**spoor** *n.* animal's track or scent.

**sporadic** *adj.* occurring only here and there or occasionally. □□ **sporadically** *adv.*

**spore** *n.* reproductive cell of ferns, fungi, protozoa, etc.

**sport** ● *n.* **1** physical activity engaged in for pleasure or competition. **2** *colloq.* fair or generous person. ● *v.* **1** play. **2** wear or exhibit, esp. ostentatiously. □ **sports car** open low-built fast car. **sports jacket** man's jacket for informal wear.

**sporting** *adj.* **1** of or interested in sport. **2** generous, fair. □ **sporting chance** some possibility of success. □□ **sportingly** *adv.*

**sportive** *adj.* playful.

**sportsground** *n.* arena for organised sport, usu. with facilities for spectators and players.

**sportsman** *n.* (*pl.* **-men**) **1** man who takes part in sport. **2** fair and generous person. □□ **sportsmanlike** *adj.* **sportsmanship** *n.*

**sportswoman** *n.* (*pl.* **-women**) woman who takes part in sport.

**sporty** *adj. colloq.* **1** fond of sport. **2** rakish, showy.

**spot** ● *n.* **1** round mark or stain; pimple. **2** a place. **3** *colloq.* small amount. **4** spotlight. ● *v.* (**spotted**) **1** mark with a spot or spots. **2** *colloq.* notice; watch for and take note of. **3** *Aust.* (of bushfire) break out in patches ahead of main fire. □ **spot-buy** pay for (currency or commodity) immediately after a sale is made. **spot check** random check. **spot-fixing** (in sport) dishonestly determining the outcome of a specific part of a match or game before it is played.

**spotless** *adj.* absolutely clean or pure. □□ **spotlessly** *adv.*

**spotlight** *n.* **1** beam of light directed on small area. **2** full attention or publicity.

**spotty** *adj.* marked with spots; patchy, irregular.

**spouse** *n.* husband or wife.

**spout** ● *n.* 1 projecting tube or lip for pouring from teapot, kettle, jug, fountain, roof gutter, etc. 2 jet of liquid. ● *v.* 1 discharge or issue forcibly in jet. 2 utter at length or pompously.

**sprain** ● *v.* wrench (ankle, wrist, etc.), causing pain or swelling. ● *n.* such injury.

**sprang** see SPRING.

**sprat** *n.* small edible marine fish.

**sprawl** ● *v.* sit, lie, or fall, with limbs spread out untidily; spread out irregularly; straggle. ● *n.* 1 sprawling movement, position, or mass. 2 straggling urban expansion.

**spray** ● *n.* 1 water etc. flying in small drops; liquid intended for spraying; device for spraying. 2 sprig of flowers or leaves, small branch; ornament in similar form. ● *v.* come or send out in small drops; wet with liquid in this way. □□ **sprayer** *n.*

**spread** ● *v.* (**spread, spreading**) 1 open, extend, unfold. 2 cause to cover larger surface; have wide or increasing extent. 3 (cause to) become widely known. 4 cover. 5 lay (table). ● *n.* 1 act, capability, or extent of spreading; diffusion. 2 breadth. 3 increased girth. 4 difference between two rates, prices, etc. 5 *colloq.* elaborate meal. 6 paste for spreading on bread etc. 7 bedspread. 8 printed matter spread across more than one column.

**spreadeagled** *adj.* with arms and legs spread.

**spreadsheet** *n.* computer program that manipulates figures in tables.

**spree** *n.* period of unrestrained indulgence in an activity.

**sprig** *n.* 1 twig; shoot. 2 stud on sole of shoe or boot.

**sprightly** *adj.* vivacious, lively.

**spring** ● *v.* (**sprang, sprung, springing**) 1 jump; move rapidly. 2 issue, arise; produce or cause to operate suddenly. 3 *Aust. colloq.* discover (concealed object, illicit activity, etc.). ● *n.* 1 act of springing, a jump. 2 device that reverts to its original position after being compressed, tightened, or stretched; elasticity. 3 place where water or oil flows naturally from ground. 4 season of year between winter and summer. □ **spring roll** fried pancake filled with vegetables etc. **spring tide** tide when there is largest rise and fall of water. □□ **springlike** *adj.*

**springboard** *n.* flexible board giving impetus to gymnast or diver; source of impetus in any activity.

**springbok** *n.* S. African gazelle.

**springy** *adj.* elastic.

**sprinkle** ● *v.* scatter small particles of (substance) over (surface); fall in this way. ● *n.* sprinkling; light shower. □□ **sprinkler** *n.*

**sprinkling** *n.* small sparse number or amount.

**sprint** ● *v.* run short distance at full speed. ● *n.* fast run; a race over short distance. □□ **sprinter** *n.*

**sprite** *n.* elf, fairy, or goblin.

**spritzer** *n.* drink of white wine and soda water.

**sprocket** *n.* projection on rim of wheel engaging with links of chain.

**sprout** ● *v.* put forth (shoots etc.); begin to grow. ● *n.* shoot of plant; beansprout; brussels sprout.

**spruce** ● *adj.* 1 trim appearance. 2 smart. ● *v.* make or become smart. ● *n.* conifer with dense conical foliage; its wood. □□ **sprucely** *adv.* **spruceness** *n.*

**spruik** *v. Aust. colloq.* hold forth in public; deliver harangue, esp. to attract customers to show etc. □□ **spruiker** *n.*

**sprung** see SPRING.

**spry** adj. lively, nimble.□□ **spryly** adv.

**spud** n. colloq. **1** potato. **2** narrow spade.

**spume** n. froth, foam.

**spun** see SPIN.

**spunk** n. colloq. **1** mettle, spirit. **2** coarse colloq. semen. **3** Aust. sexually attractive person.
□□ **spunky** adj.

**spur** ● n. **1** small spike or spiked wheel attached to rider's heel for urging horse forward; stimulus, incentive. **2** a projection.
● v. (spurred) prick (horse) with spur; incite, stimulate.□ **on the spur of the moment** on impulse; impromptu.

**spurious** adj. not genuine or authentic.□□ **spuriously** adv.

**spurn** v. reject with disdain or contempt.

**spurt** ● v. **1** (cause to) gush out in jet or stream. **2** make sudden effort.
● n. **1** sudden gushing out, jet. **2** short burst of speed, growth, etc.

**sputter** v. & n. splutter.

**sputum** n. mixed saliva and mucus.

**spy** ● n. person secretly collecting and reporting information for government, company, etc.; person watching others secretly.
● v. discern, see; act as spy.

**sq.** abbr. square.

**squabble** ● n. petty or noisy quarrel. ● v. engage in squabble.

**squad** n. small group working together.

**squadron** n. **1** basic tactical and administrative unit of airforce. **2** detachment of warships. **3** organised group etc.

**squalid** adj. filthy, dirty; morally repulsive or degraded.□□ **squalidly** adv. **squalor** n.

**squall** ● n. **1** sudden or violent gust or storm. **2** discordant cry, scream. ● v. utter (with) squall, scream.□□ **squally** adj.

**squander** v. spend wastefully.

**square** ● n. **1** rectangle with four equal sides; object of (approximately) this shape; open area surrounded by buildings. **2** product of number multiplied by itself. **3** L- or T-shaped instrument for obtaining or testing right angles. **4** colloq. conventional or old-fashioned person. ● adj. **1** square-shaped. **2** having or in form of right angle. **3** angular, not round. **4** designating unit of measure equal to area of square whose side is one of the unit specified. **5** level, parallel. **6** at right angles. **7** sturdy, squat. **8** arranged. **9** (also **all square**) with no money owed. **10** (of scores) equal. **11** fair, honest. **12** direct. **13** colloq. conventional, old-fashioned. ● adv. **1** squarely. **2** directly. **3** fairly. ● v. **1** make square. **2** multiply (number) by itself. **3** make or be consistent, reconcile. **4** mark out in squares. **5** settle (bill etc.). **6** place (shoulders etc.) squarely facing forwards. **7** colloq. bribe. **8** make scores of (match etc.) equal.□ **square dance** dance in which four couples face inwards from four sides. **square meal** substantial meal. **square root** the number of which a given number is the square. **square up to** face in fighting attitude; face resolutely.
□□ **squarely** adv.

**squash** ● v. **1** crush or squeeze flat or into pulp; force into small space, crowd. **2** silence (person) with crushing retort, bully; suppress (proposal, allegation, etc.)
● n. **1** crowd; crowded state. **2** drink made of crushed fruit. **3** (in full **squash racquets**) game played with racquets and small ball in closed court. **4** vegetable gourd.
□□ **squashy** adj.

**squat** ● v. (squatted) **1** sit on one's heels, or on ground with knees drawn up; colloq. sit down. **2** Aust. hist.

occupy tract of Crown land to graze sheep etc. **3** occupy building as squatter. ● *adj.* dumpy. ● *n.* **1** squatting posture. **2** place occupied by squatter(s). □□ **squatting** *n.*

**squatter** *n.* **1** person who inhabits unoccupied premises without permission. **2** *Aust. hist.* person occupying tract of Crown land to graze livestock, having title by licence or lease. **3** *Aust. colloq.* large-scale sheep farmer.

**squawk** ● *n.* **1** harsh cry. **2** complaint. ● *v.* utter squawk.

**squeak** ● *n.* **1** short high-pitched cry or sound. **2** (also **narrow squeak**) narrow escape. ● *v.* **1** make squeak; utter shrilly. **2** *colloq.* pass narrowly. **3** *colloq.* turn informer. □□ **squeaky** *adj.*

**squeal** ● *n.* prolonged shrill sound or cry. ● *v.* **1** make, or utter with, squeal. **2** *colloq.* turn informer. **3** *colloq.* protest vociferously.

**squeamish** *adj.* **1** easily nauseated; slightly sick; easily shocked. **2** prudish. □□ **squeamishly** *adv.* **squeamishness** *n.*

**squeegee** *n.* rubber-edged implement on handle, for cleaning windows etc.

**squeeze** ● *v.* **1** exert pressure on, esp. to extract moisture; reduce in size or alter in shape by squeezing; force or push into or through small or narrow space. **2** harass, pressure; obtain by extortion or entreaty. ● *n.* **1** squeezing, being squeezed; close embrace; crowd, crowded state. **2** small quantity produced by squeezing. **3** restriction on borrowing and investment. **4** (also **tight squeeze**) *colloq.* difficult situation.

**squelch** *v.* & *n.* (make) sucking sound like someone treading in thick mud. □□ **squelchy** *adj.*

**squib** ● *n.* **1** small hissing firework. **2** satirical essay. **3** *Aust.* horse lacking stamina; coward. **4** damp squib. ● *v.* evade (responsibility etc.); shirk; capitulate.

**squid** *n.* ten-armed marine cephalopod.

**squiggle** *n.* short curly line. □□ **squiggly** *adj.*

**squint** ● *v.* have eyes turned in different directions; look sidelong or with half-closed eyes. ● *n.* squinting condition; *colloq.* glance, look.

**squire** *n.* (in Britain) country gentleman, esp. chief landowner of district.

**squirm** ● *v.* wriggle, writhe; show or feel embarrassment. ● *n.* squirming movement.

**squirrel** *n.* small tree-climbing animal with bushy tail.

**squirt** ● *v.* eject (liquid etc.) in jet; be ejected thus; splash with squirted substance. ● *n.* **1** jet of water etc.; small quantity squirted. **2** syringe. **3** *colloq.* insignificant or short person.

**squish** *colloq.* ● *n.* slight squelching sound. ● *v.* **1** move with squish. **2** squash. □□ **squishy** *adj.*

**squiz** (also **squizz**) *Aust. colloq.* ● *n.* a look or glance. ● *v.* look or glance (at).

**SS** *abbr.* **1** steamship. **2** *hist.* Nazi special police force.

**SSE** *abbr.* south-south-east.

**SSW** *abbr.* south-south-west.

**St** *abbr.* **1** Street. **2** Saint.

**stab** ● *v.* (**stabbed**) pierce or wound with knife etc.; aim blow with sharp weapon; cause sharp pain to. ● *n.* **1** act or result of stabbing. **2** *colloq.* attempt, guess.

**stabilise** *v.* (also -**ize**) make or become stable. □□ **stabilisation** *n.* **stabiliser** *n.*

**stable** ● *adj.* firmly fixed or established; not fluctuating or changing; not easily upset or disturbed. ● n. building for keeping horses; establishment for training racehorses; horses, people, etc. from same establishment. ● v. put or keep in stable.□□ **stability** n. **stably** adv.

**staccato** Mus. ● adj. & adv. with each sound sharply distinct. ● n. staccato passage or delivery.

**stack** ● n. 1 (esp. orderly) pile or heap; colloq. large quantity. 2 tall chimney. 3 stacked group of aircraft. 4 storage section of library; storage system in computer. 5 colloq. crash in motor vehicle, etc. ● v. 1 pile in stack(s). 2 arrange (cards, circumstances, etc.) secretly for cheating. 3 manipulate meeting by attendance of one's supporters. 4 cause (aircraft) to fly in circles while waiting to land. 5 colloq. crash (motor vehicle etc.).

**stadium** n. sports ground with tiered seats for spectators.

**staff** ● n. 1 stick used as weapon, support, or symbol of authority. 2 people employed by organisation. (pl. **staffs** or **staves**) 3 set of five parallel lines on which music is written. ● v. provide with staff of people.

**stag** n. adult male deer.

**stage** ● n. 1 point or period in process or development. 2 raised platform, esp. for performing plays etc. on. 3 theatrical profession. 4 scene of action. 5 division or point reached in process or journey. ● v. 1 present (play etc.) on stage. 2 organise and carry out. □ **stage fright** nervousness on facing audience. **stage whisper** whisper meant to be overheard.□□ **staging** n.

**stagecoach** n. hist. large horse-drawn coach running on regular route by stages.

**stagflation** n. state of inflation without increase of demand and employment.

**stagger** ● v. 1 (cause to) walk unsteadily. 2 shock, confuse. 3 arrange (events etc.) so that they do not coincide; arrange (objects) so that they are not in line. ● n. tottering movement.

**staggering** adj. astonishing; bewildering.□□ **staggeringly** adv.

**staghorn** n. large epiphytic fern, having long, pendulous, much-divided leaves.

**stagnant** adj. 1 (of liquid) motionless, having no current. 2 not developing.□□ **stagnancy** n.

**stagnate** v. be or become stagnant. □□ **stagnation** n.

**staid** adj. respectable and unadventurous.

**stain** ● v. 1 discolour or be discoloured by action of liquid sinking in; spoil, damage. 2 colour (wood etc.) with penetrating substance. ● n. 1 discoloration; spot, mark; blemish. 2 dye etc. for staining.

**stainless** adj. without stains; not liable to stain. □ **stainless steel** chrome steel not liable to rust or tarnish.

**stair** n. each of set of fixed steps.

**staircase** n. set of stairs with supporting structure.

**stairway** n. staircase.

**stairwell** n. shaft in which staircase is built.

**stake** ● n. 1 pointed stick or post for driving into ground. 2 money etc. wagered; share or interest in enterprise etc. ● v. 1 secure, support, or mark with stake(s). 2 wager. □ **at stake** being risked; at issue, in question. **stake a claim** claim right to something. **stake out** place under surveillance.

**stakeholder** n. 1 independent party with whom each of those making wager deposits the money etc. wagered. 2 person with an interest or concern in something.

**stalactite** n. icicle-like deposit of calcium carbonate hanging from roof of cave etc.

**stalagmite** n. icicle-like deposit of calcium carbonate rising from floor of cave etc.

**stale** ● adj. 1 not fresh; musty, insipid, or otherwise the worse for age or use. 2 trite, unoriginal. ● v. make or become stale. □□ **staleness** n.

**stalemate** ● n. drawn position in chess; deadlock. ● v. bring to such a state.

**stalk** ● n. 1 main stem of herbaceous plant; slender attachment or support of leaf, flower, fruit, etc.; similar support for organ etc. in animal. ● v. 1 pursue (game, enemy) stealthily; harass or persecute (someone) with unwanted and obsessive attention. 2 stride, walk in haughty manner. □ **stalking horse** pretext concealing one's real intentions.

**stall** ● n. 1 stable, cowhouse; compartment in this. 2 ground floor seat in theatre. 3 booth or stand where goods are displayed for sale. ● v. 1 place or keep in stall. 2 (of engine) stop suddenly through lack of power; (of aircraft) begin to drop because speed is too low; cause to stall. 3 play for time when being questioned etc.

**stallion** n. uncastrated adult male horse.

**stalwart** ● adj. strong, sturdy; courageous, resolute, reliable. ● n. stalwart person.

**stamen** n. organ producing pollen in flower.

**stamina** n. physical or mental endurance.

**stammer** ● v. speak with involuntary pauses or repetitions of syllable. ● n. stammering speech; tendency to stammer.

**stamp** ● v. 1 bring down (one's foot) heavily, esp. on ground; crush or flatten in this way. 2 walk heavily. 3 impress (design, mark, etc.) on surface. 4 affix postage or other stamp to. 5 assign specific character to. 6 mark out. ● n. 1 instrument for stamping; mark or design made by this. 2 small adhesive piece of paper as evidence of payment, esp. postage stamp. 3 mark, label, etc. on commodity as evidence of quality etc. 4 act or sound of stamping foot. 5 characteristic mark. □ **stamping ground** favourite haunt or place of action. **stamp out** put end to, crush, destroy.

**stampede** ● n. sudden flight or hurried movement of animals or people. ● v. (cause to) take part in stampede.

**stance** n. 1 standpoint, attitude. 2 position of body.

**stanch** v. (also **staunch**) restrain flow of (esp. blood).

**stanchion** n. post or pillar, upright support.

**stand** ● v. (**stood**, **standing**) 1 have, take, or maintain upright or stationary position, esp. on feet or base; be situated; place, set upright. 2 stay firm or valid. 3 offer oneself for election. 4 endure; undergo (trial). ● n. 1 stationary condition; position taken up. 2 resistance to attack. 3 Cricket prolonged period at wicket by two batters. 4 piece of furniture to hold or display something. 5 open-fronted stall for trader, exhibitor, etc. 6 raised structure with seats at sportsground etc. □ **stand a chance** have chance of success. **stand by** 1 look on without interfering. 2 be ready for action. 3 support in difficulty. **stand down** withdraw or retire. **stand for** 1 represent. 2 colloq. tolerate. **stand in** deputise; act in place of another.

**stand-offish** cold or distant in manner. **stand one's ground** not yield. **stand up for** speak in defence of. **stand up to** resist courageously; be strong enough to endure.

**standard** ● n. 1 object, quality, or measure serving as basis, example, or principle to which others conform or should conform or by which others are judged. 2 level of excellence etc. required or specified. 3 ordinary procedure etc. 4 distinctive flag. 5 upright support or pipe. 6 shrub grafted on upright stem and trained in tree form. ● adj. 1 serving or used as standard. 2 of normal or prescribed quality, type, or size. 3 (of language) conforming to established educated usage.

**standardise** v. (also **-ize**) cause to conform to standard. □□ **standardisation** n.

**standing** ● n. 1 esteem, repute, esp. high. 2 duration. ● adj. 1 that stands, upright. 2 established, permanent. 3 (of jump, start, etc.) performed with no run-up.

**standout** n. remarkable or outstanding person or thing.

**standpoint** n. point of view.

**standstill** n. stoppage; inability to proceed.

**stank** see STINK.

**stanza** n. group of lines forming division of poem etc. □□ **stanzaic** adj.

**staphylococcus** n. (pl. **staphylococci**) bacterium sometimes forming pus. □□ **staphylococcal** adj.

**staple** ● n. 1 U-shaped piece of wire with pointed ends for holding papers together, for fixing netting to post, etc. 2 principal or standard food or product etc. 3 fibre of wool etc. with regard to its length, quality, etc. ● adj. principal, most important. ● v. fasten with staple(s). □□ **stapler** n.

**star** ● n. 1 celestial body appearing as luminous point in night sky; large luminous gaseous body such as sun. 2 celestial body regarded as influencing fortunes etc.; horoscope. 3 conventional image of star with radiating lines or points; asterisk (*); this as mark of quality. 4 famous or brilliant person; leading performer. ● adj. outstanding. ● v. (**starred**) 1 put an asterisk beside (an item). 2 appear or present as leading performer(s).

**starboard** n. right-hand side of ship or aircraft looking forward.

**starch** ● n. 1 white carbohydrate obtained chiefly from cereals and potatoes; preparation of this for stiffening fabric. 2 stiffness of manner; formality. ● v. stiffen (clothing) with starch. □□ **starchy** adj.

**stardom** n. being star actor etc.

**stare** ● v. look fixedly, esp. in curiosity, surprise, horror, etc. ● n. staring gaze.

**starfish** n. star-shaped sea creature.

**stark** ● adj. 1 sharply evident. 2 desolate, bare. 3 absolute. ● adv. completely, wholly. □□ **starkly** adv.

**starkers** adj. colloq. 1 stark naked. 2 mad, insane.

**starling** n. gregarious bird with blackish speckled lustrous plumage.

**starry** adj. full of stars; star-like. □ **starry-eyed** colloq. enthusiastic but impractical.

**start** ● v. 1 begin; set in motion or action; (cause to) begin operating; establish. 2 jump in surprise, pain, etc. ● n. 1 beginning; starting place of race etc. 2 advantageous initial position in life, business, race, etc. 3 sudden movement of surprise, pain, etc. □□ **start-up** action or process of setting something in motion; newly established business. □□ **starter** n.

**startle** v. shock or surprise.

**starve** v. 1 (cause to) die of hunger or suffer from malnourishment; *colloq.* feel very hungry. 2 feel strong craving for (sympathy, knowledge, etc.) 3 deprive of. 4 compel by starvation. □□ **starvation** n.

**stash** *colloq.* ● v. conceal; put in safe place; hoard. ● n. hiding place; thing hidden.

**state** ● n. 1 existing condition or position of person or thing; *colloq.* excited or agitated mental condition. 2 untidy condition. 3 (often **State**) political community under one government; this as part of a federation, esp. the Commonwealth of Australia; (often **State**) civil government. 4 pomp, rank, dignity. ● adj. 1 (often **State**) of, for, or concerned with a state. 2 reserved for or done on occasions of ceremony. ● v. 1 express in speech or writing. 2 fix, specify. □ **state school** *Aust.* school largely managed and funded by public authorities.

**stateless** adj. having no nationality or citizenship.

**stately** adj. dignified; imposing. □□ **stateliness** n.

**statement** n. 1 stating, being stated; thing stated. 2 expression in words. 3 declaration. 4 formal account of facts, esp. to police or in court of law. 5 record of transactions in bank account etc. 6 notification of amount due to contractor etc.

**statesman** n. experienced and respected political leader. □□ **statesmanlike** adj.

**stateswoman** n. woman who is an experienced and respected political leader.

**static** ● adj. 1 stationary; not acting or changing. 2 *Physics* concerned with bodies at rest or forces in equilibrium. ● n. electrical disturbances in air, causing interference in telecommunications; (in full **static electricity**) electricity not flowing as current.

**statics** n. branch of mechanics concerned with bodies at rest or of forces in equilibrium.

**station** ● n. 1 place where person or thing stands; place where particular activity is carried on. 2 broadcasting channel. 3 stopping place on railway; departure point for long-distance buses etc. 4 *Aust.* status. 5 *Aust. hist.* outpost of colonial government. 6 *Aust. hist.* tract of land reserved for Aboriginal people. 7 *Aust.* extensive sheep or cattle raising establishment. ● v. put at or in a certain place for a purpose. □ **station wagon** car with door at rear and extended luggage space.

**stationary** adj. not moving; not meant to be moved; unchanging.

**stationer** n. dealer in stationery.

**stationery** n. writing materials, office supplies, etc.

**statistic** n. 1 item of information expressed in numbers. 2 (**statistics**) science of collecting and interpreting numerical information. □□ **statistical** adj. **statistically** adv.

**statistician** n. expert in statistics.

**stats** n.pl. *colloq.* statistics.

**statue** n. sculptured figure of person or animal, esp. life-size or larger.

**statuesque** adj. like statue, esp. in beauty, dignity, or stillness.

**stature** n. height of (esp. human) body; calibre (esp. moral); eminence, social standing, etc.

**status** n. rank, social position, relative importance; superior social etc. position; posting on social networking website that indicates user's current situation, state of mind, or opinion about something. □ **status quo** existing state of affairs.

**statute** n. written law passed by legislative body; rule of corporation, founder, etc., intended to be permanent.

**statutory** ● *adj.* required or enacted by statute.

**staunch** ● *adj.* trustworthy; loyal. ● *v.* var. of STANCH. □□ **staunchly** *adv.*

**stave** ● *n.* 1 each of curved slats forming sides of cask. 2 *Mus.* staff. 3 stanza, verse. ● *v.* (**stove** or **staved, staving**) break hole in, damage, crush by forcing inwards. □ **stave off** avert or defer (danger or misfortune).

**stay** ● *v.* 1 continue in same place or condition; not depart or change. 2 reside temporarily. 3 postpone, stop. ● *n.* 1 period of staying. 2 postponement.

**STD** *abbr.* 1 subscriber trunk dialling. 2 sexually transmitted disease.

**stead** *n.* □ **stand in good stead** be of great service to.

**steadfast** *adj.* constant, firm, unwavering. □□ **steadfastly** *adv.* **steadfastness** *n.*

**steady** ● *adj.* (**steadier**) 1 firmly fixed or supported. 2 unwavering. 3 uniform, regular. 4 dependable, not excitable. ● *v.* make or become steady. ● *adv.* steadily. □□ **steadily** *adv.* **steadiness** *n.*

**steak** *n.* thick slice of meat (esp. beef) or fish, usu. grilled or fried.

**steal** ● *v.* (**stole, stolen, stealing**) 1 take (another's property) illegally or without right or permission, esp. in secret; obtain surreptitiously, insidiously, or artfully. 2 move, esp. silently or stealthily. ● *n.* 1 stealing. 2 *colloq.* easy task, bargain.

**stealth** *n.* secrecy.

**stealthy** *adj.* (**stealthier**) done or moving with stealth; furtive. □□ **stealthily** *adv.*

**steam** ● *n.* 1 gas into which water is changed by boiling; condensed vapour formed from this; power obtained from steam. 2 *colloq.* power, energy. ● *v.* 1 cook (food) in steam; treat with steam. 2 give off steam. 3 move under steam power; *colloq.* proceed or travel fast or with vigour. □□ **steamy** *adj.*

**steamer** *n.* 1 steam-driven ship. 2 vessel for steaming food in.

**steamroller** *n.* heavy engine with large roller, used in making roads.

**steed** *n. poet.* horse.

**steel** ● *n.* 1 strong malleable low-carbon iron alloy, used esp. for making tools, weapons, etc. 2 strength, firmness. 3 steel rod for sharpening knives. ● *adj.* of or like steel. ● *v.* harden or make resolute. □□ **steely** *adj.*

**steep** ● *adj.* 1 sloping sharply, not gradually. 2 *colloq.* exorbitant, unreasonable. 3 exaggerated, incredible. ● *v.* soak or bathe in liquid. □□ **steepen** *v.* **steeply** *adv.* **steepness** *n.*

**steeple** *n.* tall tower, esp. with spire, above roof of church.

**steeplechase** *n.* race for horses or athletes with fences to jump. □□ **steeplechaser** *n.*

**steeplejack** *n.* person who climbs tall chimneys etc. to do repairs.

**steer** ● *v.* guide (vehicle, ship, etc.) with wheel, rudder, etc.; direct or guide (one's course, other people, conversation, etc.) in specified direction. ● *n.* bullock.

**stegosaurus** *n.* large dinosaur with double row of bony plates along spine.

**stellar** *adj.* of star or stars.

**STEM** *abbr.* science, technology, engineering, and mathematics.

**stem** ● *n.* 1 main body or stalk of plant; stalk of fruit, flower, or leaf; stem-shaped part, e.g. slender part of wine glass, tobacco pipe, etc. 2 *Gram.* root or main part of noun, verb, etc., to which inflections are added. 3 main upright timber at bow of ship.

● v. (stemmed) restrain the flow of; dam. □ stem cell undifferentiated cell from which specialised cells develop. stem from have as its source.

**stench** n. foul smell.

**stencil** ● n. thin sheet in which pattern is cut, placed on surface and printed, inked over, etc.; pattern so produced. ● v. (stencilled) produce (pattern) with stencil; mark (surface) in this way.

**stenography** n. shorthand.
□□ **stenographer** n.

**stentorian** adj. (of voice) very powerful.

**step** ● n. 1 complete movement of leg in walking or running; distance so covered; pattern of steps in dancing. 2 one of a series of actions. 3 stage in a scale. 4 level surface for placing foot on in climbing; (steps) a stepladder.
● v. (stepped) lift and set down foot or alternate feet; move short distance in this way; progress.

**step-** comb. form related by remarriage of parent (stepfather; stepson).

**stepladder** n. short ladder with supporting framework.

**steppe** n. level grassy treeless plain.

**stereo** ● n. 1 stereophonic sound reproduction or equipment. 2 stereoscope. ● adj. 1 stereophonic. 2 stereoscopic.

**stereophonic** adj. (of sound recording and transmission) using two channels to give effect of naturally distributed sound.

**stereoscope** n. device for producing three-dimensional effect by viewing two slightly different photographs together. □□ **stereoscopic** adj.

**stereotype** ● n. 1 person or thing seeming to conform to widely accepted mental picture or type; such type, idea, or attitude. 2 printing plate cast from mould of composed type.
● v. standardise. □□ **stereotyped** adj.

**sterile** adj. 1 unable to produce crop, fruit, or young; barren; unproductive. 2 lacking ideas or originality. 3 free from microorganisms etc.
□□ **sterility** n.

**sterilise** v. (also -ize) 1 make sterile. 2 deprive of reproductive power.
□□ **sterilisation** n.

**sterling** ● adj. 1 of or in British money. 2 (of coin or precious metal) genuine. 3 of standard value or purity. 4 (of person etc.) genuine, reliable. 5 hist. of or pertaining to non-convict, British-born residents of Australia.
● n. 1 British money. 2 hist. non-convict, British-born resident of Australia.

**stern**¹ adj. 1 severe, grim. 2 authoritarian. ● n. rear part, esp. of ship or boat. □□ **sternly** adv. **sternness** n.

**sternum** n. (pl. **sternums** or **sterna**) breastbone.

**steroid** n. any of group of organic compounds including many hormones, alkaloids, and vitamins.

**stertorous** adj. (of breathing etc.) laboured and noisy.

**stet** v. (placed next to word that has been crossed out etc.) ignore the alteration; let original stand.

**stethoscope** n. instrument used in listening to heart, lungs, etc.

**stetson** n. American cowboy hat with wide brim and high crown.

**stevedore** n. person employed in loading and unloading ships.

**stevia** n. shrub whose leaves are used as a calorie-free substitute for sugar.

**stew** ● v. 1 cook by long simmering in closed vessel. 2 fret, be anxious. 3 colloq. swelter. 4 (of tea etc.) become bitter or strong from infusing too long. 5 (as **stewed**) colloq. drunk. ● n. 1 dish of stewed meat etc. 2 colloq. agitated or angry state.

**steward** n. 1 passengers' attendant on ship or aircraft. 2 official supervising agricultural show, race meeting, etc. **3** person whose responsibility it is to take care of something; person responsible for supplies of food etc. for club etc. □□ **stewardship** n.

**stick** ● v. (**stuck**, **sticking**) **1** thrust (thing) into something. **2** colloq. put. **3** fix or be fixed by glue or suction etc. **4** colloq. remain in specified place, not progress. **5** colloq. endure. ● n. **1** thin piece of wood; something shaped like this. **2** walking stick. **3** implement used to propel ball in hockey, polo, etc. **4** colloq. criticism. **5** (**the sticks**) Aust. remote rural areas, outback. **6** (**sticks**) AFL goalposts. □ **stick-in-the-mud** person who will not accept new ideas etc. **stick out** stand above surrounding surface; be conspicuous. **stick to** remain faithful to; keep to (subject, position, etc.)

**sticker** n. adhesive label.

**stickler** n. person who insists on something.

**sticky** ● adj. **1** tending or intended to stick or adhere. **2** (of weather) humid. **3** colloq. difficult, awkward. **4** unpleasant, painful. ● n. **1** a look. **2** Aust. sweet dessert wine. □□ **stickily** adv. **stickiness** n.

**stickybeak** n. Aust. colloq. inquisitive or prying person.

**stiff** ● adj. **1** not bending or moving easily. **2** difficult. **3** formal in manner. **4** (of wind) blowing briskly; (of drink etc.) strong; (of price or penalty) severe. ● adv. colloq. utterly, extremely. ● n. colloq. corpse. □□ **stiffly** adv. **stiffness** n.

**stiffen** v. make or become stiff.

**stifle** v. suppress; feel or make unable to breathe easily. □□ **stifling** adj. & adv.

**stigma** n. **1** mark of shame. **2** part of a flower pistil.

**stigmata** n.pl. marks corresponding to crucifixion marks on Christ's body.

**stigmatise** v. (also **-ize**) brand as unworthy or disgraceful.

**stile** n. set of steps allowing people to climb over fence, wall, etc.

**stiletto** n. **1** short dagger. **2** (in full **stiletto heel**) long tapering heel of shoe. **3** pointed instrument for making eyelets etc.

**still** ● adj. **1** with little or no movement or sound; calm, tranquil. **2** (of drink) not fizzy. ● n. **1** silence and calm. **2** photograph taken from a cinema film. **3** distilling apparatus. ● adv. **1** without moving. **2** continuing the same up to present or time mentioned (I'm still waiting). **3** nevertheless. **4** even, yet, increasingly (still more). □ **still life** picture of inanimate objects. □□ **stillness** n.

**stillborn** n. born dead.

**stilted** adj. stiffly formal.

**stilts** n.pl. pair of poles with foot supports for walking at distance above ground; piles or posts supporting building etc.

**stimulant** adj. & n. (substance) increasing body's nervous activity.

**stimulate** v. **1** act as stimulus to. **2** animate, excite, arouse; motivate. □□ **stimulation** n. **stimulative** adj. **stimulator** n.

**stimulus** n. (pl. **stimuli**) something that rouses person or thing to activity or energy.

**sting** ● n. **1** sharp wounding part of insect, nettle, etc.; wound made by this; sharp bodily or mental pain. **2** pungency, sharpness, vigour. **3** colloq. swindle. ● v. (**stung**, **stinging**) **1** wound or affect with sting. **2** feel or cause sharp pain. **3** colloq. swindle, charge exorbitantly. **4** colloq. cadge from (person).

**stingaree** n. Aust. stingray.

**stingray** n. broad flatfish with venomous spine at base of tail.

**stingy** adj. niggardly, mean.
□□ **stingily** adv. **stinginess** n.

**stink** ● v. (**stank** or **stunk**, **stinking**) 1 emit strong offensive smell. 2 colloq. be or seem very unpleasant. ● n. 1 strong or offensive smell. 2 colloq. loud complaint or fuss.

**stinker** n. colloq. 1 particularly annoying or unpleasant person. 2 difficult task. 3 unpleasantly hot day.

**stinking** adj. 1 smelling horrible. 2 colloq. very objectionable. 3 (of weather) very bad.

**stint** ● v. supply very ungenerous or inadequate amount of (something); restrict (someone) in amount of something given or permitted. ● n. 1 limitation of supply or effort. 2 allotted amount or period of work. 3 small sandpiper.

**stipend** n. fixed regular allowance or salary.

**stipendiary** ● adj. receiving stipend. ● n. person receiving stipend.

**stipple** ● v. 1 draw, paint, engrave, etc. with dots. 2 roughen surface of (paint, cement, etc.) ● n. stippling; effect of stippling.

**stipulate** v. demand or specify as part of bargain etc. □□ **stipulation** n.

**stir** ● v. (**stirred**) 1 move. 2 mix (substance) by moving spoon etc. around in it. 3 stimulate, excite. 4 colloq. cause trouble for its own sake; provoke. ● n. 1 act or process of stirring. 2 a commotion, excitement.

**stirrer** n. 1 a thing or person that stirs. 2 colloq. troublemaker.

**stirrup** n. support for horse rider's foot.

**stitch** ● n. 1 single movement of thread in and out of fabric in sewing, or of needle in knitting or crochet;

loop made in this way; method of making a stitch. 2 sharp pain in side induced by running etc. ● v. sew; make stitches (in). □ **in stitches** colloq. laughing uncontrollably.

**stoat** n. European etc. mammal of weasel family, with brown fur turning mainly white in winter.

**stobie pole** n. (in South Australia) pole of steel and concrete carrying electricity lines.

**stock** ● n. 1 store of goods etc. ready for sale or distribution; supply or quantity of things for use; equipment or raw material for manufacture, trade, etc. 2 farm animals or equipment. 3 capital of business; shares in this. 4 reputation, popularity. 5 line of ancestry. 6 liquid made by stewing bones, vegetables, etc. 7 fragrant-flowered garden plant. 8 plant on which graft is made. 9 main trunk of tree etc. 10 (**stocks**) hist. wooden frame with holes for feet in which offenders were locked as public punishment. 11 base, support, or handle for implement or machine. 12 butt of rifle etc. 13 supports for ship during building or repair. ● adj. 1 kept regularly in stock for sale or use. 2 hackneyed. ● v. have (goods) in stock; provide (shop, farm, etc.) with goods, livestock, etc. □ **stock exchange** (or **market**) institution for buying and selling stocks and shares; the transactions of this.

**stockade** n. protective fence.

**stockbroker** n. person who buys and sells shares for clients.

**stocking** n. knitted covering for leg and foot, of nylon, wool, silk, etc.

**stockman** n. person employed to tend livestock.

**stockpile** ● n. accumulated stock of goods etc., kept in reserve. ● v. accumulate stockpile of.

**stocktaking** n. 1 making inventory of stock in shop etc. 2 review of one's position and resources. □□ **stocktake** *n.* & *v.*

**stocky** *adj.* short and sturdy. □□ **stockily** *adv.* **stockiness** *n.*

**stodge** *n. colloq.* stodgy food.

**stodgy** *adj.* (**stodgier**) **1** (of food) heavy, filling. **2** dull, uninteresting. □□ **stodginess** *n.*

**stoic** *n.* person having great control in adversity. □□ **stoical** *adj.* **stoicism** *n.*

**stoke** *v.* **1** feed and tend (fire, furnace, etc.) **2** *colloq.* fill oneself with food. **3** (as **stoked** *adj.*) *colloq.* affected by alcohol or drugs. **4** (as **stoked** *adj.*) *colloq.* excited, elated.

**stole**[1] *n.* woman's garment like long wide scarf, worn over shoulders.

**stole**[2] SEE STEAL.

**stolen** SEE STEAL.

**stolid** *adj.* not easily excited or moved. □□ **stolidity** *n.* **stolidly** *adv.*

**stomach ●** *n.* internal organ in which first part of digestion occurs; abdomen; appetite. **●** *v.* endure, tolerate.

**stomp** *v.* tread or stamp heavily.

**stone ●** *n.* **1** solid non-metallic mineral matter. **2** rock; small piece of this. **3** hard case of kernel in some fruits. **4** hard morbid concretion in body. **5** unit of weight in imperial system equal to 14 lb (6.35 kg). **6** precious stone. **●** *v.* **1** pelt with stones. **2** remove stones from (fruit). □ **Stone Age** prehistoric period when weapons and tools were made of stone.

**stoned** *adj. colloq.* drunk or drugged.

**stonewall** *v.* obstruct (discussion etc.) with evasive answers etc.

**stonkered** *adj. Aust. colloq.* utterly exhausted; utterly confounded or defeated; very drunk.

**stony** *adj.* (**stonier**) **1** full of stones. **2** hard, rigid. **3** unfeeling, unresponsive. □□ **stonily** *adv.*

**stood** SEE STAND.

**stooge** *n. colloq.* **1** person acting as butt or foil, esp. for comedian. **2** assistant or subordinate, esp. for unpleasant work; lackey. **3** person used as instrument by or for someone unseen.

**stool** *n.* **1** single seat usu. without back or arms. **2** (**stools**) faeces.

**stoop ●** *v.* **1** bend down. **2** stand or walk with shoulders habitually bent forward. **3** condescend. **4** descend or lower oneself to (shameful act). **●** *n.* stooping posture.

**stop ●** *v.* (**stopped**) **1** put end to progress, motion, or operation of. **2** effectively hinder or prevent. **3** discontinue. **4** come to an end. **5** cease from motion, speaking, or action. **6** defeat. **7** remain. **8** stay for short time. **9** block, close. **10** press (violin etc. string) to obtain required pitch. **●** *n.* **1** stopping, being stopped. **2** regular stopping place for bus or train etc. **3** full stop. **4** device for stopping motion at particular point. **5** change of pitch effected by stopping string. **6** (in organ) row of pipes of one character, knob etc. operating these. **7** plosive sound.

**stopcock** *n.* valve regulating flow in pipe etc.

**stopgap** *n.* temporary substitute.

**stopover** *n.* break in one's journey.

**stoppage** *n.* **1** interruption of work owing to strike etc. **2** condition of being blocked or stopped.

**stopper** *n.* plug for closing bottle etc.

**stopwatch** *n.* watch that can be started and stopped, used for timing races etc.

**storage** *n.* storing of goods etc.; method of, space for, or cost of storing.

**store ●** *n.* **1** quantity of something kept ready for use; articles gathered for particular purpose; supply of, or place for keeping, these. **2** department store; general store. **3** device in

computer for keeping retrievable data.
● v. **1** accumulate for future use. **2** put (furniture etc.) in store. **3** stock or provide with something useful. **4** keep (data) for retrieval. □ **in store 1** kept in readiness. **2** coming in the future. **set store by** consider important or valuable.

**storehouse** n. place where things are stored.

**storeroom** n. room used for storing things.

**storey** n. (storeys or stories) each horizontal section of a building. □□ **storeyed** adj.

**stork** n. long-legged usu. white wading bird; jabiru.

**storm** ● n. **1** violent atmospheric disturbance with strong winds and usu. thunder, rain, or dust, etc. **2** violent political etc. disturbance. **3** shower of missiles or blows; outbreak of applause, hisses, etc. **4** assault on fortified place. ● v. **1** (of wind, rain, etc.) rage, be violent. **2** attack or capture by storm. **3** rush violently. **4** bluster. □□ **stormy** adj.

**story** n. **1** account of real or imaginary events; narrative, tale. **2** (in Aboriginal English) account of sacred events associated with dreaming site. **3** colloq. fib.

**stoush** n. & v. fight.

**stout** ● adj. **1** rather fat, corpulent. **2** thick, strong. **3** brave, resolute. ● n. strong dark beer. □□ **stoutly** adv. **stoutness** n.

**stove**[1] n. closed apparatus burning fuel or using electricity for heating or cooking.

**stove**[2] see STAVE.

**stow** v. pack (goods, cargo, etc.) tidily and compactly.

**stowaway** n. person who hides on board ship etc. to get free passage.

**straddle** v. sit or stand across (thing) with legs wide apart; be situated on

both sides of; spread (one's legs) wide apart. □□ **straddler** n.

**strafe** v. bombard; attack with gunfire.

**straggle** v. **1** lack or lose compactness or tidiness. **2** wander or stray from proper road; become dispersed or sporadic. □□ **straggler** n. **straggly** adj.

**straight** ● adj. **1** extending or moving in one direction, not curved or bent; correctly or tidily arranged. **2** in unbroken succession; not modified or elaborate; without additions. **3** honest, frank. **4** colloq. (of person) conventional, respectable. **5** colloq. heterosexual. ● adv. **1** in straight line; direct; without delay. **2** frankly. ● n. **1** straight part of something. **2** sequence of five cards in poker. □ **straight away** at once; immediately. **straight face** one not smiling. **straight off** immediately, without hesitation. □□ **straightness** n.

**straighten** v. make or become straight.

**straightforward** adj. honest, frank; without complications.

**strain**[1] ● v. **1** make taut; injure by overuse or excessive demands; make intense effort (with). **2** sieve to separate solids from liquid. ● n. **1** act of straining; force exerted in this; injury caused from straining. **2** severe mental or physical demand or exertion. **3** snatch of music or poetry. **4** tone or tendency in speech or in writing.

**strain**[2] n. **1** breed or stock of animals, plants, etc. **2** tendency, characteristic.

**strained** adj. **1** constrained, artificial. **2** (of relationship) distrustful or tense.

**strainer** n. device for straining liquids etc.

**strait** n. **1** (also straits) narrow channel connecting two large bodies of water. **2** (straits) difficulty or distress. □ **strait-laced** (or **straight-laced**) extremely proper in morality.

**straitened** *adj.* of or marked by poverty.

**straitjacket ●** *n.* (also **straightjacket**) strong garment put around violent person, mental patient, etc. to restrain arms.
● *v.* restrict severely.

**strand ●** *v.* 1 run aground. 2 leave in difficulties. ● *n.* 1 single thread, esp. one woven or plaited with others; one element in complex whole. 2 shore of a sea etc.

**strange** *adj.* 1 unusual, peculiar, surprising, eccentric. 2 unfamiliar, foreign. 3 unaccustomed. 4 not at ease. □□ **strangely** *adv.* **strangeness** *n.*

**stranger** *n.* person new to particular place or company; person one does not know.

**strangle** *v.* 1 squeeze windpipe or neck of, esp. so as to kill. 2 hamper, suppress. □□ **strangler** *n.*

**stranglehold** *n.* strangling grip; complete control.

**strangulation** *n.* strangling.

**strap ●** *n.* 1 strip of leather etc., often with buckle, for holding things together etc. 2 narrow strip of fabric forming part of garment. 3 loop for grasping to steady oneself in moving vehicle. 4 (**the strap**) punishment by beating with leather strap.
● *v.* (**strapped**) 1 secure or bind with strap. 2 beat with strap. □ **strapped for** *colloq.* short of. □□ **strapless** *adj.*

**strapper** *n. Aust.* person who grooms racehorses.

**strapping** *adj.* large and sturdy.

**strasburg** *n.* spiced sausage.

**strata** see STRATUM. □ **strata title** *Aust.* registered ownership of certain amount of space in multi-storey building, complex of home units, etc.

**stratagem** *n.* cunning plan or scheme.

**strategic** *adj.* 1 of or promoting strategy. 2 (of materials) essential in war. 3 (of bombing or weapons) done

or for use as longer-term military objective. □□ **strategically** *adv.*

**strategy** *n.* long-term plan or policy; planning and directing of whole operation of campaign or war. □□ **strategist** *n.*

**stratify** *v.* arrange in strata or grades etc. □□ **stratification** *n.*

**stratosphere** *n.* layer of atmosphere above troposphere, extending to about 50 km from earth's surface.

**stratum** *n.* (*pl.* **strata**) one of a series of layers or levels.

**straw** *n.* 1 dry cut stalks of grain; single stalk of straw. 2 thin tube for sucking drink through. 3 insignificant thing. 4 pale yellow colour. □ **straw man** 1 intentionally misrepresented proposition that is set up because it is easier to defeat than an opponent's real argument. 2 person regarded as having no substance or integrity. **straw vote** (or **poll**) unofficial poll as test of general feeling.

**strawberry** *n.* pulpy red fruit with seed-studded surface; plant bearing this; deep pinkish-red colour.

**stray ●** *v.* wander from right place or from one's companions; go astray; deviate. ● *n.* strayed person, animal, or thing. ● *adj.* 1 strayed, lost. 2 isolated, occasional.

**streak ●** *n.* 1 long thin usu. irregular line or band, esp. of colour. 2 strain or trait in person's character. 3 spell or series. 4 *colloq.* tall, thin person.
● *v.* 1 mark with streaks. 2 move very rapidly. 3 *colloq.* run naked in public. □□ **streaker** *n.* **streaky** *adj.*

**stream ●** *n.* 1 flowing body of water, esp. small river; current, flow. 2 *Computing* continuous flow of data or instructions; continuous flow of video and audio material transmitted or received over the Internet. 3 group of schoolchildren of similar ability taught together. ● *v.* 1 flow; move in particular direction; float in wind.

**2** run with liquid. **3** transmit or receive (data, esp. video and audio material) over the Internet as steady, continuous flow. □ **on stream** in active operation or production.

**streamer** *n.* long narrow strip of ribbon or paper; long narrow flag.

**streaming** *n.* Computing method of transmitting or receiving data of (esp. video and audio material) over computer network as steady, continuous flow.

**streamline** *v.* **1** design or provide with form that presents very little resistance to flow of air or water, increasing speed and ease of movement. **2** make simple or more efficient.

**street** *n.* public road lined with buildings.

**streetwise** *adj.* knowing how to survive in modern urban society.

**strength** *n.* **1** being strong; degree or manner of this; person or thing giving strength. **2** positive attribute. **3** number of people present or available.

**strengthen** *v.* make or become stronger.

**strenuous** *adj.* **1** requiring or using great effort. **2** energetic. □□ **strenuously** *adv.*

**streptococcus** *n.* (*pl.* **streptococci**) bacterium causing serious infections.

**stress** ● *n.* **1** pressure, tension. **2** physical or mental strain. **3** emphasis. ● *v.* **1** emphasise. **2** subject to stress. □□ **stressful** *adj.*

**stretch** ● *v.* **1** draw, be drawn, or be able to be drawn out in length or size; make or become taut. **2** place or lie at full length or spread out. **3** extend limbs and tighten muscles after being relaxed. **4** have specified length or extension, extend. **5** strain or exert extremely. **6** exaggerate. ● *n.* **1** continuous extent, expanse, or period. **2** stretching, being stretched.

**3** *colloq.* period of imprisonment etc. **4** straight side of racetrack leading to winning post. □ **stretch a point** agree to something not normally allowed. □□ **stretchy** *adj.*

**stretcher** *n.* framework for carrying sick, injured, or dead person in lying position.

**strew** *v.* (**strewn** or **strewed**, **strewing**) scatter over surface; spread (surface) with scattered things.

**striated** *adj.* marked with slight ridges or furrows. □□ **striation** *n.*

**stricken** *adj.* affected or overcome (with illness, misfortune, etc.).

**strict** *adj.* **1** precisely limited or defined. **2** without deviation. **3** requiring complete obedience or exact performance. □□ **strictly** *adv.* **strictness** *n.*

**stricture** *n.* **1** critical or censorious remark. **2** *Med.* morbid narrowing of duct etc. in body.

**stride** ● *v.* (**strode**, **stridden**, **striding**) walk with long firm steps; cross with one step; bestride. ● *n.* **1** single long step; length of this; gait as determined by length of stride; progress. **2** (**strides**) *colloq.* trousers.

**strident** *adj.* loud and harsh. □□ **stridency** *n.* **stridently** *adv.*

**strife** *n.* conflict; struggle.

**strike** ● *v.* (**struck**, **striking**) **1** hit; knock. **2** attack suddenly; afflict. **3** ignite (match) by friction. **4** agree on (bargain). **5** indicate (hour) or be indicated by sound. **6** find (gold or mineral, oil, etc.) **7** occur to mind of, produce mental impression on. **8** stop work in protest. **9** assume (attitude) dramatically. **10** take down (flag or tent etc.) **11** (of plant cutting) put forth roots. ● *n.* **1** act or instance of striking. **2** an attack. **3** employees' organised refusal to work until grievance is remedied. □ **strike home** deal an effective blow. **strike off** (or **out**) cross out. **strike up** begin playing or singing; start (friendship etc.) casually. □□ **striker** n.

**strikebound** adj. immobilised by employees' strike.

**strikebreaker** n. person working or employed in place of others who are on strike.

**striking** adj. impressive; attracting attention. □□ **strikingly** adv.

**Strine** n. colloq. Australian English, esp. as comic representation of the speech.

**string** ● n. **1** twine, narrow cord; piece of this or of similar material; piece of catgut, wire, etc. on musical instrument, producing note by vibration; (**strings**) stringed instruments in orchestra etc. **2** condition or complication attached to offer etc. **3** set of things strung together; series or line. ● v. (**strung**) fit with string(s); thread on string; arrange in or as string.

**stringent** adj. (of rules etc.) strict, precise. □□ **stringency** n. **stringently** adv.

**stringy** adj. (**stringier**) like string, fibrous. □□ **stringiness** n.

**stringybark** n. Aust. any of various eucalypts having rough furrowed bark.

**strip** ● v. (**stripped**) **1** remove (clothes, coverings, or parts, etc.); pull or tear away (from); deprive, e.g. of property or titles. **2** damage thread of (screw) or teeth of (gearwheel). ● n. long narrow piece or area.

**stripe** n. long narrow band or strip differing in colour or texture from surface on either side of it; Mil. chevron etc. denoting military rank. □□ **striped** adj. **stripy** adj.

**stripling** n. a youth.

**stripper** n. **1** device for stripping something. **2** striptease performer.

**striptease** n. entertainment in which performer gradually undresses.

**strive** v. (**strove**, **striven**, **striving**) try hard; struggle.

**strobe** ● n. stroboscope. ● v. light as if with stroboscope; flash intermittently.

**stroboscope** n. apparatus for producing rapidly flashing light. □□ **stroboscopic** adj.

**strode** see STRIDE.

**stroke** ● v. **1** pass hand gently along surface of (hair, fur, etc.) **2** act as stroke of (boat, crew). ● n. **1** act of striking something; sound of striking clock. **2** act of stroking. **3** a movement, a beat; style of swimming. **4** sudden disabling attack caused esp. by thrombosis. **5** single mark made by pen, paintbrush, etc. **6** detail contributing to general effect. **7** oarsman nearest stern, who sets time of stroke.

**stroll** ● v. walk in leisurely way. ● n. leisurely walk.

**stroller** n. lightweight folding pram.

**strong** ● adj. **1** physically, morally, or mentally powerful; vigorous; robust; (of suspicion, belief, etc.) firmly held; powerfully affecting senses or emotions. **2** (of drink, solution, etc.) containing large proportion of alcohol etc. **3** powerful in numbers or equipment etc. **4** (of verb) forming inflections by vowel changes in root syllable. ● adv. strongly. □ **going strong** colloq. continuing to be healthy or successful. **strong language** swearing. **strong-minded** determined. □□ **strongish** adj. **strongly** adv.

**stronghold** n. fortified place; centre of support for cause.

**strongroom** n. room designed for safe storage of valuables.

**strontium** n. silver-white metallic element (symbol Sr).

**strop** n. leather strip on which razor is sharpened.

**stroppy** *adj.* colloq. bad-tempered; awkward to deal with.

**strove** see STRIVE.

**struck** see STRIKE.

**structure** ● *n.* constructed unit, esp. building; way in which thing is constructed; set of interconnecting parts of complex thing; framework. ● *v.* give structure to; organise. □□ **structural** *adj.* **structurally** *adv.*

**strudel** *n.* thin leaved pastry filled esp. with fruit and baked.

**struggle** ● *v.* violently try to get free; make great efforts under difficulties; fight against; make one's way with difficulty. ● *n.* act or period of struggling; hard or confused contest.

**strum** ● *v.* (**strummed**) play on (guitar etc.) by sweeping thumb or plectrum etc. up or down strings. ● *n.* sound made by strumming.

**strumpet** *n.* arch. prostitute.

**strung** see STRING.

**strut** ● *n.* 1 bar in framework to resist pressure. 2 strutting gait. ● *v.* (**strutted**) walk in pompous self-satisfied way.

**strychnine** *n.* highly poisonous alkaloid.

**stub** ● *n.* 1 remnant of pencil, cigarette, etc. 2 counterfoil of cheque, receipt, etc. 3 stump. ● *v.* (**stubbed**) 1 strike (one's toe) against something. 2 extinguish (cigarette) by pressure.

**stubble** *n.* cut stalks of cereal crop left in ground after harvest; short stiff hair or bristles, esp. on unshaven face. □□ **stubbly** *adj.*

**stubborn** *adj.* obstinate, inflexible. □□ **stubbornly** *adv.* **stubbornness** *n.*

**stubby** ● *adj.* short and thick; squat. ● *n. Aust.* 1 (also **stubbie**) small (375 ml) squat bottle of beer. 2 (**stubbies** *propr.*) men's brief cotton shorts with elasticated waist.

**stucco** *n.* plaster or cement for coating walls or moulding into architectural decorations. □□ **stuccoed** *adj.*

**stuck** *adj.* unable to move. See also STICK. □ **stuck-up** colloq. affectedly superior and aloof, snobbish.

**stud** ● *n.* 1 projecting nail head or similar knob on surface; device for fastening, e.g. detachable shirt collar. 2 post (in building frame) to which laths are nailed. 3 livestock kept for breeding; establishment keeping these. 4 young man (esp. one noted for sexual prowess). ● *v.* (**studded**) decorate with studs or precious stones; strengthen with studs.

**student** *n.* person who is studying.

**studied** *adj.* deliberate and artificial.

**studio** *n.* workroom of painter, photographer, etc.; place for making films, recordings, or broadcast programs. □ **studio flat** flat suitable for artist or having only one main room.

**studious** *adj.* diligent in study or reading; painstaking. □□ **studiously** *adv.* **studiousness** *n.*

**study** ● *n.* 1 effort and time spent in learning; subject studied; book or article on a topic. 2 room for reading, writing, etc. 3 piece of work, esp. drawing, done for practice or as preliminary experiment. 4 portrayal, esp. in literature, of behaviour, character, etc. 5 *Mus.* composition designed to develop player's skill. 6 thing worth observing. 7 thing that is or deserves to be investigated. ● *v.* 1 make study of; scrutinise; devote time and thought to understanding subject etc. or achieving desired result. 2 (as **studied** *adj.*) deliberate, affected.

**stuff** ● *n.* 1 material. 2 unnamed things; belongings; subjects etc. ● *v.* 1 pack tightly; fill with padding or stuffing; eat greedily. 2 (as **stuffed** *adj.*) ruined; exhausted. □ **stuff-up** *Aust.* colloq. bungled action; mess.

**stuffing** n. padding for cushions etc.; mixture used to stuff food, esp. before cooking.

**stuffy** adj. (**stuffier**) **1** (of room etc.) lacking fresh air. **2** prim; formal, pompous; conventional. **3** (of nose etc.) stuffed up. □□ **stuffily** adv. **stuffiness** n.

**stultify** v. make ineffective or useless, esp. by routine or from frustration. □□ **stultification** n.

**stumble** ● v. **1** accidentally lurch forward or almost fall; walk with repeated stumbles. **2** make mistakes in speaking etc. **3** find by chance. ● n. act of stumbling. □ **stumbling block** obstacle, difficulty.

**stump** ● n. **1** part of cut or fallen tree still in ground; similar part (of limb, tooth, branch, etc.) cut off or worn down. **2** Cricket each of three uprights of wicket. ● v. **1** (of question etc.) be too difficult for, baffle. **2** (as **stumped** adj.) at a loss. **3** Cricket put batter out by dislodging bail or knocking down stump with ball while batter is out of crease. **4** walk stiffly or noisily.

**stumpy** adj. short and thick. □□ **stumpiness** n.

**stun** v. (**stunned**) knock senseless; astound.

**stung** see STING.

**stunk** see STINK.

**stunning** adj. colloq. extremely attractive or impressive. □□ **stunningly** adv.

**stunt** ● n. something unusual done to attract attention; trick, daring feat. ● v. retard growth or development of.

**stupefy** v. make stupid or insensible; astonish. □□ **stupefaction** n.

**stupendous** adj. amazing; of vast size or importance. □□ **stupendously** adv.

**stupid** adj. **1** unintelligent, slow-witted, foolish. **2** uninteresting.

**3** in a stupor. □□ **stupidity** n. **stupidly** adv.

**stupor** n. **1** dazed or torpid state. **2** utter amazement.

**sturdy** adj. robust; strongly built; vigorous. □□ **sturdily** adv. **sturdiness** n.

**sturgeon** n. large edible fish yielding caviar.

**stutter** v. & n. stammer.

**sty** n. (pl. **sties**) **1** enclosure for pigs. **2** filthy room or dwelling. **3** (also **stye**) inflamed swelling on edge of eyelid.

**style** ● n. **1** kind or sort, esp. in regard to appearance and form (of person, house, etc.); manner of writing, speaking, etc.; distinctive manner of person, artistic school, or period. **2** superior quality. **3** fashion in dress etc. **4** part of flower supporting stigma. ● v. design or make etc. in particular style; designate in specified way.

**styling** n. way in which something is made, designed, or performed; action or process of arranging hair in a particular way.

**stylish** adj. fashionable; elegant. □□ **stylishly** adv. **stylishness** n.

**stylist** n. **1** designer of fashionable styles; hairdresser. **2** stylish writer or performer.

**stylistic** adj. of literary or artistic style. □□ **stylistically** adv.

**stylus** n. (pl. **styluses** or **styli**) **1** needle-like point for cutting or following groove in a record. **2** pen-like device used to input handwritten text or drawings directly into a computer.

**stymie** (also **stimy**) ● n. Golf situation where opponent's ball lies between one's ball and hole. ● v. (**stymied**, **stymieing** or **stymying**) colloq. obstruct, thwart.

**styptic** adj. checking bleeding by causing blood vessels to contract.

**styrene** n. liquid hydrocarbon used in making plastics etc.

**suave** *adj.* smooth; polite; sophisticated.□□ **suavely** *adv.* suavity *n.*

**sub** *n. colloq.* **1** submarine. **2** subscription. **3** substitute. **4** sub-editor.

**sub-** *prefix* under; subordinate.

**subaltern** *n.* military officer.

**subatomic** *adj.* occurring in, or smaller than, an atom.

**subby** *n.* (also **subbie**) *Aust. colloq.* subcontractor.

**subcommittee** *n.* committee formed from main committee for special purpose.

**subconscious** ● *adj.* of part of mind that is not fully conscious but influences actions etc. ● *n.* this part of the mind.□□ **subconsciously** *adv.*

**subcontinent** *n.* large land mass, smaller than continent.

**subcontract** ● *v.* employ another contractor to do (work) as part of larger project; make or carry out subcontract. ● *n.* secondary contract.□□ **subcontractor** *n.*

**subculture** *n.* social group or its culture within larger culture.

**subcutaneous** *adj.* under skin.

**subdivide** *v.* divide again after first division.□□ **subdivision** *n.*

**subdue** *v.* conquer, suppress; tame. **2** (as **subdued** *adj.*) softened. **3** lacking in intensity.

**subeditor** *n.* assistant editor; person who prepares material for printing.

**subhuman** *adj.* (of behaviour, intelligence, etc.) less than human.

**subject** ● *n.* **1** person or thing being discussed or treated; branch of knowledge taught in schools, universities, etc. **2** word or phrase representing person or thing carrying out action of verb. **3** citizen, person ruled by a government etc. **4** *Philos.* thinking or feeling entity, conscious self. **5** theme, leading motif. ● *adj.*

**1** conditional on. **2** liable or exposed to. **3** owing obedience to government etc. ● *adv.* conditionally on.

● *v.* make liable or expose to; subdue (person, nation, etc.) to superior will. □ **subject matter** topic treated in book or speech etc.□□ **subjection** *n.*

**subjective** *adj.* **1** dependent on personal taste or views etc. **2** *Gram.* of subject.□□ **subjectively** *adv.* subjectivity *n.*

**sub judice** *adj. Law* under judicial consideration and therefore prohibited from public discussion.

**subjugate** *v.* conquer, bring into subjection.□□ **subjugation** *n.* subjugator *n.*

**subjunctive** *Gram.* ● *adj.* (of mood) expressing wish, supposition, or possibility (*if I were you*). ● *n.* subjunctive mood or form.

**sublimate** ● *v.* **1** divert energy (of primitive impulse, esp. sexual) into culturally higher or socially more acceptable activity. **2** sublime substance. **3** refine, purify. ● *n.* sublimated substance. □□ **sublimation** *n.*

**sublime** *adj.* **1** of most exalted kind. **2** awe-inspiring. **3** arrogantly unruffled. ● *v.* **1** convert (substance) from solid into vapour by heat (and usu. allow to solidify again). **2** make sublime. **3** become pure (as if) by sublimation. □□ **sublimely** *adv.*

**subliminal** *adj. Psychol.* below threshold of sensation or consciousness; too faint or rapid to be consciously perceived. □□ **subliminally** *adv.*

**submarine** ● *n.* vessel, esp. armed warship, which can be submerged and navigated under water. ● *adj.* existing, occurring, done, or used below surface of sea. □□ **submariner** *n.*

**submerge** v. place, go, or dive beneath water; cover, obscure. □□ **submersion** n.

**submersible** ● adj. able to submerge. ● n. submersible craft.

**submission** n. 1 submitting, being submitted; thing submitted. 2 submissive attitude.

**submissive** adj. meek, obedient. □□ **submissively** adv. **submissiveness** n.

**submit** v. (submitted) 1 cease resistance; yield. 2 present for consideration. 3 subject or be subjected to (process, treatment, etc.) 4 Law argue, suggest.

**subordinate** ● adj. of inferior importance or rank; secondary, subservient. ● n. person working under authority of another.
● v. make or treat as subordinate. □□ **subordination** n.

**suborn** v. induce by bribery etc. to commit perjury etc.

**subpoena** ● n. writ ordering person to attend law court.
● v. (subpoenaed, subpoenaing) summon with subpoena.

**subscribe** v. 1 pay (specified sum), esp. regularly, for membership of organisation or receipt of publication etc. 2 contribute to fund, for cause, etc. 3 agree with opinion etc. □□ **subscriber** n.

**subscription** n. act of subscribing; money subscribed; membership fee, esp. paid regularly.

**subsequent** adj. following specified or implied event. □□ **subsequently** adv.

**subservient** adj. 1 servile. 2 subordinate. □□ **subservience** n.

**subset** n. a set of which all the elements are contained in another set.

**subside** v. sink to lower or normal level; become less intense. □□ **subsidence** n.

**subsidiary** ● adj. 1 supplementary; additional. 2 (of company) controlled by another. ● n. subsidiary thing, person, or company.

**subsidise** v. (also -ize) pay subsidy to or for.

**subsidy** n. money contributed esp. by government to keep prices at desired level; any monetary grant.

**subsist** v. keep oneself alive; be kept alive; remain in being; exist. □□ **subsistence** n.

**subsoil** n. soil just below surface layer.

**subsonic** adj. of speeds less than that of sound.

**substance** n. 1 particular kind of material. 2 reality. 3 solidity. 4 essence of what is spoken or written. 5 wealth and possessions.

**substantial** adj. 1 of real importance or value. 2 large in size or amount. 3 solid. 4 commercially successful. 5 wealthy. 6 largely true. 7 real; existing. □□ **substantially** adv.

**substantiate** v. prove truth of (charge, claim, etc.) □□ **substantiation** n.

**substantive** adj. 1 actual, real. 2 permanent. 3 substantial.

**substitute** ● n. person or thing acting or serving in place of another. ● v. use or serve as substitute. □□ **substitution** n.

**subsume** v. include under particular rule, class, etc.

**subterfuge** n. trick or excuse used to avoid blame etc.; trickery.

**subterranean** adj. underground.

**subtext** n. underlying theme.

**subtitle** ● n. 1 secondary or additional title of book etc. 2 caption on cinema film, esp. translating dialogue. ● v. provide with subtitle(s).

**subtle** adj. hard to detect or describe; (of scent, colour, etc.) faint, delicate; capable of making fine distinctions;

perceptive; ingenious. □□ **subtletly** n. **subtly** adv.

**subtotal** n. total of part of group of figures.

**subtract** v. deduct (number etc.) from another. □□ **subtraction** n.

**subtropical** adj. of regions bordering on tropics.

**suburb** n. district of town or city, esp. residential. □□ **suburban** adj. **suburbanite** n.

**suburbia** n. suburbs and their inhabitants.

**subvention** n. subsidy.

**subvert** v. overthrow or weaken (government, religion, morality, etc.) □□ **subversion** n. **subversive** adj.

**subway** n. 1 pedestrian tunnel beneath road etc. 2 underground railway.

**succeed** v. accomplish one's purpose; have success; prosper; follow in order; come into inheritance, office, title, or property.

**success** n. accomplishment of aim; favourable outcome; attainment of wealth, fame, etc.; successful thing or person. □□ **successful** adj. **successfully** adv.

**succession** n. following in order; series of things or people following one another; succeeding to office, inheritance, or esp. throne; right to succeed to one of these; set of people with such a right.

**successive** adj. following in succession; consecutive. □□ **successively** adv.

**successor** n. person or thing that succeeds another.

**succinct** adj. concise and clear. □□ **succinctly** adv. **succinctness** n.

**succour** v. & n. (also **succor**) help.

**succulent** ● adj. 1 juicy. 2 (of plant) thick and fleshy. ● n. succulent plant. □□ **succulence** n.

**succumb** v. give way; be overcome; die (from).

**such** ● adj. 1 of kind or degree specified or suggested; similar. 2 so great or extreme. 3 of more than usual kind or degree. ● pron. such person(s) or thing(s). □ **such as** for example. **such** that with the result that. **such-and-such** particular but not needing to be specified.

**suchlike** adj. of same kind.

**suck** ● v. 1 draw (liquid) into mouth by suction; draw fluid from in this way; roll tongue around (sweet, thumb, etc.); make sucking action or sound; engulf or drown in sucking movement. 2 colloq. be bad, contemptible, or incompetent. ● n. act or period of sucking. □ **suck up to** Aust. colloq. flatter or please (person) to achieve advantage.

**sucker** n. 1 organ or device that can adhere to surface by suction. 2 colloq. person who is easily deceived. 3 adventitious growth, esp. from eucalypt branch etc. that has been severed. □ **a sucker for** colloq. very fond of or susceptible to.

**suckle** v. feed (young) from breast or udder.

**suckling** n. unweaned child or animal.

**sucrose** n. sugar.

**suction** n. 1 sucking. 2 production of partial vacuum so that atmospheric pressure forces fluid into vacant space or causes adhesion of surfaces.

**sudden** adj. done or occurring unexpectedly or abruptly. □ **all of a sudden** suddenly. □□ **suddenly** adv. **suddenness** n.

**sudoku** n. Japanese number puzzle.

**sudorific** ● adj. causing sweating. ● n. sudorific drug.

**suds** n.pl. froth of soap and water. □□ **sudsy** adj.

**sue** v. (sued, suing) take legal proceedings against.

**suede** n. leather with velvety nap on one side.

**suet** n. hard fat surrounding kidneys of cattle or sheep, used in cooking etc.

**suffer** v. undergo pain, grief, etc.; undergo punishment, or be subjected to (pain, loss, punishment, grief, etc.); tolerate. □□ **sufferer** n. **suffering** n.

**sufferance** n. tacit consent.

**suffice** v. be enough; satisfy.

**sufficient** adj. sufficing, adequate. □□ **sufficiency** n. **sufficiently** adv.

**suffix** n. letter(s) added to end of word to form new word.

**suffocate** v. choke, stifle, or kill by stopping breathing; be or feel suffocated. □□ **suffocating** adj. **suffocation** n.

**suffrage** n. right of voting in political elections.

**suffragette** n. hist. woman who agitated for women's right to vote.

**suffuse** v. (of colour, moisture, etc.) spread from within to colour or infuse. □□ **suffusion** n.

**sugar** ● n. sweet crystalline substance obtained from sugar cane and sugar beet, used in cookery etc. ● v. sweeten; make more acceptable. □ **sugar cane** tall tropical grass from which sugar is obtained. **sugar glider** Aust. gliding possum, feeding on nectar, insects, etc. **sugar soap** abrasive cleaning compound. □□ **sugary** adj.

**suggest** v. propose (theory, plan, etc.); evoke (idea etc.); hint at.

**suggestible** adj. open to suggestion; easily swayed. □□ **suggestibility** n.

**suggestion** n. 1 suggesting, thing suggested. 2 slight trace, hint.

**suggestive** adj. hinting (at); suggesting something indecent. □□ **suggestively** adv.

**suicidal** adj. (of person) liable to commit suicide; or of tending to suicide; self-destructive; very risky. □□ **suicidally** adv.

**suicide** ● n. intentional self-killing; person who commits suicide; self-destructive action or course. ● v. commit suicide.

**sui generis** adj. of its own kind; unique.

**suit** ● n. 1 set of clothes to be worn together, esp. jacket and trousers or skirt. 2 any of the four sets into which pack of cards is divided. 3 lawsuit. ● v. 1 be convenient for or acceptable to. 2 (of clothes etc.) enhance appearance of. 3 (as **suited** adj.) appropriate; well-fitted.

**suitable** adj. well-fitted for purpose; appropriate to occasion. □□ **suitability** n. **suitably** adv.

**suitcase** n. rectangular bag for carrying clothes.

**suite** n. 1 set of rooms, furniture, etc. 2 Mus. set of instrumental pieces. 3 group of attendants.

**suitor** n. 1 man who woos woman. 2 plaintiff or petitioner in lawsuit.

**sulk** ● v. be sulky. ● n. (also **the sulks**) fit of sullen silence.

**sulky** adj. 1 sullen and unsociable from resentment or bad temper. 2 (in Aboriginal English) angry, threatening. ● n. (pl. **sulkies**) light two-wheeled horse-drawn vehicle for one, esp. used in harness racing. □□ **sulkily** adv.

**sullen** adj. sulky, morose; dismal, melancholy. □□ **sullenly** adv. **sullenness** n.

**sully** v. spoil purity or splendour of (reputation etc.).

**sulphate** n. salt or ester of sulphuric acid.

**sulphide** n. binary compound of sulphur.

**sulphite** n. salt or ester of sulphurous acid.

**sulphur** n. (also **sulfur**) **1** pale yellow non-metallic element (symbol **S**). **2** burning with blue flame and suffocating smell. □□ **sulphurous** adj.

**sulphuric acid** n. strong corrosive acid.

**sultan** n. Muslim sovereign.

**sultana** n. **1** seedless raisin; small pale yellow grape producing these. **2** sultan's mother, wife, or daughter.

**sultanate** n. sultan's territory.

**sultry** adj. **1** (of weather etc.) hot and humid. **2** (of person etc.) passionate, sensual.

**sum** n. **1** total resulting from addition; amount of money. **2** arithmetical problem. □ **sum up** give total of; summarise; form opinion of.

**summarise** v. (also **-ize**) make or be summary of.

**summary** • n. brief account giving chief points. • adj. brief, without details or formalities. □□ **summarily** adv.

**summation** n. **1** finding of total or sum. **2** summing-up.

**summer** n. warmest season of year. □□ **summery** adj.

**summit** n. **1** highest point, top; highest level of achievement or status. **2** conference between heads of government, officials, etc.

**summon** v. order to come or appear, esp. in lawcourt; call on; call together; gather (courage, resources, etc.)

**summons** • n. (pl. **summonses**) authoritative call to attend or do something, esp. to appear in court. • v. serve with summons.

**sumo** n. Japanese wrestling.

**sump** n. casing holding oil in internal-combustion engine; pit, well, etc. for collecting superfluous liquid.

**sumptuous** adj. rich, lavish, costly. □□ **sumptuously** adv. **sumptuousness** n.

**sun** • n. star around which earth orbits and from which it receives light and warmth; this light or warmth; any fixed star. • v. (**sunned**) expose to sun. □□ **sunless** adj.

**Sun.** abbr. Sunday.

**sunbake** v. Aust. expose one's body to sun.

**sunbathe** v. sunbake.

**sunbeam** n. ray of sun.

**sunburn** • n. inflammation of skin caused by exposure to sun. • v. suffer sunburn. □□ **sunburnt** adj.

**suncream** n. = SUNSCREEN.

**sundae** n. a dish of ice cream and fruit, nuts, syrup, etc.

**Sunday** n. day of week following Saturday.

**sunder** v. arch. sever; separate.

**sundial** n. instrument showing time by shadow of pointer cast by sun.

**sundown** n. sunset.

**sundry** • adj. various; several. • n. **1** (**sundries**) various small items. **2** Cricket run scored otherwise than off bat.

**sung** see SING.

**sunk** see SINK.

**sunken** adj. lying below surrounding surface.

**Sunni** n. (pl. **Sunni** or **Sunnis**) (member of) one of two main branches of Islam.

**sunnies** n.pl. Aust. colloq. pair of sunglasses.

**sunny** adj. (**sunnier**) **1** bright with or warmed by sunlight. **2** cheerful. □□ **sunnily** adv.

**sunscreen** n. cream or lotion rubbed on skin to protect it from ultraviolet rays.

**sunspot** n. **1** dark patch observed on sun's surface. **2** Aust. rough scaly patch on skin caused by excessive exposure to sun; skin cancer.

**sunstroke** *n.* illness brought about by excessive exposure to sun.

**super** ● *adj.* colloq. excellent; unusually good. ● *n.* **1** colloq. superintendent. **2** supernumerary. **3** Aust. colloq. superannuation. **4** petrol of high-octane grade; leaded petrol.

**super-** *comb. form* **1** on top, over, beyond. **2** to extreme degree. **3** extra good or large of its kind. **4** of higher kind.

**superannuant** *n. Aust.* person in receipt of superannuation pension.

**superannuate** *v.* **1** pension (person) off. **2** dismiss or discard as too old. □□ **superannuated** *adj.*

**superannuation** *n.* pension or lump sum paid to retired person; payment towards this by employed person.

**superb** *adj.* **1** colloq. excellent. **2** magnificent. □□ **superbly** *adv.*

**supercharge** *v.* increase power (of engine) by device that forces extra air or fuel into it. □□ **supercharger** *n.*

**supercilious** *adj.* haughtily contemptuous. □□ **superciliously** *adv.* **superciliousness** *n.*

**superconductivity** *n. Physics* property of zero electrical resistance in some substances at very low absolute temperatures. □□ **superconductor** *n.*

**superficial** *adj.* of or on the surface; lacking depth; swift, cursory; apparent, not real; (esp. of person) shallow. □□ **superficiality** *n.* **superficially** *adv.*

**superfluous** *adj.* more than is needed or wanted; unnecessary. □□ **superfluously** *adv.* **superfluity** *n.*

**superhighway** *n.* **1** *US* broad main road for fast traffic. **2** = *information superhighway*.

---

# sunstroke | supersede

**superhuman** *adj.* exceeding normal human capacity or power.

**superimpose** *v.* place (thing) on or above something else. □□ **superimposition** *n.*

**superintend** *v.* supervise, direct (work etc.) □□ **superintendence** *n.*

**superintendent** *n.* **1** police officer above rank of inspector. **2** person who superintends.

**superior** ● *adj.* **1** higher in rank or quality etc. **2** supercilious. **3** better or greater in some respect. ● *n.* **1** person superior to another, esp. in rank. **2** head of monastery, convent, etc. □□ **superiority** *n.*

**superlative** ● *adj.* **1** of highest quality. **2** of grammatical form expressing 'most'. ● *n.* superlative form of word.

**supermarket** *n.* large self-service store selling food, household goods, etc.

**supernatural** ● *adj.* not attributable to, or explicable by, natural or physical laws; magical; mystical. ● *n.* (the supernatural) supernatural forces etc. □□ **supernaturally** *adv.*

**supernova** *n.* (pl. **supernovas** or **supernovae**) star increasing suddenly in brightness.

**supernumerary** *adj.* extra.

**superphosphate** *n.* fertiliser made from phosphate rock.

**superpower** *n.* **1** extremely powerful nation. **2** (in fiction) an exceptional or extraordinary power or ability.

**superscript** ● *adj.* written or printed above the line. ● *n.* superscript number or symbol.

**supersede** *v.* take place of; replace with another person or thing. □□ **supersession** *n.*

**supersonic** *adj.* of or having speed greater than that of sound. □□ **supersonically** *adv.*

**superstition** *n.* belief in supernatural; irrational fear of unknown or mysterious; practice or belief based on this. □□ **superstitious** *adj.*

**superstructure** *n.* part of building above its foundations; structure built on top of another.

**supervene** *v.* occur as interruption or change. □□ **supervention** *n.*

**supervise** *v.* observe and direct execution of (task, activity, etc.); keep watch over (someone). □□ **supervision** *n.* **supervisor** *n.* **supervisory** *adj.*

**supine** *adj.* 1 lying face upwards. 2 inert, indolent.

**supper** *n.* late evening snack; light evening meal taken as part of or following social event.

**supplant** *v.* take the place of, esp. by underhand means.

**supple** *adj.* flexible, pliant, easily bent. □□ **suppleness** *n.*

**supplement** ● *n.* 1 thing or part added to improve or provide further information. 2 separate section of newspaper etc. ● *v.* provide supplement for. □□ **supplemental** *adj.* **supplementary** *adj.* **supplementation** *n.*

**suppliant** ● *adj.* supplicating. ● *n.* humble petitioner.

**supplicate** *v. literary* make humble petition to or for. □□ **supplication** *n.*

**supply** ● *v.* provide; make available to; satisfy (a need). ● *n.* supplying; a stock, amount provided or available. □□ **supplier** *n.*

**support** ● *v.* 1 carry all or part of weight of. 2 keep from falling, sinking, or failing. 3 provide for. 4 strengthen, encourage. 5 give help or corroboration to; speak in favour of. 6 take secondary part to (actor etc.); perform secondary act to (main act) at pop concert etc. ● *n.* supporting, being supported; person or thing that supports. □□ **supportive** *adj.*

**supporter** *n.*

**suppose** *v.* assume; be inclined to think; take as possibility or hypothesis. □ **be supposed to** be expected to; have as duty.

**supposedly** *adv.* as is generally believed.

**supposition** *n.* what is supposed or assumed.

**suppository** *n.* solid medical preparation put into rectum or vagina to melt.

**suppress** *v.* 1 put an end to. 2 prevent (information, feelings, etc.) from being seen, heard, or known. □□ **suppression** *n.* **suppressor** *n.*

**suppurate** *v.* form or secrete pus; fester. □□ **suppuration** *n.*

**supra-** *prefix* above; beyond.

**supreme** *adj.* 1 highest in authority or rank; greatest, most important. 2 (of penalty, sacrifice, etc.) involving death. □□ **supremacy** *n.* **supremely** *adv.*

**supremo** *n.* (*pl.* **supremos**) person in overall charge.

**surcharge** ● *n.* additional charge or payment. ● *v.* exact surcharge from.

**sure** ● *adj.* 1 convinced; having or seeming to have adequate reason for belief; confident in anticipation or knowledge of. 2 reliable, unfailing. 3 certain. 4 undoubtedly true or truthful. ● *adv. colloq.* certainly. □□ **sureness** *n.*

**surely** *adv.* 1 confidently; securely. 2 added to statement to express strong belief in its correctness.

**surety** *n.* a guarantee; guarantor of another's debts etc.

**surf** ● *n.* swell of sea breaking on shore or reefs; foam produced by this. ● *v.* **1** go surfing. **2** spend time exploring (Internet). □□ **surfer** *n.*

**surface** ● *n.* the outside of a thing; any of limits of a solid; top of liquid, soil, etc.; outward or superficial aspect. ● *v.* **1** give required surface to (road, paper, etc.) **2** rise or bring to surface. **3** become visible or known. **4** *colloq.* wake up, get up. **5** *colloq.* arrive (at place), finally appear.

**surfboard** *n.* narrow board for riding over surf.

**surfeit** ● *n.* excess, esp. in eating or drinking; resulting fullness. ● *v.* overfeed; (cause to) be wearied through excess.

**surfie** *n.* (also **surfy**) *colloq.* dedicated surfer.

**surfing** *n.* sport of riding on surfboard.

**surge** ● *n.* **1** sudden rush. **2** heavy forward or upward motion. **3** sudden increase (in price etc.) **4** sudden but brief increase in voltage, pressure, etc. **5** surging motion of sea, waves, etc. ● *v.* **1** move suddenly and powerfully forwards. **2** (of electric current etc.) increase suddenly. **3** (of sea etc.) swell.

**surgeon** *n.* medical practitioner qualified to perform surgical operations.

**surgery** *n.* **1** treatment of bodily injuries or disorders by incision or manipulation etc. as opposed to drugs; branch of medicine concerned with this; operation performed by surgeon. **2** place where or time when doctor, dentist, etc. gives advice and treatment to patients. □□ **surgical** *adj.* **surgically** *adv.*

**surly** *adj.* (**surlier**) bad-tempered; unfriendly. □□ **surliness** *n.*

**surmise** ● *n.* conjecture. ● *v.* infer doubtfully; guess; suppose.

**surmount** *v.* overcome (difficulty, obstacle); be on the top of. □□ **surmountable** *adj.*

**surname** *n.* family name, usu. inherited or acquired by marriage.

**surpass** *v.* be better than; outdo.

**surplice** *n.* loose white vestment worn by clergy and choristers.

**surplus** *n.* amount left over when requirements have been met.

**surprise** ● *n.* unexpected or astonishing thing; emotion caused by this. ● *adj.* unexpected; made, done, etc. without warning. ● *v.* affect with surprise; turn out contrary to expectations; shock, scandalise; capture by surprise; come upon (person) unawares.

**surreal** *adj.* unreal; dreamlike; bizarre. □□ **surrealist** *n.* **surrealistic** *adj.*

**surrender** ● *v.* **1** hand over, relinquish; submit; esp. to enemy. **2** (often **surrender oneself**) yield to habit, emotion, influence, etc.; give up rights under (life-insurance policy) in return for smaller sum received immediately. ● *n.* surrendering.

**surreptitious** *adj.* done by stealth; clandestine. □□ **surreptitiously** *adv.*

**surrogate** *n.* deputy. □ **surrogate mother** woman who bears child on behalf of another. □□ **surrogacy** *n.*

**surround** ● *v.* come or be all around; encircle, enclose. ● *n.* border or edging.

**surroundings** *n.pl.* things in neighbourhood of, or conditions affecting, person or thing; environment.

**surtax** *n.* additional tax.

**surveil** *v.* keep (person or place) under surveillance.

**surveillance** *n.* close observation.

**survey** ● v. **1** take or present general view of; examine condition of (building etc.); determine boundaries, extent, ownership, etc. of (district etc.) **2** investigate opinions or experience of (group of people) by asking them questions. ● n. **1** general view or consideration; surveying of property; result of this; map or plan made by surveying. **2** investigation of opinions or experience of group of people, based on series of questions.

**surveyor** n. person who surveys land and buildings.

**survival** n. surviving; person, thing, or practice that has remained from former time.

**survive** v. continue to live or exist; remain alive after or continue to exist in spite of (danger, accident, etc.) □□ **survivor** n.

**sus** = SUSS.

**susceptible** adj. easily affected or influenced. □□ **susceptibility** n.

**sushi** n. Japanese dish of flavoured balls of cold rice with garnish of vegetables, raw seafood, etc. □□ **sush(bar)** n.

**suspect** ● v. **1** have impression of existence or presence of. **2** imagine or fancy something about (person, thing) with slight or no proof. **3** imagine or fancy (something) to be possible or likely. **4** doubt innocence, genuineness, or truth of. ● n. suspected person. ● adj. subject to suspicion or distrust.

**suspend** v. **1** hang up; keep from falling or sinking in air or liquid. **2** stop temporarily; deprive temporarily of position or right.

**suspender** n. attachment to hold up stocking or sock by its top.

**suspense** n. state of anxious uncertainty or expectation.

**suspension** n. **1** suspending, being suspended. **2** springs etc. supporting vehicle on its axles. **3** substance consisting of particles suspended in medium. □ **suspension bridge** bridge suspended from cables that pass over supports at each end.

**suspicion** n. **1** unconfirmed belief; distrust; suspecting, being suspected. **2** slight trace.

**suspicious** adj. prone to or feeling suspicion; indicating or justifying suspicion. □□ **suspiciously** adv.

**suss** (also **sus**) colloq. ● adj. suspicious; suspect. ● v. work out; realise.

**sustain** v. **1** support, bear weight of, esp. for long period; encourage; (of food) nourish. **2** endure, stand; undergo (defeat, loss, injury, etc.) **3** (of court etc.) decide in favour of, uphold.

**sustainable** adj. that can be sustained; (esp. of development) that conserves ecological balance by avoiding depletion of natural resources. □□ **sustainably** adv.

**sustenance** n. nourishment; food; means of support; livelihood.

**suture** ● n. joining of edges of wound or incision by stitching; thread or stitch used for this. ● v. stitch (wound, incision).

**suzerain** n. country or ruler with some authority over self-governing country; overlord. □□ **suzerainty** n.

**svelte** adj. slender and graceful.

**SW** abbr. south-west(ern).

**swab** ● n. absorbent pad used in surgery or for taking specimens; specimen of secretion taken on this; mop. ● v. (**swabbed**) cleanse with swab.

**swaddle** v. swathe in wraps or warm clothes.

**swag** ● n. 1 Aust. collection of possessions and daily necessaries carried by traveller in bush; bed roll. 2 colloq. thief's booty. 3 colloq. large number. ● v. (also swag it) Aust. carry one's swag; travel as swagman.

**swagger** ● v. walk or behave arrogantly or self-importantly. ● n. swaggering gait or manner.

**swaggie** n. Aust. swagman.

**swagman** n. Aust. person who carries swag, esp. an itinerant; tramp.

**swallow** ● v. 1 cause or let (food etc.) pass down one's throat. 2 accept meekly or gullibly. 3 repress (emotion). 4 say (words etc.) indistinctly. 5 engulf. ● n. 1 act of swallowing; amount swallowed in one action. 2 migratory swift-flying bird with forked tail.

**swam** see SWIM.

**swami** n. Hindu male religious teacher.

**swamp** ● n. (area of) waterlogged ground. ● v. overwhelm, flood, or soak with water; overwhelm with numbers or quantity.□□ **swampy** adj.

**swan** ● n. large web-footed water bird with long flexible neck. ● v. (**swanned**) colloq. move about casually with superior manner.

**swank** colloq. ● n. ostentation, swagger. ● v. show off.□□ **swanky** adj.

**swansong** n. person's last work or act before death or retirement etc.

**swap** (also **swop**) ● v. (**swapped**) exchange. ● n. an exchange; thing exchanged.

**swarm** ● n. large cluster of insects, people, etc. ● v. move in or form swarm.□ **swarm up** climb by gripping with arms and legs.

**swarthy** adj. (**swarthier**) having dark complexion.

**swashbuckling** adj. & n. showing flamboyant daring.
□□ **swashbuckler** n.

**swastika** n. ancient symbol formed by equal-armed cross with each arm continued at right angle; this with clockwise continuations as symbol of Nazi Germany.

**swat** v. (**swatted**) hit hard with something flat.

**swatch** n. sample, esp. of cloth; collection of samples.

**swathe** (also **swath**) ● n. ridge of cut grass, wheat, etc.; space left clear by mower etc. ● v. bind or wrap in bandages, garments, etc.

**sway** ● v. 1 (cause to) move unsteadily from side to side; fluctuate, waver this way and that. 2 incline in opinion, sympathy, etc. 3 cause to veer in particular direction. 4 deflect or dissuade. 5 dominate.
● n. 1 influence. 2 swaying motion.

**swear** v. (**swore, sworn, swearing**) 1 state or promise on oath; cause to take (oath); colloq. insist. 2 use profane or obscene language. 3 appeal to as witness or guarantee of oath.□ **swear by** colloq. have great confidence in. **swear word** profane or indecent word.

**sweat** ● n. moisture exuded through pores, esp. when one is hot or nervous; state or period of sweating; colloq. state of anxiety; colloq. drudgery, effort, laborious task or undertaking; condensed moisture on surface.
● v. give off sweat or as sweat; work hard; be very anxious.□ **sweated labour** labour of workers with poor pay and conditions.□□ **sweaty** adj.

**sweater** n. jumper or pullover.

**sweatshop** n. place employing sweated labour.

**sweep** ● v. (**swept, sweeping**) 1 clean or clear (room, area, etc.) (as) with broom; collect or remove (dirt etc.) by sweeping. **2** go smoothly and swiftly or majestically. **3** extend in continuous line. ● n. **1** sweeping movement or line; act of sweeping. **2** chimney sweep. **3** colloq. sweepstake. **4** marine food fish. □□ **sweeper** n.

**sweeping** adj. **1** wide in range or effect. **2** generalised, arbitrary.

**sweepstake** n. form of gambling in which money staked is divided among winners.

**sweet** ● adj. **1** having pleasant taste characteristic of sugar, honey, etc. **2** smelling pleasant like roses, perfume, etc.; fragrant. **3** melodious. **4** fresh. **5** not sour or bitter. **6** amiable; colloq. pretty, charming. **7** colloq. fond of, in love with. **8** Aust. colloq. good; all right. ● n. small shaped piece of sweet substance, usu. made with sugar or chocolate; confectionery; sweet dish forming course of meal. □ **sweet tooth** liking for sweet food. □□ **sweetly** adv.

**sweetbread** n. animal's thymus gland or pancreas used as food.

**sweetcorn** n. kind of maize with kernels having high sugar content, eaten as vegetable.

**sweeten** v. make or become sweet(er); make agreeable or less painful. □□ **sweetening** n.

**sweetener** n. **1** substance used to sweeten food or drink. **2** colloq. bribe.

**swell** ● v. (swelled, swollen or swelled, swelling) (cause to) grow bigger, louder, or more intense; rise or raise up; bulge out; (of heart etc.) feel (of joy, pride, relief, etc.; be hardly able to restrain (pride etc.) ● n. **1** act or state of swelling. **2** heaving of sea etc. with unbreaking rolling waves. **3** crescendo.
● adj. colloq. fine, excellent.

**swelling** n. abnormal swollen place, esp. on body.

**swelter** ● v. be uncomfortably hot. ● n. sweltering condition.

**swept** see SWEEP.

**swerve** ● v. (cause to) change direction, esp. suddenly.
● n. swerving movement.

**swift** ● adj. quick, rapid; prompt. ● n. swift-flying long-winged migratory bird. □□ **swiftly** adv. **swiftness** n.

**swiftie** n. colloq. **1** Aust. deceptive trick. **2** person who acts or thinks quickly.

**swill** ● v. **1** rinse, pour water over or through. **2** drink greedily.
● n. **1** swilling. **2** mainly liquid refuse as pig food.

**swim** ● v. (swam, swum, swimming) **1** travel through water by movements of body. **2** be covered with liquid. **3** seem to be whirling or waving; be dizzy. ● n. period or act of swimming. □□ **swimmer** n.

**swimmers** n.pl. Aust. swimming costume.

**swimmingly** adv. colloq. smoothly, without obstruction.

**swindle** ● v. cheat of money etc.; defraud. ● n. act of swindling; fraudulent person or thing. □□ **swindler** n.

**swine** n. **1** (as pl.) pigs. **2** colloq. derog. disgusting person; unpleasant or difficult thing. □□ **swinish** adj.

**swing** ● v. (swung, swinging) **1** (cause to) move with to-and-fro or curving motion; sway or hang like pendulum or door etc.; oscillate. **2** move by gripping something and leaping etc. **3** walk with swinging gait. **4** move to face opposite direction. **5** attempt to hit. **6** colloq. (of party etc.) be lively. **7** have decisive influence on (voting etc.) **8** colloq.

achieve, manage. ● *n.* **1** act, motion, or extent of swinging; swinging or smooth gait, rhythm, or action. **2** seat slung by ropes etc. for swinging on or in; period of swinging on this. **3** jazz or jazzy dance music. **4** means by which votes etc. change from one side to another. □ **in full swing** with activity at its height. □□ **swinger** *n.*

**swingeing** *adj.* severe; extreme.

**swipe** *colloq.* ● *v.* **1** hit hard and recklessly. **2** steal. **3** pass (swipe card) through electronic reader; swipe (one's finger) across a touchscreen in order to activate a function. ● *n.* swinging blow. □ **swipe card** credit card, security pass, etc.

**swirl** ● *v.* move, flow, or carry along with whirling motion. ● *n.* swirling motion; twist, curl. □□ **swirly** *adj.*

**swish** ● *v.* swing (scythe etc.) audibly through air, grass, etc.; move with or make this or similar sound. ● *n.* this sound. ● *adj. colloq.* smart, fashionable.

**switch** ● *n.* **1** device for making and breaking connection in electric circuit. **2** transfer, change-over, deviation. **3** flexible shoot cut from tree. **4** light tapering rod. ● *v.* **1** turn (on or off) by means of switch. **2** change or transfer (position, subject, etc.) **3** exchange. **4** whip or flick with switch.

**switchback** *n.* railway used for amusement at show etc., with alternate steep ascents and descents; road with similar slopes.

**switchboard** *n.* panel of switches for making telephone connections or operating electric circuits.

**swivel** ● *n.* coupling between two parts etc. so that one can turn freely without the other. ● *v.* (**swivelled**) turn (as) on swivel; swing around.

**swizz** *n.* (also **swiz**) *colloq.* something disappointing; a swindle.

**swollen** see SWELL.

**swoop** ● *v.* come down with rush like bird of prey; make sudden attack. ● *n.* act of swooping; sudden pounce.

**sword** *n.* weapon with long blade for cutting and thrusting.

**swordfish** *n.* (*pl.* **swordfish**) edible sea fish with long swordlike upper jaw.

**swore** see SWEAR.

**sworn** ● *v.* see SWEAR. ● *adj.* bound (as) by oath.

**swot** *colloq.* ● *v.* (**swotted**) study hard. ● *n.* person who swots.

**swum** see SWIM.

**swung** see SWING.

**swy** *n. Aust.* two-up.

**sybarite** *n.* self-indulgent or luxury-loving person. □□ **sybaritic** *adj.*

**sycamore** *n.* (in Europe) large maple tree, its wood; (in US) plane tree, its wood; (in Bible etc.) kind of fig tree.

**sycophant** *n.* flatterer; toady. □□ **sycophancy** *n.* **sycophantic** *adj.*

**Sydney silky** *n.* Australian terrier.

**syllable** *n.* unit of pronunciation forming whole or part of word, usu. consisting of vowel sound with consonant(s) before or after.

**syllabub** *n.* (also **sillabub**) dish of flavoured whipped cream.

**syllabus** *n.* (*pl.* **syllabuses** or **syllabi**) program or outline of course of study, teaching, etc.

**syllogism** *n.* form of reasoning in which from two propositions a third is deduced. □□ **syllogistic** *adj.*

**sylph** *n.* elemental spirit of air; slender graceful woman. □□ **sylphlike** *adj.*

**sylvan** *adj.* (also **silvan**) of the woods; having woods; rural.

**symbiosis** n. (pl. **symbioses**) relationship of different organisms living in close association. □□ **symbiotic** adj.

**symbol** n. thing generally regarded as typifying, representing, or recalling something; mark, sign, etc. representing object, idea, process, etc. □□ **symbolic** adj. **symbolically** adv.

**symbolise** v. (also **-ize**) be symbol of; represent by symbol(s).

**symbolism** n. use of symbols; symbols; artistic movement or style using symbols to express ideas, emotions, etc. □□ **symbolist** n.

**symmetry** n. correct proportion of parts; balance, harmony; beauty resulting from this; structure allowing object to be divided into parts of equal shape and size; repetition of exactly similar parts facing each other or a centre. □□ **symmetrical** adj. **symmetrically** adv.

**sympathetic** adj. of or expressing sympathy; inspiring sympathy and affection; (of effect) corresponding to or provoked by similar action elsewhere; inclined to favour (proposal etc.) □□ **sympathetically** adv.

**sympathise** v. (also **-ize**) feel or express sympathy; agree. □□ **sympathiser** n.

**sympathy** n. 1 feelings of pity and sorrow for someone else's misfortune. 2 understanding between people; agreement with or approval of opinion or aim.

**symphony** n. musical composition in several movements for full orchestra. □□ **symphonic** adj.

**symposium** n. (pl. **symposia**) conference, or collection of essays, on particular subject.

**symptom** n. sign of existence of something, esp. disease. □□ **symptomatic** adj.

**synagogue** n. building for Jewish religious instruction and worship.

**synapse** n. junction of two nerve cells

**synchronic** adj. concerned with subject as it exists at one point in time, not with its history.

**synchronise** v. (also **-ize**) (cause to) occur or operate at the same time or rate; agree with something else; cause (clocks etc.) to show same time; Computing cause (set of data or files) to remain identical in more than one location. □□ **synchronisation** n.

**synchronous** adj. existing or occurring at same time.

**syncopate** v. 1 displace beats or accents in (music). 2 shorten (word) by omitting syllable or letter(s) in middle. □□ **syncopation** n.

**syndicate** ● n. group of people or firms combining to achieve mutual interest. ● v. combine into syndicate; control by syndicate; arrange publication in many newspapers etc. simultaneously. □□ **syndication** n.

**syndrome** n. group of concurrent symptoms of disease; characteristic combination of opinions, emotions, etc.

**synod** n. Church council of clergy and lay people.

**synonym** n. word or phrase that means same as another. □□ **synonymous** adj.

**synopsis** n. (pl. **synopses**) summary, outline.

**synovial** adj. (of a joint) surrounded by membrane secreting thick lubricating fluid. □□ **synovial** n.

**syntax** n. way words are arranged to form phrases and sentences. □□ **syntactic** adj. **syntactically** adv.

**synthesis** n. (pl. **syntheses**) putting together of parts or elements to make up complex whole. 2 Chem. artificial production of (esp. organic) substances from simpler ones.

**synthesise** v. (also **-ize**) make synthesis of.

**synthesiser** n. electronic musical instrument producing wide variety of sounds.

**synthetic** ● adj. made by chemical synthesis, esp. to imitate natural product; not natural or genuine.
● n. synthetic substance.
□□ **synthetically** adv.

**syphilis** n. contagious venereal disease. □□ **syphilitic** adj.

**syringe** ● n. device for sucking in quantity of liquid and ejecting it in fine stream. ● v. sluice or spray with syringe.

**syrup** n. **1** thick sweet liquid. **2** excessive sweetness of style or manner. □□ **syrupy** adj.

**system** n. **1** set of connected things that form whole or work together; human or animal body as a whole. **2** set of rules or practices used together; method of classification, notation, or measurement. **3** orderliness.

**systematic** adj. **1** methodical; according to system. **2** deliberate.
□□ **systematically** adv.

**systematise** v. (also **-ize**) make systematic. □□ **systematisation** n.

**systemic** adj. **1** of or affecting whole body. **2** (of insecticide etc.) entering plant tissues via roots and shoots.
□□ **systemically** adv.

**systole** n. Physiol. contraction of heart when blood is pumped into arteries. □□ **systolic** adj.

# Tt

**T** *n.* T-shaped thing. □ **to a T** exactly; in every respect.

**ta** *int. colloq.* thank you.

**TAB** *abbr.* Totalisator Agency Board, agency controlling off-course betting; branch of this.

**tab¹** *n.* **1** small projecting flap or strip. **2** *colloq.* bill. **3** second or further document or page that can be opened on spreadsheet or web browser.

**tab²** *n.* **1** facility in computer program, or a device on a keyboard, for advancing to a sequence of set positions in tabular work. **2** = TABULATURE.

**tabard** *n.* short sleeveless tunic-like garment.

**Tabasco** *n. propr.* hot-tasting pepper sauce.

**tabbouleh** *n.* (also **tabouli**) Arab salad of cracked wheat mixed with finely chopped ingredients such as tomatoes, onions, and parsley.

**tabby** *n.* grey or brownish cat with dark stripes.

**tabernacle** *n.* (in Bible) tent for Ark of the Covenant; niche or receptacle, esp. for bread and wine of Eucharist; place used in some Nonconformist worship practices.

**tablature** *n.* form of musical notation indicating fingering rather than the pitch of notes.

**table** ● *n.* **1** flat surface on legs, used for eating, working, etc. **2** food provided. **3** group seated for dinner etc. **4** set of facts or figures arranged esp. in columns; multiplication table. ● *v.* bring forward for discussion at meeting.

**tableau** *n.* (*pl.* **tableaux**) group of silent motionless people representing stage scene.

**tablespoon** *n.* large spoon for serving food and as measure in cooking; amount (20 ml) held by this.

**tablet** *n.* **1** measured amount of a drug compressed into a solid form. **2** flat slab of stone, esp. inscribed. **3** small portable computer that accepts input directly on to its screen rather than via keyboard or mouse.

**tabloid** *n.* small-sized, often popular or sensational, newspaper.

**taboo** ● *n.* ban or prohibition made by religion or social custom. ● *adj.* prohibited by taboo.

**tabular** *adj.* of or arranged in tables or lists.

**tabulate** *v.* arrange (figures, facts) in tabular form. □□ **tabulation** *n.*

**tachograph** *n.* device in vehicle to record speed and travel time.

**tachometer** *n.* instrument measuring velocity or rate of rotation of shaft (esp. in vehicle).

**tacit** *adj.* understood or implied without being stated. □□ **tacitly** *adv.*

**taciturn** *adj.* saying little; uncommunicative. □□ **taciturnity** *n.*

**tack** ● *n.* **1** small sharp broad-headed nail. **2** long temporary stitch. **3** sailing ship's oblique course. **4** riding saddles, bridles, etc. ● *v.* **1** nail with tacks. **2** stitch with tacks. **3** add as extra thing. **4** sail zigzag course.

**tackle** *n.* **1** mechanism, esp. of ropes and pulleys, for lifting etc. **2** equipment for task or sport. **3** act of tackling in football etc. ● *v.* **1** try to deal with (problem or difficulty). **2** obstruct, intercept, or seize and stop (player running with the ball).

**tacky** *adj.* (**tackier**) **1** slightly sticky. **2** *colloq.* in poor taste, cheap; shoddy.

**taco** n. (pl. **tacos**) folded tortilla with savoury filling.

**tact** n. adroitness in dealing with people or circumstances; intuitive perception of the right thing to do or say. □□ **tactful** adj. **tactfully** adv. **tactless** adj. **tactlessly** adv.

**tactic** n. action or strategy to achieve particular end; (**tactics**) art of organising armed forces, esp. in battle; plans and means to achieve some end.

**tactical** adj. of tactics; (of weapons) for use in battle or at close quarters. □□ **tactically** adv.

**tactician** n. expert in tactics.

**tactile** adj. of or using sense of touch. □□ **tactility** n.

**tad** n. colloq. small amount.

**tadpole** n. larva, esp. of frog, toad, etc. at stage of living in water and having gills and tail.

**taekwondo** n. Korean martial art similar to karate.

**TAFE** abbr. Aust. Technical and Further Education, system of tertiary education offering courses mainly in technical and vocational subjects; institution offering such courses.

**taffeta** n. fine lustrous silk or silklike fabric.

**tag** ● n. **1** a label; electronic device that can be attached to person or thing for monitoring purposes. **2** metal point on shoelace etc. **3** much-used phrase or quotation. ● v. (**tagged**) attach label or electronic tag to. □ **tag along** accompany.

**tagine** n. (also **tajine**) North African stew of spiced meat and vegetables; dish used for cooking tagines.

**tagliatelle** n. ribbon-shaped pasta.

**tahini** n. Middle Eastern paste made from ground sesame seeds.

**t'ai chi** n. Chinese martial art and system of exercises.

**tail** ● n. **1** hindmost part of animal, esp. extending beyond body; the rear or end of something. **2** inferior, weak, or last part of anything. **3** (**tails**) tailcoat. **4** reverse of coin turning up in toss. **5** colloq. person following another. ● v. **1** remove stalks of (fruit etc.) **2** colloq. follow closely. **3** dock tail of (lamb etc.) **4** follow, herd, and tend (livestock). □□ **tailless** adj.

**tailcoat** n. man's coat with long divided flap at back.

**tailgate** v. drive (a vehicle) too closely behind another.

**tailor** ● n. **1** maker of (esp. men's) outer garments to measure. **2** (also **taylor**) Aust. marine food fish. ● v. **1** make (clothes) as tailor. **2** make or adapt for special purpose. □□ **tailor-made** adj.

**tailplane** n. horizontal aerofoil at of aircraft.

**tailspin** n. spin by aircraft with tail spiralling.

**taint** ● n. spot or trace of decay, corruption, etc.; corrupt condition, infection. ● v. affect with taint; become tainted; affect slightly.

**taipan** n. large venomous snake of northern Australia and New Guinea.

**take** ● v. (**took**, **taken**, **taking**) **1** get possession of, capture. **2** cause to come or go with one; carry, remove. **3** be effective. **4** make use of. **5** accept, endure. **6** study or teach (subject). **7** make photograph of. ● n. amount taken or caught; sequence of film or sound recorded at one time. □ **take after** resemble (parent etc.) **take back 1** withdraw (statement). **2** return a good) to the place of purchase. **take in 1** include. **2** make (a garment) smaller. **3** understand. **4** cheat; deceive. **take off 1** colloq. mimic humorously. **2** become airborne; depart, esp. hastily. **take on 1** acquire. **2** undertake. **3** engage (employee).

**4** accept as opponent. **take place** occur. **take sides** support one or other cause etc. **take up 1** become interested or engaged in (a pursuit). **2** use (time). **3** accept (offer or person making it). □□ **taker** n.

**takeaway** ● adj. (of food) bought at restaurant etc. for eating elsewhere. ● n. **1** such food; restaurant that sells such food. **2** key fact, point, or idea to be remembered.

**takeover** n. gaining control of another business etc.

**takings** n.pl. amount of money taken in a business etc.

**talc** n. talcum powder; magnesium silicate used as lubricant etc.

**talcum** n. talc. □ **talcum powder** talc powdered and usu. perfumed for use on skin.

**tale** n. **1** narrative or story, esp. fictitious. **2** allegation or gossip, often malicious.

**talent** n. special aptitude.

**talented** adj. having talent.

**talisman** n. thing believed to bring good luck or protect from harm. □□ **talismanic** adj.

**talk** ● v. converse or communicate verbally; have power of speech; express, utter, discuss; use (language); gossip. ● n. talking, conversation; style of speech; informal lecture; rumour. □ **talking book** recorded reading of book. **talking-to** reproof or reprimand. □□ **talker** n.

**talkative** adj. fond of talking.

**tall** adj. of more than average height; of specified height. □ **tall poppy** Aust. colloq. person who is conspicuously successful and whose success frequently attracts envious hostility. **tall story** colloq. exaggerated and hard to believe account.

**tallboy** n. tall chest of drawers.

**tallow** n. hard (esp. animal) fat melted down to make candles, soap, etc.

**tally** ● n. total score etc.; record of this. ● v. agree or correspond; record or reckon by tally. □ **tally room** Aust. centralised counting room for votes in election.

**tally-walka** n. Aust. division of river that rejoins it further on; anabranch.

**Talmud** n. body of Jewish civil and ceremonial law. □□ **Talmudic** adj. **Talmudist** n.

**talon** n. claw, esp. of bird of prey.

**talus** n. (pl. **tali**) ankle bone supporting tibia.

**tamarillo** n. (also **tree tomato**) egg-shaped acidic red fruit of S. American shrub.

**tamarind** n. tropical evergreen tree; its fruit pulp used as food and in drinks.

**tambour** n. hist. drum; circular frame holding fabric taut for embroidering.

**tambourine** n. small shallow drum with jingling discs in rim, shaken or banged as accompaniment.

**tame** ● adj. (of animal) domesticated, not wild or shy; unexciting. ● v. make tame or manageable. □□ **tamely** adv. **tameness** n. **tamer** n.

**tammar** n. greyish-brown wallaby of southern Australia.

**tamp** v. pack down tightly.

**tamper** v. □ **tamper with** meddle or interfere with.

**tampon** n. plug of cotton wool etc. used esp. to absorb menstrual blood.

**tan** ● n. suntan; yellowish-brown colour. ● adj. yellowish-brown. ● v. (**tanned**) **1** make or become brown by exposure to sun. **2** convert (rawhide) into leather. **3** colloq. thrash. ● abbr. tangent.

**tandem** ● n. bicycle with two or more seats one behind another. ● adv. together. □ **in tandem** one behind another; together; alongside each other.

**tandoori** n. style of Indian cooking.

**tang** n. strong taste or smell. □□ **tangy** adj.

**tangent** n. Maths **1** straight line, curve, or surface touching but not intersecting curve. **2** ratio of sides opposite and adjacent to acute angle in right-angled triangle. □ **go off at a tangent** diverge from previous course of action or thought. □□ **tangential** adj.

**tangerine** n. small sweet citrus fruit like orange; its deep orange-yellow colour.

**tangible** adj. perceptible by touch; definite; clearly intelligible; not elusive. □□ **tangibility** n. **tangibly** adv.

**tangle** ● v. intertwine or become twisted or involved in confused mass; entangle; complicate. ● n. tangled mass or state. □□ **tangly** adj.

**tango** ● n. (pl. **tangos**) ballroom dance with gliding steps. ● v. dance tango.

**tank** n. **1** large container for liquid, gas, etc.; reservoir, dam. **2** heavy armoured fighting vehicle moving on continuous tracks. □□ **tankful** n.

**tankard** n. (contents of) tall beer mug with handle.

**tanked** adj. colloq. drunk.

**tanker** n. ship, aircraft, or road vehicle for carrying liquids, esp. oil, in bulk.

**tanner** n. person who tans hides.

**tannery** n. place where hides are tanned.

**tannic acid** n. tannin.

**tannin** n. **1** any of several substances extracted from tree barks etc. and used in tanning and dyeing. **2** compound, deriving from grape skins etc., giving astringency to certain red wines.

**tantalise** v. (also **-ize**) torment with sight of unobtainable; raise and then dash the hopes of. □□ **tantalisation** n.

**tantalum** n. hard white metallic element (symbol Ta). □□ **tantalic** adj.

**tantamount** adj. equivalent.

**tantra** n. any of a class of Hindu or Buddhist mystical and devotional writings.

**tantrum** n. outburst of bad temper or petulance.

**tap** ● n. **1** device by which flow of liquid or gas from pipe or vessel can be controlled. **2** a light blow; sound of this. **3** connection for tapping telephone. ● v. (**tapped**) **1** knock gently. **2** provide with a tap; let out through tap or incision. **3** draw supplies or information from. **4** cut screw thread (in cavity). **5** connect listening device to (telephone etc.) □ **on tap** available for use. **tap and go** system for making payments with bank card, mobile phone, etc., by placing it near reader at checkout. **tap root** plant's chief root.

**tapas** n.pl. small savoury dishes, esp. in Spanish style.

**tape** ● n. **1** narrow strip of material for tying, fastening, or labelling things. **2** magnetic tape; a tape recording. **3** tape measure. ● v. **1** tie up or join with tape. **2** record on magnetic tape. □ **tape measure** strip of tape or flexible metal marked for measuring lengths. **tape recorder** apparatus for recording sounds on magnetic tape.

**taper** ● n. slender candle. ● v. **1** (cause to) diminish in thickness towards one end. **2** make or become gradually less.

**tapestry** n. thick fabric in which coloured weft threads are woven to form pictures or designs; (usu. wool) embroidery imitating this.

**tapioca** n. starchy granular foodstuff prepared from cassava.

**tapir** n. pig-like animal with long snout.

**tappet** n. projection used in machinery to tap against something.

**taproom** n. room in pub with alcoholic drinks (esp. beer) on tap.

**tar** ● *n.* dark thick liquid distilled from coal etc.; similar substance formed in combustion of tobacco. ● *v.* (**tarred**) cover with tar.

**taramasalata** *n.* (also **taramosalata**) dip made from roe, olive oil, etc.

**tarantella** *n.* whirling Italian dance.

**tarantula** *n.* large hairy tropical spider; large black S. European spider; *Aust. colloq.* huntsman spider.

**tardy** *adj.* (**tardier**) slow; late. □□ **tardily** *adv.* **tardiness** *n.*

**tare** *n.* 1 vetch, as cornfield weed or fodder. 2 allowance made for weight of container or vehicle weighed with goods it holds.

**target** ● *n.* mark fired at, esp. round object marked with concentric circles; person, objective, or result aimed at; butt of criticism etc. ● *v.* (**targeted**) aim at (as) a target.

**tariff** *n.* table of fixed charges; duty to be paid on imports or exports.

**tarmac** *n. propr.* broken stone or slag mixed with tar; area surfaced with this, e.g. runway. □□ **tarmacked** *adj.*

**tarnish** ● *v.* (cause to) lose lustre; impair (reputation etc.) ● *n.* loss of lustre; stain, blemish.

**taro** *n.* tropical plant with edible tuberous roots.

**tarot** *n.* pack of 78 cards mainly used in fortune telling.

**tarpaulin** *n.* waterproof canvas.

**tarragon** *n.* aromatic herb.

**tarsus** *n.* (*pl.* **tarsi**) set of small bones of ankle and upper foot. □□ **tarsal** *adj.*

**tart** ● *n.* 1 open pastry case containing fruit, jam, etc. 2 *colloq. derog.* prostitute; promiscuous woman. ● *adj.* acid in taste or manner. □ **tart up** *colloq.* dress gaudily; smarten up. □□ **tartlet** *n.* **tartly** *adv.*

**tartan** *n.* (woollen cloth woven in) pattern of coloured stripes crossing at right angles, esp. denoting Scottish Highland clan.

**tartar** *n.* 1 hard deposit that forms on teeth; deposit formed by fermentation in wine casks. 2 bad-tempered or difficult person.

**tartare sauce** *n.* mayonnaise with chopped gherkins, capers, etc.

**tartaric acid** *n.* acid used in baking powder.

**tartrazine** *n.* brilliant yellow dye from tartaric acid, used to colour food etc.

**Tas.** *abbr.* Tasmania.

**taser** *n.* weapon firing barbs that cause temporary paralysis.

**task** *n.* piece of work to be done.

**taskbar** *n. Computing* bar at the edge of the screen that allows quick access to current or favourite applications.

**Tasmanian** ● *n.* native or resident of Tasmania. ● *adj.* of Tasmania or its inhabitants. □ **Tasmanian devil** carnivorous marsupial found only in Tasmania. **Tasmanian tiger** extinct doglike carnivorous marsupial of Tasmania with stripes across rump.

**tassel** *n.* tuft of hanging threads etc. as decoration. □□ **tasselled** *adj.*

**taste** ● *n.* 1 (faculty of perceiving) sensation caused in mouth by contact with substance. 2 small sample of food etc.; slight experience. 3 a liking. 4 aesthetic discernment in art, clothes, conduct, etc. ● *v.* 1 perceive or sample flavour of; have specified flavour. 2 experience.

**tasteful** *adj.* done in or having good taste. □□ **tastefully** *adv.*

**tasteless** *adj.* 1 flavourless. 2 showing poor judgement of quality. □□ **tastelessly** *adv.* **tastelessness** *n.*

**tasty** *adj.* (**tastier**) of pleasing flavour; appetising. □□ **tastiness** *n.*

**tat¹** *v.* make (edging etc.) by tying knots in thread and using a small shuttle to form lace.

**tat²** *n. colloq.* tasteless or shoddy clothes, jewellery, or ornaments.

**tat³** *n.* (also **tatt**) *colloq.* tattoo.

**tattered** *adj.* ragged.

**tatters** *n.pl.* irregularly torn cloth, paper, etc.

**tatting** *n.* (process of making) kind of handmade knotted lace.

**tattle** ● *v.* prattle, chatter, gossip. ● *n.* idle talk.

**tattoo** ● *v.* mark (skin) by puncturing and inserting pigment; make (design) in this way.
● *n.* **1** tattooed design. **2** military display or pageant. **3** tapping sound. □□ **tattooer** *n.* **tattooist** *n.*

**tatty** *adj.* (**tattier**) *colloq.* tattered, shabby, inferior. □□ **tattily** *adv.* **tattiness** *n.*

**taught** SEE TEACH.

**taunt** ● *n.* insult, provocation.
● *v.* jeer at provocatively.

**taupe** *n.* grey tinged with esp. brown.

**Taurus** *n.* second sign of zodiac, the Bull. □□ **Taurean** *adj.* & *n.*

**taut** *adj.* stretched firmly, not slack. □□ **tauten** *v.* **tautly** *adv.* **tautness** *n.*

**tautology** *n.* pointless repetition of same thing in different words. □□ **tautological** *adj.* **tautologous** *adj.*

**tavern** *n.* place where alcoholic liquor is sold to be drunk on premises and that does not provide accommodation.

**taw** *n.* large marble.

**tawdry** *adj.* showy but worthless; gaudy.

**tawny** *adj.* orange-brown colour.

**tax** ● *n.* money compulsorily levied by government on person, property, business, etc.; something that makes a heavy demand. ● *v.* impose tax on; make heavy demands on. □ **tax return** declaration of income for taxation purposes. □□ **taxable** *adj.* **taxation** *n.*

**taxi** *n.* (in full **taxicab**) vehicle with driver that may be hired.
● *v.* (**taxied, taxiing**) (of aircraft) go along ground before or after flying.

**taxidermy** *n.* art of preparing, stuffing, and mounting skins of animals in lifelike form.
□□ **taxidermist** *n.*

**taxonomy** *n.* system of classification. □□ **taxonomic** *adj.* **taxonomist** *n.*

**TB** *abbr.* tuberculosis.

**TBA** *abbr.* (also **tba**) to be announced.

**T-bone** *n.* piece of loin steak containing T-shaped bone.

**tbsp** *abbr.* tablespoonful.

**T-cell** *n.* lymphocyte active in immune response.

**tchuringa** = CHURINGA.

**te** *n.* Mus. seventh note of scale in tonic sol-fa.

**tea** *n.* **1** dried leaves of Asian evergreen shrub; hot drink made by infusing these (or other substances) in boiling water. **2** light meal in morning or afternoon. **3** dinner. □ **tea bag** small porous bag holding tea for infusion. **tea chest** large wooden box in which tea is exported; this or similar used for storage or transport of goods. **tea towel** cloth for drying washed dishes etc. **tea tree** *Aust.* flowering plant with aromatic foliage.

**teach** *v.* (**taught, teaching**) give systematic information, instruction, or training to (person) or about (subject or skill). □□ **teacher** *n.*

**teacup** *n.* cup from which tea etc. is drunk.

**teak** *n.* hard durable wood of Asian evergreen tree.

**teal** *n.* (pl. **teal**) small freshwater duck.

**team** ● *n.* set of players etc. in game or sport; set of people or animals working together. ● *v.* join in team or in common action.

**teamster** *n.* driver of team of animals.

**tear¹** ● *v.* (**tore, torn, tearing**) **1** pull with some force apart or away or to

pieces; make (hole) in this way.
**2** *colloq.* go hurriedly. ● *n.* hole etc.
caused by tearing.

**tear²** *n.* drop of clear salty liquid
secreted from eye. □ **in tears** crying.
**tear gas** gas that disables by causing
severe irritation to eyes.

**tearful** *adj.* in, given to, or
accompanied by tears. □□ **tearfully**
*adv.*

**tease** ● *v.* **1** try to provoke in a
playful or unkind way. **2** pick into
separate fibres. **3** comb (hair) towards
scalp to impart fullness. ● *n. colloq.*
person fond of teasing others.

**teaspoon** *n.* small spoon for stirring
tea etc.; amount (5 ml) held by it.
□□ **teaspoonful** *n.*

**teat** *n.* nipple on a milk-secreting
organ; rubber etc. nipple for sucking
from a feeding bottle.

**tech** *n. colloq.* **1** technology;
technician. **2** technical college or
school.

**technetium** *n.* artificial radioactive
element (symbol Tc).

**technical** *adj.* **1** of mechanical arts
and applied sciences; of particular
subject, craft etc.; using technical
language. **2** in strict legal sense.
□□ **technically** *adv.*

**technicality** *n.* technical point or
detail.

**technician** *n.* **1** person doing
practical or maintenance work in
laboratory. **2** person skilled in artistic
etc. technique. **3** expert in practical
science.

**Technicolor** *n. propr.* process of
producing films in colour; *colloq.*
vivid or artificial colour.

**technique** *n.* method of doing
something; skill in an activity.

**techno** *n.* style of fast, heavy
electronic dance music.

**technocracy** *n.* rule or control by
technical experts. □□ **technocrat** *n.*

**technology** *n.* application of
scientific knowledge for practical
purposes, esp. in industry; machinery
and equipment developed from
application of scientific knowledge.
□□ **technological** *adj.* **technologically**
*adv.* **technologist** *n.*

**teddy** *n.* (in full **teddy bear**) soft toy
bear.

**tedious** *adj.* tiresomely long,
wearisome. □□ **tediously** *adv.*
**tediousness** *n.* **tedium** *n.*

**tee** ● *n.* cleared space from which
golf ball is struck at start of play for
each hole; small wood or plastic
support for this ball. ● *v.* (**teed,
teeing**) place (ball) on tee. □ **tee off**
make first stroke in golf.

**teem** *v.* be abundant; be full of or
swarming (with); (of water or rain)
pour.

**teenager** *n.* person in his or her
teens. □□ **teenage** *adj.*

**teens** *n.pl.* years of one's age from 13
to 19.

**teeny** *adj.* (**teenier**) *colloq.* tiny.

**teepee** = TEPEE.

**teeshirt** = T-SHIRT.

**teeter** *v.* stand or move unsteadily.

**teeth** *see* TOOTH.

**teethe** *v.* (of baby) have first teeth
appear through gums. □ **teething
troubles** problems in early stages of
an enterprise.

**teetotal** *adj.* advocating or practising
total abstinence from alcohol.
□□ **teetotaller** *n.*

**teflon** *n. propr.* non-stick coating for
kitchen utensils.

**tele-** *comb. form* **1** at or to a distance.
**2** television. **3** by telephone.

**telecast** ● *n.* television broadcast.
● *v.* transmit by television.
□□ **telecaster** *n.*

**telecommunications** *n.pl.*
communication by telephone, radio,
cable, etc.

**teleconference** n. conference with participants in different locations linked by telecommunication devices.

**telegram** n. message sent by telegraph.

**telegraph** ● n. (device or system for) transmitting messages to a distance by making and breaking electrical connection. ● v. send message or communicate by telegraph.

**telegraphy** n. communications by telegraph. □□ **telegraphic** adj. **telegraphically** adv. **telegraphist** n.

**telekinesis** n. movement of objects without touching them. □□ **telekinetic** adj.

**telemarketing** n. marketing of goods etc. by unsolicited telephone calls.

**telemetry** n. process of recording readings of an instrument and transmitting them by radio. □□ **telemeter** n.

**telepathy** n. communication of thoughts directly from mind to mind. □□ **telepathic** adj.

**telephone** ● n. apparatus for transmitting sound by wire or radio. ● v. send (message) or speak to (person) by telephone. □□ **telephonic** adj. **telephonically** adv. **telephony** n.

**telephonist** n. operator in telephone exchange or at switchboard.

**telephoto lens** n. photographic lens producing large image of distant object.

**teleprinter** n. device for sending, receiving, and printing telegraph messages.

**teleprompter** n. autocue.

**telesales** n.pl. selling by telephone.

**telescope** ● n. optical instrument using lenses or mirrors to magnify distant objects. ● v. make or become shorter by sliding each section inside the next; compress or become

compressed forcibly. □□ **telescopic** adj. **telescopically** adv.

**teletext** n. service transmitting written information to television screens.

**telethon** n. long television program, esp. to raise money.

**televangelist** n. evangelical preacher who uses television to promote doctrines and solicit funds.

**televise** v. transmit by television.

**television** n. system for reproducing on a screen visual images transmitted (with sound) by radio signals or cable; (in full **television set**) device with screen for receiving these signals; television broadcasting. □□ **televisual** adj.

**telex** ● n. international system of telegraphy using teleprinters and public transmission lines. ● v. send, or communicate with, by telex.

**tell** v. (**told**, **telling**) 1 make known, express in words; direct, order; divulge information, reveal secret, etc. 2 decide about, distinguish. 3 have an effect. □ **tell off** reprimand. **tell tales** reveal secrets.

**teller** n. 1 person employed to receive and pay out money in bank etc. 2 person who counts votes. 3 narrator.

**telling** adj. having a marked effect.

**tellurium** n. 1 element (symbol **Te**). 2 used in semiconductors.

**telly** n. colloq. television.

**teleopea** n. Aust. waratah.

**temerity** n. rashness, audacity.

**temp** colloq. ● n. temporary employee. ● v. work as temp.

**temper** ● n. 1 state of mind as regards calmness or anger. 2 fit of anger. ● v. 1 bring (metal, clay) to proper hardness or consistency. 2 moderate, mitigate. □ **keep** (or **lose**) **one's temper** refrain (or fail to refrain) from becoming angry.

**tempera** n. method of painting using emulsion, e.g. of pigment with egg.

**temperament** *n.* person's or animal's nature and character.

**temperamental** *adj.* regarding temperament; excitable or moody; unpredictable. □□ **temperamentally** *adv.*

**temperance** *n.* self-restraint, moderation; total abstinence from alcohol.

**temperate** *adj.* avoiding excess, moderate; not extreme.

**temperature** *n.* measured or perceived degree of heat or cold of thing, region, etc.; body temperature above normal.

**tempest** *n.* violent storm.

**tempestuous** *adj.* stormy, turbulent.

**template** *n.* pattern or gauge, esp. for cutting shapes.

**temple** *n.* 1 flat part of side of head between forehead and ear. 2 building for worship, or treated as dwelling place, of god(s).

**tempo** *n.* (*pl.* **tempos** or **tempi**) speed at which music is to be played; rate of motion or activity.

**temporal** *adj.* 1 secular. 2 of or denoting time. 3 of the temples of the head.

**temporary** *adj.* lasting or meant to last only for limited time. □□ **temporarily** *adv.*

**temporise** *v.* (also **-ize**) avoid committing oneself so as to gain time.

**tempt** *v.* persuade or try to persuade by the prospect of pleasure or advantage; arouse desire in. □□ **temptation** *n.* **tempter** *n.* **temptress** *n.*

**tempura** *n.* Japanese dish of seafood etc. fried in batter.

**ten** *adj. & n.* one more than nine (10, X). □□ **tenth** *adj. & n.*

**tenable** *adj.* able to be defended or held. □□ **tenability** *n.*

**tenacious** *adj.* holding or sticking firmly. □□ **tenaciously** *adv.* **tenacity** *n.*

**tenancy** *n.* (duration of) tenant's status or possession.

**tenant** *n.* person who rents land or property from landlord.

**tend** *v.* 1 take care of, look after. 2 have specified tendency.

**tendency** *n.* leaning, inclination.

**tendentious** *adj.* biased, not impartial. □□ **tendentiously** *adv.* **tendentiousness** *n.*

**tender** ● *adj.* 1 not tough or hard; delicate; painful when touched. 2 sensitive; gentle. ● *n.* 1 formal offer to supply goods or carry out work at stated price. 2 vessel or vehicle conveying passengers or goods to and from larger one. 3 vessel attached to steam locomotive and carrying fuel and water etc. ● *v.* offer formally; make tender for. □ **legal tender** currency that must, by law, be accepted in payment. □□ **tenderly** *adv.* **tenderness** *n.*

**tendon** *n.* tough fibrous tissue connecting muscle to bone etc.

**tendril** *n.* slender leafless shoot by which some climbing plants cling.

**tenet** *n.* doctrine, principle.

**tenfold** *adj. & adv.* ten times as much or as many.

**tennessine** *n.* chemical element (symbol **Ts**).

**tennis** *n.* ball game played with racquets on court divided by net.

**tenon** *n.* wooden projection shaped to fit into mortise of another piece.

**tenor** ● *n.* 1 male singing voice between baritone and alto. 2 general meaning. ● *adj.* of tenor pitch.

**tenosynovitis** *n.* repetitive strain injury, esp. of wrist.

**tenpin bowling** *n.* game in which ten pins or skittles are bowled at in alley.

**tense** ● *adj.* 1 stretched tightly. 2 nervous, anxious. ● *v.* make or become tense. ● *n. Gram.* form of

verb indicating time of action etc.
□□ **tensely** adv. **tenseness** n.

**tensile** adj. of tension; capable of being stretched.

**tension** n. **1** stretching, being stretched. **2** mental strain or excitement; strained state. **3** stress produced by forces pulling apart. **4** voltage.

**tent** n. portable shelter or dwelling of canvas etc.

**tentacle** n. slender flexible appendage of animal, used for feeling, grasping, or moving.
□□ **tentacled** adj.

**tentative** adj. hesitant, not definite.
□□ **tentatively** adv.

**tenterhooks** n.pl. □ **on tenterhooks** in suspense or uncertainty.

**tenuous** adj. slight; very thin; insubstantial. □□ **tenuousness** n.

**tenure** n. the holding of office or of land or accommodation etc.
□□ **tenured** adj.

**tepee** n. (also **teepee**) conical tent used by some indigenous N. Americans.

**tepid** adj. **1** lukewarm. **2** unenthusiastic.

**tequila** n. Mexican liquor made from agave.

**tera-** comb. form one trillion.

**terabyte** n. Computing unit of information equal to one million million or (strictly) $2^{40}$ bytes.

**teraglin** n. (also **trag**) Aust. marine food fish.

**terbium** n. metallic element (symbol **Tb**).

**tercentenary** n. 300th anniversary.

**tergiversate** v. **1** change one's party or principles. **2** make conflicting or evasive statements.

**term** n. **1** fixed or limited period; period of weeks during which school etc. is open; AFL a quarter. **2** word or phrase; each quantity or expression in mathematical series or ratio etc.

**3** (**terms**) conditions offered or accepted; relations between people.
□ **come to terms with** reconcile oneself to (difficulty etc.)

**termagant** n. overbearing woman.

**terminal** ● adj. **1** (of condition or disease) fatal; (of patient) dying. **2** of or forming limit or terminus.
● n. **1** terminating thing. **2** extremity. **3** bus or train terminus; air terminal. **4** point of connection for closing electric circuit. **5** apparatus for the transmission of messages to or from computer, communications system, etc. □□ **terminally** adv.

**terminate** v. end.

**termination** n. **1** terminating, being terminated. **2** induced abortion.

**terminology** n. technical terms of subject. □□ **terminological** adj.

**terminus** n. (pl. **termini** or **terminuses**) point at end of railway or bus route or of pipeline etc.

**termite** n. antlike insect destructive to timber.

**tern** n. sea bird.

**ternary** adj. composed of three parts.

**terrace** ● n. **1** flat area on slope for cultivation; level paved area next to house. **2** row of joined houses.
● v. form into or provide with terrace(s).

**terracotta** n. unglazed usu. brownish-red earthenware.

**terra firma** n. dry land, firm ground.

**terrain** n. land with regard to its natural features.

**terra nullius** n. assumption that, prior to white settlement, Australia belonged to no one and hence could be legally taken over.

**terrapin** n. freshwater tortoise.

**terrarium** n. (pl. **terrariums** or **terraria**) **1** place for keeping small land animals. **2** transparent globe containing growing plants.

**terrestrial** adj. of or on the earth; of or living on land.

**terrible** adj. causing or likely to cause terror; colloq. very great, bad, or incompetent.□□ **terribly** adv.

**terrier** n. small active hardy dog.

**terrific** adj. huge, intense, excellent. □□ **terrifically** adv.

**terrify** v. fill with terror.□□ **terrifying** adj. **terrifyingly** adv.

**terrine** n. (earthenware vessel for) pâté or similar food.

**territorial** adj. of territory or district.

**territory** n. **1** extent of land under the control of a ruler, country, etc. **2** sphere of action or thought. **3** (**the Territory**) Northern Territory.

**terror** n. **1** extreme fear; terrifying person or thing. **2** colloq. troublesome or tiresome person, esp. child.

**terrorise** v. (also **-ize**) fill with terror; use terrorism against.

**terrorism** n. unlawful use of violence and intimidation, esp. against civilians, in pursuit of political aims. □□ **terrorist** n.

**terry** n. looped pile fabric used for towels, nappies, etc.

**terse** adj. concise, curt.□□ **tersely** adv.

**tertiary** adj. next after secondary.

**tesla** n. SI unit of magnetic flux density.

**tessellated** adj. of or resembling mosaic; finely chequered.

**test** ● n. critical exam or trial of person's or thing's qualities; means, procedure, or standard for so doing; minor exam; colloq. test match.
● v. subject to a test.□□ **test drive 1** drive taken to judge performance of vehicle. **2** colloq. trial. **test match** one of a series of international cricket or rugby matches. **test tube** tube of thin glass with one end closed, used for chemical tests etc.□□ **tester** n.

**testament** n. **1** a will. **2** evidence, proof.□ **New Testament** books of Bible telling life and teachings of Christ. **Old Testament** books of Bible telling history and beliefs of Jewish people.□□ **testamentary** adj.

**testamur** n. certificate indicating that a candidate has passed a course of study.

**testate** adj. having left valid will at death.□□ **testacy** n.

**testator** n. person who has made a will.

**testatrix** n. woman who has made a will.

**testes** see TESTIS.

**testicle** n. male organ that secretes spermatozoa etc., esp. one of pair in scrotum of man and most mammals.

**testify** v. bear witness; give evidence in court; affirm, declare.

**testimonial** n. certificate of character, conduct, or qualifications; public tribute.

**testimony** n. declaration under oath etc.; supporting evidence.

**testis** n. (pl. **testes**) testicle.

**testosterone** n. male sex hormone.

**testy** adj. (**testier**) irascible, short-tempered.□□ **testily** adv.

**tetanus** n. bacterial disease causing painful spasm of voluntary muscles.

**tetchy** adj. (also **techy**) peevish, irritable.□□ **tetchily** adv.

**tête-à-tête** n. private conversation between two people.
● adv. & adj. together in private.

**tether** ● n. rope etc. tying animal to spot. ● v. **1** fasten with tether. **2** use (smartphone) in order to connect computer etc. to Internet.
□ **at the end of one's tether** having reached limit of one's patience, resources, etc.

**tetrahedron** n. (pl. **tetrahedra** or **tetrahedrons**) four-sided triangular pyramid.□□ **tetrahedral** adj.

**Teutonic** adj. dated of Germanic peoples or their languages.

**text** ● n. **1** main body of book; original document, esp. as distinct from paraphrase etc. **2** data in form of words or alphabetic characters; text message. ● *v.* send text message to. □ **text message** communication sent and received via mobile phone etc. □□ **textual** *adj.*

**textbook** *n.* book of information for use in studying subject.

**textile** ● *n.* woven or machine-knitted fabric. ● *adj.* of weaving or cloth.

**texture** *n.* feel or appearance of surface or substance; arrangement of threads in textile fabric. □□ **textural** *adj.*

**textured** *adj.* not having a smooth, plain, or regular surface.

**thalidomide** *n.* sedative drug found to cause foetal malformation when taken early in pregnancy.

**thallium** *n.* toxic metallic element (symbol Tl).

**than** *conj. & prep.* used to introduce second element in comparison.

> **Usage** *Than* is often confused with *then*.

**thank** ● *v.* **1** express gratitude to. **2** hold responsible. ● *n.* (**thanks**) expressions of gratitude; *colloq.* thank you.

**thankful** *adj.* grateful, pleased; expressive of thanks.

**thankfully** *adv.* **1** in a thankful way. **2** let us be thankful for that.

**thankless** *adj.* **1** not expressing or feeling gratitude. **2** (of task etc.) unprofitable. **3** unappreciated.

**thanksgiving** *n.* expression of gratitude, esp. to God; (**Thanksgiving** or **Thanksgiving Day**) public holiday in Canada and US.

**that** ● *adj.* (*pl.* **those**) used to describe person or thing nearby, indicated, just mentioned, or understood; used to specify further or

less immediate of two. ● *pron.* used to introduce defining relative clause. ● *adv.* to that degree. ● *conj.* used to introduce subordinate clause expressing esp. statement, purpose, or result.

**thatch** ● *n.* roof covering of straw, reeds, etc. ● *v.* cover with thatch. □□ **thatcher** *n.*

**thaw** ● *v.* pass from frozen into liquid or unfrozen state; become friendlier or less formal. ● *n.* thawing; warmth of weather that thaws; lessening of hostility etc. (between nations etc.)

**the** *adj.* (called definite article) applied to noun standing for specific person or thing, or one or all of a kind, or used to emphasise excellence or importance.

**theatre** *n.* **1** building or outdoor area for dramatic performances; writing, production, acting, etc. of plays. **2** room or hall for lectures etc. with seats in tiers. **3** cinema. **4** operating theatre. **5** scene or field of action.

**theatrical** ● *adj.* of or for the theatre or acting; calculated for effect. ● *n.* (**theatricals**) dramatic performances. □□ **theatricality** *n.* **theatrically** *adv.*

**thee** *pron.* arch. objective case of THOU.

**theft** *n.* stealing.

**their** *adj.* of or belonging to them.

**theirs** *pron.* the one(s) belonging to them.

**theism** *n.* belief in gods or a god. □□ **theist** *n.* **theistic** *adj.*

**them** *pron.* objective case of THEY.

**theme** *n.* **1** subject or topic of talk etc. **2** *Mus.* leading melody in composition. □□ **thematic** *adj.* **thematically** *adv.*

**themselves** *pron.* emphatic and reflexive form of THEY and THEM.

**then** ● *adv.* **1** at that time. **2** next. **3** after that. **4** in that case.

**5** accordingly. • *adj. & n.* (of) that time.

> **Usage** *Then* is often confused with *than*.

**thence** *adv. arch.* from that place or source.

**theocracy** *n.* form of government by god(s) directly or through priestly order etc.□□ **theocratic** *adj.*

**theodolite** *n.* surveying instrument for measuring angles.

**theology** *n.* study or system of religion.□□ **theologian** *n.* **theological** *adj.*

**theorem** *n.* mathematical statement to be proved by reasoning.

**theoretical** *adj.* concerned with knowledge but not with its practical application; based on theory rather than experience.□□ **theoretically** *adv.*

**theorise** *v.* (also **-ize**) indulge in or evolve theories.

**theorist** *n.* holder or inventor of theory.

**theory** *n.* system of ideas explaining something, esp. one based on general principles; abstract knowledge or speculative thought.

**theosophy** *n.* philosophy professing to achieve knowledge of God by direct intuition, spiritual ecstasy, etc. □□ **theosophical** *adj.* **theosophist** *n.*

**therapeutic** *adj.* of, for, or contributing to the cure of diseases; soothing, conducive to well-being. □□ **therapeutically** *adv.*

**therapy** *n.* non-surgical treatment of disease etc.□□ **therapist** *n.*

**there** • *adv.* in, at, or to that place or position; at that point; in that respect. • *n.* that place. • *int.* exclamation of satisfaction or consolation.

**thereabouts** *adv.* near there.

**thereafter** *adv.* after that.

**thereby** *adv.* by that means.

**therefore** *adv.* for that reason.

**thermal** • *adj.* of, for, producing, or retaining heat. • *n.* rising current of warm air.□□ **thermally** *adv.*

**thermocouple** *n.* device for measuring temperature by means of thermoelectric voltage.

**thermodynamics** *n.pl.* science of the relationship between heat and other forms of energy.

**thermoelectric** *adj.* producing electricity by difference of temperatures.

**thermometer** *n.* instrument for measuring temperature.

**thermonuclear** *adj.* of or using nuclear reactions that occur only at very high temperatures.

**thermoplastic** *n. & adj.* (substance) becoming plastic on heating and hardening on cooling.

**thermos** *n.* (in full **thermos flask**) *propr.* vacuum flask.

**thermosetting** *adj.* (of plastics) setting permanently when heated.

**thermostat** *n.* device for automatic regulation of temperature. □□ **thermostatic** *adj.* **thermostatically** *adv.*

**thesaurus** *n.* (*pl.* **thesauri** or **thesauruses**) book that lists words in groups of synonyms and related concepts.

**these** see THIS.

**thesis** *n.* (*pl.* **theses**) **1** proposition to be maintained or proved. **2** lengthy written essay submitted for university degree.

**thespian** • *adj.* of drama. • *n.* actor or actress.

**they** *pron.* people or things mentioned or unspecified.

**thiamine** *n.* (also **thiamin**) vitamin of B complex found in unrefined cereals, beans, and liver.

**thick** • *adj.* **1** of great or specified extent between opposite surfaces.

**2** composed of many elements; firm in consistency. **3** impenetrable, cloudy, indistinct. **4** *colloq.* stupid. **5** intimate or very friendly. ● *n.* (**the thick**) thick part of anything. ● *adv.* thickly. □ **thick-skinned** not sensitive to criticism. □□ **thickly** *adv.*
**thickness** *n.*

**thicken** *v.* make or become thick or thicker.

**thicket** *n.* tangle of shrubs or trees.

**thickset** *adj.* stocky, burly.

**thief** *n.* (*pl.* **thieves**) person who steals. □□ **thievish** *adj.*

**thieve** *v.* be a thief; steal.
□□ **thievery** *n.*

**thigh** *n.* part of leg between hip and knee.

**thimble** *n.* hard cap worn to protect finger and push needle in sewing.

**thin** ● *adj.* (**thinner**) having opposite surfaces close together; of small thickness or diameter; lean, not plump; not dense or copious; (of excuse etc.) flimsy, transparent. ● *adv.* thinly. ● *v.* (**thinned**) make or become thin(ner). □□ **thinly** *adv.*
**thinness** *n.* **thinnish** *adj.*

**thine** *adj. & pron. arch.* belonging to thee.

**thing** *n.* **1** any possible object of thought or perception including people, material objects, events, qualities, ideas, utterances, and acts. **2** *colloq.* one's special interest. **3** (**the thing**) *colloq.* what is proper, fashionable, needed, important, etc. **4** (**things**) personal belongings, clothing, equipment; circumstances.

**thingummy** *n.* (also **thingummyjig**) *colloq.* person or thing whose name one has forgotten or does not know.

**think** ● *v.* (**thought**, **thinking**) **1** be of the opinion. **2** use one's mind to form ideas etc. ● *n. colloq.* act of thinking. □ **think of 1** call to mind. **2** have opinion of. **think tank** body of experts providing advice and ideas on specific

political or economic problems. **think up** *colloq.* produce by thought.
□□ **thinker** *n.*

**thinner** *n.* solvent for diluting paint etc.

**third** ● *adj.* next after second. ● *n.* any of three equal parts of thing. □ **third-degree 1** of burns of the most severe kind. **2** *US* of the least serious category of a crime. **third party** another party besides the two principals. **third-party insurance** insurance covering damage or injury suffered by person other than the insured. **third-rate** very poor in quality. □□ **thirdly** *adv.*

**thirst** ● *n.* (discomfort caused by) need to drink; desire, craving. ● *v.* feel thirst. □□ **thirstily** *adv.*
**thirsty** *adj.*

**thirteen** *adj. & n.* one more than twelve (13, XIII). □□ **thirteenth** *adj. & n.*

**thirty** *adj. & n.* three times ten (30, XXX). □□ **thirtieth** *adj. & n.*

**this** *adj. & pron.* (*pl.* **these**) person or thing near or present or just mentioned.

**thistle** *n.* prickly plant, usu. with globular heads of purple flowers.

**thither** *adv.* to that place.

**thong** *n.* **1** narrow strip of hide or leather. **2** flat-soled sandal held on foot by thong passing between first and second toes.

**thorax** *n.* (*pl.* **thoraces** or **thoraxes**) part of body between neck and abdomen. □□ **thoracic** *adj.*

**thorium** *n.* radioactive metallic element (symbol Th).

**thorn** *n.* sharp-pointed projection on plant; thorn-bearing shrub or tree.
□□ **thorny** *adj.*

**thorough** *adj.* complete in every way; detailed; methodical. □□ **thoroughly** *adv.* **thoroughness** *n.*

**thoroughbred** *n. & adj.* (horse etc.) bred of pure or first-class stock.

**thoroughfare** n. road or path open at both ends, esp. for traffic.

**those** see THAT.

**thou** pron. arch. you.

**though** ● conj. despite the fact that; even if; and yet. ● adv. colloq. however; all the same.

**thought** ● v. see THINK.
● n. process, power, faculty, etc. of thinking; sober reflection, consideration; idea or intention, purpose.

**thoughtful** adj. 1 thinking deeply; giving signs of serious thought. 2 considerate.□□ **thoughtfully** adv. **thoughtfulness** n.

**thoughtless** adj. careless; inconsiderate.□□ **thoughtlessly** adv. **thoughtlessness** n.

**thousand** adj. & n. ten hundred (1000, M); (**thousands**) colloq. large number.□□ **thousandth** adj. & n.

**thrall** n. literary slavery.

**thrash** v. beat or whip severely; defeat thoroughly; move or fling (esp. limbs) about violently. □ **thrash out** discuss thoroughly.

**thread** ● n. 1 spun-out cotton, silk, glass, etc.; length of this. 2 continuous aspect of thing; group of linked messages posted on Internet forum that share common subject or theme. 3 spiral ridge of screw. ● v. 1 pass thread through (needle); put (beads) on thread. 2 arrange (material in strip form, e.g. film) in proper position on equipment. 3 pick (one's way) through crowded place, maze, etc.

**threadbare** adj. (of cloth) with the nap worn off and threads visible; shabbily dressed.

**threading** n. method of hair removal using twisted cotton thread.

**threadworm** n. small threadlike parasitic worm.

**threat** n. expression of intention to punish, hurt or harm; indication of something undesirable coming; person or thing regarded as dangerous.

**threaten** v. make or be a threat (to).

**three** adj. & n. one more than two (3, III).□ **three-dimensional** 1 having or appearing to have length, breadth, and depth. 2 realistic, believable.

**threefold** adj. & adv. three times as much or as many.

**threesome** n. group of three people, a trio.

**thresh** v. beat out or separate grain from (cereal plant).□□ **thresher** n.

**threshold** n. 1 plank of wood or stone forming bottom of doorway; point of entry. 2 limit below which stimulus causes no reaction.

**threw** see THROW.

**thrice** adv. arch. three times.

**thrift** n. frugality; economical management.□□ **thrifty** adj. thriftily adv.

**thrill** n. wave or nervous tremor of emotion or sensation.

**thriller** n. novel, play, or film with exciting plot, typically involving crime or espionage; very exciting contest or experience.

**thrive** v. (throve or thrived, thriven or thrived, thriving) prosper; grow vigorously.

**throat** n. front of neck; passage from mouth to lungs or oesophagus.

**throaty** adj. (throatier) uttered deep in throat; hoarsely resonant.

**throb** v. (throbbed) beat or vibrate with strong rhythm or with emotion; feel regular bursts of pain.
● n. regular pulsation.

**throes** n.pl. violent pangs of pain. □ in the throes of struggling with the task of.

**thrombosis** n. (pl. thromboses) coagulation of blood in blood vessel or organ.

**throne** n. ceremonial chair for sovereign, bishop etc.; sovereign power.

**throng | thymus**

**throng** ● *n.* crowded mass of people. ● *v.* come in great multitudes; fill (as) with crowd.

**throttle** ● *n.* valve controlling flow of fuel or steam in engine; lever controlling this. ● *v.* strangle.

**through** ● *prep.* 1 from end to end or side to side of; between; among; from start to finish; up to and including. 2 by agency, means, or fault of; by reason of. ● *adv.* 1 through something; from end to end; to the end. 2 so as to have finished. 3 so as to be connected by telephone. ● *adj.* 1 (of journey etc.) done without change of line, vehicle, etc. 2 (of traffic) going through a place to its destination. 3 (of road) open at both ends.

**throughout** *prep. & adv.* right through; from end to end (of).

**throve** see THRIVE.

**throw** ● *v.* (threw, thrown, throwing) 1 propel through space; force violently into specified position or situation; turn or move (part of body) quickly or suddenly. 2 project (light, rays, etc.); cast (shadow). 3 bring to the ground. 4 *colloq.* disconcert. 5 put (clothes etc.) carelessly or hastily on, off, etc. 6 cause to pass or extend suddenly to another state or position. 7 move (switch, lever). 8 shape pottery on wheel. 9 have (fit, tantrum, etc.) 10 give (party). 11 lose (contest, race, etc.) intentionally, esp. for bribe. ● *n.* throwing, being thrown; distance a thing is or may be thrown. □ **throw in the towel** admit defeat or failure. **throw up** 1 vomit. 2 abandon; resign from. 3 bring to notice.

**thrum** *v.* (thrummed) make continuous rhythmic humming sound; strum.

**thrush** *n.* 1 kind of songbird. 2 fungal infection of mouth, throat, or vagina.

**thrust** ● *v.* (thrust, thrusting) push with force; lunge with sword etc. ● *n.* thrusting movement or force.

**thud** ● *n.* low dull sound as of blow on non-resonant surface. ● *v.* (thudded) make thud; fall with thud.

**thug** *n.* violent ruffian. □□ **thuggery** *n.*

**thulium** *n.* metallic element (symbol Tm).

**thumb** ● *n.* short thick finger on hand, set apart from other four. ● *v.* 1 turn over pages (as) with thumb. 2 request or get (lift) by signalling with raised thumb. □ **thumb drive** = *flash drive.* **under a person's thumb** completely dominated by person.

**thumbnail** ● *n.* 1 nail of thumb. 2 *Computing* small picture of image or page layout. ● *adj.* concise, brief.

**thump** ● *v.* beat heavily, esp. with fist; throb strongly; knock loudly. ● *n.* (sound of) heavy blow.

**thunder** ● *n.* loud noise accompanying lightning; resounding loud deep noise. ● *v.* sound with or like thunder; utter loudly. □□ **thunderous** *adj.* **thundery** *adj.*

**thunderbolt** *n.* 1 lightning flash. 2 sudden unexpected event or piece of news.

**thunderclap** *n.* crash of thunder.

**thundering** *adj. colloq.* huge.

**thunderstorm** *n.* storm with thunder and lightning.

**thunderstruck** *adj.* amazed; overwhelmingly surprised or startled.

**Thurs.** *abbr.* Thursday.

**Thursday** *n.* day after Wednesday.

**thus** *adv. formal* in this way; as a result or inference; to this extent, so.

**thwack** ● *v.* hit with heavy blow. ● *n.* heavy blow.

**thwart** ● *v.* frustrate, foil. ● *n.* rower's seat.

**thy** *adj. arch.* belonging to thee.

**thylacine** *n.* = *Tasmanian tiger.*

**thyme** *n.* herb with aromatic leaves.

**thymus** *n.* (pl. thymi) ductless gland near base of neck.

**thyroid** n. (in full **thyroid gland**) large ductless gland in neck secreting hormone affecting metabolic rate.

**thyself** pron. arch. emphatic and reflexive form of THOU and THEE.

**tiara** n. jewelled ornamental band worn on front of woman's hair.

**tibia** n. (pl. **tibiae**) inner of two bones extending from knee to ankle.

**tic** n. involuntary contraction of muscles, esp. of face.

**tick** ● n. 1 slight recurring click, esp. of watch or clock. 2 colloq. moment. 3 mark (✓) to denote correctness etc. 4 parasitic arachnid or insect on animals. 5 colloq. credit. ● v. 1 make sound of ticks. 2 mark with tick. 3 (of mechanism) work, function. □ **tick off** colloq. reprimand. **tick over** (of engine) idle.

**ticket** ● n. 1 piece of paper or card entitling holder to enter place, participate in event, travel by public transport, etc. 2 Aust. document certifying membership of trade union. 3 notification of traffic offence etc. 4 price etc. label. 5 list of candidates put forward by group, esp. political party. 6 (**the ticket**) colloq. what is needed. ● v. (**ticketed**) attach ticket to.

**ticking** n. stout usu. striped material used to cover mattresses etc.

**tickle** ● v. 1 touch or stroke lightly so as to excite the nerves and usu. produce laughter and spasmodic movement; excite agreeably; amuse. ● n. act or sensation of tickling.

**ticklish** adj. 1 sensitive to tickling. 2 difficult; requiring careful handling.

**tidal** adj. related to, like, or affected by, tides.

**tiddler** n. colloq. 1 small fish, esp. minnow. 2 unusually small thing.

**tiddly** adj. (**tiddlier**) colloq. 1 slightly drunk. 2 very small.

**tiddlywinks** n. game involving flicking small counters into cup.

**tide** n. 1 periodic rise and fall of sea due to attraction of moon and sun. 2 marked trend of opinion, fortune, or events. □ **tide over** help temporarily.

**tidings** n.pl. literary news.

**tidy** ● adj. (**tidier**) neat, orderly. ● n. receptacle for holding small objects, kitchen waste, etc. ● v. make (oneself, room, etc.) tidy. □□ **tidily** adv. **tidiness** n.

**tie** ● v. (**tied**, **tying**) 1 attach or fasten with cord etc.; form into knot or bow. 2 restrict, bind. 3 make same score as another competitor. 4 Mus. unite (notes) by tie. ● n. 1 cord etc. used for fastening. 2 strip of material worn around collar and tied in knot at front. 3 thing that unites or restricts people. 4 draw, dead heat, or equality of score among competitors. 5 match between any pair of players or teams. 6 Mus. curved line above or below two notes of the same pitch indicating they are to be joined as one. □ **tie-break** means of deciding winner from competitors who have tied. **tie in** bring into or have close association or agreement.

**tier** n. row, rank, or unit of structure, as one of several placed one above another. □□ **tiered** adj.

**tiff** n. slight or petty quarrel.

**tiger** n. large Asian animal of cat family, having yellow-brown coat with black stripes.

**tight** ● adj. 1 closely held, drawn, fastened, etc.; tense, stretched; fitting closely or too closely; leaving little room; (of turn or curve) having short radius. 2 strict, thorough. 3 limited; colloq. stingy. 4 colloq. drunk. ● adv. tightly. □ **a tight corner** a difficult situation. **tighten** v. tighten. □□ **tightly** adv. **tightness** n.

**tightrope** n. tightly stretched rope on which acrobats perform.

**tights** n.pl. thin close-fitting stretch garment covering legs, feet, and lower torso.

**tigress** *n.* female tiger.

**tiki** *n. NZ* large wooden or small ornamental greenstone image representing human figure.

**tilak** *n.* mark worn by Hindu on forehead to indicate caste, status, etc., or as ornament.

**tilde** *n.* mark (~) put over letter to change its pronunciation; similar symbol used in mathematics and logic to indicate negation, inversion, etc.

**tile** ● *n.* thin slab of concrete, baked clay, etc. for roofing, paving, etc. ● *v.* cover with tiles. □□ **tiler** *n.*

**till** ● *n.* money drawer in shop, bank, etc., esp. with device recording amount of each purchase. ● *v.* cultivate (land).

**till** ● *prep.* up to, as late as. ● *conj.* 1 up to time when. 2 so long that.

> **Usage** *Till* is less formal than *until*.

**tillage** *n.* preparation of land for growing crops; tilled land.

**tiller** *n.* bar by which boat is turned.

**tilt** ● *v.* assume or cause to assume sloping position. ● *n.* sloping position. □ **at full tilt** at full speed or force.

**timber** *n.* wood for building, carpentry, etc.; trees suitable for this.

**timbered** *adj.* 1 made (partly) of timber. 2 (of country) wooded.

**timbre** *n.* distinctive character of musical sound or voice apart from its pitch and volume.

**time** ● *n.* 1 indefinite continued progress of existence, events, etc., in past, present, and future; period of this; point of time, esp. in hours and minutes; an occasion. 2 rhythm in music. 3 (**times**) expressing multiplication. ● *v.* 1 choose the time for, do at chosen or appropriate time. 2 ascertain time taken by. □ **behind the times** out of date. **for the time being** for the present. **in time** 1 not late. 2 eventually.

**timeless** *adj.* not affected by passage of time. □□ **timelessness** *n.*

**timely** *adj.* (**timelier**) coming at just the right time. □□ **timeliness** *n.*

**timetable** *n.* list of times at which events are scheduled to take place.

**timid** *adj.* lacking courage or confidence. □□ **timidity** *n.* **timidly** *adv.*

**timing** *n.* 1 way something is timed. 2 regulation of opening and closing of valves in internal combustion engine.

**timorous** *adj.* timid. □□ **timorously** *adv.*

**timpani** *n.pl.* (also **tympani**) kettledrums. □□ **timpanist** *n.*

**tin** ● *n.* 1 metallic element (symbol Sn). 2 silvery-white metal used esp. in alloys and in making tin plate. 3 (metal etc.) container, esp. for preserving food. □□ ● *v.* (**tinned**) 1 preserve (food) in tin. 2 cover or coat with tin.

**tincture** *n.* 1 slight flavour or tinge. 2 medicinal solution of drug in alcohol.

**tinder** *n.* dry substance readily catching fire from spark.

**tine** *n.* prong, tooth, or point of fork, comb, antler, etc.

**tinea** *n.* fungal disease of skin.

**tinge** ● *v.* (**tinged**, **tingeing**) colour slightly; give slight trace of element or quality to. ● *n.* slight colouring or trace.

**tingle** ● *v.* feel or cause slight pricking or stinging sensation. ● *n.* tingling sensation.

**tinker** ● *n.* itinerant mender of kettles and pans etc. ● *v.* work in amateurish or desultory way.

**tinkle** ● *v.* 1 (cause to) make short light ringing sounds. 2 *colloq.* urinate. ● *n.* tinkling sound.

**tinnitus** *n.* repeated ringing or other sounds in ears.

**tinny ●** *n.* (also **tinnie**) *Aust. colloq.* **1** can of beer; its contents. **2** small aluminium boat, usu. with outboard motor. **●** *adj.* (**tinnier**) **1** (of sound) thin and metallic. **2** *Aust. colloq.* lucky.

**tinsel** *n.* glittering decorative metallic strips, threads, etc. □□ **tinselled** *adj.*

**tint ●** *n.* a variety or slight trace of a colour. **●** *v.* **1** colour slightly. **2** apply polyester film to glass etc.

**tiny** *adj.* (**tinier**) very small.

**tip** *n.* **1** small money present. **2** useful piece of advice. **3** the end of something small or tapering. **4** place where rubbish etc. is tipped.

**●** *v.* (**tipped**) **1** tilt, topple; pour out (thing's contents) by tilting. **2** make small present of money to, esp. in acknowledgement of services. **3** name as likely winner. **4** put substance on end of (something small or tapering). □ **tip off** give warning or hint to.

**tipple** *v.* drink intoxicating liquor habitually or repeatedly in small quantities. □□ **tippler** *n.*

**tipster** *n.* person who gives tips about horseracing.

**tipsy** *adj.* (**tipsier**) slightly drunk.

**tiptoe** *v.* (**tiptoed, tiptoeing**) walk very quietly or carefully.

**tiptop** *adj. colloq.* first-rate.

**tirade** *n.* long vehement denunciation or declamation.

**tire** *v.* make or grow weary.

**tired** *adj.* ready for sleep or rest. □ **tired of** having had enough of; bored or impatient with.

**tireless** *adj.* not tiring easily, energetic. □□ **tirelessly** *adv.* **tirelessness** *n.*

**tiresome** *adj.* tedious; annoying. □□ **tiresomely** *adv.*

**tiro** *n.* = TYRO.

**tissue** *n.* **1** any of the coherent collections of cells of which animals

or plants are made. **2** tissue paper; disposable piece of thin absorbent paper for wiping, drying, etc. □ **tissue paper** thin soft paper used for packing things.

**tit** *n.* **1** any of various small birds. **2** *colloq.* breast. □ **tit for tat** blow for blow.

**titanic** *adj.* gigantic, colossal.

**titanium** *n.* grey metallic element (symbol Ti).

**titbit** *n.* small choice bit of tasty food; interesting item of information.

**tithe** *n.* one-tenth of annual produce of land or labour, formerly taken as tax for Church; (in some denominations) tenth of an individual's income pledged to Church.

**titian** *adj.* (of hair) bright auburn.

**titillate** *v.* excite or stimulate, esp. sexually. □□ **titillation** *n.*

**titivate** *v. colloq.* smarten up; put finishing touches to. □□ **titivation** *n.*

**title** *n.* **1** name of book, poem, picture, etc. **2** name indicating person's status. **3** championship in sport. **4** legal right to ownership of property. □ **title deed** legal document as evidence of right, esp. to property. **title role** character in a play etc. that gives it its name.

**ti-tree** = *tea tree.*

**titter ●** *v.* laugh covertly, giggle. **●** *n.* furtive or restrained laugh.

**tittle-tattle** *n.* & *v.* gossip, chatter.

**titular** *adj.* of or relating to title; existing or being, in name or title only.

**tizz** *n. colloq.* state of nervous agitation.

**tizzy** *adj.* gaudy, showy, in bad taste.

**tjukurpa** *n. Aust.* = DREAMING.

**T-junction** *n.* junction where one road meets another at right angles but does not cross it.

**tjuringa** *n. Aust.* = CHURINGA.

**TLC** *abbr. colloq.* tender loving care.

**TNT** *abbr.* trinitrotoluene, powerful explosive.

**to** • *prep.* **1** towards; as far as. **2** as compared with, in respect of. **3** for (person or thing) to hold or possess or be affected by. **4** (with verb) forming infinitive, or expressing purpose or consequence etc.; used alone when the infinitive is understood. • *adv.* **1** to a closed position. **2** into a state of consciousness or activity. □ **to and fro** backwards and forwards. □ **to-do** fuss or commotion.

**toa** *n. Aust.* Aboriginal direction marker.

**toad** *n.* froglike amphibian living chiefly on land.

**toadstool** *n.* mushroom-like fungus, often poisonous.

**toady** • *n.* sycophant. • *v.* behave servilely. □□ **toadyism** *n.*

**toast** • *n.* **1** sliced bread browned on both sides by radiant heat. **2** person or thing in whose honour company is requested to drink; call to drink or instance of drinking thus. • *v.* **1** brown by radiant heat. **2** drink to the health or in honour of.

**toaster** *n.* electrical device for making toast.

**tobacco** *n.* plant with leaves used for smoking, chewing, or snuff; its leaves, esp. as prepared for smoking.

**tobacconist** *n.* dealer in tobacco.

**toboggan** *n.* long light narrow sledge for sliding downhill over snow or ice. □□ **tobogganing** *n.*

**tocsin** *n.* alarm bell or signal.

**today** *adv. & n.* **1** (on) this present day; (at) the present time.

**toddle** *v.* walk with young child's short unsteady steps.

**toddler** *n.* child just learning to walk.

**toddy** *n.* sweetened drink of spirits and hot water.

**toe** • *n.* any of the divisions (five in humans) of the front part of the foot; part of footwear that covers toes. • *v.* touch with toe(s). □ **be on**

one's toes be alert or eager. **toe the line** conform, esp. unwillingly, to general policy or principle.

**toehold** *n.* **1** small foothold. **2** small beginning or advantage.

**toey** *adj. Aust. colloq.* **1** restless, nervous, touchy. **2** sexually aroused.

**toff** *n. colloq.* person of wealth and social prestige.

**toffee** *n.* firm or hard sweet made of boiled sugar, butter, etc.

**tofu** *n.* curd of mashed soybeans.

**toga** *n. hist.* ancient Roman citizen's loose flowing outer garment.

**together** • *adv.* **1** in(to) company or conjunction; towards each other. **2** simultaneously. • *adj. colloq.* **1** well-organised. **2** self-assured. □□ **togetherness** *n.*

**toggle** *n.* **1** short bar used like button for fastening clothes. **2** *Computing* key or command that alternately switches function on and off.

**togs** *n.pl. colloq.* **1** *Aust.* swimming costume. **2** clothes.

**toil** • *v.* work laboriously or incessantly. • *n.* laborious work. □□ **toilsome** *adj.*

**toilet** *n.* **1** large receptacle for urine and faeces. **2** process of washing oneself, dressing, etc. □ **toilet water** light perfume.

**toiletries** *n.pl.* articles or cosmetics used in washing, dressing, etc.

**token** *n.* **1** symbol, reminder, mark. **2** voucher; thing equivalent to something else, esp. money. • *adj.* nominal, symbolic.

**tokenism** *n.* granting of minimum concessions, esp. to minority groups.

**told** see TELL. □ **all told** counting everyone and everything.

**tolerable** *adj.* **1** endurable. **2** fairly good. □□ **tolerably** *adv.*

**tolerance** *n.* **1** willingness or ability to tolerate. **2** permitted variation in dimension, weight, etc. □□ **tolerant** *adj.* **tolerantly** *adv.*

**tolerate** v. permit without protest or interference; endure.□□ **toleration** n.

**toll** ● n. **1** charge to use bridge, road, etc. **2** cost or damage caused by disaster etc. **3** a stroke of a tolling bell. ● v. ring with slow strokes, esp. to mark a death.

**toluene** n. colourless liquid hydrocarbon, used in manufacture of explosives etc.

**tom** n. (in full **tomcat**) male cat.

**tomahawk** n. light axe formerly used by some inhabitants of N. Americans as weapon.

**tomato** n. (pl. **tomatoes**) red or yellow fleshy fruit used as vegetable.

**tomb** n. grave or other place of burial.

**tomboy** n. girl who enjoys activities conventionally associated with boys.
□□ **tomboyish** adj.

**tome** n. large book or volume.

**tomfoolery** n. foolish behaviour.

**tommy rough** n. Australian marine fish.

**tomography** n. method of radiography displaying details in selected plane within body.

**tomorrow** adv. & n. (on) the day after today; (in) the near future.

**tomtit** n. small Australian bird.

**tom-tom** n. medium-sized cylindrical drum, of which one to three may be used in drum kit.

**ton** n. (in full **long ton**) imperial unit of weight equalling 2240 lb. (1016.05 kg); (in full **short ton**) unit of weight, esp. in US, equalling 2000 lb. (907.19 kg); **tonne**; unit of volume in shipping; colloq. great weight or large number.

**tone** ● n. **1** musical or vocal sound, esp. with reference to pitch, quality, and strength; expression of feeling or mood; general character of event or place. **2** tint or shade of colour. **3** proper firmness of body. ● v. **1** give desired tone to. **2** (esp. of colour) be in harmony with.□ **tone-deaf** unable to perceive differences of musical

pitch accurately.□□ **tonal** adj. **tonality** n.

**toneless** adj. without positive tone, not expressive.□□ **tonelessly** adv.

**toner** n. **1** cosmetic for toning skin. **2** powder used in photocopier, laser printer, etc.

**tongs** n.pl. implement with two arms for grasping pieces of food etc.

**tongue** n. **1** muscular organ in mouth used in tasting, swallowing, speaking, etc.; tongue of ox etc. as food. **2** language. **3** thing like tongue in shape.□ **tongue-in-cheek** ironic, with humorous intent. **tongue-tied** too shy to speak. **tongue-twister** sequence of words difficult to pronounce quickly and correctly.

**tonic** ● n. **1** invigorating medicine. **2** tonic water. **3** Mus. keynote. ● adj. invigorating.□ **tonic water** carbonated mineral water containing quinine.

**tonic sol-fa** n. system of representing notes of musical scale by syllables doh, ray, me, etc.

**tonight** adv. & n. (on) the present or approaching evening or night.

**tonnage** n. ship's internal cubic capacity or freight-carrying capacity; charge per ton on freight or cargo.

**tonne** n. (also **metric ton**) 1000 kilograms.

**tonsil** n. either of two small organs on each side of root of tongue.

**tonsillitis** n. inflammation of tonsils.

**tonsure** n. shaving top or all of head as religious symbol; this shaven area. □□ **tonsured** adj.

**too** adv. **1** to a greater extent than is desirable or permissible; colloq. very. **2** also.

**took** see TAKE.

**tool** ● n. implement for working on something; thing used in activity; person used or exploited by another; Computing piece of software that carries out a particular function.

● v. **1** shape or ornament with tool.
**2** equip with tools.

**toolbar** n. *Computing* strip of icons used to perform certain functions.

**toot** ● n. short sharp sound as made by horn or whistle etc. ● v. make or cause to make toot.

**tooth** n. (pl. **teeth**) each of set of hard structures in jaws of most vertebrates, used for biting and chewing; toothlike part or projection, e.g. cog of gearwheel, point of saw or comb, etc. □□ **toothed** adj.

**toothpaste** n. paste for cleaning teeth.

**toothpick** n. small pointed instrument for removing food from between teeth.

**toothy** adj. (**toothier**) having or showing large, numerous, or prominent teeth.

**top** ● n. **1** highest point or part; highest rank or place, person occupying this; upper end, head; upper surface, upper part. **2** cover or cap of container etc. **3** garment for upper part of body. **4** toy spinning on point when set in motion. ● adj. highest in position, degree, or importance; greatest in amount; *colloq.* excellent, first-rate.
● v. (**topped**) **1** provide or be the top of; reach the top of; be higher than. **2** add as final thing. **3** remove the top of.□ **on top of** in addition to. **top dog** a victor or master. **top dress** apply fertiliser on the top of (earth). **top hat** man's tall hat with high cylindrical crown. **top-heavy** in danger of falling over because excessively heavy at top. **top-notch** *colloq.* first-rate. **top secret** of highest secrecy. **top up** fill up (partly full container etc.)
□□ **topmost** adj.

**topaz** n. semi-precious transparent stone, usu. yellow.

**topiary** n. art of clipping shrubs, trees, etc. into ornamental shapes.

**topic** n. subject of discourse, conversation, or argument.

**topical** adj. dealing with current affairs etc.□□ **topicality** n. **topically** adv.

**topless** adj. without a top; (of garment) leaving breasts bare.

**topography** n. detailed description, representation, etc. of features of district.□□ **topographer** n. **topographical** adj.

**topology** n. study of geometrical properties unaffected by change of shape or size.□□ **topological** adj.

**topping** n. thing that tops, esp. sauce on dessert etc.

**topple** v. (cause to) overbalance and fall.

**topside** n. outer side of round of beef.

**topsoil** n. top layer of soil.

**topspin** n. fast forward spinning motion given to ball by hitting it forward and upward.

**topsy-turvy** adv. & adj. **1** upside down. **2** in utter confusion.

**tor** n. hill, rocky peak.

**torch** n. battery-powered portable lamp; burning piece of wood etc. carried as a light.

**tore** see TEAR¹.

**toreador** n. bullfighter.

**torment** ● n. (cause of) severe physical or mental suffering.
● v. subject to torment; tease or annoy.□□ **tormentor** n.

**torn** see TEAR¹.

**tornado** n. (pl. **tornadoes**) violent destructive whirlwind.

**torpedo** ● n. (pl. **torpedoes**) self-propelled explosive underwater missile. ● v. destroy or attack with torpedo; make ineffective.

**torpid** adj. sluggish and inactive.
□□ **torpidity** n.

**torpor** n. torpid condition.

**torque** n. twisting or rotating force.

**Torrens system** n. (also **Torrens title**) system of land ownership in which

**title** to land derives from registration of documents by public official.

**torrent** n. fast and powerful stream of water etc.; outpouring; copious flow. □□ **torrential** adj.

**torrid** adj. intensely hot and dry; passionate.

**torsion** n. twisting; being twisted.

**torso** n. (pl. **torsos**) trunk of human body.

**tort** n. Law any private or civil wrong (other than breach of contract) for which damages may be claimed.

**tortilla** n. thin flat Mexican maize cake eaten hot.

**tortoise** n. slow-moving reptile with horny domed shell.

**tortoiseshell** n. mottled yellowish brown shell of certain turtles, used for making combs etc.

**tortuous** adj. full of twists and turns; excessively lengthy and complex. □□ **tortuously** adv.

**torture** ● n. infliction of severe bodily pain, esp. as punishment or means of persuasion; severe physical or mental suffering. ● v. 1 subject to torture. 2 twist, deform (words, language, etc.) □□ **torturer** n. **torturous** adj.

**toss** ● v. throw lightly or carelessly; throw (coin) into air to decide choice etc. by way it falls; (of horse etc.) throw (rider) off its back; coat (food) with dressing etc. by shaking it. ● n. tossing. □ **toss off 1** drink rapidly; compose or finish rapidly. 2 coarse colloq. masturbate.

**tot** n. 1 small child. 2 dram of liquor. □ **tot up** colloq. add up.

**total** ● adj. 1 complete, comprising the whole. 2 absolute, unqualified. ● n. whole sum or amount. ● v. (**totalled**) 1 calculate total of; amount to. 2 colloq. wreck completely. □□ **totality** n.

**totalisator** n. (also **totalizator**) device showing the number and amount of bets staked on race when total will be divided among those betting on winner(s).

**totalitarian** adj. of one-party government requiring complete subservience to the state. □□ **totalitarianism** n.

**totally** adv. 1 completely; absolutely. 2 colloq. used to emphasise a clause or statement; used to express agreement.

**tote** colloq. ● n. totalisator. ● v. carry.

**totem** n. natural object adopted as tribal emblem.

**totter** ● v. stand or walk unsteadily or feebly. ● n. unsteady or shaky movement or gait. □□ **tottery** adj.

**toucan** n. tropical American bird with large bill.

**touch** ● v. 1 be, come, or bring into contact; feel or stroke; press or strike lightly. 2 reach; affect; rouse sympathy in. 3 colloq. persuade to give or lend money. ● n. 1 an act, fact, or manner of touching; ability to perceive things through touching them. 2 manner of dealing with something. 3 a detail; a slight trace. 4 Rugby part of field outside touchlines. 5 touch football. □ **touch down** touch ball on ground behind goal line in rugby; (of aircraft) land. **touch football** variation of football with touching in place of tackling. **touch on** mention briefly. **touch up 1** improve by making small additions. 2 colloq. molest; touch sexually.

**touché** int. acknowledgement of valid criticism, or of hit in fencing.

**touching** ● adj. moving; rousing pity etc. ● prep. concerning.

**touchline** n. (in various sports) either of the lines marking side boundaries of playing field.

**touchpad** n. computer input device in the form of small panel containing different touch-sensitive areas.

**touchscreen** n. display device that allows user to interact with computer by touching areas on screen.

**touchstone** n. standard or criterion.

**touchy** adj. (**touchier**) apt to take offence; over-sensitive. □□ **touchily** adv. **touchiness** n.

**tough** ● adj. **1** hard to break, cut, tear, or chew; hardy; unyielding; resolute. **2** difficult, severe; unpleasant. ● n. rough violent person. □□ **toughen** v. **toughness** n.

**toupee** n. small wig.

**tour** ● n. journey visiting things of interest or giving performances. ● v. make tour (of).

**tour de force** n. (pl. **tours de force**) outstanding feat or performance.

**tourism** n. commercial organisation and operation of holidays.

**tourist** n. **1** holiday traveller. **2** member of touring sports team.

**tourmaline** n. mineral with unusual electric properties used as gemstone.

**tournament** n. large contest of many rounds.

**tourniquet** n. device for stopping flow of blood through artery by compression.

**tousle** v. make (esp. hair) untidy.

**tout** ● v. **1** try to sell; solicit (votes, support); pester customers. **2** spy on (racehorses in training). ● n. person who touts.

**tow** ● v. pull along by rope etc. ● n. **1** towing; being towed. **2** coarse part of flax or hemp prepared for spinning.

**towards** prep. (also **toward**) **1** in the direction of. **2** as regards, in relation to. **3** as contribution to, for. **4** near.

**towel** ● n. absorbent cloth, paper, etc. for drying things. ● v. (**towelled**) **1** wipe or dry with towel. **2** colloq. thrash or beat (person).

**towelling** n. **1** thick soft absorbent cloth, used esp. for towels. **2** colloq. thrashing.

**tower** ● n. tall narrow building; tall structure housing machinery etc. ● v. be very tall.

**town** n. **1** large collection of houses, shops, etc.; its inhabitants; Aust. any small cluster of dwellings and other buildings recognised as distinct place. **2** central business or shopping area. □ **town hall** building for administration of local government.

**toxaemia** n. (also **toxemia**) **1** blood poisoning. **2** increased blood pressure in pregnancy.

**toxic** adj. **1** of or caused by poison; very bad, unpleasant, or harmful. **2** of debt that has a high risk of default. □□ **toxicity** n.

**toxicology** n. study of poisons. □□ **toxicologist** n.

**toxin** n. poison produced by living organism.

**toy** ● n. **1** plaything. **2** diminutive breed of dog etc. □ **toy with** handle idly; deal with (thing) without seriousness.

**toyboy** n. colloq. person's much younger male lover.

**trace** ● v. **1** find signs of by investigation. **2** follow or mark track, position, or path of. **3** copy (drawing etc.) by marking its lines on superimposed translucent paper; give outline of. ● n. **1** indication of existence of something. **2** vestige; very small quantity. **3** track, footprint. **4** each of two side straps, chains, or ropes, by which horse draws vehicle. □□ **traceable** adj.

**tracery** n. decorative pattern of interlacing lines, esp. in stone.

**trachea** n. (pl. **tracheae** or **tracheas**) windpipe.

**tracheotomy** n. incision of trachea to relieve obstruction.

**trachoma** n. contagious eye disease with inflamed granulation on inner surface of lids.

**track** ● n. **1** marks left by moving person or thing. **2** course, path, rough

road; railway line. **3** recording of one song or piece of music. **4** continuous band around wheels of tank, tractor, etc. **5** strip carrying sliding fittings from which curtain is hung.
● *v.* follow track of; find or observe in this way. □ **keep** (or **lose**) **track of** fail to keep oneself informed about. **track pants** loose warm pull-on trousers. □□ **tracker** *n.*

**trackie daks** *n.pl. Aust. colloq.* track pants.

**tracksuit** *n.* loose warm set of trousers and top worn for exercise or casual wear.

**tract** *n.* **1** stretch of land. **2** system of connected parts of the body, along which something passes. **3** pamphlet with short essay, esp. on religious subject.

**tractable** *adj.* easy to deal with or control, docile. □□ **tractability** *n.*

**traction** *n.* **1** hauling, pulling. **2** grip of tyre on road, wheel on rail, etc. **3** the use of weights etc. to exert a steady pull on an injured limb etc. **4** extent to which idea, product, etc. gains popularity or acceptance.

**tractor** *n.* vehicle for pulling farm machinery etc.

**trad** *adj. colloq.* traditional.

**trade** ● *n.* **1** buying and selling; this between nations etc.; exchanging. **2** job requiring particular skill; people engaged in this. ● *v.* engage in trade; buy and sell; exchange. □ **trade deficit** extent by which country's imports exceed its exports. **trade in** exchange (used article) as part payment for another. **trade off** exchange as compromise. **trade on** take advantage of. **trade union** organised association of workers formed to protect and promote their rights and interests. □□ **trader** *n.*

**trademark** *n.* (also **trade mark**) company's registered emblem or name etc. used to identify its products.

**tradesman** *n.* male tradesperson.

**tradesperson** *n.* person engaged in trading or a trade.

**tradeswoman** *n.* female tradesperson.

**tradie** *n. Aust. colloq.* tradesperson.

**tradition** *n.* custom, opinion, or belief handed down to posterity; long established procedure.

**traditional** *adj.* of, based, or obtained by tradition; long-established; habitually done, used, or found; (of person or group) adhering to tradition, or to a particular tradition; (of jazz) in style of early 20th century. □ **traditional owner** *Aust.* Aboriginal person who is member of local descent group having certain rights etc. in relation to a tract of land or area of sea. □□ **traditionally** *adv.*

**traduce** *v.* slander. □□ **traducement** *n.*

**traffic** ● *n.* **1** vehicles, ships, or aircraft moving along a route. **2** trading. ● *v.* (**trafficked**, **trafficking**) deal, esp. illegally. □□ **trafficker** *n.*

**trag** *n. Aust.* = TERAGLIN.

**tragedian** *n.* writer of tragedies; actor in tragedy.

**tragedienne** *n.* woman who acts in tragedy.

**tragedy** *n.* serious accident, sad event; play with tragic unhappy ending.

**tragic** ● *adj.* of or in tragedy; causing great sadness. ● *n. colloq.* person devoted to specified activity, interest, etc. □□ **tragically** *adv.*

**tragicomedy** *n.* drama or event combining comedy and tragedy. □□ **tragicomic** *adj.*

**trail** ● *n.* **1** track left by moving thing, person, etc. **2** beaten path, esp. through wild region. **3** long line of people or things following behind something. **4** part dragging behind thing or person. ● *v.* **1** draw or be drawn along behind; move slowly, lag behind. **2** track. **3** hang loosely.

**trailer** *n.* **1** set of extracts from film etc. shown in advance to advertise it. **2** vehicle pulled by another.

**train** ● *v.* **1** teach (person etc.) specified skill, esp. by practice; undergo this process; bring or come to physical efficiency by exercise, diet, etc. **2** guide growth of (plant). **3** point, aim. ● *n.* **1** series of railway carriages etc. drawn by engine. **2** thing dragged along behind or forming back part of dress etc. **3** succession or series of people, things, events, etc.; retinue. □ **in train** in preparation. □□ **trainee** *n.*

**trainer** *n.* **1** person who trains horses, athletes, etc. **2** (**trainers**) soft running shoes.

**traipse** *v. colloq.* tramp or trudge wearily.

**trait** *n.* characteristic.

**traitor** *n.* person guilty of betrayal or disloyalty. □□ **traitorous** *adj.*

**trajectory** *n.* path of object moving under given forces.

**tram** *n.* electrically-powered passenger road vehicle running on rails.

**tramlines** *n.pl.* **1** rails for tram. **2** *colloq.* pair of parallel lines, sidelines in tennis etc.

**trammel** *v.* (**trammelled**) hamper.

**tramp** ● *v.* **1** walk heavily and firmly; go on walking expedition; trample. ● *n.* **1** itinerant vagrant or beggar. **2** sound of person or people walking or marching. **3** long walk. **4** *derog.* promiscuous woman.

**trample** *v.* tread under foot; crush thus.

**trampoline** ● *n.* strong fabric sheet connected by springs to horizontal frame, used by gymnasts, children, etc. ● *v.* use trampoline.

**trance** *n.* sleeplike or dreamy state.

**trannie** *n.* (also **tranny**) *colloq.* **1** transistor radio. **2** *offens.* transvestite; transexual.

**tranquil** *adj.* calm, serene, undisturbed. □□ **tranquillity** *n.* **tranquilly** *adv.*

**tranquillise** *v.* (also **-ize**) make tranquil, esp. by drug etc.

**tranquilliser** *n.* (also **-izer**) drug used to diminish anxiety.

**trans** *adj.* transsexual; transgender.

**trans-** *prefix* **1** across, beyond; on or to the other side; into another state or place; surpassing. **2** transgender.

**transact** *v.* perform or carry through (business etc.) □□ **transaction** *n.*

**transceiver** *n.* combined radio transmitter and receiver.

**transcend** *v.* be beyond or exceed limits of; excel; surpass. □□ **transcendent** *adj.* **transcendence** *n.*

**transcendental** *adj.* transcending human experience; of spiritual realm; mystical. □□ **transcendentally** *adv.*

**transcontinental** *adj.* extending across continent.

**transcribe** *v.* copy out; write out (notes etc.) in full; arrange (music) for another instrument etc. □□ **transcription** *n.*

**transcript** *n.* written copy.

**transducer** *n.* device for changing non-electrical signal (e.g. pressure) into electrical one (e.g. voltage).

**transept** *n.* part of cross-shaped church at right angles to nave.

**transfer** ● *v.* (**transferred**) move from one place, position, person, route, etc., to another. ● *n.* **1** transferring, being transferred; design etc. (to be) conveyed from one surface to another; document effecting conveyance of property, right, etc. □□ **transferable** *adj.* **transference** *n.*

**transfigure** v. change appearance of, make more elevated or idealised. □□ transfiguration n.

**transfix** v. 1 paralyse with horror or astonishment. 2 pierce with sharp implement or weapon.

**transform** v. change form, appearance, character, etc. of, esp. considerably; change voltage etc. of (alternating current). □□ transformation n.

**transformer** n. apparatus for reducing or increasing voltage of alternating current.

**transfuse** v. 1 transfer (blood or other liquid) into blood vessel to replace that lost. 2 permeate, imbue. □□ transfusion n.

**transgender** adj. of person whose sense of personal identity and gender does not correspond with their birth sex.

**transgenic** adj. (of organism) having genetic material artificially introduced from another species.

**transgress** v. break (rule or law). □□ transgression n. transgressor n.

**transient** adj. 1 of short duration. 2 passing quickly. □□ transience n.

**transistor** n. semiconductor device capable of amplification and rectification; (in full transistor radio) portable radio using transistors.

**transit** n. process of going or conveying across, over, or through.

**transition** n. passing or change from one place, state, condition, style, etc. to another. □□ transitional adj.

**transitive** adj. Gram. (of verb) requiring direct object expressed or understood.

**transitory** adj. brief, fleeting.

**translate** v. 1 express sense of in another language or in another form; be translatable. 2 transfer. □□ translatable adj. translation n.

**transliterate** v. convert to letters of another alphabet. □□ transliteration n.

**translucent** adj. allowing light to pass through; semi-transparent. □□ translucence n.

**transmigrate** v. 1 (of soul) pass into different body. 2 migrate. □□ transmigration n.

**transmission** n. 1 transmitting, being transmitted; broadcast program. 2 device transmitting power from engine to axle in vehicle.

**transmit** v. (transmitted) 1 pass or hand on; transfer. 2 communicate or be medium for (ideas, emotions, etc.) 3 allow (heat, light, sound, etc.) to pass through. □□ transmissible adj. transmittable adj. transmitter n.

**transmogrify** v. transform, esp. in magical or surprising way. □□ transmogrification n.

**transmute** v. change form, nature, or substance of. □□ transmutation n.

**transom** n. 1 horizontal bar in window or above door. 2 flat surface forming stern of boat.

**transparency** n. 1 condition of being transparent. 2 photographic slide.

**transparent** adj. 1 allowing light to pass through and giving maximum visibility possible. 2 easily understood. □□ transparently adv.

**transpire** v. 1 come to be known; happen. 2 emit (vapour, moisture) or be emitted through pores of skin, etc. □□ transpiration n.

**transplant** ● v. plant elsewhere; transfer (living tissue or organ) to another part of body or to another body. ● n. transplanting of organ or tissue; thing transplanted. □□ transplantation n.

**transport** ● v. 1 take to another place. 2 hist. deport (person sentenced in British Isles) to penal

colony in Australia. ● n. 1 process of transporting; means of conveyance. 2 (transports) strong emotion (transports of delight). 3 hist. person sentenced in British Isles to penal servitude in Australia.
□□ transportable adj.

**transportation** n. hist. deportation from British Isles to penal colony in Australia.

**transpose** v. 1 cause (two or more things) to change places; change position of (thing). 2 Mus. write or play in different key.
□□ transposition n.

**transsexual** n. (also transexual) person who emotionally and psychologically feels that they belong to opposite sex; person who has undergone physical treatment to acquire physical characteristics of opposite sex.

**transsubstantiation** n. doctrine that the bread and wine in the Eucharist are converted by consecration into the body and blood of Christ.

**transuranic** adj. having atoms heavier than those of uranium.

**transversal** adj. Math. (of a line) intersecting a set of two or more lines.

**transverse** adj. situated or extending across something.□□ transversely adv.

**transvestite** n. person deriving pleasure from dressing in clothes of opposite sex.□□ transvestism n.

**trap** ● n. 1 device, often baited, for catching animals; arrangement or trick to catch out unsuspecting person. 2 device for releasing clay pigeon, to be shot at. 3 curve in drainpipe etc. that fills with liquid and forms seal against return of gas. 4 two-wheeled carriage. 5 trapdoor. 6 Golf bunker. 7 colloq. mouth. ● v. (trapped) catch or hold in trap.

**trapdoor** n. door in floor, ceiling, or roof.

**trapeze** n. crossbar suspended by ropes as swing for acrobatics etc.; similar device enabling person to lean safely out of small sailing boat.

**trapezium** n. (pl. trapezia or trapeziums) quadrilateral with only one pair of sides parallel.

**trapezoid** n. quadrilateral with no two sides parallel.

**trapper** n. person who traps wild animals, esp. for their fur.

**trappings** n.pl. accessories; symbols of status.

**traps** n.pl. colloq. personal belongings.

**trash** n. worthless or waste stuff.
□□ trashy adj.

**trattoria** n. Italian restaurant.

**trauma** n. emotional shock; physical injury.□□ traumatic adj. traumatise v.

**travail** n. & v. labour.

**travel** ● v. (travelled) go from one place to another; journey along or through. ● n. travelling, esp. abroad.

**traveller** n. person who travels or is travelling.□ traveller's cheque cheque for fixed amount, able to be cashed in another country.

**travelogue** n. book, film, etc. about travel.

**traverse** ● v. 1 travel or lie across. 2 consider or discuss whole extent of. ● n. 1 sideways movement. 2 thing that crosses another.
□□ traversal n.

**travesty** ● n. grotesque parody, ridiculous imitation. ● v. make or be travesty of.

**trawl** ● n. large wide-mouthed fishing net. ● v. fish with trawl.

**trawler** n. boat used for trawling.

**tray** n. flat board with rim for carrying dishes etc.; open receptacle for office papers etc.; flat open part of truck on which goods are carried.

**treacherous** adj. guilty of or involving violation of faith or betrayal of trust; not to be relied on; deceptive. □□ **treacherously** adv.

**treachery** n. betrayal of a person or cause; an act of disloyalty.

**treacle** n. **1** syrup produced in refining sugar; molasses. **2** golden syrup. **3** cloying sentimentality. □□ **treacly** adj.

**tread** ● v. (**trod**, **trodden**, **treading**) set down one's foot; walk; walk on (road etc.); press down or crush with feet. ● n. **1** manner or sound of walking. **2** top surface of step or stair. **3** thick moulded part of vehicle tyre for gripping road; part of wheel or sole of shoe that touches ground. □ **tread water** keep upright in deep water by making treading movements.

**treadle** n. lever moved by foot and imparting motion to machine.

**treadmill** n. **1** a mill wheel formerly turned by people treading on steps round its edge. **2** monotonous routine work.

**treason** n. treachery to one's country.

**treasonable** adj. involving or guilty of treason.

**treasure** ● n. **1** precious metals or gems; hoard of these; accumulated wealth. **2** highly valued person or thing. ● v. value highly; store up as valuable. □ **treasure trove** treasure of unknown ownership, found hidden; collection of valuable or delightful things.

**treasurer** n. **1** person in charge of funds of society etc. **2** (**Treasurer**) minister responsible for the Treasury.

**treasury** n. **1** place where treasure is kept. **2** (**Treasury**) (offices and officers of) department managing public revenue of country.

**treat** ● v. **1** act, behave towards, or deal with in certain way; apply process or medical care or attention to. **2** provide with food, entertainment, etc., at one's own expense. ● n. something special that gives pleasure. □□ **treatable** adj.

**treatise** n. written work dealing esp. formally with subject.

**treatment** n. **1** process or manner of behaving towards or dealing with person or thing. **2** medical care or attention.

**treaty** n. formal agreement esp. between nations or peoples.

**treble** ● adj. **1** three times as much or many. **2** high-pitched. ● n. **1** treble quantity or thing. **2** high-pitched voice; person with this. **3** high-pitched instrument. **4** high-frequency sound of radio, stereo, etc. ● v. multiply or be multiplied by three. □□ **trebly** adv.

**tree** n. perennial plant with thick woody stem. □ **tree change** Aust. colloq. significant change in lifestyle, esp. by moving from city to country town.

**trefoil** n. plant with leaves of three leaflets, e.g. clover; something shaped like this.

**trek** ● v. (**trekked**) make arduous journey, esp. on foot. ● n. such journey. □□ **trekker** n.

**trellis** n. lattice of light wooden or metal bars, esp. as support for climbing plants.

**tremble** ● v. shake involuntarily from emotion, cold, etc.; be affected by extreme apprehension; quiver. ● n. trembling, quiver. □□ **trembly** adj.

**tremendous** adj. colloq. excellent; immense. □□ **tremendously** adv.

**tremolo** n. (pl. **tremolos**) **1** tremulous effect in music. **2** device in organ or on electric guitar used to produce tremolo.

**tremor** *n.* shaking, quivering; thrill (of fear, exultation, etc.).

**tremulous** *adj.* trembling.
□□ **tremulously** *adv.*

**trench** *n.* deep ditch.

**trenchant** *adj.* incisive, terse, vigorous.

**trend** ● *n.* general direction and tendency; a fashion. ● *v.* 1 change or develop in a general direction. 2 (of a topic) be the subject of many posts on social media within short period of time.

**trendy** ● *adj.* (**trendier**) following the latest fashion. ● *n.* self-consciously fashionable person.
□□ **trendily** *adv.* **trendiness** *n.*

**trepidation** *n.* fear, anxiety.

**trespass** ● *v.* enter unlawfully (on another's land, property, etc.); encroach. ● *n.* act of trespassing.
□□ **trespasser** *n.*

**tress** *n.* lock of hair.

**trestle** *n.* one of a set of supports on which a board is rested to form a table.

**trevally** *n. Aust.* marine food fish.

**tri-** *comb. form* three (times).

**triad** *n.* group of three (esp. notes in chord); Chinese secret society, usu. criminal.

**triage** *n.* act of sorting according to quality; assignment of priorities in treatment of wounds, illnesses, etc.

**trial** ● *n.* 1 judicial examination and determination of issues between parties by judge with or without jury. 2 trying thing or person. 3 test of quality, ability, performance, etc. ● *v.* test (something) to assess its suitability or performance.

**triangle** *n.* geometric figure with three sides and angles; any three things not in straight line, with imaginary lines joining them; musical instrument of steel rod bent into triangle, struck with small steel rod.

**triangular** *adj.* 1 shaped like a triangle. 2 involving three people.

**triangulation** *n.* measurement or mapping of area by means of network of triangles.

**triantelope** *n. Aust.* = HUNTSMAN.

**triathlon** *n.* athletic contest of three events.

**tribe** *n.* 1 group of families under recognised leader with blood etc. ties and usu. having common culture and dialect. 2 *Aust.* name applied to traditional Aboriginal community.
□□ **tribal** *adj.*

**tribulation** *n.* great affliction.

**tribunal** *n.* 1 a board appointed to adjudicate on particular question. 2 court of justice.

**tributary** *n. & adj.* (river) flowing into larger river or lake.

**tribute** *n.* 1 thing said or done or given as mark of respect or affection etc. 2 indication of (some praiseworthy quality). 3 *hist.* periodic payment by one nation or ruler to another; obligation to pay this.

**trice** *n.* □ **in a trice** in an instant.

**triceps** *n.* muscle (esp. in upper arm) with three points of attachment.

**triceratops** *n.* dinosaur with three horns.

**trichinosis** *n.* disease caused by hairlike worms.

**trichology** *n.* study of hair and its diseases. □□ **trichologist** *n.*

**trick** ● *n.* 1 thing done to deceive or outwit. 2 illusion. 3 knack; feat of skill or dexterity. 4 foolish or discreditable act. 5 hoax, joke. 6 cards played in one round; point gained in this. ● *v.* deceive or persuade by trick.

**trickery** *n.* deception, use of tricks.

**trickle** ● *v.* (cause to) flow in drops or small stream; come or go slowly or gradually. ● *n.* trickling flow.

**tricky** *adj.* (**trickier**) 1 requiring care and adroitness. 2 crafty, deceitful.
□□ **trickily** *adv.* **trickiness** *n.*

**tricolour** n. flag of three colours, esp. French or Irish national flag.

**tricycle** n. three-wheeled pedal-driven vehicle.

**trident** n. three-pronged spear.

**triennial** adj. lasting three years; recurring every three years.

**trier** n. person who tries hard.

**trifecta** n. Aust. form of betting in which first three placegetters in horserace must be predicted in correct sequence.

**trifle** ● n. 1 thing of slight value or importance; small amount. 2 dessert of sponge cake with custard, fruit, cream, etc. □ **trifle with** toy with.

**trifling** adj. unimportant, frivolous.

**trigger** ● n. lever releasing spring or catch, esp. to fire gun. ● v. set (action, process) in motion; precipitate. □ **trigger-happy** apt to shoot without, or with slight, provocation.

**trigonometry** n. branch of mathematics dealing with relations of sides and angles of triangles with certain functions of angles. □□ **trigonometric** adj. **trigonometrical** adj.

**trike** n. colloq. tricycle.

**trilateral** adj. having three sides or participants.

**trill** ● n. 1 quavering sound, esp. quick alternation of notes. 2 bird's warbling. ● v. sound or sing with trill.

**trillion** n. 1 million million. 2 (formerly) million million million. □□ **trillionth** adj. & n.

**trilobite** n. kind of fossil crustacean.

**trilogy** n. set of three related novels, plays, films, etc.

**trim** ● v. (trimmed) 1 make neat or tidy or the required size or shape, esp. by cutting away irregular or unwanted parts; cut off. 2 ornament. 3 adjust balance of (ship, aircraft) by arranging cargo etc. 4 arrange (sails) to suit wind. ● n. 1 state of readiness

or fitness. 2 ornament, decorative material. 3 trimming of hair etc.

**trimaran** n. vessel like catamaran, with three hulls side by side.

**trimming** n. 1 ornamental addition to dress, hat, etc. 2 (trimmings) colloq. usual accompaniments.

**trinity** n. 1 being three. 2 group of three. 3 (**the Trinity**) the three aspects of the Christian Godhead.

**trinket** n. trifling ornament, esp. piece of jewellery.

**trio** n. (pl. **trios**) group or set of three; music for three voices or instruments.

**trip** ● v. (tripped) 1 (cause to) stumble, esp. by catching foot. 2 (cause to) commit fault or blunder. 3 run lightly. 4 make excursion to place. 5 operate (mechanism) suddenly by knocking aside catch etc. 6 colloq. have drug-induced hallucinatory experience. ● n. 1 journey or excursion, esp. for pleasure. 2 stumble, blunder. 3 tripping, being tripped up. 4 nimble step. 5 colloq. drug-induced hallucinatory experience. 6 device for tripping mechanism etc.

**tripartite** adj. consisting of three parts.

**tripe** n. 1 first or second stomach of ruminant, esp. ox, as food. 2 colloq. nonsense, rubbish.

**triple** ● adj. 1 having three parts or members. 2 three times as much or as many. ● v. multiply by three. □□ **triply** adv.

**triplet** n. 1 each of three children or animals born at one birth. 2 set of three things, esp. of notes played in time of two.

**triplicate** ● adj. existing in three examples. ● n. each of a set of three copies. □ **in triplicate** as three identical copies. □□ **triplication** n.

**tripod** n. three-legged or three-footed stand, stool, table, or utensil.

**triptych** *n.* picture etc. with three panels, usu. hinged vertically together.

**trite** *adj.* hackneyed.□□ **tritely** *adv.* **triteness** *n.*

**tritium** *n.* radioactive isotope of hydrogen.

**triumph** ● *n.* a great success or achievement; joy at this. ● *v.* gain victory; be successful.

**triumphal** *adj.* of, used in, or celebrating a triumph.

**triumphant** *adj.* victorious, successful; exultant. □□ **triumphantly** *adv.*

**triumvirate** *n.* government or control by board of three.

**trivet** *n.* metal stand for kettle or hot dish etc.

**trivia** *n.pl.* trifles, trivialities.

**trivial** *adj.* of small value or importance.□□ **triviality** *n.* **trivially** *adv.*

**trod** see TREAD.

**trodden** see TREAD.

**troglodyte** *n.* cave dweller.

**troika** *n.* **1** Russian vehicle drawn by three horses abreast. **2** administrative group of three people.

**Trojan Horse** *n.* person or thing intended to undermine or secretly overthrow enemy etc.

**troll**[1] *n.* fabulous being, esp. giant or dwarf dwelling in cave.

**troll**[2] ● *v.* **1** make deliberately offensive or provocative online post with aim of upsetting someone or eliciting angry response from them. **2** carefully and systematically search area for something; fish by trailing baited line along behind boat. ● *n.* person who trolls someone online; deliberately offensive or provocative online post.

**trolley** *n.* (*pl.* **trolleys**) table, stand, or basket on wheels or castors for serving food, carrying luggage, gathering purchases in supermarket, etc.; low truck running on rails.

**trollop** *n.* disreputable girl or woman.

**trombone** *n.* brass wind instrument with sliding tube. □□ **trombonist** *n.*

**tromp l'oeil** *n.* still-life painting designed to give illusion of reality.

**troop** ● *n.* company of people or animals; cavalry or artillery unit. ● *v.* come together or move in troop.

**trooper** *n.* **1** private soldier in cavalry or armoured unit. **2** *hist.* mounted police officer, esp. on goldfields.

**trophy** *n.* cup etc. as prize in contest; memento of any success.

**tropic** *n.* parallel of latitude 23°27′ north or south of the Equator; (**the tropics**) region lying between these. □□ **tropical** *adj.*

**troposphere** *n.* layer of atmosphere extending about 6–10 km upwards from earth's surface.

**troppo** *adj.* *Aust. colloq.* mentally disturbed; mad, crazy.

**trot** ● *v.* **1** (of person) run at moderate pace; (of horse) proceed at steady pace faster than walk; traverse (distance) thus. ● *n.* **1** action or exercise of trotting. **2** (**the trots**) race meeting at which program consists of trotting and pacing races. **3** (**the trots**) *colloq.* diarrhoea.

**trotter** *n.* **1** animal's foot as food. **2** horse bred or trained for trotting.

**troubadour** *n.* medieval poet singing of love.

**trouble** ● *n.* difficulty, distress, inconvenience; cause of this; cause of annoyance or concern. **2** unrest, violence. ● *v.* **1** cause distress, disturb; be distressed, afflict, cause pain etc. to. **2** make the effort to do something.

**troubleshooter** *n.* person who deals with faults or problems. □□ **troubleshoot** *v.*

**troublesome** *adj.* causing trouble, annoying.

**troubling** adj. causing distress or anxiety.

**trough** n. **1** long narrow open receptacle for water, animal feed, etc.; channel or hollow like this. **2** elongated region of low barometric pressure.

**trounce** v. inflict severe defeat, beating, or punishment on.

**troupe** n. company of actors etc.

**trouper** n. **1** member of theatrical troupe. **2** staunch colleague.

**trousers** n.pl. two-legged outer garment reaching from waist usu. to ankles.

**trousseau** n. (pl. **trousseaus** or **trousseaux**) bride's collection of clothes etc.

**trout** n. (pl. **trout** or **trouts**) fish related to salmon; any similar Australian fish.

**trowel** ● n. flat-bladed tool for spreading mortar etc.; scoop for lifting small plants or earth. ● v. (**trowelled**) apply or spread (mortar etc.) with trowel.

**troy weight** n. imperial system of weights used for precious metals etc.

**truant** ● n. child who stays away from school. ● adj. idle, wandering. □ **play truant** stay away as truant. □□ **truancy** n.

**truce** n. temporary agreement to cease hostilities.

**truck** ● n. large powerful motor vehicle for transporting goods etc.; open railway wagon for freight. ● v. convey in or on truck.

**truckie** n. Aust. colloq. driver of truck.

**truculent** adj. aggressively defiant. □□ **truculence** n. **truculently** adv.

**trudge** ● v. walk laboriously; traverse (distance) thus. ● n. trudging walk.

**true** ● adj. **1** in accordance with fact or reality; genuine. **2** loyal, faithful.

**3** accurately conforming to (type, standard). ● adv. truly; accurately.

**truffle** n. **1** rich-flavoured underground fungus. **2** sweet made of soft chocolate mixture.

**truism** n. self-evident or hackneyed truth.

**truly** adv. **1** sincerely. **2** accurately. **3** arch. loyally.

**trump** ● n. playing card of suit temporarily ranking above others. ● v. defeat with trump; colloq. outdo.

**trumpet** ● n. brass instrument with flared mouth and bright penetrating tone; trumpet-shaped thing; sound (as) of trumpet. ● v. (**trumpeted**) blow trumpet; (of elephant) make trumpet-like cry; proclaim loudly.

**trumpeter** n. **1** person who plays or sounds trumpet. **2** Aust. marine fish.

**truncate** v. cut off top or end of; shorten. □□ **truncation** n.

**truncheon** n. short club carried by police officer.

**trundle** v. roll or move, esp. heavily or noisily.

**trunk** n. **1** main stem of tree. **2** body without limbs and head. **3** large box with hinged lid for luggage. **4** elephant's elongated prehensile nose. **5** (**trunks**) men's close-fitting shorts worn for swimming etc. □ **trunk road** important main road.

**truss** ● n. **1** framework supporting roof, bridge, etc.; surgical appliance worn to support hernia. **2** cluster of flowers or fruit. ● v. tie up securely.

**trust** ● n. **1** firm belief that person or thing may be relied on; confident expectation. **2** responsibility. **3** Law arrangement whereby person or group manages property on another's behalf, property so held, group of trustees. **4** association of companies for reducing competition.
● v. **1** place trust in; believe in;

rely on. **2** give (person) charge of. **3** hope earnestly that thing will take place. **4** entrust.□ **in trust** held on basis of legal trust. **on trust** without evidence or investigation. □□ **trustful** adj.

**trustee** n. person or member of board managing property in trust with legal obligation to administer it solely for purposes specified. □□ **trusteeship** n.

**trustworthy** adj. worthy of trust. □□ **trustworthiness** n.

**trusty** adj. (**trustier**) loyal, faithful.

**truth** n. quality or state of being true; what is (accepted as) true.

**truthful** adj. habitually speaking truth; accurate, corresponding to reality. □□ **truthfully** adv. **truthfulness** n.

**try** ● v. (**tried, trying**) **1** attempt, endeavour. **2** test by use or experiment; test qualities of. **3** make severe demands on. **4** investigate and decide (case, issue) judicially; subject (person) to trial. **5** apply or compete for; seek to attain. ● n. **1** attempt. **2** Rugby touching-down of ball by player behind opposing goal line, scoring points and entitling player's side to a kick at goal.

**trying** adj. annoying, exasperating; hard to endure.

**tsar** n. (also **czar**) hist. emperor of Russia.□□ **tsarist** n. & adj.

**tsetse** n. African fly feeding on blood and transmitting disease.

**T-shirt** n. (also **t-shirt, teeshirt**) short-sleeved casual top, usu. of knitted cotton.

**tsp** abbr. (pl. **tsps**) teaspoonful.

**tsunami** n. long high sea wave caused by underwater earthquakes etc.

**tuan** n. Aust. phascogale.

**tub** n. open flat-bottomed usu. round vessel; tub-shaped (usu. plastic) carton; colloq. bath.

**tuba** n. low-pitched brass wind instrument.

**tubby** adj. (**tubbier**) short and fat. □□ **tubbiness** n.

**tube** n. **1** long hollow cylinder; something shaped like this. **2** Aust. colloq. can of beer. **3** television. **4** Surfing hollow curve of breaking wave.

**tuber** n. thick rounded root or underground stem of plant.

**tubercle** n. small rounded swelling on part or in organ of body, esp. as characteristic of tuberculosis. □□ **tubercular** adj. **tuberculous** adj.

**tuberculosis** n. infectious bacterial disease marked by tubercles, esp. in lungs.

**tuberous** adj. having tubers; of or like tuber.

**tubing** n. length of tube, or quantity of or material for tubes.

**tubular** adj. tube-shaped.

**tuck** ● v. **1** draw, fold, or turn outer or end parts of (cloth, clothes etc.) close together; draw together into small space. **2** stow (thing) away in specified place or way. **3** make stitched fold in (cloth etc.) ● n. flattened fold sewn in garment etc.□ **tuck in** colloq. eat heartily. **tuck shop** colloq. small shop selling food at school etc.

**tucker** n. Aust. food; means of subsistence.

**Tues.** abbr. Tuesday.

**Tuesday** n. day after Monday.

**tufa** n. porous limestone rock formed around mineral springs.

**tuff** n. rock formed from volcanic ash.

**tuft** n. bunch of threads, grass, feathers, hair, etc. held or growing together at base.□□ **tufted** adj.

**tug** ● v. (**tugged**) pull hard or violently; tow. ● n. **1** hard, violent, or jerky pull. **2** small powerful boat for towing ships.□ **tug of war 1** trial of strength with two teams pulling against each other on rope. 2 decisive or severe contest.

**tuition** n. teaching; fee for this.

**tulip** n. bulbous spring-flowering plant with showy cup-shaped flowers.

**tulle** n. soft fine silk etc. net for veils and dresses.

**tumble** ● v. 1 (cause to) fall suddenly or headlong; fall rapidly in amount etc.; roll, toss; move or rush in headlong or blundering manner. 2 perform acrobatic feats, esp. somersaults. ● n. 1 fall. 2 somersault or other acrobatic feat. □ **tumble to** colloq. grasp meaning or hidden implication of.

**tumbler** n. 1 drinking glass with no handle or foot. 2 acrobat.

**tumescent** adj. swelling. □□ **tumescence** n.

**tummy** n. colloq. stomach.

**tumour** n. (also **tumor**) abnormal mass of new tissue growing in or on body.

**tumult** n. 1 uproar, din. 2 conflict of emotions etc. □□ **tumultuous** adj.

**tun** n. large cask; brewer's fermenting vat.

**tuna** n. (pl. **tuna** or **tunas**) large edible marine fish, having round body and pointed snout.

**tundra** n. vast level treeless Arctic region with permafrost.

**tune** ● n. 1 melody. 2 correct pitch or intonation. ● v. 1 put (musical instrument) in tune. 2 adjust (radio etc.) to desired frequency. 3 adjust (engine etc.) to run smoothly.

**tuneful** adj. melodious, musical.

**tungsten** n. heavy steel-grey metallic element (symbol **W**).

**tunic** n. close-fitting short coat as part of uniform; loose often sleeveless garment.

**tunnel** ● n. underground passage. ● v. (**tunnelled**) make tunnel through hill etc.; make (one's way) by tunnelling. □ **tunnel vision**

1 defective sight in which objects cannot be properly seen if not close to centre of field of view. 2 colloq. tendency to focus exclusively on a single or limited objective or view.

**tunny** n. tuna.

**turban** n. man's headdress of fabric wound around cap or head, worn esp. by Muslims and Sikhs; woman's hat resembling this.

**turbid** adj. (of liquid) muddy; not clear; confused, disordered. □□ **turbidity** n.

> **Usage** Turbid is sometimes confused with turgid.

**turbine** n. rotary motor driven by flow of water, gas, wind, etc.

**turbo-** comb. form using turbine; driven by such engine.

**turbulent** adj. 1 causing disturbance or commotion. 2 unruly. 3 (of emotions, political affairs, etc.) disturbed, agitated. 4 (of flow of air etc.) varying irregularly. 5 riotous, restless. □□ **turbulence** n. **turbulently** adv.

**turd** n. coarse colloq. lump of excrement.

**tureen** n. deep covered dish.

**turf** ● n. (pl. **turfs** or **turves**) 1 short grass with surface earth bound together by its roots; piece of this cut from ground. 2 (the turf) horseracing; racecourse. 3 colloq. area regarded as someone's territory; sphere of influence or activity. ● v. cover (ground) with turf. □ **turf out** colloq. expel, eject. □□ **turfy** adj.

**turgid** adj. 1 swollen, inflated. 2 (of language) pompous, bombastic. □□ **turgidity** n.

> **Usage** Turgid is sometimes confused with turbid.

**turkey** n. 1 large orig. American bird bred for food. 2 colloq. stupid or inept person.

**Turkish delight** n. sweet of flavoured gelatin coated in powdered sugar.

**turmeric** n. E. Indian plant of ginger family.

**turmoil** n. violent confusion; agitation; din and bustle.

**turn** ● v. 1 move around point or axis; give or receive rotary motion. 2 change from one side or state or colour to another. 3 invert, reverse. 4 give new direction to, take new direction, aim in certain way. 5 change in nature, form, or condition to. 6 set about, have recourse to, consider next. 7 become. 8 make or become hostile to. 9 pass a certain age or hour. 10 depend on. 11 send, put, cause to go. 12 make (profit). 13 shape (object) in lathe; give (esp. elegant) form to. ● n. 1 turning, rotary motion. 2 changed or change of direction or tendency; point of turning or change. 3 turning of road. 4 change of direction of tide. 5 change in course of events. 6 tendency, formation. 7 opportunity, obligation etc. that comes successively to each of several people etc. 8 short walk or ride. 9 colloq. momentary nervous shock; short illness, esp. involving giddiness. 10 Mus. ornament of principal note with those above and below it. □ in turn in succession. out of turn before or after one's proper turn; inappropriately. take turns (of two or more people) do something alternatively or in succession. to a turn so as to be perfectly cooked. turn against make or become hostile to. turn down 1 reject. 2 reduce volume of. turn in 1 hand over to authority. 2 colloq. go to bed. turn off 1 stop (machine etc.) working. 2 colloq.

(cause to) lose interest. turn on 1 start (machine etc.) 2 colloq. excite, esp. sexually. turn out 1 prove to be the case. 2 go somewhere to attend to or do something. 3 switch off (light). 4 expel; empty. 5 produce. 6 equip, dress. turn the corner pass critical point of illness, difficulty, etc. turn the tables reverse situation so that one is in superior position to those previously superior. turn the tide reverse the trend of events. turn to 1 resort to for help. 2 move on to do or consider. turn up 1 appear; be found; discover. 2 increase volume of.

**turncoat** n. person who changes sides in a dispute.

**turner** n. lathe worker.

**turnip** n. plant with globular root used as vegetable.

**turntable** n. circular revolving plate supporting a record as it is played.

**turpentine** n. 1 oil used for thinning paint and as solvent; = mineral turpentine. 2 any of several resinous or aromatic Australian shrubs or trees.

**turpitude** n. depravity, wickedness.

**turps** n. colloq. 1 turpentine. 2 Aust. alcoholic liquor.

**turquoise** n. opaque semiprecious stone, usu. greenish-blue; this colour.

**turret** n. small tower; revolving, armoured tower for gun and gunners on ship, tank, etc. □□ turreted adj.

**turtle** n. aquatic reptile with flippers and horny shell. □ turtle dove wild dove noted for its soft cooing.

**turtleneck** n. high close-fitting neck on garment; garment with such neck.

**tusk** n. long pointed tooth, esp. projecting beyond mouth as in elephant, walrus, etc. □□ tusked adj.

**tussle** n. struggle, scuffle.

**tussock** n. clump of grass etc. □□ tussocky adj.

**tute** n. colloq. tutorial.

**tutelage** n. guardianship; being under this; tuition.

**tutor** ● n. private or university teacher. ● v. act as tutor (to).
□□ **tutorship** n.

**tutorial** ● adj. of a tutor or tuition. ● n. period of tuition for single student or small group.

**tutti** adj. & adv. Mus. with all voices or instruments together.

**tut-tut** int. exclamation of annoyance, impatience, or rebuke.

**tutu** n. dancer's short skirt of stiffened frills.

**tuxedo** n. (pl. **tuxedos** or **tuxedoes**) dinner jacket.

**TV** abbr. television.

**twaddle** n. nonsense.

**twang** ● n. 1 sound made by plucked string of musical instrument, bow, etc. 2 nasal quality of voice.
● v. (cause to) emit twang.
□□ **twangy** adj.

**tweak** ● v. 1 pinch and twist sharply. 2 adjust finely. ● n. such action.

**twee** adj. affectedly dainty or quaint.

**tweed** n. rough-surfaced woollen cloth, usu. of mixed colours; (**tweeds**) clothes of tweed.

**tweet** ● n. 1 chirp of small bird. 2 posting on social media application Twitter. ● v. 1 make chirping noise. 2 make a post on Twitter.

**tweeter** n. loudspeaker for high frequencies.

**tweezers** n.pl. small pair of pincers for picking up small objects, plucking out hairs, etc.

**twelve** adj. & n. one more than eleven (12, XII). □□ **twelfth** adj. & n.

**twenty** adj. & n. twice ten (20, XX).
□□ **twentieth** adj. & n.

**twerp** n. (also **twirp**) colloq. stupid or objectionable person.

**twice** adv. two times; doubly.

**twiddle** ● v. twist or play idly about. ● n. act of twiddling.

**twig** ● n. very small thin branch of tree or shrub. ● v. (**twigged**) colloq. understand; realise.

**twilight** n. light from sky after sunset; the period of this.

**twill** n. fabric woven with surface of parallel diagonal ridges.
□□ **twilled** adj.

**twin** ● n. 1 each of closely related pair, esp. of children or animals born at a birth. 2 counterpart.
● adj. forming, or born as, twins.
● v. (**twinned**) 1 join intimately together; pair. 2 bear twins.

**twine** ● n. 1 strong coarse string of twisted strands of fibre. 2 coil, twist. ● v. twist; wind or coil.

**twinge** n. sharp momentary local pain.

**twinkle** v. shine with flickering light.

**twirl** ● v. spin, swing, or twist quickly and lightly around. ● n. 1 twirling motion. 2 flourish made with pen.

**twist** ● v. 1 wind (strands etc.) around each other, esp. to form single cord; bend around; rotate. 2 distort, pervert. ● n. 1 process of twisting; something formed by twisting. 2 unexpected development, esp. in story. 3 (**the twist**) popular 1960s dance involving twisting hips from side to side.

**twister** n. US tornado.

**twit** n. colloq. foolish person.

**twitch** ● v. 1 quiver or jerk spasmodically. 2 pull sharply at.
● n. 1 twitching. 2 colloq. state of nervousness.

**twitter** ● v. (esp. of bird) emit succession of light tremulous sounds; utter or express thus. ● n. 1 twittering. 2 colloq. tremulously excited state.
□□ **twittery** adj.

**two** adj. & n. one more than one (2, II). □ **two-dimensional** having or appearing to have length and breadth but no depth. **two-faced** insincere, deceitful. **two-time** be unfaithful to (a lover); deceive.

**twofold** *adj. & adv.* twice as much or as many.

**twosome** *n.* two people together.

**tycoon** *n.* business magnate.

**tying** see TIE.

**tyke** *n.* (also **tike**) **1** dog. **2** small child. **3** *Aust. colloq.* Roman Catholic.

**tympani** = TIMPANI.

**tympanum** *n.* (*pl.* **tympanums** or **tympana**) **1** middle ear. **2** vertical space forming centre of pediment. **3** space between lintel and arch above door etc.

**type** ● *n.* **1** sort, class, kind; person, thing, or event exemplifying class or group. **2** object, idea, or work of art, serving as model. **3** small block with raised character on upper surface for printing; printing types collectively; typeset or printed text. ● *v.* **1** write with keyboard etc. **2** classify according to type.

**typecast** *v.* assign (actor) repeatedly to same type of role.

**typeface** *n.* set of printing characters in a particular design.

**typescript** *n.* typewritten document.

**typesetter** *n.* person or machine that sets type for printing.

**typewriter** *n.* machine with keys for producing printlike characters on paper.

**typhoid** *n.* (in full **typhoid fever**) infectious bacterial fever attacking intestines.

**typhoon** *n.* hurricane.

**typhus** *n.* acute infectious fever.

**typical** *adj.* characteristic of particular person or thing. □□ **typically** *adv.*

**typify** *v.* be a representative specimen of.

**typist** *n.* user of typewriter or keyboard, esp. professionally.

**typo** *n. colloq.* typographical error.

**typography** *n.* style and art of printing. □□ **typographical** *adj.*

**tyrannical** *adj.* acting like or characteristic of tyrant.

**tyrannosaurus** *n.* very large carnivorous dinosaur with short front legs and powerful tail.

**tyranny** *n.* cruel and arbitrary use of authority; rule by tyrant; period of this; nation ruled by tyrant. □□ **tyrannous** *adj.*

**tyrant** *n.* oppressive or cruel ruler; person exercising power arbitrarily or cruelly.

**tyre** *n.* (*US* **tire**) rubber covering, usu. inflated, placed around wheel for cushioning and grip.

**tyro** *n.* (also **tiro**) (*pl.* **tyros**) beginner or novice.

**tzatziki** *n.* Greek dish of yoghurt and cucumber.

# Uu

**uber-** *prefix* denoting outstanding or extreme example of particular person or thing; to a great or extreme degree.

**ubiquitous** *adj.* found everywhere. □□ **ubiquity** *n.*

**udder** *n.* baglike milk-producing organ of cow etc.

**UFO** *n.* unidentified flying object.

**ugari** *n.* (also **yugari**) Queensland name for PIPI.

**ugg boot** *n.* (also **ugh boot**) *Aust.* boot of sheepskin with wool on inside.

**ugly** *adj.* (**uglier**) unpleasant to eye, ear, or mind etc.; discreditable; threatening; dangerous; morally repulsive. □□ **ugliness** *n.*

**UHF** *abbr.* ultra-high frequency.

**UHT** *abbr.* ultra heat treated (esp. of milk).

**UK** *abbr.* United Kingdom.

**ukulele** *n.* small four-stringed guitar.

**ulcer** *n.* open sore. □□ **ulcerous** *adj.*

**ulcerated** *adj.* affected with ulcer. □□ **ulceration** *n.*

**ulna** *n.* (*pl.* **ulnae**) thinner and longer bone in forearm, opposite to thumb. □□ **ulnar** *adj.*

**ulterior** *adj.* not evident or admitted; hidden, secret; situated beyond.

**ultimate** *adj.* 1 last, final. 2 fundamental, basic. □□ **ultimately** *adv.*

**ultimatum** *n.* (*pl.* **ultimatums**) final statement of terms, rejection of which could cause hostility etc.

**ultra-** *comb. form* extreme(ly), excessive(ly); beyond.

**ultra-high** *adj.* (of frequency) between 300 and 3000 megahertz.

**ultramarine** *adj. & n.* brilliant deep blue.

**ultrasonic** *adj.* of or using sound waves pitched above range of human hearing. □□ **ultrasonically** *adv.*

**ultrasound** *n.* ultrasonic waves; diagnostic medical procedure using such waves.

**ultraviolet** *adj.* of or using radiation with a wavelength shorter than that of visible light rays. □ **ultraviolet protection factor** measure of degree of protection provided (by sunscreen, clothing, etc.) against harmful rays of sun.

**ululate** *v.* howl, wail. □□ **ululation** *n.*

**umbel** *n.* flower cluster with stalks springing from common centre.

**umber** *n.* natural brownish colouring matter.

**umbilical** *adj.* of the navel. □ **umbilical cord** flexible tube connecting placenta to navel of foetus.

**umbra** *n.* (*pl.* **umbras** or **umbrae**) shadow cast on earth by moon during eclipse.

**umbrage** *n.* feeling of being offended. □ **take umbrage** take offence.

**umbrella** *n.* collapsible cloth canopy on central stick, for protection against rain, sun, etc.

**umlaut** *n.* mark (¨) over vowel indicating change in pronunciation, used esp. in Germanic languages.

**umpire** ● *n.* 1 person enforcing rules and settling disputes in game, contest, etc. 2 arbitrator. ● *v.* act as umpire (in).

**umpteen** *adj. colloq.* very many. □□ **umpteenth** *adj.*

**UN** *abbr.* United Nations.

**un-** *prefix* not; reversing action indicated by verb, e.g. *unlock.*

> **Usage** The number of words with this prefix is almost unlimited and many of those whose meaning is obvious are not listed below.

**unacceptable** *adj.* not satisfactory or allowable.

**unaccountable** *adj.* 1 without explanation, strange. 2 not answerable for one's actions. □□ **unaccountably** *adv.*

**unadulterated** *adj.* 1 pure. 2 complete, utter.

**unalloyed** *adj.* 1 complete. 2 utter. 3 pure.

**unanimous** *adj.* with everyone's agreement. □□ **unanimity** *n.* **unanimously** *adv.*

**unarmed** *adj.* without weapons.

**unassuming** *adj.* not pretentious; modest.

**unattended** *adj.* (of office, vehicle, etc.) without person in charge of it.

**unattractive** *adj.* not pleasing or appealing to look at; having no inviting or beneficial features.

**unauthorised** *adj.* not having official permission or approval.

**unavoidable** *adj.* unable to be avoided. □□ **unavoidably** *adv.*

**unawares** *adv.* unexpectedly; without noticing.

**unbalanced** *adj.* 1 emotionally unstable. 2 biased.

**unbeknown** *adj.* (also **unbeknownst**) without knowledge of.

**unbend** *v.* (**unbent, unbending**) straighten; relax.

**unbending** *adj.* inflexible; refusing to alter one's demands.

**unbidden** *adj.* not commanded or invited.

**unblock** *v.* remove obstruction.

**unborn** *adj.* not yet born.

**unbounded** *adj.* infinite, limitless.

**unbridled** *adj.* unrestrained.

**unburden** *v.* □ **unburden oneself** reveal one's thoughts and feelings.

**uncalled-for** *adj.* (of remark etc.) rude and unnecessary.

**uncanny** *adj.* (**uncannier**) strange and rather frightening; extraordinary. □□ **uncannily** *adv.* **uncanniness** *n.*

**uncaring** *adj.* 1 not displaying sympathy or concern for others. 2 not feeling interest in or attaching importance to something.

**unceremonious** *adj.* without proper formality or dignity. □□ **unceremoniously** *adv.*

**uncertain** *adj.* not certain; unreliable, changeable; not confident or assured, tentative. □□ **uncertainly** *adv.* **uncertainty** *n.*

**uncheck** *v.* unselect (box in electronic form, questionnaire, etc.)

**uncle** *n.* 1 parent's brother or brother-in-law. 2 (in Aboriginal English) male of parents' generation, community elder.

**unclean** *adj.* 1 not clean. 2 unchaste. 3 religiously impure.

**uncoil** *v.* unwind.

**uncommon** *adj.* unusual; remarkable. □□ **uncommonly** *adv.*

**uncompromising** *adj.* stubborn; unyielding. □□ **uncompromisingly** *adv.*

**unconcern** *n.* lack of concern.

**unconditional** *adj.* not subject to conditions. □□ **unconditionally** *adv.*

**unconscionable** *adj.* 1 unscrupulous. 2 contrary to what one's conscience feels is right.

**unconscious** ● *adj.* not conscious. ● *n.* normally inaccessible part of mind affecting emotions etc. □□ **unconsciously** *adv.* **unconsciousness** *n.*

**unconsidered** *adj.* disregarded.

**unconstitutional** *adj.* in breach of political constitution or procedural rules.

**unconventional** *adj.* not based on or conforming to what is generally done or believed.

**unconvincing** *adj.* failing to make someone believe that something is true or valid; failing to impress.

**uncork** *v.* pull the cork from.

**uncouth** *adj.* 1 lacking polish. 2 uncultured, rough.

**uncover** *v.* remove cover or covering from; reveal, expose.

**unction** *n.* 1 anointing with oil etc. as religious rite or medical treatment. 2 excessive politeness.

**unctuous** *adj.* having an oily manner; smugly virtuous. □□ **unctuously** *adv.* **unctuousness** *n.*

**uncultivated** *adj.* 1 (of land) not used for growing crops. 2 (of person) not highly educated.

**undeniable** *adj.* undoubtedly true. □□ **undeniably** *adv.*

**under** ● *prep.* 1 in or to position lower than; below; beneath; inferior to; less than. 2 undergoing, liable to. 3 controlled or bound by. 4 classified or subsumed in. ● *adv.* 1 in or to lower position or condition. 2 *colloq.* in or into unconsciousness. ● *adj.* lower.

**under-** *prefix* 1 below, lower, subordinate. 2 insufficiently.

**underarm** ● *adj. & adv.* (of throw or stroke in sport) made with arm or hand below shoulder level. ● *n.* armpit.

**underbelly** *n.* soft under surface of animal; area vulnerable to attack.

**undercarriage** *n.* wheeled retractable landing structure beneath aircraft; supporting frame of vehicle.

**underclass** *n.* subordinate social class.

**underclothes** *n.pl.* (also **underclothing**) underwear.

**undercoat** *n.* preliminary layer of paint under finishing coat.

**undercover** *adj.* done or doing things secretly.

**undercurrent** *n.* 1 current below surface. 2 underlying influence or trend.

**undercut** ● *v.* (**undercut**, **undercutting**) 1 sell or work at lower price than; undermine. 2 strike (ball) to make it rise high. ● *n.* underside of sirloin.

**underdaks** *n. Aust. colloq.* briefs, underpants.

**underdog** *n.* 1 loser or expected loser in fight etc. 2 person etc. in inferior or subordinate position.

**underdone** *adj.* not thoroughly cooked.

**underestimate** *v.* make too low an estimate (of).

**underfelt** *n.* felt laid under carpet.

**underfoot** *adv.* 1 on the ground. 2 getting in the way.

**undergo** *v.* (**undergoes, underwent, undergone, undergoing**) be subjected to; experience.

**undergraduate** *n.* person studying for first degree.

**underground** ● *adv.* 1 beneath ground. 2 in(to) secrecy or hiding. ● *adj.* 1 situated underground. 2 secret, subversive. 3 unconventional. ● *n.* underground railway.

**undergrowth** *n.* thick growth of shrubs and bushes under trees.

**underhand** *adj.* 1 deceitful; crafty. 2 secret. 3 underarm.

**underlay** *n.* material laid under another as support.

**underlie** *v.* (**underlay, underlain, underlying**) be cause or basis of. □□ **underlying** *adj.*

**underline** *v.* 1 draw line under. 2 emphasise, stress.

**underling** n. subordinate.

**undermanned** adj. having too few staff or crew.

**undermine** v. weaken gradually; weaken foundations of.

**underneath** prep. & adv. below or on inside of (thing).

**underpants** n.pl. undergarment for lower part of torso.

**underpass** n. road etc. passing under another.

**underpay** v. (underpaid, underpaying) pay too little to (person) or for (thing). □□ **underpayment** n.

**underpin** v. (underpinned) support; strengthen from beneath.

**underplay** v. make little of.

**underprivileged** adj. having below average income, rights, etc.

**underrate** v. have too low an opinion of.

**underscore** v. underline.

**undersell** v. (undersold, underselling) sell at lower price than.

**undersigned** adj. who has or have signed this document.

**underskirt** n. petticoat.

**understand** v. (understood, understanding) 1 see meaning or importance of; know ways or workings of; know explanation. 2 infer; assume without being told; interpret in particular way. □□ **understandable** adj. **understandingly** adv.

**understanding** ● adj. showing insight or sympathy. ● n. 1 ability to understand; sympathetic insight. 2 an agreement; a thing agreed.

**understate** v. 1 express in restrained terms. 2 represent as less than it really is. □□ **understatement** n.

**understudy** n. person ready to take on another's role etc. when required, esp. in theatre.

**undersubscribed** adj. without sufficient subscribers, participants, etc.

**undertake** v. (undertook, undertaken, undertaking) 1 agree to perform or be responsible for. 2 engage in. 3 promise; guarantee; affirm.

**undertaker** n. professional funeral organiser.

**undertaking** n. 1 work etc. undertaken. 2 promise, guarantee.

**undertone** n. 1 subdued tone. 2 underlying quality or feeling.

**undertow** n. current below sea surface contrary to surface current.

**underwear** n. garments worn under others, esp. next to skin.

**underwent** SEE UNDERGO.

**underworld** n. 1 those who live by organised crime. 2 mythical home of the dead.

**underwrite** v. (underwrote, underwritten, underwriting) accept liability under (insurance policy); undertake to finance or support. □□ **underwriter** n.

**undesirable** adj. objectionable, unpleasant. □□ **undesirability** n.

**undies** n.pl. colloq. underwear, underpants.

**undivided** adj. 1 not divided, separated, or broken into parts. 2 devoted completely to one object.

**undo** v. (undoes, undid, undone, undoing) 1 unfasten; unwrap. 2 cancel effects of. 3 ruin.

**undone** adj. 1 not done. 2 not fastened. 3 ruined.

**undoubted** adj. certain, not questioned. □□ **undoubtedly** adv.

**undreamed** adj. (also **undreamt**) not thought of, never imagined.

**undress** ● v. take clothes off. ● n. state of being naked or only partially clothed.

**undressed** adj. 1 naked. 2 not treated, processed, or prepared for use. 3 (of food) not having a dressing.

**undue** adj. excessive.

**undulate** v. (cause to) have wavy motion or look.□□ **undulation** n.

**unduly** adv. excessively.

**undying** adj. everlasting.

**unearned income** n. income from interest payments, rent from tenants, etc.

**unearth** v. discover by searching, digging, or rummaging.

**unearthly** adj. **1** supernatural, mysterious. **2** colloq. absurdly early or inconvenient.

**uneasy** adj. (uneasier) not comfortable; not confident; disturbing.□□ **uneasily** adv. **uneasiness** n.

**uneconomic** adj. not profitable.

**unemployable** adj. not fit for paid employment.

**unemployed** adj. **1** without paid job. **2** not in use.□□ **unemployment** n.

**unequivocal** adj. not ambiguous, plain, unmistakable.
□□ **unequivocally** adv.

**unerring** adj. making no mistake.
□□ **unerringly** adv.

**UNESCO** abbr. (also **Unesco**) United Nations Educational, Scientific, and Cultural Organisation.

**uneven** adj. not level, not smooth; not uniform.□□ **unevenly** adv.

**unexceptionable** adj. entirely satisfactory.

> **Usage** Unexceptionable is sometimes confused with unexceptional.

**unexceptional** adj. normal, ordinary.

**unexpected** adj. not expected; surprising.

**unexpurgated** adj. complete, not censored.

**unfailing** adj. constant; reliable.
□□ **unfailingly** adv.

**unfair** adj. not equitable or honest; not impartial or according to rules.
□□ **unfairly** adv. **unfairness** n.

**unfaithful** adj. not loyal; having committed adultery.
□□ **unfaithfulness** n.

**unfeeling** adj. unsympathetic, harsh.

**unfit** adj. **1** unsuitable. **2** not physically fit.

**unflappable** adj. colloq. remaining calm in crisis.

**unfold** v. **1** open out, spread. **2** become known.

**unforeseen** adj. not anticipated or predicted.

**unforgettable** adj. memorable, wonderful.

**unforgiving** adj. not willing to forgive or excuse people's faults or wrongdoings; (of place or situation) harsh or hostile.

**unfortunate** adj. unlucky; regrettable.□□ **unfortunately** adv.

**unfounded** adj. with no basis.

**unfriend** remove (someone) from list of friends or contacts on social networking website.

**unfrock** v. dismiss (priest) from priesthood.

**unfurl** v. unroll, spread out.

**ungainly** adj. awkward, clumsy.

**ungodly** adj. **1** impious, wicked. **2** colloq. outrageous.
□□ **ungodliness** n.

**ungovernable** adj. uncontrollable, violent.

**ungracious** adj. discourteous; grudging.

**unguarded** adj. **1** incautious, thoughtless. **2** not guarded.

**unguent** n. ointment, lubricant.

**ungulate** n. hoofed mammal.

**unhand** v. literary let go of.

**unhappy** adj. (unhappier) **1** not happy, sad. **2** unfortunate. **3** not satisfied.□□ **unhappily** adv. **unhappiness** n.

**unhealthy** *adj.* (**unhealthier**) in poor health; harmful to health.
□□ **unhealthily** *adv.*

**unheard-of** *adj.* not previously known or done.

**unhinge** *v.* cause to become mentally unbalanced.

**unholy** *adj.* (**unholier**) **1** profane, wicked. **2** *colloq.* dreadful.

**unicameral** *adj.* having single legislative chamber.

**UNICEF** *abbr.* United Nations Children's (orig. International Children's Emergency) Fund.

**unicorn** *n.* mythical white horse with single straight horn.

**uniform** ● *adj.* always the same.
● *n.* distinctive clothing worn by members of same organisation or group. □ **uniform resource locator** location or address identifying where documents can be found on Internet.
□□ **uniformity** *n.* **uniformly** *adv.*

**unify** *v.* unite. □□ **unification** *n.*

**unilateral** *adj.* done by or affecting one side only. □□ **unilaterally** *adv.*

**unimpeachable** *adj.* completely trustworthy.

**unimproved** *adj.* **1** (of land) not used for agriculture or building. **2** not developed. □ **unimproved value** (of land) value placed on residential block etc., excluding any improvements, buildings, etc.

**unintentional** *adj.* not done on purpose. □□ **unintentionally** *adv.*

**uninterested** *adj.* not interested; showing no concern.

**uninviting** *adj.* unattractive, repellent.

**union** *n.* **1** uniting, being united. **2** a whole formed from parts or members. **3** trade union; association. **4** rugby union.

**unionise** *v.* (also -**ize**) organise into or cause to join trade union.
□□ **unionisation** *n.*

**unionist** *n.* member of trade union; advocate of trade unions.

**unique** *adj.* **1** being the only one of its kind; unlike anything else. **2** particularly remarkable, special, or unusual. □□ **uniquely** *adv.*

**unisex** *adj.* (of clothing etc.) designed for both sexes.

**unison** *n.* agreement, concord. □ **in unison** all together.

**unit** *n.* **1** individual thing, person, or group, esp. as part of complex whole. **2** fixed quantity used as standard of measurement. **3** private residence as one of several in a building; apartment.

**Unitarian** *n.* person who believes that the Christian God is not a Trinity but one person. □□ **Unitarianism** *n.*

**unitary** *adj.* single; of a single whole.

**unite** *v.* join together, make or become one; act together, cooperate.

**unity** *n.* state of being united or coherent; complex whole; agreement.

**universal** *adj.* of, belonging to, or done by all. □□ **universally** *adv.*

**universe** *n.* all existing things, including the earth, planets, stars, etc.

**university** *n.* educational institution of advanced learning and research, conferring degrees.

**unkempt** *adj.* untidy, dishevelled.

**unkind** *adj.* cruel, harsh, hurtful.
□□ **unkindly** *adv.* **unkindness** *n.*

**unknowledgeable** *adj.* (also **unknowledgable**) not well informed or educated.

**unknown** ● *adj.* not known, unfamiliar. ● *n.* unknown thing, person, or quantity.

**unleaded** *adj.* (of petrol etc.) without added lead.

**unleash** *v.* release; let loose.

**unleavened** *adj.* (of bread) made without yeast or other raising agent.

**unless** *conj.* except when; except on condition that.

**unlettered** *adj.* illiterate.

**unlike¹** ● *adj.* not like. ● *prep.* differently from.

**unlike²** *v.* **1** (unliked) be regarded with distaste or hostility; be unpopular. **2** (in social media) withdraw one's approval of or support for (someone or something one has previously liked) by means of icon or link.

**unlikely** *adj.* (unlikelier) not likely to happen or be true or be successful.

**unlisted** *adj.* **1** not in published list. **2** (of company) not listed on stock exchange.

**unload** *v.* **1** remove load from (vehicle etc.) **2** remove ammunition from (gun etc.) **3** *colloq.* get rid of.

**unlock** *v.* release lock of; make accessible or available.

**unlooked-for** *adj.* unexpected.

**unmanned** *adj.* operated without crew.

**unmask** *v.* remove mask (from); expose true nature of.

**unmentionable** *adj.* too shocking to be spoken of.

**unmistakable** *adj.* clear, obvious, plain. □□ **unmistakably** *adv.*

**unmitigated** *adj.* not modified; absolute.

**unmoved** *adj.* not moved; not persuaded; not affected by emotion.

**unnatural** *adj.* contrary to nature; not normal. □□ **unnaturally** *adv.*

**unnecessary** *adj.* not necessary; superfluous. □□ **unnecessarily** *adv.*

**unnerve** *v.* cause to lose courage or determination.

**unobtrusive** *adj.* not making oneself or itself noticed. □□ **unobtrusively** *adv.*

**unorthodox** *adj.* contrary to what is usual, traditional, or accepted.

**unpack** *v.* open and remove contents of (suitcase etc.); take out from its packaging.

**unparalleled** *adj.* having no parallel or equal.

**unperturbed** *adj.* not perturbed or concerned.

**unpick** *v.* undo sewing of.

**unplaced** *adj.* not placed as one of first three in race etc.

**unpleasant** *adj.* disagreeable. □□ **unpleasantly** *adv.* **unpleasantness** *n.*

**unplugged** *adj.* (of music etc.) performed without electric amplification.

**unplumbed** *adj.* not fully explored or understood.

**unpopular** *adj.* not popular; disliked. □□ **unpopularity** *n.*

**unprecedented** *adj.* having no precedent; unparalleled.

**unprepossessing** *adj.* unattractive, not making good impression.

**unpretentious** *adj.* not trying to impress by artifice.

**unprincipled** *adj.* lacking or not based on moral principles, unscrupulous.

**unprintable** *adj.* too offensive or indecent to be printed.

**unproductive** *adj.* **1** not producing or able to produce large amounts of goods, crops, etc. **2** not achieving much; not very useful.

**unprofessional** *adj.* contrary to standards of behaviour for members of profession.

**unprompted** *adj.* spontaneous.

**unqualified** *adj.* **1** not qualified or competent. **2** not restricted or modified.

**unquestionable** *adj.* that cannot be disputed or doubted. □□ **unquestionably** *adv.*

**unravel** *v.* (unravelled) **1** make or become disentangled, unknotted, etc.; undo (knitted fabric). **2** probe or solve (mystery etc.).

**unreadable** adj. **1** not clear enough to read; too dull or difficult to be worth reading. **2** not capable of being processed or interpreted by a computer etc.

**unreal** adj. **1** imaginary, not real. **2** colloq. incredibly good.

**unrealistic** adj. **1** not realistic. **2** not practical or realisable.

**unreasonable** adj. excessive; not heeding reason; unfair. □□ **unreasonably** adv.

**unrelenting** adj. not becoming less in intensity.

**unreliable** adj. not able to be relied upon; erratic.

**unremitting** adj. incessant.

**unrequited** adj. (of love etc.) not returned.

**unreservedly** adv. without reservation; absolutely.

**unrest** n. disturbance, dissatisfaction.

**unrivalled** adj. having no equal, incomparable.

**unroll** v. open out from rolled-up state.

**unruly** adj. (unrulier) undisciplined, disorderly. □□ **unruliness** n.

**unsaid** adj. not spoken or expressed.

**unsaturated** adj. (of fat or oil) capable of further reaction by combining with hydrogen.

**unsavoury** adj. (also **unsavory**) **1** disagreeable to taste or smell. **2** morally disgusting.

**unscathed** adj. unharmed, uninjured.

**unscramble** v. **1** sort out. **2** make (scrambled transmission etc.) intelligible.

**unscrew** v. unfasten by removing screw(s); loosen (screw).

**unscripted** adj. (of speech etc.) delivered impromptu.

**unscrupulous** adj. not prevented by scruples of conscience.

**unseasonable** adj. not seasonable; untimely.

**unseat** v. remove from (esp. parliamentary) seat; dislodge from horseback etc.

**unseen** adj. not seen; invisible; (of translation) to be done without preparation.

**unselfish** adj. not selfish; considering others' needs before one's own. □□ **unselfishly** adv. **unselfishness** n.

**unsettle** v. make uneasy; disturb.

**unshakeable** adj. firm; obstinate.

**unsightly** adj. ugly. □□ **unsightliness** n.

**unskilled** adj. lacking or not requiring special skills or training.

**unsociable** adj. disliking company.

**unsocial** adj. not social; not conforming to normal social practices; antisocial.

**unsolicited** adj. not requested.

**unsophisticated** adj. artless, simple, natural.

**unsound** adj. not sound or strong; faulty, unreliable, invalid. □ **of unsound mind** insane.

**unsparing** adj. giving lavishly.

**unspeakable** adj. too bad to be described in words.

**unstable** adj. **1** likely to fall; mentally or emotionally unbalanced. **2** (of chemical compound) likely to decompose.

**unstick** v. (unstuck, unsticking) detach (what is stuck).

**unstinting** adj. given freely and generously. □□ **unstintingly** adv.

**unstudied** adj. natural in manner, spontaneous.

**unsung** adj. not celebrated, unrecognised.

**unsuspecting** adj. feeling no suspicion.

**unswerving** adj. steady, constant. □□ **unswervingly** adv.

**untenable** adj. (of theory or position) not valid because of strong arguments against it.

**unthinkable** adj. too bad or unlikely to be thought about.

**unthinking** adj. thoughtless. □□ **unthinkingly** adv.

**untidy** adj. (untidier) not neat or orderly. □□ **untidily** adv. **untidiness** n.

**until** prep. & conj. up to specified time; till.

> **Usage** Until, as opposed to till, is used especially at the beginning of sentence and in formal style, e.g. Until you told me, I had no idea; He resided there until his decease.

**untimely** adj. happening at unsuitable time; premature.

**unto** prep. arch. to.

**untold** adj. not told; too many or too much to be measured.

**untouchable** ● adj. that may not be touched. ● n. member of the lowest Hindu social order.

**untoward** adj. inconvenient, unexpected.

**untried** adj. not yet tried or tested.

**untruth** n. false statement; lie.

**unusual** adj. not usual; remarkable, rare. □□ **unusually** adv.

**unutterable** adj. inexpressible; beyond description; unpronounceable. □□ **unutterably** adv.

**unvarnished** adj. **1** not varnished. **2** plain, direct, simple.

**unveil** v. remove veil or drapery from; reveal, make known.

**unwarranted** adj. unjustified, unauthorised.

**unwell** adj. ill.

**unwieldy** adj. (unwieldier) cumbersome or hard to manage owing to size, shape etc.

**unwilling** adj. reluctant. □□ **unwillingly** adv. **unwillingness** n.

**unwind** v. (unwound, unwinding) **1** draw out or become drawn out after having been wound. **2** colloq. relax.

**unwise** adj. not sensible, foolish.

**unwitting** adj. unaware; unintentional. □□ **unwittingly** adv.

**unwonted** adj. not customary or usual.

**unworldly** adj. **1** spiritual; not materialistic. **2** naive. □□ **unworldliness** n.

**unworthy** adj. (unworthier) not worthy or befitting; discreditable; unseemly.

**unwrap** v. (unwrapped) remove wrapping from; open, unfold.

**unwritten** adj. not written; (of law etc.) based on custom or judicial decision, not on statute.

**unzip** v. (unzipped) open by undoing of zip fastener.

**up** ● adv. **1** at, in, or towards higher place or position; to larger size or higher level of intensity, volume, etc. **2** to vertical position; out of bed. **3** towards or as far as a stated place, position, etc. **4** so as to be closed or finished. ● prep. upwards and along, through, or into; at higher part of. ● adj. directed upwards. ● n. spell of good fortune. ● v. (upped) colloq. **1** begin abruptly to say or do something. **2** raise; increase. □ **ups and downs** alternative good and bad fortune. **up to 1** as far as; as much as. **2** capable of, fit for. **3** responsibility or choice of. **4** doing, occupied with. **up to date** modern, fashionable. **what's up?** what is going on? what is the matter?

**upbeat** ● n. Mus. unaccented beat. ● adj. colloq. optimistic, cheerful.

**upbraid** v. chide, reproach.

**upbringing** n. rearing of child.

**update** v. bring up to date.

**upend** v. set or rise up on end.

**UPF** abbr. ultraviolet protection factor.

**upfront** adj. colloq. **1** frank, direct. **2** (of payments) made in advance.

**upgrade** v. raise to higher grade; improve (equipment etc.).

**upheaval** n. sudden (esp. violent) change or disruption.

**uphill** adj. & adv. **1** going or sloping upwards. **2** difficult.

**uphold** v. (upheld, upholding) **1** support, maintain. **2** confirm.

**upholster** v. provide (furniture) with upholstery.□□ **upholsterer** n.

**upholstery** n. covering, padding, springs, etc. for furniture; upholsterer's work.

**uplift** ● v. raise. ● n. colloq. mentally elevating influence.

**upload** Computing ● v. transfer (data) from one computer to another. ● n. act or process of uploading data; file that has been uploaded.

**upmarket** adj. & adv. of or to more expensive sector of market; classy.

**upon** prep. formal on.

**upper** ● adj. higher in place, position, or rank. ● n. part of shoe above sole.□ **upper case** capital letters in printing or typing. **upper class** highest social class.

**uppermost** adj. & adv. in, on, or to the top or most prominent position.

**uppish** adj. colloq. arrogant, snobbish.

**uppity** adj. colloq. uppish.

**upright** ● adj. **1** erect, vertical. **2** (of piano) with vertical strings. **3** honourable, honest. ● n. **1** upright post or rod, esp. as structural support. **2** (of piano) with vertical strings. **3** (uprights) AFL goalposts.

**uprising** n. rebellion or revolt.

**uproar** n. tumult; violent disturbance.

**uproarious** adj. very noisy; provoking loud laughter. □□ **uproariously** adv.

**uproot** v. pull (plant etc.) up from ground; displace (person); eradicate.

**upset** ● v. (upset, upsetting) **1** overturn. **2** disturb temper, composure, or digestion of. **3** disrupt. ● n. **1** emotional disturbance. **2** surprising result.

**upshot** n. outcome, conclusion.

**upside** n. positive aspect of something; advantage.

**upside down** adv. & adj. **1** with upper and lower parts reversed. **2** inverted. **3** in(to) total disorder.

**upskill** v. teach (employee) additional skills; (of employee) learn additional skills.

**upstage** ● adj. & adv. nearer back of theatre stage. ● v. divert attention from; outshine.

**upstairs** ● adv. to or on an upper floor. ● adj. situated upstairs. ● n. upper floor.

**upstanding** adj. **1** standing up. **2** strong and healthy. **3** honest.

**upstart** n. newly successful, esp. arrogant, person.

**upstream** adv. & adj. against flow of stream etc.

**upsurge** n. upward surge; rise (esp. in feelings etc.)

**upswing** n. upward movement or trend.

**uptake** n. □ **quick on the uptake** colloq. quick to understand.

**uptight** adj. colloq. **1** nervously tense, angry. **2** rigidly conventional.

**uptime** n. time computer system etc. is available for productive use.

**upturn** ● n. upward trend; improvement. ● v. turn up or upside down.

**URL** abbr. uniform resource locator, address of World Wide Web page.

**upward** ● adv. (also **upwards**) towards what is higher, more important, etc. ● adj. moving or extending upwards. □□ **upwardly** adv.

**upwind** adj. & adv. in direction from which wind is blowing.

**uranium** *n.* 1 metallic element (symbol **U**). 2 capable of nuclear fission and used as source of nuclear energy.

**urban** *adj.* of, living in, or situated in town or city. □□ **urbanise** *v.* (also *-ize*)

**urbane** *adj.* suave; elegant; refined. □□ **urbanely** *adv.* **urbanity** *n.*

**urchin** *n.* 1 mischievous child. 2 sea urchin.

**ureter** *n.* duct carrying urine from kidney to bladder.

**urethra** *n.* duct carrying urine from bladder. □□ **urethral** *adj.*

**urge** ● *v.* encourage earnestly; advise strongly; recommend strongly; drive forcibly; hasten. ● *n.* strong desire or impulse.

**urgent** *adj.* 1 requiring immediate action or attention. 2 importunate. □□ **urgency** *n.* **urgently** *adv.*

**urinal** *n.* place or receptacle for urinating by men.

**urinate** *v.* discharge urine. □□ **urination** *n.*

**urine** *n.* waste fluid secreted by kidneys and discharged from bladder. □□ **urinary** *adj.*

**urn** *n.* 1 vase used esp. for ashes of the dead. 2 large vessel with tap, in which water etc. is heated or kept hot.

**urology** *n.* study of urinary system. □□ **urological** *adj.* **urologist** *n.*

**ursine** *adj.* of or like bear.

**urticaria** *n.* rash.

**US** *abbr.* (also **USA**) United States (of America).

**us** *pron.* the objective case of WE.

**usable** *adj.* that can be used.

**usage** *n.* 1 use; treatment. 2 customary practice, established use (esp. of language).

**USB** *abbr.* universal serial bus, standardised technology for attaching peripheral devices to computer.

**use** ● *v.* (using) 1 cause to act or serve for purpose. 2 bring into service.

3 treat in specified way. 4 exploit for one's own ends. ● *n.* 1 being used. 2 application to purpose. 3 right or power of using. 4 benefit, advantage. 5 custom, usage. □ **use-by date** latest recommended date for consumption marked on packing of, esp. perishable, food. **use up** use all or the remains of, finish.

**used** *adj.* second-hand.

**used to** ● *v.* was accustomed to (do). ● *adj.* familiar with by practice or habit.

**useful** *adj.* that can be used to advantage; helpful; beneficial. □□ **usefully** *adv.* **usefulness** *n.*

**useless** *adj.* 1 serving no purpose. 2 *colloq.* feeble or ineffectual. □□ **uselessly** *adv.* **uselessness** *n.*

**user** *n.* person who uses something; person who takes illegal drugs. □ **user-generated** of material on website that is voluntarily contributed by members of the public who use the site.

**username** *n.* identification used by person to log in to computer etc.

**usher** ● *n.* 1 person who shows people to their seats in cinema, church, etc. 2 officer walking before person of rank. 3 doorkeeper at court etc. ● *v.* act as usher to; announce, show in.

**usherette** *n.* female usher.

**USSR** *abbr. hist.* Union of Soviet Socialist Republics.

**usual** *adj.* such as commonly occurs, or is observed or done; customary, habitual. □□ **usually** *adv.*

**usurp** *v.* seize (throne, power, etc.) wrongfully. □□ **usurpation** *n.* **usurper** *n.*

**usury** *n.* lending of money at interest, esp. at exorbitant or illegal rate. □□ **usurious** *adj.*

**ute** *n. Aust. colloq.* utility truck.

**utensil** *n.* implement or vessel, esp. for kitchen use.

**uterus** *n.* hollow organ in female mammals in which young develop; womb.□□ **uterine** *adj.*

**utilise** *v.* (also **-ize**) make use of. □□ **utilisation** *n.*

**utilitarian** *adj.* **1** designed to be useful rather than attractive. **2** of utilitarianism.

**utilitarianism** *n.* doctrine that actions are right if they are useful or benefit majority.

**utility** ● *n. n.* **1** usefulness. **2** useful thing. **3** (in full **public utility**) company supplying electricity, water, gas, etc. to community. **4** (in full **utility truck**) *Aust.* small truck, having cabin and open tray in rear used for carrying light loads. **5** (in full **utility player**) person who is able to perform well in number of positions. ● *adj.* useful; functional.

**utmost** ● *adj.* furthest, extreme, greatest. ● *n.* the utmost point, degree, etc.

**utopia** *n.* (also **Utopia**) imagined perfect place or state.□□ **utopian** *adj.*

**utter** ● *adj.* complete, absolute. ● *v.* emit audibly; express in words. □□ **utterance** *n.* **utterly** *adv.* **uttermost** *adj.*

**U-turn** *n.* turning of vehicle in U-shaped course to reverse direction; reversal of policy or opinion.

**UV** *abbr.* ultraviolet.

**uvula** *n.* (*pl.* **uvulae**) fleshy part of soft palate hanging above throat. □□ **uvular** *adj.*

**uxorious** *adj.* excessively fond of one's wife.

# Vv

**V** ● *n.* (also **v**) (Roman numeral) 5. ● *abbr.* volt(s).

**v** *abbr.* (also **v.**) **1** verb. **2** verse. **3** versus. **4** very.

**vac** *n. colloq.* **1** vacation. **2** vacuum cleaner.

**vacancy** *n.* being vacant; unoccupied job; available motel room etc.

**vacant** *adj.* **1** not filled or occupied. **2** not mentally active; showing no interest.□□ **vacantly** *adv.*

**vacate** *v.* cease to occupy.

**vacation** *n.* **1** holiday. **2** vacating, being vacated.

**vaccinate** *v.* inoculate with vaccine to immunise against disease. □□ **vaccination** *n.*

**vaccine** *n.* a preparation that gives immunity from an infection.

**vacillate** *v.* keep changing one's mind.□□ **vacillation** *n.* **vacillator** *n.*

**vacuous** *adj.* expressionless; unintelligent.□□ **vacuity** *n.* **vacuously** *adv.*

**vacuum** ● *n.* (*pl.* **vacuums** or **vacua**) space from which air has been removed. ● *v. colloq.* clean with vacuum cleaner. □ **vacuum cleaner** electrical apparatus that takes up dust etc. by suction. **vacuum flask** container for keeping liquids hot or cold.

**vagabond** ● *n.* wanderer; vagrant. ● *adj.* having no settled habitation or home; *colloq.* shiftless, idle.

**vagary** *n.* capricious idea or act; a fluctuation.

**vagina** *n.* canal joining uterus and vulva of female mammals. □□ **vaginal** *adj.*

**vagrant** *n.* person without settled home.□□ **vagrancy** *n.*

**vague** *adj.* uncertain, ill-defined; not clear-thinking; inexact.□□ **vaguely** *adv.* **vagueness** *n.*

**vain** *adj.* **1** conceited. **2** useless, futile. □ **in vain** without result or success. □□ **vainly** *adv.*

**vainglory** *n.* extreme vanity. □□ **vainglorious** *adj.*

**valance** *n.* short curtain or hanging frill.

**vale** *n.* valley.

**valediction** *n. formal* a farewell. □□ **valedictory** *adj.* & *n.*

**valence** *n.* (also **valency**) combining power of atom measured by number of hydrogen atoms it can displace or combine with.

**valentine** *n.* card or letter sent, or message placed in newspaper, usu. anonymously, as mark of love on St Valentine's Day (14 Feb.); sweetheart chosen on that day.

**valet** ● *n.* man's personal servant. ● *v.* (**valeted**) **1** act as valet (to). **2** clean (out) (car).

**valetudinarian** *n.* person of poor health or who is unduly anxious about health.

**valiant** *adj.* brave.□□ **valiantly** *adv.*

**valid** *adj.* **1** (of reason, objection, etc.) sound, defensible. **2** legally acceptable. **3** not yet expired. □□ **validity** *n.*

**validate** *v.* make valid; ratify. □□ **validation** *n.*

**valise** *n.* small travelling bag.

**valley** *n.* (*pl.* **valleys**) low area between hills.

**valour** *n.* (also **valor**) courage. □□ **valorous** *adj.*

**valuable** ● *adj.* of great value, price, or worth. ● *n.* (**valuables**) valuable things.□□ **valuably** *adv.*

**valuation** *n.* estimation (esp. professional) of thing's worth; estimated value.

**value** ● *n.* 1 worth, desirability, or qualities on which these depend; worth as estimated; amount for which thing can be exchanged in open market; equivalent of thing. 2 (in full **value for money**) something well worth money spent. 3 ability of thing to serve some purpose or cause effect. 4 (**values**) one's principles, priorities, or standards. ● *v.* 1 estimate value of. 2 have high or specified opinion of. 3 attach importance to. □ **value judgement** assessment of something as good or bad in terms of one's standards or priorities.

**valve** *n.* 1 device controlling flow through pipe etc., usu. allowing movement in one direction only; structure in organ etc. allowing flow of blood etc. in one direction only. 2 thermionic valve. 3 device to vary length of tube in trumpet etc. 4 half shell of oyster, mussel, etc. □□ **valvular** *adj.*

**vamp** ● *n.* upper front part of boot or shoe. ● *v.* 1 repair, furbish, or make by patching or piecing together. 2 improvise musical accompaniment.

**vampire** *n.* 1 ghost or reanimated corpse which drinks blood of humans. 2 person who preys on others.

**van** *n.* 1 covered vehicle or closed railway truck for transporting goods etc. 2 vanguard, forefront.

**vanadium** *n.* hard grey metallic element (symbol **V**).

**vandal** *n.* person who wilfully or maliciously damages property. □□ **vandalism** *n.*

**vandalise** *v.* (also **-ize**) wilfully or maliciously destroy or damage (esp. public property).

**vane** *n.* 1 weathervane. 2 blade of windmill, ship's propeller, etc.

**vanguard** *n.* 1 foremost part of advancing army etc. 2 leaders of movement etc.

**vanilla** *n.* a flavouring, esp. obtained from pods of tropical orchid.

**vanish** *v.* disappear completely.

**vanity** *n.* 1 conceit about one's appearance or attainments. 2 futility, unreal thing. 3 bathroom unit consisting of washbasin and cupboard. □ **vanity case** small case for carrying cosmetics etc.

**vanquish** *v.* conquer, overcome.

**vantage** *n.* (also **vantage point**) place giving good view or prospect.

**vape** *colloq.* ● *v.* inhale and exhale vapour produced by electronic cigarette or similar device. ● *n.* electronic cigarette or similar device; act of vaping.

**vapid** *adj.* insipid; dull; flat. □□ **vapidity** *n.*

**vaporise** *v.* (also **-ize**) change into vapour. □□ **vaporisation** *n.*

**vapour** *n.* (also **vapor**) moisture or other substance diffused or suspended in air, e.g. mist, smoke; gaseous form of substance. □□ **vaporous** *adj.*

**variable** ● *adj.* changeable, not constant. ● *n.* variable thing or quantity. □□ **variability** *n.*

**variance** *n.* □ **at variance** in disagreement.

**variant** ● *adj.* differing. ● *n.* variant form, spelling, type, etc.

**variation** *n.* 1 varying. 2 departure from normal kind, standard, type, etc.; extent of this.

**varicose** *adj.* (esp. of vein etc.) permanently and abnormally dilated. □□ **varicosity** *n.*

**variegated** *adj.* with irregular patches of different colours. □□ **variegation** *n.*

**varietal** *adj.* (of wine) made from single designated variety of grape.

**variety** n. **1** quality of not being the same; quantity of different things. **2** a sort or kind. **3** light entertainment made up of series of short unrelated performances.

**various** adj. **1** different, diverse. **2** several.□□ **variously** adv.

Usage *Various* (unlike *several*) cannot be used with *of*, as (wrongly) in *various of the guests arrived late.*

**varlet** n. arch. menial or rascal.

**varnish** ● n. resinous solution used to give hard shiny transparent coating. ● v. **1** coat with varnish. **2** conceal with deceptively attractive appearance.

**vary** v. modify, diversify; become or be different; be of different kinds.

**vascular** adj. of or containing vessels for conveying blood, sap, etc.

**vas deferens** n. (pl. **vasa deferentia**) duct that conveys sperm from testicle to urethra.

**vase** n. vessel used as ornament or container for flowers.

**vasectomy** n. removal of part of each vas deferens, esp. for sterilisation.

**vaseline** n. propr. type of petroleum jelly used as ointment etc.

**vassal** n. humble subordinate.

**vast** adj. immense, huge; great. □□ **vastly** adv. **vastness** n.

**vat** n. large tank for liquids.

**vaudeville** n. variety entertainment.

**vault** ● n. **1** arched roof. **2** underground chamber as place of storage; burial chamber. **3** act of vaulting. **4** (in full **vaulting horse**) wooden block for vaulting over by gymnasts. ● v. leap or spring, esp. using hands or pole.

**vaunt** ● v. boast, brag. ● n. a boast.

**vax** n. colloq. vaccine; vaccination.

**VC** abbr. **1** Victoria Cross. **2** vice-chancellor.

**VCR** abbr. video cassette recorder.

**VD** abbr. venereal disease.

**VDU** abbr. visual display unit.

**veal** n. calf's flesh as food.

**vector** n. **1** Math. & Physics quantity having both magnitude and direction. **2** carrier of disease.

**veer** v. change direction.

**veg** n. colloq. vegetable(s).□ **veg out** colloq. relax, do nothing.

**vegan** n. person who does not eat meat or animal products.

**vegemite** n. propr. concentrated yeast extract used as spread.

**vegetable** ● n. **1** plant, esp. edible herbaceous plant. **2** colloq. dull or inactive person. ● adj. of, derived from, or relating to plant life or vegetables as food.

**vegetarian** ● n. person who does not eat meat or fish. ● adj. of or suitable for such people. □□ **vegetarianism** n.

**vegetate** v. **1** live a dull, monotonous life. **2** relax, do nothing.

**vegetation** n. plants collectively.

**vegies** n. pl. colloq. vegetables.

**vehement** adj. showing or caused by strong feeling.□□ **vehemence** n. **vehemently** adv.

**vehicle** n. **1** conveyance used on land or in space. **2** thing or person as medium for thought, feeling, or action. **3** liquid etc. as medium for suspending pigments, drugs, etc. □□ **vehicular** adj.

**veil** ● n. piece of fine net or other fabric worn to protect or conceal face. ● v. cover with or as if with veil.

**vein** n. **1** any of blood vessels carrying blood towards heart. **2** any threadlike structure. **3** narrow layer in rock etc. **4** specified character or tendency; mood.□□ **veined** adj.

**velcro** n. propr. fastener consisting of two strips of fabric that cling when pressed together.

**veld** n. (also **veldt**) S.Afr. open country.

**vellum** n. fine parchment; smooth writing paper.

**velocity** n. speed, esp. of inanimate things.

**velodrome** n. place or building with track for cycle racing.

**velour** n. (also **velours**) plush fabric resembling velvet.

**velvet** • n. soft fabric with thick short pile on one side. • adj. of, like, or soft as velvet.□□ **velvety** adj.

**velveteen** n. cotton fabric with pile like velvet.

**Ven.** abbr. Venerable.

**venal** adj. corrupt; able to be bribed; involving bribery.□□ **venality** n.

Usage Venal is sometimes confused with venial.

**vend** v. sell, offer for sale. □□ **vendor** n.

**vendetta** n. a feud.

**veneer** • n. 1 thin covering of fine wood. 2 deceptively pleasing appearance. • v. apply veneer to.

**venerable** adj. 1 entitled to deep respect. 2 title of high-ranking Buddhist monk or archdeacon in Anglican Church.

**venerate** v. respect deeply. □□ **veneration** n.

**venereal** adj. (of infections) contracted by sexual intercourse with infected person.

**venetian blind** n. windowblind of adjustable horizontal slats.

**vengeance** n. punishment, retribution.□ **with a vengeance** in a higher degree than expected.

**vengeful** adj. seeking vengeance.

**venial** adj. (of sin or fault) pardonable.□□ **veniality** n.

Usage Venial is sometimes confused with venal.

**venison** n. deer's flesh as food.

**Venn diagram** n. diagram using overlapping circles etc. to show relationships between sets.

**venom** n. 1 poisonous fluid secreted by snakes etc. 2 bitter feeling or language.□□ **venomous** adj. **venomously** adv.

**venous** adj. of, full of, or contained in, veins.

**vent** • n. 1 opening for passage of air etc. 2 slit in garment, esp. in back of jacket. • v. give vent to.□ **give vent to** give an outlet to.

**ventilate** v. 1 cause air to enter or circulate freely in. 2 discuss or examine publicly.□□ **ventilation** n.

**ventilator** n. 1 appliance or aperture for ventilating room etc. 2 respirator.

**ventral** adj. of or on abdomen.

**ventricle** n. cavity, esp. in brain or heart.□□ **ventricular** adj.

**ventriloquist** n. entertainer who can produce voice sounds so that they appear to come from puppet etc. □□ **ventriloquism** n.

**venture** • n. risky undertaking. • v. dare to do, make, or put forward; dare to say; expose to risk.□ **venture capital** capital invested in project in which there is substantial element of risk.□□ **venturesome** adj.

**venue** n. appointed place for match, meeting, concert, etc.

**Venus flytrap** n. flesh-consuming plant with leaves springing shut on insects etc.

**veracious** adj. truthful; true. □□ **veracity** n.

**verandah** n. (also **veranda**) open-sided roofed structure providing shelter along side of building; *Aust.* similar structure (partially) enclosed and used as additional living space.

**verb** n. word used to indicate action, event, state, or change.

**verbal** ● adj. **1** of or in words; spoken. **2** of verb. ● v. (**verballed**) *colloq.* attribute damaging statement to (suspect). □□ **verballing** n. **verbally** adv.

**verbalise** v. (also **-ize**) put into words.

**verbatim** adv. & adj. in exactly the same words.

**verbiage** n. unnecessary number of words.

**verbose** adj. using more words than are needed. □□ **verbosity** n.

**verdant** adj. (of grass etc.) green, lush. □□ **verdancy** n.

**verdict** n. decision of jury; decision, judgement.

**verdigris** n. greenish-blue substance that forms on copper or brass.

**verdure** n. green vegetation or its colour.

**verge** n. **1** edge or border. **2** brink. □ **verge on** come close to being.

**verger** n. church caretaker.

**verify** v. establish truth or correctness of. □□ **verification** n.

**verisimilitude** n. appearance of being true or real.

**veritable** adj. real; rightly so called.

**vermicelli** n. pasta in long slender threads.

**vermicide** n. drug used to kill (esp. intestinal) worms.

**vermiform** adj. worm-shaped.

**vermilion** adj. & n. brilliant scarlet.

**vermin** n. (pl. **vermin**) animals and birds harmful to crops, native wildlife, etc. □□ **verminous** adj.

**vermouth** n. wine flavoured with aromatic herbs.

**vernacular** n. language or dialect of particular country; language of particular class or group; everyday, colloquial speech.

**vernal** adj. of or in spring.

**verruca** n. (pl. **verrucas** or **verrucae**) wart or similar growth, esp. on foot.

**versatile** adj. able to do or be used for many different things. □□ **versatility** n.

**verse** n. poetry; stanza of poem or song; each of short numbered divisions of Bible.

**versed** adj. □ **versed in** experienced or skilled in.

**versify** v. turn into or express in verse; compose verses. □□ **versification** n.

**version** n. account of matter from particular point of view; particular edition or translation of book etc.

**verso** n. (pl. **versos**) left hand page of open book; back of printed leaf.

**versus** prep. against.

**vertebra** n. (pl. **vertebrae**) each segment of backbone. □□ **vertebral** adj.

**vertebrate** n. & adj. (an animal) having backbone.

**vertex** n. (pl. **vertices** or **vertexes**) highest point; apex.

**vertical** ● adj. at right angles to horizontal plane; perpendicular; in direction from top to bottom of picture etc. ● n. vertical line or plane. □□ **vertically** adv.

**vertiginous** adj. of or causing vertigo.

**vertigo** n. dizziness, esp. caused by heights.

**verve** n. enthusiasm, vigour, energy.

**very** ● adv. **1** in high degree. **2** in fullest sense. ● adj. real, true, properly so-called, etc.

**vesicle** n. small bladder, bubble, or blister.

**vessel** n. **1** hollow receptacle, esp. for liquid. **2** ship or boat, esp. large one.

**3** duct or canal etc. holding or conveying blood, sap, etc.

**vest** ● *n.* waistcoat; sleeveless jumper; singlet. ● *v.* confer (power) on as firm or legal right. □ **vested interest** personal interest in a state of affairs, usu. with expectation of gain.

**vestibule** *n.* entrance hall, lobby.

**vestige** *n.* slight amount or trace. □□ **vestigial** *adj.*

**vestment** *n.* ceremonial garment worn by priest etc.

**vet** ● *n. colloq.* veterinary surgeon. ● *v.* (vetted) make careful and critical examination of (scheme, work, candidate, etc.).

**vetch** *n.* plant of pea family used largely for fodder.

**veteran** *n.* person who has had long experience in particular field; former member of armed forces.

**veterinarian** *n.* veterinary surgeon.

**veterinary** *adj.* of or for diseases and injuries of esp. farm and domestic animals. □ **veterinary surgeon** person qualified to treat animal diseases and disorders.

**veto** ● *n.* (*pl.* vetoes) right to reject measure etc. unilaterally; rejection, prohibition. ● *v.* reject by a veto.

**vex** *v.* annoy. □□ **vexation** *n.* **vexatious** *adj.*

**vexed** *adj.* (of question) much discussed; problematic.

**VGA** *abbr.* videographics array, standard for defining colour display screens for computers.

**VHF** *abbr.* very high frequency, (in radio) 30–300 MHz.

**VHS** *abbr. propr.* format for recording video tape.

**via** *prep.* by way of, through.

**viable** *adj.* (of plan etc.) feasible; capable of surviving or living. □□ **viability** *n.*

**viaduct** *n.* long bridge over valley.

**vial** *n.* small glass vessel.

**viands** *n.pl. arch.* articles of food.

**vibes** *n.pl.* **1** *colloq.* vibrations, esp. feelings or atmosphere communicated. **2** vibraphone.

**vibrant** *adj.* full of energy and enthusiasm; (of sound) resonant; (of colour) bright. □□ **vibrancy** *n.*

**vibraphone** *n.* percussion instrument with motor-driven resonators under metal bars giving vibrato effect.

**vibrate** *v.* move rapidly to and fro; sound with rapid slight variation of pitch. □□ **vibrator** *n.*

**vibration** *n.* **1** vibrating. **2** (vibrations) mental influences; atmosphere or feeling communicated.

**vibrato** *n.* tremulous effect in musical pitch.

**vicar** *n.* **1** (in Anglican Church) incumbent of parish. **2** *RC Ch.* representative or deputy of bishop.

**vicarage** *n.* vicar's house.

**vicarious** *adj.* experienced indirectly; acting or done etc. for another. □□ **vicariously** *adv.*

**vice** *n.* **1** immoral conduct; particular form of this; bad habit. **2** clamp with two jaws holding an object being worked on.

**vice-** *comb. form* person acting in place of; next in rank to.

**vice-chancellor** *n.* chief administrator of university.

**viceregal** *adj.* of viceroy; of governor-general or governor.

**viceroy** *n.* ruler on behalf of sovereign in colony, province, etc.

**vice versa** *adv.* with order of terms changed; other way round.

**vicinity** *n.* surrounding area.

**vicious** *adj.* bad-tempered; spiteful; violent. □□ **viciously** *adv.* **viciousness** *n.*

**vicissitude** *n.* change of circumstances or luck.

**victim** *n.* person or thing injured or killed or made to suffer.

**victimise** v. (also **-ize**) single out for punishment or discrimination; make (person etc.) a victim. □□ **victimisation** n.

**victor** n. conqueror, winner of contest.

**Victorian** ● n. native or resident of Victoria. ● adj. 1 of Victoria or its inhabitants. 2 of the time of Queen Victoria. 3 prudish.

**victorious** adj. conquering, triumphant; marked by victory.

**victory** n. success in battle, war, or contest.

**victualler** n. person who supplies victuals; (in full **licensed victualler**) publican etc. licensed to sell alcohol.

**victuals** n.pl. food, provisions.

**vidcast** n. video clip that can be downloaded to computer, mobile phone, etc.

**video** ● n. (pl. **videos**) recording, reproducing, or broadcasting of moving visual images; recording of moving visual images made digitally or on videotape. ● v. make video recording of.

**videotape** ● n. magnetic tape for recording visual images and sound. ● v. record on this.

**vie** v. (**vied**, **vying**) carry on rivalry; compete.

**view** ● n. 1 range of vision; what is seen; prospect; scene; picture etc. of this. 2 attitude or opinion. ● v. 1 look at; survey visually or mentally. 2 regard in particular way. □ **in view** visible. **in view of** because of, considering. **on view** displayed for inspection. □□ **viewer** n.

**viewfinder** n. device on camera showing extent of area being photographed.

**viewpoint** n. point of view.

**vigil** n. keeping awake during night etc., esp. to keep watch or pray.

**vigilance** n. watchfulness, caution. □□ **vigilant** adj.

**vigilante** n. member of self-appointed group for keeping order etc.

**vignette** n. a short written description.

**vigoro** n. Aust. team game combining elements of baseball and cricket.

**vigour** n. (also **vigor**) activity and strength of body or mind; healthy growth; animation. □□ **vigorous** adj. **vigorously** adv.

**Viking** n. ancient Scandinavian trader and pirate.

**vile** adj. disgusting; depraved. □□ **vilely** adv. **vileness** n.

**vilify** v. speak ill of, defame. □□ **vilification** n.

**villa** n. a house; (in full **villa unit**) home unit.

**village** n. 1 small country settlement. 2 Aust. shopping centre in suburb.

**villain** n. wicked person. □□ **villainous** adj. **villainy** n.

**villein** n. hist. feudal tenant entirely subject to lord or attached to manor.

**vim** n. colloq. vigour, energy.

**vinaigrette** n. salad dressing of oil and vinegar.

**vindicate** v. clear of suspicion; establish existence, merits, or justice of. □□ **vindication** n.

**vindictive** adj. tending to seek revenge. □□ **vindictively** adv. **vindictiveness** n.

**vine** n. climbing or trailing woody-stemmed plant, esp. bearing grapes.

**vinegar** n. sour liquid produced by fermentation of malt, wine, cider, etc. □□ **vinegary** adj.

**vineyard** n. plantation of grapevines, esp. for winemaking.

**vino** n. colloq. wine, esp. of inferior kind.

**vintage** ● n. 1 wine from a season's produce of grapes. 2 date of origin or existence. ● adj. of high or peak quality, esp. from a past season.

**vintner** n. wine merchant.

**vinyl** n. any of a group of plastics made by polymerisation; vinyl record.

**viola**[1] n. musical instrument larger than violin and of lower pitch.

**viola**[2] n. any plant of the genus including pansy and violet.

**violate** v. disregard; break (oath, law, etc.); treat profanely; break in on, disturb; rape. □□ **violation** n. **violator** n.

**violent** adj. 1 involving great physical force; intense, vehement. 2 (of death) resulting from external force or poison. □□ **violence** n. **violently** adv.

**violet** ● n. small plant often with purple flowers; bluish-purple colour. ● adj. bluish-purple.

**violin** n. high-pitched musical instrument with four strings played with bow. □□ **violinist** n.

**violoncello** n. (pl. **violoncellos**) cello.

**VIP** abbr. very important person.

**viper** n. small venomous snake of Europe etc.

**virago** n. (pl. **viragos**) fierce or abusive woman.

**viral** adj. 1 of or caused by virus. 2 (of an image, video, etc.) circulated rapidly and widely from one Internet user to another.

**virgin** ● n. 1 person who has never had sexual intercourse. 2 (the Virgin) Christ's mother Mary. ● adj. 1 not yet used or explored etc. 2 never having had sexual intercourse. 3 undefiled, pure. □□ **virginal** adj. **virginity** n.

**Virgo** n. sixth sign of zodiac, the Virgin. □□ **Virgoan** adj. & n.

**virile** adj. (of a man) having strength, energy, and strong sex drive; having or characterised by strength and energy. □□ **virility** n.

**virology** n. study of viruses.

**virtual** adj. 1 almost or nearly as described, but not completely or according to strict definition. 2 not physically existing as such but made by software to appear to do so; carried out, accessed, or stored by means of computer. □ **virtual reality** computer-generated simulation of reality.

**virtually** adv. 1 nearly; almost. 2 by means of virtual reality techniques; by means of computer.

**virtue** n. moral excellence, goodness; chastity; a good quality. □ **by** (or **in**) **virtue of** because of, on the strength of.

**virtuoso** n. (pl. **virtuosos** or **virtuosi**) expert performer. □□ **virtuosity** n.

**virtuous** adj. morally good. □□ **virtuously** adv. **virtuousness** n.

**virulent** adj. (of disease or poison) violent or very strong; bitterly hostile. □□ **virulence** n. **virulently** adv.

**virus** n. 1 microscopic organism able to cause disease. 2 such disease. 3 destructive code hidden in computer program.

**visa** n. endorsement on passport etc., esp. allowing holder to enter or leave country.

**visage** n. literary face.

**vis-à-vis** prep. in relation to; in comparison with; opposite to.

**viscera** n.pl. internal organs of body. □□ **visceral** adj.

**viscid** adj. glutinous, sticky. □□ **viscidity** n.

**viscose** n. viscous cellulose; fabric made from this.

**viscount** n. nobleman ranking between earl and baron.

**viscountess** n. woman holding rank of viscount; viscount's wife or widow.

**viscous** adj. glutinous, sticky. □□ **viscosity** n.

**visibility** n. being visible; range or possibility of vision as determined by light and weather.

**visible** adj. able to be seen, perceived or discovered. □□ **visibly** adv.

**vision** n. 1 act or faculty of seeing, sight. 2 thing or person seen in dream or trance etc. **3** beautiful person etc.; imaginative insight. **4** foresight.

**visionary** ● *adj.* **1** given to seeing visions or to fanciful theories. **2** having vision or foresight. **3** not real, imaginary. **4** unpractical. ● *n.* visionary person.

**visit** ● *v.* **1** go or come to see (person, place, etc.); stay temporarily with or at. **2** (of disease, calamity, etc.) attack. ● *n.* act of visiting. □□ **visitor** *n.*

**visitation** *n.* **1** official visit or inspection. **2** trouble seen as divine punishment.

**visor** *n.* (also **vizor**) movable part of helmet covering face; shield for eyes, esp. one at top of vehicle windscreen.

**vista** *n.* extensive view, esp. seen through long opening.

**visual** *adj.* of or used in seeing. □ **visual display unit** device displaying computer output or input on screen. □□ **visually** *adv.*

**visualise** *v.* (also **-ize**) imagine visually. □□ **visualisation** *n.*

**vital** ● *adj.* **1** essential to life; essential to existence, success, etc. **2** full of life or activity. ● *n.* (**vitals**) vital organs, e.g. heart, lungs. □□ **vitally** *adv.*

**vitality** *n.* liveliness, persistent energy.

**vitamin** *n.* any of various substances present in many foods and essential to health and growth.

**vitiate** *v.* make imperfect or ineffectual.

**viticulture** *n.* cultivation of grapevines.

**vitreous** *adj.* of or like glass.

**vitrify** *v.* change into glass or glassy substance. □□ **vitrification** *n.*

**vitriol** *n.* **1** sulphuric acid or sulphate. **2** caustic speech or criticism. □□ **vitriolic** *adj.*

**vituperate** *v.* criticise abusively. □□ **vituperation** *n.* **vituperative** *adj.*

**viva**[1] *n.* viva voce examination.

**viva**[2] *int.* long live (someone or something).

**vivace** *adv. Mus.* in lively and brisk manner.

**vivacious** *adj.* lively, animated. □□ **vivacity** *n.*

**viva voce** *n.* oral university examination.

**vivid** *adj.* (of light or colour) strong, intense; (of memory, description, etc.) lively, incisive. □□ **vividly** *adv.* **vividness** *n.*

**vivify** *v.* give life to.

**viviparous** *adj.* bringing forth young alive, not egg-laying.

**vivisection** *n.* surgical experimentation on living animals. □□ **vivisectionist** *n.* & *adj.*

**vixen** *n.* female fox.

**viz.** *abbr.* in other words; namely.

**vlog** ● *n.* website etc. where person regularly posts short videos. ● *v.* add material to or regularly update vlog.

**vocabulary** *n.* words known or used by person (or group); list of words and their meanings.

**vocal** *adj.* **1** of or uttered by voice. **2** expressing opinions freely. □□ **vocally** *adv.*

**vocalise** *v.* (also **-ize**) utter. □□ **vocalisation** *n.*

**vocalist** *n.* singer.

**vocation** *n.* strong desire or feeling or fitness for certain career; employment, trade, profession. □□ **vocational** *adj.*

**vociferate** *v.* **1** utter noisily. **2** shout, bawl. □□ **vociferation** *n.*

**vociferous** *adj.* making great outcry; noisy. □□ **vociferously** *adv.*

**vodcast** = VIDCAST.

**vodka** *n.* alcoholic spirit distilled chiefly from rye etc.

**vogue** *n.* prevailing fashion; popular use. □ **in vogue** in fashion. □□ **voguish** *adj.*

**voice** ● n. 1 sound formed in larynx and uttered by mouth, esp. in speaking, singing, etc. 2 expressed opinion, right to express opinion; distinctive tone or style of literary work or author. 3 *Gram.* set of verbal forms showing whether verb is active or passive. ● v. express; utter.
□ **voice-over** narration in a film etc. without a picture of speaker.

**voicemail** n. centralised electronic system that can store messages from telephone callers.

**void** ● adj. 1 empty, vacant. 2 not valid or binding. ● n. empty space, sense of loss. ● v. invalidate; excrete.

**voile** n. fine semi-transparent fabric.

**VOIP** abbr. voice over Internet protocol, technology for making telephone calls over Internet.

**volatile** adj. 1 changeable in mood; fickle; unstable. 2 evaporating rapidly. □□ **volatility** n.

**vol-au-vent** n. small round puff pastry case, esp. with savoury filling.

**volcanic** adj. of, like, or produced by volcano.

**volcano** n. (pl. **volcanoes**) mountain or hill from which lava, steam, etc. escape through earth's crust.

**vole** n. small rodent.

**volition** n. faculty or power of using one's will.

**volley** ● n. (pl. **volleys**) 1 simultaneous firing of a number of weapons; bullets etc. so fired. 2 torrent (of abuse etc.) 3 *Tennis, Football, etc.* playing of ball before it touches ground. ● v. return or send by volley.

**volleyball** n. game for two teams sending large ball by hand over net.

**volt** n. SI unit of electromotive force.

**voltage** n. electromotive force expressed in volts.

**volte-face** n. complete change of position in one's attitude or opinion.

**voluble** adj. speaking or spoken fluently or with continuous flow of words. □□ **volubility** n. **volubly** adv.

**volume** n. 1 single book forming part or all of work. 2 solid content, bulk. 3 space occupied by gas or liquid. 4 amount or quantity of. 5 quantity or power of sound, loudness. 6 moving mass of (water, smoke etc.)

**voluminous** adj. having great volume, bulky; copious.

**voluntary** adj. 1 acting, done, or given willingly; unpaid. 2 (of muscle, limb, etc.) controlled by will. □□ **voluntarily** adv.

**volunteer** ● n. person who voluntarily undertakes task or enters military etc. service. ● v. undertake or offer voluntarily; be a volunteer.

**voluptuary** n. person who seeks luxury and sensual pleasure.

**voluptuous** adj. 1 of, tending to, occupied with, or derived from, sensuous or sensual pleasure. 2 (of woman) having full and curvaceous figure. □□ **voluptuously** adv.

**vomit** ● v. (**vomited**) eject (contents of stomach) through mouth; emit in vast quantities; eject violently, belch forth. ● n. vomited matter.

**voodoo** n. religion characterised by sorcery and spirit possession.

**voracious** adj. greedy in eating, ravenous; very eager. □□ **voraciously** adv. **voracity** n.

**vortex** n. (pl. **vortexes** or **vortices**) whirlpool or whirlwind.

**vote** ● n. formal expression of choice or opinion by ballot, show of hands, etc., in election etc.; right to vote. ● v. express one's choice by vote; elect to position by vote. □□ **voter** n.

**votive** adj. given to fulfil vow.

**vouch** v. □ **vouch for** guarantee the accuracy or reliability etc. of.

**voucher** n. document exchangeable for goods or services; receipt.

**vouchsafe** v. give or grant.

**vow** ● n. solemn, esp. religious, promise. ● v. promise solemnly; declare solemnly.

**vowel** n. **1** speech sound made by vibrations of vocal cords but without audible friction. **2** letter(s) representing this.

**vox pop** n. colloq. popular opinion as represented by informal comments.

**voyage** ● n. journey, esp. long one by sea or in space. ● v. make voyage. □□ **voyager** n.

**voyeur** n. person who derives sexual pleasure from secretly observing others' sexual activity or organs. □□ **voyeurism** n. **voyeuristic** adj.

**VPN** abbr. virtual private network, arrangement whereby secure, apparently private network is achieved using encryption over public network.

**vs.** abbr. versus.

**vulcanise** v. (also -ize) strengthen (rubber) by treating with sulphur. □□ **vulcanisation** n.

**vulcanology** n. study of volcanoes.

**vulgar** adj. lacking refinement or good taste. □ **vulgar fraction** fraction represented by numbers above and below line (rather than decimally). □□ **vulgarly** adv. **vulgarity** n.

**vulgarism** n. vulgar word, expression, or habit.

**Vulgate** n. **1** 4th c. Latin version of Bible. **2** official RC Latin text as revised in 1592.

**vulnerable** adj. **1** easily wounded or harmed. **2** open to attack, injury, or criticism. □□ **vulnerability** n.

**vulture** n. **1** large carrion-eating bird of prey. **2** rapacious person.

**vulva** n. external parts of female genital organs.

**vying** see VIE.

**W** abbr. **1** watt(s). **2** West. **3** Western.

**WA** abbr. Western Australia.

**WACA** n. (ground of) Western Australian Cricket Association.

**wacko** colloq. ● adj. crazy, weird. ● n. (pl. **wackos** or **wackoes**) derog. weird or crazy person.

**wacky** adj. colloq. crazy.
□□ **wackiness** n.

**wad** ● n. **1** pad of soft material. **2** bunch of papers or banknotes. ● v. (**wadded**) pad.

**wadding** n. soft fibrous material for stuffing quilts, packing fragile articles in, etc.

**waddle** ● v. walk with short steps and swaying motion. ● n. such a walk.

**waddy** n. (also **waddie**) Aust. Aboriginal war club made of wood.

**wade** ● v. walk through water, mud, etc.; proceed slowly and laboriously (through). ● n. spell of wading.

**wader** n. **1** long-legged water bird. **2** (**waders**) high waterproof boots.

**wadi** n. rocky watercourse, dry except in rainy season.

**wafer** n. thin light crisp biscuit; small thin slice.

**waffle** colloq. ● n. **1** aimless verbose talk or writing. **2** small crisp batter cake. ● v. talk or write waffle.
□□ **waffler** n. **waffly** adj.

**waft** ● v. convey or travel smoothly (as) through air or over water. ● n. whiff or scent.

**wag** ● v. (**wagged**) **1** shake or wave to and fro. **2** truant. colloq. play truant. ● n. **1** wagging movement. **2** facetious person.

**wage** ● n. (also **wages**) regular payment to employee for his or her work. ● v. carry on (war etc.).

**waged** adj. in regular paid employment.

**wager** n. & v. bet.

**waggle** colloq. ● v. wag. ● n. waggling motion.

**wagon** n. (also **waggon**) four-wheeled vehicle for heavy loads; open railway truck.

**Wagyu** n. breed of Japanese cattle; tender beef obtained from such cattle.

**wahlenbergia** n. Australian herb bearing blue flowers.

**waif** n. homeless child; thin and vulnerable person.

**wail** ● n. prolonged plaintive inarticulate cry of pain, grief, etc. ● v. utter wail.

**wainscot** n. (also **wainscoting**) wooden panelling on room wall.

**waist** n. part of human body between ribs and hips; narrow middle part.

**waistcoat** n. close-fitting waist-length sleeveless jacket.

**wait** ● v. **1** defer action until specified time or event occurs; be postponed; pause. **2** wait on. ● n. act or period of waiting. □ **wait on** serve food and drink to (person) at meal; fetch and carry things for.

**waiter** n. person who serves at hotel or restaurant tables etc.

**waitress** n. female waiter.

**waive** v. refrain from insisting on or using. □□ **waiver** n.

**wake** ● v. (**woke** or **waked**, **woken** or **waked**, **waking**) **1** (cause to) cease to sleep or become alert. **2** evoke. ● n. **1** track left on water's surface by moving ship etc. **2** gathering of mourners after funeral; vigil beside corpse before burial, attendant lamentation or merrymaking. □ **in the wake of** behind; following. **wake up** wake; make or become alert.

**wakeful** *adj.* unable to sleep; sleepless. □□ **wakefully** *adv.* **wakefulness** *n.*

**waken** *v.* make or become awake.

**walk** ● *v.* 1 move by lifting and setting down each foot in turn, never having both feet off ground at once. 2 travel or go on foot. 3 traverse (distance) in walking. ● *n.* act of walking; ordinary human gait; person's manner of walking; place or route for walking. □ **walk of life** social rank; occupation. **walk out on** desert. □□ **walkable** *adj.*

**walkabout** *n.* 1 *Aust.* journey on foot as undertaken by Aboriginal person in order to live in traditional manner. 2 informal stroll among crowd by visiting dignitary etc. □ **go walkabout** *Aust.* 1 take walkabout. 2 *colloq.* be lost, missing, or stolen; lose concentration.

**walker** *n.* 1 person etc. that walks. 2 framework in which baby can walk unaided. 3 walking frame.

**walkie-talkie** *n.* portable two-way radio.

**walkman** *n. propr.* type of personal stereo that is portable.

**walkout** *n.* sudden angry departure, esp. as protest or strike.

**walkover** *n.* easy victory.

**wall** ● *n.* continuous narrow upright structure of usu. brick, stone, or wood, esp. enclosing or dividing a space or supporting roof; something that divides or encloses; outermost layer of plant organ, cell, etc. ● *v.* surround or enclose with wall.

**wallaby** *n.* any of various marsupials similar to but smaller than kangaroo.

**wallaroo** *n. Aust.* large stocky kangaroo of rocky or hilly country.

**wallet** *n.* small flat case for holding banknotes etc.

**wallflower** *n.* 1 garden plant. 2 *colloq.* socially awkward person.

**wallop** *colloq.* ● *v.* (**walloped**) thrash, hit hard; defeat convincingly. ● *n.* heavy blow.

**walloper** *n.* 1 person etc. that wallops. 2 *Aust. colloq.* police officer.

**wallow** *v.* roll about in mud etc. ● *n.* act of wallowing. □ **wallow** in indulge in an unrestrained way.

**wally** *n. colloq. derog.* stupid person.

**walnut** *n.* nut containing wrinkled edible kernel; N. hemisphere tree bearing it; its wood.

**walrus** *n.* long-tusked amphibious Arctic mammal.

**waltz** ● *n.* ballroom dance in triple time; music for this. ● *v.* dance a waltz; *colloq.* move easily, lightly, casually, etc.

**wambenger** *n. Aust.* phascogale.

**WAN** *abbr. Computing* wide area network.

**wan** *adj.* pale, weary-looking. □□ **wanly** *adv.* **wanness** *n.*

**wand** *n.* a slender rod, esp. associated with working of magic.

**wander** ● *v.* go from place to place aimlessly; stray; digress. ● *n.* act of wandering. □□ **wanderer** *n.*

**wanderlust** *n.* eagerness for travelling.

**Wandjina** *n.* (also **Wondjina**) *Aust.* Aboriginal ancestral spirit of fertility and rain.

**wane** *v.* decrease in power, vigour, importance, size, etc.; (of moon) decrease in apparent size. □ **on the wane** waning.

**wangle** *v. colloq.* obtain or arrange by trickery or scheming.

**wank** *coarse colloq.* ● *n.* 1 rubbish, nonsense. 2 self-indulgent posturing. 3 act or instance of masturbation. ● *v.* masturbate. □□ **wanker** *n.*

**wannabe** *n. colloq.* person who tries to be like someone else or to fit in with particular group.

**want** ● v. desire; need; lack; fall short of. ● n. a desire, a need; a lack.

**wanting** adj. lacking in quality or quantity; deficient.

**wanton** adj. irresponsible; lacking proper restraint.□□ **wantonly** adv.

**war** ● n. armed hostilities, esp. between nations; specific period of this; hostility between people; sustained campaign against crime, poverty, etc. ● v. (**warred**) make war.

**warabi** n. Aust. smallest rock wallaby.

**waratah** n. ornamental shrub of Australian genus Telopea, having large red flowers.

**warble** ● v. sing in gentle trilling way. ● n. warbling sound.
□□ **warbler** n.

**ward** n. 1 separate division or room of hospital etc. 2 administrative division esp. for elections. 3 child under care of guardian or court.□ **ward off** keep at a distance; repel.

**warden** n. official with supervisory duties.

**warder** n. prison officer.

**wardrobe** n. large cupboard for storing clothes; a stock of clothes or costumes.

**ware** n. manufactured goods of kind specified; (**wares**) articles for sale.

**warehouse** n. building in which goods are stored.

**warfare** n. waging war, campaigning.

**warhead** n. explosive head of missile.

**warlike** adj. fond of making war; aggressive; of or for war.

**warm** ● adj. 1 of or at fairly high temperature; (of person) with skin at natural or slightly raised temperature; (of clothes) affording warmth. 2 sympathetic, friendly, loving; hearty, enthusiastic. 3 iron. dangerous, hostile. 4 colloq. (in game) near object sought, near to guessing. 5 (of colour) reddish or yellowish ● v. make or become warm.
□ **warm-blooded** having blood that

remains at constant temperature. **warm down** recover from exercise etc. by doing gentler exercise. **warm up 1** (of athlete, performer, etc.) prepare for contest, performance, etc., by practising. **2** become warmer; reheat. **3** become enthusiastic etc. □□ **warmly** adv. **warmth** n.

**warmonger** n. person who seeks to bring about or promote war.

**warn** v. 1 inform of present or future danger or misfortune etc. 2 advise (person) to take certain action.

**warning** n. what is said or done or occurs to warn person.

**warp** ● v. make or become distorted, esp. through heat, damp, etc.; make or become perverted or strange.
● n. 1 warped state. 2 lengthwise threads in loom.

**warrant** ● n. 1 thing that authorises an action; written instruction allowing police to carry out search or arrest. 2 certificate of service rank held by warrant officer. ● v. justify; guarantee.

**warranty** n. guarantee of repair or replacement of purchased article.

**warren** n. network of rabbit burrows; densely populated or labyrinthine building or district.

**warrigal** Aust. ● adj. wild, untamed.
● n. (in full **warrigal greens**) fleshy-leaved plant used as vegetable.

**warrior** n. person skilled in or famed for fighting.

**wart** n. small round growth on skin caused by virus.□□ **warty** adj.

**warthog** n. African wild pig with wart-like lumps on its face.

**wary** adj. (**warier**) cautious; looking out for possible danger or difficulty.
□□ **warily** adv. **wariness** n.

**wasabi** n. green root of plant, used ground in Japanese cookery.

**wash** ● v. 1 cleanse with water or other liquid; wash oneself or clothes etc.; be washable. 2 flow past, against, or over; carry by flowing. **3** coat thinly with paint. **4** *colloq.* (of reasoning) be valid or persuasive. ● *n.* **1** process of washing or being washed; clothes etc. to be washed. **2** disturbed water or air behind moving ship or aircraft etc. **3** thin coating of paint. □ **washed up** *colloq.* defeated; having failed. **wash out 1** make (sport) impossible by heavy rainfall. **2** *colloq.* cancel. **wash-out** complete failure. **wash up** wash (dishes etc.) after use; cast up on shore.

**washable** *adj.* able to be washed without damage.

**washbasin** *n.* bowl (usu. fixed to a wall) for washing one's hands and face.

**washer** *n.* **1** flat ring of rubber, metal, etc. placed between two surfaces to tighten joint or disperse pressure. **2** *Aust.* cloth for washing face.

**washing** *n.* clothes etc. for washing or just washed. □ **washing-up** process of washing dishes after use; such dishes now weak.

**washout** *n.* *colloq.* event or period that is spoiled by constant or heavy rain; disappointing failure.

**Wasp** *n.* (also **WASP**) middle class White (Anglo-Saxon) Protestant.

**wasp** *n.* stinging insect with black and yellow stripes.

**waspish** *adj.* irritable, snappish.

**wassail** *n.* *arch.* festive occasion; merrymaking with a lot of drinking.

**wastage** *n.* loss or diminution by waste; loss of employees by retirement or resignation.

**waste** ● *v.* **1** use to no purpose or for inadequate result or extravagantly; fail to use. **2** wear away; make or become weak. **3** devastate; *colloq.* kill, murder. ● *adj.* **1** superfluous; no longer needed. **2** uninhabited, not cultivated. ● *n.* **1** act of wasting; waste material. **2** useless by-products. **3** waste region. □□ **waster** *n.*

**wasteful** *adj.* extravagant.
□□ **wastefully** *adv.*

**watch** ● *v.* keep under observation; wait alertly; take heed; exercise protective care. ● *n.* **1** small portable timepiece for wrist or pocket. **2** act of observing or guarding; spell of duty worked by sailor, police officer, etc. □ **watch out** be careful. □□ **watcher** *n.*

**watchdog** *n.* dog kept to guard property; guardian of people's rights etc.

**watchful** *adj.* accustomed to watching; on the watch.
□□ **watchfully** *adv.* **watchfulness** *n.*

**water** ● *n.* **1** a colourless odourless tasteless liquid that is a compound of hydrogen and oxygen; this as supplied for domestic use; lake; sea; level of tide. **2** watery secretion; urine. ● *v.* **1** sprinkle, supply, or dilute with water. **2** secrete tears or saliva. **3** (as **watered** *adj.*) (of silk etc.) having irregular wavy finish. □ **by water** in boat etc. **water biscuit** thin unsweetened biscuit. **water chestnut** edible corm of a sedge. **water closet** toilet flushed by water. **water down** dilute; make less forceful. **water main** main pipe in water supply system. **water polo** ball game played by teams of swimmers. **water table** level below which ground is saturated with water.

**waterbed** *n.* mattress of rubber etc. filled with water.

**waterboarding** *n.* interrogation technique simulating experience of drowning.

**watercolour** *n.* artists' paint mixed with water (not oil); a painting done with this.

**watercourse** *n.* stream, creek, or artificial waterway; its channel.

**watercress** *n.* type of cress that grows in running water.

**waterfall** ● *n.* cascade of water falling from height. ● *adj.* of a method of project management that is characterised by sequential stages and fixed plan of work.

**waterfront** *n.* **1** part of town that borders on river, lake, or sea. **2** complex of docks, wharves, offices, etc. where ships can be loaded and unloaded.

**waterlogged** *adj.* saturated with water.

**watermark** *n.* manufacturer's design in paper, visible when paper is held against the light.

**watermelon** *n.* melon with green skin, red pulp, and sweet watery juice.

**waterproof ●** *adj.* unable to be penetrated by water. **●** *v.* make waterproof.

**watershed** *n.* **1** line of high land separating two river systems. **2** turning point in course of events.

**waterspout** *n.* column of water between sea and cloud, formed by whirlwind.

**watertight** *adj.* **1** made or fastened so that water cannot get in or out. **2** impossible to disprove.

**waterway** *n.* navigable channel, canal.

**waterwheel** *n.* wheel turned by flow of water to work machinery.

**watery** *adj.* containing too much water; too thin in consistency; of or consisting of water; vapid, uninteresting; (of colour) pale. □□ **wateriness** *n.*

**watt** *n.* SI unit of power.

**wattage** *n.* amount of electrical power expressed in watts.

**wattle** *n.* **1** *Aust.* acacia having pliant branches and profuse golden flowers. **2** interlaced rods and sticks used for making fences, walls, etc. **3** fold of skin hanging from neck or face of certain birds.

**wave ●** *v.* **1** move (hand etc.) to and fro in greeting or as signal; give such motion to; direct (person) or express (greeting etc.) by waving. **2** give undulating form to; have such form. **●** *n.* **1** moving ridge of water. **2** wavelike curve. **3** advancing group. **4** temporary increase of influence or condition. **5** act of waving. **6** wavelike motion by which heat, light, sound, or electricity is spread; single curve in this.

**waveband** *n.* a range of wavelengths.

**wavelength** *n.* **1** distance between successive crests of wave, esp. points in sound wave or electromagnetic wave. **2** *colloq.* particular mode or range of thinking and communicating.

**wavelet** *n.* small wave.

**waver** *v.* be or become unsteady; show hesitation or uncertainty.

**wavy** *adj.* (**wavier**) having waves or alternate contrary curves. □□ **waviness** *n.*

**wax ●** *n.* beeswax; polish containing this; any of various similar soft substances. **●** *v.* **1** coat, polish, or treat with wax. **2** remove hair from (legs etc.) using wax. **3** increase in vigour or importance; (of moon) show an increasingly bright area until becoming full.

**way ●** *n.* **1** road, track, path; street; course, route. **2** method, means; style, manner; habitual course of action. **3** distance (to be) travelled. **4** unimpeded opportunity or space to advance. **5** advance, progress. **6** specified condition or state. **7** particular aspect of something. **●** *adv. colloq.* by a great deal, extremely. □ **by the way** incidentally. **by way of** by means of; as a form of; passing through. **have one's way** get what one wants. **in a way** in a certain respect but not altogether or completely. **in the way** forming an obstacle. **make** (or **give**) **way** allow someone to pass. **on one's way** having progressed. **on the way** travelling; (of baby) conceived but not yet born. **out**

**of one's way** not on one's intended route; requiring extra effort.

**wayward** *adj.* childishly self-willed; capricious. □□ **waywardness** *n.*

**WC** *abbr.* water closet.

**we** *pron.* used by person to refer to herself or himself and one or more others; used instead of 'I' by sovereign in formal contexts or by editorial writer in newspaper.

**weak** *adj.* deficient in strength, power, vigour, resolution, or number; unconvincing; easily influenced. □□ **weakly** *adv.*

**weaken** *v.* make or become weaker.

**weakling** *n.* feeble person or animal.

**weakness** *n.* being weak; defect; self-indulgent liking.

**weal** *n.* ridge raised on flesh by stroke of rod or whip.

**wealth** *n.* money and valuable possessions; possession of these; great quantity.

**wealthy** *adj.* (**wealthier**) having wealth; rich.

**wean** *v.* accustom (infant or other young mammal) to food other than (mother's) milk; cause to give up gradually.

**weapon** *n.* thing designed or used for inflicting harm or damage; means for gaining advantage in a conflict.

**wear** ● *v.* (**wore**, **worn**, **wearing**) **1** have on body as clothing or ornament. **2** damage or become damaged by prolonged use. **3** endure continued use. ● *n.* **1** wearing, being worn. **2** clothing. **3** capacity for resisting wear. □ **wear down** overcome (opposition etc.) by persistence. **wear off** pass off gradually. **wear out** use or be used until useless; tire or be tired out. □□ **wearer** *n.*

**wearisome** *adj.* causing weariness.

**weary** ● *adj.* (**wearier**) very tired; tiring, tedious. ● *v.* make or grow weary. □□ **wearily** *adv.* **weariness** *n.*

**weasel** ● *n.* small carnivorous mammal of Europe etc. ● *v.* achieve something by use of cunning or deceit.

**weather** ● *n.* atmospheric conditions at specified place or time as regards heat, cloudiness, humidity, sunshine, wind, and rain, etc. ● *v.* **1** expose to or affect by weather; be discoloured or worn thus. **2** come safely through (storm). □ **make heavy weather of** have difficulty in doing. **under the weather** *colloq.* indisposed or out of sorts; drunk.

**weatherboard** *n.* each of series of overlapping horizontal boards on wall; building clad with weatherboards.

**weathervane** *n.* revolving pointer on roof etc. to show direction of wind.

**weave** ● *v.* (**wove**, **woven**, **weaving**) **1** form (fabric) by interlacing threads; form (threads) into fabric, esp. in loom. **2** compose (story etc.) **3** move in intricate course. ● *n.* style of weaving. □□ **weaver** *n.*

**web** *n.* **1** network of fine strands made by spider etc.; complex system of interconnected elements. **2** (**Web**) = World Wide Web. **3** membrane connecting toes of aquatic animal or bird. □□ **webbed** *adj.*

**webbing** *n.* strong narrow closely-woven fabric for belts etc.

**Weber** *n. propr.* barbecue kettle.

**weber** *n.* SI unit of magnetic flux.

**weblink** *n.* **1** = HYPERLINK. **2** printed address of website in book etc.

**weblog** *n.* full form of BLOG.

**webpage** *n.* document connected to World Wide Web.

**website** *n.* location connected to Internet that maintains one or more pages on World Wide Web.

**wed** *v.* marry; unite.

**Wed.** *abbr.* Wednesday.

**wedding** *n.* marriage ceremony and festivities.

**wedge** ● *n.* **1** piece of tapering wood, metal, etc. used for forcing things apart or fixing them immovably etc. **2** wedge-shaped thing. **3** golf club with wedge-shaped head. ● *v.* **1** secure or force open or apart with wedge. **2** force into a narrow space.

**wedlock** *n.* married state.

**Wednesday** *n.* day of week following Tuesday.

**wee** *colloq.* ● *adj.* little, tiny. ● *n.* act of urinating; urine. ● *v.* urinate.

**weed** ● *n.* **1** wild (or any) plant growing where it is not wanted. **2** *colloq.* feeble person etc. **3** marijuana, tobacco. ● *v.* rid of weeds or unwanted parts.□ **weed out** remove as inferior or undesirable.

**week** *n.* period of seven successive days, esp. from Monday to Sunday or Sunday to Saturday; weekdays of this; working period during week.

**weekday** *n.* day other than Saturday or Sunday.

**weekly** *adj. & adv.* (done, produced, or occurring) once a week.

**weeny** *adj.* (**weenier**) *colloq.* tiny.

**weep** *v.* (**wept, weeping**) shed (tears); shed or ooze (moisture) in drops. ● *n.* spell of weeping.

**weeping** *adj.* (of tree) having drooping branches.

**weero** *n. Aust.* cockatiel.

**weevil** *n.* destructive beetle feeding esp. on grain.

**weft** *n.* threads woven across warp to make fabric.

**weigh** *v.* **1** find weight of; have a specified weight. **2** estimate relative importance or desirability of; consider with view to choice, rejection, or preference. **3** be heavy or burdensome (to).□ **weigh anchor** raise anchor and begin voyage. **weigh down 1** bring or keep down by exerting weight. **2** be oppressive or burdensome (to). **weigh up** form estimate of.

**weighbridge** *n.* machine with plate set in road etc. for weighing vehicles.

**weight** ● *n.* **1** force on body due to earth's gravitation; heaviness of body; quantitative expression of body's weight, scale of such weights; body of known weight for use in weighing or weight training; heavy body, esp. used in mechanism etc.; load, burden. **2** influence, importance; preponderance (of evidence etc.) ● *v.* **1** attach weight to; hold down with weight; impede, burden. **2** attach importance to; bias. □□ **weightless** *adj.*

**weighting** *n.* extra pay or allowances given in special cases.

**weighty** *adj.* (**weightier**) **1** heavy. **2** momentous. **3** deserving attention. **4** influential, authoritative.

**weir** *n.* dam across river to retain water and regulate its flow.

**weird** *adj.* uncanny, supernatural; strange.□□ **weirdly** *adv.* **weirdness** *n.*

**welcome** ● *n.* kind or glad greeting or reception. ● *int.* expressing such greeting. ● *v.* receive with welcome. ● *adj.* gladly received; cordially allowed or invited to.

**weld** ● *v.* join (pieces of metal or plastic) using heat, usu. from electric arc; fashion into effectual or homogeneous whole. ● *n.* welded joint.□□ **welder** *n.*

**welfare** *n.* **1** well-being, happiness. **2** health and prosperity (of person, community etc.) **3** financial support by government.□ **welfare state** system attempting to ensure welfare of all citizens by means of government operated social services etc.

**well**[1] ● *adv.* (**better, best**) **1** in satisfactory way; with distinction; thoroughly, carefully; with heartiness or approval. **2** probably, reasonably. **3** to considerable extent. **4** fortunately. ● *adj.* in good health;

satisfactory. ● *int.* expressing surprise, resignation, etc., or continuation of talk after pause.□ **as well** in addition; desirable; desirably. **as well as** in addition to. **might as well** have no reason not to. **well-appointed** well equipped or furnished. **well-being** good health, happiness, and prosperity. **well-disposed** friendly and sympathetic. **well-executed** skilfully carried out. **well-meaning** (also **well-meant**) acting or done with good intentions. **well-nigh** almost. **well off** in satisfactory or good situation; fairly rich. **well-read** having read much literature. **well spoken** speaking in cultured way. **well-to-do** fairly rich.

**well**² ● *n.* 1 shaft sunk into ground to obtain water, oil, etc.; enclosed space like well shaft, e.g. central space in building for stairs, lift, light, or ventilation. 2 source. ● *v.* rise or flow as water from well.

**wellington** *n.* (in full **wellington boot**) waterproof boot usu. reaching knee.

**welsh** *v.* (also **welch**) avoid paying one's debts; break agreement. □□ **welsher** *n.*

**welt** ● *n.* 1 leather rim sewn to shoe upper for sole to be attached to. 2 ridge raised on flesh by stroke of rod etc. 3 ribbed or reinforced border of garment. 4 heavy blow. ● *v.* 1 provide with welt. 2 raise weals on. 3 thrash.

**welter** ● *v.* roll, wallow; be soaked in. ● *n.* 1 general confusion; disorderly mixture. 2 horserace in which minimum weight for riders is higher than usual.

**welterweight** *n.* boxing weight (63.5–67 kg).

**wen** *n.* benign tumour on skin.

**wend** *v.* □ **wend one's way** go.

**went** see GO.

**wept** see WEEP.

**werewolf** *n.* (*pl.* **werewolves**) *Mythol.* human being who changes into wolf.

**west** ● *n.* 1 point on horizon where sun sets; direction in which this lies; western part. 2 (usu. **the West**) Europe, N. America, Australia, etc., in contrast with other civilisations. ● *adj.* in the west; (of wind) coming from the west. ● *adv.* towards the west. □□ **westward** *adj., adv., & n.* **westwards** *adv.*

**westerly** *adj.* towards or blowing from the west.

**western** ● *adj.* of or in west. ● *n.* film or novel about cowboys in western N. America. □□ **westernise** *v.* (also **-ize**) **westernmost** *adj.*

**westie** *n. Aust. derog.* resident of western suburbs of Sydney etc.; person regarded as uncultured, boorish, etc.

**westringia** *n.* flowering Australian shrub.

**wet** ● *adj.* (**wetter**) 1 soaked or covered with water or other liquid; rainy; not dry. 2 *colloq.* feeble, inept. ● *n.* moisture, water, rainy weather; *Aust.* (**the wet**) rainy season. □ **wet blanket** *colloq.* gloomy person preventing enjoyment of others. **wet nurse** woman employed to suckle another's child.

**wether** *n.* castrated ram.

**wetsuit** *n.* close-fitting rubber garment worn for warmth in water sports, diving, etc.

**wettie** *n. Aust. colloq.* wetsuit.

**whack** *colloq.* ● *v.* strike with sharp blow. ● *n.* 1 sharp or resounding blow. 2 a share.

**whacked** *adj.* tired out; under influence of drugs.

**whacking** *colloq.* ● *adj.* large. ● *adv.* very.

**whale** *n.* very large sea mammal.
□ **a whale of a** *colloq.* example of exceedingly great or good thing.

**whaler** *n.* **1** whaling ship or seaman. **2** any of several sharks of Australian waters.

**whaling** *n.* hunting whales.

**wham** *int.* & *n. colloq.* sound of forcible impact.

**wharf** *n.* (*pl.* **wharves** or **wharfs**) quayside structure for loading or unloading of moored vessels.

**wharfie** *n. Aust. colloq.* waterside worker; stevedore.

**what** ● *adj.* **1** asking for something to be specified or identified. **2** how great or remarkable (*what luck!*). ● *pron.* what thing(s)? What did you say? ● *adv.* to what extent or degree. ● *int.* exclamation of surprise. □ **what for?** why?

**whatever** ● *pron.* anything or everything that; no matter what. ● *adj.* of any kind or number; of any kind at all. ● *adv.* not of any kind (*no help whatever*). ● *int. colloq.* said as response indicating reluctance to discuss something, implying indifference.

**whatnot** *n.* indefinite or trivial thing.

**whatsoever** *adj.* & *pron.* whatever.

**wheat** *n.* cereal plant bearing dense four-sided seed-spikes; its grain used for flour etc.

**wheaten** *adj.* made of wheat.

**wheedle** *v.* coax.

**wheel** ● *n.* **1** circular frame or disc revolving on axle and used to propel vehicle or other machinery; wheel-like thing. **2** motion as of wheel. **3** steering wheel. **4** (**wheels**) *colloq.* car. ● *v.* **1** turn on axis or pivot. **2** swing around in line with one end as pivot. **3** (cause to) change direction or face another way. **4** push or pull (wheeled thing, or its load or occupant). **5** go in circles or curves.

□ **wheel clamp** device for immobilising illegally parked car.

**wheelbarrow** *n.* small cart with one wheel and two shafts for carrying garden loads etc.

**wheelbase** *n.* distance between vehicle's front and rear axles.

**wheelchair** *n.* chair on wheels for person who cannot walk.

**wheelie** *n. colloq.* manoeuvre on bicycle or motorcycle with front wheel off ground.

**wheeze** ● *v.* breathe or utter with audible whistling sound. ● *n.* sound of wheezing. □□ **wheezy** *adj.*

**whelk** *n.* spiral-shelled marine mollusc.

**whelp** ● *n.* young dog. ● *v.* give birth to puppies.

**when** ● *adv.* **1** at what time; on what occasion. **2** on the occasion on which. ● *conj.* **1** at the time that; whenever; as soon as. **2** although. ● *pron.* what time.

**whence** *conj.* & *adv. formal* from where; from which.

**whenever** *conj.* & *adj.* at whatever time; on whatever occasion; every time that.

**where** ● *adv.* & *conj.* at or in which place or circumstances; from what place or source; to what place. ● *pron.* what place.

**whereabouts** ● *adv.* where or approximately where? ● *n.* person's or thing's approximate location.

**whereas** *conj.* **1** in contrast or comparison with the fact that. **2** *formal* seeing that.

**whereby** *conj.* by what or which means.

**whereupon** *conj.* immediately after which.

**wherever** *adv.* & *conj.* at or to whatever place.

**wherry** *n.* light rowing boat; large light barge.

**whet** *v.* (whetted) sharpen; stimulate (appetite or interest).

**whether** *conj.* introducing first or both of alternative possibilities.

**whetstone** *n.* shaped hard stone used for sharpening tools.

**whey** *n.* watery liquid left when milk forms curds.

**which** ● *adj. & pron.* what particular ones of a set. ● *rel. pron.* thing or animal referred to.

**whichever** *adj. & pron.* any which; no matter which.

**whiff** *n.* puff of air, smoke, etc.

**while** ● *n.* period of time; time spent in doing something. ● *conj.* 1 during the time that; for as long as. 2 although, whereas.□ **while away** pass (time) in leisurely or interesting way.

**whilst** *conj.* while.

**whim** *n.* sudden fancy.

**whimper** ● *v.* make feeble, querulous, or frightened sounds. ● *n.* such a sound.

**whimsical** *adj.* impulsive and playful; quaint, fanciful.□□ **whimsicality** *n.* **whimsically** *adv.*

**whine** ● *n.* long-drawn complaining cry or similar shrill sound; querulous tone or complaint. ● *v.* emit or utter whine(s); complain monotonously; utter in whining tone.

**whinge** *v. colloq.* ● complain peevishly. ● *n.* whining complaint.

**whinny** ● *n.* gentle or joyful neigh. ● *v.* give whinny.

**whip** ● *n.* 1 lash attached to stick for urging on or for punishing. 2 (in parliament) person appointed by political party to control its discipline and tactics. 3 dessert made with whipped cream etc. ● *v.* (whipped) 1 beat or urge on with whip. 2 beat (cream, eggs, etc.) into froth. 3 take or move suddenly or quickly. 4 make quickly.□ **whipping boy** scapegoat.

**whip-round** *colloq.* collection of money from group. **whip up 1** excite or stir up. **2** make quickly.

**whipbird** *n.* olive-green Australian bird.

**whipcord** *n.* tightly twisted cord; close-woven worsted fabric.

**whiplash** *n.* lash of whip; injury caused by jerk to head.

**whippersnapper** *n.* small child.

**whippet** *n.* crossbred dog of greyhound type, used for racing.

**whippy** *adj.* flexible, springy.

**whirl** ● *v.* 1 swing round and round; revolve rapidly; convey or go rapidly in car etc. 2 (of thoughts etc.) seem to spin round. 3 (of thoughts) be confused, follow each other in bewildering succession. ● *n.* 1 whirling movement. 2 state of intense activity or confusion. □ **give something a whirl** attempt something.

**whirlpool** *n.* current of water whirling in circle.

**whirlwind** *n.* mass of air whirling rapidly around central point.

**whirly** *n.* (also **whirly-whirly**) *Aust.* = WILLY WILLY.

**whirr** ● *n.* continuous buzzing or softly clicking sound. ● *v.* make this sound.

**whisk** ● *v.* 1 brush with sweeping movement; take suddenly. 2 whip (cream, eggs, etc.) ● *n.* 1 whisking movement. 2 utensil for whipping eggs, cream, etc.; bunch of grass, twigs, bristles, etc., for dusting or brushing.

**whisker** *n.* 1 each of bristles on face of cat etc. 2 (**whiskers**) hair on cheeks or sides of face of man. 3 *colloq.* small distance.□□ **whiskered** *adj.* **whiskery** *adj.*

**whisky** *n.* spirit distilled esp. from malted barley.

**whisper** ● *v.* speak using breath instead of vocal cords; talk or say in barely audible tone or in confidential way; rustle, murmur. ● *n.* whispering speech or sound; thing whispered; rumour.

**whisperer** n. **1** person who whispers; person who spreads gossip or rumours. **2** person skilled in taming or training specified kind of animal.

**whist** n. card game usu. for two pairs of opponents.

**whistle** ● n. **1** clear shrill sound made by forcing breath through lips contracted to narrow opening. **2** similar sound made by bird, wind, missile, etc. **3** instrument used to produce such sound. ● v. emit whistle; produce (tune) by whistling. □ **whistle-stop** politician's brief pause for electioneering speech on tour.

**white** ● adj. **1** of the colour of snow or common salt; having light-coloured skin; pale from illness, fear, etc. **2** (of coffee or tea) served with milk. ● n. **1** white colour or thing; (also **White**) member of human group having light-coloured skin. **2** transparent substance around egg yolk. □ **white ant** termite. **white elephant** useless possession. **white gold** gold mixed with platinum. **white-hot** (of metal) glowing white after heating. **white lie** harmless or trivial untruth. **white noise** noise containing many frequencies with equal intensities. **White Paper** government report giving information on proposals of an issue. **white pointer** = great white shark. □□ **whiten** v. **whitener** n. **whiteness** n. **whitish** adj.

**whitewash** n. solution of quicklime etc. for whitening walls etc.

**whither** adv. arch. to what place.

**whiting** n. (pl. **whiting**) small edible sea fish.

**whitlow** n. inflammation near fingernail or toenail.

**Whit Sunday** n. seventh Sunday after Easter.

**whittle** v. pare (wood etc.) by cutting thin slices or shavings from surface; reduce by repeated subtractions.

**whiz** (also **whizz**) ● n. **1** sound made by object moving through air at great speed. **2** colloq. person remarkably skilful at specified activity. ● v. move very quickly.

**WHO** abbr. World Health Organisation.

**who** pron. **1** what or which person(s)? **2** the particular person(s).

**whodunit** n. (also **whodunnit**) colloq. detective story, play, or film.

**whoever** pron. any or every person who, no matter who.

**whole** ● adj. uninjured, unbroken, intact, or undiminished; not less than; all. ● n. complete thing; all of a thing; all members etc. (of). □ **on the whole** considering everything; in general.

**whole number** number without fractions. □□ **wholeness** n.

**wholefood** n. food that has not been unnecessarily processed.

**wholehearted** adj. without doubts or reservations.

**wholemeal** adj. made from whole grain of wheat etc.

**wholesale** ● n. selling goods in large quantities, esp. for retail by others. ● adj. & adv. in the wholesale trade; on large scale. □□ **wholesaler** n.

**wholesome** adj. promoting physical, mental, or moral health.

**wholism** n. = HOLISM.

**wholly** adv. entirely.

**whom** pron. objective case of WHO.

**whoop** ● n. cry expressing excitement etc. ● v. utter loud cry of excitement. □ **whooping disease** cough infectious disease esp. of children, with violent convulsive cough.

**whopper** n. colloq. something very large; great lie.

**whopping** adj. & adv. colloq. huge.

**whore** n. derog. prostitute.

**whorl** n. ring of leaves etc. around stem; one turn of spiral; complete circular line in fingerprint.

**who's** who is; who has.

---

Usage Because it has an apostrophe, *who's* is easily confused with *whose*. They are each correctly used in *Who's there?* (= Who is there?), *Who's taken my pen?* (= Who has taken my pen?), and *Whose book is this?* (= Who does this book belong to?).

---

**whose** pron. & adj. belonging to whom or to which.

**whosoever** pron. whoever.

**why** ● adv. for what reason or purpose. ● int. exclamation of surprise, impatience, reflection, or protest.

**Wicca** n. religious cult of modern witchcraft.□□ **Wiccan** adj. & n.

**wick** n. strip or thread feeding flame with fuel.

**wicked** adj. 1 morally bad; offending against what is right; playfully mischievous. 2 colloq. formidable, severe. 3 colloq. excellent.
□□ **wickedly** adv. **wickedness** n.

**wicker** n. plaited osiers or thin canes as material for baskets etc.

**wicket** n. Cricket three upright stumps with bails in position defended by batter; part of cricket ground between the two wickets.

**wicketkeeper** n. Cricket fielder stationed close behind batter's wicket.

**wide** ● adj. 1 having sides far apart, broad, not narrow. 2 extending far, not restricted. 3 liberal, not specialised. 4 open to full extent. 5 not within reasonable distance of, far from. ● adv. 1 to full extent. 2 far from target etc. □ **wide awake** fully awake; colloq. alert. □□ **widely** adv. **widen** v.

**widget** n. colloq. 1 small gadget or device. 2 Computing application etc. that enables user to perform function or access service.

**widow** n. woman who has lost her spouse by death and not married again.□□ **widowhood** n.

**widowed** adj. made widow or widower.

**widower** n. man who has lost his spouse by death and not married again.

**width** n. 1 measurement from side to side. 2 large extent. 3 liberality of views etc. 4 piece of material of full width.□□ **widthways** adv.

**wield** v. hold and use (a tool etc.); control, exert.□□ **wielder** n.

**wife** n. (pl. **wives**) married woman in relation to her spouse.□□ **wifely** adj.

**Wi-Fi** abbr. propr. facility allowing computers, smartphones, etc. to connect to Internet or communicate with one another wirelessly within particular area.

**wig** ● n. 1 artificial head of hair. 2 wool that grows above and around eyes of sheep. ● v. Aust. clip wool from around sheep's eyes.

**wiggle** colloq. ● v. move from side to side etc. ● n. wiggling movement. □□ **wiggly** adj.

**wigwam** n. conical tent formerly used by some N. American indigenous peoples.

**wiki** n. collaborative website.

**wild** ● adj. 1 in original natural state; not domesticated, cultivated, or civilised. 2 (of Australian plant) resembling or acting as substitute for specified European etc. plant. 3 unrestrained, disorderly; tempestuous; intensely eager, frantic; (**wild about**) colloq. enthusiastically devoted to each other; colloq. infuriated; random, ill-aimed, rash. ● adv. in a wild way. ● *n.* wild place. □ **wild goose chase** useless quest. □□ **wildly** *adv.* **wildness** *n.*

**wilderness** *n.* wild uncultivated area.

**wildfire** *n.* □ **spread like wildfire** (of rumours etc.) spread very fast.

**wildlife** *n.* wild animals collectively.

**wile** *n.* piece of trickery.

**wilful** *adj.* **1** intentional, deliberate. **2** (of person) headstrong, obstinate. □□ **wilfully** *adv.* **wilfulness** *n.*

**will**[1] *v.aux.* used to express promises and obligations, and with other words to express future tense.

**will**[2] ● *n.* **1** mental faculty by which person decides what to do. **2** fixed desire or intention. **3** willpower. **4** legal written directions for disposal of one's property etc. after death. **5** disposition towards others. ● *v.* **1** try to cause by will power. **2** intend. **3** desire. **4** bequeath by will.

**willie** *n.* var. of WILLY.

**willies** *n.pl. colloq.* nervous discomfort.

**willing** *adj.* desiring to do what is required, not objecting; given or done readily. □□ **willingly** *adv.* **willingness** *n.*

**will-o'-the-wisp** *n.* **1** phosphorescent light seen on marshy ground. **2** delusive hope or plan.

**willow** *n.* **1** waterside tree with pliant branches yielding osiers; any similar Australian tree. **2** cricket bat.

**willowy** *adj.* lithe and slender.

**willpower** *n.* control exercised by deliberate purpose over impulse; self-control.

**willy** *n. colloq.* penis.

**willy-nilly** *adv.* whether one likes it or not.

**willy wagtail** *n.* (also **willie wagtail**) black and white bird, a fantail, widespread in Australia.

**willy willy** *n.* (also **willy-willy**) *Aust.* whirlwind or dust storm.

**wilt** ● *v.* wither, droop; lose energy. ● *n.* plant disease causing wilting.

**wily** *adj.* (**wilier**) crafty, cunning.

**wimp** *n. colloq.* feeble or ineffectual person. □□ **wimpish** *adj.*

**win** ● *v.* (**won**, **winning**) **1** secure as result of fight, contest, bet, etc. **2** be victor; be victorious in. ● *n.* victory in game etc. □ **win over** gain favour of.

**wince** ● *n.* make slight involuntary movement from pain or embarrassment etc. ● *v.* give wince.

**winch** ● *n.* machine for hoisting or pulling things by cable that winds around revolving drum. ● *v.* lift with winch.

**wind**[1] ● *n.* **1** air in natural motion; breath, esp. as needed in exercise or playing wind instrument. **2** empty talk. **3** gas generated in bowels etc. **4** wind instruments of orchestra etc. ● *v.* **1** cause to be out of breath. **2** detect by smell. □ **get wind of** *colloq.* hear a hint or rumour of. **in the wind** happening or about to happen. **put the wind up** *colloq.* alarm or frighten. **take the wind out of a person's sails** take away advantage suddenly, frustrate by anticipating person. **wind chill** cooling effect of wind. **wind farm** group of energy-producing wind turbines. **wind instrument** musical instrument sounded by current of air, esp. the breath. **wind tunnel** tunnel-like device to produce airstream past models of aircraft etc. for study of wind effects on them.

**wind**[2] ● *v.* (**wound**, **winding**) **1** go in spiral, curved, or crooked course; make (one's way) thus; wrap closely, coil. **2** provide with coiled thread etc.; surround (as) with coil; wind up (clock etc.) ● *n.* bend or turn in course.

**windbag** *n. colloq.* person who talks a lot.

**windbreak** *n.* row of trees, fence, etc., serving to break force of wind.

**winded** *adj.* having difficulty breathing because of exertion or blow to stomach.

**windfall** *n.* **1** piece of unexpected good fortune. **2** fruit blown to ground by wind.

**windlass** *n.* machine with horizontal axle for hauling or joisting.

**windmill** *n.* mill or water pump driven by action of wind on its sails.

**window** *n.* **1** opening, usu. with glass, in wall etc. to admit light; the glass itself; space for display behind window of shop; window-like aperture. **2** *Computing* framed area on computer screen allowing control and display of a number of tasks. □ **window dressing** arranging goods attractively in shop window; representing events in misleadingly favourable way.

**windscreen** *n.* glass in window at front of vehicle. □ **windscreen wiper** rubber blade on mechanical arm, for keeping windscreen clear of rain etc.

**windsock** *n.* canvas etc. cylinder on mast to show direction of wind at airfield etc.

**windsurfing** *n.* sport of riding on water on sailboard. □□ **windsurf** *v.* **windsurfer** *n.*

**windswept** *adj.* exposed to strong winds. **2** untidy after being exposed to wind.

**windward** ● *adj.* on or towards the side from which the wind is blowing. ● *n.* this direction.

**wine** ● *n.* fermented grape juice as alcoholic drink; fermented drink resembling this made from other fruits etc.; colour of red wine. ● *v.* drink wine; entertain with wine.

**wing** ● *n.* **1** each of pair of projecting parts by which bird or insect etc. is able to fly; winglike part of aircraft. **2** projecting part; bodywork above wheel of car. **3** either end of a battle array; player at either end of forward line in soccer, hockey, etc.; side part of playing area in these games; extreme section of political party; (wings) sides of theatre stage. **4** *Aust.* fence guiding stock towards stockyard entrance. ● *v.* **1** fly; travel by wings. **2** wound in wing or arm. □ **under one's wing** under one's protection. **wing collar** high stiff collar with turned-down corners. □□ **winged** *adj.*

**winger** *n.* (in sports) wing player.

**wingspan** *n.* measurement across wings from one tip to other.

**wink** ● *v.* close and open one eye quickly, esp. as signal; close eye(s) momentarily; (of light) shine or flash intermittently. ● *n.* **1** act of winking. **2** *colloq.* short sleep.

**winkle** ● *n.* edible sea snail. ● *v.* extract with difficulty.

**winning** ● *adj.* charming, persuasive. ● *n.* (winnings) money won. □ **winning post** post marking end of race. □□ **winningly** *adv.*

**winnow** *v.* expose (grain) to current of air to free it of chaff.

**winsome** *adj.* attractive, engaging.

**winter** ● *n.* coldest season of year. ● *v.* spend the winter in particular place. □□ **wintry** *adj.*

**wipe** ● *v.* **1** clean or dry surface of by rubbing; rub (cloth) over surface; spread (liquid) over surface by rubbing. **2** erase, eliminate. ● *n.* act of wiping. □ **wipe out** cancel; destroy completely.

**wiper** *n.* windscreen wiper.

**wire** ● *n.* **1** metal drawn out into thread or thin flexible rod; piece of this; length of this for fencing or to carry electric current etc. **2** *colloq.* telegram. ● *v.* **1** provide, fasten, strengthen, etc. with wire. **2** install electrical circuits in. **3** *colloq.* telegraph.

**wired** *adj.* **1** making use of computers to transfer or receive information; (of device etc.) using wires or cables rather than wireless technology. **2** *colloq.* in nervous, tense, or edgy state; under the influence of drugs or alcohol.

**wireless** ● *adj.* using radio, microwaves, etc. (as opposed to wires or cables) to transmit signals. ● *n.* **1** wireless communication. **2** *dated* radio.

**wiring** *n.* system or installation of electrical circuits.

**wiry** *adj.* (**wirier**) like wire; lean but strong.

**wisdom** *n.* experience, knowledge, and power of applying them; prudence, common sense; wise sayings. □ **wisdom tooth** hindmost molar not usu. cut before age of 20.

**wise** *adj.* showing soundness of judgement; having knowledge. □□ **wisely** *adv.*

**wisecrack** *colloq.* ● *n.* witty remark. ● *v.* make wisecrack.

**wish** ● *v.* **1** have or express desire or aspiration; want, demand; express one's hopes for. **2** *colloq.* foist. ● *n.* desire, request; expression of this; thing desired.

**wishbone** *n.* forked bone between neck and breast of bird.

**wishful** *adj.* wishing. □ **wishful thinking** belief founded on wishes rather than facts.

**wishy-washy** *adj. colloq.* weak in colour, character, etc.

**wisp** *n.* (**-ier, -iest**) small bundle or twist of straw etc.; small separate quantity of smoke, hair, etc.; small thin person. □□ **wispiness** *n.* **wispy** *adj.*

**wistful** *adj.* yearning, mournfully expectant or wishful. □□ **wistfully** *adv.* **wistfulness** *n.*

**wit** *n.* intelligence; imaginative and inventive faculty; amusing ingenuity of speech or ideas; person noted for this. □ **at one's wits' end** worried and not knowing what to do.

**witch** *n.* person (esp. a woman) who practises witchcraft; Wiccan. □ **witch doctor** magician and healer in tribal societies. **witch-hunt** *colloq.* persecution of people suspected of holding unorthodox views.

**witchcraft** *n.* practice of magic; practices of Wicca.

**witchetty** *n.* (in full **witchetty grub**) *Aust.* large, edible, wood-eating larva or pupa of any of several Australian moths and beetles.

**with** *prep.* in the company of, among; having, characterised by; by means of; of the same opinion as; at the same time as; because of; under the conditions of; by addition or possession of; in regard to, towards. □ **with it 1** fashionable, trendy. **2** expert, well-informed; alert, intelligent.

**withdraw** *v.* (**withdrew, withdrawn, withdrawing**) **1** pull or take aside or back; discontinue, cancel, retract; remove, take away; take (money) out of account. **2** retire or go apart. □□ **withdrawal** *n.*

**withdrawn** *adj.* unsociable.

**wither** *v.* **1** shrivel, lose freshness or vitality. **2** subdue with scorn etc. □□ **witheringly** *adv.*

**withhold** *v.* refuse to give, grant, or allow; hold back, restrain.

**within** ● *adv.* inside. ● *prep.* inside; not beyond or out of; not transgressing or exceeding; not further off than.

**without** ● *prep.* not having, feeling or showing; free from; in absence of; with neglect or avoidance of. ● *adv. literary* outside, out of doors.

**withstand** v. (**withstood**, **withstanding**) oppose, hold out against.

**witless** adj. foolish.

**witness** • n. eyewitness; person giving sworn testimony; person attesting another's signature to document; person or thing whose existence etc. attests or proves something. • v. be witness of.

**witter** v. colloq. speak tediously on trivial matters.

**witticism** n. witty remark.

**wittingly** adv. consciously; intentionally.

**witty** adj. (**wittier**) full of wit; clever, funny. □□ **wittily** adv. **wittiness** n.

**wives** see WIFE.

**wizard** n. 1 practitioner of magic; person of remarkable powers. 2 Computing help feature of software that automates complex tasks by asking user series of easy-to-answer questions. □□ **wizardry** n.

**wizened** adj. shrivelled-looking.

**WNW** abbr. west-north-west.

**woad** n. plant yielding blue dye; this dye.

**wobbegong** n. Aust. carpet shark.

**wobble** • v. sway from side to side; stand or go unsteadily; stagger; waver, vacillate. • n. wobbling motion.

**wobbly** • adj. (**wobblier**) unsteady; quivering. • n. Aust. colloq. fit of anger; a tantrum.

**woe** n. affliction; bitter grief. □□ **woeful** adj. **woefully** adv. **woefulness** n.

**woebegone** adj. looking unhappy.

**wog** n. colloq. 1 offens. foreigner or migrant. 2 Aust. minor illness or infection.

**wogoit** n. Aust. ringtailed rock possum.

**wok** n. bowl-shaped frying pan used in esp. Chinese cookery.

**woke** see WAKE.

**woken** see WAKE.

**wold** n. Brit. piece of high open uncultivated land or moor.

**wolf** • n. (pl. **wolves**) wild animal of dog family. • v. devour greedily. □□ **wolfish** adj.

**wolfram** n. tungsten (ore).

**woman** n. (pl. **women**) adult human female; women in general. □□ **womanish** adj. **womanly** adj.

**womanhood** n. state of being a woman.

**womanise** v. (also **-ize**) (of man) be promiscuous; philander. □□ **womaniser** n.

**womankind** n. women in general.

**womb** n. uterus.

**wombat** n. 1 burrowing, herbivorous Australian marsupial. 2 Aust. colloq. slow or stupid person.

**women** see WOMAN.

**womenfolk** n. women in general; the women of one's family.

**won** see WIN.

**wonder** • n. emotion, esp. admiration, excited by what is unexpected, unfamiliar, or inexplicable; strange or remarkable thing, specimen, event, etc. • adj. having amazing properties etc. • v. 1 feel curiosity about. 2 feel wonder and surprise.

**wonderful** adj. very remarkable or admirable. □□ **wonderfully** adv.

**wonderment** n. surprise, awe.

**wongi** Aust. • n. conversation; chat. • v. talk; tell.

**wonk** n. colloq. studious or hard-working person; person who takes excessive interest in minor details of public policy.

**wonky** adj. (**wonkier**) colloq. crooked; unsteady; unreliable.

**wont** • adj. arch. accustomed. • n. one's usual practice.

**woo** v. 1 court, seek love of; try to win; seek support of. 2 coax, importune.

**wood** n. hard fibrous substance of tree; this for timber or fuel; (also

woods) growing trees occupying tract of land; wooden-headed golf club.
□ **out of the woods** out of danger or difficulty.

**wooded** adj. having many trees.

**wooden** adj. **1** made of wood.
**2** expressionless. □□ **woodenly** adv.

**woodland** n. wooded country, woods.

**woodpecker** n. bird that clings to tree trunks and taps them with its beak to find insects.

**woodwind** n. any of the wind instruments made (or formerly made) of wood, e.g. clarinet, oboe.

**woodwork** n. making of things from wood; things made of wood.

**woody** adj. (**woodier**) like or consisting of wood.

**woof** ● n. gruff bark of dog.
● v. give woof.

**woofer** n. loudspeaker for low frequencies.

**wool** n. soft hair forming fleece of sheep etc.; woollen yarn, cloth or clothing; wool-like substance. □ **pull the wool over someone's eyes** deceive someone.

**woollen** ● adj. made of wool.
● n. woollen fabric; (**woollens**) woollen garments.

**woolly** ● adj. (**woollier**) **1** bearing or like wool; woollen. **2** indistinct; confused. ● n. colloq. woollen (esp. knitted) garment, esp. pullover.

**woomera** n. Aust. Aboriginal implement used to propel spear; spear thrower, throwing stick.

**woot** int. colloq. used to express elation, enthusiasm, or triumph.

**woozy** adj. (**woozier**) colloq. dizzy, slightly drunk.

**word** ● n. **1** sound(s) expressing meaning independently and forming basic element of speech; this represented by letters or symbols; something said; message, news; (**words**) text of song; angry talk;

**2** a promise. **3** a command. ● v. put into words; select words to express. □ **have a word** speak briefly (to).
**have words** quarrel. **word of mouth** speech (only). **word processor** computer program designed for producing and altering text and documents.

**wording** n. form of words used.

**wordy** adj. (**wordier**) using too many words.

**wore** SEE WEAR.

**work** ● n. **1** use of bodily or mental power in order to do or make something; employment; something to be done; something done or produced by work; literary or musical composition. **2** ornamentation of a certain kind, articles with this; things made of certain materials or with certain tools. **3** (**works**) operations, building, etc.; operative parts of machine; factory; defensive structure. **4** (**the works**) colloq. everything, all that is available. ● v. **1** perform work; make efforts; be employed. **2** operate, do this effectively. **3** bring about, accomplish. **4** shape, knead, or hammer etc. into a desired form or consistency. **5** make (a way) or pass gradually by effort; become (loose etc.) through repeated stress or pressure. **6** be in motion; ferment. □ **work off** get rid of (debt, fat) by work or activity. **work out** find or solve by calculation; plan details of; have specified result; take exercise. **work up** bring gradually to more developed state; excite progressively; advance (to climax).

**workable** adj. that can be worked, will work, or is worth working.
□□ **workability** n.

**workaday** adj. ordinary, everyday; practical.

**worker** n. **1** employee. **2** neuter bee or ant. **3** person who works hard. **4** Aust. draught bullock or horse.

**working** • adj. **1** engaged in work. **2** while so engaged. **3** functioning, able to function. • n. **1** activity of work. **2** functioning. **3** mine, quarry. □ **working class** the class of people who are employed for wages, esp. in manual or industrial work. **working knowledge** knowledge adequate for dealing with something.

**workman** n. (pl. -men) person employed to do manual labour.

**workmanlike** adj. showing good skill; competent.

**workmanship** n. person's skill in working; quality of thing so produced.

**workstation** n. desk with computer; the computer itself.

**world** n. **1** the earth or planetary body like it. **2** universe. **3** all that exists. **4** time, state, or scene of human existence. **5** all concerning or belonging to specific class or sphere of activity. **6** vast amount. □ **think the world of** have very high regard for. **World Wide Web** system of linked and cross-referenced documents for accessing information on Internet.

**worldly** adj. **1** of the affairs of the world, temporal, earthly, secular (opp. spiritual, religious, etc.) **2** experienced in life, sophisticated, practical. □□ **worldliness** n.

**worldwide** adj. affecting, occurring, or known in all parts of world.

**worm** • n. **1** any of various types of creeping invertebrate animal with long slender body and no limbs; larva of insect; (**worms**) internal parasites. **2** colloq. insignificant or contemptible person. **3** spiral of screw etc. **4** class of computer virus. • v. **1** crawl, wriggle; insinuate oneself (into favour etc.); obtain (secret etc.) by cunning persistence. **2** rid (dog etc.) of worms. □ **worm cast** pile of earth sent up to surface by earthworm. □□ **wormy** adj.

**wormwood** n. plant with bitter aromatic taste.

**worn** • see WEAR. • adj. damaged by use or wear; looking tired and exhausted.

**worried** adj. feeling or showing worry.

**worry** • v. **1** be anxious; be trouble or anxiety to; harass, importune. **2** shake or pull about with teeth. • n. **1** anxiety, unease; something about which one worries. **2** anxiety. □□ **worrier** n.

**worse** • adj. more bad; in or into worse health or worse condition. • adv. more badly; more ill. • n. worse thing(s). □□ **worsen** v.

**worship** • n. homage or service to deity; acts, rites, or ceremonies of this; adoration, devotion. • v. (**worshipped**) adore as divine; honour with religious rites; idolise; attend public worship; be full of adoration. □□ **worshipper** n.

**worst** • adj. & adv. most bad or badly. • n. worst part or possibility. • v. outdo, defeat.

**worsted** n. fine woollen yarn or fabric.

**worth** • adj. **1** of value equivalent to. **2** such as to justify or repay. **3** possessing property equivalent to. • n. **1** value. **2** equivalent of money etc. in commodity etc. □ **for all one is worth** colloq. with one's utmost effort; without reserve. **worth one's while** worth time or effort needed.

**worthless** adj. without value or merit. □□ **worthlessness** n.

**worthy** • adj. (**worthier**) having great merit; deserving respect or support. • n. worthy person.

**would** v.aux. used in senses corresponding to WILL[1] in the past tense, conditional statements, questions, polite requests and statements, and to express probability or something that happens from time to time. □ **would-be** desiring or pretending to be.

**wound¹** ● n. injury done by cut or blow to living tissue; pain inflicted on feelings; injury to reputation.
● v. inflict wound on.

**wound²** see WIND².

**wove** see WEAVE.

**woven** see WEAVE.

**wow** ● int. exclamation of astonishment. ● n. colloq. sensational success. ● v. colloq. impress greatly.

**wowser** n. Aust. person trying to inflict rigid or narrow morality on others, a killjoy.

**woylie** n. Aust. kangaroo rat.

**w.p.m.** abbr. words per minute.

**wrack** n. 1 seaweed. 2 ruin. 3 see RACK.

**wraith** n. ghost; spectral appearance of living person.

**wrangle** ● n. noisy argument or dispute. ● v. engage in wrangle.

**wrap** ● v. (wrapped) envelop in folded or soft encircling material; arrange or draw (pliant covering) around (person). ● n. 1 shawl, scarf, etc. 2 wrapping paper etc. 3 tortilla wrapped around cold filling.

**wrapped** see RAPT.

**wrapper** n. cover of paper etc. wrapped around something.

**wrapping** n. material used to wrap things.

**wrasse** n. bright-coloured marine food fish with thick lips and strong teeth.

**wrath** n. extreme anger. □□ **wrathful** adj.

**wreak** v. inflict (vengeance etc.)

**wreath** n. flowers or leaves wound together into ring, esp. as ornament for head or for laying on grave etc.; curl or ring of smoke, cloud, or soft fabric.

**wreathe** v. encircle (as) with or like wreath; wind, curve.

**wreck** ● n. sinking or running aground of ship; ship that has

suffered this; greatly damaged building, thing, or person.
● v. seriously damage (vehicle etc.); ruin (hopes etc.); cause wreck of (ship). □□ **wrecker** n.

**wreckage** n. remains of something wrecked.

**wren** n. very small bird.

**wrench** ● n. 1 violent twist or oblique pull or tearing off. 2 tool for gripping and turning nuts etc. 3 painful uprooting or parting etc. ● v. twist or pull violently around or sideways; pull with wrench.

**wrest** v. wrench away; obtain by effort or with difficulty.

**wrestle** ● n. contest in which two opponents grapple and try to throw each other to ground; hard struggle. ● v. have wrestling match; struggle; do one's utmost to deal with. □□ **wrestler** n.

**wretch** n. wretched or despicable person.

**wretched** adj. 1 unhappy, miserable. 2 worthless; contemptible.
□□ **wretchedly** adv. **wretchedness** n.

**wriggle** ● v. twist or turn with short writhing movements; escape from (difficulty etc.) cunningly.
● n. wriggling movement.
□□ **wriggly** adj.

**wring** ● v. (wrung, wringing) squeeze and twist, esp. to remove liquid; squeeze firmly or forcibly; obtain with effort or difficulty.
● n. act of wringing.

**wrinkle** ● n. small crease in skin or other flexible surface. ● v. form wrinkles in. □□ **wrinkly** adj.

**wrist** n. joint connecting hand and forearm; part of garment covering wrist.

**writ** n. formal written authoritative command.

**write** v. (wrote, written, writing) make letters or other symbols on surface, esp. with pen or pencil; compose in written form, esp. for publication; be author; write and send letter; commit data to computer memory. □ **write off** recognise as lost. **write-off** something written off; vehicle too damaged to be worth repairing. **write up** write account of; write entries in.

**writer** *n.* person who writes, esp. author.

**writhe** *v.* twist or roll oneself about (as) in acute pain; suffer mental torture.

**writing** *n.* handwriting; literary work. □ **in writing** in written form.

**written** see WRITE.

**wrong** ● *adj.* 1 mistaken; not true; in error. 2 unsuitable; less or least desirable. 3 contrary to law or morality. ● *adv.* 1 in wrong manner or direction. 2 with incorrect result. ● *n.* immoral or unjust action. ● *v.* treat unjustly. □□ **wrongly** *adv.* **wrongness** *n.*

**wrongdoer** *n.* person who behaves illegally or immorally. □□ **wrongdoing** *n.*

**wrongful** *adj.* contrary to what is right or legal. □□ **wrongfully** *adv.*

**wrote** see WRITE.

**wrought** *adj.* (of metals) shaped by hammering.

**wrung** see WRING.

**wry** *adj.* 1 (of the face) contorted in disgust or disappointment. 2 (of humour) dry and mocking. □□ **wryly** *adv.* **wryness** *n.*

**WSW** *abbr.* west-south-west.

**wt** *abbr.* weight.

**wurley** *n. Aust.* gunyah; any temporary shelter.

**wurrung** *n. Aust.* nail-tailed wallaby.

**wuss** *n. colloq. derog.* weak or ineffectual person; wimp.

**www** *abbr.* = *World Wide Web.*

**WYSIWYG** *adj.* indicating that text on computer screen and printout correspond exactly (What You See Is What You Get).

**X** *n.* (also **x**) **1** (Roman numeral) 10. **2** first unknown quantity in algebra.

**xanthorrhoea** *n.* plant of Australian genus of the same name, varying in form from herb-like plants to small trees. Also called **grass tree**.

**x-axis** *n.* principal or horizontal axis of system of coordinates.

**X chromosome** *n.* a sex chromosome, of which female cells have twice as many as males.

**xenon** *n.* **1** chemical element (symbol **Xe**). **2** a colourless odourless gas.

**xenophobia** *n.* hatred or fear of foreigners or strangers.
□□ **xenophobic** *adj.* **xenophobe** *n.*

**xenotransplantation** *n.* process of grafting or transplanting organs or tissues between members of different species.

**xerox** ● *n. propr.* type of photocopier; copy made by it.
● *v.* photocopy.

**X factor** *n. colloq.* noteworthy special talent or quality.

**Xmas** *n. colloq.* Christmas.

**XML** *abbr. Computing* extensible markup language, metalanguage that allows users to define their own customised languages.

**X-rated** *adj.* (of film etc.) classified as non-violent erotica for viewing by persons over 18 years of age only; indecent, pornographic.

**X-ray** ● *n.* photograph or examination made by electromagnetic radiation (**X-rays**) that can penetrate solids. ● *v.* photograph, examine, or treat by X-rays.

**xylograph** *n.* woodcut, wood engraving. □□ **xylography** *n.*

**xylophone** *n.* musical instrument of graduated wooden or metal bars struck with small wooden hammers.

**xyster** *n.* medical instrument for scraping bones.

# Yy

**Y** *n.* (also **y**) **1** second unknown quantity in algebra. **2** Y-shaped thing.

**yabber** *Aust. colloq.* ● *n.* (also **yabber-yabber**) talk, conversation; discussion; language. ● *v.* talk, converse. □□ **yabbering** *n.*

**yabby** (also **yabbie**) ● *n.* any of several Australian freshwater crayfish. ● *v.* fish for yabbies. □□ **yabbying** *n.*

**yacht** ● *n.* light sailing vessel for racing or cruising; larger usu. power-driven vessel for cruising. ● *v.* race or cruise in yacht.

**yahoo** *n.* **1** *Aust.* evil spirit. **2** *Aust.* bird of northern and eastern Australia. **3** *colloq.* lout.

**yak**[1] *n.* long-haired Tibetan ox.

**yak**[2] (also **yakker**) *colloq.* ● *n.* trivial or unduly persistent conversation. ● *v.* engage in this.

**yakka** (also **yacka**) *Aust. colloq.* work.

**yakker** = YAK[2]. ● *n.* = YAKKA.

**yam** *n.* tropical or subtropical climbing plant; edible starchy tuber of this.

**yandy** *Aust.* ● *n.* (also **yandy dish**) winnowing dish used to separate edible seeds from refuse, or particles of mineral from alluvial material. ● *v.* winnow.

**yang** *n.* (in Chinese philosophy) active male principle of universe (cf. YIN).

**Yank** *n. colloq.* inhabitant of US.

**yank** *v. & n. colloq.* pull with jerk.

**yap** ● *v.* (**yapped**) **1** bark shrilly. **2** *colloq.* talk noisily, foolishly, or complainingly. ● *n.* sound of yapping. □□ **yappy** *adj.*

**yapunyah** *n.* (also **napunyah**) *Aust.* eucalypt which occurs along watercourses.

**yard**[1] *n.* **1** a unit of linear measure (3 ft, 0.9144 m). **2** spar slung across mast for sail to hang from.

**yard**[2] ● *n.* **1** garden of house. **2** enclosure in which sheep, cattle, etc. are confined. **3** enclosed area in which business or work is carried out. ● *v.* confine (livestock) in enclosure.

**yarding** *n.* *Aust.* confining of animals in enclosure; animals so confined.

**yarmulke** *n.* (also **yarmulka**) skullcap worn by Jewish men.

**yarn** ● *n.* **1** spun thread, esp. for knitting, weaving, etc. **2** *colloq.* chat; long story, traveller's tale, anecdote. ● *v. colloq.* talk, have chat; tell yarns.

**yarran** *n.* wattle of inland eastern Australia.

**yarrow** *n.* plant with feathery leaves and strong-smelling flowers.

**yashmak** *n.* veil worn by Muslim women in certain countries.

**yaw** ● *v.* (of ship, aircraft etc.) fail to hold straight course, go unsteadily. ● *n.* yawing of ship etc. from course.

**yawl** *n.* kind of sailing boat; small fishing boat.

**yawn** ● *v.* open the mouth wide and inhale, esp. when sleepy or bored; gape, be wide open. ● *n.* **1** act of yawning. **2** *colloq.* boring idea, activity, etc.

**yaws** *n.pl.* contagious tropical skin disease.

**y-axis** *n.* secondary or vertical axis of system of coordinates.

**yay** *int. colloq.* expressing triumph, approval, or encouragement.

**Y chromosome** *n.* sex chromosome occurring only in males.

**year** *n.* time occupied by one revolution of earth around sun, approx. 365 ¼ days; (also **calendar year**) period from 1 Jan. to 31 Dec. inclusive; any consecutive period of twelve months.

**yearbook** *n.* annual publication of events or aspects of previous year.

**yearling** *n.* animal between one and two years old.

**yearly** ● *adj.* done, produced, or occurring once every year; or of lasting a year. ● *adv.* once a year.

**yearn** *v.* be filled with longing, compassion, or tenderness. □□ **yearning** *n. & adj.*

**yeast** *n.* greyish-yellow fungus, got esp. from fermenting malt liquors and used as fermenting agent, to raise bread, etc.

**yelka** *n.* (also **yalka**) any of several Australian sedges yielding small edible tuber; such tuber.

**yell** ● *n.* sharp loud cry of fright, anger, delight, etc. ● *v.* cry, shout.

**yellow** ● *adj.* 1 of the colour of ripe lemons, buttercups, etc. 2 *colloq.* cowardly. ● *n.* yellow colour or thing. ● *v.* turn yellow. □□ **yellowish** *adj.* **yellowness** *n.* **yellowy** *adj.*

**yellowtail** *n.* any of several southern Australian marine food fish having yellow caudal fin.

**yelp** ● *n.* sharp shrill bark or cry as of dog in excitement or pain. ● *v.* utter yelp.

**yen** *n.* 1 (*pl.* **yen**) chief monetary unit of Japan. 2 *colloq.* longing, yearning.

**yeoman** *n. Brit. hist.* man holding and farming small estate, or acting as servant in royal etc. household. □□ **yeomanly** *adj.*

**yes** *int. & n.* expression of agreement or consent, or of reply to summons etc. □ **yes-man** person who is always ready to agree with superior.

**yesterday** ● *adv.* on the day before today. ● *n.* day before today.

**yet** ● *adv.* 1 up to this or that time; still; besides; eventually. 2 even; nevertheless. ● *conj.* but nevertheless.

**yeti** *n.* large manlike animal said to exist in Himalayas.

**yew** *n.* dark-leaved evergreen coniferous tree of Europe etc.; its wood.

**Y-fronts** *n. propr.* men's or boys' briefs with Y-shaped seam of overlapping folds at the front.

**YHA** *abbr.* Youth Hostels Association.

**yield** ● *v.* 1 produce or return as fruit, profit, or result. 2 surrender; allow (victory, right of way, etc.) to another; be able to be forced out of the natural shape. ● *n.* amount yielded or produced.

**yin** *n.* (in Chinese philosophy) passive female principle of universe (cf. YANG).

**YMCA** *abbr.* Young Men's Christian Association.

**yob** *n.* (also **yobbo**) *colloq. derog.* lout, hooligan.

**yodel** ● *v.* (**yodelled**) 1 sing with melodious inarticulate sounds and frequent changes between falsetto and normal voice in manner of Swiss mountain dwellers. 2 *Aust. colloq.* vomit. ● *n.* 1 yodelling cry. 2 *Aust. colloq.* vomiting. □□ **yodeller** *n.*

**yoga** *n.* Hindu system of meditation and asceticism; system of physical exercises and breathing control used in yoga. □□ **yogic** *adj.*

**yoghurt** *n.* (also **yogurt**) rather sour semi-solid food made from milk fermented by added bacteria.

**yoke** ● *n.* 1 wooden crosspiece fastened over necks of two oxen etc. and attached to plough or wagon to be pulled; pair (of oxen etc.); object like yoke in form or function, e.g. wooden shoulder-piece for carrying pair of pails; top part of garment from which rest hangs. 2 sway, dominion, servitude; bond of union, esp. of marriage. ● *v.* 1 put yoke on. 2 couple or unite (pair); link (one thing) to (another); match or work together.

**yokel** *n.* a country person; a bumpkin.

**yolk** *n.* yellow inner part of an egg.

**YOLO** *abbr. colloq.* you only live once.

**Yom Kippur** *n.* most solemn religious fast day of Jewish year, Day of Atonement.

**yonder** *adv.* over there.

**yonks** *n.pl.* (also **yonkers**) *colloq.* a long time.

**yore** *n.* □ **of yore** *literary* long ago.

**york** *v. Cricket* bowl out with a yorker.

**yorker** *n. Cricket* ball that pitches immediately under bat.

**Yorkshire pudding** *n.* baked batter pudding eaten with gravy or meat.

**you** *pron.* the person(s) addressed; one, anyone, everyone.

**young** *adj.* having lived or existed for only a short time; not yet old; immature, inexperienced, youthful.

**youngster** *n.* child, young person.

**your** *adj.* of or belonging to you.

**yours** *pron.poss.* the one(s) belonging to you.

**yourself** *pron.* (*pl.* **yourselves**) the emphatic and reflexive form of 'you'.

**youse** *pron.* (also **yous**) *colloq.* used when addressing more than one person; you (*pl.*).

**youth** *n.* 1 the state or period of being young. 2 young person (esp. male); young people.

**youthful** *adj.* young; having characteristics of youth.
□□ **youthfulness** *n.*

**yowie** *n. Aust.* ape-like or humanoid monster supposed to inhabit parts of eastern Australia.

**yowl** ● *n.* loud wailing cry (as) of cat or dog in distress. ● *v.* utter yowl.

**yo-yo** ● *n.* toy consisting of pair of discs with deep groove between them in which string is attached and wound, and which can be made to fall and rise. ● *v.* move up and down; fluctuate.

**ytterbium** *n.* metallic element (symbol Yb).

**yttrium** *n.* metallic element (symbol Y).

**yuan** *n.* (*pl.* **yuan**) chief monetary unit of China.

**yuck** *int.* (also **yuk**) *colloq.* expression of strong distaste.

**yucky** *adj.* (also **yukky**) (**yuckier**) *colloq.* messy, repellent.

**yummy** *adj. colloq.* delicious.

**yuppy** *n.* (also **yuppie**) *colloq.* young ambitious professional person working in city.

**YWCA** *abbr.* Young Women's Christian Association.

**zabaglione** n. Italian dessert of whipped and heated egg-yolks, sugar, and wine.

**zac** n. (also **zack**) Aust. **1** hist. Australian sixpenny coin. **2** five-cent coin. **3** trifling sum of money.

**zambuk** n. Aust. member of the St John Ambulance Brigade, esp. one in attendance at sporting fixture.

**zany** adj. (**zanier**) comically idiotic; crazy.

**zap** v. (**zapped**) colloq. **1** kill, destroy. **2** move or act quickly.

**zeal** n. fervour, eagerness; hearty persistent endeavour. □□ **zealous** adj.

**zealot** n. extreme partisan; fanatic. □□ **zealotry** n.

**zebra** n. African black and white striped horselike animal. □ **zebra crossing** pedestrian crossing where road is marked with broad white stripes.

**Zen** n. form of Buddhism emphasising meditation and intuition.

**zenith** n. point of sky that is directly overhead; highest point (of power, prosperity, etc.).

**zephyr** n. literary mild gentle breeze.

**zero** n. (pl. **zeros**) figure 0, nought, nil; point on scale of thermometer etc. from which positive or negative quantity is reckoned. □ **zero in on** take aim at; focus attention on.

**zest** n. **1** keen enjoyment or interest, relish, gusto. **2** outer layer of orange or lemon peel.

**zettabyte** n. one million petabytes.

**zigzag** n. **1** line or course turning right and left alternately at sharp angles. ● adj. & adv. as or in a zigzag. ● v. (**zigzagged**) move in zigzag course.

**zilch** n. colloq. nothing.

**zillion** n. colloq. indefinite large number.

**zinc** n. white metallic element (symbol Zn).

**zing** colloq. ● n. vigour, energy. ● v. move swiftly, esp. with shrill sound.

**Zionism** n. movement that campaigned for Jewish homeland in Palestine. □□ **Zionist** n. & adj.

**zip** n. **1** (in full **zip fastener**) fastening device of two flexible strips with interlocking projections, closed or opened by sliding clip along them. **2** energy, vigour. ● v. (**zipped**) **1** fasten with zip fastener. **2** move with zip or at high speed. **3** Computing compress (file) so that it takes up less space.

**zip code** n. US postcode.

**zipper** n. zip fastener.

**zircon** n. bluish-white gem cut from translucent mineral.

**zirconium** n. grey metallic element (symbol Zr).

**zit** n. colloq. pimple.

**zither** n. stringed instrument with flat soundbox, placed horizontally and played by plucking.

**zodiac** n. (in astrology) band of sky divided into twelve equal parts (**signs of the zodiac**) each named from a constellation.

**zombie** n. **1** colloq. dull or apathetic person. **2** corpse said to have been revived by magic power.

**zone** ● n. area having particular characteristics, purpose, or use. ● v. divide into zones. □□ **zonal** adj.

**zonked** adj. colloq. exhausted.

**zoo** n. place where wild animals are kept for exhibition, conservation, and study.

**zoology** *n.* study of animals.
□□ **zoological** *adj.* **zoologist** *n.*

**zoom** ● *v.* **1** move quickly, esp. with buzzing sound. **2** (of camera) change rapidly from long shot to close-up (of). ● *n.* **1** aeroplane's steep climb. **2** zooming camera shot.

**zoophyte** *n.* plantlike animal, esp. coral, sea anemone, or sponge.

**zucchini** *n.* (*pl.* **zucchini** or **zucchinis**) small variety of vegetable marrow; courgette.

**zygote** *n. Biol.* cell formed by union of two gametes.

# Word games Supplement

Players of word games are often at an advantage if they have ready access to a supply of short words that can be regarded as valid for the purposes of the game. Particularly useful are words of only two letters, words with a *q* not followed by *u*, and words beginning with *x*. Many of these words are excluded from a small dictionary (which concentrates on current usage) because they are rare, obsolete, or occur only in dialects.

All the words in the following lists are attested in one of the great historical dictionaries (such as the twenty-volume *Oxford English Dictionary* and the *English Dialect Dictionary*) or are included in a major American dictionary.

Words marked with an asterisk (*) are obsolete but are subject to modern rules of inflection. Those marked with a dagger (†) are obsolete and were not in use after the Middle English period (ending in 1500); these words cannot be assumed to form plurals and verbal inflections in the modern style (for example, the plural of *ac* is *aec*, not 'acs').

Excluded from these lists are names of people and places etc. and abbreviations (such as Dr, Mr) which are not pronounced as they are spelt, and suffixes and other elements which have never been used as independent words; most word games do not regard these as valid items. An arbitrary limit of six letters has been imposed throughout.

## Two-letter words

*Note* This list does not include plurals of the names of letters of the alphabet (*bs*, *ds*, *ms*, *ts*, etc.). These are correct formations but are not always regarded by word games players as acceptable.

**aa** *n.* rough cindery lava.

**ab** *v.* (*dialect*) hinder. *n.* (*dialect*) hindrance.

†**ac** *n.* (*pl.* **aec**) oak.

**ad** *n.* (*colloquial*) advertisement.

**ae** *adj.* (*Scot.*) one.

**af** *prep.* (*dialect*) of; off.

**ah** *int.* expressing surprise.

**ai** *n.* three-toed sloth.

**ak** *n.* (*dialect*) oak.

†**al** *adj.* & *n.* all.

**am** *present tense* of be.

**an** *indefinite article* one.

**ar** *n.* letter r.

**as** *adv.* & *conj.* similarly.

**at** *prep.* having as position etc.

†**au** *n.* awe.

**aw** *n.* water wheel board.

**ax** *n.* & *v.* axe.

**ay** *int.* ah.

**ba** *n.* (*Egyptian myth*) soul.

**be** *v.* exist.

**bi** *n* & *adj.* (*slang*) bisexual (person).

**bo** *n.* a kind of fig tree.

**bu** *n.* former Japanese coin.

**by** *prep.* & *adv.* beside.

**ca** *n.* (*pl.* **caas** or **cais**) (*Scot.*) calf.

**ce** *n.* letter c.

†**co** *n.* jackdaw.

†**cu** *n.* cow.

†**cy** *n. pl.* cows.

**da** *n.* Indian fibre plant.

**de** *prep.* of; from.

**di** *n.* note in music scale.

**do** v. perform. n. performance.
*\***du** v. (Scot.) do.
*\***dw** v. (Scot.) do.
*\***dy** n. (pl. **dyce** or **dys**) gaming die.
**ea** n. (dialect) river; stream.
*\***eb** n. ebb.
**ec** adv. also, too.
*\***ed** adj. distinguished.
**ee** n. (pl. **een**) (Scot.) eye.
**ef** n. letter f.
**eg** n. egg.
**eh** int. & v. expressing surprise.
†**ei** adj. & pron. any.
*\***ek** adv. & v. eke.
**el** n. letter l.
**em** n. unit of print measure.
**en** n. half an em.
†**eo** pron. you.
**er** int. & v. expressing hesitation.
**es** n. (pl. **esses**) letter s.
†**et** prep. at.
†**eu** n. yew.
**ew** v. (dialect) owe.
**ex** n. (pl. **exes**) former spouse etc.
**ey** n. (dialect) water.
**fa** n. note in music scale.
**fe** n. (old use) note in music scale.
**fo** n. (dialect) area measure.
**fu** n. (pl. **fu**) Chinese district.
**fy** int. fie.
**ga** n. (old use) note in music scale.
**ge** n. (old use) note in music scale.
**go** v. move. n. (pl. **goes**) energy; turn.
**gu** v. (dialect) go.
**gy** n. (Scot.) guide rope. *\*v. guide.
**ha** int. & v. expressing surprise.
**he** pron. male mentioned.
**hi** int. attracting attention.
**hm** int. expressing doubt.
**ho** int. & v. expressing surprise.
**hu** n. Chinese liquid measure.
†**hv** adv. how.
†**hw** n. vew.
**hy** v. (Scot.) hie.
*\***ia** n. (Scot.) jay.
†**ic** pron. I.
**id** n. mind's impulses.
**ie** n. Pacific islands tree.

**if** conj. & n. (on) condition (that).
†**ig** pron. I.
†**ih** pron. I.
†**ik** pron. I.
†**il** n. hedgehog.
†**im** pron. him.
**in** prep. & adv. within. n. passage in.
**io** n. Hawaiian hawk.
*\***ir** n. ire.
**is** present tense of **be**.
**it** pron. thing mentioned.
**iv** prep. (dialect) in; of.
†**iw** n. yew.
**ja** v. & n. (dialect) jaw, talk.
*\***je** adv. yea.
**jo** n. (pl. **joes**) (Scot.) darling.
**ka** n. (Egyptian myth) spirit.
*\***ke** n. (Scot.) jackdaw.
**ki** n. liliaceous plant.
**ko** n. (pl. **ko**) Chinese liquid measure.
**ku** n. (dialect) ulcer in the eye.
**ky** n. pl. (Scot.) cows.
**la** n. note in music scale.
**le** n. = li.
**li** n. (pl. **li**) Chinese unit.
**lo** int. expressing surprise.
**lu** v. (Orkney) listen.
**ly** n. = li.
**ma** n. (colloquial) mother.
**me** pron. objective case of I.
**mi** n. note in music scale.
**mo** n. (colloquial) moment.
**mu** n. Greek letter m.
**my** adj. belonging to me.
**na** adv. (Scot.) no.
**ne** adv. & conj. (old use) not.
*\***ni** n. = ny.
**no** adj. not any.
**nu** n. Greek letter n.
†**nv** adj. & conj. now.
†**nw** adv. & conj. now.
*\***ny** n. brood of pheasants.
*\***ob** n. wizard.
†**oc** conj. but.
**od** n. hypnotic force.
**oe** n. small island.
**of** prep. belonging to.
**oh** int., n., & v. (give) cry of pain.

**oi** *int.* attracting attention.

**†ok** *n.* oak.

**ol** *n.* hydroxyl atom group.

**om** *n.* mantra syllable.

**on** *prep. & adv.* supported by; covering. *n.* one side of a cricket field.

**oo** *n.* (*Scot.*) wool.

**op** *n.* (*colloquial*) operation.

**or** *conj.* as an alternative.

**os**[1] *n.* (*pl.* **ora**) orifice.

**os**[2] *n.* (*pl.* **osar** or **osars**) geological ridge.

**os**[3] *n.* (*pl.* **ossa**) bone.

**ot** *n.* (*dialect*) urchin.

**ou** *int.* (*Scot.*) oh.

**†ov** *pron.* you.

**ow** *int.* expressing pain.

**ox** *n.* (*pl.* **oxen** or **oxes**) a kind of animal.

**oy** *n.* (*Scot.*) grandchild.

**pa** *n.* (*colloquial*) father.

**pe** *n.* Hebrew letter p.

**pi** *n.* Greek letter p.

**po** *n.* (*pl.* **pos**) (*colloquial*) chamber pot.

**pu** *n.* (*pl.* **pu**) Chinese measure of distance.

**\*py** *n.* pie.

**qi** *n.* (*Chinese philosophy*) life force.

**\*qu** *n.* half-farthing.

**ra** *n.* Arabic letter r.

**re** *n.* note in music scale.

**ri** *n.* (*pl.* **ri**) Japanese measure of distance.

**\*ro** *n. & v.* (*Scot.*) repose.

**†ru** *v.* rue.

**\*ry** *n.* rye.

**sa** *adv. & conj.* (*dialect*) so.

**se** *n.* Japanese measure of area.

**sh** *int.* command to silence.

**si** *n.* note in music scale.

**so**[1] *adv. & conj.* therefore.

**so**[2] *n.* note in music scale.

**st** *int.* attracting attention.

**su** *pron.* (*dialect*) she.

**sy** *n.* (*dialect*) scythe.

**ta** *n.* Arabic letter t.

**te** *n.* = ti.

**ti** *n.* note in music scale.

**to** *prep. & adv.* towards.

**tu** *n.* 250 li.

**\*ty** *n. & v.* tie.

**†ua** *n.* woe.

**ug** *v. & n.* (*dialect*) dread.

**uh** *int.* inarticulate sound.

**um** *int.* hesitation in speech.

**un** *pron.* (*dialect*) one; him.

**†uo** *n.* foe.

**†uu** *n.* yew.

**†uv** *n.* yew.

**uz** *pron.* (*dialect*) us.

**va** *n.* (*Scot.*) woe.

**vg** *v.* = ug.

**vi** *n.* Polynesian fruit.

**vo** *n.* size of book.

**\*vp** *adv.* up.

**\*vs** *pron.* us.

**\*vy** *v.* vie.

**wa** *n.* Siamese measure.

**we** *pron.* self and others.

**\*wg** *v.* (*Scot.*) = ug.

**†wi** *n.* battle; conflict.

**wo** *int.* recalling a hawk.

**\*wp** *adv.* (*Scot.*) up.

**\*wr** *pron.* our.

**\*ws** *pron.* (*Scot.*) us.

**†wu** *adv.* how.

**wy** *n.* (*Scot.*) heifer.

**\*xa** *n.* shah.

**xi** *n.* Greek letter x.

**xu** *n.* (*pl.* **xu**) Vietnamese coin.

**yu** *n.* (*Aust.*) Aboriginal shelter.

# Words with a *q* not followed by *u*

The spelling *qw* was a frequent variant of *qu* and *wh* in Middle English (c. 1150–1500), especially in Scotland and northern England. In the words listed below, most of such forms are attested in the *Oxford English Dictionary*; several hundred others are to be found in the *Dictionary of the Older Scottish Tongue*, but are excluded from the list through lack of space.

**cinq** *n.* number 5 on a die.
**eqwal** *n.* (*dialect*) green woodpecker.
**faqih** *n.* (*pl.* faqihs or fuqaha) fakir.
**faqir** *n.* fakir.
**fiqh** *n.* Islamic jurisprudence.
***liqor** *n.* liquor.
**miqra** *n.* Hebrew biblical text.
**qabab** *n.* kebab.
**qadhi** *n.* = qadi.
**qadi** *n.* Muslim civil judge.
**qaf** *n.* letter of the Arabic alphabet.
**qaid** *n.* = qadi.
**qanet** *n.* irrigation tunnel.
**qaneh** *n.* ancient Hebrew measure (= 6 ells).
**qanon** *n.* dulcimer-like instrument.
**qantar** *n.* Middle Eastern unit of weight.
**qasab** *n.* (*pl.* qasab) ancient Mesopotamian measure of length.
**qasaba** *n.* (*pl.* qasaba) ancient Arabian measure of area.
**qasida** *n.* Arabic or Persian poem.
**qat** *n.* Ethiopian bush.
**qazi** *n.* = qadi.
**qere** *n.* marginal word in Hebrew Bible.
**qeri** *n.* = qere.
**qhat** *adj.* & *pron.* what.
†**qheche** *adj.* & *pron.* which.
†**qhete** *n.* (*Scot.*) wheat.
†**qhom** *pron.* whom.
†**qhwom** *pron.* whom.
**qi** *n.* (*Chinese philosophy*) life force.
**qibla** *n.* direction towards Mecca.
**qiblah** *n.* = qibla.
**qibli** *n.* sirocco.

**qindar** *n.* (*pl.* qindarka) Albanian coin.
**qintar** *n.* Albanian coin.
***qirk** *n.* quirk.
**qirsh** *n.* (*pl.* qurush) Saudi Arabian coin.
**qiviut** *n.* belly wool of the musk-ox.
**qiyas** *n.* Islamic judgement.
**qoph** *n.* Hebrew letter q.
**qre** *n.* = qere.
***qvair** *n.* quire.
***qvan** *adv.* & *conj.* when.
***qvare** *n.* quire.
†**qvarte** *n.* quart.
†**qvayr** *n.* quire.
†**qveise** *v.* quease (= squeeze).
†**qvele** *n.* wheel.
†**qvene** *n.* queen.
†**qverel** *n.* quarrel.
†**qveyse** *v.* quease (= squeeze).
†**qvyk** *v.* quicken.
†**qvyite** *n.* quilt.
†**qwa** *pron.* who.
†**qwaint** *adj.* quaint.
***qwaire** *n.* quire.
†**qwal** *n.* (*Scot.*) whale.
†**qwalke** *n.* whelk, pimple.
†**qwall** *n.* (*Scot.*) whale.
†**qwalle** *n.* (*Scot.*) whale.
†**qwappe** *v.* quap (= quiver).
†**qwar** *adv.* & *conj.* (*dialect*) where.
†**qware** *adv.* & *conj.* (*dialect*) where.
†**qwate** *adj.* & *n.* = qwert.
†**qwarto** *adv.* whereto.
†**qwart** *adj.* & *n.* qwert.
†**qwasse** *v.* quash.

qwat v. (*dialect*) squash flat.

†quate n. divination.

†qwatte v. (*dialect*) = qwat.

qway n. whey.

†qwaylle n. (*Scot.*) whale.

†qwayer n. squire.

†qwaynt adj. quaint.

†qwe n. (*pl.* qwes) (*Scot.*) musical instrument (pipe).

†qwech adj. & pron. which.

qweche adj. & pron. which.

†qwed adj. & n. evil.

†qwede n. will or bequest.

†qwedyr n. (*dialect*) quiver.

†qweed adj. & n. evil.

†qweer n. choir.

†qwel adj. & pron. which.

*qwele n. (*dialect*) wheel.

†qwelke n. whelk.

†qwelp n. (*Scot.*) whelp.

†qwelpe n. (*Scot.*) whelp.

†qwem v. please.

†qweme v. please.

†qwen n. queen.

†qwench n. quench.

†qwene n. queen.

†qwenne adv. & conj. when.

†qwens adv. & conj. whence.

†qwent adj. quenched.

†qwer n. choir.

†qwere n. choir.

†qwerf n. wharf.

qwerk n. (*dialect*) twist; bend.

†qwerle n. whirl.

*qwern n. quern.

†qwerne n. piece of ice.

†qwert n. health. adj. healthy.

†querte adj. & adj. = qwert.

qwerty n. standard layout of typewriter keyboard.

†qweryn n. piece of ice.

*qwest n. quest.

†qwesye adj. queasy.

†qwet n. (*Scot.*) wheat.

†qwete n. (*Scot.*) wheat.

†qwey n. whey.

†qweyll n. (*dialect*) wheel.

†qweynt adj. quaint.

*qwha pron. (*Scot.*) who.

†qwhar adv. & conj. where.

†qwhare adv. & conj. where.

†qwheet n. (*Scot.*) wheat.

†qwheit n. (*Scot.*) wheat.

†qwhele n. (*dialect*) wheel.

†qwhen adv. & conj. when.

†qwhene n. queen.

†qwher adv. & conj. where.

†qwhete n. (*Scot.*) wheat.

†qwheyn adv. & conj. (*Scot.*) when.

*qwhil n. (*Scot.*) while.

†qhile n. (*Scot.*) while.

†qwhill n. (*Scot.*) while.

†qwhit adj. (*Scot.*) white.

qwhite adj. (*Scot.*) white.

†qwhois adj. & pron. (*Scot.*) which.

†qwhom pron. whom.

†qwhome pron. whom.

†qwhos pron. (*Scot.*) whose.

†qwhy adv. (*Scot.*) why.

†qwhyet n. (*Scot.*) white.

*qwhyl n. (*Scot.*) while.

†qwhyt adj. white.

†qwhyte adj. (*Scot.*) white.

†qwi adv. why.

†qwiche adj. & pron. which.

†qwike adj. quick.

†qwikk adj. quick.

†qwil n. quill.

†qwile n. (*Scot.*) while.

†qwilk adj. & pron. which.

†qwill n. (*Scot.*) while.

†qwince n. quince.

qwine n. (*dialect*) money; corner.

†qwirk n. (*dialect*) twist, bend.

†qwitte v. quit.

†qwo n. who.

†qwom pron. whom.

†qwome pron. whom.

†qwon adv. & conj. (*Scot.*) when.

qwop v. (*dialect*) throb with pain.

†qworle n. whorl.

†qwose pron. (*Scot.*) whose.

qwot v. (*dialect*) = qwat.

†qwy n. (*Scot.*) heifer.

†qwyce n. gorse.

†**qwych** adj. & pron. (Scot.) which.

†**qwyche** adj. & pron. (Scot.) which.

†**qwye** n. (Scot.) heifer.

†**qwyet** n. (Scot.) wheat.

†**qwyght** adj. white.

\***qwyk** adj. quick.

†**qwyken** v. quicken.

†**qwykyr** n. wicker.

†**qwykyn** v. quicken.

\***qwyl** n. (dialect) wheel.

†**qwyle** n. (Scot.) while.

†**qwylte** n. quilt.

†**qwylum** adv. (Scot.) whilom (= while).

†**qwylys** adv. & n. (Scot.) whiles (= while).

†**qwynce** n. quince.

†**qwyne** adv. (dialect) whence.

†**qwynn** n. whin.

†**qwynse** n. quinsy.

†**qwype** n. (Scot.) whip.

\***qwyt** adj. white.

†**qwyte** adj. white.

†**qwyuer** n. quiver.

\***qwyver** n. quiver.

†**qwytt** v. quit.

**shoq** n. Indian tree.

**suq** n. Arab marketplace.

**tariqa** n. Muslim ascetics' spiritual development.

**tariqah** n. = tariqa.

# Words beginning with x

\***xa** n. shah.

†**xal** v. shall.

†**xall** v. shall.

†**xalle** v. shall.

\***xaraf** n. Oriental money changer.

\***xaroff** n. = xaraf.

**xebec** n. sailing boat.

**xebeck** n. = xebec.

\***xel** v. shall.

**xeme** n. fork-tailed gull.

**xenia** n. (pl. **xenias**) foreign pollen effect.

**xenial** adj. of hospitality.

**xenium** n. (pl. **xenia**) gift to a guest.

**xenon** n. heavy inert gas.

**xeque** n. sheikh.

**xeric** adj. having little moisture.

**xeriff** n. Muslim title.

**xeroma** n. abnormal bodily dryness.

**xerox** v. photocopy.

**xi** n. Greek letter x.

\***xiph** n. swordfish.

\*xisti pl. of xystus.

**xoanon** n. (pl. **xoana**) carved image.

†**xowyn** v. shove.

**xu** n. (pl. **xu**) Vietnamese coin.

†**xul** v. shall.

†**xuid** v. shall.

†**xulde** v. shall.

†**xwld** v. shall.

**xylan** n. carbohydrate in plants.

**xylary** adj. of xylem.

**xylate** n. salt of xylic acid.

**xylem** n. plant tissue.

**xylene** n. hydrocarbon from wood spirit.

**xylic** adj. of a kind of acid.

**xylo** n. (colloquial) Xylonite (a kind of celluloid).

**xylol** n. xylene.

**xylose** n. substance obtained from xylan.

**xylyl** n. derivative of xylene.

**xyrid** n. sedge-like herb.

**xyst** n. xystus.

**xysta** pl. of xystum.

**xyster** n. surgeon's instrument.

**xysti** pl. of xystus.

**xyston** n. ancient Greek spear.

**xystos** n. xystus.

**xystum** n. (pl. **xysta**) xystus.

**xystus** n. (pl. **xysti**) covered portico.

# Rules of English Spelling and Punctuation

## Spelling

English spelling was largely standardised by the mid 18th century, and American variants established by the early 19th, but many conventions were fixed by printers as early as 1500, and as pronunciation has changed since then, present-day pronunciation and spelling are often at variance.

***i* before *e*** For words pronounced with an 'ee' sound, the traditional rule '*i* before *e* except after *c*' is fairly reliable. Exceptions include *seize* and *heinous*, *either* and *neither* (if you pronounce them that way), *species*, and words in which a stem ending in -*e* is followed by a suffix beginning with -*i*-, e.g. *caffeine*, *plebeian*, *protein*. Note the appearance of -*fei* in *counterfeit*, *forfeit*, *surfeit*, and that *mischief* is spelt like *chief*.

Words pronounced with an 'ay' or long 'i' (as in 'eye') sound generally have -*ei*- e.g. *beige*, *reign*, *veil*; *eiderdown*, *height*, *kaleidoscope*. Words with other sounds follow no rules and must simply become familiar to the eye, e.g. *foreign*, *friend*, *heifer*, *leisure*, *sieve*, *sovereign*, *their*, *view*, *weir*, *weird*.

**Doubling consonants** When a suffix beginning with a vowel (such as -*able*, -*ed*, -*er*, -*ing*, or -*ish*) is added to a word ending in a consonant, the consonant is usually doubled if it is a single consonant preceded by a vowel spelt with one letter, and comes at the end of a stressed syllable. So *controlled*, *dropped*, *permitted*, *transferred*, *trekked*, *bigger*, *reddish*, but *sweated*, *sweeter*, *appealing*, *greenish* (vowel spelt with more than one letter), *planting* (more than one consonant), *balloted*, *happened*, *profited*, *targeted* (not ending a stressed syllable). A secondary stress is often sufficient to give a double consonant, e.g. *caravanning*, *formatted*, *programmed*, *zigzagged*, and *kidnapped*, *worshipped*, though note *benefited*. Verbs ending in a vowel followed by -*c* generally form inflections in -*cked*, -*cking*, e.g. *bivouac*, *mimic*, *picnic*.

Derivative verbs formed by the addition of prefixes follow the pattern of the root verb, as in *inputting*, *leapfrogged*.

In Australian English, the letter *l* is doubled if it follows a single vowel, regardless of stress, e.g. *labelled*, *travelled*, *jeweller*, but *heeled*, *emailed*, *cooler* (vowel spelt with more than one letter). In American English the double *l* occurs only if ending a stressed syllable, e.g. *labeled*, *traveling*, *jeweler* in American use, but *dispelled* in both Australian and American use (the double *l* may be retained in the present tense in American use, e.g. *appall*, *enthrall*). Exceptions retaining single *l*: *paralleled*, *devilish*; exceptions having double *l* (especially in Australian use): *woollen*, *veil*; note variability of *cruel(l)er*, *cruel(l)est*.

The letter *s* is not usually doubled before the suffix -*es*, either in plural nouns, e.g. *focuses*, *gases*, *pluses*, *yeses*, or in the present tense of verbs, e.g. *focuses*, *gases*. However, verbal forms in -*s(s)ed*, -*s(s)ing* are variable, and doubling after stressed syllables is usually preferable, as in *gassed*, though with an unstressed syllable, single *-s-*, as in *biased* and *focused*, is perhaps better. The consonants *w*, *x*, and *y* are never doubled; nor are silent consonants (e.g. *crocheted*, *ricocheted*).

**Dropping silent *e*** A silent *e* is usually dropped when adding a suffix beginning with a vowel, e.g. *bluish*, *bravest*, *continuous*, *queued*, *refusal*, *writing*. However, it may be retained in certain words to preserve the sound of the preceding consonant.

The *e* is retained in *dyeing*, *singeing*, *swingeing*, to distinguish them from *dying*, *singing*, *swinging*. It is usually retained in *ageing*, *cueing*, and sometimes in *glu(e)ing*, *hing(e)ing*, *ru(e)ing*, *spong(e)ing*, *ting(e)ing*. It is also retained in *-ee*, *-oe*, *-ye*, e.g. *canoeing*, *eyeing*, *fleeing*, *shoeing*. Otherwise it is dropped: *charging*, *icing*, *staging*, etc.

The *e* is retained to preserve the sound of the consonant in words such as *advantageous*, *noticeable*, *manageable*, *peaceable*. However, the dropping of *e* before *-able* is very unpredictable, and the first (or only) spelling given in the main part of the dictionary should be preferred. The *e* is more often dropped in American English.

The *e* is usually dropped before *-age*: *cleavage*, *dosage*, *wastage*. Exceptions: *acreage* (always), *mil(e)age* (optional; note also *lineage*). It is also usually dropped before *-y*, as in *bony*, *icy*, *grimy*. Exceptions: *cagey*, *dicey*, *gluey*. The *e* is retained in *holey* to distinguish it from *holy*, and an extra *e* is added to separate two *y*s, e.g. *clayey*.

**Forming plurals** Regular plurals are formed by adding *s*, or after *s*, *sh*, *ss*, *z*, *x*, *ch* (unless pronounced 'hard') adding *es*: *books*, *boxes*, *pizzas*, *queues*, *arches*, *stomachs*. An apostrophe should not be used. Nouns ending in *-y* preceded by a consonant (or *-quy*) form plurals ending in *-ies*, e.g. *rubies*, *soliloquies*, but *boys*, *monkeys*. Nouns ending in *-f* or *-fe* (but not *-ff*, *-ffe*) may form plurals in *-ves*, either always (e.g. *halves*, *leaves*) or optionally (e.g. *hooves*, *scarves*), or they may always have regular plurals (e.g. *beliefs*, *chiefs*). Nouns ending in *-o* or *-i* should be checked; a number of words have only plurals in *-oes* (e.g. *heroes*, *potatoes*, *tomatoes*) but plurals in *-os* are common, especially among words that are less naturalised (e.g. *arpeggios*), or are formed by abbreviation (e.g. *kilos*), or have a vowel preceding the *-o* (e.g. *radios*). Nouns ending in *-ful* form regular plurals in *-fuls*. Only the letter *z* is regularly doubled in forming plurals: *fezzes*, *quizzes*. Nouns ending in *-man* form plurals in *-men*, e.g. *chairmen*, *postmen*, *pokeswomen*, but note *talismans*. Other irregular plurals are noted in the main text of the dictionary.

Most compound nouns pluralise the last element, but note exceptions such as *daughters-in-law*, *passers-by*.

Words adopted into English generally form regular English plurals. Though some words have both a regular English plural alongside a plural in the language of origin, e.g. *bureaus/bureaux*, *cherubs/cherubim*, *formulas/formulae*, *indexes/indices*, *virtuosos/virtuosi*, many nouns with similar histories regularly form only English plurals, e.g. *censures*, *octopuses*, *omnibuses*. Care should be taken with words enging in -a, e.g. *addenda, bacteria, criteria, phenomena*, and *strata* are plural, but *vertebra* is singular.

**Common suffixes** Several common suffixes occur in different forms which may cause spelling difficulties: users of the dictionary should be careful to check if unsure of accepted usage. The most frequent sources of uncertainty are: *able/-ible, -ance/-ence, -ant/-ent, -cede/-ceed, -er/-or, -er/-re, -ise/-ize, -our/-or*. Both forms of the suffix (-*ise* and -*ize*) have long histories of use in English. The -*ise* spelling is preferred in Australia, and is obligatory in certain cases: (a) where it forms part of a larger word element, such as -*mise* (= sending) in *compromise*, and -*prise* (= taking) in *surprise*; and (b) in verbs corresponding to nouns with -*s*- in the stem, such as *advertise* and *televise*. The -*ize* spelling is preferred in American English and by some British publishing houses but is only obligatory in a small number of cases, e.g. *capsize, prize* (in the sense of 'value highly').

# Punctuation

---

## apostrophe

**1**   Used to indicate the possessive case:
    singular: *a boy's book; a day's work; the boss's chair*
    plural with s: *a girls' chair; two weeks' holiday; the bosses' chairs*
    plural without s: *children's books; women's liberation*
    names: singular: *Bill's book; Thomas' coat*
       *Barnabas'* (or *Barnabas's*) *book; Nicholas'* (or *Nicholas's*) *coat*
    names ending in -*es* pronounced /-ɪz/ are treated like plurals: *Bridges'*
       *poems; Moses' mother*
    before the word *sake*: *for God's sake; for goodness' sake; for Harry's*
       *sake*
    business names often omit the apostrophe: *McDonalds, Kingsleys*
       *Chicken*
    place names often omit the apostrophe: *Kings Cross*

**2**   Used to mark an omission of one or more letters:
    *e'er* (= ever); *he's* (= he is or he has); *we'll* (= we shall or we will);
    *'88* (= 1988)

• Incorrect uses: (i) the apostrophe must not be used with a plural where there is no possessive sense, as in *tea's are served here; banana's $5 per kilo*; (ii) there is no such word as *her's, our's, their's, your's*.

• Confusions: *it's* = it is or it has (not 'belonging to it'); correct uses are *it's here* (= it is here); *it's gone* (= it has gone); but *the dog wagged its tail* (no apostrophe)
    *who's* = who is or who has; correct uses are *who's there?; who's taken my pen?*; but *whose book is this?* (*whose* = belonging to whom)

# Rules of Punctuation

## colon

**1** Used to introduce an example or a list:
*Please send the following items: passport, two photographs, the correct fee.*

**2** Used to introduce an interpretation or description of what precedes it:
*There is one thing we need: money.*
*I have news for you: we have won!*

**3** Used to introduce speech in a play or in a newspaper report where quotation marks are omitted:
*Defence lawyer: Objection!*
*Judge: Objection overruled.*

## comma

The comma marks a slight break between words or phrases etc. Among its specific uses are the following:

**1** to separate items in a list:
*red, white, and blue*
*bread, butter, jam, and cake*

**2** to separate main clauses:
*Cars will park here, buses will turn left.*

**3** after (or before and after) a vocative or a clause etc. with no finite verb:
*Reader, I married him.*
*Well, Mr Jones, we meet again.*
*Having had lunch, we went back to work.*

**4** to separate phrases etc. in order to clarify meaning:
*In the valley below, the town looked very small.*
*In 2015, 1945 seemed a long time ago.*

**5** following words that introduce direct speech, or after direct speech where there is no question mark or exclamation mark:
*They answered, 'Here we are'.*
*'Here we are', they answered.*

**6** after *Dear Sir, Dear John,* etc. in letters, and after *Yours faithfully, Yours sincerely,* etc.; after a vocative such as *My Lord.*

**7** to separate a parenthetical word, phrase, or clause:
*I am sure, however, that it will not happen.*
*Fred, who is bald, complained of the cold.*

•No comma is needed between month and year in dates (e.g. *in December 1992*) or between number and road in addresses (e.g. *17 Belsyre Court*).

## dash

**1**  Used to mark the beginning and the end of an interruption in the structure of a sentence:
*My son—where has he gone?—would like to meet you.*

**2**  In print, a line slightly longer than a hyphen is used to join pairs or groups of words where it is often equivalent to *to* or *versus*:
*the 1914–18 war; the Sydney–Canberra–Melbourne route; the Marxist–Trotskyite split*

(See also **hyphen**.)

## exclamation mark

Used after an exclamatory word, phrase, or sentence, or an interjection:
*Well! If it isn't John!*
*Order! Order!*

## full stop

**1**  Used at the end of all sentences that are not questions or exclamations.

**2**  Used after abbreviations:
*E.G. Whitlam; Sun.* (= Sunday); *Jan.* (= January); *p. 7* (= page 7); *e.g.; etc.; a.m.; p.m.*

• a full stop should not be used with the numerical abbreviations *1st, 2nd, 3rd*, etc., nor with acronyms such as *CSIRO, ASEAN*; nor with words that are colloquial abbreviations (e.g. *Co-op, demo, recap, con*).

• Full stops are not essential in abbreviations consisting entirely of capitals (e.g. *ABC, NNE, AD, BC, PLC*), nor with *C* (= Celsius), *F* (= Fahrenheit), chemical symbols, and measures of length, weight, time, etc. (except for *in.* = inch), nor for *Dr, Revd, Mr, Mrs, Ms, Mme, Mlle, St*.

## hyphen

**1**  Used to join two or more words so as to form a single expression:
*father-in-law; happy-go-lucky; non-stick; self-control*

**2**  Used to join words in an attributive compound:
*a well-known man* (but 'the man is well known')
*an out-of-date list* (but 'the list is out of date')

**3**  Used to join a prefix etc. to a proper name:
*anti-Darwinian; half-Italian*

**4**  Used to prevent misconceptions, by linking words:
*twenty-odd people; twenty odd people*
or by separating a prefix:
*re-cover/recover; re-present/represent; re-sign/resign*

**5** Used to separate two similar vowel sounds, as a help to understanding and pronunciation:
*pre-empt; pre-exist*

**6** Used to represent a common second element in the items of a list:
*two-, three-, or fourfold*

**7** Used at the end of a line of print to show that a word not usually hyphenated has had to be divided.

## question mark

**1** Used after every question that expects a separate answer:
*Why is he here? Who invited him?*

**2** Placed before a word or date etc. whose accuracy is doubted:
*Edward Redmond ?1766–1840*

• It is not used in indirect questions, e.g. *We asked why he was there and who had invited him.*

## quotation marks

Used round a direct quotation:
*'That is nonsense', she said.*

## semicolon

Used to separate those parts of a sentence between which there is a more distinct break than would be called for by a comma but which are too closely connected to be made into separate sentences:
*To err is human; to forgive, divine.*

# Independent countries of the world

| Country | Adjective and Noun |
|---|---|
| Afghanistan | Afghan |
| Albania | Albanian |
| Algeria | Algerian |
| America (*see* United States of America) | |
| Andorra | Andorran |
| Angola | Angolan |
| Antigua and Barbuda | Antiguan, Barbudan |
| Argentina | Argentinian |
| Armenia | Armenian |
| Australia | Australian |
| Austria | Austrian |
| Azerbaijan | Azerbaijani |
| Bahamas | Bahamian |
| Bahrain | Bahraini (pl. *-is*) |
| Bangladesh | Bangladeshi (*n.*, pl. *-is*) |
| Barbados | Barbadian |
| Belarus | Belorussian *or* Byelorussian |
| Belgium | Belgian |
| Belize | Belizian |
| Benin | Beninese |
| Bhutan | Bhutanese |
| Bolivia | Bolivian |
| Bosnia and Herzegovina | Bosnian, Herzegovinian |
| Botswana | Motswana, *pl.* Batswana |
| Brazil | Brazilian |
| Brunei | Bruneian |
| Bulgaria | Bulgarian |
| Burkina Faso | Burkinese |
| Burma (*see* Myanmar) | Burmese |
| Burundi | Burundian |
| Cambodia | Cambodian |
| Cameroon | Cameroonian |
| Canada | Canadian |
| Cape Verde Islands | Cape Verdean |
| Central African Republic | Central African |
| Chad | Chadian |
| Chile | Chilean |
| China | Chinese |
| Colombia | Colombian |
| Comoros | Comoran |
| Congo | Congolese |
| Congo, Democratic Republic of (formerly Zaire) | |
| Costa Rica | Costa Rican |

| Country | Adjective and Noun |
|---|---|
| Croatia | Croat or Croatian |
| Cuba | Cuban |
| Cyprus | Cypriot |
| Czech Republic | Czech |
| Denmark | Danish (a.), Dane (n.) |
| Djibouti | Djiboutian |
| Dominica | Dominican |
| Dominican Republic | Dominican |
| East Timor | East Timorese |
| Ecuador | Ecuadorean |
| Egypt | Egyptian |
| El Salvador | Salvadorean |
| Equatorial Guinea | Equatorial Guinean |
| Eritrea | Eritrean |
| Estonia | Estonian |
| Eswatini | Swazi |
| Ethiopia | Ethiopian |
| Fiji | Fijian |
| Finland | Finnish (a.), Finn (n.) |
| France | French (a.), Frenchman (n.), Frenchwoman (n.) |
| Gabon | Gabonese |
| Gambia | Gambian |
| Georgia | Georgian |
| Germany | German |
| Ghana | Ghanaian |
| Greece | Greek |
| Grenada | Grenadian |
| Guatemala | Guatemalan |
| Guinea | Guinean |
| Guinea-Bissau | Guinean |
| Guyana | Guyanese |
| Haiti | Haitian |
| Holland (see Netherlands) | |
| Honduras | Honduran |
| Hungary | Hungarian |
| Iceland | Icelandic (a.), Icelander (n.) |
| India | Indian |
| Indonesia | Indonesian |
| Iran | Iranian |
| Iraq | Iraqi (pl. -is) |
| Ireland, Republic of | Irish (a.), Irishman (n.), Irishwoman (n.) |
| Israel | Israeli (pl. -is) |
| Italy | Italian |
| Ivory Coast | Ivorian |
| Jamaica | Jamaican |

| Country | Adjective and Noun |
|---|---|
| Japan | Japanese |
| Jordan | Jordanian |
| Kazakhstan | Kazakh |
| Kenya | Kenyan |
| Kiribati | I-Kiribati |
| Korea | Korean |
| Kosovo | Kosovar |
| Kuwait | Kuwaiti (pl. -*is*) |
| Kyrgyzstan | Kyrgyz |
| Laos | Laotian |
| Latvia | Latvian |
| Lebanon | Lebanese |
| Lesotho | Mosotho (*n.*; *pl.* Basotho) |
| Liberia | Liberian |
| Libya | Libyan |
| Liechtenstein | Liechtensteiner |
| Lithuania | Lithuanian |
| Luxemburg | Luxemburger (*n.*) |
| Madagascar | Malagasy *or* Madagascan |
| Malawi | Malawian |
| Malaysia | Malaysian |
| Maldives | Maldivian |
| Mali | Malian |
| Malta | Maltese |
| Marshall Islands | Marshallese |
| Mauritania | Mauritanian |
| Mauritius | Mauritian |
| Mexico | Mexican |
| Micronesia, Federated States of | Micronesian |
| Moldova | Moldovan |
| Monaco | Monégasque *or* Monacan |
| Mongolia | Mongolian |
| Montenegro | Montenegrin |
| Morocco | Moroccan |
| Mozambique | Mozambican |
| Myanmar | Myanmarese |
| Namibia | Namibian |
| Nauru | Nauruan |
| Nepal | Nepalese |
| Netherlands, the | Dutch (*a.*), Dutchman (*n.*), Dutchwoman (*n.*) *or* Netherlander |
| New Zealand | New Zealander (*n.*) |
| Nicaragua | Nicaraguan |
| Niger | Nigerien |
| Nigeria | Nigerian |
| North Korea | North Korean |

| Country | Adjective and Noun |
|---|---|
| North Macedonia | North Macedonian |
| Norway | Norwegian |
| Oman | Omani (pl. *-is*) |
| Pakistan | Pakistani (pl. *-is*) |
| Palau | Palauan |
| Panama | Panamanian |
| Papua New Guinea | Papua New Guinean |
| Paraguay | Paraguayan |
| Peru | Peruvian |
| Philippines | Philippine (*a.*), Filipino (*n.*, *pl. -os*), Filipina (*n. fem.*) |
| Poland | Polish (*a.*), Pole (*n.*) |
| Portugal | Portuguese |
| Qatar | Qatari |
| Romania | Romanian |
| Russian Federation | Russian |
| Rwanda | Rwandan |
| St Kitts-Nevis | Kittitian, Nevisian |
| St Lucia | St Lucian |
| St Vincent and the Grenadines | Vincentian, Grenadian |
| Samoa | Samoan |
| San Marino | Sanmarinese |
| São Tomé and Príncipe | São Toméan |
| Saudi Arabia | Saudi Arabian *or* Saudi |
| Senegal | Senegalese |
| Serbia | Serb *or* Serbian |
| Seychelles | Seychellois |
| Sierra Leone | Sierra Leonean |
| Singapore | Singaporean |
| Slovak Republic | Slovak |
| Slovenia | Slovene *or* Slovenian |
| Solomon Islands | Solomon Islander (*n.*) |
| Somalia | Somali (pl. *-is*) |
| South Africa | South African |
| South Korea | South Korean |
| South Sudan | South Sudanese |
| Spain | Spanish (*a.*), Spaniard (*n.*) |
| Sri Lanka | Sri Lankan (*a.*) |
| Sudan | Sudanese |
| Suriname | Surinamese *or* Surinamer (*n.*) |
| Swaziland (*see* Eswatini) | Swazi |
| Sweden | Swedish (*a.*), Swede (*n.*) |
| Switzerland | Swiss |
| Syria | Syrian |
| Taiwan | Taiwanese |
| Tajikistan | Tajik *or* Tadjik |
| Tanzania | Tanzanian |

| Country | Adjective and Noun |
|---------|---------------------|
| Thailand | Thai |
| Togo | Togolese |
| Tonga | Tongan |
| Trinidad and Tobago | Trinidadian, Tobagonian *or* Tobagan |
| Tunisia | Tunisian |
| Turkey | Turkish (*a.*), Turk (*n.*) |
| Turkmenistan | Turkem *or* Turkomen |
| Tuvalu | Tuvaluan |
| Uganda | Ugandan |
| Ukraine | Ukranian |
| United Arab Emirates | Emirian |
| United Kingdom | British (*a.*), Briton (*n.*) |
| United States of America | American |
| Uruguay | Uruguayan |
| Uzbekistan | Uzbek |
| Vanuatu | Vanuatuan *or* Ni-Vanuatu |
| Vatican City | Vatican (*a.*) |
| Venezuela | Venezuelan |
| Vietnam | Vietnamese |
| Yemen | Yemeni (pl. -*is*) |
| Zambia | Zambian |
| Zimbabwe | Zimbabwean |